Dear CMI Fellows,

The Canadian Migration Institute is very pleased to provide this 2011 edition of *The Annotated Immigration and Refugee Protection Act of Canada*.

Henry Goslett, CCIC, FCMI, and Barbara Jo Caruso, LLB, provide an invaluable tool, which gives you the insight and technical expertise to offer the best possible advice and representation to clients.

Chers / Chères Fellows de l'ICM,

L'Institut canadien de la migration est très heureux de vous remettre un exemplaire de l'édition 2011 de la publication intitulée *Législation Canadienne en Immigration - Texte annoté.*

Henry Goslett, CCAI, FICM, et Barbara Jo Caruso, LLB, nous offrent cet outil précieux, lequel met en lumière une réflexion éclairée et une expertise technique qui vous aideront à fournir à vos clients les meilleurs services de conseil et de représentation possibles.

Imran Qayyum, KStG, CCIC,
FCMI, ICD.D, C.Dir., *ASC*
Chair
Canadian Migration
Institute

THE 2011 ANNOTATED

# IMMIGRATION AND REFUGEE PROTECTION ACT OF CANADA

*Edited & annotated by*

**Henry M. Goslett**

and

**Barbara Jo Caruso**

Formerly Frank N. Marrocco & Henry M. Goslett

*STATUTES OF CANADA ANNOTATED*

CARSWELL®

This work reproduces official English language versions of federal statutes and regulations. As this material also exists in official French language form, the reader is advised that reference to the official French language version may be warranted in appropriate circumstances.

The paper used in this publication meets the minimum requirements of American National Standard for Information Sciences — Permanence of Paper for Printed Library Materials, ANSI Z39.48-1984.

**A cataloguing record for this publication is available from Library and Archives Canada.**

ISSN 1709-2051

ISBN 978-0-7798-2669-8 (2011 edition: bound)

ISBN 978-0-7798-2668-1 (2011 edition: pbk.)

Printed in the United States by Thomson Reuters

THOMSON REUTERS

CARSWELL, A DIVISION OF THOMSON REUTERS CANADA LIMITED

One Corporate Plaza
2075 Kennedy Road
Toronto, Ontario
M1T 3V4

Customer Relations
Toronto 1-416-609-3800
Elsewhere in Canada/U.S. 1-800-387-5164
Fax 1-416-298-5082
www.carswell.com
E-mail www.carswell.com/email

To

Frank and Debbie

And to

Douglas, Allison, Jessica, Alexandra and Jacqueline

# PREFACE

The starting point for anyone interested in immigration law is the position of the alien at common law. In this regard, Lord Denning M.R.'s concise summary of the common law in the case of *R. v. The Governor of the Pentonville Prison, ex parte Azam*, [1973] 2 All E.R. 741 at 747 is most helpful:

> At common law no alien has any right to enter this country except by leave of the Crown; and the Crown can refuse leave without giving any reason: see *Schmidt v. Secretary of State for Home Affairs*, [1969] 2 Ch. 49 at 168. If he comes by leave, the Crown can impose such conditions as it thinks fit, as to his length of stay, or otherwise. He has no right whatever to remain here. He is liable to be sent home to his own country at any time if, in the opinion of the Crown, his presence here is not conducive to the public good; and for this purpose, the executive may arrest him and put him on board a ship or aircraft bound for his own country: see *R. v. Brixton Prison (Governor), ex parte Soblen*, [1963] 2 Q.B. 243 at 300, 301. The position of aliens at common law has since been covered by the various regulations; but the principles remain the same.

This annotation is directed at the question of the extent to which the common law has been affected by the *Charter of Rights and Freedoms*, the *Immigration and Refugee Protection Act of Canada* and the Regulations passed pursuant to that Act.

A number of Supreme Court of Canada decisions have confirmed that although ". . .the most fundamental principle of immigration law is that non-citizens do not have an unqualified right to enter or remain in Canada" this does not mean that the proceedings related to deportation in the immigration context are immune from scrutiny under section 7 of the *Charter*.

Bill C-11, entitled the *Balanced Refugee Reform Act*, S.C. 2010, c. 8, passed but only after significant evolution prior to Royal Assent. We fully expect the legislation will evolve further via judicial interpretation. Please note, although the provisions in Bill C-11 are to come into force immediately, the appeal provisions (section 31) in the existing legislation are to come into force within two years of Royal Assent of the Bill.

We have preserved summaries of decisions annotated under the former *Immigration Act* which dealt with the definition of a Convention Refugee. These case summaries are included under sections 96 and 108 of IRPA. Cases concerning the Schedule, Sections E and F of Article 1 of the United Nations Convention Relating to the Status of Refugees, decided under the former Act, follow the Schedule to the IRPA. In addition, procedural decisions regarding refugee hearings under the former Act are collected under the Refugee Protection Division Rules, section 61.

Cases under the former legislation dealing with the requirements to obtain a stay of a removal order are collected under section 18.2 of the *Federal Courts Act*. It is recognized that in some cases the application for a stay is made because an H&C application is pending. Such orders are perhaps inherently different than those described in section 18.2. We decided that it was better to collect all of the decisions involving judicial stays under the former Act in one place and chose section 18.2 of the *Federal Courts Act* for that purpose.

Considerable judicial resources have been applied to marking the boundary between national security obligations and individual rights. We have included, at the beginning of Part 1, Division 9, annotations of decisions taken under section 40.1 of the former *Immigration Act* and under former Division 9 of IRPA. Division 9 was replaced on March 5, 2008, as a result of the Supreme Court of Canada's decision in *Charkaoui, Re* (2007), 59 Imm. L.R. (3d) 1, that concluded there were two defects in the legislation that were inconsistent with the *Charter*. While the security provisions of the former Act and the sections under former Division 9 are differently worded, it is thought that these annotations may contribute to the development of the law in this very difficult area.

We have included the Guidelines issued by the Chairperson pursuant to section 65(3) of the former Act and section 159(1)(h) of IRPA.

On April 1, 2011, the Regulations amending the *Immigration and Refugee Protection Regulations* dealing with Temporary Foreign Workers will come into force. These amendments will significantly amend the process for, and establish factors to be considered in, assessing genuineness when Citizenship and Immigration Canada, Canada Border Services Agency and Human Resources and Skills Development Canada assess offers of employment. The amendments also allow for restrictions of an employer's eligibility to access the Temporary Foreign Worker Programs for two years, where the employer is found to not have complied with terms and conditions of the offer of employment. A list of ineligible employers will be made available on Citizenship and Immigration Canada's external website. Amendments also set a maximum cumulative duration of four years of work, for work permit applications that require a labour market opinion. Given the significant consequences for employers and temporary foreign workers, we expect negative decisions to be judicially reviewed. These amendments are shaded, as they will not come into force until several months after this 2011 edition is published.

Once again, we have observed counsel advocating and litigating various issues under the *Immigration and Refugee Protection Act* and we have been impressed with the extent to which they have pursued litigation, not only in the interest of their clients but in the interest of the evolution of the interpretation and application of this relatively new legislation. Both the Immigration Bar and the Minister's representatives have made a significant contribution in this regard. Often, it is more cost efficient to reapply or at least, to avoid the risk of having a negative decision for the client in a judicial forum; however, countless times over this past year, cases have been judicially reviewed for the benefit of all future applicants applying under the provisions of IRPA. These litigants, their counsel and the Minister's representatives should all be commended for their advocacy skills.

We wish to thank our publisher for its assistance in providing us with decisions, the citations which appear in our text and the table of cases. We also wish to thank all those who assisted in proofreading.

We are indebted once again to those members of the legal profession, Citizenship and Immigration Canada, the Canadian Border Service Agency and the Immigration and Refugee Board who have provided constructive criticism to us throughout the year. All of these comments were most gratefully received and many of them have been incorporated into this year's edition.

We wish to express our thanks to Natalie Lofeudo, Brenda Wong and Helena Labinowicz for their assistance in the preparation of the 2011 edition. We also wish to recognize the contribution of Pamela Hudson to previous editions of our text. Without the care and attention of these persons, this edition would not have been possible. This edition contains all relevant cases which have come to our attention as of June 30, 2010.

November 1, 2010
Toronto, Ontario
Henry M. Goslett
Barbara Jo Caruso

# SUMMARY TABLE OF CONTENTS

# Table of Contents

## Immigration and Refugee Protection Act

### Short Title



### Interpretation



### Objectives and Application



### Enabling Authority



### Agreements



### Part 1 — Immigration to Canada

### Division 1 — Requirements Before Entering Canada and Selection

#### *Requirements Before Entering Canada*



#### *Selection of Permanent Residents*



#### *Sponsorship of Foreign Nationals*



#### *Regulations*



### Division 2 — Examination



### Division 3 — Entering and Remaining in Canada

#### *Entering and Remaining*



#### *Status and Authorization to Enter*

### *Repeals*



### *Coming Into Force*



### SCHEDULE — SECTIONS E AND F OF ARTICLE 1 OF THE UNITED NATIONS CONVENTION RELATING TO THE STATUS OF REFUGEES



### ARTICLE 1 OF THE CONVENTION AGAINST TORTURE AND OTHER CRUEL, INHUMAN AND DEGRADING TREATMENT OR PUNISHMENT



## SOR/2002-227 — IMMIGRATION AND REFUGEE PROTECTION REGULATIONS

### PART 1 — INTERPRETATION AND APPLICATION

#### DIVISION 1 — INTERPRETATION



#### DIVISION 2 — FAMILY RELATIONSHIPS



### PART 2 — GENERAL REQUIREMENTS

#### DIVISION 1 — DOCUMENTS REQUIRED BEFORE ENTRY



#### DIVISION 2 — APPLICATIONS



#### DIVISION 3 — DOCUMENTS AND CERTIFIED COPIES



#### DIVISION 4 — REPRESENTATION FOR A FEE



### PART 3 — INADMISSIBILITY

## PRIVACY ACT

### ACCESS TO PERSONAL INFORMATION

### *Right of Access*



## APPENDIX I

## GUIDELINES ISSUED BY THE CHAIRPERSON



## APPENDIX II

## AN ACT RESPECTING IMMIGRATION TO QUÉBEC

### DIVISION I — DEFINITION



### DIVISION II — SELECTION OF FOREIGN NATIONALS



### DIVISION III — INTEGRATION OF FOREIGN NATIONALS

# APPENDIX VI
# CONSTITUTION ACT, 1982

## PART I — CANADIAN CHARTER OF RIGHTS AND FREEDOMS

## Application of Charter



## Citation

# Table of Cases

Cases are referenced to section number. Designations refer to:

Immigration and Refugee Protection Act — *IRPA*

Immigration and Refugee Protection Regulations — *IRPR*

Refugee Protection Division Rules — *RPDR*

Immigration Division Rules — *IDR*

Immigration Appeal Division Rules — *IADR*

Federal Courts Act — *FCA*

Federal Courts Rules — *FCR*

Federal Court Immigration and Refugee Protection Rules — *FCIR*

Privacy Act — *PA*

# Table of Cases

## Table of Cases

# IMMIGRATION AND REFUGEE PROTECTION ACT

## An Act respecting immigration to Canada and the granting of refugee protection to persons who are displaced, persecuted or in danger

S.C. 2001, c. 27 [ss. 73, 110, 111, 171, 194, 195, 245 not in force at date of publication.] [s. 245 repealed 2004, c. 15, s. 110.], as am. S.C. 2001, c. 27, s. 273.1(3); 2001, c. 32, s. 81(3); 2001, c. 41, s. 123; 2002, c. 8, s. 194; 2003, c. 22, ss. 172, 173, 225(z.3); 2004, c. 15, ss. 70–72, 110; 2005, c. 10, s. 34(1)(o), (2); 2005, c. 20, s. 81; 2005, c. 38, ss. 118, 119; 2008, c. 3, ss. 1–5; 2008, c. 28, ss. 116–119; 2010, c. 8, ss. 2, 3, 4(1), (2) (Fr.), 5–9, 10 (Fr.), 11–27.1, 28(1), (2) (Fr.), 29–31 [ss. 2, 7, 8, 10–12, 14.1, 15(3), (4), 17–27, 29, 30 to come into force June 29, 2012, or earlier by order; ss. 15(1), (2), (5), 16, 16.1, 27.1 to come into force June 29, 2013, or earlier by order.].

*[Editor's Note: The* Immigration Act, *R.S.C. 1985, c. I-2 has been repealed by 2001, c. 27, s. 274(a) and replaced by the* Immigration and Refugee Protection Act, *S.C. 2001, c. 27, effective June 28, 2002.*

*Despite the repeal of the* Immigration Act, *R.S.C. 1985, c. I-2, the "former Act", there are substantial transitional provisions that may apply to the particular proceeding or transaction. Reference should be made to the transitional provisions which speak to the continuing application of the former Act in certain situations in S.C. 2001, c. 27, ss. 187–201, either by express reference therein or as prescribed by the new* Immigration and Refugee Protection Regulations, *SOR/2002-227.*

*The* Immigration Regulations, 1978, *SOR/78-172, the* Refugee Claimants Designated Class Regulations, *SOR/90-40, the* Immigration Act Fees Regulations, *SOR/97-22, and the* Humanitarian Designated Classes Regulations, *SOR/97-183, the "former Regulations", have been repealed and replaced by ss. 364(a), (b), (c), (d), respectively, of the* Immigration and Refugee Protection Regulations, *SOR/2002-227, effective June 28, 2002. Despite the repeal of the former Regulations, there are substantial transitional provisions that may apply to the particular proceeding or transaction. Reference should be made to the transitional provisions which speak to the continuing application of the former Act in certain situations and as previously prescribed by the former Regulations in SOR/2002-227, ss. 316–363.]*

Her Majesty, by and with the advice and consent of the Senate and House of Commons of Canada, enacts as follows:

## SHORT TITLE

**1. Short title — This Act may be cited as the *Immigration and Refugee Protection Act.***

## INTERPRETATION

**2. (1) Definitions — The definitions in this subsection apply in this Act.**

**"Board" means the Immigration and Refugee Board, which consists of the Refugee Protection Division, Refugee Appeal Division, Immigration Division and Immigration Appeal Division.** ***("Commission")***

**"Convention Against Torture" means the Convention Against Torture and Other Cruel, Inhuman or Degrading Treatment or Punishment, signed at New York on December 10, 1984. Article 1 of the Convention Against Torture is set out in the schedule.** ***("Convention contre la torture")***

**"foreign national" means a person who is not a Canadian citizen or a permanent resident, and includes a stateless person.** ***("étranger")***

**"permanent resident" means a person who has acquired permanent resident status and has not subsequently lost that status under section 46.** ***("résident permanent")***

*[Editor's Note: SOR/2002-227, s. 328(1) provides that a person who was a permanent resident immediately before June 28, 2002 is a permanent resident under the new* Immigration and Refugee Protection Act, *S.C. 2001, c. 27.]*

**"Refugee Convention" means the United Nations Convention Relating to the Status of Refugees, signed at Geneva on July 28, 1951, and the Protocol to that Convention, signed at New York on January 31, 1967. Sections E and F of Article 1 of the Refugee Convention are set out in the schedule.** ***("Convention sur les réfugiés")***

(2) **Act includes regulations — Unless otherwise indicated, references in this Act to "this Act" include regulations made under it.**

## OBJECTIVES AND APPLICATION

3. (1) **Objectives — immigration — The objectives of this Act with respect to immigration are**

> **(a) to permit Canada to pursue the maximum social, cultural and economic benefits of immigration;**
>
> **(b) to enrich and strengthen the social and cultural fabric of Canadian society, while respecting the federal, bilingual and multi-cultural character of Canada;**
>
> **(b.1) to support and assist the development of minority official languages communities in Canada;**
>
> **(c) to support the development of a strong and prosperous Canadian economy, in which the benefits of immigration are shared across all regions of Canada;**
>
> **(d) to see that families are reunited in Canada;**
>
> **(e) to promote the successful integration of permanent residents into Canada, while recognizing that integration involves mutual obligations for new immigrants and Canadian society;**

**(f) to support, by means of consistent standards and prompt processing, the attainment of immigration goals established by the Government of Canada in consultation with the provinces;**

**(g) to facilitate the entry of visitors, students and temporary workers for purposes such as trade, commerce, tourism, international understanding and cultural, educational and scientific activities;**

**(h) to protect the health and safety of Canadians and to maintain the security of Canadian society;**

**(i) to promote international justice and security by fostering respect for human rights and by denying access to Canadian territory to persons who are criminals or security risks; and**

**(j) to work in cooperation with the provinces to secure better recognition of the foreign credentials of permanent residents and their more rapid integration into society.**



**(2) Objectives — refugees — The objectives of this Act with respect to refugees are**

**(a) to recognize that the refugee program is in the first instance about saving lives and offering protection to the displaced and persecuted;**

**(b) to fulfil Canada's international legal obligations with respect to refugees and affirm Canada's commitment to international efforts to provide assistance to those in need of resettlement;**

**(c) to grant, as a fundamental expression of Canada's humanitarian ideals, fair consideration to those who come to Canada claiming persecution;**

**(d) to offer safe haven to persons with a well-founded fear of persecution based on race, religion, nationality, political opinion or membership in a particular social group, as well as those at risk of torture or cruel and unusual treatment or punishment;**

**(e) to establish fair and efficient procedures that will maintain the integrity of the Canadian refugee protection system, while upholding Canada's respect for the human rights and fundamental freedoms of all human beings;**

**(f) to support the self-sufficiency and the social and economic well-being of refugees by facilitating reunification with their family members in Canada;**

**(g) to protect the health and safety of Canadians and to maintain the security of Canadian society; and**

**(h) to promote international justice and security by denying access to Canadian territory to persons, including refugee claimants, who are security risks or serious criminals.**

*[Editor's Note: SOR/2002-227, s. 320(1) provides that a person is inadmissible under the new* Immigration and Refugee Protection Act, *S.C. 2001, c. 27 on security grounds if, on June 28, 2002, the person had been determined to be a member of an inadmissible class described in paragraph 19(1)(e), (f), (g) or (k) of the former* Immigration Act, *R.S.C. 1985, c. I-2.]*

**(3) Application — This Act is to be construed and applied in a manner that**

**(a) furthers the domestic and international interests of Canada;**

**(b) promotes accountability and transparency by enhancing public awareness of immigration and refugee programs;**

**(c) facilitates cooperation between the Government of Canada, provincial governments, foreign states, international organizations and non-governmental organizations;**

**(d) ensures that decisions taken under this Act are consistent with the *Canadian Charter of Rights and Freedoms*, including its principles of equality and freedom from discrimination and of the equality of English and French as the official languages of Canada;**

**(e) supports the commitment of the Government of Canada to enhance the vitality of the English and French linguistic minority communities in Canada; and**

**(f) complies with international human rights instruments to which Canada is signatory.**

## Case Law

### Section 3(1)

*Shahid v. Canada (Minister of Citizenship & Immigration)* (2010), 89 Imm. L.R. (3d) 19, 2010 FC 405, 2010 CarswellNat 2897, 2010 CarswellNat 931 (F.C.) — This was an application for judicial review of the Minister's failure to take a decision on their application for landing and a remedy in the nature of *mandamus*. The applicant was granted refugee status in May 2001 and applied for permanent residence in 2002. He was notified on September 5, 2001, that he met the eligibility requirements and that a decision would be made within 18 months. No decision had been made yet.

There is no dispute that the Minister has a duty to process the applicants' application. There is also no dispute that the applicants have satisfied all conditions precedent to the performance of the Minister's duty by providing all the necessary information. Nor is there any dispute as to the fact that they have repeatedly demanded that the Minister perform the duty. The sole issue in this case is whether enough time has passed since the applicant made this demand, and whether the Minister can be inferred to have refused to act. An inference may be drawn from "unreasonable" delay in making a decision. Eight years is, *prima facie*, a much longer delay than routine background checks require. CIC's lack of diligence in the applicant's file is shocking and in direct contradiction with IRPA's objective set out in paragraph 3(1)(f): "to support, by means of consistent standards and prompt processing, the attainment of immigration goals established by the government of Canada." An order in the nature of *mandamus* requiring the respondent to process the applicant's application for permanent residence in accordance with the law was issued. A decision was to be provided to the applicant within three months of the order.

*Singh v. Canada (Minister of Citizenship & Immigration)* (2010), 89 Imm. L.R. (3d) 36, 2010 FC 378, 2010 CarswellNat 3016, 2010 CarswellNat 817, [2010] F.C.J. No. 426 (F.C.) — The applicant was recently found to be inadmissible for misrepresenting or withholding a material fact when he immigrated to Canada in 1993. At that time, he did not disclose that he had fathered a child who remained in India. His defence is that he did not know he had fathered a child. Paternity has now been scientifically established by DNA tests. As a result, the Immigration Division of the Immigration and Refugee Board of Canada issued an exclusion order and he was ordered removed from Canada. His appeal to the Immigration Appeal Division was dismissed. He sought judicial review of that decision.

The applicant's submission is that he could not have misrepresented or withheld facts within the meaning of s. 40 of IRPA or its predecessor, since subjectively he had no knowledge at the time that he was the girl Shilpa's biological father. The Minister's position is that it does not matter what the applicant knew or did not know, it is a scientifically proven fact that he is Shilpa's biological father, and that is the end of the matter.

Given that the wording "knowingly" does not appear in s. 40, it follows, that knowledge is not a prerequisite to a finding of misrepresentation or withholding material facts. Undoubtedly, the existence of a child is a material fact. In this case, the alleged misrepresentation was a misstatement of fact. Such misrepresentations may be fraudulent, negligent or innocent. The panel found that the applicant was not credible. Even if he did not know that he was Shilpa's father, the circumstances, *i.e.* his long sexual relationship with Shilpa's mother while her husband was out of India, should, at the very least, have put him on inquiry. He had a duty of candour which required him to disclose upon his arrival in Canada in 1993 the strong possibility that he had fathered a child. The panel's assessment of facts was not unreasonable and so it follows that the applicant, a permanent resident, is inadmissible for misrepresentation.

One of the objectives of IRPA, as set out in s. 3, is "to see that families are reunited in Canada," not to remove someone against his will so that he may be reunited with his wife and daughter in India. The panel noted that the applicant had been here for many years, and had been gainfully employed, however, it made no assessment of the job prospects of a 50-year-old man in India, taking into account his obligation to support his wife and child. How the couple manages their affairs is their business. It would appear that they would prefer that the applicant work in Canada. There is nothing preventing him from visiting his wife and daughter in India on a regular basis. Perhaps after he has saved more money, he will return to and retire in India. It was not for the panel to say that they would be better off if reunited in India now. This smacked of "big brotherhood." This aspect of the decision was unreasonable. The matter was referred back to a differently constituted panel for reconsideration.

*Koromila v. Canada (Minister of Citizenship & Immigration)*, 2009 CarswellNat 1167, 2009 FC 393 (F.C.) — The applicant sought judicial review of a decision to refuse an application on H&C grounds pursuant to s. 25 of the IRPA. The applicant's mother died when she was aged 3 and her father never remarried. The applicant and her sister were raised in Greece by their father and their aunt. Their father died of a heart attack when they were teenagers and their aunt continued to care for them. The applicant's sister met a Canadian citizen and immigrated to Canada. The applicant remained in Greece to live and help support her aunt. It was their intention to join her sister and her husband in Canada. Subsequently, the aunt had a very bad stroke and was paralyzed. The applicant remained in Greece to look after her aunt. The aunt died in December 2002. The applicant is alone in Greece and is currently an elderly woman. The applicant says that, as they age, it will become more difficult for her and her sister to visit each other. The applicant applied for permanent residence in Canada in June of 2007 and was refused by the officer.

The officer's stated understanding of the scope of s. 3(1)(d) of the Act is that "the objective of the law was to reunite parents with their children or children with parents or spouses." The officer either misunderstood the scope of s. 3(1)(d) and so fettered his discretion or he made a mistake of law. There was no evidence before the Court that the officer was cognizant of the principle enunciated in paragraph 3(1)(d) of the Act or of the considerations to be taken into account as enunciated in the elements of the OP 4 in considering whether a *de facto* family member should qualify for relief on humanitarian and compassionate considerations. This error was compounded by the officer's assessment that the applicant's coming to Canada permanently was simply a matter of convenience and that the applicant was not a *de facto* family member who had been left behind. The visa officer ignored the evidence of emotional dependency. There is a significant factual difference between living together and sharing day-to-day life and an occasional visit. Such matters seem to have been left entirely out of account by the officer to an unreasonable extent. The officer did not consider the application of subs. 3(1)(d) of the Act to this case. The application for judicial review was allowed.

*Khalil v. R.*, [2007] F.C.J. No. 1221, 317 F.T.R. 32, 160 C.R.R. (2d) 234, 65 Imm. L.R. (3d) 8, 2007 CarswellNat 2910, 2007 CarswellNat 5360, 2007 FC 923; affirmed (2009), 78 Imm. L.R. (3d) 1, 64 C.C.L.T. (3d) 199, 2009 CarswellNat 550, 2009 CarswellNat 1303, 2009 FCA 66 (C.A.) — The plaintiffs alleged that the defendant's delay in processing their application for permanent residence caused some harm for which they claimed damages. They asserted that their entitlement to damages arises from the defendant's negligence and the infringement of their s. 7 and 15 rights under the *Canadian Charter of Rights and Freedoms*. For this infringement, they claim a remedy under subs. 24(1) of the *Charter*. Although the plaintiffs established that there was unreasonable and inordinate delay in the processing of their applications for permanent residence, delay is not a free-standing cause of action. There was insufficient proximity between the plaintiffs and the defendant to find a private law duty of care. Additionally, there are compelling policy reasons that militate against the imposition of such a duty. Even if it were otherwise, causation was not established. Consequently, the plaintiffs could not succeed in negligence. The plaintiffs did not establish that their liberty interests under s. 7 of the *Charter* were engaged on the facts of this matter. The s. 7 security of the person interests are not engaged because the alleged harm is not state imposed.

To impose a private law duty of care on the relationship between the plaintiffs' and the defendant's officials "creates a general potential for serious and significant conflict" with the statutory duty to protect the public interest, including the health and safety of Canadians and the maintenance of the security of Canadian society. In this case, the delay in processing the plaintiffs' application for permanent residence arose in large part as a result of potential inadmissibility under paragraph 34(1)(f) of the IRPA. The purpose of the legislated inadmissibility provisions is protection of the public.

*David v. Canada (Minister of Citizenship & Immigration)*, 2007 CarswellNat 1385, 2007 FC 546 (F.C.) — This was an application for judicial review of a decision of the First Secretary, Immigration, of the Canadian Embassy in the Philippines denying an application for permanent residence based on humanitarian and compassionate grounds. The applicant filed a sponsorship application for his wife and three sons requesting that the application for his wife and eldest son be considered under humanitarian and compassionate grounds and that they be exempted from the application of paragraph 117(9)(d) of the Regulations.

The exclusion mentioned at paragraph 117(9)(d) of the Regulations is a very harsh one, but does not prevent a sponsor from invoking H&C grounds considerations. Indeed, the very reason why the Court of Appeal in *De Guzman* found that this provision is compliant with the international instruments to which Canada is a signatory is that s. 25 of the Act enables the Act to be administered in a compliant manner.

The First Secretary did not make any findings of fact with respect to the evidence tendered by the applicants, such as the relationship between the sponsor and his wife and son, the fact that the sponsor had been supporting the family financially, the frequency of their contact, as well as the letters tendered by various members of the family and others in support of their application. It is clear in this case that the First Secretary did not make a separate assessment for the oldest son's application and as such, did not address his best interest as the child of the sponsor. Instead, he simply stated that the application of the two youngest son's would proceed "but it is sponsor's choice if he wants to split his family further and take his two youngest children from their mother in the Philippines." The officer's notes do not provide a clear rationale of why any of the public policy considerations mentioned by the First Secretary (such as the past misrepresentations) should prevail here over the objective at paragraph 3(1)(d) of the Act "to see that families are reunited in Canada." Nor do they reveal whether the First Secretary considered that the *de facto* family members excluded from the family class because of paragraph 117(9)(d) of the Regulations may suffer hardship indefinitely.



*Nalbandian v. Canada (Minister of Citizenship & Immigration)* (2006), 56 Imm. L.R. (3d) 67, 2006 CarswellNat 2899, 2006 FC 1128 (F.C.) — The applicant sought judicial review of the decision that humanitarian and compassionate considerations did not justify granting the applicant permanent residence in Canada. The applicant was a citizen of Iraq in her late 60s or early 70s. She was a Christian and fled to Jordan with her daughter in 1990 due to horrific circumstances in Iraq. She did not have permanent status in Jordan. The applicant's daughter and her son subsequently fled to the Netherlands and claimed refugee status. Neither was in a position to support immigration of the applicant to the Netherlands. The applicant's three brothers and sisters all fled directly to Canada and were all citizens of Canada. They were well established in Canada and providing economic support to the applicant. They provided a detailed plan to support the applicant's settlement in Canada. The applicant also has 13 nephews and nieces who are all Canadian citizens. While the decision arrived at by the officer might well be open to her, against a standard of review of reasonableness *simpliciter*, and against the terms of paragraph 3(1)(d) of the Act and the guidance provided in OP4 to persons such as the officer, the officer erred in a reviewable manner in not documenting her decision against the prescribed criteria. The judicial review was allowed and the applicant's application for permanent residence in Canada referred back for reconsideration.

Six years elapsed between the filing of the application and a decision which represented "special circumstances" justifying an award of costs.

*R. v. Premakumaran* (2006), 53 Imm. L.R. (3d) 161, [2007] 2 F.C.R. 191, 2006 CarswellNat 1590, 2006 FCA 213 (Fed. C.A.) — The appellants were immigrants to Canada from the United Kingdom who were living comfortably when they began to investigate the idea of coming to Canada. They had relatives in Canada and they believed there was work opportunity for accountants, a field in which Mr. Premakumaran was involved. They were accepted as immigrants in the skilled immigrant category but had difficulty finding suitable work. For eight years they had to do menial work to keep them and their four children alive, causing them severe economic, physical and psychological damage. The appellants instituted a lawsuit alleging fraudulent and negligent misrepresentation causing them financial, physical and psychological harm. They also claim that the false information was disseminated about certain job categories that were supposed to be in high demand and about the use of the processing fees which were charged to applicants for immigration. As remedies, damages were sought for expenses and pain and suffering, as well as a *mandamus* ordering the Federal Court to do certain things to fix the immigration system and to apologize publicly. The defendant brought a motion for summary judgment and the motions judge dismissed the action including the claims of fraudulent and negligent misrepresentation. The Federal Court concluded the motions judge correctly exercised his discretion in dismissing the case in its entirety. There was no evidence of fraud, the complaint about the alleged misuse of the processing fees was unfounded and the unusual remedies sought were not among those available to the Court to grant. No duty of care existed as there was no special relationship of proximity and reliance in this case. There were no personal, specific representations of fact made to these particular appellants upon which they could reasonably have relied. The printed documentation and information given to them was merely general material for them to use in making an application for immigrant status. It is not correct to say that someone "who picks up a brochure or reads a poster at the High Commission is a 'neighbour'" and is owed a duty as a result. More is required. The information given to the appellants contained no guarantees of work, no guarantee of success in the licensing procedure or that any particular assistance would be forthcoming. The appeal was dismissed.

*Paszkowski v. Canada (Attorney General)* (2006), 51 Imm. L.R. (3d) 299, 2006 CarswellNat 359, 2006 FC 198 (F.C.) — The plaintiff claimed that Citizenship and Immigration officials committed torts of public misfeasance and malfeasance by delaying the processing of her June 5, 1990, permanent residence application and that her rights under the *Canadian Charter of Rights and Freedoms* were violated. As a result, the plaintiff claimed that she was deprived of opportunities to become a Canadian citizen, to travel abroad, to continue her education, to earn a living and to have more children.

The plaintiff did not establish, *prima facie*, that she was owed a duty of care by the immigration officials who dealt with her application for permanent residence. The necessary proximity required by the jurisprudence was not established. Specifically, the relationship between the plaintiff and the immigration officers arose from the implementation of the immigration policy imposed by the statute and not as a result of any misfeasance committed by the immigration officers. At the time the decision was made to deny the plaintiff's application, the legislation precluded the admissibility of the plaintiff by reason of her husband's criminal conviction. Neither the legislation nor common law imposed any duty on the immigration officers to inform the plaintiff when the law was changed such as to allow her first application to be processed or to file a fresh application.

*Medovarski v. Canada (Minister of Citizenship & Immigration)*, [2005] 2 S.C.R. 539, 50 Imm. L.R. (3d) 1, 135 C.R.R. (2d) 1, 258 D.L.R. (4th) 193, [2005] S.C.J. No. 31, 339 N.R. 1, EYB 2005-95306, 2005 CarswellNat 2943, 2005 CarswellNat 2944, 2005 SCC 51 — The appellant was a permanent resident and had been ordered deported for serious criminality. Her removal order was automatically stayed when she appealed the deportation order to the Immigration Appeal Division. The appeal was discontinued as a result of s. 196 of the IRPA (a transitional provision), which took away the right to appeal an order for removal unless a party had, under the former Act, been "granted a stay." The trial judge set aside the decision to discontinue. However, the Federal Court of Appeal allowed the Minister of Citizenship and Immigration's appeal, holding that the purpose of the IRPA transitional provision was to deny the right of appeal in the case of an automatic stay. Section 196 of the IRPA, properly interpreted, applies only to actively granted stays. The objectives of the IRPA, as expressed in s. 3, indicate an intent to prioritize security. In keeping with these objectives, the IRPA creates a new scheme whereby a person sentenced to more than six months in prison is inadmissible pursuant to s. 36; if they have been sentenced to a prison term of more than two years, they are denied a right to appeal their removal order under s. 64 of the IRPA. The purpose in enacting the IRPA, and in particular s. 64, was to efficiently remove from the country persons who have engaged in serious criminality. Since s. 196 refers explicitly to s. 64, the transitional provision should be interpreted in light of these legislative objectives.

The deportation of a non-citizen cannot in itself implicate the liberty and security interests protected by s. 7 of the *Canadian Charter of Rights and Freedoms*. Even if the liberty and security of the person were engaged, any unfairness resulting from s. 196 would be inadequate to constitute a breach of principles of fundamental justice.

*Charkaoui, Re*, 2005 CarswellNat 410, 2005 CarswellNat 5111, 2005 FC 258 (F.C.) — This judgment has to do with the fourth review of the detention of Mr. Charkaoui that is provided for in s. 83(2). The Court decided that the phrase "danger to national security" had the same meaning as the phrase "danger to the security of Canada," the meaning of which was discussed in *Suresh v. Canada (Minister of Citizenship & Immigration)*, [2002] 1 S.C.R. 3, at paragraph 90. The other phrase in subs. 83(3) "danger. . .to the safety of any person" includes awareness of danger before the terrorist act occurs. It applies to more than persons who have been convicted of a serious offence. Danger to national security or the safety of any person have in common the fact that Parliament has asked the designated judge when considering the release of the person concerned to analyse the evidence and consider whether either of these two dangers still exist. The wording of the section suggests that a danger to national security or the safety of any person may exist at one moment and not at another. There is a possibility the danger may be imminent but subsequently neutralized. The other phrase used in s. 83 is the phrase "unlikely to appear at a proceeding or for removal". This phrase indicates that Parliament intended a degree of probability to be taken into account by the designated judge when weighing the evidence.

In considering a conditional release, the designated judge must be satisfied, on reasonable grounds, that the person concerned is not a danger to national security or the safety of any person. If there is a danger, the judge cannot consider release, even with exceptional conditions.

When the Ministers signed the warrant for the arrest and detention of Mr. Charkaoui, they did so not in order to lay charges or eventually secure a conviction, but to make an arrest and detention that would prevent events that might occur. This tool, given to the Ministers by Parliament pursuant to subs. 82(1), is intended to "maintain the security of Canadian society" — one of the objectives of immigration as set out in paragraph 3(1)(h).

Detention reviews involve questions of fact peculiar to each situation. In the case at bar, the imprisonment, the passage of time, the media attention to the proceedings, the presence of the family, the community support, and the testimony of the person concerned are examples of situations to be taken into account in assessing whether a danger still exists or whether the person concerned will likely appear at a proceeding or for removal.

The Court set terms for Mr. Charkaoui's release.

*Chen v. Canada (Minister of Citizenship & Immigration)* (2003), 232 F.T.R. 118, 2003 FCT 447, 2003 CarswellNat 2908, 2003 CarswellNat 1052 (Fed. T.D.) — The applicant sought to review a negative decision on a Humanitarian and Compassionate application. In 1959 the applicant and his wife put their daughter in the care of her aunt and uncle



IRP Act

when she was only a baby. In 1961, the aunt and uncle moved from Tianjin to Hong Kong. In order to bring the little girl with them to Hong Kong the aunt and uncle needed to show authorities there a document indicating that the child had been adopted. Therefore, the applicant and his wife signed an agreement to that effect. In 1975, the aunt and uncle immigrated to Canada and brought their adopted daughter with them. The daughter was landed as a dependant daughter and not as an adopted daughter. In 1993, the applicant and his wife were reunited with their daughter. Since their reunification the applicant has been living with his daughter who was providing him with all the necessary care. The officer found that the daughter was not an eligible sponsor as she was not satisfied that a parent/child relationship existed between the applicant and daughter. Under subs. 3(c) of the *Immigration Act*, the immigration objective established is "to facilitate the reunion in Canada of Canadian citizens and permanent residents with their close relatives from abroad." In the new *Immigration and Refugee Protection Act 2001*, at subs. 3(1)(d), the related objective is "to see that families are reunited in Canada". In IRPA, s. 2, the word "relatives" means a person who is related by blood or adoption. There is room for interpretation of the law with respect to the immigration objectives and the new definition of "relative" so as not to preclude a person from sponsoring a biological parent if he or she already has an adoptive parent. There is enough evidence to show that there is a sufficient parent/child relationship to conclude that the immigration officer made a capricious finding of fact, which fettered her discretion.

## Section 3(3)

*Adolph v. Canada (Minister of Public Safety & Emergency Preparedness)* (2009), 357 F.T.R. 216 (Eng.), 2009 FC 1271, 2009 CarswellNat 4277 (F.C.) — This "sad and disturbing" case involved a minor child who remains alone in Canada after having been sent to Toronto by his mother and aunt on a one-way ticket from St. Lucia, purportedly to offer him an opportunity for a better life. To compound this unacceptable situation, two government agencies are working at cross purposes from each other in this case, each claiming to be taking into account the true best interest of the child. A motion to stay the removal procedure was brought pursuant to s. 18.2 of the *Federal Courts Act*. The applicant argued that the enforcement officer ignored compelling factors demonstrating that the best interests of the applicant were such that his removal should be deferred and that the officer failed to take into account Canada's obligations under the *Convention on the Rights of the Child* to provide protection and assistance to the applicant and act in his best interest. The Minister argued that contrary to the allegations of the Children's Aid Society of Toronto the best interests of the applicant do not include an entitlement to remain in Canada to obtain a better life than he would otherwise have in St. Lucia. The Minister also adds that non-citizen parents from foreign countries should not be encouraged to send and abandon their children in Canada in the hopes of better opportunities for them.

The interpretation and application of the *Convention on the Rights of the Child* in circumstances where a child without immigration status is abandoned, and how the Convention is to be taken into account for immigration purposes in such circumstances pursuant to paragraph 3(3)(f) of IRPA raised a serious issue including who should determine the best interest of an abandoned child in such circumstances, the Children's Aid Society or the immigration authorities? Since the Social Services Agency of St. Lucia had not been contacted in order to secure an onsite report on the applicant's family situation and on potential alternative placement solutions in St. Lucia should the return to the family not be deemed feasible, the applicant was deemed to be facing irreparable harm. In light of the fact that a minor child is involved, the Court preferred to act cautiously. Although the Court strongly supported the Minister's contention that citizens from foreign countries should not be encouraged to send and abandon their children in Canada and although the Minister must carry out a removal order as soon as reasonably practical pursuant to subs. 48(2) of IRPA, the particular circumstances of this case required a finding that the balance of convenience lies at this time with the applicant. The stay was granted.



*Okoloubu v. Canada (Minister of Citizenship & Immigration)* (2008), 75 Imm. L.R. (3d) 1, 301 D.L.R. (4th) 591, 382 N.R. 35, 2008 CarswellNat 3852, 2008 CarswellNat 5576, 2008 FCA 326 — The applicant sought an exemption to apply for permanent residence from within Canada. Were it not for a criminal conviction, he would have been entitled to remain in Canada while his application for a permanent resident visa was being considered. However, his conviction disqualified him from being a member of the Spouse or Common-law Partner in Canada class. He argued that protection of the family and the rights of his wife and the child had to be properly considered. The pre-removal risk assessment officer said she did not have jurisdiction to deal with international law and constitutional issues, and that a request for exemption from permanent resident visa requirements was not the proper venue for resolving such complex legal issues. The officer concluded that the applicant's family situation, links within Canadian society, and the risk factors upon his return to his country did not justify an exemption. The applicant successfully had the decision set aside by the Federal Court, which concluded that the officer's refusal to consider the applicant's rights and those of his wife and Canadian child under the *Charter* and the International Convention on Civil and Political Rights resulted in an unfair hearing. The Minister appealed this decision to the Federal Court of Appeal.

The Federal Court of Appeal held that paragraph 3(3)(f) of the IRPA does not require that an officer exercising discretion under s. 25 specifically refer to and analyze the international human rights instruments to which Canada is signatory. It is sufficient if the officer addresses the substance of the issues raised. While the officer stated that she did "not have jurisdiction to deal with international law" it was clear that she addressed in substance the different and important interests at stake, giving careful weight to the interest of the child and the importance of the family unit. Therefore, the Federal Court of Appeal's intervention was not warranted and it became unnecessary to address the Federal Court Judge's finding that the respondent was deprived a fair hearing. The Federal Court of Appeal found that the certified question "Does an immigration officer in charge of assessing an application under s. 25 of the *Immigration Refugee and Protection Act* (for an exemption from the obligation to present an application for an immigrant visa from outside Canada) have jurisdiction to consider whether an applicant's removal would breach the *International Covenant on Civil and Political Rights*, more specifically Article 17, 23 and 24?" was irrelevant and not dispositive of the appeal and therefore it need not be answered. The appeal was allowed, the judgment of the Federal Court set aside and the applicant's application for judicial review dismissed.

*Thiara v. Canada (Minister of Citizenship & Immigration)* (2008), 70 Imm. L.R. (3d) 80, 2008 FCA 151, 2008 CarswellNat 1220 (F.C.A.) — Paragraph 3(3)(f) of the IRPA does not require that an officer exercising discretion under s. 25 of the Act specifically refer to and analyze the international human rights instruments to which Canada is a signatory. It is sufficient if the officer addresses the substance of the issues raised.

*Charkaoui, Re* (2003), 38 Imm. L.R. (3d) 56, [2004] 3 F.C.R. 32, 253 F.T.R. 22, 2003 CarswellNat 3887, 2003 CarswellNat 4312, 2003 FC 1419 (F.C.) — The applicant was questioning the validity of several provisions of IRPA which establish a procedure for determining whether a permanent resident is a danger to national security or the safety of any person.

One of IRPA's objectives is to maintain the security of Canadian society. One method that Parliament has given the Ministers to accomplish this objective is to sign a certificate that renders the person concerned inadmissible to Canada. The signing of this certificate is a ministerial power that cannot be delegated. The certificate must be signed by the Minister of Citizenship and Immigration and by the Solicitor General, after which it is filed with the Federal Court.

Another method created by Parliament to maintain the security of Canadian society is the signing of an arrest warrant by the Ministers. The signing of this warrant is a non-delegated ministerial power. In order to sign such a warrant both Ministers must have reasonable grounds to believe that the person concerned is a danger to national security or the safety of any person or is unlikely to appear at a proceeding for removal.

Subsection 3(3) and paragraph 78(c) of the IRPA confer on the designated judge the power to decide constitutional questions. IRPA gives the designated judge jurisdiction over the person concerned and the subject matter as well as the power to order a remedy.

The judgement of a designated judge deciding constitutional questions can be appealed under s. 27 of the *Federal Courts Act*.

Given the distinction that the *Charter* draws between citizens and non-citizens, Parliament is entitled to enact a policy establishing rules that a permanent resident must follow in order to be able to enter and remain in Canada. Sections 33 *et seq.* of the IRPA provide that a permanent resident can be declared inadmissible if there are reasonable grounds to believe that the permanent resident is a danger to the security of Canada; that he has participated directly in war crimes or crimes against humanity; was a senior official in the government that committed war crimes or crimes against humanity; he has been convicted of an offence punishable by a term of imprisonment of at least 10 years, or for which a term of imprisonment of more than 6 months was imposed; he has been a member of an organization that has engaged in or is engaging in organized crime; or he made misrepresentations on his application for immigration or was sponsored by a person who made misrepresentations about him.

National security is essential for the preservation of our democratic society. We live in an era when threats to our democracy frequently come from unconventional acts that cannot be detected by unsophisticated investigations or traditional means. The methods used to obtain protected information must not be revealed. At the same time, a permanent resident must be reasonably informed of the reasons for which the Ministers have determined that he is a danger to national security. This is essential to ensure that the person concerned has the opportunity to defend himself.

The procedures established by s. 76 to 85 of the IRPA take the existence of opposing interests into consideration and strike an acceptable balance between those interests. The fact that a designated judge is involved in striking this balance adds credibility to the procedure and ensures objectivity in achieving the result.

The designated judge must analyze the evidence as a whole and determine whether it provides reasonable grounds to believe there are reasons justifying the inadmissibility or arrest warrant and continued detention of the person concerned. There must be a serious possibility that the facts exist based on reliable and credible evidence.

The system of preventative detention established by Parliament in the IRPA, in regard to persons concerned who in the opinion of the Ministers represent a danger to national security or to the safety of any person, are consistent with the *Charter*.

Sections 77, 80, 81, 82, 83 and 85 of the IRPA do not contravene the rights guaranteed by s. 15 of the *Charter* or the rights guaranteed by paragraph 1(b) of the Canadian Bill of Rights.

The expressions "danger to the national security of Canada" and "members" referred to in subs. 83(3) and paragraph 34(1)(d) of the IRPA are not vague or overbroad. Subsections 80(3) and 84 of the IRPA do not contravene s. 96 of the *British North America Act*.



## ENABLING AUTHORITY

**4. (1) Minister of Citizenship and Immigration — Except as otherwise provided in this section, the Minister of Citizenship and Immigration is responsible for the administration of this Act.**

**(1.1) Designated Minister — The Governor in Council may, by order, designate a minister of the Crown as the Minister responsible for all matters under this Act relating to special advocates. If none is designated, the Minister of Justice is responsible for those matters.**

**(2) Minister of Public Safety and Emergency Preparedness — The Minister of Public Safety and Emergency Preparedness is responsible for the administration of this Act as it relates to**

> **(a) examinations at ports of entry;**
>
> **(b) the enforcement of this Act, including arrest, detention and removal;**
>
> **(c) the establishment of policies respecting the enforcement of this Act and inadmissibility on grounds of security, organized criminality or violating human or international rights; or**
>
> **(d) determinations under any of subsections 34(2), 35(2) and 37(2).**

**(3) Specification — Subject to subsections (1) to (2), the Governor in Council may, by order,**

> **(a) specify which Minister referred to in any of subsections (1) to (2) is the Minister for the purposes of any provision of this Act; and**
>
> **(b) specify that more than one Minister may be the Minister for the purposes of any provision of this Act and specify the circumstances under which each Minister is the Minister.**

**(4) Publication — Any order made under subsection (3) must be published in Part II of the *Canada Gazette*.**

2005, c. 38, s. 118; 2008, c. 3, s. 1

### Case Law

*Paszkowski v. Canada (Attorney General)* (2006), 51 Imm. L.R. (3d) 299, 2006 CarswellNat 359, 2006 FC 198 (F.C.) — The plaintiff claimed that Citizenship and Immigration officials committed torts of public misfeasance and malfeasance by delaying the processing of her June 5, 1990, permanent residence application and that her rights under the *Canadian Charter of Rights and Freedoms* were violated. As a result, the plaintiff claimed that she was deprived of opportunities to become a Canadian citizen, to travel abroad, to continue her education, to earn a living and to have more children.

The plaintiff did not establish, *prima facie*, that she was owed a duty of care by the immigration officials who dealt with her application for permanent residence. The necessary proximity required by the jurisprudence was not established. Specifically, the relationship between the plaintiff and the immigration officers arose from the implementation of the immigration policy imposed by the statute and not as a result of any misfeasance committed by the immigration officers. At the time the decision was made to deny the plaintiff's application, the legislation precluded the admissibility of the plaintiff by reason of her husband's criminal conviction. Neither the legislation nor common law imposed any duty on the immigration officers to inform the plaintiff when the law was changed such as to allow her first application to be processed or to file a fresh application.

**5. (1) Regulations — Except as otherwise provided, the Governor in Council may make any regulation that is referred to in this Act or that prescribes any matter whose prescription is referred to in this Act.**

**(2) Tabling and referral of proposed regulations — The Minister shall cause a copy of each proposed regulation made under sections 17, 32, 53, 61, 87.2, 102, 116, 150 and 150.1 to be laid before each House of Parliament, and each House shall refer the proposed regulation to the appropriate Committee of that House.**

**(3) Alteration of proposed regulation — A proposed regulation that has been laid before each House of Parliament under subsection (2) does not need to be so laid again, whether or not it has been altered.**

**(4) Making of regulations — The Governor in Council may make the regulation at any time after the proposed regulation has been laid before each House of Parliament under subsection (2).**

2004, c. 15, s. 70; 2008, c. 3, s. 2

## Case Law

*Vaziri v. Canada (Minister of Citizenship & Immigration)* (2006), 55 Imm. L.R. (3d) 247, 52 Admin. L.R. (4th) 118, 2006 CarswellNat 3014, 2006 FC 1159 (F.C.) — A father and son jointly applied to the Court for an order of *mandamus* requiring the Minister of Citizenship and Immigration to render a decision on the father's sponsored application for permanent residence.

The applicants assert that consideration of their applications was severely and negatively impacted beginning in 2001 or 2002 when the Minister, acting administratively, established target levels for immigration to Canada that incorporated a 60:40 ratio between the economic and non-economic classes. The Minister placed further restrictions on the processing of applications for parents and grandparents by giving priority to spouses and dependent children within the family class. The effect was the sponsorship applications for parents and grandparents have been processed at much slower rates. The applicants submit that the Minister had no legal authority to establish the targets or to put into place a process that seriously detracts from the rights of parents and grandparents to become sponsored permanent residents, unless authorized by regulation made under s. 14(2) of the IRPA. There are no such regulations.

There is no dispute that the Minister and CIC, as public bodies, can only act within the constraints of their legislated jurisdiction, since their authority derives from statute. The Court concluded that there is nothing in the IRPA or the Regulations that appears to detract from the Minister's power to manage the immigration flow on the basis of social and economic policy considerations. In the absence of regulations made under s. 14(2) of the IRPA, the Minister acted lawfully in establishing the 60:40 ratio, in establishing targets for visa approvals by class and in setting procedures for prioritizing sponsored applications within the family class. While the Governor in Council may make regulations to address all of these matters, there is no obligation on the Governor in Council to do so. The existence of a non-mandatory Governor in Council regulation-making power does not preclude the Minister responsible for the administration of the IRPA from taking these policies in administrative decisions. The applicants did not satisfy the Court that the discretionary remedy of *mandamus* should be granted.

Although several questions were certified, the Federal Court of Appeal did not hear the appeal, since the Minister issued the applicant a visa, rendering the appeal moot.



**6. (1) Designation of officers — The Minister may designate any persons or class of persons as officers to carry out any purpose of any provision of this Act, and shall specify the powers and duties of the officers so designated.**

**(2) Delegation of powers — Anything that may be done by the Minister under this Act may be done by a person that the Minister authorizes in writing, without proof of the authenticity of the authorization.**

**(3) Exception — Notwithstanding subsection (2), the Minister may not delegate the power conferred by subsection 77(1) or the ability to make determinations under subsection 34(2) or 35(2) or paragraph 37(2)(a).**

## Case Law

*Khalil v. R.*, [2007] F.C.J. No. 1221, 317 F.T.R. 32, 160 C.R.R. (2d) 234, 65 Imm. L.R. (3d) 8, 2007 CarswellNat 2910, 2007 CarswellNat 5360, 2007 FC 923; affirmed (2009), 78 Imm. L.R. (3d) 1, 64 C.C.L.T. (3d) 199, 2009 CarswellNat 550, 2009 CarswellNat 1303, 2009 FCA 66 (C.A.) — The plaintiffs alleged that the defendant's delay in processing their application for permanent residence caused some harm for which they claimed damages. They asserted that their entitlement to damages arises from the defendant's negligence and the infringement of their s. 7 and 15 rights under the *Canadian Charter of Rights and Freedoms*. For this infringement, they claim a remedy under subs. 24(1) of the *Charter*. Although the plaintiffs established that there was unreasonable and inordinate delay in the processing of their applications for permanent residence, delay is not a free-standing cause of action. There was insufficient proximity between the plaintiffs and the defendant to find a private law duty of care. Additionally, there are compelling policy reasons that militate against the imposition of such a duty. Even if it were otherwise, causation was not established. Consequently, the plaintiffs could not succeed in negligence. The plaintiffs did not establish that their liberty interests under s. 7 of the *Charter* were engaged on the facts of this matter. The s. 7 security of the person interests are not engaged because the alleged harm is not state imposed.

To impose a private law duty of care on the relationship between the plaintiffs' and the defendant's officials "creates a general potential for serious and significant conflict" with the statutory duty to protect the public interest, including the health and safety of Canadians and the maintenance of the security of Canadian society. In this case, the delay in processing the plaintiffs' application for permanent residence arose in large part as a result of potential inadmissibility under paragraph 34(1)(f) of the IRPA. The purpose of the legislated inadmissibility provisions is protection of the public.

*Szebenyi v. R.*, 2007 CarswellNat 660, 2007 FCA 118 (Fed. C.A.) — This was an appeal from the Federal Court wherein the action by the appellant against the respondent seeking $6,000,000 in damages for alleged negligence in the handling of his mother's sponsorship application was dismissed. The trial judge concluded that the facts did not give rise to an action in tort against the respondent. Although the appellant had suffered depression, the trial judge was not prepared to conclude that this condition or any emotional stress suffered by the appellant was caused by the servants or agents of the respondent. The trial judge concluded that the respondent owed no duty of care to the appellant in the circumstances. The trial judge found that the appellant had no right to issuance of a visa to his mother, but only to make the sponsorship application and to appeal a negative decision in respect of the application to the Immigration Appeal Division. In these circumstances, there was an insufficiently close relationship between the respondent and the appellant to give rise to a *prima facie* duty of care. There was no basis to depart from the conclusion of the trial judge.

*Samimifar v. Canada (Minister of Citizenship & Immigration)*, [2006] F.C.J. No. 1626, 58 Imm. L.R. (3d) 24, 2006 CarswellNat 5309, 2006 FC 1301 (F.C.) — The applicant was granted approval-in-principle to accept and process an application for permanent residence from within Canada. He submitted his application in 1994 and until January 2003, his application appears to have been subject to inattention, inaction and delay for reasons which he alleges amount to negligence and breach of his s. 7 *Charter* rights. In January 2003, he was informed that his PR application was refused on the basis of inadmissibility to Canada under s. 34(1)(f) of the IRPA because there were reasonable grounds to believe he was a member of a terrorist organization.

In addition to pursuing his administrative efforts to become a permanent resident, the applicant commenced an action against the Minister of Citizenship and Immigration by filing a Statement of Claim. The respondent brought a motion seeking summary judgment to dismiss all or part of the claim. The Court concluded that the policy considerations did not preclude the imposition of the duty of care where an immigration officer completely ignores a file. At trial, it may be possible for the defendant to be able to provide a satisfactory explanation as to why this matter languished for at least seven years. However, given the unusual nature of the claim involving allegations against a particular immigration officer in the context of the harm allegedly suffered by the applicant, the action should not be summarily dismissed on broad policy grounds.

*Paszkowski v. Canada (Attorney General)* (2006), 51 Imm. L.R. (3d) 299, 2006 CarswellNat 359, 2006 FC 198 (F.C.) — The plaintiff claimed that Citizenship and Immigration officials committed torts of public misfeasance and malfeasance by delaying the processing of her June 5, 1990, permanent residence application and that her rights under the *Canadian Charter of Rights and Freedoms* were violated. As a result, the plaintiff claimed that she was deprived of opportunities to become a Canadian citizen, to travel abroad, to continue her education, to earn a living and to have more children.

The plaintiff did not establish, *prima facie*, that she was owed a duty of care by the immigration officials who dealt with her application for permanent residence. The necessary proximity required by the jurisprudence was not established. Specifically, the relationship between the plaintiff and the immigration officers arose from the implementation of the immigration policy imposed by the statute and not as a result of any misfeasance committed by the immigration officers. At the time the decision was made to deny the plaintiff's application, the legislation precluded the admissibility of the plaintiff by reason of her husband's criminal conviction. Neither the legislation nor common law imposed any duty on the immigration officers to inform the plaintiff when the law was changed such as to allow her first application to be processed or to file a fresh application.



## AGREEMENTS

**7. International agreements — The Minister, with the approval of the Governor in Council, may enter into an agreement with the government of a foreign state or with an international organization for the purposes of this Act.**

**8. (1) Federal-provincial agreements — The Minister, with the approval of the Governor in Council, may enter into an agreement with the government of any province for the purposes of this Act. The Minister must publish, once a year, a list of the federal-provincial agreements that are in force.**

**(2) Consistency with agreement — Subject to subsection (3) but despite the other provisions of this Act, the following must be consistent with the federal-provincial agreements:**

**(a) the selection and sponsorship of, and the acquisition of status by, foreign nationals under this Act; and**

**(b) regulations governing those matters, including regulations respecting the examination in Canada of applications to become a permanent resident, or respecting the foreign nationals who may be selected on the basis of an investment in Canada.**

**(3) Inadmissibility not limited — Subsection (2) is not to be interpreted as limiting the application of any provision of this Act concerning inadmissibility to Canada.**

**9. (1) Sole provincial responsibility — permanent residents — Where a province has, under a federal-provincial agreement, sole responsibility for the selection of a foreign national who intends to reside in that province as a permanent resident, the following provisions apply to that foreign national, unless the agreement provides otherwise:**

**(a) the foreign national, unless inadmissible under this Act, shall be granted permanent resident status if the foreign national meets the province's selection criteria;**

**(b) the foreign national shall not be granted permanent resident status if the foreign national does not meet the province's selection criteria;**

**(c) the foreign national shall not be granted permanent resident status contrary to the provisions of the law of the province governing the number of foreign nationals who may settle in the province as permanent residents, whether that number is an estimate or a maximum, or governing the distribution of that number among classes of foreign nationals; and**

**(d) conditions imposed in accordance with the law of the province have the same force and effect as if they were made under this Act, if they are imposed on a foreign national on or before the grant of permanent resident status.**

*[Editor's Note: SOR/2002-227, s. 328(1) provides that a person who was a permanent resident immediately before June 28, 2002 is a permanent resident under the new* Immigration and Refugee Protection Act, *S.C. 2001, c. 27.]*

**(2) Sole provincial responsibility — appeals — If a federal-provincial agreement gives a province sole responsibility to establish and apply financial criteria with respect to undertakings that sponsors living in that province may make in respect of a foreign national who applies to become a permanent resident, then, unless the agreement provides otherwise, the existence of a right of appeal under the law of that province respecting rejections by provincial officials of applications for sponsorship, for reasons of failing to meet financial criteria or failing to comply with a prior undertaking, prevents the sponsor, except on humanitarian and compassionate grounds, from appealing under this Act against a refusal, based on those reasons, of a visa or permanent resident status.**

**10. (1) Consultations with the provinces — The Minister may consult with the governments of the provinces on immigration and refugee protection policies and programs, in order to facilitate cooperation and to take into consideration the effects that the implementation of this Act may have on the provinces.**

**(2) Required consultations — The Minister must consult with the governments of the provinces respecting the number of foreign nationals in each class who will become permanent residents each year, their distribution in Canada taking into account regional economic and demographic requirements, and the measures to be undertaken to facilitate their integration into Canadian society.**

# PART 1 — IMMIGRATION TO CANADA

## DIVISION 1 — REQUIREMENTS BEFORE ENTERING CANADA AND SELECTION

### *Requirements Before Entering Canada*

**11. (1) Application before entering Canada — A foreign national must, before entering Canada, apply to an officer for a visa or for any other document required by the regulations. The visa or document may be issued if, following an examination, the officer is satisfied that the foreign national is not inadmissible and meets the requirements of this Act.**

**(2) If sponsor does not meet requirements — The officer may not issue a visa or other document to a foreign national whose sponsor does not meet the sponsorship requirements of this Act.**

2008, c. 28, s. 116

## Case Law

### Section 11(1)

*Abbasi v. Canada (Minister of Citizenship & Immigration)* (2010), 88 Imm. L.R. (3d) 174, 2010 FC 288, 2010 CarswellNat 1675, 2010 CarswellNat 560 (F.C.) — The applicant challenged a refusal of a visa officer to grant him a permanent resident visa as a member of the family class. The applicant was a Pakistan national being sponsored for landing in Canada by his wife. The refusal of the sponsorship application was based on the finding that the marriage was not genuine. Two grounds were advanced for setting aside the visa officer's decision: the finding that the marriage is not genuine is unreasonable; and that the process applied to reaching the decision offends the *Official Languages Act*, R.S.C. 1985, c. 31 (4th Supp.), because the visa officer's interview of the applicant was conducted in Urdu.

The circumstances of the marriage were unusual which, not surprisingly, raised suspicion. But the unusual circumstances should give cause for very careful consideration. A marriage is a union between two individuals, and where suspicion exists as to the genuineness of the union because an expected standard of conduct is not met, to fairly and properly deal with the suspicion, the evidence of each individual must be carefully considered. There is no evidence on the record that the visa officer provided the applicant's spouse with an opportunity to give her evidence with respect to the quality of the marriage before the decision under review was made. In a case such as this, the visa officer was required to interview both the applicant and his spouse by the best means available whether by teleconference, video conference, or personal interview. The decision under review was unreasonable.

In this case there was no breach of the *Official Languages Act*. The interview was conducted in Urdu at the applicant's request. This choice was confirmed by the visa officer at the opening of the interview. No interpreter was required as the visa officer was fluent in this language. The applicant argued that as a matter of law the visa officer was required to conduct the interview in either English or French through an interpreter who could interpret the visa officer's questions to the applicant in Urdu and his answers back in English or French to the visa officer.

Section 20(1) of the *Charter* provides a right to any member of the public in Canada to communicate with and receive available services from federal institutions in English and French. This right imposes an obligation and practical requirement on federal institutions to comply with the right. This rights based concept does not inhibit federal institutions to offer services in languages other than English or French if the members of the public involved do not wish to exercise their right under s. 20(1) of the *Charter*, and, indeed wish to conduct business in any other language to which the institution's officials are capable of reliably communicating without an interpreter. This point was made by Justice Pinard in *Toma v. Canada (Minister of Citizenships & Immigration)*, [2006] F.C.J. No.

1000 at paragraph 33 where a visa officer conducted an interview in Arabic without an interpreter:

> If the officer speaks the applicant's language — as was the case here — it would be strange indeed for the officer to use an interpreter. There would be no need to do so. The preferable options, as the Manual suggests [Overseas Processing Manual (OP) 5], is to conduct the interview in the applicant's language.

The application for judicial review was allowed on the first ground. The following question was certified:

> Is it a breach of the *Official Languages Act* for a visa officer to conduct an interview with respect to a visa application when, at the applicant's request, the language of the interview was other than English or French and the visa officer is able to comply with the request?

*Lopez v. Canada (Minister of Citizenship & Immigration)*, 2008 CarswellNat 1325, 2008 CarswellNat 1326, 2008 FC 582 — This was the judicial review of a PRRA officer's dismissal of an application for permanent residence made from within Canada. The officer failed to take into account that s. 25 of the IRPA is driven either on humanitarian and compassionate considerations or public policy considerations. Put another way, is it Canada's public policy that a person who is not inadmissible in terms of the United Nations Convention Relating to the Status of Refugees and whose record of criminality in Canada cannot be considered because of the pardon granted to him (s. 36(3) IRPA) should nevertheless have to busk in the Montreal Metro for the rest of his life without legal status? The decision of the PRRA officer was an important one which affected the applicant's life in a fundamental way. In this case, the officer failed to assure himself that there was a public policy consideration present. The question was not whether there would be an unusual, underserved or disproportionate hardship if the applicant had to leave Canada. The truth was that he cannot leave Canada since Cuba won't take him back and the authorities know it. The applicant had not applied for permanent residence from abroad because he could not. The application for judicial review was granted and the matter referred back to another officer for redetermination.

*Tantash v. Canada (Minister of Citizenship & Immigration)*, 2008 CarswellNat 1366, 2008 FC 565 — The applicant sought judicial review of a decision to refuse his application for permanent residence in Canada under the economic skilled workers class, on the ground that he had not submitted the requested documents, and he was therefore inadmissible. Although the applicant made a request for an extension of time to submit an FBI clearance, at no time did the applicant attempt to provide the officer with reasons for the lengthy wait in providing the FBI clearances, nor did he provide her with any timeframe in which he anticipated receiving the documents.

The refusal resulted from the applicant's failure to provide the officer with the evidence and documents that were reasonably required. Reasonable timeframes must be respected in order to allow that applications be processed in an expeditious manner. Therefore, the officer's decision to refuse the application and refuse any further extension of time was free of any breach of procedural fairness or natural justice.

*Tran v. Canada (Minister of Citizenship & Immigration)* (2006), 59 Imm. L.R. (3d) 217, 2006 CarswellNat 3833, 2006 FC 1377 (F.C.) — The applicant sought to overturn the decision of an immigration officer who denied his application for a study permit. The visa officer was not satisfied that he was either a *bona fide* student or a *bona fide* temporary resident, sufficiently well established in Vietnam, that he would leave Canada after his authorized stay in Canada. Procedural protection that arises in the context of a student visa application is "relaxed." In other words, there is no clear requirement that an applicant be permitted to respond to an officer's concerns as they arise. Immigration manuals are primary guidelines for the assistance of the visa officers in the assessment of applications for either permanent residence or temporary visas. As such, manuals cannot be relied upon by applicants to argue lack of fairness simply because the officer did not strictly adhere to the guidelines found in the manual in question. It is trite law that the onus is on the applicant to provide a visa officer with all relevant information and documentation to satisfy the visa officer that the applicant meets the statutory requirements of the IRPA and the Regulations. In this case, the visa officer conducted a fulsome and diligent assessment of the applicant's application for a study permit. The visa officer considered a variety of factors in her assessment, including the low income of the applicant's parents in Vietnam and no proof of their employment, income or any assets. The fact that the same type of education is available locally and at a fraction of the cost is a relevant factor in determining the credibility and intentions of a potential foreign student. It was not patently unreasonable for the visa officer to consider the availability of similar courses in Vietnam and South Asia at a much less cost. The applicant's very weak English and his inability to carry even a basic conversation in English, as was revealed during his telephone conversation with the case analyst and reflected in the CAIPS notes, was a relevant factor for the visa officer to consider, given that his acceptance into Algonquin College was conditional upon him meeting the English language requirement. There were no reviewable errors in the visa officer's refusal to issue a study permit. The application for judicial review was dismissed.

*Dhoot v. Canada (Minister of Citizenship & Immigration)*, [2006] F.C.J. No. 1625, 57 Imm. L.R. (3d) 153, 2006 CarswellNat 3480, 2006 FC 1295 (F.C.) — This is an application for judicial review of a visa officer's decision of the applicant's application for a permanent resident visa which was denied on the basis that the applicant failed to attend an interview scheduled on October 26, 2005. The applicant states that he was never informed of the interview. The visa officer insisted that the notice of the interview was provided to the applicant by letter dated August 19, 2005.

The visa officer, for whatever reason, did not send the notice by mail as would be expected given the significantly prejudicial impact non-delivery would have on the applicant's interest in obtaining a permanent resident visa. It is reasonable to expect that there will be mistakes by the respondent when dealing with thousands of immigration files. When the evidence shows that there has been such a mistake the Court expects that the respondent cure the mistake, *i.e.*, invite the applicant to attend another interview. It was wrong for the respondent, in a case such as this, to oppose the applicant's court case. The application for judicial review was allowed and the applicant was awarded legal costs.

*Wong v. Canada (Minister of Citizenship & Immigration)*, 2006 CarswellNat 3951, 2006 FC 1410 (F.C.) — In deciding whether to grant the applicant an exemption from the processing requirements under subs. 11(1) of the IRPA, the decision maker erred in placing undue emphasis on the applicant's suspected medical inadmissibility and potential for establishment in Canada. The decision maker's assessment of these factors ought to have been deferred until the second stage of the H&C application. The decision to deny the applicant's application on humanitarian and compassionate grounds for an exemption from their requirement to obtain an immigration visa before coming to Canada was quashed.

*Adegbayi v. Canada (Minister of Citizenship & Immigration)*, 2004 CarswellNat 5097, 2004 CarswellNat 3436, 2004 FC 1348 (F.C.) — This was an application to review a negative H&C decision. The officer who made the decision had concerns about whether the applicant and her spouse were in fact cohabiting. Procedural fairness dictated that the officer should have given the applicant an opportunity to address this concern.

*Khan v. Canada (Minister of Citizenship & Immigration)*, 2003 CarswellNat 113, 2003 CarswellNat 664, 2003 FCT 58, 2003 CFPI 58 (Fed. T.D.) — The applicants sought to review a negative decision by a visa officer refusing their immigration application in the investor category. At the interview, the applicants were unable to provide proof of ownership for a business that they claimed to own, nor were they able to provide balance sheets, accountants' reports or income tax returns.

There is a statutory obligation on an applicant to establish that she and her dependents are qualified for admission to Canada in accord with the Act and Regulations relating to investors. All of the instructions sent with the call-in notice did not warrant a conclusion that the visa officer failed to meet her obligation to fairly consider the application by the principal applicant. The officer had no obligation to provide an opportunity for the applicants to bolster their application by the submission of documents that in a normal course were required to be submitted before or at the interview.

## *Selection of Permanent Residents*

**12. (1) Family reunification — A foreign national may be selected as a member of the family class on the basis of their relationship as the spouse, common-law partner, child, parent or other prescribed family member of a Canadian citizen or permanent resident.**

**(2) Economic immigration — A foreign national may be selected as a member of the economic class on the basis of their ability to become economically established in Canada.**

**(3) Refugees — A foreign national, inside or outside Canada, may be selected as a person who under this Act is a Convention refugee or as a person in similar circumstances, taking into account Canada's humanitarian tradition with respect to the displaced and the persecuted.**

## *Sponsorship of Foreign Nationals*

**13. (1) Right to sponsor family member — A Canadian citizen or permanent resident may, subject to the regulations, sponsor a foreign national who is a member of the family class.**

**(2) Group right to sponsor — A group of Canadian citizens or permanent residents, a corporation incorporated under a law of Canada or of a province, and an unincorporated organization or association under federal or provincial law, or any combination of them may, subject to the regulations, sponsor a Convention refugee or a person in similar circumstances.**

**(3) Obligation — An undertaking relating to sponsorship is binding on the person who gives it.**

**(4) Instructions of Minister — An officer shall apply the regulations on sponsorship referred to in paragraph 14(2)(e) in accordance with any instructions that the Minister may make.**

## Case Law

### Section 13(3)

*Manitoba v. Barkman* (2007), 213 Man. R. (2d) 273, 2007 CarswellMan 86, 2007 MBQB 54 (Q.B.) — The plaintiff sued the defendant to recover the amount of income assistance payments which the plaintiff paid to immigrants sponsored by the defendant pursuant to an "undertaking of assistance," whereby the defendant undertook to provide and guaranteed their maintenance or support. The defendant maintains that the immigrants did not need to apply for social assistance; that any application for such was made at the instance of agents of the plaintiff. The defendant had sponsored his wife and four children. His wife and the children abruptly left. The defendant submitted that his wife and the children did not need to go on income assistance because he was always prepared to support them. The plaintiff's officials were quite right in concluding that the defendant's wife was genuinely in need of income assistance. The plaintiff did not follow their policy with respect to notifying the sponsor by registered mail (or at all) that legal action may be taken to recover the assistance as a result of the sponsor's breach of the undertaking. The plaintiff obtained judgment against the defendant.

## *Regulations*

**14. (1) Regulations — The regulations may provide for any matter relating to the application of this Division, and may define, for the purposes of this Act, the terms used in this Division.**

**(2) Regulations — The regulations may prescribe, and govern any matter relating to, classes of permanent residents or foreign nationals, including the classes referred to in section 12, and may include provisions respecting**

**(a) selection criteria, the weight, if any, to be given to all or some of those criteria, the procedures to be followed in evaluating all or some of those criteria and the circumstances in which an officer may substitute for those criteria their evaluation of the likelihood of a foreign national's ability to become economically established in Canada;**

**(b) applications for visas and other documents and their issuance or refusal, with respect to foreign nationals and their family members;**

**(c) the number of applications that may be processed or approved in a year, the number of visas and other documents that may be issued in a year, and the measures to be taken when that number is exceeded;**

**(d) conditions that may or must be imposed, varied or cancelled, individually or by class, on permanent residents and foreign nationals;**

**(e) sponsorships, undertakings, and penalties for failure to comply with undertakings;**

**(f) deposits or guarantees of the performance of obligations under this Act that are to be given by any person to the Minister; and**

**(g) any matter for which a recommendation to the Minister or a decision may or must be made by a designated person, institution or organization with respect to a foreign national or sponsor.**

## Case Law

*Vaziri v. Canada (Minister of Citizenship & Immigration)* (2006), 55 Imm. L.R. (3d) 247, 52 Admin. L.R. (4th) 118, 2006 CarswellNat 3014, 2006 FC 1159 (F.C.) — A father and son jointly applied to the Court for an order of *mandamus* requiring the Minister of Citizenship and Immigration to render a decision on the father's sponsored application for permanent residence.

The applicants assert that consideration of their applications was severely and negatively impacted beginning in 2001 or 2002 when the Minister, acting administratively, established target levels for immigration to Canada that incorporated a 60:40 ratio between the economic and non-economic classes. The Minister placed further restrictions on the processing of applications for parents and grandparents by giving priority to spouses and dependent children within the family class. The effect was the sponsorship applications for parents and grandparents have been processed at much slower rates. The applicants submit that the Minister had no legal authority to establish the targets or to put into place a process that seriously detracts from the rights of parents and grandparents to become sponsored permanent residents, unless authorized by regulation made under s. 14(2) of the IRPA. There are no such regulations.

There is no dispute that the Minister and CIC, as public bodies, can only act within the constraints of their legislated jurisdiction, since their authority derives from statute. The Court concluded that there is nothing in the IRPA or the Regulations that appears to detract from the Minister's power to manage the immigration flow on the basis of social and economic policy considerations. In the absence of regulations made under s. 14(2) of the IRPA, the Minister acted lawfully in establishing the 60:40 ratio, in establishing targets for visa approvals by class and in setting procedures for prioritizing sponsored applications within the family class. While the Governor in Council may make regulations to address all of these matters, there is no obligation on the Governor in Council to do so. The existence of a non-mandatory Governor in Council regulation-making power does not preclude the Minister responsible for the administration of the IRPA from taking these policies in administrative decisions. The applicants did not satisfy the Court that the discretionary remedy of *mandamus* should be granted.

Although several questions were certified, the Federal Court of Appeal did not hear the appeal, since the Minister issued the applicant a visa, rendering the appeal moot.

## DIVISION 2 — EXAMINATION

**15. (1) Examination by officer — An officer is authorized to proceed with an examination where a person makes an application to the officer in accordance with this Act.**

**(2) Provincial criteria — In the case of a foreign national referred to in subsection 9(1), an examination of whether the foreign national complies with the applicable selection criteria shall be conducted solely on the basis of documents delivered**

**by the province indicating that the competent authority of the province is of the opinion that the foreign national complies with the province's selection criteria.**

(3) **Inspection — An officer may board and inspect any means of transportation bringing persons to Canada, examine any person carried by that means of transportation and any record or document respecting that person, seize and remove the record or document to obtain copies or extracts and hold the means of transportation until the inspection and the examination are completed.**

*[Editor's Note: SOR/2002-227, s. 332 provides that a thing seized under the former* Immigration Act, *R.S.C. 1985, c. I-2 continues to be seized on June 28, 2002, and the seizure is governed by the provisions of the new* Immigration and Refugee Protection Act, *S.C. 2001, c. 27.]*

(4) **Instructions — The officer shall conduct the examination in accordance with any instructions that the Minister may give.**



## Case Law

### Section 15(1)

*R. v Ellis* (2009), 82 Imm. L.R. (3d) 142, 194 C.R.R. (2d) 94, 2009 ONCJ 319, 2009 CarswellOnt 4002 (Ont. C.J.) — The accused was charged with two counts of entering Canada without the required visa, and misrepresentation or withholding facts of his loss of status as a U.S. Resident Alien contrary to ss. 124(1)(a) and 127(a) of IRPA. This is a ruling on the admissibility of a disputed item of evidence sought to be tendered by the Crown. The Crown submitted that the conversation between a senior immigration officer and the accused heard in *voir dire* ought to be admitted. Defence counsel submitted that the conversation was inadmissible as it was a compelled statement taken in violation of s. 7 and s. 10(b) of the *Canadian Charter of Rights and Freedoms* before the accused could implement his right to counsel.

The *Immigration and Refugee Protection Act* requires that persons answer the questions of the immigration officials at the point of entry to Canada, and such statements are the product of statutory compulsion. It was conceded that during the initial routine questioning of the accused at the border, he was not detained for the purposes of s. 10 of the *Charter* nor was he detained when he was directed to the secondary area where he was further questioned by an officer. The referral to secondary examination is "a continuation or completion of the initial examination which takes place in the primary inspection line."

At the time that the senior immigration officer interviewed the accused he had been arrested and detained by the secondary officer. He had also indicated that he wished to exercise his right to counsel, and had not yet been afforded that call. While it was clear that the senior immigration officer had a duty to present his removal report to the accused to read, and to ask him if he wanted to add anything to it, before making a removal order; it is not so clear that he ought to ask him other questions going to the heart of the allegations here without implementing his right to counsel. The Court found that questions of the senior immigration officer were interrogatory and not merely clarification. The attempt to use those answers in the subsequent criminal proceeding runs afoul of the principle of self incrimination protected by s. 7 of the *Charter*; and in this case also infringes s. 10(b) of the *Charter*, since the accused had not yet had the opportunity to speak to counsel, although he had expressly requested to do so. There was no urgency or necessity to ask additional questions to the removal report. That could have been dealt with after the accused was permitted to speak to duty counsel. The admission of the statement was found to tend to render the trial unfair and the applicant satisfied the burden of establishing that it ought to be excluded. Therefore the statements made to the senior officer were not admissible at trial.

*Zhong v. Canada (Minister of Citizenship & Immigration)* (2009), 350 F.T.R. 43 (Eng.), 2009 FC 632, 2009 CarswellNat 1867 (F.C.) — This application exposes a fundamental fault in the refugee claim process applied at the time the applicant made his initial statements claiming refugee protection. The initial interview was conducted through a Cantonese interpreter. The applicant gave his statements in Cantonese which were in turn given in English by the interpreter and written in English by the interviewing officer. No independent means, such as a recording, was used to verify what was said by either the applicant or the interpreter, or whether the interviewing officer's writing accurately recorded what the Cantonese interpreter said. This "Record of Examination" is the centre of a fundamental controversy in the present application. Following the preparation of the Personal Information Form (PIF) by the applicant with the help of legal counsel, the Record of Examination was made available to the applicant and his counsel. The applicant immediately asserted to his counsel that the Record of Examination did not correctly record what he said in the interview, and, as a result, counsel for the applicant made this known to the Refugee Protection Division well in advance of the hearing. Nevertheless, the RPD Member who conducted the hearing chose to use the Record of Examination as accurate and relied on the statements made in it to find contradictions between it and the PIF and oral evidence produced at the hearing. This process resulted in a negative credibility finding made against the applicant. This process constituted a breach of due process.

In the absence of a verifiable record of what was said by the applicant at his interview, I find it is a breach of due process for the RPD to have accepted the Record of Examination as accurate in the face of the applicant's sworn statement that it was not accurate. The Record of Examination is the result of a fundamentally flawed record keeping process and should not be used with respect to the applicant's claim for refugee protection. The application for judicial review was allowed. Counsel for the respondents requested a question for certification, however, the applicant objected and the Court agreed that the finding of breach of due process in the present case was based on the facts.

*Toronto Coalition to Stop the War v. Canada (Minister of Public Safety & Emergency Preparedness)* (2009), 80 Imm. L.R. (3d) 72, 2009 CarswellNat 775, 2009 FC 326 (F.C.) — The applicants brought a motion to seek an order of the Federal Court to permit a Mr. Galloway to enter Canada. Mr. Galloway was a British citizen and member of Parliament of the UK. He was to speak at a public forum entitled "Resisting War from Gaza to Kandahar", hosted by the Toronto Coalition to Stop the War.

Every person seeking to enter Canada must appear for an examination to determine whether the person has a right to enter Canada or is or may become authorized to enter and remain in Canada under subs. 18(1) of the IRPA. Mr. Galloway's personal views and open sympathies for the Palestinians and their cause became a matter of public record. An official of the High Commission of Canada, Immigration Section, by letter dated March 20, 2009, advised the applicant Galloway, apparently as a matter of "courtesy", that according to the "preliminary assessment" of the CBSA, he is inadmissible to Canada on security grounds pursuant to subs. 34 of the IRPA. Mr. Galloway was invited by the letter to make submissions and that a CBSA officer will make a final determination of admissibility based on this preliminary assessment and any submissions he may make should he present himself at a port of entry.

The Court denied the applicant's request for an interim order or interlocutory injunction to enjoin the respondents and their officials from denying Mr. Galloway entry to Canada.

At one time, the Court was reluctant to grant mandatory interlocutory injunctions but, over time, has been somewhat more willing to do so. Still, some greater level of caution arises when, particularly at an interlocutory stage, the Court is asked to order somebody to take a positive action that will change the *status quo*. It is only in clear cases that mandatory injunction relief against the enforcement of a law will likely be granted by the Court before a full hearing of the application for judicial review. In such instances, public interests and the relative strength of the parties' arguments are relevant factors to consider in the assessment of balance of convenience.



A fundamental principle of immigration law is that non-citizens do not have an unqualified right to enter Canada. The admission of a foreign national to this country is a privilege determined by statute, regulation or otherwise, and not a matter of right. In this respect, Parliament has expressly given the CBSA officers legal authority to exclusively determine whether a foreign national who seeks to enter this country is admissible (s. 15 and 18 of the Act). Yet there had been no final determination made by an officer with respect to the admission in Canada of Mr. Galloway.

The Court was not prepared to exempt Mr. Galloway from the application of the provisions in the Act and Regulations respecting entry and examination, or to order the respondents' officials to allow him to come to Canada, without any final decision made on his admissibility.

*Dhoot v. Canada (Minister of Citizenship & Immigration)*, [2006] F.C.J. No. 1625, 57 Imm. L.R. (3d) 153, 2006 CarswellNat 3480, 2006 FC 1295 (F.C.) — This is an application for judicial review of a visa officer's decision of the applicant's application for a permanent resident visa which was denied on the basis that the applicant failed to attend an interview scheduled on October 26, 2005. The applicant states that he was never informed of the interview. The visa officer insisted that the notice of the interview was provided to the applicant by letter dated August 19, 2005.

The visa officer, for whatever reason, did not send the notice by mail as would be expected given the significantly prejudicial impact non-delivery would have on the applicant's interest in obtaining a permanent resident visa. It is reasonable to expect that there will be mistakes by the respondent when dealing with thousands of immigration files. When the evidence shows that there has been such a mistake the Court expects that the respondent cure the mistake, *i.e.*, invite the applicant to attend another interview. It was wrong for the respondent, in a case such as this, to oppose the applicant's court case. The application for judicial review was allowed and the applicant was awarded legal costs.

*Dehghani v. Canada (Minister of Employment & Immigration*, [1993] 1 S.C.R. 1053, 18 Imm. L.R. (2d) 245, 10 Admin. L.R. (2d) 1, 20 C.R. (4th) 34, 101 D.L.R. (4th) 654, 150 N.R. 241, 14 C.R.R. (2d) 1, 1993 CarswellNat 57, 1993 CarswellNat 1380, EYB 1993-67290, [1993] S.C.J. No. 38 — The appellant, a citizen of Iran, arrived in Canada without valid travel or identity documents and claimed Convention refugee status. He was interviewed at the secondary examination and extensive written notes were made by an immigration officer, which notes were later entered in evidence at the credible-basis hearing. At the conclusion of that hearing the first level tribunal decided that there was no credible basis to the appellant's claim.

When the appellant was taken to a secondary examination at Canadian Immigration at Pearson International Airport, he was not detained in the sense contemplated by s. 10(b) of the *Charter*. Further, the principles of s. 10(b) do not require that the appellant be provided with counsel at the pre-inquiry or pre-hearing stage of the refugee claim determination process. The secondary examination of the appellant at the port-of-entry is not analogous to a hearing. The purpose of the port-of entry interview was to aid in the processing of the appellant's application for entry and to determine the appropriate procedures which should be invoked in order to deal with the appellant's application for Convention refugee status. The principles of fundamental justice do not include a right to counsel in these circumstances of routine information gathering.

*[Editor's note: Although* Dehghani *was decided under the former Act, it may still be relevant.]*

**16. (1) Obligation — answer truthfully — A person who makes an application must answer truthfully all questions put to them for the purpose of the examination and must produce a visa and all relevant evidence and documents that the officer reasonably requires.**

**(2) Obligation — relevant evidence — In the case of a foreign national,**

> **(a) the relevant evidence referred to in subsection (1) includes photographic and fingerprint evidence; and**
>
> **(b) the foreign national must submit to a medical examination on request.**

**Proposed Amendment — 16(2)(b)**

> **(b) subject to the regulations, the foreign national must submit to a medical examination.**
>
> 2010, c. 8, s. 2 [To come into force June 29, 2012, or earlier by order.]

**(3) Evidence relating to identity — An officer may require or obtain from a permanent resident or a foreign national who is arrested, detained or subject to a removal order, any evidence — photographic, fingerprint or otherwise — that may be used to establish their identity or compliance with this Act.**

## Case Law

### Section 16(1)

*Lu v. Canada (Minister of Citizenship & Immigration)*, 2007 CarswellNat 415, 2007 FC 159 (F.C.) — This is an application for judicial review of a decision to refuse an application for permanent residence on the basis that the applicant was inadmissible to Canada due to a misrepresentation. The Consulate General made inquiries to confirm the authenticity of a capital validation report. The visa officer concluded that the applicant was inadmissible to Canada. In her letter to the applicant, the visa officer wrote ". . . because you, a person described under subs. 16(1) of IRPA and ss. 34 to 42 of the *Immigration and Refugee Protection Act* . . . you are therefore criminally inadmissible to Canada." Although the officer did overstep her role in the evaluation of the applicant's permanent resident application, her actions did not constitute an error of law. The fact that the officer wrote in her letter to the applicant that "you are therefore criminally inadmissible to Canada" was an error which can be associated to a typographical error and it was not of a conclusive nature. There was no indication in the officer's letter that she misunderstood the evidence before her and as such believed the applicant was inadmissible under s. 36 of the IRPA due to criminality, or that the officer believed that providing untruthful information made the applicant inadmissible due to criminality. The application for judicial review was dismissed.

*Li v. Canada (Minister of Citizenship & Immigration)*, 2006 CarswellNat 1300, 2006 CarswellNat 2280, 2006 FC 599 (F.C.) — The applicant applied for permanent resident status under the Canada-Quebec Investor Program. His application was denied on the basis that he failed to adequately account for the origins of his net worth. The applicant argued that the officer's decision was patently unreasonable as the decision was based on irrelevant considerations. He also argued that the information the officer requested imposed too heavy a burden on the applicant as the documents were from many years prior to the interview, and were not relevant to the current assets that had been primarily accumulated in recent years. The Court held that given the money in question was the seed money that allowed the applicant to establish his own business, it was very relevant to the application and the officer was merely doing her duty under s. 16 of IRPA when enquiring into the source of the funds.

*Shi v. Canada (Minister of Citizenship & Immigration)* (2005), 50 Imm. L.R. (3d) 277, 2005 CarswellNat 2715, 2005 CarswellNat 5376, 2005 FC 1224 (F.C.) — The applicant applied for permanent residence status to Canada as an investor in the business category. His application was refused on the basis that the visa officer was not satisfied by how the applicant accumulated his personal net worth. In applying a high degree of deference to the decision of the visa officer, it is not sufficient to show that the evidence before the visa officer could have led to a different conclusion. Rather, to show an error, the applicant would have to demonstrate that there was no evidence before the officer that could have led to the conclusion in question. The visa officer was not satisfied that the applicant had answered truthfully to all the questions put to him. Specifically, the visa officer had discovered that the tax document filed by the applicant was fraudulent. The Court upheld the visa officer's decision and concluded that s. 16(1) of the IRPA applied to the applicant even though he did not already hold a visa. Section 16(1) applies whenever an applicant under the IRPA is the subject of an examination and not just when he already holds a visa.

*Hou v. Canada (Minister of Citizenship & Immigration)*, 2005 CarswellNat 3829, 2005 CarswellNat 5466, 2005 FC 1586 (F.C.) — The applicant's application for a permanent residence visa under the skilled worker category was refused on the basis that the applicant was not credible because there were significant discrepancies between the evidence the applicant had submitted for a study permit application and the evidence she had submitted for the permanent residence application. The officer reached this decision based on the discrepancy in the evidence. The officer reviewed, but did not accept, the applicant's explanation that the misinformation was due to the activity of her consultant or her agent. The standard of review to be applied to decisions on credibility is patent unreasonableness. The officer's decision was reasonable and the application for judicial review was dismissed.

*Lan v. Canada (Ministre de la Citoyenneté & de l'Immigration)* (2004), 42 Imm. L.R. (3d) 280, 2004 CarswellNat 3167, 2004 CarswellNat 1576, 2004 FC 770 (F.C.) — This was an application to review a decision of a visa officer dismissing an application for permanent residence made by the applicant in the immigrant investor class.



IRP Act

In order to allow a visa application, the officer must be convinced that the prospective immigrant is a person admissible to Canada. The officer is bound to refuse a visa to an applicant who has not fulfilled the obligations provided in subs. 16(1).

In order for the failure to provide documents to justify the refusal of a visa, these documents must be relevant, in light of the circumstances of the file under review. Thus, the officer's request for documents must be reasonable.

The evidence in the record showed that at the hearing the applicant submitted her financial statements dating back to1996, as well as bank certificates, in order to establish the value of her current assets. The value of the applicant's shares in her company, which made up the majority of the assets declared on her application, was established by financial statements going back to 1996.

The officer did not dispute the authenticity of these documents or their probative value. Accordingly, it was possible to determine based on these documents that the applicant's current assets, primarily accumulated in recent years, were obtained legally and therefore it was not necessary to require documentary evidence for the period between 1984 and 1989. Accordingly, the application for judicial review was allowed.

**17. Regulations — The regulations may provide for any matter relating to the application of this Division, and may include provisions respecting the conduct of examinations.**

## Division 3 — Entering and Remaining in Canada

### *Entering and Remaining*

**18. (1) Examination by officer — Every person seeking to enter Canada must appear for an examination to determine whether that person has a right to enter Canada or is or may become authorized to enter and remain in Canada.**

**(2) Transit — Subsection (1) also applies to persons who, without leaving Canada, seek to leave an area at an airport that is reserved for passengers who are in transit or who are waiting to depart Canada.**

### Case Law

*Toronto Coalition to Stop the War v. Canada (Minister of Public Safety & Emergency Preparedness)* (2009), 80 Imm. L.R. (3d) 72, 2009 CarswellNat 775, 2009 FC 326 (F.C.) — The applicants brought a motion to seek an order of the Federal Court to permit a Mr. Galloway to enter Canada. Mr. Galloway was a British citizen and member of Parliament of the UK. He was to speak at a public forum entitled "Resisting War from Gaza to Kandahar", hosted by the Toronto Coalition to Stop the War.

Every person seeking to enter Canada must appear for an examination to determine whether the person has a right to enter Canada or is or may become authorized to enter and remain in Canada under subs. 18(1) of the IRPA. Mr. Galloway's personal views and open sympathies for the Palestinians and their cause became a matter of public record. An official of the High Commission of Canada, Immigration Section, by letter dated March 20, 2009, advised the applicant Galloway, apparently as a matter of "courtesy", that according to the "preliminary assessment" of the CBSA, he is inadmissible to Canada on security grounds pursuant to subs. 34 of the IRPA. Mr. Galloway was invited by the letter to make submissions and that a CBSA officer will make a final determination of admissibility based on this preliminary assessment and any submissions he may make should he present himself at a port of entry.

The Court denied the applicant's request for an interim order or interlocutory injunction to enjoin the respondents and their officials from denying Mr. Galloway entry to Canada.

At one time, the Court was reluctant to grant mandatory interlocutory injunctions but, over time, has been somewhat more willing to do so. Still, some greater level of caution arises when, particularly at an interlocutory stage, the Court is asked to order somebody to take a positive action that will change the *status quo*. It is only in clear cases that mandatory injunction relief against the enforcement of a law will likely be granted by the Court before a full hearing of the application for judicial review. In such instances, public interests and the relative strength of the parties' arguments are relevant factors to consider in the assessment of balance of convenience.

A fundamental principle of immigration law is that non-citizens do not have an unqualified right to enter Canada. The admission of a foreign national to this country is a privilege determined by statute, regulation or otherwise, and not a matter of right. In this respect, Parliament has expressly given the CBSA officers legal authority to exclusively determine whether a foreign national who seeks to enter this country is admissible (s. 15 and 18 of the Act). Yet there had been no final determination made by an officer with respect to the admission in Canada of Mr. Galloway.

The Court was not prepared to exempt Mr. Galloway from the application of the provisions in the Act and Regulations respecting entry and examination, or to order the respondents' officials to allow him to come to Canada, without any final decision made on his admissibility.

*Dehghani v. Canada (Minister of Employment & Immigration*, [1993] 1 S.C.R. 1053, 18 Imm. L.R. (2d) 245, 10 Admin. L.R. (2d) 1, 20 C.R. (4th) 34, 101 D.L.R. (4th) 654, 150 N.R. 241, 14 C.R.R. (2d) 1, 1993 CarswellNat 57, 1993 CarswellNat 1380, EYB 1993-67290, [1993] S.C.J. No. 38 — The appellant, a citizen of Iran, arrived in Canada without valid travel or identity documents and claimed Convention refugee status. He was interviewed at the secondary examination and extensive written notes were made by an immigration officer, which notes were later entered in evidence at the credible-basis hearing. At the conclusion of that hearing the first level tribunal decided that there was no credible basis to the appellant's claim.

When the appellant was taken to a secondary examination at Canadian Immigration at Pearson International Airport, he was not detained in the sense contemplated by s. 10(b) of the *Charter*. Further, the principles of s. 10(b) do not require that the appellant be provided with counsel at the pre-inquiry or pre-hearing stage of the refugee claim determination process. The secondary examination of the appellant at the port-of-entry is not analogous to a hearing. The purpose of the port-of entry interview was to aid in the processing of the appellant's application for entry and to determine the appropriate procedures which should be invoked in order to deal with the appellant's application for Convention refugee status. The principles of fundamental justice do not include a right to counsel in these circumstances of routine information gathering.

*[Editor's note: Although* Dehghani *was decided under the former Act, it may still be relevant.]*

**19. (1) Right of entry of citizens and Indians — Every Canadian citizen within the meaning of the *Citizenship Act* and every person registered as an Indian under the *Indian Act* has the right to enter and remain in Canada in accordance with this Act, and an officer shall allow the person to enter Canada if satisfied following an examination on their entry that the person is a citizen or registered Indian.**

**(2) Right of entry of permanent residents — An officer shall allow a permanent resident to enter Canada if satisfied following an examination on their entry that they have that status.**

**20. (1) Obligation on entry — Every foreign national, other than a foreign national referred to in section 19, who seeks to enter or remain in Canada must establish,**

**(a) to become a permanent resident, that they hold the visa or other document required under the regulations and have come to Canada in order to establish permanent residence; and**

**(b) to become a temporary resident, that they hold the visa or other document required under the regulations and will leave Canada by the end of the period authorized for their stay.**

**(2) Provincial criteria — A foreign national referred to in subsection 9(1) must also establish, to become a permanent resident, that they hold a document issued by the province indicating that the competent authority of the province is of the opinion that the foreign national complies with the province's selection criteria.**

## Case Law

### Section 20(1)

*Tran v. Canada (Minister of Citizenship & Immigration)* (2006), 59 Imm. L.R. (3d) 217, 2006 CarswellNat 3833, 2006 FC 1377 (F.C.) — The applicant sought to overturn the decision of an immigration officer who denied his application for a study permit. The visa officer was not satisfied that he was either a *bona fide* student or a *bona fide* temporary resident, sufficiently well established in Vietnam, that he would leave Canada after his authorized stay in Canada. Procedural protection that arises in the context of a student visa application is "relaxed." In other words, there is no clear requirement that an applicant be permitted to respond to an officer's concerns as they arise. Immigration manuals are primary guidelines for the assistance of the visa officers in the assessment of applications for either permanent residence or temporary visas. As such, manuals cannot be relied upon by applicants to argue lack of fairness simply because the officer did not strictly adhere to the guidelines found in the manual in question. It is trite law that the onus is on the applicant to provide a visa officer with all relevant information and documentation to satisfy the visa officer that the applicant meets the statutory requirements of the IRPA and the Regulations. In this case, the visa officer conducted a fulsome and diligent assessment of the applicant's application for a study permit. The visa officer considered a variety of factors in her assessment, including the low income of the applicant's parents in Vietnam and no proof of their employment, income or any assets. The fact that the same type of education is available locally and at a fraction of the cost is a relevant factor in determining the credibility and intentions of a potential foreign student.

It was not patently unreasonable for the visa officer to consider the availability of similar courses in Vietnam and South Asia at a much less cost. The applicant's very weak English and his inability to carry even a basic conversation in English, as was revealed during his telephone conversation with the case analyst and reflected in the CAIPS notes, was a relevant factor for the visa officer to consider, given that his acceptance into Algonquin College was conditional upon him meeting the English language requirement. There were no reviewable errors in the visa officer's refusal to issue a study permit. The application for judicial review was dismissed.

*Murai v. Canada (Minister of Citizenship & Immigration)* (2006), 53 Imm. L.R. (3d) 218, 2006 CarswellNat 367, 2006 FC 186 (F.C.) — The applicant came to Canada without a visa as it was not required. Her application for an extension of time to remain in Canada was refused. Her subsequent application for refugee status was denied and her leave application for judicial review was refused. Her application to defer the removal order was denied. Her pre-removal risk assessment was denied and leave for judicial review was denied. Her humanitarian and compassionate leave application was denied and leave for judicial review was also denied. She left Canada. She then made an application for a work permit as a live-in caregiver. This application was denied as the visa officer was not satisfied that the applicant would leave Canada at the end of the authorized stay period per s. 183(1)(a) of the Regulations. The officer came to this conclusion on the basis of the applicant's previous immigration history.

The officer was entitled to satisfy himself that the applicant for the Live-In Caregiver Program had an intention of leaving Canada should the application for permanent residence be refused. In this case, however, the Court concluded that the officer's decision was unreasonable since the record revealed that the applicant was a law-abiding citizen, who after exhausting her remedies returned to her home country and subsequently applied under the Live-In Caregiver Program. In fact, the evidence of her previous immigration encounters supported the applicant's contention that she was law abiding and would continue to comply with the rules in the future.

The visa officer should have asked himself "will this person stay illegally in Canada if not successful under the program?" Based on the applicant's past performance, any reasonable person would say "no, she would not stay in Canada illegally."

*Toor v. Canada (Minister of Citizenship & Immigration)*, 2006 CarswellNat 1342, 2006 FC 573 (F.C.) — The applicant applied for judicial review of a decision of an immigration officer at the New Delhi High Commission, wherein the officer refused the applicant's application for a temporary resident visa. The officer was not satisfied as to the *bona fides* of the application. The applicant had been invited to an interview by a provincial government, however, the officer noted that the letter from the province of Manitoba referred to funds claimed by the applicant which could not be verified on documents and accordingly concluded there were large inconsistencies. The officer also noted the applicant had no previous travel and only previous refusals from the United States and New Zealand.

The applicant argued that it would have been proper for the visa officer to give him an opportunity to reply to his concerns.

The Court concluded that the obligation to confront an applicant with adverse conclusions applies when the conclusions arise from material not known to the applicant. Where the issue arises out of material provided by the applicant, there is no obligation to provide an opportunity for explanation since the provider of the material is taken to know of the contents of the material. There was no breach of procedural fairness.

*Boni c. Canada (Ministre de la Citoyenneté & de l'Immigration)*, [2005] F.C.J. No. 43, 2005 CarswellNat 176, 2005 CarswellNat 4646, 2005 FC 31 (F.C.); affirmed [2006] F.C.J. No. 275, 57 Imm. L.R. (3d) 4, 2006 CarswellNat 414, 2006 FCA 68 (C.A.) — The applicant applied for judicial review of a visa officer's decision to deny the applicant's application for a study permit. The risk that study permit applicants will not leave Canada once the period of their stay ends is a very important factor to be considered. An officer may examine the applicant's long-term objective. That objective is a relevant point which carries some weight, in view of the evidence as a whole on whether a study permit would be granted. A visa officer's conclusions will not be disturbed unless they are so unreasonable as to require the Court's intervention.

*Malhi v. Canada (Minister of Citizenship & Immigration)* (2005), 53 Imm. L.R. (3d) 71, 2005 CarswellNat 2444, 2005 CarswellNat 5062, 2005 FC 1120 (F.C.) — This was an application for judicial review of an officer's decision to refuse an application for temporary resident status with a work permit. The applicant was a citizen of India and received a job offer, which was certified by Human Resources and Development Canada, to work in Ontario as a teacher. He then applied for a work permit but was refused, as the officer was not satisfied that he would leave Canada at the end of the 12-month term. The officer based his decision on the fact that the applicant had applied for a visitor visa to Canada in 2002 but had been denied, and the applicant did not have sufficient ties to India. The Court found the officer erred in concluding that the applicant did not have sufficient ties to India, given all of the presented information, mainly, that his whole family including his wife and two children would remain in India; his wife owns a trucking business in India; he completed 70% of his PhD studies and that he will not be able to complete these studies if he did not return to India; that his employment in Canada was for a duration of 12 months, after which he would become unemployed; and finally, that the assets belonging to the applicant and his wife totalled approximately $60,000, and that if the assets of his mother and father were included, that amount jumped to approximately $350,000. The officer seemed to rely mainly on the fact that the salary the applicant would receive in Canada was more than seven times that which he receives in India.

The Court found that it was patently unreasonable for the officer to determine that the applicant did not have sufficient ties to India, given all of the presented information. The application for judicial review was granted and the officer's decision quashed.

*Moghaddam v. Canada (Minister of Citizenship & Immigration)*, 39 Imm. L.R. (3d) 239, 2004 CarswellNat 2502, 2004 CarswellNat 1346, 2004 FC 680 (F.C.) — The applicant sought to review a decision by a visa officer refusing the applicant's request for a study permit. The visa officer refused the application on the basis that the applicant had weak ties with her family in Iran.

Evidence of the intention to leave Canada upon the expiry of the period authorized for a temporary stay is a requirement under the Act. Section 22(2) addresses the situation where a person seeking temporary entry also holds the intention of establishing permanent residence. The applicant's family had an outstanding application for permanent residence in which she was named as a dependent. The officer's reference to the family application for permanent residence was improper. That application was not before him for a decision and was irrelevant to the matter before him. The issue of dual intent arose only in relation to that application which did not form part of the record before the visa officer. The family's application for permanent residence was irrelevant to the assessment of the applicant's application for a study permit. By referring to that application the visa officer relied on an extraneous consideration. The decision of the visa officer was set aside.

*Thompson v. Canada (Minister of Citizenship & Immigration)* (2003), 35 Imm. L.R. (3d) 308, 2003 CarswellNat 4562 (Imm. & Ref. Bd. (App. Div.) — The appellant appealed from a departure order made against her. She was found described in paragraph 20(1)(a).

The law of residency obligations has changed under IRPA in two ways. A permanent resident complies with the residency obligation with respect to a five-year period if, for at least 730 days of that five-year period, the permanent resident is physically present in Canada. IRPA also provides recourse to humanitarian and compassionate relief. The Appeal Division considered the following factors with respect to the appellant's case: 1) the reason for the departure order; 2) the number of years the appellant lived in Canada as a landed resident and her degree of establishment here; 3) her reasons for leaving Canada and remaining outside of Canada; 4) the time of her return to Canada; 5) her ability to re-establish in Canada; 6) her ties to Canada; 7) the best interest of the appellant's daughter; 8) hardship to the appellant in having to leave Canada; 9) hardship to others if the appellant was required to leave Canada; and 10) hardship to the appellant in returning to Trinidad and Tobago.

The appellant's failure to establish residence here is not the result of malfeasance and this makes her departure order appeal different from a removal order appeal of someone whose removal is the result of criminality or misrepresentation. The appellant did not misrepresent herself to immigration in order to obtain her status and she did not commit criminal offences while she lived here.

There are three types of removal orders. For the most serious matters deportation orders are issued which require the person to obtain written permission to ever return to Canada. Exclusion orders prohibit a person returning to Canada for a two- or three-year period, but written permission is not required. A departure order is the least onerous sanction. It allows the person to leave on his or her own within 30 days of the order being made. There are no bars to applying to return to Canada.

In the circumstances of this case the Court granted humanitarian and compassionate relief.

## *Status and Authorization to Enter*

**21. (1) Permanent resident — A foreign national becomes a permanent resident if an officer is satisfied that the foreign national has applied for that status, has met the obligations set out in paragraph 20(1)(a) and subsection 20(2) and is not inadmissible.**

*[Editor's Note: SOR/2002-227, s. 328(1) provides that a person who was a permanent resident immediately before June 28, 2002 is a permanent resident under the new* Immigration and Refugee Protection Act, *S.C. 2001, c. 27.]*

**(2) Protected person — Except in the case of a person described in subsection 112(3) or a person who is a member of a prescribed class of persons, a person whose application for protection has been finally determined by the Board to be a Convention refugee or to be a person in need of protection, or a person whose application**



IRP Act

**for protection has been allowed by the Minister, becomes, subject to any federal-provincial agreement referred to in subsection 9(1), a permanent resident if the officer is satisfied that they have made their application in accordance with the regulations and that they are not inadmissible on any ground referred to in section 34 or 35, subsection 36(1) or section 37 or 38.**

*[Editor's Note: SOR/2002-227, s. 347(1) provides that if landing was not granted before June 28, 2002, an application for landing submitted under s. 46.04 of the former* Immigration Act, *R.S.C. 1985, c. I-2 is an application to remain in Canada as a permanent resident under s. 21(2) of the* Immigration and Refugee Protection Act, *S.C. 2001, c. 27 (the "new Act").*

*SOR/2002-227, s. 347(2) provides that if landing was not granted before June 28, 2002, an application for landing as a member of the undocumented Convention refugee in Canada class is an application to remain in Canada as a permanent resident under s. 21(2) of the new Act and is not subject to the requirement in s. 175(1) of the new* Immigration and Refugee Protection Regulations, *SOR/2002-227, that the application be received within 180 days after a determination is made by the Immigration and Refugee Board).*

*SOR/2002-227, s. 347(3) provides that if landing was not granted before June 28, 2002, an application for landing submitted by a person pursuant to a determination that the person is a member of the post-determination refugee claimants in Canada class is an application to remain in Canada as a permanent resident under s. 21(2) of the new Act.]*

## Case Law

### Section 21(1)

*Hamalipoor v. Canada (Minister of Citizenship & Immigration)* (2005), 47 Imm. L.R. (3d) 245, 2005 CarswellNat 1629, 2005 CarswellNat 3611, 2005 FC 803 (F.C.) — The applicant obtained refugee status in September 2000 and in November 2000 applied for permanent residence status. In February 2001, the case processing centre acknowledged receipt of his application for permanent residence. In March 2001, the applicant's CSIS check was completed and was valid for 18 months. In November 2001, the applicant was told he had to submit a certified translation of his identity card. Apparently, the translation submitted was not certified as required and it took 9½ months for the Minister to advise the applicant of this deficiency. The required certified translation was filed within weeks. At the year end of 2001, all documents had been filed and a valid CSIS clearance was in place. However, it was not until March 2004, and only after repeated requests by his counsel, that the applicant was informed that the Minister was awaiting an updated CSIS clearance, the previous one having lapsed through the passage of time. The applicant was interviewed by CSIS in February 2005.

The applicant brought an application for *mandamus* to compel the Minister to complete the processing of his application for permanent residence. The Minister claimed it had a satisfactory justification for the delay, in that it was awaiting the CSIS update. The Court pointed out that a review of the file showed a considerable amount of balancing of the file or parts of it between various parts of the respondent's organization, as well as between it and other government agencies and that this internal scurrying about with no actual progress was not a satisfactory justification for delay. Furthermore, the Court held that it was not adequate to pass the buck and avoid responsibility by blaming delays on another government organization. An applicant's right to a decision is an obligation on the Government of Canada acting through the responsible minister. It is the Minister of Citizenship and Immigration's obligation to cause the necessary steps within the government so that the rights under the statute are fulfilled. The Court concluded that there had been excessive delay beyond that which the nature of the process required, which was not attributable to the applicant, and for which there was no adequate justification; accordingly, the applicant was entitled to an order of *mandamus*.

*Rukmangathan v. Canada (Minister of Citizenship & Immigration)*, 2004 CarswellNat 1673, 2004 CarswellNat 488, 247 F.T.R. 147, 2004 FC 284, [2004] F.C.J. No. 317 (F.C.) — This was an application for judicial review of the decision of a visa officer denying an application for permanent residence.



Procedural fairness requires that an applicant be given an opportunity to respond to extrinsic evidence relied upon by the visa officer and to be apprised of the officer's concerns arising from such evidence. The duty of fairness may require immigration officials to inform applicants of their concerns with applications even where such concerns arise from evidence tendered by the applicant. A visa officer should apprise an applicant at an interview of her negative impressions of evidence tendered by the applicant. However, procedural fairness does not stretch to the point of requiring a visa officer to provide an applicant with a running score of the weaknesses in their application.

Visa officers deal with many applications. The Court was not prepared to adopt the approach that visa officers have no interest in the application and therefore their version is to be believed when it conflicts with that of an applicant. The Court observed that once a visa officer's decision is challenged, that person has an interest in justifying his or her decision. At that point the officer is not a disinterested person.

### Section 21(2)

*Starovic v. Canada (Minister of Citizenship & Immigration)*, 2004 CarswellNat 5561, 2004 CarswellNat 4398, 2004 FC 1681 (F.C.) — The applicant met the eligibility requirements to apply for permanent residence as a Convention refugee. After the applicant had been determined to be a refugee, she left the country to be with her husband.

There is no provision of the law that requires an applicant who has been found to be a Convention refugee and who has applied for permanent residence in Canada to attend an interview in Canada as a condition precedent to determination of his or her application. Undoubtedly, in circumstances where the applicant has been found to be a Convention refugee, he or she would, in most instances, remain in Canada while applying for permanent residence. This is one of those rare instances where the applicant had to leave Canada after having been found to be a refugee. Interviews of persons seeking to come to Canada as permanent residents are routinely conducted at Canada's diplomatic premises abroad. Accordingly, the decision to declare the application for permanent residence to have been abandoned by reason of the fact that the applicant could not attend in Canada for an interview was set aside.

**22. (1) Temporary resident — A foreign national becomes a temporary resident if an officer is satisfied that the foreign national has applied for that status, has met the obligations set out in paragraph 20(1)(b) and is not inadmissible.**

*[Editor's Note: SOR/2002-227, s. 329(1) provides that any of the following persons who were in Canada immediately before June 28, 2002 are temporary residents under the new*

Immigration and Refugee Protection Act, *S.C. 2001, c. 27 and are subject to its provisions:*

*(a) a visitor under the* Immigration Act, *R.S.C. 1985, c. I-2 (the "former Act"); and*

*(b) a person issued a permit under s. 37 of the former Act.]*

**(2) Dual intent — An intention by a foreign national to become a permanent resident does not preclude them from becoming a temporary resident if the officer is satisfied that they will leave Canada by the end of the period authorized for their stay.**

## Case Law

### Section 22(1)

*Boni c. Canada (Ministre de la Citoyenneté & de l'Immigration)*, [2005] F.C.J. No. 43, 2005 CarswellNat 176, 2005 CarswellNat 4646, 2005 FC 31 (F.C.); affirmed [2006] F.C.J. No. 275, 57 Imm. L.R. (3d) 4, 2006 CarswellNat 414, 2006 FCA 68 (C.A.) — The applicant applied for judicial review of a visa officer's decision to deny the applicant's application for a study permit. The risk that study permit applicants will not leave Canada once the period of their stay ends is a very important factor to be considered. An officer may examine the applicant's long-term objective. That objective is a relevant point which carries some weight, in view of the evidence as a whole on whether a study permit would be granted. A visa officer's conclusions will not be disturbed unless they are so unreasonable as to require the Court's intervention.

### Section 22(2)

*Odewole v. Canada (Minister of Citizenship & Immigration)*, 2008 CarswellNat 1667, 2008 CarswellNat 2786, 2008 FC 697 (F.C.) — The applicant sought judicial review of a visa officer's decision to refuse an application for a study permit. The application was refused because the applicant failed to demonstrate that her obligations or ties to her home country are such that they would compel her to leave Canada following the completion of her studies and because the officer was not satisfied that the applicant had dual intent pursuant to s. 22(2) of the Act. The applicant's sister had applied to sponsor the applicant's mother and the applicant was included as a dependant child in her mother's application for permanent residence.

Pursuant to subs. 22(2) of the Act, a person seeking a temporary entry into Canada may also hold the intention of establishing permanent residence. The officer was therefore required to weigh the evidence in connection with the application for a study permit and assess the applicant's intention to leave Canada at the end of her studies under paragraph 20(1)(b) of the Act and subs. 216(1) of the Regulations. The officer was not dealing with the family application for permanent residence, and the issue of dual intent arose only in relation to that application. The application for permanent residence was an irrelevant consideration for the purposes of the applicant's application for a study permit. Although in her affidavit the officer acknowledged that she lacked jurisdiction to assess the applicant's eligibility for permanent residence under the family class sponsorship, she nevertheless took this factor into account. Thus, the officer committed a reviewable error. The decision was set aside.

*Bonilla v. Canada (Minister of Citizenship & Immigration)*, 2007 CarswellNat 26, 2007 FC 20 (F.C.) — The applicant applied for a study permit. The application was refused.

The visa officer found that living in Canada during her formative high school years would have a negative impact upon the applicant's ability to function in Colombia. The applicant was therefore unable to establish that she would return to her home country following the expiration of her study permit, should she be given one. The officer concluded that the applicant's separation from her family, community, language and Colombia's education system, for such a long period of time, would result in the severance of her ties to Colombia.



The visa officer relied upon a generalization when he refused the applicant's application. The generalization in question is that all applicants who apply for a study permit which cover four years of high school should be denied, since they would automatically be unlikely to return to their home country due to long-term separation from their families and cultures. Clearly, any individual who applies to study in Canada for four years of high school would be away from the aspects of their home country noted by the visa officer. However, it is not necessarily the case that all young people in these circumstances would become unable to function in their home countries following the four-year period, and as a result, would be unlikely to leave Canada. The officer subjectively formed an opinion and should have allowed the applicant an opportunity to respond to his concerns. The applicant had no way of knowing that the visa officer would act upon his view that those in their "formative years" may not study in Canada for a four-year period, since they would be unlikely to leave the country. The visa officer's failure to give the applicant an opportunity to respond to his concerns, on the facts of this case, amounted to a breach of the rules of natural justice. The application for judicial review was allowed.

*Dang v. Canada (Minister of Citizenship & Immigration)*, 2007 CarswellNat 25, 2007 FC 15 (F.C.) — The immigration officer's decision not to grant a study permit was based on a factual finding that the applicant had not established that she would leave Canada at the end of her authorized stay. To obtain a renewal of a study permit, the Regulations require that applicants maintain good standing at their educational institution, have sufficient and available financial resources to support their studies, and establish that they will leave Canada after the expiry of their authorized stay. The evidence before the immigration officer, which included progress reports issued to the applicant by the Canadian Conversation College, indicated that the applicant maintained satisfactory standing in her classes. The immigration officer's finding of fact that the applicant was progressing slowly was patently unreasonable. Moreover, the immigration officer erroneously found that the applicant has been studying for 4 1/2 years, when in fact it was three years. The fact that the applicant had pursued an application to permanently reside in Canada with her husband does not establish that she would not leave Canada at the end of the period authorized for her study permit as required under paragraph 216(1)(b) of the Regulations. The visa officer failed to recognize that the IRPA expressly allows the applicant to simultaneously seek permanent resident status and temporary resident status as a student. Without an evidentiary basis on which to support the immigration officer's findings, the conclusion that the applicant would not leave Canada at the end of the period authorized for her stay was patently unreasonable. By determining that the applicant had taken an unreasonable amount of time to learn the English language, the immigration officer based her conclusion on irrelevant factors. The Regulations in this respect only require that an applicant maintain "good standing" at her educational institution, which she had done. The application for judicial review was allowed.

*Ogunfowora v. Canada (Minister of Citizenship & Immigration)*, 2007 CarswellNat 1022, 2007 FC 471 (F.C.) — This was an application for judicial review of a decision of a visa officer denying the applicants a temporary resident visa. The officer stated that he was not convinced the applicants would return to Nigeria at the end of the period authorized by their stay, as mandated by paragraph 20(1)(b) of the IRPA.

Legally, an officer is obligated to consider each application on its own merits. The officer was not entitled to use the fact that the applicants had an outstanding application for permanent residence to deny them their temporary resident visas and this is evident from the plain language of the legislation. Subsection 22(2) of the IRPA explicitly precludes denying an application for temporary status on the basis that there is an outstanding permanent resident application if the decision maker believes the person will return. Thus, the legislation appears to demand that a decision maker determine on the basis of objective evidence whether the person will return, irrespective of any outstanding permanent resident applications. Most of the objective evidence in this case was disregarded for no valid reason. In order to satisfy himself, the officer must look objectively at the request and all the supporting information; he should not, as he obviously did here, decide subjectively, and ignore what favoured the applicants. The officer's decision on the evidence available appears to be patently unreasonable. The application for judicial review was allowed and the matter referred back to the respondent for re-determination by a different visa officer.

*Farhat v. Canada (Minister of Citizenship & Immigration)*, 2006 CarswellNat 3418, 2006 FC 1275 (F.C.) — The Minister's delegate of the Consulate General of Canada in New York was of the opinion that the applicant's circumstances did not warrant the issuance of a temporary resident permit (TRP). The applicant sought judicial review of the decision. The applicant was married to a Canadian citizen who applied to sponsor him from within Canada. This application was refused as the applicant did not have temporary resident status at the time the application was filed. The applicant was then convicted of theft under $5,000 and a s. 44 report was prepared because the Minister was of the opinion that the applicant was inadmissible on grounds of criminality. The applicant was excluded from Canada for one year. The applicant's counsel was made aware that the applicant needed to apply for an authorization to return to Canada. The applicant then made an application for a TRP to the Canadian Consulate. The Minister concluded that the circumstances did not warrant the issuance of a TRP. The Minister was not satisfied that the applicant would leave Canada at its expiry. The Minister indicated that the applicant could apply for a pardon. The Minister also found that the applicant had to obtain an authorization to return to Canada.

The applicant has the onus of establishing the compelling reasons and did not satisfy the Minister that the particular circumstances of his case warranted the granting of a TRP. A person seeking a TRP must have the intention of staying in Canada for temporary purpose and an officer must be satisfied that such a person will leave upon the expiry of status. Albeit, it is true that an intention by a foreign national to become a permanent resident does not preclude an individual from becoming a temporary resident; nevertheless, the officer has to be satisfied that the foreign national will leave Canada by the end of the period authorized by his or her stay. Considering the applicant's history of non-compliance with the Canadian immigration laws and regulations, and his overstay in Canada, it was not patently unreasonable for the applicant to be obliged to leave at the end of the period authorized for his stay. The applicant did not present, in regard to the existence of his spouse and child, any "compelling reasons" which would allow him to be granted a TRP. It was not patently unreasonable for the Minister to consider the interest of the child, in this case, did not amount to "compelling reasons" in light of the evidence presented.

The decision of the Minister concerning the TRP application was not irrational or perverse or so gratuitous and oppressive that no reasonable person could think it justified. Consequently, this application for judicial review was dismissed.



*Murai v. Canada (Minister of Citizenship & Immigration)* (2006), 53 Imm. L.R. (3d) 218, 2006 CarswellNat 367, 2006 FC 186 (F.C.) — The applicant came to Canada without a visa as it was not required. Her application for an extension of time to remain in Canada was refused. Her subsequent application for refugee status was denied and her leave application for judicial review was refused. Her application to defer the removal order was denied. Her pre-removal risk assessment was denied and leave for judicial review was denied. Her humanitarian and compassionate leave application was denied and leave for judicial review was also denied. She left Canada. She then made an application for a work permit as a live-in caregiver. This application was denied as the visa officer was not satisfied that the applicant would leave Canada at the end of the authorized stay period per s. 183(1)(a) of the Regulations. The officer came to this conclusion on the basis of the applicant's previous immigration history.

The officer was entitled to satisfy himself that the applicant for the Live-In Caregiver Program had an intention of leaving Canada should the application for permanent residence be refused. In this case, however, the Court concluded that the officer's decision was unreasonable since the record revealed that the applicant was a law-abiding citizen, who after exhausting her remedies returned to her home country and subsequently applied under the Live-In Caregiver Program. In fact, the evidence of her previous immigration encounters supported the applicant's contention that she was law abiding and would continue to comply with the rules in the future.

The visa officer should have asked himself "will this person stay illegally in Canada if not successful under the program?" Based on the applicant's past performance, any reasonable person would say "no, she would not stay in Canada illegally."

*Patel v. Canada (Minister of Citizenship & Immigration)* (2006), 54 Imm. L.R. (3d) 180, 2006 CarswellNat 454, 2006 CarswellNat 2375, 2006 FC 224 (F.C.) — The applicant was aged 79 and a citizen of India. She had five children and 11 grandchildren living in Canada, all of whom were Canadian citizens. Her husband was deceased and she had no more family living in India. She first came to Canada to attend the wedding of her granddaughter. Subsequently, her Canadian children decided they would sponsor her to stay in Canada as she would be alone in her mother country. She obtained three extensions of her status as a temporary resident. Her request for a fourth extension was denied after consideration of dual intent and determination that she was not a *bona fide* temporary resident. An application for restoration was denied.

The standard of review applicable to a decision refusing restoration of status is that of reasonableness *simpliciter*.

A permanent residence application does not necessarily preclude a temporary purpose for being in Canada. The current statutory and regulatory scheme does not say that a person's initial temporary purpose must remain constant and unchanged. The only requirement is the existence of a temporary purpose. The application for restoration of temporary status was not refused on the basis that the applicant would not be in Canada for a temporary purpose. On the contrary, it was denied because the applicant's stay in Canada would be for a "longer" temporary purpose, that is, while awaiting a decision on the application for permanent residence. The conclusion reached by the officer contained a reviewable error. The application was granted and the matter referred back to a different officer for redetermination.

*Rebmann v. Canada (Solicitor General)*, 2005 CarswellNat 628, 2005 CarswellNat 1413, 2005 FC 310 (F.C.) — A person may have the dual intent of immigrating and of abiding by the immigration law respecting temporary entry. At the time the exclusion order was issued the applicant had a valid status of temporary resident despite the fact that the applicant was married to a Canadian citizen, was the father to a son born in Canada, owned a house and started a corporation in Toronto. It also appears that the applicant was travelling extensively inside and outside of Canada. As long as there was an intention to leave Canada when his temporary status expired, even if the applicant had been contemplating obtaining permanent residence, it was not a violation of the Act to enter Canada with dual intent. Given that the Act contemplates that persons who are married to spouses in Canada can apply for a permanent residence from within Canada it is incongruous to suggest that a person who is married to a Canadian spouse and who wishes to seek admission into Canada as a temporary resident can be inadmissible as a permanent resident without a visa. This is inconsistent with the provisions of the Act.

*Moghaddam v. Canada (Minister of Citizenship & Immigration)*, 39 Imm. L.R. (3d) 239, 2004 CarswellNat 2502, 2004 CarswellNat 1346, 2004 FC 680 (F.C.) — The applicant sought to review a decision by a visa officer refusing the applicant's request for a study permit. The visa officer refused the application on the basis that the applicant had weak ties with her family in Iran.

Evidence of the intention to leave Canada upon the expiry of the period authorized for a temporary stay is a requirement under the Act. Section 22(2) addresses the situation where a person seeking temporary entry also holds the intention of establishing permanent residence. The applicant's family had an outstanding application for permanent residence in which she was named as a dependent. The officer's reference to the family application for permanent residence was improper. That application was not before him for a decision and was irrelevant to the matter before him. The issue of dual intent arose only in relation to that application which did not form part of the record before the visa officer. The family's application for permanent residence was irrelevant to the assessment of the applicant's application for a study permit. By referring to that application the visa officer relied on an extraneous consideration. The decision of the visa officer was set aside.

**23. Entry to complete examination or hearing — An officer may authorize a person to enter Canada for the purpose of further examination or an admissibility hearing under this Part.**

*[Editor's Note: SOR/2002-227, s. 330 provides that any of the following persons who were in Canada immediately before June 28, 2002 are deemed to have been authorized under s. 23 of the new* Immigration and Refugee Protection Act, *S.C. 2001, c. 27 to enter Canada:*

> *(a) a person in respect of whom an examination remains incomplete and whose examination was adjourned and referred to another immigration officer for completion under s. 12(3) of the* Immigration Act, *R.S.C. 1985, c. I-2 (the "former Act");*
>
> *(b) a person in respect of whom an examination remains incomplete and whose examination was deferred under paragraph 13(1)(a) of the former Act;*

*(c) a person in respect of whom an examination remains incomplete and who was authorized to come into Canada for further examination under paragraph 14(2)(b) of the former Act;*

*(d) a person in respect of whom an examination remains incomplete and who was authorized to come into Canada for further examination under paragraph 23(1)(b) of the former Act; and*

*(e) a person who has made a claim to be a Convention refugee in respect of which a determination of eligibility was not made before June 28, 2002.]*



**24. (1) Temporary resident permit — A foreign national who, in the opinion of an officer, is inadmissible or does not meet the requirements of this Act becomes a temporary resident if an officer is of the opinion that it is justified in the circumstances and issues a temporary resident permit, which may be cancelled at any time.**

**(2) Exception — A foreign national referred to in subsection (1) to whom an officer issues a temporary resident permit outside Canada does not become a temporary resident until they have been examined upon arrival in Canada.**

**(3) Instructions of Minister — In applying subsection (1), the officer shall act in accordance with any instructions that the Minister may make.**

**(4) Restriction — A foreign national whose claim for refugee protection has been rejected or determined to be withdrawn or abandoned by the Refugee Protection Division or the Refugee Appeal Division may not request a temporary resident permit if less than 12 months have passed since their claim was last rejected or determined to be withdrawn or abandoned.**

*[Editor's Note: SOR/2002-227, s. 329(2) provides that a permit issued by the Minister under s. 37 of the former* Immigration Act, *R.S.C. 1985, c. I-2 is deemed to be a temporary resident permit referred to in s. 24 of the new* Immigration and Refugee Protection Act, *S.C. 2001, c. 27.]*

2010, c. 8, s. 3

## Case Law

### Section 24(1)

*Dhandal v. Canada (Minister of Citizenship & Immigration)* (2009), 82 Imm. L.R. (3d) 214, 2009 FC 865, 2009 CarswellNat 5809, 2009 CarswellNat 2582 (F.C.) — This is an application for judicial review of the decision of a visa officer in refusing to consider the issuance of a temporary resident permit (TRP). The applicants were citizens of India. They applied for permanent residence on January 9, 2007. On July 25, 2008 an immigration counsellor determined that the applicants were inadmissible pursuant to paragraph 40(1)(a) of IRPA for misrepresenting the age of Simrajit Kaur Dhandal. In accordance with paragraph 40(1)(b) of the Act, the applicants continued to be inadmissible for two years following the date of that decision. On September 4, 2008, the applicants requested that the visa officer consider issuing a TRP pursuant to s. 24 of the Act. Additional submissions supporting the request for the TRP were sent by the applicants in September 2008. The visa officer informed them that their file had been closed following the refusal in July 2008 and no further reconsideration would be given.

The applicants submit that the failure of the visa officer to even consider the TRP request was an error of law. The respondent submitted that the request for a TRP was not properly constituted as it was filed one month after the file was closed and no separate application or fee was provided.

A request for temporary residence is implicit in an application for permanent residence. A new application is not necessary if the applicant is found to be inadmissible for permanent residence. A simple letter is sufficient to trigger the request for temporary residence, based upon the existing application (for permanent residence) if the applicant has been found to be inadmissible for permanent residence. In the present instance, the permanent resident application was denied, a letter was subsequently sent to the visa officer requesting temporary residence. In refusing to consider the request, the visa officer committed an error of law. The application for judicial review was granted.

*Ali v. Canada (Minister of Citizenship & Immigration)*, [2008] F.C.J. No. 985, 73 Imm. L.R. (3d) 258, 2008 FC 784, 2008 CarswellNat 2902, 2008 CarswellNat 2061 (F.C.) — Section 24 requires an officer to decide whether a TRP is justified "in the circumstances". That phrase must mean the relevant circumstances. Both the CIC Policy Manual and the immigration officer's own analysis (as well as the applicant's submission) made family ties and the existence and interest of children a relevant circumstance. The evidence of the minor child's interest was material to this case. Therefore, the failure to address the minor child was a legal error in failing to consider the "circumstances" of this particular applicant. The application for judicial review was granted.

*Rodgers v. Canada (Minister of Citizenship & Immigration)* (2006), 56 Imm. L.R. (3d) 63, 2006 CarswellNat 2849, 2006 FC 1093 (F.C.) — The granting of TRPs under s. 24 is clearly discretionary. Depending on the circumstances, issuing a TRP may be justified or not. The mere fact that there is a provision for issuing TRPs does not mean that there cannot be circumstances where the issuing of TRPs would undermine the entire procedure for dealing with applicants under the IRPA.

The considerations under s. 24 only have to be justified under the circumstances. It is not a full-scale H&C consideration as mandated by s. 25. In this case, the applicant's immigration history was such that the immigration officer's decision was not unreasonable. The applicant came illegally to Canada and by using every available means including a false diabetes claim and an unjustified refugee claim managed to stay 15 years. Under these circumstances, the denial of the TRP was hardly unreasonable. Given that this was not a full-scale H&C assessment under s. 25, there is no requirement to consider and deal with each submission of the applicant. The application for judicial review of a decision not to grant a TRP was set aside.

*Malicia v. Canada (Minister of Citizenship & Immigration)*, 2006 CarswellNat 3208, 2006 FC 755 (F.C.) — This is an application for judicial review of the decision of an immigration officer to refuse to seek authority to issue a temporary resident permit (TRP) for the applicant. The applicant argued that a positive "stage one" H&C decision provides the foundation for considering whether to issue a TRP. The applicant claims that there is no form or formal, legislated process for applying for a TRP; in practice, an applicant is only invited to apply for a TRP after a positive "Stage One" and a negative "Stage Two" H&C decision has been made. The parties have agreed that this matter should be returned for reconsideration for lack of reasons. The applicant claims that when the decision goes back, the Court should direct that the exemption from stage one or the PR application should continue to apply.

The Court concluded that when the matter is returned for reconsideration, the officer responsible is required to re-examine all aspects of the decision, and the Court should not interfere with this process by isolating one aspect and placing it outside the scope of reconsideration. The Court should not issue a direction that has the effect of making a decision that is for the decision maker to make and, while the Court may guide the decision-making process, it cannot make the actual decision.



*Lee v. Canada (Minister of Citizenship & Immigration)* (2006), 60 Imm. L.R. (3d) 62, 2006 FC 1461, 2006 CarswellNat 4260 (F.C.) — The applicant was found to be inadmissible pursuant to s. 38(1) of the IRPA. On the basis of medical evidence, the officer found that the applicant's health conditions, which included polycystic kidney disease, hypertension, moderate mitral regurgitation and chronic renal failure, would reasonably be expected to cause "excessive demands" on Canada's health services. The applicant argued that, as he is an entrepreneur with considerable net worth, the officer erred in law by failing to consider his ability to provide for his own health care if admitted to Canada, and further, the officer breached procedural fairness by not considering his request for a temporary resident permit. Specifically, the applicant relied on the Supreme Court of Canada's decision in *Hilewitz v. Canada (Minister of Citizenship and Immigration)*. Hilewitz dealt specifically with an applicant's ability to pay for *social services* and not *health services*; therefore the applicant's argument that the reasoning in *Hilewitz* applied equally to health services was dismissed. The officer did not err in law by not considering the applicant's financial ability to pay for his own health care.

In a letter to the Canadian Consulate, the applicant requested the officer consider granting him a TRP. The officer was required to respond to this request without the necessity of a separate submission. The failure of the officer to deal with this request constituted an error in due process. A different immigration officer was ordered to assess the applicant's temporary resident permit application on the basis of the existing evidentiary record.

*Farhat v. Canada (Minister of Citizenship & Immigration)*, 2006 CarswellNat 3418, 2006 FC 1275 (F.C.) — The Minister's delegate of the Consulate General of Canada in New York was of the opinion that the applicant's circumstances did not warrant the issuance of a temporary resident permit (TRP). The applicant sought judicial review of the decision. The applicant was married to a Canadian citizen who applied to sponsor him from within Canada. This application was refused as the applicant did not have temporary resident status at the time the application was filed. The applicant was then convicted of theft under $5,000 and a s. 44 report was prepared because the Minister was of the opinion that the applicant was inadmissible on grounds of criminality. The applicant was excluded from Canada for one year. The applicant's counsel was made aware that the applicant needed to apply for an authorization to return to Canada. The applicant then made an application for a TRP to the Canadian Consulate. The Minister concluded that the circumstances did not warrant the issuance of a TRP. The Minister was not satisfied that the applicant would leave Canada at its expiry. The Minister indicated that the applicant could apply for a pardon. The Minister also found that the applicant had to obtain an authorization to return to Canada.

The applicant has the onus of establishing the compelling reasons and did not satisfy the Minister that the particular circumstances of his case warranted the granting of a TRP. A person seeking a TRP must have the intention of staying in Canada for temporary purpose and an officer must be satisfied that such a person will leave upon the expiry of status. Albeit, it is true that an intention by a foreign national to become a permanent resident does not preclude an individual from becoming a temporary resident; nevertheless, the officer has to be satisfied that the foreign national will leave Canada by the end of the period authorized by his or her stay. Considering the applicant's history of non-compliance with the Canadian immigration laws and regulations, and his overstay in Canada, it was not patently unreasonable for the applicant to be obliged to leave at the end of the period authorized for his stay. The applicant did not present, in regard to the existence of his spouse and child, any "compelling reasons" which would allow him to be granted a TRP. It was not patently unreasonable for the Minister to consider the interest of the child, in this case, did not amount to "compelling reasons" in light of the evidence presented.

The decision of the Minister concerning the TRP application was not irrational or perverse or so gratuitous and oppressive that no reasonable person could think it justified. Consequently, this application for judicial review was dismissed.

*Figueroa v. Canada (Minister of Citizenship & Immigration)*, 2003 CarswellNat 3657, 2003 CarswellNat 4507, 2003 FC 1339 (F.C.) — The applicant sought to review a decision of an immigration officer refusing the applicant's request for an extension of her temporary resident status.

The applicant is a citizen of Cuba. She met her husband, Mr. Cecil Stein, a Canadian citizen, when he was vacationing there. Mr. Stein continued to visit the applicant in Cuba after his holiday and eventually proposed to her. The applicant sought a Canadian visitor visa but was refused. Mr. Stein contacted his member of Parliament and eventually a Minister's permit was obtained for the applicant in the summer of 2002. This permit allowed the applicant temporary residence in Canada until September 30, 2002. On August 21, 2002, the applicant married Mr. Stein and on August 26, 2002, more than 30 days before the expiration of her temporary resident permit, the applicant sought an extension pending a final determination of her permanent resident application. The permanent resident application was filed in September 2002, the applicant applied as a Member of the Spouse In-Canada class. Her application was supported by Mr. Stein's sponsorship application. In December 2002, the applicant's request for an extension of her temporary resident status was refused.

The covering letter from the immigration officer indicated that she was attaching copies of the decision giving written reasons for the decision. However, it is clear that the decision did not include any written reasons.

The respondent took the position that the immigration officer acted in accordance with the instructions from the Minister. The record, however, was silent as to the content of those instructions. In the absence of any evidence as to those instructions, and without reasons, a question arose as to how the immigration officer followed the instructions. In those circumstances, the lack of reasons raised an appearance of arbitrariness on the part of the officer. Accordingly the officer's decision was set aside.

**25. (1) Humanitarian and compassionate considerations — request of foreign national — The Minister must, on request of a foreign national in Canada who is inadmissible or who does not meet the requirements of this Act, and may, on request of a foreign national outside Canada, examine the circumstances concerning the foreign national and may grant the foreign national permanent resident status or an exemption from any applicable criteria or obligations of this Act if the Minister is of the opinion that it is justified by humanitarian and compassionate**

**considerations relating to the foreign national, taking into account the best interests of a child directly affected.**

(1.1) **Payment of fees — The Minister is seized of a request referred to in subsection (1) only if the applicable fees in respect of that request have been paid.**

(1.2) **Exceptions — The Minister may not examine the request if the foreign national has already made such a request and the request is pending.**

(1.3) **Non-application of certain factors — In examining the request of a foreign national in Canada, the Minister may not consider the factors that are taken into account in the determination of whether a person is a Convention refugee under section 96 or a person in need of protection under subsection 97(1) but must consider elements related to the hardships that affect the foreign national.**

(2) **Provincial criteria — The Minister may not grant permanent resident status to a foreign national referred to in subsection 9(1) if the foreign national does not meet the province's selection criteria applicable to that foreign national.**

2008, c. 28, s. 117; 2010, c. 8, s. 4(1)

IRP Act

## Case Law

### Section 25(1)

*John v. Canada (Minister of Citizenship & Immigration)*, 2010 FC 85, 2010 CarswellNat 1134, 2010 CarswellNat 126 (F.C.) — This is a judicial review of the Immigration Officer's refusal to grant an application for permanent residence from within Canada on humanitarian and compassionate grounds. The applicant was aged 18 when she came to Canada in order to care for her ailing mother. She never left despite her visa expiring in 1991 and her mother passing away in 1994. She remained with her uncle's family which included her grandmother, of whom she takes care.

Paragraph 13.8 of the Guidelines IP-5 suggests that an important consideration is to what extent the applicant would have difficulty in meeting financial or emotional needs without the support and assistance of the family unit in Canada. "Separation of persons in such a genuine dependent relationship may be grounds for a positive decision." The Guidelines list a number of factors the officer should consider which include whether the dependency is *bona fide*, the level thereof, the stability and the length of the relationship, the ability and willingness of the family in Canada to provide support, alternatives such as siblings outside of Canada "able and willing to provide support" and whether there has been a significant degree of establishment in Canada. The facts were clearly set out in the application, and not only were staring the officer in the face, but indeed were noted by the officer and therefore it was not necessary that s. 13.8 of the Guidelines dealing with *de facto* family relationships be specifically brought to the officer's attention. The officer's decision was unreasonable. The application for judicial review was allowed.

*Kisson v. Canada (Minister of Citizenship and Immigration)* (2010), 88 Imm. L.R. (3d) 66, 2010 FC 99, 2010 CarswellNat 803, 2010 CarswellNat 161 (F.C.) — This was an application for judicial review of a visa officer's decision rejecting the applicant's application for permanent residence under the federal skilled worker category. The applicant requested a substitute evaluation and exemption from the requirements of IRPA pursuant to humanitarian and compassionate considerations. The visa officer did not demonstrate that he looked beyond the selection criteria listed at subs. 76(1) of the Regulations (*i.e.*

education, language, experience, age, arranged employment, adaptability). There was no evidence that the visa officer's substituted evaluation broadly assessed the likelihood of the ability of the applicant to become economically established in Canada according to his set of circumstances. The clear intent of subs. 76(3) is to allow the visa officer to substitute their evaluation taking into account a number of factors, and not just the factors listed in s. 76(1). In this case, the applicant had an existing employment offer and previous establishment in Canada which were indicative of the possibility that the applicant will once again be able to establish himself successfully in Canada. It was unreasonable that these factors do not appear to have been considered by the officer when he assessed the humanitarian and compassionate considerations under s. 25 of IRPA. Application for judicial review was allowed.

*Kurukkal v. Canada (Minister of Citizenship & Immigration)* (2009), 81 Imm. L.R. (3d) 263, 347 F.T.R. 60 (Eng.), 98 Admin. L.R. (4th) 242, 2009 FC 695, 2009 CarswellNat 2147, [2009] F.C.J. No. 866 (F.C.) — The application for permanent residence on H&C grounds was refused because the applicant failed to provide a death certificate for his late wife when asked to do so by the immigration officer assessing his application. The applicant provided the death certificate a few days after being notified of the negative decision and asked that the decision be reconsidered in light of the new evidence. The respondent refused to reopen or revisit the applicant's application, asserting that there was no power to do so as a result of the doctrine of *functus officio. Functus officio* does not apply in the context of H&C decisions. As a consequence, the application for judicial review was allowed. The need for flexibility and responsiveness to changing circumstances and new information in the H&C assessment process outweighs the desirability of having finality and certainty in the decision-making process. The doctrine of *functus officio* does not apply to the informal, non-adjudicative decision-making process involved in the determination of H&C applications. As a consequence, the immigration officer erred in refusing to consider the death certificate provided by the applicant in this case.

The following question was certified:

> Once a decision has been rendered in relation to an application for humanitarian and compassionate exemption, is the ability of the decision-maker to reopen or reconsider the application on the basis of further evidence provided by an applicant limited by the doctrine of *functus officio*?

*Toussaint v. Canada (Minister of Citizenship & Immigration)* (2009), 83 Imm. L.R. (3d) 51, 350 F.T.R. 109 (Eng.), 198 C.R.R. (2d) 194, 2009 FC 873, 2009 CarswellNat 2595, 2009 CarswellNat 5173, [2009] F.C.J. No. 1034 (F.C.) — The applicant, a citizen of Grenada, came to Canada in December 1999 as a visitor. Her status expired within six months of entering Canada and since then she has been without status. She made an application pursuant to s. 25(1) of IRPA for an exemption from certain requirements of the Act on the basis of H&C considerations. Specifically she wanted to be exempt from the requirements of s. 11 that she must apply for permanent residence status before entering Canada; and to be granted residence from within Canada on H&C grounds. The fee required to process her in-Canada H&C application is $550, which she claimed she could not afford. The Court considered whether the Minister's decision was reviewable on the standard of correctness. In other words, was the Minister correct in his conclusion that an exemption from the fees is contrary to s. 10(1)(d) of *IRP* Regulations?

There is no question that s. 25 is very broad and covers much more than a request for an exemption to apply for a permanent visa from Canada. However, a broad and liberal interpretation of s. 25 does not necessarily mean that this provision is available in respect of every type of obligation that arises under IRPA or the Regulations. Section 25(1) is available as a matter of right to any foreign national in Canada "who is inadmissible or who does not meet the requirements of this Act." From this phrase, it is apparent that the focus of s. 25(1) is on substantive obligations that fundamentally affect the ability of a foreign national to come to or remain in Canada. This focus is reflected in the various types of s. 25(1) decisions that have been considered by the Federal Court. Section 25(1) does not require that the Minister consider a request to exempt a foreign national from the payment of fees established pursuant to s. 89 of IRPA and the relevant *IRP* Regulations. The Minister is without authority to do so. This interpretation is apparent when s. 25(1) is read harmoniously in its entire context and in its grammatical ordinary sense together with the scheme of IRPA, the object of IRPA and the intention of Parliament.



The deportation of the applicant prior to consideration of H&C factors does not engage the liberty and security issues protected by s. 7 of the *Charter*. Since neither the assessment of H&C factors or the best interest of the child are principles of fundamental justice to which s. 7 of the *Charter* apply, it follows that there was no breach of s. 7.

The applicant and interveners advanced two different arguments under s. 15(1) of the *Charter*. First, they submitted that persons living in poverty are protected under s. 15; thus, the Minister's failure to provide a fee waiver entails an important failure to exercise the discretion available under s. 25 of IRPA. In the alternative, they asserted that, by failing to provide for a fee waiver pursuant to the regulation-making authority of s. 89 of IRPA, the government violated s. 15 of the *Charter*.

Even if the Court were to accept that persons living in a state of poverty — within in which they cannot afford the s. 25 processing fee — face a distinction as compared to the comparator group, the s. 15(1) claim fails. This is because the Court concluded that poverty is not an analogous ground. Further, and even if poverty were accepted as an analogous ground, there is insufficient evidence to persuade the Court that any distinction caused by the failure of the Minister to implement a fee waiver for foreign nationals living in poverty perpetuates the prejudice for stereotyping of persons living in poverty. The failure of the government to implement a fee waiver was not contrary to s. 15(1) of the *Charter*.

Section 25(1) provides a discretionary benefit to foreign nationals. Parliament has no obligation to provide for foreign nationals to remain in Canada on H&C grounds. Section 25 itself does not provide any right to make an in-Canada H&C application; rather it provides an opportunity to apply for an exemption from provisions of IRPA or the Regulations. The Minister is only obligated to consider H&C factors "upon request." Immigration is not a right, nor is access to s. 25 of IRPA.

The application for judicial review was dismissed.

The following questions were certified:

A. On a proper statutory interpretation of s. 25(1) of IRPA, is the Minister obligated to consider a request to grant an exemption from the requirement to pay the H&C processing fee, otherwise required under s. 307 of the *IRP* Regulations?

B. Does the failure of the government (through the GIC) to enact regulations permitting the waiver of fees for foreign nationals living in poverty who wish to make an in-Canada application for permanent residence status pursuant to s. 25(1) of IRPA infringe the applicant's rights under ss. 7 or 15 of the *Charter*?

C. Is the failure of government (through the GIC) to enact regulations permitting the waiver of fees for foreign nationals living in poverty who wish to make an in-Canada application for permanent residence status pursuant to section 25(1) of IRPA contrary to either the rule of law or the common-law constitutional right of access to the Courts?

*Kisana v. Canada (Minister of Citizenship & Immigration)*, [2010] 1 F.C.R. 360, 392 N.R. 163, 2009 FCA 189, 2009 CarswellNat 1626, 2009 CarswellNat 4008, [2009] F.C.J. No. 713 (F.C.A.) — The minor appellants were the twins of Sushil and Seema Kisana, born in India on August 20, 1991, before their parents were married. Sushil immigrated to Canada on February 16, 1993, and was landed as an unmarried dependant of his parents. He married Seema upon his return to India in 1994 and subsequently sponsored her for permanent residence in Canada. Seema was landed on April 25, 1999. Both are now Canadian citizens. Neither listed their daughters as dependants on their permanent residence applications. Seema further denied having any children during her two call-in interviews while her application was being processed. Their explanation for failing to make the disclosure is that they were ashamed of having had children out of wedlock and that they had not disclosed the fact that they had children to their parents. The girls' aunt had been caring for them in India since Seema left for Canada. An application to sponsor the girls in 2005 was made with a request that the application be considered on H&C grounds. Specifically, the appellants requested that the visa officer consider the emotional impact of continued separation and indicated that the aunt was no longer in a position to adequately care for their daughters. The Federal Court judge concluded that the officer had not erred in determining that the girls had not suffered undue hardship because of the separation from their parents and their having to live in India. The Federal Court judge also held that the parents' misrepresentation with respect to their daughters was a proper consideration for the officer in determining the H&C application. The Federal Court of Appeal reviewed whether the officer's decision was reasonable and whether adequate consideration was given to the children's best interest. The appeal was dismissed.

An officer who is "alert, alive and sensitive" to the best interest of the child will take these vulnerabilities into account. Generally officers should endeavour to ask age-appropriate questions, satisfy themselves that the questions are understood and ask open-ended questions or follow-up questions where appropriate. Particularly in cases involving very young children, it may be appropriate for an adult to accompany the child in the interview room. In short, while an officer is under no obligation to attempt to illicit all evidence that may help a child's case, being "alert, alive and sensitive" to the child's best interest requires that an interview be conducted in a manner that will allow the child to express him or herself effectively. An officer must keep in mind the linguistic, cognitive and emotional difference between children and adults when conducting an interview. A child confronted with pointed, close-ended questions will likely give simply "yes" or "no" responses and not make efforts to volunteer any additional information. He or she may be reluctant to ask for clarification if a question is not understood. Younger children may not be capable of comprehending the nature of the interview at all.

*In obiter*, Justice Trudel commented that it is wholly inappropriate to import the "best interest of the child" framework that is used in custody and access cases into immigration applications. The best interests of the child are the determinative factor in a family law case — not so in an immigration context, where it is but one factor to be weighed along with others.

*Kandhai v. Canada (Minister of Citizenship & Immigration)* (2009), 81 Imm. L.R. (3d) 144, 2009 FC 656, 2009 CarswellNat 1919, 2009 CarswellNat 5681 (F.C.) — The applicant sought judicial review of a decision refusing his application for humanitarian and compassionate exemption. The Court determined it was appropriate to consider the application, notwithstanding the applicant's history of repeatedly lying to Canadian immigration authorities. The reasons given for refusing the H&C application were also insufficient. The officer's "reasons" essentially consisted of a review of facts coupled with a statement of conclusion, without any analysis to back it up. Consequently the application for judicial review was allowed. The decision under review was the applicant's third H&C application. He admitted that he was not truthful on his most recent H&C application, as he indicated on the form that he was divorced when in fact he was living in a common-law relationship with his ex-wife. The applicant argued that while the misrepresentation as to his marital situation was undoubtedly an error in judgment, it was not made with the intent of securing an advantage in relation to his H&C application, and thus had no negative effect on the integrity of the Canadian immigration process. In fact, the presence of a common-law partner in Canada may have strengthened his H&C application. In two prior H&C applications, the applicant indicated that he had never been charged with, or convicted of, a criminal offence in another country, when that was not, in fact, the case. These misrepresentations were made in order to gain an advantage in relation to those applications, and thus had the potential to undermine the integrity of the immigration process. In this case, since the misrepresentations did not appear to be made to gain an advantage, and the applicant appeared to have come forward voluntarily with his admission of misrepresentation, the Court concluded that for the purposes of this "clean hands" analysis it was a very strong case.

The Court relied on the Federal Court of Appeal decision in *Thanabalasingham v. Canada (Minister of Citizenship & Immigration)*, [2006] F.C.J. No. 20, where the Federal Court of Appeal held that the task for the reviewing Court is to strike a balance between "maintaining the integrity of, and preventing the abuse of, judicial and administrative processes," and "the public interest in ensuring the lawful conduct of government in the protection of fundamental human rights."

*Rakheja v. Canada (Minister of Citizenship & Immigration)* (2009), 81 Imm. L.R. (3d) 219, 345 F.T.R. 159 (Eng.), 2009 FC 633, 2009 CarswellNat 5615, 2009 CarswellNat 1875 (F.C.) — An immigration officer found that the applicant did not meet the requirements of the Spouse or Common-law Partner in Canada Class as outlined in section 5.14 of the Operational Manual for Inland Processing 8 (IP8). Specifically the officer found that the applicant did not meet the requirement of possessing a valid non-expired passport, and did not qualify for the discretionary exemption available where a passport has expired during the processing of an application. During his interview, the applicant stated that he would not be able to obtain a new passport because there was an outstanding arrest warrant against him in India. The applicant argued that the immigration officer erred in concluding that he was ineligible for a passport waiver and that, under the guidelines, he should have been given an opportunity to obtain a passport before his application was refused.

Section 72(1)(e)(ii) and s. 50(1)(a) of the Regulations require that an individual must provide a passport or travel document. One reason for the passport requirement is to prove the identity of the applicant. Under the policy, individuals whose passports expire during processing may submit their expired passports if there is no question as to their identity. The guidelines in the Operational Manual IP8 do not provide that an immigra-



IRP Act

tion officer may accept an expired passport where the expired date pre-dates the application for permanent residence. However, the intent of the public policy is to facilitate family reunification of spouses under s. 25 of IRPA, even where the applicant is not in status as required by the Act.

An application for permanent residence under the Spouse or Common-law Partner in Canada Class is a discretionary exemption by the respondent under s. 25 of IRPA. The respondent has set out a policy for situations granting that exemption which include that the applicant have a valid passport at the time the application is made. According to the respondent the applicant can now make another application under s. 25 for an exemption from the requirement that he have a valid passport, and then the applicant can make another application for permanent residence under the Spouse or Common-law Partner in Canada Class. While this two-step process seems illogical, the Court acknowledges that it was reasonably open to the respondent to require that the applicant have a valid passport before bringing his current application. Accordingly, the immigration officer's decision in this matter was reasonably open to her and the application for judicial review was dismissed.

*Enabulele v. Canada (Ministry of Public Safety & Emergency Preparedness)* (2009), 81 Imm. L.R. (3d) 78, 347 F.T.R. 309 (Eng.), 2009 FC 641, 2009 CarswellNat 1876, 2009 CarswellNat 5904 (F.C.) — The applicant, a citizen of Nigeria married to a Canadian citizen, applied for permanent residence under the Spouse or Common-law Partner in Canada Class, pursuant to the Ministerial Policy, released in February 2005, and contained in Appendix H of the Citizenship and Immigration of Canada's Operational Manual for Inland Processing IP8. This policy is designed to allow spouses or common-law partners in Canada to apply for permanent residence from within Canada in accordance with the same criteria as members of the Spouse or Common-law Partner in Canada Class regardless of their immigration status. The applicant was advised, by reason of having been charged with two counts of sexual assault, that he was not entitled to a 60-day administrative deferral of removal under the policy. The applicant sought to challenge the policy on the basis that it violated his s. 7 and s. 11(d) *Charter* rights. The Court accepted the respondent's submission that the administrative deferral under the policy sought by the applicant would have expired even if the officer had found that the applicant was eligible for it. Notwithstanding this, the Court considered the *Charter* issues raised in the application.

The applicant argued that the policy compromised his security in that it did not allow him to defend his innocence of the charges laid against him. He says the policy stigmatizes those charged but not convicted of criminal charges. The Court found the applicant's argument without merit and concluded his s. 7 *Charter* rights were not engaged in the circumstances. The impugned policy renders the applicant ineligible for an administrative deferral by reason of his criminal charges. It does not follow, however that the applicant will be removed without a proper risk assessment. The PRRA process, to which the applicant is entitled, is designed to assist foreign nationals who may be required to leave Canada. It is the means by which the applicant can have his risk assessed prior to his departure. It is the very process which provides for consideration of the applicant's life, liberty and security interest in a pre-removal context. The applicant's access to that process was in no way affected by the policy. The application for judicial review was dismissed. The following question was certified:

> Does the Minister's policy on administrative deferral of removal found under IP8 offend the applicant's sections 7 and 11(d) rights of the *Canadian Charter of Rights and Freedoms*?

*Koromila v. Canada (Minister of Citizenship & Immigration)*, 2009 CarswellNat 1167, 2009 FC 393 (F.C.) — The applicant sought judicial review of a decision to refuse an application on H&C grounds pursuant to s. 25 of the IRPA. The applicant's mother died when she was aged 3 and her father never remarried. The applicant and her sister were raised in Greece by their father and their aunt. Their father died of a heart attack when they were teenagers and their aunt continued to care for them. The applicant's sister met a Canadian citizen and immigrated to Canada. The applicant remained in Greece to live and help support her aunt. It was their intention to join her sister and her husband in Canada. Subsequently, the aunt had a very bad stroke and was paralyzed. The applicant remained in Greece to look after her aunt. The aunt died in December 2002. The applicant is alone in Greece and is currently an elderly woman. The applicant says that, as they age, it will become more difficult for her and her sister to visit each other. The applicant applied for permanent residence in Canada in June of 2007 and was refused by the officer.

The officer's stated understanding of the scope of s. 3(1)(d) of the Act is that "the objective of the law was to reunite parents with their children or children with parents or spouses." The officer either misunderstood the scope of s. 3(1)(d) and so fettered his discretion or he made a mistake of law. There was no evidence before the Court that the officer was cognizant of the principle enunciated in paragraph 3(1)(d) of the Act or of the considerations to be taken into account as enunciated in the elements of the OP 4 in considering whether a *de facto* family member should qualify for relief on humanitarian and compassionate considerations. This error was compounded by the officer's assessment that the applicant's coming to Canada permanently was simply a matter of convenience and that the applicant was not a *de facto* family member who had been left behind. The visa officer ignored the evidence of emotional dependency. There is a significant factual difference between living together and sharing day-to-day life and an occasional visit. Such matters seem to have been left entirely out of account by the officer to an unreasonable extent. The officer did not consider the application of subs. 3(1)(d) of the Act to this case. The application for judicial review was allowed.

*Okoye v. Canada (Minister of Citizenship & Immigration)*, 2008 CarswellNat 4570, 2008 CarswellNat 3690, 2008 FC 1133 (F.C.) — Subsection 25 of the IRPA imposes a statutory duty on the officer to consider the best interests of a child. At the same time, the best interests of a child are not determinative of the parent's status. In the present case, Ms. Okoye expressly raised her daughter Bianca's best interests in her humanitarian and compassionate application, and provided medical evidence from Bianca's pediatrician that she requires treatment for acute asthma attacks. This distinguishes the decision of *Ahmad*, [2008] F.C.J. No. 814, where it was not clear that the parents raised as an issue their children's best interests. The officer's reference in her reasons to Bianca was almost passing in nature. While the officer referred to the doctor's letter, Bianca's medical needs were not mentioned in the analysis portion of the officer's reasons. The officer does not address how Bianca's interests will be affected by her mother's departure from Canada, does not address what hardship Bianca would face in Nigeria, and does not address Bianca's best interests. This analysis was particularly required when country condition documentation otherwise relied upon by the officer reported that in Nigeria public schools are substandard, and many children do not have access to education. Application for judicial review was allowed.

*Ferrer v. Canada (Minister of Citizenship & Immigration)*, 2009 CarswellNat 899, 2009 CarswellNat 2095, 2009 FC 356 (F.C.) — The applicant sought judicial review of a decision of the IAD which dismissed his plea for humanitarian and compassionate relief pursuant to s. 67(1)(c) of the IRPA. An exclusion order had been issued against the applicant based on a finding of inadmissibility for a misrepresentation made in September 1998 with respect to his permanent resident application. In his permanent resident application, the applicant testified that he was single with no children. It was not disputed that at the time he was the father of two dependent children living with their mother in the Philippines. The applicant married his spouse who was the mother of his two children on a trip back to the Philippines after he was granted permanent residence status in Canada. The applicant's spouse is not excluded from the family class pursuant to s. 117(9)(d) of the Regulations. Accordingly, the applicant's two children would be eligible to be included on the applicant's spouse's application for permanent residence as her dependent children, provided the applicant's appeal before the IAD was allowed as he would be in a position to sponsor his wife and both of his children as members of the family class.

The IAD considered only two possibilities with respect to the best interests of the children. The first possibility was that the children could remain in the Philippines and that their father would continue to have a geographically distant relationship with them while at the same time supporting them financially at a higher level than possible if he were returned to the Philippines. The second alternative was that the applicant could be returned to the Philippines where he would be able to better meet their emotional needs by having close contact with them, though he would not be able to provide the higher level of financial support in the event that he was removed from Canada. It was argued that the analysis was erroneous and that it did not take into consideration the most probable outcome should the applicant's appeal be allowed. The tribunal's failure to consider the likely chain of events should the appeal be allowed led to its conclusion that the best interests of the children were a neutral factor; in fact the best interests of the applicant's children were a positive factor which weighed in favour of allowing the appeal. In other words, the tribunal failed to appreciate that the applicant's children could have the best of both worlds by being reunited with him in Canada. Had the tribunal not committed this error, it would certainly have considered the best interests of the applicant's children to be a factor in favour of allowing his appeal and not a neutral factor — thereby negating its value. It appears that the IAD's reasoning was dominated by a consideration of the "integrity of the Canadian immigration system." This might be an important factor to consider, but only after the best interest of the children are properly addressed; only in this way can a fair and balanced approach be taken to this important statutory requirement. The application for judicial review was allowed and the matter sent back for redetermination.

*Okoloubu v. Canada (Minister of Citizenship & Immigration)* (2008), 75 Imm. L.R. (3d) 1, 301 D.L.R. (4th) 591, 382 N.R. 35, 2008 CarswellNat 3852, 2008 CarswellNat 5576, 2008 FCA 326 — The applicant sought an exemption to apply for permanent residence from within Canada. Were it not for a criminal conviction, he would have been entitled to remain in Canada while his application for a permanent resident visa was being considered. However, his conviction disqualified him from being a member of the Spouse or Common-law Partner in Canada class. He argued that protection of the family and the rights of his wife and the child had to be properly considered. The pre-removal risk assessment officer said she did not have jurisdiction to deal with international law and constitutional issues, and that a request for exemption from permanent resident visa requirements was not the proper venue for resolving such complex legal issues. The officer concluded that the applicant's family situation, links within Canadian society, and the risk factors upon his return to his country did not justify an exemption. The applicant successfully had the decision set aside by the Federal Court. The Federal Court agreed and concluded that the officer's refusal to consider the applicant's rights and those of his wife and Canadian child under the *Charter* and the International Convention on Civil and Political Rights resulted in an unfair hearing. The Minister appealed this decision to the Federal Court of Appeal.



The Federal Court of Appeal held that paragraph 3(3)(f) of the IRPA does not require that an officer exercising discretion under s. 25 specifically refer to and analyze the international human rights instruments to which Canada is signatory. It is sufficient if the officer addresses the substance of the issues raised. While the officer stated that she did "not have jurisdiction to deal with international law" it was clear that she addressed in substance the different and important interests at stake, giving careful weight to the interest of the child and the importance of the family unit. Therefore, the Federal Court of Appeal's intervention was not warranted and it became unnecessary to address the Federal Court Judge's finding that the respondent was deprived a fair hearing. The Federal Court of Appeal found that the certified question "Does an immigration officer in charge of assessing an application under s. 25 of the *Immigration Refugee and Protection Act* (for an exemption from the obligation to present an application for an immigrant visa from outside Canada) have jurisdiction to consider whether an applicant's removal would breach the *International Covenant on Civil and Political Rights*, more specifically Article 17, 23 and 24?" was irrelevant and not dispositive of the appeal and therefore it need not be answered. The appeal was allowed, the judgment of the Federal Court set aside and the applicant's application for judicial review dismissed.

*Alie v. Canada (Minister of Citizenship & Immigration)*, 2008 CarswellNat 2627, 2008 CarswellNat 3911, 2008 FC 925 (F.C.) — The applicants were denied permanent residency in Canada on humanitarian and compassionate grounds. When considering the best interests of the Canadian born child of the adult applicants, the officer failed to properly focus her analysis on the needs of that child; her analysis was focused on the benefit or harm to the family if they were moved from Canada. Proper focus of those considerations must be on the child herself. In this case, the officer failed to focus on the child and the hardship the removal of her family, with or without her, would have on her. Instead, the officer focused her analysis on the hardship to the family if they were removed from Canada, with or without the child. The application for judicial review was allowed.

*Odicho v. Canada (Minister of Citizenship & Immigration)* (2008), 75 Imm. L.R. (3d) 45, 2008 CarswellNat 4011, 2008 CarswellNat 3442, 2008 FC 1039 (F.C.) — Mr. and Mrs. Odicho sought judicial review of a visa officer's decision to refuse to issue a permanent resident visa to Mrs. Odicho. The applicants argued that the visa officer erred by failing to consider H&C grounds, pursuant to subs. 25 of the IRPA. They submit that they specifically requested that the wife's application for permanent residence in Canada be considered on the basis of s. 25. Mr. Odicho had been landed in Canada in January 2005 and his initial application to sponsor his wife in May 2005 was refused on the basis that he had not disclosed his marriage when he was landed. The application on behalf of a dependent child was refused for the same reason but was subsequently reversed. The visa officer, however, maintained the rejection of the application on behalf of the wife on the basis of paragraph 117(9)(d) of the Regulations.

There was no dispute that the husband failed to declare his wife as a non-accompanying dependant when he landed in Canada in January 2005. There is no evidence to challenge the *bona fides* of the marriage of the applicants. There is no evidence to challenge the status of the infant as their child. The failure of the husband to declare the change in marital status when he landed in Canada gave rise to the exclusion of his wife pursuant to the terms of paragraph 117(9)(d) of the Regulations. The Court held that the visa officer apparently ignored the material that was submitted concerning the "circumstances" of the husband's failure to declare the change in his marital status at the time he landed in Canada. The applicants carry the burden of establishing the evidence to justify an exercise of discretion, but the discharge of this burden does not require superfluity. The visa officer's decision does not demonstrate an understanding of the purpose of subs. 25(1), which is to overcome the consequences of being in breach of statutory requirements. The initial decision which excluded the child, as well as the wife, illustrates an excess of zeal on the part of that decision maker, if not a misunderstanding of s. 117 of the Regulations. The application for judicial review was allowed. The matter was remitted for reconsideration by a different member of the Canadian Embassy.

*Lopez v. Canada (Minister of Citizenship & Immigration)*, 2008 CarswellNat 1325, 2008 CarswellNat 1326, 2008 FC 582 — This was the judicial review of a PRRA officer's dismissal of an application for permanent residence made from within Canada. The officer failed to take into account that s. 25 of the IRPA is driven either on humanitarian and compassionate considerations or public policy considerations. Put another way, is it Canada's public policy that a person who is not inadmissible in terms of the United Nations Convention Relating to the Status of Refugees and whose record of criminality in Canada cannot be considered because of the pardon granted to him (s. 36(3) IRPA) should nevertheless have to busk in the Montreal Metro for the rest of his life without legal status? The decision of the PRRA officer was an important one which affected the applicant's life in a fundamental way. In this case, the officer failed to assure himself that there was a public policy consideration present. The question was not whether there would be an unusual, underserved or disproportionate hardship if the applicant had to leave Canada. The truth was that he cannot leave Canada since Cuba won't take him back and the authorities know it. The applicant had not applied for permanent residence from abroad because he could not. The application for judicial review was granted and the matter referred back to another officer for redetermination.

*Yoon v. Canada (Minister of Citizenship & Immigration)*, 2008 CarswellNat 844, 2008 CarswellNat 1862, 2008 FC 439 — The applicants, an elderly couple from Korea, applied for permanent residence from within Canada based on humanitarian and compassionate considerations. The officer refused the case stating that the applicants' daughters were "established enough to meet the LICO standards for sponsorship of their parents after eight years in Canada". A scrutiny of the record discloses that there was no evidence to support this statement. There was absolutely no evidence on the record to substantiate the notion that the applicants would only be temporarily separated from their children should they be required to return to Korea. The decision under review was unreasonable and was set aside.

*Thandal v. Canada (Minister of Citizenship & Immigration)*, 2008 CarswellNat 1085, 2008 CarswellNat 1958, 2008 FC 489 — The applicant sought judicial review of a decision to refuse her application for permanent residence as a skilled worker and her H&C

application from outside Canada. With the Supreme Court of Canada's decision in *New Brunswick (Board of Management) v. Dunsmuir*, 2008 SCC 9, it is settled that procedural fairness is to be reviewed on a correctness standard while the H&C decision is to be reviewed on a reasonableness standard. The reasonableness standard admits a range of reasonable outcomes. The Court was aware that an H&C decision is discretionary, an exception to the normal rules. The officer, by virtue of familiarity and having interviewed the applicant, was in an excellent position to assess the merits of the applicant's story.

It is well established that an applicant has the burden of establishing her case. Generally, an applicant is to do that once, rather than on the basis of some sort of rolling story of reply, sur-reply and so forth. The applicant had an interview at which all the relevant issues were canvassed. There is nothing unfair in the officer deciding the case on the evidence as provided by the applicant at that time. The judicial review was dismissed.



*Thalang v. Canada (Minister of Citizenship & Immigration)* (2008), 71 Imm. L.R. (3d) 60, 2008 CarswellNat 1270, 2008 FC 340, 2008 CarswellNat 668 — The applicant made both a PRRA application and an H&C application both of which were considered by the same officer at the same time. The officer based the H&C assessment on the wrong test. The officer's assessment was based on risk, which was a PRRA criteria, not an H&C criteria. The proper H&C criteria are unusual and undeserved or disproportionate hardship. This was an error of law in respect of which the standard of review is that of correctness.

*Johnson v. Canada (Minister of Citizenship & Immigration)*, [2008] F.C.J. No. 10, 2008 CarswellNat 1327, 2008 FC 2, 2008 CarswellNat 11 (F.C.) — The applicant's inland application for permanent residence was refused because he was found to be inadmissible on grounds of serious criminality. The criminal convictions that led to the finding of inadmissibility were later set aside. The applicant argued that the officer erred in reaching the decision to refuse his permanent residence application by ignoring relevant evidence, specifically that the applicant's conviction was under appeal and that the officer breached the duty of fairness he owed to the applicant by failing to provide the applicant with an opportunity to respond to his criminal convictions.

A deportation order has a clear and imminent effect upon a person's right to remain in Canada. If, in that context, there is no obligation to await the result of an appeal of a criminal conviction, it is the Court's view that there can be no obligation to defer consideration of a humanitarian and compassionate application because of an outstanding appeal. This is so because one may file a new inland application for permanent residence if circumstances later change as a result of a successful appeal. In the absence of compelling circumstances, it would be contrary to the scheme of the Act to require decisions about inadmissibility, made in the context of humanitarian and compassionate application, to be delayed until all criminal proceedings, including all rights of appeal are exhausted. The failure of the applicant to advise immigration of his convictions did not shift the onus to the officer to communicate with the applicant about his convictions. It was always open to the applicant to advise the officer of both his convictions and his appeal, and to request a deferral of the officer's decision until the appeal had been decided. The applicant requested no postponement of the officer's decision. The application for judicial review was dismissed.

*Montivero v. Canada (Minister of Citizenship & Immigration)*, 2008 CarswellNat 1705, 2008 CarswellNat 2802, 2008 FC 720 (F.C.) — The applicants sought to quash the decision of an immigration officer denying their application for an exemption on humanitarian and compassionate (H&C) grounds. The selection of the appropriate test in the context of an H&C application should be assessed by the Court on a correctness standard. There is an importance of holding officers to the tests prescribed by Parliament. The correctness standard should be applied here. The applicants submitted that the test for personalized risk under ss. 96 and 97 of the IRPA is different from that of undue hardship under s. 25 H&C applications. They claim that the assessment of the availability of state protection to the applicants is unnecessary under a s. 25 undue hardship analysis. They assert that the officer's assessment of this factor shows that the officer erroneously imposed the higher ss. 96 and 97 threshold to the applicants' s. 25 application. The Court concluded that the applicants did not show that the officer applied an incorrect test or threshold to their application. The Court pointed out that the applicants raised the question of state protection in their submissions on the H&C application and therefore could not now argue that such an issue was irrelevant to that assessment. In this case, the officer's analysis that the question of alleged risk on an H&C assessment revealed that it was considered in the context of hardship. Accordingly, the decision was not based on the wrong legal test and the decision was not set aside.

*Thiara v. Canada (Minister of Citizenship & Immigration)* (2008), 70 Imm. L.R. (3d) 80, 2008 CarswellNat 1220, 2008 FCA 151 (F.C.A.) — Paragraph 3(3)(f) of the IRPA does not require that an officer exercising discretion under s. 25 of the IRPA specifically refer to and analyze the international human rights instruments to which Canada is a signatory. It is sufficient if the officer addresses the substance of the issues raised.

*Phillip v. Canada (Minister of Citizenship & Immigration)* (2008), 67 Imm. L.R. (3d) 132, 2008 CarswellNat 989, 2008 CarswellNat 16, 2008 FC 19 (F.C.) — This was the case of a 64-year-old grandmother who had resided in Canada for 19 years and was the *de facto* mother of her daughter's children (if not the only caregiver). In the respondent's decision, the officer noted the applicant's accomplishments but did not regard her establishment as "exceptional". The respondent relied upon the content of the father's successful H&C application in which he included another daughter as evidence of the father's commitment to his two other children, the applicant's grandchildren. On the issue of the best interests of the children, the officer assumed that the grandchildren would be taken care of by extended family and that their father would be involved. There was no analysis of the father's ability to care for the children despite the father's admission that he had not been able to care for them. The officer's reliance on the father's H&C application and the inclusion of another daughter therein, was not only procedurally unsound but lead to a *non sequitur* of reasoning. Not only was the use of the father's H&C application a breach of fairness, it led to, or compounded, a substantive error in the consideration of the best interests of the children.

*Aguilar Espino v. Canada (Minister of Citizenship & Immigration)*, [2007] F.C.J. No. 102, 2007 CarswellNat 143, 2007 FC 74 (F.C.) — The applicant, his wife and their two children applied for permanent residence from within Canada on humanitarian and compassionate grounds. Their application was rejected by an officer. The guidelines in the Inland Processing Manual (IP 5) direct that an application to remain in Canada on humanitarian and compassionate grounds be assessed in two steps. The two-step process is explained in ss. 5.6, 5.7 and 5.9. The first step requires the applicants satisfy the decision maker that the H&C factors present in their individual circumstances are sufficient to warrant an exemption. The second step requires that the applicant must meet the requirements for permanent residence in Regulation 68, including that the applicant and their family members, whether accompanying or not, are not inadmissible and otherwise meet the requirements of the Act and Regulations. The two-step assessment process for considering humanitarian and compassionate applications set out in the guidelines applicable to subs. 25(1) of the Act is not contrary to the Act. The two-step assessment process is not contrary to the intent of the legislation but it is supportable within the terms of the Act. The application for judicial review was dismissed.

The following questions were certified:

1. Is the Minister legally entitled to fragment an application under s. 25 of the *Immigration and Refugee Protection Act* into a two-step assessment, the first step being an assessment whether individual humanitarian and compassionate circumstances are sufficient to warrant an exemption from subs. 11(1) and 20(1) of the IRPA and the second step being a determination whether the person is inadmissible?

2. Is the Minister obliged, when considering an application under s. 25 of the IRPA, to weigh or balance the degree of compelling humanitarian and compassionate circumstances on which the individual relies against the nature and extent of the legal obstacle to admissibility?

*Wong v. Canada (Minister of Citizenship & Immigration)*, 2006 CarswellNat 3951, 2006 FC 1410 (F.C.) — In deciding whether to grant the applicant an exemption from the processing requirements under subs. 11(1) of the IRPA, the decision maker erred in placing undue emphasis on the applicant's suspected medical inadmissibility and potential for establishment in Canada. The decision maker's assessment of these factors ought to have been deferred until the second stage of the H&C application. The decision to deny the applicant's application on humanitarian and compassionate grounds for an exemption from their requirement to obtain an immigration visa before coming to Canada was quashed.

*Oshurova c. Canada (Ministre de la Citoyenneté & de l'Immigration)*, 2006 CarswellNat 5301, 2006 FCA 301 (Fed. C.A.) — The Federal Court of Appeal was asked to answer whether there was an appearance of bias, *in this case*, because the same officer decided the application for a visa exemption on humanitarian and compassionate grounds as well as the pre-removal risk assessment.

There is no apprehension of institutional bias of all officers who have been or are involved with these two types of applications. The appeal was dismissed.

*Williams v. Canada (Minister of Citizenship & Immigration)*, 2006 CarswellNat 4593, 2006 FC 1474 (F.C.) — An applicant bears the onus of establishing that he or she has met the standard required to succeed in an H&C application. A successful H&C application usually requires an applicant to demonstrate that an "unusual, underserved or disproportionate hardship" would arise should he or she be required to apply for permanent resident status from outside Canada. An applicant in an H&C application is entitled to present any facts he or she believes to be relevant. The law is clear that some hardship accruing to a separation from family will not necessarily satisfy the requirements of an H&C application. The fact that one leaves behind friends or family, employment or residence, as well as the cost of or inconvenience of having to return home to apply in the normal manner would not generally be enough to constitute hardship and thus warrant a positive H&C determination. An applicant has a high threshold to meet when requesting an exemption from the IRPA.

*Yue v. Canada (Minister of Citizenship & Immigration)*, [2006] F.C.J. No. 914, 2006 CarswellNat 1600, 2006 FC 717 (F.C.) — This is an application for judicial review of a decision of a visa officer denying the applicant's request to be granted permanent residence status and exemption from a requirement of the IRPA. The applicant's mother, who is a resident and citizen of Canada, sought to sponsor her for permanent residence some years after the mother had gained permanent residence in Canada. She had not, in her application for permanent residence, included the name of the applicant as a member of the family class and is now unable to sponsor the applicant unless the applicant obtains an exemption on humanitarian and compassionate grounds under subs. 25(1) of the Act.

The applicant was born to her mother and her mother's first husband in China in 1988. In 1989, her father committed suicide. Her mother remarried in October of 1992 and had a daughter by that marriage as well. The applicant did not live with her mother after 1992 but lived with her maternal grandparents. The mother's second husband went to the United States in 1995 to study and in 1997 the mother joined him there. They immigrated to Canada in 1999. The mother, when applying for permanent residence, did not list the applicant as a family member. The mother returned to China in 2000 and 2004 to see her daughter. She talked to her daughter frequently on the telephone and sent her money regularly. The applicant lived with her maternal grandparents until she entered a boarding school where she was still a student. She visits her grandparents on weekends. The applicant is now 18 years old and her mother stated that she has not visited her daughter more often in China because while she was in the United States, she was a student who could not leave and return on a student visa, and later when in Canada she could not afford to do so.

The Court concluded that the visa officer adequately addressed herself to issues of hardship. While taking into account that it is the wish of the applicant to live with her mother she observed such facts as: that the applicant had not lived with her mother since 1992; that she was then 17 (now 18); that she lives at a boarding school and sees her grandparents on weekends; that her mother's contacts with her, at least since the mother left for the United States in 1997, have been limited to phone calls three or four times a week and two visits by her mother to China in 2000 and 2004; and that her mother sends her money periodically. The officer had no indication before her that the applicant was a needy person because of her presence in China nor was there any specific evidence as to how her life would be materially better in Canada. It is not for the Federal Court to review that balancing of factors where it is apparent that the visa officer had them in mind when she made her decision.

*Terigho v. Canada (Minister of Citizenship & Immigration)*, [2006] F.C.J. No. 1061, 2006 CarswellNat 1901, 2006 FC 835 (F.C.) — This is an application for judicial review of the decision of an immigration officer not to recommend an exemption from visa requirements due to humanitarian and compassionate considerations pursuant to subs. 25(1) of the IRPA. In her decision, the officer indicated that she had considered the applicant's case under both H&C considerations and the spousal support policy, but did not believe the marriage was genuine. The main issue in the application was whether the officer erred in her assessment that the marriage of the applicant and his Canadian wife was not genuine, and had ignored relevant evidence before her. The officer made no mention of the documentary evidence filed in support of the application. Although there is generally a presumption that a tribunal, such as an officer conducting a H&C assessment, will have considered all of the evidence that was before it, where there is relevant evidence that contradicts the tribunal's finding on a central issue, there is an obligation on the tribunal to analyze that evidence and to explain in its decision why it does not accept it or prefers other evidence on the point in question. The greater the relevance of the evidence, the greater the need for the tribunal to explain its reasons for not attributing weight to it.

In this case, there was no question that the documentary evidence was highly relevant to the issue of the genuineness of the marriage. When cross-examined on her affidavit as to why she made no mention of the documents in her decision, the officer's response was, in essence, that they were only one piece of the evidence and that she preferred to rely upon the face to face interviews and her assessment of the spouses' consistency in answer to her questions. Thus it appears that the officer totally discounted the documents and based her decision entirely upon the opinion she formed from the interviews. The Court concluded that while the interviews can be an effective tool in uncovering fraud in the H&C process, the results achieved do not relieve the officer of the responsibility to properly analyze the other evidence. The officer's failure to do so was a reviewable error and consequently the application for judicial review was allowed.

*Somasundram v. Canada (Minister of Citizenship & Immigration)* (2006), 56 Imm. L.R. (3d) 105, 2006 CarswellNat 2180, 2006 FC 925 (F.C.) — The applicant, a single, Tamil, female citizen of Sri Lanka fled Colombo where she was seized and detained by the police who abused her and demanded information as to the warring factions in her local area. Upon her release by the police she fled to Canada claiming refugee protection. Once in Canada, she took up residence with relatives in the Toronto area, has been steadily employed as a cashier in a local business and settled into the community without incident. Her refugee claim was rejected in July of 2001 and in November 2001 she made a claim for exemption from visa requirements on humanitarian and compassionate grounds. This application was dismissed in October 2005 and she sought judicial review of that decision.

The application for judicial review was allowed on the basis that the reasons for the decision did not stand up to a reasonably probative examination as required. The Court found that the last of the quotations from the reasons were nothing more than a recital of the general categories of materials reviewed following which was a recital of the criteria set out by the guidelines and of the decision made. The reasons failed to address any consideration given to the major points at issue. No issues were stated, no points of evidence were discussed, and no explanation of the thought process engaged by the officers is given.

*Malicia v. Canada (Minister of Citizenship & Immigration)*, 2006 CarswellNat 3208, 2006 FC 755 (F.C.) — This is an application for judicial review of the decision of an immigration officer to refuse to seek authority to issue a temporary resident permit (TRP) for the applicant. The applicant argued that a positive "stage one" H&C decision provides the foundation for considering whether to issue a TRP. The applicant claims that there is no form or formal, legislated process for applying for a TRP; in practice, an applicant is only invited to apply for a TRP after a positive "Stage One" and a negative "Stage Two" H&C decision has been made. The parties have agreed that this matter should be returned for reconsideration for lack of reasons. The applicant claims that when the decision goes back, the Court should direct that the exemption from stage one or the PR application should continue to apply.

The Court concluded that when the matter is returned for reconsideration, the officer responsible is required to re-examine all aspects of the decision, and the Court should not interfere with this process by isolating one aspect and placing it outside the scope of reconsideration. The Court should not issue a direction that has the effect of making a decision that is for the decision maker to make and, while the Court may guide the decision-making process, it cannot make the actual decision.

*Espino v. Canada (Minister of Citizenship & Immigration)*, [2006] F.C.J. No. 1578, 2006 CarswellNat 3331, 2006 FC 1255 (F.C.) — The Ministry showed little compassion in its decision to deny the applicant the opportunity of applying for permanent residence status from within Canada. The applicant came to Canada under a valid employment authorization as a live-in caregiver. When she completed the first phase of that program, she was entitled to and did submit an inland application for permanent residence. That application took nine years to process before it was refused. In the interim, she was given unrestricted work permits. She bettered herself and built a career with a prominent Canadian bank. A good part of her earnings go back to the Philippines to help her handicapped child. The officer was of the view that there would be only minimal adjustments to allow her to resettle, to find a job and to be self-supporting in the Philippines. The officer made no analysis as to why it took the Minister nine years to come to a final decision with respect to her initial application for permanent residence filed pursuant to the live-in caregiver program. The officer also made no analysis to contradict the applicant's assertion that a 51-year-old single woman who had not lived in the Philippines for 15 years would have difficulty finding a suitable job. The decision was unreasonable and the application for judicial review was allowed.

*Yu v. Canada (Minister of Citizenship & Immigration)* (2006), 55 Imm. L.R. (3d) 159, 2006 CarswellNat 2405, 2006 FC 956 (F.C.) — The applicant sought judicial review of a decision of the Immigration Program Manager at the Canadian Embassy in the Philippines, wherein the applicant's application for humanitarian and compassionate (H&C) consideration pursuant to subs. 25(1) of the IRPA was refused. The applicant was a 61-year-old citizen of the Philippines and was single without children. Her twin sister and she were the youngest of nine siblings, only four of whom were still alive: her and her twin sister and two other sisters. The applicant's father was killed when she was less than one year old and she was only aged 12 when her mother died. She and her twin sister moved in with their oldest brother who raised them and financed their education. When they graduated from high school, they moved into a dormitory together for their college education in Manila. After graduating, they moved back to San Pablo City to work at their oldest brother's auto supply business. After about a year, they both moved to Naga City to work at another auto supply business until 1969. They then moved to Manila and lived together for over two years. In 1974, the applicant's twin sister married and they lived separately for one year but they could not stand being away from each other and the applicant was invited to live with her twin sister and her husband. The applicant lived with them until they immigrated to Canada in 1993. The applicant applied for permanent residence to Canada as a bookkeeper shortly after her sister moved to Canada. Her application was refused in 1996. She applied again in July 2000. The applicant was advised that she would need to attend an interview at the Canadian Embassy in Manila and that the waiting period was up to 36 months. In April 2002, the applicant's sister was diagnosed with cancer and following surgery was released from hospital and the applicant was by her side following her release.

In February 2005, the applicant was interviewed by a visa officer. She subsequently received a letter from the Canadian Embassy in Manila stating that she did not meet the minimum number of points required for a permanent resident visa and therefore did not satisfy the officer that she would be able to become established in Canada.

The Court considered whether the Immigration Program Manager erred in finding no sufficient humanitarian and compassionate grounds to grant the applicant's request, specifically that she is not a *de facto* family member. The Court concluded that the decision maker did not consider the relevant H&C factors in finding that the applicant was not a *de facto* family member. This application for judicial review was allowed.

In *obiter*, the judge stated that it was not the Court's role to substitute itself for the H&C decision maker. Exceptional cases require exceptional consideration. Humanitarian and compassionate grounds are those grounds that do not fit conveniently into set parameters but rather look further to extenuating circumstances in order to address the fragility of the human condition while it can still be addressed. The anatomy of humanitarian and compassionate grounds is based on exceptional criteria in a differently constituted framework. That framework is established to examine extenuating circumstances.

It is Canada's unique response to the fragility of the human condition.

*Liang v. Canada (Minister of Citizenship & Immigration)*, 2006 CarswellNat 2412, 2006 FC 967 (F.C.) — The applicant was a citizen of China who applied for permanent residence in Canada and requested that his case be assessed on humanitarian and compassionate grounds because he is the last remaining member of his family in China. The visa officer refused the request for special relief. The application for judicial review was dismissed. The Court concluded the officer examined the evidence put before him, including that relating to the level of dependency, the impact of separation, the financial and emotional needs of the applicant in relation to the family unit, and the ability and willingness of the family in Canada to provide support. Since the officer gave tenable reasons for that conclusion, the Court was precluded from intervening on judicial review.

The applicant argued that under prior policies (specifically the Last Remaining Family Member policy) the Minister recognized that humanitarian and compassionate grounds existed in circumstances when a last remaining single son or daughter was left alone, abroad. The Court dismissed this argument stating "to argue that what amounted to sufficient humanitarian and compassionate considerations under prior guidelines must of necessity meet the current guidelines is to say that in every case where an officer finds a last remaining single son or daughter to be alone abroad when their parents are in Canada as permanent residents, an officer must find sufficient humanitarian and compassionate considerations to exist. The Court concluded this view does violence to Parliament's intent as evidenced in s. 25 of the Act. It is inconsistent with the granting of a broad discretion to the Minister in that section to say that there are circumstances which in every case must lead to a positive exercise of that discretion."

*Nalbandian v. Canada (Minister of Citizenship & Immigration)* (2006), 56 Imm. L.R. (3d) 67, 2006 CarswellNat 2899, 2006 FC 1128 (F.C.) — The applicant sought judicial review of the decision that humanitarian and compassionate considerations did not justify granting the applicant permanent residence in Canada. The applicant was a citizen of Iraq in her late 60s or early 70s. She was a Christian and fled to Jordan with her daughter in 1990 due to horrific circumstances in Iraq. She did not have permanent status in Jordan. The applicant's daughter and her son subsequently fled to the Netherlands and claimed refugee status. Neither was in a position to support immigration of the applicant to the Netherlands. The applicant's three brothers and sisters all fled directly to Canada and were all citizens of Canada. They were well established in Canada and providing economic support to the applicant. They provided a detailed plan to support the applicant's settlement in Canada. The applicant also has 13 nephews and nieces who are all Canadian citizens. While the decision arrived at by the officer might well be open to her, against a standard of review of reasonableness *simpliciter*, and against the terms of paragraph 3(1)(d) of the Act and the guidance provided in OP4 to persons such as the officer, the officer erred in a reviewable manner in not documenting her decision against the prescribed criteria. The judicial review was allowed and the applicant's application for permanent residence in Canada referred back for reconsideration.

Six years elapsed between the filing of the application and a decision which represented "special circumstances" justifying an award of costs.

*John v. Canada (Minister of Citizenship & Immigration)* (2006), 59 Imm. L.R. (3d) 314, 2006 CarswellNat 3889, 2006 FC 1422 (F.C.) — The applicant came to Canada in 1986 but was deported in 1998 after her application for humanitarian and compassionate consideration was denied. In 2002, she was allowed to return to Canada after her application was re-opened. On her return, the applicant was permitted to work while she waited for her application to be assessed. She was employed in 2002 and 2003, but then was injured in a fall. As a result, she had been on social assistance ever since. According to s. 39 of the IRPA, persons who are dependent on social assistance are inadmissible to Canada. An immigration officer denied her request for permanent residence on the ground that she was receiving social assistance.

The applicant sought judicial review and argued that the officer failed to follow guidelines applicable to applications based on humanitarian and compassionate grounds (IP5 — *Immigration Applications in Canada made on Humanitarian or Compassionate Grounds*). The only guideline that was relevant to the decision under review states that applications should not be automatically rejected on the ground that the applicant is receiving social assistance (Guideline 16.14 — see Annex). Applicants may be dependent on social assistance temporarily and may be self-sufficient by the time the application is processed. However, the guideline states that officers must reject applications where the applicant is still on social assistance after the other steps in the process had been completed. The officer in this case concluded that the applicant was inadmissible to Canada, given that she had been on social assistance since 2003 and the situation was unlikely to change. In 2005, her physician advised her not to seek employment. The officer's decision was not unreasonable.

*Bansal v. Canada (Minister of Citizenship & Immigration)* (2006), 52 Imm. L.R. (3d) 11, 2006 CarswellNat 480, 2006 CarswellNat 1356, 2006 FC 226 (F.C.) — A "prolonged inability to leave Canada" is a relevant factor in determining establishment of an applicant with respect to a H&C application. In this case, the immigration officer found that the applicant's stay in Canada had not been due to a situation beyond his control. However, the Court concluded that the only evidence was contrary to this finding in that the applicant could not get a passport although he had cooperated with removals officials attempting to arrange his departure from Canada. This evidence was relevant to the establishment of the applicant in Canada.

*Arulraj v. Canada (Minister of Citizenship & Immigration)*, 2006 CarswellNat 1106, 2006 FC 529 (F.C.) — In making a determination that the applicant be removed to Germany to apply for a visa and re-admission, the visa officer seemed to have concluded that re-entry would be a virtual certainty by referring as temporary to the negative impact of separation on the youngest child. If the granting of a visa to the applicant would be little more than a formality, the judge wondered why the officer simply did not allow him to stay in Canada. Presumably, the humanitarian and compassionate considerations would not materially change in the meantime. On the other hand, if the applicant was unsuccessful in obtaining a timely visa, the entire foundation of the visa officer's decision concerning the best interests of the children would be undermined.

The visa officer's speculation about the outcome of a future application for re-entry to Canada as part of the consideration of the children's interests constitutes a defect in the logical process by which the officer's conclusions were drawn. The officer's decision focused only on the issue of harm to the two children and not all the benefits that would accrue to them by having their father remain in Canada. In that respect as well, the decision failed to meet the standard required for considering the best interests of the children.

*Delcid v. Canada (Minister of Citizenship & Immigration)*, 2006 CarswellNat 601, 2006 FC 326 (F.C.) — The applicant applied for judicial review of a decision of an immigration officer refusing an H&C application to permit inland processing of the applicant's permanent residence application.

A humanitarian and compassionate officer must make further inquiries when a Canadian-born child is involved in order to show that he or she has been attentive and sensitive to the importance of the rights of the child, the child's best interests and the hardship that may be caused to the child by a negative decision. In this case, the immigration officer's assessment did not address how the best interests of the five- and three-year-old children would be jeopardized if their mother were removed from Canada, other than the children would have the love, support and care of the custodial parent. Specifically, the immigration officer did not consider who would care for the children when the father was at work. The immigration officer also did not address the situation of the two children should the applicant take them with her outside of Canada and specifically that English was not the first language in the foreign country and the fact that English was the children's first language. It is essential for an H&C decision to be made in a reasonable manner. The application for judicial review was allowed and the matter remitted for redetermination by a different officer.

*Keymanesh v. Canada (Minister of Citizenship & Immigration)*, 2006 CarswellNat 1392, 2006 FC 641 (F.C.) — The applicant challenged a decision made by the officer denying his application for permanent resident status because of a failure to obtain a pardon from a conviction for impaired driving in 1998. In the absence of a pardon, the applicant was ineligible for landing and, in the result, subject to removal. The Court considered whether the department owed a duty to give notice to the applicant that it was intending to determine his application for permanent residence in the absence of proof of a pardon, and if so, did it fulfill that duty. The department advised the applicant that he had been approved in principle for a visa exemption but that landing would be subject to meeting other immigration requirements including health and security assessments. When the department learned of the applicant's criminal conviction, it notified him of the need for a pardon. They also advised him that he would not be eligible to apply for a pardon for three years. This extension of time afforded by the department was generous because the applicant could have been removed immediately on the basis of his criminal conviction. The department, quite rightly, was not prepared to hold the applicant's case for landing in abeyance indefinitely. The department wrote the applicant giving him a notice to respond to its request for the pardon which was returned "undeliverable." Not hearing from the applicant they sent him a "final notice" which was also returned as "undeliverable." The department refused the application for permanent residence. The applicant claimed not to have received the three notification letters and deposed that he had advised the department of his change of address. The applicant had a clear indication that the department required proof of a pardon before his application for landing would be finalized. However, when the department began to contemplate the possibility of revoking his interim status, it did have a duty to inform him of that risk. Indeed, the department's lengthy

IRP Act

acquiescence may well have created some expectation in the mind of the applicant that time was not of the essence and that he would be informed of any change in the department's position.

It is difficult to contemplate any decision by the department which would have greater significance to the applicant than the one taken here. The finalization of his application for permanent residence without the required pardon had only one possible outcome: deportation. The obligation to give effective notice of a potentially adverse administrative decision is different than a situation involving the obligation to produce evidence or to meet a burden of proof. From the department's record, it was not clear that the officer who decided to refuse the application for landing was even aware that its notification correspondence had been returned as undelivered. Although the department need not exhaust every tracing possibility, some effort to that end is essential in cases like this, at least to the extent recognized by the Department's own guidelines.

IP5-Immigration Application in Canada Made on Humanitarian and Compassionate Grounds, s. 17.3, suggests that where contact has been lost some effort should be made to locate the subject. Those guidelines indicate that where an applicant does not respond to requests for information or fails to provide an updated address, a decision can be taken "based on information on file as long as previous correspondence has informed the applicant of how and when to apply and included the consequences of failing to respond." Those guidelines go on to indicate that officers should indicate in their computer notes any attempts to verify the applicant's current address such as looking in the local telephone directory, calling the most recent telephone number provided on the application form or calling other persons listed as contacts or representatives. The recommendations imply that where the department is aware that its notification letters have not been received there is some responsibility to make some enquiries with respect to whereabouts.

The department did not meet the duty of fairness owed to the applicant with respect to giving effective notice. The failure was entirely inadvertent but does require that the decision to refuse the applicant's application for permanent residence be set aside.

*Bajraktarevic v. Canada (Minister of Citizenship & Immigration)* (2006), 52 Imm. L.R. (3d) 5, 2006 CarswellNat 258, 2006 CarswellNat 1134, 2006 FC 123 (F.C.) — The applicant argued that the officer committed a reviewable error in failing to provide any analysis or assessment of the basis put forward by the applicant in support of her application for permanent residence on humanitarian and compassionate grounds and consequently provided inadequate and insufficient reasons. The officer's refusal letter and the notes in the applicant's Computer Assisted Immigration Processing System cannot be deemed to constitute sufficient and adequate reasons. The applicant was entitled to know why her application was rejected. Reasons must be accompanied by a sufficient analysis.

*Kim v. Canada (Minister of Citizenship & Immigration)* (2005), 51 Imm. L.R. (3d) 262, 2005 CarswellNat 3129, 2005 CarswellNat 4949, 2005 FC 1357 (F.C.) — The applicant applied for permanent residency under the skilled worker category, but was refused as he was inadmissible due to his son's medical disability. The applicant then made an H&C application, which required him to attend an oral hearing with an immigration officer. The applicant provided little in support of his application; on her own initiative, the immigration officer sought third party information concerning services available to the applicant's disabled child. The officer did not disclose this information to the applicant. After receiving that information, the officer recommended to her manager that the case be dismissed. The manager claimed that he did not consider the third party information, but that on the evidence before him, there were insufficient H&C factors present to grant the application.

The applicant's procedural fairness had been breached. The immigration officer made formal efforts to obtain third party information which was not disclosed to the applicant and she relied on this information to make her recommendation to her manager. Although the immigration officer was not the final decision maker, she had relied on that information, and the manager was found to have implicitly accepted the findings of the third party.

*Krotov c. Canada (Ministre de la Citoyenneté & de l'Immigration)*, [2005] F.C.J. No. 541, 48 Imm. L.R. (3d) 264, 2005 CarswellNat 2042, 2005 CarswellNat 826, 2005 FC 438 (Fed. C.A.) — A PRRA officer has jurisdiction under the Act to represent the Minister of Citizenship and Immigration and so act on an application for permanent residence in Canada on humanitarian and compassionate grounds pursuant to subs. 25(1) of the Act. The exercise of the decision-making power on a humanitarian and compassionate application, like the pre-removal risk assessment, has in the past been exercised from time to time by the same officer, and the case law has consistently established that this procedure is lawful.

*Kimotho v. Canada (Minister of Citizenship & Immigration)*, 2005 CarswellNat 2027, 2005 CarswellNat 2857, 2005 FC 1004 (F.C.) — An immigration officer considering an application based on humanitarian and compassionate grounds cannot demonstrate that she has been "alert, alive and sensitive" to the best interests of an affected child simply by stating in the reasons for decision that she has taken into account the interests of a child of an H&C applicant. Rather, the interests of the child must be well identified and defined and examined with a great deal of attention. The best interests of the child are an important factor and must be given substantial weight in the exercise of discretion.

*Tikaprasad v. Canada (Minister of Citizenship & Immigration)* (2005), 48 Imm. L.R. (3d) 130, 2005 CarswellNat 1689, 2005 CarswellNat 5406, 2005 FC 843 (F.C.) — The duty of fairness requires an officer who consults a third party and obtains information from that source to disclose it so that the applicant is aware of it and can respond.

*Toor v. Canada (Minister of Citizenship & Immigration)*, 2005 CarswellNat 3256, 2005 FC 1386 (F.C.) — The applicants, having been unsuccessful Convention refugees, made an application for humanitarian and compassionate consideration pursuant to s. 25 of the IRPA. They also made an application for consideration as Post-determination Refugee Claimants. Their lawyer wrote to the processing centre in Vegreville, Alberta, in anticipation that the file would be transferred to Vancouver and might be determined concurrently with the PRRA application, advising that he would make complete representations in support of their request once the applicants received their notice to make representations and file evidence in support of the PRRA. The H&C request was turned down. No additional information was supplied by the applicants' lawyer because Vegreville ignored the fact that the lawyer's address was listed as the place to communicate with the applicants, and wrote directly to the applicants instead. The decision maker's notes to file indicate that she did not appear to have focused on what was before her and consequently the decision was held to be patently unreasonable.

*Miranda v. Canada (Minister of Citizenship & Immigration)* (2005), 52 Imm. L.R. (3d) 113, 2005 CarswellNat 3691, 2005 CarswellNat 5032, 2005 FC 1533 (F.C.) — Although the Federal Court is reluctant to interfere with an H&C determination, in this case, the officer's conclusion was unreasonable. Specifically the officer concluded that the appli-



IRP Act

cant's grown children would support the applicant's wife following his removal from Canada. It was not reasonable for the officer to proceed from the presumption that the children were able and willing to support the applicant's wife. The children could be living elsewhere; they might be indigent, incapacitated, or incarcerated.

*Bui v. Canada (Minister of Citizenship & Immigration)*, 2005 CarswellNat 1636, 2005 CarswellNat 5429, 2005 FC 816 (F.C.) — The applicant was a citizen of Vietnam and Norway and he came to Canada on a visitor's visa and subsequently overstayed. He then married a Canadian citizen and he applied under the former *Immigration Act* for an exemption from the landing requirements as a sponsored spouse. Upon the coming into force of the IRPA, the application was converted to a humanitarian and compassionate application as the applicant was in Canada without status. This application was refused on the basis that the marriage was not genuine and that the applicant had not established himself in Canada. The applicant argued that his rights to procedural fairness were violated because he was not granted an oral interview. It was his responsibility to ensure the information was accurate and he bore the onus of satisfying the decision maker. An officer cannot be faulted for not convening an interview to determine what was false and what was accurate in the material.

*Singh (B.) v. Canada (Minister of Citizenship & Immigration)*, 2005 CarswellNat 1419, 2005 FC 718 (F.C.) — The applicant carries the burden of adducing evidence in support of an H&C application. When considering the best interests of the child, however, it can generally be presumed that the presence of the parent will be consistent with those interests. The applicant provided affidavit and oral evidence to the effect that he was the primary source of financial support for his child and the child's mother, the applicant's wife. Ignoring, for all practical purposes, the financial implications of the parent's removal for the child is not akin to being alert, alive and sensitive to the child's best interests.

*Adu v. Canada (Minister of Citizenship & Immigration)*, 2005 CarswellNat 1047, 2005 FC 565, [2005] F.C.J. No. 693 (F.C.) — This was an application to review a negative decision respecting an H&C application. A review of the facts and the statement by conclusion, without analysis to back it up, are not reasons at all. The officer simply reviewed the positive factors militating in favour of granting the application and concluded, without any explanation, that these factors were not sufficient to justify granting the exemption. This was not sufficient, as it leaves the applicants in the unenviable position of not knowing why their application was rejected.

*Lee v. Canada (Minister of Citizenship & Immigration)*, [2005] F.C.J. No. 507, 45 Imm. L.R. (3d) 129, 2005 CarswellNat 783, 2005 FC 413, 2005 CarswellNat 2020 (F.C.) — The decision of the ministerial delegate with respect to an H & C application is a discretionary one. The standard of review is reasonableness *simpliciter*. The onus on an application for an H&C exemption is on the applicant. The ministerial guidelines are not law and the Minister and her agents are not bound by them but they are accessible to the public and of great assistance to the Court. An H&C decision must be supported by reasons. It is inappropriate to require administrative officers to give as detailed reasons for their decisions as may be expected of an administrative tribunal that renders its decisions after an adjudicative hearing.

*Pinter v. Canada (Minister of Citizenship & Immigration)* (2005), 44 Imm. L.R. (3d) 118, 2005 CarswellNat 530, 2005 FC 296 (F.C.) — The applicants are failed refugee claimants. They applied for relief under s. 25. It was an error in law for the immigration officer to conclude that she was not required to deal with risk factors in her assessment of the humanitarian and compassionate application. She should not have closed her mind to risk factors even though a valid negative pre-removal risk assessment may have been made. There may well be risk considerations which are relevant to an application for permanent residence from within Canada.

*Raposo v. Canada (Minister of Citizenship & Immigration)* (2005), 45 Imm. L.R. (3d) 291, 2005 FC 118, 2005 CarswellNat 248 (F.C.) — The applicants sought to review a negative decision respecting their H&C application. The officer's analysis of the best interests of the Canadian-born child should deal firstly with the fact that the child is a Canadian citizen and then determine what effect his parents' removal would have on him. How would the removal affect his best interests? In the present case, the analysis dealt with the fact that the child would adapt to life in the Azores. This is not an adequate assessment of a child's best interests.



*Momcilovic v. Canada (Minister of Citizenship & Immigration)* (2005), 42 Imm. L.R. (3d) 61, 2005 CarswellNat 92, 2005 FC 79 (F.C.) — A plain reading of subs. 25(1) indicates that it is broader than the best interests of a parent's own child. The section does not use wording such as "child of the marriage" or "the applicant's child". It refers to the best interests of a "child directly affected". In this case the applicant had cared for the child for six years and was her primary caregiver. The applicant was the only mother that the child knew. The applicant looked after the child before she went to school and was there when the child returned home. The applicant did the child's laundry and took the child on outings. There was no one else caring for the child. Accordingly, the Court was of the view that the child in this case was a "child directly affected" and, therefore, her best interests must be assessed. The officer's decision was set aside.

*Cordeiro v. Canada (Minister of Citizenship & Immigration)*, 2004 CarswellNat 3116, 2004 CarswellNat 3963, 2004 FC 1231 (F.C.) — The applicants were seeking to overturn a negative decision concerning their H&C application. The applicants were citizens of Brazil. They had a nine-year-old Canadian-born child and a married daughter. The married daughter was a permanent resident of Canada having married a Canadian citizen in 2001.

The family originally came to Canada in 1989. Their son was born in this country and then the family returned to Brazil in February of 1994. They remained there until 1998 when they came back to Canada and made an unsuccessful refugee claim based upon allegations of persecution due to crime and violence in Brazil. The male applicant is a carpenter and had been employed in Canada in that trade. At the time of the application he had his own carpentry business. His wife worked as a cleaner and had completed caregiver training programs while she was in Canada. Both were active in their church and in their community. In their time in Canada, the applicants had been steadily employed, had amassed significant savings and had paid their taxes every year.

The interests of the Canadian-born child were not sufficiently well identified or defined by the officer. It was apparent that the Canadian-born child enjoyed an exceptionally close relationship with his older sister and her husband who lived next door. While the officer addressed the impact that removing the family would have on the female applicant, virtually no attention was paid to the consequences for the Canadian-born child if he were separated from his older sister. The H&C decision was set aside.

*Selliah v. Canada (Minister of Citizenship & Immigration)*, [2004] F.C.J. No. 1134, 2004 CarswellNat 2083, 256 F.T.R. 53, 2004 FC 872, 37 Imm. L.R. (3d) 263 (F.C.); affirmed 2005 CarswellNat 1146, 2005 FCA 160 (F.C.A.) — The applicants sought judicial review of the rejection of their application for protection by a pre-removal risk assessment (PRRA). The officer determined that the applicants would not face a risk of persecution or torture if returned to Sri Lanka. The applicants also sought to review a negative humanitarian and compassionate decision pursuant to subs. 25(1) of the Act.

PRRA officers have a specialized expertise in risk assessment. Their findings are usually fact driven and warrant considerable deference from a reviewing Court. The onus is on the applicants to make their case and adduce the necessary evidence. The evidence adduced here was ambiguous and in some instances contradictory. There is no suggestion that the officer was wilfully blind in the circumstances and the Court found that the officer was acting in good faith. There was therefore no obligation on the officer to gather or seek additional evidence or make further inquiries. The officer was required to consider and decide on the evidence adduced before her.

The phrase in s. 97 "believed on substantial grounds to exist" equates to a balance of probabilities test.

In this case the immigration officer who conducted the PRRA was also seized with the H&C application. Under such circumstances, it was not necessary to ensure fairness that there was a disclosure of the risk assessment to the applicant before the H&C application was made.

*Osadolor v. Canada (Minister of Citizenship & Immigration)* (2004), 36 Imm. L.R. (3d) 127, 2004 CarswellNat 1499, [2004] F.C.J. No. 895, 2004 FC 737, 2004 CarswellNat 5947, 252 F.T.R. 314 (F.C.) — IRPA changed the law and policy for immigrants married to Canadians. After June 26, 2002, a new class of persons who may apply for permanent residence within Canada was created. This class is called the "Spouse or Common-law partner In-Canada Class". To qualify as a member of this class, an applicant is required to meet the requirements of s. 124 of the Regulations.

Legal immigrants do not need to make an H&C application, if they are married to, or a common-law spouse of, a Canadian citizen.

*Khatoon v. Canada (Minister of Citizenship & Immigration)*, [2004] F.C.J. No. 1408, 39 Imm. L.R. (3d) 13, 2004 CarswellNat 4464, 2004 CarswellNat 183, 245 F.T.R. 96 (F.C.) — The applicants sought to review the denial of their request to apply from within Canada for permanent residence on humanitarian and compassionate grounds.

Due to the fact that the immigration officer adopted the PRRA officer's recommendation on risk, without analysis of her own or any comment on the applicant's responding submissions to the risk assessment, and then relied primarily on the risk opinion of the PRRA officer as the basis for her decision not to grant the applicant's request, this risk opinion can be seen as forming part of the reasons for the immigration officer's negative decision.

*Pramauntanyath v. Canada (Minister of Citizenship & Immigration)* (2004), 39 Imm. L.R. (3d) 243, 2004 CarswellNat 230, 2004 CarswellNat 2892, [2004] F.C.J. No. 184, 2004 FC 174 (F.C.) — The applicant sought to review a negative H&C decision. The applicant made an application for a humanitarian and compassionate exemption in November 2000. By letter dated January 2, 2003, Immigration Canada advised the applicant that his application was now being reviewed and he was asked to provide updated information within 30 days. The applicant's former counsel mailed updated information to the commission within the 30 day period. The H&C application was refused and a review of the officer's reasons makes it clear that the officer did not have this updated information when the H&C application was refused.

The information in question revealed that the applicant had opened a very successful restaurant in Toronto, a restaurant which employed 10 people and had received positive reviews in the Toronto media. The updated information indicated that the applicant had worked hard, lived frugally, had become fluent in English and was active in his community.

The negative decision was set aside. The applicant was directed to send supplementary information to immigration and he took advantage of this opportunity. There was no obligation on the applicant to follow-up and make sure that the information was in fact received by the immigration officer assigned to the file.

*Étienne v. Canada (Ministre de la Citoyenneté & de l'Immigration)*, 2003 CarswellNat 3527, 2003 CarswellNat 4455, 2003 FC 1314 (F.C.) — The applicants sought to review a decision refusing their request for humanitarian and compassionate exemption.

An interview is not a general requirement for decisions made on applications based on humanitarian grounds.

The doctrine of "legitimate expectation" is based on the principle that the circumstances effecting procedural fairness take into account the promises or regular practices of administrative decision makers. Generally, it will be unfair for decision makers to act in contravention of representations as to procedure, or to back track on substantive promises without according significant procedural rights.

Nothing in the record suggested that the officer had affirmed, implicitly or explicitly, that the applicants would have an interview. Nothing in the evidence established the existence of a systematic practice of granting an interview. There was no legitimate expectation of an interview established in this case.

*Jasim v. Canada (Minister of Citizenship & Immigration)*, 32 Imm. L.R. (3d) 118, 2003 CarswellNat 4413, 2003 CarswellNat 2658, 2003 FC 1017 (F.C.) — This is an application to review a negative humanitarian and compassionate decision. The existence of a humanitarian or compassionate review offers an individual special and additional consideration from an exemption from Canadian immigration laws that are otherwise universally applied. The process is highly discretionary and, as such, the onus is on the applicant to satisfy the officer that sufficient grounds exist to warrant a favourable decision. The decision of an officer not to grant a exemption takes no right away from an applicant who may still apply for landing from outside of Canada which is the usual requirement under Canadian immigration legislation.

The reasons for decision in this case consisted of a list of the factors which the officer considered. A list of factors considered does not constitute sufficient analysis. The officer thus failed to provide reasons for the decision which was a reviewable error.

**25.1 (1) Humanitarian and compassionate considerations — Minister's own initiative — The Minister may, on the Minister's own initiative, examine the circumstances concerning a foreign national who is inadmissible or who does not meet the requirements of this Act and may grant the foreign national permanent resident status or an exemption from any applicable criteria or obligations of this Act if the Minister is of the opinion that it is justified by humanitarian and compassionate considerations relating to the foreign national, taking into account the best interests of a child directly affected.**

(2) **Exemption** — The Minister may exempt the foreign national from the payment of any applicable fees in respect of the examination of their circumstances under subsection (1).

(3) **Provincial criteria** — The Minister may not grant permanent resident status to a foreign national referred to in subsection 9(1) if the foreign national does not meet the province's selection criteria applicable to that foreign national.

2010, c. 8, s. 5

25.2 (1) **Public policy considerations** — The Minister may, in examining the circumstances concerning a foreign national who is inadmissible or who does not meet the requirements of this Act, grant that person permanent resident status or an exemption from any applicable criteria or obligations of this Act if the Minister is of the opinion that it is justified by public policy considerations.

(2) **Exemption** — The Minister may exempt the foreign national from the payment of any applicable fees in respect of the examination of their circumstances under subsection (1).

(3) **Provincial criteria** — The Minister may not grant permanent resident status to a foreign national referred to in subsection 9(1) if the foreign national does not meet the province's selection criteria applicable to that foreign national.

2010, c. 8, s. 5

26. **Regulations** — The regulations may provide for any matter relating to the application of sections 18 to 25.2, and may include provisions respecting

(a) entering, remaining in and re-entering Canada;

(b) permanent resident status or temporary resident status, including acquisition of that status;

(c) the circumstances in which all or part of the considerations referred to in section 24 may be taken into account;

(d) conditions that may or must be imposed, varied or cancelled, individually or by class, on permanent residents and foreign nationals; and

(e) deposits or guarantees of the performance of obligations under this Act that are to be given to the Minister.

2010, c. 8, s. 6

## *Rights and Obligations of Permanent and Temporary Residents*

27. (1) **Right of permanent residents** — A permanent resident of Canada has the right to enter and remain in Canada, subject to the provisions of this Act.

(2) **Conditions** — A permanent resident must comply with any conditions imposed under the regulations.

*[Editor's Note: SOR/2002-227, s. 328(1) provides that a person who was a permanent resident immediately before June 28, 2002 is a permanent resident under the new* Immigration and Refugee Protection Act, *S.C. 2001, c. 27.]*

IRP Act

## Case Law

### Section 27(2)

*Chang v. Canada (Minister of Citizenship & Immigration)*, [2006] F.C.J. No. 217, 2006 CarswellNat 329, 2006 CarswellNat 2194, 2006 FC 157 (F.C.) — The legislatively established conditions of the entrepreneur category, if flaunted knowingly, without serious consequence, would make a mockery of the purpose for which they were established. The act of creating or participating in a front operation or a sham investment, if left unchecked, strikes a blow at the very integrity of the immigration system. In this case, the applicants were found to be in non-compliance with subs. 27(2) and s. 28. The applicants' children were also found to be in non-compliance with subs. 27(2) as they were dependants of an entrepreneur and bound by the same terms and conditions of landing as provided in paragraph 23.1 of the previous Regulations. Both the applicants as well as their children sought special relief on appeal in light of the circumstances of their case, specifically, that there were sufficient humanitarian and compassionate considerations that warranted the setting aside of departure orders. The IAD was of the view that the parents did not merit discretionary relief as they took part in a sham arrangement to try to fulfill the conditions of the entrepreneur category. Even though the IAD felt that the children would be excellent candidates for permanent residence, it refused to grant discretionary relief to the children, because once the children became permanent residents they would be entitled to sponsor their parents which would render the removal of the parents moot.

The granting of special relief is a weighing process. Even though there were some positive elements in favour of discretionary relief being allowed to the three children, these elements did not outweigh the importance given to the integrity of maintaining the conditions in the entrepreneur category. It was open to the IAD to find that special relief should not be granted to the children because this would benefit the parents who had not respected the conditions under which they entered Canada.

**28. (1) Residency obligation — A permanent resident must comply with a residency obligation with respect to every five-year period.**

**(2) Application — The following provisions govern the residency obligation under subsection (1):**

> **(a) a permanent resident complies with the residency obligation with respect to a five-year period if, on each of a total of at least 730 days in that five-year period, they are**
>
> > **(i) physically present in Canada,**
> >
> > **(ii) outside Canada accompanying a Canadian citizen who is their spouse or common-law partner or, in the case of a child, their parent,**
> >
> > **(iii) outside Canada employed on a full-time basis by a Canadian business or in the federal public administration or the public service of a province,**
> >
> > **(iv) outside Canada accompanying a permanent resident who is their spouse or common-law partner or, in the case of a child, their parent and who is employed on a full-time basis by a Canadian business or in the federal public administration or the public service of a province, or**
> >
> > **(v) referred to in regulations providing for other means of compliance;**

**(b) it is sufficient for a permanent resident to demonstrate at examination**

**(i) if they have been a permanent resident for less than five years, that they will be able to meet the residency obligation in respect of the five-year period immediately after they became a permanent resident;**

**(ii) if they have been a permanent resident for five years or more, that they have met the residency obligation in respect of the five-year period immediately before the examination; and**

**(c) a determination by an officer that humanitarian and compassionate considerations relating to a permanent resident, taking into account the best interests of a child directly affected by the determination, justify the retention of permanent resident status overcomes any breach of the residency obligation prior to the determination.**

*[Editor's Note: SOR/2002-227, s. 328(1) provides that a person who was a permanent resident immediately before June 28, 2002 is a permanent resident under the new* Immigration and Refugee Protection Act, *S.C. 2001, c. 27 (the "new Act").*

*SOR/2002-227, s. 328(2) provides that any period spent outside Canada within five years preceding June 28, 2002 by a permanent resident holding a returning resident permit is considered to be a period spent in Canada for the purpose of satisfying the residency obligation under s. 28 of the new Act if that period is included in the five-year period referred to in s. 28 of the new Act.*

*SOR/2002-227, s. 328(3) provides that any period spent outside Canada within the two years immediately following June 28, 2002 by a permanent resident holding a returning resident permit is considered to be a period spent in Canada for the purpose of satisfying the residency obligation under s. 28 of the new Act if that period is included in the five year period referred to in s. 28 of the new Act.]*

2003, c. 22, s. 172

## Case Law

### Section 28

*Canada (Minister of Citizenship & Immigration) v. Salem*, 2010 FC 38, 2010 CarswellNat 52, 2010 CarswellNat 732 (F.C.) — The applicant brought an application for judicial review of the Immigration Appeal Division decision to allow an appeal of a visa officer's determination that the respondent had not met the permanent resident's physical presence in Canada requirement. There was no dispute that the respondent did not meet the test of 730 days in Canada over the immediately preceding five years. The IAD found a number of factors supporting an H&C finding to overturn the visa officer's decision. Given the standard of review and recognizing the role of the IAD in this discretionary decision, the Court would be reluctant to interfere except for the reason that the decision is unreasonable, inconsistent and made without regard to the evidence or the lack thereof. The IAD's decision was unreasonable for the following reasons: the respondent did not put before it documentary evidence of his efforts to find work, the IAD seemed to accept the respondent's evidence that he had changed employer because there was an opportunity to move to Montreal yet there was not one piece of evidence from the employer; the IAD appeared to place significant weight as a mitigating factor that the respondent had to leave Canada within days of arrival to pay off hospital debt. However, that debt was paid off in approximately 2004 and could hardly be a relevant or compelling factor in 2009 when the appeal was heard; there was no supporting evidence with respect to the best interest of the children and the specific issue of the best interest of the children was never advanced or analyzed. The IAD's decision was unreasonable in these circumstances; the application for judicial review was granted and the IAD's decision quashed.

*Shaath v. Canada (Minister of Citizenship & Immigration)* (2009), 349 F.T.R. 81 (Eng.), 2009 FC 731, 2009 CarswellNat 2251, 2009 CarswellNat 4145 (F.C.) — The applicant sought judicial review of a decision dismissing his appeal from a departure order issued against him, by reason of his failure to comply with s. 28 of IRPA, which provides that a permanent resident meets his residency obligations in each five-year period if he/she was physically present in Canada at least 730 days during that period.



The tribunal reached its conclusion despite the fact counsel for the Minister appearing before the tribunal agreed the appeal should be allowed on humanitarian grounds mainly because of the family's establishment in Canada who, except for the applicant, are Canadian citizens. Counsel for the Minister also recognized his important financial investment in Canada and "he had been credible in his efforts to obtain his certification in Canada in order to get a job in his own specialty in the near future." Counsel's main reason for recommending the applicant's appeal be allowed was that she thought it was "nonsense to ask for a denial of the appeal since Mr. Shaath could apply tomorrow as a member of the family class, sponsored by his wife and it would be really easy to obtain his permanent residency and start the whole thing again." She considered that in all of the circumstances, "the punishment of losing his permanent residency would be disproportionate in all of the circumstances." The tribunal disagreed with counsel for the Minister's recommendation.

The Supreme Court of Canada's decision in *Canada (Citizenship & Immigration) v. Khosa* (2009), 77 Imm. L.R. (3d) 1, has a considerable impact upon this case because it dealt with the exercise by the IAD of its discretion under paragraph 67(1)(c) of IRPA. *Khosa* makes it clear where reasonableness standard applies, it requires deference and reviewing Courts are not allowed to substitute their own appreciation of the appropriate solution but rather must determine if the outcome falls "within a range of possible, acceptable outcomes which are defensible in respect of the facts and the law." Paragraph 67(1)(c) provides a power to grant "exceptionable relief" and calls for a fact-dependent and policy-driven assessment. An applicant has the burden of adducing proof of any claim upon which a humanitarian and compassionate application relies. The application for judicial review was dismissed.

*Dudhnath v. Canada (Minister of Citizenship & Immigration)*, 2009 CarswellNat 941, 2009 FC 386 (F.C.) — This was an application for judicial review of a decision of the IAD which dismissed the applicant's appeal of a visa officer's decision that he had failed to comply with his residency obligations as a permanent resident under s. 28 of the IRPA. The applicant placed too much reliance on "intent", both as an applicable principle and as to its application in this case. Intent may be a relevant factor under H&C considerations in s. 67 of the IRPA but it does not dominate the analysis of factors. The IAD did a thorough analysis of the relevant factors. The critical factor was the 1997 decision to deny the request for a returning resident permit. That decision, based on allegations that the applicant had sold his Record of Landing, concluded that the applicant had abandoned Canada. In the absence of any challenge to the 1997 decision, the High Commission and the IAD had to accept that finding. Given that finding, the sporadic and ineffective efforts to return to Canada are not sufficient evidence of intent to remain or to acquire residency. The IAD's consideration of the H&C factors was sufficient and comprehensive. Although the analysis of the best interests of the children may have raised issues, it is not for the Court to reweigh the evidence. The applicant's efforts to rebut any finding of abandonment or to establish H&C grounds to permit a return to Canada were "too little and too late." The applicant was left with the option of applying to enter Canada in the same way most others must. The application for judicial review was dismissed.

*Ikhuiwu v. Canada (Minister of Citizenship & Immigration)*, [2008] F.C.J. No. 35, 2008 CarswellNat 42, 2008 FC 35 — This was an application for judicial review of an IAD decision, confirming the decision of an overseas visa officer. The visa officer concluded that the applicant was inadmissible pursuant to ss. 28 and 41(b) of the IRPA as he did not reside in Canada for the required 730 days within a five-year period.

The legislative scheme under the IRPA makes it clear that the mere possession of a permanent resident card is not conclusive proof of a person's status in Canada. Pursuant to s. 31(2) of the IRPA, the presumption that the holder of a permanent resident card is a permanent resident is clearly a rebuttable one. In this case, it is clear that the permanent resident card, which was issued in error after it was determined by the visa officer in Nigeria that the applicant had lost his permanent residence status, could not possibly confer legal status on him as a permanent resident, nor could it have the effect of restoring his permanent resident status which he had previously lost because he didn't meet the residency requirements under s. 28 of the IRPA. There is no provision in the IRPA or the Regulations which suggests that the mere possession of a permanent resident card, which was improperly issued, could have the effect of restoring or reinstating a person's prior permanent resident status.

Section 59(1)(a) of the Regulations also makes it clear that an officer can only validly issue a new permanent resident card where an applicant has not lost his or her status under s. 46(1) of the IRPA. In this case, the applicant lost his permanent resident status after failing to meet the residency requirements under s. 28 of the IRPA and failed to appeal the decision within the 60 days as prescribed by Regulation 63(4). This regulatory scheme confirms that it was not possible for the issuing officer of the permanent resident card to have validly and properly issued it in light of the fact that the applicant had previously lost his permanent resident card. The application for judicial review was dismissed.

*Chen v. Canada (Minister of Public Safety & Emergency Preparedness)*, 2007 CarswellNat 2175 (Imm. & Ref. Bd. (App. Div.)) — The appellant was found to be a person described in subs. 41(b) of the IRPA as inadmissible for failing to comply with the residency obligation of s. 28 of the Act. The appellant had made no reasonable attempts to return to Canada to reside at the earliest opportunity. There were no satisfactory explanations as to why the appellant chose to spend most of his time in the last nine years in Taiwan separated from his children. His actions were consistent with the intentions of continuing to live in Taiwan, to manage his properties in Taiwan and to pursue his education in Taiwan, settling his children in Canada for a better future and attempting to maintain a potential future option to return to Canada. Even after the removal order was issued, the appellant did not remain in Canada. He had limited assets in Canada. There was no evidence of social attachments to Canada and no letters of support from friends in Canada or community or business organizations. Although he had other family members in Canada who were likely supportive of him, there was limited evidence of close relationships with other family members in Canada. The appellant's two daughters were now 22 and 23 and were Canadian citizens. They are not considered to be "dependent" children under the Act and as such the panel need not consider the best interests of children directly affected by this decision. There was limited evidence of any undue hardship that the appellant would face from losing his status in Canada. There was no credible evidence of country conditions that would create hardship to the appellant. He has close family in Taiwan as well. He had significant assets in Taiwan. While the appellant's medical condition may create some concerns or delays in future applications, there are avenues the appellant can pursue to overcome them and therefore this factor does not, in the circumstances, create undue hardship to the appellant. The removal order was valid in law. The appeal was dismissed.



*Chu v. Canada (Minister of Citizenship & Immigration)*, 2007 CarswellNat 1469, 2007 FCA 205 (Fed. C.A.) — The five-year period in s. 28 of the IRPA applies to periods prior to June 28, 2002. Applying s. 28 retroactively does not breach s. 7 of the *Canadian Charter of Rights and Freedoms*.

*Lai v. Canada (Minister of Citizenship & Immigration)* (2006), 60 Imm. L.R. (3d) 17, 2006 CarswellNat 3669, 2006 FC 1359 (F.C.) — The applicant was landed in Canada in 1996 at the age of nine. She came to Canada as a dependant but she and her family returned to Taiwan within 12 days of their arrival. The family returned to Canada on occasion but did not take up residency here. The family purchased an apartment but never occupied that property and eventually it was sold. In August 2002, the applicant returned to Canada to take up high school studies. Apart from some vacations to Taiwan, the applicant has lived continuously in British Columbia since August 2002 attending full-time high school studies. In 2004, the applicant applied for a travel document in Taiwan to permit her to return to Canada as a permanent resident. That request was denied by a visa officer because it was determined that she had not fulfilled the residency requirement of the IRPA. These provisions required that she actually reside in Canada for a minimum of 730 days in the preceding five-year period. At that point the applicant had been physically present in Canada for only 443 days during the relevant five-year period.

In the case of a dependent child of relatively tender years there is little, if any, opportunity to independently fulfil the residency obligation required to preserve landed status or to create the genuine ties to Canada that are typically necessary for H&C relief. In most cases, the child can only accomplish that which the parents are prepared to allow and support. The applicant's status in Canada may have been jeopardized by the decision of her parents, but her claim to relief should not be enhanced by those parental decisions. The application for judicial review was dismissed.

The Court adopted the decision of the Federal Court in *Chu v. Canada (Minister of Citizenship & Immigration)* (2006), [2007] 2 F.C.R. 578, 54 Imm. L.R. (3d) 216, [2006] F.C.J. No. 119, 2006 FC 893. In *Chu*, the Court concluded that the current legislative scheme represented by the IRPA is retrospective in effect, relative to compliance with the residency requirements. In this case the applicant did not have a vested legal right to the application of the previous residency rules. The status she enjoyed under the former Act was contingent upon her ability to fulfil and to establish compliance with those rules on an ongoing basis. When those rules were changed by the IRPA, she had no right to their continued application to her situation.

*Chu* certified a question: "five-year period in s. 28 of the IRPA apply to periods prior to June 28, 2002?" The Court in this case certified the same question.

*El Idrissi c. Canada (Ministre de la Citoyenneté & de l'Immigration)*, 2005 CarswellNat 2421, 2005 CarswellNat 5248, 2005 FC 1105 (F.C.) — The applicant was given permanent residence status in 1991. In 1999, the applicant left Canada to visit his sick father and manage a family business in his home country. He did not return until June 15, 2003.

He fell under the purview of s. 41 of the IRPA and a departure order was made against him by the Minister. He filed an appeal to the Immigration Appeal Division but conceded that the removal order against him was legally valid and the only issue he argued was that there were humanitarian and compassionate grounds to explain his failure to meet the residency obligation.

Simply having a wife in Canada was not sufficient for this situation to be considered a humanitarian and compassionate ground. The Appeal Division was entitled to consider that the applicant's plans for the future were vague. The applicant had the burden of establishing the existence of humanitarian and compassionate grounds.

*Yu v. Canada (Minister of Citizenship & Immigration)*, 2005 CarswellNat 2998, 2005 CarswellNat 4835, 2005 FC 1323 (F.C.) — The applicant, having been granted permanent residence status in the independent category, was denied re-admission as a resident by a visa officer in November, 2003. The visa officer's decision was appealed to the IAD who determined that the applicant failed to comply with the residency obligation under s. 28 of the IRPA. The Immigration Appeal Board determined that pursuant to s. 41 of the IRPA there was non-compliance and upheld the visa officer's determination. The Board also determined that there were insufficient humanitarian and compassionate considerations justifying the retention of permanent residence status; therefore the applicant was unable to overcome the breach of her residency obligations.

The applicant planned to work in her native land until able to retire with full pension benefits, in 2006. In 2005, the law concerning her pension benefits was changed and the applicant was able to retire earlier. This important new evidence was forwarded by way of affidavit to the Board on December 10, 2004.

The issue of "intention" should have been discussed or at least canvassed, as well as the change of circumstances regarding the applicant's retirement. The Board's decision was set aside and the matter was sent back to be reheard.

**29. (1) Right of temporary residents — A temporary resident is, subject to the other provisions of this Act, authorized to enter and remain in Canada on a temporary basis as a visitor or as a holder of a temporary resident permit.**

**(2) Obligation — temporary resident — A temporary resident must comply with any conditions imposed under the regulations and with any requirements under this Act, must leave Canada by the end of the period authorized for their stay and may re-enter Canada only if their authorization provides for re-entry.**

*[Editor's Note: SOR/2002-227, s. 329(1) provides that any of the following persons who were in Canada immediately before June 28, 2002 are temporary residents under the new* Immigration and Refugee Protection Act, *S.C. 2001, c. 27 and are subject to its provisions:*

*(a) a visitor under the* Immigration Act, *R.S.C. 1985, c. I-2 (the "former Act"); and*

*(b) a person issued a permit under s. 37 of the former Act.]*

## Case Law

### Section 29(2)

*Sui v. Canada (Minister of Public Safety & Emergency Preparedness)* (2006), 58 Imm. L.R. (3d) 135, [2007] 3 F.C.R. 218, 2006 CarswellNat 3554, 2006 FC 1314 (F.C.) — The applicant was in Canada for several years as a temporary resident on a study permit. Before his study permit expired he applied for a post-graduation work permit. He received a letter from CIC informing him that he did not meet the requirements for a work permit and that he should leave Canada immediately, failing which enforcement action would be taken against him. Within 90 days of the expiration of his study permit and within 90 days of losing his temporary resident status he applied to have his status restored pursuant to Regulation 182. While awaiting a decision on his application for restoration, two immigration officers attended his home and questioned him. Two inadmissibility reports were issued, the first based on paragraph 40(1)(a) of the IRPA and the fact that "there were reasonable grounds to believe that this foreign national was inadmissible for directly or indirectly misrepresenting or withholding material facts relating to a relevant matter that induces or could induce an error in administration of this Act." The second report was based on paragraph 41(a) and subs. 29(2) of the IRPA and the fact that the applicant was inadmissible for failing to comply with his obligation as a temporary resident to leave Canada by the end of the period authorized for his stay. A Minister's delegate decided to issue an exclusion order based on paragraph 41(a) and subs. 29(2) of the IRPA. In light of s. 225 of the Regulations, this meant that the applicant could not come back to Canada without written consent of the Minister for a period of one year following his departure. The applicant left Canada. No decision with respect to the application for restoration was ever made. In this case, the Minister's delegate had the discretion and even the duty to consider the fact that the applicant had applied for restoration well before a s. 44(1) report was issued against him in respect of his failure to leave Canada at the end of his authorized stay. It was an error of law to consider that the applicant was not entitled to make such an application for restoration simply because after the filing of his application in accordance with the Regulations, a s. 44(1) report had been issued on the sole basis of subs. 29(2) of the IRPA. The decision was set aside.

The following questions were certified:

1. Is an application for restoration pursuant to s. 182 of the Regulations a relevant consideration when the Minister's delegate considers whether or not to make an exclusion order based on a failure to comply with s. 29(2) of the IRPA?

2. foreign national who has a applied for restoration within the delay set out in s. 182 of the Regulations, automatically lose the benefit of his or her application when an enforcement officer considers issuing a report under s. 44(1) on the basis of a failure to comply with s. 29(2) of the IRPA.

*Brar v. Canada (Minister of Citizenship & Immigration)* (2006), 59 Imm. L.R. (3d) 293, 2006 CarswellNat 4324, 2006 FC 1502 (F.C.) — The applicants sought judicial review in respect of a decision by a member of the Immigration and Refugee Board of Canada given collectively, but pertaining to them. It determined that each of the applicants had contravened the terms of the work permit issued to each of them and therefore each was to be excluded from Canada. The applicants were all adult male citizens of India. They applied for and received temporary work permits. The work permit stated:

Employer: Bombay Paradise

Conditions:

- not authorized to work in any occupation other than stated;
- not authorized to work for any employer other than stated; and
- not authorized for work in any location other than stated.

When the applicants arrived in Calgary they found that the Bombay Paradise Restaurant was under construction and far from being completed. The owner of that business was a numbered company run by a person known as Vic. He placed them in another establishment known as Bombay Sweet House & Restaurant. Apparently, the ownership was not the same as Bombay Paradise, although pay cheques issued to the applicants were from the numbered company which was the owner of the Bombay Paradise business.

It came to the Minister's attention that the applicants were working for an employer whom the Minister believed to be other than that named in the work permit. As a result, an exclusion order was issued. Following that order, an admissibility hearing was held on March 1, 2006. The issue of the hearing was whether each of the applicants was inadmissible under s. 41(a) of the IRPA, as having contravened s. 29(2) of that Act.

The Court concluded that Bombay Paradise paid the applicants and the applicants worked in Calgary, and therefore, no term as set out in the work permit had been breached. A work permit should be understandable to all interested persons, not just the worker or the government, on the face of it. The Minister has the resources to ensure that the permit is complete and understandable. If it is not, the Minister cannot be seen to rely on self-created ambiguities to derive a beneficial interpretation. It is the same concept as *contra proferentum* in the interpretation of a contract. If the contract was prepared by a party, any ambiguity must be interpreted against the interests of that party.

The applicants did not breach the terms of their work permits. Their employer, the person who pays them, was Bombay Paradise. They worked in Calgary. As a result, the exclusion order was set aside and the matter was returned to be determined by a different person.

**30. (1) Work and study in Canada — A foreign national may not work or study in Canada unless authorized to do so under this Act.**

**(2) Minor children — Every minor child in Canada, other than a child of a temporary resident not authorized to work or study, is authorized to study at the preschool, primary or secondary level.**

## Case Law

### Section 30(1)

*Juneja v. Canada (Minister of Citizenship & Immigration)*, 2007 CarswellNat 636, 2007 FC 301 (F.C.) — While in Canada on a valid study permit, the applicant was observed to be working at a local car dealership in Edmonton. He was arrested for working without authorization contrary to s. 30(1) of the Act. An admissibility hearing was then convoked under s. 44(2) of the Act. The applicant was declared inadmissible and was issued an exclusion order requiring him to leave Canada. The Board was satisfied that his activity did constitute "work" under the Act and Regulations. The applicant was performing work-like tasks for the dealership but was not being paid. The employer was banking or keeping track of his hours, presumably for the purposes of paying wages if and when the applicant received an authorization to work from the department. The agreed wage was $8.00 per hour. The employer's agreement to bank the applicant's hours and to pay a wage of $8.00 per hour — albeit conditionally — was either an activity for which wages are paid or was, otherwise, in direct competition with the employment activities of

Canadians or permanent residents. The Board's finding was upheld and the application for judicial review was dismissed.

## Status Document

31. (1) **Status document — A permanent resident and a protected person shall be provided with a document indicating their status.**

*[Editor's Note: S.C. 2001, c. 27, s. 200 provides that s. 31(1) of the* Immigration and Refugee Protection Act, *S.C. 2001, c. 27 (the "new Act") does not apply with respect to persons who were permanent residents, within the meaning of the* Immigration Act, *R.S.C. 1985, c. I-2, on June 28, 2002.*

*SOR/2002-227, s. 328(1) provides that a person who was a permanent resident immediately before June 28, 2002 is a permanent resident under the new Act.]*

(2) **Effect — For the purposes of this Act, unless an officer determines otherwise**

**(a) a person in possession of a status document referred to in subsection (1) is presumed to have the status indicated; and**

**(b) a person who is outside Canada and who does not present a status document indicating permanent resident status is presumed not to have permanent resident status.**

(3) **Travel document — A permanent resident outside Canada who is not in possession of a status document indicating permanent resident status shall, following an examination, be issued a travel document if an officer is satisfied that**

**(a) they comply with the residency obligation under section 28;**

**(b) an officer has made the determination referred to in paragraph 28(2)(c); or**

**(c) they were physically present in Canada at least once within the 365 days before the examination and they have made an appeal under subsection 63(4) that has not been finally determined or the period for making such an appeal has not yet expired.**

## Regulations

32. **Regulations — The regulations may provide for any matter relating to the application of sections 27 to 31, may define, for the purposes of this Act, the terms used in those sections, and may include provisions respecting**

**(a) classes of temporary residents, such as students and workers;**

**(b) selection criteria for each class of foreign national and for their family members, and the procedures for evaluating all or some of those criteria;**

**(c) anything referred to in paragraph (b) for which a decision or recommendation may or must be made by a designated person, institution or organization;**

**(d) the conditions that must or may be imposed, varied or cancelled, individually or by class, on permanent residents and foreign nationals, including conditions respecting work or study;**

**(e) the residency obligation under section 28, including rules for calculating applicable days and periods; and**

**(f) the circumstances in which a document indicating status or a travel document may or must be issued, renewed or revoked.**

## DIVISION 4 — INADMISSIBILITY

**33. Rules of interpretation — The facts that constitute inadmissibility under sections 34 to 37 include facts arising from omissions and, unless otherwise provided, include facts for which there are reasonable grounds to believe that they have occurred, are occurring or may occur.**

### Case Law

*Tang v. Canada (Minister of Citizenship & Immigration)*, 2009 CarswellNat 1497, 2009 CarswellNat 2096, 2009 FC 292 (F.C.) — A potential permanent resident was held to be inadmissible on the grounds of organized criminality, a determination first made in 1996 and communicated to the principal applicant in 2007 after many twists and turns between federal government offices. The applicant's conviction for claiming to be a member of a triad was advanced as reasonable grounds for believing that he was in fact a member of a triad. In other cases, that might well be sufficient, but not in this case. First, there was no consideration of the circumstances surrounding the conviction which called into question whether the claim was true. The conviction arose from a guilty plea and resulted in a minimal penalty. Secondly, if the Minister of Citizenship and Immigration had a "*bona fide* belief" that the applicant was or had been a member of a triad, it had had that belief since 1997 and yet continued to permit the applicant to enter Canada on a regular basis. The Minister's actions and acquiescence belied its stated belief. Thirdly, there was a certain element of disingenuousness in the manner in which officials relied on the conviction as if the 1995 admissions by the applicant, where he denied actual membership in a triad and claimed that he had not gone through a traditional initiation ceremony but elaborated on his allegedly limited role and other aspects of his "non-membership", were never made. The Minister made no reference to the admissions and used a more convenient pretext of a conviction to ground the admissibility decision. In light of the inconsistency between what the Minister has said, done and relied upon for its decision, the decision was not reasonable. The judicial review was granted and the decision quashed, and the matter remitted back to the Minister for a proper determination.

*Thanaratnam v. Canada (Minister of Citizenship & Immigration)*, [2004] 3 F.C.R. 301, 2004 CarswellNat 2193, 2004 CarswellNat 569, 2004 FC 349, 37 Imm. L.R. (3d) 96, [2004] F.C.J. No. 395 (F.C.); reversed 45 Imm. L.R. (3d) 1, 2005 FCA 122, 2005 CarswellNat 887 (C.A.) — The words "reasonable grounds to believe" create a relatively low evidentiary threshold. "Reasonable grounds to believe" is more than mere suspicion. It connotes a degree of probability based on credible evidence. The standard of "reasonable grounds to believe" can be met by way of hearsay evidence and other forms of proof that would not normally be admissible at a trial, including evidence about a person's reputation or criminal record.

Unresolved criminal charges are, until proven otherwise, nothing more than mere allegations against the accused. They are not indicative of guilt and obviously therefore, are not indicative of a propensity to re-offend either, until they are proven beyond a reasonable doubt by the Crown in a court of law. The reasonable grounds standard operates as a protection against arbitrary, capricious or ill-founded state action.

**34. (1) Security — A permanent resident or a foreign national is inadmissible on security grounds for**

**(a) engaging in an act of espionage or an act of subversion against a democratic government, institution or process as they are understood in Canada;**

**(b) engaging in or instigating the subversion by force of any government;**

**(c) engaging in terrorism;**

**(d) being a danger to the security of Canada;**

**(e) engaging in acts of violence that would or might endanger the lives or safety of persons in Canada; or**

**(f) being a member of an organization that there are reasonable grounds to believe engages, has engaged or will engage in acts referred to in paragraph (a), (b) or (c).**

**(2) Exception — The matters referred to in subsection (1) do not constitute inadmissibility in respect of a permanent resident or a foreign national who satisfies the Minister that their presence in Canada would not be detrimental to the national interest.**

*[Editor's Note: SOR/2002-227, s. 320(1) provides that a person is inadmissible under the new* Immigration and Refugee Protection Act, *S.C. 2001, c. 27 on security grounds if, on June 28, 2002, the person had been determined to be a member of an inadmissible class described in paragraph 19(1)(e), (f), (g) or (k) of the former* Immigration Act, *R.S.C. 1985, c. I-2.]*

## Case Law

### Section 34(1)

*Saleh v. Canada (Minister of Citizenship & Immigration)*, 2010 FC 303, 2010 CarswellNat 2930, 2010 CarswellNat 645 (F.C.) — The applicant sought judicial review of a decision of an immigration officer wherein the officer determined the applicant to be inadmissible pursuant to paragraphs 36(2)(a) and 34(1)(f) of IRPA by reason, in the case of the first citation, of the applicant's conviction in Canada on March 9, 2007, for theft under $5,000 and, in the case of the second citation, for being a member of the General Union of Palestinian Students (GUPS), and the Fatah faction of the Palestinian Liberation Organization (PLO) and the Popular Committee of the PLO, organizations in which, in the view of the decision-maker, there are reasonable grounds to believe engaged, have engaged, or will engage in acts of terrorism referred to in paragraph 34(1)(c) of IRPA. The officer concluded that the applicant had been a member of GUPS, the Fatah faction of the PLO and a Popular Committee of the PLO and this finding was not disputed. The officer concluded on the issue of "engaging in terrorism" that the applicant's limited activities in the GUPS, the Fatah faction of the PLO and the Popular Committee of the PLO, as a member of such organizations, constituted his membership in organizations that there are reasonable grounds to believe have engaged in terrorism.

The burden of jurisprudence of this Court and the Federal Court of Appeal appears to be contrary to the applicant's position that mere formal membership should not inevitably constitute "membership" for the purposes of paragraph 34(1)(f) of IRPA. The Federal Court concluded "in short, if one is a 'member' then he or she is a 'member' for the purposes of paragraph 34(1)(f) with all the implications that membership carries with it and with relief, if warranted, lying in the discretion of a Minister of the Crown under subsection 34(2) of IRPA and not in the discretion of immigration officers or this Court." Therefore the decision of the officer was reasonably open to the officer in the sense that it demonstrates the existence of justification, transparency and intelligibility within the decision-making process and fell within a range of possible, acceptable outcomes which are defensible in respect of the facts underlying the matter and the applicable provisions of law. The application for judicial review was dismissed.

The following question was certified:

> Is formal membership in an organization that has engaged in acts of terrorism determinative of whether a person is to be considered inadmissible to Canada pursuant to paragraph 34(1)(f) of the *Immigration and Refugee Protection Act*?

*Gebreab v. Canada (Minister of Public Safety & Emergency Preparedness)* (2009), 85 Imm. L.R. (3d) 265, 359 F.T.R. 296 (Eng.), 2009 FC 1213, 2009 CarswellNat 5482, 2009 CarswellNat 3919 (F.C.) — This was an application for judicial review of the Immigration Division's decision pursuant to s. 44 of IRPA that the applicant was inadmissible to Canada pursuant to paragraph 34(1)(f) of IRPA for being a member of an organization in which there are reasonable grounds to believe engages, has engaged or will engage in the Acts referred to in paragraphs 34(1)(b) and (c), namely subversion by force of a government and terrorism. The applicant argued that the Board applied the wrong test for determining whether the Ethiopian Peoples' Revolutionary Party (EPRP), at the time the applicant was a member, was an organization that met the criteria of s. 34(1)(b) and (c). The Court concluded that the decision in *Sittambalam* (2006), 56 Imm. L.R. (3d) 161 (F.C.A.), does not establish any "test" for the definition of an "organization." Instead the factors are considered to be helpful, but no one of them is essential. In any event, the factors also do not address the question of changes within an organization. The Court in *Sittampalam* also favoured a broad interpretation of membership and organization — one that is not limited by temporal qualifications or changes in the organization. By finding that the EPRP is not an "organization" because at the time of the applicant's membership, it did not engage in acts of terrorism or subversion, the Board would, in effect, eliminate the words "they have occurred" from s. 33 and the words "has engaged" from s. 34(1)(f).

Having concluded that there were no required factors, the issue is whether the Board, in determining s. 37(1) issues, asked itself the right questions. In this case there was no question as to the applicant's membership in the EPRP and it was undisputed that the acts of the EPRP in the 1970s would meet the test for a terrorist or subversive organization as those terms are used in s. 34(1)(b) and (c) of IRPA. Therefore, the only issue before the Board dealt with the "organization" that called itself the EPRP in the 1970s and the "organization" that called itself the EPRP in the 1980s. The Board considered whether the organization the applicant belonged to in the 1980s was that of the 1970s, or whether there were two separate and different organizations that shared the same name. The Board correctly identified the question before it and correctly applied the test for determining whether the EPRP was an organization as contemplated by s. 34(1) of IRPA. The

Board's finding of inadmissibility under s. 34(1)(f) was not unreasonable. Accordingly, the application for judicial review was dismissed. The following question was certified:

> Is a foreign national inadmissible to Canada, pursuant to s. 34(1)(f) of IRPA, where there is clear and convincing evidence that the organization disavowed and ceased its engagement in acts of subversion or terrorism as contemplated by s. 34(1)(b) and (c) prior to the foreign national's membership in the organization?



*Toronto Coalition to Stop the War v. Canada (Minister of Public Safety & Emergency Preparedness)* (2009), 80 Imm. L.R. (3d) 72, 2009 CarswellNat 775, 2009 FC 326 (F.C.) — The applicants brought a motion to seek an order of the Federal Court to permit a Mr. Galloway to enter Canada. Mr. Galloway was a British citizen and member of Parliament of the UK. He was to speak at a public forum entitled "Resisting War from Gaza to Kandahar", hosted by the Toronto Coalition to Stop the War.

Every person seeking to enter Canada must appear for an examination to determine whether the person has a right to enter Canada or is or may become authorized to enter and remain in Canada under subs. 18(1) of the IRPA. Mr. Galloway's personal views and open sympathies for the Palestinians and their cause became a matter of public record. An official of the High Commission of Canada, Immigration Section, by letter dated March 20, 2009, advised the applicant Galloway, apparently as a matter of "courtesy", that according to the "preliminary assessment" of the CBSA, he is inadmissible to Canada on security grounds pursuant to subs. 34 of the IRPA. Mr. Galloway was invited by the letter to make submissions and that a CBSA officer will make a final determination of admissibility based on this preliminary assessment and any submissions he may make should he present himself at a port of entry.

The Court denied the applicant's request for an interim order or interlocutory injunction to enjoin the respondents and their officials from denying Mr. Galloway entry to Canada.

At one time, the Court was reluctant to grant mandatory interlocutory injunctions but, over time, has been somewhat more willing to do so. Still, some greater level of caution arises when, particularly at an interlocutory stage, the Court is asked to order somebody to take a positive action that will change the *status quo*. It is only in clear cases that mandatory injunction relief against the enforcement of a law will likely be granted by the Court before a full hearing of the application for judicial review. In such instances, public interests and the relative strength of the parties' arguments are relevant factors to consider in the assessment of balance of convenience.

A fundamental principle of immigration law is that non-citizens do not have an unqualified right to enter Canada. The admission of a foreign national to this country is a privilege determined by statute, regulation or otherwise, and not a matter of right. In this respect, Parliament has expressly given the CBSA officers legal authority to exclusively determine whether a foreign national who seeks to enter this country is admissible (s. 15 and 18 of the Act). Yet there had been no final determination made by an officer with respect to the admission in Canada of Mr. Galloway.

The Court was not prepared to exempt Mr. Galloway from the application of the provisions in the Act and Regulations respecting entry and examination, or to order the respondents' officials to allow him to come to Canada, without any final decision made on his admissibility.

*Daud v. Canada (Minister of Citizenship & Immigration)*, 2008 CarswellNat 1800, 2008 FC 701 (F.C.) — This was an application for leave for judicial review of a decision by an immigration officer in which the applicant was found to be inadmissible for permanent residence by reason of being a member of a terrorist organization pursuant to s. 34(1)(f) of the Act. The crux of the present case involves determining whether the officer committed a reviewable error when he concluded that the applicant was inadmissible on security grounds for being a member of a terrorist organization. Since the applicant was granted refugee status and thus was found to face persecution should he be returned to Pakistan, any subsequent finding of inadmissibility should be carried out with prudence, and established with the outmost clarity. Given the applicant admitted to being a member of the MQM-A organization, the Court was to review the officer's determination that the MQM-A is "an organization that there are reasonable grounds to believe engages, has engaged or will engage in acts referred to in paragraph (a), (b), or (c)" (s.34(1)(f) of the Act). The assessment of whether there are reasonable grounds to believe that an organization has engaged in acts of terrorism is a two-step analysis. The first step involves a factual determination of whether there are reasonable grounds to believe that the organization in question committed the acts of violence attributed to it. At the second step of the analysis, a determination is made as to whether those constitute acts of terrorism. The officer must provide the definition of terrorism relied upon and explain how the listed acts meet that definition.

Given the evidence before the officer, the Court was unable to conclude that the officer's determination that MQM-A committed violent acts, including murder and torture, was unreasonable.

The existence of general violence does not preclude a determination that an organization engages in terrorism. The existence of generalized violence is part of the context within which the officer conducts his analysis, but it is not dispositive of the end determination. Indeed, terrorist acts are committed during an array of country conditions ranging from periods of relative peace to those of widespread strife and conflict. In this case the officer made reference to s. 83.01 of the *Criminal Code* of Canada, as well as the annexed list of treaties to the *United Nations Convention for the Suppression of the Financing of Terrorism* as fundamental guidelines in his analysis. Furthermore, he reproduced the definition of terrorism provided by the Supreme Court of Canada in *Suresh v. Canada (Minister of Citizenship & Immigration)*, [2002] 1 S.C.R. 3. The Court was unable to conclude that the officer's analysis with respect to the second step was unreasonable. To the contrary, the "decision fell within a range of possible, acceptable outcomes which are defensible in respect of the facts in law". The application for judicial review was dismissed.

*Mekonen v. Canada (Minister of Citizenship & Immigration)* (2008), 66 Imm. L.R. (3d) 222, 2007 CarswellNat 3655, 2007 FC 1133 (F.C.) — Mr. Mekonen brought an application for judicial review of a decision of a visa officer that, as a member of the Eritrean Liberation Front ("ELF"), Mr. Mekonen was captured by paragraph 34(1)(f) of the IRPA, and therefore was inadmissible to Canada. The Court found that the officer should have provided Mr. Mekonen with a CBSA memorandum and an open source document, to allow Mr. Mekonen to make submissions that were responsive to that material. The Court adopted the Federal Court of Appeal decision in *B. (S.) v. Canada (Minister of Citizenship & Immigration)*, 2001 CarswellNat 2008, that the question is not whether the report is or contains extrinsic evidence of facts unknown to the person affected by the decision, but whether the disclosure of the report is required to provide the person with a reasonable opportunity to participate in a meaningful manner in the decision-making process. In this case, meaningful participation included the right to highlight weaknesses in the material before the officer. Because the officer breached the duty of procedural fairness, the application for judicial review was allowed.

*Jalil v. Canada (Minister of Citizenship & Immigration)*, 2007 CarswellNat 1440, 2007 FC 568 (F.C.) — While there is no legal requirement that there be evidence that an organization sanctioned or approved the terrorist acts, in making an assessment under paragraphs 34(1)(f) of the Act, an immigration officer must determine whether there is enough evidence to establish that the organization sanctions the acts.

*Golestaneh v. Canada (Minister of Public Safety & Emergency Preparedness)*, 2007 CarswellNat 1233, 2007 FC 509 (F.C.) — Pursuant to subs. 44(1) of IRPA an enforcement officer at the Canadian Border Services Agency prepared a report alleging that the applicant was inadmissible, as per paragraphs 34(1)(f) and 35(1)(a) of the Act, by reason of his involvement with a listed terrorist entity in Canada. The report prepared by the enforcement officer was referred by the Minister of Public Safety and Emergency Preparedness to the Immigration Division of the Immigration Refugee Board for an admissibility hearing. The applicant sought judicial review of the decisions made under subs. 44(1) and 44(2) of the Act.

The enforcement officer did not have access to the documentation supporting the security intelligence report prepared by the Canadian Security Intelligence Services (CSIS). The enforcement officer's decision was limited to reading the report itself. This alone was a serious error of law that justified setting aside the decision of the enforcement officer. Although the CSIS document may set out precisely the grounds on inadmissibility of the applicant, the officer who must decide whether to issue a subs. 44(1) report has a duty, when examining the file for the first time, to consult all of the reference documents, including the appendices to the CSIS report and the information on the sources underlying this report, before making a decision. This is necessary in order to ensure that the procedure followed will sufficiently guarantee the independence of the decision maker and thus protect the rights of the individual concerned.

The decision of the enforcement officer to prepare a report for the Minister, and the subsequent decision by the Minister to refer the report to the Immigration Division for an admissibility hearing, was set aside and the file was referred back to a different enforcement officer for re-determination.

*Oremade v. Canada (Minister of Citizenship & Immigration)* (2005), [2006] 1 F.C.R. 393, 2005 CarswellNat 2211, 2005 CarswellNat 2942, 2005 FC 1077 (F.C.) — For purposes of paragraph 34(1)(b) of the IRPA, the permanent resident or foreign national has to have the intention of actually using force in subverting a government. Given the context in which the words "by force" appear, the intention to subvert by force, rather than by some other means, is critical to the applicability of paragraph 34(1)(b). However, this intent to subvert by force is not to be measured solely from the subjective perspective of the applicant. It may well be that there was a hope or expectation that the coup would be bloodless but it is also reasonable for persons on the street to assume, upon seeing armed soldiers occupying lands and buildings, that force could or would be used if thought necessary. The use of force in the subversion must be more than an accident: it must be the intended means by which to affect the overthrow of the government. It is the Board's function to weigh all the subjective and objective evidence related to the impugned act. Subjective intent is but one element, albeit, in assessing all of the evidence of intent, it is appropriate to presume that a person knows or ought to have known and to have intended the natural consequences of their action.

*Poshteh v. Canada (Minister of Citizenship & Immigration)*, [2005] F.C.J. No. 381, 2005 CarswellNat 2047, 2005 CarswellNat 564, 252 D.L.R. (4th) 316, 2005 FCA 85, 331 N.R. 129 (F.C.A.); reconsideration refused 2005 CarswellNat 949, 332 N.R. 374, 252 D.L.R. (4th) 335, 2005 FCA 121 (F.C.A.) — Under subs. 34(2) of IRPA, membership in a terrorist organization does not constitute inadmissibility if the individual in question satisfies the Minister that their presence in Canada would not be detrimental to the national interest. The Court was satisfied that the term "member", under the Act, should continue to be interpreted broadly due to the fact that the Minister has the discretion to exclude an individual from the operation of paragraph 34. There is no blanket exemption for minors from the provisions of paragraph 34. An individual status as a minor is still relevant under paragraph 34(1)(f). It would be highly unusual for there to be a finding of membership in the case of a young child, say under the age of 12. Although it would depend on the evidence in each case, it would seem self evident that in the case of such children, the presumption would be that they do not possess the requisite knowledge or mental capacity to understand the nature and effect of their actions. In the case of young children, the age of the child itself would be *prima facie* evidence of an absence of the requisite knowledge or mental capacity. At common law there was an irrebuttable presumption that a child under the age of seven was incapable of possessing a criminal intent. Once a child reached the age of fourteen, the common law presumption of criminal incapacity disappeared and was replaced by a rebuttable presumption of capacity for criminal intent. For the purpose of determining membership in a terrorist organization by a minor, the requisite knowledge or mental capacity should be viewed on a continuum. Just as there would be a presumption against the requisite knowledge or mental capacity in the case of young children, there would be a presumption that the closer the minor is to eighteen years, the greater will be the likelihood that the minor possesses the requisite knowledge or mental capacity. It is open to the minor to raise issues of duress or coercion although those particular issues did not arise on the facts of this case. It would be very difficult for a minor to argue that he should not be found to be a member of a terrorist organization if he had been directly involved in violent activities or had held a leadership role in the terrorist organization. Matters such as knowledge or mental capacity are the types of considerations to be taken into account in deciding whether a determination of membership in a terrorist organization in the case of a minor is to be different than in the case of an adult.

*Abdolkhaleghi v. Canada (Minister of Citizenship & Immigration)* (2005), 46 Imm. L.R. (3d) 19, 2005 CarswellNat 1601, 2005 FC 729 (F.C.) — The applicants sought an order of *mandamus*. Their applications for permanent residence were not being processed because the respondent was waiting for the results of security checks being conducted by CSIS. The fact of an ongoing investigation by CSIS is not an absolute bar to ordering *mandamus*. If there is a long delay without adequate explanation, then *mandamus* can follow. To simply state, in response to the applicants' requests for information respecting the length of time it was taking to process their applications, that a security investigation by CSIS is ongoing, is not an adequate explanation. A blanket statement to the effect that a security check investigation is pending, prevents an analysis of the adequacy of the explanation. For security reasons, immigration authorities may not think it appropriate to disclose or provide more detailed information about why the security checks are taking so long. This concern can be addressed in the *mandamus* order itself, by providing the respondent with an opportunity to return to Court for an extension of time within which to process the application.

*Ali v. Canada (Minister of Citizenship & Immigration)* (2004), 42 Imm. L.R. (3d) 237, 2004 CarswellNat 4035, 2004 CarswellNat 2940, 2004 FC 1174 (F.C.) — Judicial review does lie from a decision of an immigration officer made pursuant to subs. 34(1). It is appropriate for the Court to entertain an application for judicial review notwithstanding that an application for Ministerial relief under subs. 34(2) is pending.

## Section 34(2)

*Agraira v. Canada (Minister of Public Safety & Emergency Preparedness)* (2009), 87 Imm. L.R. (3d) 135, 357 F.T.R. 246 (Eng.), 2009 FC 1302, 2009 CarswellNat 5509, 2009 CarswellNat 4438 (F.C.) — This was an application for judicial review of a decision by the Minister of Public Safety denying the an application for ministerial relief under subs. 34(2) of IRPA contrary to the recommendation of the Canadian Border Services Agency. The sole issue was whether the Minister's decision was unreasonable.

In a case such as this one, there might be more than one reasonable outcome. However, as long as the process adopted by the Minister and its outcome fits comfortably with the principles of justification, transparency and intelligibility, it is not open to a reviewing Court to substitute its own view of preferable outcome. Significant deference should be accorded to discretionary ministerial decisions as the power conferred on the Minister cannot be delegated, and the Minister has presumably acquired expertise in matters of national security and the national interest in the course of exercising his functions. Another consideration in favour of deference is the "political" nature of such a discretionary decision. Appendix D of the IP 10 *Refusal of National Security Cases/Processing of National Interest Request Guidelines* sets out five questions to be examined in the context of such analysis. In this case, it did not appear from the reasons that the Minister addressed the questions set out in IP 10 nor does he seem to have balanced the factors which prior decisions had identified as relevant to the determination of what is in the "national interest." These would include whether the applicant posed a threat to Canada's security; whether the applicant posed a danger to the public; the period of time the applicant had been in Canada; whether it is consistent with Canada's humanitarian reputation of allowing permanent residents to settle in Canada; the impact on both the applicant and all other members of society of the denial of permanent residence; and the adherence to all of Canada's international obligations. Furthermore the Minister's reasons did not acknowledge that the applicant had resided in Canada since 1997, that he had been a productive member of society, that he owned his own business earning over $100,000 per annum and that he had no criminal record. The application for judicial review was granted. The following question was certified:

> When determining a s. 34(2) application, must the Minister of Public Safety consider any specific factors in assessing whether a foreign national's presence in Canada would be contrary to the national interest? Specifically, must the Minister consider the five factors listed in Appendix D of IP 10?

*Miller v. Canada (Solicitor General)*, [2006] F.C.J. No. 1164, [2007] 3 F.C.R. 438, 2006 CarswellNat 2282, 2006 FC 912 — In regards to the decision to grant or deny Ministerial exemption, the standard of review is patent unreasonableness. This standard is of course dependent on the Minister's process being in accordance with fairness and natural justice and the Minister applying the correct legal test.

*John Doe v. Canada (Minister of Citizenship & Immigration)* (2006), 54 Imm. L.R. (3d) 212, 2006 CarswellNat 1105, 2006 CarswellNat 1543, 2006 FC 535 (F.C.) — The applicant came to Canada in 1984 and was granted refugee status in 1986. He then applied for permanent residence. There ensued many interviews, security checks, etc., without any decision being taken on his application. In 1998, the immigration officers raised security concerns. The applicant made an application for ministerial relief under what would now be subs. 34(2) of the IRPA, which would have the effect of relieving him of possible inadmissibility that might otherwise be a bar to grant permanent residence. In nearly eight years no decision had been taken on the application for ministerial relief. The applicant brought an application for *mandamus* to require the Minister to make a decision with respect to the applicant's permanent residence in Canada.

On the eve of the hearing, the Minister made an offer to settle. The Minister was prepared not to oppose the *mandamus* application but was to agree to an order that would set out time limits for progressive steps leading to an ultimate decision. The applicant found the proposal unacceptable as it contemplated steps totaling some 240 days and did not set out any limit as to how long the Minister of Public Security and Emergency Preparedness might take to decide the application for ministerial relief, which was first made in 1998. The Court directed that a decision on permanent residence be made by a specific date.

The Court also awarded costs, finding special reasons — specifically that the Minister failed to take a decision which was requested almost 20 years previous, while the applicant had endured interview after interview, acquired a good deal of legal advice and was forced to bring the Minister to court. Even when faced with this matter being set down for hearing the Minister waited until the afternoon of the day before the hearing to offer a settlement.

*Poshteh v. Canada (Minister of Citizenship & Immigration)*, 2005 CarswellNat 949, 332 N.R. 374, 252 D.L.R. (4th) 335, 2005 FCA 121 (F.C.A.) — There is simply no temporal aspect to subs. 34(2). Nothing in subs. 34(2) appears to fetter the discretion of the Minister respecting when he might grant a ministerial exemption.

*Hussenu v. Canada (Minister of Citizenship & Immigration)*, 38 Imm. L.R. (3d) 197, [2004] F.C.J. No. 344, 2004 CarswellNat 2092, 2004 CarswellNat 550, 247 F.T.R. 137, 2004 FC 283 (F.C.) — This was an application to review the decision of a member of the Immigration Division who determined that the applicant was inadmissible to Canada. A member had determined that the applicant was inadmissible under s. 34(1)(f) because there were reasonable grounds to believe that the applicant was a member of an organization that there are reasonable grounds to believe engages in acts of terrorism. A deportation order was issued.

The appropriate standard of review in a case such as this is correctness.

There is no obligation on the Minister to make sure that the applicant is aware of the exemption under s. 34(2). The applicant's counsel failed to raise the issue. That omission cannot be laid at the feet of the Minister by invoking a duty to provide notice of an exemption that is perfectly apparent on the face of the statute.

**35. (1) Human or international rights violations — A permanent resident or a foreign national is inadmissible on grounds of violating human or international rights for**

> **(a) committing an act outside Canada that constitutes an offence referred to in sections 4 to 7 of the *Crimes Against Humanity and War Crimes Act*;**

**(b) being a prescribed senior official in the service of a government that, in the opinion of the Minister, engages or has engaged in terrorism, systematic or gross human rights violations, or genocide, a war crime or a crime against humanity within the meaning of subsections 6(3) to (5) of the *Crimes Against Humanity and War Crimes Act*; or**

**(c) being a person, other than a permanent resident, whose entry into or stay in Canada is restricted pursuant to a decision, resolution or measure of an international organization of states or association of states, of which Canada is a member, that imposes sanctions on a country against which Canada has imposed or has agreed to impose sanctions in concert with that organization or association.**



**(2) Exception — Paragraphs (1)(b) and (c) do not apply in the case of a permanent resident or a foreign national who satisfies the Minister that their presence in Canada would not be detrimental to the national interest.**

*[Editor's Note: SOR/2002-227, s. 320(2) provides that a person is inadmissible under the new* Immigration and Refugee Protection Act, *S.C. 2001, c. 27 on grounds of violating human or international rights if, on June 28, 2002, the person had been determined to be a member of an inadmissible class described in paragraph 19(1)(j) or (l) of the former* Immigration Act, *R.S.C. 1985, c. I-2.]*

## Case Law

*Segasayo v. Canada (Minister of Citizenship & Immigration)* (2010), 89 Imm. L.R. (3d) 7, 2010 FC 173, 2010 CarswellNat 323, 2010 CarswellNat 324 (F.C.) — The applicant was Rwanda's ambassador to Canada from 1991 to 1995. After the new government in Rwanda recalled him, he and his family applied for and were given refugee status by the Immigration and Refugee Board in 1996. He submitted that as a member of the Hutu intelligentsia and as ambassador to Canada appointed by the former government he feared persecution and reprisal by the new Tutsi government. He is now subject to a deportation order because he was found inadmissible to Canada for violating human or international rights. He sought judicial review of that decision. The Board determined that the applicant was a person described in s. 35(1)(a) of IRPA. The Member was of the view that the deeming provision in s. 16 of the Regulations created an irrebuttable presumption that an ambassador in the service of a government on the Minister's list was inadmissible on the grounds of violating human or international rights. In other words, once it was shown that the applicant was the ambassador of the government designated by the Minister (facts that the applicant had never disputed), then he was inadmissible and had no defence based on lack of complicity in crimes against humanity or human rights violations. The member also dismissed the argument that the provisions in question were unconstitutional as violating s. 7 of the *Canadian Charter of Rights and Freedoms*. The Court upheld the Board's decision that the applicant was inadmissible, dismissed his *Charter* argument and dismissed the application for judicial review

The following question was certified:

> Are ss. 35(1) of the *Immigration and Refugee Protection Act* and 16 of the *Immigration and Refugee Protection Regulations* in accordance with the principles stated by the Supreme Court in *Singh v. Canada (Minister of Citizenship & Immigration), [1985] 1 S.C.R. 177* and *Charkaoui v. Canada (Citizenship & Immigration)* (2007), 59 Imm. L.R. (3d) 1, and with s. 7 of the *Canadian Charter of*

*Rights and Freedoms* when a person targeted by those provisions had already obtained the refugee or protective person status and does not have the right to defend him/herself against the allegations made against him/her under those provisions?

*Varela v. Canada (Minister of Citizenship & Immigration)* (2009), 80 Imm. L.R. (3d) 1, 2009 CarswellNat 1228, 2009 FCA 145 (C.A.); affirming [2008] F.C.J. No. 568, 72 Imm. L.R. (3d) 236, [2009] 1 F.C.R. 605, 2008 FC 436, 2008 CarswellNat 2790, 2008 CarswellNat 928 (F.C.) — This was a judicial review of a decision of the Immigration and Refugee Board which held that the applicant had violated human or international rights for having committed an act outside Canada that constituted an offence referred to in ss. 4 to 7 of the *Crimes Against Humanity and War Crimes Act*, S.C. 2000, c. 24. Section 36 of the IRPA specifically provides that inadmissibility on the grounds of serious criminality may not be based on a conviction in respect of which a pardon has been granted, or if there has been a final acquittal. Furthermore, rehabilitation is taken into account. Although s. 35, which deals with war crimes and crimes against humanity, is silent on these matters, given the international context of the case, the United Nations Guidelines cannot simply be ignored. The applicant's participation in a death squad and in the treatment of prisoners was so grave and heinous that as a matter of law the full application of s. 35 of the IRPA cannot be mitigated.

The Federal Court of Appeal determined it was not necessary to send this matter back for a new determination, as there was only one legal conclusion open to the Board. It would be a waste of resources to start the whole matter over on what is an included offence, as murder is certainly a serious crime, even if other requirements of a crime against humanity, or a war crime, were not met.

Although several questions were certified, the Federal Court of Appeal concluded there were no serious questions of general importance and dismissed the appeal.

*Golestaneh v. Canada (Minister of Public Safety & Emergency Preparedness)*, 2007 CarswellNat 1233, 2007 FC 509 (F.C.) — Pursuant to subs. 44(1) of IRPA an enforcement officer at the Canadian Border Services Agency prepared a report alleging that the applicant was inadmissible, as per paragraphs 34(1)(f) and 35(1)(a) of the Act, by reason of his involvement with a listed terrorist entity in Canada. The report prepared by the enforcement officer was referred by the Minister of Public Safety and Emergency Preparedness to the Immigration Division of the Immigration Refugee Board for an admissibility hearing. The applicant sought judicial review of the decisions made under subs. 44(1) and 44(2) of the Act.

The enforcement officer did not have access to the documentation supporting the security intelligence report prepared by the Canadian Security Intelligence Services (CSIS). The enforcement officer's decision was limited to reading the report itself. This alone was a serious error of law that justified setting aside the decision of the enforcement officer. Although the CSIS document may set out precisely the grounds on inadmissibility of the applicant, the officer who must decide whether to issue a subs. 44(1) report has a duty, when examining the file for the first time, to consult all of the reference documents, including the appendices to the CSIS report and the information on the sources underlying this report, before making a decision. This is necessary in order to ensure that the procedure followed will sufficiently guarantee the independence of the decision maker and thus protect the rights of the individual concerned.

The decision of the enforcement officer to prepare a report for the Minister, and the subsequent decision by the Minister to refer the report to the Immigration Division for an admissibility hearing, was set aside and the file was referred back to a different enforcement officer for re-determination.

*Beltran Velasquez v. Canada (Minister of Citizenship & Immigration)*, 2006 CarswellNat 2616, 2006 FC 1024 (F.C.) — A decision to deny the applicant a visa to enter Canada as a permanent resident was set aside, since the officer did not give notice of concerns respecting the nature and scope of the applicant's activities nor was the applicant given a reasonable opportunity to respond. Specifically, the visa officer concluded that the applicant was involved or complicit in crimes against humanity following disclosure by the applicant during a telephone interview that he was with Mobile Brigade #2 in a particular location in Colombia in October 1992. The applicant was never confronted with the opinion formed, and was never asked questions as to what he was doing or what others known to him were doing at the relevant time or place. The visa officer concluded he was inadmissible under subs. 35(1)(a) of the IRPA.



*Perez v. Canada (Minister of Citizenship & Immigration)* (2006), 55 Imm. L.R. (3d) 227, 2006 CarswellNat 2610, 2006 FC 1000 (F.C.) — The applicant's wife applied to sponsor the applicant, but the sponsorship was refused by a visa officer on the basis that there were reasonable grounds to believe that the applicant was inadmissible pursuant to s. 35(1)(a) of the IRPA for having violated human or international rights "by committing an act outside Canada that constitutes an offence referred to in ss. 4 to 7 of the *Crimes Against Humanity and War Crimes Act*." Although the Minister conceded that the visa officer had failed to observe principles of natural justice in rendering the decision and that consequently the matter should be sent back for re-determination, the applicant argued that the visa officer was precluded from re-examining the issue of inadmissibility pursuant to s. 35(1)(a) of the IRPA by virtue of the doctrine of *res judicata*, as an earlier binding, final decision on the issue had already been rendered in 1997. In 1997 the applicant, in the context of a refugee claim, stated that he had been a member of a Guatemalan death squad and an adjudicator held that the applicant was not inadmissible under s. 19(1)(j) of the then applicable *Immigration Act*, as there were no reasonable grounds to believe that the applicant committed an offence referred to in any of ss. 4 to 7 of the *Crimes Against Humanity and War Crimes Act*. The applicant argued that there was no new relevant evidence before the visa officer and therefore, the visa officer erred both by re-examining the issue of inadmissibility, and by reaching the unsustainable conclusion that the applicant is inadmissible.

Section 34 of the former *Immigration Act* clearly excludes res judicata in the specific context of s. 27 of the Act. Accordingly, s. 34 of the former *Immigration Act* makes it abundantly clear that the adjudicator's decision was not a final decision regarding inadmissibility. The applicant argued in the alternative that if inadmissibility could be examined, then the visa officer made his inadmissibility finding without proper regard to relevant evidence by failing to consider the adjudicator's finding that the applicant was not inadmissible for war crimes or crimes against humanity. The Court agreed with this argument and quashed the visa officer's decision, sending the matter back for a new hearing before a new visa officer and directing that the new visa officer, in rendering his or her decision, must consider all the facts and evidence of this case, including the adjudicator's decision of May 29, 1997.

*Mugesera c. Canada (Ministre de la Citoyenneté & de l'Immigration)*, [2005] 2 S.C.R. 91, 47 Imm. L.R. (3d) 1, EYB 2005-91970, [2005] S.C.J. No. 40, 197 C.C.C. (3d) 225,

254 D.L.R. (4th) 193, 30 C.R. (6th) 107, 335 N.R. 220, 15 C.P.C. (6th) 51, 2005 CarswellNat 1738, 2005 CarswellNat 1739, 2005 SCC 39 — At the secondary level of appellate review, the Federal Court of Appeal should proceed with the review of the Minister's allegations on the basis of the facts as found by the Immigration Appeal Division. On questions of law, however, the standard of review is correctness and the Immigration Appeal Division is not entitled to deference when it comes to defining the elements of a crime or whether the Minister's burden of proof has been discharged. Where the Minister relies on a crime committed abroad, a conclusion that the elements of the crime in Canadian criminal law had been made out will be deemed to be determinative in respect of the commission of crimes under the foreign criminal law. With respect to the specific allegations made pursuant to s. 27(1) of the former *Immigration Act*, the evidence adduced by the Minister must meet the civil standard of the balance of probabilities. The appellant, an active member of a hard-line Hutu political party opposed to a negotiation process then under way to end the war, spoke to about 1,000 people at a meeting of the party in Rwanda. The content of the speech eventually led the Rwandan authorities to issue the equivalent of an arrest warrant against the appellant. He fled the country and successfully applied for permanent residence in Canada. After the immigrant landed in Canada, the Minister became aware of allegations against him and commenced proceeding to deport him, on the basis that he committed criminal acts or offences. Specifically, the issue was whether a speech delivered by the appellant in Rwanda triggered a series of events that led to murder, hatred and genocide. In this case, the Minister had to prove that, on the facts of the case as found on a balance of probabilities, the speech constituted an incitement to murder, genocide or hatred. The Supreme Court of Canada upheld the validity of the deportation order on the basis that each element of the offence under the *Criminal Code* had been made out and that there were reasonable grounds to believe that the immigrant committed a crime against humanity and was therefore inadmissible under the former *Immigration Act*. The "reasonable grounds to believe" standard requires more than mere suspicion, but less than the normal civil litigation standard of proof on the balance of probabilities.

*Zazai v. Canada (Minister of Citizenship & Immigration)*, [2005] F.C.J. No. 1567, 50 Imm. L.R. (3d) 107, 259 D.L.R. (4th) 281, 339 N.R. 201, 2005 CarswellNat 2933, 2005 CarswellNat 4771, 2005 FCA 303 (Fed. C.A.) — The appellant came to Canada as a stowaway and made a refugee claim. The Refugee Board determined that he was excluded from the definition of Convention refugee under subs. 2(1) of the *Immigration Act*, R.S.C. 1985, because of section F(a) of Article 1 of the United Nations Convention relating to the status of refugees. The Board found that there were serious reasons for considering that he had committed crimes against humanity. His application for leave with respect to the Refugee Board's decision was denied. He subsequently submitted an application for landing as a post-determination refugee claimant in Canada. A report under s. 27(2) of the former Act was prepared and a s. 27(3) direction for inquiry was issued. The inquiry was held before an adjudicator who concluded that the appellant was a person described in paragraph 27(2)(a) coupled with paragraph 19(1)(j) of the former Act. As a result, the adjudicator determined that he was subject to a deportation order. The appellant successfully sought leave to apply for judicial review of the adjudicator's decision. The Federal Court Trial Division allowed the application and the Minister appealed. The appeal to the Federal Court of Appeal was allowed and the order of the applications judge was set aside and remitted back to the Federal Court for redetermination.

The Federal Court of Appeal concluded that the definition of "crime against humanity" found at subs. 6(3) of the *Crimes Against Humanity and War Crimes Act* includes complicity.

As a matter of fact, as found by the adjudicator and agreed by the reviewing judge, there was sufficient cogent evidence that the appellant was, knowingly and voluntarily, a participating and active member for five years in a secret service organization within the Ministry of State Security known as KHAD that tortured and eliminated people who were against the government. The evidence revealed that the appellant entered as a lieutenant and rose to the level of captain. Not only did he share and espouse the views of the brutal organization, he attended training sessions and provided the names of those who did not cooperate.

According to the evidence, the appellant was willingly and to his benefit a member of an organization that only existed for a limited brutal purpose. Under both Canadian and international jurisprudence, the behaviour of the appellant amounted to complicity in the commission of crimes against humanity. Consequently, the Federal Court judge properly confirmed the decision of the adjudicator that the appellant was inadmissible pursuant to paragraph 19(1)(j) of the former Act or paragraph 35(1)(a) of the new Act.

The Supreme Court's decision in *Mugesera v. Canada (Minister of Citizenship & Immigration)*, [2005] S.C.J. No. 39, was distinguished on the basis that the Supreme Court in that case was not confronted with an issue of complicity in the commission of a crime by someone else. In that case Mr. Mugesera was the actual perpetrator. Complicity is not a crime at common law and under Canadian criminal law, it was, and still is, a mode of commission of a crime. It refers to the act or omission of a person who helps, or is done for the purpose of helping, the furtherance of a crime. An accomplice is then charged with, and tried for, the crime that was actually committed and that he assisted or furthered. In other words whether one looks at it from the perspective of our domestic law or of international law, complicity contemplates a contribution to the commission of a crime. Complicity must not be confused with the inchoate crimes of conspiracy, attempt and incitement to commit a crime. Unlike complicity, they are not modes or means of committing a crime.

*Matti v. Canada (Minister of Citizenship & Immigration)*, 2005 CarswellNat 3799, 2005 CarswellNat 4785, 2005 FC 1561 (F.C.) — The visa officer refused the applicant's application for permanent residence on the basis that there were reasonable grounds to believe that the applicant, by his denial and silence with respect to certain facts based on evidence, was complicit in crimes against humanity. Although denial and silence are valid reasons for questioning credibility, they do not amount to evidence of complicity in crimes against humanity. Whether one is complicit will depend on the facts of the case, particularly the extent of knowledge of an organization's crimes and the degree of participation in or support of those crimes.

**36. (1) Serious criminality — A permanent resident or a foreign national is inadmissible on grounds of serious criminality for**

> **(a) having been convicted in Canada of an offence under an Act of Parliament punishable by a maximum term of imprisonment of at least 10 years, or of an offence under an Act of Parliament for which a term of imprisonment of more than six months has been imposed;**



IRP Act

**(b) having been convicted of an offence outside Canada that, if committed in Canada, would constitute an offence under an Act of Parliament punishable by a maximum term of imprisonment of at least 10 years; or**

**(c) committing an act outside Canada that is an offence in the place where it was committed and that, if committed in Canada, would constitute an offence under an Act of Parliament punishable by a maximum term of imprisonment of at least 10 years.**

*[Editor's Note: SOR/2002-227, s. 320(3) provides that a person is inadmissible under the* Immigration and Refugee Protection Act, *S.C. 2001, c. 27 (the "new Act") on grounds of serious criminality if, on June 28, 2002, the person had been determined to be a member of an inadmissible class described in paragraph 19(1)(c) or (c.1) of the* Immigration Act, *R.S.C. 1985, c. I-2 (the "former Act") or had been determined to be inadmissible on the basis of paragraph 27(1)(a.1) of the former Act.*

*SOR/2002-227, s. 320(5)(a) provides that a person who on June 28, 2002 had been determined to be inadmissible on the basis of paragraph 27(1)(d) of the former Act is inadmissible under the new Act on grounds of serious criminality if the person was convicted of an offence and a term of imprisonment of more than six months has been imposed or a term of imprisonment of 10 years or more could have been imposed.]*

**(2) Criminality — A foreign national is inadmissible on grounds of criminality for**

**(a) having been convicted in Canada of an offence under an Act of Parliament punishable by way of indictment, or of two offences under any Act of Parliament not arising out of a single occurrence;**

**(b) having been convicted outside Canada of an offence that, if committed in Canada, would constitute an indictable offence under an Act of Parliament, or of two offences not arising out of a single occurrence that, if committed in Canada, would constitute offences under an Act of Parliament;**

**(c) committing an act outside Canada that is an offence in the place where it was committed and that, if committed in Canada, would constitute an indictable offence under an Act of Parliament; or**

**(d) committing, on entering Canada, an offence under an Act of Parliament prescribed by regulations.**

*[Editor's Note: SOR/2002-227, s. 320(4) provides that a person is inadmissible under the* Immigration and Refugee Protection Act, *S.C. 2001, c. 27 (the "new Act") on grounds of criminality if, on June 28, 2002, the person had been determined to be a member of an inadmissible class described in paragraph 19(2)(a), (a.1) or (b) of the* Immigration Act, *R.S.C. 1985, c. I-2 (the "former Act"), or had been determined to be inadmissible on the basis of paragraph 27(1)(a.2) or (a.3) or (2)(d) of the former Act.*

*SOR/2002-227, s. 320(5)(b) further provides that a person who on June 28, 2002 had been determined to be inadmissible under the new Act on the basis of paragraph 27(1)(d) of the former Act is inadmissible under the new Act on grounds of criminality if the offence was punishable by a maximum term of imprisonment of five years or more but less than 10 years.]*

(3) **Application — The following provisions govern subsections (1) and (2):**

**(a) an offence that may be prosecuted either summarily or by way of indictment is deemed to be an indictable offence, even if it has been prosecuted summarily;**

**(b) inadmissibility under subsections (1) and (2) may not be based on a conviction in respect of which a pardon has been granted and has not ceased to have effect or been revoked under the *Criminal Records Act*, or in respect of which there has been a final determination of an acquittal;**

**(c) the matters referred to in paragraphs (1)(b) and (c) and (2)(b) and (c) do not constitute inadmissibility in respect of a permanent resident or foreign national who, after the prescribed period, satisfies the Minister that they have been rehabilitated or who is a member of a prescribed class that is deemed to have been rehabilitated;**

**(d) a determination of whether a permanent resident has committed an act described in paragraph (1)(c) must be based on a balance of probabilities; and**

**(e) inadmissibility under subsections (1) and (2) may not be based on an offence designated as a contravention under the *Contraventions Act* or an offence for which the permanent resident or foreign national is found guilty under the *Young Offenders Act*, chapter Y-1 of the Revised Statutes of Canada, 1985 or the *Youth Criminal Justice Act*.**

IRP Act

**Proposed Amendment — 36(3)(e)**

**(e) inadmissibility under subsections (1) and (2) may not be based on an offence**

**(i) designated as a contravention under the *Contraventions Act*,**

**(ii) for which the permanent resident or foreign national is found guilty under the *Young Offenders Act*, chapter Y-1 of the Revised Statutes of Canada, 1985, or**

**(iii) for which the permanent resident or foreign national received a youth sentence under the *Youth Criminal Justice Act*.**

2010, c. 8, s. 7 [To come into force June 29, 2012, or earlier by order.]

2008, c. 3, s. 3

## Case Law

### Section 36(1)

*Wajaras v. Canada (Minister of Citizenship & Immigration)* (2009), 2009 FC 200, 2009 CarswellNat 530, 2009 CarswellNat 1116 (F.C.) — The applicant sought to set aside a decision of the Immigration Division that found him to be inadmissible to Canada on the ground of serious criminality in accordance with s. 36(1)(a) of IRPA. The applicant entered Canada in 1997 as a Convention refugee and was granted permanent resident status at that time. He subsequently committed a serious assault and was criminally charged and sentenced to three years imprisonment in 2005.

The CBSA made an inadmissibility report which lead to an inadmissibility hearing before the Board under s. 44(2) of the IRPA. The applicant was advised of the CBSA's intention to have him declared a danger to the public. Notwithstanding his refugee status, such a finding would have permitted his return to Sudan in the event that he was also found to be inadmissible. The Minister determined that the applicant did not represent a danger to the public. In the result he could not be returned to Sudan even though he had been determined to be inadmissible and was the subject of a corresponding removal order. The applicant argued before the Board that it was an abuse of process for the Minister to seek a removal order against him with the resulting loss of permanent resident status in circumstances where his removal could not be lawfully effected.

The Federal Court concluded that notwithstanding that the Board erred in law by stating that the doctrine of abuse of process required evidence of malice or animus, a question remained as to whether an abuse of process argument could be sustained on this particular record. The Federal Court concluded it could not and the Board's mistake, therefore, was of no consequence. The application for judicial review was set aside. The applicant was solely responsible for the position he found himself in. He is not without potential future recourse. If administrative decisions are made which unlawfully interfere with his interests, including the opportunity to work, he would have the right to seek judicial review. If he stays out of legal trouble, enhances his Canadian establishment and continues to make positive social and economic contributions, he would be in a position at some point to pursue humanitarian and compassionate relief under s. 25 of the IRPA.

An abuse of process argument cannot be built around selective references to the purposes of the IRPA. The legislation serves many purposes, not the least of which is protecting Canadians by imposing consequences for the criminal behaviour of a few of those who have emigrated here.

The Federal Court judge certified a question and the Federal Court of Appeal in *Wajaras v. Canada (Minister of Citizenship & Immigration)* (2010), 399 N.R. 31, 2010 FCA 41, 2010 CarswellNat 266, 2010 CarswellNat 623 concluded that the Minister of Citizenship and Immigration does not engage in abuse of process in continuing to seek a removal order where the effected individual has been determined not to be a danger to the public. The Federal Court of Appeal concluded that it was not improper for the Minister to seek a deportation order for the purpose of depriving a permanent resident of this status as a result of serious criminality, even where there are impediments to removal. The appeal was dismissed.

*Capra v. Canada (Attorney General)* (2008), 76 Imm. L.R. (3d) 21, 335 F.T.R. 299 (Eng.), 2008 CarswellNat 3875, 2008 CarswellNat 5267, 2008 FC 1212 — This was an application for a declaration that subs. 128(4) of the *Corrections and Conditional Release Act*, S.C. 1992, c. 20 ("CCRA") is invalid on the ground that it breaches ss. 7, 9 and 15 of the *Canadian Charter of Rights and Freedoms*, Part 1 of the *Constitution Act, 1982*. The applicant had been granted Convention refugee status and became a permanent resident on December 2, 1992. The applicant was subsequently convicted of 80 counts of fraud in connection with credit cards and automatic bank teller machines in 2001. A deportation order was issued on the grounds of serious criminality. Both the appeal of the deportation order and his application were dismissed and the applicant lost his permanent residence status. However, because of his refugee status, he could not be removed to Romania unless the Minister of Citizenship and Immigration issued an opinion that the applicant constitutes a danger to the public. The CBSA sought the opinion of the Minister that he was a danger to the public in Canada. In the meantime, the applicant served his sentence in a medium security federal correctional facility and underwent a rehabilitation program. He became eligible for an unescorted temporary absence ("UTA") and day parole on July 2008. The CBSA informed the sentence management office of the deportation order previously issued against the applicant. As a result, by operation of subs. 128(4) of the CCRA, the applicant was ineligible for release on a UTA or day parole until his full parole eligibility date. The applicant believed that he was being treated differently in relation to day parole eligibility because he was not a Canadian citizen. He claimed that he was the subject of discrimination and regardless of whether he was allowed to stay in Canada or not, he perceived that he was being denied an opportunity to work towards his own rehabilitation simply because of his identity.



The Court held that s. 128(4) of the CCRA was directed at inmates subject to removal. The operation of the subsection is triggered by the issuance of a removal order. A stay of that removal order suspends the section's effect. The application of the section is rationally tied to its purpose and cannot be called arbitrary in relation to the objectives sought to be attained. Accordingly this was not arbitrary detention within the meaning of s. 9. Furthermore, the Supreme Court of Canada had made it clear that a "change in the form in which a sentence is served, whether it be favourable or unfavourable to the prisoner, is not, in itself, contrary to any principle of fundamental justice."

Parliament has decided that offenders subject to removal should serve their sentences in different ways from other offenders, including Canadian citizens. This is to ensure that their status as offenders does not enhance their access to Canadian society over that of non-offenders who face deportation; it is also intended to ensure that their removal status does not result in their serving shorter sentences than either Canadian citizens or non-citizens who are not subject to removal. Parliament has chosen to deal with these issues by suspending day parole and UTA for offenders who are subject to removal. It is possible to disagree with this approach and with whether it achieves the objectives it is intended to achieve, but that was not the issue before the court. What is relevant is that the variation in the form of the sentence that comes about as a result of subs. 128(4) of CCRA is triggered by the existence of a removal order and whether this fact makes it part of a deportation scheme.

The Court was not convinced that, if the purpose of parole is to protect society, that the loss of the possibility of that protection because of the loss of eligibility for day parole under subs. 128(4) was a disadvantage to the applicant, whether or not he was removed from Canada. Furthermore if parole was a benefit to offenders, the Court was not convinced that the applicant had been disadvantaged by the loss of any such benefit in a situation where the evidence showed his deportation was being actively pursued and he did not fall into one of the exceptions specifically provided for under subs. 128(6). The applicant failed to demonstrate differential treatment between citizens and non-citizens. The application was dismissed.

*Younis v. Canada (Minister of Citizenship & Immigration)* (2008), 74 Imm. L.R. (3d) 115, 332 F.T.R. 99 (Eng.), 2008 CarswellNat 2744, 2008 FC 944 — The applicant had a number of criminal convictions. The Immigration Division issued a deportation order against the applicant on the basis that he was inadmissible for serious criminality under s. 36(1)(a) of the Act because of his conviction for drug trafficking. The applicant appealed the deportation order and sought special relief on humanitarian and compassionate grounds under the Act. He did not challenge the legal validity of the deportation order. The IAD denied the applicant's appeal. He then sought judicial review of that decision. The issues raised in the application were whether the IAD erred in admitting the applicant's juvenile criminal record into evidence and whether the IAD erred in taking into consideration the report to Crown counsel. The *Youth Criminal Justice Act* ("YCJA") contains prohibitions against the release of records of convictions of young persons as well as some exceptions to the prohibition against the release of records of convictions of young persons. The question of whether or not the applicant's juvenile record fell within the period of access and is accessible turned on whether the sexual assault conviction was for a summary or indictable offence. There was no indication in the evidence before the IAD whether the applicant, as a youth, was convicted of a summary or indictable offence. Without such evidence, the IAD had no way of determining whether the applicant's juvenile conviction was releasable under the YCJA. The IAD is responsible for determining the admissibility, reliability and weight to be given to evidence presented before it. Although the IAD is not bound by the same legal or technical rules of evidence as a court of law, this does not confer upon the IAD the authority to admit a youth criminal record where the second conviction falls outside the period of access. The release of such a report would not only constitute a breach of s. 118 of the YCJA, it would also amount to a breach of the procedural fairness guarantees in hearings before the IAD. The IAD was found to have a duty to determine the admissibility of the applicant's youth criminal record before considering whether the record was credible and trustworthy and before determining the weight to be given to the record.

The IAD relied on the report to Crown counsel which contained a list of proposed criminal charges against the applicant. The IAD failed to make the necessary distinction between the fact that the proposed charges were mere allegations and that the applicant had not been convicted of the offences. Although it was open to the IAD to consider the evidence underlying the charges in question, it was not open to the IAD to conclude that this evidence was sufficient to find that the applicant was guilty of the offences proposed in the report. The IAD's decision was also void of any discussion regarding the reliability and credibility of the report. The absence of any analysis in this regard suggested that the IAD failed to turn its mind to whether the report was reliable and credible. This omission constituted an error of law. The application for judicial review was allowed.

*Johnson v. Canada (Minister of Citizenship & Immigration)*, [2008] F.C.J. No. 10, 2008 CarswellNat 1327, 2008 CarswellNat 11, 2008 FC 2 (F.C.) — The applicant's inland application for permanent residence was refused because he was found to be inadmissible on grounds of serious criminality. The criminal convictions that led to the finding of inadmissibility were later set aside. The applicant argued that the officer erred in reaching the decision to refuse his permanent residence application by ignoring relevant evidence, specifically that the applicant's conviction was under appeal and that the officer breached the duty of fairness he owed to the applicant by failing to provide the applicant with an opportunity to respond to his criminal convictions.

A deportation order has a clear and imminent effect upon a person's right to remain in Canada. If, in that context, there is no obligation to await the result of an appeal of a criminal conviction, it is the Court's view that there can be no obligation to defer consideration of a humanitarian and compassionate application because of an outstanding appeal. This is so because one may file a new inland application for permanent residence if circumstances later change as a result of a successful appeal. In the absence of compelling circumstances, it would be contrary to the scheme of the Act to require decisions about inadmissibility, made in the context of humanitarian and compassionate application, to be delayed until all criminal proceedings, including all rights of appeal are exhausted. The failure of the applicant to advise immigration of his convictions did not shift the onus to the officer to communicate with Mr. Johnson about his convictions. It was always open to the applicant to advise the officer of both his convictions and his appeal, and to request a deferral of the officer's decision until the appeal had been decided. Mr.

Johnson requested no postponement of the officer's decision. The application for judicial review was dismissed.

*Canada (Minister of Citizenship & Immigration) v. Malarski*, 2006 CarswellNat 2612, 2006 FC 1007 (F.C.) — Where a permanent resident who is subject of a deportation order which has been stayed is subsequently convicted of an offence that constitutes serious criminality under subs. 36(1), the stay is cancelled by operation of law pursuant to subs. 68(4) of the IRPA and an appeal to the IAD is terminated. Once this happens, the IAD loses jurisdiction over the matter.



*Cheddesingh v. Canada (Minister of Citizenship & Immigration)* (2006), 52 Imm. L.R. (3d) 247, 2006 CarswellNat 259, 2006 FC 124 (F.C.) — Subsection 64(2) of the IRPA is not concerned with the length of the sentence imposed on the offender, but with the punishment. It is clear from the jurisprudence that once a person is convicted of a crime, time served by that individual in pre-trial detention will be deemed to be part of the offender's punishment.

In this case, the applicant argued that the proper interpretation was to compute the time a person is sentenced to spend in custody as of the date of the sentence, and the time spent in pre-sentence custody should not be taken into account. According to this interpretation, the applicant's term of imprisonment would only amount to a year instead of 30 months. The applicant's proposed interpretation was contrary to the intent of Parliament in drafting subs. 64(2) of the Act. Accordingly, the Board did not commit a reviewable error in determining that the period the applicant spent in pre-sentence custody formed part of her "term of imprisonment."

*Medovarski v. Canada (Minister of Citizenship & Immigration)*, [2005] 2 S.C.R. 539, 50 Imm. L.R. (3d) 1, 135 C.R.R. (2d) 1, 258 D.L.R. (4th) 193, [2005] S.C.J. No. 31, 339 N.R. 1, EYB 2005-95306, 2005 CarswellNat 2943, 2005 CarswellNat 2944, 2005 SCC 51 — The appellant was a permanent resident and had been ordered deported for serious criminality. Her removal order was automatically stayed when she appealed the deportation order to the Immigration Appeal Division. The appeal was discontinued as a result of s. 196 of the IRPA (a transitional provision), which took away the right to appeal an order for removal unless a party had, under the former Act, been "granted a stay." The trial judge set aside the decision to discontinue. However, the Federal Court of Appeal allowed the Minister of Citizenship and Immigration's appeal, holding that the purpose of the IRPA transitional provision was to deny the right of appeal in the case of an automatic stay. Section 196 of the IRPA, properly interpreted, applies only to actively granted stays. The objectives of the IRPA, as expressed in s. 3, indicate an intent to prioritize security. In keeping with these objectives, the IRPA creates a new scheme whereby a person sentenced to more than six months in prison is inadmissible pursuant to s. 36; if they have been sentenced to a prison term of more than two years, they are denied a right to appeal their removal order under s. 64 of the IRPA. The purpose in enacting the IRPA, and in particular s. 64, was to efficiently remove from the country persons who have engaged in serious criminality. Since s. 196 refers explicitly to s. 64, the transitional provision should be interpreted in light of these legislative objectives.

The deportation of a non-citizen cannot in itself implicate the liberty and security interests protected by s. 7 of the *Canadian Charter of Rights and Freedoms*. Even if the liberty and security of the person were engaged, any unfairness resulting from s. 196 would be inadequate to constitute a breach of principles of fundamental justice.

*Shepherd v. Canada (Minister of Citizenship & Immigration)* (2005), 48 Imm. L.R. (3d) 118, 2005 CarswellNat 2115, 2005 CarswellNat 3490, 2005 FC 1033 (F.C.) — The IAD concluded that the pre-sentencing custodial terms that had been expressly taken into account and credited to the applicant's sentence formed part of the term of imprisonment for the purposes of subs. 64(2) of the Act. Accordingly, the IAD ruled that the applicant had lost his right on appeal in light of subs. 64(2). Subsection 719(3) of the *Criminal Code* specifically provides that pre-sentence detention can be taken into account when a court is imposing a sentence and in this case it was clear that the sentencing judge considered the pre-sentencing detention to be part of the punishment imposed on the applicant. The record showed that the applicant was punished by a term of imprisonment of at least two years and that falls within the definition of "serious criminality" pursuant to subs. 64(2). In these circumstances, the applicant had no right of appeal to the IAD.

*Magtibay v. Canada (Minister of Citizenship & Immigration)*, 2005 CarswellNat 2019, 2005 CarswellNat 757, 2005 FC 397 (F.C.) — The applicant applied for permanent residence under the live-in caregiver class. The applicant's spouse had been acquitted of a criminal offence; however, the Court in giving judgment in the Philippines had found that the offence had in fact been committed but since the victim had pardoned her aggressor, no conviction would result.

It should be made clear that paragraph 36(1)(c) of the Act does not require a conviction for the crime but simply its commission. This is in contrast to paragraph 36(1)(b) which requires a conviction and not simply that the crime was committed. It is clear that Parliament intended to allow for the inadmissibility of a permanent resident or foreign national not only on conviction but also on the commission of certain acts. The immigration officer did not err in concluding that the offence had been committed. Accordingly the judicial review application was dismissed.

*Marshall v. Canada (Minister of Citizenship & Immigration)*, 2004 CarswellNat 127, 2004 CarswellNat 877, 2004 FC 34 (F.C.) — The member conducting the hearing under s. 36(1)(a) has to make the determination that an applicant is or is not a Canadian citizen. It is the Member's decision and not the decision of Citizenship and Immigration.

*Meerza v. Canada (Minister of Citizenship & Immigration)* (2003), 34 Imm. L.R. (3d) 309, 2003 CarswellNat 4531 (Imm. & Ref. Bd. (App. Div.)) — A conditional sentence qualifies as a term of imprisonment within the meaning of that term in s. 36(1)(a).

*[Editor's note: Although decided under the former Act, the following two decisions may still be relevant.]*

*Barnett v. Canada (Minister of Citizenship & Immigration)*, [1996] F.C.J. No. 363, 33 Imm. L.R. (2d) 1, 109 F.T.R. 154, 1996 CarswellNat 319 — This was an application to set aside the decision of an adjudicator which held that the applicant was the member of an inadmissible class pursuant to paragraph 19(1)(c.1)(i). The applicant, a UK citizen, entered Canada in September 1993. In May 1994 he was reported for working without an employment authorization. An inquiry opened in May 1994 and was adjourned. The applicant was subsequently served with a report alleging that he had been convicted in the United Kingdom for impaired driving. Later, a further s. 27 report was served alleging that the applicant, in 1977, had been convicted of burglary. The applicant's position was that pursuant to the UK *Rehabilitation of Offenders Act, 1974*, his conviction for burglary was spent on October 7, 1982, and he was no longer deemed to be convicted of the offence. The adjudicator decided that although the conviction for burglary was spent under United Kingdom law, it was not spent for purposes of the Canadian *Immigration Act*.

Where another country, whose legal system is based on similar foundations and values as our own, has enacted legislation which reflects goals and objectives analogous to those encompassed within our own system, then that law should be accorded respect and recognized for purposes of Canadian immigration law. The question is not whether Canada has identical legislation in place but whether the underlying rationale of the foreign legislation is consistent with some fundamental principle of justice esteemed within our society.

The applicant has been treated in the United Kingdom as not having been convicted of the offence of burglary and there is no solid rationale for refusing to recognize the *Rehabilitation of Offenders Act, 1974* of the UK. Accordingly, the applicant had not been convicted as that term is used in paragraph 19(1)(c.1)(i) of the *Immigration Act*, and was not excluded on that basis.

*Canada (Minister of Employment & Immigration) v. Burgon* (1991), 13 Imm. L.R. (2d) 102, 78 D.L.R (4th) 103, [1991] 3 F.C. 44, (sub nom. *Burgon v. Canada (Minister of Employment & Immigration))* 122 N.R. 228, [1991] F.C.J. No. 149, 1991 CarswellNat 33, 1991 CarswellNat 777 (C.A.) — This was an appeal from a decision of the Appeal Division allowing the respondent to remain in Canada. The respondent was arrested on drug charges in the United Kingdom in 1987. While awaiting trial in prison she learned her elder son had also become involved in drug trafficking. This caused her to give a statement to the police which led to the imprisonment of her son, her father and a well-known drug dealer. The respondent had pleaded guilty in England to conspiracy to supply a controlled drug and was given a suspended sentence. In March 1987 the respondent, who had married a Canadian citizen, was the subject of a sponsorship application by her husband. On December 7, 1987, with the help of her probation officer, she received an English discharge order which had the effect of clearing her completely.

The respondent's application for permanent residence was rejected. It was refused on two bases: initially, because of her "conviction" it was the opinion of Immigration that she was caught by s. 19(1)(c) of the *Immigration Act*; and secondly, because of her previous addiction she was thought to be inadmissible by virtue of s. 19(1)(a).

The more complex question was whether the respondent was excluded pursuant to s. 19(1)(c). It is clear that the word "convicted" does not have a universal immutable meaning. This word, like so many other words, may have different meanings depending on the context in which it is used.

What must be decided is whether the policy of the *Immigration Act* predominates in arriving at the meaning of the word "convicted", whether the policy of the criminal law should be controlling, or whether the Court should seek to harmonize the legislation in these two areas. Also, in this case, there was a foreign element which required the Court to consider what recognition, if any, should be given to the laws of the foreign country in this interpretation exercise.

The policy of the criminal law in Canada in relation to criminal records has been changed in recent years to reflect altering social attitudes towards those who violated the criminal law. The first legislative response was the *Criminal Records Act*, S.C. 1969-70, c. 40, which permitted a pardon by the Governor in Council, after the lapse of a certain period of time, upon the recommendation of the National Parole Board. The effect of such a pardon was that the conviction was vacated. Not long after, the *Criminal Code* was amended to allow judges to impose absolute and conditional discharges in appropriate cases. This amendment had the effect of the accused being deemed not to have been convicted of the offence in question.

Similar provisions aimed at helping those convicted of crimes to make a new beginning were enacted in the United Kingdom as well as other countries. The British went further than Canada: in addition to allowing absolute and conditional discharges Britain enacted the *Powers of Criminal Courts Act, 1973*, to the effect that when an offender was placed on probation his conviction would be deemed not to be a conviction. It was this provision which enabled the respondent to have her conviction expunged in the UK.

When Parliament reenacted the *Immigration Act* in 1976 it must be taken to have known about its own earlier penal legislation which allowed for the elimination of criminal convictions from records of deserving individuals. In using the word "convicted" in s. 19(1)(c) Parliament meant a conviction that had not been expunged. If a conviction had been erased by the provisions of another law of Parliament, it was not meant to be treated in the same way as a conviction that had not been removed. In this way the policy of the criminal law is incorporated within the *Immigration Act*. The further question to consider was whether the UK legislation, which was similar in purpose, but not identical to the Canadian law, should be treated in the same way. In both countries certain offenders are granted the advantage of avoiding the stigma of a criminal record to facilitate their rehabilitation. There is no good reason for immigration law to thwart the goal of this British legislation which is consistent with the Canadian law. The two legal systems are based on similar foundations and share similar values. Unless there is a valid basis for deciding otherwise, the legislation of countries similar to our own, especially when their aims are identical, ought to be accorded respect. While a court is not required to go so far as to "attorn" to the law of all foreign jurisdictions, it is appropriate to do so in this case because the laws and the legal systems of the other country are similar to ours.

Accordingly, the Court ruled that there being no conviction in the United Kingdom, and there being no reason to refuse to grant recognition to the law of the United Kingdom, the respondent was not "convicted" for the purpose of s. 19(1)(c).

## Section 36(2)

*Qi v. Canada (Minister of Citizenship & Immigration)* (2009), 79 Imm. L.R. (3d) 229, 2009 CarswellNat 505, 2009 CarswellNat 1115, 2009 FC 195 (F.C.) — The applicant, a citizen of the People's Republic of China, sought leave for judicial review of a visa officer's decision refusing his application for a permanent resident visa. The visa officer found that the applicant's son was inadmissible for criminality because he committed an act in Hong Kong that is an offence in Hong Kong and that, if committed in Canada, would be an indictable offence under an Act of Parliament. The visa officer concluded that the applicant's son committed an offence under s. 42(2)(i) of the *Immigration Ordinance* of Hong Kong as a result of possessing and using an altered passport. He concluded that if committed in Canada, this would constitute an offence under s. 122(1)(b) of the IRPA, punishable by way of indictment.

The Court concluded that the visa officer could not reasonably conclude that the main applicant's son had committed acts or an offence in Hong Kong, and therefore find him criminally inadmissible in Canada, in light of the expert opinion to the contrary provided by a Mr. Blanchflower and in the absence of any contrary expert opinion. Mr. Blanchflower was of the opinion that the passport with the missing pages did not constitute an "altered travel document" within s. 42(2)(c)(i) of the Ordinance for two reasons: first, there was no evidence that the alteration was done "unlawfully", and second, the missing pages did not constitute an alteration under that provision. He relied for those propositions on the legislative history of the provision, on arguments of legislative construction, and on the case law.

This is not to say that the visa officer himself should have sought an independent legal opinion; in the normal course of events, the respondent should bear the burden of providing expert opinion supporting his position. These reasons should not be interpreted as requiring expert opinion in all circumstances where immigration officials make decisions predicated on foreign law. However, when an applicant's position is buttressed by credible and well-articulated opinions authored by an expert whose credentials are not in dispute, it will most likely be unreasonable to come to an opposite conclusion without the benefit of any expert evidence to the contrary. The application for judicial review was allowed.



*Zeon v. Canada (Minister of Citizenship & Immigration)* (2005), 49 Imm. L.R. (3d) 146, 2005 CarswellNat 3061, 2005 CarswellNat 4879, 2005 FC 1338 (F.C.) — The applicant's application for permanent residence was refused on the basis that he was inadmissible to Canada for criminality pursuant to s. 36(2)(c) of the IRPA. To render a reasonable decision under s. 36(2)(c), it is incumbent on a visa officer to provide critical analysis of how a visa applicant can be said, on reasonable grounds to believe, to have had committed an act which constitutes an offence in a foreign jurisdiction, and then to also provide critical analysis of how it can be said, on reasonable grounds to believe, that the same act would constitute an offence in Canada.

In this case, there was no evidence that this critical analysis required between the foreign law and Canadian law had been undertaken and concluded before the decision was announced during the interview.

The Court set aside the officer's decision and referred the matter back to a different visa officer for re- determination based on a fresh record of evidence and to be conducted in the presence of counsel for the applicant if the applicant so wished.

*Barnett v. Canada (Minister of Citizenship & Immigration)*, [1996] F.C.J. No. 363, 33 Imm. L.R. (2d) 1, 109 F.T.R. 154, 1996 CarswellNat 319 — See the *Barnett* case summary above, in s. 36(1) of the IRPA.

*Canada (Minister of Employment & Immigration) v. Burgon* (1991), 13 Imm. L.R. (2d) 102, 78 D.L.R (4th) 103, [1991] 3 F.C. 44, (sub nom. *Burgon v. Canada (Minister of Employment & Immigration))* 122 N.R. 228, [1991] F.C.J. No. 149, 1991 CarswellNat 33, 1991 CarswellNat 777 (C.A.) — See the *Burgon* case summary above, in s. 36(1) of the IRPA.

## Section 36(3)

*Aksenova v. Canada (Minister of Public Safety & Emergency Preparedness)*, [2006] F.C.J. No. 699, 2006 CarswellNat 1204, 2006 FC 557 (F.C.) — The immigration officer issued a report against the applicant under subs. 44(1) of the IRPA because she was deemed inadmissible to Canada pursuant to paragraph 36(2)(a), having been convicted in Canada of an offence punishable by indictment. On the basis of that report, a deportation order was then issued by the Minister's delegate under subs. 44(2). The Court considered whether in exercising its discretion to issue a report and make a deportation order, the officer and the Minister's delegate considered that the applicant was granted admission to Canada twice after she was convicted of an offence in Canada. The Court concluded that the fact that the applicant was admitted to Canada twice after being convicted of an offence in Canada is not included in the exceptions set out under subs. 36(3) of IRPA dealing with inadmissibility to Canada. Therefore, the officer and delegate made no error by not considering them before they acted as they did. The particular circumstances of a person are irrelevant considerations and at most, the delegate could have stayed or deferred the making of the order if the applicant had already been subjected to an effective removal order, if plans had been made to leave Canada or if the applicant had been a witness called to testify in proceedings held in Canada. None of these considerations were applicable in this case. "Particular circumstances of the person" were said to be irrelevant. Although both subs. 44(1) and (2) use the term "may" in enabling the officer to prepare a report and the delegate to make a removal order, the statutory scheme enacted by the IRPA limits the discretion vested in the officer and the delegate. The term "may" in subs. 44(1) and (2) must be read in conjunction with subs. 36(3), which sets out the exceptions to inadmissibility.

*Kok v. Canada (Minister of Citizenship & Immigration)*, 2005 CarswellNat 135, 2005 FC 77 (F.C.) — This was an application to review a negative decision on an application for rehabilitation. The Minister's delegate acknowledged some of the mitigating factors in a very general way in the decision but there was significant evidence in the form of supporting documentation. As well there was evidence that the applicant had not been convicted of an offence since 1985 and between 2001 and 2004 it found a religious commitment. The failure to address important issues suggests that they were not really taken into account. The delegate should have addressed the strong documentary evidence in favour of rehabilitation.

*Tessma v. Canada (Minister of Citizenship & Immigration)*, 2003 CarswellNat 4883, 2003 CarswellNat 3064, 240 F.T.R. 43, 2003 FC 1126 (F.C.) — This was an application to review the decision of the Immigration Division that the applicant was inadmissible to Canada on grounds of serious criminality. The applicant came to Canada when he was 12 years old in 1992, and at the age of 16 years was charged with several criminal offences under the *Young Offenders Act*, which was the law in effect at that time. The case was transferred to the ordinary courts and the applicant was tried and convicted as an adult of offences under the *Criminal Code* relating to pimping and assault.

The proper interpretation of the *Young Offenders Act* is that when an order is made transferring charges from youth court to ordinary court the applicant is not being tried for offences under the *Young Offenders Act*. The convictions against the applicant, in this case, were therefore convictions for indictable offences under the *Criminal Code*. Therefore, the exception contained in s. 36(3) of IRPA was not applicable and the applicant was properly found to be criminally inadmissible and the application for judicial review was dismissed.

**37. (1) Organized criminality — A permanent resident or a foreign national is inadmissible on grounds of organized criminality for**

> **(a) being a member of an organization that is believed on reasonable grounds to be or to have been engaged in activity that is part of a pattern of criminal activity planned and organized by a number of persons acting in concert in furtherance of the commission of an offence punishable under an Act of Parliament by way of indictment, or in furtherance of the commission of an offence**

**outside Canada that, if committed in Canada, would constitute such an offence, or engaging in activity that is part of such a pattern; or**

**(b) engaging, in the context of transnational crime, in activities such as people smuggling, trafficking in persons or money laundering.**

(2) **Application — The following provisions govern subsection (1):**

**(a) subsection (1) does not apply in the case of a permanent resident or a foreign national who satisfies the Minister that their presence in Canada would not be detrimental to the national interest; and**

**(b) paragraph (1)(a) does not lead to a determination of inadmissibility by reason only of the fact that the permanent resident or foreign national entered Canada with the assistance of a person who is involved in organized criminal activity.**

*[Editor's Note: SOR/2002-227, s. 320(6) provides that a person is inadmissible under the new* Immigration and Refugee Protection Act, *S.C. 2001 c. 27 on grounds of organized criminality if, on June 28, 2002, the person had been determined to be a member of an inadmissible class described in paragraph 19(1)(c.2) or subparagraph 19(1)(d)(ii) of the former* Immigration Act, *R.S.C. 1985, c. I-2.]*

IRP Act

## Case Law

*Tang v. Canada (Minister of Citizenship & Immigration)*, 2009 CarswellNat 1497, 2009 CarswellNat 2096, 2009 FC 292 — A potential permanent resident was held to be inadmissible on the grounds of organized criminality, a determination first made in 1996 and communicated to the principal applicant in 2007 after many twists and turns between federal government offices. The applicant's conviction for claiming to be a member of a triad was advanced as reasonable grounds for believing that he was in fact a member of a triad. In other cases, that might well be sufficient, but not in this case. First, there was no consideration of the circumstances surrounding the conviction which call into question whether the claim was true. The conviction arose from a guilty plea and resulted in a minimal penalty. Secondly, if the Minister of Citizenship and Immigration had a "*bona fide* belief" that the applicant was or had been a member of a triad, it had had that belief since 1997 and yet continued to permit the applicant to enter Canada on a regular basis. The Minister's actions and acquiescence belied its stated belief. Thirdly, there was a certain element of disingenuousness in the manner in which the officials relied on the conviction as if the 1995 admissions by the applicant, where he denied actual membership in a triad and claimed that he had not gone through a traditional initiation ceremony but elaborated on his allegedly limited role and other aspects of his "non-membership", were never made. The Minister made no reference to the admissions and used a more convenient pretext of a conviction to ground the admissibility decision. In light of the inconsistency between what the Minister has said, done and relied upon for its decision, the decision was not reasonable. The judicial review was granted and the decision quashed, and the matter remitted back to the Minister for a proper determination

*Castelly c. Canada (Ministre de la Citoyenneté & de l'Immigration)* (2008), 74 Imm. L.R. (3d) 209, (sub nom. *Castelly v. Canada (Minister of Citizenship & Immigration))* 329 F.T.R. 311 (Eng.), [2009] 2 F.C.R. 327, 2008 CarswellNat 2009, 2008 CarswellNat 3508, 2008 FC 788 — This was an application to consider the lawfulness of a decision dated October 24, 2007, of a member of the Immigration Division of the Immigration and

Refugee Board to make a removal order against the applicant because she was inadmissible to Canada under paragraph 37(1)(a) of the IRPA. A report was issued on July 28, 2005, under subs. 44(1) of the IRPA. The departmental official was of the opinion that the applicant should be inadmissible on grounds of "organized criminality" under paragraph 37(1)(a). The Minister referred the matter to the panel for investigation. The applicant was invited to make additional written submissions in answer to the question "are there reasonable grounds to believe that Ms. Castelly was a member of the Wolf Pack organization?" The applicant had testified before the panel that she was "simply a mother who at the time was not working outside the home, was overtaken by events, and had no knowledge about the activity of her son and his friends."

The Act does not define the term "member" and the Courts have not established a precise definition of the term or a test for "belonging to" an organization described in paragraph 37(1)(a) of the Act. In the last few years at least, case law of the Federal Court and Federal Court of Appeal has not been consistent on the issue of a test relevant to determining whether someone is a member of a criminal organization. While the evidence on the tribunal record does not demonstrate that the applicant *personally* took part in serious crimes, the panel was able to support its findings because of the fact that the applicant had direct knowledge of the criminal activity of other members of the Wolf Pack who acted on behalf of the gang. The Federal Court held that it was not unreasonable for the panel to find that the applicant was a member of the Wolf Pack, an "organization" that engaged in the types of crime described in s. 37. Moreover, it was not necessary to prove that someone belongs to a criminal organization described in s. 37; it is sufficient to have reasonable grounds to believe that he or she is or was a member of such an organization. In that regard, the panel did not have to apply the test developed by the Canadian courts concerning belonging to a criminal organization for the purposes of subs. 467.1(1) of the *Criminal Code*. The panel's decision was not unreasonable because it did not make reference to tests used by the police to determine whether someone is a member of a street gang or because it did not mention in the impugned decision the existence of an "institutional link" between the Wolf Pack and the applicant. The application for judicial review was dismissed. The following question of general importance was certified:

> For the purposes of paragraph 37(1)(a) of the *Immigration and Refugee Protection Act*, what is the general definition of "member", and what test must one apply to determine whether a person is or was a "member" of an "organization" described in that paragraph?

*Sittambalam v. Canada (Minister of Citizenship & Immigration)*, [2006] F.C.J. No. 1512, 56 Imm. L.R. (3d) 161, (sub nom. *Sittampalam v. Canada (Minister of Citizenship & Immigration))* 272 D.L.R. (4th) 1, [2007] 3 F.C.R. 198, (sub nom. *Sittampalam v. Canada (Minister of Citizenship & Immigration))* 354 N.R. 34, 2006 CarswellNat 3236, 2006 FCA 326 (C.A.) — The issue in this appeal is whether the appellant is a member of a criminal organization so as to deny him the right of appeal to the Immigration Appeal Division on the question of whether he is inadmissible pursuant to paragraph 37(1)(a) of the IRPA. The appeal was dismissed. The phrase "being a member of an organization" in paragraph 37(1)(a) includes a person who was not a member at the time of the reporting, but was a member before that time. The word "organization," as it is used in paragraph 37(1)(a), is to be given a broad unrestricted interpretation. While no precise definition can be established here, the factors listed by O'Reilly J. in *Thanaratnam v. Canada (Minister of Citizenship & Immigration)*, [2004] 3 F.C.R. 301 (T.D.) by the Board member, and possibly others, are helpful in making a determination, but no one of them is an essential element. The structure of criminal organizations is varied, and the Board must be given flexibility to evaluate all of the evidence in light of the legislative purpose of the IRPA to prioritize security in deciding whether a group is an organization for the purpose of paragraph 37(1)(a) of the IRPA.



**38. (1) Health grounds — A foreign national is inadmissible on health grounds if their health condition**

> **(a) is likely to be a danger to public health;**
>
> **(b) is likely to be a danger to public safety; or**
>
> **(c) might reasonably be expected to cause excessive demand on health or social services.**

**(2) Exception — Paragraph (1)(c) does not apply in the case of a foreign national who**

> **(a) has been determined to be a member of the family class and to be the spouse, common-law partner or child of a sponsor within the meaning of the regulations;**
>
> **(b) has applied for a permanent resident visa as a Convention refugee or a person in similar circumstances;**
>
> **(c) is a protected person; or**
>
> **(d) is, where prescribed by the regulations, the spouse, common-law partner, child or other family member of a foreign national referred to in any of paragraphs (a) to (c).**

*[Editor's Note: SOR/2002-227, s. 320(7) provides that a person — other than an applicant described in s. 7 of the* Immigration Regulations, 1978, *SOR/78-172, or s. 4 of the* Humanitarian Designated Classes Regulations, *SOR/97-183, who made an application for admission under the* Immigration Act, *R.S.C. 1985, c. I-2 (the "former Act") — is inadmissible under the new* Immigration and Refugee Protection Act, *S.C. 2001 c. 27 on health grounds if, on June 28, 2002, the person had been determined to be a member of the inadmissible class described in paragraph 19(1)(a) of the former Act.]*

## Case Law

### Section 38(1)

*Sharma v. Canada (Minister of Citizenship & Immigration)*, 2010 FC 398, 2010 CarswellNat 879, 2010 CarswellNat 2239 (F.C.) — The applicants sought a permanent resident visa and were denied on the basis that one family member, the son, had a health condition: mental retardation, which might reasonably be expected to cause excessive demand on health or social services. The applicants were asked to supply medical information to support their assertions as to the son's condition. Nothing was provided. They were asked to provide a plan as to what support would be given to the son. An offer to pay was made, but no specific plan was provided other than a suggestion that the son would be brought into whatever business the applicants would establish in Canada. The officer's rejection of these submissions was not unreasonable. The onus rests on the applicants to make out their case, including such factors as may be relevant in setting out a workable plan. The application was dismissed.

*Bichari v. Canada (Minister of Citizenship & Immigration)*, 2010 FC 127, 2010 CarswellNat 1166, 2010 CarswellNat 258 (F.C.) — The applicants were an elderly couple from Algeria with 11 children, two of whom reside in Canada. They arrived as visitors in November 1999 and applied for refugee status, which was subsequently refused. They then made an application for permanent residence on H&C grounds. Mrs. Bichari received a kidney transplant and is dependent on anti-rejection medicines for survival. On April 27, 2006, their H&C application was approved in principle. On January 22, 2007, Mrs. Bachari was informed that she was medically inadmissible due to her renal insufficiency post-transplantation. Since the prescription medicines were guaranteed by provincial health insurance, the medical officer concluded that Mrs. Bichari's medical condition might reasonably be expected to cause excessive demand on Canadian health services.

According to Operational Bulletin 021 — June 26, 2006, immigration officers are not allowed to grant exemptions from the application of s. 38 of the Act. If they are of the opinion that an exemption on humanitarian and compassionate grounds may be warranted, or if one is sought, the file must be forwarded to the Director of Case Review at National Headquarters. The Director refused the applicants' application for permanent residence status finding there were insufficient humanitarian and compassionate considerations to issue a temporary resident permit or to exempt Mrs. Bichari's medical inadmissibility. The Director relied on articles disclosed to the Bichari's counsel that renal transplantation does take place in Algeria and that 40 had been done by 1994. The Director concluded that there was adequate post-renal transplant care available in Algeria. The Court held that if the applicants wanted to question the conclusions of the inferences that could be drawn from these articles, they had ample opportunity to submit, and should have submitted their own evidence, which they failed to do. The applicants also disagreed with the Director's reliance on the medical officer's comments concerning the availability of health services in Algeria. Again, if the applicants did not agree with her conclusion it was up to them to submit documentation to the contrary. The standard on H&C applications cannot be whether the applicants will get better or more affordable treatment in Canada; if this were the case, virtually all medically and inadmissible persons would be entitled to stay. Without evidence to the contrary that the medical services were not available in Algeria, it was reasonable for the Director to decide how she did. The applicant cannot simply rest his or her case on the fact that the evidence relied upon by the decision maker is speculative when he or she has simply failed to discharge the burden of proof in establishing that proper medical care is not available in their country. The application for judicial review was dismissed.

*Mazhari v. Canada (Minister of Citizenship & Immigration)*, 2010 CarswellNat 1261, 2010 FC 467 (F.C.) — The applicant, a citizen of Iran, applied to come to Canada as a permanent resident. During his medical assessment it was discovered that he had lung cancer. The discovery of the applicant's cancer led to a request from Citizenship & Immigration for further medical examinations. The Court concluded that the medical officer's report was not generic but instead met the requirement of being individualized as stipulated by *Hilewitz v. Canada (Minister of Citizenship & Immigration); De Jong v. Canada (Minister of Citizenship & Immigration)* (2005), 50 Imm. L.R. (3d) 40 (S.C.C.). In this case, the medical assessment of the applicant was made within a few months of his original diagnosis and surgery. This made the task of evaluating the potential for recurrence more difficult; he had minimal personal history of surviving with the disease post-surgery. Accordingly, the use of statistical information as contained in the medical literature became the only reasonable way of assessing the likelihood that he will require treatment in the future. The fact that the medical officer relied on such statistical data did not necessarily make the evaluation non-personalized. The application for judicial review was dismissed.

*Rashid v. Canada (Minister of Citizenship & Immigration)* (2010), 88 Imm. L.R. (3d) 165, 2010 FC 157, 2010 CarswellNat 318, [2010] F.C.J. No. 183 (F.C.) — The visa officer found the applicant to be medically inadmissible to Canada and refused the application for permanent residence under the federal skilled worker program. The applicant was HIV positive and asymptomatic, meaning the virus was present but did not manifest any visible symptoms. He contracted HIV in 1996 from contaminated blood in Tanzania. A medical officer determined that the cost of the treatment required for the applicant's condition would likely exceed the amount spent on the average Canadian and would delay or deny provision of those services to those in Canada who might need them. Acknowledging that some HIV-infected applicants will not cross the threshold of excessive demand and thereby qualify for admittance into Canada, the medical officer found that the applicant was on a regimen of medication costing about US$10,000 per year. There is no dispute between the parties that this amount is well in excess of the health cost threshold.

The applicant relied on the Supreme Court of Canada's decision in *Hilewitz v. Canada (Minister of Citizenship & Immigration); De Jong v. Canada (Minister of Citizenship & Immigration)* (2005), 50 Imm. L.R. (3d) 40 (S.C.C.), to argue that, as in the case of social services, a person in the applicant's position can pay for his own medical health services: in this case, the cost of out-patient prescription anti-viral drugs.

The applicant would be eligible for coverage under the provincial Trillium Drug Program if he was to become resident in Ontario, as intended, once a valid Ontario health card was issued to him and upon demonstrating high prescription drug cost in relation to his net household income. The plan to pay for the prescription drugs put forward by the applicant was based upon personal commitments to pay for the required health services. Given the non-enforceability of those commitments and the expected eligibility of the applicant under Ontario's Trillium Drug Program, the visa officer's determination that the applicant did not meet the requirements for immigration to Canada pursuant to paragraph 38(1)(c) of IRPA, was reasonable and within the range of possible and acceptable outcomes.

The facts of this case were distinguishable from those in *Companioni v. Canada (Minister of Citizenship & Immigration)* (2009), 87 Imm. L.R. (3d) 271 (F.C.), where one of the two applicants had a personal insurance policy that covered prescription drug costs and the second was covered by an employer-based group policy, either or both of which might have continued to apply if the applicants relocated to Canada. In the present matter, the applicant was relying on the personal commitments of his sister and two others.

The following question was certified:

> When a medical officer has determined that an applicant will be in need of prescription drugs, the cost of which would place the applicant over the threshold of "excessive demand" as set out in the *Immigration and Refugee Protection Regulations*, must the visa officer assess the applicant's ability to pay for the prescription drugs privately when those same drugs are covered by a government program for which the applicant would be eligible in the province/territory of intended residence?

*Jafarian v. Canada (Minister of Citizenship & Immigration)* (2010), 87 Imm. L.R. (3d) 262, 360 F.T.R. 150 (Eng.), 2010 FC 40, 2010 CarswellNat 1171, 2010 CarswellNat 241

(F.C.) — The applicant, an Iranian, was selected by Quebec as an investor. His daughter was afflicted with multiple sclerosis. The visa officer came to the conclusion that the family was inadmissible because the daughter's condition might reasonably be expected to cause excess demand on health services. Although the disease is degenerative, it has been controlled by the drug Rebif. In Canada the daughter's prescription would cost some $15,000 a year. The concerns of the visa officer were certainly justified. Pursuant to the Regulations, health services include the cost of both medical personnel and prescription drugs. An "excessive demand" is one which exceeds the average annual Canadian per capita cost, which at the time was just over $5,000. However, and this is crucial to this case, a health service is one for which the majority of the funds is contributed by the governments. The officer referred to the medical diagnosis and quoted from the Health Canada doctor that Rebif ". . . is a very expensive drug which would be provided by provincial medical care plans." In the "fairness letter" the visa officer declared that the daughter's Rebif would be government funded. However, this is not necessarily the case.

The principles enunciated by the Supreme Court in *Hilewitz* and *DeJong* (2005), 50 Imm. L.R. (3d) 40, although expressly limited to social services, are equally applicable to prescription drugs and other health services as long as the majority of the funds for the prescription drug in question are not contributed by governments. The Court held that assessments must be individualized and take into account not merely eligibility for services, but also likely demand as well as the applicant's ability and intention to pay. These circumstances are quite unlike *Hilewitz*, where, as a matter of Ontario law, the cost of most if not all the social services in questions were recoverable, irrespective of Mr. Hilewitz's representations. If the majority of the cost of Rebif is not covered by the Quebec government, this issue is moot. If the majority is so covered, then his intentions and good faith are simply not relevant. The law does not permit him to opt out. If this latter scenario is the case, the refusal to grant permanent resident visas to the applicant and his family was correct in law.

The application for judicial review was granted on the basis of a procedural fairness argument. The decision as to whether the care would constitute "excessive demand" was not the Health Canada doctor's decision but rather the decision of the visa officer and he abrogated his responsibility.

*Ma v. Canada (Minister of Public Safety & Emergency Preparedness)* (2009), 84 Imm. L.R. (3d) 280, 2009 FC 1042, 2009 CarswellNat 4937, 2009 CarswellNat 3234 (F.C.) — This was an application for judicial review of a visa officer's decision to refuse the applicant's application for permanent residence under the British Columbia Provincial Nominee Program (PNP) on the basis that the visa officer was not satisfied that the applicant had both the ability and intent to offset the excessive demand on social services that would be required of his son, Jun Ma.

Jun had a moderate intellectual disability that would necessitate special education. The officer believed that Jun's health condition might cause excessive demand on health or social services in Canada. Such a finding would render the family inadmissible to Canada by virtue of ss. 38 and 42 of IRPA. The officer found that the fact that Jun had been enrolled in a public school in Canada significantly undermined the assertion that, in future, his educational and social services expenses would be paid for privately. Only recently was Jun enrolled in a private school, a fact that raised the question of whether this was done primarily for the purpose of securing immigrant visas rather than as part of a genuine plan to assume responsibility for the cost of Jun's special education services. The Court agreed with the applicant that the officer seemed to have unduly been concerned about the fact that Jun had been initially enrolled in public school. The family was under no legal obligation to proceed differently until the issue of inadmissibility was raised, and it was only then that their actions could be fairly scrutinized. The officer's pejorative characterization of the motive for enrolling Jun in private school was troubling since there is nothing inherently objectionable about taking a step with the view to improving an application for landing provided that the process is carried out openly. The officer also failed to inform the applicant that the officer was not satisfied that their future intentions were honourable. It is clear that the officer did not accept these declarations at face value and, without saying so directly, found them to be untrue and sworn only for the purpose of obtaining visas. This was an inference that was based on a negative credibility determination which itself rested upon a tenuous factual underpinning. It was also made without an interview and in the absence of an explicit warning that the credibility of the applicant and his wife and his brother were an issue. The Department has created a form of declaration for visa applicants and, in doing so, it leaves an impression that this will suffice. The fact that these declarations apparently cannot be enforced, and that there are presently no other methods to legally bind someone in the situation of the applicant, is an issue for the Department to solve. Until it does, it needs to show more patience and greater guidance to applicants than was afforded to the applicant in this case. The application for judicial review was allowed.



*Companioni v. Canada (Minister of Citizenship & Immigration)* (2009), 87 Imm. L.R. (3d) 271, 360 F.T.R. 157 (Eng.), 2009 FC 1315, 2009 CarswellNat 4596, 2009 CarswellNat 4965, [2009] F.C.J. No. 1688 (F.C.) — The officer refused to issue permanent resident visas on the grounds that the applicants were inadmissible as their condition, within the meaning of s. 38 of IRPA, might reasonably be expected to cause excessive demand on health services. Specifically, the cost of out-patient prescription drugs to control their HIV totaling some $33,500 per year made them inadmissible. The general rule in the province of Ontario is that the cost of out-patient drugs is not government funded. It follows that the cost of such drugs is not a demand on health services. There are, however, exceptions to that exception and this is where the difficulty in this case lies.

The principles annunciated in *Hilewitz* (2005), 50 Imm. L.R. (3d) 40 (S.C.C.) are equally applicable in any consideration as to whether the cost of out-patient drugs would constitute an excessive demand on health services. The fundamental distinction, however, is that when it comes to social services, at least in Ontario, as a matter of law the province is entitled to recover most, if not all, of those costs from those who can afford it. But when it comes to the supply of out-patient drugs in Ontario, by virtue of the provincial Trillium Drug Program, most of the cost of the drugs in question would be paid by the province. Promises not to access this program are simply not enforceable.

The visa officer took into account Operational Bulletin 063 which was originally designed to assess the applications of business investors who had medical or social service issues. However, since the Federal Court of Appeal held in *Colaco v. Canada (Minister of Citizenship & Immigration)* (2007), 64 Imm. L.R. (3d) 161, that individual assessments would also be required for skilled workers, hers was a perfectly sensible approach. She asked herself if the applicants had advanced a credible plan. She also asked herself if the applicants had the financial ability to cover the projected expenses over the full period. However, she was ambivalent as to whether the period was five or 10 years. It appeared to the Court that the only possible answer was 10 years, and that the visa officer attempted to give the applicants the benefit of the doubt. Absent a viable insurance plan, most of the cost of the drugs in question would be borne by the province of Ontario, would constitute an excessive demand and would render the applicants inadmissible. Although the evidence on file was far from perfect, there was specific mention of employer-based insurance. However, there was nothing in the record to substantiate the visa officer's belief that employer-based prescription drug coverage would be uninsurable due to their pre-existing condition. Accordingly, the application for judicial review was granted and the matter returned to a different officer for a fresh determination limited to medical inadmissibility. The following question was certified:

> Is the ability and willingness of applicants to defray the cost of their out-patient prescription drug medication (in keeping with the provincial/territorial regulations regulating the government payment of prescription drugs) a relevant consideration in accessing whether the demands presented by an applicant's health condition constitute an excessive demand?

*Vazirizadeh v. Canada (Minister of Citizenship & Immigration)*, [2009] F.C.J. No. 919, 2009 FC 807, 2009 CarswellNat 2387, 2009 CarswellNat 4932 (F.C.) — This was a judicial review of a decision of the IAD to dismiss the appeal of a sponsorship of a parent who was found to be medically inadmissible pursuant to paragraph 38(1)(c) of the Act because her health condition "might reasonably be expected to cause excessive demand on health or social services" in Canada. Six months after the visa officer's decision, she underwent right knee replacement surgery in Iran. The applicant argued that the IAD hearing, which was a *de novo* hearing, did not consider the appellant's changed medical status. The Court, however, concluded that the IAD analyzed the medical condition both at the time of the visa officer's decision in 2007 and the IAD hearing in 2008, including the evidence of right knee replacement surgery, physiotherapy and the opinion of the appellant's orthopedic specialist. However, the IAD reiterated or quoted the original medical opinion which, besides the likelihood of specialized knee replacement surgery, stated that the appellant's mother suffers from other medical problems, *i.e.* hypertension, obesity, osteoporosis and osteoarthritis, degenerative changes of the spine and hands and also degenerative osteoporosis of the thoracic vertebrae.

The Federal Court referred to *Mohamed v. Canada (Minister of Employment & Immigration)*, [1986] 3 F.C. 90, a Federal Court of Appeal decision which held that the medical condition at the time the visa officer refused the visa was the only relevant one and subsequent improvement in the medical condition was only relevant as to whether special relief should be granted on appeal.

The Federal Court concluded that the IAD's decision was well founded in fact and in law and amply satisfied the test of falling within an acceptable range of reasonable decisions and therefore the application for judicial review was dismissed. The Federal Court also refused to certify a question.

*Vashishat v. Canada (Minister of Citizenship & Immigration)* (2008), 77 Imm. L.R. (3d) 220, 337 F.T.R. 283 (Eng.), 2008 CarswellNat 5282, 2008 CarswellNat 4632, 2008 FC 1346 (F.C.) — The applicant applied to sponsor her father and younger brother as members of the family class. The visa officer found the brother inadmissible pursuant to paragraph 38(1)(c) of the IRPA on the ground that his state of mental development might reasonably be expected to cause excessive demands on health or social services. The applicant appealed to the IAD which dismissed her appeal and she sought judicial review of that decision. *Colaco v. Canada (Minister of Citizenship & Immigration), infra*, does not stand for the proposition that there has to be evidence of an ability to pay for the services if there is some alternative means to provide them. If a skilled worker applicant can establish that his or her admissibility in Canada cannot reasonably be expected to cause excessive demands on social services, there is no reason to exclude that applicant on that basis.

As was articulated in *Hilewitz v. Canada (Minister of Citizenship & Immigration), infra*, any anticipated burden on the public purse must be tethered to the realities of the applicants' circumstances, including the extent of the family's willingness and ability to contribute time and resources. Here, the family stated that it was prepared to make alternative arrangements to provide employment for him on a farm which would attenuate any anticipated burden or excessive demand on social services. The IAD focused on the family's ability to pay without taking into consideration the alternative arrangements they had made for the younger brother. The IAD did not properly consider the applicants' actual circumstances in determining what "demands" would be made on Canada's services.



The wording of the provision of s. 38 indicates that medical officers must assess likely *demands* on social services, not mere *eligibility* for them. In its reasons, the IAD maintained that "the Appellant might not, at this time, have the intention of using any of the social services for which her brother would be eligible; however, the applicant will have a right to these publicly funded services". This rationale does not meet the threshold required for establishing that the brother's medical condition would or might reasonably be expected to result in an excessive demand on social services. The application was allowed and the matter sent back to another panel.

*Airapetyan v. Canada (Minister of Citizenship & Immigration)*, 2007 CarswellNat 124, 2007 FC 42 (F.C.) — While the applicant stated a strong willingness to pay for the education program his dependent daughter, who suffered from moderate mental retardation, might require if allowed to immigrate to Canada, the applicant did not provide any evidence demonstrating an ability to pay for his daughter's special education in Canada. Accordingly, the applicant cannot argue that the visa officer erred in law in failing to assess his ability to pay for his daughter's special education. The application for judicial review was dismissed.

*Colaco v. Canada (Minister of Citizenship & Immigration)* (2007), 64 Imm. L.R. (3d) 161, 2007 CarswellNat 2909, 2007 FCA 282 (Fed. C.A.) — The applicants and their two children applied under the skilled worker category for permanent resident status. Their application was refused pursuant to subs. 38(1) of the IRPA on the basis that a family member whose health condition: Mental Retardation, Mild, might reasonably be expected to cause excessive demand on health or social services.

The rationale enunciated by the Supreme Court of Canada in *Hilewitz v. Canada* [2005] 2 S.C.R. 706 applied and an individualized assessment of the applicant's needs for social services support, as well as their capacity to assume the cost of them is required to determine whether the needs might reasonably be expected to cause excessive demand on these social services.

*Kirec v. Canada (Minister of Citizenship & Immigration)*, [2006] F.C.J. No. 1017, 2006 CarswellNat 1770, 2006 FC 800 (F.C.) — This was an application for judicial review of the decision of a visa officer which refused the applicant's application for permanent residence. The refusal was based on the conclusion that the applicant was inadmissible to Canada pursuant to subs. 38(1) of the IRPA because his daughter might reasonably be expected to cause excessive demand on health or social services as a result of her diagnosis of cerebral palsy. She utilizes the services of occupational and speech therapy, physiotherapy, and assistive technology equipment for communication. In school she is in a modified special education learning environment with a support worker.

Canadian social philosophy has a commitment to equality, full participation and integration of all individuals, and thus an extensive social support system is available. Currently her disability would make her eligible for intensive Special Education and support for required medical and assisted technology devices.

The applicant argued that a fairness letter was issued but did not provide detailed information relied upon by the medical officer. The Court disagreed and concluded that the letter outlined the grounds for which the applicant's daughter was found to be inadmissible due to her medical condition. The applicant also argued that the medical notification was flawed because it did not provide evidence as to the actual cost to be incurred by reason of the applicant's daughter's medical condition. The Court concluded that despite not providing an exact dollar amount of all the services the applicant's daughter would probably use, it was reasonable for the medical officer to conclude that the total cost would be in excess of the average Canadian per capita cost over a period of five years. It was perfectly reasonable for the visa officer to trust the findings of the medical officer's report in this regard.

The applicant also argued that the medical officer's conclusions were flawed because he had failed to take into consideration the applicant's daughter's personal circumstances, particularly the degree of support that would be provided by the family so as not to place excessive demand on social services. The respondent argued that the family support should not be assessed in the present matter seeing as the applicant was applying for permanent residency based on the skilled worker category and not as a business class category. The Court concluded the applicant's daughter had a long history of using social services while living in Canada. Furthermore, the applicant never made any submissions to the fact that his daughter would not place an excessive demand on such services if the family were to move back to Canada from the United States. The visa officer, therefore, clearly took into consideration the personal circumstances of the applicant's daughter. As such, the visa officer did not err in rejecting the applicant's application for permanent residence based on the medical inadmissibility of his daughter.

*Cohen v. Canada (Minister of Citizenship & Immigration)* (2006), 55 Imm. L.R. (3d) 21, 2006 CarswellNat 1745, 2006 FC 804 (F.C.) — This was an application for judicial review of the decision of a visa officer which refused the applicant's application for permanent residence. The refusal was based on the conclusion that the applicant was inadmissible to Canada pursuant to subs. 38(1) of IRPA because his wife might reasonably be expected to cause excessive demand on health and social services as a result of her diagnosis of rheumatoid arthritis.

The applicant argued that the visa officer's and medical officer's analysis of excessive demand was flawed because both failed in their obligation to calculate the health services costs and social services costs over a period of five years for the average Canadian and the applicant's spouse. The applicant argued that the officer's decision to deny permanent residency was based on the perception that the applicant's spouse needs the expensive drug Entanercept to control her medical condition. However, the applicant argued if the officer had considered the applicant's submissions in response to the fairness letter, she would have concluded that the applicant's spouse does not need this drug to control her condition.

The Court concluded that both the visa officer and the medical officer were not precise enough in their conclusions and, accordingly, the conclusions were based on imprecise assessments by both the visa and medical officers. The application for judicial review was granted.

*Newton-Juliard c. Canada (Ministre de la Citoyenneté & de l'Immigration)* (2006), 57 Imm. L.R. (3d) 15, 2006 CarswellNat 2925, 2006 FC 177 (F.C.) — This was an application for judicial review of a decision by a visa officer to deny the applicant permanent residence based on the health condition (autism) of her daughter, as admitting her to Canada might reasonably be expected to cause excessive demand on health or social services pursuant to subs. 38(1) of the IRPA. One of the grounds raised by the applicant was that the visa officer erred in failing to consider, with regard to the question of excessive demand, the financial situation of the family, which would probably be able to defray the costs of the services required by the applicant's daughter. In other words, the family would itself contribute to reduce the additional costs which would otherwise be assumed by the community in education and care for her autistic daughter through the volunteer work, for example, that the applicant would give to the school, assistance that could certainly be given a monetary value and/or through the purchase of a private insurance policy. The Court dismissed the applicant's argument on the basis that the school was a public school financed by the municipality as well as income tax. Further, the Court concluded it was purely speculative to take the applicant's volunteer work at the school into account, since nothing in the evidence would have allowed the medical doctor to quantify the time. The Court also concluded that since the case did not involve a question of health care for the daughter, but mostly of social services that she needed, the proposal to take out private insurance for health care would have nothing to do with the specialized education in the school. The application for judicial review was dismissed.

*Lee v. Canada (Minister of Citizenship & Immigration)* (2006), 60 Imm. L.R. (3d) 62, 2006 FC 1461, 2006 CarswellNat 4260 (F.C.) — The applicant was found to be inadmissible pursuant to s. 38(1) of the IRPA. On the basis of medical evidence, the officer found that the applicant's health conditions, which included polycystic kidney disease, hypertension, moderate mitral regurgitation and chronic renal failure, would reasonably be expected to cause "excessive demands" on Canada's health services. The applicant argued that, as he is an entrepreneur with considerable net worth, the officer erred in law by failing to consider his ability to provide for his own health care if admitted to Canada, and further, the officer breached procedural fairness by not considering his request for a temporary resident permit. Specifically, the applicant relied on the Supreme Court of Canada's decision in *Hilewitz v. Canada (Minister of Citizenship and Immigration)*. *Hilewitz* dealt specifically with an applicant's ability to pay for *social services* and not *health services*; therefore the applicant's argument that the reasoning in Hilewitz applied equally to health services was dismissed. The officer did not err in law by not considering the applicant's financial ability to pay for his own health care.

In a letter to the Canadian Consulate, the applicant requested the officer consider granting him a TRP. The officer was required to respond to this request without the necessity of a separate submission. The failure of the officer to deal with this request constituted an error in due process. A different immigration officer was ordered to assess the applicant's temporary resident permit application on the basis of the existing evidentiary record.

*Sarkar v. Canada (Minister of Citizenship & Immigration)* (2006), 60 Imm. L.R. (3d) 143, 2006 CarswellNat 4524, 2006 FC 1556 (F.C.) — The applicant sought to set aside a decision of an immigration officer who determined his application for permanent residence could not be accepted because his daughter was inadmissible pursuant to s. 38(1) of the IRPA as being a person whose health condition, Pervasive Development Disorder (PDD: Autism), might reasonably be expected to cause excessive demand on social services and specifically on educational services. The applicant expressed, through his counsel, a willingness and ability to pay for any social services to help his daughter. There was nothing in the record to support the conclusion that either the medical officer or the immigration officer considered, as they had to, the willingness and ability of the applicant to defray the above average educational costs, past, present and in the future his daughter would demand. There was also nothing in the record to support the conclusion that either the medical officer or the visa officer considered the extent to which, in the past, the applicant privately funded his daughter's pre-school costs and currently paid privately for her occupational therapy and speech therapy costs as well as some developmental costs at home. The judicial review application was allowed.

*Hilewitz v. Canada (Minister of Citizenship & Immigration)*, [2005] 2 S.C.R. 706, 50 Imm. L.R. (3d) 40, 33 Admin. L.R. (4th) 1, 340 N.R. 102, 259 D.L.R. (4th) 244, [2005] S.C.J. No. 58, 2005 CarswellNat 3234, 2005 CarswellNat 3235, 2005 SCC 57 — The appellant and another both applied for permanent residence, respectively, under the "investor" and "self-employed" classes set out in the *Immigration Act*. These categories require that applicants have substantial financial resources to qualify. Both qualified, but were denied admission because the intellectual disability of a dependent child "would cause or might reasonably be expected to cause excessive demands on . . . social services" in Canada, which made them inadmissible pursuant to s. 19(1)(a)(ii) of the former *Immigration Act*.

The visa officers' decisions were set aside by the Supreme Court of Canada. The Supreme Court of Canada concluded that the personal circumstances of the families of disabled dependants are relevant factors in an assessment of their anticipated impact on social services. Since the "investor" and "self-employed" categories under which the appellants were qualified for admission to Canada were, to a large extent, concerned with an individual's assets, it would be incongruous to interpret the legislation in such a way that the very assets that qualify these individuals for admission to Canada can simultaneously be ignored in determining the admissibility of their disabled children.

The applicants' ability and willingness to attenuate the burden on the public purse that would otherwise be created by their intellectually disabled children was a relevant factor in determining whether those children could reasonably be expected to cause excessive demands on Canada's social services. The fears were articulated in the rejections of the applications, such as possible bankruptcy, mobility, school closure or parental death, represent contingencies that could be raised in relation to any applicant. Using such contingencies to negate a family's genuine ability and willingness to absorb some of the burdens created by a child's disabilities anchors an applicant's admissibility to conjecture, not reality. The visa officers erred by confirming the medical officers' refusal to account for the potential impact of the families' willingness to assist. Moreover, the visa officers' failure to read the families' responses to the fairness letters sent to them meant that their decisions were not based on all the relevant available information.

*[Note: Although decided under former legislation (the Immigration Act, R.S.C. 1985, c. I-2) this decision may still be useful.]*

*Hossain v. Canada (Minister of Citizenship & Immigration)*, 2006 CarswellNat 993, 2006 FC 475 (F.C.) — The applicant's application for permanent residence under the skilled worker category was refused on the basis that he was found to have a medical condition that "would or might reasonably be expected to place excessive demands on health or social services in Canada, and thus would render him inadmissible to Canada under s. 38(1) of the IRPA." The applicant had had a kidney transplant performed in 2000 because of renal failure. His renal function was currently normal and he took medication on a daily basis. These medications were expensive and would have been paid by the provincial health care.

The applicant had personally borne all of the medical costs since his transplant and was ready to undertake not to claim medical costs from Canadian health care services relating to his current medical condition. He also was prepared to undertake to subscribe to all necessary private insurance coverage and he provided evidence of more than C$200,000 of savings that would enable him to meet the costs of his medicines from his own financial sources. There was no indication that the medical officer or the visa officer considered the applicant's offer to assume the cost of the medication relating to his current medical condition or his personal financial situation.

The decision was set aside and referred back to ensure that the next decision maker considered the financial situation of the applicant.

*Masood v. Canada (Minister of Citizenship & Immigration)*, 2003 CarswellNat 3921, 2003 CarswellNat 4446, 2003 FC 1411 (F.C.) — This is an application to review the refusal of a permanent resident application because of the nature, severity and probable duration of the applicant's dependent daughter's medical condition.

As a general rule a visa officer is bound by the medical officer's recommendations. Where the medical officer's report includes a patently unreasonable error of fact, or was generated in a manner contrary to principals of natural justice, then the visa officer's reliance on that report constitutes an error in law.

**39. Financial reasons — A foreign national is inadmissible for financial reasons if they are or will be unable or unwilling to support themself or any other person who is dependent on them, and have not satisfied an officer that adequate arrangements for care and support, other than those that involve social assistance, have been made.**

*[Editor's Note: SOR/2002-227, s. 320(8) provides that a person is inadmissible under the new* Immigration and Refugee Protection Act, *S.C. 2001 c. 27 for financial reasons if, on June 28, 2002, the person had been determined to be a member of the inadmissible class described in paragraph 19(1)(b) of the* Immigration Act, *R.S.C. 1985, c. I-2 (the "former Act") or had been determined to be inadmissible on the basis of paragraph 27(1)(f) or (2)(l) of the former Act.]*

## Case Law

*Delisa v. Canada (Minister of Citizenship & Immigration)* (2010), 87 Imm. L.R. (3d) 125, 2010 FC 88, 2010 CarswellNat 946, 2010 CarswellNat 165 (F.C.) — The immigration officer refused the applicant's application for permanent resident status under the spouse or common-law partner in Canada based on the applicant's receipt of Income Support from the Ontario Disabilities Support Program (ODSP). The phrase "social assistance" is undefined in the legislation or regulations, but the Federal Court of Appeal has held that it connotes "welfare." It is evident that social assistance is a flexible term that can include among other things "public assistance, in the form of government subsidized



IRP Act

housing." There can be no doubt that benefits under the ODSP are a form of social assistance, notwithstanding the fact that the applicant is in receipt of those benefits by virtue of being a dependant of the sponsor who receives those benefits by reason of disability. While a sponsor may be approved as a sponsor despite relying on social assistance by reason of a disability, the applicant must nevertheless satisfy the immigration officer that she is not inadmissible for any of the myriad grounds of inadmissibility pursuant to s. 11 of IRPA. One of those grounds is in s. 39 of IRPA which bars the applicant for financial reasons. Pursuant to s. 39, if applicants cannot show that they are willing and able to support themselves, they must show that adequate arrangement for their care and support have been made, other than those that involve social assistance. The officer's decision on this ground was reasonable. However, the officer breached the duty of procedural fairness by failing to alert the applicant that her receipt of ODSP benefits could render her inadmissible to Canada pursuant to s. 39 of IRPA and to give her an opportunity to address those concerns. The application for judicial review was allowed.

**40. (1) Misrepresentation — A permanent resident or a foreign national is inadmissible for misrepresentation**

> **(a) for directly or indirectly misrepresenting or witholding material facts relating to a relevant matter that induces or could induce an error in the administration of this Act;**
>
> **(b) for being or having been sponsored by a person who is determined to be inadmissible for misrepresentation;**
>
> **(c) on a final determination to vacate a decision to allow the claim for refugee protection by the permanent resident or the foreign national; or**
>
> **(d) on ceasing to be a citizen under paragraph 10(1)(a) of the *Citizenship Act*, in the circumstances set out in subsection 10(2) of that Act.**

**(2) Application — The following provisions govern subsection (1):**

> **(a) the permanent resident or the foreign national continues to be inadmissible for misrepresentation for a period of two years following, in the case of a determination outside Canada, a final determination of inadmissibility under subsection (1) or, in the case of a determination in Canada, the date the removal order is enforced; and**
>
> **(b) paragraph (1)(b) does not apply unless the Minister is satisfied that the facts of the case justify the inadmissibility.**

*[Editor's Note: SOR/2002-227, s. 320(9) provides that a person is inadmissible under the new* Immigration and Refugee Protection Act, *S.C. 2001 c. 27 for misrepresentation if, on June 28, 2002, the person had been determined to be inadmissible on the basis of paragraph 27(1)(e) or (2)(g) or (i) of the former* Immigration Act, *R.S.C. 1985, c. I-2.]*

## Case Law

### Section 40(1)

*Singh v. Canada (Minister of Citizenship & Immigration)* (2010), 89 Imm. L.R. (3d) 36, 2010 FC 378, 2010 CarswellNat 3016, 2010 CarswellNat 817, [2010] F.C.J. No. 426 (F.C.) — The applicant was recently found to be inadmissible for misrepresenting or withholding a material fact when he immigrated to Canada in 1993. At that time, he did not disclose that he had fathered a child who remained in India. His defence is that he did not know he had fathered a child. Paternity has now been scientifically established by DNA tests. As a result, the Immigration Division of the Immigration and Refugee Board of Canada issued an exclusion order and he was ordered removed from Canada. His appeal to the Immigration Appeal Division was dismissed. He sought judicial review of that decision.

The applicant's submission is that he could not have misrepresented or withheld facts within the meaning of s. 40 of IRPA or its predecessor, since subjectively he had no knowledge at the time that he was the girl Shilpa's biological father. The Minister's position is that it does not matter what the applicant knew or did not know, it is a scientifically proven fact that he is Shilpa's biological father, and that is the end of the matter.

Given that the wording "knowingly" does not appear in s. 40, it follows, that knowledge is not a prerequisite to a finding of misrepresentation or withholding material facts. Undoubtedly, the existence of a child is a material fact. In this case, the alleged misrepresentation was a misstatement of fact. Such misrepresentations may be fraudulent, negligent or innocent. The panel found that the applicant was not credible. Even if he did not know that he was Shilpa's father, the circumstances, *i.e.* his long sexual relationship with Shilpa's mother while her husband was out of India, should, at the very least, have put him on inquiry. He had a duty of candour which required him to disclose upon his arrival in Canada in 1993 the strong possibility that he had fathered a child. The panel's assessment of facts was not unreasonable and so it follows that the applicant, a permanent resident, is inadmissible for misrepresentation.

One of the objectives of IRPA, as set out in s. 3, is "to see that families are reunited in Canada," not to remove someone against his will so that he may be reunited with his wife and daughter in India. The panel noted that the applicant had been here for many years, and had been gainfully employed, however, it made no assessment of the job prospects of a 50-year-old man in India, taking into account his obligation to support his wife and child. How the couple manages their affairs is their business. It would appear that they would prefer that the applicant work in Canada. There is nothing preventing him from visiting his wife and daughter in India on a regular basis. Perhaps after he has saved more money, he will return to and retire in India. It was not for the panel to say that they would be better off if reunited in India now. This smacked of "big brotherhood." This aspect of the decision was unreasonable. The matter was referred back to a differently constituted panel for reconsideration.

*Chen v. Canada (Minister of Public Safety & Emergency Preparedness)* (2010), 2010 FC 584, 2010 CarswellNat 2957, 2010 CarswellNat 1506 (F.C.) — The applicant, a Chinese citizen, married Ms. Zou, a Canadian resident. She then sponsored him for permanent residence. When he arrived in Canada about a year later, he found her pregnant with another man's child. After a month or two, the marriage fell apart. After their divorce, he married an old flame in China and as a Canadian permanent resident endeavoured to sponsor her. At this stage, the immigration authorities became suspicious. Not only was the sponsorship of his second wife disallowed, he was also declared inadmissible for misrepresentation by directly withholding information and representing that his first marriage was genuine. The applicant appealed that decision to the Immigration Appeal Division of the Immigration and Refugee Board. His appeal was dismissed. This was the judicial review of that decision.

The basis for holding that the marriage was not genuine was that it only lasted for a short time, and that he did not immediately return to China when the marriage broke up but returned a short time later to pursue a former flame. These facts cannot establish an evidentiary basis that the marriage was not genuine in the first place. He could not know at the time of the marriage that his wife would become pregnant with another man's child a year later. As to not immediately returning to China when the marriage broke down, he said that as a cuckold he would be the laughing stock of his village. There was no evidence to contradict that statement. When he returned thereafter, it was in a different context altogether. As to not sharing the rumours regarding his wife's affair at the time of the interview, he withheld no material fact. The only fact was that he had heard rumours. Even if they were true, it did not mean that the marriage was necessarily at an end. The *Divorce Act* specifically contemplates a possible reconciliation and the divorce papers jointly signed by the parties, which are to be found in the tribunal record, contain their joint statement that reconciliation was not possible. The duty of candour did not oblige the applicant to share his worries with an immigration officer. There was no misrepresentation and no fact was withheld. The application for judicial review was granted.

*Uppal v. Canada (Minister of Citizenship & Immigration)*, 2009 CarswellNat 1209, 2009 FC 445 (F.C.) — The applicant family sought judicial review of a decision refusing their applications for permanent residence through a family sponsorship. While acknowledging that they had initially misrepresented the nature of their familial relationships, the applicants submit that the misrepresentation was withdrawn prior to a decision being made in relation to their application. Accordingly, they argued there was no material misrepresentation that induced or could induce an error in the administration of the IRPA. The applicants argued that the officer erred in failing to give any weight to the documents provided by them to demonstrate the validity of the marriage between two of them, Mr. Uppal and Ms. Kaur. It was clear that the applicants concealed the fact of Mr. Uppal's first marriage, and misrepresented the true nature of the relationship between Ms. Kaur and his two older children. The family history and the nature of the familial relationships between the various parties to the application for permanent residence were clearly both relevant and material in a family sponsorship application. Although counsel endeavoured to portray the "clarification" letter sent as a voluntary correction of the record by the applicants, the reality is that they only acknowledged the true nature of the relationships between the various individuals once it was clear that their misrepresentation was about to be revealed through DNA testing.

The misrepresentations in this case were made in the context of the applications for permanent residence that were under consideration by the officer. In such circumstances, the fact that the misrepresentations were disclosed by the applicants prior to a final decision having actually been taken in relation to their application does not assist them. The Court has previously held in *Khan v. Canada (Minister of Citizenship & Immigration, infra*, at paragraphs 27–29, that such an interpretation would lead to situations where individuals could knowingly misrepresent their circumstances, but nevertheless escape an inadmissibility finding as long as they disclose a misrepresentation right before a decision was made. Not only would such an interpretation encourage the abuse of the Act, it also ignores the requirement to provide truthful information in applications under it. The application for judicial review was dismissed.

*Nazim v. Canada (Minister of Citizenship & Immigration)*, 2009 CarswellNat 1216, 2009 FC 471 (F.C.) — The applicant sought judicial review of a decision rejecting his application for permanent residence as a member of the spouse in Canada class. The immigration officer found that the applicant had misrepresented a material fact in relation to his application. The applicant initially came to Canada in 1997 and made a refugee claim based on his alleged fear of persecution in Pakistan as a result of his membership in the Mohajir (or Muttahida) Quami Movement (or "MQM"). He was called in for an interview with the Canadian Security Intelligence Service. During questioning by these officials, the applicant changed his story, and claimed that he had never in fact been a member of the MQM. He claimed that an immigration consultant had counseled him to provide the fabricated story of the MQM membership and persecution by Pakistani forces. When the applicant was later interviewed by representatives of Citizenship and Immigration Canada, he repeated his new story and provided CIC with a revised application form that made no mention of either membership in, or association with, the MQM. An immigration officer subsequently found him to be inadmissible to Canada pursuant to s. 40(1)(a) of the IRPA for having misrepresented or withheld material facts in connection with his application for permanent residency.

This case was somewhat unusual in that rather than enhancing his application for permanent residency, the misrepresentation made by the applicant could actually have led to him having been found to be inadmissible to Canada on security grounds. As such, it was clearly material to his application. It appears, however, that the applicant only came to understand the potential implications of his misrepresentation in the course of his CSIS interview. It was at this point that he changed his story and denied ever having been a member of the MQM. The Court was satisfied that the officer's conclusion was reasonably available and the application for judicial review was dismissed.

*Mukamutara v. Canada (Minister of Citizenship & Immigration)*, 2008 CarswellNat 923, 2008 FC 451 (F.C.) — The decision challenged was a refusal by a visa officer to grant an application for permanent residence to the applicant's adopted daughters. The basis for the decision was that the officer found the two girls to be untruthful about the date of their father's death, although only one had been interviewed. The effect of the decision was to keep the daughters away from their adoptive mother. This case turns on the confusion surrounding the date of death of the girls' father. On the application it was listed as July 12, 1990. An undated death certificate was provided with the July 12, 1990 date of death filled in. One of the daughters was interviewed and she clarified that her father died on August 2, 1992. A corrected and dated death certificate was provided to the officer. The applicant claimed that when filling in the application, she had relied on the July 12, 1990 date of death from the erroneous certificate. The officer did not believe that the girls' father had died or at least not on the dates in issue, that they had lied on their application and concluded that neither of them fit within the class of persons who could be sponsored.

The issue of misrepresentation comes down to the materiality of the representation or withholding. The date of death in this case may have been material, particularly if it had any relevance to the validity of the adoption. However, there was insufficient clarity in the record to consider that the officer was questioning the validity of the adoption on the basis that the father was not dead at the time of adoption. Rather, the issue that troubled the officer was more related to the *timing* of death than the *fact* of death. Therefore, it was not possible to determine if there was some materiality to the misrepresentation other than that the officer may have felt that persons who misrepresent in any circumstance should not be admitted to Canada. As such, the officer erred in law in concluding that she had a discretion to refuse the application because of a misrepresentation, the materiality of which was never addressed. The officer never directly challenged the validity of the adoption — a most material fact.

*Koo v. Canada (Minister of Citizenship & Immigration)* (2008), 74 Imm. L.R. (3d) 99, 2008 CarswellNat 2630, 2008 CarswellNat 5631, 2008 FC 931 (F.C.) — This was an application for judicial review of an immigration officer's decision which refused the applicant's permanent residence visa under the skilled worker category. The scope of this application was limited to the officer's finding that the applicant was inadmissible to Canada on the basis that he had misrepresented or withheld material facts within the meaning of s. 40(1)(a) of the IRPA. The officer refused the applicant's application for permanent residence because she determined that he did not meet the necessary points required to be granted permanent residence in Canada and because she had found that the applicant has misrepresented or withheld material facts which could have induced errors in the administration of the Act. Specifically, she concluded that he did not admit to having previously applied for and been refused permanent residence in Canada and that he did not admit to having previously used another name. She also found that he stated on his application that the highest level of education was a trade/apprenticeship credential when in fact his highest level of education was a secondary diploma.

The applicant swore an affidavit that he believed that both his previous and current names had been provided on the forms included with his application for permanent residence submitted by his former representative. He argued that despite both names not being disclosed on the forms that the officer should have found his previous legal name as it appeared throughout the supporting documentation submitted with the application. The Court concluded that this was clear evidence that the applicant did not mislead Citizenship and Immigration authorities. At his interview, the applicant advised the officer that he had not thoroughly read the completed application forms before signing them. In light of this explanation and the fact that the applicant had clearly not attempted to conceal his previous name because he had provided numerous supporting documents in his previous name and had also disclosed his previous name at the interview, it was unreasonable for the officer to conclude that the failure to include his previous name on the application forms was not simply a human error in transcription, as his former representative recognized, and did rise to the level of misrepresentation under s. 40(1)(a) of the Act.

The applicant checked off the "yes" box to the question whether he had "previously sought refugee status in Canada or applied for a Canadian immigrant or permanent resident visa or visitor or temporary resident visa", but checked off the "no" box to the question as to whether he had been refused such status. The applicant stated that this was an oversight on both the part of himself and his former representative and it was in no way intentional. Further, when the applicant was asked at the interview about whether he had previously submitted any immigration application, the CAIPS notes reflected that he advised the officer that he had previously submitted an application for permanent residence in Canada, which was refused in 1995. The applicant's previous disclosure was found to support his claim that he misread the question on the application form and inadvertently ticked off the wrong box. Moreover, no assessment of the materiality of the inadvertent failure to disclose that the applicant had previously applied for permanent residence was conducted. Such an assessment is necessary in order to properly evaluate whether a misrepresentation was material in accordance with s. 40(1)(a) of the Act. The officer's failure to conduct such an assessment constituted a reviewable error.

Finally, the officer's finding that a misrepresentation was made with respect to the applicant's educational credentials also constituted a reviewable error. The applicant's former representative interpreted the applicant's experience and training to have constituted an apprenticeship level of education. While this may have been an inaccurate interpretation, it is not an entirely unreasonable conclusion given the fact that the applicant had undergone a significant amount of practical training and had been accredited by the government of Taiwan in the field of Chinese cuisine as the result of successfully completing a government-administered examination. The awarding of points was a matter to be evaluated by the officer and the officer did just that. She questioned the applicant about his education and he answered her honestly and openly. It is as a result of her review of his educational documentation, the information provided by the applicant himself at interview and her subsequent analysis that she came to the conclusion that the applicant should not be awarded the points requested by his former representative. This is the role of a visa officer and it is the work they conduct on a daily basis.

The inadvertent errors made by the applicant and his consultant did not in any way meet the threshold of s. 40 of the Act. Not only were they not misrepresentations, but neither were they material. The officer failed to conduct the proper analysis as to the materiality of the alleged misrepresentations, which was also a reviewable error. The officer had a duty to consider the totality of the information that was in the applicant's file with immigration for almost two years, which she did not do. The application for judicial review was granted.



*Bodine v. Canada (Minister of Citizenship & Immigration)*, 2008 CarswellNat 2300, 2008 FC 848 (F.C.) — The applicant, a citizen of the United States of America, attempted to enter Canada at the Peace Arch border crossing. The applicant stated that she was seeking entry as a visitor to stay with a friend in Canada for two or three months. The applicant was refused entry by a CBSA officer. The officer concluded that the applicant would not leave Canada at the end of her stay because she was unemployed and did not have proof of funds to support herself during her stay in Canada. Also, she did not have documents proving her ties to the United States or proof of an address in the United States to which she would return. Further, the number and nature of the items in her vehicle suggested that the applicant was coming to Canada to live. These items included personal documents (pay stubs, journals, and old mail), sheets of return address stickers with a Vancouver address, a wooden chest, bicycle and a bicycle rack, and several bags of personal goods. The applicant voluntarily withdrew her application for entry to Canada. Later, the same morning, the applicant's boyfriend, a Canadian citizen, met the applicant and transferred a number of articles from her car to his vehicle. The applicant also obtained an ATM receipt as proof of the funds in her bank account and a bank statement showing her home address in Colorado. The applicant then proceeded to the Peace Arch border crossing and was admitted into Canada without being referred to secondary examination. The officer who admitted the applicant into Canada was not aware that the applicant had voluntarily withdrawn her application earlier that morning or of the reasons for that withdrawal. Shortly thereafter, the applicant's boyfriend attempted to re-enter Canada and was referred to secondary examination. A number of articles were found in his car, including: a bicycle and bicycle rack; a wooden chest containing anti-war and cannabis literature; personal file folders filled with personal information and art work; photo albums; old letters; old bills; unopened letters; several notebooks; old books; women's clothing and shoes; a certificate of achievement for a course that was completed; and the applicant's expired passport and expired driver's license. Upon discovering that the applicant had entered Canada, the items were seized and a warrant was issued for the applicant's arrest on the grounds that she was inadmissible for a misrepresentation pursuant to

s. 40(1)(a) of the Act. The applicant was arrested and at an inadmissibility hearing, the Board found that the applicant had indirectly withheld information or made a direct misrepresentation, noting that when she entered Canada she "was not asked . . .. about the quantity of belongings she was bringing into Canada . . . because she was displaying only a minimal of personal effects". The Board held that the purpose of transferring most of her belongings to her boyfriend's car was unquestionably to mislead the examining officer into believing she was bringing into Canada less than she actually was. The Board found that this misrepresentation was material because, by removing the bulk of the belongings, the applicant foreclosed or averted further inquiries, or in other words, she cut off an avenue of investigation for the officer. The Board concluded that the misrepresentation induced, or could have induced, an error in the administration of the Act. The applicant sought judicial review of the Board's decision.

It is clear that a duty of candor exists and that the surrounding circumstances are important for deciding what that duty entails in any particular instance. This case presents the question of the extent to which an applicant must disclose information when not expressly asked for that information by an examining officer. Section 40 of the Act does not require that a person must spontaneously disclose *any* fact that could *possibly* be relevant. Instead, to determine whether the withholding of information constitutes a misrepresentation under the Act, it is necessary to consider the surrounding circumstances in each instance. Here, the applicant knew or ought to have known that the amount and the kind of goods she was bringing into Canada was a relevant fact that the examining border services officer would need to know in order to assess whether she was admissible under the Act.

On the specific facts of this case, there was an obligation on the part of the applicant to fully disclose the number of articles she was bringing into Canada, since only a few hours earlier the applicant, to her knowledge, was refused entry because of, *inter alia*, the quantity and nature of the articles in her possession. The application for judicial review was dismissed.

*Ali v. Canada (Minister of Citizenship & Immigration)*, 2008 CarswellNat 905, 2008 CarswellNat 279, 2008 FC 166 — A visa officer held a dependent of a convention refugee from Bangladesh to be inadmissible for landing in Canada due to misrepresentation under s. 40(1) of the IRPA. The visa officer's CAIPS notes disclose that, prior to the misrepresentation being detected, there was no outstanding issue with respect to the applicant's age or his family relationships. The misrepresentation issue arising thereafter was due to the fact that the applicant submitted a fraudulent school record. The applicant subsequently filed a further school record and stated that the misrepresentation was made without his knowledge.

In order for an applicant to be inadmissible due to misrepresentation, s. 40(1) of the IRPA requires that the misrepresented facts be material to the application. Therefore, by Citizenship & Immigration Canada's policy guidelines with respect to evaluating whether a misrepresentation will render an applicant inadmissible, the materiality of the misrepresentation must first be determined. The CAIPS notes do not reflect any analysis by the visa officer on the issue of the materiality of the misrepresentation under consideration. In the evaluation of the applicant's admissibility, his age, identity, and family relationships were not in doubt prior to the detection of the misrepresentation. As a result, the reasons given in the rejection letter do not constitute an analysis of materiality warranting the applicant's rejection. On this basis, the visa officer's decision was not in accordance with s. 40(1) of the IRPA, and further, is factually erroneous. The visa officer's decision was set aside and referred back for redetermination by a different visa officer.

*Walia v. Canada (Minister of Citizenship & Immigration)*, 2008 CarswellNat 1079, 2008 CarswellNat 2640, 2008 FC 486 (F.C.) — The applicants sought judicial review of a decision that they were inadmissible to Canada for directly or indirectly misrepresenting or withholding material facts contrary to paragraph 40(1)(a) of the IRPA. The principal applicant had indicated that she was divorced and did not cohabitate with one Mr. Ashok Raikhywalia. An officer from the High Commission visited the applicant's village and house and discovered that she was still in cohabitation with Mr. Ashok Raikhywalia. The applicant was given an opportunity to address the officer's concerns about the misrepresentation.



The officer's finding as to the making of a material misrepresentation within the scope of paragraph 40(2)(a) of the Act was grounded in the finding that Mrs. Raikhywalia continued to cohabitate with her former husband. The question of "cohabitation", means more than simple shared residence, if that is indeed the situation here. The word "cohabitate" has been interpreted as meaning a "marriage-like" relationship characterized by the features of financial interdependence, a sexual relationship, a common principal residence, mutual obligations to share the responsibility of running the home and the "expectation each day that there be continued mutual dependency". The evidence in the record fell short of establishing these facts. The decision of the visa officer did not meet the standard of reasonableness. The application for judicial review was allowed.

*Khan v. Canada (Minister of Citizenship & Immigration)*, 2008 CarswellNat 1153, 2008 CarswellNat 2321, 2008 FC 512 (F.C.) — The applicant was refused a permanent resident visa as a skilled worker after being found to be inadmissible on the basis of a misrepresentation pursuant to paragraph 40(1)(a) of the Act. The applicant adopted the misrepresentation made by his consultant to his benefit, but then clarified the information prior to the visa officer relying on it and making a decision. The applicant argued that paragraph 40(1)(a) does not apply to situations where the misrepresentation is corrected before a decision on the application was made. Paragraph 40(1)(a) is written very broadly in that it applies to any misrepresentation, whether direct or indirect, relating to a relevant matter that induces or could induce an error in the administration of the Act. The Court must respect the wording of the Act and give it the broad interpretation its wording demands. There is nothing in the wording of the paragraph indicating that it should not apply to a situation where a misrepresentation is adopted, but clarified prior to a decision being rendered.

*Baro v. Canada (Minister of Citizenship & Immigration)*, 2007 CarswellNat 4369, 2007 CarswellNat 5117, 2007 FC 1299 (F.C.) — The applicant was found to be inadmissible to Canada on the basis that he had misrepresented or withheld material facts from immigration authorities when his spouse, a Canadian resident, sponsored his application for permanent residence. The applicant admits that he had a previous marriage. He says that he became estranged from his spouse and then having lost touch with her entirely obtained a declaration from a court in the Philippines presuming her to be dead. He did not mention these facts to Canadian immigration officials. His second wife notified authorities after she learned, on a visit to the Philippines, that the applicant's first wife had reappeared. The Board concluded that the applicant was inadmissible to Canada. It found that the Canadian official had requested a "marriage check" in the form of a certificate from the National Statistics Office. In providing a certificate indicating that no marriage was registered in his name, the applicant had misrepresented the facts. Further, by omit-ting to mention the existence of an order recognizing that his first wife was presumed dead, he had failed to disclose a material fact. The Court considered whether the applicant had a duty to disclose his marital history in the circumstances even in the absence of a specific request from Canadian authorities.

In general terms, an applicant for permanent residence has a "duty of candour" which requires disclosure of marital facts. This duty extends to variations in his or her personal circumstances, including a change of marital status. Even an innocent failure to provide material information can result in a finding of inadmissibility. An exception arises where applicants can show that they honestly and reasonably believed that they were not withholding material information. An applicant's marital history is clearly relevant to an application for permanent residence based on a spousal sponsorship. Canadian officials will want to ensure that the union is genuine and the applicant's marital background is a valid factor for them to take into account. In this case, Mr. Baro was obligated to disclose his marital history. While he complied with the request for an official certificate of marriage registration, his compliance with that request did not absolve him of the obligation to divulge his previous marriage and the steps he took to have his first wife presumed dead. The Board's decision that the applicant had failed to comply with s. 40(1)(a) was upheld.

*Maruquin v. Canada (Minister of Citizenship & Immigration)* (2007), 68 Imm. L.R. (3d) 273, 2007 CarswellNat 4562, 2007 CarswellNat 5785, 2007 FC 1349 (F.C.) — The applicants were sponsored as permanent residents to Canada and completed their forms in April 2003. In early March 2006, the applicants' application was approved and their visas were printed. On March 21, 2006, the sponsor faxed the immigration officer advising that one of the applicants, Cheryl Maruquin, gave birth to a baby during the processing of her immigration paper. The child was born in July 2004. Cheryl was a single mother and at the time, the family had decided to leave the baby in the Philippines and petition him in the near future. When the birth of Cheryl's son was disclosed to the immigration officials, the applicants' visas had been approved but had not been delivered to the applicants. On July 14, 2006, the application for permanent residence was refused "... for directly or indirectly misrepresenting or withholding material facts relating to a relevant matter that induces or could induce an error in the administration of this Act", pursuant to paragraph 40(1)(a) of the IRPA. The basis of the misrepresentation was the failure of the principal applicant and his daughter, Cheryl, to disclose the birth of her son in a timely fashion. The applicants' principal position was that the birth of the child was disclosed on their own initiative after the printing but prior to the delivery of the visas and, in any event, prior to any of them being landed in Canada. Accordingly, in their view, the disclosure of the child's birth on March 21, 2006, some 21 months after the fact but prior to the delivery of the visas, rendered impossible any misrepresentation or withholding of a material fact that induced or could have induced an error in the administration of the Act.

The Court held, that the special circumstances of this case, the non-disclosure of the information concerning the birth of Cheryl's son until March 21, 2006 cannot be said to be the withholding of a material fact relating to a relevant matter that induced or could have induced an error in the administration of the Act. The forms made available in this proceeding could not be the basis of a requirement, in any practical sense, that Cheryl report the change of information immediately. In the end, the birth of the son was disclosed prior to any legal requirement to do so in the regulations. There was no evidence in the tribunal record that the information was "deliberately" withheld. There was no information in the CAIPS notes to suggest that the applicants had any incentive not to disclose the birth of the child, let alone the non-disclosure was deliberate.

*Lu v. Canada (Minister of Citizenship & Immigration)*, 2007 CarswellNat 415, 2007 FC 159 (F.C.) — This is an application for judicial review of a decision to refuse an application for permanent residence on the basis that the applicant was inadmissible to Canada due to a misrepresentation. The Consulate General made inquiries to confirm the authenticity of a capital validation report. The visa officer concluded that the applicant was inadmissible to Canada. In her letter to the applicant, the visa officer wrote ". . . because you, a person described under subs. 16(1) of IRPA and ss. 34 to 42 of the *Immigration and Refugee Protection Act* . . . you are therefore criminally inadmissible to Canada." Although the officer did overstep her role in the evaluation of the applicant's permanent resident application, her actions did not constitute an error of law. The fact that the officer wrote in her letter to the applicant that "you are therefore criminally inadmissible to Canada" was an error which can be associated to a typographical error and it was not of a conclusive nature. There was no indication in the officer's letter that she misunderstood the evidence before her and as such believed the applicant was inadmissible under s. 36 of the IRPA due to criminality, or that the officer believed that providing untruthful information made the applicant inadmissible due to criminality. The application for judicial review was dismissed.

*Calixto v. Canada (Minister of Citizenship & Immigration)* (2005), 49 Imm. L.R. (3d) 36, 2005 CarswellNat 2165, 2005 CarswellNat 4919, 2005 FC 1037 (F.C.) — The applicant arrived in Canada and was granted refugee status, and then applied for landed immigrant status. At a CSIS interview the applicant was confronted with information that he had lied about his past activities, including a criminal record in the United States that arose during the time he claimed he was being persecuted in Mexico. The applicant admitted this misrepresentation and as a result of the admission, the applicant's refugee status was vacated pursuant to s. 109(1) of the IRPA. A report was prepared pursuant to s. 44(1) setting out that the applicant was inadmissible pursuant to s. 40(1)(c). An immigration officer found the report well founded and consequently made a deportation order against the applicant pursuant to s. 44(2). The applicant argued that s. 40(1)(c) would render him inadmissible only if he made a misrepresentation in the course of the vacation proceeding before the Refugee Protection Division. The Court held that whether the applicant made any misrepresentations during the vacation hearing was not a relevant consideration. Instead, the use of the term "misrepresentation" in s. 40(1)(c) should be read as denoting statements of fact which operate to make a person inadmissible, that is, if either of the events mentioned in this section are proved to have occurred, a person is considered, or "deemed," inadmissible for "misrepresentation."

*Zhang c. Canada (Ministre de la Citoyenneté & de l'Immigration)*, [2005] F.C.J. No. 1594, 2005 CarswellNat 2969, 2005 CarswellNat 5557, 2005 FC 1313 (F.C.) — The applicant applied for judicial review of a decision by the immigration program manager at the Canadian Embassy in Beijing with respect to the applicant's application for permanent residence. The application was refused based on a violation of paragraph 40(1)(a) of the Act, specifically a misrepresentation as to the source of the applicant's funds. The Court concluded that where the applicant does not establish the source of her money, which is required by the Act, the visa officer is justified in denying the visa application. Therefore, misrepresenting the source of the funds is a material fact. The application for judicial review was dismissed.

*Menon v. Canada (Minister of Citizenship & Immigration)*, [2005] F.C.J. No. 1548, 53 Imm. L.R. (3d) 85, 2005 CarswellNat 2826, 2005 CarswellNat 5329, 2005 FC 1273 (F.C.) — The principal applicant misrepresented material facts in that he presented what purported to be an original certificate from the University of Bombay and an original marks transcript from the same university which were determined, following verification, to be false. During the interview, the visa officer gave the applicant notice of his concerns regarding the false educational documents. The applicant returned to Mumbai and obtained genuine evidence that he had graduated from the University of Bombay. He couriered this evidence to the High Commission in London. The Computer Assisted Immigration Processing System (CAIPS) did not reflect that the High Commission in London or the visa office in Abu Dhabi had received any further documents from the applicant after the interview. The Court concluded that the duty of fairness had not been met, since the supplementary material filed by the applicant was not entered into CAIPS by the visa officer. A very high standard of fairness is to be applied in the application of s. 40(1) where a permanent resident or a foreign national is determined to be inadmissible for misrepresentation.

*Huang v. Canada (Minister of Citizenship & Immigration)*, [2005] F.C.J. No. 1990, 52 Imm. L.R. (3d) 46, 2005 CarswellNat 3925, 2005 CarswellNat 5661, 2005 FC 1615 (F.C.) — The applicant's application for permanent residence was denied on the basis that he had made a material misrepresentation that could induce an error in the administration of the IRPA. The matter was reviewed on a patent unreasonableness standard.

*Hou v. Canada (Minister of Citizenship & Immigration)*, 2005 CarswellNat 3829, 2005 CarswellNat 5466, 2005 FC 1586 (F.C.) — The applicant's application for a permanent residence visa, under the skilled worker category, was refused on the basis that the applicant was not credible because there were significant discrepancies between the evidence the applicant had submitted for a study permit application and the evidence she had submitted for the permanent residence application. The officer reached this decision based on the discrepancy in the evidence. The officer reviewed, but did not accept, the applicant's explanation that the misinformation was due to the activity of her consultant or her agent. The standard of review to be applied to decisions on credibility is patent unreasonableness. The officer's decision was reasonable and the application for judicial review was dismissed.

**41. Non-compliance with Act — A person is inadmissible for failing to comply with this Act**

> **(a) in the case of a foreign national, through an act or omission which contravenes, directly or indirectly, a provision of this Act; and**
>
> **(b) in the case of a permanent resident, through failing to comply with subsection 27(2) or section 28.**

*[Editor's Note: SOR/2002-227, s. 320(10) provides that a person is inadmissible under the* Immigration and Refugee Protection Act, *S.C. 2001 c. 27 (the "new Act") for failing to comply with the new Act if, on June 28, 2002, the person had been determined to be a member of an inadmissible class described in paragraph 19(1)(h) or (i) or (2)(c) or (d) of the* Immigration Act, *R.S.C. 1985, c. I-2 (the "former Act") or had been determined to be inadmissible on the basis of paragraph 27(1)(b) or (2)(b), (e), (f), (h), (i) or (k) of the former Act.]*

## Case Law

*Ikhuiwu v. Canada (Minister of Citizenship & Immigration)*, [2008] F.C.J. No. 35, 2008 FC 35, 2008 CarswellNat 42 — This was an application for judicial review of an IAD decision, confirming the decision of an overseas visa officer. The visa officer concluded that the applicant was inadmissible pursuant to ss. 28 and 41(b) of the IRPA as he did not reside in Canada for the required 730 days within a five-year period.

The legislative scheme under the IRPA makes it clear that the mere possession of a permanent resident card is not conclusive proof of a person's status in Canada. Pursuant to s. 31(2) of the IRPA, the presumption that the holder of a permanent resident card is a permanent resident is clearly a rebuttable one. In this case, it is clear that the permanent resident card, which was issued in error after it was determined by the visa officer in Nigeria that the applicant had lost his permanent residence status, could not possibly confer legal status on him as a permanent resident, nor could it have the effect of restoring his permanent resident status which he had previously lost because he didn't meet the residency requirements under s. 28 of the IRPA. There is no provision in the IRPA or the Regulations which suggests that the mere possession of a permanent resident card, which was improperly issued, could have the effect of restoring or reinstating a person's prior permanent resident status.

Section 59(1)(a) of the Regulations also makes it clear that an officer can only validly issue a new permanent resident card where an applicant has not lost his or her status under s. 46(1) of the IRPA. In this case, the applicant lost his permanent resident status after failing to meet the residency requirements under s. 28 of the IRPA and failed to appeal the decision within the 60 days as prescribed by Regulation 63(4). This regulatory scheme confirms that it was not possible for the issuing officer of the permanent resident card to have validly and properly issued it in light of the fact that the applicant had previously lost his permanent resident card. The application for judicial review was dismissed.

*Ivanov v. Canada (Minister of Citizenship & Immigration)* (2006), 56 Imm. L.R. (3d) 56, 2006 CarswellNat 2335 (Imm. & Ref. Bd. (App. Div.)) — The appellant made an application for permanent residence as an independent in May 2001. At the time he disclosed that he had never been married and had no dependants. The application was successful and he was issued a permanent resident visa in June 2003. The appellant married his girlfriend on October 3, 2003. The appellant arrived in Canada on October 7, 2003. He disclosed his recent marriage to Canadian immigration officials upon his arrival in Toronto. At the time of his examination at Pearson Airport, he could not establish that his wife met the requirements of IRPA and the Regulations. His counsel wrote to the Canadian Embassy in Vienna in November 2003 advising that the immigration official at the port of entry had no objection regarding the release of the landed documents to the appellant subject to the appellant's wife meeting the medical and security requirements. The Embassy replied that there was no legal basis on which they were required to assess the wife against the admissibility criteria of IRPA. The appellant was issued an exclusion order on the basis that he was unable to establish, at the time of his examination, that his wife met the requirement of the Act and the Regulations. The appellant appealed the exclusion order.

The Appeal Board concluded that the exclusion order was valid in law. The appeal, however, was allowed under s. 67(1)(c) and the matter referred back to an immigration officer at the port of entry for reconsideration. The Board found that the appellant made an honest mistake in not informing the visa officer of his marriage prior to appearing for landing, but had disclosed the marriage immediately upon landing. As a result of the appellant's error, the Board concluded that he had suffered financial hardship upon his arrival in Canada, exhausting his savings because he could not legally work here. The Board found that the appellant had established humanitarian and compassionate considerations to warrant the granting of special relief in light of all the circumstances of the case. The Board directed that the department take all steps required to facilitate the examination of the appellant's wife and to provide the appellant with the necessary immigration documents to allow the appellant to attend before an immigration officer at a port of entry for reconsideration.

*Brar v. Canada (Minister of Citizenship & Immigration)* (2006), 59 Imm. L.R. (3d) 293, 2006 CarswellNat 4324, 2006 FC 1502 (F.C.) — The applicants sought judicial review in respect of a decision by a member of the Immigration and Refugee Board of Canada given collectively, but pertaining to each of them, that determined that each of the applicants had contravened the terms of the work permit issued to each of them and therefore each was to be excluded from Canada. The applicants were all adult male citizens of India. They applied for and received temporary work permits. The work permit stated:

> Employer: Bombay Paradise
>
> Conditions:
>
> - not authorized to work in any occupation other than stated;
> - not authorized to work for any employer other than stated; and
> - not authorized for work in any location other than stated.

When the applicants arrived in Calgary, they found that the Bombay Paradise Restaurant was under construction and far from being completed. The owner of that business was a numbered company run by a person known as Vic. He placed them in another establishment known as Bombay Sweet House & Restaurant. Apparently, the ownership was not the same as Bombay Paradise, although pay cheques issued to the applicants were from the numbered company which was the owner of the Bombay Paradise business.

It came to the Minister's attention that the applicants were working for an employer whom the Minister believed to be other than that named in the work permit. As a result, an exclusion order was issued. Following that order, an admissibility hearing was held on March 1, 2006. The issue of the hearing was whether each of the applicants was inadmissible under s. 41(a) of the IRPA, as having contravened s. 29(2) of that Act.

The Court concluded that Bombay Paradise paid the applicants and the applicants worked in Calgary, and therefore, no term as set out in the work permit had been breached. A work permit should be understandable to all interested persons, not just the worker or the government, on the face of it. The Minister has the resources to ensure that the permit is complete and understandable. If it is not, the Minister cannot be seen to rely on self-created ambiguities to derive a beneficial interpretation. It is the same concept as *contra proferentum* in the interpretation of a contract. If the contract was prepared by a party, any ambiguity must be interpreted against the interests of that party.

The applicants did not breach the terms of their work permits. Their employer, the person who pays them, was Bombay Paradise. They worked in Calgary. As a result, the exclusion order was set aside and the matter was returned to be determined by a different person.

*Chang v. Canada (Minister of Citizenship & Immigration)*, [2006] F.C.J. No. 217, 2006 CarswellNat 329, 2006 CarswellNat 2194, 2006 FC 157 (F.C.) — The legislatively established conditions of the entrepreneur category, if flaunted knowingly, without serious consequence, would make a mockery of the purpose for which they were established. The act of creating or participating in a front operation or a sham investment, if left unchecked, strikes a blow at the very integrity of the immigration system. In this case, the applicants were found to be in non-compliance with subs. 27(2) and s. 28. The applicants' children were also found to be in non-compliance with subs. 27(2) as they were dependants of an entrepreneur and bound by the same terms and conditions of landing as provided in paragraph 23.1 of the previous Regulations. Both the applicants, as well as their children, sought special relief on appeal in light of the circumstances of their case, specifically, that there were sufficient humanitarian and compassionate considerations that warranted the setting aside of departure orders. The IAD was of the view that the parents did not merit discretionary relief as they took part in a sham arrangement to try to fulfill the conditions of the entrepreneur category. Even though the IAD felt that the children would be excellent candidates for permanent residence, it refused to grant discretionary relief to the children because, once the children became permanent residents, they would be entitled to sponsor their parents which would render the removal of the parents moot.

The granting of special relief is a weighing process. Even though there were some positive elements in favour of discretionary relief being allowed to the three children, these elements did not outweigh the importance given to the integrity of maintaining the conditions in the entrepreneur category. It was open to the IAD to find that special relief should not be granted to the children because this would benefit the parents who had not respected the conditions under which they entered Canada.

*Yu v. Canada (Minister of Citizenship & Immigration)*, 2005 CarswellNat 2998, 2005 CarswellNat 4835, 2005 FC 1323 (F.C.) — The applicant, having been granted permanent residence status in the independent category, was denied re-admission as a resident by a visa officer in November, 2003. The visa officer's decision was appealed to the IAD who determined that the applicant failed to comply with the residency obligation under s. 28 of the IRPA. The Immigration Appeal Board determined that pursuant to s. 41 of the IRPA there was non-compliance and upheld the visa officer's determination. The Board also determined that there were insufficient humanitarian and compassionate considerations justifying the retention of permanent residence status; therefore, the applicant was unable to overcome the breach of her residency obligations.

The applicant planned to work in her native land until able to retire with full pension benefits, in 2006. In 2005, the law concerning her pension benefits was changed and the applicant was able to retire earlier. This important new evidence was forwarded by way of affidavit to the Board on December 10, 2004.

The issue of "intention" should have been discussed or at least canvassed, as well as the change of circumstances regarding the applicant's retirement. The Board's decision was set aside and the matter was sent back to be reheard.

*Mand v. Canada (Minister of Citizenship & Immigration)*, [2005] F.C.J. No. 2016, 51 Imm. L.R. (3d) 272, 2005 CarswellNat 3970, 2005 FC 1637 (F.C.) — The principal applicant came to Canada under the entrepreneurial category. He was accompanied to Canada by his spouse and three children. They did not meet their obligations under the terms and conditions of their landing and, as a result, deportation orders were issued against them. They filed appeals against the deportation orders and were granted a two-year stay subject to following certain terms and conditions. The appeals were subsequently rejected when the applicants did not respect the conditions. The IAD also concluded that the applicants failed to demonstrate that having regard to all the circumstances of the case, they should not be removed from Canada for humanitarian and compassionate considerations. Although the Federal Court concluded that the IAD erred in concluding that the principal applicant's daughter did have strong ties to Canada, the Federal Court concluded the IAD's decision to cancel the stay of the deportation orders was not patently unreasonable, as it would be unjust and against the principles of the Canadian immigration process to decide otherwise. The principal applicant was given a second chance and failed to respect the rules; he should not be rewarded for being able to abuse the system to the point of allowing his family to remain in Canada long enough to build strong ties and qualify for a further stay of deportation orders based on humanitarian and compassionate grounds.

*El Idrissi c. Canada (Ministre de la Citoyenneté & de l'Immigration)*, 2005 CarswellNat 2421, 2005 CarswellNat 5248, 2005 FC 1105 (F.C.) — The applicant was given permanent residence status in 1991. In 1999, the applicant left Canada to visit his sick father and manage a family business in his home country. He did not return until June 15, 2003. He fell under the purview of s. 41 of the IRPA and a departure order was made against him by the Minister. He filed an appeal to the Immigration Appeal Division but conceded that the removal order against him was legally valid and the only issue he argued was that there were humanitarian and compassionate grounds to explain his failure to meet the residency obligation.

Simply having a wife in Canada was not sufficient for this situation to be considered a humanitarian and compassionate ground. The Appeal Division was entitled to consider that the applicant's plans for the future were vague. The applicant had the burden of establishing the existence of humanitarian and compassionate grounds.

**42. Inadmissible family member — A foreign national, other than a protected person, is inadmissible on grounds of an inadmissible family member if**

**(a) their accompanying family member or, in prescribed circumstances, their non-accompanying family member is inadmissible; or**

**(b) they are an accompanying family member of an inadmissible person.**

*[Editor's Note: SOR/2002-227, s. 352 provides that a person is not required to include in an application a non-accompanying common-law partner or a non-accompanying child who is not a dependant son or a dependant daughter within the meaning of s. 2(1) of the* Immigration Regulations, 1978, *SOR/98-172 and is a dependant child as defined in s. 2 of the* Immigration and Refugee Protection Regulations, *SOR/2002-227 (the "new Regulations") if the application was made under the* Immigration Act, *R.S.C. 1985, c. I-2 (the "former Act") before June 28, 2002.*

*SOR/2002-227, s. 353 provides that if a person has made an application under the former Act before June 28, 2002, the following provisions of the new Regulations do not apply to the person in respect of any of their non-accompanying dependent children, referred to in s. 352 of the new Regulations, or their non-accompanying common-law partner:*

*(a) paragraph 70(1)(e);*

*(b) subparagraph 72(1)(e)(i); and*

*(c) paragraph 108(1)(a).*

*SOR/2002-227, s. 354 further provides that if a person makes an application before June 28, 2002, their non-accompanying dependent children, referred to in s. 352 of the new Regulations, and their non-accompanying common-law partner shall not, for the purposes of that application, be considered inadmissible non-accompanying family members referred to in paragraph 42(a) of the* Immigration and Refugee Protection Act, *S.C.*

*2001, c. 27 (the "new Act"), and are not subject to the requirements of paragraph 30(1)(a) or 51(b) of the new Regulations.*

*SOR/2002-227, s. 355 still further provides that if a person who made an application under the former Act before June 28, 2002 sponsors a non-accompanying dependent child referred to in s. 352 of the new Regulations, who makes an application as a member of the family class or the spouse or common-law partner in Canada class, or sponsors a non-accompanying common-law partner who makes such an application, paragraph 117(9)(d) of the new Regulations does not apply in respect of that dependent child or common-law partner.]*

IRP Act

**43. Regulations — The regulations may provide for any matter relating to the application of this Division, may define, for the purposes of this Act, any of the terms used in this Division, and may include provisions respecting the circumstances in which a class of permanent residents or foreign nationals is exempted from any of the provisions of this Division.**

## Division 5 — Loss of Status and Removal

### *Report on Inadmissibility*

**44. (1) Preparation of report — An officer who is of the opinion that a permanent resident or a foreign national who is in Canada is inadmissible may prepare a report setting out the relevant facts, which report shall be transmitted to the Minister.**

**(2) Referral or removal order — If the Minister is of the opinion that the report is well-founded, the Minister may refer the report to the Immigration Division for an admissibility hearing, except in the case of a permanent resident who is inadmissible solely on the grounds that they have failed to comply with the residency obligation under section 28 and except, in the circumstances prescribed by the regulations, in the case of a foreign national. In those cases, the Minister may make a removal order.**

**(3) Conditions — An officer or the Immigration Division may impose any conditions, including the payment of a deposit or the posting of a guarantee for compliance with the conditions, that the officer or the Division considers necessary on a permanent resident or a foreign national who is the subject of a report, an admissibility hearing or, being in Canada, a removal order.**

*[Editor's Note: SOR/2002-227, s. 331 provides that a performance bond posted or security deposited under the former* Immigration Act, *R.S.C. 1985, c. I-2 that remains posted or deposited immediately before June 28, 2002 continues as a deposit or a guarantee under the new* Immigration and Refugee Protection Act, *S.C. 2001, c. 27 and is governed by its provisions.]*

*[Editor's Note: SOR/2002-227, s. 321(1) provides that a report made under s. 20 or s. 27 of the* Immigration Act, *R.S.C. 1985, c. I-2 (the "former Act") is a report under s. 44(1) of the* Immigration and Refugee Protection Act, *S.C. 2001 c. 27 (the "new Act").*

*SOR/2002-227, s. 321(3) provides that a report that was forwarded to a senior immigration officer under the former Act and in respect of which a decision has not been made on June 28, 2002 is a report transmitted to the Minister.*

*SOR/2002-227, s. 321(4) further provides that the causing by a senior immigration officer of an inquiry to be held under former Act is the referring by the Minister of a report to the Immigration Division under s. 44(2) of the new Act unless s. 44(2) of the new Act allows the Minister to make a removal order.*

*SOR/2002-227, s. 321(5) still further provides that if no substantive evidence was adduced before the Adjudication Division, the causing by a senior immigration officer of an inquiry to be held under the former Act is, if s. 44(2) of the new Act allows the Minister to make a removal order, a report on the basis of which the Minister may make a removal order.]*

## Case Law

### Section 44(1)

*Kainth v. Canada (Minister of Citizenship & Immigration)*, [2009] F.C.J. No. 134, 2009 CarswellNat 278, 2009 FC 100 (F.C.) — The applicant sought judicial review of a decision of the IAD confirming an order for his removal to India, pursuant to a breach of his residency obligation set out at s. 28 of the IRPA. The applicant was a citizen of India who immigrated to Canada in June 2000. He subsequently left Canada in August 2001 to elope with an Indian woman whom he had met over the internet and who lived in the United States. He made a refugee claim in the United States based on a false name and was granted asylum there in 2002. During a police investigation of assault charges in the United States, his true name and Canadian identity documentation came to light. His U.S. refugee claim was cancelled and he was given the option of appealing the decision or being expulsed to India or Canada. He chose to return to Canada and U.S. authorities escorted him in January 2006 to the Vancouver International Airport. The officer told him that he was in breach of his residency obligation which might result in his removal to India. She explained to him that she was not convinced that he had raised sufficient humanitarian considerations to warrant the exercise of her discretion not to report him. He was asked if he had anything else to add to her consideration, in answer to which he only referred to his desire to stay in Canada. The officer gave evidence that before reporting to the Minister's delegate, she spoke with the applicant's lawyer to advise him that she would be issuing a report under subs. 44(1) of the IRPA recommending the issuance of a removal order as she had found the applicant to be inadmissible. Said counsel simply asked the officer to fax him a copy of her report after its issuance. The officer spoke to counsel regarding the terms of a bond and shortly thereafter the applicant was released on a bond.

The application for leave and judicial review of the removal order alleged a breach of the applicant's rights under subs. 10(b) of the *Charter* and of the duty of procedural fairness of a POE officer for having: (1) failed to advise him that unless he made a refugee claim before the removal order was issues, he would lose his right to do so; and (2) failed to respect his right to counsel during his interview in respect of his residency obligation.

The Court found that: (1) there are minimal participatory rights included in the duty of fairness of the POE officer in this case; (2) those rights were respected on the facts of this case; and, (3) the Court is simply not willing to say that here, the duty of fairness incumbent on the officer included expressly confirming with counsel that he had no submissions to make and felt no need for an adjournment or to speak with his client prior to the issuance of the report. Keeping in mind the undisputed findings of the IAD that the applicant properly understood the reasons for the interview, the possibility of removal to India and his answers to the POE officer's questions in respect of his refugee claim in the United States, the Court agreed that the IAD and the POE officer could, in this matter, reasonably infer that the applicant was not facing nor fearing any particular danger in India. She simply had no duty to expressly ask him if he intended to make a refugee claim in Canada. The application for judicial review was dismissed.



*Clark v. Canada (Minister of Public Safety & Emergency Preparedness)* (2009), 79 Imm. L.R. (3d) 54, 2009 CarswellNat 753, 2009 FC 311 (F.C.) — At the time of his birth, the applicant's parents ran a farm in Southern Manitoba, near the Canada-U.S. border. The applicant was born on June 5, 1947, in West Hope, North Dakota, the site of the nearest hospital. He has lived in Canada his whole life believing he was a Canadian citizen. Persons in the applicant's circumstances are sometimes referred to as "lost Canadians". Mr. Clark was convicted of various drug-related and smuggling offences in April 2006. After his conviction it came to the CBSA's attention that he had been convicted of serious criminality under the IRPA and a delegate confirmed the CBSA's finding that he was inadmissible and issued a deportation order against the applicant while he was in prison. The applicant requested that the deportation order be stayed pending the final disposition of an application for judicial review of the Minister's delegate's decision.

The applicant raised at least a serious question regarding his citizenship. The Federal Court need not resolve the dispute between the parties on the issue of the applicant's claim to Canadian citizenship. The decision maker should adjourn the proceeding to allow the person to have the citizenship issue resolved. Here, given that the delegate could only issue a deportation against a non-citizen, he should have waited until a determination of the applicant's citizenship had been made before finding him to be inadmissible. The Minister's delegate treated the applicant unfairly by failing to provide reasons for finding him inadmissible to Canada and by doing so in advance of the decision on the applicant's citizenship. Accordingly, the decision was overturned.

*Hernandez v. Canada (Minister of Public Safety & Emergency Preparedness)* (2007), 62 Imm. L.R. (3d) 236, [2008] 2 F.C.R. 450, 2007 CarswellNat 1902, 2007 CarswellNat 4085, 2007 FC 725 — The applicant was a permanent resident of Canada and was convicted of an indictable offence and was sentenced to 30 months imprisonment. An enforcement officer of Canada Border Services Agency made a report under s. 44(1) of the IRPA stating that the applicant was inadmissible to Canada pursuant to s. 36(1)(a). Neither IRPA nor its regulations define what a "report" under s. 44(1) is to comprise. The Court considered whether the failure to provide the "Recommendation and appendixes" constituted a breach of fairness that could provide a basis for setting aside the s. 44(1) or 44(2) decisions.

In the circumstances of the present case the officer prepared and delivered to the Minister not only the "report" but also a detailed "recommendation" with many appendixes. These latter documents were undoubtedly intended to provide to the Minister detail as to what was contained in the report and substantiation as to its conclusions. Having been prepared, having been sent to the Minister, being pertinent to the "report" and substantiating what is in the "report", they must be considered to be part of the "report". The issue is *not* whether there was any requirement to create the "recommendation" and appendixes. Rather, the issue was *having created* them, *having delivered them* to the Minister, and *given their pertinence* to the "report", they should have been delivered to the applicant. In particular, when a clear and specific request for delivery of such material was made by the applicant's lawyer before the admissibility hearing, there was no proper basis for withholding that material.

Where a relevant document was created and put before the Minister, yet withheld from the applicant, this is sufficient to require that the s. 44(1) determination be set aside and done again.

The following question was certified:

> What constitutes the report under s. 44(1) of the IRPA and when, if at all should that material be given to an applicant?

*Richter v. Canada (Minister of Citizenship & Immigration)*, [2008] F.C.J. No. 1033, 73 Imm. L.R. (3d) 131, [2009] 1 F.C.R. 675, 2008 CarswellNat 3180, 2008 CarswellNat 2182, 2008 FC 806 (F.C.); affirmed (2009), 79 Imm. L.R. (3d) 2, 2009 CarswellNat 593, 2009 FCA 73 (F.C.A.) — The applicant immigrated to Canada with her husband in 1970. In 2003 the applicant was arrested in Toronto and charged with trafficking in firearms and related offences. The applicant was convicted and sentenced to 37 months imprisonment. The applicant was imprisoned at Grand Valley Institute for Women where she was interviewed by at least two officers with respect to her immigration status. At some point, she was informed of her right to contact counsel and says she tried without success to contact her counsel from the criminal trial. When she was eventually informed she was being arrested on an immigration hold, she took steps to retain a lawyer specializing in immigration matters. A report on the factual grounds for proceeding with an admissibility hearing was written on May 29, 2007. The immigration officer reviewing the case interviewed the applicant and recommended that she seek legal advice on June 4th. She provided her telephone number should the applicant wish to contact her. The applicant made no contact with the officer over the next two weeks. The manager acting as a Ministerial delegate on June 18 referred the case for an admissibility hearing on the basis of the officer's report. These steps were taken pursuant to s. 44 of the IRPA. On July 4, 2007, the applicant's counsel wrote to the manager requesting the opportunity to provide further information before the s. 44 report was written. On July 11, the enforcement officer replied noting that the applicant had already been referred for an admissibility hearing and had been arrested and detained for that purpose. The officer also noted that she had been contacted by the applicant's criminal law firm and that she had offered to forward any submissions they wished to make to the enforcement office which would be scheduling the admissibility hearing. The applicant challenged the decision of the enforcement officer to prepare the report and the decision of the manager to refer the report for an admissibility hearing. The applicant alleged a heightened duty on immigration officials when dealing with the person in custody, given the restrictions on their liberty, and suggested that the officer should have contacted the criminal lawyer herself or gone back to the applicant after the two weeks to inquire whether the applicant had done anything about her situation.

While it is true that persons in the custody of the state are subject to limits on their freedom, they are not barred from seeking and obtaining legal services. Immigration officers cannot be required to act as the bridge between incarcerated persons who are the subject of s. 44 report and whatever counsel they have or may wish to have. In this case, the application was dismissed.

The Court of Appeal did not answer the general question certified by the applications Judge stating it was too vague, and that the scope and content of the duty of fairness will vary depending on the circumstances of each case. The Court of Appeal dismissed the appeal.

*Golestaneh v. Canada (Minister of Public Safety & Emergency Preparedness)*, 2007 CarswellNat 1233, 2007 FC 509 (F.C.) — Pursuant to subs. 44(1) of IRPA an enforcement officer at the Canadian Border Services Agency prepared a report alleging that the applicant was inadmissible, as per paragraphs 34(1)(f) and 35(1)(a) of the Act, by reason of his involvement with a listed terrorist entity in Canada. The report prepared by the enforcement officer was referred by the Minister of Public Safety and Emergency Preparedness to the Immigration Division of the Immigration Refugee Board for an admissibility hearing. The applicant sought judicial review of the decisions made under subs. 44(1) and 44(2) of the Act.

The enforcement officer did not have access to the documentation supporting the security intelligence report prepared by the Canadian Security Intelligence Services (CSIS). The enforcement officer's decision was limited to reading the report itself. This alone was a serious error of law that justified setting aside the decision of the enforcement officer. Although the CSIS document may set out precisely the grounds on inadmissibility of the applicant, the officer who must decide whether to issue a subs. 44(1) report has a duty, when examining the file for the first time, to consult all of the reference documents, including the appendices to the CSIS report and the information on the sources underlying this report, before making a decision. This is necessary in order to ensure that the procedure followed will sufficiently guarantee the independence of the decision maker and thus, protect the rights of the individual concerned.

The decision of the enforcement officer to prepare a report for the Minister, and the subsequent decision by the Minister to refer the report to the Immigration Division for an admissibility hearing, was set aside and the file was referred back to a different enforcement officer for re-determination.

*Sui v. Canada (Minister of Public Safety & Emergency Preparedness)* (2006), 58 Imm. L.R. (3d) 135, [2007] 3 F.C.R. 218, 2006 CarswellNat 3554, 2006 FC 1314 (F.C.) — The applicant was in Canada for several years as a temporary resident on a study permit. Before his study permit expired, he applied for a post-graduation work permit. He received a letter from CIC informing him that he did not meet the requirements for a work permit and that he should leave Canada immediately, failing which enforcement action would be taken against him. Within 90 days of the expiration of his study permit and within 90 days of losing his temporary resident status, he applied to have his status restored pursuant to Regulation 182. While awaiting a decision on his application for restoration, two immigration officers attended his home and questioned him. Two inadmissibility reports were issued, the first based on paragraph 40(1)(a) of the IRPA and the fact that "there were reasonable grounds to believe that this foreign national was inadmissible for directly or indirectly misrepresenting or withholding material facts relating to a relevant matter that induces or could induce an error in administration of this Act." The second report was based on paragraph 41(a) and subs. 29(2) of the IRPA and the fact that the applicant was inadmissible for failing to comply with his obligation as a temporary resident to leave Canada by the end of the period authorized for his stay. A Minister's delegate decided to issue an exclusion order based on paragraph 41(a) and subs. 29(2) of the IRPA. In light of s. 225 of the Regulations, this meant that the applicant could not come back to Canada without written consent of the Minister for a period of one year following his departure. The applicant left Canada. No decision with respect to the application for restoration was ever made. In this case, the Minister's delegate had the discretion and even the duty to consider the fact that the applicant had applied for restoration well before a s. 44(1) report was issued against him in respect of his failure to leave Canada at the end of his authorized stay. It was an error of law to consider that the applicant was not entitled to make such an application for restoration simply because after the filing of his application in accordance with the Regulations, a s. 44(1) report had been issued on the sole basis of subs. 29(2) of the IRPA. The decision was set aside.

The following questions were certified:

> 1. Is an application for restoration pursuant to s. 182 of the Regulations a relevant consideration when the Minister's delegate considers whether or not to make an exclusion order based on a failure to comply with s. 29(2) of the IRPA?
>
> 2. foreign national who has applied for restoration within the delay set out in s. 182 of the Regulations, automatically lose the benefit of his or her application when an enforcement officer considers issuing a report under s. 44(1) on the basis of a failure to comply with s. 29(2) of the IRPA.

*Uppal v. Canada (Minister of Citizenship & Immigration)* (2006), 53 Imm. L.R. (3d) 284, 289 F.T.R. 196, 2006 CarswellNat 697, 2006 FC 338 (F.C.) — When the applicant came from the United Kingdom claiming to be a visitor, he produced a British passport which the Canadian authorities had been notified had been obtained fraudulently. A report was written under subs. 44(1) of the IRPA alleging that the applicant was inadmissible under paragraph 36(1)(c) in that there were reasonable grounds to believe the applicant was inadmissible on grounds of serious criminality because of his commission of an act outside of Canada, that if committed in Canada would be an offence under an Act of Parliament punishable by a maximum term of at least 10 years.

The report set out the factual information upon which the report was based. It also referred to the Canadian equivalent offence of the *Criminal Code* and recited the wording of that provision. The matter was referred to an admissibility hearing. Prior to the hearing, the report was amended to substitute another section of the *Criminal Code* as the Canadian equivalent offence.

The substitution of an equivalent Canadian offence that better conforms to the offence alleged to have been committed does not affect the substance of the subs. 44(1) report. It follows that the substitution of one particular provision of the Code that better depicts or corresponds to the impugned act than another, does not necessitate a withdrawal of the report such that the subs. 44(2) decision is returned to its preliminary stage.

The applicant received formal notice of the substitution of the equivalent offence along with a supplemental disclosure package. Furthermore, no objection was taken to the amendment of the subs. 44(1) report prior to or during the hearing. The failure to make a timely objection constitutes, if not an unequivocal waiver, an implied waiver.

*Aksenova v. Canada (Minister of Public Safety & Emergency Preparedness)*, [2006] F.C.J. No. 699, 2006 CarswellNat 1204, 2006 FC 557 (F.C.) — The immigration officer issued a report against the applicant under subs. 44(1) of the IRPA because she was deemed inadmissible to Canada pursuant to paragraph 36(2)(a), having been convicted in Canada of an offence punishable by indictment. On the basis of that report, a deportation order was then issued by the Minister's delegate under subs. 44(2). The Court considered whether in exercising its discretion to issue a report and make a deportation order, the officer and the Minister's delegate considered that the applicant was granted admission to Canada twice after she was convicted of an offence in Canada. The Court concluded that the fact that the applicant was admitted to Canada twice after being convicted of an offence in Canada is not included in the exceptions set out under subs. 36(3) of IRPA dealing with inadmissibility to Canada. Therefore, the officer and delegate made no error by not considering them before they acted as they did. The particular circumstances of a person are irrelevant considerations and at most, the delegate could have stayed or deferred the making of the order if the applicant had already been subjected to an effective removal order, if plans had been made to leave Canada or if the applicant had been a witness called to testify in proceedings held in Canada. None of these considerations were applicable in this case. "Particular circumstances of the person" were said to be irrelevant. Although both subs. 44(1) and (2) use the term "may" in enabling the officer to prepare a report and the delegate to make a removal order, the statutory scheme enacted by the IRPA limits the discretion vested in the officer and the delegate. The term "may" in subs. 44(1) and (2) must be read in conjunction with subs. 36(3), which sets out the exceptions to inadmissibility.

*Awed v. Canada (Minister of Citizenship & Immigration)*, 2006 CarswellNat 1077, 2006 FC 469 (F.C.) — The purpose of the interview under s. 44(1) is simply to confirm the facts that may support the formation of an opinion by the officer that a permanent resident or foreign national present in Canada is inadmissible. The use of the word "may" in s. 44(1) does not connote discretion but merely that the officer is authorized to perform an administrative function.

While it may be more efficient to allow the officer to exercise discretion at this stage of the process, such as to decide whether a criminal conviction should be discounted because of mental illness, the officer is not empowered by the enactment to make such a determination. The formation of the officer's opinion merely initiates a process which may or may not result in removal. In every case, it remains open to the applicant to seek an exception on humanitarian and compassionate grounds or a pre-removal risk assessment.

Where an immigration officer calls a permanent resident or foreign national for an interview in order to confirm the facts that would support a s. 44(1) opinion and report, the content of the duty of fairness is minimal. However, even a minimal degree of fairness would require that the officer advise the person of the purpose of the interview if only to put the person on notice of the possible consequences and to consider his options.

The officer, in this case, breached the duty of fairness by not informing the applicant that the status of his presence in Canada was in question because of his criminal convictions. Since there was nothing in the material to indicate that the officer's opinion was incorrect, the outcome would have been the same had another officer been directed to make the same inquiry. Accordingly, the decision was not set aside.

*Mugesera c. Canada (Ministre de la Citoyenneté & de l'Immigration)*, [2005] 2 S.C.R. 91, 47 Imm. L.R. (3d) 1, [2005] S.C.J. No. 40, EYB 2005-91970, 197 C.C.C. (3d) 225, 254 D.L.R. (4th) 193, 30 C.R. (6th) 107, 335 N.R. 220, 15 C.P.C. (6th) 51, 2005 CarswellNat 1738, 2005 CarswellNat 1739, 2005 SCC 39 — At the secondary level of appellate review, the Federal Court of Appeal should proceed with the review of the Minister's allegations on the basis of the facts as found by the Immigration Appeal Division. On questions of law, however, the standard of review is correctness and the Immigration Appeal Division is not entitled to deference when it comes to defining the elements of a crime or whether the Minister's burden of proof has been discharged. Where the Minister relies on a crime committed abroad, a conclusion that the elements of the crime in Canadian criminal law had been made out will be deemed to be determinative in respect of the commission of crimes under the foreign criminal law. With respect to the specific allegations made pursuant to s. 27(1) of the former *Immigration Act*, the evidence adduced by the Minister must meet the civil standard of the balance of probabilities. The appellant, an active member of a hard-line Hutu political party opposed to a negotiation process then under way to end the war, spoke to about 1,000 people at a meeting of the party in Rwanda. The content of the speech eventually led the Rwandan authorities to issue the equivalent of an arrest warrant against the appellant. He fled the country and successfully applied for permanent residence in Canada. After the immigrant landed in Canada, the Minister became aware of allegations against him and commenced proceeding to deport him, on the basis that he committed criminal acts or offences. Specifically, the issue was whether a speech delivered by the appellant in Rwanda triggered a series of events that led to murder, hatred and genocide. In this case, the Minister had to prove that, on the facts of the case as found on a balance of probabilities, the speech constituted an incitement to murder, genocide or hatred. The Supreme Court of Canada upheld the validity of the deportation order on the basis that each element of the offence under the *Criminal Code* had been made out and that there were reasonable grounds to believe that the immigrant committed a crime against humanity and was therefore inadmissible under the former *Immigration Act*. The "reasonable grounds to believe" standard requires more than mere suspicion, but less than the normal civil litigation standard of proof on the balance of probabilities.

*Lasin v. Canada (Minister of Citizenship & Immigration)*, [2005] F.C.J. No. 1655, 2005 CarswellNat 3130, 2005 CarswellNat 4337, 2005 FC 1356 (F.C.) — The failure of the immigration officer to provide a reasonable opportunity for the applicant to present evidence on mitigating factors over the course of the subs. 44(2) proceeding, such as his two-year marriage to a Canadian citizen and his outstanding H&C application, does not constitute a breach of procedural fairness. Decisions under s. 44(1) and (2) are routine administrative decisions. Issues relating to humanitarian and compassionate considerations or the safety of the applicant are obviously vital to the applicant, however, they have no place in these routine administrative proceedings. Rather, the Act provides specific procedures for dealing with them in ss. 25 and 112, respectively.

*Hernandez v. Canada (Minister of Citizenship & Immigration)* (2005), 45 Imm. L.R. (3d) 249, 2005 CarswellNat 825, 2005 FC 429 (F.C.) — The applicant, a permanent resident of Canada, was sentenced to 30 months for possession of cocaine for the purposes of trafficking.

An immigration officer interviewed the applicant. The purpose of this interview was to decide whether to write a report under s. 44(1). The officer decided to write a report and sent it to the director of case management. The officer recommended that an admissibility hearing be held. The Minister's delegate concurred in the officer's recommendation and an admissibility hearing was held. The applicant was ordered deported.

In this application, the applicant sought to review three decisions: the officer's report; the decision to refer the matter for an admissibility hearing; and the decision to issue the deportation order. This proceeding involved a combination of three different federal court files. Sections 44(1) and 44(2) are broad enough to allow the Minister's delegate to consider the factors outlined in the relevant sections of the CIC procedure manual.

The duty of fairness required in a s. 44 decision is more relaxed. The affected person should have the right to make submissions, either orally or in writing, and to obtain a copy of the report. Implicit in the duty of fairness is a requirement that the person being interviewed is informed of the purpose of the interview. The interviewing officer should put to the person concerned any information which the person would not reasonably be expected to have. The person concerned should be offered the opportunity to have counsel present at the interview or to assist in the preparation of written submissions. An oral interview may not always be required as long as the affected person is given an opportunity to make submissions and to know the case against him or her. The duty of fairness does not require that the applicant be given a further opportunity to respond prior to the s. 44(2) referral.



*Aguillar v. Canada (Minister of Citizenship & Immigration)*, 45 Imm. L.R. (3d) 16, 2005 CarswellNat 313, 2005 FC 152 (F.C.) — The applicant sought to overturn a decision that determined that he was inadmissible and ordered his deportation. Under subs. 86(1) the Minister may make an application for non-disclosure of information. The determination is made in accordance with s. 78. The application will be allowed if the information is injurious to national security or the safety of any person.

The immunity from disclosure which is accorded in relation to information furnished to the police in the course of their performance of their duties is general in its scope. This has become recognized as a rule of law with only one recognized exception, namely, where upon the trial of the defendant for a criminal offence, disclosure of the identity of the informer could help show that the defendant was innocent. The value of informers to police investigations has long been recognized. As long as crimes have been committed, informers have played an important role in their investigation. Some informers act for compensation or for self-serving purposes. Whatever their motives, the position of informers is always precarious and their role is fraught with danger.

*Leong v. Canada (Solicitor General)*, 41 Imm. L.R. (3d) 48, 2004 CarswellNat 4848, 2004 CarswellNat 2842, 256 F.T.R. 298, 2004 FC 1126, [2004] F.C.J. No. 1369 (F.C.) — A relatively low level of procedural fairness is owed when the initial s. 44(1) report is being prepared. Consequently, the officer did not err by failing to inform the applicant that a report was being considered, nor was the applicant entitled to make written submissions before the decision was made.

*Correia v. Canada (Minister of Citizenship & Immigration)*, 36 Imm. L.R. (3d) 139, 2004 CarswellNat 2982, 2004 CarswellNat 1561, 2004 FC 782, [2004] F.C.J. No. 964, 253 F.T.R. 153 (F.C.) — The applicant was a 56-year-old citizen of Guyana who had been a permanent resident of Canada since 1968 and had a history of criminal activity. Immigration officials began the process of removing the applicant and on April 7, 2003, an officer made a report pursuant to s. 44(1) of the Act that the applicant was inadmissible by reason of serious criminality. On the next day a delegate of the Minister referred the report to the Immigration Division for an admissibility hearing. A removal order was issued by the Immigration Division and the applicant brought this application for judicial review as a result.

Section 44(1) involves two different acts by the officer: first there is the formation of an opinion concerning inadmissibility, and second, there is the decision to make a report. The discretion not to report is extremely limited and rare, otherwise, it would give officials a level of discretion not even enjoyed by the responsible Minister.

For the purposes of s. 44(1) the report is restricted to "relevant facts". In the case of serious criminality, those facts relate to the fact of the conviction. The nature of the inquiry does not involve issues of humanitarian and compassionate matters, rehabilitation or other such factors. The facts essentially involve the fact of the conviction and the length of the sentence. The officer has no jurisdiction to consider humanitarian and compassionate issues in issuing his or her report. The inquiry regarding serious criminality can be contrasted with that involving organized criminality, health grounds or misrepresentation, and on these other grounds of inadmissibility, officials are required to make judgements both as to fact and law. Therefore, the nature of those inquiries is quite different from the very straight forward inquiry as to serious criminality.

It is difficult to see what purpose an interview would serve in this type of inquiry. The fact that the interview, in this case, was held after the decision to refer was made was a breach of procedural fairness, but there was no reason to quash the decision because the applicant was unable to suggest what relevant facts could have been put to the delegate which would in any way have altered the decision to refer the matter.

## Section 44(2)

*Lee v. Canada (Minister of Citizenship & Immigration)*, [2006] F.C.J. No. 260, 2006 CarswellNat 381, 2006 FC 158 (F.C.) — Subsection 44(2) of the IRPA confers the power to refer a report to the Immigration Division in subjective terms. The test is not whether the report is well founded, but whether the Minister is "of the opinion" that the report is well founded. There is ample authority that unless the overall scheme of the Act indicated otherwise, such subjective decisions cannot be judicially reviewed except on grounds that the decision maker acted in bad faith, erred in law, or acted on the basis of irrelevant considerations. When confronted with the record which was before the decision maker and there is no evidence to the contrary, the Court must assume that the decision maker acted in good faith having regard to the material.

The fact is, under the IRPA, a permanent resident will not have his case reviewed in the same manner and with as much formality as he would have under the previous legislation. That is the clear effect of the legislation. It is consistent with the purposes of the legislation. It is more difficult under the IRPA for serious criminals to prevent their removal.

*Cha v. Canada (Minister of Citizenship & Immigration)*, [2006] F.C.J. No. 491, 53 Imm. L.R. (3d) 1, 267 D.L.R. (4th) 324, 349 N.R. 233, 2006 CarswellNat 751, 2006 FCA 126 (C.A.) — The intent of Parliament is clear. The Minister's delegate is only empowered under subs. 44(2) of the Act to make the removal orders in prescribed cases which are clear and non-controversial and where the facts simply dictate the remedy. The Minister's delegate could not look at the gravity of the offence, and the particular circumstances of the applicant and his conviction, in determining not to issue the removal order. It is simply not open to the Minister's delegate to indirectly or collaterally go beyond the actual conviction. To do so would ignore Parliament's clearly expressed intent that the breaking of the condition of non-criminality be determinative. Although the manual indicates that the personal circumstances of the offender will be considered at the front-end of the process before any decision is taken to remove an individual from Canada, these views and statements have been expressed in respect to permanent residents convicted of serious offences in Canada. No such assurances were given by specific reference to foreign nationals. A foreign national may wish to invoke humanitarian and compassionate considerations and is at liberty to make a request to the Minister pursuant to s. 25 of the Act or to stay a removal order pursuant to s. 233 of the Regulations, or avail himself of the pre-removal risk assessment proceeding pursuant to s. 112 of the Act.

Absent a *Charter* right to be notified of a right to counsel on arrest or detention, there is no authority for the proposition that a person is entitled as of right to be notified before a hearing that he or she has either a statutory right or a duty-of-fairness right to counsel. Once a person is sufficiently informed of the object and possible effects of a forthcoming hearing — absent sufficient notice, the decision rendered will in all likelihood be set aside — the decision maker is under no duty to go further.

It may be sound practice, in certain cases, to give notice in advance that counsel may be retained, but there is no duty to do so unless the statute requires it. The responsibility lies with the person to seek leave from the decision maker to be accompanied by counsel or to come to the hearing accompanied by counsel.

In the recent IRPA, the right to be informed of one's right to counsel in admissibility matters has disappeared and the right to counsel has been preserved only with respect to hearings before the Immigration Division. There is no provision concerning the right to counsel and proceedings before the immigration officer or the Minister's delegate under subs. 44(1) and (2) of the IRPA. In this case, the respondent did not seek leave to have counsel present during the interview or to attend accompanied by counsel.

If leave is denied or if counsel is not allowed to be present, that could become an issue in a judicial review of the decision ultimately rendered.

*Aksenova v. Canada (Minister of Public Safety & Emergency Preparedness)*, [2006] F.C.J. No. 699, 2006 CarswellNat 1204, 2006 FC 557 (F.C.) — The immigration officer issued a report against the applicant under subs. 44(1) of the IRPA because she was deemed inadmissible to Canada pursuant to paragraph 36(2)(a), having been convicted in Canada of an offence punishable by indictment. On the basis of that report, a deportation order was then issued by the Minister's delegate under subs. 44(2). The Court considered whether in exercising its discretion to issue a report and make a deportation order, the officer and the Minister's delegate considered that the applicant was granted admission to Canada twice after she was convicted of an offence in Canada. The Court concluded that the fact that the applicant was admitted to Canada twice after being convicted of an offence in Canada is not included in the exceptions set out under subs. 36(3) of IRPA dealing with inadmissibility to Canada. Therefore, the officer and delegate made no error by not considering them before they acted as they did. The particular circumstances of a person are irrelevant considerations and at most, the delegate could have stayed or deferred the making of the order if the applicant had already been subjected to an effective removal order, if plans had been made to leave Canada or if the applicant had been a witness called to testify in proceedings held in Canada. None of these considerations were applicable in this case. "Particular circumstances of the person" were said to be irrelevant. Although both subs. 44(1) and (2) use the term "may" in enabling the officer to prepare a report and the delegate to make a removal order, the statutory scheme enacted by the IRPA limits the discretion vested in the officer and the delegate. The term "may" in subs. 44(1) and (2) must be read in conjunction with subs. 36(3), which sets out the exceptions to inadmissibility.

*Lasin v. Canada (Minister of Citizenship & Immigration)*, [2005] F.C.J. No. 1655, 2005 CarswellNat 3130, 2005 CarswellNat 4337, 2005 FC 1356 (F.C.) — The failure of the immigration officer to provide a reasonable opportunity for the applicant to present evidence on mitigating factors over the course of the subs. 44(2) proceeding, such as his two-year marriage to a Canadian citizen and his outstanding H&C application, does not constitute a breach of procedural fairness. Decisions under s. 44(1) and (2) are routine administrative decisions. Issues relating to humanitarian and compassionate considerations or the safety of the applicant are obviously vital to the applicant. However, they have no place in these routine administrative proceedings. Rather, the Act provides specific procedures for dealing with them in ss. 25 and 112, respectively.

*El Idrissi c. Canada (Ministre de la Citoyenneté & de l'Immigration)*, 2005 CarswellNat 2421, 2005 CarswellNat 5248, 2005 FC 1105 (F.C.) — The applicant was given permanent residence status in 1991. In 1999, the applicant left Canada to visit his sick father and manage a family business in his home country. He did not return until June 15, 2003. He fell under the purview of s. 41 of the IRPA and a departure order was made against him by the Minister. He filed an appeal to the Immigration Appeal Division but conceded that the removal order against him was legally valid and the only issue he argued was that there were humanitarian and compassionate grounds to explain his failure to meet the residency obligation.

Simply having a wife in Canada was not sufficient for this situation to be considered a humanitarian and compassionate ground. The Appeal Division was entitled to consider that the applicant's plans for the future were vague. The applicant had the burden of establishing the existence of humanitarian and compassionate grounds.

*Hernandez v. Canada (Minister of Citizenship & Immigration)* (2005), 45 Imm. L.R. (3d) 249, 2005 CarswellNat 825, 2005 FC 429 (F.C.) — The applicant, a permanent resident of Canada, was sentenced to thirty months for possession of cocaine for the purposes of trafficking.

An immigration officer interviewed the applicant. The purpose of this interview was to decide whether to write a report under s. 44(1). The officer decided to write a report and sent it to the director of case management. The officer recommended that an admissibility hearing be held. The Minister's delegate concurred in the officer's recommendation and an admissibility hearing was held. The applicant was ordered deported.

In this application the applicant sought to review three decisions: the officer's report; the decision to refer the matter for an admissibility hearing; and the decision to issue the deportation order. This proceeding involved a combination of three different federal court files. Sections 44(1) and 44(2) are broad enough to allow the Minister's delegate to consider the factors outlined in the relevant sections of the CIC procedure manual.

The duty of fairness required in a s. 44 decision is more relaxed. The affected person should have the right to make submissions, either orally or in writing, and to obtain a copy of the report. Implicit in the duty of fairness is a requirement that the person being interviewed is informed of the purpose of the interview. The interviewing officer should put to the person concerned any information which the person would not reasonably be expected to have. The person concerned should be offered the opportunity to have counsel present at the interview or to assist in the preparation of written submissions. An oral interview may not always be required as long as the affected person is given an opportunity to make submissions and to know the case against him or her. The duty of fairness does not require that the applicant be given a further opportunity to respond prior to the s. 44(2) referral.

*Sogi v. Canada (Minister of Citizenship & Immigration)* (2004), 36 Imm. L.R. (3d) 1, 2004 CarswellNat 2880, 2004 CarswellNat 1599, 322 N.R. 2, 2004 FCA 212, 121 C.R.R. (2d) 137, [2005] 1 F.C.R. 171, [2004] F.C.J. No. 947 (F.C.A.); leave to appeal refused (2004), 2004 CarswellNat 4104, 2004 CarswellNat 4105, 121 C.R.R. (2d) 188 (note), [2004] S.C.C.A. No. 354 (S.C.C.) — As long as the availability of judicial review provides the appellant with an opportunity to have a Federal Court judge decide the propriety of keeping information confidential, the IRPA procedure must be found to be in accordance with the principles of fundamental justice.

Subsection 86(2) provides that the procedures set out in s. 78 apply to the determination of an application for non-disclosure before an Immigration Division member. If the member decides that the information or evidence is not relevant, or that it is relevant but should be included in the summary provided to the individual, paragraph 78(f) requires the information to be returned to the Minister. Section 78(g) allows the member to consider relevant but potentially injurious material without disclosing it. That subsection makes no mention of subsequently returning the considered material to the Minister. Any information considered by the member under paragraph 78(g) forms part of the Immigration Division's record, albeit a confidential portion.

Under Rule 14 of the *Federal Court Immigration and Refugee Protection Rules*, where a judge considers the documents in the possession or control of a tribunal are required for a proper disposition of the application for leave, the judge may order the Immigration Division to produce the documents. Once leave is granted, Rule 17 requires the Board to prepare a record including all documents in possession or control of the tribunal and submit it to the Court. When the confidential information is produced to the Court, the Minister may make an application under subs. 87(1) for continued non-disclosure.

If information is to be returned to CSIS, an undertaking must be given that the precise information that was before the Immigration Division member will be produced for judicial review purposes. The confidential information must be retained intact, in a format that allows for precise identification of what information was considered by the Immigration Division member. The information that has been considered by the member and returned to CSIS must be considered "information under the control of the tribunal for the purposes of its production to the Federal Court on judicial review." If information is returned to CSIS, the onus is on the Minister to satisfy the judge hearing the judicial review that the precise record that was before the member has been provided to the Court. In the event that the evidence was not transcribed, an affidavit attesting to the evidence given before the member would be required.

The standard of review for a decision whether information supplied by the Minister *in camera* should have been considered by the Member without completely disclosing it is correctness. Considering the correctness of the Immigration Division member's decision, the judge will make his or her own assessment of whether disclosure of the confidential information would be injurious to national security or the safety of any person.

If the judicial review is allowed, the information will not immediately be disclosed, rather, in remitting the matter to the Immigration Division, the judge may direct that some or all of the information be included in the summary to be provided to the affected individual. In such a case, it will be up to the Minister to decide whether that information should be disclosed to the individual in order to allow it to be considered by the Immigration Division member, or withdrawn from consideration in order to maintain the confidentiality of the information.

The precise record that was before the Immigration Division member will be before the judge conducting the judicial review and the member's decision not to disclose will be reviewed on a correctness standard. For these reasons, the IRPA procedure is in accordance with the principles of fundamental justice.

## *Admissibility Hearing by the Immigration Division*

**45. Decision — The Immigration Division, at the conclusion of an admissibility hearing, shall make one of the following decisions:**

**(a) recognize the right to enter Canada of a Canadian citizen within the meaning of the *Citizenship Act*, a person registered as an Indian under the *Indian Act* or a permanent resident;**

**(b) grant permanent resident status or temporary resident status to a foreign national if it is satisfied that the foreign national meets the requirements of this Act;**

**(c) authorize a permanent resident or a foreign national, with or without conditions, to enter Canada for further examination; or**

**(d) make the applicable removal order against a foreign national who has not been authorized to enter Canada, if it is satisfied that the foreign national is not inadmissible, or against a foreign national who has been authorized to enter Canada or a permanent resident, if it is satisfied that the foreign national or the permanent resident is inadmissible.**

## Case Law

*Wajaras v. Canada (Minister of Citizenship & Immigration)* (2009), 2009 FC 200, 2009 CarswellNat 530, 2009 CarswellNat 1116 (F.C.) — The applicant sought to set aside a decision of the Immigration Division that found him to be inadmissible to Canada on the ground of serious criminality in accordance with s. 36(1)(a) of IRPA. The applicant entered Canada in 1997 as a Convention refugee and was granted permanent resident status at that time. He subsequently committed a serious assault and was criminally charged and sentenced to three years imprisonment in 2005.

The CBSA made an inadmissibility report which lead to an inadmissibility hearing before the Board under s. 44(2) of the IRPA. The applicant was advised of the CBSA's intention to have him declared a danger to the public. Notwithstanding his refugee status, such a finding would have permitted his return to Sudan in the event that he was also found to be inadmissible. The Minister determined that the applicant did not represent a danger to the public. In the result he could not be returned to Sudan even though he had been determined to be inadmissible and was the subject of a corresponding removal order. The applicant argued before the Board that it was an abuse of process for the Minister to seek a removal order against him with the resulting loss of permanent resident status in circumstances where his removal could not be lawfully effected.

The Federal Court concluded that notwithstanding that the Board erred in law by stating that the doctrine of abuse of process required evidence of malice or animus, a question remained as to whether an abuse of process argument could be sustained on this particular record. The Federal Court concluded it could not and the Board's mistake, therefore, was of no consequence. The application for judicial review was set aside. The applicant was solely responsible for the position he found himself in. He is not without potential future recourse. If administrative decisions are made which unlawfully interfere with his interests, including the opportunity to work, he would have the right to seek judicial review. If he stays out of legal trouble, enhances his Canadian establishment and continues to make positive social and economic contributions, he would be in a position at some point to pursue humanitarian and compassionate relief under s. 25 of the IRPA.

An abuse of process argument cannot be built around selective references to the purposes of the IRPA. The legislation serves many purposes, not the least of which is protecting Canadians by imposing consequences for the criminal behaviour of a few of those who have emigrated here.

The Federal Court judge certified a question and the Federal Court of Appeal in *Wajaras v. Canada (Minister of Citizenship & Immigration)* (2010), 399 N.R. 31, 2010 FCA 41, 2010 CarswellNat 266, 2010 CarswellNat 623 concluded that the Minister of Citizenship and Immigration does not engage in abuse of process in continuing to seek a removal order where the effected individual has been determined not to be a danger to the public. The Federal Court of Appeal concluded that it was not improper for the Minister to seek a deportation order for the purpose of depriving a permanent resident of this status as a result of serious criminality, even where there are impediments to removal. The appeal was dismissed.

*Powell v. Canada (Minister of Citizenship & Immigration)*, 45 Imm. L.R. (3d) 210, 2005 CarswellNat 1489, 2005 FCA 202 (F.C.A.) — Assuming, without deciding, that the appellant's liberty interest is engaged, the scheme of the IRPA which may result in the removal of the appellant, a foreign national, pursuant to subs. 45(d), does not violate the principles of fundamental justice.



## Loss of Status

**46. (1) Permanent resident — A person loses permanent resident status**

**(a) when they become a Canadian citizen;**

**(b) on a final determination of a decision made outside of Canada that they have failed to comply with the residency obligation under section 28;**

**(c) when a removal order made against them comes into force; or**

**(d) on a final determination under section 109 to vacate a decision to allow their claim for refugee protection or a final determination under subsection 114(3) to vacate a decision to allow their application for protection.**

**(2) Permanent resident — A person who ceases to be a citizen under paragraph 10(1)(a) of the *Citizenship Act*, other than in the circumstances set out in subsection 10(2) of that Act, becomes a permanent resident.**

*[Editor's Note: SOR/2002-227, s. 328(1) provides that a person who was a permanent resident immediately before June 28, 2002 is a permanent resident under the new* Immigration and Refugee Protection Act, *S.C. 2001, c. 27.]*

**47. Temporary resident — A foreign national loses temporary resident status**

**(a) at the end of the period for which they are authorized to remain in Canada;**

**(b) on a determination by an officer or the Immigration Division that they have failed to comply with any other requirement of this Act; or**

**(c) on cancellation of their temporary resident permit.**

*[Editor's Note: SOR/2002-227, s. 329(1) provides that any of the following persons who were in Canada immediately before June 28, 2002 are temporary residents under the new* Immigration and Refugee Protection Act, *S.C. 2001, c. 27 and are subject to its provisions:*

*(a) a visitor under the* Immigration Act, *R.S.C. 1985, c. I-2 (the "former Act"); and*

*(b) a person issued a permit under s. 37 of the former Act.]*

## Case Law

*Zhang v. Canada (Minister of Citizenship & Immigration)* (2006), 59 Imm. L.R. (3d) 165, 2006 CarswellNat 3831, 2006 FC 1381 (F.C.) — The applicant moved to British Columbia in 2002 on a temporary student permit that was valid until August 2004. He applied for and was granted an extension to August 30, 2005. Since he wanted to continue his studies, he applied for a further extension in August 2005. The officer concluded he was not a *bona fide* student and did not intend to leave Canada at the end of his stay. The applicant did not leave Canada, nor did he seek leave of the Court to challenge the decision to refuse his extension application. Instead, the applicant submitted a restoration application seeking to re-acquire the temporary status he had lost. The applicant's restoration application was refused. The officer's letter essentially quoted paragraph 47(a) of the IRPA and s. 182 of its accompanying Regulations, and simply stated that the applicant was refused as he was not satisfied the applicant met those criteria. It was perfectly legitimate for the applicant to apply for restoration instead of judicial review of the initial decision to extend his study permit. While the immigration officer could take the extension decision into consideration, he also had to assess the applicant's new evidence in support of his claim that the initial decision was mistaken or did not reflect his true intentions. It is true that there is nothing in the IRPA requiring an immigration officer to provide reasons to an applicant. But it is well established that the duty of procedural fairness sometimes requires that explanations be given for a particular decision. In the present case, the mere recital of the relevant sections of the IRPA and the Regulations was clearly not sufficient. The applicant submitted further evidence that he was a *bona fide* student. He is certainly entitled to some explanation as to why these further documents were inadequate to show that he was a *bona fide* student. As a result of the negative restoration decision, the applicant was found to be inadmissible to Canada and the decision that he challenged before the Federal Court would have profound implications for him. The more important a decision is to the lives of those affected and the greater its impact on that person or those persons, the more stringent the procedural protections that will be mandated. Although a relatively low degree of procedural fairness is warranted in an immigration officer's decision to grant or deny an application to restore temporary resident status, a low level of procedural fairness still imposes some obligations on officers to provide reasons for negative decisions. The application for judicial review was granted.

## *Enforcement of Removal Orders*

**48. (1) Enforceable removal order — A removal order is enforceable if it has come into force and is not stayed.**

**(2) Effect — If a removal order is enforceable, the foreign national against whom it was made must leave Canada immediately and it must be enforced as soon as is reasonably practicable.**

## Case Law

### Section 48(1)

*Baron v. Canada (Minister of Public Safety & Emergency Preparedness)*, [2009] F.C.J. No. 314, 387 N.R. 278, 79 Imm. L.R. (3d) 157, 2009 CarswellNat 596, 2009 FCA 81 (C.A.) — The Court considered whether an application for judicial review of an enforcement officer's decision not to defer an applicant's scheduled removal from Canada becomes moot where the Court has stayed the removal and the applicant has remained in Canada.

The jurisprudence is conclusive that the enforcement officer's discretion is limited. However, ultimately an enforcement officer is intended to do nothing more than enforce a removal order. While enforcement officers are granted the discretion to fix new removal dates, they are not intended to defer removal to an indeterminate date. On the facts before the Court, the date of the decision on the H&C application was unknown and unlikely to be imminent, and thus, the enforcement officer was being asked to delay removal indeterminately. An indeterminate deferral was simply not within the enforcement officer's powers.

Over the years, the duties of enforcement officers have not changed, and yet, the basis upon which applicants rely to obtain deferrals have dramatically increased. The scope of the enforcement officer's discretion cannot be changed by virtue of the request made. An enforcement officer's role is not to assess the best interest of the children or the probability of success of any application. The enforcement officer's role should remain limited and deferral should be contemplated in very limited circumstances. The legislation has not provided a new step to claimants who desire yet another assessment of their circumstances. Claimants already have the refugee application process, the pre-removal risk assessment process and the H&C application in addition to judicial reviews of these processes and the stay before removal. In this case, it appears that the claimants want to open yet another avenue of review by asking the enforcement officer to reassess information that has already been examined by administrative tribunals and that was a subject of judicial review. For the enforcement officer to comply with this request for reassessment would be akin to the enforcement officer making a quasi-judicial order without the benefit of hearing from opposing counsel. It is time to stop this abusive cycle.

The appeal was dismissed. The removal date having passed, the determination of the reasonableness of the enforcement officer's refusal to defer the removal date in January 2007 was without consequence; the matter was rendered moot.

*Palka v. Canada (Minister of Public Safety & Emergency Preparedness)*, 2008 CarswellNat 1309, 2008 FCA 165 (F.C.A.) — The Palkas appealed from a decision of the Federal Court dismissing their application for judicial review of a refusal by an enforcement officer to defer their removal from Canada, until their application for permanent residence on humanitarian and compassionate grounds ("H&C") had been decided. The lower Court judge held that the application for judicial review was moot, and did not consider its merits. She based her finding of mootness on the fact that another judge of the Federal Court had stayed the Palkas' removal scheduled for June 13, 2007, pending the disposition of their application for judicial review of the officer's refusal to defer their removal. The lower Court judge rejected the position taken by both the Palkas and the respondent Minister of Public Safety & Emergency Preparedness, that the passing of the scheduled removal date did not render the application for judicial review moot because an application for permanent residence on H&C grounds was outstanding. The lower

Court judge certified a question for appeal on the mootness issue. The Palkas then brought a motion for a stay of removal to their country of nationality, pending the disposition of the appeal.

They argue that, if they are denied a stay, their appeal on the mootness decision will be nugatory. They claim that this would constitute irreparable harm. The Court did not agree. Even if their appeal was moot, the Court may decide to hear it in its discretion, on the ground that the question certified may arise repeatedly and be evasive of review. Even if a refusal of a stay does not render the appeal nugatory, this does not necessarily constitute irreparable harm. It all depends on the facts of the individual case.

Despite numerous attempts, through administrative and legal channels, the Palkas have been denied status in Canada. There has to be some finality. To grant yet another deferral of their removal is contrary to the public interest as expressed in the Act. Motion to defer removal was dismissed.

*Level (Litigation Guardian of) v. Canada (Minister of Public Safety & Emergency Preparedness)* (2008), 71 Imm. L.R. (3d) 52, 2008 CarswellNat 423, 2008 FC 227 (F.C.) — This was an application for judicial review of an enforcement officer's decision to deny the applicant's request for a deferral of removal pending a decision on his application for permanent residence based on an H&C application.

An enforcement officer is statutorily bound to remove an applicant as soon as reasonably practical. However, if the officer relies on extrinsic evidence not brought forward by the applicant, the applicant must be given an opportunity to respond to that evidence. This is a minimal duty of procedural fairness. In the application at bar, the enforcement officer relied on detailed evidence about medical conditions in Jamaica that the applicant contested in an affidavit filed in support of the applicant's successful motion for a stay of removal. With respect to tight time frames, the applicant has been in Canada for 20 years, and the duty of fairness should not be sacrificed because of an artificial deadline established by the respondent for the applicant's removal. There was no harm in allowing the applicant another week or two in order to respond to extrinsic evidence upon which the enforcement officer intends to rely. If that extrinsic evidence is incorrect, the applicant will suffer great harm. The application for judicial review was allowed.

*Maruthalingam v. Canada (Minister of Public Safety & Emergency Preparedness)*, [2007] F.C.J. No. 1079, 63 Imm. L.R. (3d) 242, 2007 CarswellNat 3088, 2007 CarswellNat 2278, 2007 FC 823 (F.C.) — The applicants were ordered to report for deportation and an enforcement officer refused the applicants' request that the removal from Canada be deferred. The applicants filed a notice of application for leave and judicial review of the enforcement officer's decision and brought a motion for a stay of their removal until the Court had disposed of the application for judicial review. The motion for the stay was granted. The applicants were not removed. By the time this judicial review application was heard by the Court, the serious issues identified in the stay motion were, in practical terms, academic. This application for judicial review was dismissed. The applicants raised the issue of whether the Court should still rule that the issue was moot where it was asked to stay the removal until the outcome of another process. The Court refused to opine as to whether the Court could grant a remedy to the applicants on a free-standing basis. The applicants had not sought an order to stay the removal until the final determination of their outstanding application on humanitarian and compassionate grounds. Instead, their sole request was that the matter be referred to another enforcement officer for reconsideration. The Court certified the following question:

> Where an applicant has filed an application for leave and judicial review of a decision not to defer the implementation of a removal order outstanding against him or her, does the fact that the applicant's removal is subsequently halted by operation of a stay order issued by this Court render the underlying judicial review application moot?

See also *Vu v. Canada (Minister of Citizenship & Immigration)*, 2007 CarswellNat 3591 (FC)



*Higgins v. Canada (Minister of Public Safety & Emergency Preparedness)*, [2007] F.C.J. No. 516, 64 Imm. L.R. (3d) 98, 2007 CarswellNat 1841, 2007 CarswellNat 832, 2007 FC 377 (F.C.) — By order dated June 29, 2006, the Court stayed the removal of the applicant from Canada pending final determination of this application for judicial review. The granting of the stay gave the applicant his remedy before the merits of the application for judicial review were addressed.

If the respondent remains determined to remove the applicant before his humanitarian and compassionate grounds application is determined, it would be open to the applicant to request a new deferral of removal, based on all of the current circumstances and evidence. If that request is denied, a further application for leave and for judicial review would be open to him together with a further motion before the Court seeking a stay of removal pending the final determination of that new application for leave and for judicial review.

The application for judicial review was moot. The Court refused to exercise discretion to hear the matter.

*Kovacs v. Canada (Minister of Public Safety & Emergency Preparedness)*, [2007] F.C.J. No. 1625, 68 Imm. L.R. (3d) 218, 2007 CarswellNat 4247, 2007 CarswellNat 5009, 2007 FC 1247 (F.C.) — There will no doubt be cases where the Court can provide an important precedent; in such a situation the Court may decide to exercise its discretion. This is not such a case. The issue in this judicial review is simply whether the enforcement officer had regard to the evidence before him. A ruling on this issue would not have any practical side effects on the rights of the parties.

The judicial review was dismissed. The following question was certified:

> Where an applicant has filed an application for leave and judicial review of a decision not to defer the implementation of a removal order outstanding against him or her, does the fact that the applicant's removal is subsequently halted by operation of a stay order issued by this Court render the underlying judicial review application moot?

See also *Islami v. Canada (Minster of Citizenship & Immigration)*, 2008 CarswellNat 702

*Tesoro v. Canada (Minister of Citizenship & Immigration)*, 2005 CarswellNat 2049, 2005 CarswellNat 1083, 2005 FCA 148, [2005] F.C.J. No. 698 (F.C.A.) — The appellant brought a motion to stay his removal pending the disposition of an appeal to the Federal Court of Appeal from a decision of a motions judge. In that decision, the motions judge dismissed his application for judicial review of the refusal of the Immigration Appeal Division to re-open its rejection of his appeal.

The IAD does not lose jurisdiction over an application for the re-opening of an appeal because the applicant, who was in Canada when the application was filed, left under a removal order before the IAD considered it.

On a motion to stay a removal pending the disposition of an application for judicial review or an appeal, the focus is limited to the effect of the deportee's temporary absence from Canada pending the disposition of the legal proceedings.

Decisions on the grant of stays tend to be fact specific. Motions can come on at very short notice and decisions are often rendered under severe time constraints. Hence, it is not surprising to find some inconsistency in the case law. Irreparable harm, in this context, may include family separation and is not limited to threats to a deportee's life and limb. The more difficult issue is to delineate the circumstances in which family separation and the disruption of personal and other important relationships constitute irreparable harm. The question is the impact of removal on the appellant and his family as a result of the separation and whether that will be more than the usual consequences of deportation. It is relevant, when considering the separation of the appellant from his parents, that his parents are getting on in years and that his mother has health problems and may not be able to travel to Italy to visit him.

If the Court had determined the appellant's removal would cause irreparable harm on the ground that the effects of family separation were more than mere inconveniences, the Court would have to balance that harm against the public interest in the prompt removal from Canada of those persons found to be inadmissible for serious criminality. If the administration of immigration law is to be credible, the prompt removal of those ordered deported must be the rule and the grant of a stay pending the disposition of legal proceedings the exception.

*Griffiths v. Canada (Minister of Citizenship & Immigration)*, 2005 CarswellNat 638, 2005 FC 329 (F.C.) — This was an application for a stay. The applicant came to Canada from Jamaica when he was six years old and has not been back since he arrived here. His mother and three siblings are all Canadian citizens. The applicant was ordered deported in 1994. He appealed and in 1995 was granted a four-year stay on conditions. One condition was that he remain crime-free. However, the applicant was convicted in 1996. In 1998, the stay of the deportation order was lifted; however, the applicant was not deported because he was facing two criminal charges. In January 2001, the applicant was acquitted of one criminal charge and pleaded guilty to the other. From that point on he could have been deported but the authorities were content to leave him alone until late 2003.

The applicant was given one working day's notice of the respondent's intention to remove him from Canada. The respondents argued that the motion for a stay should not be considered because the applicant's counsel had not submitted a full written memorandum of fact and law. Having required the applicant to seek an abridgement of the normal delays because of the extremely short notice given him, the respondents cannot be heard to complain that they were prejudiced because applicant's counsel did not have the time to generate a full set of written submissions. The Expulsion Officer refused to defer removal without considering the interests of the applicant's children. Although an Expulsion Officer is not required to carry out a full H&C analysis, he must take some account of the children.

Finally, the fact that the Minister waited three years before attempting to remove the applicant was taken into consideration in deciding to make the Minister wait for the outcome of the matters before the Federal Court before affecting removal.

*El Ouardi v. Canada (Solicitor General)*, 2005 CarswellNat 254, 2005 CarswellNat 1822, 332 N.R. 76, 2005 FCA 42, [2005] F.C.J. No. 189 (Fed. C.A.) — On the question of irreparable harm, the fact that an appeal will be rendered nugatory if a stay is not granted, will not always succeed in demonstrating irreparable harm. The difficulty with the argument is that it would apply to virtually all removal cases in which a stay is sought and would essentially deprive the Court of the discretion to decide questions of irreparable harm on the facts of each case.

*Canada (Solicitor General) v. Subhaschandran*, [2005] F.C.J. No. 107, 2005 CarswellNat 1129, 2005 FCA 27, (sub nom. *Subhaschandran v. Canada (Solicitor General))* 249 D.L.R. (4th) 269, 331 N.R. 182, 2005 CarswellNat 184 (F.C.A.) — The respondents brought a motion for a stay of the order for their deportation. At the conclusion of the argument the motions judge adjourned the motion. The Minister launched a motion for reconsideration which was dismissed. The motions judge issued a clarification and ordered that the applicants not be removed from Canada pending a determination of their motion for a stay.

It is true that, generally, interlocutory orders including adjournments cannot be appealed. An exception to this rule, however, occurs where a judge refuses to exercise his jurisdiction and deal with the case. In the present case, the motions judge, by adjourning the motion, has deprived the parties of ever having a decision on the stay motion. This amounts to a refusal to exercise his jurisdiction and a remedy must be available.

Accordingly, the Court of Appeal took jurisdiction despite the fact that there was no serious question certified by the motions judge, allowed the appeal, set aside the order of the motions judge and remitted the matter back to the motions judge to make a decision on the application for a stay.

*Mahjoub v. Canada (Minister of Citizenship & Immigration)*, 2004 CarswellNat 3440, 2004 FC 1315 (F.C.) — The applicant sought an order granting a stay of a removal order which provided for his imminent removal to Egypt, his country of nationality.

As to what constitutes at law a serious issue, the jurisprudence simply requires that an applicant show that the application is not frivolous or vexatious. This is a low threshold. The second requirement is irreparable harm. Irreparable harm must be harm which will occur in the interim between now and the time the application for leave and judicial review is adjudicated upon. Irreparable harm is harm which cannot be cured. An applicant for a stay must establish on a balance of probabilities that he or she faces a serious likelihood of harm. The existence of irreparable harm is fact-specific. The evidence must be credible and the harm non-speculative.

With respect to the balance of convenience test, the Court found that so long as the applicant remained in detention, the third branch of the test should be determined in his favour.

In this case, a stay was granted.

## Section 48(2)

*Villanueva v. Canada (Minister of Public Safety & Emergency Preparedness)*, 2010 FC 543, 2010 CarswellNat 1422, 2010 CarswellNat 2441 (F.C.) — This was an application for judicial review of a decision of an enforcement officer with the Canadian Border Services Agency, refusing the applicant's application for a deferral of the execution of the removal order against him. The officer was asked to consider the significant backlogs in the system in the case of a timely H&C application that had been outstanding for a considerable time, 15 months. The officer ignored this request and refused to defer on the basis of, *inter alia*, "imminence," *i.e.* whether a decision of the H&C grounds was about to be made, irrespective of the amount of time it had been in the system and the reasons for the delay. There was no evidence that the backlog factor was given consideration. The officer did recognize that the H&C application was timely, but in focusing upon "imminence" he neglected to consider whether significant backlogs in the system and a long-outstanding H&C application should impact his decision. This was a reviewable error and the application for judicial review was allowed.

*Vieira v. Canada (Minister of Public Safety & Emergency Preparedness)* (2007), 64 Imm. L.R. (3d) 32, 2007 CarswellNat 1637, 2007 FC 626 (F.C.) — The inconvenience, which the applicants may suffer as a result of their removal from Canada, does not outweigh the public interest in executing removal orders as soon as reasonably practicable in accordance with subs. 48(2) of the IRPA. The Minister's obligation under subs. 48(2) of the IRPA is not simply a question of administrative convenience, but implicates the integrity and fairness of, and public confidence in, Canada's system of immigration control. The motion for the stay of removal was dismissed.

*Cortes v. Canada (Minister of Citizenship & Immigration)*, 2007 CarswellNat 190, 2007 FC 78 (F.C.) — The applicants challenged a decision of a removals officer to deny of deferral of removal to Costa Rica. The Court concluded a deferral decision was not a question of fact, but is a question of mixed law and fact. The question of mixed law and fact involves the application of general principles of the statutory provision concerned to specific circumstances. The onus is on the applicants to establish that the officer's refusal to defer is untenable. A deferral decision is intricate. The legal requirement is clear: the removal is to be immediate, but enforcement is based on practicalities; that is, a removal is to occur as soon as it is "able to [be] put into practice." But there is an important additional qualifier: what is practical must be reasonable, that is, "sensible." With respect to what is practical, the line of analysis on this element of a deferral decision revolves around what is possible at the time. A decision on this factor only amounts to a conclusion being drawn on features such as: is the whereabouts of the failed refugee claimant known; is the claimant accessible; is there an available method whereby the claimant may be transported out of the country; and are there persons who can escort the claimant to the airport or drive the claimant to the border? These are not complex operational considerations. However, the factor of reasonability adds complexity to the decision-making process being conducted. It is on this factor that there is wide judicial agreement that a removals officer has discretion. There is disagreement on the scope of this discretion. Some review decisions say that only "exceptional circumstances" are reasonable, while others take in a more flexible view, and find that humanitarian considerations can be applied. In these instances, the fact that a humanitarian and compassionate application is before the Minister of Citizenship and Immigration pursuant to s. 25(1) of the IRPA can be found to make it reasonable that a claimant not be removed until the application is decided.

The applicants' main appeal to the officer on the reasonableness factor was that their removal should be deferred until their H&C application is decided. The officer analyzed the health issues which were the basis of the request. This consideration could only properly occur within the form designed for the purpose: the H&C application process which the applicants have invoked. The officer's decision was set aside and the matter referred back for re-determination before another removals officer, but with a direction that the re-determination not occur until after the applicants' outstanding H&C application is finally determined. The Court certified the following question:

> What is the correct standard of review of an officer's decision, made pursuant to the discretion set out in s. 48 of the IRPA to defer removal of persons from Canada?

*Bastien v. Canada (Minister of Citizenship & Immigration)*, 2006 CarswellNat 1598, 2006 FC 711 (F.C.) — This is an application for judicial review of the decision of an expulsion officer to refuse to stay the removal of the applicant from Canada to Dominica. The applicant came to Canada in 1996 as a visitor and her permit was extended a number of times. She was sponsored under the care-giver program, but ended up living illegally. Her claim for refugee status was denied and a PRRA application that followed was negative. She submitted an application for humanitarian and compassionate consideration under s. 25 of the IRPA, arguing that she supports her ailing mother, her sister and her sister's three children, all of whom reside in Dominica. She also argued that the three children of her employer in Canada were dependent on her as a surrogate parent. She was advised that she would be deported from Canada and an application for a motion for stay pending the current judicial review was allowed. The applicant sought judicial review of the decision of the expulsion officer to deport her. Essentially, the removals officer did not exercise her discretion to defer the applicant's request for a deferral of removal. The officer noted that she had an obligation under s. 48 of the IRPA to carry out removal orders as soon as reasonably practicable.

The application for humanitarian and compassionate consideration was processed and a negative decision was returned. Consequently the issue to be considered was now moot. Nevertheless, the Court wished to comment on the submissions regarding the exercise of discretion by a removals officer. The first issue was whether the expulsion officer had a duty to acknowledge that he or she has some discretion to defer removal. In this case, the Court concluded that the officer did acknowledge such discretion. The second issue was whether the expulsion officer was required to give reasons and elaborate a subjective analysis of the issue. The Court concluded that an expulsion officer has very limited discretion, and should not be required to give extensive reasons for a very limited decision-making process. The application for judicial review was dismissed.

*M. (R.A.) v. M (Y.Y.)*, [2005] B.C.J. No. 1507, 48 Imm. L.R. (3d) 301, 2005 CarswellBC 1604, 2005 BCPC 259 (Prov. Ct.) — The Provincial Court (B.C.) does not have jurisdiction to decide issues under the *Family Relations Act* with respect to a child who is not born in Canada, is not a Canadian citizen, and who is subject to a valid and outstanding deportation order under the *Immigration and Refugee Protection Act*. The Provincial Court's jurisdiction under the *Family Relations Act* should not be used to override the comprehensive immigration scheme created by federal legislation in order to enjoin federal authorities and the federal courts from enforcing valid removal orders. Even where there is concurrent jurisdiction between the Provincial Court and the Federal Court, the Provincial Court should decline to assume or exercise the jurisdiction in immigration matters, and leave them to the Federal Court.

*Hailu v. Canada (Solicitor General)* (2005), 27 Admin. L.R. (4th) 222, 2005 CarswellNat 362, 2005 FC 229 (F.C.) — The standard of review applied to the decisions of removal officers is a patently unreasonable standard. The decisions of a removal officer, given the very limited nature and extent of the powers of such officers, do not require a formal decision with reasons. The keeping of notes is useful and to be encouraged but is not an absolute requirement. The onus rests on the applicant to make out the case to the removals officer that would compel him or her to defer removal.

*Bharat v. Canada (Solicitor General)*, [2004] F.C.J. No. 2094, 2004 CarswellNat 4671, 2004 FC 1720 (F.C.) — The patently unreasonable standard should be applied to the decisions of removals officers, given the nature of the statutory scheme and, in particular, the limited and fact-driven discretion they exercise.

*Labiyi v. Canada (Solicitor General)*, 2004 CarswellNat 5911, 2004 CarswellNat 3808, 2004 FC 1493 (F.C.) — The applicant made a request that his removal be deferred and this request was denied in November 2003. Eight weeks later, on January 23, 2004, a further request for deferral was made. The officer declined to consider their request on the basis that her director had made a decision not to defer removal some eight weeks earlier.

The decision of the officer was set aside. In the eight weeks that passed, events could have occurred which might have justified deferring removal. It is not merely because a decision has been previously made that an enforcement officer loses his or her power to reassess a situation. The officer had an obligation and a duty to assess the situation and to make a decision whether to exercise his or her discretion. This had not been done and the decision of the officer was set aside.

*Boniowski v. Canada (Minister of Citizenship & Immigration)*, [2004] F.C.J. No. 1397, 44 Imm. L.R. (3d) 31, 2004 CarswellNat 5616, 2004 CarswellNat 2741, 2004 FC 1161 (F.C.) — The purpose of s. 48(2) is to allow for some limited discretion in the timing of a person's removal. The requirement for reasons was fulfilled in the decision letter where the officer indicated that she had received and reviewed the applicants' submissions in her decision not to defer removal. The nature of this decision is one where an officer has a very limited discretion and no actual formal decision is mandated in the legislation or regulations. The jurisprudence instructs that an officer must acknowledge that she has some discretion to defer removal, if it would not be "reasonably practicable" to enforce a removal order at a particular point in time. For example, the existence of a pending H&C application that was filed in timely manner, medical factors, and the arrangement of travel documents are some of the factors that may be considered by the officer.

The notes of the officer were filed as part of the judicial review proceeding but need not, as a regular procedure, be provided to applicants given the nature of this decision. The recording of written notes that set out the reasons for an administrative decision fosters better decision-making and provides a basis of explanation, if such a decision is challenged on judicial review. Therefore, while not obligatory, note keeping should be encouraged as a regular practice.

On the facts of this particular case, the decision of the officer not to defer removal was upheld.

**49. (1) In force — A removal order comes into force on the latest of the following dates:**

> **(a) the day the removal order is made, if there is no right to appeal;**
>
> **(b) the day the appeal period expires, if there is a right to appeal and no appeal is made; and**

**(c) the day of the final determination of the appeal, if an appeal is made.**

(2) **In force — claimants — Despite subsection (1), a removal order made with respect to a refugee protection claimant is conditional and comes into force on the latest of the following dates:**

**(a) the day the claim is determined to be ineligible only under paragraph 101(1)(e);**

**(b) in a case other than that set out in paragraph (a), seven days after the claim is determined to be ineligible;**

**(c) 15 days after notification that the claim is rejected by the Refugee Protection Division, if no appeal is made, or by the Refugee Appeal Division, if an appeal is made;**

**(d) 15 days after notification that the claim is declared withdrawn or abandoned; and**

**(e) 15 days after proceedings are terminated as a result of notice under paragraph 104(1)(c) or (d).**

*[Editor's Note: SOR/2002-227, s. 319(1), provides that subject to SOR/2002-227, s. 319(2), a removal order made under the* Immigration Act, *R.S.C. 1985, c. I-2 (the "former Act") that was unexecuted on June 28, 2002 continues in force and is subject to the provisions of the* Immigration and Refugee Protection Act, *S.C. 2001, c. 27 (the "new Act").*

*SOR/2002-227, s. 319(2) provides that the execution of a removal order that had been stayed on June 28, 2002 under paragraphs 49(1)(c) to (f) of the former Act continues to be stayed until the earliest of the events described in paragraphs 231(1)(a) to (e) of the new* Immigration and Refugee Protection Regulations, *SOR/2002-227.*

*However, SOR/2002-227, s. 319(3) provides that SOR/2002-227, s. 319(2) does not apply if*

*(a) the subject of the removal order was determined by the Convention Refugee Determination Division not to have a credible basis for his or her claim; or*

*(b) the subject of the removal order*

*(i) is subject to a removal order because he or she is inadmissible on grounds of serious criminality, or*

*(ii) resides or sojourns in the United States or St. Pierre and Miquelon and is the subject of a report prepared under s. 44(1) of the new Act on his or her entry into Canada.*

*SOR/2002-227, s. 319(4) provides that a conditional removal order made under the former Act continues in force and is subject to s. 49(2) of the new Act.]*

50. **Stay — A removal order is stayed**

**(a) if a decision that was made in a judicial proceeding — at which the Minister shall be given the opportunity to make submissions — would be directly contravened by the enforcement of the removal order;**

**(b) in the case of a foreign national sentenced to a term of imprisonment in Canada, until the sentence is completed;**



IRP Act

**(c) for the duration of a stay imposed by the Immigration Appeal Division or any other court of competent jurisdiction;**

**(d) for the duration of a stay under paragraph 114(1)(b); and**

**(e) for the duration of a stay imposed by the Minister.**

## Case Law

*Editor's Note*: *For cases dealing with judicial stays of removal orders see the cases collected under section 18.2 of the Federal Courts Act.*

*Idahosa v. Canada (Minister of Public Safety and Emergency Preparedness)* (2008), 77 Imm. L.R. (3d) 130, 385 N.R. 134, 2008 CarswellNat 4895, 2008 FCA 418 (F.C.A.) — The mother sought to stay a deportation to Nigeria indefinitely on the basis that since arriving in Canada, and while her status in Canada was uncertain, she gave birth to two children in Canada. Those children are the subject of an order of the Ontario Court precluding their removal from Ontario. That order, however, can be varied. Further, the endorsement on the record of the judge making the order makes it clear that the Ontario Court is not dealing with the immigration issues. On the basis of the decision of the Federal Court in *Alexander v. Canada (Solicitor General), infra*, the Court found that the order of the Ontario Court would not be "directly contravened" within the meaning of s. 50(a) were the removal to be carried out. The application was dismissed. The applicant appealed to the Federal Court of Appeal who dismissed the appeal and found that paragraph 50(a) does not apply to a provincial Court's order awarding custody to a parent of Canadian-born children for the purpose of delaying or preventing the enforcement of a removal order against the parent, when there is no *lis* respecting custody that is unrelated to the removal. On the facts of this case it did not make a difference that the order could be varied and that the Minister had an opportunity to speak to the order.

*Blake v. Canada (Minister of Public Safety & Emergency Preparedness)*, 2008 CarswellNat 2816, 2008 CarswellNat 1324, 2008 FC 572 (F.C.) — The applicant sought judicial review of the decision made by an enforcement officer. In that decision, the officer determined that an order of the Ontario Court of Justice granting the applicant sole custody of her children and prohibiting their removal from Ontario did not constitute a statutory stay pursuant to subs. 50(a) of the IRPA. The applicant then sought an order quashing the decision to remove her to Jamaica, a declaration that a statutory stay arises by virtue of the order of the Ontario Court of Justice for the purposes of subs. 50(a) of the Act, and an order prohibiting her removal from Canada pending the determination of her application for landing in Canada on the basis of humanitarian and compassionate grounds.

The scheme of the Act is to regulate the entry of non-citizens into Canada. At the same time the Act identifies, as one of its objectives, the reunification of families, that is in paragraph 3(1)(d). The Act also refers to the respect for international conventions in paragraph 3(3)(f). However, the Courts have repeatedly ruled that the best interest of the children are not paramount in the scheme of immigration law. The Act does not contemplate that the making of a custody order *per se* will give rise to a statutory stay pursuant to subs. 50(a). The Custody and Non-Removal Order in question was made pursuant to a provincial statute. The intent, purpose and scope of that legislation did not trump the legislative scheme set out in the IRPA. Insofar as the order in question arises under a statutory scheme enacted by the province of Ontario for the purposes and objectives that are unrelated to the purposes of the IRPA, the Court was not required to apply provincial law.

In the scheme of the IRPA, only Canadian citizens and permanent residents have an unqualified right to remain in Canada. Permanent residents may be removed, under certain circumstances. The applicant, as a result of criminal activities and convictions, became vulnerable to removal. Once the removal order against her became effective, the respondent was obligated to discharge his statutory duty pursuant to s. 48 to effect that removal as soon as practicable, unless that removal was stayed by an order of the Court or by operation of law. This statutory obligation cannot be displaced by the making of a custody order pursuant to another statutory scheme. The Custody and Non-Removal Order made by the provincial Court judge pursuant to the provincial legislation is not an "order" that gives rise to a stay pursuant to s. 50 of the IRPA. The application for judicial review was dismissed. The following questions were certified:



1. In the circumstances of this case where:

   1. A parent is a foreign national who is subject to a valid removal order;

   2. A family court issues an order, granting custody to the parent of his or her Canadian born child and prohibiting the removal of the child from the province; and

   3. The Minister is given the opportunity to make submissions before the family court before the order is pronounced;

   Would the family court order be directly contravened, within the contemplation of subs. 50(a) of the Act, if the parent, but not the child, is removed from Canada?

2. If it does not create a statutory stay pursuant to s. 50(a) of the IRPA, then does removal of the mother/parent constitute a violation of s. 7 of the *Charter*?

*H. (J.) v. A. (D.)* (2008), 290 D.L.R. (4th) 732, 51 R.F.L. (6th) 181, 89 O.R. (3d) 514, 2008 CarswellOnt 1053 (S.C.J.); affirmed (2009), 77 Imm. L.R. (3d) 123, 306 D.L.R. (4th) 496, 2009 CarswellOnt 85, 2009 ONCA 17 (Ont. C.A.) — The Minister of Citizenship & Immigration and the Minister of Public Safety & Emergency Preparedness appealed the order of the Ontario Court of Justice prohibiting the removal of a mother and one daughter, subject to a deportation order, from the province of Ontario pending a further order of the Ontario Court. The Minister sought to have the motion's judge's order vacated to the extent that its effect was to stay the deportation order.

The Court pointed out that rather than seek a stay of the deportation order from the Federal Court, which was open to the mother to do, the mother brought a motion for custody before the Ontario Court of Justice. The Ontario Court of Justice has jurisdiction to determine issues of custody and access as between the parents. The issue was whether the Court did in fact determine an issue of custody as between the parents or whether it ordered a stay of the deportation order and wrongly assumed jurisdiction. The Court concluded that the motions judge did not have jurisdiction to make the order that temporarily stayed the removal order pending the consideration of the mother's H&C claim. The motions judge committed material errors in wrongly assuming jurisdiction of an immigration proceeding; in circumventing a legitimate application of law using private custody litigation; in filling a "legislative gap" in the IRPA; and in exceeding his jurisdiction by effectively precluding the mother's removal from Canada by ordering that the child not be removed from Ontario. The order of the motions judge to the extent that it stayed the removal was vacated. There are other avenues that the mother may consider in order to properly address the question of the best interests of her children. It was open to the mother to bring a motion in Federal Court for a stay of the removal order that was issued against her.

On further appeal to the Ontario Court of Appeal, there was a finding that the appeal Court Judge did not err in vacating the non-removal order. The IRPA provides opportunities for consideration of the best interests of the children of those subject to deportation. The reasoning in *Idahosa* is consistent with the Ontario cases which indicate that non-removal orders under the CLRA should not be granted for the purpose of frustrating removal orders in immigration proceedings.

*Laranjo v. Canada (Minister of Citizenship & Immigration)*, 2007 CarswellNat 5161, 2007 FC 726 — The applicant immigrated to Canada in 1961. He never acquired Canadian citizenship. In 1981, he was convicted of first degree murder for the sexual assault and killing of a female hitchhiker. He was sentenced to a term of life imprisonment without eligibility of parole for 25 years. He filed a humanitarian and compassionate application pursuant to s. 25 of the IRPA. This application was denied. He argued that his deportation violated his s. 7 *Charter* rights because he would be deprived of the National Parole Board programs for the duration of his sentence to life imprisonment. Paragraph 50(b) of the IRPA provides that a removal order is stayed until a foreign national's sentence to a term of imprisonment is completed. However, for the purposes of paragraph 50(b) of the IRPA, the sentence of an offender on parole is deemed to be completed according to subs. 128(3) of the *Corrections and Conditional Release Act*, S.C. 1992, c. 20. Parliament's enactment of subs. 128(3) is a complete answer to the absurd consequences that would result if the applicant, because of his life sentence, could be said to have greater constitutional rights than a person in similar circumstances who had fully served a sentence of 20 years. The Supreme Court of Canada has affirmed that deportation is not a punishment. The applicant did not show that his deprivation of rehabilitation services is a punishment, let alone one that comes within the scope of s. 12 of the *Charter*. The issue of returning to their country of citizenship, persons who have lived virtually all of their lives in Canada, is a matter of policy enacted by Parliament. The constitutionality of the relevant provisions of the IRPA which enact this policy was not challenged in this proceeding. The application for judicial review was dismissed.

*Garcia c. Canada (Ministre de la Citoyenneté & de l'Immigration)*, 2007 CarswellNat 3016, 2007 CarswellNat 576, 2007 FCA 75 ((Fed. C.A.)) — A judgment by a Provincial Court refusing to order the return of a child in accordance with the Convention on the Civil Aspects of International Abduction, [1989] R.T. Can. No. 35, and s. 20 of An Act respecting the Civil aspects of international and inter-provincial child abduction, R.S.Q., c. A-23.01, cannot have the effect of directly and indefinitely preventing the enforcement of a removal order which is effective under the IRPA.

*Clark v. Canada (Minister of Public Safety & Emergency Preparedness)* (2006), 59 Imm. L.R. (3d) 299, 2006 CarswellNat 4518, 2006 FC 1512 (F.C.) — The applicant brought a motion for an order staying a deportation order against him. The applicant has lived in Canada for all of his 59 years, and was the son of Canadian-born parents. The applicant did not register the fact of his birth within two years of its occurrence as required under s. 5(1)(b) of the former *Citizenship Act*. The applicant was currently incarcerated; he was convicted of several offences. The Minister's delegate wrote a report under s. 44(1) of the IRPA stating that the applicant was a foreign national or permanent resident for whom there were reasonable grounds to believe was inadmissible. The Minister's delegate issued a deportation order stating the applicant was inadmissible on grounds of serious criminality. The applicant claimed that he is a citizen of Canada and that the issuance of the deportation order triggered a serious consequence, specifically, the automatic ineligibility for day parole for which the applicant would otherwise be eligible. The applicant raised a serious issue as to whether he was a Canadian citizen. There was a minimal prejudice to the respondents in staying the deportation order since the applicant had lived in Canada for 59 years. Therefore the balance of convenience favoured the applicant and the deportation order was stayed.

*Alexander v. Canada (Solicitor General)*, [2005] F.C.J. No. 1416, 49 Imm. L.R. (3d) 5, [2006] 2 F.C.R. 681, 279 F.T.R. 45, 2005 CarswellNat 2396, 2005 FC 1147 (F.C.); affirmed (2006), 57 Imm. L.R. (3d) 1, 360 N.R. 167, 2006 CarswellNat 4243, 2006 FCA 386 (Fed. C.A.) — An order of the Ontario Court of Justice granting sole custody of two Canadian-born children to an individual who is subject to a deportation order under the IRPA, and further ordering that the children not be removed from Ontario does not create a statutory stay pursuant to subs. 50(a) of the IRPA.

The applicant sought to have determined whether the family court order would be directly contravened, within the contemplation of subs. 50(a) of the Act, if the parent, but not the child, was removed from Canada. The application for judicial review was dismissed. The applicant obtained a stay on humanitarian and compassionate grounds, rendering the appeal moot. The conditions required for the Federal Court of Appeal to decide moot questions in special circumstances were not met. The appeal was dismissed.

*Wozniak v. Brunton* (2004), 1 R.F.L. (6th) 429, 2004 CarswellOnt 943 (Ont. S.C.J.) — The mother brought an application for temporary custody of her child with specified access to the father and a non-removal order for the child. The father brought an application for temporary joint custody, specified access and non-removal order. He argued that if the mother were removed, the child would be deprived of the social and economic benefits of Canada. There was no evidence Trinidad presented an environment harmful to the child. The Court held that separation of a child from a parent may be an unfortunate but inevitable consequence incidental to, for example, the incarceration of a parent, the deportation of a parent, or the divorce of two parents. Considerations as to whether the best interests of the child should warrant a stay of a deportation, pending an application of humanitarian and compassionate grounds, can be canvassed by the Federal Court. An order for temporary custody was awarded to the mother.

*Varvara v. Costantino*, [2003] O.J. No. 5980, 36 Imm. L.R. (3d) 256, 2003 CarswellOnt 5903 (Ont. C.J.) — The mother sought an order pursuant to paragraph 2 amending an order of the Court to include a provision preventing any persons from removing her three children from the jurisdiction. The Court ordered the non-removal of the children be an incident of custody, in spite of the pending deportation of the mother. The non-removal order was in the children's best interest because there was evidence that the children would be at risk of harm from the father if returned to Italy.

**51. Void — permanent residence — A removal order that has not been enforced becomes void if the foreign national becomes a permanent resident.**

**52. (1) No return without prescribed authorization — If a removal order has been enforced, the foreign national shall not return to Canada, unless authorized by an officer or in other prescribed circumstances.**

**(2) Return to Canada — If a removal order for which there is no right of appeal has been enforced and is subsequently set aside in a judicial review, the foreign national is entitled to return to Canada at the expense of the Minister.**

## Case Law

### Section 52(1)

*Gutierrez v. Canada (Minister of Citizenship & Immigration)*, 2010 FC 32, 2010 CarswellNat 944, 2010 CarswellNat 90 (F.C.) — This was an application for judicial review of a decision to refuse the applicant's application for Authorization to Return to Canada.

Parliament did not want anyone who had ever committed an offence against the Act to be permanently banned from Canada. On the contrary, the possibility of returning would be kept open, contingent on the authorization of an officer. The mere fact that an applicant did not comply with the Act is not a reason for rejecting the applicant's claim. The officer must take into consideration the seriousness of the offence, as noted in the "OP-1 Procedures" document.

In this case, the applicant did not leave Canada when the removal order became enforceable, before filing her PRRA application which, under a new regime, automatically imposed a stay on her departure order. Up until the date of the PRRA application, the applicant never received instructions from CIC, and was therefore never given a departure date. It was only after she withdrew her PRRA application that the 30-day deadline was reinstated. She left four days later. She failed to notify Canadian authorities of her departure and did not obtain the required certificate. Ignorance of the Act does not excuse a violation. Under the circumstances, however, it appeared to be carelessness or negligence on the applicant's part. She did not act in bad faith. It is true that this negligence allowed the applicant to return to Canada in 2003 without authorization and to work. However, the applicant was always honest with Canadian authorities and when she was given the order to leave Canada in December 2003, she complied. The technical failings of the applicant did not justify banning her from returning to Canada when in fact there was a "compelling reason" as spelled out in the CIC document for allowing her to return. The application for judicial review was allowed and the matter referred back to a different immigration officer for redetermination.

*Bravo v. Canada (Minister of Citizenship & Immigration)* (2010), 89 Imm. L.R. (3d) 123, 2010 FC 411, 2010 CarswellNat 958 (F.C.) — The applicant sought judicial review of a decision rejecting his application for a work permit. He first came to Canada in 2002 as a visitor. He overstayed his visit and subsequently made a refugee claim which gave him the ability to work in Canada. His refugee claim was rejected and he sought judicial review in the Federal Court but leave was denied. In November 2004 he left Canada. Even though his departure was voluntary under s. 240 of the *Immigration and Refugee Protection Regulations*, the removal order against him was deemed to have been enforced. This meant that s. 52(1) of IRPA required an Authorization to Return to Canada.

It is well established that one's past history with Canadian immigration officials is one of the best indicators of their likelihood of future compliance. In the applicant's case, his history is at best ambiguous, if not troubling: in 2002-2003, he first misrepresented his intentions in order to obtain a visitor's visa, then made a refugee claim only to acquire a work permit. It may or may not be that he has since learned from his mistakes, but this is what he had to show. The Court could not conclude that the decision fell outside the "range of possible, acceptable outcomes which are defensible with respect to the facts and law." The application for judicial review was dismissed.

*R. v. Beltran* (2010), 89 Imm. L.R. (3d) 1, 2010 ABPC 113, 2010 CarswellAlta 602 (Alta. Prov. Ct.) — The accused entered a guilty plea to an offence of returning to Canada without the prescribed authorization, contrary to IRPA. The Crown sought a sentence of five months' incarceration. The accused sought a conditional discharge. A discharge was not a fit disposition in this case. The offence is a problematic one in that it is difficult to detect and quantify the cost to taxpayers. The accused entered Canada unauthorized for his own personal gain and to avoid the proper and lawful mechanisms in place for application. The offence was planned, deliberate and ongoing. There were no facts presented to show that the accused intended at any time to address his unlawful act or remove himself from the country to properly apply for admission. He is currently willing to leave Canada but it appears only because he was prosecuted.



Any hardship on the accused's family was inflicted by his act. There are no exceptional circumstances in this case that would compel the Court to put the accused in a position he would have been in but for his third illegal entry. The accused was sentenced to four months and 13 days in custody. Without credit for pre-sentence custody, the jail term imposed would have been five months. The time spent in custody prior to this sentencing hearing was nine days. The amount of time credited was 18 days.

*Khakh v. Canada (Minister of Citizenship & Immigration)*, 2008 CarswellNat 1682, 2008 CarswellNat 2788, 2008 FC 710 — The applicant and his wife arrived in Canada illegally in December 2003 after three failed attempts to obtain Canadian visitor visas. In January 2004, the applicants filed a claim for refugee protection. That claim was dismissed. In November 2004 an application for leave and judicial review of that decision was dismissed. In July 2005, the applicants applied for a pre-removal risk assessment (PRRA). The applicants withdrew their PRRA application in November 2005 and left Canada in compliance with a removal order in March 2006. Prior to leaving Canada, the applicants applied as provincial nominees under the Provincial Nominee Program of Prince Edward Island. Having been accepted as provincial nominees, the applicants applied for permanent residence in Canada. Their applications were received at the Canadian High Commission in New Delhi in September 2005. Due to the fact that they had previously been subject to an enforced removal order, the applicants' permanent residence application could not be processed unless they first obtained authorization to return to Canada pursuant to subs. 52(1) of the Act. The visa officer recommended that the Immigration Program Manager refuse the applicants' request for authorization to return to Canada. The Program Manager concluded that the applicants should not be granted an authorization to return to Canada. The visa officer refused the applicants' application for permanent residence in Canada.

The Program Manager's reliance on the applicants' illegal entry into Canada in 2003, which along with their late departure in March 2006 combined to form the "multiple violations" referred to in the decision, was unreasonable in that no consideration was given to the applicants' purpose for illegally entering Canada in 2003, namely, filing a claim for refugee protection, which they were entitled to do under the law. While respecting immigration laws is a legitimate policy consideration in the Program Manager's exercise of discretion, the evidence before the Court established that the applicants' only true violation was their failure to leave Canada within the timeframe mandated. Moreover, the Program Manager's decision was not made with regard to all the circumstances of the case and the underlying objectives of Canadian immigration law. First, while the Program

Manager attempted to balance the economic benefit to Canada of granting the applicants' request for authorization, at no point did he consider the applicants' reasons for not leaving Canada until March 2006. The applicants stated that their late departure was largely due to trouble renewing their Indian passports. They explained that despite paying extra fees to have their renewal applications expedited, they could not secure renewed passports until March 2006, the very same month in which they left Canada. Further, at no time in the Program Manager's decision or the visa officer's recommendation, is any consideration given to the fact that deportation orders are often applied to those individuals who have been found inadmissible to Canada on various grounds including serious criminality, national security, or violations of human and international rights. Unlike in those situations, the applicants in the case at bar were not security risks, nor did they possess criminal records. While they entered Canada illegally, they made a valid, albeit unsuccessful claim for refugee protection. It was unreasonable that the applicants would be denied authorization to return under such circumstances, especially considering that no consideration was given to their reasons for not departing Canada before March 2006. The application for judicial review was allowed.

*Akbari v. Canada (Minister of Citizenship & Immigration)* (2006), 59 Imm. L.R. (3d) 207, 2006 CarswellNat 3882, 2006 FC 1421 (F.C.) — The applicant had a reasonably lengthy immigration history. She is an Iranian citizen and a failed refugee claimant. She had been married to a Canadian citizen since July 2002. The *bona fides* of the marriage were not in issue. An application under the spousal sponsorship provisions of the IRPA had been submitted. A previous application was refused. A spousal sponsorship application was pending.

The applicant had earlier applied for a green card in the United States although it was unclear from the record precisely when that application was made. When her green card was approved in August of 2004, she traveled to the United States. In so doing, she was deemed deported (as a failed refugee claimant) and therefore required authorization under subs. 52(1) of the IRPA and subs. 226(1) of the *Immigration and Refugee Protection Regulations*, to return to Canada.

The applicant claimed not to have been aware, at the time of her departure, that by leaving voluntarily she was effecting her deportation and would thus require authorization to return. When she returned to Canada she was intercepted at the airport. She completed a pre-removal risk assessment application, which was ultimately determined to be negative. Her passport was seized and subsequently lost by the Canada Border Services Agency officials. She was removed from Canada. She made another attempt to return in April 2005, but the applicant's application for an authorization to return to Canada was refused. She sought judicial review of the refusal alleging that the officer failed to consider the totality of the evidence upon which the application was based. The Court did not agree with the applicant's suggestion that an interview was required. Nor is there a requirement that formal reasons be provided. The notes of the immigration officer may be taken as the reasons for the decision. An authorization to return to Canada should not be construed as a mini-humanitarian and compassionate application. However, regard must be had to the various factors. This requirement necessitates that consideration be given to the totality of the factual circumstances that are presented to the immigration officer. Here, the notes of the immigration officer revealed a focus on the applicant's immigration history. The officer also indicated apprehension with respect to the applicant remaining beyond her authorization. There was no indication that consideration was given to any of the factual circumstances presented by, and of concern to the applicant — more specifically, that she had left Canada voluntarily, that she and her husband could not reunite in North America or elsewhere, and that she was not inadmissible for reasons of criminality. The immigration officer's notes did not reflect consideration of the specific submissions. Absent some indication in the notes that the officer at least turned his mind to the applicant's circumstances, it was assumed that he did not. The failure of the officer to consider the totality of the evidence resulted in a denial of procedural fairness to the applicant. The application for judicial review was allowed.



## *Regulations*

**53. Regulations — The regulations may provide for any matter relating to the application of this Division, and may include provisions respecting**

> **(a) conditions that may or must be imposed, varied, or cancelled, individually or by class, on permanent residents and foreign nationals;**
>
> **(b) the circumstances in which a removal order shall be made or confirmed against a permanent resident or a foreign national;**
>
> **(c) the circumstances in which status may be restored;**
>
> **(d) the circumstances in which a removal order may be stayed, including a stay imposed by the Minister and a stay that is not expressly provided for by this Act;**
>
> **(e) the effect and enforcement of removal orders;**
>
> **(f) the effect of a pardon under the *Criminal Records Act* on the status of permanent residents and foreign nationals and removal orders made against them; and**
>
> **(g) the financial obligations that may be imposed with respect to a removal order.**

## DIVISION 6 — DETENTION AND RELEASE

**54. Immigration Division — The Immigration Division is the competent Division of the Board with respect to the review of reasons for detention under this Division.**

**55. (1) Arrest and detention with warrant — An officer may issue a warrant for the arrest and detention of a permanent resident or a foreign national who the officer has reasonable grounds to believe is inadmissible and is a danger to the public or is unlikely to appear for examination, an admissibility hearing or removal from Canada.**

*[Editor's Note: SOR/2002-227, s. 325(1) provides that a warrant for arrest and detention made under the* Immigration Act, *R.S.C. 1985, c. I-2 (the "former Act") is a warrant for arrest and detention made under the* Immigration and Refugee Protection Act, *S.C. 2001, c. 27 (the "new Act").*

*SOR/2002-227, s. 325(2) provides that an order for the detention of a person made under the former Act is an order to detain made under the new Act.]*

**(2) Arrest and detention without warrant — An officer may, without a warrant, arrest and detain a foreign national, other than a protected person,**

> **(a) who the officer has reasonable grounds to believe is inadmissible and is a danger to the public or is unlikely to appear for examination, an admissibility hearing, removal from Canada, or at a proceeding that could lead to the making of a removal order by the Minister under subsection 44(2); or**
>
> **(b) if the officer is not satisfied of the identity of the foreign national in the course of any procedure under this Act.**

**(3) Detention on entry — A permanent resident or a foreign national may, on entry into Canada, be detained if an officer**

> **(a) considers it necessary to do so in order for the examination to be completed; or**
>
> **(b) has reasonable grounds to suspect that the permanent resident or the foreign national is inadmissible on grounds of security or for violating human or international rights.**

**(4) Notice — If a permanent resident or a foreign national is taken into detention, an officer shall without delay give notice to the Immigration Division.**

**56. Release — officer — An officer may order the release from detention of a permanent resident or a foreign national before the first detention review by the Immigration Division if the officer is of the opinion that the reasons for the detention no longer exist. The officer may impose any conditions, including the payment of a deposit or the posting of a guarantee for compliance with the conditions, that the officer considers necessary.**

*[Editor's Note: SOR/2002-227, s. 331 provides that a performance bond posted or security deposited under the former* Immigration Act, *R.S.C. 1985, c. I-2 that remains posted or deposited immediately before June 28, 2002 continues as a deposit or a guarantee under the new* Immigration and Refugee Protection Act, *S.C. 2001, c. 27 and is governed by its provisions.]*

**57. (1) Review of detention — Within 48 hours after a permanent resident or a foreign national is taken into detention, or without delay afterward, the Immigration Division must review the reasons for the continued detention.**

**(2) Further review — At least once during the seven days following the review under subsection (1), and at least once during each 30-day period following each previous review, the Immigration Division must review the reasons for the continued detention.**

**(3) Presence — In a review under subsection (1) or (2), an officer shall bring the permanent resident or the foreign national before the Immigration Division or to a place specified by it.**

## Case Law

*Canada (Minister of Citizenship & Immigration) v. Li*, 2009 CarswellNat 598, 2009 FCA 85 (C.A.) — This appeal demonstrates the delicate balancing act required when issues of criminality, long-term detention and human rights collide under the IRPA and the *Charter of Rights and Freedoms*. The Federal Court dismissed an application by the appellant for judicial review of the Immigration Division's decision that ordered the release of the respondents from detention. In the order that it issued on December 29, 2008, the Federal Court certified a question. The certified question did not lend itself to a simple "yes" or "no" answer. What was in issue in the certified question is the appropriateness of making estimates of anticipated future length of detention on a mere anticipation of available processes under the IRPA and the Regulations, including Federal Court proceedings.



The Division proceeded on a basis that was both unreasonable and erroneous in law when it determined the anticipated future length of detention of the appellants. It speculated on potential proceedings that the parties could bring rather than making its estimation on actual pending proceedings. In addition, the speculation was too far reaching, unwarranted, unreasonable and unnecessary since there was a review at least once every 30 days. It was also an error to assume that the Federal Court and the Federal Court of Appeal would entertain the speculative remedies. Finally, the Division failed to take into account and assess relevant factors as well as the impact of another appropriate available and less drastic recourse to prevent a breach of the *Charter*, i.e., expediting the proceedings. The Federal Court should have intervened to remedy these errors of law.

The Federal Court of Appeal concluded that the basis of the estimation of anticipated future length of detention should be the proceedings as they exist at the time of each monthly review and not on an anticipation of available processes not yet underway. This conclusion with others disposed of the appeal and accordingly the appeal was allowed and the decision of the Federal Court was set aside. The matter was referred back to the Immigration Division for a redetermination.

*Canada (Minister of Citizenship & Immigration) v. Sittampalam* (2004), 43 Imm. L.R. (3d) 1, 2004 CarswellNat 4867, 2004 CarswellNat 5765, 2004 FC 1756 (F.C.) — The respondent was a subject of two release orders both of which were being reviewed by the Minister in this proceeding.

Simply because the Minister established a *prima facie* case at one time does not mean it stands indefinitely. There will be a time, dependant on the facts, where a danger will be perceived to have dissipated at some point in the future. If at that point the Minister wishes the continued detention of the respondent, it is entirely reasonable that evidence of a current danger must be presented. The presiding member must decide afresh at each hearing whether continued detention is warranted. A detention review is not precisely a trial *de novo* because the member is expected to take into account the evidence and reasons pertaining to previous detention orders. The member is not entitled to rely on speculation instead of evidence. In this case, the decisions were quashed and the matter returned to be heard by a differently constituted panel.

*Canada (Minister of Citizenship & Immigration) v. Thanabalasingham*, [2004] F.C.J. No. 15, 38 Imm. L.R. (3d) 1, [2004] 3 F.C.R. 572, 2004 CarswellNat 22, 2004 CarswellNat 782, 2004 FCA 4, 247 F.T.R. 159 (note), 236 D.L.R. (4th) 329, 10 Admin. L.R. (4th) 285, 315 N.R. 91 (C.A.) — This was an appeal on a certified question from a decision of the motions judge. The certified question asked whether detention reviews were hearings *de novo* and whether the detained person bears the burden of establishing that he or she was not a danger to the public or a flight risk. The respondent was arrested in October 2001 on an immigration warrant and detained on grounds that he was a danger to the public because he was the leader of a Tamil gang. His detention was reviewed under that

Act and, after it came into force, under ss. 57 and 58 of IRPA. At his first five reviews, the continued detention of the respondent was ordered. At his sixth review, the respondent was ordered released. The Minister applied for judicial review and obtained a stay of that order until the next detention review was completed. The next detention review was completed in March 2003 and the respondent was once again ordered released. The Minister once again obtained a stay of that order and sought judicial review and it was this judicial review that was the subject of the matter in this case.

Detention reviews are the kind of essentially fact-based decisions to which deference is usually shown. While prior decisions are not binding on a Member, if a Member chooses to depart from prior decisions to detain, clear and compelling reasons for doing so must be set out. The best way for the Member to provide clear and compelling reasons would be to expressly explain what has given rise to the changed opinion. It would be unacceptable for a Member to give a cursory decision which does not advert to the prior reasons for detention in a meaningful way.

Sections 57 and 58 allow persons to be detained for potentially lengthy if not indefinite periods of time without having been charged let alone having been convicted of any crime. As a result, detention decisions must be made with s. 7 of the *Charter* in mind.

It is the Minister who must establish, on a balance of probabilities, that the respondent is a danger to the public if he wants the detention to continue. The onus is always on the Minister to demonstrate that there are reasons which warrant detention or continue detention. Once the Minister has made out a *prima facie* case for the continued detention, the individual must lead some evidence or risk continued detention. The Minister may establish a *prima facie* case in a variety of ways including reliance on reasons for prior detention.

*Canada (Minister of Citizenship & Immigration) v. Gill* (2003), 33 Imm. L.R. (3d) 204, 2003 CarswellNat 3918, 2003 CarswellNat 4422, 2003 FC 1398, 242 F.T.R. 126 (F.C.) — The Minister sought to review the decision of a member of the Immigration Division who after conducting a 48-hour first detention review ordered the respondent released. The decision of the member was set aside. The member failed to take into consideration, when exercising her discretion, the two factors, one referred to in s. 247(1)(c) of the Regulations and the other in 247(1)(e) of the Regulations. Further, the member made an erroneous finding of fact to the effect that the immigration authorities were satisfied with the respondent's identity because they decided to issue a departure order in the name reflected in the documents of doubtful authenticity. Such a finding was contrary to the opinion given by the Minister under s. 58 of the Act.

**58. (1) Release — Immigration Division — The Immigration Division shall order the release of a permanent resident or a foreign national unless it is satisfied, taking into account prescribed factors, that**

> **(a) they are a danger to the public;**
>
> **(b) they are unlikely to appear for examination, an admissibility hearing, removal from Canada, or at a proceeding that could lead to the making of a removal order by the Minister under subsection 44(2);**
>
> **(c) the Minister is taking necessary steps to inquire into a reasonable suspicion that they are inadmissible on grounds of security or for violating human or international rights; or**

**(d) the Minister is of the opinion that the identity of the foreign national has not been, but may be, established and they have not reasonably cooperated with the Minister by providing relevant information for the purpose of establishing their identity or the Minister is making reasonable efforts to establish their identity.**

*[Editor's Note: SOR/2002-227, s. 324 provides that a release from detention under the former* Immigration Act, *R.S.C. 1985, c. I-2 is the ordering of release from detention under the new* Immigration and Refugee Protection Act, *S.C. 2001, c. 27 and any terms and conditions imposed under the former Act become conditions imposed under the new Act.]*

IRP Act

**(2) Detention — Immigration Division — The Immigration Division may order the detention of a permanent resident or a foreign national if it is satisfied that the permanent resident or the foreign national is the subject of an examination or an admissibility hearing or is subject to a removal order and that the permanent resident or the foreign national is a danger to the public or is unlikely to appear for examination, an admissibility hearing or removal from Canada.**

**(3) Conditions — If the Immigration Division orders the release of a permanent resident or a foreign national, it may impose any conditions that it considers necessary, including the payment of a deposit or the posting of a guarantee for compliance with the conditions.**

*[Editor's Note: SOR/2002-227, s. 331 provides that a performance bond posted or security deposited under the former* Immigration Act, *R.S.C. 1985, c. I-2 that remains posted or deposited immediately before June 28, 2002 continues as a deposit or a guarantee under the new* Immigration and Refugee Protection Act, *S.C. 2001, c. 27 and is governed by its provisions.]*

## Case Law

### Section 58(1)

*Canada (Minister of Public Safety & Emergency Preparedness) v. Welch*, 2006 CarswellNat 2416, 2006 FC 924 (F.C.) — The Minister sought judicial review of the decision of a member of the Immigration Division of the Immigration and Refugee Board, allowing the conditional release from detention of the respondents. This was the fifth review of the detention of the respondents. The Minister argued that the member did not provide clear and compelling reasons as to why he should depart from the four previous decisions and release the respondents on terms and conditions. The Minister's view was that these terms and conditions were less stringent than those considered at the previous reviews.

The respondents are citizens of the United States and are wanted in the State of Colorado on a number of charges. They fled to Canada following release on bail pending their trial in the United States. Shortly after their arrival in Canada, they were arrested by the RCMP and a decision was made to detain them, and a removal order pursuant to s. 44 of the IRPA was issued against them. The respondents claimed refugee status and this claim had yet to be determined. At the first detention hearing, it was determined that they were a flight risk but the duration of the detention contemplated was very short. It was mentioned that they had two children. At a second detention hearing, the member came to the same conclusion and continued the detention. The two respondents' children were in the audience during the second hearing. It became clear that they had been with their parents when the latter were apprehended. The children were by then in the care of their grandmother in Canada, having been in the custody of the Ministry of Children and Families. It was argued that it was not in the best interest of the children to be separated from their parents. However, the presence of the children was not found to supersede the other factors listed in s. 245 of the Regulations. A proposal for release including a curfew and a $4,000 bond was rejected. At the third detention hearing, the member considered physical restriction to an area, $25,000 cash bond for each of the respondents, a prohibition to carry weapons, daily reporting and, alternatively, the release of only one of the respondents to enable the children, who were back in the United States with their grandmother, to visit and spend some time with her. At this hearing, the Minister argued for the first time that the respondents posed a danger to the public. This argument was rejected. The member concluded that even a release subject to cash bond and very stringent reporting conditions would not be effective considering that the respondents failed to appear for their trial in the United States, in spite of significant bail bonds in existence there (US$25,000 and US$100,000).

At the fourth hearing, the member concluded the detention was necessary to ensure the respondents would appear for their removal. At that time, in addition to the three conditions of release discussed earlier, the respondents proposed a release be made subject to a review once a decision was made on the refugee claim. They also alluded to the possibility of electronic tracking as an alternative to detention, but had been advised by the Minister that this was not a viable alternative as no such system was currently available. Despite the fact that the respondents were likely to remain in detention for several months pending the determination of their refugee claim, the member concluded that their continued detention was necessary and found he had no authority to give any direction to the Minister with respect to the quality of the detention and the electronic monitoring. At the fifth detention hearing, the respondents called a representative of the company Trace Canada as a witness to explain how Trace Canada would equip them with electronic tracking devices that would keep a record of their movements at all times. The company could then report this information to immigration officials who would know immediately if the respondents had breached their conditions of release. Their submission was that the flight risk would be considerably reduced if such a mechanism were in use. The member took the matter under advisement. When the hearing resumed, the member specified that he was not "reopening" the detention review, but simply wished to obtain some clarification with regard to the services offered by Trace Canada. He questioned the representative about the functioning of the electronic tracking system. The member concluded that he considered electronic monitoring to be more responsive than a self-monitored curfew and no-go zone. He also stated it was more responsive than periodic physical reporting where, according to him, the respondents could be long gone by the time they failed to show up to report. It was thus a more immediate form of reporting. He also noted that, in the end, if the person's intention is to abscond, they will do so whatever the type of monitoring and explained that:

> Alternatives to detention are not meant to provide absolute certainty of appearance for removal. They need only have the effect of reducing the risk to an acceptable degree. The fact that the persons concerned have proposed electronic monitoring and have made the effort to bring a proposal for consideration is an indication of their sincerity in seeking to address the Minister's concerns of flight.

The question the Court considered was not whether or not the member was justified in ordering the release on the conditions he did, but whether he had provided clear, compelling reasons for departing from the previous decisions reached at the detention reviews. Had the superiority of electronic monitoring been the sole basis of the decision, the Court would have concluded that the reasons given by the member met the low threshold set out by the Court of Appeal in *Thanabalasingham*. However, the member clearly distinguishes the situation before him from those reviewed by his colleagues on the basis of the "new evidence" with respect to the respondents' children. Since the member believed the information relating to the existence of the respondents' children was new, he could not properly turn his mind to the decisions of his colleagues on this point and consider why he should depart from the course of action they took. Since the member clearly failed to consider the contrary view expressed by the previous member on this particular point, the decision was set aside.



*Canada (Minister of Citizenship & Immigration) v. Singh (R.)* (2004), 263 F.T.R. 106, 2004 CarswellNat 5904, 2004 CarswellNat 4215, 2004 FC 1634 (F.C.) — This was an application by the Minister for judicial review of a decision of the Refugee Protection Division which ordered the applicant released. The Board member required the Minister to be satisfied with respect to the respondent's identity by a fixed date failing which the respondent would be released. Such a condition was beyond the Board member's jurisdiction.

## Section 58(2)

*Canada (Minister of Public Safety & Emergency Preparedness) v. Samuels* (2009), 85 Imm. L.R. (3d) 226, 2009 FC 1152, 2009 CarswellNat 5632, 2009 CarswellNat 3739 (F.C.) — This is an application by the Minister for judicial review of an order of a member of the Immigration Division to release the respondent from detention. The respondent was born in Panama but lived for 39 years in Jamaica. He is a citizen of both countries and came to Canada in 1991 and became a permanent resident. By September 1992, he was diagnosed as having schizophrenia. In total, the respondent has 27 or 30 criminal convictions, as well as over 10 provincial convictions. Following his last criminal conviction on March 14, 2005, he was immediately placed in immigration hold. He was released from immigration hold on October 12, 2006, under the Toronto Bail Program, for which he was supervised by Steven Sharp. Contrary to the terms of his release, the respondent repeatedly left his residence unescorted. Mr. Sharp was of the opinion that public safety would be a concern if the respondent remained in the community. The respondent was re-arrested and returned to immigration hold, remaining in detention ever since. A risk assessment officer reached a positive decision in June 2009 and the Minister then sought a danger opinion against the respondent, which would lead to his removal from Canada. Following the success of the PRRA application, the respondent sought to be released from detention. The member of the Immigration Division determined that while a danger opinion was being sought, it was likely to take a considerable time — and might yet turn out to be negative, so that it "wouldn't be fair" to keep the respondent in detention. Although the member noted that the respondent had "a pretty impressive criminal file," the member concluded that "if there's no removal in sight, the Immigration Division is not responsible to protect Canadian society anymore."

The Court held that the Immigration Division had jurisdiction to order the respondent's continued detention if it was satisfied that he was a danger to the public. The Court also found that the Immigration Division member failed to exercise its statutory duty, and quashed the decision to release the respondent. A removal order that is stayed is not void. Although it cannot be executed pending a ruling on a protected person's application for permanent residence or the passing of the deadline to file such an application, it still exists and is valid and, in the opinion of the Court, the person against whom it was issued is still "subject to it." Accordingly, the Immigration Division had jurisdiction to order the continued detention of the respondent, if it was satisfied that he was a danger to the public.

## Section 58(3)

*Canada (Minister of Public Safety & Emergency Preparedness) v. Sittampalam* (2009), 83 Imm. L.R. (3d) 147, 350 F.T.R. 101 (Eng.), 2009 FC 863, 2009 CarswellNat 5808, 2009 CarswellNat 2593 (F.C.) — This is an application for judicial review of a decision of the Immigration Refugee Board whereby the tribunal ordered changes in the terms and conditions of the respondent's release from custody. The applicant, the Minister of Public Safety and Emergency Preparedness, submits that the member's order compromises the ability of the Canadian Border Services Agency to properly monitor the respondent.

In August 2008, the respondent requested a variance to the conditions of his release to the Immigration Division. An agreement was made between counsel for the parties. The respondent requested an oral hearing to amend the conditions of release. An oral hearing was held before the member on October 8, 2008. At that hearing, the parties made submissions on the amendments requested in the respondent's motion. On November 13, 2008, the member released her order. She granted the respondent's motion and made additional amendments to the respondent's terms and conditions. The applicant sought judicial review of the decision to make additional amendments to the respondent's terms and conditions.

The member made significant changes to conditions which were not argued and which were not raised as being an issue in the hearing. In failing to provide the parties with an opportunity to make submissions and in altering and deleting conditions that were not requested by the respondent, the member breached the principles of procedural fairness, specifically the right to be heard and to know the case to be met. This error warranted the Court's intervention. The application for judicial review was allowed.

The following question was certified:

> Do the principles set forth by the Supreme Court of Canada in *Charkaoui v. M.C.I.* (2007), 59 Imm. L.R. (3d) 1, respecting a review of the conditions of release from detention, where the detention is based on a "Security Certificate," apply as well to detention reviews under subs. 58(3) of IRPA?

*Kang v. Canada (Minister of Public Safety & Emergency Preparedness)*, 2006 CarswellNat 1441, 2006 FC 652 (F.C.) — The applicant paid a cash deposit of $5,000 to secure her elderly mother's release from immigration detention. One of the release conditions was that the mother reside at her daughter's address "at all times." The mother was absent one day when Canada Border Services Agency officers visited to enquire about other family members. Several months later, after the mother had returned to Korea, the operations manager of the greater Toronto Enforcement Centre declared the $5,000 deposit forfeited. The applicant sought judicial review of that decision. The decision to forfeit a cash bond should withstand scrutiny on the reasonableness standard.

The applicant contended that the notes contained the interviewing officer's conclusions rather than statements fairly attributable to her or her mother. A close reading of the notes suggests that what may appear to be admissions against interest by the applicant and her mother are no more than a repetition of the conclusion reached by the immigration officer based on what the applicant's son may have mistakenly told the officer during the visit to the applicant's house. The case, therefore, was complicated by the involvement of other members of the family subject to arrest and removal and the language barrier. There was no fault on the part of the immigration officers, but the possibility of confusion and error should have been considered by the operations manager when there was contradictory affidavit evidence before her. The manager's factual finding that the release condition had been breached was patently unreasonable in light of that evidence. Furthermore, no rational explanation was provided as to why the evidence did not provide a justification for not forfeiting the deposit. Accordingly the decision was found to be unreasonable and was overturned.



The current Act is silent on the question of ministerial discretion for the forfeiture of security deposits or performance bonds but provides, in s. 61, for the making of regulations for the application of Division 6 with respect to detention and release. It was clear from the evidence that the operations manager did not consider whether a lesser amount, including no amount, would be sufficient to satisfy the purpose of imposing the cash deposit, particularly where, as here, the subject of the release condition had returned to her country of origin. Further, it was impossible to ascertain from the brief reasons endorsed on the applicant's submissions or from the terse letter communicating the decision what factors the manager took into consideration in deciding that the bond should be forfeited. The Court had no way to determine whether the manager relied upon considerations that were irrelevant or extraneous to the legislative purpose for which she exercised discretion. Accordingly, the manager's error in this regard amounted to another ground for concluding that the application must be granted and remitted for reconsideration by another officer.

*Khalife v. Canada (Minister of Citizenship & Immigration)*, [2006] F.C.J. No. 293, 52 Imm. L.R. (3d) 267, 2006 CarswellNat 456, 2006 CarswellNat 1135, 2006 FC 221 (F.C.) — The statute and the Regulations say little about the decisions to impose and to forfeit a cash deposit. The authority to require a cash deposit is found in the IRPA at subs. 58(3). The manager's decision to forfeit the deposit appears to have been made in accordance with the principles in the Immigration Canada Enforcement Manual. The manager exercised his statutory discretion in good faith, in accordance with the principles of natural justice and did not rely upon considerations irrelevant or extraneous to the statutory purpose. Instead, the manager verified that the applicant was fully aware of the conditions of his release and determined that the applicant had in fact breached these terms. The manager received and considered the applicant's representations and then followed the direction provided by s. 49(4) of the Regulations and the Manual and determined on the merits that it was appropriate to forfeit only part of the applicant's deposit.

*Tsang v. Canada (Minister of Public Safety & Emergency Preparedness)*, [2006] F.C.J. No. 576, 2006 CarswellNat 941, 2006 CarswellNat 2380, 2006 FC 474 (F.C.) — A regional director of the Canadian Border Services Agency decided that a performance bond granted by the applicant in the amount of $80,000 was forfeited. The bond had been provided for the release of the applicant's husband. He had violated a term of the release order and as a result was arrested. In consequence of this violation, the performance bond was forfeited. The decision to forfeit the $80,000 bond was set aside since the officer failed to appreciate that he had the discretion to make a decision that resulted in less than $80,000 being forfeited.

**59. Incarcerated foreign nationals** — If a warrant for arrest and detention under this Act is issued with respect to a permanent resident or a foreign national who is detained under another Act of Parliament in an institution, the person in charge of the institution shall deliver the inmate to an officer at the end of the inmate's period of detention in the institution.

**60. Minor children** — For the purposes of this Division, it is affirmed as a principle that a minor child shall be detained only as a measure of last resort, taking into account the other applicable grounds and criteria including the best interests of the child.

**61. Regulations** — The regulations may provide for the application of this Division, and may include provisions respecting

(a) grounds for and conditions and criteria with respect to the release of persons from detention;

(b) factors to be considered by an officer or the Immigration Division; and

(c) special considerations that may apply in relation to the detention of minor children.

## Division 7 — Right of Appeal

**62. Competent jurisdiction** — The Immigration Appeal Division is the competent Division of the Board with respect to appeals under this Division.

**63. (1) Right to appeal — visa refusal of family class** — A person who has filed in the prescribed manner an application to sponsor a foreign national as a member of the family class may appeal to the Immigration Appeal Division against a decision not to issue the foreign national a permanent resident visa.

**(2) Right to appeal — visa and removal order** — A foreign national who holds a permanent resident visa may appeal to the Immigration Appeal Division against a decision at an examination or admissibility hearing to make a removal order against them.

**(3) Right to appeal — removal order** — A permanent resident or a protected person may appeal to the Immigration Appeal Division against a decision at an examination or admissibility hearing to make a removal order against them.

**(4) Right of appeal — residency obligation** — A permanent resident may appeal to the Immigration Appeal Division against a decision made outside of Canada on the residency obligation under section 28.

*[Editor's Note: SOR/2002-227, s. 328(1) provides that a person who was a permanent resident immediately before June 28, 2002 is a permanent resident under the new* Immigration and Refugee Protection Act, *S.C. 2001, c. 27.]*

**(5) Right of appeal — Minister** — The Minister may appeal to the Immigration Appeal Division against a decision of the Immigration Division in an admissibility hearing.

## Case Law

### Section 63(1)

*Somodi v. Canada (Minister of Citizenship & Immigration)* (2009), 82 Imm. L.R. (3d) 159, 311 D.L.R. (4th) 335, 395 N.R. 270, 2009 FCA 288, 2009 CarswellNat 3062, 2009 CarswellNat 5060 (F.C.A.) — The appellant sought, in the Federal Court, judicial review of a decision of a visa officer which refused his spousal sponsorship application for permanent residence status as a member of the family class. At the same time as the appellant made his judicial review application, his sponsor appealed the decision of the visa officer. The appellant's application was dismissed by a judge of the Federal Court on the ground that paragraph 72(2)(a) of IRPA required the appellant's sponsor to exhaust her right of appeal to the Immigration Appeal Division (IAD) before an application for judicial review could be made. While the appellant's appeal was pending before the Federal Court of Appeal the IAD granted his sponsor's appeal and set aside the decision of the visa officer. In effect, the IAD, by setting aside the visa officer's decision, rendered the appellant's appeal moot since the decision which is the subject of the application for judicial review no longer exists. However, the Federal Court judge certified a question on an issue which has not been considered by the Federal Court of Appeal. Specifically the question reads:

> Does section 72 of the IRPA bar an application for judicial review by the applicant of a spousal application, while the sponsor exercises the rights of appeal pursuant to section 63 of the IRPA?

Both parties at the hearing submitted that it would be in the interest of justice that the Federal Court of Appeal answer the certified question.

It should be remembered that, on a family sponsorship application, the interest of the parties are congruent. Both the sponsor and the foreign national seek a reunification of the family. It would be illogical and detrimental to the objectives of the scheme to allow multiplicity of proceedings on the same issue, in different forms, to parties pursuing the same interest. It would also be detrimental to the administration of justice as it would open the door to conflict in decisions and fuel more litigation. This is precisely what Parliament intended to avoid. In addition, the appellant is not deprived of all remedies. He has other avenues such as an application to the Minister based on H&C considerations pursuant to s. 25 of IRPA. The appeal was dismissed for mootness and the Court answered the certified question in the affirmative.

*Sandhu v. Canada (Minister of Citizenship & Immigration)* (2005), 48 Imm. L.R. (3d) 104, 34 Admin. L.R. (4th) 307, 2005 CarswellNat 2101, 2005 CarswellNat 5263, 2005 FC 1046 (F.C.) — The Immigration Appeal Division dismissed the applicant's appeal of a visa officer's decision to refuse the applicant's application to sponsor his son as a member of the family class. The IAD concluded that the applicant had not shown that the visa officer's refusal was wrong in law. Accordingly, the IAD concluded that the person who was sponsored by the applicant was not a member of the family class and therefore under s. 65 of the IRPA, the IAD had no discretionary jurisdiction to consider humanitarian and compassionate considerations. The application for judicial review was allowed as the IAD provided no explanation or analysis whatsoever to conclude that the visa officer's refusal of the applicant's sponsorship application was wrong in law. Accordingly, the reasons provided by the IAD were entirely insufficient to allow the applicant and his family members to understand why they had been denied the opportunity to unite their family in Canada. The reasons were equally insufficient to allow the Federal Court to determine whether or not the tribunal was justified in deciding as it did.

*Singh v. Canada (Minister of Citizenship & Immigration)*, [2005] F.C.J. No. 2071, 2005 CarswellNat 4126, 2005 CarswellNat 4892, 2005 FC 1673 (F.C.) — An appeal heard under s. 63(1) of the IRPA results in a hearing *de novo*. In such a hearing, the IAD does not need to comment on every piece of new evidence that is proffered, but it must deal with evidence that directly contradicts, or at least addresses, the concerns of the original decision maker.

*de Guzman v. Canada (Minister of Citizenship & Immigration)*, [2005] F.C.J. No. 2119, 262 D.L.R. (4th) 13, 51 Imm. L.R. (3d) 17, 137 C.R.R. (2d) 20, 345 N.R. 73, 2005 CarswellNat 4381, 2005 FCA 436 (C.A.); leave to appeal to S.C.C. refused [2006] S.C.C.A. No. 70, 2006 CarswellNat 1695, 356 N.R. 399 (S.C.C.) — In 1993, the appellant came to live in Canada. When she was landed in Canada, she told the immigration officials that she was single and had no dependants, other than her daughter who was accompanying her. This was not true: she also had two sons whom she left in the Philippines with their father. Eight years later, after establishing herself in Canada and becoming a citizen, the appellant applied to sponsor her sons as members of the family class. They were refused visas under paragraph 117(9)(d) of the Regulations on the ground that they were not members of the family class because they had not been examined for immigration purposes when the appellant applied to come to Canada.

The appellant's misrepresentation was highly material to the success of her application for a visa in the family class as an unmarried daughter. Her daughter's birth certificate stated that the appellant was unmarried, unlike her sons' birth certificates.

The Immigration Appeal Division was correct in law to dismiss the appellant's appeal pursuant to paragraph 74(d) of the IRPA. Specifically, the Board concluded that since the sons were not members of the family class, the Board, under s. 65 of the IRPA, had no discretionary jurisdiction to consider humanitarian and compassionate circumstances.

The Federal Court of Appeal concluded that paragraph 117(9)(d) of the Regulations was not invalid or inoperative. It was not unconstitutional nor did it deprive the applicant of her right to liberty and/or her right to security of person, in a manner not in accordance with the principles of fundamental justice contrary to s. 7 of the *Charter*.

## Section 63(2)

*Zhang v. Canada (Minister of Citizenship & Immigration)*, 2007 CarswellNat 1498, 2007 FC 593 (F.C.) — In January 2004, the applicant received a visa in the mail from Canadian immigration authorities. Roughly one month after it was issued, her visa was revoked. She was asked to return it. Instead, she flew to Canada with the invalid document and tried to use it to enter the country. When the applicant arrived in Canada, immigration authorities realized her visa had been revoked and referred her to an admissibility hearing. An immigration officer found the applicant inadmissible to Canada under ss. 20(1)(a) and 41(a) of the *Immigration and Refugee Protection Act*. The applicant tried to appeal the officer's decision to the Immigration and Refugee Board's Immigration Appeal Division. The Board has jurisdiction to hear appeals against removal orders from admissibility hearings. However, its jurisdiction is set out specifically at s. 63(2) of the IRPA. This section limits the Board's appeal jurisdiction to foreign nationals who hold permanent resident visas.

To find that s. 63(2) of the IRPA applies to the applicants with invalid permanent resident visas would give persons, with no right to be in Canada, the right to appeal a removal order denying their ability to be in Canada. The fact the applicant still held the physical copy of her visa did not change the legal consequence of its revocation. Rather than pursuing an appeal of the immigration officer's removal order before the Board, she should have sought judicial review of the officer's decision in the Federal Court.



## Section 63(3)

*Canada (Minister of Citizenship & Immigration) v. Rumpler* (2008), 76 Imm. L.R. (3d) 237, 336 F.T.R. 285 (Eng.), 2008 CarswellNat 4258, 2008 CarswellNat 5085, 2008 FC 1264, 2008 CarswellNat 4258 — This was an application for judicial review of the decision of the IAD wherein the Division concluded it had jurisdiction to hear an appeal of the respondent's removal order. Returning to Canada from Israel, an immigration officer determined that the respondent did not satisfy the residency requirements of s. 28 of the Act, and undertook measures to have him removed. The period to appeal the removal order expired and the respondent voluntarily left Canada for the United States. The respondent then requested of the IAD an extension of the period to allow him to lodge an appeal of the removal order. The IAD decided that, according to subs. 63(3) of the Act, it did not have the competence to extend the period of appeal after its expiration, because the respondent had lost his status as permanent resident by failing to appeal. Justice Blanchard of the Federal Court granted the respondent's application for judicial review, and held that the IAD did have competence under the said provision to grant the extension. Accordingly, an extension was granted by a different member of the IAD and at a new hearing before the IAD, the Minister asked the tribunal to reject the appeal of the removal order on the ground of mootness, because the respondent had voluntarily left the country and thus executed the order. The Minister's motion was rejected and the Minister brought an application for judicial review of the IAD's decision.

The IAD erred in law in finding that it had continuing jurisdiction in spite of the fact that the respondent had left Canada and had executed the removal order before he filed a notice of appeal. It is trite law that the IAD does not have jurisdiction to reopen an appeal where the motion to reopen has been filed after an appellant is removed from Canada. Since the IAD did not have the jurisdiction to cancel the removal order once it had already been executed, it necessarily had no jurisdiction to grant a request (filed after such an execution) for an extension of time to lodge an appeal of the removal order. Consequently, the application for judicial review was allowed.

*Elias c. Canada (Ministre de la Citoyenneté & de l'Immigration)*, 2005 CarswellNat 5708, 2005 FC 1329 (F.C.) — The applicant sought judicial review of the IAD's decision dismissing their appeal from a removal order. The principal applicant was born in Lebanon and emigrated to Brazil, where he lived for 20 years and became a citizen of that country. The applicant was granted landing in Canada as an entrepreneur and accepted the conditions provided under paragraph 23.1 of the Immigration Regulations. The Immigration Division decided that the applicants were persons contemplated by s. 41 of the IRPA since the principal applicant had not respected the conditions imposed for entrepreneurs when he was granted landing. The IAD dismissed the applicant's appeal concluding that an order to stay the removal order would have the effect of not only calling into question the integrity of the program conceived to attract entrepreneurs, but also the integrity of the Canadian immigration system as a whole. The principal applicant argued that he had provided plausible explanations and reasons why he was unable to respect the conditions within the two-year time period. In this case, the Court concluded that the IAD weighed the best interests of the children directly affected as well as the other factors alleged by the applicants in support of their appeal but, considering the other circumstances of the matter, determined that special relief was not justified. The applicants' eldest son was born in Brazil while the younger son was born in Canada. The applicants did not submit any evidence regarding the effects that the removal to Brazil could have on the eldest child, or the effects of a possible migration on the younger child. The applicants' argument regarding the children amounted to saying that the presence of children in Canada automatically implies humanitarian considerations justifying special measures. The Court concluded that Parliament has not decided that the presence of children in Canada constitutes in itself an impediment to any *refoulement* of a parent illegally residing in Canada. The application for judicial review was dismissed.

**64. (1) No appeal for inadmissibility — No appeal may be made to the Immigration Appeal Division by a foreign national or their sponsor or by a permanent resident if the foreign national or permanent resident has been found to be inadmissible on grounds of security, violating human or international rights, serious criminality or organized criminality.**

**(2) Serious criminality — For the purpose of subsection (1), serious criminality must be with respect to a crime that was punished in Canada by a term of imprisonment of at least two years.**

**(3) Misrepresentation — No appeal may be made under subsection 63(1) in respect of a decision that was based on a finding of inadmissibility on the ground of misrepresentation, unless the foreign national in question is the sponsor's spouse, common-law partner or child.**

*[Editor's Note: S.C. 2001, c. 27, s. 190 provides that every application, proceeding or matter under the* Immigration Act, *R.S.C. 1985, c. I-2 (the "former Act") that is pending or in progress immediately before June 28, 2002 shall be governed by the* Immigration and Refugee Protection Act, *S.C. 2001, c. 27 (the "new Act"), effective June 28, 2002.*

*S.C. 2001, c. 27, s. 192 provides that if a notice of appeal has been filed with the Immigration Appeal Division immediately before June 28, 2002, the appeal shall be continued under the* Immigration Act, *R.S.C. 1985, c. I-2 (the "former Act") by the Immigration Appeal Division of the Immigration and Refugee Board.*

*S.C. 2001, c. 27, s. 196 provides that despite S.C. 2001, c. 27, s. 192, an appeal made to the Immigration Appeal Division before June 28, 2002 shall be discontinued if the appellant has not been granted a stay under the former Act and the appeal could not have been made because of s. 64 of the* Immigration and Refugee Protection Act, *S.C. 2001, c. 27 (the "new Act")*

*S.C. 2001, c. 27, s. 197 further provides that despite S.C. 2001, c. 27, s. 192, if an appellant who has been granted a stay under the former Act breaches a condition of the stay, the appellant shall be subject to the provisions of s. 64 and s. 68(4) of the new Act.*

*SOR/2002-227, s. 326(2) provides that a person in respect of whom s. 70(5) or paragraph 77(3.01)(b) of the former Act applied on June 28, 2002 is a person in respect of whom s. 64(1) of the new Act applies.]*

## Case Law

### Section 64(1)

*R. v. Hennessey* (2007), 63 Imm. L.R. (3d) 8, 228 O.A.C. 29, 2007 CarswellOnt 5272, 2007 ONCA 581 (C.A.) — The appellant plead guilty to five counts of robbery. In addition to seven months credit for pre-sentence custody, he was sentenced to 35 months imprisonment, concurrent, on each charge. The appellant asked the Court to vary his sentence to seven months imprisonment, consecutive, on each charge. The reason for this request was that an order was made deporting the appellant and, under s. 64(1) of the IRPA, the appellant had no right to appeal the deportation order if he received a sentence of two years imprisonment or more for any single offence. This circumstance was unknown to the appellant when he was sentenced. He had been in Canada since age five, his family is here and he wished to remain. On these particular facts, given the Crown's concession that a 35-month sentence imposed in addition to pre-sentence custody was appropriate in terms of totality, it would not circumvent the provisions and policies of the IRPA to impose sentences of 23 months on individual counts but a global sentence equivalent to that imposed by the trial judge.

*Holway v. Canada (Minister of Citizenship & Immigration)* (2005), 49 Imm. L.R. (3d) 281, 2005 CarswellNat 2927, 2005 FC 1261 (F.C.) — The applicant, a Canadian citizen, sought to sponsor his parents to come to Canada as permanent residents. A visa officer denied the sponsorship application on the basis that the applicant's father was a person described in s. 35(1)(b) of the IRPA. The applicant sought leave for judicial review and concurrently filed an appeal of the same decision with the Immigration Appeal Division (IAD). The Minister argued against leave being granted on the basis that the application was premature and that the applicant had not exhausted all rights of appeal under the IRPA, namely an appeal to the IAD. Without reasons, the Federal Court denied the application for leave. The IAD, in turn, ruled that it did not have jurisdiction to hear the applicant's appeal based on s. 64(1) of the IRPA. The plain wording of s. 64, read in the context of the IRPA as a whole, and in conjunction with the issue paper published before the IRPA, together with the clause by clause analysis prepared by the Department of Citizenship and Immigration, and provided to both the Standing Committee on Citizenship and Immigration and the Standing Senate Committee on Social Affairs, Science and Technology, confirm that Parliament's intent in enacting s. 64 of the IRPA was to foreclose any right of appeal to the IAD that may have been available to the applicant on the facts of this case.

The Minister conceded that a mistake was made by counsel in opposing the leave application that sought to challenge the visa officer's decision, specifically that the judicial review of the visa officer's decision was premature because the applicant had not exhausted his rights of appeal to the IAD. The Minister acknowledged the mistake and agreed to consent to a motion to the Federal Court to reconsider the order denying leave to review the visa officer's decision.

*Thevasagayampillai v. Canada (Minister of Citizenship & Immigration)*, 2005 CarswellNat 1094, 2005 FC 596 (F.C.) — The clear wording of s. 64(1) of IRPA together with the object of the IRPA and its scheme preclude the Appeal Division from reconsidering the finding of inadmissibility made by an authorized decision maker. If Parliament had intended to grant the right of appeal *de novo* with respect to the existence of one of the enumerated grounds mentioned in subs. 64(1), clearer language would have been used.

*R. v. Hamilton*, [2004] O.J. No. 3252, 72 O.R. (3d) 1, 186 C.C.C. (3d) 129, 241 D.L.R. (4th) 490, 189 O.A.C. 90, 22 C.R. (6th) 1, 2004 CarswellOnt 3214 (C.A.) — The risk of deportation can be a factor to be taken into consideration in choosing among the appropriate sentencing responses in tailoring the sentence to best fit the crime and the offender. However, the sentencing process cannot be used to circumvent the provisions and policies of the IRPA.

*Kroon v. Canada (Minister of Citizenship & Immigration*, [2004] F.C.J. No. 857, 36 Imm. L.R. (3d) 244, 2004 CarswellNat 2884, 2004 CarswellNat 1404, 2004 FC 697, 252 F.T.R. 257, 15 Admin. L.R. (4th) 315 (F.C.) — The IAD lacks jurisdiction to determine the constitutionality of s. 64 of IRPA. There is nothing in the legislation which either expressly or explicitly grants this jurisdiction. The challenge provisions expressly limit the jurisdiction of the IAD insofar as they remove any right of appeal to the tribunal by a permanent resident who has been found to be inadmissible on grounds of serious criminality. Parliament could not have been more clear in its intention to limit the IAD's jurisdiction with respect to individuals who fall within paragraph 36(1)(a) of the Act. Although the IAD has exclusive jurisdiction to consider questions of law and determine its own jurisdiction, its general powers do not extend to finding that a statutory section, which contain an express limitation on its jurisdiction, is unconstitutional.

### Section 64(2)

*Editor's Note: On February 22, 2010, important amendments to the Criminal Code came into force regarding sentencing. These were enacted under S.C. 2009, c. 29, the Truth in Sentencing Act. Under the new Criminal Code rules, the sentencing judge will have to state in the record whether any time of pre-sentence custody has been taken into consideration and, if so, whether the credit is granted on a 1:1 or (exceptionally) on a 1.5:1 basis. The new 1.5 credit rate will be the maximum permitted compared with the previous practice of crediting two or even three days per day detained.*

*Editor's Note: The Federal Court continues to accept CBSA's position that pre-sentence custody forms part of the period of punishment under s. 64(2) of IRPA, despite the Supreme Court of Canada's decision in* R. v. Mathieu, *[2008] 1 S.C.R. 723, which held that, as a general rule, pre-sentence custody was not part of the sentence.*

*Nguyen v. Canada (Minister of Citizenship & Immigration)*, 2010 FC 30, 2010 CarswellNat 78, 2010 CarswellNat 725 (F.C.) — The determinative issue for the IAD was whether the applicant's appeal of his deportation order was barred pursuant to subs. 64(2) of IRPA. The IAD concluded that a sentence of less than two years (in this case 18 months) does, for the purpose of subs. 64(2), become a sentence of more than two years simply because the trial judge, in imposing the sentence of less than two years, took into account the time already spent in custody as a result of the offence. Thus the sentence was 29 months (11 months of pre-sentence custody and an 18-month term of imprisonment after conviction) for the purposes of subs. 64(2). Because the IAD determined the applicant met the definition of "serious criminality," s. 64 was engaged and the IAD had no jurisdiction upon which it could consider an appeal of inadmissibility. See also *Ariri v. Canada (Minister of Public Safety & Emergency Preparedness)* (2009), 83 Imm. L.R. (3d) 162 (F.C.), where Justice Tannenbaum found that considering the pre-trial custody as part of the term of imprisonment for the purposes of determining that the applicant has serious criminality is an acceptable exemption to the ruling in *Mathieu.*

*R. v. Amon* (2009), 82 Imm. L.R. (3d) 41, 241 Man. R. (2d) 192, 2009 MBQB 163, 2009 CarswellMan 297 (Q.B.) — The accused had entered a plea of guilty to a charge of aggravated assault. The defence argued that a sentence of two years or more will affect the accused's immigration status and should be an important factor in assessing a fit and just sentence. The practice of the Court was to indicate at the time of sentence what time had been attributed to pre-sentence custody, and to record that time on the disposition sheet; it is only the measurements imposed at the time of the sentence that actually form part of the sentence. Therefore, no further time in custody was warranted in this case. Unfortunately, this did not apply to the accused because a series of Federal Court decisions have held that the time that an individual spends in pre-trial custody does form part of the "term of imprisonment" for the purposes of s. 64(2) of IRPA. Since it appears that the Immigration Appeal Division does not itself take on the task of calculating the pre-trial custody in order to determine appeal eligibility, but instead relies on how much pre-trial custody has been attributed to the sentence by the sentencing judge, the Court designated some portion of the pre-trial custody to the accused's sentence. But for the immigration issue, the Court might not have engaged in that calculation at all. However, the Crown would also want the Court to refer to a specific amount of pre-trial custody in imposing a sentence in order to provide a record of the extent of the sentence for future reference. In the event that an accused re-offends, the length of the period of incarceration attributed to an offence will be relevant in sentencing for a subsequent offence. Therefore, engaging in this calculation was not simply for the purpose of determining the accused's eligibility to appeal his removal order. The Court ordered that the disposition show pre-trial custody of two years less a day.

*Capra v. Canada (Attorney General)* (2008), 76 Imm. L.R. (3d) 21, 335 F.T.R. 299 (Eng.), 2008 CarswellNat 3875, 2008 CarswellNat 5267, 2008 FC 1212 — This was an application for a declaration that subs. 128(4) of the *Corrections and Conditional Release Act*, S.C. 1992, c. 20 ("CCRA") is invalid on the ground that it breaches ss. 7, 9 and 15 of the *Charter of Rights and Freedoms*. The applicant had been granted Convention refugee status and became a permanent resident on December 2, 1992. The applicant was subsequently convicted of 80 counts of fraud in connection with credit cards and automatic bank teller machines in 2001. A deportation order was issued on the grounds of serious criminality. Both the appeal of the deportation order and his application were dismissed and the applicant lost his permanent residence status. However, because of his refugee status, he could not be removed to Romania unless the Minister of Citizenship and Immigration issued an opinion that the applicant constitutes a danger to the public. The CBSA sought the opinion of the Minister that he was a danger to the public in Canada. In the meantime, the applicant served his sentence in a medium security federal correctional facility and underwent a rehabilitation program. He became eligible for an unescorted temporary absence ("UTA") and day parole in July 2008. The CBSA informed the sentence management office of the deportation order previously issued against the applicant. As a result, by operation of subs. 128(4) of the CCRA, the applicant was ineligible for release on a UTA or day parole until his full parole eligibility date. The applicant believed that he was being treated differently in relation to day parole eligibility because he was not a Canadian citizen. He claimed that he was the subject of discrimination and regardless of whether he was allowed to stay in Canada or not, he perceived that he was being denied an opportunity to work towards his own rehabilitation simply because of his identity.

The Court held that s. 128(4) of the CCRA was directed at inmates subject to removal. The operation of the subsection is triggered by the issuance of a removal order. A stay of that removal order suspends the section's effect. The application of the section is rationally tied to its purpose and cannot be called arbitrary in relation to the objectives sought to be attained. Accordingly this was not arbitrary detention within the meaning of s. 9. Furthermore, the Supreme Court of Canada had made it clear that a "change in the form in which a sentence is served, whether it be favourable or unfavourable to the prisoner, is not, in itself, contrary to any principle of fundamental justice."

Parliament has decided that offenders subject to removal should serve their sentences in different ways from other offenders, including Canadian citizens. This is to ensure that their status as offenders does not enhance their access to Canadian society over that of non-offenders who face deportation; it is also intended to ensure that their removal status does not result in their serving shorter sentences than either Canadian citizens or non-citizens who are not subject to removal. Parliament has chosen to deal with these issues by suspending day parole and UTA for offenders who are subject to removal. It is possible to disagree with this approach and with whether it achieves the objectives it is intended to achieve, but that was not the issue before the Court. What is relevant is that the variation in the form of the sentence that comes about as a result of subs. 128(4) of CCRA is triggered by the existence of a removal order and whether this fact makes it part of a deportation scheme.

The Court was not convinced that, if the purpose of parole is to protect society, the loss of the possibility of that protection because of the loss of eligibility for day parole under subs. 128(4) was a disadvantage to the applicant, whether or not he was removed from Canada. Furthermore if parole was a benefit to offenders, the Court was not convinced that the applicant had been disadvantaged by the loss of any such benefit in a situation where the evidence showed his deportation was being actively pursued and he did not fall into one of the exceptions specifically provided for under subs. 128(6). The applicant failed to demonstrate differential treatment between citizens and non-citizens. The application was dismissed.

*R. v. Mathieu*, [2008] S.C.J. No. 21, 292 D.L.R. (4th) 385, 373 N.R. 370, 56 C.R. (6th) 1, 231 C.C.C. (3d) 1, 2008 SCC 21, 2008 CarswellQue 3114, 2008 CarswellQue 3115 — "Pre-sentence custody is not part of the sentence, but is only one factor taken into account by the judge in determining the sentence". This means that a sentence of less than two years does not, for the purposes of s. 731(1)(b), become a sentence of more than two years simply because the trial judge, in imposing the sentence of less than two years, took into account the time already spent in custody as a result of the offence. It is not solely because of the law and s. 719 of the *Code* that pre-sentence custody is taken into account as a factor in sentencing. This result can also be inferred from a conceptual interpretation of pre-sentence custody. Pre-sentence custody generally refers to custody before the verdict is rendered, at a time when the accused is presumed innocent. In the context of these appeals, this custody is, in principle, preventive rather than punitive. Pre-sentence custody cannot really be characterized as a "sentence": if the accused is convicted, the judge does take it into account as a relevant factor in sentencing, but what if the accused is *acquitted*? Whether the pre-sentence custody was part of a sentence for the purposes of the *Code* would thus fall to be determined retroactively in light of the verdict — a subsequent and separate event.

Manifestly, the words "imprisonment for a term not exceeding two years" used by Parliament in s. 731(1)(b) refer to the custodial term imposed at the time of sentence — the actual term of imprisonment imposed by the Court after taking into account any time spent in pre-sentence custody. This interpretation of the word "sentence" is also justified by the purpose of a probation order, namely to facilitate the offender's rehabilitation. To conclude that a probation order is not available in cases where the total of the time spent in pre-sentence custody and the sentence of imprisonment imposed by the judge is more than two years, could have a harmful consequence, as the judge might decide to impose a longer period of incarceration. This interpretation must be rejected, since it would have the unfortunate effect of unjustifiably increasing the length of time to be served in prison. In addition, the probation order's effect of facilitating an offender's reintegration into society would be unavailable to offenders who might benefit from it.

*R v. Leila* (2008), 67 Imm. L.R. (3d) 82, 250 B.C.A.C. 117, 416 W.A.C. 117, 2008 BCCA 8 (C.A.) — Leave to appeal sentence is advanced on the ground that there is a serious and unintended collateral consequence to the sentence imposed by the trial judge in that a custodial sentence of two years or more results in the automatic termination of the appellant's right to appeal a deportation order to the IAD. The loss of the appellant's immigration appeal rights is a disproportionately severe collateral sanction, which was unforeseen by the appellant and his counsel at the sentencing hearing and apparently unintended by the sentencing judge. In the circumstances of this case, reducing the appellant's sentence to one which will allow him to preserve his immigration appeal rights is inconsequential to the sentencing principles relied upon by the sentencing judge. The appellant spent 57 days in pre-trial custody. The judge imposed a sentence of two years "plus time spent in custody". There was no indication that the judge gave credit beyond the 57 days spent in pre-trial custody and, therefore, the effective sentence appears to be one of two years and 57 days. Leave was granted and the appeal allowed to the extent of reducing the effective sentence so that it is one day under two years.

*Cheddesingh v. Canada (Minister of Citizenship & Immigration)* (2006), 52 Imm. L.R. (3d) 247, 2006 CarswellNat 259, 2006 FC 124 (F.C.) — Subsection 64(2) of the IRPA is not concerned with the length of the sentence imposed on the offender, but with the punishment. It is clear from the jurisprudence that once a person is convicted of a crime, time served by that individual in pre-trial detention will be deemed to be part of the offender's punishment.

In this case, the applicant argued that the proper interpretation was to compute the time a person is sentenced to spend in custody as of the date of the sentence, and the time spent in pre-sentence custody should not be taken into account. According to this interpretation, the applicant's term of imprisonment would only amount to a year instead of 30 months. The applicant's proposed interpretation was contrary to the intent of Parliament in drafting subs. 64(2) of the Act. Accordingly, the Board did not commit a reviewable error in determining that the period the applicant spent in pre-sentence custody formed part of her "term of imprisonment."

*Medovarski v. Canada (Minister of Citizenship & Immigration)*, [2005] 2 S.C.R. 539, 50 Imm. L.R. (3d) 1, 135 C.R.R. (2d) 1, 258 D.L.R. (4th) 193, [2005] S.C.J. No. 31, 339 N.R. 1, EYB 2005-95306, 2005 CarswellNat 2943, 2005 CarswellNat 2944, 2005 SCC 51 — The appellant was a permanent resident and had been ordered deported for serious criminality. Her removal order was automatically stayed when she appealed the deportation order to the Immigration Appeal Division. The appeal was discontinued as a result of s. 196 of the IRPA (a transitional provision), which took away the right to appeal an order for removal unless a party had, under the former Act, been "granted a stay." The trial judge set aside the decision to discontinue. However, the Federal Court of Appeal allowed the Minister of Citizenship and Immigration's appeal, holding that the purpose of the IRPA transitional provision was to deny the right of appeal in the case of an automatic stay. Section 196 of the IRPA, properly interpreted, applies only to actively granted stays. The objectives of the IRPA, as expressed in s. 3, indicate an intent to prioritize security. In keeping with these objectives, the IRPA creates a new scheme whereby a person sentenced to more than six months in prison is inadmissible pursuant to s. 36; if they have been sentenced to a prison term of more than two years, they are denied a right to appeal their removal order under s. 64 of the IRPA. The purpose in enacting the IRPA, and in particular s. 64, was to efficiently remove from the country persons who have engaged in serious criminality. Since s. 196 refers explicitly to s. 64, the transitional provision should be interpreted in light of these legislative objectives.

The deportation of a non-citizen cannot in itself implicate the liberty and security interests protected by s. 7 of the *Canadian Charter of Rights and Freedoms*. Even if the liberty and security of the person were engaged, any unfairness resulting from s. 196 would be inadequate to constitute a breach of principles of fundamental justice.

*Shepherd v. Canada (Minister of Citizenship & Immigration)* (2005), 48 Imm. L.R. (3d) 118, 2005 CarswellNat 2115, 2005 CarswellNat 3490, 2005 FC 1033 (F.C.) — The IAD concluded that the pre-sentencing custodial terms that had been expressly taken into account and credited to the applicant's sentence formed part of the term of imprisonment for the purposes of subs. 64(2) of the Act. Accordingly, the IAD ruled that the applicant had lost his right on appeal in light of subs. 64(2). Subsection 719(3) of the *Criminal Code* specifically provides that pre-sentence detention can be taken into account when a court is imposing a sentence and in this case it was clear that the sentencing judge considered the pre-sentencing detention to be part of the punishment imposed on the applicant. The record showed that the applicant was punished by a term of imprisonment of at least two years and that falls within the definition of "serious criminality" pursuant to subs. 64(2). In these circumstances, the applicant had no right of appeal to the IAD.

*Bouttavong v. Canada (Minister of Citizenship & Immigration)* (2005), 344 N.R. 134, 2005 CarswellNat 3527, 2005 CarswellNat 5559, 2005 FCA 341 (Fed. C.A.) — Former public danger opinions are irrelevant to the determination of danger to the public under subs. 113(d)(i). This does not mean that the underlying criminal convictions may not be taken into account, only that the danger opinions are irrelevant.

*Sherzad v. Canada (Minister of Citizenship & Immigration)*, 2005 CarswellNat 1493, 2005 FC 757 (F.C.) — In determining whether a crime was one that was punished in Canada by a term of imprisonment of at least two years, regard may be had to the time spent in pre-trial custody which resulted in a reduction of the sentence that was ultimately imposed.

*Martin v. Canada (Minister of Citizenship & Immigration)*, 42 Imm. L.R. (3d) 104, 2005 CarswellNat 86, 2005 CarswellNat 1819, 2005 FC 60, [2005] F.C.J. No. 83 (F.C.) — Section 64(2) must be interpreted as referring to the term of imprisonment for which an offender was sentenced. That is, the punishment imposed rather than the actual amount of time served prior to being granted parole.

*Canada (Minister of Citizenship & Immigration) v. Smith* (2004), 42 Imm. L.R. (3d) 254, 2004 CarswellNat 4933, 2004 CarswellNat 5740, 2004 FC 63, [2004] F.C.J. No. 2159 (F.C.) — Pre-sentence custody is included in the phrase "term of imprisonment" under s. 64(2) of the IRPA.

*Canada (Minister of Citizenship & Immigration) v. Atwal*, 2004 CarswellNat 23, 2004 CarswellNat 1623, 2004 FC 7, [2004] F.C.J. No. 63, 245 F.T.R. 170 (F.C.) — This was an application to review a decision of the Appeal Division refusing to discontinue the respondent's appeal. The respondent had received a sentence of 6 months which sentence took into account 20 months of pre-sentence custody.

The time spent in pre-sentence custody is to be taken into consideration under s. 64.

*Cartwright v. Canada (Minister of Citizenship & Immigration)*, 32 Imm. L.R. (3d) 79, 2003 CarswellNat 3179, 2003 CarswellNat 1899, 236 F.T.R. 98, 2003 FCT 792, [2003] F.C.J. No. 1024 (Fed. T.D.) — The applicant sought to review a decision of the Adjudicator declining to hear the applicant's appeal against the deportation. The applicant was born in the Bahamas and came to Canada when he was 4 years old. He never applied for Canadian citizenship. The applicant had a history of criminal offences, and was sentenced on January 25, 2001 to a four year term in a Federal Penitentiary. Section 64(2) must be interpreted as referring to the term of imprisonment for which an offender is sentenced, rather than the actual amount of time served prior to being granted parole.



**65. Humanitarian and compassionate considerations — In an appeal under subsection 63(1) or (2) respecting an application based on membership in the family class, the Immigration Appeal Division may not consider humanitarian and compassionate considerations unless it has decided that the foreign national is a member of the family class and that their sponsor is a sponsor within the meaning of the regulations.**

## Case Law

*de Guzman v. Canada (Minister of Citizenship & Immigration)*, [2005] F.C.J. No. 2119, 262 D.L.R. (4th) 13, 51 Imm. L.R. (3d) 17, 137 C.R.R. (2d) 20, 345 N.R. 73, 2005 CarswellNat 4381, 2005 FCA 436 (C.A.); leave to appeal to S.C.C. refused [2006] S.C.C.A. No. 70, 2006 CarswellNat 1695, 356 N.R. 399 (S.C.C.) — In 1993, the appellant came to live in Canada. When she was landed in Canada, she told the immigration officials that she was single and had no dependants, other than her daughter who was accompanying her. This was not true: she also had two sons whom she left in the Philippines with their father. Eight years later, after establishing herself in Canada and becoming a citizen, the appellant applied to sponsor her sons as members of the family class. They were refused visas under paragraph 117(9)(d) of the Regulations on the ground that they were not members of the family class because they had not been examined for immigration purposes when the appellant applied to come to Canada.

The appellant's misrepresentation was highly material to the success of her application for a visa in the family class as an unmarried daughter. Her daughter's birth certificate stated that the appellant was unmarried, unlike her sons' birth certificates.

The Immigration Appeal Division was correct in law to dismiss the appellant's appeal pursuant to paragraph 74(d) of the IRPA. Specifically, the Board concluded that since the sons were not members of the family class, the Board, under s. 65 of the IRPA, had no discretionary jurisdiction to consider humanitarian and compassionate circumstances.

The Federal Court of Appeal concluded that paragraph 117(9)(d) of the Regulations was not invalid or inoperative. It was not unconstitutional nor did it deprive the applicant of her right to liberty and/or her right to security of person, in a manner not in accordance with the principles of fundamental justice contrary to s. 7 of the *Charter*.

**66. Disposition — After considering the appeal of a decision, the Immigration Appeal Division shall**

**(a) allow the appeal in accordance with section 67;**

**(b) stay the removal order in accordance with section 68; or**

**(c) dismiss the appeal in accordance with section 69.**

## Case Law

*Younis v. Canada (Minister of Citizenship & Immigration)* (2008), 74 Imm. L.R. (3d) 115, 332 F.T.R. 99 (Eng.), 2008 CarswellNat 2744, 2008 FC 944 — The applicant had a number of criminal convictions. The Immigration Division issued a deportation order against the applicant on the basis that he was inadmissible for serious criminality under s. 36(1)(a) of the Act because of his conviction for drug trafficking. The applicant appealed the deportation order and sought special relief on humanitarian and compassionate grounds under the Act. He did not challenge the legal validity of the deportation order. The IAD denied the applicant's appeal. The applicant then sought judicial review of that decision. The issues raised in the application were whether the IAD erred in admitting the applicant's juvenile criminal record into evidence, and whether the IAD erred in taking into consideration the report to Crown counsel. The *Youth Criminal Justice Act* ("YCJA") contains prohibitions against the release of records of convictions of young persons as well as some exceptions to the prohibition against the release of records of convictions of young persons. The question of whether or not the applicant's juvenile record fell within the period of access and is accessible turned on whether the sexual assault conviction was for a summary or indictable offence. There was no indication in the evidence before the IAD whether the applicant, as a youth, was convicted of a summary or indictable offence. Without such evidence, the IAD had no way of determining whether the applicant's juvenile conviction was releasable under the YCJA. The IAD is responsible for determining the admissibility, reliability and weight to be given to evidence presented before it. Although the IAD is not bound by the same legal or technical rules of evidence as a court of law, this does not confer upon the IAD the authority to admit a youth criminal record where the second conviction falls outside the period of access. The release of such a report would not only constitute a breach of s. 118 of the YCJA, it would also amount to a breach of the procedural fairness guarantees in hearings before the IAD. The IAD was found to have a duty to determine the admissibility of the applicant's youth criminal record before considering whether the record was credible and trustworthy and before determining the weight to be given to the record.

The IAD relied on the report to Crown counsel which contained a list of proposed criminal charges against the applicant. The IAD failed to make the necessary distinction between the fact that the proposed charges were mere allegations and that the applicant had not been convicted of the offences. Although it was open to the IAD to consider the evidence underlying the charges in question, it was not open to the IAD to conclude that this evidence was sufficient to find that the applicant was guilty of the offences proposed in the report. The IAD's decision was also void of any discussion regarding the reliability and credibility of the report. The absence of any analysis in this regard suggested that the IAD failed to turn its mind to whether the report was reliable and credible. This omission constituted an error of law. The application for judicial review was allowed.

**67. (1) Appeal allowed — To allow an appeal, the Immigration Appeal Division must be satisfied that, at the time that the appeal is disposed of,**

**(a) the decision appealed is wrong in law or fact or mixed law and fact;**

**(b) a principle of natural justice has not been observed; or**

**(c) other than in the case of an appeal by the Minister, taking into account the best interests of a child directly affected by the decision, sufficient humanitarian and compassionate considerations warrant special relief in light of all the circumstances of the case.**

**(2) Effect — If the Immigration Appeal Division allows the appeal, it shall set aside the original decision and substitute a determination that, in its opinion, should have been made, including the making of a removal order, or refer the matter to the appropriate decision-maker for reconsideration.**



## Case Law

### Section 67(1)

*Singh v. Canada (Minister of Citizenship & Immigration)* (2010), 89 Imm. L.R. (3d) 36, 2010 FC 378, 2010 CarswellNat 3016, 2010 CarswellNat 817, [2010] F.C.J. No. 426 (F.C.) — The applicant was recently found to be inadmissible for misrepresenting or withholding a material fact when he immigrated to Canada in 1993. At that time, he did not disclose that he had fathered a child who remained in India. His defence is that he did not know he had fathered a child. Paternity has now been scientifically established by DNA tests. As a result, the Immigration Division of the Immigration and Refugee Board of Canada issued an exclusion order and he was ordered removed from Canada. His appeal to the Immigration Appeal Division was dismissed. He sought judicial review of that decision.

The applicant's submission is that he could not have misrepresented or withheld facts within the meaning of s. 40 of IRPA or its predecessor, since subjectively he had no knowledge at the time that he was the girl Shilpa's biological father. The Minister's position is that it does not matter what the applicant knew or did not know, it is a scientifically proven fact that he is Shilpa's biological father, and that is the end of the matter.

Given that the wording "knowingly" does not appear in s. 40, it follows, that knowledge is not a prerequisite to a finding of misrepresentation or withholding material facts. Undoubtedly, the existence of a child is a material fact. In this case, the alleged misrepresentation was a misstatement of fact. Such misrepresentations may be fraudulent, negligent or innocent. The panel found that the applicant was not credible. Even if he did not know that he was Shilpa's father, the circumstances, *i.e.* his long sexual relationship with Shilpa's mother while her husband was out of India, should, at the very least, have put him on inquiry. He had a duty of candour which required him to disclose upon his arrival in Canada in 1993 the strong possibility that he had fathered a child. The panel's assessment of facts was not unreasonable and so it follows that the applicant, a permanent resident, is inadmissible for misrepresentation.

One of the objectives of IRPA, as set out in s. 3, is "to see that families are reunited in Canada," not to remove someone against his will so that he may be reunited with his wife and daughter in India. The panel noted that the applicant had been here for many years, and had been gainfully employed, however, it made no assessment of the job prospects of a 50-year-old man in India, taking into account his obligation to support his wife and child. How the couple manages their affairs is their business. It would appear that they would prefer that the applicant work in Canada. There is nothing preventing him from visiting his wife and daughter in India on a regular basis. Perhaps after he has saved more money, he will return to and retire in India. It was not for the panel to say that they would be better off if reunited in India now. This smacked of "big brotherhood." This aspect of the decision was unreasonable. The matter was referred back to a differently constituted panel for reconsideration.

*Malfeo v. Canada (Minister of Citizenship & Immigration)*, 2010 CarswellNat 372, 2010 CarswellNat 2169, 2010 FC 193 (F.C.) — The main question raised by this judicial review application was whether a member of the Immigration Appeal Division (IAD) breached the principles of natural justice and/or the requirements of the law when she dismissed the applicant's request to stay his deportation to Italy. This application had been made pursuant to s. 67(1)(c) of IRPA, which enables the tribunal to grant relief if sufficient humanitarian and compassionate considerations are demonstrated in light of the circumstances.

The use of joint submissions is a concept well known in criminal law where the Crown and the defence make joint submissions, for example, in sentencing. It is not unknown in administrative law cases and has been applied by this Court in the context of immigration law (see *Nguyen v. Canada (Minister of Citizenship & Immigration)* (2000), 10 Imm. L.R. (3d) 252), a case which bears similarity with the case at hand since it involved an application by Mr. Nguyen to the then Appeal Division for the exercise of its humanitarian and compassionate jurisdiction under a provision of the now repealed *Immigration Act* similar to paragraph 67(1)(c) of IRPA. That case involved the failure of the tribunal to explain why the joint submissions of counsel proposing a five-year stay was not endorsed. The purpose of staying the deportation is, in that case as it is in this one, to give the applicant an opportunity to demonstrate, on the ground so to speak, becoming a decent law-abiding resident of the country.

Having received the joint submission albeit unexpectedly, the tribunal breached procedural fairness by rejecting it outright without asking for further input. The applicant in these circumstances was not given a fair hearing. The tribunal provided no analysis and did not even refer to the proposed terms and conditions. It was also clear that the tribunal did not give serious consideration to the joint submissions. Again, it provided no analysis of its terms and dismissed the joint submission in a perfunctory manner. The reasons put forward for rejecting the joint submission also lacked analysis. The application for judicial review was granted.

*Shaath v. Canada (Minister of Citizenship & Immigration)* (2009), 349 F.T.R. 81 (Eng.), 2009 FC 731, 2009 CarswellNat 2251, 2009 CarswellNat 4145 (F.C.) — The applicant sought judicial review of a decision dismissing his appeal from a departure order issued against him, by reason of his failure to comply with s. 28 of IRPA, which provides that a permanent resident meets his residency obligations in each five-year period if he/she was physically present in Canada at least 730 days during that period.

The tribunal reached its conclusion despite the fact counsel for the Minister appearing before the tribunal agreed the appeal should be allowed on humanitarian grounds mainly because of the family's establishment in Canada who, except for the applicant, are Canadian citizens. Counsel for the Minister also recognized his important financial investment in Canada and "he had been credible in his efforts to obtain his certification in Canada in order to get a job in his own specialty in the near future." Counsel's main reason for recommending the applicant's appeal be allowed was that she thought it was "nonsense to ask for a denial of the appeal since Mr. Shaath could apply tomorrow as a member of the family class, sponsored by his wife and it would be really easy to obtain his permanent residency and start the whole thing again." She considered that in all of the circumstances, "the punishment of losing his permanent residency would be disproportionate in all of the circumstances." The tribunal disagreed with counsel for the Minister's recommendation.



The Supreme Court of Canada's decision in *Canada (Citizenship & Immigration) v. Khosa* (2009), 77 Imm. L.R. (3d) 1, has a considerable impact upon this case because it dealt with the exercise by the IAD of its discretion under paragraph 67(1)(c) of IRPA. *Khosa* makes it clear where reasonableness standard applies, it requires deference and reviewing Courts are not allowed to substitute their own appreciation of the appropriate solution but rather must determine if the outcome falls "within a range of possible, acceptable outcomes which are defensible in respect of the facts and the law." Paragraph 67(1)(c) provides a power to grant "exceptionable relief" and calls for a fact-dependent and policy-driven assessment. An applicant has the burden of adducing proof of any claim upon which a humanitarian and compassionate application relies. The application for judicial review was dismissed.

*Vazirizadeh v. Canada (Minister of Citizenship & Immigration)*, [2009] F.C.J. No. 919, 2009 FC 807, 2009 CarswellNat 2387, 2009 CarswellNat 4932 (F.C.) — This was a judicial review of a decision of the IAD to dismiss the appeal of a sponsorship of a parent who was found to be medically inadmissible pursuant to paragraph 38(1)(c) of the Act because her health condition "might reasonably be expected to cause excessive demand on health or social services" in Canada. Six months after the visa officer's decision, she underwent right knee replacement surgery in Iran. The applicant argued that the IAD hearing, which was a *de novo* hearing, did not consider the appellant's changed medical status. The Court, however, concluded that the IAD analyzed the medical condition both at the time of the visa officer's decision in 2007 and the IAD hearing in 2008, including the evidence of right knee replacement surgery, physiotherapy and the opinion of the appellant's orthopedic specialist. However, the IAD reiterated or quoted the original medical opinion which, besides the likelihood of specialized knee replacement surgery, stated that the appellant's mother suffers from other medical problems, *i.e.* hypertension, obesity, osteoporosis and osteoarthritis, degenerative changes of the spine and hands and also degenerative osteoporosis of the thoracic vertebrae.

The Federal Court referred to *Mohamed v. Canada (Minister of Employment & Immigration)*, [1986] 3 F.C. 90, a Federal Court of Appeal decision which held that the medical condition at the time the visa officer refused the visa was the only relevant one and subsequent improvement in the medical condition was only relevant as to whether special relief should be granted on appeal.

The Federal Court concluded that the IAD's decision was well founded in fact and in law and amply satisfied the test of falling within an acceptable range of reasonable decisions and therefore the application for judicial review was dismissed. The Federal Court also refused to certify a question.

*Canlas v. Canada (Minister of Public Safety & Emergency Preparedness)*, 2009 CarswellNat 1492, 2009 FC 303 (F.C.) — This is an application for judicial review of the decision of a member of the IAD which dismissed the applicants' appeal of a removal order made against them pursuant to subs. 40(2) of the IRPA. The principal applicant obtained permanent residence status for herself and her daughters under false representations about their civil status and their identities as well as her own identity. The applicant obtained false birth certificates for her two daughters in order for them to leave the Philippines without the knowledge of their biological father, and misrepresented their paternity by indicating falsely that she was married to another man and that he was their biological father. The Canadian authorities discovered the applicants' false representations in September 2004, when the other man applied for a temporary resident visa in which he declared names of his wife and his children. The applicants requested that the exclusion orders issued against them be quashed on the basis of sufficient H&C warranting special relief supported by the best interests of her Canadian-born son.

The IAD ignored the medical report stating that since an early age, the applicant's Canadian-born son was followed and treated in a Canadian pediatric clinic with specialized multi-disciplinary care, and that two of the medications needed for his treatment were not readily available in developing countries such as the Philippines. In addition, the IAD found that there was no reason why the Canadian-born child could not remain with his father in Canada. The father, however, was not called as a witness and no material or information was filed on his behalf to confirm his willingness and/or ability to care for his son. Obligation to inquire as to whether a child will be adequately looked after if a parent is removed from Canada stems from dicta in *Adams v. Canada (Minister of Citizenship & Immigration)* (March 28, 2008), Doc. IMM-1470-08 (F.C.).

The IAD acknowledged that in *Adams*, the facts were "strikingly similar to those in the instant case", inasmuch as a Canadian-born child is concerned. In order to be able to distinguish the present case from *Adams*, the IAD erred in assuming the father was available to care for the minor child in Canada in replacement of the mother and her two daughters, and this without any evidence to support such finding. The application for judicial review was allowed.

*Ferrer v. Canada (Minister of Citizenship & Immigration)*, 2009 CarswellNat 899, 2009 CarswellNat 2095, 2009 FC 356 (F.C.) — The applicant sought judicial review of a decision of the IAD which dismissed his plea for humanitarian and compassionate relief pursuant to s. 67(1)(c) of the IRPA. An exclusion order had been issued against the applicant based on a finding of inadmissibility for a misrepresentation made in September, 1998 with respect to his permanent resident application. In his application, the applicant testified that he was single with no children. It was not disputed that at the time he was the father of two dependent children living with their mother in the Philippines. The applicant married his spouse who was the mother of his two children on a trip back to the Philippines after he was granted permanent residence status in Canada. The spouse is not excluded from the family class pursuant to s. 117(9)(d) of the Regulations. Accordingly, the applicant's two children would be eligible to be included on the spouse's application for permanent residence as her dependent children, provided the applicant's appeal before the IAD was allowed as he would be in a position to sponsor his wife and both of his children as members of the family class.

The IAD considered only two possibilities with respect to the best interests of the children. The first possibility was that the children could remain in the Philippines and that their father would continue to have a geographically distant relationship with them while at the same time supporting them financially at a higher level than possible if he were returned to the Philippines. The second alternative was that the applicant could be returned to the Philippines where he would be able to better meet their emotional needs by having close contact with them, though he would not be able to provide the higher level of financial support in the event that he was removed from Canada. It was argued that the analysis was erroneous and that it did not take into consideration the most probable outcome should the applicant's appeal be allowed. The tribunal's failure to consider this probable outcome led to its conclusion that the best interests of the children were a neutral factor when in fact the best interests of the children were a positive factor which weighed in favour of allowing the appeal. In other words, the tribunal failed to appreciate that the applicant's children could have the best of both worlds by being reunited with him in Canada. Had the tribunal not committed this error, it would certainly have considered the best interests of the applicant's children to be a factor in favour of allowing his appeal and not a neutral factor — thereby negating its value. It appears that the IAD's reasoning was dominated by a consideration of the "integrity of the Canadian immigration system". This might be an important factor to consider, but only after the best interest of the children are properly addressed; only in this way can a fair and balanced approach be taken to this important statutory requirement. The application for judicial review was allowed and the matter sent back for redetermination.



*Khosa v. Canada (Minister of Citizenship & Immigration)*, [2009] S.C.J. No. 12, 77 Imm. L.R. (3d) 1, 82 Admin. L.R. (4th) 1, 2009 SCC 12, 304 D.L.R. (4th) 1, 385 N.R. 206, 2009 CarswellNat 434, 2009 CarswellNat 435 — The applicant, a permanent resident of Canada, was convicted of criminal negligence causing death as a result of his participation in an automobile race. It ended with the death of an innocent pedestrian who was struck by the applicant's vehicle. The applicant received a conditional sentence of two years less a day with various conditions. He was declared inadmissible for serious criminality pursuant to s. 36(1)(a) of the Act and was ordered removed from Canada. He appealed. He did not challenge the validity of his removal order but rather sought special relief on the basis of humanitarian and compassionate considerations. The majority of the IAD dismissed his appeal. The application for judicial review was dismissed. The Court of Appeal concluded that the applicable standard of review should be reasonableness, essentially because the decision was not protected by a full privative clause, was not a polycentric one, related to human interest and did not, so far as the possibility of rehabilitation factors was concerned, engage the Board's expertise. The Federal Court of Appeal reviewed the Board's decision on the correct standard of review, reasonableness. Accordingly, the Board's decision was found to be unreasonable as it appeared that the Board was trying to second guess decisions of the criminal court and disagreed with the criminal sentence imposed on the applicant and saw in the H&C decision an opportunity to readdress the situation.

On appeal to the Supreme Court of Canada, the appeal restored the decision of the IAD. The majority of the Court concluded that in *New Brunswick (Board of Management) v. Dunsmuir*, [2008] S.C.J. No. 9, 69 Imm. L.R. (3d) 1, [2008] 1 S.C.R. 190, 372 N.R. 1, 69 Admin. L.R. (4th) 1, 844 A.P.R. 1, 2008 C.L.L.C. 220-020, D.T.E. 2008T-223, 329 N.B.R. (2d) 1, 170 L.A.C. (4th) 1, 291 D.L.R. (4th) 577, 2008 SCC 9, 64 C.C.E.L. (3d) 1, 95 L.C.R. 65, 2008 CarswellNB 124, 2008 CarswellNB 125, did away with the distinction between "patent unreasonableness" and "reasonableness *simpliciter*" and substituted a more context-driven view of "reasonableness" that nevertheless "does not pave the way for a more intrusive review by courts". *Dunsmuir* teaches that judicial review should be less concerned with the formation of different standards of review and more focused on substance, particularly on the nature of the issue that was before the administrative tribunal under review. Here, the decision of the IAD required the application of broad policy considerations to the facts as found to be relevant, and weighed for importance, by the IAD itself. The question whether the applicant had shown "sufficient humanitarian and compassionate considerations" to warrant relief from his removal, which all parties acknowledged to be valid, was a decision which Parliament confided to the IAD, not to the courts. On general principles of administrative law, including the Supreme Court of Canada's recent decision in *Dunsmuir*, the applications judge was right to give a high degree of deference to the IAD decision. The majority of the IAD was within a range of reasonable outcomes and the majority of the Federal Court of Appeal erred in intervening in this case to quash it. The appeal was therefore allowed and the decision of the IAD was restored.

*Tamber v. Canada (Minister of Citizenship & Immigration)*, 2008 CarswellNat 2867, 2008 CarswellNat 3913, 2008 FC 951 (F.C.) — Both the visa officer and the Board concluded that the marriage between the applicant and a Mr. Singh was not genuine. The applicant sought judicial review of the Board's decision. She had given birth to a baby boy on March 11, 2005, and DNA testing confirmed Mr. Singh as the alleged father with a 99.98% probability of paternity. The Board rejected the DNA evidence even though the supporting test documentation was on its face reliable and the respondent acknowledged that the analysis had been carried out by a reputable Canadian laboratory. That, however, was not the primary problem with the Board's approach to this highly determinative evidence. If the Board had reservations about the reliability of this testing or about the continuity of the blood samples, it had a clear duty to advise the applicant's counsel of its concerns. This was a proceeding that spanned two hearings separated by almost three months and there was no justification for ambushing the applicant by essentially ignoring the issue during the testimonial phase. It was open to the Minister to supervise the DNA testing and to control the continuity of the evidence obtained; it was not appropriate for the Minister to sit silently until all the evidence was in and then criticize the process as deficient. For the same reason it was unfair for the Board to reject this evidence as unreliable. It is a well-accepted principle of natural justice that the Board's concerns about the reliability of important documentary evidence must be put to the claimant either for an explanation or to allow for additional corroboration. The application was allowed.

*Ivanov v. Canada (Minister of Citizenship & Immigration)* (2006), 56 Imm. L.R. (3d) 56, 2006 CarswellNat 2335 (Imm. & Ref. Bd. (App. Div.)) — The appellant made an application for permanent residence as an independent in May 2001. At the time he disclosed that he had never been married and had no dependants. The application was successful and he was issued a permanent resident visa in June 2003. The appellant married his girlfriend on October 3, 2003. The appellant arrived in Canada on October 7, 2003. He disclosed his recent marriage to Canadian immigration officials upon his arrival in Toronto. At the time of his examination at Pearson Airport, he could not establish that his wife met the requirements of IRPA and the Regulations. His counsel wrote to the Canadian Embassy in Vienna in November 2003 advising that the immigration official at the port of entry had no objection regarding the release of the landed documents to the appellant subject to the appellant's wife meeting the medical and security requirements. The Embassy replied that there was no legal basis on which they were required to assess the wife against the admissibility criteria of IRPA. The appellant was issued an exclusion order on the basis that he was unable to establish at the time of his examination that his wife met the requirement of the Act and the Regulations. The appellant appealed the exclusion order.

The Appeal Board concluded that the exclusion order was valid in law. The appeal, however, was allowed under s. 67(1)(c) and the matter referred back to an immigration officer at the port of entry for reconsideration. The Board found that the appellant made an honest mistake in not informing the visa officer of his marriage prior to appearing for landing, but had disclosed the marriage immediately upon landing. As a result of the appellant's error, the Board concluded that he had suffered financial hardship upon his arrival in Canada, exhausting his savings because he could not legally work here. The Board found that the appellant had established humanitarian and compassionate considerations to warrant the granting of special relief in light of all the circumstances of the case. The Board directed that the department take all steps required to facilitate the examination of the appellant's wife and to provide the appellant with the necessary immigration documents to allow the appellant to attend before an immigration officer at a port of entry for reconsideration.

*Vong v. Canada (Minister of Citizenship & Immigration)* (2006), 60 Imm. L.R. (3d) 98, 2006 CarswellNat 4315, 2006 FC 1480 (F.C.) — The Immigration Appeal Division concluded the applicant failed to comply with the residency obligations of s. 28 of the Act during the five-year period immediately preceding August 2, 2004. The applicant appealed this decision and in the *de novo* proceedings before the Board, he produced new evidence in support of his insistence that he met the two-year residency requirement. The Board did not find the evidence credible and refused his appeal. The applicant argued the Board committed an error of law in not considering humanitarian and compassionate factors. During the Board hearing, the applicant waived his right to invoke a grant for special relief pursuant to paragraph 67(1)(c) of the Act (H&C). The applicant sought instead to provide evidence that would prove he met the residency requirements.

There is very little jurisprudence on this matter regarding the onus of the Board to consider H&C factors in spite of the stated position of the applicant not to pursue such factors. Even if the Board is required to consider H&C factors against the express wishes of the applicant, the onus will not shift from the applicant to establish exceptional reasons why he should be allowed to remain in Canada. The Board has no obligation to assume such a burden. The applicant failed to establish that the Board committed an error that would warrant intervention with respect to the H&C factors. The Court did conclude that the Board's decision regarding the credibility of the applicant and his documentary evidence should be set aside and the matter was sent back for the re-determination before a different Board member.

*Chang v. Canada (Minister of Citizenship & Immigration)*, [2006] F.C.J. No. 217, 2006 CarswellNat 329, 2006 CarswellNat 2194, 2006 FC 157 (F.C.) — The legislatively established conditions of the entrepreneur category, if flaunted knowingly, without serious consequence, would make a mockery of the purpose for which they were established. The act of creating or participating in a front operation or a sham investment, if left unchecked, strikes a blow at the very integrity of the immigration system. In this case, the applicants were found to be in non-compliance with subs. 27(2) and s. 28. The applicants' children were also found to be in non-compliance with subs. 27(2) as they were dependants of an entrepreneur and bound by the same terms and conditions of landing as provided in paragraph 23.1 of the previous regulations. Both the applicants as well as their children sought special relief on appeal in light of the circumstances of their case, specifically, that there were sufficient humanitarian and compassionate considerations that warranted the setting aside of departure orders. The IAD was of the view that the parents did not merit discretionary relief as they took part in a sham arrangement to try to fulfill the conditions of the entrepreneur category. Even though the IAD felt that the children would be excellent candidates for permanent residence, it refused to grant discretionary relief to the children because once the children became permanent residents they would be entitled to sponsor their parents which would render the removal of the parents moot.

The granting of special relief is a weighing process. Even though there were some positive elements in favour of discretionary relief being allowed to the three children, these elements did not outweigh the importance given to the integrity of maintaining the conditions in the entrepreneur category. It was open to the IAD to find that special relief should not be granted to the children because this would benefit the parents who had not respected the conditions under which they entered Canada.

*Elias c. Canada (Ministre de la Citoyenneté & de l'Immigration)*, 2005 CarswellNat 5708, 2005 FC 1329 (F.C.) — The applicant sought judicial review of the IAD's decision dismissing their appeal from a removal order. The principal applicant was born in Lebanon and emigrated to Brazil, where he lived for 20 years and became a citizen of that country. The applicant was granted landing in Canada as an entrepreneur and accepted the conditions provided under paragraph 23.1 of the Immigration Regulations. The Immigration Division decided that the applicants were persons contemplated by s. 41 of the IRPA since the principal applicant had not respected the conditions imposed for entrepreneurs when he was granted landing. The IAD dismissed the applicant's appeal concluding that an order to stay the removal order would have the effect of not only calling into question the integrity of the program conceived to attract entrepreneurs, but also the integrity of the Canadian immigration system as a whole. The principal applicant argued that he had provided plausible explanations and reasons why he was unable to respect the conditions within the two-year time period. In this case, the Court concluded that the IAD weighed the best interests of the children directly affected as well as the other factors alleged by the applicants in support of their appeal but, considering the other circumstances of the matter, determined that special relief was not justified. The applicants' eldest son was born in Brazil while the younger son was born in Canada. The applicants did not submit any evidence regarding the effects that the removal to Brazil could have on the eldest child, or the effects of a possible migration on the younger child. The applicants' argument regarding the children amounted to saying that the presence of children in Canada automatically implies humanitarian considerations justifying special measures. The Court concluded that Parliament has not decided that the presence of children in Canada constitutes in itself an impediment to any *refoulement* of a parent illegally residing in Canada. The application for judicial review was dismissed.

*Mand v. Canada (Minister of Citizenship & Immigration)*, [2005] F.C.J. No. 2016, 51 Imm. L.R. (3d) 272, 2005 CarswellNat 3970, 2005 FC 1637 (F.C.) — The principal applicant came to Canada under the entrepreneurial category. He was accompanied to Canada by his spouse and three children. They did not meet their obligations under the terms and conditions of their landing and, as a result, deportation orders were issued against them. They filed appeals against the deportation orders and were granted a two-year stay subject to following certain terms and conditions. The appeals were subsequently rejected when the applicants did not respect the conditions. The IAD also concluded that the applicants failed to demonstrate that having regard to all the circumstances of the case, they should not be removed from Canada for humanitarian and compassionate considerations. Although the Federal Court concluded that the IAD erred in concluding that the principal applicant's daughter did have strong ties to Canada, the Federal Court concluded the

IAD's decision to cancel the stay of the deportation orders was not patently unreasonable, as it would be unjust and against the principles of the Canadian immigration process to decide otherwise. The principal applicant was given a second chance and failed to respect the rules; he should not be rewarded for being able to abuse the system to the point of allowing his family to remain in Canada long enough to build strong ties and qualify for a further stay of deportation orders based on humanitarian and compassionate grounds.

*El Idrissi c. Canada (Ministre de la Citoyenneté & de l'Immigration)*, 2005 CarswellNat 2421, 2005 CarswellNat 5248, 2005 FC 1105 (F.C.) — The applicant was given permanent residence status in 1991. In 1999, the applicant left Canada to visit his sick father and manage a family business in his home country. He did not return until June 15, 2003. He fell under the purview of s. 41 of the IRPA and a departure order was made against him by the Minister. He filed an appeal to the Immigration Appeal Division but conceded that the removal order against him was legally valid and the only issue he argued was that there were humanitarian and compassionate grounds to explain his failure to meet the residency obligation.

Simply having a wife in Canada was not sufficient for this situation to be considered a humanitarian and compassionate ground. The Appeal Division was entitled to consider that the applicant's plans for the future were vague. The applicant had the burden of establishing the existence of humanitarian and compassionate grounds.

**68. (1) Removal order stayed — To stay a removal order, the Immigration Appeal Division must be satisfied, taking into account the best interests of a child directly affected by the decision, that sufficient humanitarian and compassionate considerations warrant special relief in light of all the circumstances of the case.**

**(2) Effect — Where the Immigration Appeal Division stays the removal order**

**(a) it shall impose any condition that is prescribed and may impose any condition that it considers necessary;**

**(b) all conditions imposed by the Immigration Division are cancelled;**

**(c) it may vary or cancel any non-prescribed condition imposed under paragraph (a); and**

**(d) it may cancel the stay, on application or on its own initiative.**

**(3) Reconsideration — If the Immigration Appeal Division has stayed a removal order, it may at any time, on application or on its own initiative, reconsider the appeal under this Division.**

**(4) Termination and cancellation — If the Immigration Appeal Division has stayed a removal order against a permanent resident or a foreign national who was found inadmissible on grounds of serious criminality or criminality, and they are convicted of another offence referred to in subsection 36(1), the stay is cancelled by operation of law and the appeal is terminated.**

*[Editor's Note: S.C. 2001, c. 27, s. 190 provides that every application, proceeding or matter under the* Immigration Act, *R.S.C. 1985, c. I-2 (the "former Act") that is pending or in progress immediately before June 28, 2002 shall be governed by the* Immigration and Refugee Protection Act, *S.C. 2001, c. 27 (the "new Act"), effective June 28, 2002.*

*S.C. 2001, c. 27, s. 192 provides that if a notice of appeal has been filed with the Immigration Appeal Division immediately before June 28, 2002, the appeal shall be continued*



IRP Act

*under the* Immigration Act, *R.S.C. 1985, c. I-2 (the "former Act") by the Immigration Appeal Division of the Immigration and Refugee Board.*

*S.C. 2001, c. 27, s. 196 provides that despite S.C. 2001, c. 27, s. 192, an appeal made to the Immigration Appeal Division before June 28, 2002 shall be discontinued if the appellant has not been granted a stay under the former Act and the appeal could not have been made because of s. 64 of the* Immigration and Refugee Protection Act, *S.C. 2001, c. 27 (the "new Act")*

*S.C. 2001, c. 27, s. 197 further provides that despite S.C. 2001, c. 27, s. 192, if an appellant who has been granted a stay under the former Act breaches a condition of the stay, the appellant shall be subject to the provisions of s. 64 and s. 68(4) of the new Act.*

*SOR/2002-227, s. 326(2) provides that a person in respect of whom s. 70(5) or paragraph 77(3.01)(b) of the former Act applied on June 28, 2002 is a person in respect of whom s. 64(1) of the new Act applies.]*

## Case Law

### Section 68(1)

*Ivanov v. Canada (Minister of Citizenship & Immigration)*, [2007] F.C.J. No. 1295, 64 Imm. L.R. (3d) 3, 368 N.R. 380, [2008] 2 F.C.R. 502, 2007 CarswellNat 3194, 2007 CarswellNat 4159, 2007 FCA 315 (C.A.) — The Immigration and Refugee Board, Immigration Appeal Division (the "IAD") is obligated to consider all the relevant factors raised by the applicant's evidence even if the applicant has neither referred to, nor relied on, these factors in his submissions as a basis for staying a deportation order. Once there is evidence that relates to a *Ribic* factor, the IAD must consider that *Ribic* factor in its reasons. This is not tantamount to an obligation to elicit evidence. The evidentiary burden to demonstrate why a stay ought not to be cancelled remains on the permanent resident facing deportation.

*Editor's Note: This case was decided under s. 74(3)(b)(i) of the former Act.*

*Zlobinski v. Canada (Minister of Citizenship & Immigration)*, 2006 CarswellNat 1747, 2006 FC 810 (F.C.) — The applicant came to Canada with his mother in 1992 when he was 14 years old. He is now a person who is inadmissible to Canada on grounds of serious criminality and he is the subject of a valid deportation order. As a result, the applicant moved before the IAD for an order staying the deportation order. The IAD was not satisfied that "sufficient humanitarian and compassionate considerations warranted special relief in light of all the circumstances of the case." The applicant sought judicial review.

The applicant had been convicted of nine offences. The IAD found that he was not a good candidate for rehabilitation, given his past failed attempts to do so. The IAD noted that the applicant had used heroin for 10 years and that his criminal record reflected his need to finance his drug habit. The IAD concluded that he had little establishment in Canada and a spotty work history, little money in the bank and no ownership or interest in any property. Although the IAD noted that he had no family in Ukraine, they concluded that he had not sought out the support of his family in dealing with his issues in Canada.

Although the IAD did not specifically refer in its reasons to the evidence of the applicant's father, the IAD did consider the hardship to the applicant and his family if he were to be deported to Ukraine. The Federal Court was not persuaded that this evidence was of such a nature that the failure of the IAD to mention it specifically gave rise to an inference that material evidence was ignored. Further, a misstatement as to the date in which the applicant came into Canada in 1995 was found not to be a material error. The application for judicial review was dismissed.

*Chieu v. Canada (Minister of Citizenship & Immigration)*, [2002] 1 S.C.R. 84, [2002] S.C.J. No. 1, REJB 2002-27421, 37 Admin. L.R. (3d) 252, 18 Imm. L.R. (3d) 93, 208 D.L.R. (4th) 107, 280 N.R. 268, 2002 CarswellNat 5, 2002 CarswellNat 6, 2002 SCC 3 — The Court considered whether the words "having regard to all the circumstances of the case" in s. 70(1)(b) of the *Immigration Act* allow the IAD to consider potential foreign hardship when reviewing a removal made against a permanent resident. The IAD has considered the potential foreign hardship an individual would face upon removal for well over a decade, following *Ribic v. Canada (Minister of Employment & Immigration)*, 1986 CarswellNat 135 (Imm. App. Bd.). There is no evidence that this consideration prolonged hearings before the IAD by any significant extent. The IAD is entitled to consider potential foreign hardships when exercising its discretionary jurisdiction under s. 70(1)(b) of the Act, provided that the likely country of removal has been established by the individual being removed on a balance of probabilities. The Minister should facilitate the determination of the likely country of removal before the IAD whenever possible, as this improves the efficient functioning of the Act. The factors set out in *Ribic*, *supra*, remain the proper ones for the IAD to consider during the appeal under s. 70(1)(b). On such an appeal, the onus is on the individual facing removal to establish exceptional reasons as to why they should be allowed to remain in Canada.

*Editor's note: This case was decided under the former* Immigration Act*; however, we think it continues to have relevance as the jurisprudence under the IRPA has developed.*

*Ribic v. Canada (Minister of Employment & Immigration)*, 1986 CarswellNat 1357, [1985] I.A.B.D. No. 4 (Imm. App. Bd.) — Whenever the Board exercises its equitable jurisdiction pursuant to paragraph 72(1)(b) (the former *Immigration Act*) it does so only after having found that the deportation order is valid in law. In each case the Board looks to the same general areas to determine if having regard to all the circumstances of the case, the person should not be removed from Canada. These circumstances include the seriousness of the offence or offences leading to the deportation and the possibility of rehabilitation or in the alternative, the circumstances surrounding the failure to meet the conditions of admission which led to the deportation order. The Board looks to the length of time spent in Canada and the degree to which the appellant has established; family in Canada and the dislocation to that family that deportation of the appellant would cause; the support available for the appellant not only within the family but also within the community; and the degree of hardship that would be caused to the appellant by his return to his country of nationality.

*Editor's note: This case was decided under the former* Immigration Act*; however, we think it continues to have relevance as the jurisprudence under the IRPA has developed.*

## Section 68(2)

*Canada (Minister of Citizenship & Immigration) v. Stephenson* (2008), 68 Imm. L.R. (3d) 297, 2008 CarswellNat 959, 2008 FC 82, 2008 CarswellNat 141 (F.C.) — Mr. Stephenson was a permanent resident of Canada and was ordered to be removed because he had been convicted of trafficking in a narcotic. He appealed the issuance of the removal order and the IAD stayed the removal order for a period of three years on a number of conditions. One condition was that he keep the peace and be of good behaviour. The IAD notified the parties that, pursuant to subs. 68(3) of the IRPA it would reconsider Mr. Stevenson's appeal. The IAD requested each party to provide a written statement about whether Mr. Stephenson had complied with the conditions of his stay of removal. The IAD was not convinced that three convictions in respect of the Ontario *Highway Traffic Act* offences constituted a breach of the condition to keep the peace and be of good behaviour. In order to "be of good behaviour", a person must abide by federal, provincial, and municipal statutes and regulations. In this case, given the evidence that convictions had been entered under the Ontario *Highway Traffic Act* against Mr. Stephenson, it was not, as a matter of law, open to the IAD to find that the convictions did not constitute a breach of the condition to "be of good behaviour". It was, however, open to the IAD to consider all the circumstances of Mr. Stephenson's case, including the nature and severity of his breach of conditions of the stay, and to determine how it should exercise its discretion. The application for judicial review was allowed.

*Cooper v. Canada (Minister of Citizenship & Immigration)* (2005), 49 Imm. L.R. (3d) 263, 2005 CarswellNat 2843, 2005 CarswellNat 4265, 2005 FC 1253 (F.C.) — The applicant had lived in Canada since the age of 12 and was ordered deported as a consequence of his having been convicted of four counts of armed robbery and two counts of using an imitation firearm. The IAD stayed the deportation for two years, provided that the applicant comply with a number of conditions, including the condition that he "keep the peace and be of good behaviour and not commit further criminal offences." Upon review by the IAD, evidence was provided that the applicant had been convicted of several speeding and parking offences, as well as one count of breaching the Ontario *Highway Traffic Act* and one offence contrary to the provision of the *Compulsory Automobile Insurance Act* of Ontario. The Court held the requirement that the applicant "not commit any criminal offences" was implicit in the requirement that he be of good behaviour. The Court also stated that a conditional order made in the immigration context requiring that the individual be "of good behaviour" includes, abiding by federal, provincial and municipal statutes and regulatory provisions.

## Section 68(3)

*Canada (Minister of Public Safety & Emergency Preparedness) v. Ali*, 2008 CarswellNat 1829, 2008 CarswellNat 855, 2008 FC 431 (F.C.) — The Minister challenged the decision rendered by the IAD pursuant to the transitional provision of s. 197 of the IRPA. On the facts presented to the IAD, the question was whether contraventions of the *Ontario Highway Traffic Act* (HTA) constituted a breach of a condition of the stay granted to the applicant "to keep the peace and be of good behaviour". Mr. Ali had five convictions under the HTA since his stay was imposed. The IAD panel agreed that a failure to be of "good behaviour" may result from a failure to abide by a federal, provincial or municipal statute or regulatory provision, but that a failure to abide by a federal, provincial or municipal statute or regulatory provision does not necessarily mean there has been a failure to be of "good behaviour". A relatively minor or trivial conviction under a federal, provincial or municipal statute or regulatory provision does not mean that a breach of the condition "to keep the peace and be of good behaviour" has necessarily occurred and that the appellant should be given no opportunity to argue this. While not condoning Mr. Ali's HTA offences, the incidences for which he had been convicted under the HTA were relatively minor in nature. The panel did not find they were sufficiently serious to be considered failures to "keep the peace and be of good behaviour".

In order to engage in an analysis of whether a person has breached "good behaviour", it is first necessary to establish that the person has contravened a federal, provincial or municipal statute or regulatory measure and, upon so finding, the opportunity is triggered to evaluate whether the contravention results in a further finding that a breach of "good behaviour" has occurred. Therefore, in this analysis, a person's general conduct is an important factor which must be taken into consideration. The Court found that this case was distinguishable from *Canada (Minister of Citizenship & Immigration) v. Stevenson*, 2008 FC 82, which supported the Minister's argument on the law, since it was not decided under the transition provision of the IRPA. The Court concluded that there was no reviewable error of the IAD's decision. The Court certified the following question:

> Is the condition "keep the peace and be of good behaviour" as imposed in stay of deportation orders by the IAD of the IRB breached each and every time the person concerned is convicted of an offence under and/or found to have violated any federal, provincial and/or municipal statute and regulation throughout Canada?

*Canada (Minister of Citizenship & Immigration) v. Newman* (2007), 65 Imm. L.R. (3d) 302, 2007 CarswellNat 3869, 2007 CarswellNat 5264, 2007 FC 1150 (F.C.) — Mr. Newman, a permanent resident, was ordered deported from Canada after having been convicted of welfare fraud, attempting to obstruct justice and failing to appear. The IAD granted Mr. Newman a stay of his deportation for three years on certain conditions. Three years later, the IAD decided that the original deportation order should be quashed. The Minister argued that the IAD's decision was not supported by the evidence before it. The IAD was aware that Mr. Newman had committed numerous driving offences, had failed to pay his fines, and had been sentenced to a term of imprisonment for driving while suspended. The IAD emphasized the fact that Mr. Newman had not committed any criminal offences in the preceding five years. The Court found that the IAD failed to explain how the evidence relating to Mr. Newman's conduct over recent years supported a finding of rehabilitation. The Court allowed the application for judicial review and ordered a new hearing before a different panel of the IAD.

## Section 68(4)

*Canada (Minister of Citizenship & Immigration) v. Hyde*, [2006] F.C.J. No. 1747, 57 Imm. L.R. (3d) 165, 359 N.R. 165, 2006 CarswellNat 4146, 2006 FCA 379 (Fed. C.A.) — The effect of s. 197 of IRPA is to terminate the IAD's jurisdiction with respect to a person who falls within the sections ambit. Section 197 precludes the IAD from staying a removal order in the exercise of its jurisdiction under s. 68 of IRPA. A permanent resident whose removal the IAD stayed before IRPA came into effect, and who breaches a condition of the stay, cannot continue an appeal to the IAD if either the basis of the deportation order was a criminal conviction with a sentence of two years or more, or if the offence committed after the IAD had stayed the removal was punishable by a maximum of 10 years or a sentence of more than six months was imposed.

The appellant had been ordered deported on the basis of a s. 64 offence (that is, one for which he received a sentence of two years or more). Therefore, his appeal was automatically terminated by IRPA when he breached the conditions imposed on his stay. It is irrelevant that the breaches did not involve the commission of offences referred to in subs. 68(4). The appeal was allowed.

*Canada (Minister of Citizenship & Immigration) v. Malarski*, 2006 CarswellNat 2612, 2006 FC 1007 (F.C.) — Where a permanent resident who is subject of a deportation order which has been stayed is subsequently convicted of an offence that constitutes serious criminality under subs. 36(1), the stay is cancelled by operation of law pursuant to subs. 68(4) of the IRPA and an appeal to the IAD is terminated. Once this happens, the IAD loses jurisdiction over the matter.

*Singh v. Canada (Minister of Citizenship & Immigration)*, [2006] 3 F.C.R. 70, 344 N.R. 244, 51 Imm. L.R. (3d) 49, 2005 CarswellNat 4113, 2005 CarswellNat 5141, 2005 FCA 417 (C.A.) — The appellant was a permanent resident of Canada. After being convicted of robbery he was found inadmissible on the grounds of serious criminality and ordered deported. He appealed his deportation and was granted a stay of removal that contained, among others, the condition "keep the peace and be of good behaviour." Subsequently, the appellant committed another serious offence and was convicted of that crime. It is the offence itself that constitutes the breach of the condition to keep the peace and to be of good behaviour. In this regard, a breach may be established without a conviction where there is other clear evidence of the offensive behaviour.

Between the time of the assault and the conviction, on June 28, 2002, the *Immigration Act*, R.S.C. 1985, c. I-2, was replaced by the IRPA. A provision of the IRPA addressed individuals such as the appellant, who were found inadmissible on grounds of serious criminality, had obtained a stay of their removal order, and were then convicted of another serious offence. Specifically, the IRPA mandates the cancellation of the stay and the termination of the appeal.

The appellant argued that the transitional provision of the IRPA, s. 197(1) should not apply to a breach of condition that occurred before s. 197 was enacted. The Federal Court concluded that Parliament clearly intended that the provision of the IRPA that cancels the stay and terminates the appeal apply to individuals such as the appellant, regardless of whether the condition of the stay was breached before or after the IRPA came into force.

*Leite v. Canada (Minister of Citizenship & Immigration)*, 2005 CarswellNat 2006, 2005 CarswellNat 5148, 2005 FC 984 (F.C.) — In this case, the applicant was subject to a stay order. The IAD had issued a stay of a deportation and had attached specific terms and conditions to the stay, including detailed reporting requirements and an oral review of the case. The actual stay order did not refer to a four-year term. The applicant was convicted of trafficking a controlled substance and the conviction triggered the application of s. 197 of the IRPA which required the stay to be cancelled by operation of law pursuant to subs. 68(4) of the IRPA. The applicant argued that the stay had expired at the time the conviction occurred and that the applicant should have a hearing where he could lead new evidence and the Board could determine what to do with his case on the merits. The Court concluded the stay ordered by the Board was in effect and the applicant was convicted of an offence during that time and, consequently, s. 68(4) applied.

*Ferri v. Canada (Minister of Citizenship & Immigration)*, [2005] F.C.J. No. 1941, 51 Imm. L.R. (3d) 177, [2006] 3 F.C.R. 53, 2005 CarswellNat 3878, 2005 CarswellNat 5009, 2005 FC 1580 (F.C.) — Subsection 68(4) of the IRPA limits the jurisdiction of the IAD to determining whether the factual requirements of this subsection are met. The IAD can only consider whether it has previously stayed a removal order; whether the individual in question is a permanent resident or a foreign national who was found inadmissible on grounds of serious criminality or criminality; and whether the individual has been convicted of another offence coming within subs. 36(1) of the IRPA. Once the IAD determines that the factual requirements of this subsection have been met, it then loses jurisdiction over the individual, by operation of law. The IAD does not have jurisdiction to consider the constitutionality of subs. 68(4).

**69. (1) Dismissal — The Immigration Appeal Division shall dismiss an appeal if it does not allow the appeal or stay the removal order, if any.**

**(2) Minister's Appeal — In the case of an appeal by the Minister respecting a permanent resident or a protected person, other than a person referred to in subsection 64(1), if the Immigration Appeal Division is satisfied that, taking into account the best interests of a child directly affected by the decision, sufficient humanitarian and compassionate considerations warrant special relief in light of all the circumstances of the case, it may make and may stay the applicable removal order, or dismiss the appeal, despite being satisfied of a matter set out in paragraph 67(1)(a) or (b).**

**(3) Removal order — If the Immigration Appeal Division dismisses an appeal made under subsection 63(4) and the permanent resident is in Canada, it shall make a removal order.**

**70. (1) Decision binding — An officer, in examining a permanent resident or a foreign national, is bound by the decision of the Immigration Appeal Division to allow an appeal in respect of the foreign national.**

**(2) Examination suspended — If the Minister makes an application for leave to commence an application for judicial review of a decision of the Immigration Appeal Division with respect to a permanent resident or a foreign national, an examination of the permanent resident or the foreign national under this Act is suspended until the final determination of the application.**

**71. Reopening appeal — The Immigration Appeal Division, on application by a foreign national who has not left Canada under a removal order, may reopen an appeal if it is satisfied that it failed to observe a principle of natural justice.**

## Case Law

*Nazifpour v. Canada (Minister of Citizenship & Immigration)* (2007), 60 Imm. L.R. (3d) 159, 360 N.R. 199, 278 D.L.R. (4th) 268, 2007 CarswellNat 324, 2007 FCA 35 (Fed. C.A.) — The issue in this appeal was whether the statutory context and purpose supply Parliament's omission, so that s. 71 should be interpreted as *implicitly* removing the unusual and long-established jurisdiction of the IAD to reopen a decision to consider new evidence before an appellant is deported. The appellant, a citizen of Iran, appealed from a decision of the Federal Court dismissing his application for judicial review to set aside a decision of the IAD. The applications judge held that the IAD was correct to conclude that s. 71 had removed its jurisdiction to entertain the appellant's motion to reopen its dismissal of his appeal against a deportation order on the basis of new evidence.

The Federal Court of Appeal concluded that s. 71 of the IRPA extinguishes the common law continuing "equitable jurisdiction" of the IAD to reopen an appeal except where the IAD had failed to observe a principle of natural justice. It is true that the drafter could easily have avoided all ambiguity by including the word "only" in the test of s. 71. However, the reading which best effectuates the general objects of the IRPA, and attributes a plausible function to s. 71 itself, is that the section *implicitly* removes the IAD's jurisdiction to reopen appeals on the ground of new evidence, a jurisdiction which would otherwise be judicially inferred from the nature of the statutory discretion to relieve against deportation.

*Griffiths v. Canada (Minister of Citizenship & Immigration)*, [2005] F.C.J. No. 1194, 49 Imm. L.R. (3d) 268, 2005 CarswellNat 2427, 2005 CarswellNat 4659, 2005 FC 971 (F.C.) — Under the old *Immigration Act*, the IAD had a continuing equitable jurisdiction until the moment of deportation to decide if a person should be allowed to remain in Canada upon the presentation of new evidence, as well as subsequent case law. Under s. 71 of the IRPA (no equivalent section existed in the old *Immigration Act*), the IAD's jurisdiction to reopen appeals is limited and implicitly excludes the common law jurisdiction to reopen appeals to permit the appellant to present additional or new evidence. Section 71 limits or restricts the jurisdiction of the IAD to reopen appeals with respect to breaches of the rules of natural justice.

*Ye v. Canada (Minister of Citizenship & Immigration)*, 40 Imm. L.R. (3d) 42, 2004 CarswellNat 2163, 18 Admin. L.R. (4th) 166, 254 F.T.R. 238, 2004 FC 964 (F.C.) — Section 71 limits the jurisdiction of the IAD to reopen appeals and implicitly excludes the common law jurisdiction to reopen appeals to permit the appellant to present additional or new evidence.

*Lawal v. Canada (Minister of Citizenship & Immigration)* (2002), 26 Imm. L.R. (3d) 226, 2002 CarswellNat 4340 (Imm. & Ref. Bd. (App. Div.)) — The applicant moved to reopen an appeal. The applicant was ordered deported on the basis that she had misrepresented a material fact by not declaring her dependent son when applying for permanent residence. Her appeal was dismissed and the applicant filed a motion to reopen on May 30, 2002.

The panel does not have continuing equitable jurisdiction in the matter given the changes in the immigration law. The specific language in IRPA clearly forecloses a reopening on the principle of continuing equitable jurisdiction. Section 71 explicitly defines the only grounds upon which a motion to reopen a removal order appeal by a foreign national can be made. The panel was of the view that there was no failure to observe a principle of natural justice in the appeal, and therefore, dismissed the motion to reopen.

## DIVISION 8 — JUDICIAL REVIEW

**72. (1) Application for judicial review — Judicial review by the Federal Court with respect to any matter — a decision, determination or order made, a measure taken or a question raised — under this Act is commenced by making an application for leave to the Court.**

*[Editor's Note: SOR/2002-227, s. 348(1) provides that, on June 28, 2002, any application for leave to commence an application for judicial review and any application for judicial review or appeal from an application that was brought under the* Immigration Act, *R.S.C. 1985, c. I-2 (the "former Act") that is pending before the Federal Court or the Supreme Court of Canada is deemed to have been commenced under Division 8 of Part 1 of the* Immigration and Refugee Protection Act, *S.C. 2001, c. 27 (the "new Act") and is governed by the provisions of that Division and s. 87 of the new Act.*

*SOR/2002-227, s. 348(3) provides that, despite SOR/2002-227, s. 348(1), an application for judicial review that was not subject to the requirement of an application for leave under the former Act and was pending on June 28, 2002 does not require such an application under the new Act.*

*SOR/2002-227, s. 348(4) provides that any judicial review proceeding brought in respect of any decision or order made or any matter arising under the former Act after June 28, 2002 is governed by Division 8 of Part 1 and s. 87 of the new Act.*

*SOR/2002-227, s. 348(5) provides that a person in respect of whom the 30-day period provided by s. 18.1 of the* Federal Courts Act, *R.S.C. 1985, c. F-7 for making an application for judicial review from a decision or matter referred to in s. 82.1(2) of the former Act has not elapsed on June 28, 2002 and who has not made such an application has 60 days from June 28, 2002 to file an application for leave under s. 72 of the new Act.*

*SOR/2002-227, s. 348(6) provides that the validity or lawfulness of a decision or act made under the former Act that is the subject of a judicial review procedure or appeal referred to in SOR/2002-227, s. 348(1) is determined in accordance with the provisions of the former Act.*

*SOR/2002-227, s. 349 provides that, on June 28, 2002, an appeal made under s. 102.17 of the former Act or an application for an order made under s. 102.2 of the former Act that is pending remains governed by the provisions of the former Act.]*

**(2) Application — The following provisions govern an application under subsection (1):**

**(a) the application may not be made until any right of appeal that may be provided by this Act is exhausted;**

**(b) subject to paragraph 169(f), notice of the application shall be served on the other party and the application shall be filed in the Registry of the Federal Court ("the Court") within 15 days, in the case of a matter arising in Canada, or within 60 days, in the case of a matter arising outside Canada, after the day on which the applicant is notified of or otherwise becomes aware of the matter;**

**(c) a judge of the Court may, for special reasons, allow an extended time for filing and serving the application or notice;**

**(d) a judge of the Court shall dispose of the application without delay and in a summary way and, unless a judge of the Court directs otherwise, without personal appearance; and**

**(e) no appeal lies from the decision of the Court with respect to the application or with respect to an interlocutory judgment.**

*[Editor's Note: SOR/2002-227, s. 350(1) provides that, subject to SOR/2002-227, ss. 350(2) and 350(3), if a decision or an act of the Minister or an immigration officer under the* Immigration Act, *R.S.C. 1985, c. I-2 (the "former Act") is referred back by the Federal Court or Supreme Court of Canada for determination and the determination is not made before June 28, 2002, the determination shall be made in accordance with the* Immigration and Refugee Protection Act, *S.C. 2001, c. 27 (the "new Act").*

*SOR/2002-227, s. 350(2) provides that if the decision or act was made under paragraph 46.01(1)(e), s. 70(5) or paragraph 77(3.01)(b) of the former Act and the new Act makes no provision for the decision or act, no determination shall be made.*



IRP Act

*SOR/2002-227, s. 350(3) provides that if a decision or an act of the Minister or an immigration officer under the former Act in respect of a person described in subparagraph 9(1)(b)(i) or paragraph 10(1)(b) of the* Immigration Regulations, 1978, *SOR/98-172 (the "former Regulations") is referred back by the Federal Court or Supreme Court of Canada for determination and the determination is not made before June 28, 2002, the determination shall be made in accordance with ss. 361(3) and (5) of the* Immigration and Refugee Protection Regulations, *SOR/2002-227 (the "new Regulations").*

*SOR/2002-227, s. 350(4) provides that if a decision or an act of the Minister or an immigration officer under the former Act in respect of a person described in subparagraphs 9(1)(b)(ii) or (iii) of the former Regulations is referred back by the Federal Court or Supreme Court of Canada for determination and the determination is not made before June 28, 2002, the determination shall be made in accordance with s. 361(3) of the new Regulations.*

*SOR/2002-227, s. 350(5) provides that if a decision of the Immigration Appeal Division made under the former Act is referred back by the Federal Court or Supreme Court of Canada for determination and the determination is not made before June 28, 2002, the Immigration Appeal Division shall dispose of the matter in accordance with the former Act.*

*SOR/2002-227, s. 350(6) provides that if a decision of the Adjudication Division made under the former Act is referred back by the Federal Court or Supreme Court of Canada for determination and the determination is not made before June 28, 2002, the Immigration Division shall dispose of the matter in accordance with the new Act.]*

2002, c. 8, s. 194(a)(i)

## Case Law

### Section 72(1)

*Somodi v. Canada (Minister of Citizenship & Immigration)* (2009), 82 Imm. L.R. (3d) 159, 311 D.L.R. (4th) 335, 395 N.R. 270, 2009 FCA 288, 2009 CarswellNat 3062, 2009 CarswellNat 5060 (F.C.A.) — The appellant sought, in the Federal Court, judicial review of a decision of a visa officer which refused his spousal sponsorship application for permanent residence status as a member of the family class. At the same time as the appellant made his judicial review application, his sponsor appealed the decision of the visa officer. The appellant's application was dismissed by a judge of the Federal Court on the ground that paragraph 72(2)(a) of IRPA required the appellant's sponsor to exhaust her right of appeal to the Immigration Appeal Division (IAD) before an application for judicial review could be made. While the appellant's appeal was pending before the Federal Court of Appeal, the IAD granted his sponsor's appeal and set aside the decision of the visa officer. In effect, the IAD, by setting aside the visa officer's decision, rendered the appellant's appeal moot since the decision which is the subject of the application for judicial review no longer exists. However, the Federal Court judge certified a question on an issue which has not been considered by the Federal Court of Appeal. Specifically the question reads:

> Does section 72 of the IRPA bar an application for judicial review by the applicant of a spousal application, while the sponsor exercises the rights of appeal pursuant to section 63 of the IRPA?

Both parties at the hearing submitted that it would be in the interest of justice that the Federal Court of Appeal answer the certified question.

It should be remembered that, on a family sponsorship application, the interest of the parties are congruent. Both the sponsor and the foreign national seek a reunification of the family. It would be illogical and detrimental to the objectives of the scheme to allow multiplicity of proceedings on the same issue, in different forms, to parties pursuing the same interest. It would also be detrimental to the administration of justice as it would open the door to conflict in decisions and fuel more litigation. This is precisely what Parliament intended to avoid. In addition, the appellant is not deprived of all remedies. He has other avenues such as an application to the Minister based on H&C considerations pursuant to s. 25 of IRPA. The appeal was dismissed for mootness and the Court answered the certified question in the affirmative.

*New Brunswick (Board of Management) v. Dunsmuir*, [2008] 1 S.C.R. 190, (sub nom. *Dunsmuir v. New Brunswick)* [2008] S.C.J. No. 9, 372 N.R. 1, 69 Admin. L.R. (4th) 1, 2008 C.L.L.C. 220-020, D.T.E. 2008T-223, 329 N.B.R. (2d) 1, 170 L.A.C. (4th) 1, 291 D.L.R. (4th) 577, 64 C.C.E.L. (3d) 1, 2008 CarswellNB 124, 2008 CarswellNB 125, 2008 SCC 9 — The operation of three standards of review has not been without practical and theoretical difficulties; neither has it been free of criticism. One major problem lies in distinguishing between the patent unreasonableness standard and the reasonableness símpliciter standard. The difficulty in distinguishing between those standards contributes to the problem of choosing the right standard of review. An even greater problem lies in the application of the patent unreasonableness standard, which at times seems to require parties to accept an unreasonable decision.

Even if one could conceive of a situation in which a clearly or highly irrational decision were distinguishable from a merely irrational decision, it would be unpalatable to require parties to accept an irrational decision simply because, on a deferential standard, the irrationality of the decision is not clear enough. It is also inconsistent with the rule of law to retain an irrational decision. A simpler test is needed.

In judicial review, reasonableness is concerned mostly with the existence of justification, transparency and intelligibility within the decision-making process. But it is also concerned with whether the decision falls within a range of possible, acceptable outcomes which are defensible in respect of the facts and law. The move towards a single reasonableness standard does not pave the way for a more intrusive review by courts and does not represent a return to pre-*Southam* formalism. In this respect, the concept of deference, so central to judicial review in administrative law, has perhaps been insufficiently explored in the case law.

Deference is both an attitude of the Court and a requirement of the law of judicial review. It does not mean that courts are subservient to the determinations of decision makers, or that courts must show blind reverence to their interpretations, or that they may be content to pay lip service to the concept of reasonableness review while in fact imposing their own view. Rather, deference imports respect for the decision-making process of adjudicative bodies with regard to both the facts and the law. The notion of deference "is rooted in part in a respect for governmental decisions to create administrative bodies with delegated powers". There are now only two standards, reasonableness and correctness. The process of judicial review involves two steps. First, courts ascertain whether the jurisprudence has already determined in a satisfactory manner the degree of deference to be accorded with regard to a particular category of question. Secondly, where the first inquiry proves unfruitful, courts must proceed to an analysis of the factors making it possible to identify the proper standard of review.

The existing approach to determining the appropriate standard of review has in the past commonly been referred to as "pragmatic and functional". In the future, it should simply be referred to as the "standard of review analysis". The analysis must be contextual. It is dependent on the application of a number of relevant factors, including: (1) the presence or absence of a privative clause; (2) the purpose of the tribunal as determined by interpretation of enabling legislation; (3) the nature of the question at issue; and (4) the expertise of the tribunal.

The existence of a privative or preclusive clause gives rise to a strong indication of review pursuant to the reasonableness standard. Where the question is one of fact, discretion or policy, as well as questions where the legal issues cannot be easily separated from the factual issues, a standard of reasonableness is appropriate. Where an administrative tribunal has developed particular expertise, a reasonableness test is applied. A question of law that is of "central importance to the legal system. . .and outside the. . .specialized area of expertise" of the administrative decision maker will always attract a correctness standard, while a question of law that does not rise to this level may be compatible with a reasonableness standard.

*Padda v. Canada (Minister of Citizenship & Immigration)*, 2006 CarswellNat 2516, 2006 FC 995 (F.C.) — The applicants brought a motion for an extension of time within which to perfect their record in support of their application for leave and for judicial review. Rather than bringing their motion in writing pursuant to Rule 369 of the *Federal Court Rules*, as is the norm in immigration leave applications, the applicants elected to proceed orally, making their motion returnable at the general sittings. Such practice should be discouraged. To allow an applicant to obtain an oral hearing for an interlocutory motion in a leave application that is intended to be conducted entirely in writing appears antithetical to the statutory and regulatory objectives of efficiency and expediency. It could easily be abused by an unscrupulous applicant who could obtain an extended stay of removal pending determination of the application for leave by making his or her motion for extension of time returnable in the distant future. The registry should, as a rule, seek directions from the Court with respect to any motion in an immigration leave application that is not brought in writing pursuant to Rule 369 of the *Federal Courts Rules*.

*Logeswaren v. Canada (Minister of Citizenship & Immigration)*, [2004] F.C.J. No. 1659, 43 Imm. L.R. (3d) 225, 2004 CarswellNat 5644, 2004 CarswellNat 3571, 2004 FC 1374 (F.C.) — The Court granted the Respondent Minister's motion for a reconsideration.

The Minister commenced proceedings to vacate the grant of refugee status. The Applicant filed a motion to dismiss the vacation application on the basis of *res judicata* — a previous motion to vacate having been dismissed.

The *res judicata* motion was dismissed by the Board. Leave to review that interlocutory motion was granted and the judicial review was heard on March 15, 2004.

The Court rendered its decision on June 22, 2004 and concurred with the Board's conclusion as to the inapplicability of *res judicata*; however, the Court referred the matter back to the Board for a redetermination to be made on the basis of Rule 56 of the IRB Rules.

Prior to the hearing by the Court on March 15, 2004, the Board had held its hearing on the merits of the application to vacate. This event was not brought to the attention of the Court despite the fact that counsel for the respondent had direct, personal knowledge that the hearing on the merits of the application to vacate had been held. On the same day as the judicial review hearing in this Court, but after the hearing had concluded, the applicant and his counsel received the Board's decision which granted the Minister's motion to vacate. This fact was also not brought to the Court's attention until the Minister's motion to re-open. The requirement that the Board reconsider the matter under Rule 56 is irrelevant. Accordingly, the application for judicial review was dismissed.

The adversarial system cannot properly function unless counsel conduct themselves in a professional manner and unless courts are satisfied that counsel are doing so. Lawyers must be able to confidently assume that their colleagues will not act in a fashion designed to improperly take advantage of a situation. judges must be able to assume that the merits on which they are being asked to adjudicate are, indeed, the merits. If these principles are not adhered to, the whole administration of justice is called into question. The most important and primary consideration must be to avoid subjecting the integrity of the judicial process to abuse.

*Lee v. Canada (Minister of Citizenship & Immigration)* (2004), 34 Imm. L.R. (3d) 182, 2004 CarswellNat 1380, 2004 CarswellNat 924, 320 N.R. 184, 2004 FCA 143 (F.C.A.) — Where a visa officer refuses an application for permanent residence on redetermination after a previous decision was set aside by the Court, the visa officer is not obliged to specifically state or set out the differences between the two decisions.

*Sarmis v. Canada (Minister of Citizenship & Immigration)* (2004), 40 Imm. L.R. (3d) 111, 245 F.T.R. 312, 2004 CarswellNat 167, 2004 CarswellNat 2524, 2004 FC 110 (F.C.) — The applicants failed to file their own affidavits based on personal knowledge in support of their application for leave. They filed the affidavit of a paralegal who lacked personal knowledge of the matter.

The failure of an application to be supported by affidavits based on personal knowledge is not automatically fatal to an application for judicial review. The affidavit before the Court was sufficient to establish the fact of the application and its rejection.

*Ranganathan v. Canada (Minister of Citizenship & Immigration)* (2003), 34 Imm. L.R. (3d) 302, 2003 CarswellNat 3722, 2003 CarswellNat 4418, 2003 FC 1367, [2003] F.C.J. No. 1741 (F.C.) — This was an application to challenge a decision of a panel of the Refugee Protection Division refusing to recuse a panel member.

The hearing before the Board occurred over 2 days. On the second day of the hearing the applicants agreed to proceed with a one member panel after being advised that the other panel member would be unable to attend that day. At this hearing, the member conducting the panel stated that he considered photographs tendered by the applicants not to be probative and engaged in extensive questioning of the witnesses called by the applicants. One month later, counsel for the applicants submitted a written motion in which he requested the member to remove himself due to an alleged reasonable apprehension of bias.

The applicants' counsel only brought the formal motion after having checked the case law and having sought the view of other counsel. While this may have been prudent it did not amount to raising the issue at the earliest opportunity. Counsel's failure to raise the issue of a reasonable apprehension of bias formally at the first opportunity was held to be an implied waiver of his right to raise the issue of an apprehension of bias.

*Waraich v. Canada (Minister of Citizenship & Immigration)*, 33 Imm. L.R. (3d) 78, 2003 CarswellNat 4268, 2003 CarswellNat 2951, 2003 FC 1099 (F.C.) — This was a motion by an immigration consultant seeking leave to intervene in the judicial review application. The applicant applied for recognition as a Convention refugee and was rejected. The applicant applied for leave to judicially review the negative decision. The proposed intervener in his capacity as an immigration consultant and a citizen of Canada suggests that he has a juridical interest which clearly requires him to intervene in the present debate. Applicants for intervener status must have an interest of more than a jurisprudential nature. This application was rejected. Whatever decision the Court was going to give on the application, it could have no direct impact on the rights of the proposed intervener. The immigration consultant was also denied a status as *"amicus curiae"* because he failed to satisfy the Court as to the nature of his expertise and how this expertise would be of assistance to the Court. The application was dismissed.

*Kalachnikov v. Canada (Minister of Citizenship & Immigration)*, [2003] F.C.J. No. 1016, 2003 CarswellNat 1950, 2003 CFPI 777, 236 F.T.R. 142, 2003 FCT 777, 2003 CarswellNat 3436 (Fed. T.D.) — This is an application for an order of *mandamus* directing the respondent to process the application of the applicant and issue a final decision within 60 days.

*Mandamus* is a discretionary equitable remedy subject to the following conditions precedent:

1. There is a public duty to act.
2. This duty must be owed to the applicant.
3. There is a clear right to performance of that duty, in particular:
   (a) The applicant must have satisfied all conditions precedent giving rise to the duty;
   (b) There must have been a prior demand for performance of the duty, a reasonable time to comply with the demand and a subsequent refusal which can either be expressed or implied.
4. There must be no other adequate remedy.
5. The balance of convenience must favour the applicant.

If the applicant tends to rely on the fact that there has been an implied refusal to perform the duty due to an unreasonable delay, then the following conditions must be met:

1. The delay must have been longer than the nature of the process required.
2. The applicant and his counsel must not be responsible for the delay; and
3. The authority responsible for the delay must not have provided a satisfactory justification.

Prior jurisprudence is not particularly helpful except for the purposes of outlining the parameters in which the Court has issued an order in the nature of *mandamus* where it has found an unusual delay. Based on the facts of this case *mandamus* issued.

The Court declined to order costs, finding that special reasons as contemplated by Rule 22 of the *Federal Court Immigration and Refugee Protection Rules* have not been demonstrated.

*Marshall v. R.*, 2002 CarswellNat 2901, 2002 CarswellNat 3965, 2002 FCT 1099, 2002 CFPI 1099 (Fed. T.D.) — The applicant applied to the Court for an order restraining an adjudicator from continuing a hearing against the applicant until the action commenced by the applicant was heard and determined. The Court concluded that it did not have jurisdiction to issue the order requested because no application for judicial review had been filed with the Court. Section 18(1) of the *Federal Court Act* grants the Federal Court the jurisdiction to grant certain remedies, but subs. 18(3) requires that the application for judicial review be commenced. In the present motion, the motion for an interim injunction is made incidental to an action, not an application for judicial review. The Court has jurisdiction to grant a stay pursuant to s. 18.2 of the *Federal Court Act*, but only if a judicial review application has been filed. Subsection 50(1) of the *Federal Court Act* gives the Court jurisdiction to grant a stay, but only provides for stays in proceedings being conducted before the Federal Court. Accordingly, the motion for an injunction was dismissed.



## Section 72(2)

*Somodi v. Canada (Minister of Citizenship & Immigration)* (2009), 82 Imm. L.R. (3d) 159, 311 D.L.R. (4th) 335, 395 N.R. 270, 2009 FCA 288, 2009 CarswellNat 3062, 2009 CarswellNat 5060 (F.C.A.) — See the *Somodi* summary under s. 72(1).

*Canada (Minister of Citizenship & Immigration) v. Edwards*, 2005 CarswellNat 1238, 2005 FCA 176 (F.C.A.) — The Minister appealed the decision of a motions judge granting the respondent a stay of a departure order. The motions judge had the requisite jurisdiction to entertain the stay motion and make an order disposing of that motion. Paragraph 72(2)(e) precludes the Court of Appeal from entertaining an appeal from that judgement without a certified question.

*Mabrouki c. Canada (Ministre de la Citoyenneté & de l'Immigration)*, 2003 CarswellNat 3854, 2003 CarswellNat 2948, 2003 FC 1104, 242 F.T.R. 171 (F.C.) — A motions judge does not have jurisdiction to hear an appeal from a decision of a prothonotary which dismissed an application for an extension of time.

*Dydyuk v. Canada (Minister of Citizenship & Immigration)*, 2003 CarswellNat 1687, 2003 CarswellNat 2807, 2003 FCT 717, 2003 CFPI 717, 245 F.T.R. 161 (Fed. T.D.) — The applicant was seeking to review a negative determination of her refugee claim. Six days before the application for judicial review was to be heard in the Federal Court, a letter was sent by a person purporting to be counsel for the applicant requesting a short adjournment because counsel was unable to attend due to a family emergency. Counsel was overseas and would be returning on June 10, 2003, one day after the date scheduled for the judicial review application.

The request for an adjournment was refused. On February 17, 1993, the Trial Division issued a practice direction advising parties that scheduled trials and hearings would only be adjourned in exceptional cases. The practice direction advises that the Federal Court does not overbook its trial sittings. Adjournments, therefore, cause serious inconvenience and expense. It is therefore expected that all counsel will be able to proceed on the date fixed. Requests to adjourn must be made to the Associate Chief Justice and, unless made promptly after the fixing of a hearing date, will be considered only in the most exceptional circumstances.

Accordingly, the request for an adjournment was refused and the judicial application proceeded.

*Yogalingam v. Canada (Minister of Citizenship & Immigration)* (2003), 27 Imm. L.R. (3d) 198, 2003 CarswellNat 1175, 2003 FCT 540, 2003 CarswellNat 2696, [2003] F.C.J. No. 697, 233 F.T.R. 74, 2003 CFPI 540 (Fed. T.D.) — The applicant sought an extension of time to file an application record. This motion was dismissed by the Prothonotary and the applicant appealed. Section 72(2)(e) of the IRPA removes jurisdiction to hear an appeal of the Prothonotary's decision.

**Unproclaimed Text — 73**

**73. Right of Minister — The Minister may make an application for leave to commence an application for judicial review with respect to any decision of the Refugee Appeal Division, whether or not the Minister took part in the proceedings before the Refugee Protection Division or Refugee Appeal Division.**

**74. Judicial review — Judicial review is subject to the following provisions:**

**(a) the judge who grants leave shall fix the day and place for the hearing of the application;**

**(b) the hearing shall be no sooner than 30 days and no later than 90 days after leave was granted, unless the parties agree to an earlier day;**

**(c) the judge shall dispose of the application without delay and in a summary way; and**

**(d) an appeal to the Federal Court of Appeal may be made only if, in rendering judgment, the judge certifies that a serious question of general importance is involved and states the question.**

## Case Law

*Felipa v. Canada (Minister of Citizenship & Immigration)* (2010), 87 Imm. L.R. (3d) 1, 357 F.T.R. 253 (Eng.), 3 Admin. L.R. (5th) 77, 2010 FC 89, 2010 CarswellNat 123, 2010 CarswellNat 124 (F.C.) — The applicant in this interlocutory motion challenged the jurisdiction of a deputy judge over 75 years of age to preside over the hearing of two related applications for judicial review under the *Immigration and Refugee Protection Act*. The applicant challenged the two decisions refusing the relief he sought for H&C consideration and for pre-removal risk assessment. The mandatory age of retirement of 75 years in s. 99(2) of the *Constitution Act, 1867* does not apply to deputy judges of the Federal Court. Section 8(2) of the *Federal Courts Act* does not preclude a person over age 75 from acting as a deputy judge of the Federal Court. This conclusion is consistent with the principles of statutory interpretation, with the limited legislative history and the *obiter* statement of Deputy Judge Grant in *Addy v. Canada*, [1985] 2 F.C. 452. There is no conflict between ss. 8(2) and 10(1.1) of the *Federal Courts Act*. The Court held that the motion was a "separate, divisible judicial act" not subject to s. 74(d) of IRPA. Either party may appeal the interlocutory judgment pursuant to s. 27 of the *Federal Courts Act* without the necessity of a certified question. The applicant's motion was dismissed.

*Ismail v. Canada (Minister of Citizenship & Immigration)* (2006), 58 Imm. L.R. (3d) 179, 358 N.R. 160, 2006 CarswellNat 4247, 2006 FCA 396 (Fed. C.A.) — The statutory prohibition on appeals in immigration matters, unless a question is certified pursuant to paragraph 74(d) of the IRPA, would be meaningless if it could be circumvented simply by filing a motion under Rule 397 or 399 (Federal Court Rules).

*Lazareva v. Canada (Minister of Citizenship & Immigration)* (2005), 335 N.R. 21, 2005 CarswellNat 1240, 2005 FCA 181 (F.C.A.) — This was the second attempt in two days by the Minister to appeal a decision of the Federal Court in the absence of a certified question. It is not open to the Court to disregard the provisions of the *Immigration and Refugee Protection Act* that preclude an appeal or an appeal without a certified question. Accordingly, the appeal was quashed and costs were awarded to the respondent.

*Canada (Solicitor General) v. Subhaschandran*, [2005] F.C.J. No. 107, 2005 CarswellNat 184, 2005 CarswellNat 1129, 2005 FCA 27, (sub nom. *Subhaschandran v. Canada (Solicitor General))* 249 D.L.R. (4th) 269, 331 N.R. 182 (F.C.A.) — The respondents brought a motion for a stay of the order for their deportation. At the conclusion of the argument, the motions judge adjourned the motion. The Minister launched a motion for reconsideration which was dismissed. The motions judge issued a clarification and ordered that the applicants not be removed from Canada pending a determination of their motion for a stay.

It is true that, generally, interlocutory orders including adjournments cannot be appealed. An exception to this rule, however, occurs where a judge refuses to exercise his jurisdiction and deal with the case. In the present case, the motions judge, by adjourning the motion, has deprived the parties of ever having a decision on the stay motion. This amounts to a refusal to exercise his jurisdiction and a remedy must be available.

Accordingly, the Court of Appeal took jurisdiction despite the fact that there was no serious question certified by the motions judge, allowed the appeal, set aside the order of the motions judge and remitted the matter back to the motions judge to make a decision on the application for a stay.

*Li v. Canada (Minister of Citizenship & Immigration)* (2004), 40 Imm. L.R. (3d) 161, 2004 CarswellNat 2338, 2004 CarswellNat 3952, 2004 FCA 267, 327 N.R. 253, [2004] F.C.J. No. 1264 (F.C.A.); leave to appeal refused (2004), 2004 CarswellNat 4253, 2004 CarswellNat 4254 (S.C.C.) — The IRB applied to intervene in an appeal before the Federal Court of Appeal. The Board intended to address a substantive issue raised in the appeal, namely the standard of proof under s. 97 of IRPA and to add fresh evidence with respect to this issue. Where the parent or authorizing statute is silent as to the role or status of the tribunal in appeal or review proceedings, the tribunal is confined to the issue of its jurisdiction to make the order in question. Even where the right to appear is given by statute, the Supreme Court of Canada has held that the administrative tribunal's role in such a situation is limited to an explanatory role with reference to the record and to making representations relating to jurisdiction. In this case, therefore, the Board was denied permission to intervene.

*Khalil v. R.* (2004), 252 F.T.R. 292, 2004 CarswellNat 3067, 2004 CarswellNat 1451, 2004 FC 732 (F.C.) — The standard of review applicable to appeals from a prothonotary requires that unless the decision is clearly wrong, insofar as it was based upon a wrong legal principle or a misapprehension of the facts, involved the misuse of judicial discretion, or raised issues vital to the final disposition of the action, the decision should remain undisturbed on appeal. The Court decided that a *de novo* standard should apply when the decision could terminate the plaintiff's action. It was that standard which was applied in this case.

The plaintiffs have a right to frame their action. It is not open to the defendant to impute a different manner of proceeding, that is, an application for judicial review, when the plaintiffs themselves did not choose that forum.

*Joseph v. Canada (Minister of Citizenship & Immigration)*, [2004] F.C.J. No. 838, 2004 CarswellNat 3074, 2004 CarswellNat 1347, 2004 FC 682 (F.C.) — Any lack of fairness in the hearing process generally voids a hearing and requires that a new hearing be held unless the demerits of the claim are such that the remission of the claim would be hopeless.

IRP Act

*Amado-Cordeiro v. Canada (Minister of Citizenship & Immigration)* (2004), 36 Imm. L.R. (3d) 35, 2004 CarswellNat 1515, 2004 CarswellNat 742, 2004 FCA 120, 320 N.R. 319 (F.C.A.) — The Court of Appeal will not overrule its own prior decisions in the absence of manifest error.

*Zazai v. Canada (Minister of Citizenship & Immigration)* (2004), 36 Imm. L.R. (3d) 167, 2004 CarswellNat 544, 318 N.R. 365, 2004 FCA 89, 2004 CarswellNat 4792, (sub nom. *Canada (Minister of Citizenship & Immigration) v. Zazai)* 247 F.T.R. 320 (note) (F.C.A.) — The certification of a question of general importance allows for an appeal from the judgement of the Trial Division which would otherwise not be permitted. Such an appeal does not confine the Court to answering the stated question or issues directly related to it. All issues raised by the appeal may be considered.

The threshold for certifying a question is this: is there a serious question of general importance which would be dispositive of an appeal? The corollary of the fact that a question must be dispositive of the appeal is that it must be a question which has been raised and dealt with in the decision below. In this case, the certified question was not dealt with by the applications judge, so the court remitted the matter for a decision by a Federal Court judge.

**75. (1) Rules — Subject to the approval of the Governor in Council, the rules committee established under section 45.1 of the *Federal Courts Act* may make rules governing the practice and procedure in relation to applications for leave to commence an application for judicial review, for judicial review and for appeals. The rules are binding despite any rule or practice that would otherwise apply.**

**(2) Inconsistencies — In the event of an inconsistency between this Division and any provision of the *Federal Courts Act*, this Division prevails to the extent of the inconsistency.**

2002, c. 8, s. 194(b)(i), (c)

## Division 9 — Certificates and Protection of Information

[Heading amended 2008, c. 3, s. 4.]

## *Interpretation*

[Heading amended 2005, c. 10, s. 34(1)(o)(i); 2008, c. 3, s. 4.]

### Author's Note

*[Included below are the annotations of decisions taken under section 40.1 of the former Immigration Act. While the security provisions of the former Act are differently worded than the security provisions of IRPA, it is thought that these annotations may still be of assistance.]*

### Case Law

#### Section 40.1(1) of the Former Act

*Canada (Minister of Citizenship & Immigration) v. Singh (I.)* (1998), 44 Imm. L.R. (2d) 309, 151 F.T.R. 101 (Fed. T.D.) — This was a decision on the merits under paragraph 40.1(4)(d) dealing with whether a certificate filed by the applicants in relation to the respondent was reasonable. In s. 40.1 proceedings, where there are reasonable grounds to believe that a person is a member of an organization, there must also be reasonable grounds to believe that the organization is engaged in subversion or terrorism. Standard of proof is on a balance of probabilities.

In his testimony, a supervisor with the counter-terrorist branch of CSIS expressed the opinion that terrorism included politically motivated violence often with an indiscriminate target. A politically motivated organization, which sets off bombs killing innocent people or which engages in assassinations, is an organization engaged in terrorism.

The Court concluded that the term "member" incorporated into s. 40.1 by reference to s. 19 was to be interpreted broadly. The context of this provision in immigration legislation is public safety and national security, the most serious concerns of government. Terrorist organizations do not issue membership cards, there is no formal test for membership and members are therefore not easily identifiable. In this context, it is obvious that Parliament intended that the term "member" be given an unrestricted and broad interpretation.

*Ahani v. R.* (1996), 37 C.R.R. (2d) 181, 201 N.R. 233, 119 F.T.R. 80 (note) (Fed. C.A.); leave to appeal to S.C.C. refused [1997] 2 S.C.R. v, 44 C.R.R. (2d) 376 (note), 223 N.R. 72 (note) (S.C.C.) — The Court adopted the reasons of the trial judge in this matter and affirmed her decision.

Between a determination by the designated judge that the s. 40.1 certificate is reasonable and a possible removal of the person concerned to the country where he or she fears persecution, there must be a second opinion formed by the Minister of Immigration, based on a determination that the person constitutes "a danger to the public in Canada," or "a danger to the security of Canada". Such a determination will have to be made in accordance with the principles of fundamental justice and will be subject to judicial review.

Section 40.1 is in no way akin to a criminal proceeding. In a s. 40.1 proceeding there exists an alien who may lose the qualified right to stay in Canada that he or she gained by being given refugee status, but whose liberty will not then be otherwise impeded. While it is true that the filing of the certificate has the immediate unfortunate effect of leading to the arrest and detention of the person concerned, it must not be forgotten that this detention is not imposed as a punishment, but rather as a means of providing preventative protection to the Canadian public. This detention is not arbitrary or excessive. The test for the issuance of the certificate is the reasoned opinion of two Ministers based on security information. The scheme provides for the obligatory judicial scrutiny of the reasonableness of those opinions within an acceptably short period of time; further, at any time, the person can agree to leave the country and thereby end his or her detention. Finally, this procedure deals with a type or class of individual who is believed to be associated with terrorism.

*Baroud, Re* (1995), 98 F.T.R. 99 (Fed. T.D.) — The purpose of subparagraphs 19(1)(f)(ii) and 19(1)(f)(iii) of the *Immigration Act*, in very general terms, is to prevent the arrival of persons considered to be a danger to Canadian society. The term terrorism must therefore receive an unrestrictive interpretation and will unavoidably include the political connotations which it entails. In the light of the evidence submitted to the Court, there existed reasonable grounds to believe that the applicant was described in s. 19(1)(f)(iii).

### Section 40.1(4) of the Former Act

*Suresh, Re* (1997), 40 Imm. L.R. (2d) 247, 140 F.T.R. 88 (Fed. T.D.) — These were the reasons of the court determining that reasonable grounds existed for the Solicitor General and the Minister of Employment and Immigration to have issued a certificate pursuant to s. 40.1 of the *Immigration Act*. It was not necessary to define the content of the term "terrorist" or "terrorist act" as it is referred to in s. 19. The Act "must be seen through the eyes of a Canadian for the purposes of a s. 40.1 application." The term "terrorism or terrorist act" must receive a wide and unrestricted interpretation for the purposes of a s. 40.1 application.

Membership in an organization cannot and should not be narrowly interpreted when it involves the issue of Canada's national security. Membership does not only refer to persons who have engaged in or who might engage in terrorist activities. The Court looked at the nature of Mr. Suresh's activities in support of the organization that he was supposed to be a member of and his own admission of his close association with that organization.

*Singh (H.), Re* (1994), 83 F.T.R. 219 (Fed. T.D.) — This case dealt with a certificate signed pursuant to s. 40.1. The Court's role in this type of case is difficult, for it is not to concede or find that the Ministers were correct in their assessment of the evidence presented to them, but rather to find whether or not, based on the facts and evidence presented to them, their opinion was a reasonable one.

*Farahi-Mahdavieh, Re* (1993), 19 Imm. L.R. (2d) 222, 63 F.T.R. 120 (Fed. T.D.) — Robab Farahi-Mahdavieh illegally entered Canada from the United States at the border near Vancouver. While preparing to fly to Toronto, she was stopped and detained by immigration officials acting under a certificate issued under s. 40.1(1) and (2) of the *Immigration Act*. The certificate stated that Ms. Mahdavieh was a member of an inadmissible class described in s. 19(1)(g).

The Court must determine whether on the basis of the evidence and information available, the certificate is reasonable when it identifies Ms. Mahdavieh as a person who, there is reasonable grounds to believe, will engage in acts of violence that would or might endanger the lives or safety of persons in Canada, or is a member of, or likely to participate in the unlawful activities of, an organization that is likely to engage in such acts of violence (s. 19(1)(g)).

As the person named in such a certificate is subject to mandatory detention, a higher standard of reasonableness should be applied in reviewing this type of administrative action. Actual membership in an organization described in s. 19(1)(g) is not required. It is sufficient to meet the statutory requirement that the evidence show that there are reasonable grounds to believe that the person is a member of such an organization. The test is the one understood in *Canada (Attorney General) v. Jolly*, [1975] F.C. 216 (C.A.). In this case the Court found the certificate to be reasonable.

*Editor's Note: Although the sections in question have been amended, the principles in this case may still be applicable.*

*Smith v. R.*, [1991] 3 F.C. 3, 14 Imm. L.R. (2d) 57, 4 Admin. L.R. (2d) 97, 42 F.T.R. 81 (Fed. T.D.) — The applicants applied to be admitted to Canada as refugees. They were detained as possible security risks and then brought before an adjudicator who reviewed the circumstances of their detention and ordered that they were to be released. The Minister then issued a certificate pursuant to s. 40.1 stating the opinion that the applicants were members of classes described in s. 19(1)(f) and 19(1)(g) of the *Immigration Act*.

The issuance of this certificate caused the adjudicator to order the applicants' detention. Once the certificate is issued, the Court is to determine whether the certificate is reasonable on the evidence and information provided to the judge. Until this determination is made, an inquiry into the refugee status of the applicant may not be commenced or, if already commenced, must be adjourned. The applicants were referred to in the proceedings as Joseph Smith and Sarah Smith, which were pseudonyms. The Court concluded that the word "shall" in s. 40.1(3)(b) was directory and not mandatory. Further, the Court ruled that compliance with the notice provision was not a pre-condition to the exercise by the Court of its review function under s. 40.1(4) having concluded that the Court had jurisdiction to consider the reasonableness of the certificate. The Court concluded that s. 40.1(4)(a) provided it with jurisdiction to proceed *ex parte* to extend the time to serve the applicants with notice of the proceedings. The Court ruled as well that s. 40.1(4)(a) authorizes the Court to hear oral evidence *in camera*. The Court also determined that the word "forthwith" as required by s. 40.1(3)(a) meant "as soon as was reasonably possible in the circumstances". The Court found that in this particular case the reference to the Court was made forthwith in all circumstances.

Section 40.1(4) gives the Court sitting on review of the certificate discretion to determine whether any part of the information or evidence put before the Court should not be disclosed on the grounds that the disclosure would be injurious to national security or the safety of persons. The Court concluded that disclosure of the sealed file material would be injurious to national security. The Court noted that an "informed reader," that is, a person who is both knowledgeable regarding security matters and is a member or associate of a group which constitutes a threat or potential threat to the security of Canada, may, at times, by fitting pieces of apparently innocuous information into a general picture, be in a position to arrive at damaging deductions regarding the investigation conducted by our security services. This damage could be an understanding of the duration, scope, intensity and degree of success of an investigation, the investigative techniques of CSIS, the typographic and teleprinter systems employed by CSIS, the internal security procedures, the nature and content of classified documents and the identity of personnel involved in the investigation. Applying this consideration to the case at bar, the Court concluded that certain information should not be made public.

On the ultimate issue, the Court determined that the word "reasonable" in s. 40.1(4)(d) adopted a standard of reasonableness set out in *R. v. Secretary of State for Home Department*, [1984] 1 A.C. 74 (U.K. H.L.). There, the Court said that in cases of restraint put by the executive upon the liberty of an individual the civil standard should be flexibly applied. It was not necessary to import the formula devised by judges for the guidance of juries in criminal cases. Liberty is at stake and that is a grave matter. The reviewing Court must be satisfied that the facts which are required for the justification of the restraint do exist. The Court will require a high degree of probability which is appropriate to what is at stake. Applying that standard in this case, the Court concluded that it was not reasonable to issue a certificate. The certificate was quashed and the applicants were set free.

## Section 40.1(8) of the Former Act

*Ahani v. Canada (Minister of Citizenship & Immigration)* (1998), 48 Imm. L.R. (2d) 308, 159 F.T.R. 252 (Fed. T.D.) — The Court had previously determined in this matter that a certificate issued by the two Ministers involved was reasonable. The applicant was not removed from Canada within the 120 days set out in s. 40.1(8) with the result that he filed a motion for release from detention.



IRP Act

The judge hearing this matter was the same judge who determined that the certificate was reasonable. In the course of that determination, the judge made a general finding that the applicant lacked credibility. Accordingly, counsel for the applicant asked the judge to recuse himself.

The Court dismissed the motion, concluding that a fully informed person well aware of the requirements of the Act and of the certificate previously issued against the applicant, would appreciate the narrow parameters to be observed by the designated judge under this section and, therefore, not have a reasonable apprehension of bias relative to this application.

## Section 40.1(9) of the Former Act

*Ahani v. Canada (Minister of Citizenship & Immigration)* (2000), 7 Imm. L.R. (3d) 1, 77 C.R.R. (2d) 144, 261 N.R. 40, 24 Admin. L.R. (3d) 171, 184 F.T.R. 320 (note), 2000 CarswellNat 1485 (Fed. C.A.) — Merely because the trial judge was involved in an earlier decision involving this appellant did not impair his ability to be impartial. While a finding of lack of credibility in an earlier case, on the same factual issues, may create problems, there was no such situation in this case. The issues before the trial judge here were mainly legal along with factual ones that, with one exception, did not depend on findings of credibility.

Sections 40.1(7), (8) and (9) establish that it is the applicant who bears the onus of showing that his removal will not occur within a reasonable time and that his release would not be injurious to national security or the safety of persons.

Subject to two exceptions, Parliament meant people who are the subject of security certificates under s. 40.1 are to remain in custody until removed. A person may be released in order to permit his or her departure from Canada, and the other exception is meant to be available in only very limited circumstances outlined in the legislation in s. 40.1(9). Release under this subsection cannot be an automatic or easy thing to achieve. A review of this detention is permitted after 120 days, and release is allowed, but only if the person will not be removed within a reasonable period of time, and if the person's release would not be injurious to national security or to the safety of persons. Normally, one would expect an individual to show some significant change in circumstances or new evidence not previously available to obtain his release.

The onus of proof on the applicant is the ordinary standard of proof in civil cases, the balance of probabilities. The judge should not order the release of the individual unless he or she is satisfied by the applicant, on a balance of probabilities, that the applicant has met the statutory criteria. The balance of probability standard in these circumstances does not violate s. 7 of the *Charter of Rights and Freedoms*.

The trial judge considered that the appellant was the cause of the delay in his own removal because he was exercising his legal rights. No one can deny an appellant his right to exhaust every legal avenue open to him, but neither can one say that the removal of such a person is not taking place within a reasonable period of time, when the time necessary to hear all of the appellant's applications and appeals stretches into months and years.

*Singh (I.) v. Canada (Minister of Citizenship & Immigration)* (1999), 1999 CarswellNat 1077 (Fed. T.D.) — The applicant applied for release from detention. The Court found that the Minister was ready and willing to remove the applicant to India. The bar to removal was a Court imposed stay which was granted at the instance of the applicant. Section 40.1(9) is a relieving provision for individuals who, through no fault or action of their own, are not being removed by the Minister expeditiously. An individual is free to take those steps available to him at law to remain in Canada. If he does so, however, he may not claim that on the basis of his own actions that he will not be removed from Canada within a reasonable time for the purpose of paragraph 40.1(9)(a).

*Baroud v. Canada (Minister of Citizenship & Immigration)* (1995), 121 D.L.R. (4th) 308, 22 O.R. (3d) 255, 77 O.A.C. 26, 26 C.R.R. (2d) 318 (Ont. C.A.) — The appellant, a stateless refugee claimant who had been detained pursuant to a certificate issued under s. 40.1, applied for release from detention by means of a writ of *habeas corpus* with *certiorari* in aid. The appellant was a Palestinian who entered Canada and claimed refugee status in 1991. About 3 years later the Minister of Employment and Immigration and the Solicitor General of Canada certified their belief that the appellant was not admissible to Canada under s. 19(1)(f) of the *Immigration Act*. The appellant was detained in June, 1994 and remained in detention when this application was heard.

The Federal Court trial division has no jurisdiction to grant *habeas corpus*. The hearing, available under s. 40.1, would take place approximately the same time as the argument on the return of *habeas corpus* and, accordingly, the Federal Court trial procedure was an adequate and effective alternative remedy which provided relief to the appellant in a forum where proceedings relating to the appellant's detention were in progress. The mandatory language of s. 10 of the *Charter* was subject to s. 1 of the *Charter*. Once there is a finding that an alternative remedy is equally effective, it is axiomatic that the denial of the right to the issuance of a writ of *habeas corpus* is a justifiable limit. Accordingly, the *habeas corpus* application was dismissed.

### Author's Note

[*Included below are the annotations of decisions taken under the former Division 9 of Part I of the IRPA which was replaced on March 5, 2008, as a result of the Supreme Court of Canada's decision in* Charkaoui, Re, *[2007] S.C.J. No. 9, that concluded there were two defects in the legislation that were inconsistent with the Charter.*]

## Case Law

### Former Section 77(1)

*Charkaoui, Re*, [2004] F.C.J. No. 2060, 42 Imm. L.R. (3d) 165, 2004 CarswellNat 4849, 2004 CarswellNat 4495, 2004 FCA 421, 247 D.L.R. (4th) 405, 328 N.R. 201 (F.C.A.) — Parliament's intention in creating the concept of a "designated judge" was to ensure the presence of judges who are sufficiently informed to hear matters pertaining to national security. It is an added value for a judge of the Federal Court to be a designated judge and his general expertise as a judge is enhanced by his specialization. The designated judge is a representative of the Chief Justice. A decision on the constitutional validity of the IRPA has to do with the jurisdiction of the Court and not the reasonableness of the security certificate. Such a decision is a separate divisible judicial act and it is appealable.

It is the Ministers who brought the originating proceeding, the application for judicial examination, and the appellant, in challenging his detention, is simply pleading in his defence that some provisions of the IRPA are unconstitutional. This defence is arguable by a motion within the framework of the original proceeding without the need to initiate a parallel proceeding. The motion is an independent and distinct proceeding that, by its nature and its effects, escapes the rules of procedure established for the original proceeding and the rules of procedure established for the presentation of ordinary motions. Both the parties and the judge are entitled to require the application of the ordinary rules of evidence and adjudication.

The designated judge has jurisdiction to determine constitutional questions and he did not commit any reviewable error by doing so in the context of a motion.

Sections 77 and 78 of the IRPA do not contravene the rights under the *Charter* with respect to a fair trial before an independent and impartial tribunal.

Parliament weighed the interests at stake, those of the litigant and those of the community. It made a choice that recognizes the right to collective security while prescribing a procedure in which a judge, endowed with the necessary independence and impartiality, decides whether the disclosure of information or evidence would be injurious to national security or to the safety of any person.

The detention of a permanent resident awaiting the determination of the reasonableness of the security certificate issued against him is not an unjustified measure where there is proof of a danger to national security or that he might not appear at the proceedings taken against him.

The protection of national security is not a caprice. It is a necessity for the purpose of protecting the social order which allows the exercise and development of the individual rights conferred by the Constitution. This necessity to protect national security can justify derogations from the system or process that normally prevails. The process established for the review of protected information, by which the Chief Justice, or judge he designates, examines the denial of access to that information, fulfills the minimum requirements of the principles of fundamental justice.

The provisions relating to the preventive detention of the appellant, while awaiting the determination on the reasonableness of the security certificate, meet the requirements of the *Charter* and the Bill of Rights. The grounds for detention are serious and limited. They have a close and direct relationship to the objectives of IRPA, the obligation to ensure the protection of national security and the right of the Parliament of Canada to control the access to, and sojourn in, Canada of permanent residents.

The detention of a permanent resident, pursuant to a security certificate, is not unjustified and unconstitutional when the evidence discloses that he might be a danger to national security or the safety of any person or that he might thwart the pursuit of justice by avoiding the proceedings against him.

The expressions "reasonable grounds to believe" and "danger to the security of Canada" are not vague, overly broad or discriminatory.

Paragraph 3(3)(f) of the IRPA requires that the Act be construed and applied in a manner that complies with international human rights instruments to which Canada is a signatory. The Universal Declaration is a resolution of the General Assembly. It is of no binding effect, although it plays an important role in customary international law. The European Convention on Human Rights has a limited role in our domestic law. Insofar as its provisions are similar to those of the European Covenant on Human Rights and our *Charter*, its interpretation by the European tribunals offers an additional and relevant perspective.

*Richard C.J.* (Concurring)

Canada has a legitimate and compelling interest in protecting national security. The task of the law is to find ways to maintain national security without unduly sacrificing individual liberties. It is the designated judge, ultimately, who determines the need to withhold information from the party named in the certificate, not the Ministers. By ensuring that decisions regarding the withholding of evidence and information are made by the designated judge and not by the Ministers, the Act endeavours to grant protection to the rights of the party named in the certificate while maintaining national security.

Counsel, appearing on behalf of the Ministers in *ex parte* proceedings under s. 78, is under a duty of utmost good faith in the representations made to the judge. No relevant information may be withheld. The principle of full and frank disclosure in an *ex parte* proceeding is a fundamental principle of justice. Counsel for the Ministers are obliged to put before the designated judge not only the protected evidence that serves to incriminate the subject of the security certificate, but also any and all information that could serve to exculpate that person.



## Former Section 78

*Charkaoui, Re*, [2007] S.C.J. No. 9, 59 Imm. L.R. (3d) 1, 54 Admin. L.R. (4th) 1, 44 C.R. (6th) 1, 358 N.R. 1, 276 D.L.R. (4th) 594, 2007 CarswellNat 325, 2007 SCC 9 (S.C.C.) — Mr. Charkaoui is a permanent resident, while Messrs. Harkat and Almrei are foreign nationals who had been recognized as Convention refugees. All were living in Canada when they were arrested and detained. At the time of the decisions on appeal, all had been detained for some time — since 2003, 2002 and 2001 respectively. In 2001, a judge of the Federal Court determined Mr. Almrei's certificate to be reasonable; another determined Mr. Harkat's certificate to be reasonable in 2005. The reasonableness of Mr. Charkaoui's certificate had not yet been determined. Messrs. Charkaoui and Harkat were released on conditions in 2005 and 2006 respectively, but Mr. Harkat has been advised that he will be deported to Algeria, which he is contesting in other proceedings. Mr. Almrei remains in detention. In all three cases, the detentions were based on allegations that the individuals constituted a threat to the security of Canada by reason of involvement in terrorist activities. In the course of their detentions, all three appellants challenged, unsuccessfully, the constitutionality of the IRPA's certificate scheme and detention review processes.

The IRPA's procedure for determining whether a certificate is reasonable does not conform to the principles of fundamental justice as embodied in s. 7 of the *Charter*. The same conclusion necessarily applies to the detention review procedures under ss. 83 and 84 of the IRPA. The secrecy required by the scheme denies the named person the opportunity to know the case put against him or her, and hence to challenge the government's case. This, in turn, undermines the judge's ability to come to a decision based on all the relevant facts and law. Despite the best efforts of judges of the Federal Court to breathe judicial life into the IRPA procedure, it fails to assure the fair hearing that s. 7 of the *Charter* requires before the state deprives a person of life, liberty or security of the person.

While the deportation of a non-citizen in the immigration context may not in *itself* engage s. 7 of the *Charter*, some features associated with deportation, such as detention in the course of the certificate process or the prospect of deportation to torture, may do so.

The IRPA's procedures for determining whether a certificate is reasonable and for detention cannot be justified as minimal impairments of the individual's right to a judicial determination on the facts and the law and right to know and meet the case. Mechanisms developed in Canada and abroad illustrate that the government can do more to protect the individual while keeping critical information confidential than it has done in the IRPA. Precisely what more should be done is a matter for Parliament to decide.

Permanent residents, who pose a danger to national security, are also meant to be removed expeditiously. If this objective can be pursued while providing permanent residents with a mandatory detention review within 48 hours, then how can a denial of review for foreign nationals for 120 days after the certificate is confirmed be considered a minimal impairment? The lack of timely review of the detention of foreign nationals violates s. 9 and s. 10(c) and cannot be saved by s. 1.

Extended periods of detention under the certificate provisions of the IRPA do not violate ss. 7 and 12 of the *Charter* if accompanied by a process that provides regular opportunities for review of detention, taking into account all relevant factors, including the following: reasons for detention; length of detention; reasons for the delay in deportation; anticipated future length of detentions; availability of alternatives to detention.

The IRPA, interpreted in conformity with the *Charter*, permits robust ongoing judicial review of the continued need for, and justice of, the detainee's detention pending deportation. On this basis, extended periods of detention pending deportation under the certificate provisions of the IRPA do not violate s. 7 or s. 12 of the *Charter*, provided that reviewing courts adhere to the guidelines set out above. Thus, the IRPA procedure itself is not unconstitutional on this ground. However, this does not preclude the possibility of a judge concluding at a certain point that a particular detention constitutes cruel and unusual treatment or is inconsistent with the principles of fundamental justice, and therefore, infringes the *Charter* in a manner that is remediable under s. 24(1) of the *Charter*.

Mr. Charkaoui argued that the IRPA certificate scheme discriminated against non-citizens, contrary to s. 15(1) of the *Charter*. However, s. 6 of the *Charter* specifically allows for different treatment of citizens and non-citizens in deportation matters: only citizens are accorded the right to enter, remain or leave Canada (s. 6(1)). A deportation scheme that applies to non-citizens, but not to citizens, does not, for that reason alone, violate s. 15 of the *Charter*.

The scheme set up under Division 9 of Pt.1 of the IRPA suffers from two defects that are inconsistent with the *Charter*. The first is that s. 78(g) allows for the use of evidence that is never disclosed to the named person without providing adequate measures to compensate for this non-disclosure and the constitutional problems it causes. It is clear from approaches adopted in other democracies, and in Canada itself in other security situations, that solutions can be devised that protect confidential security information and at the same time are less intrusive on the person's rights. It follows that the IRPA's procedure for judicial confirmation of certificates and review of detention violates s. 7 of the *Charter* and has not been shown to be justified under s. 1 of the *Charter*.

In order to give Parliament time to amend the law, the Supreme Court of Canada suspended its declaration for one year from the date of its judgment. After one year, the certificates of any individuals whose certificates have been deemed reasonable will lose the "reasonable" status that has been conferred on them, and it will be open to them to apply to have the certificates quashed. If the government intends to employ a certificate after the one-year delay, it will need to seek a fresh determination of reasonableness under the new process devised by Parliament. Any detention review occurring after the delay will be subject to the new process.

The second defect is found in s. 84(2) of the IRPA, which denies a prompt hearing to foreign nationals by imposing a 120-day embargo, after confirmation of the certificate, on applications for release. Section 84(2) was struck and "foreign nationals" was read into s. 83 and the words "until a determination is made under subs. 80(1)" were struck from s. 83(2).

*Harkat, Re*, [2004] F.C.J. No. 2101, 2004 CarswellNat 5369, 2004 CarswellNat 4688, 259 F.T.R. 98 (Eng.), 2004 FC 1717 (F.C.) — The Federal Court is not a court of general or inherent jurisdiction. It is a statutory court, constituted pursuant to Parliament's authority under s. 101 of the *Constitution Act*, 1867. Section 3 of the *Federal Courts Act* provides that the Court is a court of law, equity, and admiralty and a superior court of record having civil and criminal jurisdiction. The designation of the Federal Court, as a superior court, has been held to confer no jurisdiction by itself. The Federal Court can only exercise those powers that are given to it by Parliament.

A power may be conferred by implication to the extent that the existence and exercise of such power is necessary for the Court to properly and fully exercise the jurisdiction expressly conferred upon it. The evidence does not establish that the appointment of an *amicus curiae* is necessary in order for the Court to exercise its responsibility under ss. 78 and 80.

In security proceedings, the Court is obliged to isolate the facts relied upon to support the security certificate and then review such evidence with intense scrutiny and weigh the evidence with an eye to the quality and number of sources of information. Such an exercise will require the Court to consider the potential for error caused by a number of factors including misidentification, mistake, misdirection, incompetence and malevolence.

The Court denied the applicant's request for an *amicus curiae* to assist the Court.

*Harkat, Re*, [2003] F.C.J. No. 400, 27 Imm. L.R. (3d) 47, 2003 CarswellNat 556, 2003 FCT 285, 2003 CarswellNat 3392, 2003 CFPI 285, 231 F.T.R. 19 (Fed. T.D.) — This proceeding was instituted by the Solicitor General of Canada and the Minister of Citizenship and Immigration for a determination as to whether the certificate signed by them, stating that Mohamed Harkat is inadmissible to Canada under s. 34 of the IRPA, was reasonable. Mr. Harkat made a motion for an order directing the disclosure of relevant information in order to make full answer in defence. In the absence of a judicial determination, a disclosure of information put before the judge would be injurious to national security or the safety of any person. The information or evidence put before the judge should be disclosed to the subject of the certificate. The right of the subject of the certificate to be reasonably informed of the circumstances, giving rise to the certificate, is subject to the restriction that the disclosure would be injurious to national security or the safety of any person. Criminal law principles as articulated in Stinchcombe are not applicable. The Court approved of the statement of Lord Denning in *R. v. Secretary of State for the Home Department*, [1977] 3 All. E.R. 452 (Eng. C.A.); affirmed [1977] 1 W.L.R. 789 (Eng. H.L.): "The information supplied to the Home Secretary by the Security Service is, and must be, highly confidential. The public interest in the security of the realm is so great that the sources of information must not be disclosed, nor should the nature of the information itself be disclosed, if there is any risk that it would lead to the sources being discovered. The reason is because, in this very secretive field, our enemies might try to eliminate the source of information."

In security matters, there is a requirement to not only protect the identity of human sources of information but to recognize that the following types of information might require to be protected, with due regard, of course, to the administration of justice and more particularly to the openness of proceedings: (1) information pertaining to the identity of targets of surveillance whether they be individuals or groups; (2) the technical means and sources of surveillance; (3) the methods of operation of the service; (4) the identity of certain members of the service; (5) the telecommunications and cypher systems; (6) the fact that a surveillance is being, or is not being, carried out. Evidence which of itself might not be of any particular use in actually identifying the threat might nevertheless require to be protected if the divulging of the fact that CSIS is in possession of such information would alert the targeted organization to the fact that it is subject to electronic surveillance or to a wiretap or to a leak from some human source within the organization. An informed reader of information, that is a person who is both knowledgeable regarding security matters and a member of, or associated with a group which constitutes a threat or potential threat to the security of Canada, will be quite familiar with the minute details of its organization and of the ramifications of its operations. As a result, such an informed reader may, by fitting a piece of apparently innocuous information into the general picture, be in a position to arrive at some damaging deductions regarding the investigation being conducted by CSIS. The target or targeted group might for instance be in a position to determine: (1) the duration, scope, intensity and degree of success or lack of success of an investigation; (2) the investigative techniques of the service; (3) the typographic and teleprinter systems employed by this service; (4) internal security procedures; (5) the nature and content of other classified documents; (6) the identities of service personnel or other persons involved in an investigation.

## Former Section 80(1)

*Harkat, Re*, [2005] F.C.J. No. 481, 45 Imm. L.R. (3d) 65, 2005 FC 393, 2005 CarswellNat 737 (F.C.) — The Court decided that the security certificate in this case was reasonable. Courts both here and abroad have recognized the need for security intelligence information to be kept secret in order to protect national security. The need to preserve the secrecy of security information flows from the fact that security intelligence investigations are directed towards future events. They attempt to predict future events by discovering from past and present events patterns of occurrences and relationships. This requires piecing together bits of information that may, at first, not appear to be related.

A group or organization with hostile intentions has an ongoing existence with a continuity of operations. A security intelligence investigation does not end with the detention or apprehension of one member, rather investigations are long range and ongoing. This is one of the principal factors that distinguishes intelligence investigations from criminal investigations. Furthermore, there is no completed offence to provide a framework for the investigation. Criminal law principles and policies do not apply to security certificate proceedings.

When security information is disclosed it must be assumed that the information will reach persons who have knowledge about the suspect of an investigation and his activities. In the hands of an informed reader, unrelated pieces of information can provide an insight into the scope or progress of an ongoing intelligence operation. Equally, disclosure of the fact that certain information is not known by the authorities may allow an informed reader to learn about subjects of investigation, methods of investigation, sources of information or that certain activities are not under investigation.

The designated judge is responsible to ensure the confidentiality of the information upon which the security certificate is based and of any other evidence provided to the judge which disclosure would be injurious to national security or the safety of any person. This obligation and its companion obligation to provide a summary to the person concerned, reflect the tension between the democratic requirement of open court proceedings and the equally compelling necessity of keeping security information secret.

If confidential information is provided by a human source, some relevant inquiries and areas for examination by the Court include matters such as the origin and length of the relationship between the service and the human source, whether the source was paid for the information, what is known about the source's motive for providing information, whether the source has provided information about other persons and if so, particulars of that, the extent to which information provided by the source has been corroborated, the citizenship/immigration status of the source and whether that status has changed throughout the source's relationship with the service, whether the source has been subject to any form of pressure to provide information, if so, why and by whom, whether the source was or is under investigation by the service or any other intelligence agency or police force, whether the source has a criminal record or any outstanding criminal charges, the nature of any relationship between the source and the subject of the investigation, whether there is any known or inferred motive for the source to provide false information.

If any confidential information is provided from another agency, some relevant inquiries are: the manner in which the service assesses the reliability of information, the extent to which the information is corroborated, is there any suggestion the agency may have a motive for colouring the information provided, what is the human rights record of the agency and the agency's home country, how does the foreign agency itself assess the reliability of the information it has provided, and is the agency a conduit for information originating from a less reliable agent.

If confidential information is provided through technical sources, relevant inquiries may include: the accuracy of any document that records intercepted information, the accuracy of any translation, the objectivity or bias of any summary made of the intercepted information, and how the parties to any conversation are identified.

Reasons delivered in security intelligence cases cannot fully justify and explain a result publicly when the evidence the Court relies upon cannot be disclosed.

## Former Section 82(1)

*Charkaoui, Re*, 2005 CarswellNat 410, 2005 FC 258, 2005 CarswellNat 5111 (F.C.) — This judgment has to do with the fourth review of the detention of Mr. Charkaoui that is provided for in s. 83(2). The Court decided that the phrase "danger to national security" had the same meaning as the phrase "danger to the security of Canada," the meaning of which was discussed in *Suresh v. Canada (Minister of Citizenship & Immigration)*, [2002] 1 S.C.R. 3 (S.C.C.) at paragraph 90. The other phrase in subs. 83(3) "danger. . .to the safety of any person" includes awareness of danger before the terrorist act occurs. It applies to more than persons who have been convicted of a serious offence. Danger to national security or the safety of any person have in common the fact that Parliament has asked the designated judge, when considering the release of the person concerned, to analyse the evidence and consider whether either of these two dangers still exist. The wording of the section suggests that a danger to national security or the safety of any person may exist at one moment and not at another. There is a possibility the danger may be imminent but subsequently neutralized. The other phrase used in s. 83 is the phrase "unlikely to appear at a proceeding or for removal". This phrase indicates that Parliament intended a degree of probability to be taken into account by the designated judge when weighing the evidence.

In considering a conditional release, the designated judge must be satisfied, on reasonable grounds, that the person concerned is not a danger to national security or the safety of any person. If there is a danger, the judge cannot consider release, even with exceptional conditions.

When the Ministers signed the warrant for the arrest and detention of Mr. Charkaoui, they did so not in order to lay charges or eventually secure a conviction, but to make an arrest and detention that would prevent events that might occur. This tool, given to the Ministers by Parliament pursuant to subs. 82(1), is intended to "maintain the security of Canadian society" — one of the objectives of immigration as set out in paragraph 3(1)(h).

Detention reviews involve questions of fact peculiar to each situation. In the case at bar, the imprisonment, the passage of time, the media attention to the proceedings, the presence of the family, the community support, and the testimony of the person concerned are examples of situations to be taken into account in assessing whether a danger still exists or whether the person concerned will likely appear at a proceeding or for removal.

The court set terms for Mr. Charkaoui's release.

## Former Section 83

*Jaballah v. Canada (Attorney General)*, [2005] O.J. No. 3681, 258 D.L.R. (4th) 161, 49 Imm. L.R. (3d) 305, 2005 CarswellOnt 3869 (S.C.J.) — The applicant sought declaratory and other just and appropriate relief because, in his submission, his continued detention pursuant to ss. 82 to 85 of the IRPA, which provide for the automatic and mandatory detention of a foreign national subject to a security certificate issued under s. 77 and which prohibit any possibility of review of the need to detain the foreign national until the security certificate is upheld and the person is not removed within the next 120 days, was unconstitutional. The Ontario Superior Court of Justice refused to deal with the *habeas corpus* application as it could lead to a decision on the constitutional validity of any impugned provisions of the IRPA that is inconsistent with any decisions of the Federal Court dealing with the same, or similar, issues. The Federal Court has the expertise and experience that is necessary to develop a coherent body of law on these constitutional issues. The Ontario Superior Court should defer to that expertise and experience where the constitutionality of the IRPA is at issue, since the danger of inconsistent decisions between the Ontario Superior Court and the Federal Court must be avoided as any such inconsistencies are not in the public interest and may undermine the public confidence in the administration of justice.

*Charkaoui, Re*, 2005 CarswellNat 410, 2005 FC 258 (F.C.) — This judgment has to do with the fourth review of the detention of Mr. Charkaoui that is provided for in s. 83(2). The Court decided that the phrase "danger to national security" had the same meaning as the phrase "danger to the security of Canada," the meaning of which was discussed in *Suresh v. Canada (Minister of Citizenship & Immigration)*(2002), 18 Imm. L.R. (3d) 1 (S.C.C.) at paragraph 90. The other phrase in subs. 83(3) "danger. . .to the safety of any person" includes awareness of danger before the terrorist act occurs. It applies to more than persons who have been convicted of a serious offence. Danger to national security or the safety of any person have in common the fact that Parliament has asked the designated judge when considering the release of the person concerned to analyse the evidence and consider whether either of these two dangers still exist. The wording of the section suggests that a danger to national security or the safety of any person may exist at one moment and not at another. There is a possibility the danger may be imminent but subsequently neutralized. The other phrase used in s. 83 is the phrase "unlikely to appear at a proceeding or for removal". This phrase indicates that Parliament intended a degree of probability to be taken into account by the designated judge when weighing the evidence.

In considering a conditional release, the designated judge must be satisfied, on reasonable grounds, that the person concerned is not a danger to national security or the safety of any person. If there is a danger, the judge cannot consider release, even with exceptional conditions.

When the Ministers signed the warrant for the arrest and detention of Mr. Charkaoui, they did so not in order to lay charges or eventually secure a conviction, but to make an arrest and detention that would prevent events that might occur. This tool, given to the Ministers by Parliament pursuant to subs. 82(1), is intended to "maintain the security of Canadian society" — one of the objectives of immigration as set out in paragraph 3(1)(h).

Detention reviews involve questions of fact peculiar to each situation. In the case at bar, the imprisonment, the passage of time, the media attention to the proceedings, the presence of the family, the community support, and the testimony of the person concerned are examples of situations to be taken into account in assessing whether a danger still exists or whether the person concerned will likely appear at a proceeding or for removal.

The Court set terms for Mr. Charkaoui's release.

*Zündel, Re* (2004), 39 Imm. L.R. (3d) 271, 2004 CarswellNat 66, 2004 CarswellNat 439, 2004 FC 86, 245 F.T.R. 61 (F.C.) — The Minister of Citizenship and the Solicitor General signed a certificate stating that Mr. Zundel was inadmissible on grounds of security. A warrant for Mr. Zundel's arrest was issued and, in this case, the judge sitting as a designated judge pursuant to s. 76 and subs. 83(1) was reviewing the continued detention of Mr. Zundel.

The grounds to continue detention are much narrower than the grounds of inadmissibility. Inadmissibility covers more than security and includes such grounds as human rights violations or criminality. The test for continued detention requires the designated judge to consider whether the person is a danger to national security or the safety of any person and whether the person is unlikely to appear at a proceeding for removal. The onus is on the Ministers to prove that the permanent resident presents a danger. The standard of proof is "a *bona fide* belief in a serious possibility based on credible evidence."

A person constitutes a danger to the security of Canada if he or she poses a serious threat the security of Canada, whether direct or indirect, and one must bear in mind the fact that the security of one country is often dependent on the security of other nations. The threat must be serious in the sense that it must be grounded on objectively reasonable suspicion based on evidence and in the sense that the threat and harm must be substantial rather than negligible.

The Court found that the threat to national security in this case was sufficient to justify the applicant's detention.

*Charkaoui, Re*, [2003] F.C.J. No. 1119, [2004] 1 F.C.R. 528, 37 Imm. L.R. (3d) 1, 2003 CarswellNat 2240, 2003 CarswellNat 2360, 237 F.T.R. 143, 2003 FC 882 (F.C.); affirmed (2003), 37 Imm. L.R. (3d) 20, (sub nom. *Charkaoui v. Canada (Minister of Citizenship & Immigration))* [2004] 1 F.C.R. 451, 2003 CarswellNat 3356, 2003 CarswellNat 4012, 2003 FCA 407, 245 F.T.R. 160 (note), 236 D.L.R. (4th) 91, 315 N.R. 1 (F.C.A.); leave to appeal refused (2004), 2004 CarswellNat 1270, 2004 CarswellNat 1271, 330 N.R. 393 (note) (S.C.C.) — One of the purposes of IRPA is to maintain the security of Canadians. The Ministers concluded that the respondent should be declared inadmissible because in their opinion he was, or is, a member of the Osama Bin Laden network and consequently he constituted, or will constitute, a danger to a security of Canada. The Ministers also signed a warrant to arrest the respondent and within 48 hours of the respondent's arrest, the Court commenced a review of that detention.

A designated judge, carrying out this responsibility, must ask himself or herself whether there is any evidence in support of the Ministers' position that the respondent remains a danger to national security. The designated judge is not to look for proof of the existence of facts but rather to analyze the proof as a whole, while asking himself or herself whether it is sufficient for a person to have a reasonable belief that there is a danger to national security. The standard of proof must tend toward a serious possibility of the existence of facts based on reliable and justifiable evidence.

In reviewing protected records and hearing witnesses, in the absence of the respondent, the judge must be curious, concerned by what is advanced and must maintain a sceptical attitude with the objective of conducting a critical review of facts. He or she must verify the human, technical and documentary sources, their reliability and the truth of what they may relate. The designated judge must seriously test the protected documentation and information. The designated judge must analyze the evidence taking into account the danger to national security.

## Former Section 84(2)

*Harkat v. Canada (Minister of Citizenship & Immigration)*, 2006 CarswellNat 1310, 2006 CarswellNat 2434, 2006 FC 628 (F.C.) — The applicant applied to the Court for release from incarceration following a determination that a security certificate signed by the Minister of Citizenship and Immigration and the Solicitor General of Canada was reasonable. The certificate stated that the applicant, a foreign national, was inadmissible to Canada on grounds of security because there were reasonable grounds to believe that he has engaged in terrorism by supporting terrorist activities.

The applicant established a material or substantial change of circumstances since his previous application. The applicant also met the onus placed upon him by subs. 84(2) of the Act, to satisfy the Court that he would not be removed from Canada within a reasonable time and that his release would not pose a danger to national security or to the safety of any person.

The Court concluded that if the delay in appointing a delegate and the resultant delay in considering whether the applicant may be removed from Canada were known in December of 2005, the previous decision of the Federal Court made by Mr. Justice Lemieux may well have been different. Mr. Justice Lemieux set out seven factors that led him to conclude that the applicant had not discharged the onus upon him to satisfy the Court that he would not be removed in a reasonable time. The unexpected delay in the appointment of the Minister's delegate, and the consequent failure of the delegate to begin to consider his decision, are facts that are inconsistent with Justice Lemieux's conclusions that the authorities were "proceeding expeditiously in this matter" and that the Minister's delegate's decision is pending.

The Court also concluded that no cogent evidence of imminent removal had been put before it. Instead, the Court pointed out that the advice from the Canadian Border Services Agency to the applicant's counsel was that the delegate's decision would not be made within the time originally contemplated.

Finally, the Court concluded it would be erroneous to reject the applicant's application for release if there were conditions that, on a balance of probabilities, would neutralize or contain the danger posed by his release. In that circumstance, his continued incarceration could not be justified because of Canada's respect for human and civil rights, and the values protected by our *Charter*.

In considering whether there were terms and conditions that would neutralize and contain the danger posed by the applicant's release, the Court considered the need for terms and conditions to be specific and tailored to the applicant's precise circumstances. These terms and conditions had to be designed to prevent his involvement in any activity that commits, encourages, facilitates, assists or instigates an act of terrorism or any similar activity. The terms and conditions had to be proportionate to the risk posed by the applicant.



The applicant, having satisfied the Court that there had been a material or substantive change of circumstance since his previous application, that he would not be removed from Canada within a reasonable time and that his release would not pose a danger to national security or the safety of any person, was ordered released.

*Canada (Minister of Citizenship & Immigration) v. Mahjoub* (2005), 270 F.T.R. 101, 2005 CarswellNat 3933, 2005 FC 1596 (F.C.) — The applicant sought to be released from detention. The presence of sureties and the imposition of conditions would not be sufficient to neutralize the danger posed by the release of the applicant. The applicant did not satisfy the Court he could be trusted to abide by those conditions. Furthermore, the medical evidence did not support that the applicant would comply with the conditions and the sureties did not know the applicant sufficiently well to have the ability to control his actions.

*Almrei v. Canada (Attorney General)* (2005), 50 Imm. L.R. (3d) 310, 2005 CarswellOnt 6822, (Ont. S.C.J.) — There is a long line of authority in Ontario's Superior Court and in the Ontario Court of Appeal that holds that the Ontario courts should decline to assume jurisdiction in matters relating to immigration, except in the rarest of cases, because of the expertise and experience that the Federal Court possesses in immigration matters. The Court issued a stay of the applicant's application for a writ of *habeas corpus* and *certiorari* and other declaratory relief pertaining to his conditions of detention.

*Almrei v. Canada (Minister of Citizenship & Immigration)*, [2005] F.C.J. No. 1994, 270 F.T.R. 1, 50 Imm. L.R. (3d) 160, 2005 CarswellNat 4022, 2005 CarswellNat 5881, 2005 FC 1645 (F.C.) — On an application for relief brought under subs. 84(2) of the IRPA, the onus of proof is on the applicant to establish, on a balance of probabilities, that he will not be removed within a reasonable time and that he is not a danger to national security or to the safety of any person. The statutory criteria in the provision are conjunctive. In this case, the applicant premised his application wholly on the grounds that he will not be removed within a reasonable time and that he is not such a danger. The applicant only met one criteria but not the other. Accordingly, the statute mandates that the application be dismissed.

*Almrei v. Canada (Minister of Citizenship & Immigration)* (2005), 45 Imm. L.R. (3d) 163, 2005 CarswellNat 319, 2005 CarswellNat 869, 2005 FCA 54, 330 N.R. 73, 251 D.L.R. (4th) 13, [2005] F.C.J. No. 213 (F.C.A.) — This was an appeal against a decision dismissing an application for a judicial release from detention. Subsection 27(1) of the *Federal Courts Act* gives the appellant a right of appeal against a decision on a subs. 84(2) application for judicial release. The onus of proof rests with the person who brings the application for judicial release and it has to be discharged on a balance of probabilities. The decision on the reasonableness of the security certificate is not determinative of the merit, opportunity and legality of the detention of the person concerned.

Where the removal of a foreign national is delayed so as to bring into play the reasonable time requirement, the judge hearing the judicial release application must consider the delay and look at the causes of such delay. Judicial remedies have to be pursued diligently and in a timely fashion. The same goes for the Government's responses and the judicial hearing of these remedies. Courts, as they must do, have given priority to the hearing of challenges to the legality of detention. Thus, in determining whether there will be execution or enforcement of the removal order within a reasonable period of time, a judge must look at the delay generated by the parties as well as the institutional delay which is inherent in the exercise of a remedy. Where an applicant, rightly or wrongly, tries to prevent his removal from Canada and delay ensues as a result of his action, he cannot be heard to complain that his removal has not occurred within a reasonable period of time, unless the delay is unreasonable or inordinate and not attributable to him.

Section 78, which deals with the protection of information relating to national security, applies to an application for judicial release under subs. 84(2) of IRPA.

The test for granting or refusing a subs. 84(2) application is future-oriented. Evidence has to be provided that the applicant will not be removed within a reasonable period of time. If the government produces, at the hearing, credible and compelling evidence of an imminent removal, the time already served and the conditions of detention lose much of their significance. The length and conditions of past detention are relevant in assessing the credibility of the evidence submitted that the removal of the person concerned is imminent. The history of events may cast doubt on the reliability of the assertion and evidence submitted that the moment of removal is close. Conditions of detention, especially when coupled with a lengthy detention, may cause the phrase "within a reasonable time" to take on some urgency. The removal would then have to be effected more expeditiously in order to be in compliance with the requirements of subs. 84(2).

The possibility that the removal of a detainee may be to a country where the detainee may face torture and serious violations of human rights requires that more substantial procedural protections and safeguards be given in the preparation of the danger opinion. The person facing deportation to torture must be informed of the case to be met and must be given an opportunity to respond to the case presented by the Minister. He or she is entitled to disclosure, subject to privilege and other lawful exceptions. He or she has a right to present evidence both on the issue of lack of danger to the security of Canada and on the risk of torture. Consultations with other government departments and with the countries to which the person could be removed may be necessary to obtain and implement safeguards for the life and integrity of the individual.

*Canada (Minister of Citizenship & Immigration) v. Mahjoub*, [2004] F.C.J. No. 1335, 2004 CarswellNat 2644, 260 F.T.R. 226 (Eng.), 2004 FC 1028, 2004 CarswellNat 5396 (F.C.) — The respondent was seeking an order releasing him from detention and was requesting an order, during the course of that proceeding, to give part of his evidence *in camera*. It is a fundamental principle that the proceedings of Canadian courts are open and accessible to the public. The Court is obliged to determine where such a restriction is necessary to prevent a real and substantial risk to the fairness of the hearing, because reasonably available alternative measures will not prevent the risk, and secondly whether the salutary effects of the restriction outweigh the deleterious effects of the free expression of those affected by the ban. The respondent's request that he be permitted to testify *in camera* was dismissed.

*Charkaoui, Re*, 2004 CarswellNat 3253, 2004 CarswellNat 1222, 255 F.T.R. 199, 2004 FC 624 (F.C.) — In adopting the IRPA, Parliament contemplated that the judge designated by the Chief Justice would be able to decide the reasonableness of the certificate and the continued detention of the person concerned. The Chief Justice designates certain judges from among the Federal Court judges to perform such duties in accordance with s. 76. The designated judge has the duty to examine the information and any other evidence within seven days after the referral of the certificate and prepare a summary of the circumstances giving rise to the certificate and forward it to the person concerned. He or she also has a duty, within 48 hours of detention, to review the reasons for the continued detention. For at least once every six months, the person concerned must appear for an evaluation of whether he or she is still a danger to national security or the safety of any person or is unlikely to appear at a proceeding or for removal.

Parliament has expressly contemplated the possibility that the designated judge would hear the matter, that is, determine the reasonableness of the certificate, and undertake a review of the reasons justifying the detention. Accordingly, there can be no apprehension of bias when the designated judge performs these functions.

*Almrei v. Canada (Minister of Citizenship & Immigration)*, [2004] F.C.J. No. 509, 38 Imm. L.R. (3d) 117, 2004 CarswellNat 5580, [2004] 4 F.C.R. 327, 249 F.T.R. 53, 2004 CarswellNat 787, 2004 FC 420 (F.C.); affirmed 45 Imm. L.R. (3d) 163, 2005 CarswellNat 319, 2005 CarswellNat 869, [2005] F.C.J. No. 213, 2005 FCA 54, 330 N.R. 73, 251 D.L.R. (4th) 13 (F.C.A.) — The provisions of s. 78, which govern the determination of the reasonableness of the certificate, are also applicable to a detention review. The designated judge is required by these provisions to ensure the confidentiality of the information on which the certificate is based and of any other evidence that may be provided to the judge, if, in the opinion of the judge, its disclosure would be injurious to national security or to the safety of any person.

The reference to the period of 120 days reflects Parliament's intent that removal should occur expeditiously once a certificate has been determined to be reasonable. The length of time that the applicant has remained in detention since the certificate was determined to be reasonable and the conditions of the applicant's detention are matters of great concern to the Court.

Where a risk of torture is asserted by a person who has been found to be a Convention refugee, more time rather than less will reasonably be required to ensure that the principles of fundamental justice are not breached. In this case, much of the delay was necessary for the due process required for applications brought by the applicant during the proceeding.

The conditions of the applicant's detention are not ideal. The Court must be mindful that the legislative scheme provides for preventative detention upon the issuance of a security certificate and ongoing detention until release is ordered or removal is effected. The applicant stated that solitary detention was necessary for his own protection within the institution. The circumstances of the applicant's detention are a factor to be considered but are insufficient to warrant the applicant's release.

The Court accepted that the jurisprudence relating to s. 40.1 of the former Act remain relevant to the provisions of the IRPA. The Court declined to order the applicant's release.

*Jaballah v. Canada (Minister of Citizenship & Immigration)*, [2004] F.C.J. No. 420, 38 Imm. L.R. (3d) 179, 2004 CarswellNat 645, (sub nom. *Jaballah, Re)* 247 F.T.R. 68, 2004 FC 299 (F.C.) — This was an application for release made more than 120 days after the determination by the Court that a certificate signed by the two respondent Ministers was reasonable in stating that Mr. Jaballah was inadmissible to Canada on the grounds of national security.

The applicant applied for release under s. 84(2) of IRPA. This provision carries forward a process established under s. 40.1(8) and (9) of the former *Immigration Act*. Jurisprudence under the former Act remains relevant to applications under subsection 84(2). The standard of proof is the ordinary civil standard. The certificate is conclusive proof that the person is inadmissible to Canada. Release under subs. 84(2) is not automatic. A person cannot be detained indefinitely, at least without good reason. The 120-day detention, which must occur before an application for release can be initiated, is measured from the date the Minister's certificate is found to be reasonable so that time spent in detention before that is not ordinarily a factor. Similarly, the 120 days after the certificate is upheld is also not a factor in assessing whether release in the future will not be in a reasonable time.

The burden to establish the requirements under subs. 84(2) is that of the applicant. Release under subs. 84(2) is not automatic nor is it easily achieved. One would expect the applicant to show change in circumstances or new evidence not previously available to obtain release.

While the applicant was entitled to pursue his legal rights in Canada, he is not entitled to rely on any uncertainty in predicting when those matters may be determined as a basis to claim uncertainty about when his removal would be effective.

This type of application is not similar to a bail application in a criminal proceeding. Such a comparison ignores the basic principles of immigration law that the state may control access to Canada by foreign nationals and may distinguish between them, permanent residents and citizens. It has long been recognized that the state may preclude admission, particularly for those who are reasonably believed on the information available to the Ministers to a present danger to national security. Release from detention of a person certified as one who presents a threat to national security is simply not comparable to release on bail of one detained in regular criminal or extradition proceedings.

*Almrei v. Canada (Minister of Citizenship & Immigration)* (2003), 245 F.T.R. 27, 2003 CarswellNat 4425, 2003 FC 1523, 2003 CarswellNat 4152 (F.C.) — The applicant made an application for an order pursuant to s. 84(2) that he should be released from detention (s. 84(2) does not contain any provision with respect to the procedure to be followed in the detention review). The proceedings commenced by the issuance of the security certificate continue so long as the subject of the certificate remains in detention or is released on bail pending removal. If a certificate is determined to be reasonable under subs. 80(1), it is conclusive proof that the permanent resident or foreign national is inadmissible. Conclusive proof of inadmissibility is not conclusive proof that the person will pose a danger to national security or the safety of any person. The second branch of the detention review test is not automatically met where there is, in existence, a valid security certificate.

The requirements of subs. 84(2) necessitate incorporation of s. 78 procedures. Consideration of the second branch of the test, that release will not pose a danger to national security or to the safety of any person, requires that the judge assess the basis upon which the applicant is detained.

*Canada (Minister of Citizenship & Immigration) v. Mahjoub* (2003), [2004] 1 F.C.R. 493, 2003 CarswellNat 3857, 2003 CarswellNat 2332, [2003] F.C.J. No. 1183, 2003 FC 928, 238 F.T.R. 12 (F.C.) — This is an application by Mr. Mahjoub for an order releasing him from detention. The applicant entered Canada on December 30, 1995 and immediately claimed refugee status. In October 1996, he was found to be a refugee. On June 27, 2000 under the former Act, the Solicitor General and Minister of Citizenship and Immigration caused a copy of a security certificate signed by them to be referred to the Court for determination, as to whether the certificate should be quashed. On the basis of the certificate, Mr. Mahjoub was detained on June 26, 2000 and has been in custody ever since. In October 2001, the certificate was found to be reasonable and in March 2002 the adjudication division found Mr. Mahjoub to be inadmissible based on the security certificate and issued a deportation order. On June 28, 2002, the present Act came into effect and on October 28, 2002, this motion was commenced.

The wording now found in subs. 84(2) is not to be construed in a significantly different fashion than the similar provisions under the former Act.

The applicant bears the onus of showing that he meets the statutory criteria for release. The criteria require a judge to be satisfied that the applicant will not be removed within a reasonable time and that the release of the applicant will not pose a danger to the public. The standard of proof is the ordinary civil standard. The certificate is conclusive proof that the person is inadmissible on the grounds of security. Release under subs. 84(2) cannot be automatic because the persons to whom that section applies had been found to be inadmissible on the grounds of security, violating human or international rights, serious criminality or organized criminality. Finally, a person cannot be detained indefinitely without good reason.

The applicant has a right to be reasonably informed as to the basis upon which his release from detention is opposed. Such right must be viewed against the state's interest to protect information which, if disclosed, would be injurious to national security or the safety of any person. The Court's duty to ensure that national security is protected is not lessened on an application for release from detention.

The reference to a period of 120 days in subs. 84(2) reflects Parliament's intent, that once a certificate has been determined to be reasonable, the person named in the certificate should be removed expeditiously by requiring as one of the criteria for release that the Court consider whether removal will take place within a reasonable time. Parliament contemplated that in some circumstances removal will not have occurred within 120 days. The right to apply for release after 120 days undoubtedly acts as an impetus to officials to assure an expeditious removal, and at the same time assures that any post 120-day delay can be the subject of judicial scrutiny.

While it is the applicant's right to exhaust all avenues of legal recourse, the time required for those challenges cannot be relied upon by the applicant for the purpose of arguing that he or she will not be removed from Canada within a reasonable time. An individual is free to take those steps available to him or her at law to remain in Canada. If he or she does so however, they may not claim that, on the basis of their own actions, they will not be removed from Canada within a reasonable time.

The Court, having regard to the fact that the uncertainty about when the applicant may be removed from Canada was in a large part the result of pending and contemplated Court challenges initiated by the applicant, concluded that the applicant had not met the burden on a balance of probabilities of proving that he would not be removed from Canada within a reasonable time.

For the purpose of subs. 84(2), evidence which grounds an objectively reasonable suspicion of substantial threatened harm, would establish a danger to national security. Because the onus is on the applicant for release to satisfy the Court on a balance of probabilities, that his or her release will not pose a danger to national security or the safety of any person, the onus may be difficult to meet given that an objectively reasonable suspicion of substantial threatened harm may establish the danger.

**76. Definitions — The following definitions apply in this Division.**

**"information" means security or criminal intelligence information and information that is obtained in confidence from a source in Canada, the government of a foreign state, an international organization of states or an institution of such a government or international organization.** ***("renseignements")***

**"judge" means the Chief Justice of the Federal Court or a judge of that Court designated by the Chief Justice.** ***("juge")***

2002, c. 8, s. 194(d); 2008, c. 3, s. 4

## *Certificate*

[Heading added 2008, c. 3, s. 4.]

**77. (1) Referral of certificate — The Minister and the Minister of Citizenship and Immigration shall sign a certificate stating that a permanent resident or foreign national is inadmissible on grounds of security, violating human or international rights, serious criminality or organized criminality, and shall refer the certificate to the Federal Court.**

**(2) Filing of evidence and summary — When the certificate is referred, the Minister shall file with the Court the information and other evidence on which the certificate is based, and a summary of information and other evidence that enables the person who is named in the certificate to be reasonably informed of the case made by the Minister but that does not include anything that, in the Minister's opinion, would be injurious to national security or endanger the safety of any person if disclosed.**

**(3) Effect of referral — Once the certificate is referred, no proceeding under this Act respecting the person who is named in the certificate — other than proceedings relating to sections 82 to 82.3, 112 and 115 — may be commenced or continued until the judge determines whether the certificate is reasonable.**

2002, c. 8, s. 194(a)(ii); 2005, c. 10, s. 34(1)(o)(ii); 2008, c. 3, s. 4

### Case Law

*Jaballah, Re* (2010), 88 Imm. L.R. (3d) 268, 2010 FC 224, 2010 CarswellNat 1174, 2010 CarswellNat 448 (F.C.) — Mahmoud Jaballah was named in a security certificate signed by the Minister of Citizenship & Immigration and the Minister of Public Safety and Emergency Preparedness. Mr. Jaballah moved for an order to restrict the Ministers from using his evidence given in previous proceedings. What was in issue was a very unique situation: where there had been three prior reasonableness hearings, and a number of associated detention review hearings, years later the question arose whether the Ministers could use Mr. Jaballah's prior testimony against him in support of their case in the Court proceeding. The Court held that the evidence could not be used to build the Ministers' case in chief, but could be used in cross examination should Mr. Jaballah decide to testify. This finding represented a balance between protecting Mr. Jaballah's right to a fair hearing and protecting the public's right to have all relevant evidence available in search of the truth.



*Almrei, Re* (2009), 86 Imm. L.R. (3d) 212, 355 F.T.R. 222 (Eng.), [2009] F.C.J. No. 1579, 2009 FC 1263, 2009 CarswellNat 4286, 2009 CarswellNat 5657 (F.C.) — On February 22, 2008, the Ministers signed a certificate in which they stated that Hassan Almrei was a foreign national inadmissible to Canada on security grounds. Pursuant to s. 77(1) of IRPA, the certificate was referred to the Court for determination as to whether it was reasonable. The Court held the reasons for determining the certificate were not reasonable.

The duties of utmost good faith and candour imply that the party relying upon the presentation of *ex parte* evidence will conduct a thorough review of the information in its possession and make representations based on all of the information including that which is unfavourable to their case. That was not done in this instance. The 2008 security intelligence report was assembled with information that could only be construed as unfavourable to Mr. Almrei without any serious attempt to include information to the contrary, or to update their assessment.

The Court held that Hassan Almrei of 2009 was not the same person as in 2001 when the certificate was initially issued. The service's assessment in a February 2008 Security Intelligence Review was prepared, in the Court's view, without sufficient consideration of all the information within its possession and without considering whether the state of knowledge about the risk to national security posted by Islamic extremists had evolved since Mr. Almrei was detained in 2001. That task fell on the Court with the assistance of counsel for both parties and the special advocates. The Federal Court struck down the national security certificate.

*Charkaoui, Re*, [2008] 2 S.C.R. 326, (sub nom. *Charkaoui v. Canada (Minister of Citizenship & Immigration))* 70 Imm. L.R. (3d) 1, [2008] S.C.J. No. 39, 175 C.R.R. (2d) 120, 294 D.L.R. (4th) 478, 58 C.R. (6th) 45, 376 N.R. 154, 2008 CarswellNat 1898, 2008 CarswellNat 1899, 2008 SCC 38 — The appellant appealed against the dismissal in Federal Court of his application for a stay of proceedings relating to the security certificate issued against him under s. 77 of the IRPA. He alleged that the government breached its duty to disclose relevant information in its possession, and its auxiliary duty to do so in a timely manner. He alleged as well that the respondent Ministers relied impermissibly on evidence obtained subsequent to the issuance of the security certificate. They did so, he alleged, upon the designated judge's review of reasonableness of the certificate and again during the judge's review of the appellant's applications for release from custody. The Court concluded that the appellant's appeal should succeed. The Canadian Security Intelligence Service ("CSIS") is bound to disclose to the Ministers responsible all information in its possession regarding the person named in a security certificate. The Ministers must convey this information to the designated judge. The judge must then disclose the information to the person named in the security certificate, except to the extent that disclosure might, in the judge's view, endanger Canada's security. These obligations of disclosure cannot be properly discharged when CSIS has destroyed what it was bound to disclose.

As a matter of text and context, the Court concluded that CSIS was bound to retain the information it gathers within the limits established by the legislation governing its activities. In accordance with its prior practice, it did not do so here. Nevertheless, the Court was satisfied that a stay of proceedings would not be an appropriate remedy in this case. It would be premature at this stage of the proceedings for the Court to determine how the destruction of the notes affects the reliability of the evidence. The designated judge will be in a position to make that determination as he will have all of the evidence before him and will be able to summon and question as witnesses those who took the interview notes. If he concludes that there is a reasonable basis for the security certificate but that the destruction of the notes had a prejudicial effect, he will then consider whether the appellant should be granted a remedy. A stay would be an inappropriate remedy here. The only appropriate remedy is to confirm the duty to disclose the appellant's entire file to the designated judge and, after the judge has filtered it, to the appellant and his counsel. The appeal from the decision of the Federal Court of Appeal was allowed in part. The application for a stay of proceedings was dismissed.

**78. Determination — The judge shall determine whether the certificate is reasonable and shall quash the certificate if he or she determines that it is not.**

2005, c. 10, s. 34(2); 2008, c. 3, s. 4

**79. Appeal — An appeal from the determination may be made to the Federal Court of Appeal only if the judge certifies that a serious question of general importance is involved and states the question. However, no appeal may be made from an interlocutory decision in the proceeding.**

2002, c. 8, s. 194(b)(ii); 2008, c. 3, s. 4

**80. Effect of certificate — A certificate that is determined to be reasonable is conclusive proof that the person named in it is inadmissible and is a removal order that is in force without it being necessary to hold or continue an examination or admissibility hearing.**

2008, c. 3, s. 4

## *Detention and Release*

[Heading added 2008, c. 3, s. 4.]

**81. Ministers' warrant — The Minister and the Minister of Citizenship and Immigration may issue a warrant for the arrest and detention of a person who is named in a certificate if they have reasonable grounds to believe that the person is a danger to national security or to the safety of any person or is unlikely to appear at a proceeding or for removal.**

2008, c. 3, s. 4

[Heading repealed 2008, c. 3, s. 4.]

**82. (1) Initial review of detention — A judge shall commence a review of the reasons for the person's continued detention within 48 hours after the detention begins.**

(2) **Further reviews of detention — before determining reasonableness** — **Until it is determined whether a certificate is reasonable, a judge shall commence another review of the reasons for the person's continued detention at least once in the six-month period following the conclusion of each preceding review.**

(3) **Further reviews of detention — after determining reasonableness** — **A person who continues to be detained after a certificate is determined to be reasonable may apply to the Federal Court for another review of the reasons for their continued detention if a period of six months has expired since the conclusion of the preceding review.**

(4) **Reviews of conditions** — **A person who is released from detention under conditions may apply to the Federal Court for another review of the reasons for continuing the conditions if a period of six months has expired since the conclusion of the preceding review.**

(5) **Order** — **On review, the judge**

> **(a) shall order the person's detention to be continued if the judge is satisfied that the person's release under conditions would be injurious to national security or endanger the safety of any person or that they would be unlikely to appear at a proceeding or for removal if they were released under conditions; or**
>
> **(b) in any other case, shall order or confirm the person's release from detention and set any conditions that the judge considers appropriate.**

2005, c. 10, s. 34(1)(o)(iii); 2008, c. 3, s. 4

## Case Law

*Almrei, Re* (2009), 78 Imm. L.R. (3d) 167, 337 F.T.R. 160 (Eng.), 2009 CarswellNat 17, 2009 FC 3 (F.C.) — The applicant had been detained since October 2001 for his removal from the country as a risk to Canada's national security. The Court concluded that his continued detention could no longer be justified and that he should be released under strict conditions pending a determination of the reasonableness of the security certificate under which he was presently detained, and if the certificate should be found to be reasonable, until a determination whether he can be removed from Canada to his country of nationality or some other country.

The length of detention in the applicant's case exceeded seven years. It is difficult to find any comparable cases in the common law world where a person detained on security grounds has been held for so long. While this factor does not outweigh all other considerations, it must count heavily in favour of his release. The government's case against the applicant had remained substantially unchanged for seven years. The Minister conceded that there was no certain date in relation to the applicant's removal. This factor will weigh in favour of release "if there will be a lengthy detention before deportation or if the future detention cannot be ascertained". The applicant's principle difficulty thus far had been the fact that he had no family network in Canada and had thus far been unable to come up with a proposal for supervising sureties similar to those that were relied upon in the release decisions respecting the other security certificate detainees.

The Court did not agree with the view expressed by the Ministers that it was in some way an inappropriate delegation of supervisory responsibility to government. The Court held that it is a responsibility which stems from the legislative scheme in the same way that the burden of supervision of an offender on probation or parole is borne by the state. It is the Ministers who seek the restriction of the applicant's liberty and are prepared to accept the responsibility of detaining him. They must equally accept the responsibility of supervising his release on conditions. The applicant was released from detention subject to conditions imposed.

**82.1 (1) Variation of orders — A judge may vary an order made under subsection 82(5) on application of the Minister or of the person who is subject to the order if the judge is satisfied that the variation is desirable because of a material change in the circumstances that led to the order.**

**(2) Calculation of period for next review — For the purpose of calculating the six-month period referred to in subsection 82(2), (3) or (4), the conclusion of the preceding review is deemed to have taken place on the day on which the decision under subsection (1) is made.**

2008, c. 3, s. 4

**82.2 (1) Arrest and detention — breach of conditions — A peace officer may arrest and detain a person released under section 82 or 82.1 if the officer has reasonable grounds to believe that the person has contravened or is about to contravene any condition applicable to their release.**

**(2) Appearance before judge — The peace officer shall bring the person before a judge within 48 hours after the detention begins.**

**(3) Order — If the judge finds that the person has contravened or was about to contravene any condition applicable to their release, the judge shall**

> **(a) order the person's detention to be continued if the judge is satisfied that the person's release under conditions would be injurious to national security or endanger the safety of any person or that they would be unlikely to appear at a proceeding or for removal if they were released under conditions;**
>
> **(b) confirm the release order; or**
>
> **(c) vary the conditions applicable to their release.**

**(4) Calculation of period for next review — For the purpose of calculating the six-month period referred to in subsection 82(2), (3) or (4), the conclusion of the preceding review is deemed to have taken place on the day on which the decision under subsection (3) is made.**

2008, c. 3, s. 4

**82.3 Appeal — An appeal from a decision made under any of sections 82 to 82.2 may be made to the Federal Court of Appeal only if the judge certifies that a serious question of general importance is involved and states the question. However, no appeal may be made from an interlocutory decision in the proceeding.**

2008, c. 3, s. 4

**82.4 Minister's order to release — The Minister may, at any time, order that a person who is detained under any of sections 82 to 82.2 be released from detention to permit their departure from Canada.**

2008, c. 3, s. 4



## *Protection of Information*

[Heading added 2008, c. 3, s. 4.]

**83. (1) Protection of information — The following provisions apply to proceedings under any of sections 78 and 82 to 82.2:**

**(a) the judge shall proceed as informally and expeditiously as the circumstances and considerations of fairness and natural justice permit;**

**(b) the judge shall appoint a person from the list referred to in subsection 85(1) to act as a special advocate in the proceeding after hearing representations from the permanent resident or foreign national and the Minister and after giving particular consideration and weight to the preferences of the permanent resident or foreign national;**

**(c) at any time during a proceeding, the judge may, on the judge's own motion — and shall, on each request of the Minister — hear information or other evidence in the absence of the public and of the permanent resident or foreign national and their counsel if, in the judge's opinion, its disclosure could be injurious to national security or endanger the safety of any person;**

**(d) the judge shall ensure the confidentiality of information and other evidence provided by the Minister if, in the judge's opinion, its disclosure would be injurious to national security or endanger the safety of any person;**

**(e) throughout the proceeding, the judge shall ensure that the permanent resident or foreign national is provided with a summary of information and other evidence that enables them to be reasonably informed of the case made by the Minister in the proceeding but that does not include anything that, in the judge's opinion, would be injurious to national security or endanger the safety of any person if disclosed;**

**(f) the judge shall ensure the confidentiality of all information or other evidence that is withdrawn by the Minister;**

**(g) the judge shall provide the permanent resident or foreign national and the Minister with an opportunity to be heard;**

**(h) the judge may receive into evidence anything that, in the judge's opinion, is reliable and appropriate, even if it is inadmissible in a court of law, and may base a decision on that evidence;**

**(i) the judge may base a decision on information or other evidence even if a summary of that information or other evidence is not provided to the permanent resident or foreign national; and**

**(j) the judge shall not base a decision on information or other evidence provided by the Minister, and shall return it to the Minister, if the judge determines that it is not relevant or if the Minister withdraws it.**

**(1.1) Clarification — For the purposes of paragraph (1)(h), reliable and appropriate evidence does not include information that is believed on reasonable grounds to have been obtained as a result of the use of torture within the meaning of section 269.1 of the *Criminal Code*, or cruel, inhuman or degrading treatment or punishment within the meaning of the Convention Against Torture.**

**(1.2) Appointment of special advocate — If the permanent resident or foreign national requests that a particular person be appointed under paragraph (1)(b), the judge shall appoint that person unless the judge is satisfied that**

> **(a) the appointment would result in the proceeding being unreasonably delayed;**
>
> **(b) the appointment would place the person in a conflict of interest; or**
>
> **(c) the person has knowledge of information or other evidence whose disclosure would be injurious to national security or endanger the safety of any person and, in the circumstances, there is a risk of inadvertent disclosure of that information or other evidence.**

**(2) For greater certainty — For greater certainty, the judge's power to appoint a person to act as a special advocate in a proceeding includes the power to terminate the appointment and to appoint another person.**

2008, c. 3, s. 4

## Case Law

### Section 83(1)

*Harkat, Re*, [2009] F.C.J. No. 1242, 312 D.L.R. (4th) 464, 350 F.T.R. 143 (Eng.), 198 C.R.R. (2d) 275, 2009 FC 1050, 2009 CarswellNat 5823, 2009 CarswellNat 3192 — CSIS failed to include relevant information in the source matrix. Three CSIS witnesses were given the opportunity to explain their failure to provide important information to the Court. The Court recognized the importance of human source information to Canada's national security and the need to protect the identity of sources. The importance of human sources to intelligence gathering is not in question. However, when human source information is used to support serious allegations against an individual, the Court and the special advocates must be able to effectively test the credibility and reliability of that information. To conform to the law, CSIS and the Ministers must give the Court all the information necessary to test the credibility of the source and not just the information that a witness, trained as an intelligence officer, considers operationally necessary. CSIS must also ensure that nothing prevents its legal counsel from fulfilling his role as legal advisor to CSIS or his ability to act as an officer of the Court. A lawyer has an obligation to represent his client to the utmost subject to an overriding duty to the Court and to the administration of justice. Without access to all the information available, counsel is unable to effectively advise his or her client and is unable to ensure that the administration of justice is being served. It is also clear that despite his best efforts, counsel for CSIS had been overwhelmed by the magnitude of this file. Adequate administrative and legal resources must be dedicated to these complex and time-consuming files.

The evolution of the security certificate proceedings post-*Charkaoui 1* (2007), 59 Imm. L.R. (3d) 1 and *Charkaoui 2* (2008), 70 Imm. L.R. (3d) 1, require the Ministers to adapt to the requirements of the law as propounded by the Supreme Court of Canada and as set out by Parliament. Counsel representing the Ministers must thoroughly understand the evolving jurisprudence and law and be able to adequately prepare CSIS employees who have been asked to appear as witnesses before the Court. The Ministers' decision in relation to what evidence must be adduced should not be left in the hands of a legally inexperienced witness. A process must be put in place to ensure that decisions are made after a proper consultation with all stakeholders and upon receipt of legal advice. Such a process must be followed by the institution and its employees.

The Court found that Mr. Harkat's rights as guaranteed by the *Charter* had not been violated and consequently s. 24(1) was not engaged. However, the Court found the failure of CSIS, and of its witnesses, to act in accordance with the obligations of utmost good faith recognized in *Charkaoui* has undermined the integrity of the Court's process. By failing to make full and frank disclosure, CSIS and the Ministers do not protect the confidentiality of their human sources; they put it at risk. The judge, not the Ministers, is charged with determining the reasonableness of a security certificate pursuant to s. 78 of IRPA. With the coming into force of Bill C-3, Special Advocates are appointed by the Court to protect Mr. Harkat's interest by, among other things, testing the reliability of the information that is heard in closed proceedings. The Ministers and CSIS intelligence officers may have their own views as to the reliability of the human source information but they may not impose that view by limiting the information provided to the Court and the Special Advocates. Filtering evidence even with the best of intentions is unacceptable.

The explanations provided by the three witnesses did not convince the Court that all the relevant evidence was before it. Accordingly, the Court determined it was necessary to order the production of the files of other human sources relied on by the Ministers in this proceeding. Such an order will ensure that there is no further concern in relation to the Special Advocate's ability to fully test the evidence; it is necessary to repair the damage done to the administration of justice and to reestablish the necessary climate of trust and confidence which must be present in such an exceptional legal proceeding.

*Harkat, Re* (2008), 78 Imm. L.R. (3d) 303, 306 D.L.R. (4th) 269, 2008 CarswellNat 5335, 2008 CarswellNat 5667, 2009 FC 204 (F.C.) — In September, 2008, during a closed hearing, the special advocates sought an order of the Court compelling the Ministers to produce for cross-examination covert human intelligence source(s) who provided information about the applicant to the Canadian Security and Intelligence Services. They proposed to conduct their cross-examination during a closed hearing before the Court. They also requested that they be granted an opportunity to interview the source(s) prior to any evidence being given during a closed hearing. The special advocates wished to test the credibility of the source(s) and possibly corroborate future explanations which may be testified to by the applicant in relation to his motives for coming to Canada in the mid-1990s. They provided no further justification to the Court beyond this general objective.

Analogous to police informer privilege, the Court found that covert human intelligence source(s) privilege cannot be renounced unilaterally either by the source(s) or the Crown. Any renunciation must be a joint decision based on a full understanding of the consequences. Until such time as proof of a joint and informed waiver is provided to it, the Court has an obligation to protect the asserted privilege subject only to the exception set out in *Bisaillon*, [1983] 2 S.C.R. 60, 2 D.L.R. (4th) 193, 51 N.R. 81, 4 Admin. L.R. 205, 7 C.C.C. (3d) 385, 37 C.R. (3d) 289, 1983 CarswellQue 384, 1983 CarswellQue 28, which confirmed that if the identity of the informer is admitted, then there is no reason for pretended concealment of his identity. This is a situation where the reason for the rule no longer exists, as other police informers, knowing that the disclosure was made by the informer himself or with his consent, would no longer feel threatened. The Supreme Court found that the privilege in the context of a police informer is ". . . a legal rule of public order by which the judge is bound".

The request by the special advocates that the covert intelligence source(s) be identified and made available to them for cross-examination was denied.

*Harkat, Re*, [2009] F.C.J. No. 228, 80 Imm. L.R. (3d) 89, 2009 CarswellNat 436, 2009 FC 167 — Special advocates do not have the jurisdiction to act in public on behalf of a named person, nor are they permitted to communicate with him while acting as special advocate. They are not counsel of record in the proceeding. They do not, therefore, have standing to seek a confidentiality order which would prevent public access to court records; only counsel for the applicant may seek such an order. The objection made by the special advocates that the three summaries of conversation be kept confidential was granted on an interim basis. The three summaries of conversations were disclosed to the applicant and his counsel. The applicant and his counsel were given 10 days to serve and file a motion asking the Court to continue treating the three summaries of conversations confidentially. In the absence of any such motion, the summaries would become part of the public amended security intelligence report.

*Canada (Minister of Citizenship & Immigration) v. Jaballah*, 2009 CarswellNat 840, 2009 FC 279 — This decision explains why the Court allowed an employee of the Canadian Security Intelligence Service to testify in public under the name "David" without disclosing his proper legal name.

The open court principle requires a witness to be identified by their proper legal name. However, in s. 83 of the IRPA, Parliament has evidenced its intent that the open court principle be infringed to the extent necessary to protect Canada's national security and the safety of persons. Such infringement is only warranted, however, where the designated judge forms the opinion that the disclosure of information that the Ministers seek to protect would be injurious to national security or endanger the safety of any person. In order to ascertain the need to protect information, the designated judge may hold a hearing in the absence of the person concerned and the public to hear pertinent evidence and submissions. It is the Ministers who bear the burden of establishing that disclosure not only could, but would, be injurious to national security, or endanger the safety of a person. Once satisfied that the disclosure would be injurious to national security, or endanger the safety of any person, the designated judge must, pursuant to paragraph 83(1)(d) of the Act, ensure the confidentiality of the information. The designated judge is given no discretion in this regard. This renders irrelevant the balancing of interests test.

Of particular importance to this case was the fact that the applicant was unable to properly name the officer in an Ontario court lawsuit even though the officer gave evidence that he had identified himself to the applicant on two occasions. On the basis of this evidence, which supported the conclusion that the applicant did not know the officer's identity, the Court concluded that the officer's identity retained the necessary quality of confidentiality such that it was appropriate to protect it. For these reasons, an order issued permitting the officer to testify publicly in court identifying himself only as "David".

*Almrei, Re*, 2009 CarswellNat 690, 2009 FC 240 (F.C.) — By order dated January 2, 2009, the Chief Justice ordered that the Court adjudicate upon two common issues of law that have arisen in four proceedings. The two common issues were identified in the order as follows:

(a) What is the role of the designated judge with respect to the additional information disclosed by the Ministers pursuant to the decision of the Supreme Court of Canada in *Charkaoui v. Canada (Citizenship & Immigration) (Charkaoui 2)*, [2008] 2 S.C.R. 326, 70 Imm. L.R. (3d) 1, [2008] S.C.J. No. 39, 2008 SCC 38, 175 C.R.R. (2d) 120, 294 D.L.R. (4th) 478, 58 C.R. (6th) 45, 376 N.R. 154, 2008 CarswellNat 1898, 2008 CarswellNat 1899? More specifically, does paragraph 62 of that decision require the judge to "verify" all information disclosed by the Ministers if the special advocates and counsel for the Ministers all agree that a portion of that information is irrelevant to the issues before the Court?

(b) Should the information disclosed to the named persons and their counsel be placed on the Court's public files in these proceedings? If so, when?

The Federal Court concluded that:

(a) Where the Ministers and the special advocate agree that the material disclosed by the Ministers pursuant to *Charkaoui 2* is irrelevant to the issues before the Court, the Court may rely upon that agreement. In such a case, the Court need not verify information that the Ministers and the special advocates agree to be irrelevant.

(b) No information filed with the Court in confidence pursuant to *Charkaoui 2* can be disclosed to the person named in a security certificate without the prior approval of the Court.

(c) Information or evidence disclosed to the named persons pursuant to *Charkaoui 2* should be disclosed directly to counsel for each person named in a security certificate. The *Charkaoui 2* disclosure should not be placed on the Court's public file. Such information or evidence would only become public if it is relied upon by a party and placed into evidence.

(d) Summaries of evidence or information made pursuant to paragraph 83(1)(e) of the Act must be placed on the Court's public file because they relate to information relied upon by the Ministers and to what transpired in the *in camera* proceedings.

**84. Protection of information on appeal — Section 83 — other than the obligation to provide a summary — and sections 85.1 to 85.5 apply to an appeal under section 79 or 82.3, and to any further appeal, with any necessary modifications.**

2008, c. 3, s. 4

## *Special Advocate*

[Heading added 2008, c. 3, s. 4.]

**85. (1) List of persons who may act as special advocates — The Minister of Justice shall establish a list of persons who may act as special advocates and shall publish the list in a manner that the Minister of Justice considers appropriate to facilitate public access to it.**

**(2) Statutory Instruments Act — The *Statutory Instruments Act* does not apply to the list.**

(3) **Administrative support and resources — The Minister of Justice shall ensure that special advocates are provided with adequate administrative support and resources.**

2008, c. 3, s. 4

## Case Law

### Section 85(3)

*Harkat, Re*, 2009 CarswellNat 626, 2009 FC 173 (F.C.) — The special advocates sought the ability to communicate with an administrative support person to assist them with the organization of the documents which were to be disclosed pursuant to a previous order in this proceeding. They indicated that they had identified a person who was prepared to commence work at any time and who was already security cleared. They also provided an email to the Court which indicated that the Minister of Justice was prepared to provide funding for that administrative support. The Minister's objections were two-fold. Firstly, the Ministers argued that the special advocates had not established a need for the assistance of an administrative assistant. Second, the Ministers asserted that the appointment of such a person was impermissible under the current legislative scheme set out in the IRPA. They argued that the entire scheme of the Act is premised on a general rule that the protected information be given to a specific, limited number of people and that further circulation of the information is prohibited.

The Court concluded that where a person is not representing the interest of a named person, has the requisite security clearance, agrees to become permanently bound to secrecy and is subject to the same restrictions on communication as other participants in the proceeding, the disclosure of the confidential information to her by the Court for administrative support purposes will not injure national security or endanger the safety of an individual.

### Author's Note

[*These cases pertain to the former s. 86 which was replaced on March 5, 2008. The previous jurisprudence may still be relevant.*]

## Case Law

### Former Section 86

*Sogi v. Canada (Minister of Citizenship & Immigration)* (2004), 36 Imm. L.R. (3d) 1, 2004 CarswellNat 2880, 2004 CarswellNat 1599, 322 N.R. 2, 2004 FCA 212, [2004] F.C.J. No. 947, 121 C.R.R. (2d) 137, [2005] 1 F.C.R. 171 (F.C.A.); leave to appeal refused (2004), [2004] S.C.C.A. No. 354, 2004 CarswellNat 4104, 2004 CarswellNat 4105, 121 C.R.R. (2d) 188 (note) (S.C.C.) — As long as the availability of judicial review provides the appellant with an opportunity to have a Federal Court judge decide the propriety of keeping information confidential, the IRPA procedure must be found to be in accordance with the principles of fundamental justice.

Subsection 86(2) provides that the procedures set out in s. 78 apply to the determination of an application for non-disclosure before an Immigration Division member. If the member decides that the information or evidence is not relevant, or that it is relevant but should be included in the summary provided to the individual, paragraph 78(f) requires the information to be returned to the Minister. Section 78(g) allows the member to consider relevant but potentially injurious material without disclosing it. That subsection makes no mention of subsequently returning the considered material to the Minister. Any information considered by the member under paragraph 78(g) forms part of the Immigration Division's record, albeit a confidential portion.

Under Rule 14 of the *Federal Court Immigration and Refugee Protection Rules*, where a judge considers the documents in the possession or control of a tribunal are required for a proper disposition of the application for leave, the judge may order the Immigration Division to produce the documents. Once leave is granted, Rule 17 requires the Board to prepare a record including all documents in possession or control of the tribunal and submit it to the Court. When the confidential information is produced to the Court, the Minister may make an application under subs. 87(1) for continued non-disclosure.

If information is to be returned to CSIS, an undertaking must be given that the precise information that was before the Immigration Division member will be produced for judicial review purposes. The confidential information must be retained intact, in a format that allows for precise identification of what information was considered by the Immigration Division member. The information that has been considered by the member and returned to CSIS must be considered "information under the control of the tribunal for the purposes of its production to the Federal Court on judicial review." If information is returned to CSIS, the onus is on the Minister to satisfy the judge hearing the judicial review that the precise record that was before the member has been provided to the Court. In the event that the evidence was not transcribed, an affidavit attesting to the evidence given before the member would be required.

The standard of review, for a decision on whether information supplied by the Minister *in camera* should have been considered by the Member without completely disclosing it, is correctness. Considering the correctness of the Immigration Division member's decision, the judge will make his or her own assessment of whether disclosure of the confidential information would be injurious to national security or the safety of any person.

If the judicial review is allowed, the information will not immediately be disclosed, rather, in remitting the matter to the Immigration Division, the judge may direct that some or all of the information be included in the summary to be provided to the affected individual. In such a case, it will be up to the Minister to decide whether that information should be disclosed to the individual in order to allow it to be considered by the Immigration Division member or withdrawn from consideration in order to maintain the confidentiality of the information.

The precise record that was before the Immigration Division member will be before the judge conducting the judicial review and the member's decision not to disclose will be reviewed on a correctness standard. For these reasons, the IRPA procedure is in accordance with the principles of fundamental justice.

**85.1 (1) Special advocate's role — A special advocate's role is to protect the interests of the permanent resident or foreign national in a proceeding under any of sections 78 and 82 to 82.2 when information or other evidence is heard in the absence of the public and of the permanent resident or foreign national and their counsel.**

**(2) Responsibilities — A special advocate may challenge**

> **(a) the Minister's claim that the disclosure of information or other evidence would be injurious to national security or endanger the safety of any person; and**
>
> **(b) the relevance, reliability and sufficiency of information or other evidence that is provided by the Minister and is not disclosed to the permanent resident or foreign national and their counsel, and the weight to be given to it.**

**(3) For greater certainty — For greater certainty, the special advocate is not a party to the proceeding and the relationship between the special advocate and the permanent resident or foreign national is not that of solicitor and client.**

**(4) Protection of communications with special advocate — However, a communication between the permanent resident or foreign national or their counsel and the special advocate that would be subject to solicitor-client privilege if the relationship were one of solicitor and client is deemed to be subject to solicitor-client privilege. For greater certainty, in respect of that communication, the special advocate is not a compellable witness in any proceeding.**

2008, c. 3, s. 4

## Case Law

*Harkat, Re* (2009), 80 Imm. L.R. (3d) 252, 345 F.T.R. 143 (Eng.), 2009 FC 553, 2009 CarswellNat 1681 (F.C.) — A request was made by the special advocates to access the human source file in question. Access to the file would inevitably result in the special advocates learning the identity of the source in question.

The Court found that as a result of the review of the Minister's letter, the special advocates have a "need to know" the contents of the human source file even if this results in a revelation of the source's identity. The rule of law requires no less. Once the Court has evidence that leads it to question the completeness of the information being provided to it by the Ministers, in apparent violation of their obligation of utmost good faith, it must allow the special advocates access to all information which they have a need to know. To do otherwise would bring the administration of justice into disrepute.

*Almrei, Re*, 2009 CarswellNat 690, 2009 FC 240 (F.C.) — By order dated January 2, 2009, the Chief Justice ordered that the Court adjudicate upon two common issues of law that have arisen in four proceedings. The two common issues were identified in the order as follows:

> (a) What is the role of the designated judge with respect to the additional information disclosed by the Ministers pursuant to the decision of the Supreme Court of Canada in *Charkaoui v. Canada (Citizenship & Immigration) (Charkaoui 2)*, [2008] 2 S.C.R. 326, 70 Imm. L.R. (3d) 1, [2008] S.C.J. No. 39, 2008 SCC 38, 175 C.R.R. (2d) 120, 294 D.L.R. (4th) 478, 58 C.R. (6th) 45, 376 N.R. 154, 2008 CarswellNat 1898, 2008 CarswellNat 1899? More specifically, does paragraph 62 of that decision require the judge to "verify" all information disclosed by the Ministers if the special advocates and counsel for the Ministers all agree that a portion of that information is irrelevant to the issues before the Court?
>
> (b) Should the information disclosed to the named persons and their counsel be placed on the Court's public files in these proceedings? If so, when?

IRP Act

The Federal Court concluded that:

(a) Where the Ministers and the special advocate agree that the material disclosed by the Ministers pursuant to *Charkaoui 2* is irrelevant to the issues before the Court, the Court may rely upon that agreement. In such a case, the Court need not verify information that the Ministers and the special advocates agree to be irrelevant.

(b) No information filed with the Court in confidence pursuant to *Charkaoui 2* can be disclosed to the person named in a security certificate without the prior approval of the Court.

(c) Information or evidence disclosed to the named persons pursuant to *Charkaoui 2* should be disclosed directly to counsel for each person named in a security certificate. The *Charkaoui 2* disclosure should not be placed on the Court's public file. Such information or evidence would only become public if it is relied upon by a party and placed into evidence.

(d) Summaries of evidence or information made pursuant to paragraph 83(1)(e) of the Act must be placed on the Court's public file because they relate to information relied upon by the Ministers and to what transpired in the *in camera* proceedings.

**85.2 Powers — A special advocate may**

**(a) make oral and written submissions with respect to the information and other evidence that is provided by the Minister and is not disclosed to the permanent resident or foreign national and their counsel;**

**(b) participate in, and cross-examine witnesses who testify during, any part of the proceeding that is held in the absence of the public and of the permanent resident or foreign national and their counsel; and**

**(c) exercise, with the judge's authorization, any other powers that are necessary to protect the interests of the permanent resident or foreign national.**

2008, c. 3, s. 4

## Case Law

*Almrei, Re*, 2009 CarswellNat 1491, 2009 CarswellNat 2098, 2009 FC 314 (F.C.) — This decision concerns the exclusion of the special advocates from a closed hearing in which the Court heard evidence from a witness presented by the Ministers with respect to one of the conditions of the applicant's release from detention. A redacted version of the transcript of the evidence heard on that occasion was provided to the special advocates and the Court invited submissions from them and counsel for the Ministers as to whether the procedure adopted was correct. The Court concluded that a complete transcript of the evidence from the hearing must be provided to the special advocates and an opportunity provided to them to cross-examine the witness and make further submissions. The transcript of evidence was to remain confidential pending any further determination by the Court, but this decision was entered on the public record of proceedings.

In general, information which could cause injury to national security should only be assessed by persons who have a genuine need to know the information in order to carry out their responsibilities. The statute does not contain an explicit "need to know" test that would restrict the special advocates' participation in the closed hearing in which the Minister presents information or other evidence to the Court which may affect the named person's interests. Nor does the law implicitly recognize such a test that would override the express terms of the statute. Special advocates are not empowered to have access to all information within the possession of the government, particularly privileged information. The special advocates have not requested that the government provide access to privileged information which is not before the Court, but are asking that they be allowed to perform the role which Parliament has assigned to them to question evidence that the Ministers have chosen to present in Court. The Court may need to review information provided by the Ministers in the absence of the special advocates to determine whether it pertains to the proceedings or is privileged for reasons other than national security claims. The summary and the redacted transcript of the testimony given to the special advocates did not serve as an adequate substitute for the right to "participate in and cross-examine witnesses who testify during any part of the proceeding that is held in the absence of the public" as set out in subs. 85.2(b) of IRPA.

**85.3 Immunity — A special advocate is not personally liable for anything they do or omit to do in good faith under this Division.**

2008, c. 3, s. 4

**85.4 (1) Obligation to provide information — The Minister shall, within a period set by the judge, provide the special advocate with a copy of all information and other evidence that is provided to the judge but that is not disclosed to the permanent resident or foreign national and their counsel.**

**(2) Restrictions on communications — special advocate — After that information or other evidence is received by the special advocate, the special advocate may, during the remainder of the proceeding, communicate with another person about the proceeding only with the judge's authorization and subject to any conditions that the judge considers appropriate.**

**(3) Restrictions on communications — other persons — If the special advocate is authorized to communicate with a person, the judge may prohibit that person from communicating with anyone else about the proceeding during the remainder of the proceeding or may impose conditions with respect to such a communication during that period.**

2008, c. 3, s. 4

## Case Law

*Almrei, Re*, 2009 CarswellNat 690, 2009 FC 240 (F.C.) — By order dated January 2, 2009, the Chief Justice ordered that the Court adjudicate upon two common issues of law that have arisen in four proceedings. The two common issues were identified in the order as follows:

> (a) What is the role of the designated judge with respect to the additional information disclosed by the Ministers pursuant to the decision of the Supreme Court of Canada in *Charkaoui v. Canada (Citizenship & Immigration) (Charkaoui 2)*, [2008] 2 S.C.R. 326, 70 Imm. L.R. (3d) 1, [2008] S.C.J. No. 39, 2008 SCC 38, 175 C.R.R. (2d) 120, 294 D.L.R. (4th) 478, 58 C.R. (6th) 45, 376 N.R. 154, 2008 CarswellNat 1898, 2008 CarswellNat 1899? More specifically, does paragraph 62 of that decision require the judge to "verify" all information disclosed by the Ministers if the

special advocates and counsel for the Ministers all agree that a portion of that information is irrelevant to the issues before the Court?

(b) Should the information disclosed to the named persons and their counsel be placed on the Court's public files in these proceedings? If so, when?

The Federal Court concluded that:

(a) Where the Ministers and the special advocate agree that the material disclosed by the Ministers pursuant to *Charkaoui 2* is irrelevant to the issues before the Court, the Court may rely upon that agreement. In such a case, the Court need not verify information that the Ministers and the special advocates agree to be irrelevant.

(b) No information filed with the Court in confidence pursuant to *Charkaoui 2* can be disclosed to the person named in a security certificate without the prior approval of the Court.

(c) Information or evidence disclosed to the named persons pursuant to *Charkaoui 2* should be disclosed directly to counsel for each person named in a security certificate. The *Charkaoui 2* disclosure should not be placed on the Court's public file. Such information or evidence would only become public if it is relied upon by a party and placed into evidence.

(d) Summaries of evidence or information made pursuant to paragraph 83(1)(e) of the Act must be placed on the Court's public file because they relate to information relied upon by the Ministers and to what transpired in the *in camera* proceedings.

*Harkat, Re*, 2009 CarswellNat 540, 2009 CarswellNat 99 (F.C.) — The special advocates in this proceeding sought judicial authorization to communicate with special advocates appointed in other certificate proceedings "concerning the Orders that should be issued in IRPA proceedings where special advocates are appointed". The special advocates submitted that one of the goals of the amendments made to the IRPA by Parliament in Bill C-3 was to put the special advocates in the same position as counsel for the Ministers, that is, provide for an equity of arms in the closed portion of security certificate proceedings. It was therefore asserted that special advocates should be authorized to discuss common issues since it is believed that ministerial counsel have that ability. The Ministers opposed the request on the grounds that the authorization sought is overly vague and seeks to displace the designated judge's role to authorize specific communication requests by special advocates appointed in a proceeding. The order sought, according to the Ministers, goes against the intent of the legislation which is to prevent the inadvertent disclosure of confidential information by constant judicial supervision.

The Court held that the request was not so vague that it was impossible to determine what can be discussed. A person with legal training, who is qualified to be a special advocate, has the knowledge necessary to determine the meaning of "common issues and questions of jurisdiction, procedure, and substantive law". He or she is also capable of distinguishing legal from factual issues although whenever there is a doubt, the guidance of the Court should be sought. The Court granted permission for the special advocates to communicate with other special advocates (who have obtained the same judicial authorization from their respective designated judge) appointed in other security certificate proceedings to discuss common issues related to questions of jurisdiction, procedure, and substantive law and orders rendered or orders to be sought. They are not authorized to refer directly or indirectly to any information or evidence which has been provided to them or to which they have been privy in their capacity as special advocates. These communications were only authorized at meetings organized by the support resources group for special advocates.

**85.5 Disclosure and communication prohibited — With the exception of communications authorized by a judge, no person shall**

**(a) disclose information or other evidence that is disclosed to them under section 85.4 and that is treated as confidential by the judge presiding at the proceeding; or**

**(b) communicate with another person about the content of any part of a proceeding under any of sections 78 and 82 to 82.2 that is heard in the absence of the public and of the permanent resident or foreign national and their counsel.**

2008, c. 3, s. 4

**85.6 (1) Rules — The Chief Justice of the Federal Court of Appeal and the Chief Justice of the Federal Court may each establish a committee to make rules governing the practice and procedure in relation to the participation of special advocates in proceedings before the court over which they preside. The rules are binding despite any rule of practice that would otherwise apply.**

**(2) Composition of committees — Any committee established shall be composed of the Chief Justice of the Federal Court of Appeal or the Chief Justice of the Federal Court, as the case may be, the Attorney General of Canada or one or more representatives of the Attorney General of Canada, and one or more members of the bar of any province who have experience in a field of law relevant to those types of proceedings. The Chief Justices may also designate additional members of their respective committees.**

**(3) Chief Justices shall preside — The Chief Justice of the Federal Court of Appeal and the Chief Justice of the Federal Court — or a member designated by them — shall preside over their respective committees.**

2008, c. 3, s. 4

## *Other Proceedings*

[Heading amended 2008, c. 3, s. 4.]

**86. Application for non-disclosure — The Minister may, during an admissibility hearing, a detention review or an appeal before the Immigration Appeal Division, apply for the non-disclosure of information or other evidence. Sections 83 and 85.1 to 85.5 apply to the proceeding with any necessary modifications, including that a reference to "judge" be read as a reference to the applicable Division of the Board.**

2008, c. 3, s. 4

[Heading repealed 2008, c. 3, s. 4.]

**87. Application for non-disclosure — judicial review — The Minister may, during a judicial review, apply for the non-disclosure of information or other evidence. Section 83 — other than the obligations to appoint a special advocate and**

**to provide a summary — applies to the proceeding with any necessary modifications.**

2008, c. 3, s. 4

### Author's Note

[*These cases pertain to the former s. 87 which was replaced on March 5, 2008. The previous jurisprudence may still be relevant.*]



## Case Law

### Former Section 87

*Gariev v. Canada (Minister of Citizenship & Immigration)*, 2004 CarswellNat 1159, 2004 FC 531, 2004 CarswellNat 3389 (F.C.) — Section 87 of the Act permits the Minister, in the course of a judicial review application, to apply to a judge for the non-disclosure of information considered by an officer in the course of determining whether a foreign national who has applied for a visa or other document is inadmissible. The procedure to be followed on such an application is the procedure provided in s. 78 modified to the extent that no summary of the withheld information need be provided to the party opposite to the Minister. There is no prescribed time limit within which the judge must examine the information.

When considering whether disclosure of confidential information would be injurious to national security or to the safety of persons, the principles applied were those articulated in *Henrie v. Canada (Security Intelligence Review Committee)* (1988), [1989] 2 F.C. 229, 53 D.L.R. (4th) 568, 1988 CarswellNat 160, 24 F.T.R. 24 (Fed. T.D.); affirmed (1992), 88 D.L.R. (4th) 575, 1992 CarswellNat 194, 5 Admin. L.R. (2d) 269, 140 N.R. 315, (sub nom. *Henrie v. Security Intelligence Review Committee)* 55 F.T.R. 96 (note) (Fed. C.A.).

*Sogi v. Canada (Minister of Citizenship & Immigration)* (2004), 36 Imm. L.R. (3d) 1, 2004 CarswellNat 2880, 2004 CarswellNat 1599, 322 N.R. 2, 2004 FCA 212, [2004] F.C.J. No. 947, 121 C.R.R. (2d) 137, [2005] 1 F.C.R. 171 (F.C.A.); leave to appeal refused (2004), [2004] S.C.C.A. No. 354, 2004 CarswellNat 4104, 2004 CarswellNat 4105, 121 C.R.R. (2d) 188 (note) (S.C.C.) — As long as the availability of judicial review provides the appellant with an opportunity to have a Federal Court judge decide the propriety of keeping information confidential, the IRPA procedure must be found to be in accordance with the principles of fundamental justice.

Subsection 86(2) provides that the procedures set out in s. 78 apply to the determination of an application for non-disclosure before an Immigration Division member. If the member decides that the information or evidence is not relevant, or that it is relevant but should be included in the summary provided to the individual, paragraph 78(f) requires the information to be returned to the Minister. Section 78(g) allows the member to consider relevant but potentially injurious material without disclosing it. That subsection makes no mention of subsequently returning the considered material to the Minister. Any information considered by the member under paragraph 78(g) forms part of the Immigration Division's record, albeit a confidential portion.

Under Rule 14 of the *Federal Court Immigration and Refugee Protection Rules*, where a judge considers the documents in the possession or control of a tribunal are required for a proper disposition of the application for leave, the judge may order the Immigration Division to produce the documents. Once leave is granted, Rule 17 requires the Board to prepare a record including all documents in possession or control of the tribunal and submit it to the Court. When the confidential information is produced to the Court, the Minister may make an application under subs. 87(1) for continued non-disclosure.

If information is to be returned to CSIS, an undertaking must be given that the precise information that was before the Immigration Division member will be produced for judicial review purposes. The confidential information must be retained intact, in a format that allows for precise identification of what information was considered by the Immigration Division member. The information that has been considered by the member and returned to CSIS must be considered "information under the control of the tribunal for the purposes of its production to the Federal Court on judicial review." If information is returned to CSIS, the onus is on the Minister to satisfy the judge hearing the judicial review that the precise record that was before the member has been provided to the Court. In the event that the evidence was not transcribed, an affidavit attesting to the evidence given before the member would be required.

The standard of review, for a decision whether information supplied by the Minister *in camera* should have been considered by the Member without completely disclosing it, is correctness. Considering the correctness of the Immigration Division member's decision, the judge will make his or her own assessment of whether disclosure of the confidential information would be injurious to national security or the safety of any person.

If the judicial review is allowed, the information will not immediately be disclosed, rather, in remitting the matter to the Immigration Division, the judge may direct that some or all of the information be included in the summary to be provided to the affected individual. In such a case, it will be up to the Minister to decide whether that information should be disclosed to the individual in order to allow it to be considered by the Immigration Division member or withdrawn from consideration in order to maintain the confidentiality of the information.

The precise record that was before the Immigration Division member will be before the judge conducting the judicial review and the member's decision not to disclose will be reviewed on a correctness standard. For these reasons the IRPA procedure is in accordance with the principles of fundamental justice.

**87.1 Special advocate — If the judge during the judicial review, or a court on appeal from the judge's decision, is of the opinion that considerations of fairness and natural justice require that a special advocate be appointed to protect the interests of the permanent resident or foreign national, the judge or court shall appoint a special advocate from the list referred to in subsection 85(1). Sections 85.1 to 85.5 apply to the proceeding with any necessary modifications.**

2008, c. 3, s. 4

## Case Law

*Farkhondehfall v. Canada (Minister of Citizenship & Immigration)* (2009), 2 Admin. L.R. (5th) 240, 2009 FC 1064, 2009 CarswellNat 3344 (F.C.) — The Minister of Citizenship & Immigration brought motions for the non-disclosure of portions of a certified tribunal record in accordance with s. 87 of IRPA. The Minister asserted that the disclosure of the redacted information would be injurious to national security or to the safety of any person. In response to the Minister's s. 87 motions, the applicant brought motions of his own seeking the appointment of a special advocate to protect his interest in the s. 87 proceedings in each application. The Court concluded that considerations of fairness and natural justice do not require the appointment of a special advocate to protect the applicant's interest in either application and dismissed the applicant's motion seeking a special advocate.

While the amendments made to IRPA in the wake of *Charkaoui* (2007), 59 Imm. L.R. (3d) 1 (S.C.C.), made the appointment of special advocates mandatory in security certificate proceedings, the appointment of special advocates in other types of cases under the Act is left to the discretion of the presiding designated judge. That is, s. 87.1 of IRPA gives the Court the discretion to appoint a special advocate if it "is of the opinion that considerations of fairness and natural justice require" such an appointment in order to protect the interest of an applicant. A number of factors should be weighed by the Court in accessing whether considerations of fairness and natural justice require the appointment of a special advocate to protect the interests of the individual. No one factor will necessarily be determinative; rather, the task for the Court should be to balance all of the competing considerations in order to arrive at a just result. One set of related factors to be considered involves the importance of the decision in issue to the individual, the nature of the interests affected, and the degree of procedural fairness to which the individual is entitled in the case at hand. Other relevant considerations are the amount of information that has been disclosed and the extent to which the affected individual has been made aware of the case that they have to meet.

*Malkine v. Canada (Minister of Citizenship & Immigration)*, 2009 CarswellNat 1390, 2009 FC 496 (F.C.) — The officer found that Mr. Malkine was inadmissible to Canada for being a member of a group engaged in organized or transnational crime. The Minister brought a motion for non-disclosure of portions of the certified tribunal record, in accordance with the provisions of s. 87 of the IRPA, asserting that the disclosure of the redacted information would be injurious to national security or to the safety of any person. In response to the Minister's motion, Mr. Malkine brought a motion seeking the appointment of a special advocate to protect his interests in the s. 87 proceedings. The appointment of a special advocate was not necessary in this case and Mr. Malkine's motion was dismissed.

While the amendments to the IRPA make the appointment of special advocates mandatory in security certificate proceedings, the appointment of special advocates in other types of cases under the Act is left to the discretion of the presiding designated judge. Unlike security certificate proceedings, no *Charter* rights were at stake in this case. Mr. Malkine was not in detention, and there was no issue of his potential removal to a place where his life or freedom would be at risk. The only reason that Mr. Malkine had given for wanting to come to Canada was to protect his economic interests in this country. As such, the *Charter's* "fundamental justice" guarantees were not engaged. Instead, the issue was one of common-law procedural fairness. Considerations of fairness and natural justice do not require the appointment of a special advocate in this case.

## *Regulations*

[Heading added 2008, c. 3, s. 4.]

**87.2 (1) Regulations — The regulations may provide for any matter relating to the application of this Division and may include provisions respecting conditions and qualifications that persons must meet to be included in the list referred to in**

**subsection 85(1) and additional qualifications that are assets that may be taken into account for that purpose.**

(2) **Requirements — The regulations**

> **(a) shall require that, to be included in the list, persons be members in good standing of the bar of a province, not be employed in the federal public administration, and not otherwise be associated with the federal public administration in such a way as to impair their ability to protect the interests of the permanent resident or foreign national; and**
>
> **(b) may include provisions respecting those requirements.**

2008, c. 3, s. 4

## DIVISION 10 — GENERAL PROVISIONS

### *Instructions on Processing Applications and Requests*

[Heading added 2008, c. 28, s. 118.]

87.3 (1) **Application — This section applies to applications for visas or other documents made under subsection 11(1), other than those made by persons referred to in subsection 99(2), sponsorship applications made by persons referred to in subsection 13(1), applications for permanent resident status under subsection 21(1) or temporary resident status under subsection 22(1) made by foreign nationals in Canada and to requests under subsection 25(1) made by foreign nationals outside Canada.**

(2) **Attainment of immigration goals — The processing of applications and requests is to be conducted in a manner that, in the opinion of the Minister, will best support the attainment of the immigration goals established by the Government of Canada.**

(3) **Instructions — For the purposes of subsection (2), the Minister may give instructions with respect to the processing of applications and requests, including instructions**

> **(a) establishing categories of applications or requests to which the instructions apply;**
>
> **(b) establishing an order, by category or otherwise, for the processing of applications or requests;**
>
> **(c) setting the number of applications or requests, by category or otherwise, to be processed in any year; and**
>
> **(d) providing for the disposition of applications and requests, including those made subsequent to the first application or request.**

(4) **Compliance with instructions — Officers and persons authorized to exercise the powers of the Minister under section 25 shall comply with any instructions before processing an application or request or when processing one. If an application or request is not processed, it may be retained, returned or otherwise disposed of in accordance with the instructions of the Minister.**

**(5) Clarification — The fact that an application or request is retained, returned or otherwise disposed of does not constitute a decision not to issue the visa or other document, or grant the status or exemption, in relation to which the application or request is made.**

**(6) Publication — Instructions shall be published in the *Canada Gazette*.**

**(7) Clarification — Nothing in this section in any way limits the power of the Minister to otherwise determine the most efficient manner in which to administer this Act.**

*[Editor's Note: According to section 120 of 2008, c. 28, section 87.3 applies only to applications and requests made on or after February 27, 2008.]*

2008, c. 28, s. 118



## Case Law

*Jin v. Canada (Minister of Citizenship & Immigration)* (2009), 86 Imm. L.R. (3d) 13, 357 F.T.R. 309 (Eng.), 2009 FC 1234, 2009 CarswellNat 4162 (F.C.) — This was an application for judicial review concerning the interpretation of ministerial instructions issued in 2008 pursuant to s. 87.3 of IRPA introduced into the Act by s. 118 of the *Budget Implementation Act, 2008*. The applicant sought to have the Court interpret the words "[a]pplications submitted [. . .] by foreign nationals residing legally in Canada for at least one year as [. . .] International Students" set out in the instructions as including foreign nationals who, *at any time in the past*, resided legally in Canada for at least one year as International Students. This interpretation would allow an International Student who resided in Canada for at least one year at any time in the past to benefit from priority processing for Federal Skilled Workers permanent residence applications.

The terms of the instructions are clear on the residency requirements. The words "applications submitted by foreign nationals residing legally in Canada for at least one year as Temporary Foreign Workers or International Students" suffer no ambiguity. The choice of verb tense makes it abundantly clear that the Temporary Foreign Worker or the International Student must have been residing legally in Canada for at least one year immediately prior to his or her application. The French wording is also unambiguous and conveys the same meaning. Where the ministerial instructions wish to convey that a past period of time can be considered, they state so clearly, such as in the footnote concerning applications from skilled workers with evidence of experience which clearly provides for recognition of past experience in the following terms: "[a]t least one year of continuous full-time or equivalent paid work experience in the last ten years." The Court also commented that the unfortunate use of form letters in responding to applications where multiple fact situations are involved can easily lead to ambiguity and misunderstanding. In this case the whole litigation could have easily been avoided had a proper and cogent response been provided to the applicant setting out in unambiguous terms the basis for which her application could not be processed as an International Student. The form letter stated that the applicant did not indicate in her application that she was legally residing in Canada for at least one year as an International Student. The true reason for not processing the application is thus stated, but in such a convoluted and ambiguous manner as to render the decision almost impossible to understand without further inquiry. Although the decision was legally correct, the communication of the reasons for which it was made were deficient. Nevertheless, returning the matter to the decision maker on the basis of the original application would not provide the applicant with the result she sought. The application for judicial review was dismissed.

## *Loans*

**88. (1) Loans — The Minister of Finance may, from time to time, advance to the Minister out of the Consolidated Revenue Fund, up to the maximum amount that is prescribed, sums that the Minister may require in order to make loans for the purposes of this Act.**

**(2) Regulations — The regulations may provide for any matter relating to the application of this section, and may include provisions respecting classes of persons to whom, and the purposes for which, the loans may be made.**

## *Fees*

**89. Regulations — The regulations may govern fees for services provided in the administration of this Act, and cases in which fees may be waived by the Minister or otherwise, individually or by class.**

### Case Law

*Toussaint v. Canada (Minister of Citizenship & Immigration)* (2009), 83 Imm. L.R. (3d) 51, 350 F.T.R. 109 (Eng.), 198 C.R.R. (2d) 194, 2009 FC 873, 2009 CarswellNat 2595, 2009 CarswellNat 5173, [2009] F.C.J. No. 1034 (F.C.) — The applicant, a citizen of Grenada, came to Canada in December 1999 as a visitor. Her status expired within six months of entering Canada and since then she has been without status. She made an application pursuant to s. 25(1) of IRPA for an exemption from certain requirements of the Act on the basis of H&C considerations. Specifically she wanted to be exempt from the requirements of s. 11 that she must apply for permanent residence status before entering Canada; and to be granted residence from within Canada on H&C grounds. The fee required to process her in-Canada H&C application is $550, which she claimed she could not afford. The Court considered whether the Minister's decision was reviewable on the standard of correctness. In other words, was the Minister correct in his conclusion that an exemption from the fees is contrary to s. 10(1)(d) of *IRP* Regulations?

There is no question that s. 25 is very broad and covers much more than a request for an exemption to apply for a permanent visa from Canada. However, a broad and liberal interpretation of s. 25 does not necessarily mean that this provision is available in respect of every type of obligation that arises under IRPA or the Regulations. Section 25(1) is available as a matter of right to any foreign national in Canada "who is inadmissible or who does not meet the requirements of this Act." From this phrase, it is apparent that the focus of s. 25(1) is on substantive obligations that fundamentally affect the ability of a foreign national to come to or remain in Canada. This focus is reflected in the various types of s. 25(1) decisions that have been considered by the Federal Court. Section 25(1) does not require that the Minister consider a request to exempt a foreign national from the payment of fees established pursuant to s. 89 of IRPA and the relevant *IRP* Regulations. The Minister is without authority to do so. This interpretation is apparent when s. 25(1) is read harmoniously in its entire context and in its grammatical ordinary sense together with the scheme of IRPA, the object of IRPA and the intention of Parliament.

The deportation of the applicant prior to consideration of H&C factors does not engage the liberty and security issues protected by s. 7 of the *Charter*. Since neither the assessment of H&C factors or the best interest of the child are principles of fundamental justice to which s. 7 of the *Charter* apply, it follows that there was no breach of s. 7.

The applicant and interveners advanced two different arguments under s. 15(1) of the *Charter*. First, they submitted that persons living in poverty are protected under s. 15; thus, the Minister's failure to provide a fee waiver entails an important failure to exercise the discretion available under s. 25 of IRPA. In the alternative, they asserted that, by failing to provide for a fee waiver pursuant to the regulation-making authority of s. 89 of IRPA, the government violated s. 15 of the *Charter*.



Even if the Court were to accept that persons living in a state of poverty — within in which they cannot afford the s. 25 processing fee — face a distinction as compared to the comparator group, the s. 15(1) claim fails. This is because the Court concluded that poverty is not an analogous ground. Further, and even if poverty were accepted as an analogous ground, there is insufficient evidence to persuade the Court that any distinction caused by the failure of the Minister to implement a fee waiver for foreign nationals living in poverty perpetuates the prejudice for stereotyping of persons living in poverty. The failure of the government to implement a fee waiver was not contrary to s. 15(1) of the *Charter*.

Section 25(1) provides a discretionary benefit to foreign nationals. Parliament has no obligation to provide for foreign nationals to remain in Canada on H&C grounds. Section 25 itself does not provide any right to make an in-Canada H&C application; rather it provides an opportunity to apply for an exemption from provisions of IRPA or the Regulations. The Minister is only obligated to consider H&C factors "upon request." Immigration is not a right, nor is access to s. 25 of IRPA.

The application for judicial review was dismissed.

The following questions were certified:

A. On a proper statutory interpretation of s. 25(1) of IRPA, is the Minister obligated to consider a request to grant an exemption from the requirement to pay the H&C processing fee, otherwise required under s. 307 of the *IRP* Regulations?

B. Does the failure of the government (through the GIC) to enact regulations permitting the waiver of fees for foreign nationals living in poverty who wish to make an in-Canada application for permanent residence status pursuant to s. 25(1) of IRPA infringe the applicant's rights under ss. 7 or 15 of the *Charter*?

C. Is the failure of government (through the GIC) to enact regulations permitting the waiver of fees for foreign nationals living in poverty who wish to make an in-Canada application for permanent residence status pursuant to section 25(1) of IRPA contrary to either the rule of law or the common-law constitutional right of access to the Courts?

## *Social Insurance Number Cards*

**90. Minister directs special cards to be issued — The Minister may direct the Canada Employment Insurance Commission to issue to persons, other than Canadian citizens or permanent residents, Social Insurance Number Cards, by which**

**the holders of such cards are identified as persons who may be required under this Act to obtain authorization to work in Canada.**

## *Representation*

**91. Regulations — The regulations may govern who may or may not represent, advise or consult with a person who is the subject of a proceeding or application before the Minister, an officer or the Board.**

**Proposed Amendment — 91**

**91. Regulations — The regulations may govern who may or may not represent, advise or consult with a person who is the subject of a proceeding or application before the Minister, an officer or any Division of the Board, including an interview before an official referred to in subsection 100(4.1).**

2010, c. 8, s. 8 [To come into force June 29, 2012, or earlier by order.]

## *Material Incorporated in Regulations*

**92. (1) Incorporated material — A regulation may incorporate by reference the following material:**

> **(a) material produced by a person or body other than the Governor in Council;**
>
> **(b) material referred to in paragraph (a) that has been subsequently adapted or edited in order to facilitate its incorporation for the purposes of the regulation;**
>
> **(c) material that has been developed jointly with another government or government agency for the purpose of harmonizing the regulation with other laws; and**
>
> **(d) material that is technical or explanatory in nature, such as specifications, classifications, illustrations or graphs, as well as examples that may assist in the application of the regulation.**

**(2) Amended from time to time — Material may be incorporated by reference on a specified date or as amended from time to time.**

**(3) Incorporated material is not a regulation — For greater certainty, material that is incorporated by reference in a regulation made under this Act is not a regulation for the purposes of the *Statutory Instruments Act*.**

**93. Statutory Instruments Act — Instructions given by the Minister under this Act and guidelines issued by the Chairperson under paragraph 159(1)(h) are not statutory instruments for the purposes of the *Statutory Instruments Act*.**

## Report to Parliament

**94. (1) Annual report to Parliament** — The Minister must, on or before November 1 of each year or, if a House of Parliament is not then sitting, within the next 30 days on which that House is sitting after that date, table in each House of Parliament a report on the operation of this Act in the preceding calendar year.

**(2) Contents of report** — The report shall include a description of

(a) the instructions given under section 87.3 and other activities and initiatives taken concerning the selection of foreign nationals, including measures taken in cooperation with the provinces;

(b) in respect of Canada, the number of foreign nationals who became permanent residents, and the number projected to become permanent residents in the following year;

(b.1) in respect of Canada, the linguistic profile of foreign nationals who became permanent residents;

(c) in respect of each province that has entered into a federal-provincial agreement described in subsection 9(1), the number, for each class listed in the agreement, of persons that became permanent residents and that the province projects will become permanent residents there in the following year;

(d) the number of temporary resident permits issued under section 24, categorized according to grounds of inadmissibility, if any;

(e) the number of persons granted permanent resident status under each of subsections 25(1), 25.1(1) and 25.2(1); and

(f) a gender-based analysis of the impact of this Act.

2008, c. 28, s. 119; 2010, c. 8, s. 9

# Part 2 — Refugee Protection

## Division 1 — Refugee Protection, Convention Refugees and Persons in Need of Protection

**95. (1) Conferral of refugee protection** — Refugee protection is conferred on a person when

(a) the person has been determined to be a Convention refugee or a person in similar circumstances under a visa application and becomes a permanent resident under the visa or a temporary resident under a temporary resident permit for protection reasons;

(b) the Board determines the person to be a Convention refugee or a person in need of protection; or

(c) except in the case of a person described in subsection 112(3), the Minister allows an application for protection.

**(2) Protected person — A protected person is a person on whom refugee protection is conferred under subsection (1), and whose claim or application has not subsequently been deemed to be rejected under subsection 108(3), 109(3) or 114(4).**

*[Editor's Note: SOR/2002-227, s. 338 provides that refugee protection under the* Immigration and Refugee Protection Act, *S.C. 2001, c. 27 (the "new Act") is conferred on a person who*

*(a) has been determined in Canada before June 28, 2002 to be a Convention refugee and*

*(i) no determination was made to vacate that determination, or*

*(ii) no determination was made that the person ceased to be a Convention refugee;*

*(b) as an applicant or an accompanying dependant was granted landing before June 28, 2002 after being issued a visa under*

*(i) s. 7 of the* Immigration Regulations, 1978, *SOR/78-172 (the "former Regulations"), or*

*(ii) s. 4 of the* Humanitarian Designated Classes Regulations, *SOR/97-183; or*

*(c) was determined to be a member of the post-determination refugee claimants in Canada class before June 28, 2002 and was granted landing under s. 11.4 of the former Regulations or who becomes a permanent resident under s. 21(2) of the new Act.*

*SOR/2002-227, s. 339 further provides that a determination made in Canada before June 28, 2002 that a person is not a Convention refugee is deemed to be a claim for refugee protection rejected by the Immigration and Refugee Board.]*

## Case Law

### Section 95(1)

*Seyoboka v. Canada (Minister of Citizenship & Immigration)*, 2009 CarswellNat 237, 2009 FC 104 (F.C.) — This was an application for judicial review of a decision of the Immigration and Refugee Board dismissing the applicant's motion to reopen his claim for refugee protection pursuant to s. 72(1) of the IRPA. The applicant contends that the Minister had a duty to disclose exculpatory evidence in vacation proceedings and the Minister breached her duty to disclose the exculpatory evidence.

The Refugee Protection Division of the Board is an administrative tribunal with specialized knowledge, not bound by legal or technical rules of evidence. As a result, the disclosure to standards delineated in *Stinchcombe*, [1991] 3 S.C.R. 326, do not necessarily apply automatically in the context of a refugee hearing and may require some adaptation. On the other hand, the level of disclosure owed to an applicant cannot be decided by a simple invocation of the distinction between criminal and administrative proceedings, and the consequences of an adverse finding on the applicant must be taken into consideration. The application for judicial review was dismissed. The following four questions were certified:

1. Within the context of the judicial review hearing where the Minister intervenes to seek the exclusion of the claimant, is the Minister under a duty to disclose all relevant evidence in his possession including exculpatory evidence subject only to any claims to privilege which would be assessed by the tribunal?

2. Is that duty contingent on any request from the claimant or does the duty exist independently of any request from the claimant?

3. Can the right to disclosure be waived? If so, must the waiver be explicit, or can it be inferred from the conduct of the claimant?

4. If there is a duty to disclose, does that duty include a duty to disclose evidence in the possession of other government agencies when Minister's counsel is aware that that government agency has a file on the person which might contain relevant evidence?

*Quintanilla v. Canada (Minister of Citizenship & Immigration)* (2006), 55 Imm. L.R. (3d) 112, 2006 CarswellNat 1595, 2006 FC 726 (F.C.) — The applicants were citizens of El Salvador. They lost their permanent residence status and currently face removal from Canada. The applicants contested the validity of the direction to report for removal issued against them on the grounds that they are protected from *refoulement.*

The applicants were granted permanent residence status in December 1995 under the *Political Prisoners and Oppressed Persons Designated Class Regulations* (PPOP). The applicants sought re-settlement in Canada on the basis of a well-founded fear of persecution on a Convention ground. Four months after their arrival in Canada as permanent residents in December 1995, the applicants returned to El Salvador. They stayed for more than six years in El Salvador until their second return to Canada in June 2002. In July 2002, the applicants were issued removal orders for failing to comply with their residency obligations. The applicants' appeals of these removal orders were denied by the IAD in July 2003. As a result, the applicants lost their permanent residence status and their removal orders came into force.

The Court concluded that the applicants did not have a vested right not to be returned to El Salvador. The concept of "protected person" was created by IRPA. The determinative factor is that the applicants entered Canada in 1995 as permanent residents under the PPOP Designated Class. The applicants were subject to the same rights and obligations as any other permanent resident. In 1996, the applicants voluntarily returned to El Salvador and remained there for six years. The only right the applicants acquired under the *PPOP Regulations* was permanent resident status and that status was lost in light of the applicants' failure to comply with their residency requirements. Upon their second entry to Canada, the applicants were found to be inadmissible. The argument made by the applicants that the members of the PPOP Designated Class are permanently protected from *refoulement*, unless steps are taken by the Minister to cease or vacate their status under s. 108(3) or 109(3) of the IRPA, was dismissed by the Federal Court.

A question was certified: Under the *Immigration and Refugee Protection Act* and Regulations, is "refugee protection" conferred on a person who was landed in Canada as a member of the Political Prisoners and Oppressed Persons Designated Class but who has never been determined to be a Convention refugee or a person in need of protection?

*Ha v. Canada (Minister of Citizenship & Immigration)*, 34 Imm. L.R. (3d) 157, 2004 CarswellNat 247, [2004] F.C.J. No. 174, 11 Admin. L.R. (4th) 306, 2004 FCA 49, 236 D.L.R. (4th) 485, 316 N.R. 299, 2004 CarswellNat 5581, [2004] 3 F.C.R. 195, 247 F.T.R. 314 (note) (F.C.A.) — This was an appeal from a decision of a motions judge dismissing the appellants' application for judicial review of the decision of a visa officer at the Canadian High Commission in Singapore denying the appellants' application for permanent residents as Convention refugees seeking resettlement.

The duty of fairness owed to the appellants, in the particular circumstances of this case, entitled them to have counsel attend and observe their interviews. The respondent's refusal to allow counsel to be present, accordingly, breached the appellants' right to procedural fairness.

The policy contained in the operations memorandum stating that counsel should not attend interviews is invalid because it fettered the visa officer's discretion and duty to consider the particular facts of each case when deciding whether counsel should be permitted to attend interviews.

**96. Convention refugee — A Convention refugee is a person who, by reason of a well-founded fear of persecution for reasons of race, religion, nationality, membership in a particular social group or political opinion,**

> **(a) is outside each of their countries of nationality and is unable or, by reason of that fear, unwilling to avail themself of the protection of each of those countries; or**
>
> **(b) not having a country of nationality, is outside the country of their former habitual residence and is unable or, by reason of that fear, unwilling to return to that country.**

## Case Law

*Smith v. Canada (Minister of Citizenship & Immigration)* (2009), 86 Imm. L.R. (3d) 114, 358 F.T.R. 189 (Eng.), 2009 FC 1194, 2009 CarswellNat 3800, 2009 CarswellNat 3801 (F.C.) — The applicant, an American citizen, claimed refugee protection pursuant to ss. 96 and 97(1) of IRPA as a homosexual member of the U.S. Army, from which she had deserted. She alleged a fear of persecution on the part of a colleague and superiors because of her sexual orientation. She also claimed that she would be personally facing a risk to her life or cruel and unusual treatment or punishment if she were returned to the United States. Her claim was rejected by the Refugee Board on the ground that she failed to seek state protection that would have been adequate.

Contrary to the situation in *Hinzman, Re* (2006), 55 Imm. L.R. (3d) 54 (F.C.), where the appellants had not made an adequate attempt to avail themselves of the protections afforded by the Uniform Code of Military Justice (UCMJ), the applicant in this case provided evidence that she did approach her superiors to try to obtain a discharge. According to the evidence, she went so far as to ask her superior for permission to speak to a higher authority, but was denied. She also testified that one supervisor scoffed at her and said they would figure out the paper work when she returned from her tour of duty in Afghanistan. The case law of this Court requires more than one attempt to obtain state protection. It is often said that an applicant must usually follow up with his complaint, and seek assistance from higher authorities if unsuccessful at the first stage. Yet, one must take into account the particular environment that an applicant finds himself in. It is clear that in the Army there is an atmosphere of unconditional obedience to the hierarchy. The Board member did not seem to be sensitive to this special context.

The duty of the Board member was to determine whether she would suffer persecution as a result of the relevant substantive law or of the process whereby the law would be applied to her. It was not enough for the Board member to state that he is "not in a position to defend or criticize." It is part of the assessment of a refugee claim to determine whether a claimant has a well-founded fear of persecution for reasons, *inter alia*, of her membership in a particular social group, if he/she is returned to his/her home country. The applicant provided evidence to the Board that the punishment she would be exposed to under the court-martial process relates to a breach of a law that is in conflict with a fundamental human right and therefore adversely differentiates on a Convention ground in its application. This evidence could not simply be ignored by the Board member and had to be properly discussed and analyzed before he could conclude that the UCMJ was a law of general application and applied in a non-discriminatory fashion. It was therefore the duty of the Board member to assess the fairness of the court-martial process in light of the particular set of facts and of the evidence that was before him. The application for judicial review was allowed.

*R. v. Laboucan*, [2010] S.C.J. No. 12, 73 C.R. (6th) 235, (sub nom. *R. v. Briscoe)* 400 N.R. 200, 22 Alta. L.R. (5th) 62, 253 C.C.C. (3d) 129, [2010] 6 W.W.R. 13, 316 D.L.R. (4th) 590, (sub nom. *R. v. Briscoe)* 477 A.R. 70, 483 W.A.C. 70, 2010 SCC 12, 2010 CarswellAlta 591, 2010 CarswellAlta 590 — The fact that a witness has an interest in the outcome of the proceedings is common sense and a relevant factor, among others, to take into account when assessing the credibility of the witness's testimony. A trier of fact, however, should not place undue weight on the status of a person in the proceeding as a factor going to credibility. For example, it would be improper to base a finding of credibility regarding a parent's or a spouse's testimony solely on the basis of a witness's relationship to the complainant or to the accused. Regard should be given to all relevant factors in assessing credibility.

*Alexander v. Canada (Minister of Citizenship & Immigration* (2009), 88 Imm. L.R. (3d) 75, 357 F.T.R. 222 (Eng.), 2009 FC 1305, 2009 CarswellNat 5510, 2009 CarswellNat 4566, [2009] F.C.J. No. 1682 (F.C.) — The Refugee Protection Panel accepted that the applicant had been beaten up by her boyfriend, that she had taken refuge with her aunt on one of the Grenadian Islands, that her boyfriend had threatened to burn down her mother's house if she did not return to Kingstown and that he continued to make terrifying threats by telephone. The only issue was that of state protection. The panel found that St. Vincent and the Grenadines was a democracy and that the applicant did not "take all reasonable steps in the circumstances of this case to pursue the available state protection," and that she "did not provide any persuasive evidence of similarly-situated individuals let down by the state protection arrangements." The conclusion was that she had failed to rebut the presumption of state protection with clear and convincing evidence.

Taken at its face value, the decision appears to be reasonable. This Court is supposed to show deference to the RPD panels that allegedly have greater expertise in country conditions than the Court itself. However, there comes a time when it becomes obvious that deference should be earned, particularly when the panel apparently pays no attention to the cases coming out of this Court which specifically deal with St. Vincent and the Grenadines. The analysis of country conditions was clearly a *pro forma* one, or a "cookie cutter analysis." This Court does not sit in a *de novo* appeal and so cannot do its own country analysis. It was "absolutely astonishing" that the IRB publishes information on country conditions but failed to mention that the Consul General has admitted that the state cannot guarantee the effectiveness of a restraining order. That would be relevant information in any assessment as would an analysis of the types of threats the applicant received. The application for judicial review was granted.

*Perez v. Canada (Minister of Citizenship & Immigration)* (2009), 85 Imm. L.R. (3d) 118, 2009 FC 1065, 2009 CarswellNat 5598, 2009 CarswellNat 3345 (F.C.) — Refugee law does not require altruism from those who seek protection from persecution nor does it exclude those who publicize their fears. In this case, the board member repeatedly criticized the applicant's recourse to the media to call attention to her victimization. The member's comments that the applicant "failed frequently to address corruption before it affected her," used "duplicity and threats" to press her case and lacked "altruistic intent," reflect judgments about the applicant's integrity that are legally irrelevant and taint the entire decision. The application for judicial review was allowed.

*Key v. Canada (Minister of Citizenship & Immigration)*, [2008] F.C.J. No. 1003, 73 Imm. L.R. (3d) 278, 331 F.T.R. 137, 85 Admin. L.R. (4th) 157, 2008 CarswellNat 3031, 2008 CarswellNat 2152, 2008 FC 838 (F.C.) — It is clear that officially condoned military misconduct falling well short of a war crime may support a claim to refugee protection. Indeed, authorities indicate that military action which *systematically* degrades, abuses or humiliates either combatants or noncombatants is capable of supporting a refugee claim where that is the proven reason for refusing to serve. The Board erred in this case by imposing a too restrictive legal standard upon the applicant. The Board's assertion that his past combat participation would not be sufficient to support his claim to asylum unless it constituted excludible conduct cannot be correct. This would give rise to an unacceptable "Catch-22" situation where the factual threshold for obtaining protection would necessarily exclude a claimant from that protection. That, however, does not end the matter because the Court has made it very clear in *Hinzman* (C.A.), *infra*, that soldiers facing punishment in the United States for desertion must, as a rule, pursue the available options for state protection at home before seeking protection in Canada. In light of this decision, there is no question that the Board erred by adopting the "state of persecutor" principle as a basis for finding that state protection was not available to the applicant. There is not much doubt that he would likely face some form of punishment for desertion if he returned to the United States and, indeed, the Board found that he would, in all probability, be court martialled and sentenced to a year of imprisonment. While the *Hinzman* decision has certainly set the bar very high for deserters from the United States military seeking refuge in Canada, the Court of Appeal acknowledged in that case that one's failure to fully pursue state protection opportunities will not always be fatal to a refugee claim. Clear and convincing evidence about similarly situated individuals who unsuccessfully sought to be excused from combat duty or who were persecuted and imprisoned for a refusal to serve, may be sufficient to rebut the presumption of state protection in the United States. Since the applicant would have been deployed back to Iraq within two weeks of his arrival in the United States, the opportunity to pursue a release or re-assignment may not have been realistic. Because the outcome of this case could not be considered to be a foregone conclusion, the applicant was given the opportunity to address fully the issue of state protection in a rehearing before the Board. The application for judicial review was allowed and the matter remitted to a differently constituted panel of the Board for reconsideration on the merits.

*Guney v. Canada (Minister of Citizenship & Immigration)*, 2008 CarswellNat 5579, 2008 CarswellNat 3687, 2008 FC 1134 (F.C.) — The applicant tried to bolster his claim for refugee status more than a year later, by inventing an additional basis for protection. The Board found that this new lie rendered the applicant's evidence, as a whole, not to be credible and thus did no real analysis of the rest of his story. The fact that a witness has been caught in one lie, in itself, is insufficient to discredit all of his evidence where, as here, the evidence is otherwise plausible and consistent. This approach was unreasonable and the decision was set aside.

*Munderere v. Canada (Minister of Citizenship & Immigration)* (2008), 69 Imm. L.R. (3d) 129, 291 D.L.R. (4th) 68, 2008 CarswellNat 600, 2008 CarswellNat 601, 2008 FCA 84 (C.A.) — Considering s. 53 of the United Nations Handbook on Procedures and Criteria for Determining Refugee Status, and in particular the last sentence of that paragraph, "This will necessarily depend on all the circumstances, including the particular geographical, historical and ethnological context", it is not an error in law to limit the analysis of the cumulative grounds to the events that occurred within one country of nationality or habitual residence, when the claimant alleges persecution on the basis of the same Convention ground in the two (or more) countries, and where the claimant's subject fear is related to events that occurred in more than one country, except where the events which occur in a country other than that in respect of which a claimant seeks refugee status are relevant to the determination of whether the country where a claimant seeks refugee status can protect him or her from persecution.

*Carrillo v. Canada (Minister of Citizenship & Immigration)*, [2008] F.C.J. No. 399, 69 Imm. L.R. (3d) 309, 2008 CarswellNat 1953, 2008 CarswellNat 605, 2008 FCA 94 (C.A.) — A refugee who claims that the state protection is inadequate or non-existent bears the evidentiary burden of adducing evidence to that effect and the legal burden of persuading the trier of fact that his or her claim in this respect is founded. The standard of proof applicable is the balance of probabilities and there is no requirement of a higher degree of probability than what that standard usually requires. As for the quality of the evidence required to rebut the presumption of state protection, the presumption is rebutted by clear and convincing evidence that the state protection is inadequate or non-existent. The appeal was allowed, the decision of the Federal Court set aside and the decision of the Board restored.

*Sanchez v. Canada (Minister of Citizenship & Immigration)* (2007), 360 N.R. 344, 2007 CarswellNat 572, 2007 FCA 99 (Fed. C.A.) — The appellants, a husband and wife, were Colombian nationalists. One appellant was employed full-time by the Colombian Ministry of Agriculture as an engineer, with a specialty in environmental clean-up. In addition, he ran a side-line business with his brother that reported violations of signage by-laws to the city authorities. He and his brother received a percentage of the fine that was levied against the guilty person or business. The appellant was threatened by the Fuerzas Armadas Revolucionarias de Colombia ("FARC") due to his part-time business. The appellant sought refugee status. The Board found no indication that the lives or well being of the appellants would have been at risk had the appellant simply chosen to comply with the warning and cease his side business. The Board was of the view that it was not unreasonable to expect him to cease his side business and that his inability to continue this endeavour was not a denial of his core human rights or of his general ability to earn a living. The applications judge found the Board's decision to be reasonable and legally correct with respect to this part-time business.

Although it was not possible in the context of this case to attempt to develop an exhaustive list of the factors that should be taken into account in assessing whether a person is in need of protection, persons claiming to be in need of protection solely because of the nature of the occupation or business in which they are engaged in their own country generally will not be found to be in need of protection unless they can establish that there is no alternative occupation or business reasonably open to them in their own country that it would eliminate the risk of harm.

*Hinzman, Re*, [2006] F.C.J. No. 521, 55 Imm. L.R. (3d) 54, (sub nom. *Hinzman v. Canada (Minister of Citizenship & Immigration))* [2007] 1 F.C.R. 561, (sub nom.

*Hinzman v. Canada (Minister of Citizenship & Immigration))* 290 F.T.R. 8 (Eng.), 266 D.L.R. (4th) 582, 2006 CarswellNat 1779, 2006 FC 420; affirmed [2007] F.C.J. No. 584, 2007 CarswellNat 950, 2007 FCA 171 (Fed. C.A.) — The applicant is an American soldier who deserted the United States Army after his unit was deployed to fight in Iraq. He says he deserted because of his strong moral objections to the war in Iraq, and his belief that the American-led military action in that country is illegal. The applicant made a refugee claim which was rejected. He then sought judicial review of the Board's decision, asserting that the Board erred in refusing to allow him to lead evidence with respect to the alleged illegality of the American military action in Iraq. He also argued that in ignoring evidence with respect to the alleged condoning of ongoing human rights violations perpetrated by the American military in Iraq, and with respect to the systemic nature of those violations, the Board further erred. Finally, he argued that the Board imposed too heavy a burden on him to demonstrate that he would have been involved in unlawful acts had he gone to Iraq and that the Board erred in failing to properly consider the fact that an objection to a particular war is not recognized as a legitimate basis on which to grant conscientious objector status in the United States.

The application for judicial review was dismissed. The Court concluded that there was no internationally recognized right to object to a particular war, other than in the circumstances specifically identified in paragraph 171 of the United Nations High Commission for Refugees Handbook on Procedures and Criteria for Determining Refugee Status. The Court stated that the reality is that states, including Canada, can and do punish their citizens for acting in accordance with their sincerely held moral, political and religious views when those individuals break laws of general application.

Note: The Federal Court of Appeal refused to answer the certified question, since the appellants failed to satisfy the fundamental requirement that claimants seek protection from their home state before going abroad to obtain protection through the refugee system. It was impossible for a Canadian Court or tribunal to assess the availability of protections in the United States.

*Hughey v. Canada (Minister of Citizenship & Immigration)*, [2006] F.C.J. No. 522, 52 Imm. L.R. (3d) 192, 2006 CarswellNat 808, 2006 FC 421 (F.C.) — The applicant was a private in the United States Army who deserted after his unit was deployed to Iraq. The applicant claimed he deserted because of his strong moral objections to the war in Iraq, and his belief that the American-led military action in that country is illegal. The applicant came to Canada and claimed refugee protection asserting a well-founded fear of persecution in the United States, based upon his political opinion.

There is currently no internationally recognized right to object to a particular war, other than the circumstances specifically identified in the United Nations High Commission for Refugees *Handbook on Procedures and Criteria for Determining Refugee Status*. While the applicant may face prosecution in the United States for having acted in accordance with his conscience, this does not amount to persecution on the basis of his political opinion. The reality is that states, including Canada, can and do punish their citizens for acting in accordance with their sincerely held moral, political and religious views when those individuals break laws of general application.

*Rey Nunez v. Canada (Minister of Citizenship & Immigration)* (2005), 51 Imm. L.R. (3d) 291, 2005 CarswellNat 4127, 2005 FC 1661 (F.C.) — The Board's conclusion that the applicants had not rebutted the presumption of state protection available to them in Bolivia was unreasonable in light of the evidence before it. With regard to the standard of review applicable to a state protection determination, it is clear that the findings of fact can only be set aside if made in a perverse and capricious manner, or without regard to the material before the tribunal. Once the findings of fact are made, they must be assessed to determine if they constitute "clear and convincing confirmation of a state's inability to protect." That is a question of mixed fact and law for which less deference should be shown to the tribunal's decision. The appropriate standard of review for a finding of state protection is reasonableness *simpliciter*. Therefore, the decision of the Board will be set aside only if there is no line of analysis within the given reasons that could reasonably lead the tribunal from the evidence before it to the conclusion at which it arrived. If any of the reasons that are sufficient to support the conclusion are tenable in the sense that they can stand up to a somewhat probing examination, then the decision will not be unreasonable and a reviewing court must not interfere.



In the case at hand, the principal applicant and his family had made at least four attempts at seeking protection from state authorities and there was no analysis in the Board's reasons as to why these efforts were not enough to demonstrate a lack of state protection.

*Manzi Williams v. Canada (Minister of Citizenship & Immigration)*, 2005 CarswellNat 950, 2005 CarswellNat 1805, 253 D.L.R. (4th) 449, 2005 FCA 126 (F.C.A.) — Refugee protection will be denied where it is shown that an applicant is entitled to acquire, by mere formalities, the citizenship of a particular country with respect to which he has no well founded fear of persecution.

If it is within the control of the applicant to acquire the citizenship of a country with respect to which he has no well founded fear of persecution, the claim for refugee status will be denied. The control test also reflects the notion, which is transparent in the definition of a refugee, namely that the unwillingness of an applicant to take steps required from him to gain state protection is fatal to his refugee claim unless that unwillingness results from the very fear of persecution itself.

Whether the citizenship of another country was obtained at birth, by naturalization, or by state succession is of no consequence provided it is within the control of the applicant to obtain it.

The condition of not having a country of nationality must be one that is beyond the power of the applicant to control.

*Fernandopulle v. Canada (Minister of Citizenship & Immigration)*, 2005 CarswellNat 610, 253 D.L.R. (4th) 425, 2005 FCA 91, 331 N.R. 385 (F.C.A.) — Evidence of past persecution may support a finding of fact that a claimant has a well-founded fear of persecution. Whether such a finding is made in a particular case will depend on all of the evidence including evidence of current country conditions. There is, however, no rebuttable legal presumption to this effect.

*De Barros v. Canada (Minister of Citizenship & Immigration)*, 2005 CarswellNat 535, 2005 FC 283 (F.C.) — A basic principle of refugee law is to grant status to those requiring surrogate protection and not to those who have a ready and automatic right to another country's nationality and protection. A person who is able to obtain citizenship in another country by complying with mere formalities is not entitled to avail themselves of protection in Canada.

*Chaves v. Canada (Minister of Citizenship & Immigration)* (2005), 45 Imm. L.R. (3d) 58, 2005 CarswellNat 333, 2005 FC 193, [2005] F.C.J. No. 232 (F.C.) — This was an application to review a negative decision respecting the applicant's application for protection. The onus lies on the applicant to rebut the presumption of state protection. The claimant's subjective fear of persecution is not at issue. The issue is whether the fear is objectively justifiable and that requires an examination into the existence or non-existence of state protection. The mere refusal by the police or authorities to aid a claimant will not suffice to displace the presumption of state protection. The burden of proof on the individual increases in proportion to the democratic nature of the particular state's institutions. An individual will not be required to exhaust all avenues before the presumption of state protection is rebutted. Where agents of the state are themselves the source of the persecution in question, and where the applicant's credibility is not undermined, the applicant can successfully rebut the presumption without exhausting every conceivable recourse in the country. The very fact that agents of the state are the alleged perpetrators of persecution undercuts the apparent democratic nature of the state's institutions, and correspondingly, the burden of proof.

*Ozdemir v. Canada (Minister of Citizenship & Immigration)*, [2004] F.C.J. No. 1242, 38 Imm. L.R. (3d) 237, 2004 CarswellNat 2232, 2004 FC 1008, 256 F.T.R. 154 (F.C.) — Pursuant to s. 97(1) of the IRPA, the Board is required to evaluate whether a claimant is in need of protection owing to the danger of torture or risk of cruel and unusual punishment. The separate analysis of a claimant's refugee claim under s. 96 and the enumerated risks under s. 97(1) is required. Further, a negative credibility determination in respect of a refugee claim under s. 96 is not necessarily dispositive of the considerations under s. 97(1).

*Kadoura v. Canada (Ministre de la Citoyenneté & de l'Immigration)*, [2003] F.C.J. No. 1328, 2003 CarswellNat 4831, 2003 CarswellNat 2789, 2003 FC 1057 (F.C.) — The terms "refugee" and "person in need of protection" apply in particular to persons who do not have a country of nationality and who find themselves outside the country of their former "habitual residence." If a claimant resided in more than one country, it is not necessary to prove that he or she was persecuted in each of those countries. The claimant must show that he or she was persecuted in at least one of these countries and that he or she is unable or unwilling to return to the countries where he had his habitual residence.

The definition of "country of habitual residence" should not be so unduly restrictive as to pre-empt providing shelter to a stateless person who has demonstrated a well-founded fear of persecution on any of the grounds listed in the Convention. The claimant does not have to be legally able to return to a country of a habitual residence. The denial of the right to return, in fact, may in itself constitute an act of persecution by the State.

*Ranjha v. Canada (Minister of Citizenship & Immigration)* (2003), 29 Imm. L.R. (3d) 59, 2003 CarswellNat 4495, 2003 CarswellNat 1686, 234 F.T.R. 132, 2003 CFPI 637, 2003 FCT 637 (Fed. T.D.) — The applicant sought to overturn a negative determination of his refugee claim. The tribunal determined, in part, that the applicant had not suffered past persecution. The tribunal analyzed separately the incidents of persecution but found that they were not repetitive, persistent and systematic and therefore, did not cumulatively amount to persecution.

Security measures to unmask terrorists can never justify torture of and physical violence to innocent civilians. While the tribunal made an error in its analysis, the panel had found the applicant to be a credible witness. It had to determine whether the quality of the incidents constituted a fundamental violation of human dignity. Reading the tribunal's decision as a whole, the Court concluded that the tribunal took the view that the absence of past persecution necessarily impacted on its view as to whether the applicant would be persecuted should he return and accordingly set aside the decision of the panel.

*Kovacs v. Kovacs*, [2002] O.J. No. 3074, 59 O.R. (3d) 671, 2002 CarswellOnt 1429, 21 Imm. L.R. (3d) 205, 212 D.L.R. (4th) 711, [2002] O.T.C. 287 (S.C.J.) — The respondent arrived at Pearson Airport from Hungary with her 3-year-old son and immediately claimed refugee status for herself and on behalf of her child. Eventually, the applicant learned of the respondent's whereabouts and launched this application for an order for the immediate return of the child to Hungary.

An order for the immediate return of the child can be made despite the fact there is a refugee claim pending.

*Editor's note: The following case summaries were collected under the provisions of the former Act relating to the definition of Convention refugee. The previous jurisprudence interpreting refugee concepts may still be relevant.*

*Bin v. Canada (Minister of Citizenship & Immigration)* (2001), 213 F.T.R. 47, 2001 FCT 1246, 2001 CarswellNat 2600 (Fed. T.D.) — The applicant was aged 17 at the time the refugee claim was made. The applicant was transported to Canada by human smugglers or "snakeheads". The applicant also claimed that he was a refugee *sur place* on the basis that the Chinese government will view his illegal exit and the refugee claim as expressing a political opinion.

There are few guidelines and little jurisprudence on the proper evaluation of *sur place* claims. A person can become a refugee *sur place* for reasons other than a change in circumstances in her or his country of origin. The person can become such a refugee as a result of his own actions such as associating with refugees already recognized or expressing his political views in his country of residence. Regard should be had in particular to whether such actions may have come to the notice of the authorities of the person's country of origin and how they are likely to be viewed by those authorities.

There was no evidence before the panel, documentary or otherwise, that substantiated the *sur place* allegation. The panel limited its analysis to documentary evidence of punishment for illegal exit in China. The Court did not agree that the panel should have determined how the Chinese government might view making a claim for refugee status, even in the absence of specific documentary evidence. If there is a distinction to be made respecting the treatment given to returnees who have claimed refugee status in Canada and other returnees, and if that amounts to discrimination based on imputed political opinion, it should have been a matter of evidence before the panel. In the absence of such evidence it was reasonable for the panel to draw no conclusion based upon evidence of publicity. It was not open to the panel to engage in speculation whether it is to the applicant's benefit or detriment.

*Reul v. Canada (Minister of Citizenship & Immigration)* (2000), 9 Imm. L.R. (3d) 79, 2000 CarswellNat 2318 (Fed. T.D.) — The applicants sought to review a negative determination of their claim for refugee status. The applicants are Jehovah's Witnesses. The principal applicant's mother was also a Jehovah's Witness. During her final illness, she and the principal applicant received advice that she required a blood transfusion. The principal applicant's mother declined to accept the transfusion. The principal applicant supported her in this decision. The principal applicant's mother died. The principal applicant's siblings accused him of causing their mother's death. They sent threatening letters and made threatening phone calls to the principal applicant.

The principal applicant and his family members feared persecution by reason of the principal applicant's choice to live his conviction, flowing from his religious beliefs, a conviction shared by his mother based on her religious beliefs, that it was inappropriate to receive a blood transfusion. The principal applicant thus established a subjectively and objectively well-founded fear of persecution in Mexico on the ground of religious belief. Religion encompasses both the beliefs that one may choose to hold and behaviour which stems from those beliefs.

*Ranganathan v. Canada (Minister of Citizenship & Immigration)* (2000), 11 Imm. L.R. (3d) 142, [2001] 2 F.C. 164, 266 N.R. 380, 193 F.T.R. 320 (note), 2000 CarswellNat 3134, 2000 CarswellNat 3459 (Fed. C.A) — The sole issue before the panel of the Immigration and Refugee Board was whether there was an internal flight alternative in Colombo that was reasonably available to the respondent. In order for an IFA to be unreasonable, it requires nothing less than the existence of conditions which would jeopardize the life and safety of a claimant in travelling or temporarily relocating to a safe area. In addition, it requires actual and concrete evidence of such conditions. The absence of relatives in a safe place, whether taken alone or in conjunction with other factors, can only amount to such a condition if it meets that threshold, that is to say, if it establishes that, as a result, a claimant's life or safety would be jeopardized. This is in sharp contrast with undue hardship resulting from loss of employment, loss of status, reduction in quality of life, loss of aspirations, loss of loved ones and frustration of one's wishes and expectations.

*Zhuravlvev v. Canada (Minister of Citizenship & Immigration)*, [2000] 4 F.C. 3, 187 F.T.R. 110, 2000 CarswellNat 706, 2000 CarswellNat 3264, [2000] F.C.J. No. 507 (Fed. T.D.) — The applicant sought to overturn a negative decision of a panel of the CRDD. The question of state protection must be considered two times: the first time, in relation to the question of a well-founded fear of persecution; and the second time, in relation to the claimant's unwillingness or inability to avail him- or herself of state protection. Given that a lack of state protection is inherent in the finding of a well-founded fear of persecution, it is unlikely that the question of willingness or inability to avail oneself of state protection will require serious inquiry.

Refugees are generally not political scientists who can establish systemic lack of state protection. The object of the refugee system is to deal with state failure to protect its citizens. The Convention refugee system was designed to deal with the failure of national governments to protect their citizens from persecution.

When the agent of persecution is not the state, the lack of state protection has to be assessed as a matter of state capacity to provide protection rather than from the perspective of whether the local apparatus provided protection in a given circumstance. Local failures to provide effective policing do not amount to a lack of state protection. Where the evidence, including the documentary evidence, situates the individual claimant's experience as part of a broader pattern of state inability or refusal to extend protection, then the absence of state protection is made out. The question of a refusal to provide protection should be addressed on the same basis as the inability to provide protection. A local refusal to provide protection is not a state refusal in the absence of evidence of a broader state policy not to extend state protection to a target group.

There is an additional element in the question of refusal which is that the refusal by the state to extend protection may not be overt. The state organs may justify their failure to act by reference to various factors which, in their view, would make any state action ineffective. It is for the CRDD to assess the bona fides of those assertions in light of all the evidence.

The issue of internal flight alternative must be considered in relation to the state's inability or refusal to provide protection. A reasonable response to a local failure to provide protection is the internal migration to an area where state protection is available. Where internal movement is restricted, a failure to remedy local conditions may amount to state failure to provide protection. If state policy restricts a claimant's access to the whole of the state's territory, then the state's failure to provide local protection can be seen as a state failure to provide protection and not a mere local failure.

In this case, the CRDD's analysis of state protection was perfunctory with the result that the decision of the panel was set aside.

*Klinko v. Canada (Minister of Citizenship & Immigration)*, [2000] 3 F.C. 327, 184 D.L.R. (4th) 14, 251 N.R. 388, 179 F.T.R. 253 (note), 2000 CarswellNat 283, 2000 CarswellNat 3251, [2000] F.C.J. No. 228 (Fed. C.A.) — This was an appeal against the decision of a motions judge dismissing an application for judicial review of a decision denying the appellant's refugee status. The central issue was whether the opinion expressed by the appellants in this case was a political opinion or not. The standard of review of such decisions is that of correctness. In the present case, while the motions judge did not explicitly discuss the standard, the Court was satisfied that he applied the standard of correctness in reviewing the Convention Refugee Division's interpretation of the law with respect to the notion of political opinion. An opinion can be political for the purposes of subs. 2(1) of the Act whether or not that opinion accorded with the official government position. The words "political opinion" were broad enough to cover all instances where the political opinion expressed or imputed attracted persecution, including those where the government officially agreed with that opinion. The Court declined to follow *Femenia v. Canada (Minister of Citizenship & Immigration)*, [1995] F.C.J. No. 1455 (T.D.).

*Montchak v. Canada (Minister of Citizenship & Immigration)* (1999), 1999 CarswellNat 1323 (Fed. T.D.) — The applicant was a citizen of Ukraine, claimed refugee status and stated that he was a successful businessman and for that reason organized criminals stole his property, extorted money from him and attempted to kill him. He further alleged that he received no adequate protection from the Ukrainian police.

There is ample authority for the proposition that those who had made money in business do not comprise a particular social group and therefore if they attract the attention of criminals by virtue of their wealth they cannot be said to fear persecution on a Convention ground.

*Serrano v. Canada (Minister of Citizenship & Immigration)* (1999), 166 F.T.R. 227(1999), 1999 CarswellNat 636, [1999] F.C.J. No. 57 (Fed. T.D.) — This was an application to review a decision of a panel of the CRDD. The applicants were citizens of Mexico who claim to be at risk of being killed or seriously injured if returned there. The applicant operated a small trucking business in Acapulco. In 1996, he hired a new driver who introduced him to people who wished to hire his truck for the purpose of transporting drugs. The applicant refused to deal with them and a few days later his truck was found abandoned and damaged. Subsequently, the applicant and his family received threatening phone calls and a threatening letter. A friend of the applicant's who had agreed to work for drug traffickers was killed after he changed his mind.

The applicants' claims initially were based on a fear of persecution by reason of membership in a particular social group or political opinion. The CRDD concluded that as a matter of law the applicants were not members of a particular social group. In this case, the social group was described as "law abiding Mexican citizens". The Court agreed with the CRDD that "law abiding citizens of Mexico" were not a particular social group within the meaning of the Convention.

The Court found that to hold that everyone who fears persecution solely because of a family connection may be entitled to the protection of the Convention, would be to stretch the category of "particular social group" far beyond its proper limits. The Court did not accept that family connection was an attribute requiring Convention protection in the absence of an underlying Convention ground for the claimed protection. Accordingly, the application for judicial review was dismissed.

*Ali v. Canada (Minister of Citizenship & Immigration)* (1999), 235 N.R. 316, 160 F.T.R. 292 (note), 1999 CarswellNat 128 (Fed. C.A.) — The appeal in this matter was dismissed. The Court of Appeal noted that the test for persecution in a civil war context was set out in *Salibian v. Canada (Minister of Employment & Immigration)*, [1990] 3 F.C. 250, 11 Imm. L.R. (2d) 165 (Fed. C.A.) and *Rizkallah v. Canada (Minister of Citizenship & Immigration)* (1992), 156 N.R. 1 (Fed. C.A.). The Court also approved page 6 of the Refugee Board Guidelines issued on March 7, 1996, pursuant to s. 65(3) of the *Immigration Act*, dealing with refugee claims of civilian non-combatants in a civil war situation.

*Canada (Minister of Citizenship & Immigration) v. Bob Smith* (1998), 47 Imm. L.R. (2d) 305, [1999] 1 F.C. 310, 154 F.T.R. 92 (Fed. T.D.); additional reasons at 1998 CarswellNat 2423 (Fed. T.D.) — The respondent, Bob Smith, aged 14, is a citizen of the United States and the United Kingdom. He was a victim of ongoing sexual abuse. The principal aggressor was his natural father. The Minister sought judicial review of the determination by the CRDD that the respondent, his mother and his step-father were Convention refugees. The quantum of clear and convincing evidence required to rebut the presumption of a state's ability to protect depends on its democratic processes. In a democracy such as the United States with a free and independent judicial system, it would be necessary to impeach substantially the relevant jury selection process for the independence and fair-mindedness of the judiciary.

In this case, the evidence was simply insufficient to rebut the presumption of state protection. The tribunal's finding of no state protection in the United Kingdom and the United States was made in a perverse manner and without regard to the evidence. Accordingly, the decision of the tribunal was set aside.

*Ramanathan v. Canada (Minister of Citizenship & Immigration)* (1998), 44 Imm. L.R. (2d) 294, 152 F.T.R. 305 (Fed. T.D.) — This was an application to review a decision of the CRDD. The Board acknowledged that the applicant would probably not be able to attend to his daily living activities without the aid of his son, daughter-in-law and grandchildren. Notwithstanding this fact, the Board found a viable IFA in Columbo. There was no issue with respect to the fact that Colombo was a place where the applicant could live without fear of persecution. The panel refused to consider humanitarian and compassionate considerations in applying the second branch of the IFA test. A test of whether the IFA is unreasonable or unduly harsh in all the circumstances is bound to involve the consideration of some factors, at least, which will undoubtedly be the same sort of considerations that are taken into account in humanitarian and compassionate relief.

*Thabet v. Canada (Minister of Citizenship & Immigration)* (1998), 48 Imm. L.R. (2d) 195, [1998] 4 F.C. 21, 151 F.T.R. 160 (note), 227 N.R. 42, 160 D.L.R. (4th) 666 (Fed. C.A.) — The appellant was born in Kuwait and is a stateless Palestinian. He lived in

Kuwait on a residency permit sponsored by his father. In 1983, the appellant left Kuwait to study in the United States where he obtained an engineering degree. In 1986, his residency status in Kuwait came to an end, and he returned to Kuwait to make an independent application to renew his residency permit, which was denied. The appellant then returned to the United States on a visitor's visa, where he lived for 11 years. After the outbreak of the Gulf War the appellant sought asylum in the United States. His application was rejected and he was ordered deported. He filed an appeal, but abandoned it and came to Canada where he applied for refugee status. Before a panel of the IRB, the appellant based his claim on the ground that Kuwait was his country of formal habitual residence and that he feared persecution if returned there. He also claimed to fear persecution in the United States, because while living in Louisiana he experienced harassment threats and violence at the hands of the Ku Klux Klan.

A panel of the IRB found that both Kuwait and the U.S. were countries of formal habitual residence and that the appellant had to demonstrate a well-founded fear of persecution against both in order to be granted refugee status. According to the Board, the appellant had not made out his fear of persecution in either country, and denied his claim.

The Trial Division judge found that the Board had erred in not asking itself whether the denial of a right to return to Kuwait was in itself an act of persecution. The Trial Division judge went on to find that a stateless person who has habitually resided in more than one country before making a refugee claim must establish his or her claim by reference to the last country of formal habitual residence. Accordingly, notwithstanding the error made by the panel in this matter the application for judicial review was dismissed.

On appeal, it was held that a stateless person must show on a balance of probabilities that he or she would suffer persecution in any country of formal habitual residence. In addition, the Court observed that so long as a claimant does not face persecution in a country of formal habitual residence that will take him or her back, he or she could not be determined to be a refugee.

*Shahpari v. Canada (Minister of Citizenship & Immigration)* (1998), 44 Imm. L.R. (2d) 139, 146 F.T.R. 102 (Fed. T.D.) — The applicants sought to review the question of whether section E of Article I of the *Geneva Convention* applied to them. The applicants were citizens of Iran. In 1984 they moved to France and after seven years of temporary residence were issued a "Carte de Résident" which was valid for 10 years. After residing in France until 1994, the applicants came to Canada and within one month made a refugee application.

The burden of proving that section E applies rests with the party asserting it, in this case the respondent. It did not assist the applicant in this case that she allowed her visa to expire. The evidence allowed the panel to conclude that the visa could be renewed. Applicants should remember that actions they themselves take, which are intended to result in their not being able to return to a country which has already granted them refugee status, may well evidence an absence of the subjective fear of persecution in their original country. Further, if applicants are entitled to renounce the protection they receive from one country and claim protection from another, it gives them a right to emigrate to another country without complying with the usual requirements, solely by reason of their unilateral renunciation of the protection that they have been afforded by the country they are leaving.

*Pour-Shariati v. Canada (Minister of Employment & Immigration)* (1997), 39 Imm. L.R. (2d) 103, 215 N.R. 174 (Fed. C.A.) — Indirect persecution does not constitute persecution within the meaning of Convention refugee. The concept of indirect persecution goes directly against the decision of the Court of Appeal in *Rizkallah v. Canada (Minister of Employment & Immigration)* (1992), 156 N.R. 1 (Fed. C.A.), where it was held that there had to be a personal nexus between the claimant and the alleged persecution on one of the Convention grounds. The Convention ground of "membership in a particular social group" is a ground which allows for family concerns in an appropriate case. In addition s. 46.04(1) and 46.04(3) allow for the landing of dependants of refugees.

*Kadenko v. Canada (Solicitor General)* (1996), 143 D.L.R. (4th) 532, 206 N.R. 272, 124 F.T.R. 160 (note) (Fed. C.A.); leave to appeal to S.C.C. refused (sub nom. *Kadenko v. Canada (Solliciteur général))* 218 N.R. 80 (note) (S.C.C.) — Once it is assumed that the state has political and judicial institutions capable of protecting its citizens, it is clear that the refusal of certain police officers to take action cannot in itself make the state incapable of doing so. If the refusal to take action could be said to be that of the police as an institution or to be more or less a general refusal by the police force to provide the protection conferred by the country's political and judicial institutions the answer might have been different.

When the state in question is a democratic state the claimant must do more than simply show that he or she went to see some members of the police force and that his or her efforts were unsuccessful. The burden of proof that rests on the claimant is in a way directly proportional to the level of democracy in the state in question: the more democratic the state's institutions, the more the claimant must have done to exhaust all the courses of action open to him or her.

*Martinez v. Canada (Minister of Citizenship & Immigration)* (1996), 114 F.T.R. 113 (Fed. T.D.) — The applicant sought to review a negative decision of the CRDD. The applicant is a citizen of El Salvador, by reason of his mother's nationality, and of Belize, by reason of his birth. The applicant's mother alleged before the CRDD a well-founded fear of persecution in El Salvador based on her membership in a particular social group.

The applicant's mother and two of her three children were found to be Convention refugees as against El Salvador, but the applicant as a citizen of Belize was found not to have a well-founded fear of persecution in that country.

It is unnecessary to extend the plain meaning of the words Convention refugee to include the principle of family unity. The principle of family unity is enshrined in the *Immigration Act* by s. 46.04(1) and (3). None of the exceptions or limitations provided for in the two subsections in any way limit the applicant's mother's right to apply for landing in Canada for herself and the applicant, or the obligation of an immigration officer to grant landing in the event of such an application is made. Accordingly the application for judicial review was dismissed.

*Wassiq v. Canada (Minister of Citizenship & Immigration)* (1996), 33 Imm. L.R. (2d) 238, 112 F.T.R. 143 (T.D.) — The applicants applied to review a negative decision of the IRB. The applicants were citizens of Afghanistan. In 1981, they successfully applied as Convention refugees in Germany. In 1991, they left Germany and came to Canada and sought refugee status here.

A panel of the IRB had decided that the applicants had a well-founded fear of persecution in respect of Afghanistan, but that Canada had assumed responsibility for them and that Germany was obliged to allow them to return. Therefore, the Board found that the convention did not apply to the applicants by virtue of section E of Article 1.

Refugee claims were never meant to allow a claimant to seek out better protection than that from which he or she already benefitted. If by reason of their absence from Germany and sojourn in Canada, the applicants were in effect entitled to renounce the protection they received from Germany and claim protection from Canada, such a result would be anomalous. In substance, it would give a person who had Convention refugee status in one country the right to emigrate to another country without complying with the usual requirements.

Whether Canada or Germany should be responsible for the applicants should ideally be determined as between the governments of Canada and Germany. A decision of a panel of IRB, that Germany should have responsibility for the applicants which is in effect the decision in this case, is not binding on Germany. The real issue is whether Germany recognizes that the applicants may return.

On the evidence before it, the panel could not have arrived at such a conclusion and therefore could not have found that section E of Article 1 was applicable to the applicants. Accordingly, the application for judicial review was allowed and the matter remitted back to a differently constituted panel.

*Badran v. Canada (Minister of Citizenship & Immigration)* (1996), 111 F.T.R. 211 (Fed. T.D.) — The applicant sought judicial review of a negative decision of the IRB. The applicant in the instant case was a member of a particular social group: his family. He was also a member of a group which can be labelled "The Children of Police Officers Who Are Anti-terrorist Supporters". The evidence before the tribunal established that the authorities were effectively unable to protect the children of police officers and the documentary evidence supported that statement.

It is very difficult for a state to effectively protect its citizens against terrorism. In most cases, the inability to protect against random terrorist attacks will not constitute an inability of the state to protect. There is a limited exception to this however, where past, personal incidents qualify an individual as a member of the particular social group which the state is unable to protect. In the present case, there was a specifically and directly targeted applicant who was a member of a small targeted group and this distinguished the applicant's case from most cases which involved random instances of terrorism.

The negative decision of the IRB was set aside and the matter sent back to the same panel on the same record for a redetermination in the manner not inconsistent with the court's reasons.

*Kanagaratnam v. Canada (Minister of Employment & Immigration)* (1996), 36 Imm. L.R. (2d) 180, 194 N.R. 46 (Fed. C.A.) — The Refugee Board determined that the appellant, a native of Sri Lanka, had an internal flight alternative (IFA) within her country, and did not think it necessary to decide that the appellant otherwise had a well-founded fear of persecution. A motion was brought for judicial review and the trial Judge dismissed the motion but certified a question for appeal, namely, whether a determination of whether a claimant has a well-founded fear of persecution in the area from which he or she originates, is a prerequisite to the consideration of an IFA.

In assessing whether a viable IFA exists, the Board, of course, must have regard to all the appropriate circumstances. Since an IFA existed, therefore, the claimant, by definition, could not have a well-founded fear of persecution in her country of nationality. Thus, while the Board may certainly do so if it chooses, there was no need, as a matter of law, for the Board to decide whether there was persecution in the area of origin as a prerequisite to the consideration of an IFA.

*Chan v. Canada (Minister of Employment & Immigration)*, [1995] 3 S.C.R. 593, 187 N.R. 321, 128 D.L.R. (4th) 213 (S.C.C.) — The appellant held a managerial position at a manufacturing company, and owned a restaurant business. He fled to Hong Kong in 1990 and proceeded to Canada where he sought Convention refugee status based on his fear of persecution because of his political opinion and membership in a particular social group. The panel found that the appellant did not have good grounds for fearing persecution based on his membership in a particular social group, relying on the fact that there was no evidence adduced to suggest that the appellant was persecuted beyond the period of the Cultural Revolution. A panel of the CRDD also found that the appellant did not have good grounds for fearing persecution by reason of his political opinion manifested through his pro-democracy activities.

The appellant, who was a male, also claimed to fear sterilization due to the fact that he had fathered more children than the government of China's family planning policy permitted. Sterilization was found by the panel not, in itself, to be a form of persecution. Further, due to the fact that the appellant testified that he did not wish to have any more children, and due to a lack of evidence to suggest that the appellant would be physically abused during the sterilization process, the CRDD panel found that the appellant's fear of persecution was not well founded. The appellant appealed only on the issue of forced sterilization. The appeal was dismissed with one justice dissenting.

The appellant was required to demonstrate a well-founded fear of sterilization. The majority accepted the fact that the United Nations Handbook on Procedures and Criteria for Determining Refugee Status (Geneva 1979) although not binding on the Court was highly persuasive authority in Canada. The appellant was not required to prove that persecution would be more likely than not in order to meet the objective portion of the refugee test. That test is more appropriately described as requiring the appellant to demonstrate a serious possibility of persecution.

The appellant testified with the assistance of an interpreter. The task of an interpreter in a judicial or quasi-judicial hearing is an extremely difficult one. Simultaneous translation can lead to minor infelicities of style. The Board and the Court, when reviewing the written record, are well equipped to look past grammatical errors and to grasp the general import of a claimant's testimony, particularly when that testimony is considered as a whole. This is a fundamental part of the sympathetic approach to the evidence. It is the responsibility of the presiding member of the Board to ensure that the interpretation provided to the Board and reflected in the written record is as accurate as possible. The appellant's testimony, even with respect to his own fear of forced sterilization, was equivocal and inconsistent.

The evidence of the appellant with respect to his subjective fear of forced sterilization was equivocal, however, in the absence of an explicit finding by the Board on this point, it would not be appropriate for the Supreme Court of Canada to determine that the appellant did not have a subjective fear. Even if the appellant is given the benefit of the doubt on the question of his subjective fear it is the responsibility of the appellant to lay an evidentiary foundation upon which the Board can conclude not only that the fear existed in the mind of the appellant, but also that it was objectively well founded.

The objective component of the refugee test requires an examination of the objective situation and the relevant factors include the conditions in the appellant's country of origin, and the laws in that country, together with the manner in which they are applied. The appellant did not meet the burden of proof on the objective aspect of the test. The appellant failed to adduce any evidence that his fear of forced sterilization was objectively well founded. The appellant failed to adduce any evidence that forced sterilization was actually carried out and not merely threatened by the local authorities in his area. Evidence with respect to the enforcement procedures utilized in the particular region where the appellant lives, at the relevant time, should be presented to the Board. Where such evidence is not available in documentary form, the appellant may still be able to establish that the fear was objectively well founded by providing testimony with respect to similarly situated individuals. This liberal approach to establishing the facts represents a relaxation of the usual rules of evidence and is intended to grant the appellant the benefit of the doubt in cases where strict documentary evidence may be lacking.

The appellant failed to provide either documentary evidence or anecdotal evidence to substantiate his claim that the pressure from the Chinese authorities to submit to sterilization would extend beyond psychological and financial pressure to actual physical coercion. The benefit of the doubt should only be given to a refugee claimant when all available evidence has been obtained and checked and a panel is satisfied as to the claimant's general credibility. The refugee claimant's statements must be coherent and plausible, and must not run counter to generally known facts.

With respect to sterilization the available evidence shows that the Chinese authorities attempt to persuade couples with more than one child to submit to sterilization by psychological, social and financial pressure, including heavy fines. The primary agent of enforcement is the woman's work unit, but such measures can include other family members, specifically, in the case of government control licenses such as driver's licenses. The generally known facts suggest that some, but not all local authorities exceed these measures and resort to physical compulsion primarily against women.

In light of the fact that not all persons who have breached the one-child policy in China face a reasonable chance of forced sterilization, the appellant was required to establish a well-founded fear of forced sterilization before he could attempt to rely on that type of persecutory treatment. On the basis of the oral testimony, and the documentary evidence presented, forced sterilization remained no more than a mere possibility. In the absence of that evidence it was open to the Board to conclude that it could not determine that the appellant had a well-founded fear of persecution in the form of a forced sterilization. Accordingly, in the opinion of the majority, the appeal was dismissed.

*Al-Maisri v. Canada (Minister of Employment & Immigration)* (1995), 183 N.R. 234 (Fed. C.A.) — The appellant, a citizen of Yemen, claimed a well-founded fear of persecution by reason of political opinion. Yemen had supported Iraq during the invasion of Kuwait and the appellant, when he was called up to serve in the Yemenese army, deserted rather than go to Iraq by way of Jordan, to fight in the Iraqi Army.

The Refugee Division rejected the claim on the ground that the appellant would face prosecution in Yemen for deserting his country's military rather than persecution for political opinion.

Iraq's invasion of Kuwait was condemned by the United Nations and the annexation of Kuwait by Iraq was declared by the U.N. to be null and void.

The Court was persuaded that Iraq's actions were contrary to the basic rules of human conduct and following the guidance afforded by paragraph 171 of the UNHCR Handbook, concluded that any punishment for desertion visited upon the appellant if he returned to Yemen would amount to persecution of which the appellant had a well-founded fear.

The appeal was allowed and the applicant was declared to be a Convention refugee.

*Isa v. Canada (Secretary of State)* (1995), 91 F.T.R. 71 (T.D.) — The applicant comes from Somalia. The applicant fled Mogadishu and went to live in the Gedo region of Somalia. Subsequent to that the applicant and his family fled to Kenya and then eventually came to Canada. The applicant's claim was dismissed on the basis that the applicant demonstrated merely a general fear arising out of civil war and anarchy, and not persecution for a Convention reason.

A situation of civil war does not preclude an individual being found a Convention refugee. The individual must demonstrate that his or her fear arose because reprehensible acts were likely to be committed against members of a group to which he or she belonged, or against all citizens as a result of one of the reasons identified in the Convention definition of a refugee. A case will fail if it falls short of establishing that the applicants were collectively targeted differently from the general victims of a civil war. Many, if not most, civil war situations are racially or ethnically based. If racially motivated attacks in civil war circumstances alone could constitute grounds for Convention refugee status, then all individuals on either side of the conflict would qualify for refugee status.

*Castellanos v. Canada (Minister of Citizenship & Immigration)* (1994), 84 F.T.R. 316 (T.D.) — The applicant was a Cuban citizen as were his two daughters. His wife was a citizen of what was formerly the Soviet Union and she lived with her husband and children in Cuba on a renewable five-year visa.

The husband was found to be a Convention refugee; his wife and two daughters were not. With respect to the wife of the principal applicant the Board erred in finding that she was a Ukrainian citizen. The decision refusing her claim was quashed and an order was made directing a new hearing.

The status of the two daughters raised the question of whether family unity was a concept recognized by Canadian refugee law. The principle of family unity requires that persons granted refugee status should not be separated from their closest family members, particularly when a situation of dependency exists. The Court found that there was no mention of family unity in the current definition of a Convention refugee, and that therefore, in order to apply the principle of family unity, it would have to extend the definition. The Court found no justification for doing so.

For a person to be considered a Convention refugee it must be shown that the person is a member of one of five enumerated classes. The class of membership in a particular social group is the basket clause of this definitional provision. The family has been accepted as a social group for purposes of a Refugee definition. One will not be deemed a Convention refugee just because one has a relative that is being persecuted. There has to be a clear nexus between the persecution that is being levelled against one of the family members and that which is taking place against the others. A family can only be considered a social group in cases where there is evidence that the persecution is taking place against the family members as a social group. Here the Board found no evidence that any persecutory activity had been levelled against the mother or the daughters, let alone any based upon their being members of the principal applicant's family. Their claims were not well founded. Finally, the Court was not prepared to accept the principle of indirect persecution as defined in *Bhatti v. Canada (Secretary of State)* (1994), 25 Imm. L.R. (2d) 275, 84 F.T.R. 145 (Fed. T.D.) as part of our refugee law. The Court held that indirect persecution did not constitute persecution within the meaning of the definition of Convention refugee.

The Court found that s. 46.04 was the legislative response to the principle of family unity.

*Ramirez v. Canada (Solicitor General)* (1994), 88 F.T.R. 208 — This was an application to review a negative decision of the CRDD. The panel declined to describe the harm suffered by the applicant in her native Nicaragua as persecution. The Court noted that discrimination will only amount to persecution where it is serious or systematic enough to be characterized as persecution and, secondly, that the dividing line between discrimination and persecution is difficult to establish with the result that the Court will not intervene unless the conclusion reached by the panel "appears to be capricious or unreasonable".

In this case the conclusion reached by the panel was neither and the application for judicial review was dismissed.

*Fosu v. Canada (Minister of Employment & Immigration)* (1994), 27 Imm. L.R. (2d) 95, 90 F.T.R. 182 — The applicant is a Jehovah's Witness and claimed religious persecution based on the enforcement of legislation in Ghana restricting the public activities of the applicant's religion. The claim was unsuccessful because a panel determined that the legislation prohibited religious services but did not prevent individual members from worshipping God.

The right to freedom of religion also includes the right to demonstrate one's religion or belief in public or in private by teaching, practise, worship and the performance of rites. The persecution of the practise of religion can take various forms such as prohibiting worshipping in public, or giving or receiving religious instruction or the implementation of serious discriminatory practises against persons on account of their religion. The prohibition against Jehovah's Witnesses to practice their religion could amount to persecution and the panel was obliged to consider this matter which it failed to do. Accordingly, the decision of the panel was set aside and the matter remitted for determination.

*Gil v. Canada (Minister of Employment & Immigration)* (1994), 25 Imm. L.R. (2d) 209, 174 N.R. 292, 119 D.L.R. (4th) 497, [1995] 1 F.C. 508 (C.A.) — This case raised the question of what is meant by the phrase a "serious non-political crime" in section F of Article 1 of the Convention.

The appellant is an Iranian citizen, the son of a wealthy family which had been an active supporter of the Shah's regime. The family experienced considerable difficulties after the coming into power of the government that overthrew the Shah. The appellant joined an underground student group and, in due course, became associated with a larger militant group of anti-government activists. In the years 1980 and 1981 the appellant personally took part in five or six incidents of bombing and arson. Those attacks were directed against wealthy supporters of the regime. These incidents led to the injury and death of innocent bystanders. The appellant was arrested and interrogated by the authorities but never confessed to his activities and he was ultimately released by the authorities, without being charged, and eventually fled to Canada.

A panel of the CRDD found that the appellant had a well-founded fear of persecution but that he was excluded by the provision in section 1F(b) of the Convention.

A panel of the CRDD concluded that the appellant's crimes were non-political. Accordingly, the appeal raised the question of what was meant by political crime. The characterization of crimes as political is found in both extradition and refugee law. The Court noted that there was a need for even greater caution characterizing the crime as political for the purposes of applying section 1F(b) than for the purpose of denying extradition. The Court developed an incidence test as a means of resolving whether a crime is political. The appellant met the first branch of the test because Iran, in the years in question, was a turbulent society in which a number of armed groups were in conflict with the regime and the appellant's testimony that he was a member of one such group was accepted as credible. The appellant's claim failed the second branch of the test. There was no objective rational connection between injuring the commercial interests of certain wealthy supporters of the government and any realistic goal of forcing the regime itself to fall or change. Further, the means used by the appellant excluded his crimes from any claim to be political in nature. The attacks were not carried out against armed adversaries and were bound to injure innocent bystanders. The use of deadly force against unarmed civilian commercial targets in circumstances where serious injury or death to innocent bystanders was inevitable rendered the violence used wholly disproportionate to any legitimate political objective.

*Khatib v. Canada (Minister of Citizenship & Immigration)* (1994), 83 F.T.R. 310 — The Court noted that in *Ward v. Canada (Minister of Employment & Immigration)*, [1993] 2 S.C.R. 689, the applicant was a citizen of a state which admitted that it could not provide protection. The discussion and conclusions reached in *Ward*, in the opinion of the Court, applied only to citizens of a state, and not to stateless people. A stateless person is not expected to avail himself or herself of state protection when there is no duty on the state to provide such protection.

*Bediako v. Canada (Minister of Employment & Immigration)*, 1994 CarswellNat 1590 (Fed. T.D.) — The applicant had a well-founded subjective and objective fear of persecution when he left Ghana. The Board concluded that the objective fear of the applicant had been removed by changes in the country conditions between December 31, 1991, when the applicant left that country, and December 30, 1992, when the Board heard evidence of the applicant's claim.

The Board, in deciding whether there has been a change in country conditions, is required to give a sufficient analysis of the conflicting documentary evidence before it. There was, in this case, a very extensive analysis of the change in country conditions and, accordingly, that aspect of the Board's decision cannot be criticized.

Country changes have to be meaningful, effective and durable. In this case there was documentary evidence that showed that democracy was not working perfectly in Ghana, however, the Board addressed in detail the changes in country conditions and found them to be fundamental and durable enough to eliminate the objective basis for the applicant's fear. Accordingly, the application was dismissed.

*Hassan v. Canada (Minister of Employment & Immigration)* (1994), 174 N.R. 74 (Fed. C.A.) — The appellant claimed refugee status for herself and for her four children. She was a member of the Issaq clan. She and her husband operated a small grocery store in Northern Somalia. She and her husband suffered at the hands of police in the months leading up to the outbreak of hostilities in 1988. After that time their grocery store was destroyed and her husband fled the country never to be seen again. The appellant herself fled to Canada and claimed refugee status in 1989.

The decision of the Board was set aside. The issue was not whether the difficulties the appellant had experienced in the past constituted persecution, nor was it whether the appellant had been singled out for harassment while in Somalia. The issue was whether the appellant could reasonably fear persecution in the future simply by being a member of the Issaq clan.

It is clear that the status of refugee is attached to an individual and is granted on the basis that this individual needs protection from personal harm and persecution that he or she may suffer in his or her country over and above what would come from a state of general oppression affecting all the inhabitants of the country. This principle relates to the objective fear, not to its well-foundedness or reasonability. It has nothing to do with the question of whether one may have a reasonable fear of being personally a victim of persecution for the sole reason that he or she belongs to a specific targeted group whose members are indiscriminately subject to persecution. It is this question which was at the heart of the appellant's claim. The Board missed the point and as a result its decision did not dispose of the real issue.



*Papu v. Canada (Minister of Employment & Immigration)*, 1994 CarswellNat 1587 (Fed. T.D.) — It is well established that the determination of whether an individual's treatment is sufficiently serious to constitute persecution is to be left to the members of the Board. Most states have measures which provide for the derogation of civil rights temporarily in a time of emergency. This derogation of civil rights does not necessarily amount to "persecution".

*Chun v. Canada (Minister of Employment & Immigration)*, 1994 CarswellNat 1605 (Fed. T.D.) — The Court construed the Federal Court of Appeal decision in *Cheung v. Canada (Minister of Employment & Immigration)* (1993), 19 Imm. L.R. (2d) 81 (Fed. C.A.), as standing for the proposition that women in China who have more than one child and are faced with forced sterilization form a particular social group so as to come within the meaning of the definition Convention refugee. The Court also determined that the Court of Appeal found in *Cheung* that even if forced sterilization was accepted as a law of general application, that fact would not necessarily prevent a claim to Convention refugee status.

The Court allowed this application for judicial review because the panel that reached a negative decision in this case did not have the benefit of the decision of the Court of Appeal in *Cheung*.

*Equizabal v. Canada (Minister of Employment & Immigration)*, [1994] 3 F.C. 514, 24 Imm. L.R. (2d) 277, 170 N.R. 329 (Fed. C.A.) — The appellant was denied refugee status on the basis that he was included in Article 1F of the Convention and therefore excluded from the definition of refugee. The specific finding of the CRDD was that the appellant had committed crimes against humanity by torturing civilians. The appellant sought and obtained leave to apply for judicial review, which application was dismissed. The Trial Division judge certified a serious question of general importance.

The appellant was a citizen of Guatemala who was forcibly recruited by the Guatemalan military. He described in his evidence before the CRDD four military missions which involved the torture of civilians. A crime against humanity is not only a domestic offence, but is rather an offence with the additional component of barbarous cruelty. On the uncontradicted evidence of the appellant, it is obvious that he was guilty of barbarous cruelty in the four incidents he described in his evidence.

The defence of obedience to the orders of a superior based on compulsion was also considered. The first matter to be assessed was whether the orders in issue were manifestly unlawful. A manifestly unlawful order must be one that offends the conscience of every reasonable right-thinking person. It must be an order which is obviously and flagrantly wrong. The Court had no difficulty in concluding that the orders here in issue were manifestly unlawful. The appellant and two other soldiers were ordered on one occasion to beat four persons and torture them over a period of three hours. Torturing the truth out of someone is manifestly unlawful, by any standard.

On the question of compulsion, the issue was whether the appellant faced an imminent, real and inevitable threat to his life. Stern punishment or demotion would not be sufficient. The appellant's evidence summarized two reasons why, notwithstanding his understanding that the penalty for desertion was only 12 months in jail, he would be killed: first, he knew of three other deserters who were apprehended and never heard from again; second, he believed he would be killed by his lieutenant because of his knowledge of relatives of persons whom the lieutenant had tortured personally. The first reason was dismissed as it was pure speculation without any credible evidence to support it. The second reason was not supported by the record. The record established that before the third mission, the appellant advised his lieutenant that he would no longer participate in such torture. As a result he was never forced to torture anyone again. He was thereafter, on two occasions, assigned to act as a guard while others did the torturing. There was, therefore, no evidence that the appellant was facing an imminent, real and inevitable threat to his life.

Accordingly, the appeal was dismissed and the decision that the appellant had committed a crime against humanity, as that expression appears in Article 1F of the Convention relating to the status of refugees, was upheld.

*Gonzalez v. Canada (Minister of Employment & Immigration)*, [1994] 3 F.C. 646, 24 Imm. L.R. (2d) 229, 170 N.R. 302, 115 D.L.R. (4th) 403 (C.A.) — This was an appeal from a decision of the Refugee Division, which found the appellant excluded from the definition of Convention refugee by reason of section F(a) of Article 1 of The United Nations Convention Relating to the Status of Refugees because the Board found there was serious reason to believe that the appellant had committed a crime against humanity. The Board proceeded directly to that finding and made no finding on the merits of the refugee claim. The appellant had admitted to killing civilians on two occasions when his military unit in Nicaragua encountered armed counter-revolutionaries. The Court noted that as a practical matter it would have been better had the Refugee Division dealt with the merits of the claim as well as the applicability of the exclusion. The Court noted that if the claim was well founded but for the application of the exclusion and if it were found on appeal that the exclusion had been wrongly applied to the appellant, then the Court could have made the necessary declaration without requiring the Refugee Division to deal with the matter again. The Court found that, on the particular facts and circumstances of this case, the appellant was a soldier engaged in an action against an armed enemy and that his actual participation in the killing of innocent civilians fell short of a crime against humanity. The Court indicated that it did not wish to be understood as saying that the killing of civilians by a soldier while engaged in an action against an armed enemy could never amount to a war crime or a crime against humanity; each case will depend on its own individual facts and circumstances.

*Roble v. Canada (Minister of Employment & Immigration)* (1994), 169 N.R. 125 (Fed. C.A.) — The appellant was born in Somalia and claimed a fear of persecution if he were returned at the hands of the National Security Service, which had been the security service used by former President Mohammed Siad Barre. The Board found as a fact that the National Security Service was no longer a factor in Somalia because the Barre government had been toppled.

The appellant submitted that when the political situation in a country is unstable and uncertain and an interim government is not yet in control, it is inappropriate for the appellant to be required to seek the protection of his state. There are situations in which the political and military circumstances in a country at a given time are such that it is impossible to speak of a government with control of the territory and able to provide effective protection. The non-existence of a government is not an obstacle to an application for refugee status. However, this statement of the law only applies to cases where a claimant has demonstrated a prospective risk of persecution based on one of the grounds enumerated in the definition. The finding that the agent of persecution — the NSS — was no longer a factor meant that the inability of the state to protect the appellant was not in itself sufficient basis for his claim.



*Fathi-Rad v. Canada (Secretary of State)* (1994), 77 F.T.R. 41 — The applicant sought review of a decision determining that she was not a Convention refugee. The applicant was a 51-year-old woman whose family supported the pre-revolutionary government and the People's Democratic Front in Iran. The applicant was arrested, detained and questioned approximately once every two months between 1985 and 1988 for her failure to conform to the Islamic dress code. In overruling the Board's decision, the Court concluded that the Islamic dress code in Iran was not a law of general application. The dress code applied only to women. It dictated the manner in which women must dress to comply with the religious beliefs of the governing regime and prescribed punishments for violation of that law. A law which specifically targets the manner in which women dress may not properly be characterized, as it was in this case, as a law of general application which applies to all citizens.

For this and other reasons the decision of the Board was set aside and the matter returned to a differently constituted panel for rehearing and redetermination.

*Rodriguez-Hernandez v. Canada (Secretary of State)* (1994), 76 F.T.R. 107 — The applicant, a citizen of Cuba, claimed persecution on the basis of religion and political opinion. The applicant left Cuba for Canada while he was in possession of a valid travel permit, which allowed him to be absent for 30 days. In determining whether the applicant faced persecution for overstaying his exit visa, the Board considered that Cuban exit laws are of general application. This finding alone did not end the matter, however, for the law must still be examined to determine whether it is persecutory. One indication that a general law is persecutory is a penalty which is disproportionate to the offence. The Board did not err in concluding that the potential punishment for violation of the Cuban exit laws by the applicant did not amount to persecution. The onus was on the applicant to bring evidence before the Board of the punishment to be faced upon return and to demonstrate that the punishment is disproportionate to the offence. This onus had not been met, and the application for judicial review was dismissed.

*Maarouf v. Canada (Minister of Employment & Immigration)* (1993), [1994] 1 F.C. 723, 23 Imm. L.R. (2d) 163, 72 F.T.R. 6 — The applicant lived in both Lebanon and Kuwait before going to the United States to study and then coming to Canada and claiming refugee status. The Board concluded that the applicant had neither a country of nationality nor a country of former habitual residence. The Board found that Kuwait was not a country of former habitual residence. Even though the claimant lived in that state for most of his life, on the claimant's uncontradicted evidence, there was no way he could return there. It was the claimant's evidence that Palestinians who left Kuwait prior to the Gulf War were not allowed to return. With respect to Lebanon, the Board found that the claimant only lived there for five years during his infancy and, that while he did visit Lebanon for a short period of time, there was no significant period of *de facto* residence.

The decision of the Board was quashed. The definition of country of former habitual residence should not be unduly restrictive so as to pre-empt the provision of surrogate shelter to a stateless person who has demonstrated a well-founded fear of persecution on any of the enumerated grounds in the definition. A country of former habitual residence should not be limited to the country where the claimant initially feared persecution. The claimant does not have to be legally able to return a country of former habitual residence as a denial of a right of return may in itself constitute an act of persecution by the state. The claimant must, however, have established a significant period of *de facto* residence in the country in question.

*Thirunavukkarasu v. Canada (Minister of Employment & Immigration)* (1993), [1994] 1 F.C. 589, 22 Imm. L.R. (2d) 241, 109 D.L.R. (4th) 682, 163 N.R. 232 (C.A.) — The appellant was a citizen of Sri Lanka and a Tamil. The appellant's claim that he faced serious risk to his life in the north of Sri Lanka was accepted but his claim for refugee status was refused on the basis that there was an internal flight alternative (IFA) available to him.

The Court had occasion to review the law on the question of IFAs in this judgment.

The notion of an IFA is not a legal defence and it is not a legal doctrine. It is a convenient, short-hand way of describing a fact situation in which a person may be in danger of persecution in one part of a country, but not in another. The idea of an IFA is inherent in the definition of a Convention refugee; it is not something separate. The definition requires that claimants have a well-founded fear of persecution which renders them unwilling or unable to return to their home country. If claimants are able to seek refuge within their own country, there is no basis for finding that they are unable or unwilling to avail themselves of the protection of that country.

The burden of proof with respect to an IFA is on the claimant. The claimant must show, on a balance of probabilities, a serious possibility of persecution throughout the country, including the area which is alleged to afford an IFA.

There is an obligation on the Minister or the Board to warn a claimant that the IFA issue will be raised. If the possibility of an IFA is raised, the claimant must demonstrate that there is a serious possibility of persecution in the area alleged to constitute an IFA. A refugee claimant enjoys the benefit of the privilege of natural justice in hearings before the Refugee Division. A basic and well-established component of the right to be heard includes notice of the case to be met. The purpose of this notice is to allow a person to prepare an adequate response. The right to notice of the case against the claimant is acutely important where the claimant may be called upon to provide evidence to show that no valid IFA exists in response to an allegation by the Minister. Therefore, neither the Minister nor the Refugee Division may spring the allegation of an IFA upon a complainant without notice that an IFA will be in issue at the hearing.

A claimant must seek and resort to an IFA if it is not unreasonable to do so in the circumstances of the individual claimant. This aspect of the test is a flexible one, that takes into account the particular situation of the claimant and the particular country involved. It is an objective test and the onus of proof rests on the claimant on this issue, just as it does with all other aspects of a refugee claim. Consequently, if there is a safe haven for claimants in their own country, where they would be free of persecution, they are expected to avail themselves of it unless they can show that it is objectively unreasonable for them to do so. It is not a question of whether the IFA is more or less appealing to the claimant than a new country. The question is whether, given the persecution in the claimant's part of the country, it is objectively reasonable to expect him or her to seek safety in a different part of that country before seeking a haven in Canada or elsewhere. Stated another way, the question to be answered is, would it be unduly harsh to expect the claimant, who is being persecuted in one part of his country, to move to another less hostile part of the country before seeking refugee status abroad?

An IFA cannot be speculative or theoretical. The alternative place of safety must be realistically accessible to the claimant. Any barriers getting there should be reasonably surmountable. The claimant cannot be required to encounter great physical danger or undergo undue hardship in travelling there or staying there. For example, claimants should not be required to cross battle lines where fighting is going on at great risk to their lives in order to reach a place of safety. Similarly, claimants should not be compelled to hide out in isolated regions of their country, like a cave in the mountains, or in a desert or in a jungle, if those are the only areas of internal safety. Neither is it enough for refugee claimants to say that they do not like the weather in a safe area, or that they have no friends or relatives there, or that they may not be able to find suitable work there. If it is objectively reasonable in these latter situations to live in those places, without fear of persecution, then an IFA exists and the claimant is not a refugee.

It is not a matter of a claimant's convenience or the attractiveness of the IFA, but whether one should be expected to make do in that location, before travelling half-way around the world to seek a safe haven in another country.

The finding of an IFA, in this case, by the IRB was not sustained. The Country Profile of Sri Lanka and the Amnesty International Reports on the country did not show "quite clearly" that Tamils were safe in the southwest of the country. The reports, at the time this case was argued, spoke of several violent incidents in which Tamils were persecuted by the Sri Lankan government in the southwest in retaliation for the activities of the LTTE and other Tamil groups. Accordingly, there was no IFA for this appellant and the appeal was allowed.

*Osoble v. Canada (Minister of Employment & Immigration)* (1993), 69 F.T.R. 184 — This was an application to review a negative determination of the applicant's refugee claim. The applicant was from Somalia and based his fear of persecution on his religious convictions, political opinion and membership in a particular social group.

The test for applicants who are from a country where a civil war is going on was set out in *Salibian v. Canada (Minister of Employment & Immigration)*, [1990] 3 F.C. 250, 11 Imm. L.R. (2d) 165, 73 D.L.R. (4th) 551, 113 N.R. 123 (Fed. C.A.). A situation of civil war is not an obstacle to a claim provided the fear felt is not that felt indiscriminately by all citizens as a consequence of the civil war, but a fear felt by the applicant himself or herself, or by a group of which he or she is associated, or on account of a risk of persecution based on one of the reasons stated in the definition.

*Petrescu v. Canada (Solicitor General) (sub nom. Petrescu c. Canada (Solliciteur général))* (1993), 73 F.T.R. 1. — The applicant was a Romanian claiming refugee status on account of his political opinion and membership in a particular social group. The Court elaborated on what was meant by a reasonable possibility of persecution and referred to

*Ponniah v. Canada (Minister of Employment & Immigration)* (1991), 13 Imm. L.R. (2d) 241, 132 N.R. 32 (Fed. C.A.):

> "Good grounds" or "reasonable chance" is defined in *Adjei* as occupying the field between upper and lower limits; it is less than a 50% chance (*i.e.* a probability), but more than a minimal or mere possibility. There is no intermediate ground: what falls between the two limits is "good grounds".
>
> If the claimant, as the Board said, "... may face slightly more than a mere possibility ..." of persecution, he had crossed the lower limit and had made his case of "good grounds" or a "reasonable chance" for fearing persecution.

In this case, it was said that the claimant, when he argued that he feared a repetition of what he had suffered if he returned home and that he was in danger of losing his liberty or being the victim of a staged accident, did not persuade the panel. The Refugee Division imposed too high a standard of proof. Accordingly, the decision of the Refugee Division was quashed.

*Kahlon v. King* (1993), 66 F.T.R. 219 — The CRDD determined that the applicant was not a Convention refugee because a viable internal flight alternative (IFA) existed. The applicant was a citizen of India who feared persecution in his native Punjab State. The CRDD accepted, as a fact, the assertion that it was unrealistic for the applicant to consider a return to the Punjab. The risk of persecution, if he were to return to that state, was not in question, but the CRDD found that there existed a viable IFA. The criteria relevant to an IFA were reviewed by the Federal Court of Appeal in *Rasaratnam v. Canada (Minister of Employment & Immigration)*, [1992] 1 F.C. 706, 140 N.R. 138 (Fed. C.A.). The IFA concept is inherent in the Convention refugee definition. The Board must be satisfied on a balance of probabilities that there is no serious possibility of the claimant being persecuted in that part of the country to which it finds an IFA exists. By definition a Convention refugee must be a refugee from a country, not from some subdivision or region of a country. Therefore, a claimant cannot be a Convention refugee if there is an IFA. Whether or not there is an IFA is integral to the determination of whether an applicant is or is not a refugee. The CRDD erred in failing to take into account the situations of individuals who were similarly situated to the applicant. It was not sufficient to take into account Sikhs in general living in India outside the Punjab or all Sikh men living in India outside the Punjab. The question before the tribunal was whether there was a serious possibility of the applicant being persecuted elsewhere in India. Accordingly, the decision of the CRDD was set aside and the matter referred back for rehearing before a differently constituted panel.

*Chan v. Canada (Minister of Employment & Immigration)*, [1993] 3 F.C. 675, 20 Imm. L.R. (2d) 181, 156 N.R. 279 (C.A.); affirmed [1995] 3 S.C.R. 593, 128 D.L.R. (4th) 213, 187 N.R. 321 — This was an appeal with leave from a decision of the Convention Refugee Determination Division of the Immigration and Refugee Board deciding that the appellant was not a Convention refugee.

The appellant was a citizen of the People's Republic of China (PRC). During the Cultural Revolution the appellant's family was persecuted due to his father's background as a landowner. During the students' pro-democracy demonstrations in 1989 the appellant expressed his support of the movement by giving food and drink to the students from his restaurant in Guangzhou Province. After the students' movement was crushed by the authorities and the appellant voluntarily reported his pro-democracy activities to the Public Security Bureau (PSB); officers visited his restaurant at least 13 times, interrogating him, his staff and his customers. In November 1989, the appellant's wife gave birth to a second child. When the PSB learned of this birth, they accused the appellant of violating the birth control policy of the PRC. Officers visited his home on a number of occasions after the birth of his child. The appellant was advised that either he or his wife would have to undergo sterilization. The appellant agreed to be sterilized but fled the PRC before the operation took place. The appellant claimed that after his departure his family continued to be harassed for violating the one-child policy.

There were three decisions given by the Court, namely: the majority (Heald J.A. and Desjardins J.A.) dismissed the appeal; the minority (Mahoney J.A.) would have allowed the appeal.

Heald J.A. was not convinced on the evidence that the appellant had a well-founded fear of persecution and this determination would normally have been sufficient to dispose of the appeal. However, His Lordship went on to discuss the meaning of the phrase "particular social group" and "political opinion" in his judgment. The particular social group was defined to be parents in China with more than one child, who disagree with forced sterilization. This group was found by Heald J.A. not to be encompassed by any of the categories identified by the Supreme Court of Canada in the *Ward* decision (*Ward v. Canada (Minister of Employment & Immigration)* (1993), 20 Imm. L.R. (2d) 85, [1993] 2 S.C.R. 689). This group was found to be defined solely by the fact that its members face a particular form of persecutory treatment. Membership in the group was dictated by the finding of persecution. This logic reversed the statutory definition and voided enumerated grounds of content. The appellant's fear stemmed from what he did and not from what he was.

Disagreement with the one-child policy is a political statement. There was no evidence that persons who simply voiced their opposition to this policy or to forced sterilization were not tolerated. On the question of whether the appellant who had breached the policy and failed to submit to the resulting demand for sterilization faced a well-founded fear of persecution, Heald J.A. answered in the negative. The persecutory treatment emanated not from a refusal to submit to sterilization, but from a breach of the policy. There was no indication that a breach of the one-child policy and a reluctance to undergo sterilization would be perceived by the central government or the local authorities as anything more than a breach of a law and a reluctance to undergo the ensuing penalty. The one-child policy is well within the jurisdiction of the Chinese government and there was a plethora of documentary evidence which articulated the rationale for this policy in China. Sanctions, in general, imposed for a breach of the policy must be accepted. A finding of persecution would have to be based uniquely on an abhorrence of the penalty. In other words the persecution alone motivates the determination of refugee status. Heald J.A. found that the definition of Convention refugee did not permit such a conclusion.

Desjardins J.A. agreed in the result and noted that, with respect to the phrase "particular social group", what links the members of the group together must be so fundamental that it cannot be changed and if it were to be changed, would destroy the person as a person. The unchangeable characteristic of a particular social group must be distinguished from the basic human right which the group might decide to defend. The innate characteristic must be so strong a factor that it makes a group of individuals what they are and it must exist independently of what they are fighting for. The appellant was one of a number of persons who, individually, had resisted the one-child policy and, like the others of his category, faced the general sanction, namely forced sterilization. This was not a group that was affiliated in a fundamental way so as to qualify as a particular social group. The group of which the appellant claimed to be a member was cognizable by the decision of the local Chinese authorities to use forced sterilization as a means of enforcing government policy. Thus, what linked the group together was an external factor and this was insufficient to meet the definition of the term particular social group.

With respect to the ground of "political opinion", Desjardins J.A. accepted that any opinion on any matter related to state affairs expressed or imputed to a claimant may constitute the basis for a claim under political opinion. Her Lordship, however, was unable to infer that the local authorities would impute to the appellant a political opinion in this case on account of his resistance to a general government policy. The evidence showed that there was continuing popular resistance to family planning in China and that birth rates soared the moment the pressure was eased. Her Lordship noted that the treatment, in the case at bar, related to forced sterilization. The Court assumed that this was carried out through normal procedures currently in use by those who voluntarily opt for this procedure elsewhere, including Canada. What was objected to was the absence of consent. Her Lordship concluded that, unless amended, the *Convention Relating to the Status of Refugees* would not cover violations of human rights imposed by local authorities in the pursuit of what the record showed is a legitimate state objective, namely population control.

Mahoney J.A. dissented and found this case undistinguishable from *Cheung v. Canada (Minister of Employment & Immigration)* (1993), 19 Imm. L.R. (2d) 81, [1993] 2 F.C. 314 (Fed. C.A.). He further found that none of the reasons which would justify a Court departing from its previous decisions were present in this case and therefore *Cheung* had to be followed. Thus, the appellant could not be said not to belong to a particular social group. Further, he was in profound disagreement with the notion that the legitimacy of population control excluded persecution in pursuit of it from the Convention refugee definition.

*Zolfagharkhani v. Canada (Minister of Employment & Immigration)*, 20 Imm. L.R. (2d) 1, [1993] 3 F.C. 540, 155 N.R. 311 (C.A.) — This was an appeal of a decision denying Convention refugee status to the appellant.

The appellant was an Iranian citizen who had served 27 months in the Iranian military during the Iran Iraq war. Subsequent to his discharge, the Revolutionary Guards requested him to report for a further six months of military service as a paramedic. The appellant reported for a one-month training course and during the last week of training discovered the apparent intention of his government to engage in chemical warfare against the Kurds. His conscience being troubled by this, he deserted and fled the country.

No issue was raised as to conscientious objection in relation to war in general. Since the appellant had no objection to serving in an active capacity in the Iranian military in the Iran/Iraq war, the issue as to conscientious objection relates solely to participation in chemical warfare.

The probable use of chemical weapons, which the Board accepted as a fact, was clearly judged by the international community to be contrary to basic rules of human conduct. Consequently, the ordinary Iranian conscription law of general application, as applied to a conflict in which Iran intended to use chemical weapons, amounted to persecution for political opinion.

The Court set forth the following general propositions relating to the status of an ordinary law of general application in determining the question of persecution:

1. The statutory definition of Convention refugee makes the intent or any principal effect of an ordinary law of general application, rather than the motivation of the claimant, relevant to the existence of persecution.

2. The neutrality of an ordinary law of general application, *vis-à-vis* the five grounds for refugee status, must be judged objectively by Canadian tribunals and courts when required.

3. In such consideration, an ordinary law of general application, even in non-democratic societies, should be given a presumption of validity and neutrality, and the onus should be on a claimant, as is generally the case in refugee cases, to show that the laws are either inherently or for some other reason persecutory.

4. It will not be enough for the claimant to show that a particular regime is generally oppressive, but rather that the law in question is persecutory in relation to a Convention ground.

The Court referred to *Abarca v. Canada (Minister of Employment & Immigration)*, 1986 CarswellNat 867, to the effect that a conscientious objector from El Salvador was a Convention refugee on the basis of political opinion because he probably would have been forced to participate in violent acts of persecution against non-combatant civilians, which conduct is contrary to recognized basic international principles of human rights. The Court also referred to *Cruz v. Canada (Minister of Employment & Immigration)* (1988), 10 Imm. L.R. (2d) 47 (Imm. App. Bd.), involving a deserter from the Mexican army. In the instant case there could be no doubt that the appellant's refusal to participate in the military action against the Kurds would be treated by the Iranian government as the expression of an unacceptable political opinion.

The appeal was allowed and the matter returned to a differently constituted panel for reconsideration not inconsistent with the reasons of the Court.

*Bouianova v. Canada (Minister of Employment & Immigration)* (1993), 67 F.T.R. 74 — The applicant was born in Komi, near Moscow in the former USSR. The applicant's place of birth is located in what is now Russia. Before coming to Canada the applicant had lived in Latvia for 14 years. The applicant claimed a well-founded fear of persecution in Latvia based on discrimination against ethnic Russians in that country. Latvia had been her country of habitual residence. The panel found that the applicant was a citizen of the Russian Federation and that there was no evidence that she had a well-founded fear of persecution in Russia. In order to become a Russian citizen, all that the applicant had to do was make an application to the Russian Embassy requesting Russian citizenship and have her USSR passport so stamped. The applicant did not do this and her counsel in this proceeding sought to claim that she was therefore stateless.

Statelessness was not an option for the applicant. The condition of not having a country of nationality must be one that is beyond the power of the applicant to control. Otherwise, a person could claim statelessness merely by renouncing his or her former citizenship.

*Ward v. Canada (Minister of Employment & Immigration)* (1993), 20 Imm. L.R. (2d) 85, [1993] 2 S.C.R. 689, (sub nom. *Canada (Attorney General) v. Ward)* 103 D.L.R. (4th) 1, 153 N.R. 321, [1993] S.C.J. No. 74, [1997] I.N.L.R. 42, 1993 CarswellNat 1382, 1993 CarswellNat 90 — The appellant was born in Northern Ireland in 1955. He joined the Irish National Liberation Army (INLA) in 1983 as a volunteer. The INLA is a paramilitary organization, more violent than the Irish Republican Army (IRA), with a military-like hierarchy and strict discipline. The appellant's first task as a member of the INLA was to assist in guarding two of the organization's hostages. After he commenced his duties the INLA ordered the hostages executed. The appellant underwent what he described as "a predicament of moral conscience" and released the hostages without revealing himself to the INLA. Sometime later the police let slip to an INLA member that one of their own had assisted the hostages in their escape. The appellant was court-martialled and sentenced to death, but managed to escape. He was charged in the hostage incident and while in police custody the INLA kidnapped his wife and children to prevent him from becoming an informant.

The appellant was sentenced to three years in prison. He did not become an informant and never publicly admitted having released the hostages. Toward the end of his prison sentence he obtained a Republic of Ireland passport and on his release entered Canada as a visitor in December, 1985. He claimed refugee status in 1986. Under the procedures that were in effect at that time the Minister determined that the appellant was not a Convention refugee. The appellant applied for redetermination of his claim to the Immigration Appeal Board, as it was then known. The Board allowed the redetermination and found him to be a Convention refugee.

The Attorney General brought an application in the Federal Court to set aside the Board's decision, which decision was successful. The result of the Federal Court decision was that the appellant's case was referred back to the Immigration Appeal Board for reconsideration.

The Board again found the appellant to be a Convention refugee. The Minister appealed the Board's decision to the Federal Court of Appeal, which set aside the Board's decision. The appellant then appealed that decision to the Supreme Court of Canada.

International refugee law was formulated to serve as a back-up to the protection one expects from the state of which an individual is a national. It was meant to come into play only in situations when that protection is unavailable, and then only in certain situations. The international community intended that persecuted individuals be required to approach their home state for protection before the responsibility of other states became engaged.

The onus of proof in a refugee proceeding is on the claimant and it is for the claimant to show a well-founded fear of persecution in all countries of which the claimant is a national. In this case the appellant was a national not only of the Republic of Ireland, but also of Great Britain and there was therefore a burden upon him to prove that he was a refugee from both countries before Canada's obligation could be engaged.

State complicity in persecution is not a prerequisite to a valid refugee claim. The claimant must establish a "well-founded fear". The claimant must be outside his or her country of nationality because of that fear and unable to avail him- or herself of its protection. Alternatively, the claimant must be both outside his or her country of nationality and unwilling to avail himself or herself of its protection by reason of that well-founded fear. If a state is able to protect a claimant, then his or her fear is not, objectively speaking, well founded. Persecution under the Convention includes situations where the state is not an accomplice to the persecution, but is simply unable to protect its citizens.

Being unable to avail oneself of state protection implies circumstances that are beyond the will of the person concerned. There may, for example, be a state of war, civil war or other grave disturbance which prevents the country of nationality from extending protection. Protection by the country of nationality may also have been denied to the claimant. Such denial may confirm or strengthen the claimant's fear of persecution and may indeed be an element of the persecution. The term "unwilling" in the definition refers to refugees who refuse to accept the protection of the country of nationality. Where a person is willing to avail himself or herself of the protection of his or her home country, such willingness would be incompatible with a claim that he or she is outside that country owing to a well-founded fear of persecution. Whenever the protection of the country of nationality is available and there is no ground based on well-founded fear for refusing it, the person concerned is not in need of international protection and is not a refugee. Ineffective state protection is encompassed within the concept of "unable" and "unwilling". In cases of "inability", protection is denied to the claimant, whereas when the claimant is "unwilling", he or she opts not to approach the state by reason of his or her fear on one of the enumerated bases. In either case, the state's involvement in the persecution is not a necessary consideration.



Where the existence of a fear is established and where the state's inability to protect is established, it is not assuming too much to say that the fear is well founded. The burden of showing a state's inability to protect rests on the claimant and can only be discharged by the adducing of clear and convincing confirmation of this inability to protect. In this particular case the proof was unnecessary as representatives of the state authorities conceded their inability to protect the appellant. Nations should be presumed to be capable of protecting their citizens. Security of nationals is the essence of sovereignty. Absent a situation where the state apparatus has completely broken down, such as that recognized in Lebanon in the *Zalzali* case, [1991] 3 F.C. 605, it should be assumed that the state is capable of protecting its nationals.

The appellant justified his claim to refugee status on the basis of a well-founded fear of persecution at the hands of the INLA by reason of his membership in a particular social group, *i.e.*, the INLA. A good working rule to determine the meaning of "particular social group" is set out in the test proposed in *Canada (Minister of Employment & Immigration) v. Mayers* (1992), 97 D.L.R. (4th) 729; *Acosta, Re* 2986, 919850 WL 56042 (B.I.A.); and *Cheung v. Canada (Minister of Employment & Immigration)*, (1993), 19 Imm. L.R. (2d) 81 (Fed. T.D.). Those cases identify three possible categories:

1. groups defined by an innate or unchangeable characteristic;
2. groups whose members voluntarily associate for reasons so fundamental to their human dignity that they should not be forced to forsake the association; and
3. groups associated by a former voluntary status, unalterable due to its historical permanence.

The INLA did not meet these three tests and was therefore not a particular social group.

However, it is for the examiner to decide whether the Convention definition is met; usually there will be more than one ground for the well-founded fear of persecution. In this case the Court considered whether the appellant had a well-founded fear of persecution for reasons of his political opinion. He believed that the killing of innocent people to achieve political change was unacceptable and thus his persecution by the INLA stemmed from that belief, which was held by the Supreme Court of Canada to be a political opinion. Any opinion on any matter in which the machinery of state, government and policy may be engaged is a political opinion. The political opinion need not have been expressed outright by the claimant and need not conform to the claimant's true beliefs.

Not just any dissent to any organization will unlock the gates to Canadian asylum; the disagreement has to be rooted in political conviction.

The appeal was allowed. The decision of the Court of Appeal was set aside. The case was remitted back to the Immigration and Refugee Board so that it could determine whether the appellant was also a refugee from Great Britain, his second country of nationality.

*Ling v. Canada (Minister of Employment & Immigration)* (1993), 64 F.T.R. 182 — The expression "a reasonable chance of persecution" has been held by the Appeal Division of the Federal Court to be an apt equivalent for a "well-founded fear of persecution".

The Court approved the following comments of MacGuigan J.A. in *Adjei v. Canada (Minister of Employment & Immigration)*, [1989] 2 F.C. 680, 7 Imm. L.R. (2d) 169, 57 D.L.R. (4th) 153, 132 N.R. 24 (C.A.):

> The fear of persecution in the definition has a two-fold aspect. On the one hand, the applicant must experience a subjective fear. A man with great fortitude may not have a subjective fear of persecution until adverse circumstances are worse for him than for his less courageous fellow countryman; nevertheless such a fear must be present in the mind of the applicant for the definition of Convention refugee to be met. The appropriate test as to whether or not a subjective fear exists is that appropriate for determining the existence of other matters of fact in a case of this kind, namely balance of probabilities.
>
> The second aspect is the objective element. The subjective fear of the applicant ... must have an objective basis.

The decision of the Board was unexceptionable, and not to be disturbed. Accordingly, the application to quash the decision of the Convention Refugee Determination Division was dismissed.

*Ghazizadeh v. Canada (Minister of Employment & Immigration)* (1993), 154 N.R. 236 (Fed. C.A.) — The whole concept of a refugee "*sur place*" requires an assessment of the situation in the applicant's country of origin after she or he has left it. The fact that the departure may have been perfectly legal is nothing to the point.

*Cheung v. Canada (Minister of Employment & Immigration)* (1993), 19 Imm. L.R. (2d) 81, 153 N.R. 145 (Fed. C.A.) — In 1984 Ting Ting Cheung gave birth to a baby boy in the People's Republic of China. She had another child in 1987 and came to the attention of the Family Planning Bureau in her native province. Shortly after the pro-democracy demonstrations in Beijing she came to Canada and claimed to be a refugee.

The first question was whether women in China who have more than one child and are faced with forced sterilization constitute a social group within the meaning of the definition of "Convention refugee". The Court indicated that the following criteria provide a useful basis for consideration in constructing a test for being a particular social group:

> (1) a natural or non-natural group of persons with (2) similar shared background, habits, social status, political outlook, education, values, aspirations, history, economic activity or interests, often interests contrary to those of the prevailing government, and (3) sharing basic, innate, unalterable characteristics, consciousness, and solidarity or (4) sharing a temporary but voluntary status, with the purpose of their association being so fundamental to their human dignity that they should not be required to alter it.

The Court concluded that women in China who have one child and are faced with forced sterilization satisfy enough of the above criteria to be considered a particular social group. This did not mean that all women in China who have more than one child may automatically claim Convention refugee status. It is only those women who also have a well-founded fear of persecution as a result of membership in that social group who can claim such status.

The next question was whether forced or strongly coerced sterilization in the context of China's one-child policy constituted persecution. The Immigration and Refugee Board had concluded that forced sterilization in that context was not persecution. The Court disagreed.

The Court noted that forced sterilization of women was a violation of Articles 3 and 5 of the United Nations Universal Declaration of Human Rights. This declaration was adopted and proclaimed December 10, 1948 by the General Assembly of the United Nations.

Karen Lee Cheung was the second child, whose birth was contrary to the one-child policy. The Court found that the minor could also claim the benefit of Convention refugee status on the principle of family unity. Finally, there being no problems as to the credibility of the adult claimant, nor any factual questions that needed to be resolved by the Board, the Court exercised its discretion under subs. 52(c)(i) of the *Federal Court Act* and declared both appellants to be Convention refugees.

*Canada (Minister of Employment & Immigration) v. Villafranca* (1992), 18 Imm. L.R. (2d) 130, 99 D.L.R. (4th) 334, 150 N.R. 232 (Fed. C.A.) — The respondent was a Philippine national who served in his home country as a policeman. He fled because he had been marked for death by a communist terrorist guerilla group and he feared for his life. The Refugee Division found him credible and held that he did have a well-founded fear of persecution by reason of his political opinion.

The Refugee Division failed to address the question of whether the respondent was unable or unwilling to avail himself of the protection of the Philippines. Where the claimant is himself an agent of the state, it makes no sense to speak of him as being unwilling to seek the state's protection. The claim can only succeed if he shows that he is unable to do so. The burden of showing that one is not able to avail oneself of the protection of one's own state is not easily satisfied. The test is an objective one and involves the claimant showing either that he is physically prevented from seeking his government's aid or that the government itself is in some way prevented from giving it. No government that makes any claim to democratic values can guarantee the protection of all of its citizens at all times. Thus, it is not enough for a claimant to show that his government has not always been effective at protecting persons in his particular situation. Where the state is so weak and its control over all or part of its territories so tenuous as to make it a government in name only, a refugee may justly claim to be unable to avail himself of its protection. Situations of civil war, invasion or the total collapse of internal order will normally be required. The Refugee Division having failed to address this question, its decision was quashed and the matter referred back to a differently constituted panel of the Board for a new hearing.

*Orelien v. Canada (Minister of Employment & Immigration)* (1991), [1992] 1 F.C. 592, 15 Imm. L.R. (2d) 1, 135 N.R. 50 (Fed. C.A.) — Canada's obligations in the area of refugees stem from the 4th Geneva Convention of August 12, 1949, and protocol due to the Geneva Convention of August 12, 1949, both approved by Acts of Parliament (*Geneva Conventions Act*, R.S.C. 1985, c. G-3, s. 2, as am. S.C. 1990, c. 14, s. 1), as well as a customary norm of temporary refuge. To return a person to Haiti in the circumstances that presently exist and have existed at relevant times in this case would have violated

Canada's obligations under the Convention, the protocol and the customary norm of international law prohibiting the forceable repatriation of foreign nationals who have fled generalized violence and other threats to their lives and security arising out of internal armed conflict within their state of nationality. The Convention, the protocol and the customary norm of international law have the force of domestic law in Canada and can be enforced in the courts of Canada at the suit of a private individual. The intention to execute a deportation order, which if executed would breach those laws, does not colour the process under the *Immigration Act* by which a person from such a country may be ordered deported. This is not to denigrate the importance of the Convention, the protocol and the customary norms of international law. It would be a grave and justiciable matter if Canada were to execute deportation orders in circumstances which breached obligations under international law and put the life, liberty or security of persons in peril.

*Rasaratnam v. Canada (Minister of Employment & Immigration)* (1991), [1992] 1 F.C. 706 (Fed. C.A.) — The internal flight alternative (IFA) concept is inherent in the Convention refugee definition. First, in order to conclude an IFA exists the Board must be satisfied on a balance of probabilities that there is no serious possibility of a claimant being persecuted in the part of the country which is viewed upon as the internal flight alternative. Second, conditions in that part of the country to which the IFA applies must be such that it would not be unreasonable for the claimant to seek refuge there. Third, the determination of whether there is an IFA is integral to the determination of whether the claimant is a refugee. Fourth, the claimant is not expected to raise the question of an IFA nor is an allegation that none exists simply to be inferred from the claim itself. The question of an IFA must be expressly raised at the hearing by the refugee hearing officer or the Board and the claimant afforded the opportunity to address it with evidence and argument.

In this case, the Board did not err in concluding the appellant was not a Convention refugee because the appellant could have lived free from persecution in Colombo, Sri Lanka.

*Canada (Minister of Employment & Immigration) v. Obstoj*, [1992] 2 F.C. 739, 93 D.L.R. (4th) 144, 142 N.R. 81 (Fed. C.A.) — The Minister applied to set aside a credible basis determination. The first-level tribunal found that given the present day change of circumstances in Poland there was no realistic possibility of the respondent suffering persecution if she would return. They found, however, that the respondent fell under the provisions of s. 2(3) of the *Immigration Act* and that there were compelling reasons for her refusing to avail herself of the protection of Poland and that therefore her claim had a credible basis. The three judges of the Court of Appeal that heard the matter gave three different judgments. Hugessen J. ruled that since the Refugee Division, when conducting the hearing into the claim for refugee status, was able to hear evidence and consider questions raised by s. 2(3), the credible basis tribunal, when deciding whether or not there is credible or trustworthy evidence on which the division could decide in a claimant's favour, is likewise able to consider such evidence. Subs. 2(2) and (3) were found to deal not only with the loss of a refugee status which had already been acquired, but also to have been incorporated into the definition of a Convention refugee by virtue of paragraph (b) of the definition.

Section 2(3) extends to anyone who has been recognized as a refugee at any time, even long after the date of the Convention. It should also be read as requiring Canadian authorities to give recognition to refugee status on humanitarian grounds to a special and limited category of persons, in particular, those persons who have suffered such appalling persecution that the experience alone is a compelling reason not to return them even though they may no longer have reason to fear further persecution.

Desjardins J.A. was of the view that paragraph (b) contained in the definition of a Convention refugee was an integral part of that definition and that a claimant must meet the requirements of both paragraphs (a) and (b) at the time that status is claimed and continuously thereafter. There is a constant relationship between the cases mentioned in paragraph (b) and the requirement of a well-founded fear mentioned in paragraph (a). Subsection (2) referred to in paragraph (b) contains five categories. Paragraphs (a), (b), (c) and (d) presuppose the case of an individual who does something contrary to the idea of a Convention refugee. Such an individual could then never claim that his or her fear was well founded. Such a person ceases to be a refugee first because of the requirements in paragraph (b) of the definition, and second because the fear of such a person is not well founded. Paragraph 2(2)(e) does not deal with an act committed by a claimant which conflicts with the idea of a well-founded fear, but rather with changes that occurred in the country of origin so that the reasons for the fear have ceased. Such a claimant does not meet paragraph (b) of the definition and further his fear is no longer well founded as required by paragraph (a) of the definition. Subsection 2(3) creates justification which excludes the application of paragraph 2(2)(e). While the fear of a person described in s. 2(3) is not well founded, Parliament intended to recognize that such persons could claim refugee status despite this fact. Such a claim could only initially be made at a first-level tribunal, and accordingly a first-level tribunal can consider whether there is credible evidence of the justification set out in s. 2(3).

Pratte J.A. dissented and would have allowed the application and ruled that a foreigner who no longer has a reason to fear persecution in his country may not be determined to be a Convention refugee for the sole reason that the persecution he suffered in the past justifies his refusal to avail himself of the protection of that country.

*Editor's Note: Although decided under a different statutory framework the principles discussed may still be of interest.*

*Zalzali v. Canada (Minister of Employment & Immigration)* (1991), 14 Imm. L.R. (2d) 81, 126 N.R. 126, [1991] 3 F.C. 605 (Fed. C.A.) — The appellant, a Lebanese national, claimed he was persecuted on account of his nationality, political opinion and membership in a particular social group. In most cases of claims for refugee status, the state, while it may not itself be the agent of persecution, makes itself an accomplice by tolerance or inertia. It is then possible to speak in terms of persecution attributable to the state and to conclude that the refugee claimant had good reason to be unwilling to claim protection which the state was, in all likelihood, not going to give him. There can be persecution within the meaning of the convention and the *Immigration Act* where there is no form of guilt, complicity or participation by the state. The definition of a refugee refers to "the fear of persecution without saying that this persecution must be by the government." The natural meaning of the words "is unable" assumes an objective inability on the part of the complainant and the fact that "is unable" is not qualified by "reason of that fear" confirms that the inability in question is governed by objective criteria which can be verified independently of the fear experienced. Seeing a connection of any kind between "is unable" and "complicity by the government" would be a misreading of the definition. Persecution by someone other than the government is possible when the government is unable to offer protection. There are several reasons beyond the person's control why he or she might be unable to claim the protection of the state. One of those reasons is the non-existence of a government to which that person may resort. In this case, the decision of the Refugee Division was set aside and the matter was remitted back for a rehearing in accordance with the reasoning of the Court.

*Editor's Note: The cases which discuss the phrase "is unwilling" are Rajudeen (1984), 55 N.R. 129; Surujpal (1985), 60 N.R. 73; Satiacum (1985), 99 N.R. 171.*

*Hilo v. Canada (Minister of Employment & Immigration)* (1991), 15 Imm. L.R. (2d) 199, 130 N.R. 236 (Fed. C.A.) — The Refugee Division was under a duty to give its reasons for casting doubt upon the appellant's credibility in clear and unmistakeable terms. The Board's credibility assessment was defective because it was couched in vague and general terms. The claimant had only attended informal meetings of a political group inside Syria. The Refugee Division viewed this group as loosely knit with apparently charitable aims, no official title or status and noted further that the claimant was only 14 years of age at the time of his attendance. The Court found that characterizing the group in this way was irrelevant. The Syrian authorities had sought to persecute the appellant because of his perceived political opinion. The proper test for evaluating political activities is not whether the division or members considered that the appellant had engaged in political activities but whether the ruling government of the country from which he claimed to be a refugee so considered his conduct.

*Hoang v. Canada (Minister of Employment & Immigration)* (1990), 13 Imm. L.R. (2d) 35, 120 N.R. 193 (Fed. C.A.) — The appellant was ordered deported because he was a permanent resident who had been convicted of an offence for which a term of imprisonment of more than six months had been imposed; he had also been convicted of an offence for which the maximum term was five years or greater. The appellant had come to Canada as a stateless person from Vietnam and had been determined by the Minister in 1986 to be a Convention refugee. The Court noted that the Immigration Appeal Board (which had decided this matter) correctly determined that its jurisdiction is only over whether a person should be removed from Canada and not as to the country of removal. Until the issue of deportation is settled the Minister cannot make a decision as to the country of removal. Thus, a statement by the Minister's representative as to the Minister's disposition to deport the appellant to Vietnam was not taken as a formal expression of the Minister's decision since the Minister was not, at the date of that statement, empowered to make the decision.

The Court determined that in dealing with the "double jeopardy" provisions of s. 11(h) of the *Charter*, deportation was not to be seen as a punishment of the person deported but a protection of those who remained. Further, deportation for serious offences affects neither s. 7 nor s. 12 of the *Charter of Rights and Freedoms* since it is not to be conceptualized as either a deprivation of liberty or a punishment. Finally, the Court noted that with respect to Canada's international obligations the United Nations convention relating to the status of refugees contained an exception to the prohibition against *refoulement* where the deportee had been convicted in the country where he was making the refugee claim of a particularly serious crime. The Court noted that the phrase "particularly serious crime" and "danger to the community" were not defined in the convention and therefore presumed that Parliament responsibly fulfilled its obligation when it enacted the *Immigration Act*.

Accordingly, the appellant's appeal was dismissed.

*Adjei v. Canada (Minister of Employment & Immigration)*, [1989] 2 F.C. 680, 7 Imm. L.R. (2d) 169, 57 D.L.R. (4th) 153, 132 N.R. 24 (Fed. C.A.) — This application focuses on the proper interpretation of the definition of Convention refugee. An accurate way of describing the requisite test is in terms of "reasonable chance": is there a reasonable chance that persecution would take place were the applicant returned to his country of origin. There need not be more than a 50 per cent chance that persecution will occur (that is, a probability). On the other hand, there must be more than a minimal possibility of persecution. This application was allowed because the Board, in describing the test set out in the definition, stated that it was whether there was a reasonable chance or "substantial grounds" for thinking that the persecution may take place. The use of the term "substantial grounds" introduced an element of ambiguity into the Board's formulation of the correct test under the refugee definition. Accordingly, the Board's decision was set aside and the matter remitted back to the Board for reconsideration.



*Surujpal v. Canada (Minister of Employment & Immigration)* (1985), 60 N.R. 73 (Fed. C.A.) — The applicant brought an application to quash a decision of the Immigration Appeal Board finding that the applicant was not a Convention refugee. The decision of the Immigration Appeal Board was quashed because the evidence disclosed that the police were complicit in the broader sense in the persecution and harassment of the applicant. It is not required that state participation in persecution be direct; it is sufficient that it is indirect provided that there is proof of state complicity.

*Rajudeen v. Canada (Minister of Employment & Immigration)* (1984), 55 N.R. 129 (Fed. C.A.) — The definition of Convention refugee does not include a definition of persecution. "Persecute" was defined by reference to a dictionary as "to harass or afflict with repeated acts of cruelty or annoyance; to afflict persistently; to afflict or punish because of particular opinions or adherence to a particular creed or mode of worship." "Persecution" was defined as "a particular course or period of systematic infliction of punishment directed against those holding a particular (religious belief); persistent injury or annoyance from any source."

There is a subjective and objective component necessary to satisfy the definition of Convention refugee. The subjective component relates to the existence of the fear of persecution in the mind of the refugee. The objective component requires that the refugee's fear be evaluated objectively to determine if there is a valid basis for that fear.

In determining whether refugee status has been extended to cover a particular case, reference should be made to the expression of underlying policy in s. 3(g) of the Act. To satisfy the definition, the persecution complained of must have been committed or been condoned by the state itself and consist either of conduct directed by the state toward the individual or in the state knowingly tolerating the behaviour of private citizens or refusing or being unable to protect the individual from such behaviour.

*Naredo v. Canada (Minister of Employment & Immigration)* (1981), 130 D.L.R. (3d) 752, 40 N.R. 436 (Fed. C.A.) — The Federal Court held that the Immigration Appeal Board erred in imposing upon the applicant and his wife the requirement that they be subject to persecution. The statutory definition requires only that they establish a well-founded fear of persecution.

*Inzunza v. Canada (Minister of Employment & Immigration)* (1979), 103 D.L.R. (3d) 105 (Fed. C.A.) — Whether a person has engaged in political activity must be determined by considering the opinion of the government of the country of his nationality and not by the Immigration Appeal Board's consideration of whether the applicant has engaged in such activity.

## Author's Note

*[Refugee decisions summarized under the former Act are reproduced in a separate section of this text, immediately after the Immigration Appeal Division Rules.]*

**97. (1) Person in need of protection — A person in need of protection is a person in Canada whose removal to their country or countries of nationality or, if they do not have a country of nationality, their country of former habitual residence, would subject them personally**

> **(a) to a danger, believed on substantial grounds to exist, of torture within the meaning of Article 1 of the Convention Against Torture; or**
>
> **(b) to a risk to their life or to a risk of cruel and unusual treatment or punishment if**
>
> > **(i) the person is unable or, because of that risk, unwilling to avail themself of the protection of that country,**
> >
> > **(ii) the risk would be faced by the person in every part of that country and is not faced generally by other individuals in or from that country,**
> >
> > **(iii) the risk is not inherent or incidental to lawful sanctions, unless imposed in disregard of accepted international standards, and**
> >
> > **(iv) the risk is not caused by the inability of that country to provide adequate health or medical care.**

**(2) Person in need of protection — A person in Canada who is a member of a class of persons prescribed by the regulations as being in need of protection is also a person in need of protection.**

## Case Law

*R. v. Laboucan*, [2010] S.C.J. No. 12, 73 C.R. (6th) 235, (sub nom. *R. v. Briscoe)* 400 N.R. 200, 22 Alta. L.R. (5th) 62, 253 C.C.C. (3d) 129, [2010] 6 W.W.R. 13, 316 D.L.R. (4th) 590, (sub nom. *R. v. Briscoe)* 477 A.R. 70, 483 W.A.C. 70, 2010 SCC 12, 2010 CarswellAlta 591, 2010 CarswellAlta 590 — The fact that a witness has an interest in the outcome of the proceedings is common sense and a relevant factor, among others, to take into account when assessing the credibility of the witness's testimony. A trier of fact, however, should not place undue weight on the status of a person in the proceeding as a factor going to credibility. For example, it would be improper to base a finding of credibility regarding a parent's or a spouse's testimony solely on the basis of a witness's relationship to the complainant or to the accused. Regard should be given to all relevant factors in assessing credibility.

*Smith v. Canada (Minister of Citizenship & Immigration)* (2009), 86 Imm. L.R. (3d) 114, 358 F.T.R. 189 (Eng.), 2009 FC 1194, 2009 CarswellNat 3800, 2009 CarswellNat 3801 (F.C.) — The applicant, an American citizen, claimed refugee protection pursuant to ss. 96 and 97(1) of IRPA as a homosexual member of the U.S. Army, from which she had deserted. She alleged a fear of persecution on the part of a colleague and superiors because of her sexual orientation. She also claimed that she would be personally facing a risk to her life or cruel and unusual treatment or punishment if she were returned to the United States. Her claim was rejected by the Refugee Board on the ground that she failed to seek state protection that would have been adequate.

Contrary to the situation in *Hinzman, Re* (2006), 55 Imm. L.R. (3d) 54 (F.C.), where the appellants had not made an adequate attempt to avail themselves of the protections afforded by the Uniform Code of Military Justice (UCMJ), the applicant in this case provided evidence that she did approach her superiors to try to obtain a discharge. According to the evidence, she went so far as to ask her superior for permission to speak to a higher authority, but was denied. She also testified that one supervisor scoffed at her and said they would figure out the paper work when she returned from her tour of duty in Afghanistan. The case law of this Court requires more than one attempt to obtain state protection. It is often said that an applicant must usually follow up with his complaint, and seek assistance from higher authorities if unsuccessful at the first stage. Yet, one must take into account the particular environment that an applicant finds himself in. It is clear that in the Army there is an atmosphere of unconditional obedience to the hierarchy. The Board member did not seem to be sensitive to this special context.

The duty of the Board member was to determine whether she would suffer persecution as a result of the relevant substantive law or of the process whereby the law would be applied to her. It was not enough for the Board member to state that he is "not in a position to defend or criticize." It is part of the assessment of a refugee claim to determine whether a claimant has a well-founded fear of persecution for reasons, *inter alia*, of her membership in a particular social group, if he/she is returned to his/her home country. The applicant provided evidence to the Board that the punishment she would be exposed to under the court-martial process relates to a breach of a law that is in conflict with a fundamental human right and therefore adversely differentiates on a Convention ground in its application. This evidence could not simply be ignored by the Board member and had to be properly discussed and analyzed before he could conclude that the UCMJ was a law of general application and applied in a non-discriminatory fashion. It was therefore the duty of the Board member to assess the fairness of the court-martial process in light of the particular set of facts and of the evidence that was before him. The application for judicial review was allowed.

*Alexander v. Canada (Minister of Citizenship & Immigration* (2009), 88 Imm. L.R. (3d) 75, 357 F.T.R. 222 (Eng.), 2009 FC 1305, 2009 CarswellNat 5510, 2009 CarswellNat 4566, [2009] F.C.J. No. 1682 (F.C.) — The Refugee Protection Panel accepted that the applicant had been beaten up by her boyfriend, that she had taken refuge with her aunt on one of the Grenadian Islands, that her boyfriend had threatened to burn down her mother's house if she did not return to Kingstown and that he continued to make terrifying threats by telephone. The only issue was that of state protection. The panel found that St. Vincent and the Grenadines was a democracy and that the applicant did not "take all reasonable steps in the circumstances of this case to pursue the available state protection," and that she "did not provide any persuasive evidence of similarly-situated individuals let down by the state protection arrangements." The conclusion was that she had failed to rebut the presumption of state protection with clear and convincing evidence.

Taken at its face value, the decision appears to be reasonable. This Court is supposed to show deference to the RPD panels that allegedly have greater expertise in country conditions than the Court itself. However, there comes a time when it becomes obvious that deference should be earned, particularly when the panel apparently pays no attention to the cases coming out of this Court which specifically deal with St. Vincent and the Grenadines. The analysis of country conditions was clearly a *pro forma* one, or a "cookie cutter analysis." This Court does not sit in a *de novo* appeal and so cannot do its own country analysis. It was "absolutely astonishing" that the IRB publishes information on country conditions but failed to mention that the Consul General has admitted that the state cannot guarantee the effectiveness of a restraining order. That would be relevant information in any assessment as would an analysis of the types of threats the applicant received. The application for judicial review was granted.

*Perez v. Canada (Minister of Citizenship & Immigration)* (2009), 85 Imm. L.R. (3d) 118, 2009 FC 1065, 2009 CarswellNat 5598, 2009 CarswellNat 3345 (F.C.) — Refugee law does not require altruism from those who seek protection from persecution nor does it exclude those who publicize their fears. In this case, the board member repeatedly criticized the applicant's recourse to the media to call attention to her victimization. The member's comments that the applicant "failed frequently to address corruption before it affected her," used "duplicity and threats" to press her case and lacked "altruistic intent," reflect judgments about the applicant's integrity that are legally irrelevant and taint the entire decision. The application for judicial review was allowed.

*Odetoyinbo v. Canada (Minister of Citizenship & Immigration)*, 2009 CarswellNat 1328, 2009 FC 501 (F.C.) — The applicant, a citizen of Nigeria, challenged the legality of a decision of the Refugee Protection Division of the Immigration and Refugee Board wherein the Board held he was not a Convention refugee or a person in need of protection. The applicant's claim is based on his alleged bisexuality. Since homosexuality is illegal in Nigeria, the applicant feared persecution because of his sexual orientation.

The Board's failure to make an explicit determination as to the applicant's bisexuality constituted a reviewable error and justified a redetermination of the applicant's claim. It is well settled that an adverse credibility finding, though it may be conclusive of a refugee claim under s. 96 of the IRPA, is not necessarily conclusive of a claim under s. 97(1). The reason is that the evidence necessary to establish a claim under s. 97 differs from that required under s. 96. When considering s. 97, the Board must decide whether the claimant's removal would subject him personally to the dangers and risks stipulated in paragraph 97(1)(a) and (b) of the Act. Further, there are objective and subjective components to s. 96, which is not the case for paragraph 97(1)(a): a person relying on this paragraph must show on a balance of probabilities that he or she is more likely than not to be persecuted.

In the case at bar, the Board did not explicitly state in its reasons that it did not believe that the applicant was bisexual. Accordingly, it could not ignore compelling objective evidence on record demonstrating the abuses which gay men are subjected to in Nigeria. Therefore, even if the Board rejected the applicant's account of what happened to him in Nigeria, it still had a duty to consider whether the applicant's sexual orientation would put him personally at risk in his country. The application was allowed and returned to the Board for redetermination by a different member.

*Guney v. Canada (Minister of Citizenship & Immigration)*, 2008 CarswellNat 5579, 2008 CarswellNat 3687, 2008 FC 1134 (F.C.) — The applicant tried to bolster his claim for refugee status more than a year later, by inventing an additional basis for protection. The Board found that this new lie rendered the applicant's evidence, as a whole, not to be credible and thus did no real analysis of the rest of his story. The fact that a witness has been caught in one lie, in itself, is insufficient to discredit all of his evidence where, as here, the evidence is otherwise plausible and consistent. This approach was unreasonable and the decision was set aside.

*Carrillo v. Canada (Minister of Citizenship & Immigration)*, [2008] F.C.J. No. 399, 69 Imm. L.R. (3d) 309, 2008 CarswellNat 1953, 2008 CarswellNat 605, 2008 FCA 94

(C.A.) — A refugee who claims that the state protection is inadequate or non-existent bears the evidentiary burden of adducing evidence to that effect and the legal burden of persuading the trier of fact that his or her claim in this respect is founded. The standard of proof applicable is the balance of probabilities and there is no requirement of a higher degree of probability than what that standard usually requires. As for the quality of the evidence required to rebut the presumption of state protection, the presumption is rebutted by clear and convincing evidence that the state protection is inadequate or non-existent. The appeal was allowed, the decision of the Federal Court set aside and the decision of the Board restored.



*Prophète v. Canada (Minister of Citizenship & Immigration)*, [2009] F.C.J. No. 143, 78 Imm. L.R. (3d) 163, 387 N.R. 149, 2009 FCA 31, 2009 CarswellNat 282, 2009 CarswellNat 1393 (C.A.) — The Refugee Protection Division of the Immigration and Refugee Board determined that the applicant was not a Convention refugee. The appellant, a citizen of Haiti, claimed to have been the target of gang violence on multiple occasions. The appellant submitted that kidnapping was rampant in Haiti, but businessmen are especially at risk because the goal of kidnapping for ransom is to obtain money. The appellant argued, given the fact that in Haiti most of the population is poor, those with money or those perceived to have money are at a greater risk than the general population. He claimed s. 97 of the Act was to be interpreted as indicating that there can be a subgroup within a generalized group that faces an even more acute risk than the larger group. The lower Court concluded that the appellant did not face a personalized risk that is not faced generally by other individuals in or from Haiti. The risk of all forms of criminality is general and felt by all Haitians. While a specific number of individuals may be targeted more frequently because of their wealth, all Haitians are at risk of becoming the victims of violence. The application for judicial review was dismissed by the Federal Court and the following question was certified:

> Where the population of a country faces a generalized risk of crime, does the limitation of s. 97(1)(b)(ii) of the IRPA apply to a subgroup of individuals who face a significantly heightened risk of such crime.

The Federal Court of Appeal concluded that unlike s. 96, s. 97 of the Act is meant to afford protection to an individual whose claim "is not predicated on the individual demonstrating that he or she is [at risk] . . . for any enumerated grounds of s. 96". The examination of a claim under subs. 97(1) necessitates an individualized inquiry, which is to be conducted on the basis of the evidence adduced by a claimant "in the context of a *present* or *prospective* risk" for him. As drafted, the Court of Appeal found the certified question was too broad. Taking into consideration the broader federal scheme of which s. 97 is a part, answering the certifying question in a factual vacuum would, depending on the circumstances of each case, result in unduly narrowing or widening the scope of subparagraph 97(1)(b)(ii) of the Act. The Federal Court of Appeal declined to answer the certified question and dismissed the appeal.

*Sanchez v. Canada (Minister of Citizenship & Immigration)* (2007), 360 N.R. 344, 2007 CarswellNat 572, 2007 FCA 99 (Fed. C.A.) — The appellants, a husband and wife, were Colombian nationalists. One appellant was employed full-time by the Colombian Ministry of Agriculture as an engineer, with a specialty in environmental clean-up. In addition, he ran a side-line business with his brother that reported violations of signage by-laws to the city authorities. He and his brother received a percentage of the fine that was levied against the guilty person or business. The appellant was threatened by the Fuerzas Armadas Revolucionarias de Colombia ("FARC") due to his part-time business. The appellant sought refugee status. The Board found no indication that the lives or well being of the appellants would have been at risk had the appellant simply chosen to comply with the warning and cease his side business. The Board was of the view that it was not unreasonable to expect him to cease his side business and that his inability to continue this endeavour was not a denial of his core human rights or of his general ability to earn a living. The applications judge found the Board's decision to be reasonable and legally correct with respect to this part-time business.

Although it was not possible in the context of this case to attempt to develop an exhaustive list of the factors that should be taken into account in assessing whether a person is in need of protection, persons claiming to be in need of protection solely because of the nature of the occupation or business in which they are engaged in their own country generally will not be found to be in need of protection unless they can establish that there is no alternative occupation or business reasonably open to them in their own country that it would eliminate the risk of harm.

*Covarrubias v. Canada (Minister of Citizenship & Immigration)*, [2006] F.C.J. No. 1682, 56 Imm. L.R. (3d) 178, 354 N.R. 367, 148 C.R.R. (2d) 45, [2007] 3 F.C.R. 169, 2006 CarswellNat 3653, 2006 FCA 365 (C.A.) — The male appellant had a serious health condition and required life-sustaining medical treatment which he is unable to afford in his native Mexico, and which he says his country will not freely provide. The Federal Court of Appeal declined to consider the certified question of whether the exclusion of a risk to life caused by the inability of a country to provide adequate medical care to a person suffering a life-threatening illness under s. 97 of the IRPA infringed the *Canadian Charter of Rights and Freedoms* in a manner that does not accord with the principles of fundamental justice, and which cannot be justified under s. 1 of the *Charter*. Since the appellant had failed to provide sufficient evidence of a risk to his life on account of inadequate medical care should he be deported to Mexico? The allegations of specific *Charter* violation were without evidentiary foundation. Hence, there was no factual basis for entering into a *Charter* analysis in this case.

The provision in issue (s. 97) is meant to be broadly interpreted so that only in rare cases would the onus on the applicant be met. The applicant must establish on the balance of probabilities, not only that there is a personalized risk to his or her life, but that this was not caused by the inability of his or her country to provided adequate health care. Proof of a negative is required, that is, that the country is not able to furnish medical care that is adequate for this applicant. This is no easy task and the language and the history of the provision show that it was not meant to be. The words "inability to provide adequate medical services" must include situations where a foreign government decides to allocate its limited funds in a way that obliges some of its less prosperous citizens to defray part or all of their medical expenses. The exclusion in subparagraph 97(1)(b)(iv) should not be interpreted so broadly as to exclude any claim in respect of health care. The wording of the provision clearly leaves open the possibility for protection where an applicant can show that he faces a personalized risk to life on account of his country's unjustified unwillingness to provide him with adequate medical care, where the financial ability is present.

The phrase "not caused by the inability of that country to provide adequate health care or medical care" in subparagraph 97(1)(b)(iv) of the IRPA excludes from protection persons whose claims are based on evidence that their native country is unable to provide adequate medical care because it chooses in good faith, for legitimate, political and financial priority reasons, not to provide such care to its nationals. If it can be proved that there is an illegitimate reason for denying the care, such as persecutorial reasons, that may suffice to avoid the operation of the exclusion.

*Kandiah v. Canada (Minister of Citizenship & Immigration)*, [2005] F.C.J. No. 275, 2005 CarswellNat 390, 2005 FC 181 (F.C.) — There may well be instances where a refugee claimant, whose identity is not disputed, is found to not have a valid basis for his subjective fear of persecution, but the country conditions are such that the claimant's particular circumstances, make him or her a person in need of protection. A negative subjective fear determination is not necessarily determinative of a claim under s. 97. A claim under s. 97 requires that the Board determine whether a claimant's removal would subject him personally to the dangers and risks stipulated in paragraphs 97(1)(a) and (b).



*Li v. Canada (Minister of Citizenship & Immigration)*, [2005] F.C.J. No. 1, 41 Imm. L.R. (3d) 157, 2005 CarswellNat 30, 2005 CarswellNat 1128, 2005 FCA 1, 329 N.R. 346, 249 D.L.R. (4th) 306 (F.C.A.); leave to appeal refused (2005), 2005 CarswellNat 1112, 2005 CarswellNat 1113, [2005] S.C.C.A. No. 119 (S.C.C.) — Section 97 requires that a person establish, on a balance of probabilities, that he or she will face the danger or risks described in paragraphs 97(1)(a) and (b). The test for the degree of danger of torture in paragraph 97(1)(a) is a balance of probabilities or "more likely than not". Proof on a balance of probabilities is the standard of proof that the panel will apply in assessing the evidence adduced before it for the purposes of making its factual findings. The test for determining the danger of torture is whether, on the facts found by the panel, the panel is satisfied that it is more likely than not the individual would be personally subjected to a danger of torture.

*Ozdemir v. Canada (Minister of Citizenship & Immigration)*, [2004] F.C.J. No. 1242, 38 Imm. L.R. (3d) 237, 2004 CarswellNat 2232, 2004 FC 1008, 256 F.T.R. 154 (F.C.) — Pursuant to s. 97(1) of the IRPA, the Board is required to evaluate whether a claimant is in need of protection owing to the danger of torture or risk of cruel and unusual punishment. The separate analysis of a claimant's refugee claim under s. 96 and the enumerated risks under s. 97(1) is required. Further, a negative credibility determination in respect of a refugee claim under s. 96 is not necessarily dispositive of the considerations under s. 97(1).

*Selliah v. Canada (Minister of Citizenship & Immigration)*, [2004] F.C.J. No. 1134, 37 Imm. L.R. (3d) 263, 2004 CarswellNat 2083, 256 F.T.R. 53, 2004 FC 872 (F.C.); affirmed 2005 CarswellNat 1146, 2005 FCA 160 (F.C.A.) — The applicants sought judicial review of the rejection of their application for protection by a pre-removal risk assessment (PRRA). The officer determined that the applicants would not face a risk of persecution or torture if returned to Sri Lanka. The applicants also sought to review a negative humanitarian and compassionate decision pursuant to subs. 25(1) of the Act.

PRRA officers have a specialized expertise in risk assessment. Their findings are usually fact driven and warrant considerable deference from a reviewing Court. The onus is on the applicants to make their case and adduce the necessary evidence. The evidence adduced here was ambiguous and in some instances contradictory. There is no suggestion that the officer was wilfully blind in the circumstances and the Court found that the officer was acting in good faith. There was, therefore, no obligation on the officer to gather or seek additional evidence or make further inquiries. The officer was required to consider and decide on the evidence adduced before her.

The phrase in s. 97 "believed on substantial grounds to exist" equates to a balance of probabilities test.

In this case the immigration officer who conducted the PRRA was also seized with the H&C application. Under such circumstances it was not necessary to ensure fairness that there was a disclosure of the risk assessment to the applicant before the H&C application was made.

*Xie v. Canada (Minister of Citizenship & Immigration)* (2004), 37 Imm. L.R. (3d) 163, 2004 CarswellNat 2036, 2004 CarswellNat 3972, 325 N.R. 255, [2005] 1 F.C.R. 304, 243 D.L.R. (4th) 385, 2004 FCA 250, [2004] F.C.J. No. 1142 (F.C.A.); leave to appeal refused (2005), 2005 CarswellNat 748, 2005 CarswellNat 749 (S.C.C.) — The appellant, a citizen of the People's Republic of China, was a senior official in the Guangzhou Commission for Foreign Economic Relations and Trade. She fled China and arrived in Canada in 2001 and made a claim for refugee protection. In the course of processing her claim, two facts emerged. Firstly, the appellant and her daughter had to their names bank accounts containing $2.7 million. Second, at the request of the Chinese authorities, there was an international warrant for the arrest of the appellant and a charge of embezzlement. On the basis of the appellant's unexplained wealth, the Board applied the exclusion in Article 1(F)(b) of the Convention. The Board also decided that, in light of the offence with which the appellant was charged, she faced a risk of torture at the hands of the Chinese authorities if she were to return to China.

The Board was entitled to presume that the warrant for the appellant's arrest was issued in the belief that she was guilty of misconduct. The presumption of innocence does not apply so as to prevent the Board from taking the Chinese State's belief in the appellant's guilt into account in deciding if there are serious reasons to consider that she committed the crime with which she is charged. There are three ways in which refugee protection can be obtained. Refugee protection is extended to persons falling within the definition of Convention refugee which has not been changed by the new Act. Refugee protection is also extended to those persons who are found to be in the need of protection, a class defined by the risk of harm as opposed to the motivation of those inflicting harm. The grounds upon which such an application can be made are found in s. 97 and include those who are in "danger, believed on substantial grounds to exist, of torture within the meaning of Article 1 of the Convention Against Torture". Finally, a person can be extended refugee protection by means of an application for protection pursuant to s. 112 of the Act. Persons facing deportation may apply to the Minister for protection on the basis that they face a risk of harm if they return to their country of origin. If the application for protection is granted, such persons acquire refugee protection pursuant to paragraph 95(1)(c) of the Act. Subsection 112(3) of the Act lists those persons who are ineligible for refugee protection, including persons who are described in Article 1, Section F of the Convention. The exclusion from refugee protection is not an exclusion from protection altogether. Section 113 stipulates that persons described in 112(3) are to have their applications for protection decided on the basis of the factors set out in s. 97, with additional consideration given to the issue of whether such persons are a danger to the public in Canada or to the security of Canada. For all except those described in subs. 112(3), a successful application for protection results in the grant of refugee protection in the status of protected person. For persons described in subs. 112(3) the result is a stay of the deportation order in force against them. One consequence of the distinction is that protected persons have access to the status of permanent residence and are subject to the principle of non-refoulement.

Thus, the structure of the Act has two streams, claims for refugee protection and claims for protection in the context of pre-removal risk assessments. The person who is excluded from refugee protection is eligible to apply for protection at the PRRA stage. The basis on which the claim for protection may be advanced is the same, but the Minister can have regard to whether the granting of protection would affect the safety of the public or the security of Canada. If protection is granted, the result is a stay of the deportation order. The claimant does not have the same access to permanent resident status as does a successful claimant for refugee protection.

Once a panel of the Refugee Protection Division found that the appellant was excluded pursuant to Section F of Article 1, it had done everything that it was required to do. The appellant was, thereby, excluded from refugee protection, a matter within the Board's confidence, and was limited to applying for protection, a matter within the Minister's jurisdiction. Accordingly, the Board's conclusions as to the appellant's risk of torture were gratuitous and were an infringement upon the Minister's responsibilities.

*Singh (H.) v. Canada (Solicitor General)*, [2004] 3 F.C.R. 323, (sub nom. *Singh v. Canada (Minister of Citizenship & Immigration))* 39 Imm. L.R. (3d) 261, 248 F.T.R. 114, (sub nom. *Singh v. Canada (Minister of Citizenship & Immigration) (No. 2))* 117 C.R.R. (2d) 239, 2004 CarswellNat 2091, 2004 CarswellNat 549, 2004 FC 288 (F.C.) — A risk to life under s. 97 does not include having to assess whether there is appropriate health and medical care available in the country in question.

Pre-removal risk assessment officers do not have the jurisdiction to consider constitutional questions.

*Kadoura v. Canada (Ministre de la Citoyenneté & de l'Immigration)*, [2003] F.C.J. No. 1328, 2003 CarswellNat 4831, 2003 CarswellNat 2789, 2003 FC 1057 (F.C.) — The terms "refugee" and "person in need of protection" apply in particular to persons who do not have a country of nationality and who find themselves outside the country of their former "habitual residence". If a claimant resided in more than one country, it is not necessary to prove that he or she was persecuted in each of those countries. The claimant must show that he or she was persecuted in at least one of these countries and that he or she is unable or unwilling to return to the countries where he had his habitual residence.

The definition of "country of habitual residence" should not be so unduly restrictive as to pre-empt providing shelter to a stateless person who has demonstrated a well-founded fear of persecution on any of the grounds listed in the Convention. The claimant does not have to be legally able to return to a country of a habitual residence. The denial of the right to return, in fact, may in itself constitute an act of persecution by the State.

*Li v. Canada (Minister of Citizenship & Immigration)* (2003), 39 Imm. L.R. (3d) 216, [2004] 3 F.C.R. 501, 2003 CarswellNat 4150, 2003 CarswellNat 4739, [2003] F.C.J. No. 1934, 2003 FC 1514, 243 F.T.R. 261 (F.C.); affirmed 41 Imm. L.R. (3d) 157, 2005 CarswellNat 30, [2005] F.C.J. No. 1, 2005 CarswellNat 1128, 2005 FCA 1, 329 N.R. 346, 249 D.L.R. (4th) 306 (F.C.A.); leave to appeal refused (2005), 2005 CarswellNat 1112, 2005 CarswellNat 1113, [2005] S.C.C.A. No. 119 (S.C.C.) — The applicant was seeking to quash a negative decision with respect to his refugee claim.

Pursuant to subs. 97(1), there must be persuasive evidence (that is a balance of probabilities) establishing the facts on which a claimant relies to say that he or she faces a substantial danger of being tortured on his or her return. Second, the danger or risk must be such that it is more likely than not that he or she would be tortured or subjected to other cruel or other degrading treatments. This does not mean that the Refugee Protection Division will not continue to give the benefit of the doubt to the claimant, in fact, it must do so.

*Bouaouni v. Canada (Minister of Citizenship & Immigration)*, [2003] F.C.J. No. 1540, 2003 CarswellNat 3266, 2003 CarswellNat 3267, 2003 FC 1211 (F.C.) — This is an application to review a negative decision of a panel of the Refugee Protection Division.

A claim under s. 97 must be evaluated with respect to all the relevant considerations and with a view to the country's human rights record. While the Board must assess the applicant's claim objectively, the analysis must still be individualized. There may well be instances where a refugee claimant, whose identity is not disputed, is found to be not credible with respect to his subjective fear of persecution but the country conditions are such that the claimant's particular circumstances make him a person in need of protection. A negative credibility determination which may be determinative of a refugee claim under s. 96 is not necessarily determinative of a claim under s. 97(1).

A claim under s. 97 requires that the Board determine whether the applicant's removal would subject him or her personally to the dangers and risks stipulated in paragraphs 97(1)(a) and (b) of the Act.

**98. Exclusion — Refugee Convention — A person referred to in section E or F of Article 1 of the Refugee Convention is not a Convention refugee or a person in need of protection.**

## Case Law

*Liu v. Canada (Minister of Citizenship & Immigration)* (2009), 83 Imm. L.R. (3d) 228, 353 F.T.R. 132 (Eng.), 2009 FC 877, 2009 CarswellNat 2750, 2009 CarswellNat 4523, [2009] F.C.J. No. 1110 (F.C.) — This was an application for judicial review of a decision of a Minister's delegate refusing the applicant's pre-removal risk assessment decision. The PRRA officer concluded that the applicant was a person described under Article 1F(b) of the Convention based on an analysis of the criminal charges against him. The charges include: criminal fraud in China; immigration fraud in the United States of America; criminal fraud in the US; and immigration fraud in Canada. However, the PRRA officer concluded that "if the applicant is returned to China he will more likely than not be at risk of cruel or unusual treatment or punishment due to his being denied his right to a fair trial guaranteed under the *Universal Declaration of Human Rights and the International Covenant on Civil Political Rights*." The Minister's delegate disagreed with the assessment and concluded that there were no humanitarian and compassionate grounds to consider in this matter.

The applicant says that the decision is wrong because there is no basis in the Act or the Regulations that allows a PRRA officer to consider a claim for refugee protection and reject it on the basis of section F of Article 1 of the Convention. The applicant imposed upon the PRRA officer a full consideration of his ss. 96 and 97 rights without the benefit of a determination by the RPD. The Act appears to contemplate this alternative approach, but it was the applicant's choice to use the PRRA system and was not something that was forced upon him. He was not made to relinquish rights and safeguards he would otherwise have had. He then argued that since the PRRA officer made a positive risk assessment under s. 97, the effect of that decision was to confer refugee protection on him by virtue of subs. 114(1) of the Act. The Court concluded it was not Parliament's intent to provide a means for a claimant to bypass the RPD and to have his or her ss. 96 and 97 rights considered *de novo* by the PRRA officer, without any reference to serious criminality and 1F(b) of the Convention. Neither the PRRA officer nor the delegate acted without jurisdiction or committed an error of law in their determination of the applicant's claim insofar as it related to serious criminality outside of Canada in the Article 1F(b) exclusion issue. The application for judicial review was dismissed. The following questions were certified:

> Do pre-removal risk assessment officers have the jurisdiction to exclude persons from refugee protection under s. 98 of IRPA and find them described in s. 112(3)(c) of IRPA?
>
> Does s. 112(3)(c) of the IRPA only apply to rejections by the Refugee Protection Division on the basis of section F of Article 1 of the *Refugee Convention* or does it apply to rejections by pre-removal risk assessment officers on the basis of section F of Article 1 of the *Refugee Convention*?



*Murillo v Canada (Minister of Citizenship & Immigration)* (2008), 333 F.T.R. 149 (Eng.), 2008 FC 966, 2008 CarswellNat 3002, 2008 CarswellNat 3705 — There is no obligation or requirement on the Refugee Protection Division of the Immigration and Refugee Board to conduct a "balancing" exercise to determine whether a claimant is excludable under Article 1F(b) of the *United Nations Convention Relating to the Status of Refugees*. It is reasonable for the RPD to use as a measurement of a "serious" crime, the view which Canadian law takes of that offence. Any offence for which a maximum sentence of 10 years could be imposed under Canadian law is a "serious" crime. There is also no requirement that the RPD consider a claimant's "good character" under Article 1F(b) of the Refugee Convention. The only consideration that may be salient to the RPD's determination is whether the claimant already served a sentence outside of Canada for the crime in question. The application for judicial review to set aside the RPD's decision was dismissed.

*Jayasekara v. Canada (Minister of Citizenship & Immigration)* (2008), 76 Imm. L.R. (3d) 159, 305 D.L.R. (4th) 630, 384 N.R. 293, 2008 CarswellNat 5525, 2008 CarswellNat 4718, 2008 FCA 404 (C.A.) — The Board excluded the appellant from refugee protection under s. 98 of the IRPA and Article 1F(b) of the Convention because there were serious reasons for considering that he had committed a serious non-political crime outside of Canada and that he had not completed his sentence, as he fled the United States during his probation. Moreover, it found that, even if the appellant were not excludable under Article 1F(b) of the Convention, he did not meet the criteria for either Convention refugee status or as a person requiring protection. These findings based on credibility were not contested. The appellant sought judicial review before the Federal Court only of his exclusion under s. 98 of the IRPA and Article 1F(b) of the Convention.

The Federal Court of Appeal confirmed that the Federal Court judge did not commit an error when he concluded that it was reasonable for the Board to conclude on these facts that the appellant's conviction in the United States gave it a serious reason to believe that he had committed a serious non-political crime outside the country. Serving a sentence for a serious crime prior to coming to Canada does not allow one to avoid the application of Article 1F(b) of the Convention relating to the Status of Refugees.

*Parshottam v. Canada (Minister of Citizenship & Immigration)* (2008), 75 Imm. L.R. (3d) 165, 303 D.L.R. (4th) 672, 382 N.R. 186, 2008 CarswellNat 4154, 2008 CarswellNat 5358, 2008 FCA 355 (C.A.) — This was an appeal of a decision to dismiss an application for judicial review of a rejection of the appellant's application for protection by a pre-removal risk assessment ("PRRA") officer. The question certified by Justice Mosley was found not to be dispositive of the appeal and the Court declined to answer the question.

The Court did add that they did not share Justice Mosley's view that it was "settled law" that whether a claimant for protection in Canada is a permanent resident of a third country for the purpose of Article 1E and s. 98 of the IRPA is invariably determined as of the time of the claimant's arrival in Canada and that subsequent events are irrelevant. It was common ground that if the appellant was a permanent resident of the United States at the relevant time, he was excluded by Article IE from claiming refugee status in Canada. Counsel for the appellant argued that the PRRA officer had erred in law by applying the wrong standard of proof. That is, the officer required the appellant to prove as a matter of certainty that he had lost his permanent residence status in the United States. The Court found that although the PRRA officer did not articulate the standard of proof that she was applying, it was to be assumed in the absence of indications to the contrary that she applied the correct one, namely, a balance of probabilities. The officer's reasons, including her observation that whether the appellant was still a permanent resident would ultimately be determined by an immigration judge in the United States, did not establish that she had applied some standard other than a balance of probabilities. The appeal was dismissed. However, Justice Sharlow would have answered the certified question even though the issue may not have been dispositive of the appeal. He would have answered the certified question as follows:

> If the claimant presents new evidence (as contemplated by paragraph 113(a) of IRPA that Article 1E does not apply as of the date of the pre-removal risk assessment, the PRRA officer may determine on the basis of the new evidence that Article 1E currently applies, in which case the claim for protection is barred. Alternatively, the PRRA officer may determine on the basis of the new evidence that Article 1E does not currently apply although it did apply at the time of the claimant's admission to Canada (or at the date of the RPD decision). If such a change of status has occurred, the PRRA officer should consider why the change of status occurred and what steps, if any, the claimant took or might have taken to cause or fail to prevent the change of status. If the acts or omissions of the claimant indicate asylum shopping, Article 1E may be held to apply despite the change in status.

*Al Husin v. Canada (Minister of Citizenship & Immigration)* (2006), 59 Imm. L.R. (3d) 142, 2006 CarswellNat 4250, 2006 FC 1451 (F.C.) — The applicant's refugee claim was denied on the basis of the exclusion in Article 1F(b) of the *United Nations Convention Relating to the Status of Refugees*. The Board found that it had serious grounds to believe that the applicant had committed a serious non-political crime and that he had not completed his sentence for that crime before entering Canada. The Board's decision was overturned.

The applicant was a citizen of Jordan and while studying in the United States was convicted of an offence and upon being released on probation was arrested by federal Immigration and Naturalization Services and deported to Jordan. A bench warrant for his arrest was issued for involuntarily violating his probation by leaving the country. The Board erred in concluding that the American offence was the equivalent of a Canadian offence of aiding and abetting. It is clear that the applicant's probation imposed under state law was rendered impossible by action of U.S. federal authorities to deport him. The Board's conclusion that the applicant had not served his sentence was correct.

The following questions were certified:

1. Does serving a sentence for a serious crime prior to coming to Canada allow one to avoid the application of Article 1F of the Convention?

2. If the answer to Question 1 is affirmative, when and in what circumstances is a sentence deemed served, specifically does a deportation have the effect of deeming a sentence served?



*Xie v. Canada (Minister of Citizenship & Immigration)* (2004), 37 Imm. L.R. (3d) 163, 2004 CarswellNat 2036, 2004 CarswellNat 3972, 325 N.R. 255, [2005] 1 F.C.R. 304, 243 D.L.R. (4th) 385, 2004 FCA 250, [2004] F.C.J. No. 1142 (F.C.A.); leave to appeal refused (2005), 2005 CarswellNat 748, 2005 CarswellNat 749 (S.C.C.) — The appellant is a citizen of the People's Republic of China where she was a senior official in the Guangzhou Commission for Foreign Economic Relations and Trade. She fled China and arrived in Canada in 2001 and made a claim for refugee protection. In the course of processing her claim, two facts emerged. The first was that the appellant and her daughter had to their names bank accounts containing $2.7 million dollars. Second was, at the request of the Chinese authorities, an international warrant for the arrest of the appellant and a charge of embezzlement. On the basis of the appellant's unexplained wealth, the Board applied the exclusion in Article 1(F)(b) of the Convention. The Board also decided that in light of the offence with which the appellant was charged she faced a risk of torture at the hands of the Chinese authorities if she were to return to China.

The Board was entitled to presume that the warrant for the appellant's arrest was issued in the belief that she was guilty of misconduct. The presumption of innocence does not apply so as to prevent the Board from taking the Chinese State's belief in the appellant's guilt into account in deciding if there are serious reasons to consider that she committed the crime with which she is charged. There are three ways in which refugee protection can be obtained. Refugee protection is extended to persons falling within the definition of Convention Refugee which has not been changed by the new Act. Refugee protection is also extended to those persons who are found to be in the need of protection, a class defined by the risk of harm as opposed to the motivation of those inflicting harm. The grounds upon which such an application can be made are found in s. 97 and include those who are in "danger, believed on substantial grounds to exist, of torture within the meaning of Article 1 of the Convention Against Torture". Finally, a person can be extended refugee protection by means of an application for protection pursuant to s. 112 of the Act. Persons facing deportation may apply to the Minister for protection on the basis that they face a risk of harm if they return to their country of origin. If the application for protection is granted, such persons acquire refugee protection pursuant to paragraph 95(1)(c) of the Act. Subsection 112(3) of the Act lists those persons who are ineligible for refugee protection, including persons who are described in Article 1, Section F of the Convention. The exclusion from refugee protection is not an exclusion from protection altogether. Section 113 stipulates that persons described in 112(3) are to have their applications for protection decided on the basis of the factors set out in s. 97 with additional consideration given to the issue of whether such persons are a danger to the public in Canada or to the security of Canada. For all except those described in subs. 112(3), a successful application for protection results in the grant of refugee protection in the status of protected person. For persons described in subs. 112(3), the result is a stay of the deportation order in force against them. One consequence of the distinction is that protected persons have access to the status of permanent residence and are subject to the principle of non-refoulement.

Thus, the structure of the Act has two streams, claims for refugee protection and claims for protection in the context of pre-removal risk assessments. The person who is excluded from refugee protection is eligible to apply for protection at the PRRA stage. The basis on which the claim for protection may be advanced is the same, but the Minister can have regard to whether the granting of protection would affect the safety of the public or the security of Canada. If protection is granted, the result is a stay of the deportation order. The claimant does not have the same access to permanent resident status as does a successful claimant for refugee protection.

Once a panel of the Refugee Protection Division found that the appellant was excluded pursuant to Section F of Article 1, it had done everything that it was required to do. The appellant was thereby excluded from refugee protection, a matter within the Board's confidence, and was limited to applying for protection, a matter within the Minister's jurisdiction. Accordingly, the Board's conclusions as to the appellant's risk of torture were gratuitous and were an infringement upon the Minister's responsibilities.

*Chowdhury v. Canada (Minister of Citizenship & Immigration)* (2003), 28 Imm. L.R. (3d) 299, 2003 CarswellNat 1797, 2003 CarswellNat 2640, 2003 FCT 744, 2003 CFPI 744, 235 F.T.R. 271 (Fed. T.D.) — This is an application to review a negative decision of the Refugee Protection Division. The applicant was found not be a refugee or a "person in need of protection" because he was referred to in Article 1F(c) of the refugee Convention and was excluded from claiming asylum by s. 98 of IRPA. The question of the applicant's exclusion refugee process was first raised by the presiding member during the course of the applicant's hearing. No objection was raised by the applicant's counsel, however, in oral submissions counsel objected to the fact that the Minister's representative had not committed to invoking or not invoking the exclusion clause.

The decision of the panel was set aside. There had been no notice provided to the claimant prior to the hearing that the exclusion issue was to be raised. The presiding member raised the issue and the Minister's counsel replied that the exclusion "could be raised". This was a tentative answer and did not meet the requirements of procedural fairness. Notice in advance of the hearing or an adjournment of the hearing, once the issue was raised, would have given the applicant and his counsel time to prepare submissions. In the circumstances, the presiding member only allowed for written submissions to be filed after the hearing. This was insufficient to ensure procedural fairness at the hearing. Accordingly, the decision of the panel was set aside.

## DIVISION 2 — CONVENTION REFUGEES AND PERSONS IN NEED OF PROTECTION

### *Claim for Refugee Protection*

**99. (1) Claim — A claim for refugee protection may be made in or outside Canada.**

**(2) Claim outside Canada — A claim for refugee protection made by a person outside Canada must be made by making an application for a visa as a Convention refugee or a person in similar circumstances, and is governed by Part 1.**

**(3) Claim inside Canada — A claim for refugee protection made by a person inside Canada must be made to an officer, may not be made by a person who is subject to a removal order, and is governed by this Part.**

(4) **Permanent resident — An application to become a permanent resident made by a protected person is governed by Part 1.**

## *Examination of Eligibility to Refer Claim*

100. (1) **Referral to Refugee Protection Division — An officer shall, within three working days after receipt of a claim referred to in subsection 99(3), determine whether the claim is eligible to be referred to the Refugee Protection Division and, if it is eligible, shall refer the claim in accordance with the rules of the Board.**

*[Editor's Note: SOR/2002-227, s. 342 provides that a claim made in Canada to be a Convention refugee in respect of which a determination of eligibility was not made before June 28, 2002 is deemed to be a claim for refugee protection made in Canada that is received on June 28, 2002.*

*SOR/2002-227, s. 343 provides that, subject to s. 191 of the* Immigration and Refugee Protection Act, *S.C. 2001, c. 27 (the "new Act"), a claim of a person who was determined eligible before June 28, 2002 to have a claim to be a Convention refugee determined by the Convention Refugee Determination Division, and in respect of which no determination was made by the Convention Refugee Determination Division, is a claim that:*

> *(a) is referred under the new Act to the Refugee Protection Division unless an officer gives notice under s. 104(1) of the new Act; and*
>
> *(b) is subject to the provisions of the new Act.]*

**Proposed Addition — 100(1.1)**

(1.1) **Burden of proof — The burden of proving that a claim is eligible to be referred to the Refugee Protection Division rests on the claimant, who must answer truthfully all questions put to them.**

2010, c. 8, s. 11(1) [To come into force June 29, 2012, or earlier by order.]

(2) **Decision — The officer shall suspend consideration of the eligibility of the person's claim if**

> **(a) a report has been referred for a determination, at an admissibility hearing, of whether the person is inadmissible on grounds of security, violating human or international rights, serious criminality or organized criminality, or**
>
> **(b) the officer considers it necessary to wait for a decision of a court with respect to a claimant who is charged with an offence under an Act of Parliament that is punishable by a maximum term of imprisonment of at least 10 years.**

(3) **Consideration of claim — The Refugee Protection Division may not consider a claim until it is referred by the officer. If the claim is not referred within the three-day period referred to in subsection (1), it is deemed to be referred, unless there is a suspension or it is determined to be ineligible.**

(4) **Duty of claimant — The burden of proving that a claim is eligible to be referred to the Refugee Protection Division rests on the claimant, who must answer truthfully all questions put to them. If the claim is referred, the claimant must produce all documents and information as required by the rules of the Board.**

**Proposed Amendment — 100(4)**

**(4) Duty of claimant — A person whose claim is referred to the Refugee Protection Division must attend an interview with an official of the Board on a date fixed by the referring officer in accordance with the rules of the Board and must at the interview produce all documents and information required by those rules. The date fixed for the interview must not be earlier than 15 days after the day on which the claim is referred, unless the claimant consents to an earlier date.**

2010, c. 8, s. 11(2) [To come into force June 29, 2012, or earlier by order.]

**Proposed Addition — 100(4.1)**

**(4.1) Hearing — Refugee Protection Division — The official of the Board who conducts the interview must, in accordance with the regulations and any directions of the Chairperson of the Board, fix the date on which the claimant is to attend a hearing before the Refugee Protection Division.**

2010, c. 8, s. 11(2) [To come into force June 29, 2012, or earlier by order.]

**(5) Quarantine Act — If a traveller is detained or isolated under the *Quarantine Act*, the period referred to in subsections (1) and (3) does not begin to run until the day on which the detention or isolation ends.**

2005, c. 20, s. 81

**101. (1) Ineligibility — A claim is ineligible to be referred to the Refugee Protection Division if**

**(a) refugee protection has been conferred on the claimant under this Act;**

**(b) a claim for refugee protection by the claimant has been rejected by the Board;**

**(c) a prior claim by the claimant was determined to be ineligible to be referred to the Refugee Protection Division, or to have been withdrawn or abandoned;**

**(d) the claimant has been recognized as a Convention refugee by a country other than Canada and can be sent or returned to that country;**

**(e) the claimant came directly or indirectly to Canada from a country designated by the regulations, other than a country of their nationality or their former habitual residence; or**

**(f) the claimant has been determined to be inadmissible on grounds of security, violating human or international rights, serious criminality or organized criminality, except for persons who are inadmissible solely on the grounds of paragraph 35(1)(c).**

*[Editor's Note: SOR/2002-227, s. 340 provides that a determination made before June 28, 2002 that a person is not eligible to have his or her Convention refugee claim determined by the Convention Refugee Determination Division is deemed to be a determination that the claim is ineligible to be referred to the Refugee Protection Division.*

*SOR/2002-227, s. 341 further provides that a claim to be a Convention refugee that was withdrawn or declared to be abandoned before June 28, 2002 is deemed to be a claim determined to be withdrawn or abandoned under the* Immigration and Refugee Protection Act, *S.C. 2001, c. 27.]*

(2) **Serious criminality — A claim is not ineligible by reason of serious criminality under paragraph (1)(f) unless**

**(a) in the case of inadmissibility by reason of a conviction in Canada, the conviction is for an offence under an Act of Parliament punishable by a maximum term of imprisonment of at least 10 years and for which a sentence of at least two years was imposed; or**

**(b) in the case of inadmissibility by reason of a conviction outside Canada, the Minister is of the opinion that the person is a danger to the public in Canada and the conviction is for an offence that, if committed in Canada, would constitute an offence under an Act of Parliament that is punishable by a maximum term of imprisonment of at least 10 years.**

*[Editor's Note: SOR/2002-227, s. 326(1) provides that a claim to be a Convention Refugee by a person described in subparagraph 19(1)(c.1)(i) of the* Immigration Act, *R.S.C. 1985, c. I-2 (the "former Act") in respect of whom the Minister was of the opinion under subparagraph 46.01(1)(e)(i) of the former Act that the person constitutes a danger to the public in Canada is deemed, if no determination was made by a senior immigration officer under s. 45 of the former Act, to be a claim for refugee protection made by a person described in paragraph 101(2)(b) of the new* Immigration and Refugee Protection Act, *S.C. 2001, c. 27 who is inadmissible and in respect of whom the Minister is of the opinion that the person is a danger to the public.]*

IRP Act

## Case Law

### Section 101(1)

*Tsering v. Canada (Minister of Citizenship & Immigration)*, 2008 CarswellNat 3295, 2008 CarswellNat 2054, 2008 FC 799 (F.C.) — In 2007, the applicant tried to come to Canada from the United States where she had been living and working. She was stopped at the border and found to be ineligible to make a refugee claim in Canada. Normally, a person entering Canada from the United States is ineligible because Canada recognizes the United States as a "safe third country" in which to make a refugee claim. However, stateless persons who are former habitual residents of the United States are exempted from the safe third country rule. Similarly, persons who are family members of permanent residents of Canada are exempted. The immigration officer found the applicant to be stateless and neither a former habitual resident of the United States nor a family member of a permanent resident of Canada. The officer's findings did not constitute adequate reasons for deciding that the applicant was not a former habitual resident of the United States. The officer's notes mention only a few of the many factors that might have been relevant to an assessment of whether the applicant had formed any significant attachment to the United States, but which do not, in themselves, suggest that she had not been a habitual resident there. The fact is that she lived and worked in the United States for seven years. The proper test is whether the claimant has established a significant period of actual residence in the country in question. The application for judicial review was allowed.

*Wangden v. Canada (Minister of Citizenship & Immigration)* (2008), 76 Imm. L.R. (3d) 52, 336 F.T.R. 242 (Eng.), 2008 CarswellNat 4077, 2008 CarswellNat 5516, 2008 FC 1230 (F.C.); affirmed (2009), 86 Imm. L.R. (3d) 165, 398 N.R. 265, 2009 FCA 344, 2009 CarswellNat 3878, 2009 CarswellNat 4975 (F.C.A.) — The Minister's delegate determined that the applicant was ineligible to be referred to the Refugee Protection Division pursuant to paragraph 101(1)(d) as he had been "recognized as a Convention refugee by the U.S.A. and to which [he] could be sent and returned". The delegate signed an exclusion order against the applicant. Pursuant to paragraph 49(2)(b) of the IRPA, the order did not come into force for seven days and the applicant was not required to return to the U.S. immediately. His removal to the United States was stayed until the final disposition of this application by the order of the Chief Justice issued on April 8, 2008.

In the case at bar, the delegate's ineligibility decision is consistent with the primary objective of the IRPA, which is about saving lives and offering protection to the displaced and persecuted, since the applicant can be returned to the United States where he will not be at risk of persecution. Based on the objectives of the IRPA and on the wording of paragraph 101(1)(d), the Court concluded that Parliament did not intend for this provision to include consideration of whether a person could *remain* indefinitely in the country in which he or she has been recognized as a Convention refugee and to which he or she can be returned. Of importance is whether the individuals are protected from risk, not whether they have the full panoply of rights provided for under the 1951 Convention. It would be incompatible with the expeditious and relatively straightforward administrative process of screening certain claims out of the RPD's jurisdiction to require front line immigration officers to conduct a more expansive review of claimants' status in another country to determine whether the particular features of that jurisdiction's domestic law satisfies the definition of "refugee" under the Convention. This is not their role; the Refugee Protection Division level is tasked with this assessment. In this case, the decision makers acted reasonably and within the scope of their authority. The application was dismissed. The following question was certified:

> Is the legal remedy or status of "withholding of removal" in the United States of America equivalent to being "recognized as a Convention refugee", pursuant to s. 101(1)(d) of the IRPA?

The Federal Court of Appeal agreed with the decision of Justice Mosley and dismissed the appeal. The Federal Court of Appeal answered the certified question positively. The legal remedy or status of "withholding of removal" in the United States of America is equivalent to being "recognized as a Convention refugee," pursuant to s. 101(1)(d) of IRPA.

*Bouttavong v. Canada (Minister of Citizenship & Immigration)* (2005), 344 N.R. 134, 2005 CarswellNat 3527, 2005 CarswellNat 5559, 2005 FCA 341 (Fed. C.A.) — Former public danger opinions are irrelevant to the determination of danger to the public under subs. 113(d)(i). This does not mean that the underlying criminal convictions may not be taken into account, only that the danger opinions are irrelevant.

**102. (1) Regulations — The regulations may govern matters relating to the application of sections 100 and 101, may, for the purposes of this Act, define the terms used in those sections and, for the purpose of sharing responsibility with governments of foreign states for the consideration of refugee claims, may include provisions**

> **(a) designating countries that comply with Article 33 of the Refugee Convention and Article 3 of the Convention Against Torture;**
>
> **(b) making a list of those countries and amending it as necessary; and**

**(c) respecting the circumstances and criteria for the application of paragraph 101(1)(e).**

**(2) Factors — The following factors are to be considered in designating a country under paragraph (1)(a):**

**(a) whether the country is a party to the Refugee Convention and to the Convention Against Torture;**

**(b) its policies and practices with respect to claims under the Refugee Convention and with respect to obligations under the Convention Against Torture;**

**(c) its human rights record; and**

**(d) whether it is party to an agreement with the Government of Canada for the purpose of sharing responsibility with respect to claims for refugee protection.**



**(3) Review — The Governor in Council must ensure the continuing review of factors set out in subsection (2) with respect to each designated country.**

## Case Law

*Canadian Counsel for Refugees v. R.* (2008), 74 Admin. L.R. (4th) 79, 2008 CarswellNat 1995, 2008 CarswellNat 2197, 2008 FCA 229 (F.C.A.); leave to appeal to S.C.C. refused 2008 CarswellNat 5170, 2008 CarswellNat 5171 (S.C.C.) — This was an appeal from a decision of Phelan J. (the "applications judge"), granting an application for judicial review by the Canadian Council of Refugees, the Canadian Council of Churches, Amnesty International and John Doe ("the respondents"), declaring invalid sections of 159.1 to 159.7 of the Immigration and Refugee Protection Regulations, and the Agreement between the Government of Canada and the Government of the United States of America for Co-operation in the Examination of Refugee Status Claims from Nationals of Third Countries (the "Safe Third Country Agreement"). The Regulations at issue implement into domestic law a Safe Third Country Agreement between Canada and the United States whereby if a refugee enters Canada from the U.S. at a land border port-of-entry, Canada will, subject to specified exceptions, send the refugee back to the U.S. The same applies for refugees crossing by land from Canada to the U.S. The appeal was allowed and the decision of the applications judge set aside. The appropriate standard of review in respect of the decision of the Governor In Council ("GIC") to designate the United States as a "Safe Third Country" pursuant to s. 102 of the Immigration and Refugee Protection Act is correctness. The Federal Court of Appeal took issue with the applications judge's suggestion that unless "compliance" is made a condition precedent to the designation of a country, the GIC would have discretion to designate a country that does not comply. Subsection 101(2) does not refer to "actual" compliance or compliance "in absolute terms" nor does it otherwise specify the type and extent of compliance contemplated. However, Parliament has specified the four factors to be considered in determining whether a country can be designated. These factors are general in nature and are indicative of Parliament's intent that the matter of compliance be assessed on the basis of an appreciation by the GIC of the country's policies, practices and human rights record. Once it is accepted, as it must be in this case, that the GIC has given due consideration to these four factors, and formed the opinion that the candidate country is compliant with the relevant articles of the Conventions, there is nothing left to be reviewed judicially. The Federal Court of Appeal concluded there was no factual basis on which to assess the alleged *Charter* breaches. The respondents' main contention was directed at a border officer's lack of discretion to forego returning a claimant to the U.S. for reasons other than the enumerated exceptions set out in s. 159.5 of the Regulations. This challenge, however, should be assessed in a proper factual context - that is, when advanced by a refugee who has been denied asylum in Canada pursuant to the Regulations and faces a real risk of *refoulement* in being sent back to the U.S. pursuant to the Safe Third Country Agreement. In this case the refugee never came to Canada, and instead claimed that he would have sought asylum in Canada but for the Regulations.

## *Suspension or Termination of Consideration of Claim*

**103. (1) Suspension — Proceedings of the Refugee Protection Division and of the Refugee Appeal Division are suspended on notice by an officer that**

> **(a) the matter has been referred to the Immigration Division to determine whether the claimant is inadmissible on grounds of security, violating human or international rights, serious criminality or organized criminality; or**
>
> **(b) an officer considers it necessary to wait for a decision of a court with respect to a claimant who is charged with an offence under an Act of Parliament that may be punished by a maximum term of imprisonment of at least 10 years.**

**(2) Continuation — On notice by an officer that the suspended claim was determined to be eligible, proceedings of the Refugee Protection Division and of the Refugee Appeal Division shall continue.**

### Case Law

*Tjiueza v. Canada (Minister of Safety & Emergency Preparedness)* (2009), 86 Imm. L.R. (3d) 176, 357 F.T.R. 179 (Eng.), 2009 FC 1247, 2009 CarswellNat 4168, 2009 CarswellNat 5296 (F.C.) — This was an application for judicial review of a notice given by an enforcement officer of the Pacific Region Enforcement Centre of the Canadian Border Services Agency under s. 104(1)(b) of the Act. The officer found the applicant's claim for refugee protection ineligible to be referred to the Refugee Protection Division because the Immigration Division had determined the applicant to be inadmissible on grounds of security. The issue raised by the applicant is reviewable on a correctness standard. Determining whether or not the officer had the discretion to issue the notice requires statutory interpretation and is therefore a question of law. If he had discretion, whether he failed to exercise it was either an issue of law or of procedural fairness, both of which are reviewable against the standard of correctness. Finally, where it is found that he had discretion and exercised it, whether he exercised that discretion properly is reviewable on a standard of reasonableness.

While s. 104 of IRPA does generally give an officer discretion as to whether or not to redetermine the eligibility of the claim, that discretion does not exist in the case of a claim that has been suspended under s. 103. In the case of a claim that has been suspended, any discretion that may exist regarding re-determining the eligibility of a claim would have been exercised in making the decision under s. 103 to suspend the RPD proceeding. Once a claim is suspended, IRPA only provides for two possible results: either the proceedings are continued because an officer notifies the RPD that the claim is eligible, or the proceedings are terminated because an officer notifies the RPD that the claim is not eligible.

The Manual confirms that the officer generally has discretion under s. 104. However, it states that the officer would only exercise his discretion because situations may arise where the RPD ought to make a decision on the claim (for example, in cases involving exclusion clauses). Since a claim that has been suspended under s. 103 will remain suspended indefinitely, the RPD will never make a decision on this sort of claim. Thus it seems that the discretion in s. 104 was never meant to apply to this situation. This is consistent with the provisions of IRPA and the objective of this Act that require refugee protection claims to be dealt with efficiently and expeditiously. Furthermore, this interpretation is supported by the fact that an indefinite suspension would not give any practical benefit to the applicant. Having come to the conclusion that the officer had no discretion, and was required to determine the eligibility of the applicant's claim according to the ID finding and to notify the RPD of his determination, there is no need to address the other questions raised by the applicant. He may still have his risk assessed by making a PRRA application. The application for judicial review was dismissed. The following question was certified:

> After an RPD hearing has been suspended under s. 103 of the *Immigration and Refugee Protection Act* pending the outcome of an ID hearing and re-determination of a claim's eligibility, if the ID determines that the claimant is inadmissible for security reasons, does the officer have discretion under the *Immigration and Refugee Protection Act* to not re-determine the claim's eligibility and to not notify the RPD of the officer's decision on eligibility, and thereby suspend the RPD hearing indefinitely?

**104. (1) Notice of ineligible claim — An officer may, with respect to a claim that is before the Refugee Protection Division or, in the case of paragraph (d), that is before or has been determined by the Refugee Protection Division or the Refugee Appeal Division, give notice that an officer has determined that**

> **(a) the claim is ineligible under paragraphs 101(1)(a) to (e);**
>
> **(b) the claim is ineligible under paragraph 101(1)(f);**
>
> **(c) the claim was referred as a result of directly or indirectly misrepresenting or withholding material facts relating to a relevant matter and that the claim was not otherwise eligible to be referred to that Division; or**
>
> **(d) the claim is not the first claim that was received by an officer in respect of the claimant.**

**(2) Termination and nullification — A notice given under the following provisions has the following effects:**

> **(a) if given under any of paragraphs (1)(a) to (c), it terminates pending proceedings in the Refugee Protection Division respecting the claim; and**
>
> **(b) if given under paragraph (1)(d), it terminates proceedings in and nullifies any decision of the Refugee Protection Division or the Refugee Appeal Division respecting a claim other than the first claim.**

## Case Law

*Tjiueza v. Canada (Minister of Safety & Emergency Preparedness)* (2009), 86 Imm. L.R. (3d) 176, 357 F.T.R. 179 (Eng.), 2009 FC 1247, 2009 CarswellNat 4168, 2009 CarswellNat 5296 (F.C.) — This was an application for judicial review of a notice given by an enforcement officer of the Pacific Region Enforcement Centre of the Canadian Border Services Agency under s. 104(1)(b) of the Act. The officer found the applicant's claim for refugee protection ineligible to be referred to the Refugee Protection Division because the Immigration Division had determined the applicant to be inadmissible on grounds of security. The issue raised by the applicant is reviewable on a correctness standard. Determining whether or not the officer had the discretion to issue the notice requires statutory interpretation and is therefore a question of law. If he had discretion, whether he failed to exercise it was either an issue of law or of procedural fairness, both of which are reviewable against the standard of correctness. Finally, where it is found that he had discretion and exercised it, whether he exercised that discretion properly is reviewable on a standard of reasonableness.

While s. 104 of IRPA does generally give an officer discretion as to whether or not to re-determine the eligibility of the claim, that discretion does not exist in the case of a claim that has been suspended under s. 103. In the case of a claim that has been suspended, any discretion that may exist regarding re-determining the eligibility of a claim would have been exercised in making the decision under s. 103 to suspend the RPD proceeding. Once a claim is suspended, IRPA only provides for two possible results: either the proceedings are continued because an officer notifies the RPD that the claim is eligible, or the proceedings are terminated because an officer notifies the RPD that the claim is not eligible.

The Manual confirms that the officer generally has discretion under s. 104. However, it states that the officer would only exercise his discretion because situations may arise where the RPD ought to make a decision on the claim (for example, in cases involving exclusion clauses). Since a claim that has been suspended under s. 103 will remain suspended indefinitely, the RPD will never make a decision on this sort of claim. Thus it seems that the discretion in s. 104 was never meant to apply to this situation. This is consistent with the provisions of IRPA and the objective of this Act that require refugee protection claims to be dealt with efficiently and expeditiously. Furthermore, this interpretation is supported by the fact that an indefinite suspension would not give any practical benefit to the applicant. Having come to the conclusion that the officer had no discretion, and was required to determine the eligibility of the applicant's claim according to the ID finding and to notify the RPD of his determination, there is no need to address the other questions raised by the applicant. He may still have his risk assessed by making a PRRA application. The application for judicial review was dismissed. The following question was certified:

> After an RPD hearing has been suspended under s. 103 of the *Immigration and Refugee Protection Act* pending the outcome of an ID hearing and re-determination of a claim's eligibility, if the ID determines that the claimant is inadmissible for security reasons, does the officer have discretion under the *Immigration and Refugee Protection Act* to not re-determine the claim's eligibility and to not notify the RPD of the officer's decision on eligibility, and thereby suspend the RPD hearing indefinitely?

## *Extradition Procedure*

**105. (1) Suspension if proceeding under *Extradition Act* — The Refugee Protection Division and Refugee Appeal Division shall not commence, or shall sus-**

**pend, consideration of any matter concerning a person against whom an authority to proceed has been issued under section 15 of the *Extradition Act* with respect to an offence under Canadian law that is punishable under an Act of Parliament by a maximum term of imprisonment of at least 10 years, until a final decision under the *Extradition Act* with respect to the discharge or surrender of the person has been made.**

(2) **Continuation if discharge under *Extradition Act* — If the person is finally discharged under the *Extradition Act*, the proceedings of the applicable Division may be commenced or continued as though there had not been any proceedings under that Act.**

(3) **Rejection if surrender under *Extradition Act* — If the person is ordered surrendered by the Minister of Justice under the *Extradition Act* and the offence for which the person was committed by the judge under section 29 of that Act is punishable under an Act of Parliament by a maximum term of imprisonment of at least 10 years, the order of surrender is deemed to be a rejection of a claim for refugee protection based on paragraph (b) of Section F of Article 1 of the Refugee Convention.**

(4) **Final decision — The deemed rejection referred to in subsection (3) may not be appealed, and is not subject to judicial review except to the extent that a judicial review of the order of surrender is provided for under the *Extradition Act*.**

(5) **Limit if no previous claim — If the person has not made a claim for refugee protection before the order of surrender referred to in subsection (3), the person may not do so before the surrender.**

## *Claimant Without Identification*

106. **Credibility — The Refugee Protection Division must take into account, with respect to the credibility of a claimant, whether the claimant possesses acceptable documentation establishing identity, and if not, whether they have provided a reasonable explanation for the lack of documentation or have taken reasonable steps to obtain the documentation.**

### Case Law

*Flores v. Canada (Minister of Citizenship & Immigration)*, 2005 CarswellNat 2332, 2005 FC 1138 (F.C.) — The applicant claimed refugee protection in Canada, but a panel of the Immigration and Refugee Board dismissed his claim because it felt he had not provided acceptable evidence of identity. On the day of his hearing, the applicant provided two documents he hoped would constitute good evidence of his identity and nationality. The first was a photocopy of one page of a Salvadoran passport. The second was a faxed copy of a birth certificate. The Board found that the applicant had failed to prove his identity and, therefore, that it was unnecessary to consider the merits of the claim. The Board stated that it "rejected" the applicant's identity documents for the following reasons: the photocopy of the passport did not resemble the applicant; the documents were mere photocopies; the originals were not available, and the applicant could not provide a reasonable explanation why he could not get them; the applicant had nearly a year between making his refugee claim and the date of his hearing to obtain acceptable identity documents;

the documents were filed very late, on the date of the hearing; and the applicant claimed to have spent a period of time in the United States but, without a complete passport, it was impossible to verify the duration of his stay there. Since the Board did not reject the documents solely because they were photocopies, its decision was not out of keeping with the requirements of the IRPA or the Rules.

*Rasheed v. Canada (Minister of Citizenship & Immigration)*, [2004] F.C.J. No. 715, 35 Imm. L.R. (3d) 299, 2004 CarswellNat 1086, 2004 FC 587, 2004 CarswellNat 4478, 251 F.T.R. 258 (F.C.) — The determination made by a panel with respect to the identity of the applicant should be examined on the reasonableness *simpliciter* standard.

*Gasparyan v. Canada (Minister of Citizenship & Immigration)*, [2003] F.C.J. No. 1103, 2003 CarswellNat 2140, 2003 FC 863, 2003 CarswellNat 5121, 2003 CFPI 863 (F.C.) — The appropriate standard for reviewing the Refugee Division's assessment of identity documents is patent unreasonableness. The panel had firsthand access to the identity documents and the testimony of the applicants and also possesses a high level of expertise in this area.

## Decision on Claim for Refugee Protection

### Author's Note

*[Procedural decisions regarding refugee hearings under the former Act are collected and tabbed separately for your information. Decisions concerning the sufficiency of reasons in a refugee case are collected under Refugee Protection Division Rule 61.]*

**107. (1) Decision — The Refugee Protection Division shall accept a claim for refugee protection if it determines that the claimant is a Convention refugee or person in need of protection, and shall otherwise reject the claim.**

*[Editor's Note: SOR/2002-227, s. 343 provides that, subject to s. 191 of the* Immigration and Refugee Protection Act, *S.C. 2001, c. 27 (the "new Act"), a claim of a person who was determined eligible before June 28, 2002 to have a claim to be a Convention refugee determined by the Convention Refugee Determination Division, and in respect of which no determination was made by that Division, is a claim that:*

*(a) is referred under the new Act to the Refugee Protection Division unless an officer gives notice under s. 104(1) of the new Act; and*

*(b) is subject to the provisions of the new Act.]*

**(2) No credible basis — If the Refugee Protection Division is of the opinion, in rejecting a claim, that there was no credible or trustworthy evidence on which it could have made a favourable decision, it shall state in its reasons for the decision that there is no credible basis for the claim.**

### Case Law

#### Section 107(1)

*Avci v. Canada (Minister of Citizenship & Immigration)*, 35 Imm. L.R. (3d) 19, 2003 CarswellNat 3039, 244 F.T.R. 320 (note), 2003 FCA 359, 313 N.R. 307, [2003] F.C.J. No. 1424 (F.C.A.) — If the Board reserves its decision at the end of the Refugee determination hearing, it renders its decision and becomes *functus officio* when it signs written reasons for the decision and transmits them to the registrar.

*Yu v. Canada (Minister of Citizenship & Immigration)*, 2003 CarswellNat 1694, 2003 CarswellNat 2639, [2003] F.C.J. No. 932, 2003 FCT 720, 2003 CFPI 720 (Fed. T.D.) — The applicant sought to review a negative decision of his refugee claim. The appropriate standard of review is one of patent unreasonableness, which means that findings of credibility and of fact must be supported by the evidence and must not be made capriciously. These findings must not be based on erroneous findings of fact or made without regard to the evidence. When the Board finds a claimant not credible based on implausibility findings which are open to it on the evidence, the Court should not interfere unless an overriding error has been made.

The panel did not commit a reviewable error when it failed to confront the applicant with the inconsistencies in his testimony regarding his arrival in Canada. The Board was not obligated by the duty of fairness to put all of its concerns regarding credibility before the applicant.

Contradictions or discrepancies in the evidence of a refugee claimant are a well-accepted basis for a finding of a lack of credibility. The application in this case was dismissed.



**Proposed Addition — 107.1**

**107.1 Manifestly unfounded — If the Refugee Protection Division rejects a claim for refugee protection, it may state in its reasons for the decision that the claim is manifestly unfounded if it is of the opinion that the claim is clearly fraudulent.**

2010, c. 8, s. 11.1 [To come into force June 29, 2012, or earlier by order.]

## *Cessation of Refugee Protection*

**108. (1) Rejection — A claim for refugee protection shall be rejected, and a person is not a Convention refugee or a person in need of protection, in any of the following circumstances:**

**(a) the person has voluntarily reavailed themself of the protection of their country of nationality;**

**(b) the person has voluntarily reacquired their nationality;**

**(c) the person has acquired a new nationality and enjoys the protection of the country of that new nationality;**

**(d) the person has voluntarily become re-established in the country that the person left or remained outside of and in respect of which the person claimed refugee protection in Canada; or**

**(e) the reasons for which the person sought refugee protection have ceased to exist.**

*[Editor's Note: SOR/2002-227, s. 339 provides that a determination made in Canada before June 28, 2002 that a person is not a Convention refugee is deemed to be a claim for refugee protection rejected by the Immigration and Refugee Board.]*

(2) **Cessation of refugee protection — On application by the Minister, the Refugee Protection Division may determine that refugee protection referred to in subsection 95(1) has ceased for any of the reasons described in subsection (1).**

(3) **Effect of decision — If the application is allowed, the claim of the person is deemed to be rejected.**

*[Editor's Note: SOR/2002-227, s. 344 provides that a determination made in Canada before June 28, 2002 that a person has ceased to be a Convention refugee is deemed to be a determination by the Immigration and Refugee Board that refugee protection has ceased.]*

(4) **Exception — Paragraph (1)(e) does not apply to a person who establishes that there are compelling reasons arising out of previous persecution, torture, treatment or punishment for refusing to avail themselves of the protection of the country which they left, or outside of which they remained, due to such previous persecution, torture, treatment or punishment.**

## Case Law

### Section 108(1)

*Editor's note: The following case summaries were collected under the provisions of the former Act relating to the cessation of Convention Refugee status. The previous jurisprudence interpreting refugee concepts may still be relevant.*

*Chandrakumar v. Canada (Minister of Employment & Immigration)*, 1997 CarswellNat 792 (Fed. T.D.) — The applicant sought to review a negative decision of the CRDD. A panel of the CRDD found that the applicant's renewal of his Sri Lanka passport indicated that he had re-availed himself of the protection of Sri Lanka. A person who applies for a passport must have the intention to re-avail himself or herself of the protection of the state. Such an intention cannot simply be assumed. The panel of the CRDD in this case did not engage in an analysis of the intention of the principal applicant in renewing his passport. The panel seems to have assumed that the simple action of renewing the passport without more was sufficient to establish re-availment of the protection of Sri Lanka. Such an inference is unreasonable. Accordingly, the decision of the CRDD was set aside.

*Yusuf v. Canada (Minister of Employment & Immigration)* (1995), 179 N.R. 11 (Fed. C.A.) — A change in the political situation in the claimant's country of origin is only relevant if it may help in determining whether or not there is, at the date of the hearing, a reasonable and objectively foreseeable possibility that the claimant will be persecuted in the event of a return there. The use of words such as meaningful, effective or durable are only helpful if one keeps clearly in mind that the only question, and therefore the only test, is that derived from the definition of Convention refugee. The issue of so-called change in circumstances is simply one of fact. It is not a question of law.

See annotation for *Canada (Minister of Employment & Immigration) v. Obstoj*, [1992] 2 F.C. 739, 93 D.L.R. (4th) 144, 142 N.R. 81 (Fed. C.A.), under s. 96, *supra*.

## Case Law

### Section 108(2)

See annotation for *Canada (Minister of Employment & Immigration) v. Obstoj*, [1992] 2 F.C. 739, 93 D.L.R. (4th) 144, 142 N.R. 81 (Fed. C.A.), under s. 96, *supra.*



## Case Law

### Section 108(4)

*Brovina v. Canada (Minister of Citizenship & Immigration)*, [2004] F.C.J. No. 771, 2004 CarswellNat 2841, 2004 CarswellNat 1243, 2004 FC 635, 254 F.T.R. 244 (F.C.) — For a panel to embark on a compelling reasons analysis, it must first find that there was a valid refugee or protected person claim and that the reasons for the claim have ceased to exist. It is only then that the Board should consider whether the nature of the claimant's experiences in the former country were so appalling that he or she should not be expected to return and put himself or herself under the protection of that state.

*Editor's note: The following case summaries were collected under the provisions of the former Act relating to the cessation of Convention Refugee status. The previous jurisprudence interpreting refugee concepts may still be relevant.*

*Elemah v. Canada (Minister of Citizenship & Immigration)*, 2001 CarswellNat 1530, 2001 FCT 779 (Fed. T.D.) The applicant sought to review a negative decision of a panel of the CRDD. The decision of the panel was set aside. The panel determined that the applicant had not suffered appalling persecution which would bring him within the ambit of subs. 2(3). Subsection 2(3) does not establish a test which necessitates that persecution reach a level to qualify it as atrocious and appalling. Rather, the subsection requires that the Board must thoroughly canvass all the documentary and oral evidence, including the nature of the incidents of torture and the medical reports provided by the parties, in order to determine, as stated in the legislation, if there are "compelling reasons" not to return the claimant.

*Kulla v. Canada (Minister of Citizenship & Immigration)* (2000), 2000 CarswellNat 1912, [2000] F.C.J. No. 1347 (Fed. T.D.) — The applicant's claim for refugee status was rejected by a panel of the CRDD. The panel also concluded that subs. 2(3) of the *Immigration Act* was not of any assistance to the applicant. The panel found that the claimant's past experience, at the hands of the authorities in Albania, was "cruel and harsh" but not "atrocious" and "appalling" and, therefore, not caught by s. 2(3). The issue is not whether a claimant's past experience can be characterized as "atrocious" and "appalling", adjectives used in other jurisprudence, but rather, if the person has established that there are compelling reasons arising out of any previous persecution for the applicant refusing to avail himself or herself of the protection of the country that he or she has left.

*Yamba v. Canada (Minister of Citizenship & Immigration)* (2000), 254 N.R. 388, 181 F.T.R. 132 (note), 2000 CarswellNat 543, [2000] F.C.J. No. 457 (Fed. C.A.) — The motions judge was correct in holding that the Refugee Division is under an obligation to consider the applicability of subs. 2(3) once it is satisfied that refugee status cannot be claimed because of a change in country conditions under paragraph 2(2)(e). The evidentiary burden is upon the claimant to establish that there are compelling reasons for not returning to the country in which the past persecution arose.

*Jiminez v. Canada (Minister of Citizenship & Immigration)* (1999), 162 F.T.R. 177 (Fed. T.D.) — In order to bring himself within the provisions of s. 2(3) of the *Immigration Act*, the applicant is not required to show that he is suffering continual psychological after-effects from the persecution which he suffered in his country of nationality. The Board accepted as a fact that the applicant had been beaten, burned, raped, shot and left for dead. However, it did not comment on whether the nature of the applicant's persecution was sufficiently appalling and atrocious to warrant the application of s. 2(3), rather it focused exclusively on whether the applicant was currently suffering from "the continued effect of past persecution". In so deciding, the Board erred in law, and the matter was remitted back for redetermination.

*Shahid v. Canada (Minister of Citizenship & Immigration)* (1995), 89 F.T.R. 106 (Fed. T.D.) — The applicant claimed that by virtue of s. 2(3) of the *Immigration Act* he should not be returned to Pakistan. The Board, in refusing to apply s. 2(3) determined that it required an ongoing fear of persecution. For this reason the decision was set aside. The Board, once it embarked upon the assessment of the applicant's claim under s. 2(3) had the duty to consider the level of atrocity of the acts inflicted upon the applicant, the repercussions upon his physical and mental state, and determine whether this experience alone constituted a compelling reason not to return him to his country of origin. The panel failed to do this and accordingly its decision was quashed and the matter returned for a new hearing before a differently constituted tribunal.

*Hassan v. Canada (Minister of Employment & Immigration)* (1994), 77 F.T.R. 309 (Fed. T.D.) — The respondent conceded that the Board had erred in this case. However, counsel for the applicants was of the view that the panel had erred in its interpretation of s. 2(3) of the *Immigration Act* and that if it had not been for this error the applicants would have been found to be Convention refugees.

Before the Court will refer a matter back for redetermination in accordance with a direction that the applicants be found to be Convention refugees, the following circumstances must apply:

1. the evidence must be so clearly conclusive that the only possible conclusion is that the claimant is a Convention refugee;
2. the sole issue to be decided must be a pure question of law which will be dispositive of the case;
3. the legal issue must be based on uncontroverted evidence and accepted facts; and
4. there must be no factual issues which involve conflicting evidence which are central to the claim.

To require that before s. 2(3) could apply, there would have to be a Convention refugee determination in respect of an applicant, would make the application of s. 2(3) dependent on timing alone. Section 2(3) does not require an on-going fear of persecution. It only applies to a tiny minority of present day claimants who can demonstrate that they have suffered such appalling persecution that their experience alone is a compelling reason not to return them to the country in which they suffered the persecution. Section 2(3) only applies to extraordinary cases in which the persecution is relatively so exceptional that, even in the wake of changed circumstances, it would be wrong to return refugee claimants. The Court did not direct that on a rehearing of the matter the Board find the applicants to be Convention refugees. The Board with its experience and expertise was best able to assess whether, having regard to the special and limited application of s. 2(3), the applicants fell within its ambit.

*Arguello-Garcia v. Canada (Minister of Employment & Immigration)* (1993), 21 Imm. L.R. (2d) 285, 64 F.T.R. 307, 70 F.T.R. 1 — The Refugee Division found the applicant not to be a Convention refugee. The Board erred in law when it found that the facts did not amount to previous persecution. The Court noted that it had accepted a broad range of harassment and ill-treatment as constituting persecution and, furthermore, that neither deprivation of physical liberty nor physical mistreatment were essential elements of persecution.

The Board, notwithstanding its findings that there was no persecution, found that there had been a change of circumstance in El Salvador. The second issue before the Court was whether the applicant fell within the special or limited category of persons to which s. 2(3) of the *Immigration Act* applies. Section 2(3) is based on a general humanitarian principle which permits a person who has suffered serious past persecution to retain or obtain Convention refugee status despite fundamental changes in his or her country of origin.

The Court referred to the Concise Oxford Dictionary of Current English, Clarendon Press, Oxford, 1990 definition of atrocious and appalling. Atrocious was defined as very bad or unpleasant or alternatively extremely savage or wicked. An atrocity was defined as an extremely wicked or cruel act, especially one involving physical violence or injury. Appalling was defined as shocking, unpleasant or bad.

In this case, the torture and sexual assault experienced by the applicant qualified as atrocious and appalling acts as defined above. The right not to be subject to torture and cruel, inhuman and degrading treatment is a fundamental right which enjoys the highest international protection.

Further, there was ample evidence before the Board to show that the applicant continued to suffer severe psychological hardship as a result of the very serious persecution which he and his family members suffered in El Salvador. A psychiatric report entered in evidence stated that the applicant was suffering from post-traumatic stress disorder, related to his personal and family history of violent persecution, torture and massacre. The finding by the Board that the applicant did not fit within the criteria set out in s. 2(3) was on a misconstruction of the applicable test and constituted an error in law.

The application was granted and the matter returned to a differently constituted panel of the IRB to reconsider the evidence in accordance with the reasons of the Court.

## *Applications to Vacate*

**109. (1) Vacation of refugee protection — The Refugee Protection Division may, on application by the Minister, vacate a decision to allow a claim for refugee protection, if it finds that the decision was obtained as a result of directly or indirectly misrepresenting or witholding material facts relating to a relevant matter.**

*[Editor's Note: SOR/2002-227, s. 345 provides that a decision made in Canada before June 28, 2002 to approve an application to reconsider and vacate a determination that a person is a Convention refugee is deemed to be a determination by the Immigration and Refugee Board to vacate a decision to allow a claim for refugee protection.]*

**(2) Rejection of application — The Refugee Protection Division may reject the application if it is satisfied that other sufficient evidence was considered at the time of the first determination to justify refugee protection.**



IRP Act

*[Editor's Note: SOR/2002-227, s. 339 provides that a determination made in Canada before June 28, 2002 that a person is not a Convention refugee is deemed to be a claim for refugee protection rejected by the Immigration and Refugee Board.]*

**(3) Allowance of application — If the application is allowed, the claim of the person is deemed to be rejected and the decision that led to the conferral of refugee protection is nullified.**

## Case Law

*Bortey v. Canada (Minister of Citizenship & Immigration)*, 2006 CarswellNat 327, 2006 CarswellNat 2422, 2006 FC 190 (F.C.) — The Board found that the applicant obtained refugee status on the basis of misrepresentations and the withholding of material facts. The Board also concluded that once these misrepresentations were set aside, there was no other sufficient evidence considered at the time of the first determination on which a decision in favour of the applicant could have been based. The Board was required, under subs. 109(2) of the IRPA, to decipher whether any of the evidence cited in support of the original positive determination is left "untainted" by the fact of the newly discovered material misrepresentations.

*Iliev v. Canada (Minister of Citizenship & Immigration)*, 2005 CarswellNat 2010, 2005 FC 395 (F.C.) — The applicant, a citizen of Bulgaria, made a claim to be a Convention refugee and was found to be a Convention refugee. However, the Minister of Citizenship and Immigration obtained leave to vacate the determination of the Convention Refugee Determination Division pursuant to s. 109 of the IRPA on the basis that the applicant had obtained refugee status on fraudulent means, misrepresentation, suppression and concealment of material facts, specifically with respect to the entry of two criminal convictions in Bulgaria. The Minister relied on certificates of conviction that had been issued by the Bulgarian court. The Board accepted the Minister's argument and concluded that pursuant to Article 1F(b) of the *Refugee Convention*, the applicant was a person who was excluded from consideration as a Convention refugee as a result of having committed a serious non-political offence. The Board's conclusion was set aside by the Federal Court as it was made in the absence of any evidence about the equivalency between the Bulgarian criminal law and the Canadian criminal law. A factual finding made without evidence is a ground for judicial intervention, pursuant to s. 18.1(4) of the *Federal Courts Act*, R.S.C. 1985, c. F-7, as amended.

*Calixto v. Canada (Minister of Citizenship & Immigration)* (2005), 49 Imm. L.R. (3d) 36, 2005 CarswellNat 2165, 2005 CarswellNat 4919, 2005 FC 1037 (F.C.) — The applicant arrived in Canada and was granted refugee status, and then applied for landed immigrant status. At a CSIS interview, the applicant was confronted with information that he had lied about his past activities, including a criminal record in the United States that arose during the time he claimed he was being persecuted in Mexico. The applicant admitted this misrepresentation and as a result of the admission, the applicant's refugee status was vacated pursuant to s. 109(1) of the IRPA. A report was prepared pursuant to s. 44(1) setting out that the applicant was inadmissible pursuant to s. 40(1)(c). An immigration officer found the report well founded and consequently made a deportation order against the applicant pursuant to s. 44(2). The applicant argued that s. 40(1)(c) would render him inadmissible only if he made a misrepresentation in the course of the vacation proceeding before the Refugee Protection Division. The Court held that whether the applicant made any misrepresentations during the vacation hearing was not a relevant consideration. Instead, the use of the term "misrepresentation" in s. 40(1)(c) should be read as denoting statements of fact which operate to make a person inadmissible, that is, if either of the events mentioned in this section are proved to have occurred, a person is considered, or "deemed," inadmissible for "misrepresentation."



**Proposed Addition — 109.1**

## *Designated Countries of Origin*

**[Heading added 2010, c. 8, s. 12. To come into force June 29, 2012, or earlier by order.]**

**109.1 (1) Designation of countries of origin — The Minister may, by order, for the purposes of section 111.1, designate a country or part of a country or a class of nationals of a country.**

**(1.1) Limitation — The Minister may make a designation only if**

**(a) the number of claims for refugee protection made in Canada by nationals of the country in question is equal to or greater than the number set out in the regulations; and**

**(b) the rate of acceptance by the Refugee Protection Division of claims made by nationals of the country in question is equal to or lower than the rate set out in the regulations.**

**(1.2) Criteria to be considered — In making a designation, the Minister must take the following criteria into account:**

**(a) the human rights record of the country in question as it relates to**

**(i) the factors set out in sections 96 and 97, and**

**(ii) the international human rights instruments specified in the regulations and any other international instrument that the Minister considers relevant;**

**(b) the availability in the country in question of mechanisms for seeking protection and redress;**

**(c) the number of claims for refugee protection made in Canada by nationals of the country in question;**

**(d) the rate of acceptance by the Refugee Protection Division of claims made by nationals of the country in question and the rate of appeals allowed by the Refugee Appeal Division in respect of appeals made by nationals of the country in question; and**

**(e) any other criteria set out in the regulations.**

**(2) Statutory Instruments Act — An order referred to in subsection (1) is not a statutory instrument for the purposes of the *Statutory Instruments Act*. However, it must be published in the *Canada Gazette*.**

2010, c. 8, s. 12 [To come into force June 29, 2012, or earlier by order.]

**Unproclaimed Text — 110, 111**

## *Appeal to Refugee Appeal Division*

**110. (1) Appeal — A person or the Minister may appeal, in accordance with the rules of the Board, on a question of law, of fact or of mixed law and fact, to the Refugee Appeal Division against a decision of the Refugee Protection Division to allow or reject the person's claim for refugee protection, or a decision of the Refugee Protection Division rejecting an application by the Minister for a determination that refugee protection has ceased or an application by the Minister to vacate a decision to allow a claim for refugee protection.**

**(2) Restriction on appeals — A determination that a refugee protection claim has been withdrawn or abandoned may not be appealed.**

**(2.1) Making of appeal — The appeal must be filed and perfected within the time limits set out in the regulations.**

**(3) Procedure — Subject to subsections (3.1), (4) and (6), the Refugee Appeal Division must proceed without a hearing, on the basis of the record of the proceedings of the Refugee Protection Division, and may accept documentary evidence and written submissions from the Minister and the person who is the subject of the appeal and written submissions from a representative or agent of the United Nations High Commissioner for Refugees and any other person described in the rules of the Board.**

**(3.1) Time limits — Unless a hearing is held under subsection (6), the Refugee Appeal Division must make a decision within the time limits set out in the regulations.**

**(4) Evidence that may be presented — On appeal, the person who is the subject of the appeal may present only evidence that arose after the rejection of their claim or that was not reasonably available, or that the person could not reasonably have been expected in the circumstances to have presented, at the time of the rejection.**

**(5) Exception — Subsection (4) does not apply in respect of evidence that is presented in response to evidence presented by the Minister.**

**(6) Hearing — The Refugee Appeal Division may hold a hearing if, in its opinion, there is documentary evidence referred to in subsection (3)**

> **(a) that raises a serious issue with respect to the credibility of the person who is the subject of the appeal;**
>
> **(b) that is central to the decision with respect to the refugee protection claim; and**
>
> **(c) that, if accepted, would justify allowing or rejecting the refugee protection claim.**

***[Editor's Note: S.C. 2001, c. 27, s. 191 provides that every application, proceeding or matter before the Convention Refugee Determination Division under the* Immigration Act, *R.S.C. 1985, c. I-2 (the "former Act") that is pending or in progress imme-***

*diately before June 28, 2002, in respect of which substantive evidence has been adduced but no decision has been made, shall be continued under the former Act by the Refugee Protection Division of the Immigration and Refugee Board.*

*S.C. 2001, c. 27, s. 194 [not in force at date of publication] provides that in cases referred to in S.C. 2001, c. 27, s. 191, a decision by the Refugee Protection Division following a hearing that has been commenced by the Convention Refugee Determination Division is not subject to an appeal under s. 110 of the* **Immigration and Refugee Protection Act**, *S.C. 2001, c. 27 (the "new Act").*

*S.C. 2001, c. 27, s. 195 [not in force at date of publication] further provides that a decision made by the Convention Refugee Determination Division before June 28, 2002 is not subject to an appeal under s. 110 of the new Act.*

*S.C. 2001, c. 27, s. 198 provides that the Refugee Protection Division has jurisdiction to consider decisions of the Convention Refugee Determination Division that are set aside by the Federal Court or the Supreme Court of Canada, and shall dispose of those matters in accordance with the provisions of the new Act.*

*S.C. 2001, c. 27, s. 199 still further provides that sections 112 to 114 of the new Act apply to a redetermination of a decision set aside by the Federal Court with respect to an application for landing as a member of the post-determination refugee claimants in Canada class within the meaning of the* **Immigration Regulations, 1978**, *SOR/78-172.]*

2010, c. 8, s. 13

**111. (1) Decision — After considering the appeal, the Refugee Appeal Division shall make one of the following decisions:**

**(a) confirm the determination of the Refugee Protection Division;**

**(b) set aside the determination and substitute a determination that, in its opinion, should have been made; or**

**(c) refer the matter to the Refugee Protection Division for re-determination, giving the directions to the Refugee Protection Division that it considers appropriate.**

**(1.1) Manifestly unfounded — For greater certainty, if the Refugee Appeal Division does not set it aside, the Refugee Protection Division's determination under section 107.1 is confirmed.**

**(2) Referrals — The Refugee Appeal Division may make the referral described in paragraph (1)(c) only if it is of the opinion that**

**(a) the decision of the Refugee Protection Division is wrong in law, in fact or in mixed law and fact; and**

**(b) it cannot make a decision under paragraph 111(1)(a) or (b) without hearing evidence that was presented to the Refugee Protection Division.**

2010, c. 8, s. 14

IRP Act

**Proposed Addition — 111.1**

## *Regulations*

**[Heading added 2010, c. 8, s. 14.1. To come into force June 29, 2012, or earlier by order.]**

**111.1 (1) Regulations — The regulations may provide for any matter relating to the application of this Division, and may include provisions**

> **(a) relating to the criteria referred to in subsection 109.1(1.2) and the process to be followed with respect to a designation made under subsection 109.1(1);**
>
> **(b) establishing criteria for the purposes of paragraph 109.1(1.2)(e); and**
>
> **(c) respecting the time limits**
>
> > **(i) for the hearing referred to in subsection 100(4.1),**
> >
> > **(ii) for the filing and perfecting of an appeal under subsection 110(2.1), and**
> >
> > **(iii) for the making of a decision by the Refugee Appeal Division, the extension of those time limits and the circumstances under which they do not apply.**

**(2) Clarification — regulations made under subparagraph (1)(c)(i) — Regulations made under subparagraph (1)(c)(i) may provide for time limits for any of the following claimants that are different from the time limits for other claimants:**

> **(a) claimants who are nationals of a country that is, on the date of their interview referred to in subsection 100(4), a country designated under subsection 109.1(1);**
>
> **(b) claimants who are nationals of a country of which a part is, on the date of their interview referred to in subsection 100(4), a part designated under subsection 109.1(1); or**
>
> **(c) claimants who belong to a class of nationals of a country that is, on the date of their interview referred to in subsection 100(4), a class designated under subsection 109.1(1).**

**(3) Clarification — regulations made under subparagraph (1)(c)(ii) — Regulations made under subparagraph (1)(c)(ii) may provide for time limits for the filing and perfecting of appeals by any of the following claimants that are different from the time limits for other claimants:**

> **(a) claimants whose claims are found by the Refugee Protection Division to be manifestly unfounded under section 107.1;**
>
> **(b) claimants who are nationals of any country that is, on the day on which the decision being appealed is made, a country designated under subsection 109.1(1);**
>
> **(c) claimants who are nationals of a country of which a part is, on the day on which the decision being appealed is made, a part designated under that**

subsection and who lived in that designated part before they left the country; or

(d) claimants who belong to a class of nationals of a country that is, on the day on which the decision being appealed is made, a class designated under that subsection.

(4) **Clarification — regulations made under subparagraph (1)(c)(iii)** — Regulations made under subparagraph (1)(c)(iii) may provide for time limits for making decisions in respect of appeals by claimants referred to in paragraphs (3)(a) to (d) that are different from the time limits for other claimants.

2010, c. 8, s. 14.1 [To come into force June 29, 2012, or earlier by order.]



## Division 3 — Pre-removal Risk Assessment

### *Protection*

112. (1) **Application for protection** — A person in Canada, other than a person referred to in subsection 115(1), may, in accordance with the regulations, apply to the Minister for protection if they are subject to a removal order that is in force or are named in a certificate described in subsection 77(1).

**Proposed Amendment — 112(1)**

(1) **Application for protection** — Subject to subsection (1.1), a person in Canada, other than a person referred to in subsection 115(1), may, in accordance with the regulations and the rules of the Board, apply to the Refugee Protection Division for protection if they are subject to a removal order that is in force.

2010, c. 8, s. 15(1) [To come into force June 29, 2013, or earlier by order.]

**Proposed Addition — 112(1.1)–(1.7)**

(1.1) **Application to Minister** — In the case of a person described in subsection (3), the application for protection must be made to the Minister in accordance with the regulations.

(1.2) **Suspension of application** — Proceedings of the Refugee Protection Division in respect of an application are suspended on notice by an officer that

(a) a report has been referred to the Immigration Division for a determination of whether the applicant is inadmissible on grounds of security, violating human or international rights, serious criminality — as referred to in paragraph (3)(b) — or organized criminality; or

(b) the applicant is the subject of an authority to proceed issued under section 15 of the *Extradition Act*.

(1.3) **Transfer — inadmissibility** — On notice by an officer that the Immigration Division has made a determination that the applicant is inadmissible on the grounds referred to in paragraph (1.2)(a), consideration of the application is transferred to the Minister.

**(1.4) Continuation — On notice by an officer that the Immigration Division has made a determination that the applicant is not inadmissible on the grounds referred to in paragraph (1.2)(a), consideration of the application is continued by the Refugee Protection Division.**

**(1.5) Termination after surrender under *Extradition Act* — If the applicant is ordered surrendered by the Minister of Justice under the *Extradition Act*, consideration of the application is terminated.**

**(1.6) Continuation — If the applicant is finally discharged under the *Extradition Act*, consideration of the application is continued by the Refugee Protection Division.**

**(1.7) Transfer: Refugee Convention — If the Refugee Protection Division makes a determination that the applicant is referred to in section F of Article 1 of the Refugee Convention, consideration of the application is transferred to the Minister.**

2010, c. 8, s. 15(1) [To come into force June 29, 2013, or earlier by order.]

**(2) Exception — Despite subsection (1), a person may not apply for protection if**

**Proposed Amendment — 112(2) opening words**

**(2) Exception — Despite subsections (1) and (1.1), a person may not apply for protection if**

2010, c. 8, s. 15(2) [To come into force June 29, 2013, or earlier by order.]

**(a) they are the subject of an authority to proceed issued under section 15 of the *Extradition Act*;**

**(b) they have made a claim to refugee protection that has been determined under paragraph 101(1)(e) to be ineligible;**

**Proposed Addition — 112(2)(b.1)**

**(b.1) subject to subsection (2.1), less than 12 months have passed since their claim for refugee protection was last rejected — unless it was rejected on the basis of section E or F of Article 1 of the Refugee Convention — or determined to be withdrawn or abandoned by the Refugee Protection Division or the Refugee Appeal Division;**

2010, c. 8, s. 15(3) [To come into force June 29, 2012, or earlier by order.]

**(c) in the case of a person who has not left Canada since the application for protection was rejected, the prescribed period has not expired; or**

**(d) in the case of a person who has left Canada since the removal order came into force, less than six months have passed since they left Canada after their claim to refugee protection was determined to be ineligible, abandoned, withdrawn or rejected, or their application for protection was rejected.**

**Proposed Addition — 112(2.1)–(2.3)**

**(2.1) Exemption — The Minister may exempt from the application of paragraph (2)(b.1)**

**(a) the nationals — or, in the case of persons who do not have a country of nationality, the former habitual residents — of a country;**

**(b) the nationals or former habitual residents of a country who, before they left the country, lived in a given part of that country; and**

**(c) a class of nationals or former habitual residents of a country.**

**(2.2) Application — However, an exemption made under subsection (2.1) does not apply to persons in respect of whom, after the day on which the exemption comes into force, a decision is made respecting their claim for refugee protection by the Refugee Protection Division or, if an appeal is made, by the Refugee Appeal Division.**

**(2.3) Regulations — The regulations may govern any matter relating to the application of subsection (2.1) or (2.2) and may include provisions establishing the criteria to be considered when an exemption is made.**

2010, c. 8, s. 15(4) [To come into force June 29, 2012, or earlier by order.]

**(3) Restriction — Refugee protection may not result from an application for protection if the person**

**(a) is determined to be inadmissible on grounds of security, violating human or international rights or organized criminality;**

**(b) is determined to be inadmissible on grounds of serious criminality with respect to a conviction in Canada punished by a term of imprisonment of at least two years or with respect to a conviction outside Canada for an offence that, if committed in Canada, would constitute an offence under an Act of Parliament punishable by a maximum term of imprisonment of at least 10 years;**

**(c) made a claim to refugee protection that was rejected on the basis of section F of Article 1 of the Refugee Convention; or**

**Proposed Amendment — 112(3)(c)**

**(c) made a claim to refugee protection that was rejected on the basis of section F of Article 1 of the Refugee Convention;**

2010, c. 8, s. 15(5) [To come into force June 29, 2013, or earlier by order.]

**Proposed Addition — 112(3)(c.1)**

**(c.1) made an application for protection and the consideration of that application was transferred to the Minister under subsection (1.7); or**

2010, c. 8, s. 15(5) [To come into force June 29, 2013, or earlier by order.]

**(d) is named in a certificate referred to in subsection 77(1).**

*[Editor's Note: S.C. 2001, c. 27, s. 199 provides that sections 112 to 114 of the* Immigration and Refugee Protection Act, *S.C. 2001, c. 27 (the "new Act") apply to a redetermination of a decision set aside by the Federal Court with respect to an application for landing as a member of the post-determination refugee claimants in Canada class within the meaning of the* Immigration Regulations, 1978, *SOR/78-172.*

*SOR/2002-227, s. 346(1) provides that an application for landing as a member of the post-determination refugee claimants in Canada class in respect of which no determination of whether the applicant is a member of that class was made before June 28, 2002 is an application for protection under sections 112 to 114 of the new Act and those sections apply to the application.*

*SOR/2002-227, s. 346(2) provides that before a decision is made on the application, the applicant shall be notified that he or she may make additional submissions in support of his or her application.*

*SOR/2002-227, s. 346(3) provides that a decision on the application shall not be made until 30 days after notification is given to the applicant.*

*SOR/2002-227, s. 346(4) provides that notification is given*

> *(a) when it is given by hand to the applicant; or*
>
> *(b) if it is sent by mail, seven days after the day on which it was sent to the applicant at the last address provided by him or her to the Department.]*

## Case Law

### Section 112(1)

*Krohmalnik v. Canada (Minister of Citizenship & Immigration)*, 2009 CarswellNat 1635, 2009 FC 589 (F.C.) — The applicant sought judicial review of a negative decision made in relation to her application for a pre-removal risk assessment. It is clearly the role of the PRRA officer to weigh the available information relating to the issues of risk and the availability of state protection. However, where, as here, there is important evidence that runs directly contrary to the officer's finding on a central issue, there is an obligation on the officer to analyze that evidence, and to explain why he or she prefers other evidence on the point in question. The failure of the officer to do so means that the decision lacks the justification, transparency and intelligibility required of a reasonable decision. The application for judicial review was allowed.

*Perez v. Canada (Minister of Citizenship & Immigration)* (2009), 82 Imm. L.R. (3d) 167, 393 N.R. 332, 2009 FCA 171, 2009 CarswellNat 1522, 2009 CarswellNat 5164, [2009] F.C.J. No. 691 (F.C.A.) — This is an appeal from a decision of Justice Martineau dated May 26, 2008 wherein he dismissed the appellants' application for judicial review of a pre-removal risk assessment (PRRA) officer's decision on the ground that the matter was moot because the appellant was no longer in Canada. The Court further held that it would not exercise its discretion to hear the judicial review. After having sought, without success, to stay the removal order issued subsequent to the negative decision of the PRRA officer, the appellant returned to Mexico. Subsequently, leave to seek judicial review of the decision of the PRRA officer was granted. Justice Martineau dismissed the application on the grounds of mootness, applying the decision in *Borowski v. Canada (Attorney General)*, [1989] 1 S.C.R 342. The Federal Court of Appeal agreed with Justice Martineau that the judicial review was moot.

Parliament intended that the PRRA should be determined before the PRRA applicant was removed from Canada, to avoid putting her or him at risk in her or his country of origin. To this extent, if a PRRA applicant is removed from Canada before a determination is made on the risks to which the person would be subject to in her or his country of origin, the intended objective of the PRRA system cannot be met. This explains why s. 112 of the Act specifies that a person applying for protection is a "person in Canada."

By the same logic, a review of a negative decision of a PRRA officer after the subject person has been removed from Canada, is without object. The appeal was dismissed.

*Oshurova c. Canada (Ministre de la Citoyenneté & de l'Immigration)*, 2006 CarswellNat 5301, 2006 FCA 301 (Fed. C.A.) — The Federal Court of Appeal was asked to answer whether there was an appearance of bias, *in this case*, because the same officer decided the application for a visa exemption on humanitarian and compassionate grounds as well as the pre-removal risk assessment.

There is no apprehension of institutional bias of all officers who have been or are involved with these two types of applications. The appeal was dismissed.

*Varga v. Canada (Minister of Citizenship & Immigration)*, [2006] F.C.J. No. 1828, 57 Imm. L.R. (3d) 159, 357 N.R. 333, 277 D.L.R. (4th) 762, 2006 CarswellNat 4183, 2006 FCA 394 (Fed. C.A.) — A PRRA officer has no obligation to consider, in the context of the PRRA, the interests of a Canadian-born child when assessing the risks involved in removing at least one of the parents of that child.

*Ragupathy v. Canada (Minister of Public Safety & Emergency Preparedness)* (2006), 58 Imm. L.R. (3d) 101, 2006 CarswellNat 3734, 2006 FC 1370 (F.C.) — The applicant was a Convention refugee and became a permanent resident of Canada. He then became inadmissible on grounds of serious criminality within the meaning of s. 36 of the IRPA. The Minister's delegate issued an opinion concluding that the applicant was a danger to the public in Canada (the Danger Opinion). The applicant was subject to removal from Canada under paragraph 115(2)(a) of the Act. The enforcement officer had discretion to defer the applicant's removal. The enforcement officer stated in her affidavit that the reason for not deferring removal was because there was no specific reason to do so. The enforcement officer also stated that she relied on the risk assessment provided by the Minister's delegate in the Danger Opinion. Both statements indicated that the enforcement officer was not alert and alive to the possibility that the alleged change in country conditions gave rise to an enhanced risk of torture or persecution upon the applicant's return to Sri Lanka. By relying on the existing risk assessment pre-dating the events identified by the applicant in his request for deferral, the enforcement officer failed to acknowledge the basis for the applicant's concern. The applicant was entitled to an updated risk assessment before removal. Recognizing an applicant's right under s. 7 of the *Charter* to a risk assessment before removal requires that the risk assessment occur proximate in time to the removal and is not incompatible with the need for finality in the system. Whatever the period of delay between the issuance of a Danger Opinion and the scheduled removal, the onus is on the applicant to demonstrate that there has been a material change in circumstances warranting a re-assessment of his risk upon removal. If an enforcement officer declines to exercise the discretion to defer the removal of a deportee pending re-assessment, a judicial stay of the removal order will only be granted where the deportee can satisfy the well-established tri-partite test. The requirements of a serious issue, irreparable harm and the balance of convenience are appropriate safeguards to ensure that vexatious attempts to forestall removal are dealt with accordingly.

The applicant was entitled to an updated risk assessment in light of the considerable passage of time since the issuance of the Danger Opinion. The application for judicial review was allowed in part. The enforcement officer was correct in determining that the applicant was not eligible for a PRRA under subs. 112(1) of the Act. However, the enforcement officer erred in declining to suspend the applicant's removal pending a re-assess-



IRP Act

ment of the risk faced by him on removal in light of the significant change of circumstances alleged by the applicant.

*Qazi v. Canada (Minister of Citizenship & Immigration)*, [2005] F.C.J. No. 2069, 2005 CarswellNat 4129, 2005 CarswellNat 5566, 2005 FC 1667 (F.C.) — The question of when a PRRA becomes unreasonably stale is not solely dependent on the length of time that has passed, but also depends on the applicant establishing that he has been prejudiced by the delay. In this case, nearly two years had elapsed from the time the applicant replied to the negative risk assessment. While the delay was unfortunate, nevertheless there was no evidence that the applicant had been prejudiced by it. The Court concluded that he had not been denied procedural fairness or natural justice.

*Say v. Canada (Solicitor General)*, 2005 CarswellNat 1510, 2005 FC 739 (F.C.) — This application raised the issue of institutional bias or lack of independence on the part of PRRA assessment officers during the period from December 12, 2003 to October 8, 2004 when such officers were situated, in an organizational sense, within the Canada Border Services Agency. The Pre-Removal Risk Assessment Program was first created on the coming into force of the *Immigration and Refugee Protection Act* on the 28th of June, 2002.

The policy basis for assessing risk prior to removal is found in Canada's domestic and international commitments to the principle of non-refoulement. This principle holds that persons should not be removed from Canada to a country where they would be at risk of persecution, torture, risk to life or risk of cruel and unusual treatment or punishment. Such commitments require that risk be reviewed prior to removal.

While a first-time application for a pre-removal risk assessment is being reviewed and assessed, a statutory stay of removal is in effect by virtue of s. 232 of the IRPA Regulations.

The Canada Border Services Agency was created within the Canadian Public Service on the 12th of December, 2003. On that same day, control and supervision of pre-removal risk assessments was transferred to the agency. On the 8$^{th}$ of October 2004, control and supervision of pre-removal risk assessments was transferred back to the Department of Citizenship and Immigration. The fact that the Government, within ten months of transferring the PRRA Program from the Department of Citizenship and Immigration to the CBSA, determined to transfer it back because it concluded the function was more in the nature of a protection function than an enforcement and removal function, does not lead to a presumption that while the program was with CBSA, it was subject to institutional bias. Accordingly, the application for judicial review was dismissed.

*Thamotharampillai v. Canada (Solicitor General)*, 2005 CarswellNat 1503, 2005 FC 756 (F.C.) — A judicial review application directed against a negative PRRA decision is moot where the applicant for judicial review has been removed from Canada following a finding by a judge that the applicant is not entitled to a stay of removal by reason that he or she has failed to meet the "irreparable harm" element of the test for a stay.

*Ratnasingham v. Canada (Minister of Citizenship & Immigration)*, 2005 CarswellNat 1504, 2005 FC 740 (F.C.) — This was an application to review a decision of a pre-removal risk assessment officer. The analysis of the Officer of the impact of changed country conditions is extensive and detailed. The failure, however, to in any way relate that analysis to the risk of forced recruitment of the children by the Tamil Tigers amounts to a reviewable error. The Court was satisfied that the deference owed to a PRRA Officer was minimal. The decision of the Officer was set aside.

*Hausleitner v. Canada (Minister of Citizenship & Immigration)*, 2005 CarswellNat 1202, 2005 FC 641 (F.C.) — The risk assessment to be carried out at the PRRA stage is not to be a reconsideration of the Board's decision, but instead, is limited to an evaluation of new evidence that either arose after the applicant's refugee hearing or was not previously reasonably available to the applicant. An extensive risk assessment should be carried out where a PRRA applicant has not already had their claim to be at risk assessed by the Refugee Protection Division.

*Rasiah v. Canada (Minister of Citizenship & Immigration)*, 2005 CarswellNat 1073, 2005 FC 583 (F.C.) — The purpose of a PRRA application is to assess whether the applicant is in need of protection in Canada because removal to her country of nationality would subject her personally to a danger of torture, a risk to her life or a risk of cruel and unusual treatment or punishment. The PRRA officer should focus the assessment on risk, and not whether the applicant has the personal financial resources to care for herself, if she is removed from Canada.

*Sherzady v. Canada (Minister of Citizenship & Immigration)*, 2005 CarswellNat 971, 2005 FC 516 (F.C.) — A pre-removal risk assessment officer has the delegated authority to decide a properly constituted H&C application. However, when a person applies for a PRRA and appends a request for H&C consideration, without making the H&C application through the appropriate channels, it does not follow that the PRRA officer must consider H&C factors.

*Vasquez v. Canada (Minister of Citizenship & Immigration)*, 2005 CarswellNat 89, 2005 FC 91, [2005] F.C.J. No. 96 (F.C.) — This was an application for a judicial review of the decision of the PRRA Officer. The Officer had no duty to disclose the analysis of the risk of return and to give the applicant an opportunity to make comments before reaching a final decision because the same Officer is making both the PRRA risk assessment and the H&C decision.

*Canada (Minister of Citizenship & Immigration) v. Jaballah* (2004), 38 Imm. L.R. (3d) 157, 2004 CarswellNat 3451, 2004 CarswellNat 2123, (sub nom. *Jaballah, Re)* 325 N.R. 90, 242 D.L.R. (4th) 490, 2004 FCA 257 (F.C.A.) — This was an appeal by the Minister from a decision of the designated judge that the delay by the MCI in deciding the protection application constituted an abuse of process. A protection application involves two risk assessments. One relates to the risk faced by the individual if removed from Canada, and the other assesses the risk the individual poses to the security of Canada. Based on these two assessments and any submissions made by the individual, the Minister decides the protection application.

The decision of the designated judge, made in the course of security certificate proceedings under ss. 78 and 80, is not a judicial review and therefore paragraph 74(d) of IRPA is not applicable.

A decision by a designated judge made under s. 80 is subject to the privative clause in subs. 80(3). The finding that the MCI's delay in deciding the application for protection constituted an abuse of process is not protected from review.

Pursuant to s. 112, a person named in a security certificate may make an application for protection to the MCI. The application must be made before the certificate is determined to be reasonable. If the individual in question makes an application for protection, the designated judge is required to suspend the security certificate proceedings.

In remedying abuses of their process, courts are to be flexible and provide a remedy that is suitable to the circumstances. The decision of how best to remedy an abuse is a discretionary one. An appellate court may only overturn such a decision if it reaches the clear conclusion that there has been a wrongful exercise of discretion.

*Zamora v. Canada (Minister of Citizenship & Immigration)* (2004), 41 Imm. L.R. (3d) 276, 2004 CarswellNat 5619, 2004 CarswellNat 3709, 260 F.T.R. 155 (Eng.), 2004 FC 1414 (F.C.) — The unilateral use of internet information by a PRRA officer is unfair unless the applicant has been given an opportunity to examine the material and make submissions respecting it.

*Nosa v. Canada (Solicitor General)* (2004), 41 Imm. L.R. (3d) 32, 2004 CarswellNat 5095, 2004 CarswellNat 3180, 2004 FC 1248 (F.C.) — On December 12, 2003, the Governor General-in-Council transferred various duties from the Minister of Citizenship and Immigration to the Canada Border Services Agency. A pre-removal risk assessment was one of these functions. The Canada Border Services Agency is presided over by the Solicitor General with the result that the style of cause in this matter was amended removing the Minister of Citizenship and Immigration and adding the Solicitor General of Canada.

This was an application to review a negative decision made by a Pre-Removal Risk Assessment officer. The applicant included in her submissions her husband's personal information form and the favourable determination that his refugee application had received from Canadian immigration. The applicant had taken the position with the PRRA officer that she faced persecution from this same group of people, namely the State Security Service. The officer's failure to consider and explain her analysis of this separate risk made her finding that the applicant had an IFA patently unreasonably. Accordingly, the officer's decision was set aside.

*Harkat v. Canada (Minister of Citizenship & Immigration)*, 2004 CarswellNat 2870, 2004 CarswellNat 1957, (sub nom. *Harkat, Re)* 325 N.R. 298, 2004 FCA 244 (F.C.A.) — After a security certificate was issued against the appellant, he brought a motion requesting that the hearing into the reasonableness of the certificate be suspended pursuant to subs. 79(1) in order that he might make an application for protection under s. 112(1). The designated judge declined to suspend the proceedings into the reasonableness of the security certificate on the grounds that the appellant was not entitled to apply for protection under subs. 112(1) because he had already been determined to be a Convention refugee and therefore was already a protected person under subs. 95(2) of the Act. In the Court of Appeal's opinion the designated judge's decision in this regard was correct.

The appeal with respect to the second order, having to do with the production of a CSIS employee as a witness, was not pursued although the issue of whether there had been an abuse of process was left to the Court of Appeal for its decision. The Court of Appeal decided that there had been no abuse of process to this point in the proceedings against the appellant.

*Singh (H.) v. Canada (Solicitor General)*, [2004] 3 F.C.R. 323, (sub nom. *Singh v. Canada (Minister of Citizenship & Immigration))* 39 Imm. L.R. (3d) 261, 248 F.T.R. 114, (sub nom. *Singh v. Canada (Minister of Citizenship & Immigration) (No. 2))* 117 C.R.R. (2d) 239, 2004 CarswellNat 2091, 2004 CarswellNat 549, 2004 FC 288 (F.C.) — A risk to life under s. 97 does not include having to assess whether there is appropriate health and medical care available in the country in question.

pre-removal risk assessment officers do not have the jurisdiction to consider constitutional questions.

*Sidhu v. Canada (Minister of Citizenship & Immigration)*, [2004] F.C.J. No. 30, 2004 CarswellNat 4182, 2004 CarswellNat 118, 2004 FC 39 (F.C.) — The standard of review to be applied to a Pre-Removal Risk Assessment officer's determination is one of reasonableness *simpliciter*.

*Kaybaki v. Canada (Solicitor General)*, [2004] F.C.J. No. 27, 2004 CarswellNat 149, 2004 CarswellNat 5940, 2004 FC 32 (F.C.) — This was an application to review the decision of a Pre-Removal Risk Assessment (PRRA) officer.

The decision of a PRRA officer is to be accorded deference since it involves findings of fact; however, the decision must be supported by the evidence. The presumption that the decision maker has considered all the evidence is a rebuttable one, and where the evidence in question is of significant probative value, the Court can make a negative inference from the decision maker's failure to mention it.



*Zolotareva v. Canada (Minister of Citizenship & Immigration)* (2003), 2003 CarswellNat 5082, 2003 CarswellNat 3360, [2003] F.C.J. No. 1596, 2003 FC 1274, 241 F.T.R. 289 (F.C.) — The applicant sought to review a decision of a Pre-Removal Risk Assessment Officer (PRRA Officer) which found insufficient humanitarian and compassionate grounds to permit the applicant to remain. The PRRA Officer has jurisdiction to make a determination under subs. 25(1). The PRRA Officer had no duty to disclose the analysis of the risk of return and to give the applicant an opportunity to make comments before reaching a final decision. There is no obligation on the PRRA officer to do so where there is no third party involved in the decision making.

## Section 112(3)

*Liu v. Canada (Minister of Citizenship & Immigration)* (2009), 83 Imm. L.R. (3d) 228, 353 F.T.R. 132 (Eng.), 2009 FC 877, 2009 CarswellNat 2750, 2009 CarswellNat 4523, [2009] F.C.J. No. 1110 (F.C.) — This was an application for judicial review of a decision of a Minister's delegate refusing the applicant's pre-removal risk assessment decision. The PRRA officer concluded that the applicant was a person described under Article 1F(b) of the Convention based on an analysis of the criminal charges against him. The charges include: criminal fraud in China; immigration fraud in the United States of America; criminal fraud in the US; and immigration fraud in Canada. However, the PRRA officer concluded that "if the applicant is returned to China he will more likely than not be at risk of cruel or unusual treatment or punishment due to his being denied his right to a fair trial guaranteed under the *Universal Declaration of Human Rights and the International Covenant on Civil Political Rights*." The Minister's delegate disagreed with the assessment and concluded that there were no humanitarian and compassionate grounds to consider in this matter.

The applicant says that the decision is wrong because there is no basis in the Act or the Regulations that allows a PRRA officer to consider a claim for refugee protection and reject it on the basis of section F of Article 1 of the Convention. The applicant imposed upon the PRRA officer a full consideration of his ss. 96 and 97 rights without the benefit of a determination by the RPD. The Act appears to contemplate this alternative approach, but it was the applicant's choice to use the PRRA system and was not something that was forced upon him. He was not made to relinquish rights and safeguards he would otherwise have had. He then argued that since the PRRA officer made a positive risk assessment under s. 97, the effect of that decision was to confer refugee protection on him by virtue of subs. 114(1) of the Act. The Court concluded it was not Parliament's intent to provide a means for a claimant to bypass the RPD and to have his or her ss. 96 and 97 rights considered *de novo* by the PRRA officer, without any reference to serious criminality and 1F(b) of the Convention. Neither the PRRA officer nor the delegate acted without jurisdiction or committed an error of law in their determination of the applicant's claim insofar as it related to serious criminality outside of Canada in the Article 1F(b) exclusion issue. The application for judicial review was dismissed. The following questions were certified:

> Do pre-removal risk assessment officers have the jurisdiction to exclude persons from refugee protection under s. 98 of IRPA and find them described in s. 112(3)(c) of IRPA?
>
> Does s. 112(3)(c) of the IRPA only apply to rejections by the Refugee Protection Division on the basis of section F of Article 1 of the *Refugee Convention* or does it apply to rejections by pre-removal risk assessment officers on the basis of section F of Article 1 of the *Refugee Convention*?

*Sogi v. Canada (Minister of Citizenship & Immigration)*, 2004 CarswellNat 1908, 254 F.T.R. 129, 2004 FC 853 (F.C.) — The Minister's delegate denied an application made by the applicant for protection under s. 112 of IRPA. The applicant claimed refugee status; however, he became the subject of a report under subs. 44(1) of IRPA. This report led to an admissibility hearing where a decision was made that the applicant was inadmissible because he was a member of a Sikh terrorist organization.

Since the applicant was found to be inadmissible, two assessments were prepared pursuant to subs. 172(2). The first was a pre-removal risk assessment. The PRRA was conducted under paragraphs 112(3)(a) and 113(d)(ii) of IRPA. These paragraphs provide that applicants who were inadmissible on security grounds will have their PRRA applications considered based only on the factors in s. 97 of IRPA. The PRRA concluded that the applicant would be at risk of torture if deported to India. There was a second assessment which determined that the applicant represented a present and future danger to the security of Canada. The Minister's delegate balanced these two assessments, decided to deport the applicant to India, despite the likelihood that the applicant would be tortured.

Canadian jurisprudence does not suggest that Canada may never deport a person to face treatment elsewhere that would be unconstitutional if imposed by Canada directly, on Canadian soil.

The Minister's delegate erred in determining that the applicant should be deported. The decision did not address any alternatives to deportation to torture. A decision to deport to torture must consider, in the balancing exercise, any alternatives proposed to reduce the threat.

In the circumstances of this case, it was patently unreasonable to decide to deport the applicant without considering the applicant's proposal to observe curfews, reporting requirements and wear a tracking device.

*Xie v. Canada (Minister of Citizenship & Immigration)* (2004), 37 Imm. L.R. (3d) 163, 2004 CarswellNat 2036, 2004 CarswellNat 3972, 325 N.R. 255, [2005] 1 F.C.R. 304, 243 D.L.R. (4th) 385, 2004 FCA 250, [2004] F.C.J. No. 1142 (F.C.A.); leave to appeal refused (2005), 2005 CarswellNat 748, 2005 CarswellNat 749 (S.C.C.) — The appellant is a citizen of the People's Republic of China where she was a senior official in the Guangzhou Commission for Foreign Economic Relations and Trade. She fled China and arrived in Canada in 2001 and made a claim for refugee protection. In the course of processing her claim, two facts emerged. The first was that the appellant and her daughter had to their names bank accounts containing $2.7 million dollars. Second was, at the request of the Chinese authorities, an international warrant for the arrest of the appellant and a charge of embezzlement. On the basis of the appellant's unexplained wealth, the Board applied the exclusion in Article 1(F)(b) of the Convention. The Board also decided that, in light of the offence with which the appellant was charged, she faced a risk of torture at the hands of the Chinese authorities if she were to return to China.

The Board was entitled to presume that the warrant for the appellant's arrest was issued in the belief that she was guilty of misconduct. The presumption of innocence does not apply so as to prevent the Board from taking the Chinese State's belief in the appellant's guilt into account in deciding if there are serious reasons to consider that she committed the crime with which she is charged. There are three ways in which refugee protection can be obtained. Refugee protection is extended to persons falling within the definition of Convention Refugee which has not been changed by the new Act. Refugee protection is also extended to those persons who are found to be in the need of protection, a class defined by the risk of harm as opposed to the motivation of those inflicting harm. The grounds upon which such an application can be made are found in s. 97 and include those who are in "danger, believed on substantial grounds to exist, of torture within the meaning of Article 1 of the Convention Against Torture". Finally, a person can be extended refugee protection by means of an application for protection pursuant to s. 112 of the Act. Persons facing deportation may apply to the Minister for protection on the basis that they face a risk of harm if they return to their country of origin. If the application for protection is granted, such persons acquire refugee protection pursuant to paragraph 95(1)(c) of the Act. Subsection 112(3) of the Act lists those persons who are ineligible for refugee protection including persons who are described in Article 1, Section F of the Convention. The exclusion from refugee protection is not an exclusion from protection altogether. Section 113 stipulates that persons described in 112(3) are to have their applications for protection decided on the basis of the factors set out in s. 97 with additional consideration given to the issue of whether such persons are a danger to the public in Canada or to the security of Canada. For all except those described in subs. 112(3), a successful application for protection results in the grant of refugee protection in the status of protected person. For persons described in subs. 112(3) the result is a stay of the deportation order in force against them. One consequence of the distinction is that protected persons have access to the status of permanent residence and are subject to the principle of non-refoulement.

Thus, the structure of the Act has two streams, claims for refugee protection and claims for protection in the context of pre-removal risk assessments. The person who is excluded from refugee protection is eligible to apply for protection at the PRRA stage. The basis on which the claim for protection may be advanced is the same, but the Minister can have regard to whether the granting of protection would affect the safety of the public or the security of Canada. If protection is granted, the result is a stay of the deportation order. The claimant does not have the same access to permanent resident status as does a successful claimant for refugee protection.

Once a panel of the Refugee Protection Division found that the appellant was excluded pursuant to Section F of Article 1, it had done everything that it was required to do. The appellant was thereby excluded from refugee protection, a matter within the Board's confidence, and was limited to applying for protection, a matter within the Minister's jurisdiction. Accordingly, the Board's conclusions as to the appellant's risk of torture were gratuitous and were an infringement upon the Minister's responsibilities.

**113. Consideration of application — Consideration of an application for protection shall be as follows:**

**(a) an applicant whose claim to refugee protection has been rejected may present only new evidence that arose after the rejection or was not reasonably available, or that the applicant could not reasonably have been expected in the circumstances to have presented, at the time of the rejection;**

**Proposed Amendment — 113(a)**

**(a) an applicant whose claim for refugee protection or whose most recent application for protection, as the case may be, has been rejected may present only evidence that arose after the rejection or was not reasonably available, or that the applicant could not reasonably have been expected in the circumstances to have presented, at the time of the rejection;**

2010, c. 8, s. 16 [To come into force June 29, 2013, or earlier by order.]

**(b) a hearing may be held if the Minister, on the basis of prescribed factors, is of the opinion that a hearing is required;**

**Proposed Amendment — 113(b)**

**(b) in the case of an applicant described in subsection 112(3), a hearing may be held if the Minister, on the basis of prescribed factors, is of the opinion that a hearing is required;**

2010, c. 8, s. 16 [To come into force June 29, 2013, or earlier by order.]

**Proposed Addition — 113(b.1)–(b.3)**

**(b.1) subject to paragraphs (a) and (b.3), in the case of an applicant not described in subsection 112(3), the Refugee Protection Division must proceed without a hearing and may accept documentary evidence and written submissions from the Minister and the applicant;**

**(b.2) in the case of an applicant not described in subsection 112(3), paragraph (a) does not apply in respect of evidence that is presented in response to evidence presented by the Minister;**

**(b.3) in the case of an applicant not described in subsection 112(3), the Refugee Protection Division may hold a hearing if, in its opinion, there is documentary evidence referred to in paragraph (b.1)**

**(i) that raises a serious issue with respect to the credibility of the applicant,**

**(ii) that is central to the decision with respect to the application, and**

**(iii) that, if accepted, would justify allowing the application;**

2010, c. 8, s. 16 [To come into force June 29, 2013, or earlier by order.]

**(c) in the case of an applicant not described in subsection 112(3), consideration shall be on the basis of sections 96 to 98;**

**(d) in the case of an applicant described in subsection 112(3), consideration shall be on the basis of the factors set out in section 97 and**

**(i) in the case of an applicant for protection who is inadmissible on grounds of serious criminality, whether they are a danger to the public in Canada, or**

**(ii) in the case of any other applicant, whether the application should be refused because of the nature and severity of acts committed by the applicant or because of the danger that the applicant constitutes to the security of Canada.**

*[Editor's Note: S.C. 2001, c. 27, s. 199 provides that sections 112 to 114 of the* Immigration and Refugee Protection Act, *S.C. 2001, c. 27 (the "new Act") apply to a redetermination of a decision set aside by the Federal Court with respect to an application for landing as a member of the post-determination refugee claimants in Canada class within the meaning of the* Immigration Regulations, 1978, *SOR/78-172.*

*SOR/2002-227, s. 346(1) provides that an application for landing as a member of the post-determination refugee claimants in Canada class in respect of which no determination of whether the applicant is a member of that class was made before June 28, 2002 is an application for protection under sections 112 to 114 of the new Act and those sections apply to the application.*

*SOR/2002-227, s. 346(2) provides that before a decision is made on the application, the applicant shall be notified that he or she may make additional submissions in support of his or her application.*

*SOR/2002-227, s. 346(3) provides that a decision on the application shall not be made until 30 days after notification is given to the applicant.*

*SOR/2002-227, s. 346(4) provides that notification is given*

*(a) when it is given by hand to the applicant; or*

*(b) if it is sent by mail, seven days after the day on which it was sent to the applicant at the last address provided by him or her to the Department.]*

## Case Law

*Chen v. Canada (Minister of Citizenship & Immigration)*, 2009 CarswellNat 973, 2009 FC 379 (F.C.) — The applicant sought judicial review of a decision of a pre-removal risk assessment ("PRRA") officer. The basis of the officer's decision appears to be that nothing submitted with the PRRA application changed what the Refugee Protection Division decided. However, the PRRA officer did proceed further because she recognized an obligation to go beyond the applicant's evidence and review country condition documents. The officer was correct to conclude that, notwithstanding the continuing identity problems, she was still obliged to assess risk against the country of removal. The failure to establish identity means that there is no need to proceed further with an analysis of persecution. This does not mean that the PRRA officer need not go further in assessing risk if identity is a continuing problem. In this case the officer proceeded beyond the identity issue. That being the case, the officer's analysis of the country conditions documents was inadequate. There was reliable documentation before the officer of the torture mistreatment of Falun Gong supporters in China that was not referred to and that directly contradicted the officer's conclusions. This means that important evidence was overlooked and the reasons do not provide an adequate assessment of that evidence. For these reasons, the decision was unreasonable. The application for judicial review was allowed and the matter returned for reconsideration.

*Raza v. Canada (Minister of Citizenship & Immigration)*, [2007] F.C.J. No. 1632, 68 Admin. L.R. (4th) 225, 370 N.R. 344, 289 D.L.R. (4th) 675, 2007 CarswellNat 4905, 2007 FCA 385 (C.A.) — This was an appeal from a judgment ((2006), 304 F.T.R. 46) dismissing the appellants' application for judicial review of the decision of a pre-removal risk assessment officer, who rejected their application for protection under subs. 112(1) of the *Immigration Refugee Protection Act* (The "IRPA"). An application under s. 112(1) IRPA is referred to as a "Pre-removal Risk Assessment application" or a "PRRA application". The principal issue in this appeal is the interpretation of paragraph 113(a) of the IRPA.

Paragraph 113(a) deals with the circumstances in which a failed refugee claimant who makes a PRRA application may present evidence to the PRRA officer that was not before the refugee protection division ("RPD") of the Immigration and Refugee Board. A PRRA application is not an appeal or reconsideration of the decision of the RPD to reject a claim for refugee protection; nevertheless, it may require consideration of some or all of the same factual or legal issues as a claim for refugee protection. In such cases, there is an obvious risk of wasteful and potentially abusive relitigation. The IRPA mitigates that risk by limiting the evidence that may be presented to the PRRA officer. The limitation is found in paragraph 113(a) of the IRPA.

Paragraph 113(a) is based on the premise that a negative refugee determination by the RPD must be respected by the PRRA officer, unless there is new evidence of facts that might have affected the outcome of the RPD hearing if the evidence had been presented to the RPD. Paragraph 113(a) asks a number of questions, some expressly and some by necessary implication, about the proposed new evidence. Those questions are summarized as follows:

1. *Credibility*: Is the evidence credible, considering its source and the circumstances in which it came into existence? If not, the evidence need not be considered.

2. *Relevance*: Is the evidence relevant to the PRRA application, in the sense that it is capable of proving or disproving a fact that is relevant to the claim for protection? If not, the evidence need not be considered.

3. *Newness*: Is the evidence new in the sense that it is capable of:

(a) proving the current state of affairs in the country of removal or an event that occurred, or a circumstance that arose after the hearing in the RPD, or

(b) proving a fact that was unknown to the refugee claimant at the time of the RPD hearing, or

(c) contradicting a finding of fact by the RPD (including a credibility finding)?

If not, the evidence need not be considered.

4. *Materiality*: Is the evidence material, in the sense that the refugee claim probably would have succeeded if the evidence had been made available to the RPD? If not, the evidence need not be considered.

5. *Express statutory conditions*:

(a) If the evidence is capable of proving only an event that occurred or circumstances that arose prior to the RPD hearing, then has the applicant established either that the evidence was not reasonably available to him or her for presentation at the RPD hearing, or that he or she could not reasonably have been expected, in the circumstances, to have presented the evidence at the RPD hearing? If not, the evidence need not be considered.

(b) If the evidence is capable of proving an event that occurred or circumstances that arose after the RPD hearing, then the evidence must be considered (unless it is rejected because it is not credible, not relevant, not new or not material).

The first four questions, relating to credibility, relevance, newness and materiality, are necessarily implied from the purpose of paragraph 113(a) within the statutory scheme of the IRPA relating to refugee claims and pre removal risk assessments. The remaining questions are asked expressly by paragraph 113(a).

The questions listed above need not be asked in any particular order. It is not necessary that the PRRA officer ask each question. What is important is that the PRRA officer must consider all evidence that is presented, unless it is excluded on one of the grounds stated above.

In this case, Mr. Raza and his family submitted a number of documents in support of their PRRA application. All of the documents were created after the rejection of their claim for refugee protection. The PRRA officer concluded that the information in the documents was essentially a repetition of the same information that was before the RPD. This conclusion was reasonable. The documents were not capable of establishing that state protection in Pakistan, which had been found by the RPD to be adequate, was no longer adequate as of the date of the PRRA application. Therefore, the proposed new evidence fails at the fourth question listed above.

The appeal was dismissed.

*Elezi v. Canada (Minister of Citizenship & Immigration)*, 2007 CarswellNat 577, 2007 FC 240 (F.C.) — The applicant applied for refugee status after escaping Albania. His claim was dismissed. He applied for pre-removal risk assessment (PRRA). A PRRA officer rejected his application. The applicant sought judicial review of the PRRA officer's decision. The proper standard of review for a PRRA decision, when considered globally and as a whole, is reasonableness. When assessing the issue of new evidence under subs. 113(a) of IRPA, two separate questions must be addressed. The first one is whether the officer erred in interpreting the section itself. This is a question of law, which must be reviewed against a standard of correctness. If he made no mistake interpreting the provision, the Court must still determine whether he erred in his application of the section to the particular facts of the case. This is a question of mixed fact and law, to be reviewed on a standard of reasonableness. The applicant submitted to the PRRA officer various documents that predated the Board's decision. All of this evidence was obviously extremely probative, and to a large extent, refutes all of the Board's conclusions against the applicant. Had he submitted this evidence at his Board hearing, the Board may have written a very different decision. These documents did not raise any "new" risks, *per se*. The risks outlined were the same as those the applicant claimed during his hearing before the Board. It was not reasonable for the PRRA officer to exclude all these documents on that basis.

The nature of the information, its significance for the case, the credibility of its source, are all factors that can and should be taken into consideration in determining whether it can be considered "new evidence," when it appears to have been created after the Board's decision. The letters created after the Board's decision qualified as "new evidence." As for the evidence that predated the Board's decision, the PRRA officer erred in excluding it. The error related to the second and third branches of subs. 113(a). Not only were all these documents extremely helpful in assessing the applicant's claim but he could not reasonably have been expected, in the circumstances, to have presented them to the Board. The Board's hearing took place only three months after he arrived in Canada, and it does not require a stretch of the imagination to consider that this is not much time to gather that kind of evidence. The application for judicial review was granted. The Court certified four questions:

1. Is "new evidence" for the purposes of s. 113(a) of the IRPA limited to evidence that postdates and is "substantially different" from the evidence that was before the RPD?

2. Does the standard for the reception of "new evidence" under s. 113(a) of the IRPA require the PRRA officer to accept any evidence created after the RPD determination, even where that evidence was reasonably available to the applicant or he/she could reasonably have been expected to present it at the refugee hearing?

3. In determining whether evidence has arisen after the Board rejects a refugee claim and is therefore "new," must the PRRA officer look only for new facts or new risks, or can he or she take into consideration other factors like the nature of the information, its significance for the case, and the credibility of its source?

4. In light of paragraphs 3(3)(d) and (f) of the IRPA, is the PRRA officer precluded from considering personalized evidence that goes to the heart of an applicant's claim and establishes that he would be at risk if returned, when that evidence could conceivably have been presented to the Board?

*Sing v. Canada (Minister of Citizenship & Immigration)*, [2006] F.C.J. No. 851, 2006 CarswellNat 1420, 2006 FC 672 (F.C.) — The applicants were accused by the Chinese government of masterminding a massive smuggling and bribery operation. It wants the couple returned home to face prosecution for their alleged crimes. The applicants have consistently maintained that China has fabricated all the allegations against them. The applicants and their three children claimed refugee status. The Board found the parents were excluded from Convention refugee status under Article 1F(b) of the *United Nations Convention Relating to the Status of Refugees*. The Board also found the parents not to be Convention refugees because there was no nexus between their claims and any Convention refugee grounds. The Board described the couple as criminals fleeing from justice, not persecution. In their PRRA application, the applicants made submissions alleging bias, charter violations and breaches of procedural fairness. Their submissions on risk included a number of challenges to the Chinese legal system. They maintained the same theory raised at their Board hearing. They argued that they could not get a fair trial in China, and that they faced torture and the death penalty despite a diplomatic note from China assuring the contrary. After a probing review of their submissions, the PRRA officer rejected all of their claims.

The applicants' PRRA decision, although well reasoned and quite comprehensive in its assessment of the facts and of the submissions made by both counsel, was deficient in its assessment of the risk of torture. The application for judicial review was granted. The following questions were certified:

1. Where the Minister takes a public position on pre-removal risk to an applicant before a pre-removal risk assessment application is decided, is there a reasonable

apprehension that the Minister's decision on pre-removal risk assessment application will be biased?

2. What is the appropriate standard of review for the interpretation of a diplomatic note providing assurances against the death penalty or the infliction of torture or other cruel or unusual treatment?

3. Is it appropriate to rely on assurances against torture in assessing an applicant's risk under s. 97 of the IRPA, when there are credible reports that torture prevails in the country where the applicant is to be removed? If so, under what circumstances?

4. If there is a risk of torture in an individual case, what are the requirements that an assurance against torture should fulfil to make that risk less likely than not? Should the assurance provide for monitoring to allow for verification of compliance for that assurance to be found reliable? In the absence of a monitoring mechanism, is the notoriety of the person to be removed a relevant, and a sufficient, consideration for the PRRA officer in determining whether it is more likely than not that the assuring state will adhere to the diplomatic assurance?



*Jaballah v. Canada (Minister of Citizenship & Immigration)*, [2006] F.C.J. No. 747, 353 N.R. 6, (sub nom. *Jaballah, Re*) 2006 CarswellNat 1362, 2006 CarswellNat 2227, 2006 FCA 179 (C.A.) — A principle of international law acknowledged by a treaty to which Canada is a signatory, such as the prohibition against deportation to death or torture, may be relevant in interpretation of Canadian law, but it is not determinative of that interpretation unless it is specifically incorporated by legislation. The prohibition in this case is not expressly incorporated in the IRPA or other legislation.

*Chudal v. Canada (Minister of Citizenship & Immigration)*, 2005 CarswellNat 2227, 2005 CarswellNat 4713, 2005 FC 1073 (F.C.) — A PRRA officer has an obligation to receive all evidence which may affect the decision until the time that such decision is made. It is reasonable to consider that such decision is not made until it has been written and signed and notice of the decision, even if not its contents, has been delivered to the applicant.

*Bouttavong v. Canada (Minister of Citizenship & Immigration)* (2005), 344 N.R. 134, 2005 CarswellNat 3527, 2005 CarswellNat 5559, 2005 FCA 341 (Fed. C.A.) — Former public danger opinions are irrelevant to the determination of danger to the public under subs. 113(d)(i). This does not mean that the underlying criminal convictions may not be taken into account, only that the danger opinions are irrelevant.

*Jaballah, Re* (2005), 44 Imm. L.R. (3d) 181, 2005 CarswellNat 754, 2005 FC 399 (F.C.) — This decision was the Court's reasons for finding that the decision on behalf of the Minister on the application of protection by the applicant was not lawfully made. There was no question that the applicant faced a substantial risk of death or torture if he were returned to Egypt.

The Minister's delegate erred in law by undue reliance on certain matters, *i.e.* (1) an earlier decision by the Court that the Minister's opinion was reasonable, a decision quashed by the Court of Appeal and (2) by failing to describe the danger to Canada's security that the applicant represented. Further, the delegate failed to consider as a factor the effect of the applicant's continued restraint, in one form or another, while he remains in Canada. Finally, the delegate failed to consider adequately the best interests of the applicant's children.

*Mojzisik v. Canada (Minister of Citizenship & Immigration)*, [2004] F.C.J. No. 33, 40 Imm. L.R. (3d) 204, 245 F.T.R. 183, 2004 CarswellNat 68, 2004 CarswellNat 872, 2004 FC 48 (F.C.) — The applicant was denied refugee status under the former *Immigration Act*. He submitted a Post-Determination Refugee Claim In-Canada application which was converted to a pre-removal risk assessment (PRRA) application on the coming into effect of the Immigration and Refugee Protection Act. This application was dismissed and the applicant now sought to judicially review that refusal.

The PRRA is an innovation in the new Act which is designed to ensure that the vast majority of individuals facing removal from Canada are given a full but expedited chance to establish that they face a risk of torture or gross mistreatment on their return to a home country.

This case was caught in the transition from the former Act to the *Immigration and Refugee Protection Act*.

The definition of "new evidence" in the kit which accompanied the PRRA application form was woefully inadequate. The letter informing the applicant of the conversion of his application should have informed him that the PRRA officer now had additional authority to determine whether the applicant was in need of protection and that any evidence in that respect would qualify as new evidence and should be presented.

**114. (1) Effect of decision — A decision to allow the application for protection has**

> **(a) in the case of an applicant not described in subsection 112(3), the effect of conferring refugee protection; and**
>
> **(b) in the case of an applicant described in subsection 112(3), the effect of staying the removal order with respect to a country or place in respect of which the applicant was determined to be in need of protection.**

**(2) Cancellation of stay — If the Minister is of the opinion that the circumstances surrounding a stay of the enforcement of a removal order have changed, the Minister may re-examine, in accordance with paragraph 113(d) and the regulations, the grounds on which the application was allowed and may cancel the stay.**

**(3) Vacation of determination — If the Minister is of the opinion that a decision to allow an application for protection was obtained as a result of directly or indirectly misrepresenting or witholding material facts on a relevant matter, the Minister may vacate the decision.**

**(4) Effect of vacation — If a decision is vacated under subsection (3), it is nullified and the application for protection is deemed to have been rejected.**

*[Editor's Note: SOR/2002-227, s. 339 provides that a determination made in Canada before June 28, 2002 that a person is not a Convention refugee is deemed to be a claim for refugee protection rejected by the Immigration and Refugee Board.]*

*[Editor's Note: S.C. 2001, c. 27, s. 199 provides that sections 112 to 114 of the* Immigration and Refugee Protection Act, *S.C. 2001, c. 27 (the "new Act") apply to a redetermination of a decision set aside by the Federal Court with respect to an application for landing as a member of the post-determination refugee claimants in Canada class within the meaning of the* Immigration Regulations, 1978, *SOR/78-172.*

*SOR/2002-227, s. 346(1) provides that an application for landing as a member of the post-determination refugee claimants in Canada class in respect of which no determination of whether the applicant is a member of that class was made before June 28, 2002 is an application for protection under sections 112 to 114 of the new Act and those sections apply to the application.*

*SOR/2002-227, s. 346(2) provides that before a decision is made on the application, the applicant shall be notified that he or she may make additional submissions in support of his or her application.*

*SOR/2002-227, s. 346(3) provides that a decision on the application shall not be made until 30 days after notification is given to the applicant.*

*SOR/2002-227, s. 346(4) provides that notification is given*

> *(a) when it is given by hand to the applicant; or*
>
> *(b) if it is sent by mail, seven days after the day on which it was sent to the applicant at the last address provided by him or her to the Department.]*

**Proposed Addition — 114.1**

**114.1 (1) Limitation — Subsections 114(3) and (4) apply in respect of a decision to allow an application for protection only if the application was made to the Minister under subsection 112(1.1) or transferred to the Minister under subsection 112(1.3) or (1.7).**

**(2) Application of section 109 — Section 109 applies to a decision made by the Refugee Protection Division to allow an application for protection as if it were a decision to allow a claim for refugee protection.**

2010, c. 8, s. 16.1 [To come into force June 29, 2013, or earlier by order.]

## *Principle of Non-refoulement*

**115. (1) Protection — A protected person or a person who is recognized as a Convention refugee by another country to which the person may be returned shall not be removed from Canada to a country where they would be at risk of persecution for reasons of race, religion, nationality, membership in a particular social group or political opinion or at risk of torture or cruel and unusual treatment or punishment.**

**(2) Exceptions — Subsection (1) does not apply in the case of a person**

> **(a) who is inadmissible on grounds of serious criminality and who constitutes, in the opinion of the Minister, a danger to the public in Canada; or**
>
> **(b) who is inadmissible on grounds of security, violating human or international rights or organized criminality if, in the opinion of the Minister, the person should not be allowed to remain in Canada on the basis of the nature and severity of acts committed or of danger to the security of Canada.**

*[Editor's Note: SOR/2002-227, s. 326(3) provides that a person whose removal on June 28, 2002 was allowed by the application of paragraphs 53(1)(a) to (d) of the former* Immigration Act, *R.S.C. 1985, c. I-2 is a person referred to in s. 115(2) of the new* Immigration and Refugee Protection Act, *S.C. 2001, c. 27.]*



IRP Act

**(3) Removal of refugee — A person, after a determination under paragraph 101(1)(e) that the person's claim is ineligible, is to be sent to the country from which the person came to Canada, but may be sent to another country if that country is designated under subsection 102(1) or if the country from which the person came to Canada has rejected their claim for refugee protection.**

## Case Law

### Section 115(2)

*Canada (Minister of Public Safety & Emergency Preparedness) v. Samuels* (2009), 85 Imm. L.R. (3d) 226, 2009 FC 1152, 2009 CarswellNat 5632, 2009 CarswellNat 3739 (F.C.) — This is an application by the Minister for judicial review of an order of a member of the Immigration Division to release the respondent from detention. The respondent was born in Panama but lived for 39 years in Jamaica. He is a citizen of both countries and came to Canada in 1991 and became a permanent resident. By September 1992, he was diagnosed as having schizophrenia. In total, the respondent has 27 or 30 criminal convictions, as well as over 10 provincial convictions. Following his last criminal conviction on March 14, 2005, he was immediately placed in immigration hold. He was released from immigration hold on October 12, 2006, under the Toronto Bail Program, for which he was supervised by Steven Sharp. Contrary to the terms of his release, the respondent repeatedly left his residence unescorted. Mr. Sharp was of the opinion that public safety would be a concern if the respondent remained in the community. The respondent was re-arrested and returned to immigration hold, remaining in detention ever since. A risk assessment officer reached a positive decision in June 2009 and the Minister then sought a danger opinion against the respondent, which would lead to his removal from Canada. Following the success of the PRRA application, the respondent sought to be released from detention. The member of the Immigration Division determined that while a danger opinion was being sought, it was likely to take a considerable time — and might yet turn out to be negative, so that it "wouldn't be fair" to keep the respondent in detention. Although the member noted that the respondent had "a pretty impressive criminal file," the member concluded that "if there's no removal in sight, the Immigration Division is not responsible to protect Canadian society anymore."

The Court held that the Immigration Division had jurisdiction to order the respondent's continued detention if it was satisfied that he was a danger to the public. The Court also found that the Immigration Division member failed to exercise its statutory duty, and quashed the decision to release the respondent. A removal order that is stayed is not void. Although it cannot be executed pending a ruling on a protected person's application for permanent residence, or the passing of the deadline to file such an application, it still exists and is valid and, in the opinion of the Court, the person against whom it was issued is still "subject to it." Accordingly, the Immigration Division had jurisdiction to order the continued detention of the respondent, if it was satisfied that he was a danger to the public.

*Villanueva Cruz v. Canada (Minister of Citizenship & Immigration)* (2008), 78 Imm. L.R. (3d) 68, 2008 CarswellNat 5281, 2008 CarswellNat 4628, 2008 FC 1341 (F.C.) — The applicant was found to be a Convention refugee in 1999. He was subsequently convicted of trafficking in a controlled substance and sentenced to serve three years and 10 months. A delegate of the Minister of Citizenship and Immigration determined that the applicant constituted a danger to the public in Canada pursuant to s. 115(2)(a) of the IRPA. The applicant sought judicial review of that decision.

The test to be used by the Minister in forming a danger opinion was summarized by Justice Strayer in *Williams v. Canada (Minister of Citizenship & Immigration)*, [1997] 2 F.C. 646 (C.A.) at paragraph 29:

> In the context the meaning of "public danger' is not a mystery: it must refer to the possibility that a person who has committed a serious crime in the past may seriously be thought to be a potential re-offender. It need not be proven — indeed it cannot be proven — that the person will reoffend. What I believe the subs. adequately focusses the Minister's mind on is consideration of *whether, given what she knows about the individual and what that individual has had to say in his own behalf, she can form an opinion in good faith that he is a possible re-offender whose presence in Canada creates an unacceptable risk to the public.*

Justice Beaudry offered further comments on this standard as it related to individuals convicted of narcotics-related offences *Do v. Canada (Minister of Citizenship & Immigration)*, [2003] 2 F.C. 493 at paragraphs 42-43:

> This Court has consistently held, including in cases dealing with narcotics-related offences, that the mere fact of conviction on one or more criminal offences does not itself support a determination that a person is, may be, or is likely to pose a danger to the public, although some offences by their nature may be of a type that invite such conclusion: *Salilar v. Canada (Minister of Citizenship & Immigration)* [1995] 3 F.C. 150 at page 159 (T.D.); *Thai v. Canada (Minister [page 510] of Citizenship & Immigration)* (1998), 42 Imm. L.R. (2d) 28 at para. 16 (F.C.T.D.); *Tewelde v. Canada (Minister of Citizenship & Immigration)* (2000), 89 F.T.R. 206 (F.C.T.D.).
>
> Rather, in forming an opinion as to whether an individual constitutes a danger to the public, natural justice and procedural fairness require the Minister to take into account all of the relevant and particular circumstances of each case, and the circumstances of each case must, over and above the conviction, indicate a danger to the public: *Fairhurst v. Canada (Minister of Citizenship & Immigration)* (1996), 124 F.T.R. 142 at para. 10 (F.C.T.D.); *Thompson v. Canada (Minister of Citizenship & Immigration)* (1996), 41 Admin. L.R. (2d) 10 at para. 19 (F.C.T.D.).

The Court concluded that the Minister's delegate misconstrued the evidence and did not have regard to the evidence before her. The application for judicial review was allowed.

*Hasan v. Canada (Minister of Citizenship & Immigration)* (2008), 75 Imm. L.R. (3d) 64, 180 C.R.R. 286, 2008 CarswellNat 3445, 2008 FC 1069 (F.C.) — The applicant was reported as an inadmissible permanent resident because of serious criminality pursuant to s. 44 of the IRPA. The Canadian Border Services Agency informed the applicant of their intention to seek the opinion, pursuant to s. 115(2)(a), from the Minister of Citizenship and Immigration that he was a danger to the public and, thus, could be returned to Iraq. There is no requirement in s. 115(2) that the Minister must assess the risk to the person who has been found to be a danger. That obligation arises from the operation of s. 7 of the *Charter*, as decided by the Supreme Court of Canada in *Suresh*, [2002] 1 S.C.R. 3. Thus, there is no parallel between the cessation provisions of s. 108, which explicitly require the Minister to demonstrate that the reasons for which the person sought refugee protection have ceased to exist, and s. 115, where the only obligation arises as a result of the *Charter*. The jurisprudence is clear that, once the applicant is found to be a danger to the public, he must establish that he would be at risk.

Therefore, the delegate did not erroneously place the onus on the applicant to prove that he faced the risk of torture or risk to life if returned to Iraq. The delegate properly engaged in an assessment of the current risks facing the applicant should he be removed to Iraq. The applicant was told that he could make written representations or arguments deemed necessary and relevant, including those related to whether his life or freedoms were threatened by removal from Canada. This was adequate notice to the applicant.

The applicant also argued that the delegate failed to have regard to the fact that the Minister had imposed a stay on removals to Iraq pursuant to s. 230 of the Regulations. Not only had the applicant not initially raised this argument in his submissions to the CBSA, but more importantly, the s. 230(1) moratorium does not apply to the applicant since s. 230(3) explicitly states that the stay under s. 230(1) does not apply to a person who is inadmissible on grounds of serious criminality or criminality. In this case, the applicant had been found to be inadmissible on grounds of serious criminality and he could not rely on the stay provisions of s. 230. The application for judicial review was dismissed.

*Nagalingam v. Canada (Minister of Citizenship & Immigration)* (2008), 292 D.L.R. (4th) 463, 70 Imm. L.R. (3d) 54, 2008 CarswellNat 1221, 2008 FCA 153 (C.A.) — In the preparation of an opinion under paragraph 115(2)(b) of the IRPA, where the Minister finds that a refugee who is inadmissible on grounds of organized criminality does not face a risk of persecution, torture, cruel and unusual punishment or treatment upon return to his country of origin, such a finding does not render the Minister's consideration of the "nature and severity of acts committed" under paragraph 115(2)(b) unnecessary.

The exception of paragraph 115(2)(b) regarding organized criminality will apply to a Convention refugee or a protected person if, in the opinion of the Minister, that person should not be allowed to remain in Canada on the basis of the nature and substantial gravity of acts committed (in the context of organized criminality) personally or through complicity, as defined by Canadian domestic laws, but established on a standard of reasonable grounds. In this case, the Delegate had to reasonably link the appellant to the acts of the organization in which he was a member, taking into consideration, if applicable, his role and responsibilities within the criminal organization. In doing so, the Delegate had to caution himself that it is only in exceptional cases that a Convention refugee or a protected person will lose the benefit of subs. 115(1). Only acts which are of substantial gravity will meet this high threshold. The appeal was allowed and the matter remitted back to the Delegate for re-determination.

*Balathavarajan v. Canada (Minister of Citizenship & Immigration)*, [2006] F.C.J. No. 1550, 56 Imm. L.R. (3d) 1, 354 N.R. 320, 2006 CarswellNat 3297, 2006 FCA 340 (Fed. C.A.) — The Court considered whether the IAD must consider hardship to a permanent resident who had been issued a deportation order, and who had been declared a Convention refugee, where the deportation order did not specify the country of removal, and where it is uncertain what that country might be. The Minister had not specified the country of deportation, and at the time of the IAD appeal had not taken the necessary steps under subs. 115(2) of the IRPA to remove the appellant. It was, at the time of the IAD appeal, not only unlikely but legally improper to remove the appellant to Sri Lanka. For the IAD to consider potential hardship the appellant might face if deported to Sri Lanka would have been a hypothetical and a speculative exercise. Therefore it did not need to do this. Accordingly, the certified question was answered in the negative by the Court of Appeal.

Section 173 of the IRPA permits the IAD to receive and base a decision on evidence adduced in immigration proceedings that it considers to be credible and trustworthy in the circumstances. It is up to the IAD, not the Court, to decide the weight to be given to the evidence. Therefore the appellant also failed to demonstrate that the judge had committed a palpable and overriding error in upholding the IAD's decision. The appeal was dismissed.

*Ragupathy v. Canada (Minister of Public Safety & Emergency Preparedness)* (2006), 58 Imm. L.R. (3d) 101, 2006 CarswellNat 3734, 2006 FC 1370 (F.C.) — The applicant was a Convention refugee and became a permanent resident of Canada. He then became inadmissible on grounds of serious criminality within the meaning of s. 36 of the IRPA. The Minister's delegate issued an opinion concluding that the applicant was a danger to the public in Canada (the Danger Opinion). The applicant was subject to removal from Canada under paragraph 115(2)(a) of the Act. The enforcement officer had discretion to defer the applicant's removal. The enforcement officer stated in her affidavit that the reason for not deferring removal was because there was no specific reason to do so. The enforcement officer also stated that she relied on the risk assessment provided by the Minister's delegate in the Danger Opinion. Both statements indicated that the enforcement officer was not alert and alive to the possibility that the alleged change in country conditions gave rise to an enhanced risk of torture or persecution upon the applicant's return to Sri Lanka. By relying on the existing risk assessment pre-dating the events identified by the applicant in his request for deferral, the enforcement officer failed to acknowledge the basis for the applicant's concern. The applicant was entitled to an updated risk assessment before removal. Recognizing an applicant's right under s. 7 of the *Charter* to a risk assessment before removal requires that the risk assessment occur proximate in time to the removal and is not incompatible with the need for finality in the system. Whatever the period of delay between the issuance of a Danger Opinion and the scheduled removal, the onus is on the applicant to demonstrate that there has been a material change in circumstances warranting a re-assessment of his risk upon removal. If an enforcement officer declines to exercise the discretion to defer the removal of a deportee pending re-assessment, a judicial stay of the removal order will only be granted where the deportee can satisfy the well-established tri-partite test. The requirements of a serious issue, irreparable harm and the balance of convenience are appropriate safeguards to ensure that vexatious attempts to forestall removal are dealt with accordingly.

The applicant was entitled to an updated risk assessment in light of the considerable passage of time since the issuance of the Danger Opinion. The application for judicial review was allowed in part. The enforcement officer was correct in determining that the applicant was not eligible for a PRRA under subs. 112(1) of the Act. However, the enforcement officer erred in declining to suspend the applicant's removal pending a re-assessment of the risk faced by him on removal in light of the significant change of circumstances alleged by the applicant.

*Ragupathy v. Canada (Minister of Citizenship & Immigration)*, 2006 CarswellNat 1100, 2006 FCA 151 (Fed. C.A.) — The applicant was recognized as a refugee and was granted permanent residence status. He was subsequently convicted of criminal offences. Following a report by immigration officials requesting a "danger opinion," the delegate of the Minister of Citizenship and Immigration formed the opinion that the applicant's continued presence in Canada presented a high level of danger to the public and that this outweighed the small chance he would be persecuted or tortured if he was returned to Sri Lanka.

Since a finding that a protected person is a danger to the public by virtue of his criminality is a prerequisite of removal, this is a logical starting point in a delegate's analysis. Without a positive opinion on this issue, the delegate's inquiry must end, because the person cannot be deported. Proceeding in this manner also avoids the possibility that the delegate will assess whether a protected person is a "danger to the public" by having regard to the risk of persecution.

Neither the text of the IRPA nor the jurisprudence dictates, as a matter of law, in what order the Minister's delegates' reasons must deal with the various elements of the "danger opinion." This is more a matter of elegance than substance and does not rise to the level of a legal requirement, especially given the degree of discretion entrusted to delegates in the formation of their opinion. The preferred ordering is not required either for a protected person to understand the bases of a delegate's opinion, or for a court to determine whether the delegate had committed reviewable error in performing the legal tasks entrusted to her. While analytical clarity will generally be enhanced if the delegate considers the criminal aspects of the "danger opinion" before opining on the gravity of the risk of persecution, if necessary, and balancing one against the other, there is no legal requirement to follow this format.

*Akuech v. Canada (Minister of Citizenship & Immigration)*, 2005 CarswellNat 624, 2005 FC 337 (F.C.) — The delegate's opinion was quashed. Nowhere in her reasons did the Minister's delegate conclude that the applicant was a danger to the public in Canada. Rather, she decided "on balance" that the applicant's ongoing presence in Canada was a greater danger to the public than the risk he might face upon his return to Sudan. It is incumbent on the Minister's delegate to develop a clear, distinct and separate rationale and decision respecting whether the applicant was a danger to the public in Canada. She is required to make this determination separate from, and prior to, any analysis of the risks which may result from the applicant's return to Sudan. A discrete finding under s. 115(2) that the applicant is a danger to the public in Canada must be made before the non-refoulement rights the applicant has under s. 115(1) can be said not to apply to him.

*Almrei v. Canada (Minister of Citizenship & Immigration)* (2005), 262 F.T.R. 7, 2005 CarswellNat 653, 2005 FC 355 (F.C.) — The applicant applied for judicial review of the PRAA decision determining that the applicant was not at risk if returned to Syria.

In making her decision, the Minister's delegate considered both secret evidence and evidence which was publicly disclosed. The secret evidence consisted of the narrative portion of the report (SIR) which led to the issuance of the security certificate. The delegate did not have before her the secret appendices which contained the information that supported the SIR.

Section 115(2) requires that the applicant establish that there are substantial grounds upon which to believe that, if removed to Syria, he would be at risk of persecution on a Convention ground or at risk of torture, death, or cruel or unusual treatment or punishment. If the risk is not established, there is no need to pursue the analysis since the applicant is not entitled to the protection afforded by subs. 115(1). The risk that must be assessed goes beyond mere theory or suspicion. The risk, however, can be something less than highly probable. The risk of torture must be personal and present.

The delegate could not rely on the SIR, the ensuing security certificate, and the motion judge's decision that the certificate was reasonable as proof that the applicant posed a danger to Canada.

A reviewing in court must be able to know and assess the evidentiary basis upon which findings are made in order to determine if they are properly based on the evidence. In making her decision, the delegate could not substitute the beliefs of the security service or the opinions of the designated judge for her own. The decision maker must independently consider and assess all of the evidence upon which she relies relating to the danger posed to Canada's security. The delegate must be in a position to weigh the factors which go to the reliability, cogency and value of that information.

The decision of the delegate was set aside.

*Mahjoub v. Canada (Minister of Citizenship & Immigration)* (2005), 45 Imm. L.R. (3d) 135, 2005 CarswellNat 339, 2005 CarswellNat 1058, 2005 FC 156 (F.C.) — In the spring of 2000, the Solicitor General of Canada and the Minister of Citizenship and Immigration signed a security certificate, evincing their opinion that the applicant was a member of an inadmissible class of persons. The security certificate was found to be reasonable. Finally, by a decision dated July 22, 2004, a delegate of the Minister decided that the applicant should be removed to Egypt. The applicant sought to review that decision.

Section 115(1) generally prohibits the government from returning a protected person to a country where he or she would be at risk of persecution or torture or cruel or unusual treatment or punishment. Subsection 115(2) sets out certain exceptions to that general principle. One such exception is in the case of a person who poses a danger to the security of Canada.

Both the decision whether the applicant constitutes a danger to the security of Canada and the decision whether the applicant faces a substantial risk of torture if deported to Egypt ought not to be set aside unless patently unreasonable. Whether there is a real possibility of an adverse effect on Canada if the individual remained in Canada must be weighed against the possible injustice to the individual if deported. Anyone exercising discretion under s. 115(2) must have evidence that allows the conclusion that the person concerned poses a danger to the security of Canada. The decision maker cannot rely simply upon the fact that the person is described in subs. 34(1) of the Act. The decision maker must carefully analyse all of the relevant evidence. The delegate must consider all of the evidence before him or her relating to the danger posed to Canada's security, and weigh the factors which go to the reliability of that information.

Conflicting evidence relating to danger must be weighed and reasons given for rejecting evidence of significance. The effect of the passage of time, and the effect of the person's apprehension and detention, should be considered so that not just the person's past actions but their future behaviour may be assessed. The fact of apprehension and disclosure may neutralize the future ability of the person concerned to conduct clandestine activities. After considering these factors, the nature of the danger posed by the person concerned should be articulated. By articulating the nature of the danger posed, the decision maker may, at the final stage of the analysis, properly balance the competing interests.

*Thuraisingam v. Canada (Minister of Citizenship & Immigration)*, [2004] F.C.J. No. 746, 40 Imm. L.R. (3d) 145, 251 F.T.R. 282, 2004 CarswellNat 2725, 2004 CarswellNat 1179, 2004 FC 607 (F.C.) — There are two elements that must be established in order to support the issuance of a danger opinion under s. 115. The individual must be inadmissible on the basis of serious criminality and in the opinion of the Minister must constitute a danger to the public in Canada. The phrase "danger to the public" is not a mystery. It must refer to the possibility that the person who has committed a serious crime in the past may seriously be thought to be a potential re-offender. The subsection adequately focuses the Minister's mind on the question of whether, given what the Minister knows about the individual and what the individual had to say in his or her own behalf, the Minister can form an opinion in good faith that the individual is a possible re-offender whose presence in Canada creates an unacceptable risk.

The fact that an individual has been convicted of a serious offence is not, in and of itself, a sufficient foundation for the opinion.

The fact that someone has been charged with an offence proves nothing. It is simply an allegation. The evidence underlying the charge may indeed be sufficient to provide the foundation for a good faith opinion that the individual poses a present or future danger to others in Canada.

Section 115 creates an exception to the principle of non-refoulement, that is, a person who has been found to be a Convention refugee should not be returned to the country where they would be at risk of persecution. Determining whether the return of such a person offends s. 7 of the *Charter*, a balancing exercise must be carried out weighing the protection of Canada's security interest against the refugee's interest in not being deported or tortured. A similar exercise must be carried out when the danger opinion is based on serious criminality.

The assessment of risk is largely outside the expertise of reviewing courts and does not possess a significant legal dimension. As such, significant deference must be accorded to the risk assessment.

**116. Regulations — The regulations may provide for any matter relating to the application of this Division, and may include provisions respecting procedures to be followed with respect to applications for protection and decisions made under section 115, including the establishment of factors to determine whether a hearing is required.**

## PART 3 — ENFORCEMENT

### *Human Smuggling and Trafficking*

**117. (1) Organizing entry into Canada — No person shall knowingly organize, induce, aid or abet the coming into Canada of one or more persons who are not in possession of a visa, passport or other document required by this Act.**

**(2) Penalties — fewer than 10 persons — A person who contravenes subsection (1) with respect to fewer than 10 persons is guilty of an offence and liable**

**(a) on conviction on indictment**

**(i) for a first offence, to a fine of not more than $500,000 or to a term of imprisonment of not more than 10 years, or to both, or**

**(ii) for a subsequent offence, to a fine of not more than $1,000,000 or to a term of imprisonment of not more than 14 years, or to both; and**

**(b) on summary conviction, to a fine of not more than $100,000 or to a term of imprisonment of not more than two years, or to both.**

**(3) Penalty — 10 persons or more — A person who contravenes subsection (1) with respect to a group of 10 persons or more is guilty of an offence and liable on conviction by way of indictment to a fine of not more than $1,000,000 or to life imprisonment, or to both.**

**(4) No proceedings without consent — No proceedings for an offence under this section may be instituted except by or with the consent of the Attorney General of Canada.**



## Case Law

### Section 117(1)

*R. v. Toor*, 2009 CarswellOnt 8881 (Ont. S.C.J.) — The accused was a licensed taxi driver in 2002. On seven occasions he drove people from Toronto to the Windsor area and left them there. Arrangements had been made by others to smuggle the passengers into the United States. The accused was charged with conspiring to illegally smuggle the immigrants into the United States and was found guilty under s. 117 of IRPA. When relying on s. 117 the Crown has to establish that the accused knew or was willfully blind as to whether the migrants had the required documents to enter the United States. The American legislation makes it an offence to bring someone into the United States at a location other than a regular border crossing location or someone who the accused knows or in reckless disregard of the fact that an alien has not received prior official authorization to come to, enter or reside in the United States. The Canadian legislation makes it an offence to enter Canada without reporting immediately to Canadian authorities. Accordingly, tha accused was presumed by law to have known that he agreed to participate in a human smuggling offence in which people were taken to the United States at a port of entry after a lawful inspection and authorization by an immigration officer or at a location other than a port of entry. In those circumstances, he would know or at the very least be willfully blind to the fact that the migrants did not have prior authorization to enter the United States. That prior authorization could be given in advance of the attendance at the port of entry. Knowing that they were to be secreted into the United States he knew or was at least willfully blind that they did not have prior official authorization.

*R. v. Alzehrani* (2008), 75 Imm. L.R. (3d) 304, 237 C.C.C. (3d) 471, 2008 CarswellOnt 6556 (Ont. S.C.J.) — This was a trial alleging a conspiracy between one or both of the accused, together with others, to smuggle people across the border between Canada and the United States. The defence moved for a directed verdict and the trial judge found on 23 of the 30 counts there was no evidence on one or more of the essential elements of the offence and that those counts could not be left to the jury. The remaining seven counts went to the jury and the jury convicted on all of them.

An issue arose during the course of the trial as to whether the Crown was required to prove that the persons being brought into Canada did not have the required documents to enter, and if so, the means by which that could be proven. Initially, the issue was cast by the defence simply as an admissibility of evidence issue on the final telephone intercept relied upon by the Crown in respect of Count 11 on the indictment. However, it became apparent in the course of argument that the defence position related to all counts on the indictment. The defence argument was that the failure of the Crown to tender any direct evidence as to the lack of documentation and knowledge of the accused was fatal to the Crown's case, that no reasonable inferences of guilt could be drawn from the limited circumstantial evidence on these points, and that there was, therefore, no case to go to the jury on any of the counts before the Court.

In the majority of the charges before the Court, the Crown presented no direct evidence as to whether the persons being smuggled had the required documents for legal entry, and also no evidence of the knowledge or belief of the accused. All of the counts on the indictment involved some surreptitious manner of crossing the border so as to avoid the scrutiny of border crossing authorities. However, even though in some of these cases the persons crossing illegally were apprehended, there was no evidence as to their status in the country they were entering and whether they had any documentation that would permit their entry. In respect of those counts, the position of the Crown was that both the lack of documentation and the knowledge of the accused could be determined by drawing inferences from the manner in which the persons involved were taken across the border.

The statute is very explicit about requiring proof that the person being brought into the country does not have appropriate documentation. Parliament could have made it an offence to assist any person to cross the border surreptitiously. If that was the language of the statute, there would be no problem with these 23 counts. However, the statute is not worded that way, and ought not to be interpreted as if it was. The plain meaning of the statute is clear. It is only the assisting of persons who do not have passports or similar documents that is the subject matter of this offence. Something beyond surreptitious entry is required in order to establish a lack of documentation.

There was also no evidence of the accused's state of knowledge with respect to the 23 counts. Wilful blindness is not a route for imputing knowledge unless the true facts to which the accused has shut his eyes are known. Therefore, unless there was some evidence that the people being transported did not have documents, the doctrine of wilful blindness had no application. Why s. 117 of the IRPA was limited to the smuggling of persons across the border who are without the required documents, as opposed to simply smuggling people across the border for whatever reason, is not apparent. However, if the manner in which the legislation is drafted makes it difficult to prosecute wrongdoers (which it does), and the wrongdoing is serious (which it is), the remedy lies in legislative reform, not by judicial interpretation that violates the plain meaning of the existing statutory language.

## Section 117(2)

*R v. Ng* (2008), 241 C.C.C. (3d) 340, 263 B.C.A.C. 300, 2008 CarswellBC 2823, 2008 BCCA 535 (C.A.) — The appellant kept a common bawdy house for almost two years and employed more than two prostitutes. He was convicted of procuring two of them to have illicit sexual intercourse, one of them over a lengthy period of time. He ran a prostitution business from which he profited. Deterrence is a significant factor in sentencing for these offences. Because of the moral turpitude involved, denunciation is an equally significant factor. The sentences imposed for the prostitution offences do not adequately speak to these factors and are unfit. The global sentence was inadequate. The Crown's leave to appeal to increase the global sentence by one year to 27 months was allowed. The Court did not disturb the sentences for the immigration offences. Mr. Ng had been convicted under s. 117(1) of the IRPA for inducing, aiding or abetting the coming into Canada of a person who was not in possession of a valid visa, passport or other document required by the IRPA and of inducing, aiding or abetting or attempting to counsel, induce, aid or abet a person, to directly or indirectly misrepresent or withhold material facts relating to a relevant matter that induces or could induce an error in the administration of the IRPA under s. 126 of the IRPA.

The immigration sentencing cases relied upon by the Crown involved more serious circumstances and, in some cases at least, offenders with existing criminal records. The appellant, who had no prior record, assisted one person to illegally enter Canada, apparently without compromising her physical safety. It seems that there are no reported sentencing decisions in immigration cases that involve comparable facts. If the two immigration offences were the only offences for which the appellant had been convicted, it would have been the Court's opinion that the concurrent nine-month sentences were at the low end of the scale but not unfit. The sentences for the immigration offences were not varied on appeal.



*R. v. Wasiluk*, 2005 CarswellOnt 4728, 2005 ONCJ 407 (Ont. C.J.) — The increase in the maximum penalty to life imprisonment for organizing entry into Canada of a group of 10 persons or more is reflective of the seriousness with which Parliament views these types of activities and the need to increase the sentences for these types of offences. Accordingly, a statutorily increased penalty is a legislative signal that the sentencing paradigm has shifted towards a regime of tougher sentences than that which previously existed.

The accused transported three migrants across the river to the United States. Their role was limited to transporting the migrants across the river in their boat and they were not involved in the arrangements which resulted in the migrants coming to Canada. A sentence of 14 months' house arrest was imposed with the exception of attending work.

**Section 117(3)**

*R. v. Hallal*, 2008 ONCA 210, 2008 CarswellOnt 1644 (C.A.) — The defendant pleaded guilty to Count 22, which concerned the conspiracy in relation to the newly enacted *Immigration and Refugee Protection Act*. Approximately 200 persons were smuggled from Canada to the United States and charged between $2,500 and $3,000 U.S. The evidence showed that in less than four months following that the defendant was involved in the movement of 30 migrants and those 30 migrants were part of 10 different operations. The evidence showed that the defendant was actively involved and he was assertive with other members of the conspiracy about business being directed to him and not to others. As far as this defendant was concerned, his actions were planned and deliberate. It was done for profit.

Unless a conditional sentence is an obvious outcome on sentencing there is an evidentiary burden on the defendant to show that he is not a risk in the community for re-offending. It is true that the Court has greater concern with respect to this factor when one is dealing with violent offences, but being involved in a non-violent offence alone is not a ticket to a conditional sentence. Looking at the bigger picture, this is a serious offence. It has international implications. In mitigation there was a plea of guilty. The plea was significant. A term of custody of 18 months is appropriate. In light of the defendant's financial circumstances and length of time in jail, the victim fine surcharge was waived. The Ontario Federal Court of Appeal affirmed the lower Court's decision with respect to the sentencing.

**118. (1) Offence — trafficking in persons — No person shall knowingly organize the coming into Canada of one or more persons by means of abduction, fraud, deception or use or threat of force or coercion.**

**(2) Definition of "organize" — For the purpose of subsection (1), "organize", with respect to persons, includes their recruitment or transportation and, after their entry into Canada, the receipt or harbouring of those persons.**

## Case Law

*R. v. Ng*, 2006 CarswellBC 723, 2006 BCPC 111 (B.C. Prov. Ct.) — The defendant was charged with committing offences under s. 118 of the IRPA and challenged the constitutionality of the section. Specifically, he submitted that inclusion of the terms fraud and deception as means of committing the offence renders the section vague or overly broad or both.

The use of the terms fraud and deception as legislative means of achieving the object of the IRPA are not grossly disproportionate to the section's objective. Accordingly, s. 118(1) of the IRPA is neither vague nor overly broad, and as such, this section does not violate s. 7 of the *Charter of Rights and Freedoms*.

**119. Disembarking persons at sea — A person shall not disembark a person or group of persons at sea for the purpose of inducing, aiding or abetting them to come into Canada in contravention of this Act.**

**120. Penalties — A person who contravenes section 118 or 119 is guilty of an offence and liable on conviction by way of indictment to a fine of not more than $1,000,000 or to life imprisonment, or to both.**

**121. (1) Aggravating factors — The court, in determining the penalty to be imposed under subsection 117(2) or (3) or section 120, shall take into account whether**

**(a) bodily harm or death occurred during the commission of the offence;**

**(b) the commission of the offence was for the benefit of, at the direction of or in association with a criminal organization;**

**(c) the commission of the offence was for profit, whether or not any profit was realized; and**

**(d) a person was subjected to humiliating or degrading treatment, including with respect to work or health conditions or sexual exploitation as a result of the commission of the offence.**

**(2) Definition of "criminal organization" — For the purposes of paragraph (1)(b), "criminal organization" means an organization that is believed on reasonable grounds to be or to have been engaged in activity that is part of a pattern of criminal activity planned and organized by a number of persons acting in concert in furtherance of the commission of an offence punishable under an Act of Parliament by way of indictment or in furtherance of the commission of an offence outside Canada that, if committed in Canada, would constitute such an offence.**

## *Offences Related to Documents*

**122. (1) Documents — No person shall, in order to contravene this Act,**

**(a) possess a passport, visa or other document, of Canadian or foreign origin, that purports to establish or that could be used to establish a person's identity;**

**(b) use such a document, including for the purpose of entering or remaining in Canada; or**

**(c) import, export or deal in such a document.**

**(2) Proof of offence — Proof of the matters referred to in subsection (1) in relation to a forged document or a document that is blank, incomplete, altered or not genuine is, in the absence of evidence to the contrary, proof that the person intends to contravene this Act.**

**123. (1) Penalty — Every person who contravenes**

**(a) paragraph 122(1)(a) is guilty of an offence and liable on conviction on indictment to a term of imprisonment of up to five years; and**

**(b) paragraph 122(1)(b) or (c) is guilty of an offence and liable on conviction on indictment to a term of imprisonment of up to 14 years.**

**(2) Aggravating factors — The court, in determining the penalty to be imposed, shall take into account whether**

**(a) the commission of the offence was for the benefit of, at the direction of or in association with a criminal organization as defined in subsection 121(2); and**

**(b) the commission of the offence was for profit, whether or not any profit was realized.**

## Case Law

*R. v. Zelaya* (2009), 77 Imm. L.R. (3d) 163, 2009 CarswellAlta 37, 2009 ABPC 7 (Alta. Prov. Ct.) — Although the *Immigration and Refugee Protection Act* was enacted in 2001, there have been few prosecutions taken in Alberta. The penalty provisions are a guide as to how seriously Parliament (and thus, the Canadian people) consider the current offences. The accused was sentenced with respect to four guilty pleas entered including: possession of a false passport — s. 123(1)(a); using a false passport to wrongfully enter Canada — s. 123(1)(b); lying about his identity and nationality to gain entry to Canada — s. 128(a); and, return to Canada without the correct authorization — s. 124(1)(a).

In this case, a conditional sentence order would not address the fundamental principle of proportionality found in s. 718.1 of the *Code*, or the principles of denunciation, punishment and deterrence. The sentence must account for relevant aggravating and mitigating circumstances and be tailored to fit the individual accused before the Court. The accused received four months in jail for having a false passport; 7 ½ months for using a false passport to enter Canada; six months for lying about his identity and nationality to enter Canada; and three months for merely returning to Canada without authorization. All of these terms of imprisonment were concurrent one to another for a global sentence of one year in jail; however, accounting for pre-sentence custody credit of 140 days (70 actual days), the sentence of 7½ months was made consecutive to any other sentence imposed by any Court, should there be any.

*R. v. Lin*, 2006 CarswellNfld 371 (N.L. T.D.); affirmed [2007] N.J. No. 74, 263 Nfld. & P.E.I.R. 273, 798 A.P.R. 273, 2007 CarswellNfld 155, 2007 NLCA 13 (N.L. C.A.) — The facts established that the accused was a Chinese national who used a forged Korean passport. When individuals use false passports to enter Canada they undermine the *Immigration and Refugee Protection Act*. Authorities have the right to run background on all persons wishing to enter Canada in order to ensure compliance with Canadian laws and regulations. Authorities also have the duty to screen persons entering our country for the purposes of national security and public safety. There needs to be a message sent that using a false passport for the purpose of illegally entering Canada will result in a deterrent sentence of imprisonment. A sentence that was considered a mere slap on the wrist would only be encouragement for like-minded individuals to illegally enter our country. Deterrence has to be the guiding principle in sentencing such individuals. A sentence of one year is appropriate.

## *General Offences*

**124. (1) Contravention of Act — Every person commits an offence who**

**(a) contravenes a provision of this Act for which a penalty is not specifically provided or fails to comply with a condition or obligation imposed under this Act;**

**(b) escapes or attempts to escape from lawful custody or detention under this Act; or**

**(c) employs a foreign national in a capacity in which the foreign national is not authorized under this Act to be employed.**

**(2) Deemed knowledge — For the purposes of paragraph (1)(c), a person who fails to exercise due diligence to determine whether employment is authorized under this Act is deemed to know that it is not authorized.**

**(3) Due diligence defence — A person referred to in subsection 148(1) shall not be found guilty of an offence under paragraph (1)(a) if it is established that they exercised all due diligence to prevent the commission of the offence.**

### Case Law

*R. v. Beltran* (2010), 89 Imm. L.R. (3d) 1, 2010 ABPC 113, 2010 CarswellAlta 602 (Alta. Prov. Ct.) — The accused entered a guilty plea to an offence of returning to Canada without the prescribed authorization, contrary to IRPA. The Crown sought a sentence of five months' incarceration. The accused sought a conditional discharge. A discharge was not a fit disposition in this case. The offence is a problematic one in that it is difficult to detect and quantify the cost to taxpayers. The accused entered Canada unauthorized for his own personal gain and to avoid the proper and lawful mechanisms in place for application. The offence was planned, deliberate and ongoing. There were no facts presented to show that the accused intended at any time to address his unlawful act or remove himself from the country to properly apply for admission. He is currently willing to leave Canada but it appears only because he was prosecuted.

Any hardship on the accused's family was inflicted by his act. There are no exceptional circumstances in this case that would compel the Court to put the accused in a position he would have been in but for his third illegal entry. The accused was sentenced to four months and 13 days in custody. Without credit for pre-sentence custody, the jail term imposed would have been five months. The time spent in custody prior to this sentencing hearing was nine days. The amount of time credited was 18 days.

*R. v. Zelaya* (2009), 77 Imm. L.R. (3d) 163, 2009 CarswellAlta 37, 2009 ABPC 7 (Alta. Prov. Ct.) — Although the *Immigration and Refugee Protection Act* was enacted in 2001, there have been few prosecutions taken in Alberta. The penalty provisions are a guide as to how seriously Parliament (and thus, the Canadian people) consider the current offences. The accused was sentenced with respect to four guilty pleas entered including: possession of a false passport — s. 123(1)(a); using a false passport to wrongfully enter Canada — s. 123(1)(b); lying about his identity and nationality to gain entry to Canada — s. 128(a); and, return to Canada without the correct authorization — s. 124(1)(a).

In this case, a conditional sentence order would not address the fundamental principle of proportionality found in s. 718.1 of the *Code*, or the principles of denunciation, punishment and deterrence. The sentence must account for relevant aggravating and mitigating circumstances and be tailored to fit the individual accused before the Court. The accused received four months in jail for having a false passport; 7 ½ months for using a false passport to enter Canada; six months for lying about his identity and nationality to enter Canada; and three months for merely returning to Canada without authorization. All of these terms of imprisonment were concurrent one to another for a global sentence of one year in jail; however, accounting for pre-sentence custody credit of 140 days (70 actual days), the sentence of 7½ months was made consecutive to any other sentence imposed by any Court, should there be any.

**125. Penalties — A person who commits an offence under subsection 124(1) is liable**

> **(a) on conviction on indictment, to a fine of not more than $50,000 or to imprisonment for a term of not more than two years, or to both; or**
>
> **(b) on summary conviction, to a fine of not more than $10,000 or to imprisonment for a term of not more than six months, or to both.**

**126. Counselling misrepresentation — Every person who knowingly counsels, induces, aids or abets or attempts to counsel, induce, aid or abet any person to directly or indirectly misrepresent or withhold material facts relating to a relevant matter that induces or could induce an error in the administration of this Act is guilty of an offence.**

## Case Law

*R. v. Dhalla*, 2007 CarswellOnt 2095 (Ont. S.C.J.) — The respondent was sentenced on one count of counseling, aiding or abetting contrary to s. 126 of the IRPA to a fine of $5,000. The appellant appealed the sentence. At the sentencing hearing, the Crown counsel had asked for six months incarceration due to the seriousness of child smuggling, the abandonment of the child, and the financial benefit to the respondent. Defence counsel took no position during the sentencing hearing.

While it was open to the trial judge to impose a custodial sentence, the sentence imposed was within the appropriate range for this type of offence, taking into account both the nature and gravity of the offence as well as the particular circumstances and antecedents of the respondent. The appeal was dismissed.

127. **Misrepresentation — No person shall knowingly**

**(a) directly or indirectly misrepresent or withhold material facts relating to a relevant matter that induces or could induce an error in the administration of this Act;**

**(b) communicate, directly or indirectly, by any means, false or misleading information or declarations with intent to induce or deter immigration to Canada; or**

**(c) refuse to be sworn or to affirm or declare, as the case may be, or to answer a question put to the person at an examination or at a proceeding held under this Act.**

## Case Law

*Kandhai v. Canada (Minister of Citizenship & Immigration)* (2009), 81 Imm. L.R. (3d) 144, 2009 FC 656, 2009 CarswellNat 1919, 2009 CarswellNat 5681 (F.C.) — The applicant sought judicial review of a decision refusing his application for humanitarian and compassionate exemption. The Court determined it was appropriate to consider the application, notwithstanding the applicant's history of repeatedly lying to Canadian immigration authorities. The reasons given for refusing the H&C application were also insufficient. The officer's "reasons" essentially consisted of a review of facts coupled with a statement of conclusion, without any analysis to back it up. Consequently the application for judicial review was allowed. The decision under review was the applicant's third H&C application. He admitted that he was not truthful on his most recent H&C application, as he indicated on the form that he was divorced when in fact he was living in a common-law relationship with his ex-wife. The applicant argued that while the misrepresentation as to his marital situation was undoubtedly an error in judgment, it was not made with the intent of securing an advantage in relation to his H&C application, and thus had no negative effect on the integrity of the Canadian immigration process. In fact, the presence of a common-law partner in Canada may have strengthened his H&C application. In two prior H&C applications, the applicant indicated that he had never been charged with, or convicted of, a criminal offence in another country, when that was not, in fact, the case. These misrepresentations were made in order to gain an advantage in relation to those applications, and thus had the potential to undermine the integrity of the immigration process. In this case, since the misrepresentations did not appear to be made to gain an advantage, and the applicant appeared to have come forward voluntarily with his admission of misrepresentation, the Court concluded that for the purposes of this "clean hands" analysis it was a very strong case.

The Court relied on the Federal Court of Appeal decision in *Thanabalasingham v. Canada (Minister of Citizenship & Immigration)*, [2006] F.C.J. No. 20, where the Federal Court of Appeal held that the task for the reviewing Court is to strike a balance between "maintaining the integrity of, and preventing the abuse of, judicial and administrative processes," and "the public interest in ensuring the lawful conduct of government in the protection of fundamental human rights."

*Koo v. 5220459 Manitoba Inc.* (2010), 89 Imm. L.R. (3d) 140, 2010 MBQB 132, 2010 CarswellMan 248 (Man. Q.B.) — The issue on this *de novo* hearing under the *Court of Queen's Bench Small Claims Practices Act* was whether the Labour Market Opinion (LMO) obtained by the defendant and furnished to the plaintiff for submission by him in support of his application for a work permit gives the plaintiff the right to recover from the defendant in contract or tort for failure to pay him the wage referred to in the document. The LMO refers to a salary of $14.50 per hour. The defendant paid less than that to the plaintiff and it was agreed that if the plaintiff succeeded in his claim he was entitled to judgment for $9,057.06.

There is no provision in the statute or regulation expressly spelling out the consequences if incorrect information is given in the application for an LMO or if the employer chooses to pay the foreign national a salary less than indicated in the application.

It would be difficult to find that the LMO in itself or the providing of the LMO creates a contract, express or implied, between the plaintiff and defendant. The LMO is an expression of opinion by Service Canada of the matter set out therein. None of the essentials of a contract is present: offer, acceptance, privity, consideration and intention to create legal relations. The fundamental policy being to protect Canadian citizens or persons who are landed immigrants, it would be impossible for a member of that class to sustain an action against the defendant if the defendant had paid the plaintiff a salary greater than $14.50 per hour. It would be impossible for Service Canada to sustain an action against either party for breach of the terms of the document. There is no basis in contract for allowing the plaintiff to recover on the facts of this case. Nor is there a duty of care sufficient to support a tort action.

Is an employer free to disregard the salary set out in the LMO? Perhaps, perhaps not. If there is a false statement in the LMO, it may make it impossible for the employer to justify a finding of genuineness in a second or later application for an LMO. If there is a misrepresentation made knowingly, an employer may be subject to prosecution. Whatever the answer to the question, the plaintiff could have discussed the proposed salary with the defendant before receiving the LMO. He could have sought clarification from the defendant or refused to come to Canada. As it happens, the Court found the parties did have a discussion, and the plaintiff agreed to accept a lesser salary. He was not entitled to recover from the defendant the difference between the salary stated in the LMO and the salary paid. The claim was dismissed.

*R. v. Pandher* (2009), 83 Imm. L.R. (3d) 322, 2009 CarswellOnt 5198 (Ont. C.J.) — The accused entered a plea to two counts of making a material misrepresentation by including falsified documents in applications for sponsorship under s. 127(a) of the IRPA and the Crown proceeded by indictment. The accused did so as a consultant to clients who retained him to file the applications on their behalf. The Court concluded that it is people like the accused who give immigration consultants such a bad name and why they are held in such low regard and with such great suspicion. Accordingly, any sentence, because of the significant criminal acts, should reflect not only the Court's extreme denunciation of his actions, which again strike at the heart of the security of this country, but also take advantage of desperate people who are trying to get their families into the country, and expose them to prosecution, all for the almighty dollar. Normally any sentence for these offences should be considerable jail sentences. The accused had suffered a heart attack and had some significant health issues in 2007 and accordingly the Court acceded to the joint submission and conditional sentence. The accused was sentenced to 18 months conditional; for the first six months he was subject to house arrest, save and except traveling to and from his place of employment in a schedule to be provided to his supervisor at least once a week and to any medical appointments and medical emergencies for himself or his immediate family. For the remaining 12 months he was to observe a curfew except for medical emergencies or medical appointments. During the entire conditional sentence he will not be involved directly or indirectly with any sponsorship matters whatsoever. He was also prohibited from working in any form as a consultant on immigration matters.

*R. v. Zhong*, [2008] B.C.J. No. 723, 2008 CarswellBC 815, 2008 BCSC 514 (S.C.) — Mr. Zhong appealed his conviction for making false statements on his immigration application to renew his student visa. He was charged and convicted of one count under s. 128 of the IRPA for misrepresenting facts relating to a relevant matter that could induce an error in the administration of the Act, by providing false transcripts and acceptance documents in support of his study permit renewal application, contrary to s. 127(a) of the Act.

Mr. Zhong testified that he was not aware that something illegal would happen with his application, that it was not his signature on the application document, that he never lived, at and was unaware of, the Surrey address given on the application, and that he did not see the fraudulent documents until his arrest in July 2007. He acknowledged that all of his previous study permit applications had been prepared with the assistance of the staff at the college that he was attending and they did not charge a large fee. Any fee charged was considerably less than the $8,000 he had paid the consultant who prepared this application. Intent was the only issue before the trial judge. The trial judge concluded that it was incredible that Mr. Zhong did not know that his payment of $8,000 was to obtain fraudulent papers. He questioned why a $2,000 deposit would be paid for something that had cost "next to nothing" on other occasions. He concluded that it was "probable" that the $8,000 was for obtaining false documents, that this is what $8,000 would get you, that anybody who did not realize that was "beyond willfully blind", and that Zhong was desperate.

On appeal, the Court found it was a reasonable inference on the whole of the evidence that a payment of $8,000 must have been for more than completion of an application. The fact that Mr. Zhong had paid a minimum amount on several occasions previously was evidence of a reasonable amount to be paid for an application. The Appeal Court did not accept that the trial judge had to consider that the immigration consultant's self description as an immigration consultant automatically put his fees into a different service category than the school-based consultant. Accordingly, the reasons of the trial judge, taken as a whole, did not reflect a reversible error.

*R. v. Hupang*, 2007 CarswellBC 3491 (B.C. Prov. Ct.); varied (2008), 76 Imm. L.R. (3d) 1, 261 B.C.A.C. 298, 440 W.A.C. 298, 2008 CarswellBC 2498, 2008 BCCA 4 (C.A.) — The accused pled guilty to a charge under s. 127(a) of the IRPA that he knowingly misrepresented material facts relevant to the administration of the Act. In this case the accused, through searching the Internet, found an individual who was prepared to provide false university or college transcripts and false acceptance letters for a fee. The accused paid $3,000 to receive the false documentation.

It is incumbent on the Court to impose a sentence that is fit in all the circumstances, including the circumstances of the accused. The accused had no criminal history in Canada, and the Court accepted that he probably had no criminal history where he came from. By all accounts, he was seeking to improve his life. However, the Court had to consider the issue of general deterrence and that issue, with respect to this case, is the issue of people lying to either get into or stay in this country. Once somebody does that they become a security risk, not only to Canada but to the US. It is unquestionable that security is a major concern in these times. The Court has to send a message, not only to the accused, but to anybody who may be willing to search the Internet to get false documentation to stay in the country.

Although a discharge might well have been in the accused's best interests, it would be contrary to the public interest. The public interest in this case was paramount. The Court stated: "the public interest includes the issue of national security and international security. Canada must be seen as a nation that will not tolerate illegal immigrants. It must be seen as a nation that will protect the integrity of our national security and the security of our neighbour to the south. If we do not do that, all of our borders will be closed, the walls will be built, and we will be in a very isolated and dangerous situation".

The accused was sentenced to two months in jail as well as a $2,500 fine. The Court of Appeal varied the sentence by setting aside the custodial sentence and imposing a sentence of 17 days imprisonment, representing time already served. The fine was not altered.

*R. v. Tongo*, 2002 CarswellBC 2657, 2002 BCPC 463 (B.C. Prov. Ct.) — The accused pleaded guilty under s. 127(a) of the IRPA. IRPA was a strong response by Parliament to a growing problem of illegal migration. Part 3 recognizes the role of organized crime and persons who would profit from such activity and establishes severe penalties which are considered to be aggravated by profit, by involvement of organized crime and by the inhuman treatment of the migrants, including humiliation, degradation, death or bodily harm. The Act establishes a number of general offences to discourage persons from engaging in enabling activities such as employing illegal migrants and withholding relevant information. The accused were charged, and plead guilty to, the general enabling offence of withholding material facts relating to a relevant matter. The material fact, in this case, was the presence onboard the ship of the three Chinese migrants who were being transported to Canada for illegal entry. The accused were sentenced to two months incarceration, in addition to the equivalent of six weeks already spent, for their involvement in this activity.

**128. Penalties — A person who contravenes a provision of section 126 or 127 is guilty of an offence and liable**

> **(a) on conviction on indictment, to a fine of not more than $100,000 or to imprisonment for a term of not more than five years, or to both; or**
>
> **(b) on summary conviction, to a fine of not more than $50,000 or to imprisonment for a term of not more than two years, or to both.**

## Case Law

*R. v. Zelaya* (2009), 77 Imm. L.R. (3d) 163, 2009 CarswellAlta 37, 2009 ABPC 7 (Alta. Prov. Ct.) — Although the *Immigration and Refugee Protection Act* was enacted in 2001, there have been few prosecutions taken in Alberta. The penalty provisions are a guide as to how seriously Parliament (and thus, the Canadian people) consider the current offences. The accused was sentenced with respect to four guilty pleas entered including: possession of a false passport — s. 123(1)(a); using a false passport to wrongfully enter Canada — s. 123(1)(b); lying about his identity and nationality to gain entry to Canada — s. 128(a); and, return to Canada without the correct authorization — s. 124(1)(a).

In this case, a conditional sentence order would not address the fundamental principle of proportionality found in s. 718.1 of the *Code*, or the principles of denunciation, punishment and deterrence. The sentence must account for relevant aggravating and mitigating circumstances and be tailored to fit the individual accused before the Court. The accused received four months in jail for having a false passport; 7 ½ months for using a false passport to enter Canada; six months for lying about his identity and nationality to enter Canada; and three months for merely returning to Canada without authorization. All of these terms of imprisonment were concurrent one to another for a global sentence of one year in jail; however, accounting for pre-sentence custody credit of 140 days (70 actual days), the sentence of 7½ months was made consecutive to any other sentence imposed by any Court, should there be any.

*R. v. Pandher* (2009), 83 Imm. L.R. (3d) 322, 2009 CarswellOnt 5198 (Ont. C.J.) — The accused entered a plea to two counts of making a material misrepresentation by including falsified documents in applications for sponsorship under s. 127(a) of the IRPA and the Crown proceeded by indictment. The accused did so as a consultant to clients who retained him to file the applications on their behalf. The Court concluded that it is people like the accused who give immigration consultants such a bad name and why they are held in such low regard and with such great suspicion. Accordingly, any sentence, because of the significant criminal acts, should reflect not only the Court's extreme denunciation of his actions, which again strike at the heart of the security of this country, but also take advantage of desperate people who are trying to get their families into the country, and expose them to prosecution, all for the almighty dollar. Normally any sentence for these offences should be considerable jail sentences. The accused had suffered a heart attack and had some significant health issues in 2007 and accordingly the Court acceded to the joint submission and conditional sentence. The accused was sentenced to 18 months conditional; for the first six months he was subject to house arrest, save and except traveling to and from his place of employment in a schedule to be provided to his supervisor at least once a week and to any medical appointments and medical emergencies for himself or his immediate family. For the remaining 12 months he was to observe a curfew except for medical emergencies or medical appointments. During the entire conditional sentence he will not be involved directly or indirectly with any sponsorship matters whatsoever. He was also prohibited from working in any form as a consultant on immigration matters.

*R v. Ng* (2008), 241 C.C.C. (3d) 340, 263 B.C.A.C. 300, 2008 CarswellBC 2823, 2008 BCCA 535 (C.A.) — The appellant kept a common bawdy house for almost two years and employed more than two prostitutes. He was convicted of procuring two of them to have illicit sexual intercourse, one of them over a lengthy period of time. He ran a prostitution business from which he profited. Deterrence is a significant factor in sentencing for these offences. Because of the moral turpitude involved, denunciation is an equally significant factor. The sentences imposed for the prostitution offences do not adequately speak to these factors and are unfit. The global sentence was inadequate. The Crown's leave to appeal to increase the global sentence by one year to 27 months was allowed. The Court did not disturb the sentences for the immigration offences. Mr. Ng had been convicted under s. 117(1) of the IRPA for inducing, aiding or abetting the coming into Canada of a person who was not in possession of a valid visa, passport or other document required by the IRPA and of inducing, aiding or abetting or attempting to counsel, induce, aid or abet a person, to directly or indirectly misrepresent or withhold material facts relating to a relevant matter that induces or could induce an error in the administration of the IRPA under s. 126 of the IRPA.

The immigration sentencing cases relied upon by the Crown involved more serious circumstances and, in some cases at least, offenders with existing criminal records. The appellant, who had no prior record, assisted one person to illegally enter Canada, apparently without compromising her physical safety. It seems that there are no reported sentencing decisions in immigration cases that involve comparable facts. If the two immigration offences were the only offences for which the appellant had been convicted, it would have been the Court's opinion that the concurrent nine-month sentences were at the low end of the scale but not unfit. The sentences for the immigration offences were not varied on appeal.

*R. v. Dhalla*, 2007 CarswellOnt 2095 (Ont. S.C.J.) — The respondent was sentenced on one count of counseling, aiding or abetting contrary to s. 126 of the IRPA to a fine of $5,000. The appellant appealed the sentence. At the sentencing hearing, the Crown counsel had asked for six months incarceration due to the seriousness of child smuggling, the abandonment of the child, and the financial benefit to the respondent. Defence counsel took no position during the sentencing hearing.

While it was open to the trial judge to impose a custodial sentence, the sentence imposed was within the appropriate range for this type of offence, taking into account both the nature and gravity of the offence as well as the particular circumstances and antecedents of the respondent. The appeal was dismissed.



**129. (1) Offences relating to officers — Every person is guilty of an offence who**

**(a) being an officer or an employee of the Government of Canada, knowingly makes or issues any false document or statement, or accepts or agrees to accept a bribe or other benefit, in respect of any matter under this Act or knowingly fails to perform their duties under this Act;**

**(b) gives or offers to give a bribe or consideration to, or makes an agreement or arrangement with, an officer to induce the officer not to perform their duties under this Act;**

**(c) falsely personates an officer or by any act or omission leads any person to believe that the person is an officer; or**

**(d) obstructs or impedes an officer in the performance of the officer's duties under this Act.**

**(2) Punishment — Every person who is guilty of an offence under subsection (1) is liable**

**(a) on conviction on indictment, to a fine of not more than $50,000 or to imprisonment for a term of not more than five years, or to both; or**

**(b) on summary conviction, to a fine of not more than $10,000 or to imprisonment for a term of not more than six months, or to both.**

## *Proceeds of Crime*

**130. [Repealed 2001, c. 32, s. 81(3)(a).]**

**131. Counselling offence** — Every person who knowingly induces, aids or abets or attempts to induce, aid or abet any person to contravene section 117, 118, 119, 122, 124 or 129, or who counsels a person to do so, commits an offence and is liable to the same penalty as that person.

2001, c. 32, s. 81(3)(b)

**132.** [Repealed 2001, c. 32, s. 81(3)(c).]

## *Prosecution of Offences*

**133. Deferral** — A person who has claimed refugee protection, and who came to Canada directly or indirectly from the country in respect of which the claim is made, may not be charged with an offence under section 122, paragraph 124(1)(a) or section 127 of this Act or under section 57, paragraph 340(c) or section 354, 366, 368, 374 or 403 of the *Criminal Code*, in relation to the coming into Canada of the person, pending disposition of their claim for refugee protection or if refugee protection is conferred.

**134. Defence — incorporation by reference** — No person may be found guilty of an offence or subjected to a penalty for the contravention of a provision of a regulation that incorporates material by reference, unless it is proved that, at the time of the alleged contravention,

(a) the material was reasonably accessible to the person;

(b) reasonable steps had been taken to ensure that the material was accessible to persons likely to be affected by the regulation; or

(c) the material had been published in the *Canada Gazette*.

**135. Offences outside Canada** — An act or omission that would by reason of this Act be punishable as an offence if committed in Canada is, if committed outside Canada, an offence under this Act and may be tried and punished in Canada.

**136. (1) Venue** — A proceeding in respect of an offence under this Act may be instituted, tried and determined at the place in Canada where the offence was committed or at the place in Canada where the person charged with the offence is or has an office or place of business at the time of the institution of those proceedings.

**(2) Where commission outside Canada** — A proceeding in respect of an offence under this Act that is committed outside Canada may be instituted, tried and determined at any place in Canada.

## *Forfeiture*

**137. (1) Forfeiture** — A court that convicts a person of an offence under this Act may, in addition to any other punishment imposed, order that any offence-related property seized in relation to the offence be forfeited to Her Majesty in right of Canada.

(2) **Regulations** — The regulations may define the expression "offence-related property" for the purposes of this section, may provide for any matter relating to the application of this section, and may include provisions respecting the return to their lawful owner, disposition, or disposition of the proceeds of disposition, of offence-related property that has been seized.

## *Officers Authorized to Enforce Act*



138. (1) **Powers of peace officer** — An officer, if so authorized, has the authority and powers of a peace officer — including those set out in sections 487 to 492.2 of the *Criminal Code* — to enforce this Act, including any of its provisions with respect to the arrest, detention or removal from Canada of any person.

(2) **Temporary assistants** — An officer may, in cases of emergency, employ a person to assist the officer in carrying out duties under this Act. That person has the authority and powers of the officer for a period of no more than 48 hours, unless approved by the Minister.

139. (1) **Search** — An officer may search any person seeking to come into Canada and may search their luggage and personal effects and the means of transportation that conveyed the person to Canada if the officer believes on reasonable grounds that the person

(a) has not revealed their identity or has hidden on or about their person documents that are relevant to their admissibility; or

(b) has committed, or possesses documents that may be used in the commission of, an offence referred to in section 117, 118 or 122.

(2) **Search by person of same sex** — A search of a person under this section must be performed by a person of the same sex as the person being searched. If an officer of the same sex is not available, any suitable person of the same sex may be authorized by an officer to perform the search.

140. (1) **Seizure** — An officer may seize and hold any means of transportation, document or other thing if the officer believes on reasonable grounds that it was fraudulently or improperly obtained or used or that the seizure is necessary to prevent its fraudulent or improper use or to carry out the purposes of this Act.

*[Editor's Note: SOR/2002-227, s. 332 provides that a thing seized under the former* Immigration Act, *R.S.C. 1985, c. I-2 continues to be seized on June 28, 2002, and the seizure is governed by the provisions of the new* Immigration and Refugee Protection Act, *S.C. 2001, c. 27.]*

(2) **Interpretation** — Despite subsection 42(2) of the *Canada Post Corporation Act*, a thing or document that is detained under the *Customs Act* and seized by an officer is not in the course of post for the purposes of the *Canada Post Corporation Act*.

(3) **Regulations** — The regulations may provide for any matter relating to the application of this section and may include provisions respecting the deposit of security as a guarantee to replace things that have been seized or that might otherwise

**be seized, and the return to their lawful owner, and the disposition, of things that have been seized.**

*[Editor's Note: SOR/2002-227, s. 331 provides that a performance bond posted or security deposited under the former* Immigration Act, *R.S.C. 1985, c. I-2 that remains posted or deposited immediately before June 28, 2002 continues as a deposit or a guarantee under the new* Immigration and Refugee Protection Act, *S.C. 2001, c. 27 and is governed by its provisions.]*

**141. Oaths and evidence — Every officer has the authority to administer oaths and to take and receive evidence under oath on any matter arising out of this Act.**

## *Peace Officers*

**142. Duties of peace officers to execute orders — Every peace officer and every person in immediate charge or control of an immigrant station shall, when so directed by an officer, execute any warrant or written order issued under this Act for the arrest, detention or removal from Canada of any permanent resident or foreign national.**

**143. Authority to execute warrants and orders — A warrant issued or an order to detain made under this Act is, notwithstanding any other law, sufficient authority to the person to whom it is addressed or who may receive and execute it to arrest and detain the person with respect to whom the warrant or order was issued or made.**

## *Ticketable Offences*

**144. (1) Prosecution of designated offences — In addition to other procedures set out in this Act or in the *Criminal Code* for commencing a proceeding, proceedings in respect of any offence that is prescribed by regulation may be commenced in accordance with this section.**

**(2) Procedure — An officer may commence a proceeding by**

**(a) completing a ticket that consists of a summons portion and an information portion;**

**(b) delivering the summons portion of the ticket to the accused or mailing it to the accused at the accused's latest known address, and**

**(c) filing the information portion of the ticket with a court of competent jurisdiction before or as soon as practicable after the summons portion has been delivered or mailed.**

**(3) Content of ticket — The summons and information portions of a ticket must**

**(a) set out a description of the offence and the time and place of its alleged commission;**

**(b) include a statement, signed by the officer, that there are reasonable grounds to believe that the accused committed the offence;**

(c) set out the amount of the prescribed fine for the offence and the manner in which and period within which it must be paid;

(d) include a statement that, if the accused pays the fine within the period set out in the ticket, a conviction will be entered and recorded against the accused; and

(e) include a statement that if the accused wishes to plead not guilty or for any other reason fails to pay the fine within the period set out in the ticket, the accused must appear in the court and at the time set out in the ticket.



(4) **Consequences of payment** — Payment of the fine by the accused within the period set out in the ticket constitutes a plea of guilty to the offence described in the ticket and, following the payment,

(a) a conviction shall be entered against the accused and no further action shall be taken against the accused in respect of that offence; and

(b) any thing seized from the accused under this Act relating to the offence described in the ticket, or any proceeds realized from its disposition, are forfeited to Her Majesty in right of Canada and may be disposed of as the Minister directs.

(5) **Regulations** — The regulations may provide for any matter relating to the application of this section, and may include provisions prescribing

(a) the offences referred to in subsection (1) and the manner in which those offences may be described in tickets; and

(b) the amount of the fine, not exceeding $10,000, for a prescribed offence.

## *Debt Due to Her Majesty*

145. (1) **Debts due** — The following amounts are debts due to Her Majesty in right of Canada payable on demand:

(a) a debt incurred by Her Majesty for which any person is liable under this Act;

(b) an amount that a person has agreed to pay as a deposit or guarantee of performance of an obligation under this Act;

(c) the costs incurred in removing a prescribed foreign national from Canada;

(d) an amount that is ordered to be paid under section 147 on account of an unpaid liability; and

(e) an amount referred to in paragraph 148(1)(g).

*[Editor's Note: SOR/2002-227, s. 331 provides that a performance bond posted or security deposited under the former* Immigration Act, *R.S.C. 1985, c. I-2 that remains posted or deposited immediately before June 28, 2002 continues as a deposit or a guarantee under the new* Immigration and Refugee Protection Act, *S.C. 2001, c. 27 and is governed by its provisions.]*

(2) **Debts due — sponsors** — Subject to any federal-provincial agreement, an amount that a sponsor is required to pay under the terms of an undertaking is payable on demand to Her Majesty in right of Canada and Her Majesty in right of the

**province concerned and may be recovered by Her Majesty in either or both of those rights.**

**(3) Recovery of debt — A debt may be recovered at any time.**

*[Editor's Note: SOR/2002-227, s. 333 provides that any debt under s. 118(3) of the former* Immigration Act, *R.S.C. 1985, c. I-2 continues as a debt on June 28, 2002 and is governed by the provisions of the new* Immigration and Refugee Protection Act, *S.C. 2001, c. 27.]*

## Case Law

*Mavi v. Canada (Attorney General)* (2009), 85 Imm. L.R. (3d) 1, 98 O.R. (3d) 1, 313 D.L.R. (4th) 137, 259 O.A.C. 33, 2009 ONCA 794, 2009 CarswellOnt 6992 (C.A.); additional reasons (2009), 85 Imm. L.R. (3d) 83, 2009 ONCA 909, 2009 CarswellOnt 8048 (Ont. C.A.) — The main issues on this appeal were whether the governments must exercise discretion on a case-by-case basis and comply with a duty of procedural fairness when enforcing undertakings given by citizens or permanent residents of Canada to sponsor a relative's immigration to Canada. The appellants' sponsored relatives all received social assistance in Ontario during the period of their sponsorships and Ontario has requested payment of their sponsorship debts. The appellants claim that circumstances beyond their control left them unable to honour their undertakings. On this basis, each of the appellants applied for a declaration that they are discharged from their sponsorship obligations. The appellants argued that, properly interpreted, the language of the Acts stating that sponsorship debt "may be recovered" indicates the governments have discretion to forgive sponsorship debt. In support of their argument, the appellants relied on the terms of their undertakings which state that the government may choose not to recover in circumstances involving "abuse" or in "other appropriate circumstances." The lower Court judge rejected their contractual defences. She found that the words "may be recovered" are merely enabling in the sense that they do no more than permit the government to enforce the debt. She concluded that they do not impose either an obligation on government to consider appellants' circumstances on a case-by-case basis, or a duty of procedural fairness. On appeal, the appellants claim that the application judge erred in rejecting their arguments concerning discretion and procedural fairness and in failing to make declarations in that regard. The appeal was allowed, and the lower Court decision set aside and the following four declarations were made:

(i) Canada and Ontario have a case-by-case discretion whether to enforce sponsorship debt taking into account a sponsor's submissions concerning the sponsor's circumstances and those of their sponsored relatives:

(ii) Ontario fettered its discretion by adopting policies that are inconsistent with the provisions of the family class immigration regime;

(iii) Canada and Ontario owe the sponsors a duty of procedural fairness when enforcing sponsorship debt; and

(iv) the duty of procedural fairness includes: a) an obligation to provide sponsors with a process for explaining their own and their sponsored relative's relevant personal and financial circumstances; b) an obligation to consider those circumstances; and c) an obligation to inform any sponsor who makes submissions that their submissions have been considered and of the decision that was made.

*Editor's note: The Ontario Government has appealed this decision to the Supreme Court, with leave allowed 2010 CarswellOnt 2435, 2010 CarswellOnt 2436.*

## Collection of Debts Due to Her Majesty



**146. (1) Certificates — An amount or part of an amount payable under this Act that has not been paid may be certified by the Minister**

**(a) without delay, if the Minister is of the opinion that the person liable for that amount is attempting to avoid payment; and**

**(b) in any other case, on the expiration of 30 days after the default.**

**(2) Judgments — The certificate is to be filed and registered in the Federal Court and, when registered, has the same force and effect, and all proceedings may be taken, as if the certificate were a judgment obtained in the Court for a debt of the amount specified in the certificate plus interest to the day of payment.**

**(3) Costs — The costs of registering the certificate are recoverable in the same manner as if they had been included in the certificate.**

*[Editor's Note: SOR/2002-227, s. 333 provides that any debt under s. 118(3) of the former* Immigration Act, *R.S.C. 1985, c. I-2 continues as a debt on June 28, 2002 and is governed by the provisions of the new* Immigration and Refugee Protection Act, *S.C. 2001, c. 27.]*

**147. (1) Garnishment — If the Minister is of the opinion that a person is or is about to become liable to make a payment to a person liable to make a payment under this Act, the Minister may, by written notice, order the first person to pay to the Receiver General, on account of the second person's liability, all or part of the money otherwise payable to the second person.**

**(2) Applicability to future payments — If the Minister, under subsection (1), orders an employer to pay to the Receiver General money otherwise payable to an employee as remuneration,**

**(a) the order is applicable to all future payments of remuneration until the liability is satisfied; and**

**(b) the employer shall pay to the Receiver General out of each payment of remuneration the amount that the Minister stipulates in the notice.**

**(3) Discharge of liability — The receipt of the Minister is a good and sufficient discharge of the original liability to the extent of the payment.**

**(4) Regulations — The regulations may provide for any matter relating to the application of this section.**

## *Transportation Companies*

**148. (1) Obligation of operators of vehicles and facilities — A person who owns or operates a vehicle or a transportation facility, and an agent for such a person, must, in accordance with the regulations,**

**(a) not carry to Canada a person who is prescribed or does not hold a prescribed document, or who an officer directs not be carried;**

**(b) hold the prescribed documentation of a person whom it carries to Canada until an examination begins, present the person for examination and hold the person until the examination is completed;**

**(c) arrange for a medical examination and medical treatment and observation of a person it carries to Canada;**

**(d) provide prescribed information, including documentation and reports;**

**(e) provide facilities for the holding and examination of persons being carried to Canada;**

**(f) carry from Canada a person whom it has carried to or caused to enter Canada and who is prescribed or whom an officer directs to be carried;**

**(g) pay for all prescribed costs and fees relating to paragraphs (a), (b), (c) and (f); and**

**(h) provide security for compliance with its obligations under paragraphs (a) to (g).**

**(2) Seizure of security for compliance — If a person who owns or operates a vehicle or a transportation facility, or an agent of such a person, fails to comply with an obligation under this Act, all or part of any security provided by the person and any vehicle or other prescribed good owned or operated by the person may be detained, seized or forfeited to Her Majesty in right of Canada.**

*[Editor's Note: SOR/2002-227, s. 332 provides that a thing seized under the former* Immigration Act, *R.S.C. 1985, c. I-2 continues to be seized on June 28, 2002, and the seizure is governed by the provisions of the new* Immigration and Refugee Protection Act, *S.C. 2001, c. 27.]*

## Case Law

*KLM Royal Dutch Airlines v. Canada (Soliciteur général)*, 2004 CarswellNat 5196, 2004 CarswellNat 536, 2004 FC 308, (sub nom. *KLM Royal Dutch Airlines v. Canada (Attorney General))* 258 F.T.R. 261 (Eng.) (F.C.) — This was an application to review a decision by Citizenship and Immigration Canada that the applicant owes $114,000.00 to the respondent for removal costs of one Mohamed Moussa Mouhoumed. Mr. Mouhoumed came to Canada on January 19, 1999 from France. He arrived with a false passport. A deportation order was issued the same day but stayed because Mr. Mouhoumed claimed refugee status. The respondent advised the applicant that it had an obligation to transport Mr. Mouhoumed to Djibouti. The applicant agreed to transport Mr. Mouhoumed but could not because of Mr. Mouhoumed's resistance and violent behaviour. The applicant refused to pay the cost of chartering a private plane and finally the respondent removed Mr. Mouhoumed of its own initiative and asked the applicant to reimburse the costs which request was refused. The respondent advised the applicant that unless the amount was paid the amount of the security provided by the applicant could be forfeited under subs. 148(2) of IRPA.

The applicable standard of review is that of reasonableness *simpliciter*.

On the facts of this case, the decision by the respondent that the applicant had not been prompt in fulfilling its obligation to remove Mr. Mouhoumed was reasonable. The application for judicial review was dismissed.



**149. Use of information — The following provisions govern information provided under paragraph 148(1)(d):**

**(a) the information may be used only for the purposes of this Act or the *Department of Citizenship and Immigration Act* or to identify a person for whom a warrant of arrest has been issued in Canada; and**

**(b) notice regarding use of the information must be given to the person to whom it relates.**

2004, c. 15, s. 71

**150. Regulations — The regulations may provide for any matter relating to the purposes of sections 148 and 149, may define, for the purposes of this Act, terms used in those sections and may include provisions respecting**

**(a) the requirements and procedures applicable to a person who owns or operates a vehicle or a transportation facility;**

**(b) the costs and fees for which a person who owns or operates a vehicle or a transportation facility is liable;**

**(c) the procedures to be followed when a vehicle or other security is detained, seized, forfeited to Her Majesty in right of Canada or returned; and**

**(d) the procedures by which a person may make claim that their interest in a vehicle or other good is not affected by it being detained, seized or forfeited to Her Majesty in right of Canada.**

## *Sharing of Information*

[Heading added 2004, c. 15, s. 72.]

**150.1 (1) Regulations — The regulations may provide for any matter relating to**

**(a) the collection, retention, use, disclosure and disposal of information for the purposes of this Act or for the purposes of program legislation as defined in section 2 of the *Canada Border Services Agency Act*; and**

**(b) the disclosure of information for the purposes of national security, the defence of Canada or the conduct of international affairs, including the implementation of an agreement or arrangement entered into under section 5 of the *Department of Citizenship and Immigration Act* or section 13 of the *Canada Border Services Agency Act*.**

**(2) Conditions — Regulations made under subsection (1) may include conditions under which the collection, retention, use, disposal and disclosure may be made.**

2004, c. 15, s. 72; 2005, c. 38, s. 119

# PART 4 — IMMIGRATION AND REFUGEE BOARD

## *Composition of Board*

151. **Immigration and Refugee Board** — The Immigration and Refugee Board consists of the Refugee Protection Division, the Refugee Appeal Division, the Immigration Division and the Immigration Appeal Division.

152. **Composition** — The Board is composed of a Chairperson and other members as are required to ensure the proper functioning of the Board.

**Proposed Addition — 152.1**

152.1 **Oath or affirmation of office** — The Chairperson and other members of the Board must swear the oath or give the solemn affirmation of office set out in the rules of the Board.

2010, c. 8, s. 17 [To come into force June 29, 2012, or earlier by order.]

153. (1) **Chairperson and other members** — The Chairperson and members of the Refugee Protection Division, Refugee Appeal Division and Immigration Appeal Division

**Proposed Amendment — 153(1) opening words**

(1) **Chairperson and other members** — The Chairperson and members of the Refugee Appeal Division and Immigration Appeal Division

2010, c. 8, s. 18(1) [To come into force June 29, 2012, or earlier by order.]

(a) are appointed to the Board by the Governor in Council, to hold office during good behaviour for a term not exceeding seven years, subject to removal by the Governor in Council at any time for cause, to serve in a regional or district office of the Board;

(b) shall swear the oath or give the solemn affirmation of office set out in the rules of the Board;

**Proposed Repeal — 153(1)(b)**

(b) [Repealed 2010, c. 8, s. 18(2). To come into force June 29, 2012, or earlier by order.]

(c) are eligible for reappointment in the same or another capacity;

(d) shall receive the remuneration that may be fixed by the Governor in Council;

(e) are entitled to be paid reasonable travel and living expenses incurred while absent in the course of their duties, in the case of a full-time member, from their ordinary place of work or, in the case of a part-time member, while absent from their ordinary place of residence;

(f) are deemed to be employed in the public service for the purposes of the *Public Service Superannuation Act* and in the federal public administration for

**the purposes of the *Government Employees Compensation Act* and any regulations made under section 9 of the *Aeronautics Act*;**

**(g) may not accept or hold any office or employment or carry on any activity inconsistent with their duties and functions under this Act; and**

**(h) if appointed as full-time members, must devote the whole of their time to the performance of their duties under this Act.**



**(2) Deputy Chairperson and Assistant Deputy — One Deputy Chairperson for each Division referred to in subsection (1) and not more than 10 Assistant Deputy Chairpersons are to be designated by the Governor in Council from among the full-time members of those Divisions.**

**(3) Full-time and part-time appointments — The Chairperson and the Deputy Chairpersons and Assistant Deputy Chairpersons of the Divisions referred to in subsection (1) are appointed on a full-time basis and the other members are appointed on a full-time or part-time basis.**

**(4) Qualification — The Deputy Chairperson of the Immigration Appeal Division and a majority of the Assistant Deputy Chairpersons of that Division and at least 10 per cent of the members of the Divisions referred to in subsection (1) must be members of at least five years standing at the bar of a province or notaries of at least five years standing at the Chambre des notaires du Québec.**

2003, c. 22, s. 173

## Case Law

*Mroshaj v. Canada (Minister of Citizenship & Immigration)*, 2004 CarswellNat 5302, 2004 CarswellNat 3635, 262 F.T.R. 118, 2004 FC 1395 (F.C.) — The applicant sought to review a negative determination of his claim for protection. The member who dismissed the claim was on extended medical leave at the time she decided the case.

Section 153(1)(h) does not deprive a full-time member who, is on extended medical leave, from deciding cases that she heard before her leave began.

**154. Disposition after member ceases to hold office — A former member of the Board, within eight weeks after ceasing to be a member, may make or take part in a decision on a matter that they heard as a member, if the Chairperson so requests. For that purpose, the former member is deemed to be a member.**

**155. Disposition if member unable to take part — If a member of a three-member panel is unable to take part in the disposition of a matter that the member has heard, the remaining members may make the disposition and, for that purpose, are deemed to constitute the applicable Division.**

**156. Immunity and no summons — The following rules apply to the Chairperson and the members in respect of the exercise or purported exercise of their functions under this Act:**

**(a) no criminal or civil proceedings lie against them for anything done or omitted to be done in good faith; and**

**(b) they are not competent or compellable to appear as a witness in any civil proceedings.**

## Case Law

*Bourbonnais c. Canada (Procureur général)* (2006), 267 D.L.R. (4th) 120, (sub nom. *Bourbonnais v. Canada (Attorney General))* 348 N.R. 28, 2006 CarswellNat 318, 2006 CarswellNat 1030, 2006 FCA 62 (Fed. C.A.) — Close to 100 charges were laid against a member of the IRB for fraud against the government, breach of trust, and obstruction of justice. More particularly, the charges were with respect to having solicited and accepted money for the purpose of issuing favourable decisions to certain persons in cases that were being heard by the Board member.

The Board member claimed the right to be indemnified for his legal costs and fees incurred in defending himself on the charges against him. His claim was premised on the principle of judicial independence and its essential components: security of tenure, financial security and institutional independence. The Board member in this case was charged with soliciting and accepting money in exchange for favourable decisions. Consequently, the sole purpose of the trial he would have to undergo was to determine his guilt on those charges. Those proceedings do not challenge the notion of security of tenure, an essential component of judicial independence. The Board member was not entitled to obtain from the IRB the payment of legal costs and fees he would have to incur in defending himself against the charges laid against him. The Board member did not act in good faith, and accordingly, was not entitled to immunity.

## *Head Office and Staff*

**157. (1) Head office — The head office of the Board shall be in the National Capital Region as described in the Schedule to the *National Capital Act*.**

**(2) Residence — Chairperson — The Chairperson must live in the National Capital Region or within reasonable commuting distance of it.**

**158. Personnel — The Executive Director and other personnel necessary for the proper conduct of the business of the Board shall be appointed in accordance with the *Public Service Employment Act*, and the personnel are deemed to be employed in the public service for the purposes of the *Public Service Superannuation Act*.**

*[Editor's Note: S.C. 2001, c. 27, s. 188(4) provides that the person who, on June 28, 2002, held the office of Executive Director of the Immigration and Refugee Board is deemed to have been appointed to that office under section 158 of the new* Immigration and Refugee Protection Act, *S.C. 2001, c. 27, without prejudice to any salary and benefits he or she may receive by virtue of having held that office before June 28, 2002.]*

2003, c. 22, s. 225(z.3)

## *Duties of Chairperson*

**159. (1) Chairperson — The Chairperson is, by virtue of holding that office, a member of each Division of the Board and is the chief executive officer of the Board. In that capacity, the Chairperson**

**(a) has supervision over and direction of the work and staff of the Board;**

**(b) may at any time assign a member appointed under paragraph 153(1)(a) to the Refugee Protection Division, the Refugee Appeal Division and the Immigration Appeal Division;**

**Proposed Amendment — 159(1)(b)**

**(b) may at any time assign a member appointed under paragraph 153(1)(a) to the Refugee Appeal Division or the Immigration Appeal Division;**

2010, c. 8, s. 19(1) [To come into force June 29, 2012, or earlier by order.]

**(c) may at any time, notwithstanding paragraph 153(1)(a), assign a member, other than a member of the Immigration Division, to work in another regional or district office in order to satisfy operational requirements, but an assignment may not exceed 90 days without the approval of the Governor in Council;**

**Proposed Amendment — 159(1)(c)**

**(c) may at any time, despite paragraph 153(1)(a), assign a member of the Refugee Appeal Division or the Immigration Appeal Division to work in another regional or district office to satisfy operational requirements, but an assignment may not exceed 120 days without the approval of the Governor in Council;**

2010, c. 8, s. 19(1) [To come into force June 29, 2012, or earlier by order.]

**(d) designates from among the full-time members of the Board coordinating members for a Division, other than the Immigration Division;**

**Proposed Amendment — 159(1)(d)**

**(d) may designate, from among the full-time members appointed under paragraph 153(1)(a), coordinating members for the Refugee Appeal Division or the Immigration Appeal Division;**

2010, c. 8, s. 19(1) [To come into force June 29, 2012, or earlier by order.]

**(e) assigns administrative functions to the members of the Board;**

**(f) apportions work among the members of the Board and fixes the place, date and time of proceedings;**

**(g) takes any action that may be necessary to ensure that the members of the Board carry out their duties efficiently and without undue delay;**

**(h) may issue guidelines in writing to members of the Board and identify decisions of the Board as jurisprudential guides, after consulting with the Deputy Chairpersons and the Director General of the Immigration Division, to assist members in carrying out their duties; and**

**Proposed Amendment — 159(1)(h)**

**(h) may issue guidelines in writing to members of the Board and identify decisions of the Board as jurisprudential guides, after consulting with the Deputy Chairpersons, to assist members in carrying out their duties; and**

2010, c. 8, s. 19(2) [To come into force June 29, 2012, or earlier by order.]

**(i) may appoint and, subject to the approval of the Treasury Board, fix the remuneration of experts or persons having special knowledge to assist the Divisions in any matter.**

**(2) Delegation — The Chairperson may delegate any of his or her powers under this Act to a member of the Board, other than a member of the Immigration Division, except that**

**(a) powers conferred under subsection 161(1) may not be delegated;**

**(b) powers referred to in paragraphs (1)(a) and (i) may be delegated to the Executive Director of the Board; and**

**(c) powers in relation to the Immigration Division may only be delegated to the Director General, directors or members of that Division.**

**Proposed Amendment — 159(2)**

**(2) Delegation — The Chairperson may delegate any of his or her powers under this Act to a member of the Board, except that**

**(a) powers referred to in subsection 161(1) may not be delegated;**

**(b) powers referred to in paragraphs (1)(a) and (i) may be delegated to the Executive Director of the Board;**

**(c) powers in relation to the Immigration Appeal Division and the Refugee Appeal Division may only be delegated to the Deputy Chairperson, the Assistant Deputy Chairpersons, or other members, including coordinating members, of either of those Divisions; and**

**(d) powers in relation to the Immigration Division or the Refugee Protection Division may only be delegated to the Deputy Chairperson, the Assistant Deputy Chairpersons or other members, including coordinating members, of that Division.**

2010, c. 8, s. 19(3) [To come into force June 29, 2012, or earlier by order.]

## Case Law

### Section 159(1)

*Benitez v. Canada (Minister of Citizenship & Immigration)*, 2007 CarswellNat 1393, 2007 FCA 199 (Fed. C.A.) — The Federal Court consolidated a number of applications for judicial review impugning the validity of Guideline 7. Guideline 7 was issued by the Chairperson of the Board in 2003, pursuant to the power conferred by paragraph 159(1)(h) of the Immigration and Refugee Protection Act, S.C. 2001, c. 27, to issue guidelines to assist members of the Board in carrying out their duties ("the Guideline 7 issue"). Guideline 7 provides that the standard order of questioning at a refugee protection hearing by the Refugee Protection Division of the Board will be that the claimant is questioned first by the Refugee Protection officer and/or by the Refugee Protection Division member conducting the hearing. However, in exceptional cases members may permit claimants to be questioned first by their own counsel.

Guideline 7 does not breach the duty of fairness by either denying the claimants an effective opportunity to make representations or so distorting the role of the member of the Refugee Protection Division hearing the claim as to give rise to a reasonable apprehension of bias. Nor is it an unlawful fetter on members' discretion, and it was not legally required to have been issued under the Chairperson's statutory power to issue rules of procedure, subject to cabinet approval.

*Thamotharem v. Canada (Minister of Citizenship & Immigration)*, 2006 CarswellNat 1588, 2006 FCA 218 (Fed. C.A.) — This appeal concerns the validity of Guideline 7 (preparation and conduct of a hearing in the Refugee Protection Division) issued in 2003 by the Chairperson of the Board pursuant to the statutory power to "issue guidelines. . .to assist members in carrying out their duties": Immigration and Refugee Protection Act, S.C. 2001, c. 27, paragraph 159(1)(h). The key paragraphs of Guideline 7 provide as follows:

> "In a claim for refugee protection, the standard practice will be for the Refugee Protection Officer to start questioning the claimant," although the member of the Refugee Protection Division ("RPD") hearing the claim "may vary the order of questioning in exceptional circumstances."

Guideline 7 is not, on its face, invalid on the ground of procedural unfairness, although, as the Minister and the Board conceded, fairness may require that, in certain circumstances particular claimants should be questioned first by their own counsel. Guideline 7 is not incompatible with the impartiality required of a member when conducting a hearing which is inquisitorial in form. Guideline 7 is not an unlawful fetter on the exercise of members' discretion on the conduct of refugee protection hearings. The Guideline expressly directs members to consider the facts of the particular case before them to determine whether there are exceptional circumstances warranting a deviation from the standard order of questioning. The evidence did not establish that members disregarded this aspect of Guideline 7 and slavishly adhered to the standard order of questioning, regardless of the facts of the case before them. Nor does it follow that the fact that Guideline 7 could have been issued as a statutory rule of procedure that it is invalid because it was not approved by the Governor in Council. The Minister's appeal was allowed, the appellant's cross-appeal was dismissed, the order of the Federal Court set aside, and the application for judicial review dismissed.

*Karanja v. Canada (Minister of Citizenship & Immigration)*, 2006 CarswellNat 1265, 2006 CarswellNat 2533, 2006 FC 574 (F.C.) — Pursuant to the Gender Guidelines (*Women Refugee Claimants Fearing Gender-Related Persecution*, 9 March 1993, by the chairperson of the Immigration and Refugee Board pursuant to paragraph 159(1)(h) of the *Immigration Act*), the Board should be particularly sensitive to a female applicant's difficulty in testifying. However, the gender guidelines, in and of themselves, are not intended to serve as a cure for all deficiencies in the applicant's claim or evidence. The applicant bears the onus of proving her claim. The Guidelines cannot be treated as corroborating any evidence of gender-based persecution so that the giving of the evidence becomes proof of its truth.

Instead, the Guidelines are an aid for the panel in the assessment of the evidence of women who allege that they have been victims of gender-based persecution. The Guidelines do not create new grounds for finding a person to be a victim of persecution. A board's failure to specifically mention the Gender Guidelines does not mean that they were not considered and is not material or fatal to the Board's decision.

The Gender Guidelines specifically state that the female refugee claimant must demonstrate that the harm feared is sufficiently serious to amount to persecution. In this case, there were numerous negative credability findings by the Board and such findings are open to the Board to make. Accordingly, the applicant failed to demonstrate that the Board's decision was patently unreasonable so as to warrant the intervention of the Court.

**160. Absence, incapacity or vacancy — In the event of the absence or incapacity of the Chairperson, or if the office of Chairperson is vacant, the Minister may authorize one of the Deputy Chairpersons or any other member of the Board to act as Chairperson.**

## *Functioning of Board*

**161. (1) Rules — Subject to the approval of the Governor in Council, and in consultation with the Deputy Chairpersons and the Director General of the Immigration Division, the Chairperson may make rules respecting**

**Proposed Amendment — 161(1) opening words**

**(1) Rules — Subject to the approval of the Governor in Council, and in consultation with the Deputy Chairpersons, the Chairperson may make rules respecting**

2010, c. 8, s. 20 [To come into force June 29, 2012, or earlier by order.]

**(a) the activities, practice and procedure of each of the Divisions of the Board, including the periods for appeal, the priority to be given to proceedings, the notice that is required and the period in which notice must be given;**

**Proposed Amendment — 161(1)(a)**

**(a) the referral of a claim for refugee protection to the Refugee Protection Division and the conduct of the interview referred to in subsection 100(4);**

2010, c. 8, s. 20 [To come into force June 29, 2012, or earlier by order.]

**Proposed Addition — 161(1)(a.1), (a.2)**

**(a.1) the factors to be taken into account in fixing or changing the date of an interview referred to in subsection 100(4);**

**(a.2) the activities, practice and procedure of each of the Divisions of the Board, including the periods for appeal, other than in respect of appeals of decisions of the Refugee Protection Division, the priority to be given to proceedings, the notice that is required and the period in which notice must be given;**

2010, c. 8, s. 20 [To come into force June 29, 2012, or earlier by order.]

**(b) the conduct of persons in proceedings before the Board, as well as the consequences of, and sanctions for, the breach of those rules;**

**(c) the information that may be required and the manner in which, and the time within which, it must be provided with respect to a proceeding before the Board; and**

**(d) any other matter considered by the Chairperson to require rules.**

**(2) Tabling in Parliament — The Minister shall cause a copy of any rule made under subsection (1) to be laid before each House of Parliament on any of the first 15 days on which that House is sitting after the approval of the rule by the Governor in Council.**



## *Provisions that Apply to All Divisions*

**162. (1) Sole and exclusive jurisdiction — Each Division of the Board has, in respect of proceedings brought before it under this Act, sole and exclusive jurisdiction to hear and determine all questions of law and fact, including questions of jurisdiction.**

**(2) Procedure — Each Division shall deal with all proceedings before it as informally and quickly as the circumstances and the considerations of fairness and natural justice permit.**

### Case Law

*Kamtasingh v. Canada (Minister of Citizenship & Immigration)* (2010), 87 Imm. L.R. (3d) 118, 2010 FC 45, 2010 CarswellNat 801, 2010 CarswellNat 101 (F.C.) — This was an application for judicial review challenging a decision of the Immigration Appeal Division which determined the applicant's marriage was not genuine. The applicant states that the IAD member denied him procedural fairness by preventing him from calling all of his proposed witnesses.

The IAD has the right to limit repetitive testimony, but not by effectively excluding witnesses who could offer evidence going to the central issues of the case. The place to control excessive or repetitive evidence on issues of controversy which are central or determinate is generally not at the entrance to the witness box, but once the witness is testifying — and even then the member must grant some latitude to ensure that all important matters are covered. The IAD can, of course, limit the scope of evidence by stipulating certain points that are not in dispute. In a case like this one where the credibility of the applicant is clearly an issue and where the genuineness of a marriage is in doubt, the evidence of immediate family and close acquaintances is highly relevant and should be heard without reservation. Indeed, it was difficult to see how this matter could be fairly determined after only two hours of evidence, particularly when the applicant was self-represented and was initially intending to lead evidence from several witnesses. This was a situation where the duty to allow the applicant to fully present his case was sacrificed for the desire for administrative efficiency. That is not a permissible trade-off. The application for judicial review was allowed.

*Canada (Minister of Citizenship & Immigration) v. Peirovdinnabi* (2010), 87 Imm. L.R. (3d) 162, 2010 FC 64, 2010 CarswellNat 108, 2010 CarswellNat 726 (F.C.) — The issue considered was whether, in 2010, the respondent made a misrepresentation by answering "yes" to the question "are you living with your spouse," posed in a form entitled "Supplemental Information Spouse in Canada." This issue arose in the course of the respondent's sponsorship of his second wife to Canada in 2005. In the course of that application he was questioned about his living circumstances with his first wife three years before and he answered that he thought that the question posed at the time required an answer as to whether he and his first wife were living "together." To this question the respondent said that, while they were living together, he and his first wife maintained separate residences and lived in both after their marriage. The problem that arose was that the applicant interpreted the question answered by the respondent to mean "are you living together with your wife in the same residence." This conflict in interpretation set a course of decision making in motion which has resulted in the present application for judicial review of an IAD decision that found that the respondent did not make a misrepresentation.

The central argument advanced by the applicant in the present review of the IAD decision is that, as a matter of law, the IAD was required to determine the genuineness of the respondent's first marriage. The position that the applicant takes is that since the hearing before the IAD was *de novo*, all issues with respect to the respondent's first marriage were required to be determined. The Court rejected this argument and found that the IAD took the appeal as it came: there was only one question to be addressed and that was whether the respondent made a misrepresentation. The question of whether the marriage was genuine was not determined in the first and second level decisions, and it was not in play in the IAD decision. The IAD's decision was upheld and the application for judicial review dismissed. The following question was certified:

> Does the IAD have an obligation in law to determine the genuineness of a marriage on a *de novo* appeal brought with respect to an issue of misrepresentation when the issue of the genuineness of the marriage concerned was not specifically raised for determination in the appeal?

*Ferri v. Canada (Minister of Citizenship & Immigration)*, [2005] F.C.J. No. 1941, 51 Imm. L.R. (3d) 177, [2006] 3 F.C.R. 53, 2005 CarswellNat 3878, 2005 CarswellNat 5009, 2005 FC 1580 (F.C.) — Subsection 68(4) of the IRPA limits the jurisdiction of the IAD to determining whether the factual requirements of this subsection are met. The IAD can only consider whether it has previously stayed a removal order; whether the individual in question is a permanent resident or a foreign national who was found inadmissible on grounds of serious criminality or criminality; and whether the individual has been convicted of another offence coming within subs. 36(1) of the IRPA. Once the IAD determines that the factual requirements of this subsection have been met, it then loses jurisdiction over the individual, by operation of law. The IAD does not have jurisdiction to consider the constitutionality of subs. 68(4).

*Alwan v. Canada (Minister of Citizenship & Immigration)*, 2004 CarswellNat 5221, 2004 CarswellNat 1689, 2004 FC 807 (F.C.) — The applicant's refugee claim was rejected under Article 1(F)(a) of the Refugee Convention. At the end of the hearing, the Refugee Protection Division panel asked counsel for the applicant, the refugee protection officer and the Minister's counsel for written submissions concerning the exclusion under Article 1(F). Counsel for the Minister indicated that he would not be providing written submissions as he was of the view that the evidence before the Board in this respect was not compelling and that the test had not been made out. He left it to the RPD to draw its own conclusions. The Refugee Protection officer and counsel for the applicant provided written submissions. The Refugee Protection Division found that the test had been met and excluded the applicant.

The Refugee Protection Division was not required to defer to the opinion of the Minister's counsel. Subsection 162(1) vests the Refugee Protection Division with sole and exclusive jurisdiction to hear and determine all questions of law and fact including questions of jurisdiction.

**163. Composition of panels — Matters before a Division shall be conducted before a single member unless, except for matters before the Immigration Division, the Chairperson is of the opinion that a panel of three members should be constituted.**

**Proposed Amendment — 163**

**163. Composition of panels — Matters before a Division must be conducted before a single member unless, with respect to a matter before the Refugee Appeal Division or the Immigration Appeal Division, the Chairperson is of the opinion that a panel of three members should be constituted.**

2010, c. 8, s. 21 [To come into force June 29, 2012, or earlier by order.]

**164. Presence of parties — Where a hearing is held by a Division, it may, in the Division's discretion, be conducted in the presence of, or by a means of live telecommunication with, the person who is the subject of the proceedings.**

## Case Law

*Sundaram v. Canada (Minister of Citizenship & Immigration)*, 2006 CarswellNat 499, 2006 CarswellNat 2426, 2006 FC 291 (F.C.) — When the IRB receives requests for a change of venue because a person cannot attend at a scheduled hearing location, it has an obligation to consider all relevant matters including its own discretionary powers relevant to the request. In this case, the applicant had moved from Toronto to Vancouver. As there was no indication in the conclusionary reasons that the Refugee Protection Division ever turned its mind to the issue of alternative means and locations of hearing, the decision not to reopen the dismissal of the applicant's refugee claim was quashed.

**165. Powers of a commissioner — The Refugee Protection Division and the Immigration Division and each member of those Divisions have the powers and authority of a commissioner appointed under Part I of the *Inquiries Act* and may do any other thing they consider necessary to provide a full and proper hearing.**

**Proposed Amendment — 165**

**165. Powers of a commissioner — The Refugee Protection Division, the Refugee Appeal Division and the Immigration Division and each member of those Divisions have the powers and authority of a commissioner appointed under Part I of the *Inquiries Act* and may do any other thing they consider necessary to provide a full and proper hearing.**

2010, c. 8, s. 22 [To come into force June 29, 2012, or earlier by order.]

## Case Law

*Canada (Minister of Public Safety & Emergency Preparedness) v. Kahlon* (2005), 35 Admin. L.R. (4th) 213, 2005 CarswellNat 2255, 2005 CarswellNat 5610, 2005 FC 1000 (F.C.) — The proper procedure when there is a requirement to produce documents, whether by subpoena or otherwise, and there is a genuine dispute as to their relevance or as to whether they are privileged, is to have the documents produced, so that the tribunal charged with determining their relevance will have them available for examination. If any of the documents then turned out to be irrelevant, the privacy interest of the owner would be protected as the documents would not then be provided to the party making the demand. In this case, the Refugee Protection Division improperly exercised its powers to compel evidence and did not follow its own procedural rules.

**166. Proceedings — all Divisions — Proceedings before a Division are to be conducted as follows:**

**(a) subject to the other provisions of this section, proceedings must be held in public;**

**(b) on application or on its own initiative, the Division may conduct a proceeding in the absence of the public, or take any other measure that it considers necessary to ensure the confidentiality of the proceedings, if, after having considered all available alternate measures, the Division is satisfied that there is**

**(i) a serious possibility that the life, liberty or security of a person will be endangered if the proceeding is held in public,**

**(ii) a real and substantial risk to the fairness of the proceeding such that the need to prevent disclosure outweighs the societal interest that the proceeding be conducted in public, or**

**(iii) a real and substantial risk that matters involving public security will be disclosed;**

**(c) subject to paragraph (d), proceedings before the Refugee Protection Division and the Immigration Division concerning a claimant of refugee protection, proceedings concerning cessation and vacation applications and proceedings before the Refugee Appeal Division must be held in the absence of the public;**

**(d) on application or on its own initiative, the Division may conduct a proceeding in public, or take any other measure that it considers necessary to ensure the appropriate access to the proceedings if, after having considered all available alternate measures and the factors set out in paragraph (b), the Division is satisfied that it is appropriate to do so;**

**(e) despite paragraphs (b) and (c), a representative or agent of the United Nations High Commissioner for Refugees is entitled to observe proceedings concerning a protected person or a person who has made a claim to refugee protection; and**

**(f) despite paragraph (e), the representative or agent may not observe any part of the proceedings that deals with information or other evidence in respect of which an application has been made under section 86, and not rejected, or with information or other evidence protected under that section.**

2008, c. 3, s. 5

**167. (1) Right to counsel — Both a person who is the subject of Board proceedings and the Minister may, at their own expense, be represented by a barrister or solicitor or other counsel.**

**Proposed Amendment — 167(1)**

**(1) Right to counsel — A person who is the subject of proceedings before any Division of the Board, including the interview referred to in subsection 100(4), and the Minister may, at their own expense, be represented by legal or other counsel.**

2010, c. 8, s. 23 [To come into force June 29, 2012, or earlier by order.]

**(2) Representation — If a person who is the subject of proceedings is under 18 years of age or unable, in the opinion of the applicable Division, to appreciate the nature of the proceedings, the Division shall designate a person to represent the person.**



## Case Law

### Section 167(1)

*Cha v. Canada (Minister of Citizenship & Immigration)*, [2006] F.C.J. No. 491, 53 Imm. L.R. (3d) 1, 267 D.L.R. (4th) 324, 349 N.R. 233, 2006 CarswellNat 751, 2006 FCA 126 (C.A.) — The intent of Parliament is clear. The Minister's delegate is only empowered under subs. 44(2) of the Act to make the removal orders in prescribed cases which are clear and non-controversial and where the facts simply dictate the remedy. The Minister's delegate could not look at the gravity of the offence, and the particular circumstances of the applicant and his conviction, in determining not to issue the removal order. It is simply not open to the Minister's delegate to indirectly or collaterally go beyond the actual conviction. To do so would ignore Parliament's clearly expressed intent that the breaking of the condition of non-criminality be determinative. Although the manual indicates that the personal circumstances of the offender will be considered at the front-end of the process before any decision is taken to remove an individual from Canada, these views and statements have been expressed in respect to permanent residents convicted of serious offences in Canada. No such assurances were given by specific reference to foreign nationals. A foreign national may wish to invoke humanitarian and compassionate considerations and is at liberty to make a request to the Minister pursuant to s. 25 of the Act or to stay a removal order pursuant to s. 233 of the Regulations, or avail himself of the pre-removal risk assessment proceeding pursuant to s. 112 of the Act.

Absent a *Charter* right to be notified of a right to counsel on arrest or detention, there is no authority for the proposition that a person is entitled, as of right, to be notified before a hearing that he or she has either a statutory right or a duty of fairness right to counsel. Once a person is sufficiently informed of the object and possible effects of a forthcoming hearing — absent sufficient notice, the decision rendered will in all likelihood be set aside — the decision maker is under no duty to go further.

It may be sound practice, in certain cases, to give notice in advance that counsel may be retained, but there is no duty to do so unless the statute requires it. The responsibility lies with the person to seek leave from the decision maker to be accompanied by counsel or to come to the hearing accompanied by counsel.

In the recent IRPA, the right to be informed of one's right to counsel in admissibility matters has disappeared and the right to counsel has been preserved only with respect to hearings before the Immigration Division. There is no provision concerning the right to counsel and proceedings before the immigration officer or the Minister's delegate under subs. 44(1) and (2) of the IRPA. In this case, the respondent did not seek leave to have counsel present during the interview or to attend accompanied by counsel.

If leave is denied or if counsel is not allowed to be present, that could become an issue in a judicial review of the decision ultimately rendered.

*Mallette v. Canada (Minister of Citizenship & Immigration)* (2005), 51 Imm. L.R. (3d) 267, 2005 CarswellNat 3224, 2005 FC 1400 (F.C.) — The applicant was ordered deported because she had been convicted of possession of narcotics for purposes of trafficking. She was granted a stay of execution of the deportation order for five years on 10 expressed conditions. The Minister's representative requested an early review of the stay of execution alleging breaches of the conditions imposed. The breaches included further criminal offences, the use of illegal drugs, sale of drugs including problems with keeping the peace and being of good behaviour. The Board did not cancel the stay but modified the initial conditions imposed on the applicant. The Board advised the applicant that an oral interim reconsideration of the case would take place the next year and that a final reconsideration would take place four years later or at such date as it determined. The applicant received a notice of the hearing date, however, arrived at the hearing without a lawyer and testified on her own behalf. The Board cancelled the order staying the applicant's removal and directed that she be removed from Canada as soon as reasonably possible.

The right to counsel is not absolute. Immigration case law indicates that a decision is invalid should the absence of counsel deprive the applicant of his or her right to a fair hearing. In *Mervilus v. Canada (Minister of Citizenship & Immigration)*, [2004] F.C.J. No. 1460, the law from the Federal Court and the Federal Court of Appeal was reviewed and summarized as follows at page 25:

> The following principles can therefore be drawn from the case law: although the right to counsel is not absolute in an administrative proceeding, refusing an individual the possibility to retain counsel by not allowing a postponement is reviewable if the following factors are in play: the case is complex, the consequences of the decision are serious, the individual does not have the resources — whether in terms of intellect or legal knowledge — to properly represent his interests.

The Court found all of the above factors present in this case and that it was clear the applicant was not capable of representing herself.

The applicant was formerly notified twice of the Board's intention to review her compliance with the conditions; it was evident that she understood the purpose of the hearing to be a yearly review of her progress and recovery, similar to her monthly stay interviews. It was for this reason she claimed that she did not bring in a lawyer. The Board's failure to provide an adjournment in order that the applicant might retain counsel deprived her of the right to a fair hearing.

*Hak v. Canada (Minister of Citizenship & Immigration)*, 2005 CarswellNat 3669, 2005 CarswellNat 5007, 2005 FC 1488 (F.C.) — The law is clear that an individual must bear the consequences of hiring poor counsel. There may be circumstances where the negligent or incompetent actions of an individual's representative may result in the person being denied a fair hearing. In this case the applicant claimed that the failure of her immigration consultant to notify her of the date for her interview resulted in her being denied procedural fairness in the process. The applicant failed to persuade the Court that she had been denied procedural fairness in the process.

*Toor v. Canada (Minister of Citizenship & Immigration)*, 2005 CarswellNat 3256, 2005 FC 1386 (F.C.) — The applicants, having been unsuccessful Convention refugees, made an application for humanitarian and compassionate consideration pursuant to s. 25 of the IRPA. They also made an application for consideration as Post-determination Refugee Claimants. Their lawyer wrote to the processing centre in Vegreville, Alberta, in anticipation that the file would be transferred to Vancouver and might be determined concurrently with the PRRA application, advising that he would make complete representations in support of their request once the applicants received their notice to make representations and file evidence in support of the PRRA. The H&C request was turned down. No additional information was supplied by the applicants' lawyer because Vegreville ignored the fact that the lawyer's address was listed as the place to communicate with the applicants, and wrote directly to the applicants instead. The decision maker's notes to file indicate that she did not appear to have focused on what was before her and consequently the decision was held to be patently unreasonable.

*Shirvan v. Canada (Minister of Citizenship & Immigration)*, [2005] F.C.J. No. 1864, 2005 CarswellNat 3744, 2005 CarswellNat 5233, 2005 FC 1509 (F.C.) — Before examining allegations of incompetence, the Court must first determine whether the applicants have met their preliminary burden of giving notice of the allegations to their former counsel. In this case, new counsel for the applicants wrote to the Canadian Society of Immigration Consultants to complain of their former counsel's treatment and to request that he immediately be prohibited from practising as an immigration consultant. The letter provided sufficient corroborating evidence and provided sufficient notice of the allegation to the applicants' former counsel.

Although the Immigration Appeal Division transcript demonstrated that the former counsel was unfamiliar with the hearing procedure, the applicants were still able to present their case. The only major ground the applicants claimed their former counsel should have raised was the best interest of the child consideration. Since the child was aged 19 or older at the time of the initial determination and at the time of the Immigration Appeal Division hearing, the Immigration Appeal Division did not err in its decision not to consider the best interest of the applicant's daughter. Accordingly, the applicants failed to demonstrate the result of their hearing would have been different but for their former counsel's alleged incompetence.

*Mervilus v. Canada (Ministre de la Citoyenneté & de l'Immigration)*, 2004 CarswellNat 5673, 2004 CarswellNat 3104, 262 F.T.R. 186, 2004 FC 1206 (F.C.) — The applicant was ordered to leave Canada in 1996. The execution of that order was stayed by order of the Appeal Division in March 1997. The stay was for a five year period with a review six months later and every year thereafter. On September 16, 2003 the Immigration Appeal Division set aside the stay of the deportation order and dismissed the appeal of this order.

The applicant appeared before the Appeal Division for the annual review of the stay. For the first time since the proceedings began he did not have counsel. At the outset of the proceedings he requested a postponement. The applicant explained that he had been in Haiti and that he had only arrived back in Canada a few days before the review of his appeal. The member presiding over the hearing decided to proceed.

Although the right to counsel is not absolute in an administrative proceeding, refusing an individual the possibility to retain counsel by not allowing a postponement is reviewable if the following factors are in play: the case is complex, the consequences of the decision are serious, the individual does not have resources whether in terms of intellect or legal knowledge to properly represent his interests. The decision of the Board member was quashed and the matter referred for re-determination by a differently constituted panel.

*Robles v. Canada (Minister of Citizenship & Immigration)*, [2003] F.C.J. No. 520, 2003 CarswellNat 815, 2003 CarswellNat 1819, 2003 FCT 374, 2003 CFPI 374, 2 Admin. L.R. (4th) 315 (Fed. T.D.) — This was an application to review a negative decision of a panel of the CRDD. The applicants argued that they were denied natural justice due to the incompetence of their former counsel who was himself an immigration consultant and not a lawyer. *Law Society (British Columbia) v. Mangat* (2001), 16 Imm. L.R. (3d) 1, [2001] 3 S.C.R. 113, 2001 CarswellBC 2168, 2001 CarswellBC 2169, [2001] S.C.J. No. 66, 2001 SCC 67, 205 D.L.R. (4th) 577, 157 B.C.A.C. 161, 256 W.A.C. 161, 96 B.C.L.R. (3d) 1, 276 N.R. 339, [2002] 2 W.W.R. 201 (S.C.C.), established that the participation of non-lawyer consultants as a matter within federal, not provincial, jurisdiction. A precise factual foundation must exist in order for the Court to find that prejudice resulted to a person as a result of the incompetence of counsel. Incompetence is determined by a reasonableness standard. The analysis proceeds upon a strong presumption that counsel's conduct fell within the wide range of reasonable professional assistance. The onus is on the applicant to establish the acts or omissions of counsel that are alleged not to have been the result of reasonable professional judgment. The wisdom of hindsight has no place in this assessment.

Miscarriages of justice may take many forms. In some instances, counsel's performance may have resulted in procedural unfairness. In others, the reliability of the trial's result may have been compromised.

In the present case, the principal applicant filed an affidavit in which he addressed the alleged incompetent performance of his immigration consultant. The applicant also filed the affidavit of a person with expertise in the immigration area who attested to the fact that the immigration consultant was incompetent.

In this case the evidence was held not to have been sufficient and the application was dismissed.

*Dehghani v. Canada (Minister of Employment & Immigration*, [1993] 1 S.C.R. 1053, 18 Imm. L.R. (2d) 245, 10 Admin. L.R. (2d) 1, 20 C.R. (4th) 34, 101 D.L.R. (4th) 654, 150 N.R. 241, 14 C.R.R. (2d) 1, 1993 CarswellNat 57, 1993 CarswellNat 1380, EYB 1993-67290, [1993] S.C.J. No. 38 — The appellant, a citizen of Iran, arrived in Canada without valid travel or identity documents and claimed Convention refugee status. He was interviewed at the secondary examination and extensive written notes were made by an immigration officer, which notes were later entered in evidence at the credible-basis hearing. At the conclusion of that hearing the first level tribunal decided that there was no credible basis to the appellant's claim.

When the appellant was taken to a secondary examination at Canadian Immigration at Pearson International Airport, he was not detained in the sense contemplated by s. 10(b) of the *Charter*. Further, the principles of s. 10(b) do not require that the appellant be provided with counsel at the pre-inquiry or pre-hearing stage of the refugee claim determination process. The secondary examination of the appellant at the port-of-entry is not analogous to a hearing. The purpose of the port-of entry interview was to aid in the processing of the appellant's application for entry and to determine the appropriate procedures which should be invoked in order to deal with the appellant's application for Convention refugee status. The principles of fundamental justice do not include a right to counsel in these circumstances of routine information gathering.

*[Editor's note: Although* Dehghani *was decided under the former Act, it may still be relevant.]*

### Section 167(2)

*Duale v. Canada (Minister of Citizenship & Immigration)*, [2004] F.C.J. No. 178, 40 Imm. L.R. (3d) 165, 2004 CarswellNat 198, 2004 CarswellNat 2401, 2004 FC 150 (F.C.) — The obligation to designate a representative for a claimant who is a minor, or who is otherwise unable to appreciate the nature of the proceedings, arises at the earliest point in time at which the Refugee Protection Division becomes aware of facts which reveal the need for the designated representative. The need for the designation of a representative applies to the entirety of the proceedings in respect of a refugee claim and not just to the actual hearing of the claim.

The duties of the designated representative are:

a) to retain counsel;

b) to instruct counsel or to assist the child in instructing counsel;

c) to make other decisions with respect to the proceedings or to help the child make those decisions;

d) to inform the child about the various stages and proceedings of the claim;

e) to assist in obtaining evidence in support of the claim;

f) to provide evidence and be a witness in the claim;

g) to act in the best interest of the child.

**168. (1) Abandonment of proceeding — A Division may determine that a proceeding before it has been abandoned if the Division is of the opinion that the applicant is in default in the proceedings, including by failing to appear for a hearing, to provide information required by the Division or to communicate with the Division on being requested to do so.**

**Proposed Amendment — 168(1)**

**(1) Abandonment of proceeding — A Division may determine that a proceeding before it has been abandoned if the Division is of the opinion that the applicant is in default in the proceedings, including by failing to attend the interview referred to in subsection 100(4), to appear for a hearing, to provide information required by the Division or to communicate with the Division on being requested to do so.**

2010, c. 8, s. 24 [To come into force June 29, 2012, or earlier by order.]

**(2) Abuse of process — A Division may refuse to allow an applicant to withdraw from a proceeding if it is of the opinion that the withdrawal would be an abuse of process under its rules.**

## Case Law

### Section 168(1)

*Revich v. Canada (Ministre de la Citoyenneté & de l'Immigration)* (2004), 44 Imm. L.R. (3d) 129, 2004 CarswellNat 5036, 2004 CarswellNat 2631, 2004 FC 1064 (F.C.) — The

*Refugee Protection Division Rules* clearly provide how the Division must proceed in order to declare a claim abandoned. The Division must give the claimant the opportunity to explain why the claim should not be declared abandoned, must take into account the claimant's explanations and must take into account any other relevant factor, in particular the claimant's intention to pursue the matter. The standard of review to apply to abandonment claim decisions is that of reasonableness *simpliciter*. The case law provides that the question the Division must ask itself is whether the applicant truly intended to abandon the claim.

The claimant did not behave like a person indifferent to the outcome of her claim. She informed her counsel of her absence, consulted a physician who confirmed the seriousness of her state of health. She came to the abandonment proceeding with the necessary documentary evidence. The chairperson dismissed the applicant's explanation but did not explain why. The chairperson drew an invalid inference from the evidence in declaring that the claim had been abandoned.

*Aslam v. Canada (Minister of Citizenship & Immigration)*, [2004] F.C.J. No. 620, 35 Imm. L.R. (3d) 100, 2004 CarswellNat 920, 2004 FC 514, 250 F.T.R. 307 (F.C.) — This is an application to judicially review a decision that a refugee claim had been abandoned. The member declared that the applicant had abandoned his claim because the applicant would not proceed to a hearing without his counsel. Approximately 3 weeks before the hearing of the applicant's application, his immigration consultant informed him that he would be unable to assist him. The applicant made other arrangements but the new counsel could not proceed on the day set for the hearing. A day before the hearing the applicant was informed that his counsel's request for a postponement was denied. The applicant's consultant was unable to proceed and the applicant refused to proceed without counsel with the result that the applicant's claim was declared abandoned.

The decision of the member was set aside.

Rules of procedure are to be interpreted and to be applied to bring about the most expeditious and least expensive determination of proceedings on their merits. Fundamental rights can never be sacrificed at the altar of administrative efficiency and the right to a full and fair hearing cannot be compromised.

*Gapchenko v. Canada (Minister of Citizenship & Immigration)*, 2004 CarswellNat 767, 2004 FC 427 (F.C.) — In order for the Board to find that a claim has been abandoned, the claimant must be in default either because he/she failed to appear for a hearing, failed to provide information, or failed to communicate with the Board. In addition, the Board must give the claimant an opportunity to be heard at the hearing, unless the circumstances provided for in subs. 58(1) of the Rules exist.

There is an onus on the applicant to act diligently in pursuing his/her refugee claim.

The decided cases of the Court on a review of abandonment claim decisions indicate the test or question to be asked is whether the refugee claimant's conduct amounts to an expression of intention by that person that he or she did not wish, or had shown no interest, to pursue the refugee claim with diligence.

It is the duty of the applicants at the last minute, before changing counsel, to verify that a new one is available.

**169. Decisions and reasons — In the case of a decision of a Division, other than an interlocutory decision:**

**(a) the decision takes effect in accordance with the rules;**

**(b) reasons for the decision must be given;**

**(c) the decision may be rendered orally or in writing, except a decision of the Refugee Appeal Division, which must be rendered in writing;**

**(d) if the Refugee Protection Division rejects a claim, written reasons must be provided to the claimant and the Minister;**

**(e) if the person who is the subject of proceedings before the Board or the Minister requests reasons for a decision within 10 days of notification of the decision, or in circumstances set out in the rules of the Board, the Division must provide written reasons; and**

**(f) the period in which to apply for judicial review with respect to a decision of the Board is calculated from the giving of notice of the decision or from the sending of written reasons, whichever is later.**



**Proposed Amendment — 169**

**169. (1) Decisions and reasons — In the case of a decision of a Division, other than an interlocutory decision:**

**(a) the decision takes effect in accordance with the rules;**

**(b) reasons for the decision must be given;**

**(c) the decision may be rendered orally or in writing, except for a decision of the Refugee Protection Division in respect of an application for protection under subsection 112(1), which must be rendered in writing;**

**(d) if the Refugee Protection Division rejects a claim, written reasons must be provided to the claimant and the Minister;**

**(e) if the person who is the subject of proceedings before the Board or the Minister requests reasons for a decision within 10 days of notification of the decision, or in circumstances set out in the rules of the Board, the Division must provide written reasons;**

**(e.1) notice of a decision of the Refugee Protection Division in respect of an application for protection, as well as written reasons for the decision, must, in accordance with the regulations, be provided to the Minister, who must then provide the notice and reasons to the applicant in accordance with the regulations; and**

**(f) the period in which to apply for judicial review with respect to a decision of the Board is calculated from the giving of notice of the decision or from the sending of written reasons, whichever is later.**

**(2) Regulations — The regulations may govern the time within which and the manner in which notice of a decision of the Refugee Protection Division in respect of an application for protection, as well as written reasons for the decision, must be provided.**

2010, c. 8, s. 25 [To come into force June 29, 2012, or earlier by order.]

## Case Law

### Section 169(b)

*Bajraktarevic v. Canada (Minister of Citizenship & Immigration)* (2006), 52 Imm. L.R. (3d) 5, 2006 CarswellNat 258, 2006 CarswellNat 1134, 2006 FC 123 (F.C.) — The applicant argued that the officer committed a reviewable error in failing to provide any analysis or assessment of the basis put forward by the applicant, in support of her application for permanent residence on humanitarian and compassionate grounds, and consequently provided inadequate and insufficient reasons. The officer's refusal letter and the notes in the applicant's Computer Assisted Immigration Processing System cannot be deemed to constitute sufficient and adequate reasons. The applicant was entitled to know why her application was rejected. Reasons must be accompanied by a sufficient analysis.

*Agalliu v. Canada (Minister of Citizenship & Immigration)* (2005), 49 Imm. L.R. (3d) 1, 34 Admin. L.R. 1 (4th) 214, 2005 CarswellNat 2112, 2005 FC 1035 (F.C.) — The Board's reasons disclosed a number of superficial errors, in footnotes and in references to the documentary evidence. However, the Board's other errors and its failure to explain its conclusions adequately disclosed more fundamental problems. Taken together, these errors led to the conclusion that the Board's decision was out of keeping with the evidence before it. Sometimes, little errors in a written decision represent no more than a lack of final polishing. Other times, they are symptomatic of inadequate care on the part of the decision maker.

*Torres v. Canada (Minister of Citizenship & Immigration)*, [2005] F.C.J. No. 812, 45 Imm. L.R. (3d) 313, 2005 CarswellNat 1206, 2005 FC 660 (F.C.) — The applicant expressed her fear of the lack of police support and the difficulty of her taking advantage and having recourse to the existing legislative and procedural framework of state protection in Nicaragua. The Board never engaged with the applicant's concern that the police and other support groups could not provide effective protection. The applicant's evidence was clear and convincing that the state could not protect her against her father in the past and would not be able to do so in the future. The Board should have turned its mind to this issue and addressed it directly in its reasons.

*Yontem v. Canada (Minister of Citizenship & Immigration)*, 2005 CarswellNat 197, 26 Admin. L.R. (4th) 115, 2005 FC 41 (F.C.) — It is well established that a Board may draw a negative inference from inconsistencies between statements made at the port of entry and the content of subsequent testimony. The Board acted appropriately by notifying the applicant that the port of entry notes were an issue and providing him with a reasonable opportunity to explain the inconsistency before it drew an adverse inference. The Board also provided cogent reasons for rejecting the applicant's explanation. There was nothing in the applicant's port of entry notes to suggest that the Board translation was faulty. Many of the details recorded in the notes appear to be accurate since they were repeated and relied on by the applicant during the hearing. It was reasonably open to the Board to reject the applicant's explanation regarding the inconsistencies arising from the port of entry notes.

If the applicant had wanted to challenge the accuracy of the notes, he could have subpoenaed both the immigration officer and the interpreter to testify at the hearing.

*Cobo v. Canada (Minister of Citizenship & Immigration)*, 2005 CarswellNat 93, 2005 CarswellNat 1553, 2005 FC 69 (F.C.) — This was an application to review a negative decision on an application for protection. The Board's bare statement that the Board "was not satisfied with the explanation" (of the applicant) does not provide satisfactory reasons for not accepting the applicant's evidence.

*Ahmed v. Canada (Minister of Citizenship & Immigration)*, 2004 CarswellNat 5683, 2004 CarswellNat 2586, 2004 FC 1076 (F.C.) — It is an error for a Board not to deal with the applicants' reasonable explanations for the tribunal's concerns in its reasons. While it is open to the Board to disbelieve explanations which appear reasonable on their face, the Board has an obligation to address them in its reasons and explain why it did not find the explanations convincing.

*Coitinho v. Canada (Minister of Citizenship & Immigration)*, [2004] F.C.J. No. 1269, 2004 CarswellNat 3892, 2004 FC 1037, 2004 CarswellNat 2577 (F.C.) — In the absence of stating that the applicant's evidence was not credible, the Board concluded that it would give more weight to the documentary evidence because it came from knowledgeable sources, none of whom had any interest in the outcome of the particular hearing. This statement was tantamount to stating that documentary evidence should always be preferred to that of a refugee claimant. Further, the decision did not inform the reader why the applicant's evidence was considered suspect. The decision of the Board was overturned.

*Shahid v. Canada (Minister of Citizenship & Immigration)*, 2004 CarswellNat 5919, 2004 CarswellNat 4311, 2004 FC 1607 (F.C.) — This was an application to review a decision of a Board member dismissing the applicant's motion to reopen his refugee claim. The decision not to reopen a refugee claim is a final decision. Reasons are required by s. 169(b).

*Sawyer v. Canada (Minister of Citizenship & Immigration)*, [2004] F.C.J. No. 1140, 37 Imm. L.R. (3d) 114, 2004 CarswellNat 4460, 2004 CarswellNat 2104, 2004 FC 935 (F.C.) — The applicant sought to judicially review the rejection of his claim to refugee protection. The Minister's operating manual instructs officers, to whom a claim for refugee status is made, to ask the standard questions on the refugee claim and record the answers of the claimant. The officers are instructed not to ask the claimant to elaborate on the basis of the claim unless the information relates to admissibility and eligibility. In the face of this instruction, it was patently unreasonable for the panel to reject, summarily, the applicant's evidence that he was told by an immigration officer not to give his full story and that it is was for that reason that everything the applicant claimed he told the officer was not found in the officer's notes.

*Muliri v. Canada (Ministre de la Citoyenneté & de l'Immigration)*, [2004] F.C.J. No. 1376, 42 Imm. L.R. (3d) 139, 2004 CarswellNat 5052, 2004 CarswellNat 2813, 2004 FC 1139 (F.C.) — Judicial deference does not amount to a blind acceptance of the findings of fact drawn by a panel, without any critical analysis by the Court. The judicial review process exists to ensure that administrative tribunals do not venture into the absurd, thinking that they can make findings of fact which simply do not stand up.

The applicant, a citizen of the Democratic Republic of Congo, obtained a visa to come to Canada from South Africa. The visa application contains facts which contradicted the applicant's testimony before the panel. The applicant told the panel that he lied to Canadian authorities at the Canadian Embassy in South Africa in order to obtain a Canadian visa. The panel did not believe the applicant because it was of the view that the information he submitted to the Canadian authorities would have been easy for them to verify. There was nothing in the record to indicate that the information had been verified and accordingly the panel's finding of credibility was unreasonable and its decision set aside.

*Hussain v. Canada (Ministre de la Citoyenneté & de l'Immigration)*, 2004 CarswellNat 3996, 2004 CarswellNat 766, 2004 FC 430 (F.C.) — This is an application to judicially review a negative decision respecting the applicants' request for protection.

An initial hearing took place on July 29, 2002. During this hearing, the panel asked the refugee protection officer for information about the applicants' passage through the United States. A second hearing took place on August 7, 2002. On August 9, 2002, the officer received a report from the American authorities which indicated that they had no indication that the applicants had crossed the American border. The officer informed the panel of this and it was evident that additional evidence would be required. On September 27, 2002, the applicants' counsel gave birth to a child. On October 16, two months after the report was received, the panel asked the officer to contact counsel to ask her to respond within six days. Counsel was informed of this letter at home by her secretary and submitted a written reply informing that it was not necessary to reconvene because her client had informed her that it had been a smuggler who had made the arrangements. Three months later the panel rendered its decision.

The panel was aware that counsel was on maternity leave for several months due to the fact that she had appeared before the panel in the final months of her pregnancy and had discussed it with the panel informally. Further, the panel had been informed by the officer of the receipt of the report in August, while counsel was still available. Despite this, it was only two months later that, at the panel's request, the officer wrote to counsel giving her only six days to respond, knowing that she was on maternity leave. There was no urgency in this matter. The panel did not render its decision until three months later. The short time given to reply was totally unjustified given that counsel was at home with a newborn and not in a position to make an enlightened decision about how to deal with the file and present the applicants' position fully and fairly. The decision of the panel was set aside.

*Nagulesan v. Canada (Minister of Citizenship & Immigration)*, [2004] F.C.J. No. 1690, 44 Imm. L.R. (3d) 99, 2004 CarswellNat 5903, 2004 CarswellNat 3637, 2004 FC 1382 (F.C.) — The applicant sought to review a negative decision respecting his claim under ss. 96 and 97. A few days after his hearing, the applicant delivered to the RPD a letter addressed to the member presiding at his hearing indicating that he wished to file additional evidence to corroborate his testimony. The proposed evidence was attached to the letter. The letter and the documents attached thereto were not in the certified copy of Tribunal Record and RPD did not refer to the evidence at all in its decision.

The applicant's letter satisfied the requirement of Rule 37. This meant that the RPD had to deal with the applicant's request. It could simply mention that having reviewed the letter, it decided not to consider the evidence because of factors listed in Rule 37(3), or it could accept the new evidence and deal with it in its decision. The failure to deal with the matter at all was a breach of procedural fairness and the decision was set aside.

*Begollari v. Canada (Minister of Citizenship & Immigration)*, [2004] F.C.J. No. 1613, 2004 CarswellNat 5098, 2004 CarswellNat 3437, 2004 FC 1340 (F.C.) — The reviewing Court could not determine whether the Board had applied a balance of probabilities test to the objective component of a well founded fear of persecution, or the reasonable chance or serious possibility of a fear of persecution test. The balance of probabilities test was an erroneous test and since the Court could not determine whether it was used or not, the decision was set aside.

*Mann v. Canada (Minister of Citizenship & Immigration)* (2004), 43 Imm. L.R. (3d) 230, 2004 CarswellNat 5099, 2004 CarswellNat 3438, (sub nom. *Canada (Minister of Citizenship & Immigration) v. Mann)* 258 F.T.R. 139 (Eng.), 2004 FC 1338 (F.C.) — This is an application to review a decision of the Immigration Appeal Division wherein the Appeal Division allowed an appeal from a visa officer's refusal to grant the respondent's wife an immigrant visa.

In dealing with the adequacy of reasons, the Court relied upon the Federal Court of Appeal decision in *VIA Rail Canada Inc. v. Canada (National Transportation Agency)* (2000), [2001] 2 F.C. 25, 2000 CarswellNat 2531, 2000 CarswellNat 3453, 261 N.R. 184, 193 D.L.R. (4th) 357, 26 Admin. L.R. (3d) 1, [2000] F.C.J. No. 1685 (Fed. C.A.). Reasons foster better decision making. By ensuring that issues and reasoning are well articulated and therefore more carefully thought out, the process of writing reasons for a decision by itself may be a guarantee of a better decision. Reasons provide the parties with the assurance that their representations have been considered.

Reasons allow the parties to effectuate any right of appeal or judicial review that they might have. They provide a basis for an assessment of possible grounds of appeal or review. They allow the appellate or reviewing body to determine whether the decision maker erred and thereby render him or her accountable. This is particularly important when the decision is subject to a deferential standard of review.

In a case of a regulated industry, the regulator's reasons provide guidance to others who are subject to the regulator's jurisdiction.

The duty to give reasons is only fulfilled if the reasons provided are adequate. What constitutes adequate reasons is a matter to be determined in the light of the circumstances of each case. As a general rule, adequate reasons are those that serve the functions for which the duty to provide them was imposed.

The obligation to provide adequate reasons is not satisfied by merely reciting the submissions and evidence of the parties and stating a conclusion. The decision maker must set out its findings of fact and the principal evidence upon which those findings were based. The reasons must address the major points at issue. The reasoning process followed by the decision maker must be set out and must reflect consideration of the main relevant factors.

In this case, s. 4 of the *Hindu Marriage Act* was an important factor in the case. The interpretation of this section is a matter on which the IAD's reasons are silent, and due to this silence, the reasons are inadequate.

*Machedon v. Canada (Minister of Citizenship & Immigration)*, [2004] F.C.J. No. 1331, 2004 CarswellNat 3551, 2004 CarswellNat 2665, 256 F.T.R. 211, 2004 FC 1104 (F.C.) — The Board found that the fact that the applicants, who were citizens of Romania, had abandoned refugee claims in Ireland lacked a subjective fear of persecution. The applicants explained their abandonment of their Irish refugee claims by stating that their initial intention was to come to Canada and that they were told Romanian refugee claimants were not successful in obtaining protection from Irish authorities.

The standard of review on this issue is patent unreasonableness. An applicant's failure to seek refugee status in transit countries is relevant to a determination of their subjective fear of persecution. In this case the Board did not analyze the explanation offered by the applicants for the abandonment of their Irish claims, nor did it state that it disbelieved their explanation for abandoning the Irish claims. The Board simply stated that there was no persuasive, trustworthy and reliable evidence to show that Ireland would not fulfil its obligations. The Board did not make a negative finding of credibility and therefore drew a negative inference with regard to the evidence before it. The decision of the Board was set aside.

*Eminidis v. Canada (Ministre de la Citoyenneté & de l'Immigration)*, 2004 CarswellNat 2769, 2004 CarswellNat 1403, 2004 FC 700 (F.C.) — The fact that the panel preferred the documentary evidence even though the applicants had been considered credible was not an error. It was within the panel's jurisdiction to do so and open to the panel to decide what weight to give the evidence before it.

## *Refugee Protection Division*

**Proposed Addition — 169.1**

**169.1 (1) Composition — The Refugee Protection Division consists of the Deputy Chairperson, Assistant Deputy Chairpersons and other members, including coordinating members, necessary to carry out its functions.**

**(2) Public Service Employment Act — The members of the Refugee Protection Division are appointed in accordance with the *Public Service Employment Act*.**

2010, c. 8, s. 26 [To come into force June 29, 2012, or earlier by order.]

**170. Proceedings — The Refugee Protection Division, in any proceeding before it,**

**Proposed Amendment — 170 opening words**

**170. Proceedings — Except in respect of an application for protection made under subsection 112(1), the Refugee Protection Division, in any proceeding before it,**

2010, c. 8, s. 27(1) [To come into force June 29, 2012, or earlier by order.]

**(a) may inquire into any matter that it considers relevant to establishing whether a claim is well-founded;**

**(b) must hold a hearing;**

**(c) must notify the person who is the subject of the proceeding and the Minister of the hearing;**

**(d) must provide the Minister, on request, with the documents and information referred to in subsection 100(4);**

**Proposed Addition — 170(d.1)**

**(d.1) may question the witnesses, including the person who is the subject of the proceeding;**

2010, c. 8, s. 27(2) [To come into force June 29, 2012, or earlier by order.]

**(e) must give the person and the Minister a reasonable opportunity to present evidence, question witnesses and make representations;**

**(f) may, despite paragraph (b), allow a claim for refugee protection without a hearing, if the Minister has not notified the Division, within the period set out in the rules of the Board, of the Minister's intention to intervene;**

**(g) is not bound by any legal or technical rules of evidence;**

**(h) may receive and base a decision on evidence that is adduced in the proceedings and considered credible or trustworthy in the circumstances; and**

**(i) may take notice of any facts that may be judicially noticed, any other generally recognized facts and any information or opinion that is within its specialized knowledge.**



## Case Law

### Section 170(b)

*Reyes v. Canada (Minister of Citizenship & Immigration)*, 2005 CarswellNat 806, 2005 FC 418 (F.C.) — It is open to the Board to ask for corroborating evidence if such evidence is material and could reasonably be expected to be available. If an applicant is unwilling or unable to comply with such a request, he or she bears the onus of explaining the non-compliance.

*Balson v. Canada (Minister of Citizenship & Immigration)*, 2005 CarswellNat 311, 2005 FC 197 (F.C.) — The applicant sought to review a negative decision respecting her application for protection. On August 24, 2002 the applicant received a notice which informed her that if her counsel was unable to proceed on the hearing date, she should find another counsel who is able to proceed and warned her that she may have to proceed without counsel if no counsel attended with her on the date of her hearing. In September 2002, the applicant identified her counsel. In July 2003 the applicant and her counsel were asked to attend in August 2003 to set a hearing date. In August 2003 the applicant attended, set a hearing date and received a form entitled "A Notice to Appear" which advised her that her claim would be heard in November 2003. In September 2003 the applicant and her counsel were asked to confirm their readiness to proceed in November. The day before the hearing, the applicant's counsel faxed a letter to the Board requesting an adjournment. On the date set for the hearing the request for an adjournment was denied and the applicant's refugee claim proceeded.

It was made very clear to the applicant that her case would proceed on the date set, with or without counsel. It was open to the Board to exercise its discretion to refuse the request for an adjournment and accordingly the application for judicial review was dismissed.

*Herrera v. Canada (Minister of Citizenship & Immigration)* (2005), 2005 CarswellNat 2128, 2005 CarswellNat 140, 2004 FC 1724 (F.C.) — The applicant sought to overturn a negative decision respecting his application for protection. At the hearing, the applicant was not allowed to lead his evidence, but instead the Refugee Protection Officer was instructed to question first, and then the RPD followed with its own questions. The applicant's lawyer consented to the procedure but the consent was not binding. There was no way that the lawyer would have known the nature and intensity of the questioning to come. As the procedure was highly unusual it was incumbent on the RPD to state a reason why the procedure was adopted. The decision of the RPD was set aside.

*Guermache v. Canada (Ministre de la Citoyenneté & de l'Immigration)*, [2004] F.C.J. No. 1058, 43 Imm. L.R. (3d) 195, 2004 CarswellNat 3999, 2004 CarswellNat 1853, *(sub* nom. *Guermache v. Canada (Minister of Citizenship & Immigration))* 257 F.T.R. 272 (Eng.), 21 Admin. L.R. (4th) 37, 2004 FC 870 (F.C.) — The applicant sought to review the negative decision of his protection application. The applicant successfully maintained that the member's conduct at the hearing was such that it raised a reasonable apprehension of bias. Members have a difficult but essential role to play. Because of their workload, the stress is enormous. Nevertheless, even if they may have heard the same "story" hundreds of times, individuals are different, each application for protection deserves the same degree of care. Canada offers protection to those who have well-founded fears of persecution for a Convention reason, as well as those in danger of torture or risk of cruel and unusual treatment or punishment. At the same time, the objectives of the Act grant, as a fundamental expression of Canada's humanitarian ideals, fair consideration to those seeking protection. The scale of the members' tasks must not cause them to lose sight of the fact that the rules of natural justice must be observed and that their conduct during hearings and applications for protection must be irreproachable. There is neither place for intimidation, contempt, and offensive innuendo, nor for harshness or inappropriate language. The neutral attitude expected from members during hearings suggests that they adhere to their own responsibilities as much as possible, and let the claimant's counsellor, the refugee claim officer and, if applicable, the Minister's representative, play their respective roles.

The Court found that the chairperson had crossed the line from the role of an impartial adjudicator by his constant interference which prevented the applicant from presenting his case. Accordingly, the decision was set aside.

*Upul v. Canada (Minister of Citizenship & Immigration)* (2004), 41 Imm. L.R. (3d) 284, 2004 CarswellNat 4747, 2004 CarswellNat 3741, (sub nom. *Kankanagme v. Canada (Minister of Citizenship & Immigration))* 259 F.T.R. 268 (Eng.), 2004 FC 1451 (F.C.) — Where the full extent of the member's animus towards the applicant was not entirely evident until the decision was rendered, the failure of counsel to object to the conduct of the Board member is not fatal to the applicant's right to argue that there exists a reasonable apprehension of bias.

*Geza v. Canada (Minister of Citizenship & Immigration)* (2004), 44 Imm. L.R. (3d) 57, 2004 CarswellNat 5179, 2004 CarswellNat 2970, 20 Admin. L.R. (4th) 79, 257 F.T.R. 114 (Eng.), 2004 FC 1039, 2004 FC 1163, 244 D.L.R. (4th) 218, [2004] F.C.J. No. 1401 (F.C.) — In 1998, the Immigration and Refugee Board decided to produce a precedent, coined a "lead case," out of concern for growing numbers of Roma refugee claimants from Hungary. The stated purpose of the exercise was to establish a base line of legal and factual issues to promote consistency in subsequent claim decisions. The Applicants agreed to participate in the test case on the advice of counsel, however, after their claims were rejected, they challenged the jurisdiction of the Board to conduct such an exercise.

No reasonable apprehension of bias was created on the part of the Board when the lead case idea was conceived and conducted.

A lead case conducted to promote consistency in decision-making is a matter of procedure that was clearly within the jurisdiction of the Board on the basis of the common-law and by necessary implication by virtue of the *Immigration Act*. No reasonable apprehension of bias is created by the Board acting in this manner.

The evidence does not prove that there was a decline in acceptance rates for Hungarian Roma directly as result of the lead case.

*Caceres v. Canada (Minister of Citizenship & Immigration)*, 2004 CarswellNat 2539, 2004 CarswellNat 1821, 2004 FC 843 (F.C.) — The applicant sought to review a negative decision of a panel of the Refugee Protection Division. The panel concluded that there was no credible or trustworthy evidence on which the applicant could establish his claim. The applicant forwarded written submissions to the Board by fax after the hearing had been concluded but before the Board had rendered its decision. The fax transmission sheet shows that seven pages of material were sent to the Board in a sensible timeframe and to the Board's correct fax number. The Court, therefore, presumed that the submission was received at the Board's fax machine. The faxed material correctly described the case and the hearing date. There is no evidence that this submission reached the relevant panel members. They did not mention it in their decision and it does not appear in the tribunal records.

The Court concluded that on a balance of probabilities that through error at the Board's offices, the panel did not receive the submission. To disregard written submissions on the sole basis of the delay of their delivery would be absurd. Such a breach of natural justice is, in itself, sufficient to warrant intervention by the Court.



## Section 170(e)

*Chohan v. Canada (Minister of Citizenship & Immigration)*, 2006 CarswellNat 819, 2006 CarswellNat 2501, 2006 FC 390 (F.C.) — The Board has an obligation to deal with a request for an adjournment in a principled way. To have denied the applicant the benefit of a short adjournment was manifestly unfair and contravened the requirement of s. 170 of the IRPA that the applicant be given a reasonable opportunity to present evidence.

The Board's reasons for denying the adjournment request also failed to address the factors required by s. 48 of the *Refugee Protection Division Rules*. Had these factors been considered and applied, the adjournment would also certainly have been granted.

*Canada (Ministre de la Citoyenneté & de l'Immigration) c. Deffo*, 2005 CarswellNat 3924, 2005 CarswellNat 5117, 2005 FC 1589 (F.C.) — The Refugee Protection Division of the Immigration and Refugee Board has a duty to formally notify the counsel representing the Minister pursuant to s. 170(e) of the IRPA and s. 22 of the Rules. There is no discretionary authority for the Board to dispense of this duty. In failing to notify the counsel of record for the Minister after he had filed a notice of intervention in accordance with subs. 25(1) of the Rules, the Board erred in law.

*Bokhari v. Canada (Minister of Citizenship & Immigration)*, 2005 CarswellNat 1092, 2005 FC 574 (F.C.) — The applicants sought to review a negative decision concerning their application for refugee status. At the hearing, after counsel had finished questioning the applicant, the Board member made a statement to counsel which suggested that credibility, objective and subjective fear, had been established and that state protection and the IFA were the issues that the Board member was concerned about.

The claim was dismissed, however, on the basis that there was insufficient credible and trustworthy evidence to establish the principal claimant's allegation that he was a high profile Shia leader in Peshawar.

Such misleading of counsel, thereby effectively depriving an applicant from making submissions on crucial points, amounts to a denial of natural justice.

## Section 170(h)

*Kovacs v. Canada (Minister of Citizenship & Immigration)* (2005), [2006] 2 F.C.R. 455, 2005 CarswellNat 3524, 2005 CarswellNat 4487, 2005 FC 1473 (F.C.) — The principle applicant, a citizen of Hungary, arrived in Canada and claimed protection in Canada for herself and two minor children: a daughter, who subsequently returned to Hungary, and a son. The refugee claim was refused. Subsequent to the applicant's arrival in Canada, and prior to the refugee determination hearing, the applicant's husband brought an application in the Ontario Superior Court of Justice, pursuant to the Hague Convention on the Civil Aspects of International Child Abduction (October 25, 1980) for the removal of his son, in accordance with a Hungarian custody order. The Ontario Superior Court judge made several findings with respect to the credibility of both parties and findings that the applicant's husband was a wanted fugitive with a history of criminal behaviour.

Upon judicial review of the decision to refuse the applicant's refugee claim, the Court considered the extent to which the Refugee Protection Board was bound by or could rely on the decision of the Ontario Superior Court. The Ontario Superior Court's decision was not binding on the Refugee Protection Board. Nevertheless, it was relevant and important evidence and the Board was entitled to and, in fact, should have taken into account the findings of the Ontario Superior Court where they were directly relevant to the facts before the Refugee Protection Board. The Refugee Protection Board must carry out its own analysis and reach its own conclusions on the matters before it and cannot be bound by the actions of the Ontario Superior Court, particularly where the issues and questions are different.

*Application Under s. 83.28 of the Criminal Code, Re*, [2004] S.C.J. No. 40, 2004 CarswellBC 1378, 2004 CarswellBC 1379, [2004] 2 S.C.R. 248, 33 B.C.L.R. (4th) 195, 121 C.R.R. (2d) 1, [2005] 2 W.W.R. 605, 21 C.R. (6th) 82, 322 N.R. 205, (sub nom. *R. v. Bagri)* 184 C.C.C. (3d) 449, (sub nom. *R. v. Bagri)* 240 D.L.R. (4th) 81, 199 B.C.A.C. 45, 2004 SCC 42 (S.C.C.) — The appeal raised, for the first time in the Supreme Court, fundamental questions about the Constitutional validity of provisions of the *Anti-Terrorism Act*. The Act was a legislative component of Canada's response to the tragedy of September 11, 2001. The appellant was ordered to attend a judicial investigative hearing. This case dealt with the Constitutional validity of the "judicial investigative hearing" provision.

There were essentially two acts of alleged terrorism. Firstly, an explosion killed two baggage handlers, and injured four others at Narita Airport, as baggage was being transferred onto Air India Flight 301. A second explosion occurred just one hour later, causing Air India Flight 182 to crash off the west coast of Ireland, killing all passengers and crew.

The first accused, Inderjit Singh Reyat, was arrested in England and extradited to Canada where he was convicted in connection with the explosion at Narita Airport. Mr. Reyat pleaded guilty to manslaughter in connection with the explosion of Air India Flight 182. Two other accused were jointly charged with offences in relation to both explosions and while their trial was ongoing, the Crown brought an application to examine the appellant in this matter pursuant to s. 83.28.

The challenge for democracies in the battle against terrorism is not whether to respond, but rather how to do so. Canadians value the importance of human life and liberty and the protection of society through respect for the rule of law. A democracy cannot exist without the rule of law. Terrorism challenges the context in which the rule of law must operate, but does not call for the abdication of the law. At the same time, the Constitution must not become a suicide pact. The challenge for a democratic state's answer to terrorism calls for a balancing of what is required for an effective response to terrorism in a way that appropriately recognizes the fundamental values of the rule of law. In a democracy, not every response is available to meet the challenge of terrorism.

The international scope of terrorism raised concerns about the potential uses of information gathered pursuant to s. 83.28. Section 83.28 specifically provides use and derivative use immunity in the context of criminal proceedings. The legislation did not speak to the safeguards in relation to other types of hearings. Deportation and extradition hearings must accord with the principles of fundamental justice. In order to meet the requirements of s. 7 of the *Charter of Rights*, use and derivative use immunity respecting information gathered under s. 83.28 must be extended to extradition and deportation hearings. Therefore, the hearing judge must make and, if necessary, vary the terms of an order to properly provide use and derivative use immunity in extradition and deportation proceedings.



## Section 170(i)

*Sadeghi-Pari v. Canada (Minister of Citizenship & Immigration)* (2004), 37 Imm. L.R. (3d) 150, 2004 CarswellNat 1672, 2004 CarswellNat 483, 2004 FC 282 (F.C.) — The applicant sought to review a negative decision of a panel of the Refugee Protection Division. The Board may rely on its general expertise on country conditions in evaluating the plausibility of an applicant's testimony. Documentary evidence on the standardized country file that is not specifically relied on by the Board does not necessarily need to be reproduced on the tribunal record. The Board's power, in this regard, is not open ended. In this case, the Board relied on several specific observations about life in Tehran without referring to any sociological, human rights or other country evidence in support of its conclusions. Accordingly, the decision of the Board was set aside.

### Proposed Addition — 170.1

**170.1 Application for protection — In respect of an application for protection under subsection 112(1), the Refugee Protection Division**

**(a) may inquire into any matter that it considers relevant to establishing whether an application is well-founded;**

**(b) must provide the Minister, on request, with the documentary evidence and written submissions of the applicant that are referred to in paragraph 113(b.1);**

**(c) must give notice of any hearing to the Minister and the applicant;**

**(d) subject to paragraph 113(a), must — if a hearing is held — give the applicant and the Minister the opportunity to present evidence, question witnesses and make submissions;**

**(e) may question the witnesses, including the applicant;**

**(f) is not bound by any legal or technical rules of evidence;**

**(g) may receive and base a decision on evidence that is adduced in the proceedings and considered credible or trustworthy in the circumstances; and**

**(h) may take notice of any facts that may be judicially noticed and of any other generally recognized facts and any information or opinion that is within its specialized knowledge.**

2010, c. 8, s. 27.1 [To come into force June 29, 2013, or earlier by order.]

**Unproclaimed Text — 171**

## *Refugee Appeal Division*

**171. Proceedings — In the case of a proceeding of the Refugee Appeal Division,**

**(a) the Division must give notice of any hearing to the Minister and to the person who is the subject of the appeal;**

**(a.1) subject to subsection 110(4), if a hearing is held, the Division must give the person who is the subject of the appeal and the Minister the opportunity to present evidence, question witnesses and make submissions;**

**(a.2) the Division is not bound by any legal or technical rules of evidence;**

**(a.3) the Division may receive and base a decision on evidence that is adduced in the proceedings and considered credible or trustworthy in the circumstances;**

**(a.4) the Minister may, after giving notice in accordance with the rules, intervene in the appeal, including for the purpose of filing submissions;**

**(b) the Division may take notice of any facts that may be judicially noticed and of any other generally recognized facts and any information or opinion that is within its specialized knowledge; and**

**(c) a decision of a panel of three members of the Refugee Appeal Division has, for the Refugee Protection Division and for a panel of one member of the Refugee Appeal Division, the same precedential value as a decision of an appeal court has for a trial court.**

2010, c. 8, s. 28(1)

## *Immigration Division*

**172. (1) Composition — The Immigration Division consists of the Director General and other directors and members necessary to carry out its functions and who are employed in accordance with the *Public Service Employment Act*.**

**(2) Powers — The Director General and the directors of the Immigration Division have all the powers and may carry out the duties and functions of members of the Division.**

**Proposed Amendment — 172**

**172. (1) Composition — The Immigration Division consists of the Deputy Chairperson, Assistant Deputy Chairpersons and other members necessary to carry out its functions.**

**(2) Public Service Employment Act — The members of the Immigration Division are appointed in accordance with the *Public Service Employment Act.***

2010, c. 8, s. 29 [To come into force June 29, 2012, or earlier by order.]

**173. Proceedings — The Immigration Division, in any proceeding before it,**

**(a) must, where practicable, hold a hearing;**

**(b) must give notice of the proceeding to the Minister and to the person who is the subject of the proceeding and hear the matter without delay;**

**(c) is not bound by any legal or technical rules of evidence; and**

**(d) may receive and base a decision on evidence adduced in the proceedings that it considers credible or trustworthy in the circumstances.**



## Case Law

*Balathavarajan v. Canada (Minister of Citizenship & Immigration)*, [2006] F.C.J. No. 1550, 56 Imm. L.R. (3d) 1, 354 N.R. 320, 2006 CarswellNat 3297, 2006 FCA 340 (Fed. C.A.) — The Court considered whether the IAD must consider hardship to a permanent resident who had been issued a deportation order, and who had been declared a Convention refugee, where the deportation order did not specify the country of removal, and where it is uncertain what that country might be. The Minister had not specified the country of deportation, and at the time of the IAD appeal had not taken the necessary steps under subs. 115(2) of the IRPA to remove the appellant. It was, at the time of the IAD appeal, not only unlikely but legally improper to remove the appellant to Sri Lanka. For the IAD to consider potential hardship the appellant might face if deported to Sri Lanka would have been a hypothetical and a speculative exercise. Therefore it did not need to do this. Accordingly, the certified question was answered in the negative by the Court of Appeal.

Section 173 of the IRPA permits the IAD to receive and base a decision on evidence adduced in immigration proceedings that it considers to be credible and trustworthy in the circumstances. It is up to the IAD, not the Court, to decide the weight to be given to the evidence. Therefore the appellant also failed to demonstrate that the judge had committed a palpable and overriding error in upholding the IAD's decision. The appeal was dismissed.

*Application Under s. 83.28 of the Criminal Code, Re*, [2004] S.C.J. No. 40, 2004 CarswellBC 1378, 2004 CarswellBC 1379, [2004] 2 S.C.R. 248, 33 B.C.L.R. (4th) 195, 121 C.R.R. (2d) 1, [2005] 2 W.W.R. 605, 21 C.R. (6th) 82, 322 N.R. 205, (sub nom. *R. v. Bagri*) 184 C.C.C. (3d) 449, (sub nom. *R. v. Bagri*) 240 D.L.R. (4th) 81, 199 B.C.A.C. 45, 2004 SCC 42 (S.C.C.) — The appeal raised, for the first time in the Supreme Court, fundamental questions about the Constitutional validity of provisions of the *Anti-Terrorism Act*. The Act was a legislative component of Canada's response to the tragedy of September 11, 2001. The appellant was ordered to attend a judicial investigative hearing. This case dealt with the Constitutional validity of the "judicial investigative hearing" provision.

There were essentially two acts of alleged terrorism. Firstly, an explosion killed two baggage handlers, and injured four others at Narita Airport, as baggage was being transferred onto Air India Flight 301. A second explosion occurred just one hour later, causing Air India Flight 182 to crash off the west coast of Ireland, killing all passengers and crew.

The first accused, Inderjit Singh Reyat, was arrested in England and extradited to Canada where he was convicted in connection with the explosion at Narita Airport. Mr. Reyat pleaded guilty to manslaughter in connection with the explosion of Air India Flight 182. Two other accused were jointly charged with offences in relation to both explosions and while their trial was ongoing, the Crown brought an application to examine the appellant in this matter pursuant to s. 83.28.

The challenge for democracies in the battle against terrorism is not whether to respond, but rather, how to do so. Canadians value the importance of human life and liberty and the protection of society through respect for the rule of law. A democracy cannot exist without the rule of law. Terrorism challenges the context in which the rule of law must operate, but does not call for the abdication of the law. At the same time, the Constitution must not become a suicide pact. The challenge for a democratic state's answer to terrorism calls for a balancing of what is required for an effective response to terrorism in a way that appropriately recognizes the fundamental values of the rule of law. In a democracy, not every response is available to meet the challenge of terrorism.

The international scope of terrorism raised concerns about the potential uses of information gathered pursuant to s. 83.28. Section 83.28 specifically provides use and derivative use immunity in the context of criminal proceedings. The legislation did not speak to the safeguards in relation to other types of hearings. Deportation and extradition hearings must accord with the principles of fundamental justice. In order to meet the requirements of s. 7 of the *Charter of Rights*, use and derivative use immunity respecting information gathered under s. 83.28 must be extended to extradition and deportation hearings. Therefore, the hearing judge must make and, if necessary, vary the terms of an order to properly provide use and derivative use immunity in extradition and deportation proceedings.

## *Immigration Appeal Division*

**174. (1) Court of record — The Immigration Appeal Division is a court of record and shall have an official seal, which shall be judicially noticed.**

**(2) Powers — The Immigration Appeal Division has all the powers, rights and privileges vested in a superior court of record with respect to any matter necessary for the exercise of its jurisdiction, including the swearing and examination of witnesses, the production and inspection of documents and the enforcement of its orders.**

### Case Law

*Canada (Minister of Citizenship & Immigration) v. Peirovdinnabi* (2010), 87 Imm. L.R. (3d) 162, 2010 FC 64, 2010 CarswellNat 108, 2010 CarswellNat 726 (F.C.) — The issue considered was whether, in 2010, the respondent made a misrepresentation by answering "yes" to the question "are you living with your spouse," posed in a form entitled "Supplemental Information Spouse in Canada." This issue arose in the course of the respondent's sponsorship of his second wife to Canada in 2005. In the course of that application he was questioned about his living circumstances with his first wife three years before and he answered that he thought that the question posed at the time required an answer as to whether he and his first wife were living "together." To this question the respondent said that, while they were living together, he and his first wife maintained separate residences and lived in both after their marriage. The problem that arose was that the applicant interpreted the question answered by the respondent to mean "are you living together with your wife in the same residence." This conflict in interpretation set a course of decision making in motion which has resulted in the present application for judicial review of an IAD decision that found that the respondent did not make a misrepresentation.

The central argument advanced by the applicant in the present review of the IAD decision is that, as a matter of law, the IAD was required to determine the genuineness of the respondent's first marriage. The position that the applicant takes is that since the hearing before the IAD was *de novo*, all issues with respect to the respondent's first marriage were required to be determined. The Court rejected this argument and found that the IAD took the appeal as it came: there was only one question to be addressed and that was whether the respondent made a misrepresentation. The question of whether the marriage was genuine was not determined in the first and second level decisions, and it was not in play in the IAD decision. The IAD's decision was upheld and the application for judicial review dismissed. The following question was certified:

> Does the IAD have an obligation in law to determine the genuineness of a marriage on a *de novo* appeal brought with respect to an issue of misrepresentation when the issue of the genuineness of the marriage concerned was not specifically raised for determination in the appeal?



**175. (1) Proceedings — The Immigration Appeal Division, in any proceeding before it,**

> **(a) must, in the case of an appeal under subsection 63(4), hold a hearing;**
>
> **(b) is not bound by any legal or technical rules of evidence; and**
>
> **(c) may receive and base a decision on evidence adduced in the proceedings that it considers credible or trustworthy in the circumstances.**

**(2) Presence of permanent resident — In the case of an appeal by a permanent resident under subsection 63(4), the Immigration Appeal Division may, after considering submissions from the Minister and the permanent resident and if satisfied that the presence of the permanent resident at the hearing is necessary, order the permanent resident to physically appear at the hearing, in which case an officer shall issue a travel document for that purpose.**

## Case Law

*Kamtasingh v. Canada (Minister of Citizenship & Immigration)* (2010), 87 Imm. L.R. (3d) 118, 2010 FC 45, 2010 CarswellNat 801, 2010 CarswellNat 101 (F.C.) — This was an application for judicial review challenging a decision of the Immigration Appeal Division which determined the applicant's marriage was not genuine. The applicant states that the IAD member denied him procedural fairness by preventing him from calling all of his proposed witnesses.

The IAD has the right to limit repetitive testimony, but not by effectively excluding witnesses who could offer evidence going to the central issues of the case. The place to control excessive or repetitive evidence on issues of controversy which are central or determinate is generally not at the entrance to the witness box, but once the witness is testifying — and even then the member must grant some latitude to ensure that all important matters are covered. The IAD can, of course, limit the scope of evidence by stipulating certain points that are not in dispute. In a case like this one where the credibility of the applicant is clearly an issue and where the genuineness of a marriage is in doubt, the evidence of immediate family and close acquaintances is highly relevant and should be heard without reservation. Indeed, it was difficult to see how this matter could be fairly determined after only two hours of evidence, particularly when the applicant was self-represented and was initially intending to lead evidence from several witnesses. This was a situation where the duty to allow the applicant to fully present his case was sacrificed for the desire for administrative efficiency. That is not a permissible trade-off. The application for judicial review was allowed.

*Ayele v. Canada (Minister of Citizenship & Immigration)* (2007), 60 Imm. L.R. (3d) 197, 2007 CarswellNat 253, 2007 FC 126 (F.C.) — The duty of fairness requires that a party to a proceeding should have the opportunity to present his or her case fully and fairly. This generally includes the right to call witnesses in order to establish the evidentiary basis of a claim or defence. The applicant applied to sponsor his wife. A visa officer rejected the wife's application for permanent residence on the ground that the marriage was not genuine and was entered into for immigration purposes. The applicant appealed to the Immigration Appeal Division (IAD). After hearing the applicant's testimony, the IAD was anxious to conclude the hearing and to dismiss the appeal. In the words of the presiding member, "[i]t will be a waste of the tribunal's time to continue to indulge the appellant in this waste of taxpayer's money." The IAD refused to hear a witness that the applicant wished to call. The Minister claimed that the IAD refused to allow the witness to testify because the applicant was in breach of Rule 37 of the *Immigration Appeal Division Rules* which required the applicant to have provided, in writing, witness information.

The Minister's reliance upon Rule 37 in order to justify the refusal of the IAD to hear the witness was misplaced. At the outset of the hearing, after hearing submissions with respect to the applicant's late disclosure of information, including late disclosure of witness information, the presiding member ruled "I will allow you to deal with the witness, but obviously the identity and credibility of the witness will be an issue." Any hurdle posed by Rule 37 was overcome when the IAD ruled it would exercise its discretion to allow the witness to testify. When the IAD later ruled it would not allow the witness to testify, it did not refer to Rule 37. Instead, the presiding member stated, "Even if the witness corroborates the testimony, in assessing the testimony it's not credible. So, there's no point in calling the witness and even if it is characterized as a breach of natural justice, there is no prejudice suffered when the evidence is of no use and calling the witness is futile."

It is not within the purview of a tribunal bound by the requirement of procedural fairness to dispense with those requirements because, in its view, the result of the hearing will be the same. Rather, it is for a court reviewing a decision of the tribunal that has erred to determine whether, as a matter of administrative law, the consequences of a failure to comply with the requirements of procedural fairness are such that the discretionary remedy available to the reviewing court should be withheld.

The withholding of relief in the face of a breach of procedural fairness is exceptional. One can never rule on the credibility of evidence that has not yet been heard. The presiding member violated the principle when he stated that even if the witness corroborated the applicant's testimony, that subsequent testimony would not be credible.

The essence of adjudication is the ability to keep an open mind until all evidence has been heard. The reliability of evidence is to be determined in light of all the evidence in a particular case. The application for judicial review was allowed.

*Canada (Ministre de la Citoyenneté & de l'Immigration) c. Nkunzimana* (2005), 54 Admin. L.R. (4th) 122, 2005 CarswellNat 177, 2005 CarswellNat 4820, 2005 FC 29 (F.C.) — The applicant, a Canadian citizen, successfully appealed a visa officer's decision to refuse an application to sponsor five orphaned children of whom he claimed to be the uncle. The mothers of the children were the applicant's two deceased sisters. The key evidence the applicant relied on was a letter from the Burundian Ambassador to Canada, attesting that, following a verification of the adopting father's attestation of family composition and the birth certificates of the children to be adopted, the applicant was the uncle of the children he wanted to sponsor. On judicial review the Minister argued the Appeal Division erred in law by stating it was bound by the legal and technical rules of evidence of the *Civil Code of Quebec* and *Code of Civil Procedure* when determining that the contents of the letter from the Ambassador of Burundi was true. This approach incorporated a form of evidentiary rigidity that was not intended by Parliament and in this case had the effect of reversing the burden of proof and placing it on the Minister's shoulders. Section 175(1)(c) of the current Act "has the purpose and effect of freeing the Board's hearings from all technical rules of evidence and particularly the 'best evidence' and 'hearsay' rules."

Although the Federal Court agreed that the Appeal Division panel erred, it decided that the panel's decision should not be set aside, since on a balance of probabilities, the Federal Court concluded the children were members of the family class.

*Application Under s. 83.28 of the Criminal Code, Re*, [2004] S.C.J. No. 40, 2004 CarswellBC 1378, 2004 CarswellBC 1379, [2004] 2 S.C.R. 248, 33 B.C.L.R. (4th) 195, 121 C.R.R. (2d) 1, [2005] 2 W.W.R. 605, 21 C.R. (6th) 82, 322 N.R. 205, (sub nom. *R. v. Bagri)* 184 C.C.C. (3d) 449, (sub nom. *R. v. Bagri)* 240 D.L.R. (4th) 81, 199 B.C.A.C. 45, 2004 SCC 42 (S.C.C.) — The appeal raised, for the first time in the Supreme Court, fundamental questions about the Constitutional validity of provisions of the *Anti-Terrorism Act*. The Act was a legislative component of Canada's response to the tragedy of September 11, 2001. The appellant was ordered to attend a judicial investigative hearing. This case dealt with the Constitutional validity of the "judicial investigative hearing" provision.

There were essentially two acts of alleged terrorism. Firstly, an explosion killed two baggage handlers, and injured four others at Narita Airport, as baggage was being transferred onto Air India Flight 301. A second explosion occurred just one hour later, causing Air India Flight 182 to crash off the west coast of Ireland, killing all passengers and crew.

The first accused, Inderjit Singh Reyat, was arrested in England and extradited to Canada where he was convicted in connection with the explosion at Narita Airport. Mr. Reyat pleaded guilty to manslaughter in connection with the explosion of Air India Flight 182. Two other accused were jointly charged with offences in relation to both explosions and while their trial was ongoing, the Crown brought an application to examine the appellant in this matter pursuant to s. 83.28.

The challenge for democracies in the battle against terrorism is not whether to respond, but rather, how to do so. Canadians value the importance of human life and liberty and the protection of society through respect for the rule of law. A democracy cannot exist without the rule of law. Terrorism challenges the context in which the rule of law must operate, but does not call for the abdication of the law. At the same time, the Constitution must not become a suicide pact. The challenge for a democratic state's answer to terrorism calls for a balancing of what is required for an effective response to terrorism in a way that appropriately recognizes the fundamental values of the rule of law. In a democracy, not every response is available to meet the challenge of terrorism.

The international scope of terrorism raised concerns about the potential uses of information gathered pursuant to s. 83.28. Section 83.28 specifically provides use and derivative use immunity in the context of criminal proceedings. The legislation did not speak to the safeguards in relation to other types of hearings. Deportation and extradition hearings must accord with the principles of fundamental justice. In order to meet the requirements of s. 7 of the *Charter of Rights*, use and derivative use immunity respecting information gathered under s. 83.28 must be extended to extradition and deportation hearings. Therefore, the hearing judge must make and, if necessary, vary the terms of an order to properly provide use and derivative use immunity in extradition and deportation proceedings.

## *Remedial and Disciplinary Measures*

**176. (1) Request — The Chairperson may request the Minister to decide whether any member, except a member of the Immigration Division, should be subject to remedial or disciplinary measures for a reason set out in subsection (2).**

**Proposed Amendment — 176(1)**

**(1) Request — The Chairperson may request the Minister to decide whether any member of the Immigration Appeal Division or the Refugee Appeal Division should be subject to remedial or disciplinary measures for a reason set out in subsection (2).**

2010, c. 8, s. 30 [To come into force June 29, 2012, or earlier by order.]

**(2) Reasons — The request is to be based on the reason that the member has become incapacitated from the proper execution of that office by reason of infirmity, has been guilty of misconduct, has failed in the proper execution of that office or has been placed, by conduct or otherwise, in a position that is incompatible with due execution of that office.**

**177. Measures — On receipt of the request, the Minister may take one or more of the following measures:**

**(a) obtain, in an informal and expeditious manner, any information that the Minister considers necessary;**

**(b) refer the matter for mediation, if the Minister is satisfied that the issues in relation to the request may be appropriately resolved by mediation;**

**(c) request of the Governor in Council that an inquiry be held under section 178; or**

**(d) advise the Chairperson that the Minister considers that it is not necessary to take further measures under this section or sections 178 to 185.**

**178. Appointment of inquirer — On receipt of a request referred to in paragraph 177(c), the Governor in Council may, on the recommendation of the Minister of Justice, appoint a judge of a superior court to conduct an inquiry.**

179. **Powers** — The judge has all the powers, rights and privileges that are vested in a superior court, including the power

(a) to issue a summons requiring any person to appear at the time and place mentioned in the summons to testify about all matters within that person's knowledge relative to the inquiry and to produce any document or thing relative to the inquiry that the person has or controls; and

(b) to administer oaths and examine any person on oath.

180. **Staff** — The judge may engage the services of counsel and other persons having technical or specialized knowledge to assist the judge in conducting the inquiry, establish the terms and conditions of their engagement and, with the approval of the Treasury Board, fix and pay their remuneration and expenses.

181. (1) **Exceptions to public hearing** — An inquiry must be held in public. However, the judge may, on application, take any appropriate measures and make any order that the judge considers necessary to ensure the confidentiality of the inquiry if, after having considered all available alternate measures, the judge is satisfied that there is

(a) a real and substantial risk that matters involving public security will be disclosed;

(b) a real and substantial risk to the fairness of the inquiry such that the need to prevent disclosure outweighs the societal interest that the inquiry be conducted in public; or

(c) a serious possibility that the life, liberty or security of a person will be endangered.

(2) **Confidentiality of application** — If the judge considers it appropriate, the judge may take any measures and make any order that the judge considers necessary to ensure the confidentiality of a hearing held in respect of an application under subsection (1).

182. (1) **Rules of evidence** — In conducting an inquiry, the judge is not bound by any legal or technical rules of evidence and may receive, and base a decision on, evidence presented in the proceedings that the judge considers credible or trustworthy in the circumstances of the case.

(2) **Intervenors** — An interested party may, with leave of the judge, intervene in an inquiry on any terms and conditions that the judge considers appropriate.

183. **Right to be heard** — The member who is the subject of the inquiry shall be given reasonable notice of the subject-matter of the inquiry and of the time and place of any hearing and shall be given an opportunity, in person or by counsel, to be heard at the hearing, to cross-examine witnesses and to present evidence.

184. (1) **Report to Minister** — After an inquiry has been completed, the judge must submit a report containing the judge's findings and recommendations, if any, to the Minister.

(2) **Recommendations** — The judge may, for any of the reasons set out in subsection 176(2), recommend in the report that the member be suspended without pay or removed from office or that any other disciplinary measure or any remedial measure be taken.

185. **Transmission of report to Governor in Council** — If the Minister receives a report of an inquiry in which the judge makes a recommendation, the Minister shall send the report to the Governor in Council who may, if the Governor in Council considers it appropriate, suspend the member without pay, remove the member from office or impose any other disciplinary measure or any remedial measure.

186. **Rights not affected** — Nothing in sections 176 to 185 affects any right or power of the Governor in Council in relation to the removal of a member from office for cause.

# PART 5 — TRANSITIONAL PROVISIONS, CONSEQUENTIAL AND RELATED AMENDMENTS, COORDINATING AMENDMENTS, REPEALS AND COMING INTO FORCE

## *Transitional Provisions*

187. **Definition of "former Act"** — For the purposes of sections 188 to 201, "former Act" means the *Immigration Act*, chapter 1-2 of the Revised Statutes of Canada, 1985, and, where applicable, the regulations and rules made under it.

188. (1) **Continuation** — The Immigration and Refugee Board continued by section 57 of the former Act is hereby continued.

(2) **Chairpersons, Deputy Chairpersons, Assistant Deputy Chairpersons** — The Chairperson, Deputy Chairpersons and Assistant Deputy Chairpersons appointed under the former Act continue in the same capacity with the Board until the expiry or revocation of their respective appointments.

(3) **Continuation — members** — A member appointed under the former Act to the Convention Refugee Determination Division or the Immigration Appeal Division continues in office as a member of the Board until the expiry or revocation of their appointment.

(4) **Executive Director** — The person who, on the coming into force of this section, held the office of Executive Director of the Board is deemed to have been appointed to that office under section 158, without prejudice to any salary and benefits he or she may receive by virtue of having held that office before that coming into force.

189. **Powers** — Sections 94.6, 102.001 to 102.003 and 107.1 of the former Act are, despite paragraph 274(a), deemed not to be repealed and the Minister may exercise

**any of the powers described in those sections with respect to any business or fund that was approved by the Minister before the coming into force of paragraph 274(a).**

**190. Application of this Act — Every application, proceeding or matter under the former Act that is pending or in progress immediately before the coming into force of this section shall be governed by this Act on that coming into force.**



## Case Law

*Lopez v. Canada (Minister of Citizenship & Immigration)*, 2003 CarswellNat 4893 (Imm. & Ref. Bd. (App. Div.)) — The appellant made an application to re-open his removal order appeal. This application is governed by s. 190 of the Act. Section 192 applies only in proceedings where a Notice of Appeal has been filed with the Appeal Division. Filing a Notice of Appeal involves a standard practice related to the filing of a recognized form in an appeal from a refused sponsorship or the issuance of a removal order. Once filed, a Notice of Appeal serves to create or initiate an appeal where before there was none. A re-opening application seeks to re-open an already existing appeal and as such is governed by s. 190 of IRPA.

*Mafuala v. Canada (Minister of Citizenship & Immigration)*, 2003 CarswellNat 3291, 2003 CarswellNat 4685, 2003 FC 1221 (F.C.) — The applicant came to Canada from Congo in 1966. He made a refugee claim which was dismissed, subsequently left Canada for the United States and returned in 1999 when he made another refugee claim which was also dismissed. He then went back to the United States and returned to Canada in 2001 and once again applied for refugee status. The former *Immigration Act* permitted repeat claims so long as the applicant spent more than 90 days outside of Canada between each one. The applicant was informed that his third claim could not be heard because he was no longer eligible under the new *Immigration and Refugee Protection Act*. This decision was upheld. The *Immigration and Refugee Protection Regulations* state the general rule that applicants for refugee protection who are eligible to make claims under the former Act are entitled to have their claims determined under the new Act, unless, an immigration officer notifies them that they are no longer eligible. The Act specifically provides that the person is no longer eligible if his or her claim has already been rejected even if it was dealt with under the former legislation.

Section 90 of the IRPA Regulations does not permit the applicant's claim to go forward despite the fact that he was told in October 2001 that he was eligible to have his third claim heard.

*Dragan v. Canada (Minister of Citizenship & Immigration)*, [2003] 4 F.C. 189, 27 Imm. L.R. (3d) 157, 2003 CarswellNat 467, 2003 CarswellNat 1525, 2003 FCT 211, 2003 CFPI 211, 227 F.T.R. 272, 224 D.L.R. (4th) 738, [2003] F.C.J. No. 260; additional reasons at 27 Imm. L.R. (3d) 185, 2003 CarswellNat 588, 2003 CarswellNat 1580, 2003 FCT 281, 2003 CFPI 281, 228 F.T.R. 52, [2003] F.C.J. No. 404; affirmed 27 Imm. L.R. (3d) 194, 2003 CarswellNat 1419, 2003 FCA 233, 224 D.L.R. (4th) 764, [2003] F.C.J. No. 813 (C.A.) — This consolidated application involved 124 applicants who applied for permanent residence in Canada before June 28, 2002, the day that the IRPA came into force. The applicants sought a writ of *mandamus* requiring the respondent to assess them in accordance with the former Act and the former Regulations. Sections 190 and 201 of the IRPA indicate that Parliament intended the new Act to apply retrospectively and to authorize regulations with retrospective effect. Parliament can expressly enact retroactive or retrospective legislation. The clear expression of Parliamentary intent in this regard overrides the presumption against retroactivity or retrospectively in s. 43 of the *Interpretation Act*. Section 361 of the IRPA Regulations is validly authorized respective legislation and operates according to its terms, which means that applications filed after January 1, 2002, are to be assessed under the new Regulations and applications filed before January 1, 2002 are to be assessed under the old Regulations up until March 31, 2003.

The following conditions need to be satisfied for the Court to issue a writ of *mandamus*:

1. There must be a public legal duty to act.
2. The duty must be owed to the applicant.
3. There must be a clear right to the performance of that duty, in particular,
    (a) the applicant must have satisfied all conditions precedent giving rise to the duty and;
    b) there was a prior demand for the performance of the duty, a reasonable time to comply with the demand and a subsequent refusal which can either be expressed or implied, e.g. unreasonable delay.
4. No other adequate remedy is available to the applicant.
5. The order sought will be of some practical value or effect.
6. The Court finds no equitable bar to the relief sought.
7. On a balance of convenience an order should issue.

The Court found all of these conditions satisfied and granted a writ of *mandamus* with respect to 102 of the applicants requiring the respondent on or before March 31, 2003 to assess the 102 applicants and award units of assessment in accordance with the former Regulations. Applications for judicial review with respect to applicants who filed after January 1, 2002 will be assessed under the selection criteria in the IRPA. The applicants who applied in this category had notice of the new selection criteria at the time of their application.

*Karmali v. Canada (Minister of Citizenship & Immigration)* (2003), 30 Imm. L.R. (3d) 90, 2003 CarswellNat 800, 2003 CarswellNat 2109, 2003 FCT 358, 230 F.T.R. 140 (T.D.) — Section 190 of IRPA and s. 350 of the Regulations do not apply retroactively. They do not state that IRPA should govern as though it was enforced in 1997, rather they state that applications still pending, and specifically applications sent back for re-determination after IRPA came into force, are to be dealt with under IRPA.

The applicant does not have a vested right to have his application re-determined under the law as it existed at the date of the application. Section 190 of IRPA and s. 350 of the Regulations deal with, in clear terms, the manner in which a matter sent back for re-determination is to be re-considered.

The language of s. 190 is not permissive. When s. 190 of IRPA and s. 350 of the Regulations are read together they clearly provide a complete framework for dealing with applications that are referred back by the Court for re-determination.

Section 350 of the Regulations is not *ultra vires* the framework of s. 190. Section 201 of the IRPA allows for Regulations regarding the transition between the former Act and IRPA.

Finally s. 190 of IRPA does not offend subs. 2(e) of the *Canadian Bill of Rights* as it does not deprive a person of the right to a fair hearing.

**191. Convention Refugee Determination Division — Every application, proceeding or matter before the Convention Refugee Determination Division under the former Act that is pending or in progress immediately before the coming into force of this section, in respect of which substantive evidence has been adduced but no decision has been made, shall be continued under the former Act by the Refugee Protection Division of the Board.**

## Case Law

*Molnar v. Canada (Minister of Citizenship & Immigration)*, 2004 CarswellNat 5334, 2004 CarswellNat 1840, 254 F.T.R. 221, 2004 FC 834 (F.C.) — The filing of a PIF does not constitute "substantive evidence adduced in the proceeding" for the purposes of s. 191, because evidence is only "adduced" when it is identified on the record and entered as an exhibit at the hearing.

*Borcsok v. Canada (Minister of Citizenship & Immigration)*, 2004 CarswellNat 1516, [2004] F.C.J. No. 552, 2004 CarswellNat 799, 2004 FC 445 (F.C.) — The filing of a Personal Information Form does not constitute substantive evidence for the purpose of s. 191.

**192. Immigration Appeal Division — If a notice of appeal has been filed with the Immigration Appeal Division immediately before the coming into force of this section, the appeal shall be continued under the former Act by the Immigration Appeal Division of the Board.**

## Case Law

*Lopez v. Canada (Minister of Citizenship & Immigration)* (2003), 2003 CarswellNat 4893 (Imm. & Ref. Bd. (App. Div.)) — The appellant made an application to re-open his removal order appeal. This application is governed by s. 190 of the Act. Section 192 applies only in proceedings where a Notice of Appeal has been filed with the Appeal Division. Filing a Notice of Appeal involves a standard practice related to the filing of a recognized form in an appeal from a refused sponsorship or the issuance of a removal order. Once filed, a Notice of Appeal serves to create or initiate an appeal where before there was none. A re-opening application seeks to re-open an already existing appeal and as such is governed by s. 190 of IRPA.

**193. Continuation by Immigration Division — Every application, proceeding or matter before the Adjudication Division under the former Act that is pending or in progress immediately before the coming into force of this section, in respect of which substantive evidence has been adduced but no decision has been made, shall be continued under this Act by the Immigration Division of the Board.**

### Unproclaimed Text — 194, 195

**194. Refugee Protection Division — In cases referred to in section 191, a decision by the Refugee Protection Division following a hearing that has been commenced by the Convention Refugee Determination Division is not subject to an appeal under section 110.**

**195. Convention Refugee Determination Division — A decision made by the Convention Refugee Determination Division before the coming into force of this section is not subject to an appeal under section 110.**

**196. Appeals — Despite section 192, an appeal made to the Immigration Appeal Division before the coming into force of this section shall be discontinued if the appellant has not been granted a stay under the former Act and the appeal could not have been made because of section 64 of this Act.**

## Case Law

*Medovarski v. Canada (Minister of Citizenship & Immigration)*, [2005] 2 S.C.R. 539, 50 Imm. L.R. (3d) 1, 135 C.R.R. (2d) 1, 258 D.L.R. (4th) 193, [2005] S.C.J. No. 31, 339 N.R. 1, EYB 2005-95306, 2005 CarswellNat 2943, 2005 CarswellNat 2944, 2005 SCC 51 — The appellant was a permanent resident and had been ordered deported for serious criminality. Her removal order was automatically stayed when she appealed the deportation order to the Immigration Appeal Division. The appeal was discontinued as a result of s. 196 of the IRPA (a transitional provision), which took away the right to appeal an order for removal unless a party had, under the former Act, been "granted a stay." The trial judge set aside the decision to discontinue. However, the Federal Court of Appeal allowed the Minister of Citizenship and Immigration's appeal, holding that the purpose of the IRPA transitional provision was to deny the right of appeal in the case of an automatic stay. Section 196 of the IRPA, properly interpreted, applies only to actively granted stays. The objectives of the IRPA, as expressed in s. 3, indicate an intent to prioritize security. In keeping with these objectives, the IRPA creates a new scheme whereby a person sentenced to more than six months in prison is inadmissible pursuant to s. 36; if they have been sentenced to a prison term of more than two years, they are denied a right to appeal their removal order under s. 64 of the IRPA. The purpose in enacting the IRPA, and in particular s. 64, was to efficiently remove from the country persons who have engaged in serious criminality. Since s. 196 refers explicitly to s. 64, the transitional provision should be interpreted in light of these legislative objectives.

The deportation of a non-citizen cannot in itself implicate the liberty and security interests protected by s. 7 of the *Canadian Charter of Rights and Freedoms*. Even if the liberty and security of the person were engaged, any unfairness resulting from s. 196 would be inadequate to constitute a breach of principles of fundamental justice.

*Kang v. Canada (Minister of Citizenship & Immigration)*, 2005 CarswellNat 531, 2005 FC 297, [2005] F.C.J. No. 367 (F.C.) — Section 196 applies to sponsorship appeals. The jurisdictional question for the IAD is not whether the foreign national is in fact inadmissible but rather whether the individual in question has been found to be inadmissible on one of the enumerated bases. Once that question is answered in the affirmative, the statute is clear. The IAD is without jurisdiction to deal further with the matter.

*Canada (Minister of Citizenship & Immigration) v. Bhalrhu*, [2004] F.C.J. No. 1498, 40 Imm. L.R. (3d) 238, 2004 CarswellNat 3184, 2004 FC 1236 (F.C.) — The Minister sought to review a decision of the IRB not to discontinue the respondent's appeal.

Section 196 applies to sponsorship appeals. The legislator excluded from the application of s. 196, appellants who were granted a stay under the former Act out of deference to the IAD and therefore only appeals where the IAD has in fact been involved and granted a stay are excluded by s. 196.

*Williams v. Canada (Minister of Citizenship & Immigration)*, [2004] F.C.J. No. 814, 36 Imm. L.R. (3d) 235, 2004 CarswellNat 2979, 2004 CarswellNat 1310, 2004 FC 662, 254 F.T.R. 224 (F.C.) — Section 196 is designed to put the appellants, including sponsors, under the provisions of the new legislation.

*Canada (Minister of Citizenship & Immigration) v. Sohal*, [2004] F.C.J. No. 813, 36 Imm. L.R. (3d) 91, 2004 CarswellNat 1309, 2004 FC 660, 2004 CarswellNat 4467, 252 F.T.R. 267 (F.C.) — Section 196 does not apply to sponsorship appeals.

*Medovarski v. Canada (Minister of Citizenship & Immigration)*, [2004] F.C.J. No. 366, 35 Imm. L.R. (3d) 161, 2004 CarswellNat 2709, 2004 CarswellNat 543, 318 N.R. 252, 238 D.L.R. (4th) 328, 2004 FCA 85, (sub nom. *Medovarski c. Canada (Minister of Citizenship & Immigration))* [2004] 4 F.C.R. 48, 119 C.R.R. (2d) 187 (note), 248 F.T.R. 319 (note), 116 C.R.R. (2d) 268 (F.C.A.); leave to appeal allowed (2004), 2004 CarswellNat 4019, 2004 CarswellNat 4020 (S.C.C.); leave to appeal allowed (2004), 2004 CarswellNat 4021, 2004 CarswellNat 4022, 119 C.R.R. (2d) 187 (S.C.C.); affirmed (2005), 2005 CarswellNat 1533, 2005 CarswellNat 1534 (S.C.C.); affirmed (2005), 2005 CarswellNat 1535, 2005 CarswellNat 1536 (S.C.C.) — With respect to the statutory transitional scheme, the general rule is that IRPA applies to every application, proceeding or matter under the former Act that is pending or in progress immediately before the coming into force of s. 190. Section 192 creates an exception to s. 190 by enacting the opposite general rule for appeals to the IAD. If the Notice of Appeal has been filed immediately before the coming into force of s. 190 then the appeal shall be continued under the former Act.

Section 196 carves a specific exception out of s. 192 by providing that appeals to the IAD filed before the coming into force of s. 192 shall be discontinued if the appellant has not been granted a stay under the former Act and the appeal could not have been made because of s. 64. Section 196 discontinues appeals only when a stay has not been granted on the disposition of an appeal under the former Act paragraph 73(1)(c). Section 196 does not include an automatic statutory stay.

*Esteban v. Canada (Minister of Citizenship & Immigration)*, [2003] F.C.J. No. 1181, 31 Imm. L.R. (3d) 47, 2003 CarswellNat 4360, 2003 CarswellNat 2279, 2003 FC 930 (F.C.); reversed 35 Imm. L.R. (3d) 161, 2004 CarswellNat 2709, 2004 CarswellNat 543, [2004] F.C.J. No. 366, 318 N.R. 252, 238 D.L.R. (4th) 328, 2004 FCA 85, (sub nom. *Medovarski c. Canada (Minister of Citizenship & Immigration))* [2004] 4 F.C.R. 48, 119 C.R.R. (2d) 187 (note), 248 F.T.R. 319 (note), 116 C.R.R. (2d) 268 (F.C.A.); leave to appeal allowed (2004), 2004 CarswellNat 4019, 2004 CarswellNat 4020 (S.C.C.); leave to appeal allowed (2004), 2004 CarswellNat 4021, 2004 CarswellNat 4022, 119 C.R.R. (2d) 187 (S.C.C.); affirmed (2005), 2005 CarswellNat 1533, 2005 CarswellNat 1534 (S.C.C.); affirmed (2005), 2005 CarswellNat 1535, 2005 CarswellNat 1536 (S.C.C.) — The applicant, since 1990, had been convicted of a number of criminal offences. In consequence of his last conviction he was reported under the former *Immigration Act* and ordered deported. The applicant had a right of appeal from the issuance of the deportation order because he was a permanent resident of Canada and filed a Notice of Appeal at the end of the hearing. On June 28, 2002 the IRPA was proclaimed and the Appeal Division advised the applicant that his appeal was discontinued. The applicant in this action is reviewing the decision of the IAD to treat his appeal as discontinued.

Section 192 is the general transitional provision applicable to appeals pending before the IAD when the IRPA came into force. This section generally continues, under the former

Act, appeals before the IAD. Section 196 limits this provision. Section 196 only has any meaning if it contemplates a statutory stay. Sections 196 and 197 should be read together because they both limit the general provision in s. 192, continuing appeals under the former Act. Section 196 applies to appeals launched but not heard or disposed of, while s. 197 applies to appeals heard but still extant because a stay was issued by the IAD.

The interpretation that s. 196 contemplates a statutory stay, avoids the result that there would never be a granted stay in respect of an appeal pending with the IAD but not heard. Under this interpretation there are some cases where s. 196 of the Act would operate to remove an appeal pending to the IAD.

Accordingly, the decision of the registrar concluding that the applicant's appeal was discontinued was set aside.

*Jones v. Canada (Minister of Citizenship & Immigration)*, 2003 CarswellNat 1655, 2003 FCT 661 (Fed. T.D.); reversed [2004] F.C.J. No. 366, 35 Imm. L.R. (3d) 161, 2004 CarswellNat 543, 2004 CarswellNat 2709, 318 N.R. 252, 238 D.L.R. (4th) 328, 2004 FCA 85, (sub nom. *Medovarski c. Canada (Minister of Citizenship & Immigration))* [2004] 4 F.C.R. 48, 119 C.R.R. (2d) 187 (note), 248 F.T.R. 319 (note), 116 C.R.R. (2d) 268 (F.C.A.); leave to appeal allowed (2004), 2004 CarswellNat 4019, 2004 CarswellNat 4020 (S.C.C.); leave to appeal allowed (2004), 2004 CarswellNat 4021, 2004 CarswellNat 4022, 119 C.R.R. (2d) 187 (S.C.C.); affirmed (2005), 2005 CarswellNat 1533, 2005 CarswellNat 1534 (S.C.C.); affirmed (2005), 2005 CarswellNat 1535, 2005 CarswellNat 1536 (S.C.C.) — The word "stay" in s. 196 contemplates a stay that came into effect as a result of the operation of paragraph 49(1)(b) of the former Act.

*Medovarski v. Canada (Minister of Citizenship & Immigration)*, [2003] 4 F.C. 227, 28 Imm. L.R. (3d) 50, [2003] F.C.J. No. 811, 234 F.T.R. 101, 2003 CarswellNat 1486, 2003 FCT 634 (Fed. T.D.); reversed 35 Imm. L.R. (3d) 161, 2004 CarswellNat 2709, 2004 CarswellNat 543, [2004] F.C.J. No. 366, 318 N.R. 252, 238 D.L.R. (4th) 328, 2004 FCA 85, (sub nom. *Medovarski c. Canada (Minister of Citizenship & Immigration))* [2004] 4 F.C.R. 48, 119 C.R.R. (2d) 187 (note), 248 F.T.R. 319 (note), 116 C.R.R. (2d) 268 (F.C.A.); leave to appeal allowed (2004), 2004 CarswellNat 4019, 2004 CarswellNat 4020 (S.C.C.); leave to appeal allowed (2004), 2004 CarswellNat 4021, 2004 CarswellNat 4022, 119 C.R.R. (2d) 187 (S.C.C.); affirmed (2005), 2005 CarswellNat 1533, 2005 CarswellNat 1534 (S.C.C.); affirmed (2005), 2005 CarswellNat 1535, 2005 CarswellNat 1536 (S.C.C.) — This is an application to review a decision of the IAD which had discontinued the applicant's appeal for lack of jurisdiction. The applicant, a permanent resident of Canada, had appealed her deportation order to the IAD. She received a notice to appear dated April 24, 2002 stating that her appeal would be heard on September 26, 2002. On June 28, 2002 the *Immigration and Refugee Protection Act* and its accompanying regulations came into force. On August 12, 2002 the IAD advised the applicant that her appeal would be discontinued pursuant to ss. 196 and 64 of the IRPA.

Parliament acknowledges that a change from one legislative framework to another will affect parties who have commenced some actions under the appeal legislation. This group of affected parties is usually easily defined. While those caught in the transition are subject to the new statute as a whole, they form a unique group to whom the general objectives of both the new law and the old law will apply. Thus, almost every statute that is intended to replace an existing statute contains transitional provisions. The objective of Parliament is to treat those caught by the transition as fairly as possible. Where a right previously held is being affected, the transitional provisions should be interpreted in a manner that respects not only the overall intent of the IRPA, but also the more limited intent of treating those individuals fairly. Where the right to an appeal is being removed, the context requires an interpretation that minimizes the negative impact on the applicant.

The word "stay" in s. 196 of the IRPA contemplates a stay that came into effect as a result of the operation of paragraph 49(1)(b) of the former Act. As a result, the IAD was held to have erred in concluding that s. 196 had the effect of extinguishing the applicant's appeal rights under s. 192.



**197. Stays — Despite section 192, if an appellant who has been granted a stay under the former Act breaches a condition of the stay, the appellant shall be subject to the provisions of section 64 and subsection 68(4) of this Act.**

## Case Law

*Canada (Minister of Citizenship & Immigration) v. Hyde*, [2006] F.C.J. No. 1747, 57 Imm. L.R. (3d) 165, 359 N.R. 165, 2006 CarswellNat 4146, 2006 FCA 379 (Fed. C.A.) — The effect of s. 197 of IRPA is to terminate the IAD's jurisdiction with respect to a person who falls within the sections ambit. Section 197 precludes the IAD from staying a removal order in the exercise of its jurisdiction under s. 68 of IRPA. A permanent resident whose removal the IAD stayed before IRPA came into effect, and who breaches a condition of the stay, cannot continue an appeal to the IAD if either the basis of the deportation order was a criminal conviction with a sentence of two years or more, or if the offence committed after the IAD had stayed the removal was punishable by a maximum of 10 years or a sentence of more than six months was imposed.

The appellant had been ordered deported on the basis of a s. 64 offence (that is, one for which he received a sentence of two years or more). Therefore, his appeal was automatically terminated by IRPA when he breached the conditions imposed on his stay. It is irrelevant that the breaches did not involve the commission of offences referred to in subs. 68(4). The appeal was allowed.

*Singh v. Canada (Minister of Citizenship & Immigration)*, [2006] 3 F.C.R. 70, 344 N.R. 244, 51 Imm. L.R. (3d) 49, 2005 CarswellNat 4113, 2005 CarswellNat 5141, 2005 FCA 417 (C.A.) — The appellant was a permanent resident of Canada. After being convicted of robbery he was found inadmissible on the grounds of serious criminality and ordered deported. He appealed his deportation and was granted a stay of removal that contained, among others, the condition "keep the peace and be of good behaviour." Subsequently, the appellant committed another serious offence and was convicted of that crime. It is the offence itself that constitutes the breach of the condition to keep the peace and to be of good behaviour. In this regard, a breach may be established without a conviction where there is other clear evidence of the offensive behaviour.

Between the time of the assault and the conviction, on June 28, 2002, the *Immigration Act*, R.S.C. 1985, c. I-2, was replaced by the IRPA. A provision of the IRPA addressed individuals such as the appellant, who were found inadmissible on grounds of serious criminality, had obtained a stay of their removal order, and were then convicted of another serious offence. Specifically, the IRPA mandates the cancellation of the stay and the termination of the appeal.

The appellant argued that the transitional provision of the IRPA, s. 197(1) should not apply to a breach of condition that occurred before s. 197 was enacted. The Federal Court concluded that Parliament clearly intended that the provision of the IRPA that cancels the stay and terminates the appeal apply to individuals such as the appellant, regardless of whether the condition of the stay was breached before or after the IRPA came into force.

*Leite v. Canada (Minister of Citizenship & Immigration)*, 2005 CarswellNat 2006, 2005 CarswellNat 5148, 2005 FC 984 (F.C.) — In this case, the applicant was subject to a stay order. The IAD had issued a stay of a deportation and had attached specific terms and conditions to the stay, including detailed reporting requirements and an oral review of the case. The actual stay order did not refer to a four-year term. The applicant was convicted of trafficking a controlled substance and the conviction triggered the application of s. 197 of the IRPA which required the stay to be cancelled by operation of law pursuant to subs. 68(4) of the IRPA. The applicant argued that the stay had expired at the time the conviction occurred and that the applicant should have a hearing where he could lead new evidence and the Board could determine what to do with his case on the merits. The Court concluded the stay ordered by the Board was in effect and the applicant was convicted of an offence during that time and, consequently, s. 68(4) applied.

*Ferri v. Canada (Minister of Citizenship & Immigration)*, [2005] F.C.J. No. 1941, 51 Imm. L.R. (3d) 177, [2006] 3 F.C.R. 53, 2005 CarswellNat 3878, 2005 CarswellNat 5009, 2005 FC 1580 (F.C.) — Subsection 68(4) of the IRPA limits the jurisdiction of the IAD to determining whether the factual requirements of this subsection are met. The IAD can only consider whether it has previously stayed a removal over order; whether the individual in question is a permanent resident or a foreign national who was found inadmissible on grounds of serious criminality or criminality; and whether the individual has been convicted of another offence coming within subs. 36(1) of the IRPA. Once the IAD determines that the factual requirements of this subsection have been met, it then loses jurisdiction over the individual, by operation of law. The IAD does not have jurisdiction to consider the constitutionality of subs. 68(4).

**198. Refugee Protection Division — The Refugee Protection Division has jurisdiction to consider decisions of the Convention Refugee Determination Division that are set aside by the Federal Court, the Federal Court of Appeal or the Supreme Court of Canada, and shall dispose of those matters in accordance with the provisions of this Act.**

2002, c. 8, s. 194(e)

**199. Redetermination — Sections 112 to 114 apply to a redetermination of a decision set aside by the Federal Court with respect to an application for landing as a member of the post-determination refugee claimants in Canada class within the meaning of the *Immigration Regulations, 1978*.**

**200. Exclusion — Subsection 31(1) does not apply with respect to persons who were permanent residents, within the meaning of the former Act, on the coming into force of this section.**

**201. Regulations — The regulations may provide for measures regarding the transition between the former Act and this Act, including measures regarding classes of persons who will be subject in whole or in part to this Act or the former Act and measures regarding financial and enforcement matters.**

. . . . .

## *Repeals*

**274. Repeals — The following Acts are repealed:**

**(a) the *Immigration Act*, chapter I-2 of the Revised Statutes of Canada, 1985;**

*[Editor's Note: S.C. 2001, c. 27, s. 189 provides that sections 94.6, 102.001, 102.002, 102.003 and 107.1 of the* Immigration Act, *R.S.C. 1985, c. I-2 (the "former Act") are, despite paragraph 274(a) of the* Immigration and Refugee Protection Act, *S.C. 2001, c. 27 (the "new Act"), deemed not to be repealed and the Minister may exercise any of the powers described in sections 94.6, 102.001, 102.002, 102.003 and 107.1 with respect to any business or fund that was approved by the Minister before the repeal of the former Act on June 28, 2002.*

*However, S.C. 2001, c. 27, s. 190 provides that every application, proceeding or matter under the former Act that is pending or in progress immediately before June 28, 2002 shall be governed by the new Act.]*

**(b) *An Act to amend the Immigration Act and other Acts in consequence thereof*, chapter 49 of the Statutes of Canada, 1992;**

**(c) *An Act to amend the Immigration Act and the Citizenship Act and to make a consequential amendment to the Customs Act*, chapter 15 of the Statutes of Canada, 1995; and**

**(d) *An Act to amend the Citizenship Act and the Immigration Act*, chapter 22 of the Statutes of Canada, 1997.**

## *Coming Into Force*

**275. Coming into force — Sections 73, 110, 111, 171, 194 and 195 come into force two years after the day on which the *Balanced Refugee Reform Act* receives royal assent or on any earlier day that may be fixed by order of the Governor in Council.**

2010, c. 8, s. 31

## SCHEDULE — SECTIONS E AND F OF ARTICLE 1 OF THE UNITED NATIONS CONVENTION RELATING TO THE STATUS OF REFUGEES

**(Subsection 2(1))**

**E. This Convention shall not apply to a person who is recognized by the competent authorities of the country in which he has taken residence as having the rights and obligations which are attached to the possession of the nationality of that country.**

**F. The provisions of this Convention shall not apply to any person with respect to whom there are serious reasons for considering that:**

**(a) he has committed a crime against peace, a war crime, or a crime against humanity, as defined in the international instruments drawn up to make provision in respect of such crimes;**

**(b) he has committed a serious non-political crime outside the country of refuge prior to his admission to that country as a refugee;**

**(c) he has been guilty of acts contrary to the purposes and principles of the United Nations.**

## Case Law

### Section E

*Zeng v. Canada (Minister of Citizenship & Immigration)* (2010), 402 N.R. 154, 2010 FCA 118, 2010 CarswellNat 1295, 2010 CarswellNat 2439 (F.C.A.) — This appeal concerns Section E of Article 1 (Article 1E) of the *United Nations Convention Relating to the Status of Refugees* and more particularly, the issue of asylum shopping. Article 1E is an exclusion clause. It precludes the conferral of refugee protection if an individual has surrogate protection in a country where the individual enjoys substantially the same rights and obligations as nationals of that country. Asylum shopping refers to circumstances where an individual seeks protection in one country, from alleged persecution, torture, or cruel or unusual punishment in another country (the home country), while entitled to stay in a "safe" country (the third country). The appellant Minister of Citizenship and Immigration appealed the judgment of Justice Gibson of the Federal Court on an application for judicial review of a decision of the Refugee Protection Division of the Immigration and Refugee Board. The RPD determined that the respondents, Zeng and Feng, were excluded from refugee protection pursuant to Article 1E. In allowing the application for judicial review, Justice Gibson identified a discrepancy in the jurisprudence regarding the appropriate date for assessing the applicability of Article 1E exclusion (date of application or date of hearing). He concluded that a more fluid approach was required and proposed a three-step test to be followed in Article 1E exclusion determinations. The applicants were citizens of the PRC. The daughter was born in China and has always lived there. Their son was born in Chile. Mr. Zeng obtained permanent residence status in Chile and his wife obtained temporary residence status. Upon their return to China, they faced persecution for breaching the one-child policy. On their return trip to Chile, they remained in Toronto where they made refugee claims.

The Federal Court of Appeal allowed the appeal and set aside the decision of the application judge and dismissed the application for judicial review. The Federal Court of Appeal set out a test to be applied to Article 1E determinations as follows:

> Considering all relevant factors to the date of the hearing, does the claimant have status, substantially similar to that of its nationals, in the third country? If the answer is yes, the claimant is excluded. If the answer is no, the next question is whether the claimant previously had such status and lost it, or had access to such status and failed to acquire it? If the answer is no, the claimant is not excluded under Article 1E. If the answer is yes, the RPD must consider and balance various factors. These include, but are not limited to, the reason for the loss of status (voluntary or involuntary), whether the claimant could return to the third country, the risk the claimant would face in the country, Canada's international obligations, and any other relevant factors.

It will be for the RPD to weigh the factors and arrive at a determination as to whether the exclusion will apply in the particular circumstances.

*Parshottam v. Canada (Minister of Citizenship & Immigration)* (2008), 75 Imm. L.R. (3d) 165, 303 D.L.R. (4th) 672, 382 N.R. 186, 2008 CarswellNat 4154, 2008 CarswellNat 5358, 2008 FCA 355 (C.A.) — This was an appeal of a decision to dismiss an application for judicial review of a rejection of the appellant's application for protection by a pre-removal risk assessment ("PRRA") officer. The question certified by Justice Mosley was found not to be dispositive of the appeal and the Court declined to answer the question. The Court did add that they did not share Justice Mosley's view that it was "settled law" that whether a claimant for protection in Canada is a permanent resident of a third country for the purpose of Article 1E and s. 98 of the IRPA is invariably determined as of the time of the claimant's arrival in Canada and that subsequent events are irrelevant. It was common ground that if the appellant was a permanent resident of the United States at the relevant time, he was excluded by Article IE from claiming refugee status in Canada. Counsel for the appellant argued that the PRRA officer had erred in law by applying the wrong standard of proof. That is, the officer required the appellant to prove as a matter of certainty that he had lost his permanent residence status in the United States. The Court found that although the PRRA officer did not articulate the standard of proof that she was applying, it was to be assumed in the absence of indications to the contrary that she applied the correct one, namely, a balance of probabilities. The officer's reasons, including her observation that whether the appellant was still a permanent resident would ultimately be determined by an immigration judge in the United States, did not establish that she had applied some standard other than a balance of probabilities. The appeal was dismissed. However, Justice Sharlow would have answered the certified question even though the issue may not have been dispositive of the appeal. He would have answered the certified question as follows:

> If the claimant presents new evidence (as contemplated by paragraph 113(a) of IRPA that Article 1E does not apply as of the date of the pre-removal risk assessment, the PRRA officer may determine on the basis of the new evidence that Article 1E currently applies, in which case the claim for protection is barred. Alternatively, the PRRA officer may determine on the basis of the new evidence that Article 1E does not currently apply although it did apply at the time of the claimant's admission to Canada (or at the date of the RPD decision). If such a change of status has occurred, the PRRA officer should consider why the change of status occurred and what steps, if any, the claimant took or might have taken to cause or fail to prevent the change of status. If the acts or omissions of the claimant indicate asylum shopping, Article 1E may be held to apply despite the change in status.

*Shahpari v. Canada (Minister of Citizenship & Immigration)* (1998), 44 Imm. L.R. (2d) 139, 146 F.T.R. 102 (Fed. T.D.) — The applicants sought to review the question of whether Section E of Article I of the *Convention* applied to them. The applicants were citizens of Iran. In 1984 they moved to France and after seven years of temporary residence in France were issued a "Carte de Resident" which was valid for 10 years. After residing in France until 1994, the applicants came to Canada and within one month made a refugee application.

The burden of proving that Section E applies rests with the party asserting it, in this case the respondent. It did not assist the applicant in this case that she allowed her visa to expire. The evidence allowed the panel to conclude that the visa could be renewed. Applicants should remember that actions they themselves take, which are intended to result in their not being able to return to a country which has already granted them refugee status, may well evidence an absence of the subjective fear of persecution in their original country. Further, if applicants are entitled to renounce the protection they receive from one country and claim protection from another, it gives them a right to emigrate to another country without complying with the usual requirements, solely by reason of their unilateral renunciation of the protection that they have been afforded by the country they are leaving.

*Hamdan v. Canada (Minister of Citizenship & Immigration)* (1997), 38 Imm. L.R. (2d) 20 (Fed. T.D.) — This was an application to review a negative decision of the CRDD. The applicant, a citizen of Iraq, claimed refugee status in February 1995. Before coming to Canada the applicant had resided in the Philippines since May 1986. From 1986 until 1992 he had legal status in the Philippines as a student. After the expiry of his student visa, he stayed in the Philippines illegally for approximately one year. He tried to come to Canada with false travel documents, but was turned back in Hong Kong. He returned to the Philippines and subsequently filed a refugee claim with the United Nations High Commissioner for Refugees. His claim was accepted. The fact that the applicant has a well-founded fear of persecution in Iraq was confirmed by the Board and was not at issue in this application. The Board determined that the applicant was not a convention refugee on the basis of the exclusion in Article 1(E) of the Convention.

Article 1(E) is incorporated into Canadian law under s. 2 of the *Immigration Act* under the definition of convention refugee. The primary source for understanding the meaning and application of Article 1(E) must be the text of the article itself. It is clear that the article is intended to operate where a person has been recognized "as having the rights and obligations which are attached to the possession of the nationality" of the country in which he has taken residence. With respect to the criteria in *Shamlou v. Canada* (1995), 103 F.T.R. 241, the Court observed that the relevant criteria would change depending on the rights which normally accrue to citizens in the country which is being scrutinized. The Court did not comment on whether all the criteria set out in the *Shamlou* case must be satisfied for exclusion under Article 1(E). In this case, the Court found it to be critical that the applicant had neither the right to work nor the right to receive social services in the Philippines.

Accordingly, the Court concluded that the Board had applied the wrong test in determining that the applicant had the rights and obligations attaching to nationality of the Philippines. The decision of the Board was set aside and the matter remitted back for rehearing by a freshly constituted panel.

*Wassiq v. Canada (Minister of Citizenship & Immigration)* (1996), 33 Imm. L.R. (2d) 238, 112 F.T.R. 143 (T.D.) — The applicants applied to review a negative decision of the IRB. The applicants were citizens of Afghanistan. In 1981, they successfully applied as Convention refugees in Germany. In 1991, they left Germany and came to Canada and sought refugee status here.

A panel of the IRB had decided that the applicants had a well-founded fear of persecution in respect of Afghanistan, but that Canada had assumed responsibility for them and that Germany was obliged to allow them to return. Therefore, the Board found that the Convention did not apply to the applicants by virtue of Section E of Article 1.

Refugee claims were never meant to allow a claimant to seek out better protection than that from which he or she already benefitted. If by reason of their absence from Germany and sojourn in Canada, the applicants were in effect entitled to renounce the protection they received from Germany and claim protection from Canada, such a result would be anomalous. In substance, it would give a person who had Convention refugee status in one country the right to emigrate to another country without complying with the usual requirements.

Whether Canada or Germany should be responsible for the applicants should ideally be determined as between the governments of Canada and Germany. A decision of a panel of the IRB that Germany should have responsibility for the applicants, which is in effect the decision in this case, is not binding on Germany. The real issue is whether Germany recognizes that the applicants may return.

On the evidence before it, the panel could not have arrived at such a conclusion and therefore could not have found that Section E of Article 1 was applicable to the applicants. Accordingly, the application for judicial review was allowed and the matter remitted back to a differently constituted panel.

*Kanesharan v. Canada (Minister of Citizenship & Immigration)* (1996), 35 Imm. L.R. (2d) 185, 120 F.T.R. 67 (T.D.) — The applicant, a Sri Lankan Tamil, fled Sri Lanka and went to the United Kingdom in 1990. In 1991, the applicant unsuccessfully applied for Convention refugee status in the U.K. The applicant was however given permission to remain in the U.K. until September 1993. This right to remain included the right to make trips from and to the United Kingdom during that period. This right was extended to May 1997. The applicant eventually made his way to Canada where he made a claim which was the subject of this application.

A panel of the IRB decided that Article 1(E) of the 1951 U.N. Convention applied to the applicant. Thus, the issue before the Federal Court was whether, with respect to the United Kingdom, the applicant had the rights and obligations which are normally attached to persons possessing U.K. nationality.

The Court noted that in the United Kingdom, the home office reserved the right to remove persons similarly situated to the applicant to their country of nationality should the prevailing circumstances change significantly in a positive manner. Further, the Court noted it was only in 1997, when the applicant's extended right to remain in the U.K. had concluded that the applicant would be considered by the home office to be eligible for indefinite leave to remain in that country.

Accordingly, the Court found that Article 1(e) of the U.N. Convention did not apply to the applicant, quashed the decision of the IRB and remitted the matter back for reconsideration.

*Kroon v. Canada (Minister of Employment & Immigration)* (1995), 89 F.T.R. 236 — The applicant, his wife and children sought to set aside a negative decision of the CRDD. The panel concluded that although the claimants may subjectively fear persecution in Estonia, what they suffered or might suffer is discrimination at most. Their claims that they face a reasonable chance of persecution were held to be not well-founded. The purpose of Article 1E of the U.N. Convention is to support regular immigration laws of countries in the international community. If a person faces threat of persecution in his own country but is living in another country, with or without refugee status, and there faces no threat of persecution, but rather enjoys the same basic rights as nationals of the second country, then the function of Article 1E is to exclude such a person as a potential refugee claimant in Canada. The panel did not err by considering the basic rights which the applicant was apparently entitled to under the Constitution and laws of Estonia, and comparing those with the rights acknowledged for Estonian nationals. The tribunal's assessments of the rights to which the male applicant would be entitled were he to return and register in

Estonia as a foreign national cannot be said to be in error. In light of the special role and expertise of the CRDD the Court should defer to the tribunal's assessment on issues of this sort which fall within its particular specialized capacities, unless the tribunal's finding is found to be patently unreasonable.

## Section F

*Jayasekara v. Canada (Minister of Citizenship & Immigration)* (2008), 76 Imm. L.R. (3d) 159, 305 D.L.R. (4th) 630, 384 N.R. 293, 2008 CarswellNat 5525, 2008 CarswellNat 4718, 2008 FCA 404 (C.A.) — The Board heard the appellant's refugee claim and found that he was excluded from refugee protection under s. 98 of the IRPA and Article 1F(b) of the Convention because there were serious reasons for considering that he had committed a serious non-political crime outside of Canada and that he had not completed his sentence as he fled the United States during his probation. Moreover, it found that, even if the appellant was not excludable under Article 1F(b) of the Convention, he did not meet the criteria for either Convention refugee status or as a person requiring protection. These findings based on credibility were not contested. The appellant sought judicial review before the Federal Court only of his exclusion under s. 98 of the IRPA and Article 1F(b) of the Convention.

The Federal Court of Appeal confirmed that the Federal Court judge did not commit an error when he concluded that it was reasonable for the Board to conclude on these facts that the appellant's conviction in the United States gave it a serious reason to believe that he had committed a serious non-political crime outside the country. Serving a sentence for a serious crime prior to coming to Canada does not allow one to avoid the application of Article 1F(b) of the Convention relating to the Status of Refugees.

*Zazai v. Canada (Minister of Citizenship & Immigration)*, [2005] F.C.J. No. 1567, 50 Imm. L.R. (3d) 107, 259 D.L.R. (4th) 281, 339 N.R. 201, 2005 CarswellNat 2933, 2005 CarswellNat 4771, 2005 FCA 303 (Fed. C.A.) — The appellant came to Canada as a stowaway and made a refugee claim. The Refugee Board determined that he was excluded from the definition of Convention refugee under subs. 2(1) of the *Immigration Act*, R.S.C. 1985, because of Section F(a) of Article 1 of the United Nations Convention relating to the status of refugees. The Board found that there were serious reasons for considering that he had committed crimes against humanity. His application for leave with respect to the Refugee Board's decision was denied. He subsequently submitted an application for landing as a post-determination refugee claimant in Canada. A report under s. 27(2) of the former Act was prepared and a s. 27(3) direction for inquiry was issued. The inquiry was held before an adjudicator who concluded that the appellant was a person described in paragraph 27(2)(a) coupled with paragraph 19(1)(j) of the former Act. As a result, the adjudicator determined that he was subject to a deportation order. The appellant successfully sought leave to apply for judicial review of the adjudicator's decision. The Federal Court Trial Division allowed the application and the Minister appealed. The appeal to the Federal Court of Appeal was allowed and the order of the applications judge was set aside and remitted back to the Federal Court for redetermination.

The Federal Court of Appeal concluded that the definition of "crime against humanity" found at subs. 6(3) of the *Crimes Against Humanity and War Crimes Act* includes complicity.

As a matter of fact, as found by the adjudicator and agreed by the reviewing judge, there was sufficient cogent evidence that the appellant was, knowingly and voluntarily, a participating and active member for five years in a secret service organization within the Ministry of State Security known as KHAD that tortured and eliminated people who were against the government. The evidence revealed that the appellant entered as a lieutenant and rose to the level of captain. Not only did he share and espouse the views of the brutal organization, he attended training sessions and provided the names of those who did not cooperate.

According to the evidence, the appellant was willingly and to his benefit a member of an organization that only existed for a limited brutal purpose. Under both Canadian and international jurisprudence, the behaviour of the appellant amounted to complicity in the commission of crimes against humanity. Consequently, the Federal Court judge properly confirmed the decision of the adjudicator that the appellant was inadmissible pursuant to paragraph 19(1)(j) of the former Act or paragraph 35(1)(a) of the new Act.

The Supreme Court's decision in *Mugesera vs. Canada (Minister of Citizenship & Immigration)*, [2005] S.C.J. No. 39, was distinguished on the basis that the Supreme Court in that case was not confronted with an issue of complicity in the commission of a crime by someone else. In that case, Mr. Mugesera was the actual perpetrator. Complicity is not a crime at common law and under Canadian criminal law, it was, and still is, a mode of commission of a crime. It refers to the act or omission of a person who helps, or is done for the purpose of helping, the furtherance of a crime. An accomplice is then charged with, and tried for, the crime that was actually committed and that he assisted or furthered. In other words, whether one looks at it from the perspective of our domestic law or of international law, complicity contemplates a contribution to the commission of a crime. Complicity must not be confused with the inchoate crimes of conspiracy, attempt and incitement to commit a crime. Unlike complicity, they are not modes or means of committing a crime.

*Lai v. Canada (Minister of Citizenship & Immigration)*, 2005 CarswellNat 886, 332 N.R. 344, 2005 FCA 125 (F.C.A.) — This was an appeal from a decision of an applications judge who dismissed the appellants' application for judicial review of their failed refugee claims. While various purposes of Article 1F have been identified, the primary purpose of the Article is to ensure that perpetrators of serious, non-political crimes are not entitled to international protection. The exclusion hearing under Article 1F is not in the nature of a criminal trial. In both the extradition and criminal law context, signed foreign statements taken in accordance with foreign procedural law are not inadmissible on the ground that the foreign procedural requirements are different than Canadian procedural requirements if the admission would not make the trial unfair. Enforcement processes on foreign soil are governed by the laws and codes of the foreign jurisdiction. In order for the Board to admit interrogation statements produced abroad by foreign government agencies, the Minister need only provide general evidence as to the credible or trustworthy nature of the statements offered. The Board may take into consideration specific evidence presented by the Minister or by the applicant as to the voluntariness or involuntariness of a particular statement. The legal rules normally associated with the criminal process, when dealing with the voluntariness of a statement, simply do not apply in a refugee context. Subsection 20(3) of the *Refugee Protection Division Rules* requires the Minister to state in the notice the facts and law on which he relies if he believes that Section E or F of Article 1 applies to a claim.

One of the purposes of Article 1F(b) is to protect the integrity of the refugee determination system of the receiving state by screening out serious ordinary criminals because of their criminal activities in a foreign state.

Whether a crime is political for the purposes of Article 1F(b) is determined by the motivation of the offender at the time the crime was committed.

Once excluded under Article 1F(b), claimants are not entitled to have their inclusionary claims determined. Because in this appeal the children's actions were not subject to Article 1F(b) their derivatives claims must be determined. Accordingly, it was proper for the Board to conduct an inclusionary analysis with respect to all five of the appellants in order to determine if the children's derivative claims could be successful.

*Bitaraf v. Canada (Minister of Citizenship & Immigration)*, 2004 CarswellNat 2909, 2004 CarswellNat 1941, 254 F.T.R. 277, 2004 FC 898 (F.C.) — This application for judicial review raised issues concerning the interpretation of the exclusion found in Article 1(F)(c) of the United Nations Convention Relating to the Status of Refugees.

The purpose of Article 1(F)(c) can be characterized in the following terms: to exclude those individuals responsible for serious, sustained or systemic violations of fundamental human rights which amount to persecution in a non-war setting. Two categories of acts qualify as being contrary to the purposes and principles of the United Nations: (i) those acts which have been expressly determined by the United Nations or the International Court of Justice to be contrary to the purposes and principles of the United Nations; and (ii) certain types of serious, sustained and systemic violations of human rights constituting persecution.

In order to make a finding under Article 1(F)(c) given its potential breadth, the panel ought to have had regard for such matters as the United Nations Security Council Resolution 1377, both as regards to the MEK and, more importantly, the specific conduct of the applicant.

Mere membership in an organization is insufficient to incur exclusion except where the organization is one of limited brutal purpose and absence of membership is likewise insufficient where there is personal and knowing participation. It is essential that the panel focus on the specific acts of the person, their nature, quality and the circumstances thereof and their relationship of those acts to the offending acts or practices of the subject organization.

In order for the applicant to be an accomplice, the Board has to address whether he had a shared common purpose with MEK and whether there was personal and knowing participation in the organization.

*Xie v. Canada (Minister of Citizenship & Immigration)* (2003), [2004] 2 F.C.R. 372, 34 Imm. L.R. (3d) 220, 2003 CarswellNat 4640, 2003 CarswellNat 2942, 239 F.T.R. 59, 2003 FC 1023 (F.C.); affirmed (2004), 37 Imm. L.R. (3d) 163, 2004 CarswellNat 2036, 2004 FCA 250, [2004] F.C.J. No. 1142, 2004 CarswellNat 3972, 325 N.R. 255, [2005] 1 F.C.R. 304, 243 D.L.R. (4th) 385 (F.C.A.); leave to appeal refused (2005), 2005 CarswellNat 748, 2005 CarswellNat 749 (S.C.C.) — This is an application to review a negative decision of a panel of the Refugee Protection Division. The applicant was excluded under Article 1F(b) of the 1951 Convention. The standard of review for decisions under Article 1F(b) was described as follows: 1) the standard of patent unreasonableness will be applied to the panel's finding of fact and its credibility finding; 2) the determination that there were serious reasons for considering the applicant to have committed fraud or embezzlement will be reviewed according to a standard of reasonableness *simpliciter*; and 3) the standard of review of correctness will be applied to the determination that a purely economic offence can constitute a serious non-political crime, because interpreting Articles of the Convention is a determination of law. The Court determined that a serious crime should be determined by having reference to the applicable maximum sentence that could have been imposed had the crime had been committed in Canada. An examination of all the relevant surrounding circumstances can still be conducted. The fact that the offence is punishable in this case by a maximum sentence of 10 years is not the end of the analysis. Surrounding circumstances can be looked at to determine whether Article 1F(b) is applicable.

On the facts of this case, the finding of the panel that a serious non-political crime had been committed was upheld.

*Zrig c. Canada (Ministre de la Citoyenneté & de l'Immigration)*, [2003] 3 F.C. 761, 32 Imm. L.R. (3d) 1, 2003 CarswellNat 924, 2003 CarswellNat 1978, (sub nom. *Zrig v. Canada (Minister of Citizenship & Immigration))* 229 D.L.R. (4th) 235, 307 N.R. 201, 239 F.T.R. 319 (note), 2003 FCA 178, [2003] F.C.J. No. 565 (Fed. C.A.) — The appellant sought to review the dismissal of his application for judicial review of a decision of the Immigration and Refugee Board. A panel of the Refugee Division had concluded that the applicant was not a refugee on the grounds that he should be excluded because of the provisions of Articles 1(F)(b)(c). The question on appeal was whether the rules laid down by the Court in *Sivakumar v. Canada (Minister of Employment & Immigration)*, [1993] F.C.J. No. 1145, [1994] 1 F.C. 433, 1993 CarswellNat 242, 163 N.R. 197 (C.A.), on complicity by association for the purposes of implementing Article 1F(a) of the Convention were applicable in connection with an exclusion under Article 1F(b). The majority of the Court concluded that the rules laid down in Sivakumar on complicity by association were applicable for the purpose of an exclusion under Article 1F(b). Decary J.A. concurred in the result but found that the rules complicity by association developed with respect to Article 1F(a) of the Convention did not apply, as such, to Article 1F(b).

*Harb v. Canada (Ministre de la Citoyenneté & de l'Immigration)*, [2003] F.C.J. No. 108, 27 Imm. L.R. (3d) 1, 2003 CarswellNat 1279, 2003 CarswellNat 180, 2003 FCA 39, 302 N.R. 178, 238 F.T.R. 194 (note) (Fed. C.A.) — Article 1 F(a) of the United Nations Convention relating to the status of refugees should be interpreted so as to include international instruments concluded since it was adopted.

*Chitrakar v. Canada (Minister of Citizenship & Immigration)*, 2002 CarswellNat 2172, 2002 FCT 888, 222 F.T.R. 247 (T.D.) — The tribunal found that the applicant was not a refugee because he was excluded from its application by Article 1, Section F(a). It was open to the tribunal to make this finding because (1) the applicant joined the UPF and knew of the atrocities committed by the UPF's militant wing; (2) he shared the purpose of those acts and such acts constituted crimes against humanity; and (3) he did not withdraw his financing of the UPF at the earliest opportunity.

*Baqri v. Canada (Minister of Citizenship & Immigration)* (2001), [2002] 2 F.C. 85, 2001 CarswellNat 2315, 2001 FCT 1096, 2001 CarswellNat 3520, 212 F.T.R. 275 (T.D.) — The applicant sought to review a negative decision of a panel of the CRDD. The panel found the applicant complicit in crimes against humanity as a result of his involvement with the MQM Movement in Pakistan.

Absent a finding that the organization to which an applicant belongs is principally directed to a limited, brutal purpose, the Minister seeking to exclude an applicant under article 1F(a) must show that the applicant had knowledge of the crimes in question and shared the organization's purpose in committing them. Complicity in this type of situation requires evidence of a shared common purpose. A leadership position, while not necessarily justifying a conclusion of complicity, may support the inference of a knowing participation in the organization's plan and purpose to commit the international crimes in question.

The panel's decision was set aside. The panel did not characterize the MQM as an organization principally directed to a limited, brutal purpose. Neither the evidence nor the panel's decision suggested that the applicant was personally involved in the commission of the violent acts in question. The exclusion finding was linked only to the applicant's leadership role in the MQM and the inference of complicity drawn from his admitted knowledge of the violent acts committed by MQM members, despite his denial that the acts were the result of any plan or participation by the MQM.

The applicant was cross-examined by the Minister's representative, the refugee claims officer and the panel members. He was never challenged with respect to his denial of any involvement in the kidnapping or torture that was the subject of the evidence. Not a single question in this regard by any of the persons who cross-examined him was put. Their questioning focused principally on his leadership role with little, if any, probing of his advanced knowledge, planning or participation with respect to the international crimes.

Accordingly, the panel's negative finding in this regard cannot be said to have been expressed in clear and unmistakable terms. The decision was set aside.

*Zrig c. Canada (Ministre de la Citoyenneté & de l'Immigration)*, 2001 CarswellNat 2228, 2001 CarswellNat 2782, 2001 CFPI 1043, 2001 FCT 1043 (Fed. T.D.) — A majority of the judges in the House of Lords in *T. v. Secretary of State for the Home Department*, [1996] 2 All E.R. 865 (U.K. H.L.), defined a non-political [sic] crime for purposes of paragraph 1F(b) as follows: a crime is a political crime for the purposes of article 1F(b) if and only if (1) it is committed for a political purpose, that is to say with the object of overthrowing or subverting or changing the government of the State or inducing it to change its policy; and (2) there is a sufficiently close and direct link between the crime and the alleged political purpose. The Court will bear in mind the means used to achieve the political end and will have particular regard to whether the crime was aimed at a military or government target on the one hand, or a civilian target on the other, and in either event, whether it was likely to involve the indiscriminate killing or injuring of members of the public.

The word "serious" means that these are crimes that warrant an especially severe punishment thus making clear the commitment of signatories of the Convention to withhold protection from those who have committed truly abhorrent wrongs.

*Bermudez v. Canada (Minister of Citizenship & Immigration)* (2000), 6 Imm. L.R. (3d) 135, 24 Admin. L.R. (3d) 65, 191 F.T.R. 72, 2000 CarswellNat 1174 (T.D.); additional reasons at (2001), 17 Imm. L.R. (3d) 273, 2001 CarswellNat 1335, 35 Admin. L.R. (3d) 145, 206 F.T.R. 188 (T.D.) — The applicant sought to review an unsuccessful decision of a panel of the CRDD. In that decision, the panel found that the female applicant and her minor children did not have a well-founded fear of persecution. The panel also found that the male applicant did have a fear of persecution but was excluded from status as a convention refugee by Article 1(F)(A) as a person who had committed war crimes in Nicaragua.

The panel did not give the applicants notice that an exclusion based on the commission of war crimes would be considered. There are two possible grounds for exclusion under clause 1(F)(A), namely, crimes against humanity and war crimes. These two types of crimes are sufficiently different to require different evidence in argument and different submissions in response. Accordingly, the panel was required to give the applicants proper notice of the ground on which the exclusion would be considered.

War crimes have come to be understood internationally in the context of international conflict. The foundation documents for the concept of the international war crime are the London Agreement of August 8, 1945 and the *Charter* of the International Military Tribunal, Article 6. An inhumane action that would be a war crime, during war time, may well be a crime against humanity in the absence of international war. In this case, the activities of the applicant have to do with the mistreatment of prisoners in the course of a civil war. The ill treatment of civilians as a war crime is limited to crimes against the population of, or in the territory of, a country other than that of the perpetrator in the course of an international war. The CRDD made an erroneous determination of the law in relation to war crimes. The applicant may have committed a crime against humanity. The Trial Division however does not accord the CRDD deference on a matter of law. The standard is correctness and the panel erred. The decision of the panel was overturned.

*Chan v. Canada (Minister of Citizenship & Immigration)*, [2000] 4 F.C. 390, 190 D.L.R. (4th) 128, 260 N.R. 376, 10 Imm. L.R. (3d) 167, 2000 CarswellNat 1512, 2000 CarswellNat 3277 (Fed. C.A.) — Article 1F(b) cannot be invoked in cases where a refugee claimant has been convicted of a crime and served his/her sentence outside Canada prior to his or her arrival in this country.

*Wajid v. Canada (Minister of Citizenship & Immigration)* (2000), 185 F.T.R. 308, 2000 CarswellNat 978 (T.D.) — The applicant sought to overturn a negative decision of a panel of the Convention Refugee Determination Division (CRDD). The applicant was the general secretary of the TNSM in his village in Pakistan. The TNSM described itself as a peaceful movement seeking the imposition of traditional Islamic law upon certain administrative units of the northwest frontier in Pakistan. When it became clear to the TNSM that the central government was not able to satisfy its demands more militant activity resulted in the course of which hostages were taken, the local airport seized and closed and people killed. The applicant was excluded from being considered a Convention refugee because there were "serious reasons to consider that he had committed a crime against peace, a war crime or a crime against humanity. . .." It was incumbent upon the panel to identify the crime in question and to show what made it an international crime instead of merely a domestic crime. The onus of establishing that a person is excluded lies on the person asserting the exclusion. It is not for the applicant to show that the acts did not constitute international crimes.

*Sumaida v. Canada (Minister of Citizenship & Immigration)*, 3 Imm. L.R. (3d) 169, 183 D.L.R. (4th) 713, 252 N.R. 380, [2000] 3 F.C. 66, 179 F.T.R. 148, 2000 CarswellNat 23, 2000 CarswellNat 1751 (Fed. C.A.) — The respondent was a citizen of Iraq and Tunisia. He claimed to be a Convention refugee by reason of a well-founded fear of persecution in Iraq and Tunisia on the ground of his political opinion. The applicant's claim was rejected because a panel of the Convention Refugee Determination Division (CRDD) found serious reasons for believing that the respondent had committed crimes against humanity. The panel's finding that civilians were targeted victims of the respondent's crimes against humanity referred to two classes of civilians, students in the United Kingdom and their families in Iraq. Such a finding was sufficient to meet the definition "crime against humanity."

When an informant such as the respondent has knowingly directed those at the most violent point in the chain of command to their victims, it hardly lies in his mouth to say, "you can't prove anyone I informed on was actually killed or tortured." Evidence that any harm befell the alleged victims or that any crime was committed specifically against them was not required.

*Brzezinski v. Canada (Minister of Citizenship & Immigration)*, [1998] 4 F.C. 525, 45 Imm. L.R. (2d) 262, 148 F.T.R. 296 (T.D.) — The applicants claimed Convention refugee status and they were determined by the tribunal to be excluded from the definition by reason of the fact that they had committed serious non-political crimes outside the country of refuge.

The evidence was that the applicants, who described themselves as gypsies, supported themselves by stealing, both prior to seeking refuge in Canada and subsequently. Their stealing was by way of shoplifting.

The extent of theft and shoplifting in Canada may be a serious social problem. The acts of stealing acknowledged by the applicants are crimes. They are serious matters. They are not, however, serious crimes within the meaning of Article 1(F)(b), which is part of the laws of Canada through its incorporation in the *Immigration Act*. On the evidence in this case it appears that the applicants were charged with summary conviction offences in Canada. Their sentences ranged between fines and one 14-day period of detention. The sanction against the applicants' repeated conduct, should they succeed in establishing their well-founded fear of persecution in Poland, must be found in Canada's Criminal and Immigration laws. The response, however, cannot be Article 1(F)(b).

*Bamlaku v. Canada (Minister of Citizenship & Immigration)* (1998), 142 F.T.R. 140 (T.D.) — The applicant sought to review a negative decision of the CRDD, which was based on the applicant being excluded from protection pursuant to Section F(a) of Article 1 of the Convention. The applicant joined the Marine Transportation Authority in Ethiopia where he was assigned to security duties at a strategic facility comprised of a port and oil refinery. The applicant informed on some or all of the individuals he investigated to security forces of the government notwithstanding his opposition to the government. He also secretly joined the Ethiopian People's Revolutionary Party. The applicant then informed against persons who were enemies of the Ethiopian People's Revolutionary Party and turned them over to the security forces of the Ethiopian government. The result was that these persons were arrested, detained and probably tortured. The applicant expressed no remorse at this result. He acknowledged that his motivation was mixed — partly they were enemies of the Ethiopian People's Revolutionary Party, and partly he feared they represented threats of terrorist activity against the oil refinery in respect of which he was employed. The applicant testified that any such terrorist activity would have resulted in significant civilian casualties.

The CRDD made no reviewable error. The applicant in informing on the persons in question was not motivated by humanitarian considerations alone. The applicant was also motivated by the fact that such persons were enemies of the Ethiopian People's Revolutionary Party. The tribunal had reasons for considering that the applicant was a person within the scope of Section F and accordingly its decision was not reviewable.

*Pushpanathan v. Canada (Minister of Employment & Immigration)* (1998), 43 Imm. L.R. (2d) 117, (sub nom. *Pushpanathan v. Canada (Minister of Citizenship & Immigration))* [1998] 1 S.C.R. 982, 226 N.R. 201, (sub nom. *Pushpanathan v. Canada (Minister of Citizenship & Immigration))* 160 D.L.R. (4th) 193, 11 Admin. L.R. (3d) 1 (S.C.C.);

amended (sub nom. *Pushpanathan v. Canada (Minister of Citizenship & Immigration))* [1998] 1 S.C.R. 1222, 11 Admin. L.R. (3d) 130 (S.C.C.) — This appeal raised two questions: first, the standard of judicial review over decisions of the IRB and second, the meaning of the exclusion from refugee status set out in Article 1F(c) of the *United Nations Convention Relating to the Status of Refugees*. The appellant left Sri Lanka in 1983 and spent time in India and France before arriving in Canada via Italy in March 1985. He claimed Convention refugee status. The claim was never adjudicated because the appellant was granted permanent resident status in May 1987 under an administrative program. In December 1987, the appellant was arrested and charged with conspiracy to traffic in heroin. The appellant was convicted and sentenced to eight years in prison.



In September 1991, the appellant, then on parole, renewed his claim to Convention refugee status. In June 1992, a conditional deportation order was issued against the appellant. Deportation was conditional upon a determination that the claimant was not a Convention refugee and accordingly the appellant's claim was referred to the CRDD. The Board decided that the appellant was not a Convention refugee. The Federal Court Trial Division and the Federal Court of Appeal refused to reverse that decision on an application for judicial review.

A correctness standard applies to the determinations of law by the IRB.

Conspiracy to traffic in a narcotic is not a violation of Article 1F(c) of the *United Nations Convention Relating to the Status of Refugees.*

Even though international trafficking in drugs is an extremely serious problem that the United Nations has taken extraordinary measures to eradicate, in the absence of clear indications that the international community recognizes drug trafficking as a sufficiently serious and sustained violation of fundamental human rights as to amount to persecution, either through a specific designation, as an act contrary to the purposes and principles of the United Nations, or through international instruments which otherwise indicate that trafficking is a serious violation of fundamental human rights, individuals should not be deprived of the essential protections contained in the Convention for having committed those acts.

*Ledezma v. Canada (Minister of Citizenship & Immigration)*, [1997] F.C.J. No. 1664, 1997 CarswellNat 2277 (T.D.) — The applicants sought to review a negative decision with respect to their claim for refugee status.

The Board rejected the refugee claim because of a lack of credible and trustworthy evidence from the principal applicant with respect to his persecution for his political beliefs. In addition, the Board concluded that the applicant was excluded under Article 1(F)(a) of the UN convention for being an accomplice to crimes against humanity.

The Court elected to review the exclusion order to ensure that it was error free, even though the decision about the exclusion would not be dispositive of the judicial review application. Exclusion by Canada under Article 1(F)(a) of the Convention is a serious matter which could affect the applicant for the rest of his life and accordingly, even though the Board's decision would stand on the basis of its credibility findings, the Court agreed to undertake a review of the exclusion order.

*Suliman v. Canada (Minister of Citizenship & Immigration)* (1997), 133 F.T.R. 178 (T.D.) — The applicants sought to review a negative decision of a panel of the CRDD. The Board found that the male applicant was excluded under Article 1(F)(a) of the Convention on the basis that he committed crimes against humanity. The decision of the panel was set aside. The Board did not expressly consider whether the crimes committed by the police constituted crimes against humanity. Crimes against humanity must generally be committed in a wide spread systematic fashion. This requirement does not mean that a crime against humanity cannot be committed against one person, but in order to elevate a domestic crime such as murder or assault to the realm of international law an additional element will have to be found. This element is that the person who has been victimized is a member of a group which has been targeted systematically and in a widespread manner for one of the crimes of murder, extermination, enslavement, deportation or other inhuman acts. The Board should have considered whether the victims of police abuse in this case were "...members of a group which have been targeted systematically and in a widespread manner for one of the crimes mentioned...."

*Bazargan v. Canada (Ministre de l'Emploi & de l'Immigration)* (1996), 205 N.R. 282, 119 F.T.R. 240 (note) (Fed. C.A.) — The respondent joined the Iranian national police in 1960 and pursued his career there until 1980. Between 1960 and 1977, he climbed the ranks of the military hierarchy and became a colonel. From 1974 to 1977, he worked in Tehran as the officer in charge of liaison between the police forces and SAVAK. SAVAK, from which the respondent had received some of his training, was an internal security agency under the Shah's personal authority. During that period, the respondent was in charge of the network for exchanging classified information between the police forces and SAVAK. The respondent was appointed to that position because of his knowledge of intelligence, espionage and counterespionage. In 1977, the respondent became a chief of the police forces in a province in southwestern Iran and held that position until the fall of the monarchist regime in 1979.

A panel of the IRB had determined that the respondent was a refugee within the meaning of subs. 2(1) but that he was excluded from Convention protection due to Article 1(F). This decision was overturned by the motions judge on a judicial review application. A court of appeal allowed the appeal and reinstated the decision of the panel of the IRB.

The Court has expressly refused to make formal membership in an organization a condition for the exclusion to apply. Membership in an organization that committed atrocities helps to determine whether the condition of personal and knowing participation has been met. It is important not to turn what is actually a factual presumption into a legal condition.

The Minister does not have to prove the respondent's guilt. The minister has to show that there is serious reason for considering that the respondent is guilty, the burden of proof resting on a minister is "less than a balance of probabilities."

In this appeal the inferences and the conclusions of the panel were based on the evidence and were reasonable. The IRB is a specialized tribunal and it has complete jurisdiction to draw the inferences that can reasonably be drawn.

*Pushpanathan v. Canada (Minister of Citizenship & Immigration)* (1995), 191 N.R. 247 (Fed. C.A.) — The appellant left Sri Lanka in May 1983 and spent nearly two years in India. He then proceeded to Canada by way of France and Italy arriving here on March 21, 1985 where upon he made a claim for Convention refugee status. In December, 1987 the appellant was among 8 individuals arrested on charges of conspiracy to traffic in heroin. He received an 8 year sentence and was released on parole. A panel of the IRB determined that the appellant was excluded from entitlement to claim the status of a Convention refugee due to paragraph F(c) of Article 1 of the *International Convention on the Status of Refugees*.

The Court of Appeal upheld the decision of the Trial Division and concluded that paragraph F(c) of Article 1 can apply to acts committed by a refugee claimant after his arrival in Canada. It was also held that the paragraph can apply to persons otherwise within its terms, even with respect to acts not committed in the name of, or on behalf of a state. Article 1 of the Convention is dedicated to defining which individuals may have the right, in international law, to be recognized as refugees. The exceptions, found in paragraph F, deny refugee status to certain individuals who might otherwise be within the global definition. Finally, the Court concluded that trafficking in narcotics was an act contrary to the purposes and principles of the United Nations. The Court pointed out that the United Nations adopted a Convention against the illicit traffic in narcotics in 1988 and that this Convention was ratified by Canada in 1988. This Convention called upon Canada and other signatory states to establish criminal offenses domestically to prevent, among other things, trafficking in narcotics. In Canada, such a measure was the *Narcotic Control Act*, which is the law under which the appellant was convicted. Accordingly, trafficking in narcotics is contrary to the purposes and principles of the United Nations and the appellant was properly excluded from the refugee process. Accordingly, the appeal was dismissed.



*Atef v. Canada (Minister of Citizenship & Immigration)*, [1995] 3 F.C. 86, 96 F.T.R. 217, 32 Imm. L.R. (2d) 106 — This was an application to review a negative decision of a panel of the CRDD which had concluded that the applicant was a person to whom Section F(c) of Article 1 of the *United Nations Convention Relating to the Status of Refugees* applied.

The applicant, a citizen of Iran, was convicted in Canada of possession of heroin for the purpose of trafficking.

It was not necessary for the panel to determine whether the applicant was a Convention refugee within the meaning of the definition. There is no requirement for the Board to determine this question when applying Article 1F(c) of the Convention. The panel could have conducted an inclusion analysis, but there was no error in not so doing.

The applicant raised arguments suggesting that his rights under ss. 7 and 12 of the *Charter* had been infringed. The panel correctly determined that these arguments were premature. The panel was dealing with the question of whether the applicant was entitled to claim refugee status and not with the execution of the deportation order. The exclusion of an individual from claiming such status does not, by itself, imply or lead to any positive act which may affect the life, liberty or security of the person. This type of reasoning also lead to a conclusion that the applicant's arguments with respect to s. 12 of the *Charter* were also premature.

Finally, the applicant contended that the definition of Convention refugee, which incorporated Article 1F(c) of the Convention, violated the applicant's right to fundamental justice under s. 7 of the *Charter* on account of vagueness. It was argued that Article 1F(c) provided no substantive notice to society in the sense that society was given no notice of what actions are contrary to the principles and purposes of the United Nations. Further, it was argued that Article 1F(c) did not provide meaningful boundaries of conduct or delineate areas of risk because the general public is unaware of the initiatives taken by the United Nations to curb drug trafficking.

The doctrine of vagueness is founded on the principles of fair notice to citizens and the limitation of enforcement discretion. Fair notice comprises two aspects:

1. A formal aspect, namely, an acquaintance with the actual text of the statute; and,

2. A substantive aspect, namely, an understanding that certain conduct is the subject of legal restrictions.

The limitation of enforcement discretion relates to the fact that a law must not be so imprecise that the power to decide becomes fused with the power to prosecute. The various factors to be considered in determining whether a law is vague are:

A. The need for flexibility and the interpretative role of the Courts;

B. The impossibility of achieving absolute certainty, a standard of intelligibility being more appropriate; and,

C. The possibility that many varying judicial interpretations of a given disposition may exist and perhaps co-exist.

Applying those factors, the Court concluded that Article 1F(c) was not unconstitutionally vague.

*Arica v. Canada (Minister of Employment & Immigration)* (1995), 182 N.R. 392 (Fed. C.A.) — The appellant was denied refugee status because there were serious reasons for considering that he had been involved in acts constituting crimes against humanity.

Under s. 69.1(5) there is no obligation on the Minister to give notice to claimants of the former's intention to participate in the hearing. The purpose of the notice, which is directed solely at the Board, is to empower the Minister to question a claimant and other witnesses and to make representations, otherwise the Minister's participation is limited to the presentation of evidence.

Further, the Board was not required to balance the nature of the crimes committed by the appellant against the fate that awaits him should he be returned to Peru. This was the finding of the Court in *Gonzalez v. Canada (Minister of Employment & Immigration)* (1994), 24 Imm. L.R. (2d) 229. Section 7 of the *Charter*, which was not argued in the *Gonzalez* case, does not alter the extant law. A decision in which it was found that the appellant was not entitled to claim refugee status does not, by itself, imply or lead to any positive act which may affect the life, liberty or security of the person.

*Kabirian v. Canada (Solicitor General)* (1995), 93 F.T.R. 222 (T.D.) — The panel of the CRDD concluded that there was a reasonable possibility that the applicant would be persecuted if he were to return to Iran. Despite this conclusion, the tribunal found that the applicant was excluded from the definition of Convention refugee under Section F(c) of Article 1 of the Convention.

The applicant deserted the Iranian Army and took refuge in Canada in 1985. In October, 1986 he was convicted of trafficking 26 grams of heroin and sentenced to 3 years in prison. In view of the unresolved ambiguity concerning the intention of the signatories to the Convention with respect to the scope of Section F(c), the subsequent conventions and protocols of the United Nations concerning the struggle against drug trafficking should be considered when interpreting the words ". . .contrary to the purposes and principles of the United Nations."

Section F(c) of Article 1 of the Convention is applicable to someone convicted of heroin trafficking in Canada, even in the absence of proof of an international aspect to his crime. The activities of the United Nations in the struggle against illegal drug trafficking are conducted both internationally and nationally. Further, a trafficker constitutes an indispensable link in the chain of distribution of drugs.

The panel did not err in concluding that Section F(c) of Article 1 of the Convention applied to the applicant.

*Srour v. Canada (Solicitor General)* (1995), 91 F.T.R. 24 — The applicant, a citizen of Lebanon, was denied refugee status on the basis that he was a person covered by Section F(a) of Article 1 of the U.N. Convention. The Court reviewed the principles that govern this exclusion and reaffirmed that it was unnecessary to analyze the validity of the applicant's fear of persecution if the exclusion applied.

After reviewing the principles the Court applied them in this case and concluded that the applicant was rightly excluded from the definition.

*Malouf v. Canada (Minister of Citizenship & Immigration)* (1994), 26 Imm. L.R. (2d) 20, 86 F.T.R. 124, [1995] 1 F.C. 537 — The applicant sought to overturn an unfavourable decision of the CRDD. The applicant, who was a citizen of Lebanon, left there in 1977 and obtained permanent resident status in the United States. The applicant pleaded guilty to possession of cocaine for the purpose of trafficking and fled to Canada before his sentencing.

The panel excluded the applicant from the refugee process by applying the exclusion in Section F(b) of Article 1 of the Convention. That section excluded the applicant from the protection of the Geneva Convention on the basis that he had committed a serious, non-political crime outside of Canada and prior to his admission to Canada. Once the panel concluded that the exclusion clause might apply to the applicant, it should have, through the Refugee Hearing Officer, given notice to the Minister and provided an opportunity for the Minister to make representations. Then, whether or not the Minister intervened, it would have been open to the panel to conclude that the exclusion clause applied to the applicant.

For purposes of Section F(b) the country of refuge was Canada, notwithstanding the fact that there was more than one country of refuge. There were reasons for considering that the applicant had committed a serious non-political crime outside of Canada, prior to his admission to Canada as a refugee claimant, that is, in the United States.

The CRDD erred in failing to consider the applicant's Convention refugee claim as against Lebanon and in failing to balance the risk to the applicant that would flow from his return to Lebanon by reason of the exclusion clause against the seriousness of the non-political crime here at issue. Once that balancing was conducted, the panel would have been in a position to determine whether the serious non-political crimes were of such a nature as to warrant the application of the exclusion clause, and the imposition on the applicant of the risk that would flow from his return to Lebanon. No balancing would be required had the panel concluded that the applicant was not, in fact, a refugee from Lebanon.

*Gil v. Canada (Minister of Employment & Immigration)* (1994), 25 Imm. L.R. (2d) 209, 174 N.R. 292, 119 D.L.R. (4th) 497, [1995] 1 F.C. 508 (C.A.) — This case raises the question of what is meant by the phrase a "serious non-political crime" in Section F of Article 1 of the Convention.

The appellant is an Iranian citizen, the son of a wealthy family which had been an active supporter of the Shah's regime. The family experienced considerable difficulties after the coming into power of the government that overthrew the Shah. The appellant joined an underground student group and, in due course, became associated with a larger militant group of anti-government activists. In the years 1980 and 1981 the appellant personally took part in five or six incidents of bombing and arson. Those attacks were directed against wealthy supporters of the regime. These incidents lead to the injury and death of innocent bystanders. The appellant was arrested and interrogated by the authorities but never confessed to his activities and he was ultimately released by the authorities, without being charged, and eventually fled to Canada.

A panel of the CRDD found that the appellant had a well-founded fear of persecution but that he was excluded by the provision in Section 1F(b) of the Convention.

A panel of the CRDD concluded that the appellant's crimes were non-political. Accordingly, the appeal raised the question of what was meant by political crime. The characterization of crimes as political is found in both extradition and refugee law. The Court noted that there was a need for even greater caution characterizing the crime as political for the purposes of applying Section 1F(b) than for the purpose of denying extradition. The Court developed an incidence test as a means of resolving whether a crime is political. The appellant met the first branch of the test because Iran, in the years in question, was a turbulent society in which a number of armed groups were in conflict with the regime and the appellant's testimony that he was a member of one such group was accepted as credible. The appellant's claim failed the second branch of the test. There was no objective rational connection between injuring the commercial interests of certain wealthy supporters and any realistic goal of forcing the regime itself to fall or change. Further, the means used by the appellant excluded his crimes from any claim to be political in nature. The attacks were not carried out against armed adversaries and were bound to injure innocent bystanders. The use of deadly force against unarmed civilian commercial targets in circumstances where serious injury or death to innocent bystanders was inevitable rendered the violence used wholly disproportionate to any legitimate political objective.

*Randhawa v. Canada (Minister of Employment & Immigration)* (1994), 93 F.T.R. 151 — The applicant was found to have a well-founded fear for a Convention reason but was excluded as an accomplice in the commission of crimes against humanity. The applicant was a member of the Punjab State Police Force. He testified that he was aware that that organization regularly tortured and murdered suspects in the course of its investigation. The applicant testified about 3 instances where he refused to abuse prisoners with whom he was involved. Ultimately, he was asked to resign by reason of irreconcilable differences of opinion with the police.

There was no evidence before the Board about why the applicant did not resign until he was asked. He was not questioned about this issue, thus to draw an inference from the fact that he did not resign earlier, and to make a finding of a shared common purpose based on that inference, was an error. The preponderance of evidence was to the effect that the applicant shared no common purpose with the police force, notwithstanding the fact that he knew about its activities.

The finding that the applicant was an accomplice was a perverse finding because it was not supported by the evidence. Accordingly, the application was allowed and the matter was directed to be redetermined, without a hearing, in accordance with the reasons of the Court.

*Thamotharampillai v. Canada (Minister of Employment & Immigration)*, [1994] 3 F.C. 99, 77 F.T.R. 114 — This was an application for judicial review of a negative decision of the CRDD. The applicant was found, by the relevant minister of the Government of Canada in February of 1985, to be a Convention refugee. On the 30th day of August, 1990 he was convicted of conspiracy to traffic in a narcotic and sentenced to three years. The

CRDD found the applicant to have a well-founded fear of persecution. It found the applicant not to have an internal flight alternative. Despite these findings, it found the applicant not to be a Convention refugee as he was a person to whom the Convention did not apply because, in the terms of Article 1F(c) of the Convention, he was a person with respect to whom there were serious reasons for considering that he had been guilty of acts contrary to the purposes and principles of the United Nations. The crime committed by the applicant was one with international implications. Heroin was not a locally-produced narcotic. The crime in question was a crime against which the United Nations has initiated, coordinated and undertaken a range of international initiatives. It was a crime within Canada that potentially had fearful social, cultural and humanitarian, to say nothing of its economic, repercussions. Accordingly, the CRDD was correct in concluding that Article 1F(c) of the Convention excluded the applicant from Convention refugee status.



*Gonzalez v. Canada (Minister of Employment & Immigration)*, [1994] 3 F.C. 646, 24 Imm. L.R. (2d) 229, 170 N.R. 302, 115 D.L.R. (4th) 403 (C.A.) — This was an appeal from a decision of the Refugee Division, which found the appellant excluded from the definition of Convention refugee by reason of Section F(a) of Article 1 of the *United Nations Convention Relating to the Status of Refugees* because the Board found that there was serious reason to believe that the appellant had committed a crime against humanity. The Board proceeded directly to that finding and made no finding on the merits of the refugee claim. The appellant had admitted to killing civilians on two occasions when his military unit in Nicaragua encountered armed counter-revolutionaries. The Court noted that as a practical matter it would have been better had the Refugee Division dealt with the merits of the claim as well as the applicability of the exclusion. The Court noted that if the claim was well-founded but for the application of the exclusion and if it were found on appeal that the exclusion had been wrongly applied to the appellant, then the Court could have made the necessary declaration without requiring the Refugee Division to deal with the matter again. The Court found that, on the particular facts and circumstances of this case, the appellant was a soldier engaged in an action against an armed enemy and that his actual participation in the killing of innocent civilians fell short of a crime against humanity. The Court indicated that it did not wish to be understood as saying that the killing of civilians by a soldier while engaged in an action against an armed enemy could never amount to a war crime or a crime against humanity, rather, each case will depend on its own individual facts and circumstances.

*Equizabal v. Canada (Minister of Employment & Immigration)*, [1994] 3 F.C. 514, 24 Imm. L.R. (2d) 277, 170 N.R. 329 (Fed. C.A.) — The appellant was denied refugee status on the basis that he was included in Article 1(F) of the Convention and therefore excluded from the definition of refugee. The specific finding of the CRDD was that the appellant had committed crimes against humanity by torturing civilians. The appellant sought and obtained leave to apply for judicial review, which application was dismissed. The Trial Division judge certified a serious question of general importance.

The appellant was a citizen of Guatemala who was forcibly recruited by the Guatemalan military. He described in his evidence before the CRDD four military missions which involved the torture of civilians. A crime against humanity is not only a domestic offence, but is rather an offence with the additional component of barbarous cruelty. On the uncontradicted evidence of the appellant, it is obvious that he was guilty of barbarous cruelty in the four incidents he described in his evidence.

The defence of obedience to the orders of a superior based on compulsion was also considered. The first matter to be assessed was whether the orders in issue were manifestly unlawful. A manifestly unlawful order must be one that offends the conscience of every reasonable right-thinking person. It must be an order which is obviously and flagrantly wrong. The Court had no difficulty in concluding that the orders here in issue were manifestly unlawful. The appellant and two other soldiers were ordered on one occasion to beat four persons and torture them over a period of three hours. Torturing the truth out of someone is manifestly unlawful, by any standard.

On the question of compulsion, the issue was whether the appellant faced an imminent, real and inevitable threat to his life. Stern punishment or demotion would not be sufficient. The appellant's evidence summarized two reasons why, notwithstanding his understanding that the penalty for desertion was only twelve months in jail, he would be killed: first, he knew of three other deserters who were apprehended and never heard from again; second, he believed he would be killed by his lieutenant because of his knowledge of relatives of persons whom the lieutenant had tortured personally. The first reason was dismissed as it was pure speculation without any credible evidence to support it. The second reason was not supported by the record. The record established that before the third mission, the appellant advised his lieutenant that he would no longer participate in such torture. As a result he was never forced to torture anyone again. He was thereafter, on two occasions, assigned to act as a guard while others did the torturing. There was, therefore, no evidence that the appellant was facing an imminent, real and inevitable threat to his life.

Accordingly, the appeal was dismissed and the decision that the appellant had committed a crime against humanity, as that expression appears in Article 1F of the *Convention Relating to the Status of Refugees*, was upheld.

*Cardenas v. Canada (Minister of Employment & Immigration)* (1994), 74 F.T.R. 214 — The applicant was unsuccessful in his claim for refugee status because he was found to have been an accomplice to crimes against humanity. The applicant was from Chile and had an association with the political faction, the Manuel Rodriguez Patriotic Front. In quashing the Board's decision, the Court noted that the Board had made little effort to link the applicant to specific criminal activities. Rather, it chose to refer only in general terms to shootings and bombings. The Board should have endeavoured to carefully detail the criminal acts which it considered the applicant to have committed.

The Board's decision was quashed on this and other grounds.

*Sivakumar v. Canada (Minister of Employment & Immigration)* (1993), 163 N.R. 197, [1994] 1 F.C. 433 (Fed. C.A.); leave to appeal to S.C.C. refused (1996), 175 N.R. 324 (note) (S.C.C.) — The appellant was found to have a well-founded fear of persecution at the hands of the Sri Lankan government on the basis of his political opinion. The Refugee Division decided to exclude the appellant on the basis of Section 1(F)(a) of Article 1 of the *United Nations Convention Relating to the Status of Refugees* as someone who had committed crimes against humanity.

It is possible to be liable for war crimes as an accomplice even though one has not personally committed the acts amounting to the crime. The starting point for complicity in an international crime is "personal and knowing participation." Mere bystanders or onlookers are not accomplices. A person who aids in or encourages the commission of a crime, or a person who willingly stands guard while it is being committed, is usually responsible, although each case will depend upon its own facts. Further, those involved in planning or conspiring to commit a crime, even though not personally present at the scene, might also be accomplices, depending on the facts of the case. Additionally, a commander may be responsible for international crimes committed by those under his command, but only if there is knowledge or reason to know about the crimes. There can also be complicity through association. Individuals may be rendered responsible for the acts of others because of their close association with the principal actors. An individual's complicity in international crimes committed by his or her organization is stronger if the individual member in questions holds a position of importance within the organization. The closer one is to being a leader rather than an ordinary member, the more likely it is that an inference will be drawn that one knew of the crime and shared the organization's purpose in committing that crime. Remaining in an organization in a leadership position with knowledge that the organization was responsible for crimes against humanity may constitute complicity. An important factor in this type of association is whether the individual protested against the crime or tried to stop its commission or attempted to withdraw from the organization.



Association with a person or organization responsible for international crimes may constitute complicity if there is personal and knowing participation or toleration of the crimes. Mere membership in a group responsible for international crimes is not enough unless the purpose of the organization is the commission of international crimes.

Crimes against humanity are defined in Article 6 of the *Charter* of the International Military Tribunal. Crimes against humanity must generally be committed in a wide-spread, systematic fashion. Further, historically, a crime against humanity was generally committed against a country's own nationals.

The Court of Appeal on the facts of this case concluded that the appellant was properly excluded in the factual context of this case and dismissed his appeal.

*Moreno v. Canada (Minister of Employment & Immigration)* (1993), 21 Imm. L.R. (2d) 221, [1994] 1 F.C. 298, 159 N.R. 210, 107 D.L.R. (4th) 424 (Fed. C.A.) — The appellants appealed the rejection of their refugee claims because of the applicability of the exclusion clause appended to the definition of a Convention refugee. The application of the exclusion clause was premised on the Board's finding that there were serious reasons for considering that Mr. Moreno had committed crimes against humanity during the four months he served in the Salvadoran army.

In early January, 1988, the appellant, having just completed grade nine, was forcibly recruited into the army. He was sixteen years old. He spent four months in military service immersed in the army's training program. During this period he was assigned to general guard duty. On one occasion he was required to stand watch outside of a prisoner's cell — a cell to which the appellant had not been given a key — while the prisoner was interrogated, tortured and eventually killed. Later, the appellant participated in five armed confrontations with guerrilla forces over a 20-day period. As part of their training the recruits pledged their willingness to kill all guerrillas, as well as civilians believed to be guerrilla supporters. Immediately following the military campaign against the guerilla forces the appellant was granted a three-day leave. He returned home, deserted the army and fled El Salvador.

The exclusion clause does not depend on whether a claimant has been charged or convicted. The Minister's burden is merely to meet the standard of proof embraced by the term "serious reasons for considering." The standard of proof is only relevant to questions of fact. Whether the act of killing civilians can be classified as a crime against humanity is a question of law. It is also a question of law whether the appellant's acts or omissions as a guard constituted a crime against humanity. Further, it is a question of law whether membership in a military organization, such as the Salvadoran army, constitutes sufficient complicity to warrant application of the exclusion clause.

Mere membership in an organization involved in international offences is not sufficient basis on which to invoke the exclusion clause. An exception to this rule arises where the organization is one whose very existence is premised on achieving political or social ends by any means deemed necessary. Membership in a secret police force may be deemed sufficient grounds for invoking the exclusion clause. Membership in a military organization involved in armed conflict with guerrilla forces comes within the ambit of the general rule and not the exception.

With respect to a guard, mere presence at the scene of a crime (torture) is not sufficient to invoke the exclusion clause. The act, however, of keeping watch with a view to preventing the intended victim from escaping may well attract criminal liability. The Court applied the criteria in *R. v. Dunlop*, [1979] 2 S.C.R. 881 (S.C.C.) to determine this aspect of the appeal and concluded that the appellant's acts or omissions would not have been sufficient to attract criminal liability as a matter of law. Criminal liability, however, was not the only issue to be determined. The Court had to decide whether the appellant's conduct satisfied the criteria set out in *Ramirez*, namely, "personal and knowing participation in persecutory acts." A person forcibly conscripted into the military, and who on one occasion witnessed the torture of a prisoner while on assigned guard duty, cannot be considered at law to have committed a crime against humanity because *mens rea* remains an essential element of the crime. Complicity rests on the existence of a shared common purpose as between principal and accomplice. In this case, the appellant disassociated himself from the actual perpetrators by deserting the army within a relatively short period after his forcible enlistment. The closer a person is involved in the decision-making process and the less he or she does to thwart the commission of inhumane acts, the more likely criminal responsibility will attach. Sixteen year-old foot soldiers should not be accorded the same legal treatment as those who commanded the war.

The Court noted that it would have been preferable for the Board to make a determination with respect to the appellant's refugee claim, notwithstanding its decision to apply the exclusion clause.

Finally, the Court considered whether the female appellant's claim, which was dependent upon that of her husband, should fail as a result of the application of the exclusion clause. Normally, if there is a likelihood that the principal claimant will be exposed to persecution, then it is as likely that those who are dependent on that claimant will also be persecuted on the basis of that relationship. Thus, even where the exclusion clause applies to one claimant, it cannot be said that those persons dependent on that claimant will therefore no longer be subject to persecution.

Accordingly, the appeal was allowed and the matter referred to a differently constituted panel for consideration on the basis that Section F of Article 1 of the Convention had no application to the claims of these appellants.

*Nehru, Re* (1993), 21 Imm. L.R. (2d) 53 (Imm. & Ref. Bd. (Ref. Div.)) — The issue before the Refugee Division was whether the claimant was described in Schedule F as referred to in the definition of a Convention refugee. The Minister's representative referred to the fact that the claimant had been convicted of trafficking in a narcotic and sentenced to four months' imprisonment and that trafficking in narcotics was contrary to the purposes and principles of the United Nations.

The panel was of the opinion that countering world drug trafficking was a purpose of the United Nations. The panel was prepared to find that persons who committed acts that are contrary to this initiative do not deserve international protection by countries who are signatories to the 1951 Convention and the 1967 Protocol.

In this case, however, the panel viewed the claimant's involvement in the illicit drug trafficking as marginal. It noted that the length of sentence (four months) did not persuade it of the seriousness of the offence committed by the claimant. Further, the Court that convicted the claimant recommended that monies possessed by the police at the time of his arrest be returned to him. Thus, the panel concluded that the claimant should not be excluded from protection and that he was not a person described in Schedule F of the definition.

*Ramirez v. Canada (Minister of Employment & Immigration)* (1992), 85 D.L.R. (4th) 173, 135 O.R. 390 (Fed. C.A.) — The Refugee Division determined that the appellant was not a Convention refugee even though he had a well-founded fear of persecution by reason of his political opinion. The appellant was found to be excluded from the definition by virtue of Section F of Article 1 of the *United Nations Convention Relating to the Status of Refugees*. The appellant had engaged in criminal acts which were either war crimes or crimes against humanity.

The Court determined that the phrase "serious reasons for considering" appearing in Section F of Article 1 established a lower standard of proof than the balance of probabilities. The Court saw no great difference between the phrases "serious reasons for considering" and "reasonable grounds to believe" appearing in ss. 19(1)(j) and 27(1)(g) and (h).

There was no issue as to which party bore the onus. The government must establish that it has reasonable grounds for excluding claimants and accordingly bore the burden of establishing serious reasons for considering that the claimant was excluded by Section F of Article 1. Finally, the Court concluded that accomplices as well as principal actors are included in the exclusion. In order to be an accomplice the individual must be shown to be a personal and knowing participant in the crimes against peace, war crimes or crimes against humanity which are referred to in Section F. The appellant was, by his own evidence, an accomplice in acts which were either war crimes or crimes against humanity and accordingly his appeal was dismissed.

IRP Regulations

## Article 1 of the Convention Against Torture and Other Cruel, Inhuman and Degrading Treatment or Punishment

**1. For the purposes of this Convention, torture means any act by which severe pain or suffering, whether physical or mental, is intentionally inflicted on a person for such purposes as obtaining from him or a third person information or a confession, punishing him for an act he or a third person has committed or is suspected of having committed, or intimidating or coercing him or a third person, or for any reason based on discrimination of any kind, when such pain or suffering is inflicted by or at the instigation of or with the consent or acquiescence of a public official or other person acting in an official capacity. It does not include pain or suffering arising only from, inherent in or incidental to lawful sanctions.**

**2. This article is without prejudice to any international instrument or national legislation which does or may contain provisions of wider application.**

# CAN. REG. 2002-227 — IMMIGRATION AND REFUGEE PROTECTION REGULATIONS

## made under the *Immigration and Refugee Protection Act* and the *Financial Administration Act*

SOR/2002-227, as am. S.C. 2002, c. 8, s. 182(3)(a); SOR/2002-326; SOR/2002-332; SOR/2003-97; SOR/2003-197; SOR/2003-260; SOR/2003-383; SOR/2004-34; SOR/2004-59; SOR/2004-111; SOR/2004-167, ss. 1(1), (2) (Fr.), 2–4, 5(1), (2) (Fr.), 6–9, 10–14 (Fr.), 15–19, 20(1), (2), (3) (Fr.), 21, 22(1) (Fr.), (2), 23, 24 (Fr.), 25, 26(1)–(4), (5) (Fr.), (6), (7), 27, 28(1) (Fr.), (2), 29, 30(1)–(3), (4) (Fr.), (5)–(7), 31–43, 44(1) (Fr.), (2), 45, 46 (Fr.), 47–49, 50(1), (2), (3) (Fr.), 51 (Fr.), 52 (Fr.), 53–63, 64(1) (Fr.), (2)–(4), 65–73, 74(1), (2), (3) (Fr.), 75–79, 80 (Fr.); SOR/2004-217; SOR/2005-61; SOR/2005-63; SOR/2006-89; SOR/2006-116; SOR/2006-228; SOR/2007-238; SOR/2008-54; SOR/2008-188; SOR/2008-193; SOR/2008-202, ss. 1–8, 9 (Fr.), 10 (Fr.), 11; SOR/2008-253; SOR/2008-254; SOR/2008-308; SOR/2008-309; SOR/2009-105; SOR/2009-163, ss. 1, 2–13 (Fr.), 14–17, 18 (Fr.); SOR/2009-164; SOR/2009-207; SOR/2009-208; SOR/2009-210; SOR/2009-290, ss. 1, 2, 3–5 (Fr.), 6; SOR/2010-54; SOR/2010-78; SOR/2010-121, ss. 1, 2, 3 (Fr.); SOR/2010-172 [To come into force April 1, 2011.]; SOR/2010-195, ss. 1–6 (Fr.), 7, 8 (Fr.), 9, 10 (Fr.), 11(1)–(3), (4) (Fr.), (5), (6), 12, 13, 14(1), (2) (Fr.), 15 (Fr.); SOR/2010-208; SOR/2010-118.

*[Editor's Note: The* Immigration Act, *R.S.C. 1985, c. I-2 has been repealed by 2001, c. 27, s. 274(a) and replaced by the* Immigration and Refugee Protection Act, *2001, c. 27, effective June 28, 2002.*

*Despite the repeal of the* Immigration Act, *R.S.C. 1985, c. I-2, the "former Act", there are substantial transitional provisions that may apply to the particular proceeding or transaction. Reference should be made to the transitional provisions which speak to the continuing application of the former Act in certain situations in 2001, c. 27, ss. 187–201, either by express reference therein or as prescribed by the new* Immigration and Refugee Protection Regulations, *SOR/2002-227.*

*The* Immigration Regulations, 1978, *SOR/78-172, the* Refugee Claimants Designated Class Regulations, *SOR/90-40, the* Immigration Act Fees Regulations, *SOR/97-22, and the* Humanitarian Designated Classes Regulations, *SOR/97-183, the "former Regulations", have been repealed by ss. 364(a), (b), (c), (d), respectively, of the* Immigration and Refugee Protection Regulations, *SOR/2002-227, effective June 28, 2002. Despite the repeal of the former Regulations, there are substantial transitional provisions that may apply to the particular proceeding or transaction. Reference should be made to the transitional provisions which speak to the continuing application of the former Act in certain situations and as previously prescribed by the former Regulations in SOR/2002-227, ss. 316–363.]*

# PART 1 — INTERPRETATION AND APPLICATION

## DIVISION 1 — INTERPRETATION

**1. (1) Definitions — The definitions in this subsection apply in the Act and in these Regulations.**

**"common-law partner" means, in relation to a person, an individual who is cohabiting with the person in a conjugal relationship, having so cohabited for a period of at least one year.** *("conjoint de fait")*

**"excessive demand" means**

> **(a) a demand on health services or social services for which the anticipated costs would likely exceed average Canadian per capita health services and social services costs over a period of five consecutive years immediately following the most recent medical examination required by these Regulations, unless there is evidence that significant costs are likely to be incurred beyond that period, in which case the period is no more than 10 consecutive years; or**
>
> **(b) a demand on health services or social services that would add to existing waiting lists and would increase the rate of mortality and morbidity in Canada as a result of an inability to provide timely services to Canadian citizens or permanent residents.**

*("fardeau excessif")*

**"health services" means any health services for which the majority of the funds are contributed by governments, including the services of family physicians, medical specialists, nurses, chiropractors and physiotherapists, laboratory services and the supply of pharmaceutical or hospital care.** *("services de santé")*

**"social services" means any social services, such as home care, specialized residence and residential services, special education services, social and vocational rehabilitation services, personal support services and the provision of devices related to those services,**

> **(a) that are intended to assist a person in functioning physically, emotionally, socially, psychologically or vocationally; and**
>
> **(b) for which the majority of the funding, including funding that provides direct or indirect financial support to an assisted person, is contributed by governments, either directly or through publicly-funded agencies.**

*("services sociaux")*

**"student" means a person who is authorized by a study permit or these Regulations to engage in studies in Canada and who is studying or intends to study in Canada.** *("étudiant")*

**"studies" means studies undertaken at a university or college, or any course of academic, professional or vocational training.** *("études")*

**"study permit" means a written authorization to engage in studies in Canada issued by an officer to a foreign national.** *("permis d'études")*

IRP Regulations

**(2) Interpretation — common-law partner — For the purposes of the Act and these Regulations, an individual who has been in a conjugal relationship with a person for at least one year but is unable to cohabit with the person, due to persecution or any form of penal control, shall be considered a common-law partner of the person.**

**(3) Definition of "family member" — For the purposes of the Act, other than section 12 and paragraph 38(2)(d), and for the purposes of these Regulations, other than sections 159.1 and 159.5, "family member" in respect of a person means**

**(a) the spouse or common-law partner of the person;**

**(b) a dependent child of the person or of the person's spouse or common-law partner; and**

**(c) a dependent child of a dependent child referred to in paragraph (b).**

SOR/2004-217, s. 1; SOR/2009-163, s. 1

## Case Law

### Section 1(1)

#### *Common-Law Partner*

*Walia v. Canada (Minister of Citizenship & Immigration)*, 2008 CarswellNat 1079, 2008 CarswellNat 2640, 2008 FC 486 (F.C.) — The applicants sought judicial review of a decision that they were inadmissible to Canada for directly or indirectly misrepresenting or withholding material facts contrary to paragraph 40(1)(a) of the IRPA. The principal applicant had indicated that she was divorced and did not cohabitate with one Mr. Ashok Raikhywalia. An officer from the High Commission visited the applicant's village and house and discovered that she was still in cohabitation with Mr. Ashok Raikhywalia. The applicant was given an opportunity to address the officer's concerns about the misrepresentation.

The officer's finding as to the making of a material misrepresentation within the scope of paragraph 40(2)(a) of the Act was grounded in the finding that Mrs. Raikhywalia continued to cohabitate with her former husband. The question of "cohabitation", means more than simple shared residence, if that is indeed the situation here. The word "cohabitate" has been interpreted as meaning a "marriage-like" relationship characterized by the features of financial interdependence, a sexual relationship, a common principal residence, mutual obligations to share the responsibility of running the home and the "expectation each day that there be continued mutual dependency". The evidence in the record fell short of establishing these facts. The decision of the visa officer did not meet the standard of reasonableness. The application for judicial review was allowed.

*Cai v. Canada (Minister of Citizenship & Immigration)*, 2007 CarswellNat 2274, 2007 CarswellNat 5843, 2007 FC 816 — The applicant's application for permanent resident status under the Spouse or Common-Law Partner in Canada Class was refused on the basis that the applicant did not comply with Regulation 125(1)(d). At the time of the sponsor's application for permanent residence, she did not list the applicant as a non-accompanying family member and the applicant was not examined. The Court considered whether the immigration officer erred in determining that the applicant was his sponsor's common-law partner when the sponsor applied to be a permanent resident of Canada. In her application to sponsor an undertaking, the applicant's sponsor stated that her relationship with the applicant began on June 1, 2002. The applicant argued that, despite the fact that the relationship with the sponsor traces back to 2002, his relationship with his sponsor did not meet the requirements of common-law relationship as of that date. When the applicant and his sponsor began living together they were young students, and as such, they may not have made a "mutual commitment to a shared life" when they decided to live together. There was accordingly no basis on which the immigration officer could reasonably conclude that the applicant was a common-law partner of his sponsor when she submitted her application for permanent residence in January, 2005 and did not identify the applicant as a non-accompanying family member. The meaning of "common-law partner" means that the conjugal relationship is one of some permanence where the couple has made a serious commitment to one another. The applicant's application for judicial review was allowed.



**2. Interpretation — The definitions in this section apply in these Regulations.**

**"Act" means the *Immigration and Refugee Protection Act. ("Loi")***

**"administration fee" means an administration fee that represents a portion of the total average costs incurred by Her Majesty in right of Canada in respect of foreign nationals referred to in subsection 279(1), and includes the costs relating to**

**(a) examinations;**

**(b) detention;**

**(c) investigations and admissibility hearings in respect of inadmissible foreign nationals;**

**(d) fingerprinting, photographing and the verification of documents with other governments and national or international police agencies;**

**(e) translation and interpretation; and**

**(f) proceedings before the Immigration Division.**

*("frais administratifs")*

**"agent" includes**

**(a) for the purposes of section 148 of the Act, any person in Canada who provides services as a representative of a vehicle owner, a vehicle operator or a charterer; and**

**(b) for the purposes of paragraph 148(1)(d) of the Act, in addition to the person referred to in paragraph (a), a travel agent, a charterer, and an operator or owner of a reservation system.**

*("mandataire")*

**"authorized representative" means a member in good standing of a bar of a province, the Chambre des notaires du Québec or the Canadian Society of Immigration Consultants incorporated under Part II of the *Canada Corporations Act* on October 8, 2003. *("représentant autorisé")***

**"Canadian citizen" means a citizen referred to in subsection 3(1) of the *Citizenship Act*. *("citoyen canadien")***

**"commercial transporter" means a transporter who operates a commercial vehicle.** *("transporteur commercial")*

**"commercial vehicle" means a vehicle that is used by a commercial transporter for commercial purposes.** *("véhicule commercial")*

**"conjugal partner" means, in relation to a sponsor, a foreign national residing outside Canada who is in a conjugal relationship with the sponsor and has been in that relationship for a period of at least one year.** *("partenaire conjugal")*

**"Department" means the Department of Citizenship and Immigration.** *("ministère")*

**"dependent child", in respect of a parent, means a child who**

**(a) has one of the following relationships with the parent, namely,**

**(i) is the biological child of the parent, if the child has not been adopted by a person other than the spouse or common-law partner of the parent, or**

**(ii) is the adopted child of the parent; and**

**(b) is in one of the following situations of dependency, namely,**

**(i) is less than 22 years of age and not a spouse or common-law partner,**

**(ii) has depended substantially on the financial support of the parent since before the age of 22 — or if the child became a spouse or common-law partner before the age of 22, since becoming a spouse or common-law partner — and, since before the age of 22 or since becoming a spouse or common-law partner, as the case may be, has been a student**

**(A) continuously enrolled in and attending a post-secondary institution that is accredited by the relevant government authority, and**

**(B) actively pursuing a course of academic, professional or vocational training on a full-time basis, or**

**(iii) is 22 years of age or older and has depended substantially on the financial support of the parent since before the age of 22 and is unable to be financially self-supporting due to a physical or mental condition.**

*("enfant à charge")*

**"guardianship" [Repealed SOR/2005-61, s. 1.]**

**"Hague Convention on Adoption" means the Convention on the Protection of Children and Cooperation in respect of Inter-Country Adoption that was concluded on May 29, 1993 and came into force on May 1, 1995.** *("Convention sur l'adoption")*

**"Indian" means any person registered as an Indian under the *Indian Act*.** *("Indien")*

**"in-transit passenger" means a person who arrives by aircraft at a Canadian airport from any country for the sole purpose of reboarding their flight or boarding a connecting flight departing from that airport to a country other than Canada.** *("passager en transit")*

**"in-transit preclearance passenger" means an in-transit passenger who is subject to a preclearance procedure in accordance with the *Preclearance Act*.** *("passager en transit bénéficiant d'un précontrôle")*

**"live-in caregiver" means a person who resides in and provides child care, senior home support care or care of the disabled without supervision in the private household in Canada where the person being cared for resides.** ***("aide familial")***

**"marriage", in respect of a marriage that took place outside Canada, means a marriage that is valid both under the laws of the jurisdiction where it took place and under Canadian law.** ***("mariage")***

**"minimum necessary income" means the amount identified, in the most recent edition of the publication concerning low income cut-offs that is published annually by Statistics Canada under the *Statistics Act*, for urban areas of residence of 500,000 persons or more as the minimum amount of before-tax annual income necessary to support a group of persons equal in number to the total number of the following persons:**

> **(a) a sponsor and their family members,**
>
> **(b) the sponsored foreign national, and their family members, whether they are accompanying the foreign national or not, and**
>
> **(c) every other person, and their family members,**
>
> > **(i) in respect of whom the sponsor has given or co-signed an undertaking that is still in effect, and**
> >
> > **(ii) in respect of whom the sponsor's spouse or common-law partner has given or co-signed an undertaking that is still in effect, if the sponsor's spouse or common-law partner has co-signed with the sponsor the undertaking in respect of the foreign national referred to in paragraph (b).**

***("revenu vital minimum")***

**"Minister" means the Minister referred to in section 4 of the Act.** ***("ministre")***

**"National Occupational Classification" means the *National Occupational Classification* published by the Department of Human Resources Development, as amended from time to time.** ***("Classification nationale des professions")***

**Proposed Amendment — 2 "National Occupational Classification"**

**"National Occupational Classification" means the *National Occupational Classification* published by the Department of Human Resources and Skills Development, as amended from time to time.** ***("Classification nationale des professions")***

SOR/2010-172, s. 5(a) [To come into force April 1, 2011.]

**"officer" means a person designated as an officer by the Minister under subsection 6(1) of the Act.** ***("agent")***

**"port of entry" means**

> **(a) a place set out in Schedule 1; and**
>
> **(b) a place designated by the Minister under section 26 as a port of entry, on the dates and during the hours of operation designated for that place by the Minister.**

***("point d'entrée")***

**"relative" means a person who is related to another person by blood or adoption.** ***("membre de la parenté")***

**"social assistance" means any benefit in the form of money, goods or services provided to or on behalf of a person by a province under a program of social assistance, including a program of social assistance designated by a province to provide for basic requirements including food, shelter, clothing, fuel, utilities, household supplies, personal requirements and health care not provided by public health care, including dental care and eye care.** ***("assistance sociale")***

**"sterile transit area" means an area in an airport where in-transit passengers, in-transit preclearance passengers or goods that are in transit or precontrolled are physically separated from other passengers and goods.** ***("espace de transit isolé")***

**"transporter" means**

> **(a) a person who owns, operates, charters or manages a vehicle or a fleet of vehicles and an agent for that person;**
>
> **(b) a person who owns or operates an international tunnel or bridge and an agent for that person; or**
>
> **(c) a designated airport authority within the meaning of subsection 2(1) of the** ***Airport Transfer (Miscellaneous Matters) Act*** **and an agent for that authority.**

***("transporteur")***

**"vehicle" means a means of transportation that may be used for transportation by water, land or air.** ***("véhicule")***

**"vessel" means a vessel within the meaning of section 2 of the** ***Canada Shipping Act.*** ***("bâtiment")***

**"work" means an activity for which wages are paid or commission is earned, or that is in direct competition with the activities of Canadian citizens or permanent residents in the Canadian labour market.** ***("travail")***

**"work permit" means a written authorization to work in Canada issued by an officer to a foreign national.** ***("permis de travail")***

*[Editor's Note: SOR/2002-227, s. 352 provides that a person is not required to include in an application a non-accompanying common-law partner or a non-accompanying child who is not a dependant son or a dependant daughter within the meaning of s. 2(1) of the* Immigration Regulations, 1978, *SOR/78-172 (the "former Regulations") and is a dependant child as defined in s. 2 of the* Immigration and Refugee Protection Regulations, *SOR/2002-227 if the application was made under the* Immigration Act, *R.S.C. 1985, c. I-2 (the "former Act") before June 28, 2002.*

*SOR/2002-227, s. 356 provides that if a person referred to in paragraph (f) of the definition "member of the family class" in s. 2(1) of the former Regulations made an application under the former Regulations for a permanent resident visa before June 28, 2002, the application is governed by the former Act.]*

SOR/2004-59, s. 1; SOR/2004-167, s. 1(1); SOR/2005-61, s. 1

## Case Law

### Section 2

#### *Authorized Representative*

*Chinese Business Chamber of Canada v. R.* (2005), 45 Imm. L.R. (3d) 40, 2005 CarswellNat 250, 2005 FC 142 (F.C.) — On April 13, 2004, regulations came into effect that governed who may represent, advise or consult with persons subject to immigration proceedings or those making immigration applications. Since that date, only lawyers, members of the Chambre des Notaries du Québec or members of the Canadian Society of Immigration Consultants may act for a fee in immigration matters.

Notwithstanding that the *Immigration Act* conferred the statutory power to regulate who could appear before the Immigration and Refugee Board or the Governor-in-Council, there was some question as to whether the federal government could in fact legislate in this area, or whether this would be an encroachment on provincial jurisdiction. In 2001, the Supreme Court of Canada decided that while the provinces do indeed have the power to regulate professions, including the legal profession, it is Parliament that has jurisdiction over the areas of immigration and naturalization. Flowing from this is the authority to provide for the powers of immigration tribunals. One of these powers is the power to regulate who may appear. In June 2002, the *Immigration and Refugee Protection Act* came into effect. With the jurisdiction question resolved, the regulations determining who could act in immigration matters were passed.

There has been a long recognized need to regulate immigration consultants. Unqualified and unscrupulous consultants have been known to take advantage of vulnerable prospective immigrants and refugees. On October 8, 2003, CSIC was incorporated. The mandate of CSIC was to regulate immigration consultants in the public interest and, in so doing, to establish a code of conduct, a complaints and disciplinary process and a compensation fund. In January 2004, CSIC published an announcement advising that non-lawyer immigration consultants could file an "intent to register" in order to be recognized as a registered consultant at the time the regulations came into force. CSIC's by-laws, which contain the details of the regulatory scheme governing immigration consultants, were published on March 29, 2004. On April 1, 2004, the immigration consultant regulations were approved by the Governor-in-Council and came into force on April 13, 2004.

In accordance with its by-laws, CSIC has developed membership requirements, a code of conduct and a complaints and discipline process. CSIC has established errors and omissions insurance requirements and competency testing. Of the estimated 6,000–7,000 immigration consultants, approximately 1,400 have become "transitional" members.

This application for a stay of the enforcement of the regulations was refused because the applicants could not demonstrate irreparable harm.

#### *Conjugal Partner*

*Leroux v. Canada (Minister of Citizenship & Immigration)* (2007), 64 Imm. L.R. (3d) 123, 2007 FC 403, 2007 CarswellNat 2813, 2007 CarswellNat 984 (F.C.) — The applicant in this proceeding alleged that the applicant for permanent residence, a 26-year-old Moroccan citizen, was his conjugal partner. An immigration officer concluded that the applicant for permanent residence was excluded from the family class under s. 4 of the Regulations. The applicant appealed to the IAD. In dismissing the appeal, the IAD concluded that "the Appellant had failed to establish on the preponderance of the evidence,

IRP Regulations

that his relationship with the Applicant is a conjugal relationship within the meaning of s. 2 of the *Regulations*" and reaffirmed the immigration officer's opinion that the relationship was not genuine.

The Federal Court has not rendered any decision about the criteria to be used in an immigration context to determine whether there is a conjugal relationship; however, several IAD decisions have recognized the criteria in *M. v. H.*, [1999] 2 S.C.R. 3, which specifies seven non-exhaustive factors used to identify a conjugal relationship, namely, shared shelter, sexual and personal behaviour, services, social activities, economic support, children, and the societal perception of the couple. The IAD decisions recognize that the criteria in *M. v. H.* were established for couples living in Canada and must be modified for couples living in different countries. The Federal Court agreed with this approach stating that it was important to keep in mind the restrictions which apply because the partners live in different countries, some of which have different moral standards and customs which may have an impact on the degree of tolerance for conjugal relationships, especially where same-sex partners are concerned. Nevertheless, the alleged conjugal relationship must have a sufficient number of features of a marriage to show that it is more than just a means of entering Canada as a member of the family class. A conjugal relationship is more than a precursor, or plan, to share a conjugal relationship in future.

The application for judicial review was allowed. The IAD erred in law in its interpretation of s. 2 of the Regulations by restricting its analysis to the one-year period preceding the filing of the application for permanent residence. It was also impossible on reading the reasons to conclude that the IAD applied the criteria in a flexible manner on the basis of all the relevant facts in order to determine whether or not the relationship was genuine.

*Canada (Ministre de la Citoyenneté & de l'Immigration) c. Savard*, [2006] F.C.J. No. 126, 292 F.T.R. 10 (Eng.), 2006 CarswellNat 4609, 2006 FC 109 (F.C.) — The respondent, a Canadian citizen, met Mr. Samadi, a citizen of Morocco, through the internet. The respondent filed a sponsorship application to sponsor Mr. Samadi in the family reunification class as a "conjugal partner." The visa officer rejected the sponsorship application. The visa officer found Mr. Samadi did not belong in the family class as he was not maintaining a conjugal relationship with the applicant within the meaning of ss. 2 and 121 of the *Immigration and Refugee Protection Regulations*. She appealed the visa officer's decision before the Immigration Appeal Division (IAD). The IAD found that the respondent had discharged her burden of proof and that there was a conjugal relationship between her and Mr. Samadi. The IAD also found the record indicated that the couple were in love and intended to live together once he was in Canada.

The Minister argued that the IAD erred in law and in fact in finding the couple had discharged their onus of establishing that they are conjugal partners within the meaning of the IRPA and ss. 2 and 121 of the IRPR. Section 2 of the IRPR requires that the individuals be in a conjugal relationship for a period of at least one year at the time of filing of the sponsorship application. A conjugal partner need not cohabitate for at least one year. The IAD may in fact consider all of the evidence that is adduced before it. However, in this case, the IAD made no distinction between the evidence pertaining to the relevant period and the subsequent evidence. The Minister argued that the IAD considered the subsequent evidence in order to determine that the two were indeed conjugal partners, and that the IAD did not correctly interpret the language in s. 2 of the IRPR, which requires that the individuals have been in a conjugal relationship for a period of at least one year at the time of filing of this sponsorship application. The problem in this case was that it is impossible to determine from the IAD's reasons how the decision maker arrived at the finding that the respondent and Mr. Samadi were conjugal partners within the meaning of s. 2 of the IRPR. Absent a precise distinction between the evidence relating to the sponsorship period and the evidence subsequent to the application, the Court must assume that the subsequent evidence was considered. The application for judicial review was allowed.

*Gibbs v. Canada (Minister of Citizenship & Immigration*, [2004] I.A.D.D. No. 1221, 2004 CarswellNat 6212 (Imm. & Ref. Bd. (App. Div.)) — The appellant applied to sponsor the applicant to Canada as a permanent resident under the family class category. The application was refused because the visa officer concluded that the appellant and applicant had not established a conjugal relationship.

The definition of "conjugal partner" sets out three basic requirements. Firstly, the foreign national must reside outside Canada; second, the relationship must be conjugal in nature; and third, the conjugal relationship has subsisted for a one-year period.

The Board stated that in looking at other relevant factors it is significant that the parties, although living within reasonable proximity of each other in the United Kingdom and apparently able to reside together, consciously chose not to do so for economics and other reasons of convenience. The couple did not have any routine joint habits with respect to meals, housekeeping, shopping, household maintenance or other domestic duties. With respect to their financial interdependence there was none. Each was responsible for his/her own financial affairs and adequately managed their respective separate income and debt issues. The couple did not own property together and, in the relevant period, did not have any particular plans in place for the future acquisition of joint property.

The balance of evidence did not support the conclusion that the relationship between the appellant and applicant was of a conjugal nature for one year or more, as required by the legislation. While the relationship may have had some conjugal characteristics, when all was taken together, the relationship as between the appellant and applicant during the applicant's period of residence overseas was at best a precursor, or plan, to have a conjugal relationship in the future.

### Dependent Child

*Sha v. Canada (Minister of Citizenship & Immigration)*, 2010 FC 434, 2010 CarswellNat 1109, 2010 CarswellNat 2281 (F.C.) — The applicant sought judicial review of a decision to reject the inclusion of Quan Sha as a dependent child on his father's permanent residence application. The basis for the rejection was the officer's determination that the vocational school Quan Sha was attending did not meet the requirements of the *Immigration and Refugee Protection Regulations*. The officer was clearly concerned with whether Quan Sha's school met the requirements described under the "dependent child" definition in the Regulations. The Regulations require that the post-secondary institution to be "accredited by the relevant government authority." The officer's request for a China Academic Degrees and Graduate Education Development Center (CADGEDC) report was in relation to this accreditation.

In this case, the applicants were given an opportunity to respond to the officer's concerns. Consequently, the reasons were adequate and the officer satisfied the duty of fairness. What was problematic, in the Court's view, was the officer's reliance on the lack of a CADGEDC report. Neither the Regulations nor the respondent's guidelines stipulate how an officer is to determine whether a post-secondary institution "is accredited by the relevant authority." In this case, the applicants provided an answer as to why the report

IRP Regulations

would not be forthcoming, and tendered evidence that Quan's school was "accredited by the relevant government authority." The officer failed to explain why this evidence, a copy of the school's licence from the Ministry of Education, was rejected. The application for judicial review was allowed.

*Yao v. Canada (Minister of Citizenship & Immigration)*, 2009 CarswellNat 271, 2009 FC 114 (F.C.) — The applicants sought judicial review of the decision of a visa officer to exclude the son from his father's application for permanent residence on the basis that he did not meet the definition of "dependent child" in s. 2 of the Regulations. The father applied for permanent residence under the economic class including himself, his wife and his son shortly after May 2, 2007. In December 2003, the son turned 22. At that time, he was enrolled and studying at the Language College of the Immigration Services Society of British Columbia ("ISS"). He completed these programs in April 2004 and in the fall of 2004 he started the Arts and Science Program at Langara College, where he studied until August 2007, obtaining a total of 67 credits in the process.

The visa officer informed the applicants that the son was not eligible for inclusion in the application as a "dependent child" because the ISS was not a post-secondary institution and the courses in which he was enrolled from December 24, 2003, to April 15, 2004, did not constitute "a course of academic, professional or vocation training" within the meaning of s. 2 of the Regulations, and from April 16, 2004, to at least August 31, 2004, he was not enrolled and studying in any educational institution. As well, in the fall semester of 2006, the son concluded only one four credit course at Langara College and therefore was not pursuing a course on a full-time basis as defined in subs. 78(1) of the Regulations or by Langara College.

The requirement of dependency contained at s. 2 of the Regulations under the definition of "dependent child" is a public recognition of the value which our society and Parliament places on higher education. These requirements are susceptible to being applied to a number of different countries and educational systems. It is thus understandable that the definition of "dependent child" at s. 2 refers to concepts that include some flexibility in order to achieve its goals. In that sense, although an officer applies objective criteria, he or she has some discretion in their application. Although there is no obligation on a visa officer to provide a running account to the applicants of concerns with any specific answers or impressions they have given, a visa officer should provide an opportunity to applicants to comment when he or she comes to a conclusion based on their own specific standards or tests for interpreting the documentary evidence before them with a view of applying the Regulations. In the present instance, this entails that, for example, before reaching any conclusion based on s. 78 of the Regulations which is expressly said to apply only to the part of the Regulations dealing with the "federal skilled workers class", the officer should have given an opportunity to the applicants to comment in respect of her concerns that their son was not studying full time. The same reasoning would apply to the particular interpretation given by the officer to Langara College policy, as this institution offers its programs on a flexible three-semester basis as opposed to a traditional two-semester basis. If there were any doubts as to whether or not "Learn English Now" and "TOEFL Preparation" courses qualified as "courses of academic, professional or vocational training", the answer may well lie in whether these courses were part of a study plan or were prerequisites to the ability of a foreign student to enroll in a college or university in Canada. The application of the Regulations in such respects raises important policy issues which should be clarified for it appears to be dealt with differently depending on the officer. The officer should have raised her concerns with respect to these courses. The Court also found that the decision did not disclose adequate reasons, specifically as to why the officer concluded that ISS was not a post-secondary institution and whether or not the "Learn English Now" and "TOEFL Preparation" courses fell within the meaning of the expression used in clause (b)(ii)(B) of the definition of "dependent child" at s. 2 of the Regulations. The application for judicial review was granted.

*Gill v. Canada (Minister of Citizenship & Immigration)*, 2008 CarswellNat 793, 2008 CarswellNat 2416, 2008 FC 365 — The applicant indicated to the visa officer that she had taken leave from school on certain occasions — the period of her grandmother's illness — to assist in preparing for her sister's wedding. These leaves or absences from studies, however, did not, in and of themselves, constitute a sufficient period of time for her to abandon her studies. Her school transcripts and certificates attested she continued with her studies, uninterrupted; neither of the educational institutions specified considered that she had either withdrawn or abandoned her studies for any given year. No intention existed, on the part of the applicant, to withdraw or abandon her studies. Following an interview by a visa officer at the High Commission of Canada, in New Delhi, India, the applicant was deleted from the application as she was found not to have been in continuous studies nor was she found to be actively pursuing post-secondary education prior to the age of 22. The fact that the applicant had failed one year of her studies was not due to her absence or withdrawal from her studies, but was the result of poor marks and, more particularly, to "difficult personal circumstance". The visa officer was unreasonable in determining that the applicant was not "continuously enrolled in and attending a post-secondary institution" and that she was not a "dependent child" within the meaning of s. 2 of the Regulations. The application for judicial review was allowed.

*Dehar v. Canada (Minister of Citizenship & Immigration)*, 2007 CarswellNat 1401, 2007 FC 558 (F.C.) — The applicant sought judicial review of the decision of a visa officer that she no longer met the definition of a "dependent child" in s. 2 of the Immigration Refugee Protection Regulations. The officer correctly determined that the applicant did not meet the criteria in s. 2(b)(ii) of the definition of "dependent child" because she was married after the age of 22. This would be sufficient to dismiss the application for judicial review. Nevertheless, the Court commented on the second ground raised by the applicants for the purpose of assessing whether questions should be certified. The applicant submitted that the reasons of the visa officer do not adequately explain why attending a distant education wing of a post-secondary institution offends the definition of "dependent child."

The evidence *prima facie* suggests that the applicant was continuously enrolled and attending a post-secondary institution. The officer's notes and the decision letter made no reference to any of those documents nor did they provide an explanation for the officer's conclusion that attending a distant education program does not amount to "attending a post secondary institution" within the meaning of the definition of "dependent child." The officer's decision that the applicant was not attending full-time classes was therefore unreasonable. However, since the applicant had to meet all the requirements set out in the definition of a "dependent child," the application for judicial review was dismissed.

*Dhillon v. Canada (Minister of Citizenship & Immigration)*, 2006 CarswellNat 3928, 2006 FC 1430 (F.C.) — The applicant sought to include his two children — each of whom is older than 22 years of age — as accompanying family members in his visa application. To do so, it must be established that each were "continuously enrolled in and attending" and "actively pursuing" their education in a post-secondary institution.

The parties agreed that a decision issued prior to IRPA by the Federal Court of Appeal in *Sandhu v. Canada (Minister of Citizenship & Immigration)*, [2002] F.C.J. No. 299, 287 N.R. 97, 211 D.L.R. (4th) 567, 23 Imm. L.R. (3d) 8, [2002] 3 F.C. 280, 2002 CarswellNat 454, 2002 FCA 79, is instructive in the application of the definition of "dependent child" to the fact situation in this case. The visa officer must make "sufficient enquiries" to assure that the student understood the courses and made a *bona fide* attempt to assimilate the material. On the other hand, the student need not have "a mastery of the subject."

*Shah v. Canada (Minister of Citizenship & Immigration)* (2006), 56 Imm. L.R. (3d) 43, 2006 CarswellNat 2957, 2006 FC 1131 (F.C.) — This was an application for judicial review of a decision by a visa officer that the applicant was not a dependent child according to the *Immigration and Refugee Protection Regulations*; she was deleted from the permanent residence application of her parents, her brother and herself — sponsored by her sister — and her sister's husband, both citizens of Canada. The application for permanent residence was filed in November 2002. The applicant turned 22 years of age on July 27, 2001, prior to the sponsorship being filed. The applicant alleged that she was in full-time attendance at an educational institution in India and was completely dependent upon her parents for support at all times since her 22nd birthday. The only issue arising on this application was whether the post-secondary institution that the applicant had been enrolled in and attending since before the age of 22 was "accredited" by the relevant government authority. The shorter Oxford English Dictionary defines "accredited" to mean "furnished with credentials; authoritatively sanctioned." It does not equate to "recognized" in some informal sense. The onus is on the applicant to establish that she fills the criteria that entitled her to a visa to enter Canada. On a standard of review of reasonableness *simpliciter*, and taking into account the totality of evidence before the decision maker, the decision maker made no reviewable error in determining that the school was not a post-secondary institution accredited by the relevant government authority in India. The fact that graduates of the school may be "recognized" by certain government institutions in India as possessing certain academic or technical qualifications for employment simply does not equate to "accreditation by a relevant government authority."

*Hamid v. Canada (Minister of Citizenship & Immigration)*, 2006 CarswellNat 1592, 2006 FCA 217 (Fed. C.A.) — The applicant applied for permanent residence and included his accompanying family members in his application. His oldest two sons qualified as dependent children because they were financially dependent on him and full-time students. However, when the officer assessed the application 2½ years after it had been received, both sons had graduated and were no longer enrolled in full-time studies. The question to be decided in this appeal was whether the visa officer was correct to remove them from the applicant's application on the ground that they did not meet the eligibility requirement of being students when the visa application was both made and assessed.

The Federal Court of Appeal found a child of a federal skilled worker who has applied for a visa, who was 22 years of age or over, and who was considered dependent on the skilled worker on the date of the application by virtue of his or her financial dependence and full time study, but who does not meet the requirements of "a dependent child" within the meaning of paragraph 2(b)(ii) of the *Immigration and Refugee Protection Regulations*, when the visa application is determined, cannot be included as part of his or her parent's application for permanent residence in Canada. The appeal by the Minister was allowed and the order of the Federal Court was set aside and the application for judicial review was dismissed.

*Gilani v. Canada (Minister of Citizenship & Immigration)* (2005), 51 Imm. L.R. (3d) 190, 2005 CarswellNat 3692, 2005 CarswellNat 4513, 2005 FC 1522 (F.C.) — The relevant portions of the definition "dependent child" simply do not require that an applicant demonstrate that a "physical or mental" condition causing an applicant child to be unable to be financially self-supporting has existed at all times since the applicant became 22 years of age and that the condition was diagnosed before the applicant reached that age. A question was certified which read as follows: "must the condition of the inability of the child to be financially self-supporting due to a physical or mental condition be established only at the time the claim to dependency is being asserted or must it be established that such condition existed and was diagnosed prior to the child attaining the age of 22 years?"

*Lee v. Canada (Minister of Citizenship & Immigration)* (2004), 38 Imm. L.R. (3d) 220, 2004 CarswellNat 2213, 2004 CarswellNat 4989, [2005] 2 F.C.R. 3, 256 F.T.R. 172, 2004 FC 1012, [2004] F.C.J. No. 1232 (F.C.) — The definition of dependent child in the regulations expresses the intent to codify the test articulated by the Court of Appeal in Sandhu. Sub-part (A) of the definition carries forward the requirement of full-time enrolment and attendance in an educational program. Sub-part (B) articulates the requirement for a mental presence in the educational program in the form of a genuine, *bona fide* effort on the part of a student.



### *Marriage*

*Manuvelpillai v. Canada (Minister of Citizenship & Immigration)* (2010), 88 Imm. L.R. (3d) 156, 2010 FC 286, 2010 CarswellNat 2340, 2010 CarswellNat 558 (F.C.) — The applicant was a citizen of Sri Lanka who intended to marry a man who was a lawful landed immigrant resident in Canada. This man traveled to Sri Lanka where he and the applicant engaged in a ceremony in a church including exchange of rings. The evidence is equivocal as to whether the ceremony was "registered as a marriage in Sri Lanka." The Board seems to have found that it was. In any event the applicant and this man came to Canada, in particular Ontario, where, within 90 days a marriage ceremony took place and the marriage was "registered in Ontario." Later there was a falling out between the two spouses and they divorced. An appropriate order of divorce was granted by the appropriate Ontario Court. The applicant remarried a man who is a citizen of Sri Lanka. She sought to sponsor him so that he may obtain a permanent resident visa and enter Canada as a member of the family class as her husband. This application was refused and came before the Immigration Refugee Board. The Board concluded that the applicant's first marriage had taken place in Sri Lanka and since it was not "dissolved" in Sri Lanka she could not sponsor a second husband. The Board did not state any basis for its determination as to why a dissolution of the first marriage had to be obtained in Sri Lanka. It did not state why it would not consider the Ontario divorce adequate to terminate the marriage.

The *Divorce Act* does not restrict the appropriate Canadian Court from granting a divorce only in respect of marriages performed in Canada. Once a divorce has been granted it is effective throughout Canada, including, for the purposes of the *Immigration and Refugee Protection Act*. The Board, therefore, was in error in not finding that the applicant's first marriage had been terminated by the divorce.

The following question was certified:

> Whether a person legally married outside Canada who has come to Canada and subsequently receives a divorce from an appropriate court of the Canadian province in which they reside, must also secure a divorce from the country in which they were married before they can sponsor the new spouse who is resident outside Canada to enter Canada as an applicant for permanent residence in Canada.

### Relative

*Chen v. Canada (Minister of Citizenship & Immigration)* (2003), 232 F.T.R. 118, 2003 FCT 447, 2003 CarswellNat 2908, 2003 CarswellNat 1052 (Fed. T.D.) — The applicant sought to review a negative decision on a Humanitarian and Compassionate application. In 1959 the applicant and his wife put their daughter in the care of her aunt and uncle when she was only a baby. In 1961, the aunt and uncle moved from Tianjin to Hong Kong. In order to bring the little girl with them to Hong Kong the aunt and uncle needed to show authorities there a document indicating that the child had been adopted. Therefore, the applicant and his wife signed an agreement to that effect. In 1975, the aunt and uncle immigrated to Canada and brought their adopted daughter with them. The daughter was landed as a dependent daughter and not as an adopted daughter. In 1993, the applicant and his wife were reunited with their daughter. Since their reunification the applicant has been living with his daughter who was providing him with all the necessary care. The officer found that the daughter was not an eligible sponsor as she was not satisfied that a parent/child relationship existed between the applicant and daughter. Under subs. 3(c) of the *Immigration Act*, the immigration objective established is "to facilitate the reunion in Canada of Canadian citizens and permanent residents with their close relatives from abroad." In the new *Immigration and Refugee Protection Act 2001*, at subs. 3(1)(d), the related objective is "to see that families are reunited in Canada". In IRPA, s. 2, the word "relatives" means a person who is related by blood or adoption. There is room for interpretation of the law with respect to the immigration objectives and the new definition of "relative" so as not to preclude a person from sponsoring a biological parent, if he or she already has an adoptive parent. There is enough evidence to show that there is a sufficient parent/child relationship to conclude that the immigration officer made a capricious finding of fact, which fettered her discretion.

### Work

*Juneja v. Canada (Minister of Citizenship & Immigration)*, 2007 CarswellNat 636, 2007 FC 301 (F.C.) — While in Canada on a valid study permit, the applicant was observed to be working at a local car dealership in Edmonton. He was arrested for working without authorization contrary to s. 30(1) of the Act. An admissibility hearing was then convoked under s. 44(2) of the Act. The applicant was declared inadmissible and was issued an exclusion order requiring him to leave Canada. The Board was satisfied that his activity did constitute "work" under the Act and Regulations. The applicant was performing work-like tasks for the dealership but was not being paid. The employer was banking or keeping track of his hours, presumably for the purposes of paying wages if and when the applicant received an authorization to work from the department. The agreed wage was $8.00 per hour. The employer's agreement to bank the applicant's hours and to pay a wage of $8.00 per hour — albeit conditionally — was either an activity for which wages are paid or was, otherwise, in direct competition with the employment activities of

Canadians or permanent residents. The Board's finding was upheld and the application for judicial review was dismissed.

**3. (1) Interpretation — member of a crew — For the purposes of these Regulations,**

**(a) "member of a crew" means a person who is employed on a means of transportation to perform duties during a voyage or trip, or while in port, related to the operation of the means of transportation or the provision of services to passengers or to other members of the crew, but does not include**

**(i) any person whose fare is waived in exchange for work to be performed during the voyage or trip,**

**(ii) any person who performs maintenance or repairs under a service contract with a transporter during the voyage or trip or while the means of transportation is in Canada, or**

**(iii) any other person who is on board the means of transportation for a purpose other than to perform duties that relate to the operation of the means of transportation or to provide services to passengers or other members of the crew; and**

**(b) a person ceases to be a member of a crew if**

**(i) they have deserted;**

**(ii) an officer believes on reasonable grounds that they have deserted;**

**(iii) they have been hospitalized and have failed to return to the means of transportation or leave Canada after leaving the hospital, or**

**(iv) they have been discharged or are otherwise unable or unwilling to perform their duties as a member of a crew and failed to leave Canada after the discharge or after they first became unable or unwilling to perform those duties.**

**(2) Interpretation — adoption — For the purposes of these Regulations, "adoption", for greater certainty, means an adoption that creates a legal parent-child relationship and severs the pre-existing legal parent-child relationship.**

SOR/2004-167, s. 2

## DIVISION 2 — FAMILY RELATIONSHIPS

**4. (1) Bad faith — For the purposes of these Regulations, a foreign national shall not be considered a spouse, a common-law partner or a conjugal partner of a person if the marriage, common-law partnership or conjugal partnership**

**(a) was entered into primarily for the purpose of acquiring any status or privilege under the Act; or**

**(b) is not genuine.**

IRP Regulations

(2) **Adopted children — A foreign national shall not be considered an adopted child of a person if the adoption**

**(a) was entered into primarily for the purpose of acquiring any status or privilege under the Act; or**

**(b) did not create a genuine parent-child relationship.**

(3) **Sponsorship of adopted children — Subsection (2) does not apply to adoptions referred to in paragraph 117(1)(g) and subsections 117(2) and (4).**

SOR/2004-167, s. 3; SOR/2010-208, s. 1

## Case Law

*Abbasi v. Canada (Minister of Citizenship & Immigration)* (2010), 88 Imm. L.R. (3d) 174, 2010 FC 288, 2010 CarswellNat 1675, 2010 CarswellNat 560 (F.C.) — The applicant challenged a refusal of a visa officer to grant him a permanent resident visa as a member of the family class. The applicant was a Pakistan national being sponsored for landing in Canada by his wife. The refusal of the sponsorship application was based on the finding that the marriage was not genuine. Two grounds were advanced for setting aside the visa officer's decision: the finding that the marriage is not genuine is unreasonable; and that the process applied to reaching the decision offends the *Official Languages Act*, R.S.C. 1985, c. 31 (4th Supp.), because the visa officer's interview of the applicant was conducted in Urdu.

The circumstances of the marriage were unusual which, not surprisingly, raised suspicion. But the unusual circumstances should give cause for very careful consideration. A marriage is a union between two individuals, and where suspicion exists as to the genuineness of the union because an expected standard of conduct is not met, to fairly and properly deal with the suspicion, the evidence of each individual must be carefully considered. There is no evidence on the record that the visa officer provided the applicant's spouse with an opportunity to give her evidence with respect to the quality of the marriage before the decision under review was made. In a case such as this, the visa officer was required to interview both the applicant and his spouse by the best means available whether by teleconference, video conference, or personal interview. The decision under review was unreasonable.

In this case there was no breach of the *Official Languages Act*. The interview was conducted in Urdu at the applicant's request. This choice was confirmed by the visa officer at the opening of the interview. No interpreter was required as the visa officer was fluent in this language. The applicant argued that as a matter of law the visa officer was required to conduct the interview in either English or French through an interpreter who could interpret the visa officer's questions to the applicant in Urdu and his answers back in English or French to the visa officer.

Section 20(1) of the *Charter* provides a right to any member of the public in Canada to communicate with and receive available services from federal institutions in English and French. This right imposes an obligation and practical requirement on federal institutions to comply with the right. This rights based concept does not inhibit federal institutions to offer services in languages other than English or French if the members of the public involved do not wish to exercise their right under s. 20(1) of the *Charter*, and, indeed wish to conduct business in any other language to which the institution's officials are capable of reliably communicating without an interpreter. This point was made by Justice

Pinard in *Toma v. Canada (Minister of Citizenships & Immigration)*, [2006] F.C.J. No. 1000 at paragraph 33 where a visa officer conducted an interview in Arabic without an interpreter:

> If the officer speaks the applicant's language — as was the case here — it would be strange indeed for the officer to use an interpreter. There would be no need to do so. The preferable options, as the Manual suggests [Overseas Processing Manual (OP) 5], is to conduct the interview in the applicant's language.

The application for judicial review was allowed on the first ground. The following question was certified:

> Is it a breach of the *Official Languages Act* for a visa officer to conduct an interview with respect to a visa application when, at the applicant's request, the language of the interview was other than English or French and the visa officer is able to comply with the request?



*Chen v. Canada (Minister of Public Safety & Emergency Preparedness)* (2010), 2010 FC 584, 2010 CarswellNat 2957, 2010 CarswellNat 1506 (F.C.) — The applicant, a Chinese citizen, married Ms. Zou, a Canadian resident. She then sponsored him for permanent residence. When he arrived in Canada about a year later, he found her pregnant with another man's child. After a month or two, the marriage fell apart. After their divorce, he married an old flame in China and as a Canadian permanent resident endeavoured to sponsor her. At this stage, the immigration authorities became suspicious. Not only was the sponsorship of his second wife disallowed, he was also declared inadmissible for misrepresentation by directly withholding information and representing that his first marriage was genuine. The applicant appealed that decision to the Immigration Appeal Division of the Immigration and Refugee Board. His appeal was dismissed. This was the judicial review of that decision.

The basis for holding that the marriage was not genuine was that it only lasted for a short time, and that he did not immediately return to China when the marriage broke up but returned a short time later to pursue a former flame. These facts cannot establish an evidentiary basis that the marriage was not genuine in the first place. He could not know at the time of the marriage that his wife would become pregnant with another man's child a year later. As to not immediately returning to China when the marriage broke down, he said that as a cuckold he would be the laughing stock of his village. There was no evidence to contradict that statement. When he returned thereafter, it was in a different context altogether. As to not sharing the rumours regarding his wife's affair at the time of the interview, he withheld no material fact. The only fact was that he had heard rumours. Even if they were true, it did not mean that the marriage was necessarily at an end. The *Divorce Act* specifically contemplates a possible reconciliation and the divorce papers jointly signed by the parties, which are to be found in the tribunal record, contain their joint statement that reconciliation was not possible. The duty of candour did not oblige the applicant to share his worries with an immigration officer. There was no misrepresentation and no fact was withheld. The application for judicial review was granted.

*Tamber v. Canada (Minister of Citizenship & Immigration)*, 2008 CarswellNat 2867, 2008 CarswellNat 3913, 2008 FC 951 (F.C.) — Both the visa officer and the Board concluded that the marriage between the applicant and a Mr. Singh was not genuine. The applicant sought judicial review of the Board's decision. She had given birth to a baby boy on March 11, 2005, and DNA testing confirmed Mr. Singh as the alleged father with a 99.98% probability of paternity. The Board rejected the DNA evidence even though the supporting test documentation was on its face reliable and the respondent acknowledged that the analysis had been carried out by a reputable Canadian laboratory. That, however, was not the primary problem with the Board's approach to this highly determinative evidence. If the Board had reservations about the reliability of this testing or about the continuity of the blood samples, it had a clear duty to advise the applicant's counsel of its concerns. This was a proceeding that spanned two hearings separated by almost three months and there was no justification for ambushing the applicant by essentially ignoring the issue during the testimonial phase. It was open to the Minister to supervise the DNA testing and to control the continuity of the evidence obtained; it was not appropriate for the Minister to sit silently until all the evidence was in and then criticize the process as deficient. For the same reason it was unfair for the Board to reject this evidence as unreliable. It is a well-accepted principle of natural justice that the Board's concerns about the reliability of important documentary evidence must be put to the claimant either for an explanation or to allow for additional corroboration. The application was allowed.

*Chen v. Canada (Minister of Citizenship & Immigration)* (2008), 75 Imm. L.R. (3d) 282, 2008 FC 1227, 2008 CarswellNat 4076 (F.C.) — The applicant applied for permanent residence as a member of the skilled worker category. Included as family members were his wife and her son by a previous marriage. The visa officer refused the application because the officer was not satisfied the applicant answered truthfully about his marriage to Ms. Zhao. The applicant was inadmissible pursuant to s. 40(1) of the IRPA because he misrepresented material facts relating to his marriage. Accordingly, the officer was concerned whether the marriage was entered into in order for the applicant to serve as a "courier" husband and stepfather and thereby assist Ms. Zhao and her son to gain admission to Canada as family members. The officer did not advise the applicant or Ms. Zhao that the purpose for the scheduled interview was to ascertain whether their marriage was genuine.

The question of whether the officer had jurisdiction to look at the question of the *bona fides* of a marriage in a skilled worker application involves a matter of statutory interpretation. This question goes to the fundamental issue of whether s. 4 of the *Immigration and Refugee Protection Regulations*, confers jurisdiction upon an officer processing an application in the skilled worker class. The applicant had never been married before his marriage to Ms. Zhao 2½ months before applying for permanent residence and the circumstances of the marriage were inconsistent with local and Chinese customs that an unmarried young man should marry a woman 11 years his senior with a dependent child.

The Court concluded that s. 4 was not limited to family class sponsorships. Section 4 applied to family members of an applicant in the skilled worker class. However, the Court concluded that the officer denied the applicant's procedural fairness when, having not given advance notice of the purpose of the examination, she did not afford the applicants the opportunity to supply further documentation and submissions. Had the applicants been notified in advance about this issue, the potential for being denied a permanent resident visa, and the consequence of being ruled inadmissible, they could have had the opportunity to obtain additional documents and make focused submissions to the officer. The application for judicial review of both the decision of the visa officer and the immigration program manager was granted and the matter referred back for reconsideration.

*Leroux v. Canada (Minister of Citizenship & Immigration)* (2007), 64 Imm. L.R. (3d) 123, 2007 CarswellNat 2813, 2007 CarswellNat 984, 2007 FC 403 (F.C.) — The applicant in this proceeding alleged that the applicant for permanent residence, a 26-year-old Moroccan citizen, was his conjugal partner. An immigration officer concluded that the applicant for permanent residence was excluded from the family class under s. 4 of the Regulations. The applicant appealed to the IAD. In dismissing the appeal, the IAD concluded that "the Appellant had failed to establish on the preponderance of the evidence, that his relationship with the applicant is a conjugal relationship within the meaning of section 2 of the *Regulations*" and reaffirmed the immigration officer's opinion that the relationship was not genuine.

The Federal Court has not rendered any decision about the criteria to be used in an immigration context to determine whether there is a conjugal relationship; however, several IAD decisions have recognized the criteria in *M. v. H.*, [1999] 2 S.C.R. 3, which specifies seven non-exhaustive factors used to identify a conjugal relationship, namely, shared shelter, sexual and personal behaviour, services, social activities, economic support, children, and the societal perception of the couple. The IAD decisions recognize that the criteria in *M. v. H.* were established for couples living in Canada and must be modified for couples living in different countries. The Federal Court agreed with this approach stating that it was important to keep in mind the restrictions which apply because the partners live in different countries, some of which have different moral standards and customs which may have an impact on the degree of tolerance for conjugal relationships, especially where same-sex partners are concerned. Nevertheless, the alleged conjugal relationship must have a sufficient number of features of a marriage to show that it is more than just a means of entering Canada as a member of the family class. A conjugal relationship is more than a precursor, or plan, to share a conjugal relationship in future.



The application for judicial review was allowed. The IAD erred in law in its interpretation of s. 2 of the Regulations by restricting its analysis to the one-year period preceding the filing of the application for permanent residence. It was also impossible on reading the reasons to conclude that the IAD applied the criteria in a flexible manner on the basis of all the relevant facts in order to determine whether or not the relationship was genuine.

*Canada (Minister of Citizenship & Immigration) v. Nahal*, 2007 CarswellNat 178, 2007 FC 92 (F.C.) — The IAD found that the adoption was genuine because it was legally solemnized, without considering other factors to determine the *bona fides* of the adoption. This interpretation ". . . to interpret 'genuine' as 'legal' would render s. 4 of the *Regulations* redundant." The IAD erroneously addressed the questions of whether the adoption was valid or legal in the local country and did not analyze whether there was a genuine parent-child relationship created. Relevant factors to be considered under the s. 4 analysis such as the circumstances of the adoption, the whereabouts of the child's natural parents and their personal and living circumstances, financial and emotional support provided by the adoptive parents, the reasons for the adoption, and the social and legal practices in the local country, were not considered. The IAD's decision was set aside and the matter sent back for re-determination.

*Owusu v. Canada (Minister of Citizenship & Immigration)*, 2006 CarswellNat 3100, 2006 FC 1195 (F.C.) — The applicant's application for permanent residence based on a spousal sponsorship was denied on the basis that the marriage was not genuine. The Immigration and Appeal Division came to the same conclusion. The applicant sought judicial review of the Immigration and Appeal Division's decision.

"Sometimes it can be difficult to realize that many of our attitudes derive from our own culture and may not be universally shared. If these attitudes, or bias if you will, are not recognized, it is impossible to cast them aside and try to walk a mile in someone else's shoes. That is what happened in this case.

. . . . .

"Reweighing evidence is improper within the limits of the scales of justice. Those limits are set by the functional and pragmatic approach to judicial review. The range or swing of deference is narrow if the scale has been set to correctness, broader if based on reasonableness, and broader yet if based on patent unreasonableness. In this case, the simplest probing, or weighing if you will, shows that the decision cannot stand up to scrutiny.

"The panel's focus was on this being a marriage of convenience. No fault was given to the inconvenience to [the applicant] if the marriage was not genuine. The analysis was woefully inadequate. The panel engaged in conjecture, which cannot serve as an evidentiary basis for finding that the marriage was not genuine or entered into '*primarily*' for the purpose of acquiring status in Canada."

The application for judicial review was granted.

*Apaza v. Canada (Minister of Citizenship & Immigration)*, 2006 CarswellNat 606, 2006 CarswellNat 1415, 2006 FC 313 (F.C.) — The applicant's inland application for permanent residence based on humanitarian and compassionate grounds was rejected. The decision letter also stated that the case had been assessed under the spouse or common-law partner in Canada class and was rejected on that ground as well. In the opinion of the immigration officer, there was little evidence to show there was a genuine marriage and that the marriage had not been entered into primarily for the purpose of acquiring permanent residence status in Canada. The refusal letter provided no detailed reasons. The immigration officer's lengthy notes were produced only in the course of the application for judicial review. The Court concluded that the officer ignored relevant evidence that, if believed, would have significant probative value. Specifically, the immigration officer ignored evidence about the ages of the applicants, the period of cohabitation before marriage, and supporting documents, including doctors' notes, employer reference letters and the filing of joint income tax returns, in reaching her conclusion about the genuineness of the marriage. Instead, the officer focused on irrelevant matters, for example the contents of bedside tables and the timing of the wife's divorce from her previous husband, and details of the mode of transportation used for their first date, in assessing the genuineness of the marriage. The application for judicial review was allowed and referred to a different officer for redetermination.

*Gavino v. Canada (Minister of Citizenship & Immigration)*, [2006] F.C.J. No. 385, 2006 CarswellNat 561, 2006 FC 308 (F.C.) — Section 4 of the Regulations requires the focus of the inquiry to be the "marriage," its genuineness and its primary purpose. In deciding these issues, the evidence of both spouses is relevant.

*Mohammed c. Canada (Ministre de la Citoyenneté & de l'Immigration)*, [2005] F.C.J. No. 1786, 2005 CarswellNat 3499, 2005 CarswellNat 4868, 2005 FC 1442 (F.C.) — In November of 1998, a visa officer rejected an application to sponsor the applicant as a spouse on the basis that the marriage was not *bona fide*. The Appeal Division, on a balance of probability, also concluded that the marriage was not *bona fide* and dismissed the appeal. In July 2001, a second spousal sponsorship application was filed and in February 2003 a visa officer rejected that application again on the grounds that the marriage was not *bona fide*. On appeal to the Appeal Division, the Minister's representative filed a motion to dismiss the second appeal on the ground that there was *res judicata*. The doctrine of *res judicata* applies when three conditions are satisfied: the parties in the previous proceeding are the same as those in the second proceeding; the previous decision was final; and the issue is the same. The Appeal Division properly concluded that the issue to be decided was the same, after having compared the meaning of subs. 4(3) of the *Immigration Regulations*, 1978 and s. 4 of the *Immigration Refugee Protection Regulations*. Both subs. 4(3) of the old Regulations and subs. (4) of the new Regulations are intended to exclude spouses whose spousal status is not based on the creation of a *bona fide* marriage.

**4.1 New relationship — For the purposes of these Regulations, a foreign national shall not be considered a spouse, a common-law partner or a conjugal partner of a person if the foreign national has begun a new conjugal relationship with that person after a previous marriage, common-law partnership or conjugal partnership with that person was dissolved primarily so that the foreign national, another foreign national or the sponsor could acquire any status or privilege under the Act.**

SOR/2004-167, s. 4

**5. Excluded relationships — For the purposes of these Regulations, a foreign national shall not be considered**

> **(a) the spouse or common-law partner of a person if the foreign national is under the age of 16 years; or**
>
> **(b) the spouse of a person if**
>
> > **(i) the foreign national or the person was, at the time of their marriage, the spouse of another person, or**
> >
> > **(ii) the person has lived separate and apart from the foreign national for at least one year and is the common-law partner of another person.**

IRP Regulations

## PART 2 — GENERAL REQUIREMENTS

### DIVISION 1 — DOCUMENTS REQUIRED BEFORE ENTRY

**6. Permanent resident — A foreign national may not enter Canada to remain on a permanent basis without first obtaining a permanent resident visa.**

**7. (1) Temporary resident — A foreign national may not enter Canada to remain on a temporary basis without first obtaining a temporary resident visa.**

**(2) Exception — Subsection (1) does not apply to a foreign national who**

> **(a) is exempted under Division 5 of Part 9 from the requirement to have a temporary resident visa;**
>
> **(b) holds a temporary resident permit issued under subsection 24(1) of the Act; or**
>
> **(c) is authorized under the Act or these Regulations to re-enter Canada to remain in Canada.**

**(3) When certificat d'acceptation du Québec required — In addition to any visa required under this section, a foreign national who is seeking to enter and remain in Canada on a temporary basis to receive medical treatment in the Prov-**

**ince of Quebec must hold a *certificat d'acceptation du Québec* if the laws of that Province require the foreign national to hold that document.**

**8. (1) Work permit — A foreign national may not enter Canada to work without first obtaining a work permit.**

**(2) Exception — Subsection (1) does not apply to a foreign national who is authorized under section 186 to work in Canada without a work permit.**

**9. (1) Study permit — A foreign national may not enter Canada to study without first obtaining a study permit.**

**(2) Exception — Subsection (1) does not apply to a foreign national who is authorized under section 188 or 189 to study in Canada without a study permit.**

## DIVISION 2 — APPLICATIONS

**10. (1) Form and content of application — Subject to paragraphs 28(b) to (d), an application under these Regulations shall**

**(a) be made in writing using the form provided by the Department, if any;**

**(b) be signed by the applicant;**

**(c) include all information and documents required by these Regulations, as well as any other evidence required by the Act;**

**(d) be accompanied by evidence of payment of the applicable fee, if any, set out in these Regulations; and**

**(e) if there is an accompanying spouse or common-law partner, identify who is the principal applicant and who is the accompanying spouse or common-law partner.**

**(2) Required information — The application shall, unless otherwise provided by these Regulations,**

**(a) contain the name, birth date, address, nationality and immigration status of the applicant and of all family members of the applicant, whether accompanying or not, and a statement whether the applicant or any of the family members is the spouse, common-law partner or conjugal partner of another person;**

**(b) indicate whether they are applying for a visa, permit or authorization;**

**(c) indicate the class prescribed by these Regulations for which the application is made; and**

**(c.1) include the name, postal address and telephone number of any person who represents the applicant, and the person's fax number and electronic mail address, if any;**

**(c.2) if the person who represents the applicant is charging a fee for representation, include**

**(i) the name of the organization referred to in the definition "authorized representative" of which the person is a member, and**

**(ii) the membership identification number issued by that organization to the person; and**

**(d) include a declaration that the information provided is complete and accurate.**

**(3) Application of family members — The application is considered to be an application made for the principal applicant and their accompanying family members.**

**(4) Sponsorship application — An application made by a foreign national as a member of the family class must be preceded or accompanied by a sponsorship application referred to in paragraph 130(1)(c).**

**(5) Multiple applications — No sponsorship application may be filed by a sponsor in respect of a person if the sponsor has filed another sponsorship application in respect of that same person and a final decision has not been made in respect of that other application.**

**(6) Invalid sponsorship application — A sponsorship application that is not made in accordance with subsection (1) is considered not to be an application filed in the prescribed manner for the purposes of subsection 63(1) of the Act.**

SOR/2004-59, s. 2; SOR/2004-167, s. 5(1)

## Case Law

*Wang v. Canada (Minister of Citizenship & Immigration)*, 2008 CarswellNat 3897, 2008 CarswellNat 2051, 2008 FC 798 (F.C.) — The officer concluded that the applicant had insufficient points to qualify for immigration to Canada. She noted that no points were awarded for the male applicant's brother living in Canada. She determined that the evidence provided by the applicants in support of this allegation was insufficient to establish that the brother resided in Canada at the time of the decision, based on the fact that the majority of the documentation provided related to the brother's wife and not him. The brother's notice of assessment was the only document which specifically related to him. It indicated he earned a total of $2,000 in 2006. The officer noted that her records indicated that the brother had prolonged absences from Canada in the past. The Notice of Assessment was therefore insufficient evidence to convince her that he was a resident of Canada at the time the decision was made. The officer's decision was based on the insufficiency of evidence establishing the brother's residence in Canada. The burden of adducing sufficient evidence to support the application falls to the applicant. The application for judicial review was dismissed.

**11. (1) Place of application for permanent resident visa — An application for a permanent resident visa — other than an application for a permanent resident visa made under Part 8 — must be made to the immigration office that serves**

**(a) the country where the applicant is residing, if the applicant has been lawfully admitted to that country for a period of at least one year; or**

**(b) the applicant's country of nationality or, if the applicant is stateless, their country of habitual residence other than a country in which they are residing without having been lawfully admitted.**

**(2) Place of application for temporary resident visa, work permit or study permit — An application for a temporary resident visa — or an application for a work permit or study permit that under these Regulations must be made outside of Canada — must be made to an immigration office that serves as an immigration office for processing the type of application made and that serves, for the purpose of the application,**

> **(a) the country in which the applicant is present and has been lawfully admitted; or**
>
> **(b) the applicant's country of nationality or, if the applicant is stateless, their country of habitual residence other than a country in which they are residing without having been lawfully admitted.**

**(3) Applications to remain in Canada as permanent residents — An application to remain in Canada as a permanent resident as a member of one of the classes referred to in section 65 or subsection 72(2), and an application to remain in Canada referred to in subsection 175(1), must be made to the Department's Case Processing Centre in Canada that serves the applicant's place of habitual residence.**

**(4) Applications for permanent resident cards — An applicant for a permanent resident card must send the application to the Department's Case Processing Centre in Canada that serves the applicant's place of habitual residence.**

**(5) Sponsorship applications — A person who applies to sponsor a foreign national must send the application to the Department's Case Processing Centre in Canada that serves the applicant's place of habitual residence.**

*[Editor's Note: SOR/2002-227, s. 358(1) provides that a fee paid for processing an application in respect of which no decision has been made before June 28, 2002 or an application that has been refused but the refusal has not been communicated to the applicant before June 28, 2002 shall be applied to the cost of completing the processing of the application under the new* Immigration and Refugee Protection Act, *2001, c. 27.*

*SOR/2002-227, s. 358(2) provides, however, that SOR/2002-227, s. 358(1) does not apply in respect of an application for a returning resident permit.]*

SOR/2004-167, s. 6

## Case Law

*Lopez v. Canada (Minister of Citizenship & Immigration)*, 2008 CarswellNat 1325, 2008 CarswellNat 1326, 2008 FC 582 — This is the judicial review of a PPRA officer's dismissal of Mr. Lopez's application for permanent residence made from within Canada. The officer failed to take into account that s. 25 of the IRPA is driven either on humanitarian and compassionate considerations or public policy considerations. Put another way, is it Canada's public policy that a person who is not inadmissible in terms of the United Nations Convention Relating to the Status of Refugees and whose record of criminality in Canada cannot be considered because of the pardon granted to him (s. 36(3) IRPA) should nevertheless have to busk in the Montreal Metro for the rest of his life without legal status? The decision of the PPRA officer was an important one which affected Mr. Lopez's life in a fundamental way. In this case, the officer failed to assure himself that there was a public policy consideration present. The question is not whether there would be an unusual, underserved or disproportionate hardship if Mr. Lopez had to leave Canada. The truth is he cannot leave Canada since Cuba won't take him back and the authorities know it. Mr. Lopez had not applied for permanent residence from abroad because he could not. The application for judicial review was granted and the matter referred back to another officer for redetermination.

*Ramos-Frances v. Canada (Minister of Citizenship & Immigration)*, [2007] F.C.J. No. 192, 2007 CarswellNat 278, 2007 FC 142 (F.C.) — The applicant, a citizen of Spain, applied for permanent residence as a skilled worker. At the time of his application, he was working in Canada as authorized by a work permit. Therefore, his application for permanent residence was filed at the Canadian Consulate in Buffalo. The applicant received a letter advising that he was required to attend a personal interview at the Canadian Consulate in Detroit, Michigan. He responded advising that he no longer had legal status in the United States so would be unable to attend an interview in Detroit. He stated that he was now living in Chile and requested his file be transferred to the Canadian Embassy in Santiago, Chile, to attend an interview there. This request was refused.



The applicant claimed he was denied procedural fairness because his request for the transfer of his file was unfairly and unreasonably refused. The requirements of s. 11 of the Regulations applied to this application. Chile is not the applicant's country of nationality and he provided no information in his request for file transfer with respect to how long he had been in Chile, or what his legal status in Chile was.

The applicant did not attend the scheduled interview and his application was based on the information contained within his file. The application was rejected. Given that there is no absolute entitlement to an interview, and the fact that the onus is on the applicant for permanent residence to ensure that his or her file is complete, the officer did not breach the duty of fairness, either by failing to advise about her concerns under subs. 11(1) of the Regulations or by failing to transfer the file. The application was dismissed.

*Ponomarenko v. Canada (Minister of Citizenship & Immigration)* (2003), 26 Imm. L.R. (3d) 315, 2003 CarswellNat 562, 2003 CarswellNat 1906, 2003 FCT 259 (Fed. T.D.) — The applicant, originally from Russia, applied for permanent residence at the Canadian Consulate General in Buffalo, USA. The file was transferred to New York for an interview and a visa officer there decided to transfer the file to Moscow. The applicant failed to attend his interview in Moscow with the result that the application for permanent residence was dismissed. The applicant's attempt to quash that decision failed. Visa applicants have no statutory right to have their applications processed at any particular visa post. While efforts should be made to accommodate applicants, in the end the place of the interview must remain at the discretion of the visa officer.

**12. Return of an application — If the requirements of sections 10 and 11 are not met, the application and all documents submitted in support of the application shall be returned to the applicant.**

## Case Law

*Mashtouli v. Canada (Minister of Citizenship & Immigration)*, 2006 CarswellNat 205, 2006 FC 94 (F.C.) — The Regulations set out a 180-day deadline for successful refugee claimants to file an application for permanent residence. The Regulations, however, do not stipulate that incomplete applications submitted on time should be rejected. On the contrary, s. 12 of the Regulations simply says that incomplete applications should be returned to the applicants. Had the Governor in Council intended that incomplete applications be rejected entirely, it would have said so. In contrast, a sponsorship application that is deficient is considered not to be an application filed in the prescribed manner: see s. 10(6) of the *Immigration and Refugee Protection Regulations*.

## Division 3 — Documents and Certified Copies

**13. (1) Production of documents — Subject to subsection (2), a requirement of the Act or these Regulations to produce a document is met**

**(a) by producing the original document;**

**(b) by producing a certified copy of the original document; or**

**(c) in the case of an application, if there is an application form on the Department's website, by completing and producing the form printed from the website or by completing and submitting the form on-line, if the website indicates that the form can be submitted on-line.**

**(2) Exception — Unless these Regulations provide otherwise, a passport, a permanent resident visa, a permanent resident card, a temporary resident visa, a temporary resident permit, a work permit or a study permit may be produced only by producing the original document.**

## Division 4 — Representation for a Fee

[Heading added SOR/2004-59, s. 3.]

**13.1 (1) Representation for a fee — Subject to subsection (2), no person who is not an authorized representative may, for a fee, represent, advise or consult with a person who is the subject of a proceeding or application before the Minister, an officer or the Board.**

**(2) Exception — A person who is not an authorized representative may, for a period of four years after the coming into force of this section, continue for a fee to represent, advise or consult with a person who is the subject of a proceeding or application before the Minister, an officer or the Board, if**

**(a) the person was providing any of those services to the person who is the subject of the proceeding or application on the coming into force of this section; and**

**(b) the proceeding or application is the same proceeding or application that was before the Minister, an officer or the Board on the coming into force of this section.**

**(3) Students-at-law — A student-at-law shall not be deemed under subsection (1) to be representing, advising or consulting for a fee if the student-at-law is acting under the supervision of a member in good standing of a bar of a province or the Chambre des notaires du Québec who represents, advises or consults with the person who is the subject of the proceeding or application.**

SOR/2004-59, s. 3

## Case Law

*Onuschak v. Canadian Society of Immigration Consultants* (2009), 86 Imm. L.R. (3d) 78, 357 F.T.R. 22 (Eng.), 3 Admin. L.R. (5th) 214, 2009 FC 1135, 2009 CarswellNat 5491, 2009 CarswellNat 4214 (F.C.) — The applicant was a member of the Canadian Society of Immigration Consultants and a would-be director. She applied to the Court for various declarations pertaining to her eligibility to run for office and as to the validity of the nomination and election procedures currently in place and other relief. The issue was whether the society is a federal board, commission or other tribunal within the meaning of the *Federal Courts Act* and, if so, whether the activities in question had a public aspect or a connotation to them or whether they were merely incidental to the society's status as a corporation incorporated under the *Canada Corporations Act.*

The Minister delegated to the society the power to set the rules to license third parties on standards set by the Minister and has prohibited immigration consultants from charging fees or having a right of standing in administrative proceedings unless they are members of the society. Thus licensing, standards and membership all form part of a single whole. A society is a federal board, commission or other tribunal, and was acting as such with respect to all aspects of the application for judicial review. Whether the Federal Court has any jurisdiction over the society other than by way of judicial review was a question to be left to another day.



*Domantay v. Canada (Minister of Citizenship & Immigration)* (2008), 73 Imm. L.R. (3d) 241, 2008 CarswellNat 3997, 2008 CarswellNat 1968, 2008 FC 755 (F.C.) — The sole issue raised by this application was whether by allowing the applicant's former representative, allegedly someone who was not a "member in good standing of a bar of a province, Chamber des notaires du Québec or the Canadian Society of Immigration Consultants", as required by the *Immigration and Refugee Protection Regulations*, to represent the applicant, the Board committed a breach of procedural fairness or natural justice. The Court concluded that there is an onus on the applicant to choose his representative. It is not the obligation of the Board to police the applicant's right to counsel, while the applicant bears the onus of establishing the circumstances surrounding his allegation that any duty owed to him was not met, and that as a result he suffered a breach of natural justice. The applicant retained the office of a Max Chaudhary to act on his behalf in his appeal before the Board and someone was sent by Chaudhary's office to act on his behalf at his hearing. That person was neither a member of the Law Society nor a member of the Canadian Society of Immigration Consultants. The Court concluded that the applicant accepted the representative delegated to him by Chaudhary's firm and that the Board fulfilled any verification duties that were incumbent upon it and that applicant had not established that the Board failed to meet its verification obligations pursuant to the Regulations, or that it committed a breach of procedural fairness or natural justice. Therefore the application was dismissed.

*Shapovalov v. Canada (Minister of Citizenship & Immigration)* (August 27, 2007), IMM-784-06 (F.C.) — The applicant sought judicial review of an immigration officer's decision to refuse the applicant's request to have counsel present at his inadmissibility interview. The respondent relied primarily on the fact that the questions posed to the applicant were not of a legal or complex nature and did not warrant the presence of counsel at the interview. The Court held that other factors identified by the applicant outweighed this consideration. Specifically, this interview was not occurring at the early stages of the process, since the applicant had previously been interviewed and a finding had been made that he met the selection criteria; the interview was to determine whether he was inadmissible and was a last crucial step in the process. Further, the rejection of an application on the ground of inadmissibility identified in this case may well hinder any future chance of success and therefore was of importance to the applicant. Thirdly, permitting counsel to attend in these circumstances to observe would not unduly encumber the efficient administration of the process. Finally, given the nature of the inquiry at which the questions were directed coupled with the fact that the application had already been the subject of a judicial review proceeding weighed in favour of concluding that the duty of fairness in these circumstances encompasses the right to have counsel present at the interview. The application for judicial review was allowed.

*Law Society of Upper Canada v. Canada (Minister of Citizenship & Immigration)* (2006), 55 Imm. L.R. (3d) 238, 2006 CarswellNat 2717, 2006 FC 1042 (F.C.) — The applicant Law Society of Upper Canada sought a declaration that the *Regulations Amending the Immigration and Refugee Protection Regulations* are *ultra vires*. The Regulations at issue provided that, subject to certain "grandfathering," only the certain persons may, for a fee, represent, advise or consult with a person who is the subject of an IRPA proceeding, before the Minister, an officer or the Board.

The Regulations were not discriminatory. The federal government has the power to choose persons who can represent others for the IRPA purposes including representations before the Board, and such persons need not be lawyers. Not to select a group of persons such as lawyers' employees, is not, in itself, discriminatory.

The following question has been certified: Are the *Regulations Amending the Immigration & Refugee Protection Regulations* (SOR/2004-59), which were enacted pursuant to s. 91 of the *Immigration and Refugee Protection Act, ultra vires*?

*Hak v. Canada (Minister of Citizenship & Immigration)* (2005), 54 Imm. L.R. (3d) 98, 2005 CarswellNat 3669, 2005 CarswellNat 5007, 2005 FC 1488 (F.C.) — The law is clear that an individual must bear the consequences of hiring poor counsel. There may be circumstances where the negligent or incompetent actions of an individual's representative may result in the person being denied a fair hearing. In this case, the applicant claimed that the failure of her immigration consultant to notify her of the date for her interview resulted in her being denied procedural fairness in the process. The applicant failed to persuade the Court that she had been denied procedural fairness in the process.

*Toor v. Canada (Minister of Citizenship & Immigration)*, 2005 CarswellNat 3256, 2005 FC 1386 (F.C.) — The applicants, having been unsuccessful Convention refugees, made an application for humanitarian and compassionate consideration pursuant to s. 25 of the IRPA. They also made an application for consideration as Post-determination Refugee Claimants. Their lawyer wrote to the processing centre in Vegreville, Alberta, in anticipation that the file would be transferred to Vancouver and might be determined concurrently with the PRRA application, advising that he would make complete representations in support of their request once the applicants received their notice to make representations and file evidence in support of the PRRA. The H&C request was turned down. No additional information was supplied by the applicants' lawyer because Vegreville ignored the fact that the lawyer's address was listed as the place to communicate with the applicants, and wrote directly to the applicants instead. The decision maker's notes to file indicate that she did not appear to have focused on what was before her and consequently the decision was held to be patently unreasonable.

*Khan v. Canada (Minister of Citizenship & Immigration)* (2005), 47 Imm. L.R. (3d) 278, 2005 CarswellNat 1716, 2005 CarswellNat 5405, 2005 FC 833 (F.C.) — There is no doubt that the onus of notifying immigration of change of addresses rests with the refugee claimant. However, where the negligence of counsel is egregious and there has been no contributing negligence or fault on the part of the applicant, the Immigration Refugee Board's decision to refuse to reopen the applicant's claim after it had been declared abandoned when the applicant failed to appear for a hearing and failed to appear at an abandonment show cause hearing can be set aside. In this case, the applicants put their trust in a consultant who led them to believe that he would take care of all correspondence with the Board, that they need not contact the Board directly and that he would advise them of any scheduled proceedings. Consequently, the Court was prepared to accept that their fault was not of such a degree that the applicants should be held accountable for their counsel's failures.

*Shirvan v. Canada (Minister of Citizenship & Immigration)*, [2005] F.C.J. No. 1864, 2005 CarswellNat 3744, 2005 CarswellNat 5233, 2005 FC 1509 (F.C.) — Before examining allegations of incompetence, the Court must first determine whether the applicants have met their preliminary burden of giving notice of the allegations to their former counsel. In this case, new counsel for the applicants wrote to the Canadian Society of Immigration Consultants to complain of their former counsel's treatment and to request that he immediately be prohibited from practising as an immigration consultant. The letter provided sufficient corroborating evidence and provided sufficient notice of the allegation to the applicants' former counsel.

Although the Immigration Appeal Division transcript demonstrated that the former counsel was unfamiliar with the hearing procedure, the applicants were still able to present their case. The only major ground the applicants claimed their former counsel should have raised was the best interest of the child consideration. Since the child was aged 19 or older at the time of the initial determination and at the time of the Immigration Appeal Division hearing, the Immigration Appeal Division did not err in its decision not to consider the best interest of the applicant's daughter. Accordingly, the applicants failed to demonstrate the result of their hearing would have been different but for their former counsel's alleged incompetence.

## PART 3 — INADMISSIBILITY

**14. Application of par. 34(1)(c) of the Act — For the purpose of determining whether a foreign national or permanent resident is inadmissible under paragraph 34(1)(c) of the Act, if either the following determination or decision has been rendered, the findings of fact set out in that determination or decision shall be considered as conclusive findings of fact:**

> **(a) a determination by the Board, based on findings that the foreign national or permanent resident has engaged in terrorism, that the foreign national or permanent resident is a person referred to in section F of Article 1 of the Refugee Convention; or**
>
> **(b) a decision by a Canadian court under the *Criminal Code* concerning the foreign national or permanent resident and the commission of a terrorism offence.**

**15. Application of par. 35(1)(a) of the Act — For the purpose of determining whether a foreign national or permanent resident is inadmissible under paragraph**

IRP Regulations

**35(1)(a) of the Act, if any of the following decisions or the following determination has been rendered, the findings of fact set out in that decision or determination shall be considered as conclusive findings of fact:**

**(a) a decision concerning the foreign national or permanent resident that is made by any international criminal tribunal that is established by resolution of the Security Council of the United Nations, or the International Criminal Court as defined in the *Crimes Against Humanity and War Crimes Act*;**

**(b) a determination by the Board, based on findings that the foreign national or permanent resident has committed a war crime or a crime against humanity, that the foreign national or permanent resident is a person referred to in section F of Article 1 of the Refugee Convention; or**

**(c) a decision by a Canadian court under the *Criminal Code* or the *Crimes Against Humanity and War Crimes Act* concerning the foreign national or permanent resident and a war crime or crime against humanity committed outside Canada.**

**16. Application of par. 35(1)(b) of the Act — For the purposes of paragraph 35(1)(b) of the Act, a prescribed senior official in the service of a government is a person who, by virtue of the position they hold or held, is or was able to exert significant influence on the exercise of government power or is or was able to benefit from their position, and includes**

**(a) heads of state or government;**

**(b) members of the cabinet or governing council;**

**(c) senior advisors to persons described in paragraph (a) or (b);**

**(d) senior members of the public service;**

**(e) senior members of the military and of the intelligence and internal security services;**

**(f) ambassadors and senior diplomatic officials; and**

**(g) members of the judiciary.**

## Case Law

*Segasayo v. Canada (Minister of Citizenship & Immigration)* (2010), 89 Imm. L.R. (3d) 7, 2010 FC 173, 2010 CarswellNat 323, 2010 CarswellNat 324 (F.C.) — The applicant was Rwanda's ambassador to Canada from 1991 to 1995. After the new government in Rwanda recalled him, he and his family applied for and were given refugee status by the Immigration and Refugee Board in 1996. He submitted that as a member of the Hutu intelligentsia and as ambassador to Canada appointed by the former government he feared persecution and reprisal by the new Tutsi government. He is now subject to a deportation order because he was found inadmissible to Canada for violating human or international rights. He sought judicial review of that decision. The Board determined that the applicant was a person described in s. 35(1)(a) of IRPA. The Member was of the view that the deeming provision in s. 16 of the Regulations created an irrebuttable presumption that an ambassador in the service of a government on the Minister's list was inadmissible on the grounds of violating human or international rights. In other words, once it was shown that the applicant was the ambassador of the government designated by the Minister (facts that the applicant had never disputed), then he was inadmissible and had no defence based on lack of complicity in crimes against humanity or human rights violations. The member also dismissed the argument that the provisions in question were unconstitutional as violating s. 7 of the *Canadian Charter of Rights and Freedoms*. The Court upheld the Board's decision that the applicant was inadmissible, dismissed his *Charter* argument and dismissed the application for judicial review

The following question was certified:

> Are ss. 35(1) of the *Immigration and Refugee Protection Act* and 16 of the *Immigration and Refugee Protection Regulations* in accordance with the principles stated by the Supreme Court in *Singh v. Canada (Minister of Citizenship & Immigration)*, [1985] 1 S.C.R. 177 and *Charkaoui v. Canada (Citizenship & Immigration)* (2007), 59 Imm. L.R. (3d) 1, and with s. 7 of the *Canadian Charter of Rights and Freedoms* when a person targeted by those provisions had already obtained the refugee or protected person status and does not have the right to defend him/herself against the allegations made against him/her under those provisions?

*Sungu v. Canada (Ministre de la Citoyenneté & de l'Immigration)* (2002), 26 Imm. L.R. (3d) 242, [2003] 3 F.C. 192, 2002 CarswellNat 3326, 2002 CarswellNat 4178, 2002 FCT 1207, 230 F.T.R. 67 (T.D.) — The male applicant was an elected deputy or member of Parliament for the city of Kinshasa in the Congo from 1982 to 1987. From 1987 to 1990 he remained an active but unpaid cadre within the MPR as an honorary deputy and member of a political judicial committee. The applicant participated in foreign missions to Brussels, France and Portugal as well as participating, while he was a deputy, in a subcommission on national defence and security. The panel determined that the applicant had not demonstrated a well-founded fear of persecution, that his testimony lacked credibility and that he was excluded from refugee protection pursuant to paragraph 1(F)(a) of the Convention because of his complicity with the Mobutu regime and crimes against humanity that were committed by that regime. The position of deputy or member of Parliament is not listed in s. 16 of the Regulations. Deputies are not persons who, by virtue of the position they hold or held, are or were necessarily persons able to exert significant influence on the exercise of governmental power. This does not exclude a situation in which such influence could be established in light of the evidence, where appropriate. There is no evidence to show that the applicant, as a deputy, participated in the promotion or preparation of laws supporting the criminal objectives of the Mobutu regime.

**17. Prescribed period — For the purposes of paragraph 36(3)(c) of the Act, the prescribed period is five years**

> **(a) after the completion of an imposed sentence, in the case of matters referred to in paragraphs 36(1)(b) and (2)(b) of the Act, if the person has not been convicted of a subsequent offence other than an offence designated as a contravention under the *Contraventions Act* or an offence under the *Young Offenders Act*; and**
>
> **(b) after committing an offence, in the case of matters referred to in paragraphs 36(1)(c) and (2)(c) of the Act, if the person has not been convicted of a subsequent offence other than an offence designated as a contravention under the *Contraventions Act* or an offence under the *Young Offenders Act*.**

IRP Regulations

**18. (1) Rehabilitation — For the purposes of paragraph 36(3)(c) of the Act, the class of persons deemed to have been rehabilitated is a prescribed class.**

**(2) Members of the class — The following persons are members of the class of persons deemed to have been rehabilitated:**

**(a) persons who have been convicted outside Canada of no more than one offence that, if committed in Canada, would constitute an indictable offence under an Act of Parliament, if all of the following conditions apply, namely,**

**(i) the offence is punishable in Canada by a maximum term of imprisonment of less than 10 years,**

**(ii) at least 10 years have elapsed since the day after the completion of the imposed sentence,**

**(iii) the person has not been convicted in Canada of an indictable offence under an Act of Parliament,**

**(iv) the person has not been convicted in Canada of any summary conviction offence within the last 10 years under an Act of Parliament or of more than one summary conviction offence before the last 10 years, other than an offence designated as a contravention under the *Contraventions Act* or an offence under the *Youth Criminal Justice Act*,**

**(v) the person has not within the last 10 years been convicted outside Canada of an offence that, if committed in Canada, would constitute an offence under an Act of Parliament, other than an offence designated as a contravention under the *Contraventions Act* or an offence under the *Youth Criminal Justice Act*,**

**(vi) the person has not before the last 10 years been convicted outside Canada of more than one offence that, if committed in Canada, would constitute a summary conviction offence under an Act of Parliament, and**

**(vii) the person has not committed an act described in paragraph 36(2)(c) of the Act;**

**(b) persons convicted outside Canada of two or more offences that, if committed in Canada, would constitute summary conviction offences under any Act of Parliament, if all of the following conditions apply, namely,**

**(i) at least five years have elapsed since the day after the completion of the imposed sentences,**

**(ii) the person has not been convicted in Canada of an indictable offence under an Act of Parliament,**

**(iii) the person has not within the last five years been convicted in Canada of an offence under an Act of Parliament, other than an offence designated as a contravention under the *Contraventions Act* or an offence under the *Youth Criminal Justice Act*,**

**(iv) the person has not within the last five years been convicted outside Canada of an offence that, if committed in Canada, would constitute an offence under an Act of Parliament, other than an offence designated as a contravention under the *Contraventions Act* or an offence under the *Youth Criminal Justice Act*,**

**(v) the person has not before the last five years been convicted in Canada of more than one summary conviction offence under an Act of Parliament, other than an offence designated as a contravention under the *Contraventions Act* or an offence under the *Youth Criminal Justice Act*,**

**(vi) the person has not been convicted of an offence referred to in paragraph 36(2)(b) of the Act that, if committed in Canada, would constitute an indictable offence, and**

**(vii) the person has not committed an act described in paragraph 36(2)(c) of the Act; and**

**(c) persons who have committed no more than one act outside Canada that is an offence in the place where it was committed and that, if committed in Canada, would constitute an indictable offence under an Act of Parliament, if all of the following conditions apply, namely,**

**(i) the offence is punishable in Canada by a maximum term of imprisonment of less than 10 years,**

**(ii) at least 10 years have elapsed since the day after the commission of the offence,**

**(iii) the person has not been convicted in Canada of an indictable offence under an Act of Parliament,**

**(iv) the person has not been convicted in Canada of any summary conviction offence within the last 10 years under an Act of Parliament or of more than one summary conviction offence before the last 10 years, other than an offence designated as a contravention under the *Contraventions Act* or an offence under the *Youth Criminal Justice Act*,**

**(v) the person has not within the last 10 years been convicted outside of Canada of an offence that, if committed in Canada, would constitute an offence under an Act of Parliament, other than an offence designated as a contravention under the *Contraventions Act* or an offence under the *Youth Criminal Justice Act*,**

**(vi) the person has not before the last 10 years been convicted outside Canada of more than one offence that, if committed in Canada, would constitute a summary conviction offence under an Act of Parliament, and**

**(vii) the person has not been convicted outside of Canada of an offence that, if committed in Canada, would constitute an indictable offence under an Act of Parliament.**

SOR/2004-167, s. 7

**18.1** (1) **Prescribed class** — **The class of foreign nationals who are inadmissible solely on the basis of having been convicted in Canada of two or more offences that may only be prosecuted summarily, under any Act of Parliament, is a prescribed class for the application of paragraph 36(2)(a) of the Act.**

(2) **Exemption** — **A member of the class prescribed in subsection (1) is exempt from the application of paragraph 36(2)(a) of the Act if it has been at least five years since the day after the completion of the imposed sentences.**

SOR/2004-167, s. 8

**19. Transborder crime** — For the purposes of paragraph 36(2)(d) of the Act, indictable offences under the following Acts of Parliament are prescribed:

(a) the *Criminal Code*;

(b) the *Immigration and Refugee Protection Act*;

(c) the *Firearms Act*;

(d) the *Customs Act*; and

(e) the *Controlled Drugs and Substances Act*.

**20. Assessment of inadmissibility on health grounds** — An officer shall determine that a foreign national is inadmissible on health grounds if an assessment of their health condition has been made by an officer who is responsible for the application of sections 29 to 34 and the officer concluded that the foreign national's health condition is likely to be a danger to public health or public safety or might reasonably be expected to cause excessive demand.

**21. Financial reasons** — Protected persons within the meaning of subsection 95(2) of the Act are exempted from the application of section 39 of the Act.

**22. Misrepresentation** — Persons who have claimed refugee protection, if disposition of the claim is pending, and protected persons within the meaning of subsection 95(2) of the Act are exempted from the application of paragraph 40(1)(a) of the Act.

**23. Prescribed circumstances — family members** — For the purposes of paragraph 42(a) of the Act, the prescribed circumstances in which the foreign national is inadmissible on grounds of an inadmissible non-accompanying family member are that

(a) the foreign national has made an application for a permanent resident visa or to remain in Canada as a permanent resident; and

(b) the non-accompanying family member is

(i) the spouse of the foreign national, except where the relationship between the spouse and foreign national has broken down in law or in fact,

(ii) the common-law partner of the foreign national,

(iii) a dependent child of the foreign national and either the foreign national or an accompanying family member of the foreign national has custody of that child or is empowered to act on behalf of that child by virtue of a court order or written agreement or by operation of law, or

(iv) a dependent child of a dependent child of the foreign national and the foreign national, a dependent child of the foreign national or any other accompanying family member of the foreign national has custody of that child or is empowered to act on behalf of that child by virtue of a court order or written agreement or by operation of law.

24. **Exception to excessive demand** — For the purposes of subsection 38(2) of the Act, a foreign national who has been determined to be a member of the family class is exempted from the application of paragraph 38(1)(c) of the Act if they are

(a) in respect of the sponsor, their conjugal partner, their dependent child or a person referred to in paragraph 117(1)(g); or

(b) in respect of the spouse, common-law partner or conjugal partner of the sponsor, their dependent child.

SOR/2005-61, s. 2

# PART 4 — PROCEDURES

## DIVISION 1 — VISA ISSUANCE

25. **When unenforced removal order** — A visa shall not be issued to a foreign national who is subject to an unenforced removal order.

## DIVISION 2 — AUTHORIZATION TO ENTER CANADA

26. **Designation of ports of entry** — The Minister may, on the basis of the following factors, designate a place as a port of entry as well as the port of entry's dates and hours of operation:

(a) the frequency or anticipated frequency of persons arriving from abroad in the area under consideration;

(b) the need for the Department's services in that area;

(c) the operational requirements of commercial transporters; and

(d) administrative arrangements with other departments or agencies of the Government of Canada.

27. (1) **Obligation on entry** — Unless these Regulations provide otherwise, for the purpose of the examination required by subsection 18(1) of the Act, a person must appear without delay before an officer at a port of entry.

(2) **Seeking entry at a place other than a port of entry** — Unless these Regulations provide otherwise, a person who seeks to enter Canada at a place other than a port of entry must appear without delay for examination at the port of entry that is nearest to that place.

(3) **Refused entry elsewhere** — For the purposes of section 18 of the Act, every person who has been returned to Canada as a result of the refusal of another country to allow that person entry is a person seeking to enter Canada.

## DIVISION 3 — CONDUCT OF EXAMINATION

### *General*

**28. Examination — For the purposes of subsection 15(1) of the Act, a person makes an application in accordance with the Act by**

**(a) submitting an application in writing;**

**(b) seeking to enter Canada;**

**(c) seeking to transit through Canada as provided in section 35; or**

**(d) making a claim for refugee protection**

**29. Medical examination — For the purposes of paragraph 16(2)(b) of the Act, a medical examination includes any or all of the following:**

**(a) physical examination;**

**(b) mental examination;**

**(c) review of past medical history;**

**(d) laboratory test;**

**(e) diagnostic test; and**

**(f) medical assessment of records respecting the applicant.**

**30. (1) Medical examination required — For the purposes of paragraph 16(2)(b) of the Act, the following foreign nationals are requested to submit, and must submit, to a medical examination:**

**(a) foreign nationals who are applying for a permanent resident visa or applying to remain in Canada as a permanent resident as well as their family members, whether accompanying or not;**

*[Editor's Note: SOR/2002-227, s. 354 provides that if a person makes an application before June 28, 2002, his or her non-accompanying dependent children, referred to in s. 352 of the* Immigration and Refugee Protection Regulations, *SOR/2002-227 (the "new Regulations"), and his or her non-accompanying common-law partner shall not, for the purposes of that application, be considered inadmissible non-accompanying family members referred to in paragraph 42(a) of the new* Immigration and Refugee Protection Act, *S.C. 2001, c. 27, and are not subject to the requirements of paragraph 30(1)(a) or 51(b) of the new Regulations.]*

**(b) foreign nationals who are seeking to work in Canada in an occupation in which the protection of public health is essential;**

**(c) foreign nationals who**

**(i) are seeking entry into Canada or applying for renewal of their work or study permit or authorization to remain in Canada as a temporary resident for a period in excess of six consecutive months, including an actual or proposed period of absence from Canada of less than 14 days, and**

**(ii) have resided or sojourned for a period of six consecutive months, at any time during the one-year period immediately preceding the date they**

**sought entry or made their application, in an area that the Minister determines, after consultation with the Minister of Health, has a higher incidence of serious communicable disease than Canada;**

**(d) foreign nationals who an officer, or the Immigration Division, has reasonable grounds to believe are inadmissible under subsection 38(1) of the Act;**

**(e) foreign nationals who claim refugee protection in Canada; and**

**(f) foreign nationals who are seeking to enter or remain in Canada and who may apply to the Minister for protection under subsection 112(1) of the Act, other than foreign nationals who have not left Canada since their claim for refugee protection or application for protection was rejected.**

(2) **Exception** — **Subsection (1) does not apply to**

**(a) a person described in paragraph 186(b) who is entering or is in Canada to carry out official duties, unless they seek to engage or continue in secondary employment in Canada;**

**(b) a family member of a person described in paragraph 186(b), unless that family member seeks to engage or continue in employment in Canada;**

**(c) a member of the armed forces of a country that is a designated state for the purposes of the *Visiting Forces Act*, who is entering or is in Canada to carry out official duties, other than a person who has been designated as a civilian component of those armed forces, unless that member seeks to engage or continue in secondary employment in Canada;**

**(d) a family member of a protected person, if the family member is not included in the protected person's application to remain in Canada as a permanent resident; and**

**(e) a non-accompanying family member of a foreign national who has applied for refugee protection outside Canada.**

(2.1) **Exception** — **A foreign national who has applied for permanent resident status and is a member of the live-in caregiver class is not required to submit to a medical examination under subsection (1).**

(3) **Subsequent examination** — **Every foreign national who has undergone a medical examination under subsection (1) is requested to submit, and must submit, to a new medical examination before entering Canada if, after being authorized to enter and remain in Canada, they have resided or stayed for a period in excess of six months in an area that the Minister determines, after consultation with the Minister of Health, has a higher incidence of serious communicable disease than Canada.**

(4) **Medical certificate** — **Every foreign national referred to in subsection (1) who seeks to enter Canada must hold a medical certificate, based on the most recent medical examination to which they were required to submit under that subsection within the previous 12 months, that indicates that their health condition is not likely to be a danger to public health or public safety and, unless subsection 38(2) of the Act applies, is not reasonably expected to cause excessive demand.**

SOR/2004-167, s. 9; SOR/2010-78, s. 1

IRP Regulations

**31. Public health — Before concluding whether a foreign national's health condition is likely to be a danger to public health, an officer who is assessing the foreign national's health condition shall consider**

> **(a) any report made by a health practitioner or medical laboratory with respect to the foreign national;**
>
> **(b) the communicability of any disease that the foreign national is affected by or carries; and**
>
> **(c) the impact that the disease could have on other persons living in Canada.**

**32. Conditions — In addition to the conditions that are imposed on a foreign national who makes an application as a member of a class, an officer may impose, vary or cancel the following conditions in respect of any foreign national who is requested to and must submit to a medical examination under subsection 16(2) of the Act or section 30 of these Regulations:**

> **(a) to report at the specified times and places for medical examination, surveillance or treatment; and**
>
> **(b) to provide proof, at the specified times and places, of compliance with the conditions imposed.**

**33. Public safety — Before concluding whether a foreign national's health condition is likely to be a danger to public safety, an officer who is assessing the foreign national's health condition shall consider**

> **(a) any reports made by a health practitioner or medical laboratory with respect to the foreign national; and**
>
> **(b) the risk of a sudden incapacity or of unpredictable or violent behaviour of the foreign national that would create a danger to the health or safety of persons living in Canada.**

**34. Excessive demand — Before concluding whether a foreign national's health condition might reasonably be expected to cause excessive demand, an officer who is assessing the foreign national's health condition shall consider**

> **(a) any reports made by a health practitioner or medical laboratory with respect to the foreign national; and**
>
> **(b) any condition identified by the medical examination.**

## Case Law

*Hossain v. Canada (Minister of Citizenship & Immigration)*, 2006 CarswellNat 993, 2006 FC 475 (F.C.) — The applicant's application for permanent residence under the skilled worker category was refused on the basis that he was found to have a medical condition that "would or might reasonably be expected to place excessive demands on health or social services in Canada, and thus would render him inadmissible to Canada under s. 38(1) of the IRPA." The applicant had had a kidney transplant performed in 2000 because of renal failure. His renal function was currently normal and he took medication on a daily basis. These medications were expensive and would have been paid by the provincial health care.

The applicant had personally borne all of the medical costs since his transplant and was ready to undertake not to claim medical costs from Canadian health care services relating to his current medical condition. He also was prepared to undertake to subscribe to all necessary private insurance coverage and he provided evidence of more than C$200,000 of savings that would enable him to meet the costs of his medicines from his own financial sources. There was no indication that the medical officer or the visa officer considered the applicant's offer to assume the cost of the medication relating to his current medical condition or his personal financial situation.

The decision was set aside and referred back to ensure that the next decision maker considered the financial situation of the applicant.

*Hilewitz v. Canada (Minister of Citizenship & Immigration)*, [2005] 2 S.C.R. 706, 50 Imm. L.R. (3d) 40, 33 Admin. L.R. (4th) 1, 340 N.R. 102, 259 D.L.R. (4th) 244, [2005] S.C.J. No. 58, 2005 CarswellNat 3234, 2005 CarswellNat 3235, 2005 SCC 57 — The appellant and another both applied for permanent residence, respectively, under the "investor" and "self-employed" classes set out in the *Immigration Act*. These categories require that applicants have substantial financial resources to qualify. Both qualified, but were denied admission because the intellectual disability of a dependent child "would cause or might reasonably be expected to cause excessive demands on . . . social services" in Canada, which made them inadmissible pursuant to s. 19(1)(a)(ii) of the former *Immigration Act*.



The visa officers' decisions were set aside by the Supreme Court of Canada. The Supreme Court of Canada concluded that the personal circumstances of the families of disabled dependants are relevant factors in an assessment of their anticipated impact on social services. Since the "investor" and "self-employed" categories under which the appellants were qualified for admission to Canada were, to a large extent, concerned with an individual's assets, it would be incongruous to interpret the legislation in such a way that the very assets that qualify these individuals for admission to Canada can simultaneously be ignored in determining the admissibility of their disabled children.

The applicants' ability and willingness to attenuate the burden on the public purse that would otherwise be created by their intellectually disabled children was a relevant factor in determining whether those children could reasonably be expected to cause excessive demands on Canada's social services. The fears were articulated in the rejections of the applications, such as possible bankruptcy, mobility, school closure or parental death, represent contingencies that could be raised in relation to any applicant. Using such contingencies to negate a family's genuine ability and willingness to absorb some of the burdens created by a child's disabilities anchors an applicant's admissibility to conjecture, not reality. The visa officers erred by confirming the medical officers' refusal to account for the potential impact of the families' willingness to assist. Moreover, the visa officers' failure to read the families' responses to the fairness letters sent to them meant that their decisions were not based on all the relevant available information.

*[Note: Although decided under former legislation (the* Immigration Act, *R.S.C. 1985, c. I-2) this decision may still be useful.]*

35. (1) **Transit** — Subject to subsection (2), the following persons are not seeking to enter Canada but are making an application under subsection 15(1) of the Act to transit through Canada:

(a) in airports where there are United States' in-transit preclearance facilities, in-transit preclearance passengers; and

(b) in any airport, passengers who are arriving from any country and who are transiting to a country other than Canada and remain in a sterile transit area.

(2) **Obligatory examination** — Any person seeking to leave a sterile transit area must appear immediately for examination.

36. **Actions not constituting a complete examination** — An inspection carried out aboard a means of transportation bringing persons to Canada or the questioning of persons embarking on or disembarking from a means of transportation, or the examination of any record or document respecting such persons before they appear for examination at a port of entry, is part of an examination but does not constitute a complete examination.

37. **End of examination** — The examination of a person who seeks to enter Canada, or who makes an application to transit through Canada, ends only when

(a) a determination is made that the person has a right to enter Canada, or is authorized to enter Canada as a temporary resident or permanent resident, the person is authorized to leave the port of entry at which the examination takes place and the person leaves the port of entry;

(b) if the person is an in-transit passenger, the person departs from Canada;

(c) the person is authorized to withdraw their application to enter Canada and an officer verifies their departure from Canada; or

(d) a decision in respect of the person is made under subsection 44(2) of the Act and the person leaves the port of entry.

## *Alternative Means of Examination*

38. **Means** — For the purposes of subsection 18(1) of the Act, the following persons may — unless otherwise directed by an officer — be examined by the means indicated as alternative to appearing for an examination by an officer at a port of entry:

(a) persons who have previously been examined and hold an authorization issued under section 11.1 of the *Customs Act*, in which case examination is effected by the presentation of the authorization by those persons at a port of entry;

(b) persons who are seeking to enter Canada at a port of entry where facilities are in place for automatic screening of persons seeking to enter Canada, in which case examination is performed by automatic screening;

(c) persons who leave Canada and proceed directly to a marine installation or structure to which the *Oceans Act* applies, and who return directly to Canada from the installation or structure without entering the territorial waters of a foreign state, in which case examination is conducted by an officer by telephone or other means of telecommunication;

(d) members of a crew of a ship that transports oil or liquid natural gas and that docks at a marine installation or structure to which the *Oceans Act* applies, for the purpose of loading oil or liquid natural gas, in which case examination is conducted by an officer by telephone or other means of telecommunication;

(e) members of a crew of a ship registered in a foreign country, other than members of a crew referred to in paragraph (d), in which case examination is conducted by an officer by telephone or other means of telecommunication;

(f) members of a crew of a ship registered in Canada, in which case examination is conducted by an officer by telephone or other means of telecommunication;

(g) citizens or permanent residents of Canada or the United States who are seeking to enter Canada at remote locations where no officer is assigned or where there are no means by which the persons may report for examination, in which case examination is conducted by an officer by telephone or other means of telecommunication; and

(h) citizens or permanent residents of Canada or the United States who seek to enter Canada at places, other than a port of entry, where no officer is assigned, in which case examination is conducted by an officer by telephone or other means of telecommunication.



## *Permitted Entry*

39. **Entry permitted** — An officer shall allow the following persons to enter Canada following an examination:

(a) persons who have been returned to Canada as a result of a refusal of another country to allow them entry after they were removed from or otherwise left Canada after a removal order was made against them;

(b) persons returning to Canada under a transfer order made under the *Mutual Legal Assistance in Criminal Matters Act* and who, immediately before being transferred to a foreign state under the transfer order, were subject to an unenforced removal order; and

(c) persons who are in possession of refugee travel papers issued to them by the Minister of Foreign Affairs that are valid for return to Canada.

## *Conduct of Examination Measures*

40. (1) **Direction to leave** — Except in the case of protected persons within the meaning of subsection 95(2) of the Act and refugee protection claimants, an officer who is unable to examine a person who is seeking to enter Canada at a port of entry shall, in writing, direct the person to leave Canada.

(2) **Service** — A copy of the direction shall be served on the person as well as on the owner or person in control of the means of transportation, if any, that brought the person to Canada.

(3) **Ceasing to have effect** — The direction ceases to have effect when the person appears again at a port of entry and an officer proceeds to examine the person.

41. **Direct back** — Unless an authorization has been given under section 23 of the Act, an officer who examines a foreign national who is seeking to enter Canada from the United States shall direct them to return temporarily to the United States if

(a) no officer is able to complete an examination;

(b) the Minister is not available to consider, under subsection 44(2) of the Act, a report prepared with respect to the person; or

(c) an admissibility hearing cannot be held by the Immigration Division.

42. (1) **Withdrawing application** — Subject to subsection (2), an officer who examines a foreign national who is seeking to enter Canada and who has indicated that they want to withdraw their application to enter Canada shall allow the foreign national to withdraw their application and leave Canada.

(2) **Exception — report** — If a report is being prepared or has been prepared under subsection 44(1) of the Act in respect of a foreign national who indicates that they want to withdraw their application to enter Canada, the officer shall not allow the foreign national to withdraw their application or leave Canada unless the Minister does not make a removal order or refer the report to the Immigration Division for an admissibility hearing.

(3) **Obligation to confirm departure** — A foreign national who is allowed to withdraw their application to enter Canada must appear without delay before an officer at a port of entry to confirm their departure from Canada.

## *Application of Section 23 of the Act*

43. (1) **Conditions** — An officer must impose the following conditions on every person authorized to enter Canada under section 23 of the Act:

(a) to report in person at the time and place specified for the completion of the examination or the admissibility hearing;

(b) to not engage in any work in Canada;

(c) to not attend any educational institution in Canada; and

(d) to report in person to an officer at a port of entry if the person withdraws their application to enter Canada.

(2) **Effect of authorization to enter** — A foreign national who is authorized to enter Canada under section 23 of the Act does not, by reason only of that authorization, become a temporary resident or a permanent resident.

## Obligation to Appear at an Admissibility Hearing

44. (1) **Class** — The class of persons who are the subject of a report referred for an admissibility hearing under subsection 44(2) of the Act is prescribed as a class of persons.

(2) **Members** — The members of the class of persons who are the subject of a report referred for an admissibility hearing under subsection 44(2) of the Act are the persons who are the subject of such a report.

(3) **Obligation** — Every member of the class prescribed under subsection (1) must appear at their admissibility hearing before the Immigration Division if they are given notice of the hearing by the Division.



## Deposits or Guarantees

45. (1) **Deposit or guarantee required on entry** — An officer can require, in respect of a person or group of persons seeking to enter Canada, the payment of a deposit or the posting of a guarantee, or both, to the Minister for compliance with any conditions imposed.

(2) **Amount** — The amount of the deposit or guarantee is fixed by an officer on the basis of

(a) the financial resources of the person or group;

(b) the obligations that result from the conditions imposed;

(c) the costs that would likely be incurred to locate and arrest the person or group, to detain them, to hold an admissibility hearing and to remove them from Canada; and

(d) in the case of a guarantee, the costs that would likely be incurred to enforce it.

46. **Application** — Sections 47 to 49 apply to deposits and guarantees required under subsection 44(3), section 56 and subsection 58(3) of the Act and section 45 of these Regulations.

47. (1) **General requirements** — A person who pays a deposit or posts a guarantee

(a) must not have signed or co-signed another guarantee that is in default; and

(b) must have the capacity to contract in the province where the deposit is paid or the guarantee is posted.

(2) **Requirements if guarantee posted** — A person who posts a guarantee must

(a) be a Canadian citizen or a permanent resident, physically present and residing in Canada;

(b) be able to ensure that the person or group of persons in respect of whom the guarantee is required will comply with the conditions imposed; and

(c) present to an officer evidence of their ability to fulfil the obligation arising from the guarantee.

(3) **Money illegally obtained** — If an officer has reasonable grounds to believe that a sum of money offered by a person as a deposit was not legally obtained, or that a sum of money that a person may be obliged to pay under a guarantee would not be legally obtained, the officer shall not allow that person to pay a deposit or post a guarantee.

48. (1) **Conditions if guarantee posted** — In addition to any other conditions that are imposed, the following conditions are imposed on a person or group of persons in respect of whom a guarantee is required:

(a) to provide the Department with the address of the person posting the guarantee and to advise the Department before any change in that address; and

(b) to present themself or themselves at the time and place that an officer or the Immigration Division requires them to appear to comply with any obligation imposed on them under the Act.

(2) **Conditions if deposit paid** — In addition to any other conditions that are imposed, the following conditions are imposed on a person or group of persons in respect of whom a deposit is required:

(a) to provide the Department with their address and to advise the Department before any change in that address; and

(b) to present themself or themselves at the time and place that an officer or the Immigration Division requires them to appear to comply with any obligation imposed on them under the Act.

49. (1) **Acknowledgment of consequences of failure to comply with conditions** — A person who pays a deposit or posts a guarantee must acknowledge in writing

(a) that they have been informed of the conditions imposed; and

(b) that they have been informed that non-compliance with any conditions imposed will result in the forfeiture of the deposit or enforcement of the guarantee.

(2) **Receipt** — An officer shall issue a receipt for the deposit or a copy of the guarantee, and a copy of the conditions imposed.

(3) **Return of deposit** — The Department shall return the deposit paid on being informed by an officer that the person or group of persons in respect of whom the deposit was required has complied with the conditions imposed.

(4) **Breach of condition** — A sum of money deposited is forfeited, or a guarantee posted becomes enforceable, on the failure of the person or any member of the group of persons in respect of whom the deposit or guarantee was required to comply with a condition imposed.

## Case Law

### Section 49(4)

*Ferzly v. Canada (Minister of Citizenship & Immigration)* (2007), 65 Imm. L.R. (3d) 293, 2007 CarswellNat 3440, 2007 CarswellNat 4426, 2007 FC 1064 (F.C.) — The applicant paid a cash deposit of $10,000 to secure the release of Mr. Bassolé from immigration detention. One of the conditions of release imposed by the Canadian Border Services Agency (CBSA) Enforcement Officer, was for Mr. Bassolé to report to the Pierre Elliott Trudeau Airport in Montreal, on June 28, 2006, to board a flight, bound for Burkina Faso. This condition was imposed on him as a result of the airline ticket which Mr. Bassolé had purchased and presented in order to secure his release from detention. Instead, Mr. Bassolé unilaterally chose to attempt to leave Canada, on June 28, 2006, via Ottawa, on a flight for Boston, United States, thereby breaching a term of his release. As a result of this breach, the Director of the Investigations and Removal Section of the CBSA declared the $10,000 deposit forfeited. The applicant sought judicial review of that decision. The standard of review for whether the Director's decision to forfeit the security deposit was properly made is reasonableness. This decision is a question of mixed law and fact that attracts considerable deference by the Court. The decision was made in good faith. There was no evidence of malice. The Director considered several factors which are referenced in his decision. Under the circumstances, the decision was logical and reasonably sound as it was based on all of the evidence on the record before the Director. The decision was exercised in good faith, in accordance with the principles of natural justice; none of the considerations were irrelevant nor extraneous to the statutory purpose. Therefore, the Court did not intervene.

*Kang v. Canada (Minister of Public Safety & Emergency Preparedness)*, 2006 CarswellNat 1441, 2006 FC 652 (F.C.) — The applicant paid a cash deposit of $5,000 to secure her elderly mother's release from immigration detention. One of the release conditions was that the mother reside at her daughter's address "at all times." The mother was absent one day when Canada Border Services Agency officers visited to enquire about other family members. Several months later, after the mother had returned to Korea, the operations manager of the Greater Toronto Enforcement Centre declared the $5,000 deposit forfeited. The applicant sought judicial review of that decision. The decision to forfeit a cash bond should withstand scrutiny on the reasonableness standard.

The applicant contended that the notes contained the interviewing officer's conclusions rather than statements fairly attributable to her or her mother. A close reading of the notes suggests that what may appear to be admissions against interest by the applicant and her mother are no more than a repetition of the conclusion reached by the immigration officer based on what the applicant's son may have mistakenly told the officer during the visit to the applicant's house. The case, therefore, was complicated by the involvement of other members of the family subject to arrest and removal and the language barrier. There was no fault on the part of the immigration officers, but the possibility of confusion and error should have been considered by the operations manager when there was contradictory affidavit evidence before her. The manager's factual finding that the release condition had been breached was patently unreasonable in light of that evidence. Furthermore, no rational explanation was provided as to why the evidence did not provide a justification for not forfeiting the deposit. Accordingly the decision was found to be unreasonable and was overturned.

The current Act is silent on the question of ministerial discretion for the forfeiture of security deposits or performance bonds but provides, in s. 61, for the making of regulations for the application of Division 6 with respect to detention and release. It was clear from the evidence that the operations manager did not consider whether a lesser amount, including no amount, would be sufficient to satisfy the purpose of imposing the cash deposit, particularly where, as here, the subject of the release condition had returned to her country of origin. Further, it was impossible to ascertain from the brief reasons endorsed on the applicant's submissions or from the terse letter communicating the decision what factors the manager took into consideration in deciding that the bond should be forfeited. The Court had no way to determine whether the manager relied upon considerations that were irrelevant or extraneous to the legislative purpose for which she exercised discretion. Accordingly, the manager's error in this regard amounted to another ground for concluding that the application must be granted and remitted for reconsideration by another officer.

*Khalife v. Canada (Minister of Citizenship & Immigration)*, [2006] F.C.J. No. 293, 52 Imm. L.R. (3d) 267, 2006 CarswellNat 456, 2006 CarswellNat 1135, 2006 FC 221 (F.C.) — The statute and the Regulations say little about the decisions to impose and to forfeit a cash deposit. The authority to require a cash deposit is found in the IRPA at subs. 58(3). The manager's decision to forfeit the deposit appears to have been made in accordance with the principles in the Immigration Canada Enforcement Manual. The manager exercised his statutory discretion in good faith, in accordance with the principles of natural justice and did not rely upon considerations irrelevant or extraneous to the statutory purpose. Instead, the manager verified that the applicant was fully aware of the conditions of his release and determined that the applicant had in fact breached these terms. The manager received and considered the applicant's representations and then followed the direction provided by s. 49(4) of the Regulations and the Manual and determined on the merits that it was appropriate to forfeit only part of the applicant's deposit.

*Tsang v. Canada (Minister of Public Safety & Emergency Preparedness)*, [2006] F.C.J. No. 576, 2006 CarswellNat 941, 2006 CarswellNat 2380, 2006 FC 474 (F.C.) — A regional director of the Canadian Border Services Agency decided that a performance bond granted by the applicant in the amount of $80,000 was forfeited. The bond had been provided for the release of the applicant's husband. He had violated a term of the release order and as a result was arrested. In consequence of this violation, the performance bond was forfeited. The decision to forfeit the $80,000 bond was set aside since the officer failed to appreciate that he had the discretion to make a decision that resulted in less than $80,000 being forfeited.

## Documents Required

**50. (1) Documents — permanent residents — In addition to the permanent resident visa required of a foreign national who is a member of a class referred to in subsection 70(2), a foreign national seeking to become a permanent resident must hold**

> **(a) a passport, other than a diplomatic, official or similar passport, that was issued by the country of which the foreign national is a citizen or national;**
>
> **(b) a travel document that was issued by the country of which the foreign national is a citizen or national;**

**(c) an identity or travel document that was issued by a country to non-national residents, refugees or stateless persons who are unable to obtain a passport or other travel document from their country of citizenship or nationality or who have no country of citizenship or nationality;**

**(d) a travel document that was issued by the International Committee of the Red Cross in Geneva, Switzerland, to enable and facilitate emigration;**

**(e) a passport or travel document that was issued by the Palestinian Authority;**

**(f) an exit visa that was issued by the Government of the Union of Soviet Socialist Republics to its citizens who were compelled to relinquish their Soviet nationality in order to emigrate from that country;**

**(g) a British National (Overseas) passport that was issued by the Government of the United Kingdom to persons born, naturalized or registered in Hong Kong; or**

**(h) a passport that was issued by the Government of Hong Kong Special Administrative Region of the People's Republic of China.**

**(2) Exception — protected persons — Subsection (1) does not apply to a person who is a protected person within the meaning of subsection 95(2) of the Act and holds a permanent resident visa when it is not possible for the person to obtain a passport or an identity or travel document referred to in subsection (1).**

**(3) [Repealed SOR/2010-54, s. 1.]**

SOR/2008-253, s. 1; SOR/2010-54, s. 1

IRP Regulations

## Case Law

*Andryanov v. Canada (Minister of Citizenship & Immigration)* (2007), 60 Imm. L.R. (3d) 202, 2007 CarswellNat 429, 2007 FC 186 (F.C.) — The applicant and his wife attended a marriage interview at an inland immigration office. The officer who conducted the interview was satisfied the marriage was genuine. A considerable amount of correspondence then ensued between the applicant and the respondent's officials with respect to paragraph 50(1)(a) or (b) of the *Immigration and Refugee Protection Regulations*, namely that he provide a passport or a travel document issued by his country of origin. The result was a "Catch 22" situation. The respondent's officials refused to accept that the applicant was who he said he was without the passport, and the Russian Embassy refused to give him one without a request from the respondent's officials. The respondent's officials refused to make such a request as the onus to provide the passport rested on the applicant. As a result, the applicant's application was denied.

At no point in either the refusal letter or the FOSS notes was it explained how the officer reached his conclusion that the applicant had not provided a passport, a travel document or other suitable identification, or reasonable explanation. Though this conclusion was ultimately open to the officer, in light of the fact that the applicant provided his Seaman's Passport, internal identity card, his birth certificate, and his valid Russian driver's licence, in addition to multiple explanations, something further was required on the part of the officer to meet the adequacy test for his reasons. The officer had a duty to explain why the evidence and explanations were insufficient. At no time did CIC indicate that they had a concern regarding the validity of the Seaman's Passport. It had been issued by the country of which the applicant was a citizen, and it was subsisting at the time it was submitted.

It was also not clear why the applicant's internal identity card was not accepted as sufficient identification. Although CIC had concerns regarding whether or not the document was subsisting, in light of the fact it did not have an expiry date, the applicant clearly explained that the document was issued for life. Absent a conclusion on the part of CIC that either the document was fraudulent or that they did not believe the explanation of the applicant, it was not open to them to conclude that the document was not subsisting. No analysis was provided for CIC's conclusion that the document was not subsisting. Moreover, neither paragraph 50(1)(a) nor (b) include the words "valid and subsisting" as had been the case in subs. 46.4(8) of the former *Immigration Act*.

The decision to refuse the application on the ground that the applicant had been unable to provide a passport or suitable identifications to satisfy CIC officials as to his identity was unreasonable. The decision was set aside and was remitted for reconsideration.

**50.1 (1) Designation of unreliable travel documents — The Minister may designate, individually or by class, passports or travel or identity documents that do not constitute reliable proof of identity or nationality.**

**(2) Factors — The Minister shall consider the following factors in determining whether to designate any passport or travel or identity document, or class of passport or travel or identity document, as not being reliable proof of identity or nationality:**

> **(a) the adequacy of security features incorporated into the passport or document for the purpose of deterring its misuse or unauthorized alteration, reproduction or issuance; and**
>
> **(b) information respecting the security or integrity of the process leading to the issuance of the passport or document.**

**(3) Effect of designation — A passport or travel or identity document that has been designated under subsection (1) is not a passport or travel or identity document for the purpose of subsection 50(1) or 52(1).**

**(4) Public notice — The Minister shall make available to the public a list of all passports or travel or identity documents designated under subsection (1).**

SOR/2010-54, s. 2

**51. Examination — permanent residents — A foreign national who holds a permanent resident visa and is seeking to become a permanent resident must, at the time of their examination,**

> **(a) inform the officer if**
>
> > **(i) the foreign national has become a spouse or common-law partner or has ceased to be a spouse, common-law partner or conjugal partner after the visa was issued, or**
> >
> > **(ii) material facts relevant to the issuance of the visa have changed since the visa was issued or were not divulged when it was issued; and**

**(b) establish that they and their family members, whether accompanying or not, meet the requirements of the Act and these Regulations.**

*[Editor's Note: SOR/2002-227, s. 354 provides that if a person makes an application before June 28, 2002, his or her non-accompanying dependent children, referred to in s. 352 of the* Immigration and Refugee Protection Regulations, *SOR/2002-227 (the "new Regulations"), and his or her non-accompanying common-law partner shall not, for the purposes of that application, be considered inadmissible non-accompanying family members referred to in paragraph 42(a) of the new* Immigration and Refugee Protection Act, *S.C. 2001, c. 27, and are not subject to the requirements of paragraph 30(1)(a) or 51(b) of the new Regulations.]*

SOR/2008-253, s. 2



## Case Law

*Ivanov v. Canada (Minister of Citizenship & Immigration)* (2006), 56 Imm. L.R. (3d) 56, 2006 CarswellNat 2335 (Imm. & Ref. Bd. (App. Div.)) — The appellant made an application for permanent residence as an independent in May 2001. At the time he disclosed that he had never been married and had no dependants. The application was successful and he was issued a permanent resident visa in June 2003. The appellant married his girlfriend on October 3, 2003. The appellant arrived in Canada on October 7, 2003. He disclosed his recent marriage to Canadian immigration officials upon his arrival in Toronto. At the time of his examination at Pearson Airport, he could not establish that his wife met the requirements of IRPA and the Regulations. His counsel wrote to the Canadian Embassy in Vienna in November 2003 advising that the immigration official at the port of entry had no objection regarding the release of the landed documents to the appellant subject to the appellant's wife meeting the medical and security requirements. The Embassy replied that there was no legal basis on which they were required to assess the wife against the admissibility criteria of IRPA. The appellant was issued an exclusion order on the basis that he was unable to establish at the time of his examination that his wife met the requirement of the Act and the Regulations. The appellant appealed the exclusion order.

The Appeal Board concluded that the exclusion order was valid in law. The appeal, however, was allowed under s. 67(1)(c) and the matter referred back to an immigration officer at the port of entry for reconsideration. The Board found that the appellant made an honest mistake in not informing the visa officer of his marriage prior to appearing for landing, but had disclosed the marriage immediately upon landing. As a result of the appellant's error, the Board concluded that he had suffered financial hardship upon his arrival in Canada, exhausting his savings because he could not legally work here. The Board found that the appellant had established humanitarian and compassionate considerations to warrant the granting of special relief in light of all the circumstances of the case. The Board directed that the department take all steps required to facilitate the examination of the appellant's wife and to provide the appellant with the necessary immigration documents to allow the appellant to attend before an immigration officer at a port of entry for reconsideration.

**52. (1) Documents — temporary residents — In addition to the other requirements of these Regulations, a foreign national seeking to become a temporary**

**resident must hold one of the following documents that is valid for the period authorized for their stay:**

**(a) a passport that was issued by the country of which the foreign national is a citizen or national, that does not prohibit travel to Canada and that the foreign national may use to enter the country of issue;**

**(b) a travel document that was issued by the country of which the foreign national is a citizen or national, that does not prohibit travel to Canada and that the foreign national may use to enter the country of issue;**

**(c) an identity or travel document that was issued by a country, that does not prohibit travel to Canada, that the foreign national may use to enter the country of issue and that is of the type issued by that country to non-national residents, refugees or stateless persons who are unable to obtain a passport or other travel document from their country of citizenship or nationality or who have no country of citizenship or nationality;**

**(d) a laissez-passer that was issued by the United Nations;**

**(e) a passport or travel document that was issued by the Palestinian Authority;**

**(f) a document that was issued by the Organization of American States and is entitled "Official Travel Document";**

**(g) a passport that was issued by the Government of the United Kingdom to a British Overseas Citizen;**

**(h) a British National (Overseas) passport that was issued by the Government of the United Kingdom to persons born, naturalized or registered in Hong Kong; and**

**(i) a passport that was issued by the Government of Hong Kong Special Administrative Region of the People's Republic of China.**

**(1.1) [Repealed SOR/2003-260, s. 1(1).]**

**(2) Exceptions — Subsection (1) does not apply to**

**(a) citizens of the United States;**

**(b) persons seeking to enter Canada from the United States or St. Pierre and Miquelon who have been lawfully admitted to the United States for permanent residence;**

**(c) residents of Greenland seeking to enter Canada from Greenland;**

**(d) persons seeking to enter Canada from St. Pierre and Miquelon who are citizens of France and residents of St. Pierre and Miquelon;**

**(e) members of the armed forces of a country that is a designated state for the purposes of the *Visiting Forces Act* who are seeking entry in order to carry out official duties, other than persons who have been designated as a civilian component of those armed forces;**

**(f) persons who are seeking to enter Canada as, or in order to become, members of a crew of a means of air transportation and who hold an airline flight crew licence or crew member certificate issued in accordance with International Civil Aviation Organization specifications; or**

**(g) persons seeking to enter Canada as members of a crew who hold a seafarer's identity document issued under International Labour Organization conventions and are members of the crew of the vessel that carries them to Canada.**

**(3) [Repealed SOR/2010-54, s. 3.]**

SOR/2003-197, s. 1; SOR/2003-260, s. 1; SOR/2010-54, s. 3

# PART 5 — PERMANENT RESIDENTS

## DIVISION 1 — PERMANENT RESIDENT CARDS

**53. (1) Document indicating status — For the purposes of subsection 31(1) of the Act, the document indicating the status of a permanent resident is a permanent resident card that is**

**(a) provided by the Department to a person who has become a permanent resident under the Act; or**

**(b) issued by the Department, on application, to a permanent resident who has become a permanent resident under the Act or a permanent resident who obtained that status under the *Immigration Act*, chapter I-2 of the Revised Statutes of Canada, 1985, as it read immediately before the coming into force of section 31 of the Act.**

**(2) Property of Her Majesty — A permanent resident card remains the property of Her Majesty in right of Canada at all times and must be returned to the Department on the Department's request.**

SOR/2004-167, s. 15

### Case Law

### Section 53(2)

*Salewski v. Canada (Minister of Citizenship & Immigration)* (2008), 74 Imm. L.R. (3d) 57, 83 Admin. L.R. (4th) 167, 2008 CarswellNat 2565, 2008 CarswellNat 5094, 2008 FC 899 (F.C.) — This was an application for judicial review of Citizenship and Immigration Canada's ("CIC") decision to recall and cancel the permanent resident card issued to the applicant. The applicant, a citizen of Germany, became a permanent resident of Canada in 1958. She left Canada in 1968 following the breakup of her marriage. There was no indication that the applicant returned to Canada at any time from 1968 to 2007. The applicant entered Canada in February 2007. It is not clear whether she entered Canada as a visitor or a permanent resident. However, on June 19, 2007, she sought to extend her visitor's status. She also made an application for a permanent resident card on June 4, 2007. During that application process she informed CIC that she had resided in Canada for 10 years (from 1958 to 1968); she had three Canadian born children; she returned to Germany in June 1968 for personal reasons and had remained there until February 5, 2007. She currently intends to remain in Canada to be with her children, who are residents and citizens of Canada, and she requested the card be issued on H&C grounds. The card was issued on August 16, 2007. In September 2007, CIC discovered that no residency determination had been made with respect to the applicant and according to

CIC the residency card had been issued in error. The applicant was asked to return her card and she refused, and requested CIC's reasons for recalling the card.

Neither the Act nor the Regulations provide that a holder of a permanent resident card is to be provided an opportunity to make submissions before his or her card is recalled. Instead, Regulation 53(2) explicitly states that the card "remains the property of Her Majesty . . . at all times and must be retuned to the Department on the Department's request". There is a general common law principle, a duty of procedural fairness, lying on every public authority making an administrative decision which is not of a legislative nature and which affects the rights, privileges or interests of an individual. Where a permanent resident card has been issued in error, the canceling or rendering the card void is not beyond the jurisdiction of an officer or, more generally, the issuing department. It was not Parliament's intent to confer the authority upon CIC to recall a permanent resident card but to limit its power to cancel or render null a permanent resident card, especially where the card has been issued in error and the person to whom it was issued has refused to return it. The officer did not act beyond his jurisdiction by recalling, canceling and rendering void the applicant's permanent resident card in this case. The applicant has no entitlement to the card and she is simply refusing to return it. The application for judicial review was dismissed.

**54. (1) Period of validity — Subject to subsection (2), a permanent resident card is valid for five years from the date of issue.**

**(2) Exception — A permanent resident card is valid for one year from the date of issue if, at the time of issue, the permanent resident**

**(a) is subject to the process set out in paragraph 46(1)(b) of the Act;**

**(b) is the subject of a report prepared under subsection 44(1) of the Act;**

**(c) is subject to a removal order made by the Minister under subsection 44(2) of the Act and the period for filing an appeal from the decision has not expired or, if an appeal is filed, there has been no final determination of the appeal; or**

**(d) is the subject of a report referred to the Immigration Division under subsection 44(2) of the Act and the period for filing an appeal from the decision of the Immigration Division has not expired or, if an appeal is filed, there has been no final determination of the appeal.**

**55. Delivery — A permanent resident card shall only be provided or issued in Canada.**

**56. (1) [Repealed SOR/2008-188, s. 1(1).]**

**(2) Application for a card — An application for a permanent resident card must be made in Canada and include**

**(a) an application form that contains the following information, namely,**

**(i) the applicant's name and date and place of birth,**

**(ii) the applicant's gender, height and eye colour,**

**(iii) the date on which and the place where the applicant became a permanent resident,**

(iv) the applicant's mailing address,

(v) the addresses of all of the applicant's places of residence during the previous five years,

(vi) the names and addresses of the applicant's employers and educational institutions attended, during the previous five years,

(vii) the periods during the previous five years that the applicant was absent from Canada,

(viii) [Repealed SOR/2008-188, s. 1(2).]

(ix) whether a report under subsection 44(1) of the Act has been made in respect of the applicant or whether a decision was made outside of Canada that they have failed to comply with the residency obligation under section 28 of the Act, and

(x) whether the applicant has lost their permanent resident status or has been issued a removal order;

(b) [Repealed SOR/2008-188, s. 1(3).]

(c) a copy of

(i) any document described in paragraphs 50(1)(a) to (h) — or, if the applicant does not hold one of those documents, any document described in paragraphs 178(1)(a) and (b) — that is currently held by the applicant or was held by the applicant at the time they became a permanent resident,

(ii) a certificate of identity issued in Canada to the applicant by the Minister of Foreign Affairs, or

(iii) refugee travel papers issued in Canada to the applicant by the Minister of Foreign Affairs;

(d) a copy of

(i) the form IMM1000, entitled "Record of Landing", held by the applicant,

(ii) a provincial driver's license held by the applicant,

(iii) a photo-identity card held by the applicant and issued by a province,

(iv) a student card held by the applicant and issued by a provincially accredited college or university, or

(v) the most recent notice of assessment within the meaning of the *Income Tax Act* received in relation to the applicant's income tax return; and

(e) two identical photographs that

(i) were taken not more than 12 months before the application was made,

(ii) [Repealed SOR/2008-188, s. 1(4).]

(iii) are in black and white or colour on paper,

(iv) show a full front view of the applicant's head and shoulders and have a white background,

(v) have a view of the applicant's head that is at least 25 mm (one inch) and at most 35 mm (1.375 inches) in length,

**(vi) show the applicant's face unobscured by sunglasses or any other object, and**

**(vii) have a dimension of 35 mm (1.375 inches) by 45 mm (1.75 inches).**

**(3) [Repealed SOR/2008-188, s. 1(5).]**

SOR/2004-167, s. 16; SOR/2008-188, s. 1

**57. (1) Applicants — Subject to subsection (3), every person who applies for a permanent resident card must make and sign the application on their own behalf.**

**(2) Minor applicants 14 years of age or more — The application of a child who is 14 years of age or more but less than 18 years of age must be signed by the applicant and one of their parents unless**

**(a) a Canadian court has made another person responsible for the child, in which case that person must co-sign the application; or**

**(b) the parents are deceased, in which case the person legally responsible for the child must co-sign the application.**

**(3) Minor applicants less than 14 years of age — The application of a child who is less than 14 years of age must be signed by one of their parents unless**

**(a) a Canadian court has made another person responsible for the child, in which case that person must sign the application; or**

**(b) the parents are deceased, in which case the person legally responsible for the child must sign the application.**

**58. (1) Providing address within 180 days — In order to allow the Department to provide a permanent resident card, a permanent resident referred to in paragraph 53(1)(a) must provide to the Department, within 180 days after their entry into Canada, their address in Canada and, on the request of an officer,**

**(a) a photograph of the permanent resident that satisfies the requirements of subparagraphs 56(2)(e)(i) and (iii) to (vii); and**

**(b) the signature of the permanent resident or, if the permanent resident is a child less than 14 years of age, the signature of one of their parents unless**

**(i) a Canadian court has made another person responsible for the child, in which case the signature of that person must be provided, or**

**(ii) the parents are deceased, in which case the signature of the person legally responsible for the child must be provided.**

**(2) Issuance after 180 days — If the permanent resident does not comply with subsection (1), they must make an application for a permanent resident card in accordance with section 56.**

**(3) Attendance required — A permanent resident who applies for a permanent resident card under section 56 must, in order to be provided with the card, attend at the time and place specified in a notice mailed by the Department. If the permanent resident fails to attend within 180 days after the Department first mails a notice, the card shall be destroyed and the applicant must make a new application in order to be issued a permanent resident card.**

(4) **Document verification** — When attending in accordance with subsection (3), a permanent resident must produce the original documents copies of which were included in their application as required by paragraphs 56(2)(c) and (d).

SOR/2004-167, s. 17

59. (1) **Issuance of new permanent resident card** — An officer shall, on application, issue a new permanent resident card if

(a) the applicant has not lost permanent resident status under subsection 46(1) of the Act;

(b) the applicant has not been convicted under section 123 or 126 of the Act for an offence related to the misuse of a permanent resident card, unless a pardon has been granted and has not ceased to have effect or been revoked under the *Criminal Records Act*;

(c) the applicant complies with the requirements of sections 56 and 57 and subsection 58(4); and

(d) the applicant returns their last permanent resident card, unless the card has been lost, stolen or destroyed, in which case the applicant must produce all relevant evidence in accordance with subsection 16(1) of the Act.

(2) **Issuance of new permanent resident card — effect** — A previously issued permanent resident card is revoked on the issuance of a new permanent resident card.

SOR/2004-167, s. 18

60. **Revocation** — A permanent resident card is revoked if

(a) the permanent resident becomes a Canadian citizen or otherwise loses permanent resident status;

(b) the permanent resident card is lost, stolen or destroyed; or

(c) the permanent resident is deceased.

## DIVISION 2 — RESIDENCY OBLIGATION

61. (1) **Canadian business** — Subject to subsection (2), for the purposes of subparagraphs 28(2)(a)(iii) and (iv) of the Act and of this section, a Canadian business is

(a) a corporation that is incorporated under the laws of Canada or of a province and that has an ongoing operation in Canada;

(b) an enterprise, other than a corporation described in paragraph (a), that has an ongoing operation in Canada and

(i) that is capable of generating revenue and is carried on in anticipation of profit, and

(ii) in which a majority of voting or ownership interests is held by Canadian citizens, permanent residents, or Canadian businesses as defined in this subsection; or



IRP Regulations

(c) an organization or enterprise created under the laws of Canada or a province.

(2) **Exclusion** — For greater certainty, a Canadian business does not include a business that serves primarily to allow a permanent resident to comply with their residency obligation while residing outside Canada.

(3) **Employment outside Canada** — For the purposes of subparagraphs 28(2)(a)(iii) and (iv) of the Act, the expression "employed on a full-time basis by a Canadian business or in the public service of Canada or of a province" means, in relation to a permanent resident, that the permanent resident is an employee of, or under contract to provide services to, a Canadian business or the public service of Canada or of a province, and is assigned on a full-time basis as a term of the employment or contract to

(a) a position outside Canada;

(b) an affiliated enterprise outside Canada; or

(c) a client of the Canadian business or the public service outside Canada.

(4) **Accompanying outside Canada** — For the purposes of subparagraphs 28(2)(a)(ii) and (iv) of the Act and this section, a permanent resident is accompanying outside Canada a Canadian citizen or another permanent resident — who is their spouse or common-law partner or, in the case of a child, their parent — on each day that the permanent resident is ordinarily residing with the Canadian citizen or the other permanent resident.

(5) **Compliance** — For the purposes of subparagraph 28(2)(a)(iv) of the Act, a permanent resident complies with the residency obligation as long as the permanent resident they are accompanying complies with their residency obligation.

(6) **Child** — For the purposes of subparagraphs 28(2)(a)(ii) and (iv) of the Act, a child means a child of a parent referred to in those subparagraphs, who is not and has never been a spouse or common-law partner and is less than 22 years of age.

SOR/2009-290, s. 1

62. (1) **Calculation — residency obligation** — Subject to subsection (2), the calculation of days under paragraph 28(2)(a) of the Act in respect of a permanent resident does not include any day after

(a) a report is prepared under subsection 44(1) of the Act on the ground that the permanent resident has failed to comply with the residency obligation; or

(b) a decision is made outside of Canada that the permanent resident has failed to comply with the residency obligation.

(2) **Exception** — If the permanent resident is subsequently determined to have complied with the residency obligation, subsection (1) does not apply.

## DIVISION 3 — PERMIT HOLDERS

**63. Period of permit's validity** — A temporary resident permit is valid until any one of the following events occurs:

(a) the permit is cancelled under subsection 24(1) of the Act;

(b) the permit holder leaves Canada without obtaining prior authorization to re-enter Canada;

(c) the period of validity specified on the permit expires; or

(d) a period of three years elapses from its date of validity.

## DIVISION 4 — PERMIT HOLDER CLASS

[Heading amended SOR/2004-167, s. 19.]

**64. Permit holder class** — The permit holder class is prescribed as a class of foreign nationals who may become permanent residents on the basis of the requirements of this Division.

SOR/2004-167, s. 19



**65. Member of class** — A foreign national is a permit holder and a member of the permit holder class if

(a) they have been issued a temporary resident permit under subsection 24(1) of the Act;

(b) they have continuously resided in Canada as a permit holder for a period of

(i) at least three years, if they

(A) are inadmissible on health grounds under subsection 38(1) of the Act,

(B) are inadmissible under paragraph 42(a) of the Act on grounds of an accompanying family member who is inadmissible under subsection 38(1) of the Act, or

(C) are inadmissible under paragraph 42(b) of the Act on grounds of being an accompanying family member of a foreign national who is inadmissible

(I) under subsection 38(1) of the Act, or

(II) under paragraph 42(a) of the Act on grounds of an accompanying family member who is inadmissible under subsection 38(1) of the Act,

(ii) at least five years, if they are inadmissible on any other grounds under the Act, except sections 34 and 35 and subsections 36(1) and 37(1) of the Act;

(c) they have not become inadmissible on any ground since the permit was issued; and

(d) in the case of a foreign national who intends to reside in the Province of Quebec and is not a member of the family class or a person whom the Board

**has determined to be a Convention refugee, the competent authority of that Province is of the opinion that the foreign national meets the selection criteria of the Province.**

SOR/2004-167, s. 20(1), (2)

**65.1 (1) Becoming a permanent resident — A foreign national in Canada who is a permit holder and a member of the permit holder class becomes a permanent resident if, following an examination, it is established that**

**(a) they have applied to remain in Canada as a permanent resident as a member of that class;**

**(b) they are in Canada to establish permanent residence;**

**(c) they meet the selection criteria and other requirements applicable to that class;**

**(d) they hold**

**(i) subject to subsection (4), a document described in any of paragraphs 50(1)(a) to (h), and**

**(ii) a medical certificate, based on the most recent medical examination to which they were required to submit under these Regulations within the previous 12 months, that indicates that their health condition is not likely to be a danger to public health or public safety and is not reasonably expected to cause excessive demand; and**

**(e) they and their family members, whether accompanying or not, are not inadmissible on any ground other than the grounds on which an officer, at the time the permit was issued, formed the opinion that the foreign national was inadmissible.**

**(2) Criteria in the Province of Quebec — For the purposes of paragraph (1)(c), the selection criterion applicable to a foreign national who intends to reside in the Province of Quebec as a permanent resident and who is not a person whom the Board has determined to be a Convention refugee is met by evidence that the competent authority of that Province is of the opinion that the foreign national meets the selection criteria of the Province.**

**(3) Foreign nationals without a passport or other travel document — The following foreign nationals who are not holders of a document described in any of paragraphs 50(1)(a) to (h) may submit with their application a document described in paragraph 178(1)(a) or (b):**

**(a) a protected person within the meaning of subsection 95(2) of the Act;**

**(b) a person who was determined to be a Convention refugee seeking resettlement under the *Immigration Regulations, 1978*, as enacted by Order in Council P.C. 1978-486 dated February 23, 1978 and registered as SOR/78-172, if under the Act or section 69.2 of the former Act, within the meaning of section 187 of the Act,**

**(i) no determination has been made to vacate that determination, or**

**(ii) no determination has been made that the person ceased to be a Convention refugee; and**

(c) a member of the country of asylum class or the source country class under the *Humanitarian Designated Classes Regulations*, as enacted by Order in Council P.C. 1997-477 dated April 8, 1997 and registered as SOR/97-183.

(4) **Alternative documents** — A document submitted under subsection (3) shall be accepted in lieu of a document described in any of paragraphs 50(1)(a) to (h) if it satisfies the requirements of paragraphs 178(2)(a) or (b).

SOR/2004-167, s. 21

## Division 5 — Humanitarian and Compassionate Considerations

66. **Request** — A request made by a foreign national under subsection 25(1) of the Act must be made as an application in writing accompanied by an application to remain in Canada as a permanent resident or, in the case of a foreign national outside Canada, an application for a permanent resident visa.



67. **Applicant outside Canada** — If an exemption from paragraphs 70(1)(a), (c) and (d) is granted under subsection 25(1) of the Act with respect to a foreign national outside Canada who has made the applications referred to in section 66, a permanent resident visa shall be issued to the foreign national if, following an examination, it is established that the foreign national meets the requirement set out in paragraph 70(1)(b) and

(a) in the case of a foreign national who intends to reside in the Province of Quebec and is not a member of the family class, the competent authority of that Province is of the opinion that the foreign national meets the selection criteria of the Province;

(b) the foreign national is not otherwise inadmissible; and

(c) the family members of the foreign national, whether accompanying or not, are not inadmissible.

68. **Applicant in Canada** — If an exemption from paragraphs 72(1)(a), (c) and (d) is granted under subsection 25(1) of the Act with respect to a foreign national in Canada who has made the applications referred to in section 66, the foreign national becomes a permanent resident if, following an examination, it is established that the foreign national meets the requirements set out in paragraphs 72(1)(b) and (e) and

(a) in the case of a foreign national who intends to reside in the Province of Quebec and is not a member of the family class or a person whom the Board has determined to be a Convention refugee, the competent authority of that Province is of the opinion that the foreign national meets the selection criteria of the Province;

(b) the foreign national is not otherwise inadmissible; and

(c) the family members of the foreign national, whether accompanying or not, are not inadmissible

SOR/2004-167, s. 22(2)

**69. (1) Accompanying family member outside Canada — A foreign national who is an accompanying family member of a foreign national to whom a permanent resident visa is issued under section 67 shall be issued a permanent resident visa if, following an examination, it is established that**

**(a) the accompanying family member is not inadmissible; and**

**(b) in the case of an accompanying family member who intends to reside in the Province of Quebec and is not a member of the family class or a person whom the Board has determined to be a Convention refugee, the competent authority of that Province is of the opinion that the family member meets the selection criteria of the Province.**

**(2) Accompanying family member in Canada — A foreign national who is an accompanying family member of a foreign national who becomes a permanent resident under section 68 shall become a permanent resident if the accompanying family member is in Canada and, following an examination, it is established that**

**(a) the accompanying family member is not inadmissible; and**

**(b) in the case of an accompanying family member who intends to reside in the Province of Quebec and is not a member of the family class or a person whom the Board has determined to be a Convention refugee, the competent authority of that Province is of the opinion that the family member meets the selection criteria of the Province.**

SOR/2004-167, s. 23

## Division 6 — Permanent Resident Visa

**70. (1) Issuance — An officer shall issue a permanent resident visa to a foreign national if, following an examination, it is established that**

**(a) the foreign national has applied in accordance with these Regulations for a permanent resident visa as a member of a class referred to in subsection (2);**

*[Editor's Note: SOR/2002-227, s. 356 provides that if a person referred to in paragraph (f) of the definition "member of the family class" in s. 2(1) of the* Immigration Regulations, 1978, *SOR/78-172 (the "former Regulations") made an application under the former Regulations for a permanent resident visa before June 28, 2002, the application is governed by the former* Immigration Act, *R.S.C. 1985, c. I-2.]*

**(b) the foreign national is coming to Canada to establish permanent residence;**

**(c) the foreign national is a member of that class;**

**(d) the foreign national meets the selection criteria and other requirements applicable to that class; and**

**(e) the foreign national and their family members, whether accompanying or not, are not inadmissible.**

*[Editor's Note: SOR/2002-227, s. 353 provides that if a person has made an application under the former* Immigration Act, *R.S.C. 1985, c. I-2 before June 28, 2002, the following provisions of the* Immigration and Refugee Protection Regulations, *SOR/2002-227 (the "new Regulations") do not apply to the person in respect of any*

*of his or her non-accompanying dependent children, referred to in s. 352 of the new Regulations, or his or her non-accompanying common-law partner:*

*(a) paragraph 70(1)(e);*

*(b) subparagraph 72(1)(e)(i); and*

*(c) paragraph 108(1)(a).]*

(2) **Classes** — **The classes are**

**(a) the family class;**

**(b) the economic class, consisting of the federal skilled worker class, the transitional federal skilled worker class, the Quebec skilled worker class, the provincial nominee class, the Canadian experience class, the investor class, the entrepreneur class, the self-employed persons class, the transitional federal investor class, the transitional federal entrepreneur class and the transitional federal self-employed persons class; and**

**(c) the Convention refugees abroad class, the country of asylum class and the source country class.**

(3) **Criteria in the Province of Quebec** — **For the purposes of paragraph (1)(d), the selection criterion for a foreign national who intends to reside in the Province of Quebec as a permanent resident and is not a member of the family class is met by evidence that the competent authority of that Province is of the opinion that the foreign national complies with the provincial selection criteria.**

(4) **Accompanying family members** — **A foreign national who is an accompanying family member of a foreign national who is issued a permanent resident visa shall be issued a permanent resident visa if, following an examination, it is established that**

**(a) the accompanying family member is not inadmissible; and**

**(b) in the case of a family member who intends to reside in the Province of Quebec and is not a member of the family class, the competent authority of that Province is of the opinion that the family member complies with the provincial selection criteria.**

(5) **Family member** — **If a permanent resident visa is not issued to a child as an accompanying family member of a foreign national or the foreign national's spouse or common law partner, a permanent resident visa shall not be issued to a child of that child as an accompanying family member of the foreign national.**

SOR/2003-383, s. 1; SOR/2008-254, s. 1

71. **Issuance — particular Quebec selection cases** — **An officer shall issue a permanent resident visa to a foreign national outside Canada who intends to reside in the Province of Quebec as a permanent resident and does not satisfy the requirements of paragraphs 70(1)(a), (c) and (d) if, following an examination, it is established that**

**(a) the foreign national has applied for a permanent resident visa in accordance with these Regulations, other than paragraph 10(2)(c);**

**(b) the foreign national may not be issued a permanent resident visa under subsection 176(2) and is not a member of any class of persons prescribed by these Regulations who may become permanent residents or be issued permanent resident visas;**

**(c) the foreign national is named in a *Certificat de sélection du Québec* issued by that Province indicating that the foreign national, under the regulations made under *An Act respecting immigration to Québec*, R.S.Q., c. I-0.2, as amended from time to time, is a foreign national in a particularly distressful situation; and**

**(d) the foreign national and their family members, whether accompanying or not, are not inadmissible.**

## DIVISION 7 — BECOMING A PERMANENT RESIDENT

[Heading added SOR/2008-253, s. 3.]

**71.1 (1) Foreign nationals outside Canada — A foreign national who is a member of a class referred to in subsection 70(2) and is outside Canada must, to become a permanent resident, present their permanent resident visa to an officer at a port of entry.**

**(2) Foreign nationals in Canada as temporary residents — A foreign national who is a member of a class referred to in paragraph 70(2)(a) or (b) and who is a temporary resident in Canada must, to become a permanent resident, present their permanent resident visa to an officer at a port of entry or at an office of the Department in Canada.**

SOR/2008-253, s. 3

[Heading repealed SOR/2008-253, s. 4.]

**72. (1) Obtaining status — A foreign national in Canada becomes a permanent resident if, following an examination, it is established that**

**(a) they have applied to remain in Canada as a permanent resident as a member of a class referred to in subsection (2);**

**(b) they are in Canada to establish permanent residence;**

**(c) they are a member of that class;**

**(d) they meet the selection criteria and other requirements applicable to that class;**

**(e) except in the case of a foreign national who has submitted a document accepted under subsection 178(2) or of a member of the protected temporary residents class,**

**(i) they and their family members, whether accompanying or not, are not inadmissible,**

*[Editor's Note: SOR/2002-227, s. 353 provides that if a person has made an application under the former* Immigration Act, *R.S.C. 1985, c. I-2 before June 28, 2002, the following provisions of the* Immigration and Refugee Protection

Regulations, *SOR/2002-227 (the "new Regulations") do not apply to the person in respect of any of his or her non-accompanying dependent children, referred to in s. 352 of the new Regulations, or his or her non-accompanying common-law partner:*

*(a) paragraph 70(1)(e);*

*(b) subparagraph 72(1)(e)(i); and*

*(c) paragraph 108(1)(a).]*

**(ii) they hold a document described in any of paragraphs 50(1)(a) to (h), and**

**(iii) they hold a medical certificate, based on the most recent medical examination to which they were required to submit under these Regulations within the previous 12 months, that indicates that their health condition is not likely to be a danger to public health or public safety and, unless subsection 38(2) of the Act applies, is not reasonably expected to cause excessive demand; and**

**(f) in the case of a member of the protected temporary residents class, they are not inadmissible.**

(2) **Classes — The classes are**

**(a) the live-in caregiver class;**

**(b) the spouse or common-law partner in Canada class; and**

**(c) the protected temporary residents class.**

(3) **Criteria in the Province of Quebec — For the purposes of paragraph (1)(d), the selection criterion applicable to a foreign national who intends to reside in the Province of Quebec as a permanent resident, and who is not a member of the family class or a person whom the Board has determined to be a Convention refugee, is met by evidence that the competent authority of that Province is of the opinion that the foreign national meets the selection criteria of the Province.**

(4) **Accompanying family members — A foreign national who is an accompanying family member of a foreign national who becomes a permanent resident under this section shall be issued a permanent resident visa or become a permanent resident, as the case may be, if following an examination it is established that**

**(a) the accompanying family member is not inadmissible;**

**(b) in the case of a family member who intends to reside in the Province of Quebec and is not a member of the family class or a person whom the Board has determined to be a Convention refugee, the competent authority of that Province is of the opinion that the family member meets the selection criteria of the Province.**

SOR/2004-167, s. 26(1)–(4), (6), (7); SOR/2008-253, s. 5

IRP Regulations

# PART 6 — ECONOMIC CLASSES

## DIVISION 1 — SKILLED WORKERS

### *Interpretation*

**73. Definitions — The following definitions apply in this Division, other than section 87.1.**

**"educational credential" means any diploma, degree or trade or apprenticeship credential issued on the completion of a program of study or training at an educational or training institution recognized by the authorities responsible for registering, accrediting, supervising and regulating such institutions in the country of issue. *("diplôme")***

**"former Regulations" has the same meaning as in subsection 316(1). *("ancien règlement")***

**"restricted occupation" means an occupation designated as a restricted occupation by the Minister, taking into account labour market activity on both an area and a national basis, following consultation with the Department of Human Resources Development, provincial governments and any other relevant organizations or institutions. *("profession d'accès limité")***

**Proposed Amendment — 73 "restricted occupation"**

**"restricted occupation" means an occupation designated as a restricted occupation by the Minister, taking into account labour market activity on both an area and a national basis, following consultation with the Department of Human Resources and Skills Development, provincial governments and any other relevant organizations or institutions. *("profession d'accès limité")***

SOR/2010-172, s. 5(b) [To come into force April 1, 2011.]

SOR/2003-383, s. 2; SOR/2008-254, s. 2

[Heading repealed SOR/2008-253, s. 6.]

**74. [Repealed SOR/2008-253, s. 6.]**

### *Federal Skilled Workers*

#### Federal Skilled Worker Class

**75. (1) Class — For the purposes of subsection 12(2) of the Act, the federal skilled worker class is hereby prescribed as a class of persons who are skilled workers and who may become permanent residents on the basis of their ability to become economically established in Canada and who intend to reside in a province other than the Province of Quebec.**

(2) **Skilled workers — A foreign national is a skilled worker if**

**(a) within the 10 years preceding the date of their application for a permanent resident visa, they have at least one year of continuous full-time employment experience, as described in subsection 80(7), or the equivalent in continuous part-time employment in one or more occupations, other than a restricted occupation, that are listed in Skill Type 0 Management Occupations or Skill Level A or B of the *National Occupational Classification* matrix;**

**(b) during that period of employment they performed the actions described in the lead statement for the occupation as set out in the occupational descriptions of the *National Occupational Classification*; and**

**(c) during that period of employment they performed a substantial number of the main duties of the occupation as set out in the occupational descriptions of the *National Occupational Classification*, including all of the essential duties.**

(3) **Minimal requirements — If the foreign national fails to meet the requirements of subsection (2), the application for a permanent resident visa shall be refused and no further assessment is required.**

*[Editor's Note: SOR/2002-227, s. 361(1) provides that if, before June 28, 2002, a foreign national referred to in SOR/2002-227, s. 361(2) has been assessed by a visa officer and awarded the number of units of assessment required by the* Immigration Regulations, 1978, *SOR/78-172 (the "former Regulations"), that assessment is, for the purpose of the* Immigration and Refugee Protection Regulations, *SOR/2002-227 (the "new Regulations"), an award of points equal or superior to the minimum number of points required of*

*(a) a skilled worker, in the case of a foreign national described in paragraph (2)(a) of the new Regulations;*

*(b) an investor, in the case of a foreign national described in paragraph (2)(b) of the new Regulations;*

*(c) an entrepreneur, in the case of a foreign national described in paragraph (2)(c) of the new Regulations; or*

*(d) a self-employed person, in the case of a foreign national described in paragraph (2)(a) of the new Regulations.*

*SOR/2002-227, s. 361(2) provides that SOR/2002-227, s. 361(1) applies in respect of a foreign national who submitted an application under the former Regulations, as one of the following, for an immigrant visa that is pending immediately before June 28, 2002:*

*(a) a person described in subparagraph 9(1)(b)(i) or paragraph 10(1)(b) of the former Regulations;*

*(b) an investor; or*

*(c) an entrepreneur.*

*SOR/2002-227, s. 361(5) provides that if a foreign national referred to in paragraph 2(a) of the new Regulations made an application before January 1, 2002 for an immigrant visa and has not, before April 1, 2003, been awarded the number of units of assessment required by the former Regulations, he or she must obtain a minimum of 70 points based*

IRP Regulations

*on the factors set out in paragraph 76(1)(a) of the new Regulations to become a permanent resident as a member of the federal skilled worker class.]*

SOR/2004-167, s. 27

## Case Law

*Shangguan v. Canada (Minister of Citizenship & Immigration)*, 2007 CarswellNat 181, 2007 FC 75 (F.C.) — The applicant sought judicial review of a decision of a visa officer refusing his application for permanent residence in the skilled worker category on the basis that she did not meet the requirements under paragraph 75(2) of the Regulations. The onus is on the applicant to fully satisfy the visa officer of the existence of all the positive elements in her application. The visa officer dismissed the idea that the applicant had a managerial position, in part because she found that the applicant was not privy to financial reports or profit/loss statements and that she was not tasked with the responsibility of conducting daily banking transactions or general accounting. The NOC states that persons who fit within the occupation "Restaurant and Food Service Managers" perform some or all of the duties listed under this occupation. None of the listed duties referred to financial reports or responsibility for banking transaction or general accounting. The list does include monitoring revenue; however, since an applicant need only have performed some of the duties listed, monitoring revenues is not a mandatory requirement. The officer interpreted the NOC duties relevant to the occupation in an unreasonable manner by importing extraneous criteria into the occupation's duties. The officer's error of law was sufficient to warrant setting the decision aside for reconsideration by a different officer.

*Mercado v. Canada (Minister of Citizenship & Immigration)* (2006), 60 Imm. L.R. (3d) 88, 2006 CarswellNat 4484, 2006 FC 1527 (F.C.) — The applicant argued the immigration officer incorrectly assessed his experience under s. 75 of the Regulations. He argued that he presented evidence of employment with a landscaping company. He contended that the evidence established that he met the requirements for Landscape Contractor as set out in NOC 8255. He argued that the immigration officer incorrectly rejected such evidence as it was evidence of contracting for services and not evidence of employment. Under cross-examination, the immigration officer admitted that she applied s. 75 as if it only applied to employment situations. This was a questionable interpretation as s. 75(2) applies to "continuous full-time employment experience" which could be broad enough to cover contracting. However, this was immaterial, since the applicant had to first establish that he qualified as a skilled worker.

The applicant also argued that his arranged employment should have been assessed under s. 82(2)(c) instead of s. 82(2)(a). He made his application from Canada on March 18, 2005, and went back to Mexico for his interview on October 25, 2005. While by his own admission he had worked illegally in Canada for many years and never paid any taxes, at the time of the assessment, he was in Mexico. Given that the applicant was making the application while working illegally in Canada, none of the provisions of s. 82(2) were available to him. The immigration officer rightly disqualified him under s. 82(2)(a). She could have done so equally under s. 82(2)(c).

The applicant also argued that the immigration officer erred by not employing a substituted evaluation scheme under s. 76(3). Section 76(3) only comes into play once an immigration officer has found that an applicant qualifies as a skilled worker, but does not acquire the requisite minimum number of points. Here the applicant never qualified as a skilled worker, thus the immigration officer could never invoke s. 76(3). The application for judicial review was dismissed.

**76. (1) Selection criteria — For the purpose of determining whether a skilled worker, as a member of the federal skilled worker class, will be able to become economically established in Canada, they must be assessed on the basis of the following criteria:**

**(a) the skilled worker must be awarded not less than the minimum number of required points referred to in subsection (2) on the basis of the following factors, namely,**

**(i) education, in accordance with section 78,**

**(ii) proficiency in the official languages of Canada, in accordance with section 79,**

**(iii) experience, in accordance with section 80,**

**(iv) age, in accordance with section 81,**

**(v) arranged employment, in accordance with section 82, and**

**(vi) adaptability, in accordance with section 83; and**

**(b) the skilled worker must**

**(i) have in the form of transferable and available funds, unencumbered by debts or other obligations, an amount equal to half the minimum necessary income applicable in respect of the group of persons consisting of the skilled worker and their family members, or**

**(ii) be awarded the number of points referred to in subsection 82(2) for arranged employment in Canada within the meaning of subsection 82(1).**

**(2) Number of points — The Minister shall fix and make available to the public the minimum number of points required of a skilled worker, on the basis of**

**(a) the number of applications by skilled workers as members of the federal skilled worker class currently being processed;**

**(b) the number of skilled workers projected to become permanent residents according to the report to Parliament referred to in section 94 of the Act; and**

**(c) the potential, taking into account economic and other relevant factors, for the establishment of skilled workers in Canada.**

**(3) Circumstances for officer's substituted evaluation — Whether or not the skilled worker has been awarded the minimum number of required points referred to in subsection (2), an officer may substitute for the criteria set out in paragraph (1)(a) their evaluation of the likelihood of the ability of the skilled worker to become economically established in Canada if the number of points awarded is not a sufficient indicator of whether the skilled worker may become economically established in Canada.**

**(4) Concurrence — An evaluation made under subsection (3) requires the concurrence of a second officer.**

SOR/2004-167, s. 28(2)

## Case Law

### Section 76(1)

*Hussain v. Canada (Minister of Citizenship & Immigration)* (2009), 80 Imm. L.R. (3d) 124, 2009 CarswellNat 546, 2009 CarswellNat 1117, 2009 FC 209 (F.C.) — The applicant sought judicial review of a visa officer's decision to refuse an application for permanent residence under the skilled worker class. The applicant was awarded 68 points out of a minimum of 67. Nonetheless, the officer undertook a negative substituted evaluation pursuant to subs. 76(3).

The officer failed to take into account the applicant's settlement funds. This is an essential element when an assessment is conducted pursuant to subs. 76(1) of the Regulations. Although an officer is presumed to have considered all the evidence, the failure in this case to refer to these funds raises the suspicion that she did not do so. This is a reviewable error.

Insofar as the exercise of discretion pursuant to subs. 76(4) is concerned, there was another error. The second officer apparently took into account the marital status of the applicant who, in accordance with Pakistan law, has two wives. His application for permanent residence showed that he intended to be accompanied by one wife if granted status in Canada. The second officer referred to his "peculiar/polygamist family situation". The Court found that this was an irrelevant consideration in relation to the application before her. The application for judicial review was allowed.

*Wang v. Canada (Minister of Citizenship & Immigration)*, 2008 CarswellNat 3897, 2008 CarswellNat 2051, 2008 FC 798 (F.C.) — The officer concluded that the applicant had insufficient points to qualify for immigration to Canada. She noted that no points were awarded for the male applicant's brother living in Canada. She determined that the evidence provided by the applicants in support of this allegation was insufficient to establish that the brother resided in Canada at the time of the decision, based on the fact that the majority of the documentation provided related to the brother's wife and not him. The brother's notice of assessment was the only document which specifically related to him. It indicated he earned a total of $2,000 in 2006. The officer noted that her records indicated that the brother had prolonged absences from Canada in the past. The Notice of Assessment was therefore insufficient evidence to convince her that he was a resident of Canada at the time the decision was made. The officer's decision was based on the insufficiency of evidence establishing the brother's residence in Canada. The burden of adducing sufficient evidence to support the application falls to the applicant. The application for judicial review was dismissed.

*Zheng v. Canada (Minister of Citizenship & Immigration)*, 2008 CarswellNat 1864, 2008 CarswellNat 880, 2008 FC 430 — A visa officer rejected an application for landing by a skilled worker from China. The visa officer's entry in the CAIPS system identifies a stark conflict in the evidence the applicant tendered in obvious error: the standard application form was completed to say that the applicant attended Kunming University at the same time she completed high school there, which, of course, is impossible. Because of the conflict, and the fact that the applicant failed to file a diploma to prove her attendance at the university, the application was rejected. It was remarkably unfair for the visa officer not to have asked for clarification of the obvious error which drove the rejection of the applicant's application. The visa officer's decision was set aside.

*Gay v. Canada (Minister of Citizenship & Immigration)* (2007), 69 Imm. L.R. (3d) 245, 320 F.T.R. 132, 2007 FC 1280, 2007 CarswellNat 5403, 2007 CarswellNat 4277 (F.C.) — The applicant, an accountant by profession, applied for permanent residence under the skilled worker category. He forwarded proof of his financial situation to the Canadian Embassy, claiming US$19,592.10 as his available financial resources. A letter from the Embassy was sent to the applicant requesting that he provide evidence of availability of his financial resources in the amount of C$10,168, for the purpose of establishment in Canada for his file to be finalized. The applicant forwarded to the Canadian Embassy a certified copy of a property deed, showing his title to the land, a statement of his net assets and new bank statements. The financial evidence provided at this time had a total value of approximately C$22,000.00. The application was refused pursuant to paragraph 76(1)(b) of the Regulations. The visa officer did not consider the applicant's land assets in the calculation of his settlement funds, as the applicant did not establish that this property amounted to funds that were available, transferable and unencumbered by debts or other obligations, as required by subs. 76(1) of the Regulations. The officer did not provide the applicant with the opportunity to provide more complete information in order to address her concerns that the assets from the land were transferable and unencumbered by debts and other obligations. Her failure to mention important pieces of evidence resulted in her having made an erroneous finding of fact "without regard to the evidence" before her (i.e. the certified copy of a property deed showing the applicant's title to the land, a statement of the applicant's net assets and new bank statements). The application for judicial review was granted.

*Hernandez v. Canada (Minister of Citizenship & Immigration)* (2004), 43 Imm. L.R. (3d) 63, 2004 CarswellNat 5382, 2004 CarswellNat 3658, 2004 FC 1398 (F.C.) — The applicant applied for admission as a member of the skilled worker class. The operations manual purports to assist a visa officer in assessing an application of this type. The manual requires a visa officer to give an applicant the opportunity to supply missing documentation concerning settlement funds. The officer failed to comply with this guideline and the officer's decision was set aside.

## Section 76(3)

*Kisson v. Canada (Minister of Citizenship and Immigration)* (2010), 88 Imm. L.R. (3d) 66, 2010 FC 99, 2010 CarswellNat 803, 2010 CarswellNat 161 (F.C.) — This was an application for judicial review of a visa officer's decision rejecting the applicant's application for permanent residence under the federal skilled worker category. The applicant requested a substitute evaluation and exemption from the requirements of IRPA pursuant to humanitarian and compassionate considerations. The visa officer did not demonstrate that he looked beyond the selection criteria listed at subs. 76(1) of the Regulations (*i.e.* education, language, experience, age, arranged employment, adaptability). There was no evidence that the visa officer's substituted evaluation broadly assessed the likelihood of the ability of the applicant to become economically established in Canada according to his set of circumstances. The clear intent of subs. 76(3) is to allow the visa officer to substitute their evaluation taking into account a number of factors, and not just the factors listed in s. 76(1). In this case, the applicant had an existing employment offer and previous establishment in Canada which were indicative of the possibility that the applicant will once again be able to establish himself successfully in Canada. It was unreasonable that these factors do not appear to have been considered by the officer when he assessed the humanitarian and compassionate considerations under s. 25 of IRPA. Application for judicial review was allowed.

*Hussain v. Canada (Minister of Citizenship & Immigration)* (2009), 80 Imm. L.R. (3d) 124, 2009 CarswellNat 546, 2009 CarswellNat 1117, 2009 FC 209 (F.C.) — The applicant sought judicial review of a visa officer's decision to refuse an application for permanent residence under the skilled worker class. The applicant was awarded 68 points out of a minimum of 67. Nonetheless, the officer undertook a negative substituted evaluation pursuant to subs. 76(3).

The officer failed to take into account the applicant's settlement funds. This is an essential element when an assessment is conducted pursuant to subs. 76(1) of the *Regulations*. Although an officer is presumed to have considered all the evidence, the failure in this case to refer to these funds raises the suspicion that she did not do so. This is a reviewable error.

In so far as the exercise of discretion pursuant to subs. 76(4) is concerned, there was another error. The second officer apparently took into account the marital status of the applicant who, in accordance with Pakistan law, has two wives. His application for permanent residence showed that he intended to be accompanied by one wife if granted status in Canada. The second officer referred to his "peculiar/polygamist family situation". The Court found that this was an irrelevant consideration in relation to the application before her. The application for judicial review was allowed.

*Lackhee v. Canada (Minister of Citizenship & Immigration)*, [2008] F.C.J. No. 1615, 76 Imm. L.R. (3d) 283, 337 F.T.R. 299 (Eng.), 2008 CarswellNat 5316, 2008 CarswellNat 4270, 2008 FC 1270 (F.C.) — The designated immigration officer who rendered the impugned decision rejected the application for permanent residence because he "obtained insufficient points to qualify for immigration to Canada, the minimum requirement being 67 points". The applicant did not contest the points awarded to him by the officer. Nor did the applicant argue that the officer did not turn her mind to his request for substituted evaluation. Instead, the applicant argued that the officer exercised her discretion in a capricious manner without due regard to the evidence in determining that the units of assessment assigned were an accurate indication of his prospects of becoming established in Canada.

Written reasons explaining why the request for substituted evaluation was denied are not required. The Court was sympathetic to the applicant's position: he was a skilled tradesman with expertise in a field that is in high demand in Canada, and his profile was compelling. It was unclear why his relative lack of formal education and modest score on his language assessment have any bearing on the question of his ability to become economically settled in Canada. However, it is not the role of the Court to substitute its own view for that of the decision maker, whom the legislation has imbued with broad discretion over this matter.

Although the immigration officer referred in her notes to $25,000 initially noted in the applicant's application, the updated information indicating the availability of dramatically more assets for establishment is nowhere mentioned in either her notes or her refusal letter. It is not enough that she was aware of this information: she had a duty to reflect this awareness in her notes and/or reasons in the interests of "justification, transparency and intelligibility". The jurisprudence of the Federal Court leaves no doubt that settlement income is among the considerations pertinent to assessing "the likelihood of the ability of the skilled worker to become economically established in Canada". The officer's failure to make any reference to the considerable assets available to the applicant in either her decision or her notes constituted a reviewable error warranting court intervention. The application was set aside.

*Esguerra v. Canada (Minister of Citizenship & Immigration)*, 2008 CarswellNat 864, 2008 FC 413 — Discretion under subs. 76(3) of the IRPR is clearly exceptional and applies only in cases where the points awarded are not a sufficient indicator of whether the skilled worker will become economically established. The fact that the applicant or even the Court would have weighed the factors differently is not a sufficient ground for judicial review.

*Fernandes v. Canada (Minister of Citizenship & Immigration)* (2008), 71 Imm. L.R. (3d) 134, 2008 FC 243, 2008 CarswellNat 465 (F.C.) — When it is said that an officer need give no reasons for refusing to exercise a discretion, what is meant is that an officer need give no reasons for exercising the discretion negatively. But it must be clear that the visa officer did consider whether the discretion should be exercised in favour of the applicant. There was nothing to indicate that the visa officer considered exercising the discretion under subs. 76(3). Therefore, she erred in law and the decision was set aside.

*Choi v. Canada (Minister of Citizenship & Immigration)*, 2008 CarswellNat 1372, 2008 FC 577 — The applicant applied for permanent residence under the economic class, skilled worker category, as a secondary school teacher. The applicant received an offer of employment as a music teacher at Cambridge International College of Canada in Toronto. The offer required both oral and written proficiency in English and was open for a two-year period from the date of issue. The applicant submitted the results of her language proficiency exams. The language results established that the applicant had "no proficiency" in English with respect to speaking, listening and writing, and that she possessed only "basic" English proficiency with respect to reading. The visa officer concluded that since the arranged employment opinion specified that both oral and written English was a requirement, and the applicant's IELTS score indicated that she had no proficiency in speaking, listening, and writing, and only basic proficiency in reading of English, she did not warrant any points for arranged employment in Canada.

Under subs. 76(3) of the Regulations, a visa officer may substitute the points assessment with his or her own evaluation of an applicant's likelihood of becoming economically established in Canada. Such a power is discretionary under the Regulations and may be performed "if the number of points awarded is not a sufficient indicator of whether the skilled worker may become economically established in Canada." The applicant argued that the visa officer did not give any weight to the principal's letter, which assured the visa officer that the applicant would be able to fulfill the requirements of the job, and that her English ability would soon rise to the requirements of the job. In the Court's view, it was unreasonable for the visa officer not to give this letter some weight as a sufficient indicator of the applicant's ability to perform this job to the satisfaction of the principal of the school. The applicant also argued that she had settlement funds totalling approximately C$699,000 and that it was impossible for a reasonable person to conclude that a person arriving in Canada with these funds and an offer of employment would not be able to become "economically established in Canada." The Court concluded that consideration under subs. 76(3) should not be limited to the assessment of points, but rather, should be open to all factors identified in subs. 76(1), including the settlement funds possessed by the applicant. In this case, there was no evidence that the visa officer considered those funds in refusing to exercise his discretion to substitute his evaluation. The visa officer's decision was set aside and the matter remitted to another visa officer for redetermination.

*Eslamieh v. Canada (Minister of Citizenship & Immigration)*, 2008 CarswellNat 1701, 2008 CarswellNat 2799, 2008 FC 722 — The applicant's application for permanent residence status as a skilled worker was rejected. She scored 66 out of a possible 100 points. The applicant contended that the visa officer should have considered her discretion to grant the applicant permanent residence status despite her failure to reach the threshold set by the Minister pursuant to subs. 76(3) of the IRPA Regulations.

Given that the decision of the visa officer is highly discretionary, it is to be reviewed on a standard of reasonableness with great deference shown by the Court. Visa officers have the authority to consider an alternative evaluation under subs. 76(3) by their own motion. That said, it is clear from the jurisprudence that they are under no obligation to exercise that discretion unless specifically requested to do so. The applicant concedes that she did not make such a request, and therefore, the Court could not find that the visa officer was unreasonable in her decision.

The applicant also raised a question of natural justice inferentially in her reply brief and at the hearing. She asserted that the officer should have considered her application in the context of her self-representation and extremely narrow failure to reach the point target. From that perspective, the officer had an obligation in the name of fairness to consider her discretion under subs. 76(3). While the Court was sympathetic to this contention, it is trite law that the applicant is restricted, also for reasons of natural justice and procedural fairness, to arguing issues raised in her application for leave. She sought leave solely on the ground that the officer had erred in law. The Court could not now substitute a ground which was not contained therein. The application was dismissed.

*Tathgur v. Canada (Minister of Citizenship & Immigration)*, [2007] F.C.J. No. 1662, 321 F.T.R. 102, 2007 FC 1293, 68 Imm. L.R. (3d) 258, 2007 CarswellNat 4354, 2007 CarswellNat 4954 — The failure by the visa officer to consider exercising the statutory discretion when requested to do so is a failure to carry out a statutory responsibility the visa officer was obligated to do. Under IRPA Regulations, a visa officer may substitute the evaluation criteria if the number of points awarded is not a sufficient indicator of whether the applicant will become economically established in Canada. The respondent argued that the applicant, in requesting the exercise of discretion, did not specify the reason for believing he would become successfully established in Canada despite not meeting the assessment requirements. The Court concluded that the applicant did offer "good reason" for the consideration of positive discretion, and that in any event it is clear that the Regulations impose no such requirement. The request for judicial review was granted.

*Nayyar v. Canada (Minister of Citizenship & Immigration)*, 2007 CarswellNat 559, 2007 FC 199 (F.C.) — The applicant sought judicial review of a decision to refuse his application for permanent residence as a skilled worker. The applicant alleged a breach of procedural fairness in that the officer failed to consider the exercise of positive discretion or substituted evaluation when specifically requested to do so in the applicant's application for permanent residence. It was not in dispute before the Court that: there is nothing on the face of the officer's decision or of the CAIPS notes supporting that decision that the officer considered the exercise of positive discretion or substituted evaluation notwithstanding the fact that the applicant was within one (1) unit of assessment from a successful score under the *Immigration and Refugee Protection Act* and related *Regulations* assessment; there was absolutely no evidence before the Court that the applicant reiterated his request for an exercise of positive discretion or substituted evaluation during his interview with the officer before the decision under review was arrived at; and notwithstanding the fact a request for reconsideration of the decision under review was made, that request made no reference to the question of exercise of positive discretion or substituted evaluation.

In the application for a permanent resident visa filed on behalf of the applicant under the former Act, the applicant's immigration consultant sets out at some length the applicant's personal background and an assessment of the units of assessment the consultant thinks are justified for the applicant, and provides a rationale for the units of assessment that he urges in respect of the education and training factor, the work experience factor, the knowledge of English and other languages factor and the personal suitability factor. The Court was satisfied that the consultant's presentation constitutes the "some good reasons" why a units of assessment determination made by the officer that he did not reach the threshold justifying the issuance of a permanent resident visa would not reflect the chances of successful establishment in Canada by the applicant and would therefore justify the exercise of positive discretion or positive substituted evaluation. The application for judicial review was allowed and was referred back for consideration of the exercise of positive discretion by a different officer.

*Mercado v. Canada (Minister of Citizenship & Immigration)* (2006), 60 Imm. L.R. (3d) 88, 2006 CarswellNat 4484, 2006 FC 1527 (F.C.) — The applicant argued the immigration officer incorrectly assessed his experience under s. 75 of the Regulations. He argued that he presented evidence of employment with a landscaping company. He contended that the evidence established that he met the requirements for Landscape Contractor as set out in NOC 8255. He argued that the immigration officer incorrectly rejected such evidence as it was evidence of contracting for services and not evidence of employment. Under cross-examination, the immigration officer admitted that she applied s. 75 as if it only applied to employment situations. This was a questionable interpretation as s. 75(2) applies to "continuous full-time employment experience" which could be broad enough to cover contracting. However, this was immaterial, since the applicant had to first establish that he qualified as a skilled worker.

The applicant also argued that his arranged employment should have been assessed under s. 82(2)(c) instead of s. 82(2)(a). He made his application from Canada on March 18, 2005, and went back to Mexico for his interview on October 25, 2005. While by his own admission he had worked illegally in Canada for many years and never paid any taxes, at the time of the assessment, he was in Mexico. Given that the applicant was making the application while working illegally in Canada, none of the provisions of s. 82(2) were available to him. The immigration officer rightly disqualified him under s. 82(2)(a). She could have done so equally under s. 82(2)(c).

The applicant also argued that the immigration officer erred by not employing a substituted evaluation scheme under s. 76(3). Section 76(3) only comes into play once an immigration officer has found that an applicant qualifies as a skilled worker, but does not acquire the requisite minimum number of points. Here, the applicant never qualified as a skilled worker, thus the immigration officer could never invoke s. 76(3). The application for judicial review was dismissed.

*Poblado v. Canada (Minister of Citizenship & Immigration)*, 2005 CarswellNat 2399, 2005 CarswellNat 4425, 2005 FC 1167 (F.C.) — A visa officer merely has to inform the applicant that they have considered the request for substitution of evaluation, where the applicant asked that favourable discretion be exercised.

*Yan v. Canada (Minister of Citizenship & Immigration* (2003), 35 Imm. L.R. (3d) 93, 2003 CarswellNat 1111, 2003 FCT 510, 2003 CarswellNat 2795, 233 F.T.R. 161

(T.D.) — The applicant sought to review the refusal of his application for permanent residence. The applicant specifically sought the exercise of positive discretion under s. 11(3) of the Regulations of the former *Immigration Act*. The refusal letter contained no reference to this request. The decision of the visa officer was set aside because the officer failed to consider the applicant's request for positive discretion. The applicant sought an order that the consideration of his application be pursuant to the former *Immigration Act* and Regulations. The Court was not prepared to make this order. The former Act and Regulations are no longer in force. An order that this application be reconsidered with respect to that Act and Regulations would be inconsistent with the law. Furthermore, there is discretion to overlook the fact that a skilled worker has not obtained the minimum number of points, if the visa officer believes that the number of points awarded is not a sufficient indicator of the skilled workers ability to become economically established in Canada.

**77. Conformity — applicable times — For the purposes of Part 5, the requirements and criteria set out in sections 75 and 76 must be met at the time an application for a permanent resident visa is made as well as at the time the visa is issued.**

## Selection Grid

**78. (1) Definitions — The definitions in this subsection apply in this section.**

**"full-time" means, in relation to a program of study leading to an educational credential, at least 15 hours of instruction per week during the academic year, including any period of training in the workplace that forms part of the course of instruction. *("temps plein")***

**"full-time equivalent" means, in respect of part-time or accelerated studies, the period that would have been required to complete those studies on a full-time basis. *("équivalent temps plein")***

**(2) Education (25 points) — A maximum of 25 points shall be awarded for a skilled worker's education as follows:**

**(a) 5 points for a secondary school educational credential;**

**(b) 12 points for a one-year post-secondary educational credential, other than a university educational credential, and a total of at least 12 years of completed full-time or full-time equivalent studies;**

**(c) 15 points for**

**(i) a one-year post-secondary educational credential, other than a university educational credential, and a total of at least 13 years of completed full-time or full-time equivalent studies, or**

**(ii) a one-year university educational credential at the bachelor's level and a total of at least 13 years of completed full-time or full-time equivalent studies;**

**(d) 20 points for**

**(i) a two-year post-secondary educational credential, other than a university educational credential, and a total of at least 14 years of completed full-time or full-time equivalent studies, or**

**(ii) a two-year university educational credential at the bachelor's level and a total of at least 14 years of completed full-time or full-time equivalent studies;**

**(e) 22 points for**

**(i) a three-year post-secondary educational credential, other than a university educational credential, and a total of at least 15 years of completed full-time or full-time equivalent studies, or**

**(ii) two or more university educational credentials at the bachelor's level and a total of at least 15 years of completed full-time or full-time equivalent studies; and**

**(f) 25 points for a university educational credential at the master's or doctoral level and a total of at least 17 years of completed full-time or full-time equivalent studies.**

**(3) Multiple educational achievements — For the purposes of subsection (2), points**

**(a) shall not be awarded cumulatively on the basis of more than one single educational credential; and**

**(b) shall be awarded**

**(i) for the purposes of paragraphs (2)(a) to (d), subparagraph (2)(e)(i) and paragraph (2)(f), on the basis of the single educational credential that results in the highest number of points, and**

**(ii) for the purposes of subparagraph (2)(e)(ii), on the basis of the combined educational credentials referred to in that paragraph.**

**(4) Special circumstances — For the purposes of subsection (2), if a skilled worker has an educational credential referred to in paragraph (2)(b), subparagraph (2)(c)(i) or (ii), (d)(i) or (ii) or (e)(i) or (ii) or paragraph (2)(f), but not the total number of years of full-time or full-time equivalent studies required by that paragraph or subparagraph, the skilled worker shall be awarded the same number of points as the number of years of completed full-time or full-time equivalent studies set out in the paragraph or subparagraph.**

## Case Law

*Shahid v. Canada (Minister of Citizenship & Immigration)*, 2010 FC 130, 2010 CarswellNat 847, 2010 CarswellNat 278 (F.C.) — The application for permanent residence as a skilled worker was refused on the basis that the applicant scored only 63 points. The officer gave the applicant no credit for his spouse's education. The evidence showed that the spouse had completed a two-year university degree and wrote exams in her first and second years. The officer, however, concluded that she was an external candidate at the university and, therefore, did not meet the requirement that she demonstrate completion of 14 years of full-time or full-time equivalent studies.

The Court held that the Minister's position overlooked the definition of "full-time equivalent." Even without the evidence of 14 years of full-time study, the officer had to consider, on the evidence before him, whether the spouse met the definition of full-time equivalent. The Court held that an applicant would meet the criteria where he or she actually takes either more or less than 14 years to acquire a bachelor's degree but, nevertheless shows that the degree would ordinarily take 14 years of full-time study to obtain. The Court held even if she studied elsewhere, or on her own, whether part-time or on an accelerated basis, she could meet the definition of "full-time equivalent" if she proved the degree she obtained would ordinarily take 14 years of full-time study to obtain. The evidence showed that she took exams over two years and obtained a degree that ordinarily takes two years of full-time study to achieve, and that she provided proof of 12 years of full-time study preceding her university credential. In these circumstances, another officer should consider whether this evidence satisfies the applicable regulatory requirements. The Court ordered the application to be reviewed by another officer.

*Espinosa v. Canada (Minister of Citizenship & Immigration)* (2009), 82 Imm. L.R. (3d) 135, 2009 FC 609, 2009 CarswellNat 1785, 2009 CarswellNat 5750 (F.C.) — A visa officer in Manila assessed the application under IRPA and granted the applicant 66 points, one short of the threshold for success. The officer's notes revealed that he considered exercising his discretion but decided it would be inappropriate to do so. The applicant suggested he ought to be awarded 9 points in the "adaptability" category. This suggestion was based on two facts: first, that the applicant's spouse's parents and two sisters lived in Canada and are Canadian citizens; and second, that his spouse had completed a total of 14 years of full-time education. The applicant had proposed that he be awarded 5 points for the former and 4 points for the latter. The officer granted the applicant 8 points for adaptability: 5 for his family connections in Canada and 3 for his spouse's education.

The evidence before the officer showed that the applicant's spouse had completed secondary school (10 years of study), a two-year college program leading to a medical secretary diploma, and a further two years of study at Centro Escolar University. The latter period of study led to her recognition as an Associate in Arts (Pre-Dentistry) and entitled her to receive a Certificate of Eligibility for Admission into the Dental Course. Thus, it is clear that the applicant's spouse had completed 14 years of full-time study.

The Minister argued that the highest educational credential obtained by the applicant's spouse was her medical secretary diploma. Her further two years of study did not lead to an additional educational credential, and therefore should not be considered in the calculation of the educational points in her favour.

The applicant argued that the Regulations do not stipulate that the years of full-time study must precede or lead up to the educational credential obtained by an applicant. They simply set out a dual requirement of an educational credential and a minimal number of years of full-time study. The purpose of these requirements is to ensure consistent treatment of applicants who come from various countries with different educational assistance and requirements. The applicant also argued that s. 78(4) of the Regulations provide that an applicant who has a particular credential but not the required number of years of study should be "awarded the same number of points as the number of years of completed full-time or full-time equivalent studies." This provision suggests that the total number of years of full-time study should be counted, not just the years preceding the grant of the certificate or diploma.

On the record there was no basis for concluding that the officer's decision was justified, transparent or intelligible. The Court could not conclude that the decision fell within a range of acceptable outcomes. The application for judicial review was allowed.

*McLachlan v. Canada (Minister of Citizenship & Immigration)* (2009), 85 Imm. L.R. (3d) 90, 354 F.T.R. 176 (Eng.), 2009 FC 975, 2009 CarswellNat 5869, 2009 CarswellNat

2936 (F.C.) — This was an application for judicial review of a decision rejecting the applicant's request for permanent residence under the skilled worker category. The applicant was a citizen of the United Kingdom, aged 42 at the time of his application and a police officer with the British Transport Police since 1992. He completed Scottish Ordinary Grades and had a further two years of training as a police officer. He had 13 years of experience as a police officer. His application was not approved because of the shortfall in points, 65, two short of 67 necessary for acceptance in the skilled worker category. The applicant expected to receive 20 points on the basis of having 12 years of study in completing Scottish Ordinary Grades together with two years of post secondary education. He had repeated his final year of Scottish Ordinary Grades in order to achieve higher marks. He relied on subsection 78(2)(d)(i). The immigration officer stated that the Scottish Ordinary Grades could be completed in 11 years and is counted as such regardless of how many years it takes to complete. Relying on s. 78(2)(c)(i), she considered the applicant as scoring 11 years of study together with two years post secondary for a total of 13 years of study equating to 15 points under the educational criteria.

The immigration officer did not look beyond the words of subs. 78(2)(c) and (d) and consider all of s. 78 of the Regulations or indeed the scheme of the skilled worker provisions. Her analysis focused on a tallying of effective years of studies without regard to the level of educational attainment. Educational attainment is usually, but not always, achieved by methodical progression of years of study. The legislators were alive to the possibility of a shortfall in years of study in situations where the educational credential is valid and that special circumstance was addressed in subs. 78(4) of the *IRPA* Regulations.

The trigger of subs. 78(4) is the attainment of an educational credential. The special circumstances subsection recognizes the educational attainment of skilled workers with *bona fide* educational credentials but not the specified years of study. Special circumstances could include those who attended state educational systems with shorter primary and secondary programs than in Canada. In this case, the applicant clearly had attained the two-year educational credential in subs. 78(2)(d)(i) by virtue of his successful completion of two years of police training. It was a substantive educational accomplishment, the merit of which is amply demonstrated by his 13 years as a police officer. The Court concluded that the applicant came within subs. 78(2)(d)(i) by application of subs. 78(4). The application for judicial review was granted.

*Healey v. Canada (Minister of Citizenship & Immigration)* (2009), 80 Imm. L.R. (3d) 138, 2009 CarswellNat 891, 2009 FC 355 (F.C.) — This was an application for judicial review of a decision of a visa officer refusing the applicant's application for permanent residence under the federal skilled worker category. There was an error made on the applicant's application in that two years of college were not accurately indicated in the educational history boxes on the application form. The applicant accidentally wrote "0" instead of "2" in the box labeled "University/College." The officer concluded that the applicant had only completed 13 years of education, and 15 points was appropriate. Counsel for the applicant attempted to clarify the mistake but received no response.

It was not possible to tell from the record why the officer felt the applicant only had 13 years of education, and the fact that the officer had recently provided a detailed affidavit justifying his calculations is a clear confirmation that the letter and CAIPS notes do not explain that issue. The officer's affidavit was given no weight by the Court as it went well beyond an elaboration of the reasons and instead provided an after-the-fact rationale for the central issue in this application concerning the way that the points were calculated.

In all the circumstances of this case, the reasons were inadequate. This was a decision of importance for the applicant's future. He could not surmise from the decision why the Thurrock and BTEC certificates had been awarded 0 points. The officer's position was simply that he had no obligation to explain to the applicant why he had taken a position on the facts that the two certificates in question would not be credited. This prevented any understanding or questioning of the officer's position on the facts. It was a denial of the applicant's right to comprehend why he had been refused and an attempt to thwart any action he might take to question the officer's decision. It left him to choose between incomprehension and legal action. In fairness to the applicant, he should have the matter reviewed by someone else who will explain to him what his certificates represent and how they merit, or do not merit, points under the Regulations. A simple explanation by the officer could have prevented what became a significant waste of time and resources on both sides. The application for judicial review was allowed.

*Hameed v. Canada (Minister of Citizenship & Immigration)* (2009), 80 Imm. L.R. (3d) 109, 2009 FC 527, 2009 CarswellNat 1416 (F.C.) — The applicant's application for permanent residence as a skilled worker was turned down. The officer's assessment was based on the applicant's completion of secondary education. The applicant was given no points for his Bachelor's degree because, according to the officer, he had failed to provide conclusive proof that he had attended classes on a full-time or full-time equivalent basis on the way to achieving that degree.

The officer's conclusion was unreasonable. The Regulations do not require proof of attendance. Even if the officer was concerned that the applicant had not proved how many hours of classes he was supposed to have attended each week, his evidence showed that "the period that would have been required to complete" his degree was 14 years, according to the Higher Education Commission. In other words, even if the applicant had failed to show that his studies met the definition of "full-time", he had proved that he had obtained a degree based on a full-time equivalent of 14 years of study. Accordingly, he met the dual requirements of the Regulations. The officer's decision to the contrary is out of keeping with the law and the relevant facts and, therefore, is unreasonable. The application for judicial review was allowed.

*Bhuiya v. Canada (Minister of Citizenship & Immigration)*, [2008] F.C.J. No. 1110, 2008 CarswellNat 2554, 2008 FC 878 — The applicant held a Master's degree in Commerce. She completed 16 years of full-time education leading up to this degree. After obtaining it she returned to school and took a one-year course which resulted in her receiving a diploma in personnel management. The visa officer awarded her only 22 points for the education factor, based upon the 16 years of education spent by the applicant earning the highest educational credential she had obtained, namely her Master's. The visa officer determined that the applicant's post-graduate diploma in personnel management was "not in the line of progression towards the highest credential", namely the Master's degree. As a result, the visa officer did not include the year that the applicant spent working towards this diploma in the calculation of her years of education. Had the applicant been credited with an additional year of education she would have received 25 points for the education factor and would have thereby met the 67-point threshold required to obtain a permanent resident visa.

Subs. 78(3) of the Regulations provides that points are to be awarded on the basis of the single educational credential that results in the highest number of points. It was not disputed that the highest education credential held by the applicant was her Master's degree, and that she had completed 16 years of education prior to obtaining this degree. As a result, the provisions of subs. 78(4) came into play, that is, since the applicant had 16 years of education leading up to her Master's degree, rather than the 17 years contemplated by paragraph 78(2)(f), she was only entitled to the number of points set out in paragraph 78(2)(e), namely 22 points. Such an interpretation of the Regulations is consistent with both the Immigration Manual, and the policy objectives described in the Regulatory Impact Assessment Statement relating to the Regulations. The visa officer, therefore, did not err in her assessment of the applicant's education. The application for judicial review was dismissed.

*Tiwana v. Canada (Minister of Citizenship & Immigration)*, 2008 CarswellNat 526, 2008 CarswellNat 154, 2008 FC 100 — The applicant argued that the visa officer erred in assessing the qualification of the applicant's spouse. The applicant argued that his wife should have been awarded 4 points because she was eligible to receive 20 points for her education qualifications, pursuant to subparagraph 78(2)(d)(ii). The visa officer awarded no points for the two-years university level studies completed by the applicant's spouse. The definition of "educational credential" in the IRPA Regulations makes it clear that an award of points in that regard, pursuant to subparagraph 78(2)(d)(ii), requires completion of a programme and the grant of a diploma or degree.

IRP Regulations

## Section 78(4)

*McLachlan v. Canada (Minister of Citizenship & Immigration)* (2009), 85 Imm. L.R. (3d) 90, 354 F.T.R. 176 (Eng.), 2009 FC 975, 2009 CarswellNat 5869, 2009 CarswellNat 2936 (F.C.) — This was an application for judicial review of a decision rejecting the applicant's request for permanent residence under the skilled worker category. The applicant was a citizen of the United Kingdom, aged 42 at the time of his application and a police officer with the British Transport Police since 1992. He completed Scottish Ordinary Grades and had a further two years of training as a police officer. He had 13 years of experience as a police officer. His application was not approved because of the shortfall in points, 65, two short of 67 necessary for acceptance in the skilled worker category. The applicant expected to receive 20 points on the basis of having 12 years of study in completing Scottish Ordinary Grades together with two years of post secondary education. He had repeated his final year of Scottish Ordinary Grades in order to achieve higher marks. He relied on subsection 78(2)(d)(i). The immigration officer stated that the Scottish Ordinary Grades could be completed in 11 years and is counted as such regardless of how many years it takes to complete. Relying on s. 78(2)(c)(i), she considered the applicant as scoring 11 years of study together with two years post secondary for a total of 13 years of study equating to 15 points under the educational criteria.

The immigration officer did not look beyond the words of subs. 78(2)(c) and (d) and consider all of s. 78 of the Regulations or indeed the scheme of the skilled worker provisions. Her analysis focused on a tallying of effective years of studies without regard to the level of educational attainment. Educational attainment is usually, but not always, achieved by methodical progression of years of study. The legislators were alive to the possibility of a shortfall in years of study in situations where the educational credential is valid and that special circumstance was addressed in subs. 78(4) of the *IRPA* Regulations.

The trigger of subs. 78(4) is the attainment of an educational credential. The special circumstances subsection recognizes the educational attainment of skilled workers with *bona fide* educational credentials but not the specified years of study. Special circumstances could include those who attended state educational systems with shorter primary and secondary programs than in Canada. In this case, the applicant clearly had attained the two-year educational credential in subs. 78(2)(d)(i) by virtue of his successful completion of two years of police training. It was a substantive educational accomplishment, the merit of which is amply demonstrated by his 13 years as a police officer. The Court concluded that the applicant came within subs. 78(2)(d)(i) by application of subs. 78(4). The application for judicial review was granted.

**79. (1) Proficiency in English and French (20 points) — A skilled worker must specify in their application for a permanent resident visa which of English or French is to be considered their first official language in Canada and which is to be considered their second official language in Canada and must**

> **(a) have their proficiency in those languages assessed by an organization or institution designated under subsection (3); or**
>
> **(b) provide other evidence in writing of their proficiency in those languages.**

*[Editor's Note: Section 79(1) of SOR/2002-227,* Immigration and Refugee Protection Regulations, *appears to include a legislative drafting error. "Proficiency in English and French (20 points)" should read "Proficiency in English and French (24 points)". This apparent drafting error in the Regulation has not been amended to date.]*

**(2) 24 Points — Assessment points for proficiency in the official languages of Canada shall be awarded up to a maximum of 24 points based on the benchmarks referred to in *Canadian Language Benchmarks 2000* for the English language and *Niveaux de compétence linguistique canadiens 2006* for the French language, as follows:**

> **(a) for the ability to speak, listen, read or write with high proficiency**
>
> > **(i) in the first official language, 4 points for each of those abilities if the skilled worker's proficiency corresponds to a benchmark of 8 or higher, and**
> >
> > **(ii) in the second official language, 2 points for each of those abilities if the skilled worker's proficiency corresponds to a benchmark of 8 or higher;**
>
> **(b) for the ability to speak, listen, read or write with moderate proficiency**
>
> > **(i) in the first official language, 2 points for each of those abilities if the skilled worker's proficiency corresponds to a benchmark of 6 or 7, and**
> >
> > **(ii) in the second official language, 2 points for each of those abilities if the skilled worker's proficiency corresponds to a benchmark of 6 or 7; and**
>
> **(c) for the ability to speak, listen, read or write**
>
> > **(i) with basic proficiency in either official language, 1 point for each of those abilities, up to a maximum of 2 points, if the skilled worker's proficiency corresponds to a benchmark of 4 or 5, and**
> >
> > **(ii) with no proficiency in either official language, 0 points if the skilled worker's proficiency corresponds to a benchmark of 3 or lower.**

**(3) Designated organization — The Minister may designate organizations or institutions to assess language proficiency for the purposes of this section and shall, for the purpose of correlating the results of such an assessment by a particular designated organization or institution with the benchmarks referred to in subsection (2), establish the minimum test result required to be awarded for each ability and**

**each level of proficiency in the course of an assessment of language proficiency by that organization or institution in order to meet those benchmarks.**

(4) **Conclusive evidence — The results of an assessment of the language proficiency of a skilled worker by a designated organization or institution and the correlation of those results with the benchmarks in accordance with subsection (3) are conclusive evidence of the skilled worker's proficiency in the official languages of Canada for the purposes of subsections (1) and 76(1).**

SOR/2004-167, s. 29; SOR/2008-253, s. 7

## Case Law

### Section 79(1)

*Khan v. Canada (Minister of Citizenship & Immigration)* (2009), 88 Imm. L.R. (3d) 61, 2009 FC 1312, 2009 CarswellNat 5532, 2009 CarswellNat 4569 (F.C.) — The applicant applied for a permanent resident visa as a federal skilled worker. He only listed English, and professed no proficiency in French. The application needed to be accompanied by test results by an accredited language institution or by other evidence in writing of the applicant's proficiency in his selected language. The High Commission requested further documentation and strongly advised the applicant to provide the International English Language Testing System (IELTS) test results. The applicant was unable to secure a seat for the exam until February 2009. He requested a 60-day extension, through his consultant, to supply the IELTS test results. The CAIPS notes reflect the request but do not state if the consultant gave a reason for the request. The refusal to grant an extension of time was unreasonable. Administrative efficiency is important, and necessary. The underlying consideration on an application to extend time is that justice be done. Consideration should be given to the reason for the requested delay and whether there is an arguable case on the merits. Certainly the applicant had a continuing intention to pursue his application, his application had some merit, there was no prejudice to the Minister arising from the delay and a reasonable explanation existed. Thus the decision arises from procedural unfairness, upon which no deference is owed. However, in any event, the decision on the merits not to award any points for English language ability was also unreasonable. The applicant obtained both an undergraduate degree and a Masters of Administration in England, and had worked in Dubai for a number of years in English. The Regulation does not require an IELTS report and so the visa officer failed to discharge his duty by not accessing the material which was on hand. Not only did the applicant study in the UK, he was awarded 25 out of 25 points for education. It was "ludicrous" to suggest that someone who has obtained both an undergraduate and a Master's degree in England from an English language university has no ability in the English language. The application for judicial review was allowed.

*Shaker v. Canada (Minister of Citizenship & Immigration)*, [2006] F.C.J. No. 201, 2006 CarswellNat 271, 2006 CarswellNat 2244, 2006 FC 185 (F.C.) — The applicant submitted an application for permanent residence as a skilled worker in December 1999. An interview date was set for July 2004 and the applicant was instructed to submit additional information regarding his financial situation, employment history and identity. However, before the applicant received the notice, his counsel sent a letter to the embassy requesting that his file be transferred to the Canadian High Commission in Singapore. The Canadian Embassy in Manila sent the file to the Canadian High Commission in Singapore, returned the documents the applicant's counsel had submitted and instructed him to send them directly to the High Commission in Singapore. The applicant was then informed by the High Commission of the coming into effect of the IRPA and that his application would be processed under the new requirements. The applicant was asked to provide proof of his current level of official language proficiency. In August 2004, the applicant sent the High Commission in Singapore the documents that had been sent back by the embassy in Manila, as well as proof of his English language proficiency in the form of school transcripts, a letter from a company stating that he had taken an English course, and six pages of manuscript narrative regarding his use of English in the workplace and at home.

In September 2004, the officer stated in her assessment under the old and new Acts and Regulations that under the old Act she was not satisfied the applicant had performed the essential duties of his intended occupation in Canada, and she consequently would not award him any units of assessment under the "occupational factor" or "experience" headings. In addition to the overall pass mark of 70 units, at least one unit under these headings was necessary for an application to be granted. The officer also stated that in the context of her assessment under the new Act, there was insufficient evidence to determine the applicant's work experience or his proficiency in the English language. She instructed the applicant to submit employment references, work contracts, or any other information/documentation which demonstrates experience in the occupation described by the National Occupational Classification No. 0611, and either IELTS test results or more written evidence that can permit measurement of proficiency in the English language. In addition, the visa officer asked the applicant to pay the cost recovery fee for his wife and child and to submit proof of financial capacity to resettle in Canada. In fact, the High Commission had already sent the applicant a receipt for payment of the processing fees regarding his spouse and child on August 28, 2004.

Since the applicant had sent documents regarding all four of these subjects in August of 2004, he inferred that the officer did not have them when she assessed his application. The Minister argued that the officer did not violate procedural fairness, in that her letter of September 2, 2004, gave the applicant a chance to respond to her concerns regarding his professional qualifications and his proficiency in English. The Court disagreed and held that the fact that the officer requested items that the applicant had already submitted reasonably led him to believe that she did not have any of the evidence he had submitted in the same package. In light of the ambiguity caused by her letter and the applicant's effort to notify her that he had already sent the items she requested, the duty of procedural fairness required the officer to inform the applicant that the evidence he submitted regarding his employment history and proficiency in English was still insufficient, and that she explain the confusion. The officer's decision was found to be unreasonable as she failed to offer any explanation as to why the applicant was awarded no points under the "experience" and "arranged employment" headings. Furthermore, the visa officer's decision to award zero points for English was found to be patently unreasonable. While the presence of mistakes in the applicant's manuscript evidencing his English skills and the relatively poor grades he obtained while studying English may not have warranted the attribution of full marks for English skills, he clearly demonstrated the ability to communicate in English at some level.

*Islam v. Canada (Minister of Citizenship & Immigration)*, 2006 CarswellNat 1073, 2006 FC 424 (F.C.) — Rather than have his language proficiency assessed as provided by s. 79(1)(a) of the Regulations, the applicant opted to submit written evidence of his proficiency in the English language under s. 79(1)(b). The applicant was notified in a letter that the written submissions he provided did not support the level of proficiency he claimed in his application for permanent residency, and that further written submissions would not be accepted. He was given the option of submitting language test results from an approved organization. The applicant did not provide the test results requested. Nevertheless, he did attend an immigration interview at which the visa officer administered a "writing test," and found his level of proficiency in English to be at a "basic" level. The visa officer subsequently issued a negative decision.

The Regulations do not grant the visa officer the authority to administer their own "writing test" in lieu of the prescribed test.

### Section 79(2)

*Al-Kassous v. Canada (Minister of Citizenship & Immigration)*, 2007 CarswellNat 1324, 2007 FC 541 (F.C.) — The applicant sought judicial review of an immigration officer's decision to refuse his application for permanent residence as a member of the skilled worker class. The applicant submitted international language testing system results as evidence of his language proficiency and a written submission as evidence of his French proficiency. In a letter dated November 26, 2005, the visa officer informed the applicant that his submissions with respect to his French language ability were inconclusive and that he was being given the opportunity to submit language proficiency test results before the final assessment of points for his French ability would be done. The letter also noted that further written submissions by the applicant would not be accepted.

If a second chance to meet the requirements of s. 79 is provided then it is a breach to preclude an applicant from exercising one of the options provided in s. 79. Here, it was clear from the letter of November 26, 2005, that no decision had been made and that applicant was being given his second chance to meet the requirements of s. 79. Therefore, the officer breached the duty of procedural fairness.

The officer's notes contain no analysis of the applicant's writing sample, nor any analysis as to the issue of only six points being awarded for speaking, listening, reading and writing. The officer's conclusion appears to be based entirely on the fact of the applicant's studies in France were concluded 17 years ago. The applicant's writing sample was an important part of his submission. The officer was required to assess the applicant's French language ability with reference to the information about the applicant's experience with French as well as on the writing sample provided. The failure to assess the writing sample in accordance with the Canadian language benchmarks makes the decision unreasonable. The application for judicial review was allowed.

**80. (1) Experience (21 points) — Up to a maximum of 21 points shall be awarded to a skilled worker for full-time work experience, or the full-time equivalent for part-time work experience, within the 10 years preceding the date of their application, as follows:**

> **(a) for one year of work experience, 15 points;**
>
> **(b) for two years of work experience, 17 points;**
>
> **(c) for three years of work experience, 19 points; and**
>
> **(d) for four or more years of work experience, 21 points.**

**(2) Listed occupation — For the purposes of subsection (1), points are awarded for work experience in occupations, other than a restricted occupation, that are**

IRP Regulations

**listed in Skill Type 0 Management Occupations or Skill Level A or B of the *National Occupational Classification* matrix.**

**(3) Occupational experience — For the purposes of subsection (1), a skilled worker is considered to have experience in an occupation, regardless of whether they meet the employment requirements of the occupation as set out in the occupational descriptions of the *National Occupational Classification*, if they performed**

**(a) the actions described in the lead statement for the occupation as set out in the occupational descriptions of the *National Occupational Classification*; and**

**(b) at least a substantial number of the main duties of the occupation as set out in the occupational descriptions of the *National Occupational Classification*, including all the essential duties.**

**(4) Work in excess — A period of work experience that exceeds full-time work in one occupation, or simultaneous periods of work experience in more than one full-time occupation, shall be evaluated as a single period of full-time work experience in a single occupation.**

**(5) Classification code — A skilled worker must specify in their application for a permanent resident visa the four-digit code of the *National Occupational Classification* that corresponds to each of the occupations engaged in by the applicant and that constitutes the skilled worker's work experience.**

**(6) Officer's duty — An officer is not required to consider occupations that have not been specified in the application.**

**(7) Full-time — For the purposes of this section, full-time work is equivalent to at least 37.5 hours of work per week.**

SOR/2010-195, s. 7

## Case Law

*Kaur v. Canada (Minister of Citizenship & Immigration)*, 2010 FC 442, 2010 CarswellNat 2241, 2010 CarswellNat 1305 (F.C.) — The application for permanent residence was refused. The visa officer found the supporting documents with respect to work experience insufficient. The applicant claimed that she provided a "detailed letter" stating that she performed the duties of a cook for 3 1/2 years in India. The applicant complained that the visa officer's concern that the letter was insufficient could easily have been addressed had he notified the applicant. The question of whether an applicant has the relevant experience as required by the Regulations and is thus qualified for the trade or profession in which he or she claims to be a skilled worker is "based directly on the requirements of the legislation and regulations." Therefore, it is up to the applicant to submit sufficient evidence on this question, and the visa officer was not under a duty to apprise her of his concerns. It did not help that the applicant's own description of her duties appeared to be copied from the National Occupational Classification. It was open to the visa officer on the basis of the scant evidence before him to find the applicant had not established that she had sufficient work experience in her stated occupation, and to reject her application on that basis. The application for judicial review was dismissed.

*Rodrigues v. Canada (Minister of Citizenship & Immigration)*, 2009 CarswellNat 864, 2009 CarswellNat 240, 2009 FC 111 (F.C.) — This was a judicial review of the decision of a visa officer to reject the applicant's application for permanent residence as a member of the skilled worker class. The only issue argued in this matter was with respect to the officer's evaluation of the applicant's experience under job category NOC 1221 Administrative Officers. The visa officer's function in this matter is to make a largely factual determination, which is informed by particular experience in this area. The officer concluded that the applicant worked "in customer service and logistics (not as a supervisor)." The officer found that the applicant's real functions were the coordination of cargo and some financial management. The best that could be said in respect of the applicant's qualifications under NOC 1221 is that he performed some element of oversight in an indirect manner. The function of oversight was only one element in the NOC 1221 main duties requirements. In the Federal Court of Appeal's decision in *Noman v. Canada (Minister of Citizenship & Immigration)* (2002), 24 Imm. L.R. (3d) 131, while the Court outlined that an applicant was not required to perform all the main duties in an NOC job category, they did require that an applicant perform a few, meaning more than one.

The real function of the visa officer is to determine what is the pith and substance of the work performed by an applicant. Tangential performance of one or more functions under one or more job categories does not convert the job or the functions from one NOC category to another. On the evidence, it was open to the officer to reach the conclusion that the applicant did not have sufficient experience to match the requirements of NOC 1221 for the skilled worker application. The application for judicial review was dismissed.



*McHugh v. Canada (Minister of Citizenship & Immigration)*, 2006 CarswellNat 3095, 2006 FC 1181 (F.C.) — In assessing an application for permanent residence in the skilled worker class, visa officers are required to give the NOC categories a liberal interpretation, and the requirements of the job in question have to be assessed with flexibility. Job requirements also have to be assessed in the operational context in which the individual has actually worked. In this case, although the visa officer found that the evidence did not demonstrate the applicant had performed all of the essential duties of an administrative officer, NOC 1221 does not identify any essential duties for the position. It should also be noted that NOC 1221 required that applicants have performed *some or all* of the duties in question. This allows a visa officer to give greater weight to certain duties contained in the job description over others, but does not require that applicants must perform all of the duties listed in the NOC. The applicant's documented financial management skills demonstrate that she would satisfy several of the criteria for the administrative officer category, in particular as they relate to the administration of the internal financial management of the bank, the preparation of reports, and the duties in budgetary administration. While visa officers have considerable discretion in determining whether an applicant satisfies the requirements of a given occupation, and in interpreting the provisions of a NOC, in this case the officer's conclusion that there was "no comparison" between the list of the applicant's duties provided by her employer and the duties of administrative officers was patently unreasonable. The officer's decision was set aside.

*Kniazeva v. Canada (Minister of Citizenship & Immigration)* (2006), 52 Imm. L.R. (3d) 298, 2006 CarswellNat 472, 2006 FC 268 (F.C.) — The applicant filed an application for permanent residence under the skilled worker class. New legislation was enacted following the applicant's application having been filed. Under subs. 361(4) of the *Immigration and Refugee Protection Regulations*, the applicant could have become a permanent resident as a member of the federal skilled worker class by qualifying under either the former Act's regulation or under the new legislation. Once the visa officer decided to assess the applicant under both the old and new Act, he had to inform the applicant of the new requirements with respect to language proficiency. The visa officer's failure to conduct a thorough review of her application under the new Act and failure to provide the applicant with an opportunity to provide him with the language assessment amounted to a clear breach of duty of fairness owed to the applicant.

The visa officer contacted the applicant's former employer with a view to verifying her employment. The employer confirmed the applicant had "practical training at the plant while she was a student and had worked intervals during the period between June 1997 and July 1998. Accordingly, the visa officer had a duty to inform the applicant that he only considered this work experience as part-time and therefore the experience was being disqualified as relevant work experience.

The visa officer breached the duty of procedural fairness and the application for judicial review was allowed.

**81. Age (10 points) — Points shall be awarded up to a maximum of 10 for a skilled worker's age, as of the date of their application, as follows:**

**(a) 10 points for 21 years of age or older but less than 50 years of age;**

**(b) 8 points, for 20 or 50 years of age;**

**(c) 6 points, for 19 or 51 years of age;**

**(d) 4 points, for 18 or 52 years of age;**

**(e) 2 points, for 17 or 53 years of age; and**

**(f) 0 points, for less than 17 years of age or 54 years of age or older.**

**82. (1) Definition — arranged employment — In this section, "arranged employment" means an offer of indeterminate employment in Canada.**

**(2) Arranged employment (10 points) — Ten points shall be awarded to a skilled worker for arranged employment in Canada in an occupation that is listed in Skill Type 0 Management Occupations or Skill Level A or B of the *National Occupational Classification* matrix if they are able to perform and are likely to accept and carry out the employment and**

**(a) the skilled worker is in Canada and holds a work permit and**

**(i) there has been a determination by an officer under section 203 that the performance of the employment by the skilled worker would be likely to result in a neutral or positive effect on the labour market in Canada,**

**(ii) the skilled worker is currently working in that employment,**

**(iii) the work permit is valid at the time an application is made by the skilled worker for a permanent resident visa as well as at the time the permanent resident visa, if any, is issued to the skilled worker, and**

**(iv) the employer has made an offer to employ the skilled worker on an indeterminate basis once the permanent resident visa is issued to the skilled worker;**

**(b) the skilled worker is in Canada and holds a work permit referred to in paragraph 204(a) or 205(a) or subparagraph 205(c)(ii) and the circumstances referred to in subparagraphs (a)(ii) to (iv) apply;**

**(c) the skilled worker does not intend to work in Canada before being issued a permanent resident visa and does not hold a work permit and**

**(i) the employer has made an offer to employ the skilled worker on an indeterminate basis once the permanent resident visa is issued to the skilled worker, and**

**(ii) an officer has approved that offer of employment based on an opinion provided to the officer by the Department of Human Resources Development at the request of the employer or an officer that**

**Proposed Amendment — 82(2)(c)(ii) opening words**

**(ii) an officer has approved that offer of employment based on an opinion provided to the officer by the Department of Human Resources and Skills Development at the request of the employer or an officer that**

SOR/2010-172, s. 5(c) [To come into force April 1, 2011.]

**(A) the offer of employment is genuine,**

**(B) the employment is not part-time or seasonal employment, and**

**(C) the wages offered to the skilled worker are consistent with the prevailing wage rate for the occupation and the working conditions meet generally accepted Canadian standards; or**

**(d) the skilled worker holds a work permit and**

**(i) the circumstances referred to in subparagraphs (a)(i) to (iv) and paragraph (b) do not apply, and**

**(ii) the circumstances referred to in subparagraphs (c)(i) and (ii) apply.**

SOR/2004-167, s. 30(1)–(3), (5)–(7)



## Case Law

*Gill v. Canada (Minister of Citizenship & Immigration)*, 2010 FC 466, 2010 CarswellNat 1153, 2010 CarswellNat 3278 (F.C.) — The application for permanent residence was refused on the basis that the applicant did not meet the required 67 points. Had he demonstrated that his spouse's brother was a permanent resident of Canada, living in Canada, he would have been assessed 5 further points. Had he "arranged employment" he would have received 10 additional points.

It was procedurally unfair for the visa officer to render her decision without bringing to the applicant's attention concerns that the applicant's brother in law may or may not be a permanent resident living in Canada. This was not a case where there had been a bald statement of a relative living in Canada, without any evidence whatsoever. There was evidence. If the officer wanted more, she should have asked for it.

Having reached the conclusion with respect to the points for a relative in Canada, the Court did not need to consider the arranged employment issue as it was moot. Nevertheless, *in obiter*, the Court held that, read in conjunction with s. 82(2) of the Regulations, which requires the officer to assess whether a skilled worker is able to perform and is likely to accept and carry out the employment, a visa officer must determine whether the applicant is up to the job. In this case, the officer not only found that the applicant was not up to the job, but was also of the view that the job offer was not genuine. That a visa officer in India is entitled to override the Department of Human Resources and Development's opinion based on an investigation in Canada of whether the offer is genuine is best left for another day.

*Singh v. Canada (Minister of Citizenship & Immigration)*, [2008] F.C.J. No. 65, 2008 CarswellNat 92, 2008 FC 58 (F.C.) — The applicant argued that the visa officer erred in finding that he did not have a work permit allowing him to work in Canada and refusing to award him any points for "arranged employment" or "adaptability." The applicant was a Sikh priest and an Indian citizen who came to Canada on a visitor's visa. His visa explicitly prohibited him from being employed while he was in Canada, but did allow him to perform religious duties in the country. The applicant contended that religious workers do not require a work permit to be allowed to work in Canada, and the fact that he did not have such a permit should not have precluded the consideration of his job offer.

The applicant's argument ignored the explicit condition contained in his visitor's visa that he was "prohibited from engaging in employment in Canada." In the face of this language, the visa cannot reasonably be interpreted as amounting to "a written authorization to work in Canada." There was no evidence that the applicant had complied with the application process required under Divisions 2 and 3 of the Regulations containing extensive provisions governing the granting of work permits. Finally, the applicant's offer of employment was never validated by Human Resources and Skills Development Canada. Consequently, there was no error in the visa officer's assessment.

*Nathoo v. Canada (Minister of Citizenship & Immigration)*, 2007 CarswellNat 2277, 2007 CarswellNat 4924, 2007 FC 818 — The applicant was an assistant manager at a hotel in Tanzania. She was offered a similar job at the Holiday Inn Express in Calgary, Alberta. A visa officer refused her application as a skilled worker on the basis that she was not persuaded that the applicant could perform the job she had been offered. The officer noted that the applicant had no direct contact with her putative employer, knew little about the Holiday Inn Express, and knew nothing about the hotel industry in Canada. As a result, the officer gave the applicant no credit for arranged employment.

The officer took into account extraneous factors. There was nothing in the NOC, or in the description of the job the applicant was being offered, that required her to know in advance all of the various items cited by the officer. The Court noted that the applicant had indirect contact with the hotel through her brother, a staffing consultant, and her mother who resided in Calgary and was acquainted with the president of the hotel. This degree of contact was not so inadequate as to deny the applicant credit for the position that she was offered. The application for judicial review was allowed.

*Singh v. Canada (Minister of Citizenship & Immigration)*, 2007 CarswellNat 142, 2007 FC 69 (F.C.) — The applicant first arrived in Canada on a visitor's visa, allowing him to temporarily perform religious duties. He subsequently applied for permanent residence as a skilled worker. The applicant fell short of the required 67 points.

The applicant was correct in noting that he was exempt from the requirement to obtain a work permit before coming to Canada to work as a Sikh priest as per subs. 186(l) of the Regulations. However, no further accommodations are made in the Regulations that would grant special privileges for workers that meet the requirements of s. 186 when applying for a permanent resident visa. Given the various scenarios considered under s. 82 of the Regulations to be awarded points for arranged employment, had such an exemption been contemplated by the Canadian Government, it could easily have been included in the Regulations. The applicant argued that no such accommodations were made because the occupations listed under s. 186 have already been determined to have a "neutral and positive affect on the labour market in Canada," as required to issue a work permit under s. 203 of the Regulations, and thus, an exemption is implied from a joint reading of ss. 186, 203, and 82 of the Regulations. The Court dismissed this argument. The Court found it was clear on the face of the record that the applicant possessed neither a work permit nor an offer of employment validated by HRSDC, and that the decision of the visa officer not to grant the applicant any points for adaptability or arranged employment, and ultimately to refuse the application for permanent residence, was reasonable pursuant to the existing Regulations. Nevertheless, since it appeared at the time that the applicant submitted his application for permanent residence, that there was confusion at Citizenship and Immigration Canada concerning the proper awarding of points for arranged employment for priests, whose job offers were not validated by HRSDC as evidenced by the visa officer's affidavit and the email from a third party submitted by the applicant, this was sufficient to raise serious concerns that all individuals applying for permanent residence in Canada under circumstances similar to that of the applicant may not be treated alike, a situation contrary to the rules of procedural fairness. On this basis alone, the judicial review was granted.

The Court strongly encouraged the Minister of Citizenship and Immigration to clarify the guidelines concerning the allocation of points in permanent resident applications, for both arranged employment and adaptability, for individuals who are permitted to work in Canada without a work permit under s. 186, and who later seek to become permanent residents under the skilled worker class.

*Mercado v. Canada (Minister of Citizenship & Immigration)* (2006), 60 Imm. L.R. (3d) 88, 2006 CarswellNat 4484, 2006 FC 1527 (F.C.) — The applicant argued the immigration officer incorrectly assessed his experience under s. 75 of the Regulations. He argued that he presented evidence of employment with a landscaping company. He contended that the evidence established that he met the requirements for Landscape Contractor as set out in NOC 8255. He argued that the immigration officer incorrectly rejected such evidence as it was evidence of contracting for services and not evidence of employment. Under cross-examination, the immigration officer admitted that she applied s. 75 as if it only applied to employment situations. This was a questionable interpretation as s. 75(2) applies to "continuous full-time employment experience" which could be broad enough to cover contracting. However, this was immaterial, since the applicant had to first establish that he qualified as a skilled worker.

The applicant also argued that his arranged employment should have been assessed under s. 82(2)(c) instead of s. 82(2)(a). He made his application from Canada on March 18, 2005, and went back to Mexico for his interview on October 25, 2005. While by his own admission he had worked illegally in Canada for many years and never paid any taxes, at the time of the assessment, he was in Mexico. Given that the applicant was making the application while working illegally in Canada, none of the provisions of s. 82(2) were available to him. The immigration officer rightly disqualified him under s. 82(2)(a). She could have done so equally under s. 82(2)(c).

The applicant also argued that the immigration officer erred by not employing a substituted evaluation scheme under s. 76(3). Section 76(3) only comes into play once an immigration officer has found that an applicant qualifies as a skilled worker, but does not acquire the requisite minimum number of points. Here the applicant never qualified as a skilled worker, thus the immigration officer could never invoke s. 76(3). The application for judicial review was dismissed.

*Bellido v. Canada (Minister of Citizenship & Immigration)*, 2005 CarswellNat 889, 2005 FC 452 (F.C.) — HRDC validation is not sufficient evidence of arranged employment. Such validation does not remove the obligation of the visa officer to assess whether the applicant is able to perform the job described in the validation.

**83. (1) Adaptability (10 points) — A maximum of 10 points for adaptability shall be awarded to a skilled worker on the basis of any combination of the following elements:**

> **(a) for the educational credentials of the skilled worker's accompanying spouse or accompanying common-law partner, 3, 4 or 5 points determined in accordance with subsection (2);**
>
> **(b) for any previous period of study in Canada by the skilled worker or the skilled worker's spouse or common-law partner, 5 points;**
>
> **(c) for any previous period of work in Canada by the skilled worker or the skilled worker's spouse or common-law partner, 5 points;**
>
> **(d) for being related to a person living in Canada who is described in subsection (5), 5 points; and**
>
> **(e) for being awarded points for arranged employment in Canada under subsection 82(2), 5 points.**

**(2) Educational credentials of spouse or common-law partner — For the purposes of paragraph (1)(a), an officer shall evaluate the educational credentials of a skilled worker's accompanying spouse or accompanying common-law partner as if the spouse or common-law partner were a skilled worker, and shall award points to the skilled worker as follows:**

> **(a) for a spouse or common-law partner who would be awarded 25 points, 5 points;**
>
> **(b) for a spouse or common-law partner who would be awarded 20 or 22 points, 4 points; and**
>
> **(c) for a spouse or common-law partner who would be awarded 12 or 15 points, 3 points.**

**(3) Previous study in Canada — For the purposes of paragraph (1)(b), a skilled worker shall be awarded 5 points if the skilled worker or their accompanying spouse or accompanying common-law partner, by the age of 17 or older, completed a program of full-time study of at least two years' duration at a post-secondary institution in Canada under a study permit, whether or not they obtained an educational credential for completing that program.**

**(4) Previous work in Canada — For the purposes of paragraph (1)(c), a skilled worker shall be awarded 5 points if they or their accompanying spouse or accompanying common-law partner engaged in at least one year of full-time work in Canada under a work permit.**

**(5) Family relationships in Canada — For the purposes of paragraph (1)(d), a skilled worker shall be awarded 5 points if**

**(a) the skilled worker or the skilled worker's accompanying spouse or accompanying common-law partner is related by blood, marriage, common-law partnership or adoption to a person who is a Canadian citizen or permanent resident living in Canada and who is**

**(i) their father or mother,**

**(ii) the father or mother of their father or mother,**

**(iii) their child,**

**(iv) a child of their child,**

**(v) a child of their father or mother,**

**(vi) a child of the father or mother of their father or mother, other than their father or mother, or**

**(vii) a child of the child of their father or mother; or**

**(b) the skilled worker has a spouse or common-law partner who is not accompanying the skilled worker and is a Canadian citizen or permanent resident living in Canada.**



## Case Law

### Section 83(2)

See the summary for *McLachlan v. Canada (Minister of Citizenship & Immigration)* (2009), 85 Imm. L.R. (3d) 90, 354 F.T.R. 176 (Eng.), 2009 FC 975, 2009 CarswellNat 5869, 2009 CarswellNat 2936 (F.C.) annotated at Reg. 78(2).

### Section 83(4)

*Singh v. Canada (Minister of Citizenship & Immigration)*, [2008] F.C.J. No. 65, 2008 CarswellNat 92, 2008 FC 58 — The applicant argued that the visa officer erred in finding that he did not have a work permit allowing him to work in Canada and refusing to award him any points for "arranged employment" or "adaptability". The applicant was a Sikh priest and an Indian citizen who came to Canada on a visitor's visa. His visa explicitly prohibited him from being employed while he was in Canada, but did allow him to perform religious duties in the country. The applicant contended that religious workers do not require a work permit to be allowed to work in Canada, and the fact that he did not have such a permit should not have precluded the consideration of his job offer.

The applicant's argument ignored the explicit condition contained in his visitor's visa that he was "prohibited from engaging in employment in Canada." In the face of this language, the visa cannot reasonably be interpreted as amounting to "a written authorization to work in Canada." There was no evidence that the applicant had complied with the application process required under Divisions 2 and 3 of the Regulations containing extensive provisions governing the granting of work permits. Finally, the applicant's offer of employment was never validated by Human Resources and Skills Development Canada. Consequently, there was no error in the visa officer's assessment.

*Singh v. Canada (Minister of Citizenship & Immigration)*, 2007 CarswellNat 142, 2007 FC 69 (F.C.) — The applicant first arrived in Canada on a visitor's visa, allowing him to temporarily perform religious duties. He subsequently applied for permanent residence as a skilled worker. The applicant fell short of the required 67 points.

The applicant was correct in noting that he was exempt from the requirement to obtain a work permit before coming to Canada to work as a Sikh priest as per subs. 186(l) of the Regulations. However, no further accommodations are made in the Regulations that would grant special privileges for workers that meet the requirements of s. 186 when applying for a permanent resident visa. Given the various scenarios considered under s. 82 of the Regulations to be awarded points for arranged employment, had such an exemption been contemplated by the Canadian Government, it could easily have been included in the Regulations. The applicant argued that no such accommodations were made because the occupations listed under s. 186 have already been determined to have a "neutral and positive affect on the labour market in Canada," as required to issue a work permit under s. 203 of the Regulations, and thus an exemption is implied from a joint reading of ss. 186, 203, and 82 of the Regulations. The Court dismissed this argument. The Court found it was clear on the face of the record that the applicant possessed neither a work permit nor an offer of employment validated by HRSDC, and that the decision of the visa officer not to grant the applicant any points for adaptability or arranged employment, and ultimately to refuse the application for permanent residence, was reasonable pursuant to the existing Regulations. Nevertheless, since it appeared at the time that the applicant submitted his application for permanent residence, that there was confusion at Citizenship and Immigration Canada concerning the proper awarding of points for arranged employment for priests, whose job offers were not validated by HRSDC as evidenced by the visa officer's affidavit and the email from a third party submitted by the applicant, this was sufficient to raise serious concerns that all individuals applying for permanent residence in Canada under circumstances similar to that of the applicant may not be treated alike, a situation contrary to the rules of procedural fairness. On this basis alone, the judicial review was granted.

The Court strongly encouraged the Minister of Citizenship and Immigration to clarify the guidelines concerning the allocation of points in permanent resident applications, for both arranged employment and adaptability, for individuals who are permitted to work in Canada without a work permit under s. 186, and who later seek to become permanent residents under the skilled worker class.

## Section 83(5)

*Gill v. Canada (Minister of Citizenship & Immigration)*, 2010 FC 466, 2010 CarswellNat 1153, 2010 CarswellNat 3278 (F.C.) — The application for permanent residence was refused on the basis that the applicant did not meet the required 67 points. Had he demonstrated that his spouse's brother was a permanent resident of Canada, living in Canada, he would have been assessed 5 further points. Had he "arranged employment" he would have received 10 additional points.

It was procedurally unfair for the visa officer to render her decision without bringing to the applicant's attention concerns that the applicant's brother-in-law may or may not be a permanent resident living in Canada. This was not a case where there had been a bald statement of a relative living in Canada, without any evidence whatsoever. There was evidence. If the officer wanted more, she should have asked for it.

Having reached the conclusion with respect to the points for a relative in Canada, the Court did not need to consider the arranged employment issue as it was moot. Nevertheless, *in obiter*, the Court held that, read in conjunction with s. 82(2) of the Regulations, which requires the officer to assess whether a skilled worker is able to perform and is likely to accept and carry out the employment, a visa officer must determine whether the applicant is up to the job. In this case, the officer not only found that the applicant was not up to the job, but was also of the view that the job offer was not genuine. That a visa officer in India is entitled to override the Department of Human Resources and Development's opinion based on an investigation in Canada of whether the offer is genuine is best left for another day.

*Wang v. Canada (Minister of Citizenship & Immigration)*, 2008 CarswellNat 3897, 2008 CarswellNat 2051, 2008 FC 798 — The officer concluded that the applicant had insufficient points to qualify for immigration to Canada. She noted that no points were awarded for the male applicant's brother living in Canada. She determined that the evidence provided by the applicants in support of this allegation was insufficient to establish that the brother resided in Canada at the time of the decision, based on the fact that the majority of the documentation provided related to the brother's wife and not him. The brother's notice of assessment was the only document which specifically related to him. It indicated he earned a total of $2,000 in 2006. The officer noted that her records indicated that the brother had prolonged absences from Canada in the past. The Notice of Assessment was therefore insufficient evidence to convince her that he was a resident of Canada at the time the decision was made. The officer's decision was based on the insufficiency of evidence establishing the brother's residence in Canada. The burden of adducing sufficient evidence to support the application falls to the applicant. The application for judicial review was dismissed.



## Requirements

**84. [Repealed SOR/2008-202, s. 1.]**

**85. Permanent resident status — A foreign national who is an accompanying family member of a person who makes an application as a member of the federal skilled worker class shall become a permanent resident if, following an examination, it is established that**

> **(a) the person who made the application has become a permanent resident; and**
>
> **(b) the foreign national is not inadmissible.**

SOR/2008-202, s. 1

## Case Law

*Hamid v. Canada (Minister of Citizenship & Immigration)*, 2006 CarswellNat 1592, 2006 FCA 217 (Fed. C.A.) — The applicant applied for permanent residence and included his accompanying family members in his application. His oldest two sons qualified as dependent children because they were financially dependent on him and full-time students. However, when the officer assessed the application 2½ years after it had been received, both sons had graduated and were no longer enrolled in full-time studies. The question to be decided in this appeal was whether the visa officer was correct to remove them from the applicant's application on the ground that they did not meet the eligibility requirement of being students when the visa application was both made and assessed.

The Federal Court of Appeal found a child of a federal skilled worker who has applied for a visa, who was 22 years of age or over, and who was considered dependent on the skilled worker on the date of the application by virtue of his or her financial dependence and full time study, but who does not meet the requirements of "a dependent child" within the meaning of paragraph 2(b)(ii) of the *Immigration and Refugee Protection Regulations*, when the visa application is determined, cannot be included as part his or her parent's application for permanent residence in Canada. The appeal by the Minister was allowed and the order of the Federal Court was set aside and the application for judicial review was dismissed.

## *Transitional Federal Skilled Workers*

[Heading added SOR/2003-383, s. 3.]

### Transitional Federal Skilled Worker Class

[Heading added SOR/2003-383, s. 3.]

**85.1 (1) Class — For the purposes of subsection 12(2) of the Act, the transitional federal skilled worker class is hereby prescribed as a class of persons who are transitional skilled workers and who may become permanent residents on the basis of their ability to become economically established in Canada and who intend to reside in a province other than the Province of Quebec.**

**(2) Transitional skilled workers — A foreign national is a transitional skilled worker if they made an application before January 1, 2002 under the former Regulations for an immigrant visa as a person described in subparagraph 9(1)(b)(i) or paragraph 10(1)(b) of those Regulations, other than a self-employed person within the meaning of subsection 2(1) of those Regulations, that was**

**(a) refused after March 31, 2003 and before June 20, 2003; or**

**(b) withdrawn by the foreign national on or after January 1, 2002 and before December 1, 2003.**

SOR/2003-383, s. 3

**85.2 (1) Application before January 1, 2005 — Subject to subsection (2), an application for a permanent resident visa as a member of the transitional federal skilled worker class must be made in accordance with sections 10 and 11 and must be received by the applicable immigration office referred to in subsection 11(1) not later than December 31, 2004.**

**(2) Alternate place of application — An application referred to in subsection (1) may be made to the immigration office at the location where the application referred to in subsection 85.1(2) was made, instead of to the immigration office referred to in subsection 11(1).**

SOR/2003-383, s. 3

**85.3 Criteria —** For the purpose of determining whether a transitional skilled worker, as a member of the transitional federal skilled worker class, will be able to become economically established in Canada, they must

(a) be awarded the number of units of assessment required by the former Regulations for a person described in subparagraph 9(1)(b)(i) or paragraph 10(1)(b) of those Regulations, other than a self-employed person within the meaning of subsection 2(1) of those Regulations; or

(b) meet the requirements of subsection 75(2) and paragraph 76(1)(b) of these Regulations and obtain a minimum of 67 points based on the factors set out in paragraph 76(1)(a) of these Regulations.

SOR/2003-383, s. 3

### Requirements

[Heading added SOR/2003-383, s. 3.]

85.4 [Repealed SOR/2008-253, s. 8.]

85.5 [Repealed SOR/2008-202, s. 2.]

**85.6 Permanent resident status —** A foreign national who is a family member of a person who makes an application for a permanent resident visa as a member of the transitional federal skilled worker class shall become a permanent resident if, following an examination, it is established that the family member is not inadmissible.

SOR/2003-383, s. 3

## *Quebec Skilled Worker Class*

**86. (1) Class —** For the purposes of subsection 12(2) of the Act, the Quebec skilled worker class is hereby prescribed as a class of persons who may become permanent residents on the basis of their ability to become economically established in Canada.

**(2) Member of the class —** A foreign national is a member of the Quebec skilled worker class if they

(a) intend to reside in the Province of Quebec; and

(b) are named in a *Certificat de sélection du Québec* issued to them by that Province.

(3) [Repealed SOR/2008-253, s. 9.]

(4) [Repealed SOR/2008-253, s. 9.]

**(5) Requirements for accompanying family members —** A foreign national who is an accompanying family member of a person who makes an application as a member of the Quebec skilled worker class shall become a permanent resident if, following an examination, it is established that

(a) the person who made the application has become a permanent resident; and

(b) the foreign national is not inadmissible.

SOR/2008-202, s. 3; SOR/2008-253, s. 9

## *Provincial Nominee Class*

**87.** (1) **Class** — For the purposes of subsection 12(2) of the Act, the provincial nominee class is hereby prescribed as a class of persons who may become permanent residents on the basis of their ability to become economically established in Canada.

(2) **Member of the class** — A foreign national is a member of the provincial nominee class if

(a) subject to subsection (5), they are named in a nomination certificate issued by the government of a province under a provincial nomination agreement between that province and the Minister; and

(b) they intend to reside in the province that has nominated them.

(3) **Substitution of evaluation** — If the fact that the foreign national is named in a certificate referred to in paragraph (2)(a) is not a sufficient indicator of whether they may become economically established in Canada and an officer has consulted the government that issued the certificate, the officer may substitute for the criteria set out in subsection (2) their evaluation of the likelihood of the ability of the foreign national to become economically established in Canada.

(4) **Concurrence** — An evaluation made under subsection (3) requires the concurrence of a second officer.

(5) **Exclusion** — Subject to subsection (6), a foreign national who is named in a certificate referred to in paragraph (2)(a) shall not be considered a member of the provincial nominee class if

(a) the nomination was based on the provision of capital by the foreign national; or

(b) the foreign national intends to participate in, or has participated in, an immigration-linked investment scheme.

(6) **Exception** — Subsection (5) does not apply if

(a) the capital is provided by the foreign national to a business in the province that nominated them, other than a business operated primarily for the purpose of deriving investment income such as interest, dividends or capital gains;

(b) the foreign national controls or will control

(i) a percentage of equity in the business equal to or greater than 33⅓%, or

(ii) an equity investment in the business of at least $1,000,000;

(c) the foreign national provides or will provide active and ongoing management of the business from within the province that nominated them; and

(d) the terms of the investment in the business do not include a redemption option.

**(7) [Repealed SOR/2008-253, s. 10.]**

**(8) [Repealed SOR/2008-253, s. 10.]**

**(9) Definitions — The following definitions apply in this section.**

**"immigration-linked investment scheme" means a strategy or plan**

> **(a) where one of the objectives of the strategy or plan is to facilitate immigration to Canada and one of the objectives of the promoters of the strategy or plan is to raise capital; or**
>
> **(b) where the agreement or arrangement in respect of the strategy or plan was entered into primarily for the purpose of acquiring a status or privilege under the Act.**

***("projet de placement lié à l'immigration")***

**"percentage of equity" has the same meaning as in subsection 88(1). *("pourcentage des capitaux propres")***

**(10) Non-application — Subsections (5), (6) and (9) do not apply in respect of a foreign national who is issued a nomination certificate referred to in paragraph (2)(a) before September 2, 2008.**

**(11) Transitional — Subsections (5) and (6) as they read immediately before September 2, 2008 apply in respect of a foreign national referred to in subsection (10).**

**(12) Requirements for accompanying family members — A foreign national who is an accompanying family member of a person who makes an application as a member of the provincial nominee class shall become a permanent resident if, following an examination, it is established that**

> **(a) the person who made the application has become a permanent resident; and**
>
> **(b) the foreign national is not inadmissible.**

SOR/2008-202, ss. 4, 5; SOR/2008-253, s. 10; SOR/2009-164, s. 1

## Case Law

*Wai v. Canada (Minister of Citizenship & Immigration)* (2009), 348 F.T.R. 85 (Eng.), 2009 FC 780, 2009 CarswellNat 2481, [2009] F.C.J. No. 1015 (F.C.) — This was an application for judicial review of a decision of a visa officer, refusing the applicant's application for permanent residence in Canada under the provincial nominee class. The officer requested additional information from the applicant, including: evidence of his current legal status in Canada; employment letter(s) and pay stubs; evidence of current funds; and a written personal statement explaining how he was supporting himself. The applicant indicated to the officer that he had been living with his mother and grandmother since his arrival and had been supported by his mother for the entire time. The officer concluded that the applicant named in the certificate issued by Manitoba, was not likely to become economically established in Canada. The officer points out that the fact that a foreign national is named in the certificate is not a sufficient indicator of whether they may become economically established in Canada. An officer who has consulted with the provincial government that issued the certificate may substitute, for the criteria set out in subs. (2), their own evaluation of the likelihood of the ability of the foreign national to become economically established in Canada. The officer in this case was not satisfied that, just because the applicant was named in the certificate issued by Manitoba, he was likely to become economically established in Canada.

Under the relevant legislation, as well as the agreement between Manitoba and Canada, it is clear that the province will, in the normal course, be afforded deference once it has issued a nomination certificate, and it is also clear under s. 87(2)(b) of the Regulations that an applicant must intend to reside in Manitoba. However, s. 87(3) makes it clear that an officer can substitute their own evaluation on the likelihood of economic establishment. As Canada has the ultimate responsibility for immigration matters, the intent of this provision appears clear. Accordingly, the real issue was whether the decision was reasonable. The Court found justification, transparency and intelligibility throughout the decision-making process and the decision falls within the required range.

Subsection 87(4) of the Regulations stipulates that a substitute evaluation under subs. 87(3) "requires the concurrence of a second officer." In this context "concurrence" can only mean "agreement." Concurrence requires that the second officer must read the evaluation and indicate that he or she agrees with it. The second officer adopted the reasons and conclusions of the first officer. Nothing further was required to satisfy subs. 87(4) of the Regulations or to provide adequate reasons. The application for judicial review was dismissed.

## *Canadian Experience Class*

[Heading added SOR/2008-254, s. 3.]

**87.1 (1) Class — For the purposes of subsection 12(2) of the Act, the Canadian experience class is prescribed as a class of persons who may become permanent residents on the basis of their experience in Canada and who intend to reside in a province other than the Province of Quebec.**

**(2) Member of the class — A foreign national is a member of the Canadian experience class if**

**(a) they**

**(i) have acquired in Canada within the 24 months before the day on which their application for permanent residence is made at least 12 months of full-time work experience, or the equivalent in part-time work experience, in one or more occupations that are listed in Skill Type 0 Management Occupations or Skill Level A or B of the *National Occupational Classification* matrix, and have acquired that work experience after having obtained**

**(A) a diploma, degree or trade or apprenticeship credential issued on the completion of a program of full-time study or training of at least two years' duration at a public, provincially recognized post-secondary educational or training institution in Canada,**

**(B) a diploma or trade or apprenticeship credential issued on the completion of a program of full-time study or training of at least two years' duration at a private, Quebec post-secondary institution that operates under the same rules and regulations as public Quebec post-secondary institutions and that receives at least 50 per cent of**

its financing for its overall operations from government grants, subsidies or other assistance,

(C) a degree from a private, provincially recognized post-secondary educational institution in Canada issued on the completion of a program of full-time study of at least two years' duration, or

(D) a graduate degree from a provincially recognized post-secondary educational institution in Canada issued on the completion of a program of full-time study of at least one year's duration and within two years after obtaining a degree or diploma from an institution referred to in clause (A) or (C), or

(ii) have acquired in Canada within the 36 months before the day on which their application for permanent residence is made at least 24 months of full-time work experience, or the equivalent in part-time work experience, in one or more occupations that are listed in Skill Type 0 Management Occupations or Skill Level A or B of the *National Occupational Classification* matrix; and

(b) they have had their proficiency assessed in the English or French language by an organization or institution designated under subsection (4), or have provided other evidence in writing of their proficiency in either language, and have obtained proficiencies for their abilities to speak, listen, read and write that correspond to benchmarks, as referred to in Canadian Language Benchmarks 2000 for the English language and *Niveaux de compétence linguistique canadiens 2006* for the French language, of

(i) in the case of a foreign national who has acquired work experience in one or more occupations that are listed in Skill Type 0 Management Occupations or Skill Level A of the *National Occupational Classification* matrix,

(A) 7 or higher for each of those abilities, or

(B) 6 for any one of those abilities, 7 or higher for any other two of those abilities and 8 or higher for the remaining ability, and

(ii) in the case of a foreign national who has acquired work experience in one or more occupations that are listed in Skill Level B of the *National Occupational Classification* matrix,

(A) 5 or higher for each of those abilities, or

(B) 4 for any one of those abilities, 5 or higher for any other two of those abilities and 6 or higher for the remaining ability.

(3) **Application** — For the purposes of subsection (2),

(a) full-time work is equivalent to at least 37.5 hours of work per week;

(b) any period of self-employment or unauthorized work shall not be included in calculating a period of work experience;

(c) the foreign national must have had temporary resident status during their period of work experience and any period of full-time study or training;

(d) the foreign national must have been physically present in Canada for at least two years of their full-time study or training;

**(e) any period during which the foreign national was engaged in a full-time program of study or training in English or French as a second language — and any period of full-time study or training in respect of which study or training in English or French as a second language amounted to most of the full-time study or training — shall not be included in calculating the period of full-time study or training;**

**(f) any period of study or training during which the foreign national was a recipient of a Government of Canada scholarship or bursary, or participated in an exchange program sponsored by the Government of Canada, a purpose or condition of which was that the foreign national return to their country of origin or nationality on completion of their studies or training shall not be included in calculating the period of full-time study or training; and**

**(g) in the case of a foreign national whose work experience is referred to in both subparagraphs (2)(b)(i) and (ii), the foreign national must obtain a proficiency in the English or French language that corresponds to the benchmarks required for the skill type, as set out in subparagraph (2)(b)(i) or (ii), in which the foreign national has acquired most of their work experience.**

**(4) Designated organization — The Minister may designate organizations or institutions to assess language proficiency for the purposes of this section and shall, for the purpose of correlating the results of such an assessment by a particular designated organization or institution with the benchmarks referred to in subsection (2), establish the minimum test result required to be awarded for each ability and each level of proficiency in the course of an assessment of language proficiency by that organization or institution in order to meet those benchmarks.**

**(5) Conclusive evidence — The results of an assessment of the language proficiency of a foreign national by a designated organization or institution and the correlation of those results with the benchmarks in accordance with subsection (4) are conclusive evidence of the foreign national's proficiency in an official language of Canada for the purposes of this section.**

SOR/2008-254, s. 3

## DIVISION 2 — BUSINESS IMMIGRANTS

### *Interpretation*

**88. (1) Definitions — The definitions in this subsection apply in this Division.**

**"agent" means, in respect of a fund, the Minister acting as an agent on behalf of a fund that has been approved by a province. *("mandataire")***

**"allocation period" means, in respect of the provincial allocation of an investor, the period of five years beginning on the first day of the second month after the month in which the agent receives the investment. *("période de placement")***

**"approved fund" means a fund that is approved by the Minister under section 91. *("fonds agréé")***

**"business experience", in respect of**

**(a) an investor, other than an investor selected by a province, means a minimum of two years of experience consisting of**

**(i) two one-year periods of experience in the management of a qualifying business and the control of a percentage of equity of the qualifying business during the period beginning five years before the date of application for a permanent resident visa and ending on the day a determination is made in respect of the application,**

**(ii) two one-year periods of experience in the management of at least five full-time job equivalents per year in a business during the period beginning five years before the date of application for a permanent resident visa and ending on the day a determination is made in respect of the application, or**

**(iii) a combination of a one-year period of experience described in subparagraph (i) and a one-year period of experience described in subparagraph (ii);**

**(b) an entrepreneur, other than an entrepreneur selected by a province, means a minimum of two years of experience consisting of two one-year periods of experience in the management of a qualifying business and the control of a percentage of equity of the qualifying business during the period beginning five years before the date of application for a permanent resident visa and ending on the day a determination is made in respect of the application; and**

**(c) an investor selected by a province or an entrepreneur selected by a province, has the meaning provided by the laws of the province and is calculated in accordance with the laws of the province.**

***("expérience dans l'exploitation d'une entreprise")***

**"debt obligation" has the same meaning as in subsection 2(1) of the *Canada Business Corporations Act*. *("titre de créance")***

**"entrepreneur" means a foreign national who**

**(a) has business experience;**

**(b) has a legally obtained minimum net worth; and**

**(c) provides a written statement to an officer that they intend and will be able to meet the conditions referred to in subsections 98(1) to (5).**

***("entrepreneur")***

**"entrepreneur selected by a province" means an entrepreneur who**

**(a) intends to reside in a province the government of which has, under subsection 8(1) of the Act, entered into an agreement referred to in subsection 9(1) of the Act with the Minister whereby the province has sole responsibility for the selection of entrepreneurs; and**

**(b) is named in a selection certificate issued to them by that province.**

***("entrepreneur sélectionné par une province")***

**"former Regulations" has the same meaning as in subsection 316(1). *("ancien règlement")***

**“full-time job equivalent” means 1,950 hours of paid employment.** *(“équivalent d’emploi à temps plein”)*

**“fund” means a corporation that is controlled by the government of a province and is authorized to create or continue employment in Canada in order to foster the development of a strong and viable economy.** *(“fonds”)*

**“investment” means, in respect of an investor, a sum of $800,000 that**

> **(a) in the case of an investor other than an investor selected by a province, is paid by the investor to the agent for allocation to all approved funds in existence as of the date the allocation period begins and that is not refundable during the period beginning on the day a permanent resident visa is issued to the investor and ending at the end of the allocation period; and**
>
> **(b) in the case of an investor selected by a province, is invested by the investor in accordance with an investment proposal within the meaning of the laws of the province and is not refundable for a period of at least five years, as calculated in accordance with the laws of the province.**

*(“placement”)*

**“investor” means a foreign national who**

> **(a) has business experience;**
>
> **(b) has a legally obtained net worth of at least $1,600,000; and**
>
> **(c) indicates in writing to an officer that they intend to make or have made an investment.**

*(“investisseur”)*

**“investor selected by a province” means an investor who**

> **(a) intends to reside in a province the government of which has, under subsection 8(1) of the Act, entered into an agreement referred to in subsection 9(1) of the Act with the Minister whereby the province has sole responsibility for the selection of investors; and**
>
> **(b) is named in a selection certificate issued to them by that province.**

*(“investisseur sélectionné par une province”)*

**“minimum net worth” means**

> **(a) in respect of an entrepreneur, other than an entrepreneur selected by a province, $300,000; and**
>
> **(b) in respect of an entrepreneur selected by a province, the minimum net worth required by the laws of the province.**

*(“avoir net minimal”)*

**“net assets”, in respect of a qualifying business or a qualifying Canadian business, means the assets of the business, minus the liabilities of the business, plus shareholder loans made to the business by the foreign national who is making or has made an application for a permanent resident visa and their spouse or common-law partner.** *(“actif net”)*

**"net income", in respect of a qualifying business or a qualifying Canadian business, means the after tax profit or loss of the business plus remuneration by the business to the foreign national who is making or has made an application for a permanent resident visa and their spouse or common-law partner.** *("revenu net")*

**"net worth", in respect of**

**(a) an investor, other than an investor selected by a province, means the fair market value of all of the assets of the investor and their spouse or common-law partner minus the fair market value of all of their liabilities;**

**(b) an entrepreneur, other than an entrepreneur selected by a province, means the fair market value of all of the assets of the entrepreneur and their spouse or common-law partner minus the fair market value of all of their liabilities; and**

**(c) an investor selected by a province or an entrepreneur selected by a province, has the meaning provided by the laws of the province and is calculated in accordance with the laws of the province.**

*("avoir net")*

**"percentage of equity" means**

**(a) in respect of a sole proprietorship, 100 per cent of the equity of the sole proprietorship controlled by a foreign national or their spouse or common-law partner;**

**(b) in respect of a corporation, the percentage of the issued and outstanding voting shares of the capital stock of the corporation controlled by a foreign national or their spouse or common-law partner; and**

**(c) in respect of a partnership or joint venture, the percentage of the profit or loss of the partnership or joint venture to which a foreign national or their spouse or common-law partner is entitled.**

*("pourcentage des capitaux propres")*

**"provincial allocation" means the portion of an investor's investment in an approved fund calculated in accordance with subsection (2).** *("quote-part provinciale")*

**"qualifying business" means a business — other than a business operated primarily for the purpose of deriving investment income such as interest, dividends or capital gains — for which, during the year under consideration, there is documentary evidence of any two of the following:**

**(a) the percentage of equity multiplied by the number of full-time job equivalents is equal to or greater than two full-time job equivalents per year;**

**(b) the percentage of equity multiplied by the total annual sales is equal to or greater than $500,000;**

**(c) the percentage of equity multiplied by the net income in the year is equal to or greater than $50,000; and**

**(d) the percentage of equity multiplied by the net assets at the end of the year is equal to or greater than $125,000.**

*("entreprise admissible")*

**"qualifying Canadian business" means a business operated in Canada by an entrepreneur — other than a business operated primarily for the purpose of deriving investment income, such as interest, dividends or capital gains — for which there is in any year within the period of three years after the day the entrepreneur becomes a permanent resident documentary evidence of any two of the following:**

**(a) the percentage of equity multiplied by the number of full-time job equivalents is equal to or greater than two full-time job equivalents per year;**

**(b) the percentage of equity multiplied by the total annual sales is equal to or greater than $250,000;**

**(c) the percentage of equity multiplied by the net income in the year is equal to or greater than $25,000; and**

**(d) the percentage of equity multiplied by the net assets at the end of the year is equal to or greater than $125,000.**

***("entreprise canadienne admissible")***

**"relevant experience", in respect of**

**(a) a self-employed person, other than a self-employed person selected by a province, means a minimum of two years of experience, during the period beginning five years before the date of application for a permanent resident visa and ending on the day a determination is made in respect of the application, consisting of**

**(i) in respect of cultural activities,**

**(A) two one-year periods of experience in self-employment in cultural activities,**

**(B) two one-year periods of experience in participation at a world class level in cultural activities, or**

**(C) a combination of a one-year period of experience described in clause (A) and a one-year period of experience described in clause (B),**

**(ii) in respect of athletics,**

**(A) two one-year periods of experience in self-employment in athletics,**

**(B) two one-year periods of experience in participation at a world class level in athletics, or**

**(C) a combination of a one-year period of experience described in clause (A) and a one-year period of experience described in clause (B), and**

**(iii) in respect of the purchase and management of a farm, two one-year periods of experience in the management of a farm; and**

**(b) a self-employed person selected by a province, has the meaning provided by the laws of the province.**

***("expérience utile")***

**"self-employed person" means a foreign national who has relevant experience and has the intention and ability to be self-employed in Canada and to make a signifi-**

**cant contribution to specified economic activities in Canada. *("travailleur autonome")***

**"self-employed person selected by a province" means a self-employed person**

> **(a) who intends to reside in a province the government of which has, under subsection 8(1) of the Act, entered into an agreement referred to in subsection 9(1) of the Act with the Minister whereby the province has sole responsibility for the selection of self-employed persons; and**
>
> **(b) is named in a selection certificate issued to them by that province.**

***("travailleur autonome sélectionné par une province")***

**"specified economic activities", in respect of**

> **(a) a self-employed person, other than a self-employed person selected by a province, means cultural activities, athletics or the purchase and management of a farm; and**
>
> **(b) a self-employed person selected by a province, has the meaning provided by the laws of the province.**

***("activités économiques déterminées")***



(2) **Provincial allocation — For the purposes of the definition "provincial allocation" in subsection (1), the provincial allocation shall be calculated as of the first day of the allocation period in accordance with the formula**

$$A + B$$

**where**

**A equals $400,000 divided by the number of approved funds that are not suspended; and**

**B equals $400,000 multiplied by the gross domestic product at market prices of the province that has approved the non-suspended fund, divided by the total of the gross domestic products at market prices of all of the provinces that have approved a non-suspended fund.**

(3) **Gross domestic product — For the purposes of subsection (2), the gross domestic product is the one for the calendar year before the calendar year that immediately precedes the date of provincial allocation, as set out in the table entitled "Provincial accounts GDP at market prices by province (millions of dollars)" in the *Canadian Economic Observer Historical Statistical Supplement*, published by Statistics Canada.**

SOR/2003-383, s. 4; SOR/2004-167, s. 31; SOR/2010-218

## Case Law

### Section 88(1)

#### *Business Experience*

*Rahim v. Canada (Minister of Citizenship & Immigration)* (2008), 69 Imm. L.R. (3d) 120, 375 N.R. 210, 2008 CarswellNat 610, 2008 CarswellNat 1456, 2008 FCA 87 (F.C.A.) — The issue in this appeal related to the appropriate test to be applied with respect to the determination of whether the appellant had control of certain shares of a corporation, a condition of the definition of business experience that he was obligated to meet to succeed in his application for a permanent resident visa as a member of the entrepreneur class. The visa officer stated that the documentary evidence showed that the appellant had set up a trust whereby he had turned over his rights, titles and 60% interest in the issued shares of the corporation to a Mr. Ali and accordingly, the visa officer considered that Mr. Rahim had relinquished his equity in the corporation. The visa officer concluded that Mr. Rahim did not meet the business experience requirement of the definition of an entrepreneur in subs. 88(1) of the Regulations and, therefore, rejected his application. The Federal Court upheld the visa officer's decision, holding that the test was whether the applicant had legal or *de jure* control over the shares in question.

The Federal Court of Appeal concluded that the *de jure* control test with respect to the determination of who, if anyone, controls a corporation for income tax purposes does not provide authority for the proposition that a *de jure* control test is applicable with respect to the determination of whether a person controls shares for the purposes of the definition of business experience in subs. 88(1) of the Regulations. Income tax legislation and immigration legislation are based upon significantly different considerations. Instead, the Federal Court of Appeal concluded that the effective control test in *Cloutier v. Canada (Minister of National Revenue)*, 1986 F.C.J. No. 788, [1987] 2 F.C. 222 was consistent with the language of the definitions of business experience and percentage of equity that are found in subs. 88(1) of the Regulations, as well as the purpose of the provisions of the Regulations that deal with immigration by entrepreneurs.

In the present circumstances, the appellant had always been in a position to have the shares of the corporation transferred to him by revoking the trust. His power to do so was unfettered and could be freely exercised. Accordingly, he had and always had effective control over the shares of the corporation that were held in trust for him by Mr. Ali and, therefore, demonstrated that he met the requirement of control of a percentage of equity of the qualifying business in subs. 88(1) of the Regulations. The appeal was allowed.

### Entrepreneur

*Rahim v. Canada (Minister of Citizenship & Immigration)* (2008), 69 Imm. L.R. (3d) 120, 375 N.R. 210, 2008 CarswellNat 610, 2008 CarswellNat 1456, 2008 FCA 87 (F.C.A.) — The issue in this appeal related to the appropriate test to be applied with respect to the determination of whether Mr. Rahim had control of certain shares of a corporation, a condition of the definition of business experience that Mr. Rahim was obligated to meet to succeed in his application for a permanent resident visa as a member of the entrepreneur class. The visa officer stated that the documentary evidence showed that Mr. Rahim set up a trust whereby he had turned over his rights, titles and 60% interest in the issued shares of the corporation to Mr. Ali and accordingly, the visa officer considered that Mr. Rahim had relinquished his equity in the corporation. The visa officer concluded that Mr. Rahim did not meet the business experience requirement of the definition of an entrepreneur in subs. 88(1) of the *Regulations* and, therefore, rejected Mr. Rahim's application. The Federal Court upheld the visa officer's decision holding that the test was whether the applicant had legal or *de jure* control over the shares in question.

The Federal Court of Appeal concluded that the *de jure* control test with respect to the determination of who, if anyone, controls a corporation for income tax purposes does not provide authority for the proposition that a *de jure* control test is applicable with respect to the determination of whether a person controls shares for the purposes of the definition of business experience in subs. 88(1) of the *Regulations*. Income tax legislation and immigration legislation are based upon significantly different considerations. Instead the Federal Court of Appeal concluded that the effective control test in *Cloutier v. Canada (Minister of National Revenue)*, [1987] 2 F.C. 222, 1986 F.C.J. No. 788 was consistent with the language of the definitions of business experience and percentage of equity that are found in subs. 88(1) of the *Regulations*, as well as the purpose of the provisions of the *Regulations* which deal with immigration by entrepreneurs.

In the present circumstances, Mr. Rahim had always been in a position to have the shares of the corporation transferred to him by revoking the trust. His power to do so was unfettered and could be freely exercised. Accordingly, Mr. Rahim had and always had, effective control over the shares of the corporation that were held in trust for him by Mr. Ali and, therefore, he demonstrated that he met the requirement of control of a percentage of equity of the qualifying business in subs. 88(1) of the *Regulations*. The appeal was allowed.

*Li v. Canada (Minister of Citizenship & Immigration)*, 2006 CarswellNat 1300, 2006 CarswellNat 2280, 2006 FC 599 (F.C.) — The applicant applied for permanent resident status under the Canada-Quebec Investor Program. His application was denied on the basis that he failed to adequately account for the origins of his net worth. The applicant argued that the officer's decision was patently unreasonable as the decision was based on irrelevant considerations. He also argued that the information the officer requested imposed too heavy a burden on the applicant as the documents were from many years prior to the interview, and were not relevant to the current assets that had been primarily accumulated in recent years. The Court held that given the money in question was the seed money that allowed the applicant to establish his own business, it was very relevant to the application and the officer was merely doing her duty under s. 16 of IRPA when enquiring into the source of the funds.

*Bharaj v. Canada (Minister of Citizenship & Immigration)*, [2005] F.C.J. No. 1821, 2005 CarswellNat 3571, 2005 CarswellNat 5028, 2005 FC 1462 (F.C.) — The applicant submitted an application for a permanent resident visa as a member of the "entrepreneur class." The visa officer determined that the applicant did not meet the definition of "entrepreneur" as set out in s. 88(1) of the Regulations. In determining that the applicant did not satisfy the visa officer that Bharaj & Co. is a "qualified business," he only cited one reason, that being that the applicant indicated that the total sales of the business were 35,686,302 rupees and the auditor's report showed the actual total annual sales as 3,568,302 rupees. The single explanation or reason cited by the visa officer did not even stipulate which part of the "qualifying business" test the applicant did not meet and, accordingly, the Federal Court concluded that it could not be certain that a visa officer had considered all the relevant facts.

*Zhang c. Canada (Ministre de la Citoyenneté & de l'Immigration)*, [2005] F.C.J. No. 1594, 281 F.T.R. 35, 2005 CarswellNat 2969, 2005 CarswellNat 5557, 2005 FC 1313 (F.C.) — The applicant applied for judicial review of a decision by the immigration program manager at the Canadian Embassy in Beijing with respect to the applicant's application for permanent residence. The application was refused based on a violation of paragraph 40(1)(a) of the Act, specifically a misrepresentation as to the source of the applicant's funds. The Court concluded that where the applicant does not establish the source of her money, which is required by the Act, the visa officer is justified in denying the visa application. Therefore, misrepresenting the source of the funds is a material fact. The application for judicial review was dismissed.

### Investor

*Ahmed v. Canada (Minister of Citizenship & Immigration)*, 2006 CarswellNat 3202, 2006 FC 1203 (F.C.) — This was an application for judicial review of a decision of a visa officer rejecting the applicant's application for permanent residence under the Investor category. The visa officer expressed concerns about how the applicant had accumulated his wealth and asked if the applicant could provide further documentation to satisfy her of the sources of his funds. The visa officer states in her decision that the applicant replied that he did not have any further documentation and at no time did he advise that he would be sending, within 30 days of the interview, the necessary proof from his accountant showing that he was exempt from filing and paying personal income tax.

The visa officer was under no obligation to apprise the applicant of concerns unless these concerns dealt with extrinsic evidence. Although there was no obligation to do so, the visa officer did express her misgivings and invited the applicant to provide further documentation to persuade her that his wealth was not gleaned from illegitimate sources. Unfortunately, the applicant said he had no further information. The information the applicant subsequently provided was simply too late and arrived after the decision was made. There was no request from the applicant to reopen the case. The application for judicial review was dismissed as the applicant had failed to discharge himself of the onus to respect the terms of his application for permanent residence under the Investor program. Specifically, the applicant failed to clearly establish that his net worth was not gained by illegitimate means.

*Li v. Canada (Minister of Citizenship & Immigration)*, 2006 CarswellNat 1300, 2006 CarswellNat 2280, 2006 FC 599 (F.C.) — The applicant applied for permanent resident status under the Canada-Quebec Investor Program. His application was denied on the basis that he failed to adequately account for the origins of his net worth. The applicant argued that the officer's decision was patently unreasonable as the decision was based on irrelevant considerations. He also argued that the information the officer requested imposed too heavy a burden on the applicant as the documents were from many years prior to the interview, and were not relevant to the current assets that had been primarily accumulated in recent years. The Court held that given the money in question was the seed money that allowed the applicant to establish his own business, it was very relevant to the application and the officer was merely doing her duty under s. 16 of IRPA when enquiring into the source of the funds.

*Zhang c. Canada (Ministre de la Citoyenneté & de l'Immigration)*, [2005] F.C.J. No. 1594, 281 F.T.R. 35, 2005 CarswellNat 2969, 2005 CarswellNat 5557, 2005 FC 1313 (F.C.) — The applicant applied for judicial review of a decision by the immigration program manager at the Canadian Embassy in Beijing with respect to the applicant's application for permanent residence. The application was refused based on a violation of paragraph 40(1)(a) of the Act, specifically a misrepresentation as to the source of the applicant's funds. The Court concluded that where the applicant does not establish the source of her money, which is required by the Act, the visa officer is justified in denying the visa application. Therefore, misrepresenting the source of the funds is a material fact. The application for judicial review was dismissed.

### Net Worth

*Li v. Canada (Minister of Citizenship & Immigration)*, 2006 CarswellNat 1300, 2006 CarswellNat 2280, 2006 FC 599 (F.C.) — The applicant applied for permanent resident status under the Canada-Quebec Investor Program. His application was denied on the basis that he failed to adequately account for the origins of his net worth. The applicant argued that the officer's decision was patently unreasonable as the decision was based on irrelevant considerations. He also argued that the information the officer requested imposed too heavy a burden on the applicant as the documents were from many years prior to the interview, and were not relevant to the current assets that had been primarily accumulated in recent years. The Court held that given the money in question was the seed money that allowed the applicant to establish his own business, it was very relevant to the application and the officer was merely doing her duty under s. 16 of IRPA when enquiring into the source of the funds.

*Zhang c. Canada (Ministre de la Citoyenneté & de l'Immigration)*, [2005] F.C.J. No. 1594, 281 F.T.R. 35, 2005 CarswellNat 2969, 2005 CarswellNat 5557, 2005 FC 1313 (F.C.) — The applicant applied for judicial review of a decision by the immigration program manager at the Canadian Embassy in Beijing with respect to the applicant's application for permanent residence. The application was refused based on a violation of paragraph 40(1)(a) of the Act, specifically a misrepresentation as to the source of the applicant's funds. The Court concluded that where the applicant does not establish the source of her money, which is required by the Act, the visa officer is justified in denying the visa application. Therefore, misrepresenting the source of the funds is a material fact. The application for judicial review was dismissed.



### *Qualifying Business*

*Thomas v. Canada (Minister of Citizenship & Immigration)*, 2006 CarswellNat 607, 2006 CarswellNat 1875, 2006 FC 334 (F.C.) — A visa officer refused the application of the applicant and his dependants for permanent residence in Canada under the entrepreneur class. The officer concluded that the applicants had not established that any of the applicants' businesses met the definition of a "qualifying business" as required by s. 88(1) of the Regulations. The visa officer did not consider the aggregate of the applicants' businesses' results under the Regulations but instead, looked at each corporate entity on its own in determining whether the applicants' business met the definition of a "qualifying business."

Since the issue of whether s. 88(1) of the Regulations authorizes the aggregation of the results of the two corporations was a question of law to which the Court has greater experience than a visa officer, the appropriate standard of review was correctness.

A business is not defined in the Act or Regulations but is generally an activity carried out for the purpose of profit. The legal vehicle by which businesses are conducted is a different issue. In dealing with the term "qualifying business," the Regulation not only does not define a "business" but does not stipulate how it is structured. The definition simply excludes a business whose purpose is deriving investment income. The purpose of the definition is to ensure that the business in which the entrepreneur has management experience is an "active" business. The Regulation does not address and is not intended to address the structure or legal vehicle used to conduct the business, whether by a "business name," partnership, joint venture, trust, or corporation.

In this case, the proper question to ask was what were the results of the active businesses managed by the applicant? The visa officer put undue emphasis on the legal structure of the businesses, and ignored the results of the active business in all its components. The result was to ignore the reality of the scope of the businesses managed by the entrepreneur. Such an approach could lead to the unreasonable result that an entrepreneur who has structured his/her business through many corporations — for legitimate reasons such as liability, tax planning and so forth — is penalized for using the very business acumen that the Act and Regulations seeks to attract to Canada (see s. 3(1)(c) of the IRPA which identifies one of the objectives of the IRPA to "support the development of a strong and prosperous Canadian economy, in which the benefits of immigration are shared by all regions of Canada.")

It is more consistent with the purposes of the legislative provisions to focus the consideration of the entrepreneur on the overall results of the business activities managed by him/her. This leads to a result in keeping with the very aim of the statutory provision and the Regulations. The term "qualifying business" is not restricted to each legal entity conducting the non-investment income activity. It is more consistent with the purposes of the Act and the Regulations to include the financial results of the entrepreneur's non-investment income activities.

*Bharaj v. Canada (Minister of Citizenship & Immigration)*, [2005] F.C.J. No. 1821, 2005 CarswellNat 3571, 2005 CarswellNat 5028, 2005 FC 1462 (F.C.) — The applicant submitted an application for a permanent resident visa as a member of the "entrepreneur class." The visa officer determined that the applicant did not meet the definition of "entrepreneur" as set out in s. 88(1) of the Regulations. In determining that the applicant did not satisfy the visa officer that Bharaj & Co. is a "qualified business," he only cited one reason, that being that the applicant indicated that the total sales of the business were 35,686,302 rupees and the auditor's report showed the actual total annual sales as 3,568,302 rupees. The single explanation or reason cited by the visa officer did not even stipulate which part of the "qualifying business" test the applicant did not meet and accordingly the Federal Court concluded that it could not be certain that a visa officer had considered all the relevant facts.

### *Self-employed person*

*Rolfe v. Canada (Minister of Citizenship & Immigration)*, 2005 CarswellNat 3686, 2005 CarswellNat 4784, 2005 FC 1514 (F.C.) — The obligation to provide adequate reasons is not satisfied by merely stating a conclusion. In this case, the officer concluded the applicant did not meet the definition of a "self-employed person" because she was not satisfied that his experience as an explorer, leader of northern expeditions, and husky trainer was recognized as a form of cultural activity, sports, or farming under the intent of s. 88 of the Regulations. Since the applicant was presented with a conclusion without meaningful explanation, the Court concluded the officer had failed to fulfill the duty of procedural fairness owed to the applicant and set aside the decision of the immigration officer.

**89. Artificial transactions — For the purposes of this Division, an investor, an entrepreneur and a self-employed person are not considered to have met the applicable requirements of this Division if the fulfillment of those requirements is based on one or more transactions the purpose of which is to circumvent, directly or indirectly, the requirements of this Division.**

## *Investors*

### Investors Class

**90. (1) Members of the class — For the purposes of subsection 12(2) of the Act, the investor class is hereby prescribed as a class of persons who may become permanent residents on the basis of their ability to become economically established in Canada and who are investors within the meaning of subsection 88(1).**

**(2) Minimal requirements — If a foreign national who makes an application as a member of the investor class is not an investor within the meaning of subsection 88(1), the application shall be refused and no further assessment is required.**

*[Editor's Note: SOR/2002-227, s. 361(1) provides that if, before June 28, 2002, a foreign national referred to in SOR/2002-227, s. 361(2), has been assessed by a visa officer and awarded the number of units of assessment required by the* Immigration Regulations, 1978, *SOR/78-172 (the "former Regulations"), that assessment is, for the purpose of the* Immigration and Refugee Protection Regulations, *SOR/2002-227 (the "new Regulations"), an award of points equal or superior to the minimum number of points required of*

*(a) a skilled worker, in the case of a foreign national described in paragraph (2)(a) of the new Regulations;*

*(b) an investor, in the case of a foreign national described in paragraph (2)(b) of the new Regulations;*

*(c) an entrepreneur, in the case of a foreign national described in paragraph (2)(c) of the new Regulations; or*

*(d) a self-employed person, in the case of a foreign national described in paragraph (2)(a) of the new Regulations.*

*SOR/2002-227, s. 361(2) provides that SOR/2002-227, s. 361(1) applies in respect of a foreign national who submitted an application under the former Regulations, as one of the following, for an immigrant visa that is pending immediately before June 28, 2002:*

*(a) a person described in subparagraph 9(1)(b)(i) or paragraph 10(1)(b) of the former Regulations;*

*(b) an investor; or*

*(c) an entrepreneur.]*

### Fund

**91. Approval by the Minister — The Minister shall approve a fund if**

**(a) the fund has been approved by a province;**

**(b) the province provides documentation to the Minister stating that, if the fund fails to transfer the provincial allocation to the agent in accordance with paragraph 92(g), the province will be liable to transfer to the agent an amount equal to the provincial allocation in order to repay the investor in accordance with paragraph 92(i);**

**(c) the fund will be the only non-suspended approved fund in the province; and**

**(d) the fund has entered into an agreement with the Minister designating the Minister as agent for the purpose of**

**(i) receiving the provincial allocation and keeping it until the beginning of the allocation period, unless the provincial allocation is repaid under paragraph 92(b),**

**(ii) transferring the provincial allocation to the approved fund at the beginning of the allocation period in accordance with paragraph 92(d), unless the approval of the fund is suspended under subsection 93(1),**

**(iii) preparing and delivering to the investor a debt obligation and notifying the investor of the date of receipt of the provincial allocation at the beginning of the allocation period in accordance with paragraph 92(e),**

**(iv) receiving the provincial allocation transferred by the approved fund at the end of the allocation period in accordance with paragraph 92(g),**

**(v) if the approved fund fails to transfer the provincial allocation under paragraph 92(g), receiving the provincial allocation from the province in accordance with paragraph 92(h), and**

**(vi) repaying the provincial allocation to the investor in accordance with paragraph 92(i).**

SOR/2010-195, s. 9

**92. Terms and conditions — An approved fund is subject to the following terms and conditions:**

**(a) it must receive the provincial allocation through the agent;**

**(b) it must repay the provincial allocation through the agent to the investor within 90 days after the date of receipt by the agent of the request for repayment by the investor, if the request for repayment is received before a permanent resident visa is issued to the investor;**

**(c) it must repay the provincial allocation to the agent within 30 days after the agent informs the fund that the investor has chosen to withdraw their investment before the issuance of a permanent resident visa;**

**(d) if the approval of the fund has not been suspended, it must receive the provincial allocation through the agent on the first day of the allocation period;**

**(e) when it receives the provincial allocation it must**

**(i) on the first day of the allocation period, issue to the investor, through the agent, a debt obligation that is in an amount equal to the provincial allocation, is due and payable 30 days after the expiry of the allocation period, can be pledged as security and cannot be transferred before the expiry of the allocation period without the written consent of the approved fund provided by the agent, and**

**(ii) notify the investor through the agent of the date of receipt of the provincial allocation;**

**(f) during the allocation period, it must use the provincial allocation for the purpose of creating or continuing employment in Canada to foster the development of a strong and viable economy;**

**(g) at the end of the allocation period, it must transfer the provincial allocation to the agent for repayment in accordance with paragraph (i);**

**(h) if the approved fund fails to transfer the provincial allocation to the agent under paragraph (g), the province must transfer an amount equal to the provincial allocation to the agent for repayment in accordance with paragraph (i); and**

**(i) 30 days after the expiry of the allocation period, the agent must repay the provincial allocation to the investor thereby extinguishing the debt obligation in respect of that provincial allocation.**

SOR/2004-167, s. 32

**93. (1) Suspension — The Minister shall suspend the approval of a fund if**

**(a) the province that approved the fund withdraws its approval;**

**(b) the fund no longer qualifies as a fund within the meaning of subsection 88(1);**

**(c) the documentation provided by the province to the Minister in accordance with paragraph 91(b) is no longer valid and no valid documentation has been provided by the province to replace it;**

**(d) the agreement between the fund and the Minister referred to in paragraph 91(d) is no longer valid; or**

**(e) the fund is not in compliance with the terms and conditions set out in section 92.**

**(2) Lifting of suspension — The Minister shall lift the suspension if the circumstances that gave rise to the suspension cease to exist.**

**94. Revocation — The Minister shall revoke the approval of a fund if**

**(a) the approved fund has repaid the provincial allocation to all of its investors; and**

**(b) the approval of the fund has been suspended.**

**95. Reports — Every approved fund must submit to the Minister, until all investors in that fund have been repaid in accordance with paragraph 92(i), the following periodic reports for the purpose of demonstrating compliance with paragraph 92(f):**

**(a) a quarterly report on the use of provincial allocations, including**

**(i) the names of the recipients of the portion of the provincial allocations invested,**

**(ii) a description of and the terms of the security received for that investment,**

**(iii) the date on which the portion of the provincial allocations is invested,**

**(iv) the date on which the portion of the provincial allocations invested is recovered by the approved fund,**

**(v) a brief description of the use of the portion of the provincial allocations invested,**

IRP Regulations

**(vi) the number of full-time job equivalents created by the portion of the provincial allocations invested, and**

**(vii) the code for each recipient of the investment as set out in the *Canadian Standard Industrial Classification for Companies and Enterprises, 1980*; and**

**(b) audited annual financial statements for the approved fund, submitted within 180 days after the end of each financial year.**

### Investor Selected by a Province

**96. Exception — A foreign national who is an investor selected by a province shall not be assessed in accordance with section 102.**

SOR/2004-167, s. 33

## *Entrepreneurs*

### Entrepreneur Class

**97. (1) Members of the class — For the purposes of subsection 12(2) of the Act, the entrepreneur class is hereby prescribed as a class of persons who may become permanent residents on the basis of their ability to become economically established in Canada and who are entrepreneurs within the meaning of subsection 88(1).**

**(2) Minimal requirements — If a foreign national who makes an application as a member of the entrepreneur class is not an entrepreneur within the meaning of subsection 88(1), the application shall be refused and no further assessment is required.**

*[Editor's Note: SOR/2002-227, s. 361(1) provides that if, before June 28, 2002, a foreign national referred to in SOR/2002-227, s. 361(2), has been assessed by a visa officer and awarded the number of units of assessment required by the* Immigration Regulations, 1978, *SOR/78-172 (the "former Regulations"), that assessment is, for the purpose of the* Immigration and Refugee Protection Regulations, *SOR/2002-227 (the "new Regulations"), an award of points equal or superior to the minimum number of points required of*

*(a) a skilled worker, in the case of a foreign national described in paragraph (2)(a) of the new Regulations;*

*(b) an investor, in the case of a foreign national described in paragraph (2)(b) of the new Regulations;*

*(c) an entrepreneur, in the case of a foreign national described in paragraph (2)(c) of the new Regulations; or*

*(d) a self-employed person, in the case of a foreign national described in paragraph (2)(a) of the new Regulations.*

*SOR/2002-227, s. 361(2) provides that SOR/2002-227, s. 361(1) applies in respect of a foreign national who submitted an application under the former Regulations, as one of the following, for an immigrant visa that is pending immediately before June 28, 2002:*

> *(a) a person described in subparagraph 9(1)(b)(i) or paragraph 10(1)(b) of the former Regulations;*
>
> *(b) an investor; or*
>
> *(c) an entrepreneur.]*

## Case Law

### Section 97(2)

*Bharaj v. Canada (Minister of Citizenship & Immigration)*, [2005] F.C.J. No. 1821, 2005 CarswellNat 3571, 2005 CarswellNat 5028, 2005 FC 1462 (F.C.) — The applicant submitted an application for a permanent resident visa as a member of the "entrepreneur class." The visa officer determined that the applicant did not meet the definition of "entrepreneur" as set out in s. 88(1) of the Regulations. In determining that the applicant did not satisfy the visa officer that Bharaj & Co. is a "qualified business," he only cited one reason, that being that the applicant indicated that the total sales of the business were 35,686,302 rupees and the auditor's report showed the actual total annual sales as 3,568,302 rupees. The single explanation or reason cited by the visa officer did not even stipulate which part of the "qualifying business" test the applicant did not meet and accordingly the Federal Court concluded that it could not be certain that a visa officer had considered all the relevant facts.

### Conditions

**98. (1) Permanent residence — Subject to subsection (2), an entrepreneur who becomes a permanent resident must meet the following conditions:**

> **(a) the entrepreneur must control a percentage of the equity of a qualifying Canadian business equal to or greater than 33 1/3 per cent;**
>
> **(b) the entrepreneur must provide active and on-going management of the qualifying Canadian business; and**
>
> **(c) the entrepreneur must create at least one incremental full-time job equivalent in the qualifying Canadian business for Canadian citizens or permanent residents, other than the entrepreneur and their family members.**

**(2) Conditions — par. 9(1)(d) of the Act — If at the time an entrepreneur selected by a province provides the written statement referred to in paragraph (c) of the definition "entrepreneur" in subsection 88(1) the province has established the conditions required to be met by such an entrepreneur, that statement must refer to those conditions instead of the conditions set out in subsection (1) and the entrepreneur must meet those conditions instead of the conditions set out in subsection (1).**

**(3) Applicable time — The entrepreneur must meet the conditions for a period of at least one year within the period of three years after the day on which the entrepreneur becomes a permanent resident.**

**(4) Evidence of compliance — An entrepreneur who becomes a permanent resident must provide to an officer evidence of compliance with the conditions within the period of three years after the day on which the entrepreneur becomes a permanent resident.**

**(5) Report and evidence of efforts to comply — An entrepreneur must provide to an officer**

> **(a) not later than six months after the day on which the entrepreneur becomes a permanent resident, their residential address and telephone number; and**
>
> **(b) during the period beginning 18 months after and ending 24 months after the day on which the entrepreneur becomes a permanent resident, evidence of their efforts to comply with the conditions.**

**(6) Family members — The family members of an entrepreneur are subject to the condition that the entrepreneur meets the conditions set out in this section.**

SOR/2004-167, s. 34

## Case Law

### Section 98(1)

*Gjoka v. Canada (Minister of Citizenship & Immigration)* (2009), 84 Imm. L.R. (3d) 198, 352 F.T.R. 303, 2009 FC 943, 2009 CarswellNat 3058, 2009 CarswellNat 5358 (Eng.) (F.C.) — The applicant was selected on September 16, 2002, for permanent residence under the entrepreneur category and was issued a permanent resident visa on February 4, 2003, and landed on March 12, 2003. On May 28, 2004, in response to a letter from Canadian Immigration and Citizenship, the applicant submitted a monitoring report and an application to cancel his terms and conditions of landing. No other monitoring reports were submitted. A report alleging that the applicant had failed to comply with the terms and conditions of his landing was issued on March 18, 2008. An inadmissibility hearing was held before the ID on May 7, 2008. The respondent submitted that the applicant had not met the conditions imposed on him under the *Immigration Regulations* (the former Regulations), specifically paragraphs 23.1(1)(a) to (d). The applicant made his application for permanent residency under the former Act but the selection decision and his permanent resident visa were issued after the coming into force of the current Act. Furthermore, the Confirmation of Permanent Residence form signed by the applicant upon landing specified that the conditions to be met were those of the former Regulations and s. 23.1 of those Regulations was attached to the form. At the admissibility hearing, the ID member found that the conditions imposed on the applicant were of s. 98 of the current Regulations and as such, this subs. 44(1) report alleging a failure to meet the conditions under the former Regulations was unfounded. Following an appeal by the Minister, the IAD set aside the ID's decision and referred the matter back for reconsideration. The IAD accepted the conclusion that the applicant was subject to the conditions set out in s. 98 of the current Regulations and referred the matter back to the ID to determine whether or not the applicant had met the conditions imposed under the Act.

Because of the transitional provisions and s. 318 of the current Regulations, the Court found that the entrepreneur class selected applicants under the former *Immigration Act* are required to comply with post-admission to Canada terms and conditions as set out in paragraphs 23(a) to (d) of the former *Immigration Regulations*. The interpretation of the transitional provisions of the IAD is too restrictive. It implies that s. 98 of the current Regulations can be applied retroactively to entrepreneurial applicants who filed their application prior to January 1, 2002, and were assessed and issued visas as entrepreneur under the former *Immigration Act* and Regulations. Nothing in the Act, the current Regulations or the transitional provisions support such a proposition. The application for judicial review was allowed.

*Chang v. Canada (Minister of Citizenship & Immigration)*, [2006] F.C.J. No. 217, 2006 CarswellNat 329, 2006 CarswellNat 2194, 2006 FC 157 (F.C.) — The legislatively established conditions of the entrepreneur category, if flaunted knowingly, without serious consequence, would make a mockery of the purpose for which they were established. The act of creating or participating in a front operation or a sham investment, if left unchecked, strikes a blow at the very integrity of the immigration system. In this case, the applicants were found to be in non-compliance with subs. 27(2) and s. 28. The applicants' children were also found to be in non-compliance with subs. 27(2) as they were dependants of an entrepreneur and bound by the same terms and conditions of landing as provided in paragraph 23.1 of the previous Regulations. Both the applicants as well as their children sought special relief on appeal in light of the circumstances of their case, specifically, that there were sufficient humanitarian and compassionate considerations that warranted the setting aside of departure orders. The IAD was of the view that the parents did not merit discretionary relief as they took part in a sham arrangement to try to fulfill the conditions of the entrepreneur category. Even though the IAD felt that the children would be excellent candidates for permanent residence, it refused to grant discretionary relief to the children because once the children became permanent residents they would be entitled to sponsor their parents which would render the removal of the parents moot.

The granting of special relief is a weighing process. Even though there were some positive elements in favour of discretionary relief being allowed to the three children, these elements did not outweigh the importance given to the integrity of maintaining the conditions in the entrepreneur category. It was open to the IAD to find that special relief should not be granted to the children because this would benefit the parents who had not respected the conditions under which they entered Canada.

*Elias c. Canada (Ministre de la Citoyenneté & de l'Immigration)*, 2005 CarswellNat 5708, 2005 FC 1329 (F.C.) — The applicant sought judicial review of the IAD's decision dismissing their appeal from a removal order. The principal applicant was born in Lebanon and emigrated to Brazil, where he lived for 20 years and became a citizen of that country. The applicant was granted landing in Canada as an entrepreneur and accepted the conditions provided under paragraph 23.1 of the *Immigration Regulations*. The Immigration Division decided that the applicants were persons contemplated by s. 41 of the IRPA since the principal applicant had not respected the conditions imposed for entrepreneurs when he was granted landing. The IAD dismissed the applicant's appeal concluding that an order to stay the removal order would have the effect of not only calling into question the integrity of the program conceived to attract entrepreneurs, but also the integrity of the Canadian immigration system as a whole. The principal applicant argued that he had provided plausible explanations and reasons why he was unable to respect the conditions within the two-year time period. In this case, the Court concluded that the IAD weighed the best interests of the children directly affected as well as the other factors alleged by the applicants in support of their appeal but, considering the other circumstances of the matter, determined that special relief was not justified. The applicants'

IRP Regulations

eldest son was born in Brazil while the younger son was born in Canada. The applicants did not submit any evidence regarding the effects that the removal to Brazil could have on the eldest child, or the effects of a possible migration on the younger child. The applicants' argument regarding the children amounted to saying that the presence of children in Canada automatically implies humanitarian considerations justifying special measures. The Court concluded that Parliament has not decided that the presence of children in Canada constitutes in itself an impediment to any *refoulement* of a parent illegally residing in Canada. The application for judicial review was dismissed.

### Entrepreneur Selected by a Province

**99. Exception — A foreign national who is an entrepreneur selected by a province shall not be assessed in accordance with section 102.**

SOR/2004-167, s. 35

## *Self-employed Persons*

### Self-employed Persons Class

**100. (1) Members of the class — For the purposes of subsection 12(2) of the Act, the self-employed persons class is hereby prescribed as a class of persons who may become permanent residents on the basis of their ability to become economically established in Canada and who are self-employed persons within the meaning of subsection 88(1).**

**(2) Minimal requirements — If a foreign national who applies as a member of the self-employed persons class is not a self-employed person within the meaning of subsection 88(1), the application shall be refused and no further assessment is required.**

*[Editor's Note: SOR/2002-227, s. 361(1) provides that if, before June 28, 2002, a foreign national referred to in SOR/2002-227, s. 361(2), has been assessed by a visa officer and awarded the number of units of assessment required by the* Immigration Regulations, 1978, *SOR/78-172 (the "former Regulations"), that assessment is, for the purpose of the* Immigration and Refugee Protection Regulations, *SOR/2002-227 (the "new Regulations"), an award of points equal or superior to the minimum number of points required of*

*(a) a skilled worker, in the case of a foreign national described in paragraph (2)(a) of the new Regulations;*

*(b) an investor, in the case of a foreign national described in paragraph (2)(b) of the new Regulations;*

*(c) an entrepreneur, in the case of a foreign national described in paragraph (2)(c) of the new Regulations; or*

*(d) a self-employed person, in the case of a foreign national described in paragraph (2)(a) of the new Regulations.*

*SOR/2002-227, s. 361(2) provides that SOR/2002-227, s. 361(1) applies in respect of a foreign national who submitted an application under the former Regulations, as one of the following, for an immigrant visa that is pending immediately before June 28, 2002:*

*(a) a person described in subparagraph 9(1)(b)(i) or paragraph 10(1)(b) of the former Regulations;*

*(b) an investor; or*

*(c) an entrepreneur.]*

## Case Law

### Section 100(2)

*Rolfe v. Canada (Minister of Citizenship & Immigration)*, 2005 CarswellNat 3686, 2005 CarswellNat 4784, 2005 FC 1514 (F.C.) — The obligation to provide adequate reasons is not satisfied by merely stating a conclusion. In this case, the officer concluded the applicant did not meet the definition of a "self-employed person" because she was not satisfied that his experience as an explorer, leader of northern expeditions, and husky trainer was recognized as a form of cultural activity, sports, or farming under the intent of s. 88 of the Regulations. Since the applicant was presented with a conclusion without meaningful explanation, the Court concluded the officer had failed to fulfill the duty of procedural fairness owed to the applicant and set aside the decision of the immigration officer.



### Self-employed Person Selected by a Province

**101. Exception — A foreign national who is a self-employed person selected by a province shall not be assessed in accordance with section 102.**

SOR/2004-167, s. 36

## *Selection Criteria*

### General

**102. (1) Criteria — For the purpose of determining whether a foreign national, as a member of the investor class, the entrepreneur class or the self-employed persons class, and the foreign national's family members will be able to become economically established in Canada, an officer shall assess that foreign national on the basis of the following factors:**

**(a) age, in accordance with section 81, on the same basis as for skilled workers;**

**(b) education, in accordance with section 78, on the same basis as for skilled workers;**

**(c) proficiency in the official languages of Canada, in accordance with section 79, on the same basis as for skilled workers;**

**(d) experience, in accordance with section 103; and**

**(e) adaptability, in accordance with section 104 in the case of a member of the investor class or the entrepreneur class, and in accordance with section 105 in the case of a member of the self-employed persons class.**

(2) **Units of assessment** — **A foreign national who is assessed on the basis of the factors set out in paragraphs (1)(a) to (e) shall be awarded the applicable number of assessment points for each factor set out in the provision referred to in each of those paragraphs, subject to the maximum number set out in that provision for that factor.**

SOR/2004-167, s. 37

## Experience

**103. (1) Investor — A member of the investor class shall be awarded assessment points up to a maximum of 35 points for business experience during the period beginning five years before the date of their application for a permanent resident visa and ending on the day a determination is made in respect of the application as follows:**

> **(a) for two one-year periods of experience described in subparagraph (a)(i) or (ii) of the definition "business experience" in subsection 88(1) or for a combination of two one-year periods of such experience, 20 points;**
>
> **(b) for three one-year periods of experience described in subparagraph (a)(i) or (ii) of the definition "business experience" in subsection 88(1) or for any combination of three one-year periods of such experience, 25 points;**
>
> **(c) for four one-year periods of experience described in subparagraph (a)(i) or (ii) of the definition "business experience" in subsection 88(1) or for any combination of four one-year periods of such experience, 30 points; and**
>
> **(d) for five one-year periods of experience described in subparagraph (a)(i) or (ii) of the definition "business experience" in subsection 88(1) or for any combination of five one-year periods of such experience, 35 points.**

**(2) Entrepreneur — A member of the entrepreneur class shall be awarded assessment points up to a maximum of 35 points for business experience during the period beginning five years before the date of their application for a permanent resident visa and ending on the day a determination is made in respect of the application as follows:**

> **(a) for two one-year periods of experience described in paragraph (b) of the definition "business experience" in subsection 88(1), 20 points;**
>
> **(b) for three one-year periods of experience described in paragraph (b) of the definition "business experience" in subsection 88(1), 25 points;**
>
> **(c) for four one-year periods of experience described in paragraph (b) of the definition "business experience" in subsection 88(1), 30 points; and**
>
> **(d) for five one-year periods of experience described in paragraph (b) of the definition "business experience" in subsection 88(1), 35 points.**

**(3) "Self-employed person" — A member of the self-employed persons class shall be awarded assessment points up to a maximum of 35 points for relevant experience during the period beginning five years before the date of their application for**

**a permanent resident visa and ending on the day a determination is made in respect of the application as follows:**

**(a) 20 points for**

**(i) two one-year periods of experience described in clause (a)(i)(A) or (B) of the definition "relevant experience" in subsection 88(1) or a combination of two one-year periods of such experience,**

**(ii) two one-year periods of experience described in clause (a)(ii)(A) or (B) of the definition "relevant experience" in subsection 88(1) or a combination of two one-year periods of such experience, or**

**(iii) two one-year periods of experience described in subparagraph (a)(iii) of the definition "relevant experience" in subsection 88(1);**

**(b) 25 points for**

**(i) three one-year periods of experience described in clause (a)(i)(A) or (B) of the definition "relevant experience" in subsection 88(1) or any combination of three one-year periods of such experience,**

**(ii) three one-year periods of experience described in clause (a)(ii)(A) or (B) of the definition "relevant experience" in subsection 88(1) or any combination of three one-year periods of such experience, or**

**(iii) three one-year periods of experience described in subparagraph (a)(iii) of the definition "relevant experience" in subsection 88(1);**

**(c) 30 points for**

**(i) four one-year periods of experience described in clause (a)(i)(A) or (B) of the definition "relevant experience" in subsection 88(1) or any combination of four one-year periods of such experience,**

**(ii) four one-year periods of experience described in clause (a)(ii)(A) or (B) of the definition "relevant experience" in subsection 88(1) or any combination of four one-year periods of such experience, or**

**(iii) four one-year periods of experience described in subparagraph (a)(iii) of the definition "relevant experience" in subsection 88(1); and**

**(d) 35 points for**

**(i) five one-year periods of experience described in clause (a)(i)(A) or (B) of the definition "relevant experience" in subsection 88(1) or any combination of five one-year periods of such experience,**

**(ii) five one-year periods of experience described in clause (a)(ii)(A) or (B) of the definition "relevant experience" in subsection 88(1) or any combination of five one-year periods of such experience, or**

**(iii) five one-year periods of experience described in subparagraph (a)(iii) of the definition "relevant experience" in subsection 88(1).**

SOR/2004-167, s. 38

IRP Regulations

## Adaptability

**104. Investor and entrepreneur — A member of the investor class or the entrepreneur class shall be awarded assessment points up to a maximum of six points for adaptability on the basis of the following elements:**

**(a) for a business exploration trip to Canada in the period beginning five years before the date of their application for a permanent resident visa and ending on the day on which a determination is made in respect of the application, 6 points; and**

**(b) for participation in joint federal-provincial business immigration initiatives, 6 points.**

**105. (1) Self-employed person — A member of the self-employed persons class shall be awarded assessment points up to a maximum of 6 points for adaptability on the basis of any combination of the following elements:**

**(a) for the educational credentials of the member's accompanying spouse or common-law partner, 3, 4 or 5 points determined in accordance with subsection (2);**

**(b) for any previous period of study in Canada by the member or their spouse or common-law partner, 5 points;**

**(c) for any previous period of work in Canada by the member, 5 points; and**

**(d) for being related to a person living in Canada who is described in subsection (5), 5 points.**

**(2) Educational credentials of spouse or common-law partner — For the purposes of paragraph (1)(a), an officer shall evaluate the educational credentials of the accompanying spouse or accompanying common-law partner of the member of the self-employed persons class as if the spouse or common-law partner were the member, and shall award points to the member as follows:**

**(a) for a spouse or common-law partner who would be awarded 25 points, 5 points;**

**(b) for a spouse or common-law partner who would be awarded 20 or 22 points, 4 points; and**

**(c) for a spouse or common-law partner who would be awarded 12 or 15 points, 3 points.**

**(3) Previous study in Canada — For the purposes of paragraph (1)(b), a member of the self-employed persons class shall be awarded 5 points if the member or their accompanying spouse or accompanying common-law partner, by the age of 17 or older, completed a program of full-time study of at least two years' duration at a post-secondary institution in Canada under a study permit, whether or not they obtained an educational credential for completing that program.**

**(4) Previous work in Canada — For the purpose of paragraph (1)(c), a member of the self-employed persons class shall be awarded 5 points if the member or their accompanying spouse or accompanying common-law partner engaged in at least one year of full-time work in Canada under a work permit.**

(5) **Family relationships in Canada** — For the purposes of paragraph (1)(d), a member of the self-employed persons class shall be awarded 5 points if

(a) the member or their accompanying spouse or accompanying common-law partner is related by blood, marriage, common-law partnership or adoption to a person who is a Canadian citizen or permanent resident living in Canada and who is

(i) their father or mother,

(ii) the father or mother of their father or mother,

(iii) their child,

(iv) a child of their child,

(v) a child of their father or mother,

(vi) a child of the father or mother of their father or mother, other than their father or mother, or

(vii) a child of the child of their father or mother; or

(b) the member has a spouse or common-law partner who is not accompanying them and is a Canadian citizen or permanent resident living in Canada.

SOR/2004-167, s. 39



## *Requirements*

106. [Repealed SOR/2008-202, s. 6.]

107. **Permanent resident status** — A foreign national who is an accompanying family member of a person who makes an application as a member of the investor class, the entrepreneur class or the self-employed persons class shall become a permanent resident if, following an examination, it is established that

(a) the person who made the application has become a permanent resident; and

(b) the foreign national is not inadmissible.

SOR/2008-202, s. 6

## *Selection*

108. (1) **Application for visa** — Subject to subsection (5), if a foreign national makes an application as a member of the investor class, the entrepreneur class or the self-employed persons class for a permanent resident visa, an officer shall issue the visa to the foreign national and their accompanying family members if

(a) the foreign national and their family members, whether accompanying or not, are not inadmissible and meet the requirements of the Act and these Regulations;

*[Editor's Note: SOR/2002-227, s. 353 provides that if a person has made an application under the former* Immigration Act, *R.S.C. 1985, c. I-2 before June 28, 2002, the following provisions of the* Immigration and Refugee Protection Regulations, *SOR/2002-227 (the "new Regulations") do not apply to the person in respect of any*

*of his or her non-accompanying dependent children, referred to in s. 352 of the new Regulations, or his or her non-accompanying common-law partner:*

*(a) paragraph 70(1)(e);*

*(b) subparagraph 72(1)(e)(i); and*

*(c) paragraph 108(1)(a).]*

**(b) where the foreign national and their accompanying family members intend to reside in a place in Canada other than a province the government of which has, under subsection 8(1) of the Act, entered into an agreement referred to in subsection 9(1) of the Act with the Minister whereby the province has sole responsibility for selection, the foreign national is awarded the minimum number of points referred to in subsection (2), (3) or (4), as the case may be, and, if they are a member of the investor class, they have made an investment; and**

**(c) where the foreign national and their accompanying family members intend to reside in a province the government of which has, under subsection 8(1) of the Act, entered into an agreement referred to in subsection 9(1) of the Act with the Minister whereby the province has sole responsibility for selection, the foreign national is named in a selection certificate issued by that province and, if the foreign national is a member of the investor class, they have made an investment.**

**(2) Minimum points — investors — The Minister shall fix and make available to the public the minimum number of points required of an investor, on the basis of**

**(a) the number of applications made by members of the investor class currently being processed;**

**(b) the number of investors projected to become permanent residents according to the report to Parliament referred to in section 94 of the Act; and**

**(c) the potential, taking into account economic and other relevant factors, for the establishment of investors in Canada.**

**(3) Minimum points — entrepreneurs — The Minister shall fix and make available to the public the minimum number of points required of an entrepreneur, on the basis of**

**(a) the number of applications by members of the entrepreneur class currently being processed;**

**(b) the number of entrepreneurs projected to become permanent residents according to the report to Parliament referred to in section 94 of the Act; and**

**(c) the potential, taking into account economic and other relevant factors, for the establishment of entrepreneurs in Canada.**

**(4) Minimum points — self-employed persons — The Minister shall fix and make available to the public the minimum number of points required of a self-employed person, on the basis of**

**(a) the number of applications by members of the self-employed persons class currently being processed;**

(b) the number of self-employed persons projected to become permanent residents according to the report to Parliament referred to in section 94 of the Act; and

(c) the potential, taking into account economic and other relevant factors, for the establishment of self-employed persons in Canada.

(5) **Federal-provincial agreement** — A permanent resident visa shall not be issued to an investor selected by a province, or to that investor's accompanying family members, if the Minister is engaged in consultations with the province in respect of the interpretation or implementation of the agreement, referred to in subsection 9(1) of the Act and entered into under subsection 8(1) of the Act, between the province and the Minister in respect of the selection of investors and the consultations have not been successfully completed.

SOR/2004-167, s. 40

109. (1) **Substitution of evaluation** — Whether or not a foreign national has been awarded the minimum number of required points referred to in subsection 108(1), an officer may substitute for the factors set out in subsection 102(1) their evaluation of the likelihood of the foreign national's ability to become economically established in Canada if the number of points awarded is not a sufficient indicator of whether the foreign national may become economically established in Canada.

(2) **Concurrence** — An evaluation made under subsection (1) requires the concurrence of a second officer.

## *Transitional Federal Investors, Entrepreneurs and Self-employed Persons*

[Heading added SOR/2003-383, s. 5.]

### Transitional Federal Business Classes

[Heading added SOR/2003-383, s. 5.]

109.1 (1) **Classes** — For the purposes of subsection 12(2) of the Act, the transitional federal investor class, the transitional federal entrepreneur class and the transitional federal self-employed persons class are hereby prescribed as classes of persons who are transitional investors, transitional entrepreneurs or transitional self-employed persons, respectively, and who may become permanent residents on the basis of their ability to become economically established in Canada and who intend to reside in a province other than the Province of Quebec.

(2) **Transitional federal business immigrants** — A foreign national is a transitional investor, a transitional entrepreneur or a transitional self-employed person if they made an application before January 1, 2002 under the former Regulations for an immigrant visa as an investor, an entrepreneur or a self-employed person, respectively, within the meaning of subsection 2(1) of those Regulations that was

(a) refused after March 31, 2003 and before June 20, 2003; or

**(b) withdrawn by the foreign national on or after January 1, 2002 and before December 1, 2003.**

SOR/2003-383, s. 5

**109.2 (1) Application before January 1, 2005 — Subject to subsection (2), an application for a permanent resident visa as a member of the transitional federal investor class, the transitional federal entrepreneur class or the transitional federal self-employed persons class must be made in accordance with sections 10 and 11 and must be received by the applicable immigration office referred to in subsection 11(1) not later than December 31, 2004.**

**(2) Alternate place of application — An application referred to in subsection (1) may be made to the immigration office at the location where the application referred to in subsection 109.1(2) was made, instead of to the immigration office referred to in subsection 11(1).**

SOR/2003-383, s. 5

**109.3 Criteria — For the purpose of determining whether**

**(a) a transitional investor, as a member of the transitional federal investor class, will be able to become economically established in Canada, they must be**

**(i) an investor within the meaning of subsection 2(1) of the former Regulations and be awarded the number of units of assessment required by those Regulations for an investor, or**

**(ii) an investor within the meaning of subsection 88(1) and obtain a minimum of 35 points based on the factors set out in subsection 102(1) to become a permanent resident as a member of the investor class;**

**(b) a transitional entrepreneur, as a member of the transitional federal entrepreneur class, will be able to become economically established in Canada, they must be**

**(i) an entrepreneur within the meaning of subsection 2(1) of the former Regulations and be awarded the number of units of assessment required by those Regulations for an entrepreneur, or**

**(ii) an entrepreneur within the meaning of subsection 88(1) and obtain a minimum of 35 points based on the factors set out in subsection 102(1) to become a permanent resident as a member of the entrepreneur class; and**

**(c) a transitional self-employed person, as a member of the transitional federal self-employed persons class, will be able to become economically established in Canada, they must be**

**(i) a self-employed person within the meaning of subsection 2(1) of the former Regulations and be awarded the number of units of assessment required by those Regulations for a self-employed person, or**

**(ii) a self-employed person within the meaning of subsection 88(1) and obtain a minimum of 35 points based on the factors set out in subsection 102(1) to become a permanent resident as a member of the self-employed persons class.**

SOR/2003-383, s. 5

### Requirements

[Heading added SOR/2003-383, s. 5.]

**109.4 [Repealed SOR/2008-202, s. 7.]**

**109.5 Permanent resident status — A foreign national who is a family member of a person who makes an application for a permanent resident visa as a member of the transitional federal investor class, the transitional federal entrepreneur class or the transitional federal self-employed persons class shall become a permanent resident if, following an examination, it is established that the family member is not inadmissible.**

SOR/2003-383, s. 5

## DIVISION 3 — LIVE-IN CAREGIVERS



**110. Live-in caregiver class — The live-in caregiver class is prescribed as a class of foreign nationals who may become permanent residents on the basis of the requirements of this Division.**

**111. Processing — A foreign national who seeks to enter Canada as a live-in caregiver must make an application for a work permit in accordance with Part 11 and apply for a temporary resident visa if such a visa is required by Part 9.**

**112. Work permits — requirements — A work permit shall not be issued to a foreign national who seeks to enter Canada as a live-in caregiver unless they**

**(a) applied for a work permit as a live-in caregiver before entering Canada;**

**(b) have successfully completed a course of study that is equivalent to the successful completion of secondary school in Canada;**

**(c) have the following training or experience, in a field or occupation related to the employment for which the work permit is sought, namely,**

**(i) successful completion of six months of full-time training in a classroom setting, or**

**(ii) completion of one year of full-time paid employment, including at least six months of continuous employment with one employer, in such a field or occupation within the three years immediately before the day on which they submit an application for a work permit;**

**(d) have the ability to speak, read and listen to English or French at a level sufficient to communicate effectively in an unsupervised setting; and**

**(e) have an employment contract with their future employer.**

### Case Law

*Nazir v. Canada (Minister of Citizenship & Immigration)* (2010), 89 Imm. L.R. (3d) 131, 2010 FC 553, 2010 CarswellNat 2246, 2010 CarswellNat 1421 (F.C.) — A visa officer determined that the applicant did not meet the requirements for a work permit as a live-in caregiver pursuant to s. 112 of the Regulations. The visa officer was not satisfied that the applicant's intentions were *bona fide* and temporary in nature, and that she was a genuine temporary worker in Canada. While noting that there is no legislative restriction preventing family members from offering relatives jobs as live-in caregiver, the visa officer was not convinced that the job offer was not made primarily for the purposes of facilitating the applicant's admission in Canada.

There is nothing in the Act or Regulations to prevent family ties between future employer and employee. Furthermore, the caregiver program specifically provides that these individuals can apply for permanent residence afterward. A candidate with no intention of applying for permanent residence would be ineligible for the program (see 5.2 of the Manual). The Manual also points out that with these individuals, it is difficult to apply the normal requirement that temporary residents will leave Canada by the end of the authorized period (at section 8.4). The officer's determination was therefore clearly erroneous; he quite simply disregarded the type of program involved in this case. The application for judicial review was allowed.

*Bondoc v. Canada (Minister of Citizenship & Immigration)*, [2008] F.C.J. No. 1063, 2008 CarswellNat 4247, 2008 CarswellNat 2327, 2008 FC 842 — The application for a work permit in Canada as a "live-in caregiver" was refused on the basis that the employment offer was not genuine, the applicant was unable to demonstrate that she had sufficient knowledge and skills to adequately provide care without supervision and that the job offer was made primarily for the purpose of facilitating the applicant's admission to Canada and that the applicant's intentions in coming to Canada were not for a temporary purpose. The HRSDC deals exclusively with the employer in Canada and is therefore not responsible for assessing the *bona fides* of the employment contract. The visa officer has the responsibility to assess the intent of both parties to the contract. As to the duties envisaged by the employment contract, the visa officer committed no unreasonable error in concluding that the applicant's duties were more in line with domestic duties, rather than providing unsupervised care to the children. With regards to the officer's consideration of the applicant's familial relationship with her future employer, the Court noted that this is not the only pertinent factor considered in the officer's assessment of the *bona fides* of the employment offer. This consideration should not be isolated from the other factors that were considered in support of this finding. Nothing in the Act or its Regulations prevents employment offers between family members. On the other hand, nothing prevented the officer from considering the family relationship with the other factors that were considered to be able to convince herself that the applicant's offer of employment was not genuine. It is within the power of a visa officer to assess the genuineness of an employer's offer, and there is no requirement for her to give deference to the HRSDC officer's assessment of the validity of the employment offer.

The Court agreed with the applicant that the finding that she was not a genuine visitor was not supported by the evidence and the visa officer had no basis to make it. While there is a provision entitling applicants for the LIC Program to have a dual intent in entering Canada, the visa officer must still be satisfied that ultimately the applicant would depart Canada and not remain here illegally if their application for permanent residence was denied. The visa officer in this case appeared to ignore the applicant's close ties to the Philippines, including the fact that her husband and young child resided there. It was also an error for the visa officer to ignore in her decision the dual intent nature of the LIC Program. The visa officer does not have to be satisfied that the applicant has a temporary purpose in coming to Canada, but instead, that the applicant will not remain illegally in Canada if her application for permanent residence under the LIC class is rejected.

While the visa officer did err in her finding that the applicant did not seek to come to Canada for a temporary purpose, this error had no serious consequence on the impugned decision, since the Court found that the first two issues were determinative of the visa officer's decision that the applicant did not meet the LIC Program's requirements, and that this finding was reasonable. The application for judicial review was dismissed.

*Duroseau v. Canada (Minister of Citizenship & Immigration)*, 2008 CarswellNat 130, 2008 CarswellNat 957, 2008 FC 72 — The officer refused to issue a work permit for two reasons:

> (1) She referred to the prohibition against issuing a work permit under subparagraph 200(3)(e)(i) to persons having engaged in unauthorized work in Canada in the past six months. The officer believed that the applicant had engaged in such work since her arrival in Canada by helping Ms. Darius with her children.
>
> (2) The officer determined that the applicant did not meet the requirements of s. 112 of the Regulations because the employment contract was not genuine and constituted an offer of convenience aimed at facilitating the applicant's acquisition of status in Canada.

The definition of "work" set forth in the Regulations does not require compensation to have been received in order for an activity to be considered work. The activity merely has to be "in direct competition with the activities of Canadian citizens or permanent residents in the Canadian labour market." Child care meets the definition of work. The friendship between the applicant and the employer was just one fact among many justifying the officer's doubts as to the *bona fide* character of the contract. The fact that the applicant lived in Ms. Darius' home prior to submitting her application, the length of time before she submitted it, and the fact that the applicant was engaged in child-care activity all provided sufficient support for the officer's decision.

*Salman v. Canada (Minister of Citizenship & Immigration)*, [2007] F.C.J. No. 1142, 63 Imm. L.R. (3d) 285, 2007 FC 877, 2007 CarswellNat 3464, 2007 CarswellNat 2749 (F.C.) — A visa officer determined that the applicant was not a member of the live-in caregiver class and denied his application for a work permit. He sought judicial review. The visa officer was not satisfied that the applicant had completed the equivalent of a secondary school education, as required by s. 112 of the Regulations. Following this rejection, the applicant's future employer in Canada obtained an evaluation by the Comparative Education Service of the University of Toronto, confirming that the programme of study in which the applicant was enrolled was the academic equivalent of the Ontario Secondary School Diploma. This letter was faxed to the Embassy, and the applicant was granted a second interview with a different visa officer. Even though the officer refers to the evaluation in his CAIPS notes, he made no analysis or comments as to why he rejected that evidence. With the evidence before him, the visa officer had a duty to investigate this point more thoroughly. The error was sufficient to justify the intervention of the Court. The application for judicial review was allowed.

*Singh v. Canada (Minister of Citizenship & Immigration)*, 2006 CarswellNat 2573, 2006 CarswellNat 1474, 2006 FC 684 (F.C.) — The applicant challenged a decision of the visa officer who refused his application for a work permit as a live-in caregiver. The applicant was offered a position at the home of his sister and brother-in-law. The position involved looking after the needs of two young children. The applicant's request for a work permit was refused on the basis that he did not have the requisite training or work experience in the field of child care. The applicant's employment experience had been in the field of



IRP Regulations

health care. He had successfully passed his examination in nursing and had been employed as a ward nurse at a well known geriatric hospital in Vienna. Although the applicant had a wealth of experience as a geriatric caregiver, he presented no evidence of experience in the area of child care. Due to the absence of child-care experience his application for a work permit was refused. The visa officer's decision was based on an interpretation that s. 112 of the Regulations required the applicant to have specific employment experience in the field of child care. The Court held that the language of s. 112 was sufficiently ambiguous that it could support either of the interpretations advanced by the parties. The CIC operational guidelines applicable to s. 112 offered some limited assistance in understanding how the department applies the eligibility criteria for issuing a live-in caregiver work permit. Although the provisions of the guidelines lack clarity, the tenor of these provisions suggest that it is not the labels that are attached to the training or experience factors that are instructive, but rather the relevant skills that one acquires against which work permit eligibility is to be measured.

The adoption of a purposive approach to the interpretation of s. 112 leads to the same result. Clearly what is intended by these provisions is that caregivers have the capacity to adequately perform the tasks expected of them. There is no question that a well qualified nurse would have considerable knowledge and experience in the field of caregiving. The fact that beneficiaries of that prior work experience may not have been children does not mean that such an applicant has no transferable skills which could be applied in a child-care setting. The record in this case suggests that the applicant did enjoy a number of skills which could have been readily applied to the care of children, including those of nutrition, hygiene, first aid, supervision, home care and social skills.

What is required in the application of s. 112 to any given fact situation is to assess the applicant's employment experience with a view of identifying the transferable skills that are available to the fulfillment of the proposed Canadian employment. It could very well be that in a single household there will be children needing typical care, along with elderly or disabled individuals whose needs may be different or unique. A too-rigid approach to the interpretation of work experience or training requirements of s. 112 could deprive a family of the support that this provision was intended to accommodate.

The visa officer should have considered the caregiving skills acquired by the applicant during his more than 10 years of hospital nursing employment to determine if they would be adequate to meet the employment demands for the position he had been offered. It is not sufficient in assessing prior experience to focus only on the characteristics or the age of the intended beneficiaries of care. It is difficult to believe that more than 10 years of experience as a hospital nurse would not result in the acquisition of many skills and aptitudes which would be readily applicable to the provision of child care in a home setting.

The matter was remitted to a different visa officer for reconsideration of the application.

*Ouafae c. Canada (Ministre de la Citoyenneté & de l'Immigration)*, [2005] F.C.J. No. 592, 2005 CarswellNat 899, 2005 CarswellNat 5098, 2005 FC 459 (F.C.) — The applicant's application for a work permit as a live-in caregiver was refused on the basis that she did not meet the requirements of s. 112 of the Regulations. Section 112 requires that the applicant show they have training or experience in a field or occupation related to the employment for which the work permit is sought. The applicant stated in the interview that she had worked as a teacher for two years. On that basis, the officer concluded that the applicant had failed to show she had any recent experience as a housekeeper. The officer was, therefore, not satisfied that she really was a domestic worker. The officer also concluded that since the applicant's brother was her future employer in Canada, the application was being made to facilitate her entry to Canada and she would not return to Morocco.

According to the department's manual, training and experience must be in a field or occupation related to the employment sought, and it specifies that caregivers may have training or experience in early childhood education, which was precisely the applicant's case. The visa officer's decision to disregard that experience was therefore unreasonable and inconsistent with the provisions of the manual. Both the training and the experience may be acquired in a field or occupation related to the employment.

The officer's conclusion with respect to the applicant's brother being the intended employer and the conclusion that she would not return to Morocco were purely speculative and without evidence. Furthermore, there was nothing in the Act or Regulations to prevent family ties between future employer and employee. The caregiver programs specifically provide that these individuals can apply for permanent residence afterwards. A candidate with no intention of applying for permanent residence would be ineligible for the program. The manual also points out that it is difficult with these individuals to apply the normal requirement that temporary residents will leave Canada by the end of the authorized period. The officer's determination was, therefore, clearly erroneous because he disregarded the type of program the applicant was applying under.



**113. (1) Permanent residence — A foreign national becomes a member of the live-in caregiver class if**

**(a) they have submitted an application to remain in Canada as a permanent resident;**

**(b) they are a temporary resident;**

**(c) they hold a work permit as a live-in caregiver;**

**(d) they entered Canada as a live-in caregiver and for at least two of the four years immediately following their entry or, alternatively, for at least 3,900 hours during a period of not less than 22 months in those four years,**

**(i) resided in a private household in Canada, and**

**(ii) provided child care, senior home support care or care of a disabled person in that household without supervision;**

**(e) they are not, and none of their family members are, the subject of an enforceable removal order or an admissibility hearing under the Act or an appeal or application for judicial review arising from such a hearing;**

**(f) they did not enter Canada as a live-in caregiver as a result of a misrepresentation concerning their education, training or experience; and**

**(g) where they intend to reside in the Province of Quebec, the competent authority of that Province is of the opinion that they meet the selection criteria of the Province.**

**(2) Calculation — For the purposes of paragraph (1)(d),**

**(a) the periods of two years and 3,900 hours may be in respect of more than one employer or household, but may not be in respect of more than one employer or household at a time; and**

**(b) the 3,900 hours are not to include more than 390 hours of overtime.**

SOR/2010-78, s. 2

**114. Family members — requirement — The requirement with respect to a family member of a live-in caregiver applying to remain in Canada as a permanent resident is that the family member was included in the live-in caregiver's application to remain in Canada as a permanent resident at the time the application was made.**

SOR/2008-202, s. 8

**114.1 Family members — permanent residence — A foreign national who is a family member of a live-in caregiver who makes an application to remain in Canada as a permanent resident shall become a permanent resident if, following an examination, it is established that**

**(a) the live-in caregiver has become a permanent resident; and**

**(b) the foreign national is not inadmissible.**

SOR/2008-202, s. 8

**115. Conformity — applicable times — The applicable requirements set out in sections 112 to 114.1 must be met when an application for a work permit or temporary resident visa is made, when the permit or visa is issued and when the foreign national becomes a permanent resident.**

SOR/2008-202, s. 8

### Case Law

*Pacis v. Canada (Minister of Citizenship & Immigration)*, 2005 CarswellNat 1973, 2005 CarswellNat 4901, 2005 FC 931 (F.C.) — The live-in caregiver program requires an applicant to work a minimum of 24 months out of a 36-month period. The evidence submitted indicated that the applicant was only able to work approximately 16 months, well short of the required amount. After reviewing her work background, the officer confronted the applicant with her inability to keep steady employment and the fact she had been unemployed for more than half of her time in Canada. The officer was not satisfied with the applicant's answers and denied a fifth work permit. The Court dismissed this application for judicial review, stating that if the applicant was allowed to continually apply for temporary work permits this would allow her to be permitted to stay in Canada as a live-in caregiver perpetually, without ever meeting the requirements set out for that program.

## PART 7 — FAMILY CLASSES

### DIVISION 1 — FAMILY CLASS

**116. Family class — For the purposes of subsection 12(1) of the Act, the family class is hereby prescribed as a class of persons who may become permanent residents on the basis of the requirements of this Division.**

**117. (1) Member — A foreign national is a member of the family class if, with respect to a sponsor, the foreign national is**

**(a) the sponsor's spouse, common-law partner or conjugal partner;**

**(b) a dependent child of the sponsor;**

*[Editor's Note: SOR/2002-227, s. 357 provides that the fee set out in column III of item 19 of the schedule to the* Immigration Act Fees Regulations, *SOR/97-22 is remitted and shall be repaid by the Minister to the person who paid it if the fee is paid in respect of a person before he or she becomes a permanent resident under the new* Immigration and Refugee Protection Act, *S.C. 2001, c. 27 and the person, at the time he or she made an application for landing under the* Immigration Regulations, 1978, *SOR/78 172 (the "former Regulations"), was:*

*(a) a member of the family class and 19 years of age or older and, on June 28, 2002, is a foreign national referred to in paragraph 117(1)(b) or (e) of the new* Immigration and Refugee Protection Regulations, *SOR/2002-227; or*

*(b) an accompanying dependant of an immigrant, within the meaning of s. 2(1) of the former Regulations, 19 years of age or older and not a spouse of the principal applicant.]*

**(c) the sponsor's mother or father;**

**(d) the mother or father of the sponsor's mother or father;**

**(e) [Repealed SOR/2005-61, s. 3(1).]**

*[Editor's Note: SOR/2002-227, s. 357 provides that the fee set out in column III of item 19 of the schedule to the* Immigration Act Fees Regulations, *SOR/97-22 is remitted and shall be repaid by the Minister to the person who paid it if the fee is paid in respect of a person before he or she becomes a permanent resident under the new* Immigration and Refugee Protection Act, *S.C. 2001, c. 27 and the person, at the time he or she made an application for landing under the* Immigration Regulations, 1978, *SOR/78-172 (the "former Regulations"), was:*

*(a) a member of the family class and 19 years of age or older and, on June 28, 2002, is a foreign national referred to in paragraph 117(1)(b) or (e) of the new* Immigration and Refugee Protection Regulations, *SOR/2002-227; or*

*(b) an accompanying dependant of an immigrant, within the meaning of s. 2(1) of the former Regulations, 19 years of age or older and not a spouse of the principal applicant.]*

**(f) a person whose parents are deceased, who is under 18 years of age, who is not a spouse or common-law partner and who is**

**(i) a child of the sponsor's mother or father,**

**(ii) a child of a child of the sponsor's mother or father, or**

**(iii) a child of the sponsor's child;**

**(g) a person under 18 years of age whom the sponsor intends to adopt in Canada if**

**(i) the adoption is not being entered into primarily for the purpose of acquiring any status or privilege under the Act,**

**(ii) where the adoption is an international adoption and the country in which the person resides and their province of intended destination are**

**parties to the Hague Convention on Adoption, the competent authority of the country and of the province have approved the adoption in writing as conforming to that Convention, and**

**(iii) where the adoption is an international adoption and either the country in which the person resides or the person's province of intended destination is not a party to the Hague Convention on Adoption**

**(A) the person has been placed for adoption in the country in which they reside or is otherwise legally available in that country for adoption and there is no evidence that the intended adoption is for the purpose of child trafficking or undue gain within the meaning of the Hague Convention on Adoption, and**

**(B) the competent authority of the person's province of intended destination has stated in writing that it does not object to the adoption; or**

**(h) a relative of the sponsor, regardless of age, if the sponsor does not have a spouse, a common-law partner, a conjugal partner, a child, a mother or father, a relative who is a child of that mother or father, a relative who is a child of a child of that mother or father, a mother or father of that mother or father or a relative who is a child of the mother or father of that mother or father**

**(i) who is a Canadian citizen, Indian or permanent resident, or**

**(ii) whose application to enter and remain in Canada as a permanent resident the sponsor may otherwise sponsor.**

(2) **Adoption — under 18** — **A foreign national who is the adopted child of a sponsor and whose adoption took place when the child was under the age of 18 shall not be considered a member of the family class by virtue of the adoption unless**

**(a) the adoption was in the best interests of the child within the meaning of the Hague Convention on Adoption; and**

**(b) the adoption was not entered into primarily for the purpose of acquiring any status or privilege under the Act.**

(3) **Best interests of the child** — **The adoption referred to in subsection (2) is considered to be in the best interests of a child if it took place under the following circumstances:**

**(a) a competent authority has conducted or approved a home study of the adoptive parents;**

**(b) before the adoption, the child's parents gave their free and informed consent to the child's adoption;**

**(c) the adoption created a genuine parent-child relationship;**

**(d) the adoption was in accordance with the laws of the place where the adoption took place;**

**(e) the adoption was in accordance with the laws of the sponsor's place of residence and, if the sponsor resided in Canada at the time the adoption took place, the competent authority of the child's province of intended destination has stated in writing that it does not object to the adoption;**

(f) if the adoption is an international adoption and the country in which the adoption took place and the child's province of intended destination are parties to the Hague Convention on Adoption, the competent authority of the country and of the province have stated in writing that they approve the adoption as conforming to that Convention; and

(g) if the adoption is an international adoption and either the country in which the adoption took place or the child's province of intended destination is not a party to the Hague Convention on Adoption, there is no evidence that the adoption is for the purpose of child trafficking or undue gain within the meaning of that Convention.

(4) **Adoption — over 18** — A foreign national who is the adopted child of a sponsor and whose adoption took place when the child was 18 years of age or older shall not be considered a member of the family class by virtue of that adoption unless it took place under the following circumstances:

(a) the adoption was in accordance with the laws of the place where the adoption took place and, if the sponsor resided in Canada at the time of the adoption, the adoption was in accordance with the laws of the province where the sponsor then resided, if any, that applied in respect of the adoption of a child 18 years of age or older;

(b) a genuine parent-child relationship existed at the time of the adoption and existed before the child reached the age of 18; and

(c) the adoption was not entered into primarily for the purpose of acquiring any status or privilege under the Act.

(5) [Repealed SOR/2005-61, s. 3(2).]

(6) [Repealed SOR/2005-61, s. 3(2).]

(7) **Provincial statement** — If a statement referred to in clause (1)(g)(iii)(B) or paragraph (3)(e) or (f) has been provided to an officer by the competent authority of the foreign national's province of intended destination, that statement is, except in the case of an adoption that was entered into primarily for the purpose of acquiring any status or privilege under the Act, conclusive evidence that the foreign national meets the following applicable requirements:

(a) [Repealed SOR/2005-61, s. 3(4).]

(b) in the case of a person referred to in paragraph (1)(g), the requirements set out in clause (1)(g)(iii)(A); and

(c) in the case of a person referred to in paragraph (1)(b) who is an adopted child described in subsection (2), the requirements set out in paragraphs (3)(a) to (e) and (g).

(8) **New evidence** — If, after the statement is provided to the officer, the officer receives evidence that the foreign national does not meet the applicable requirements set out in paragraph (7)(b) or (c) for becoming a member of the family class, the processing of their application shall be suspended until the officer provides that evidence to the competent authority of the province and that authority confirms or revises its statement.

**(9) Excluded relationships — A foreign national shall not be considered a member of the family class by virtue of their relationship to a sponsor if**

**(a) the foreign national is the sponsor's spouse, common-law partner or conjugal partner and is under 16 years of age;**

**(b) the foreign national is the sponsor's spouse, common-law partner or conjugal partner, the sponsor has an existing sponsorship undertaking in respect of a spouse, common-law partner or conjugal partner and the period referred to in subsection 132(1) in respect of that undertaking has not ended;**

**(c) the foreign national is the sponsor's spouse and**

**(i) the sponsor or the foreign national was, at the time of their marriage, the spouse of another person, or**

**(ii) the sponsor has lived separate and apart from the foreign national for at least one year and**

**(A) the sponsor is the common-law partner of another person or the sponsor has a conjugal partner, or**

**(B) the foreign national is the common-law partner of another person or the conjugal partner of another sponsor; or**

**(d) subject to subsection (10), the sponsor previously made an application for permanent residence and became a permanent resident and, at the time of that application, the foreign national was a non-accompanying family member of the sponsor and was not examined.**

*[Editor's Note: SOR/2002-227, s. 355 provides that if a person who made an application under the former* Immigration Act, *R.S.C. 1985, c. I-2 before June 28, 2002 sponsors a non-accompanying dependent child referred to in s. 352 of the* Immigration and Refugee Protection Regulations, *SOR/2002-227 (the "new Regulations"), who makes an application as a member of the family class or the spouse or common-law partner in Canada class, or sponsors a non-accompanying common-law partner who makes such an application, paragraph 117(9)(d) of the new Regulations does not apply in respect of that dependent child or common-law partner.]*

**(10) Exception — Subject to subsection (11), paragraph (9)(d) does not apply in respect of a foreign national referred to in that paragraph who was not examined because an officer determined that they were not required by the Act or the former Act, as applicable, to be examined.**

**(11) Application of par. (9)(d) — Paragraph (9)(d) applies in respect of a foreign national referred to in subsection (10) if an officer determines that, at the time of the application referred to in that paragraph,**

**(a) the sponsor was informed that the foreign national could be examined and the sponsor was able to make the foreign national available for examination but did not do so or the foreign national did not appear for examination; or**

**(b) the foreign national was the sponsor's spouse, was living separate and apart from the sponsor and was not examined.**

**(12) Definition of "former Act" — In subsection (10), "former Act" has the same meaning as in section 187 of the Act.**

SOR/2004-59, s. 4; SOR/2004-167, s. 41; SOR/2005-61, s. 3; SOR/2010-195, s. 11(1)–(3), (5), (6); SOR/2010-208, s. 2

## Case Law

### Section 117(1)

*Canada (Minister of Citizenship & Immigration) v. Vong* (2005), [2006] 1 F.C.R. 404, 47 Imm. L.R. (3d) 213, 2005 CarswellNat 1701, 2005 CarswellNat 3724, 2005 FC 855 (F.C.) — The respondent applied to sponsor his stepmother (the widow of the respondent's father). The visa officer refused the sponsorship application on the grounds that the stepmother was not a member of the family class as described in the *Immigration and Refugee Protection Regulations*. Upon appeal, the IAD determined that the absence of the definition of the word "mother" in the Regulations indicated Parliament's intention that the term be accorded a broad and liberal interpretation, in order to accommodate the changing dynamics of the modern family. It concluded that a stepmother could, in appropriate circumstances, fall within the definition of "mother." According to its reasons, the IAD considered that the presence of mutual benefits and dependencies could constitute such "appropriate circumstances."

The Minister sought judicial review of the IAD's decision on the basis that the issue to be determined was a question of statutory interpretation and the word "mother" was not defined and appeared only in the English version of the Regulations. The Federal Court held that the stepmother did not fall within the definition of "parents." The absence of an English definition of "mother" or "parents" does not indicate that Parliament intended that step-parents be included in the family class.

The following questions were certified:

- Are step-parents included in the family class and, in particular, does the word "mother" in paragraph 117(1)(c) of the *Immigration and Refugee Protection Regulations* include a stepmother?
- Does the word "parent" in French include a "step-parent"?

### Section 117(9)

*Lau v. Canada (Minister of Citizenship & Immigration)* (2009), 84 Imm. L.R. (3d) 261, 356 F.T.R. 206 (Eng.), 2009 FC 1089, 2009 CarswellNat 3343 (F.C.) — This was an application for judicial review of a decision of the Immigration Appeal Division of the Immigration and Refugee Board dismissing the appeal of a decision of a visa officer refusing to approve the permanent resident visa application made to sponsor the applicant's spouse. The IAD dismissed the appeal on the basis that the divorce in question between the applicant and Huang was not undertaken in compliance with Canadian law and was not deemed to be a valid divorce according to the laws of Canada. The Board made no determination whatsoever as to whether the divorce at issue was legally valid in the place where it was granted. Accordingly, the application for judicial review was allowed, the decision under review set aside and the applicant's appeal to the IAD referred back to the Board for rehearing and redetermination.

*Sultana v. Canada (Minister of Citizenship & Immigration)*, 2009 CarswellNat 1418, 2009 FC 533 — The applicants contended that the immigration officer failed to adequately assess the best interests of the children affected by the decision to deny them family reunification with the sponsor, and that it did not mention, refer to or analyze the level of dependency between the child and the sponsor and how the humanitarian and compassionate decision would affect them.

The Court agreed with the applicants that the decision fell far short of the duty to consider the best interests of the children and to be "alive, alert and sensitive" to those interests. The immigration officer failed to have regard to the children's specific gender, age and education related needs; that two of the children are boys and require a father figure; that the mother only had a Grade 8 education and no paid labour force experience; that Pakistan is a male-dominated society where single female households are looked down upon and how all of this would impact the children. Moreover, there was no evidence to support the immigration officer's bald assertion and presumption that the mother and her children could turn to her parents/siblings and in-laws for emotional and other support, when the evidence indicated otherwise as they lived a few hours away. There was no consideration of the consequences of growing up without their father and it was not explained why the policy consideration underlying s. 117(9)(d) of the Regulations should outweigh the hardships faced by these children when there is no indication that they would have been inadmissible if listed and have already suffered seven years away from their father.

While an immigration official should not be left to speculate as to how a child will be impacted by his or her decision, it would be preposterous to require from an applicant a detailed and minute demonstration of the negative consequences of such a decision when they can reasonably be deducted from the facts brought to his or her attention. The application for judicial review was allowed.

*Ferrer v. Canada (Minister of Citizenship & Immigration)*, 2009 CarswellNat 899, 2009 CarswellNat 2095, 2009 FC 356 (F.C.) — The applicant sought judicial review of a decision of the IAD which dismissed his plea for humanitarian and compassionate relief pursuant to s. 67(1)(c) of the IRPA. An exclusion order had been issued against the applicant based on a finding of inadmissibility for a misrepresentation made in September 1998 with respect to his permanent resident application. In his permanent resident application, the applicant testified that he was single with no children. It was not disputed that at the time he was the father of two dependent children living with their mother in the Philippines. The applicant married his spouse who was the mother of his two children on a trip back to the Philippines after he was granted permanent residence status in Canada. The applicant's spouse is not excluded from the family class pursuant to s. 117(9)(d) of the Regulations. Accordingly, the applicant's two children would be eligible to be included on the applicant's spouse's application for permanent residence as her dependent children, provided the applicant's appeal before the IAD was allowed as he would be in a position to sponsor his wife and both of his children as members of the family class.

The IAD considered only two possibilities with respect to the best interests of the children. The first possibility was that the children could remain in the Philippines and that their father would continue to have a geographically distant relationship with them while at the same time supporting them financially at a higher level than possible if he were returned to the Philippines. The second alternative was that the applicant could be returned to the Philippines where he would be able to better meet their emotional needs by having close contact with them, though he would not be able to provide the higher level of financial support in the event that he was removed from Canada. It was argued that the analysis was erroneous and that it did not take into consideration the most probable outcome should the applicant's appeal be allowed. The tribunal's failure to consider the likely chain of events should the appeal be allowed led to its conclusion that the best interests of the children were a neutral factor; in fact the best interests of the applicant's children were a positive factor which weighed in favour of allowing the appeal. In other words, the tribunal failed to appreciate that the applicant's children could have the best of both worlds by being reunited with him in Canada. Had the tribunal not committed this error, it would certainly have considered the best interests of the applicant's children to be a factor in favour of allowing his appeal and not a neutral factor — thereby negating its value. It appears that the IAD's reasoning was dominated by a consideration of the "integrity of the Canadian immigration system." This might be an important factor to consider, but only after the best interest of the children are properly addressed; only in this way can a fair and balanced approach be taken to this important statutory requirement. The application for judicial review was allowed and the matter sent back for redetermination.



*Odicho v. Canada (Minister of Citizenship & Immigration)* (2008), 75 Imm. L.R. (3d) 45, 2008 CarswellNat 4011, 2008 CarswellNat 3442, 2008 FC 1039 (F.C.) — The applicants sought judicial review of a visa officer's decision to refuse to issue a permanent resident visa to the wife. The applicants argued that the visa officer erred by failing to consider H&C grounds, pursuant to subs. 25 of the IRPA. They submit that they specifically requested that the wife's application for permanent residence in Canada be considered on the basis of s. 25. The husband had been landed in Canada in January 2005 and his initial application to sponsor his wife in May 2005 was refused on the basis that he had not disclosed his marriage when he was landed. The application on behalf of a dependent child was refused for the same reason but was subsequently reversed. The visa officer, however, maintained the rejection of the application on behalf of the wife on the basis of paragraph 117(9)(d) of the Regulations.

There was no dispute that the husband failed to declare his wife as a non-accompanying dependant when he landed in Canada in January 2005. There is no evidence to challenge the *bona fides* of the marriage of the applicants. There is no evidence to challenge the status of the infant as their child. The failure of the husband to declare the change in marital status when he landed in Canada gave rise to the exclusion of his wife pursuant to the terms of paragraph 117(9)(d). The Court held that the visa officer apparently ignored the material that was submitted concerning the "circumstances" of the husband's failure to declare the change in his marital status at the time he landed in Canada. The applicants carry the burden of establishing the evidence to justify an exercise of discretion, but the discharge of this burden does not require superfluity. The visa officer's decision does not demonstrate an understanding of the purpose of subs. 25(1) of the Act, which is to overcome the consequences of being in breach of statutory requirements. The initial decision which excluded the child, as well as the wife, illustrates an excess of zeal on the part of the original decision maker, if not a misunderstanding of s. 117 of the Regulations. The application for judicial review was allowed. The matter was remitted for reconsideration by a different member of the Canadian Embassy.

*David v. Canada (Minister of Citizenship & Immigration)*, 2007 CarswellNat 1385, 2007 FC 546 (F.C.) — This was an application for judicial review of a decision of the First Secretary, Immigration, of the Canadian Embassy in the Philippines denying an application for permanent residence based on humanitarian and compassionate grounds. The applicant filed a sponsorship application for his wife and three sons requesting that the application for his wife and eldest son be considered under humanitarian and compassionate grounds and that they be exempted from the application of paragraph 117(9)(d) of the Regulations.

The exclusion mentioned at paragraph 117(9)(d) of the Regulations is a very harsh one, but does not prevent a sponsor from invoking H&C grounds considerations. Indeed, the very reason why the Court of Appeal in De Guzman found that this provision is compliant with the international instruments to which Canada is a signatory is that s. 25 of the Act enables the Act to be administered in a compliant manner.

The First Secretary did not make any findings of fact with respect to the evidence tendered by the applicants, such as the relationship between the sponsor and his wife and son, the fact that the sponsor had been supporting the family financially, the frequency of their contact, as well as the letters tendered by various members of the family and others in support of their application. It is clear in this case that the First Secretary did not make a separate assessment for the oldest son's application and as such, did not address his best interest as the child of the sponsor. Instead, he simply stated that the application of the two youngest son's would proceed "but it is sponsor's choice if he wants to split his family further and take his two youngest children from their mother in the Philippines." The officer's notes do not provide a clear rationale of why any of the public policy considerations mentioned by the First Secretary (such as the past misrepresentations) should prevail here over the objective at paragraph 3(1)(d) of the Act "to see that families are reunited in Canada." Nor do they reveal whether the First Secretary considered that the *de facto* family members excluded from the family class because of paragraph 117(9)(d) of the Regulations may suffer hardship indefinitely.

*Woldeselassie v. Canada (Minister of Citizenship & Immigration)* (2006), 60 Imm. L.R. (3d) 119, 2006 CarswellNat 4497, 2006 FC 1540 (F.C.) — The applicant sought judicial review of a decision by the Immigration Appeals Division (IAD) wherein the IAD affirmed the decision of a visa officer that the applicant's illegitimate daughter was not a member of the family class pursuant to paragraph 117(9)(d) of the *Immigration and Refugee Protection Regulations*, as the applicant had not disclosed her existence both at the time of the processing of his application, and at the time of his landing in Canada.

The applicant was born in Ethiopia (now Eritrea). He became a refugee in Sudan and then left Sudan and settled as a stateless refugee in Rome, Italy in 1989. His wife did not join him as a stateless refugee until August 1990. During this period of separation from his wife, the applicant had an extra-marital affair in Rome. The young woman was pregnant when she left Rome and gave birth to a girl. Shortly after the birth, she took the child to the applicant's mother and told her the child was her granddaughter and asked her to raise the girl. This girl was the subject of the failed sponsorship application by the applicant. The applicant applied for permanent residence in May 1990. He listed his wife as a dependant. They had no children. They became permanent residents and subsequently the applicant became a Canadian citizen. The issue before the IAD was whether the applicant was precluded from sponsoring his daughter after having failed to disclose her existence at the time of his application for permanent residence in Canada. The applicant argued that one can only declare or disclose information that is known. He claimed that he did not know the existence of the child at the time that he applied for permanent residence or at the time that he landed in Canada. The IAD did not make any credibility findings or question the veracity of the applicant's testimony with respect to his explanation as to why he did not know about the pregnancy and subsequent birth of his daughter until after he arrived in Canada with his wife. Having not called into question the applicant's explanation regarding the country conditions and the communication problems in and out of

Eritrea in 1991, it was not reasonable for the IAD to simply state its sense of incredulity at the applicant's story without providing reasons to support this reaction. The application for judicial review was granted and the matter sent back for re-determination.

The Court certified the following question:

> Does subs. 117(9)(d) of the Immigration Refugee Protection Regulations (IRPR) apply to exclude non-accompanying family members from membership from the family class in circumstances where the sponsor was unaware of their existence at the time of his/her application for Permanent Residence and Landing in Canada?

*dela Fuente v. Canada (Minister of Citizenship & Immigration)*, [2006] F.C.J. No. 774, 2006 CarswellNat 1334, 2006 CarswellNat 2749, 2006 FCA 186 (Fed. C.A.) — The respondent and her mother applied for a permanent resident visa in the family class in 1992. A visa was issued to the respondent on the basis that she was an unmarried accompanying family member of her mother. The respondent arrived in Canada on October 23, 1992, made an application for landing upon arrival and was granted landing and permanent resident status following an examination. She indicated on her landing form that she was single (unmarried) and had no dependants. She has lived and remained a permanent resident in Canada since that time. The respondent, however, was engaged to be married in October 1986, and in fact did marry on October 12, 1992, approximately two weeks before entering Canada. She and her husband have a child born in Canada in September 1994. The respondent applied to sponsor her husband on January 27, 2002; this application was received by Citizenship and Immigration Canada on January 30, 2002.

After it was noted that the respondent had not declared her marriage when she was examined on her application for landing, she was called in for her sponsorship interview which took place on April 9, 2002. The interviewer, after consultation with other officers, told her she would be permitted to sponsor her husband in spite of the misrepresentation made on her application for landing. The respondent subsequently received a letter dated April 17, 2002, which confirmed that her sponsorship application was approved. The respondent's husband applied for a permanent resident visa by application dated July 23, 2002. The visa officer reviewed the husband's application and determined he was excluded under paragraph 117(9)(d) of the Regulations because he was a spouse who was not declared at the time of the respondent's entry to Canada. The respondent appealed to the IAD which upheld the visa officer's decision, finding that the husband was excluded from eligibility in the family class. The respondent then applied for judicial review before the Federal Court. The Trial Division judge found that although s. 190 of the IRPA was applicable to the matter before him, since the respondent's husband made his application one month after IRPA came into force he and his wife had a legitimate expectation that the application would be processed under the former *Immigration Act*. The Federal Court judge held that s. 190 was inapplicable because the immigration authorities had failed to forewarn the respondent that her husband might fall in an excluded class upon the coming into force of IRPA. Had this warning been given, the respondent would have taken "every conceivable step" to have the application processed in the 2½ month period that was open to them.

The Court of Appeal concluded that s. 190 is clear and unambiguous. It provides that if an application is pending or in progress on June 28, 2002, IRPA applies without condition. The doctrine of legitimate expectations is a procedural doctrine which has its source in common law. As such, it does not create substantive rights and cannot be used to counter Parliament's clearly expressed intent. There was no basis in law imposing a positive duty on the immigration officials to forewarn the respondent and her husband of the pending legislations impact on the husband's status.

The Court also considered the meaning of "time of that application" referred to in paragraph 117(9)(d) of the Regulations. The Federal Court adopted the interpretation proposed in *Dave v. Canada (M.C.I.)* (2005), 272 F.T.R. 168, 2005 FC 510, [2005] F.C.J. No. 686, 2005 CarswellNat 4680, which held that the application process for permanent residence encompasses not only the application for a visa, but also the application for admission at the port-of-entry. Accordingly, the argument that the phrase "at the time of that application" comprises only the point in time when the application form was completed and submitted must fail. This interpretation was preferred as it was consistent with the objective of family unification under IRPA.

The Legislative scheme requires that a prospective immigrant's family members be identified so that the family unit may be assessed as a whole as well as the eligibility of each member. Reading the phrase "at the time of that application" as referring to the life of the application allows foreign nationals to define their family unit and make appropriate changes right up to the moment when they seek to enter Canada, which in turn, facilitates the admission of disclosed family members who may seek to come to Canada in the future. This is how family unification is achieved under IRPA.

Since the respondent was married during the life of the application from the time it was initiated by the filing of the authorized form to the time when permanent resident status was granted at the port-of-entry and since she failed to disclose this relationship, her husband was excluded from the family class by virtue of paragraph 117(9)(d) of Regulations.

*Azizi v. Canada (Minister of Citizenship & Immigration)*, [2006] 3 F.C.R. 118, 344 N.R. 174, 51 Imm. L.R. (3d) 6, 2005 CarswellNat 4119, 2005 CarswellNat 5068, 2005 FCA 406 (F.C.A.) — The applicant applied to sponsor his wife and daughters in April 2003. A visa officer determined that the applicant's wife was not eligible for sponsorship because she was not a member of the family class. At the time the applicant applied for permanent residence he failed to declare her as a non-accompanying family member and she was not examined. That decision applied to the applicant's two daughters as well. He appealed to the Immigration Appeal Division. He claimed that before coming to Canada he lived in a refugee camp in Pakistan, having fled the Taliban regime in Afghanistan. He had no way to leave Pakistan other than through the World University Service Canada sponsorship and scholarship program, which required him to be single, so he did not disclose his wife and children. The Immigration Appeal Division found that the visa officer was correct to decide that the applicant's wife and children were not members of the family class because of the operation of paragraph 117(9)(d) of the Regulations. This decision was upheld by the Federal Court and on appeal to the Federal Court of Appeal it was decided that paragraph 117(9)(d) of the Regulations applies to exclude Convention refugees abroad, or Convention refugees seeking resettlement, as members of the family class by virtue of their relationship to a sponsor who previously became a permanent resident and at that time failed to declare them as non-accompanying family members.

*de Guzman v. Canada (Minister of Citizenship & Immigration)*, [2005] F.C.J. No. 2119, 262 D.L.R. (4th) 13, 51 Imm. L.R. (3d) 17, 137 C.R.R. (2d) 20, 345 N.R. 73, 2005 CarswellNat 4381, 2005 FCA 436 (C.A.); leave to appeal to S.C.C. refused [2006] S.C.C.A. No. 70, 2006 CarswellNat 1695, 356 N.R. 399 (note) (S.C.C.) — In 1993, the appellant came to live in Canada. When she was landed in Canada, she told the immigration officials that she was single and had no dependants, other than her daughter who was accompanying her. This was not true: she also had two sons whom she left in the Philippines with their father. Eight years later, after establishing herself in Canada and becoming a citizen, the appellant applied to sponsor her sons as members of the family class. They were refused visas under paragraph 117(9)(d) of the Regulations on the ground that they were not members of the family class because they had not been examined for immigration purposes when the appellant applied to come to Canada.

The appellant's misrepresentation was highly material to the success of her application for a visa in the family class as an unmarried daughter. Her daughter's birth certificate stated that the appellant was unmarried, unlike her sons' birth certificates.

The Immigration Appeal Division was correct in law to dismiss the appellant's appeal pursuant to paragraph 74(d) of the IRPA. Specifically, the Board concluded that since the sons were not members of the family class, the Board, under s. 65 of the IRPA, had no discretionary jurisdiction to consider humanitarian and compassionate circumstances.

The Federal Court of Appeal concluded that paragraph 117(9)(d) of the Regulations was not invalid or inoperative. It was not unconstitutional nor did it deprive the applicant of her right to liberty and/or her right to security of person, in a manner not in accordance with the principles of fundamental justice contrary to s. 7 of the *Charter*.

*Natt v. Canada (Minister of Citizenship & Immigration)*, [2004] F.C.J. No. 997, 36 Imm. L.R. (3d) 292, 254 F.T.R. 122, 2004 FC 810, 2004 CarswellNat 1693 (F.C.) — This was an application to review a decision of the Immigration Appeal Division. The applicant married a Canadian citizen who then sponsored her application for permanent residence. The applicant did not disclose that she had two children and on this basis was granted permanent residence. In May 2001, the applicant sponsored applications for permanent residence for her two children. A visa officer refused these applications and the applicant appealed to the Appeal Division who dismissed her appeal.

The central issue was whether Regulation 117(9)(d) applied to the two children as members of the family class. The purpose of this provision is to ensure that foreign nationals seeking permanent residence do not omit non-accompanying dependent members from their application, thereby avoiding their examination for admissibility at that time, and then, once having obtained their own permanent residence status, seek to sponsor their dependants and benefit from the preferential processing as well as admission treatments given to members of the family class. The sole exception is with respect to the children of sponsors whose applications for permanent residence were made before June 28, 2002, where those children meet the definition of "dependent child" under the Act but do not meet the definition of "dependent child" under the former act. This exception is articulated in ss. 352 and 355 of the Regulations and reflects the fact that the Act changed the definition of dependent child to include unmarried children as old as age 21, whereas the former Act's definition included only unmarried children up to age 18. The purpose of the exception is to enable family members to sponsor dependants who would have been considered too old to be eligible before the Act came into force.

**118. Medical condition — A foreign national who is an adopted dependent child or is a person referred to in paragraph 117(1)(f) or (g) shall not be issued a permanent resident visa as a member of the family class unless the sponsor has provided a**

**statement in writing confirming that they have obtained information about the medical condition of the child or of the foreign national.**

SOR/2005-61, s. 4; SOR/2010-195, s. 12

**119. Withdrawal of sponsorship application — A decision shall not be made on an application for a permanent resident visa by a member of the family class if the sponsor withdraws their sponsorship application in respect of that member.**

**120. Approved sponsorship application — For the purposes of Part 5,**

**(a) a permanent resident visa shall not be issued to a foreign national who makes an application as a member of the family class or to their accompanying family members unless a sponsorship undertaking in respect of the foreign national and those family members is in effect; and**

**(b) a foreign national who makes an application as a member of the family class and their accompanying family members shall not become permanent residents unless a sponsorship undertaking in respect of the foreign national and those family members is in effect and the sponsor who gave that undertaking still meets the requirements of section 133 and, if applicable, section 137.**

**121. Requirements — The requirements with respect to a person who is a member of the family class or a family member of a member of the family class who makes an application under Division 6 of Part 5 are the following:**

**(a) the person is a family member of the applicant or of the sponsor both at the time the application is made and, without taking into account whether the person has attained 22 years of age, at the time of the determination of the application;**

**(b) [Repealed SOR/2004-167, s. 42.]**

SOR/2004-167, s. 42

**122. Requirements for accompanying family members — A foreign national who is an accompanying family member of a person who makes an application as a member of the family class shall become a permanent resident if, following an examination, it is established that**

**(a) the person who made the application has become a permanent resident; and**

**(b) the family member is not inadmissible.**

## Division 2 — Spouse or Common-law Partner in Canada Class

**123. Class — For the purposes of subsection 12(1) of the Act, the spouse or common-law partner in Canada class is hereby prescribed as a class of persons who may become permanent residents on the basis of the requirements of this Division.**

**124. Member — A foreign national is a member of the spouse or common-law partner in Canada class if they**

**(a) are the spouse or common-law partner of a sponsor and cohabit with that sponsor in Canada;**

**(b) have temporary resident status in Canada; and**

**(c) are the subject of a sponsorship application.**

## Case Law

*Ally v. Canada (Minister of Citizenship & Immigration)*, 2008 CarswellNat 1869, 2008 CarswellNat 853, 2008 FC 445 — The applicant's application for permanent residence as a member of the Spouse or Common-law Partner in Canada Class was denied. Immigration received information that he had been charged by police with assault and threats; conditions of his bail release stated that he must stay away from his wife and reside with his uncle when in Canada. The onus was upon the applicant to establish that s. 124 of the Regulations was satisfied and that any separation was only temporary and short.

**125. (1) Excluded relationships — A foreign national shall not be considered a member of the spouse or common-law partner in Canada class by virtue of their relationship to the sponsor if**

**(a) the foreign national is the sponsor's spouse or common-law partner and is under 16 years of age;**

**(b) the foreign national is the sponsor's spouse or common-law partner, the sponsor has an existing sponsorship undertaking in respect of a spouse or common-law partner and the period referred to in subsection 132(1) in respect of that undertaking has not ended;**

**(c) the foreign national is the sponsor's spouse and**

**(i) the sponsor or the spouse was, at the time of their marriage, the spouse of another person, or**

**(ii) the sponsor has lived separate and apart from the foreign national for at least one year and**

**(A) the sponsor is the common-law partner of another person or the sponsor has a conjugal partner, or**

**(B) the foreign national is the common-law partner of another person or the conjugal partner of another sponsor; or**

**(d) subject to subsection (2), the sponsor previously made an application for permanent residence and became a permanent resident and, at the time of that application, the foreign national was a non-accompanying family member of the sponsor and was not examined.**

**(2) Exception — Subject to subsection (3), paragraph (1)(d) does not apply in respect of a foreign national referred to in that paragraph who was not examined because an officer determined that they were not required by the Act or the former Act, as applicable, to be examined.**

**(3) Application of par. (1)(d) — Paragraph (1)(d) applies in respect of a foreign national referred to in subsection (2) if an officer determines that, at the time of the application referred to in that paragraph,**

> **(a) the sponsor was informed that the foreign national could be examined and the sponsor was able to make the foreign national available for examination but did not do so or the foreign national did not appear for examination; or**
>
> **(b) the foreign national was the sponsor's spouse, was living separate and apart from the sponsor and was not examined.**

**(4) Definition of "former Act" — In subsection (2), "former Act" has the same meaning as in section 187 of the Act.**

SOR/2004-167, s. 43; SOR/2010-195, s. 13

## Case Law

### Section 125(1)

*Cai v. Canada (Minister of Citizenship & Immigration)*, 2007 CarswellNat 2274, 2007 CarswellNat 5843, 2007 FC 816 — The applicant's application for permanent resident status under the Spouse or Common-Law Partner in Canada Class was refused on the basis that the applicant did not comply with s. 125(1)(d) of the Regulation. At the time of the sponsor's application for permanent residence, she did not list the applicant as a non-accompanying family member and the applicant was not examined. The Court considered whether the immigration officer erred in determining that the applicant was his sponsor's common-law partner when the sponsor applied to be a permanent resident of Canada. In her application to sponsor an undertaking, the applicant's sponsor stated that her relationship with the applicant began on June 1, 2002. The applicant argued that, despite the fact that the relationship with the sponsor traces back to 2002, his relationship with his sponsor did not meet the requirements of common-law relationship as of that date. When the applicant and her sponsor began living together they were young students, and as such, they may not have made a "mutual commitment to a shared life" when they decided to live together. There was, accordingly, no basis on which the immigration officer could reasonably conclude that the applicant was a common-law partner of his sponsor when she submitted her application for permanent residence in January, 2005 and did not identify the applicant as a non-accompanying family member. The meaning of "common-law partner" means that the conjugal relationship is one of some permanence where the couple has made a serious commitment to one another. The applicant's application for judicial review was allowed.

**126. Withdrawal of sponsorship application — A decision shall not be made on an application for permanent residence by a foreign national as a member of the spouse or common-law partner in Canada class if the sponsor withdraws their sponsorship application in respect of that foreign national.**

**127. Approved sponsorship application — For the purposes of Part 5, a foreign national who makes an application as a member of the spouse or common-law partner in Canada class and their accompanying family members shall not become a permanent resident unless a sponsorship undertaking in respect of the foreign na-**

**tional and those family members is in effect and the sponsor who gave that undertaking still meets the requirements of section 133 and, if applicable, section 137.**

**128. Requirement — The requirements with respect to a person who is a family member of a member of the spouse or common-law partner in Canada class who makes an application under Division 6 of Part 5 are the following:**

**(a) the person is a family member of the applicant both at the time the application is made and, without taking into account whether the person has attained 22 years of age, at the time of the determination of the application; and**

**(b) at the time it is made, the application includes a request for the family member to remain in Canada as a permanent resident.**

**129. Requirements for accompanying family members — A foreign national who is an accompanying family member of a person who makes an application as a member of the spouse or common-law partner in Canada class shall become a permanent resident if, following an examination, it is established that**

**(a) the person who made the application has become a permanent resident; and**

**(b) the family member is not inadmissible.**



## DIVISION 3 — SPONSORS

**130. (1) Sponsor — Subject to subsection (2), a sponsor, for the purpose of sponsoring a foreign national who makes an application for a permanent resident visa as a member of the family class or an application to remain in Canada as a member of the spouse or common-law partner in Canada class under subsection 13(1) of the Act, must be a Canadian citizen or permanent resident who**

**(a) is at least 18 years of age;**

**(b) resides in Canada; and**

**(c) has filed a sponsorship application in respect of a member of the family class or the spouse or common-law partner in Canada class in accordance with section 10.**

**(2) Sponsor not residing in Canada — A sponsor who is a Canadian citizen and does not reside in Canada may sponsor an application referred to in subsection (1) by their spouse, common-law partner, conjugal partner or dependent child who has no dependent children if the sponsor will reside in Canada when the applicant becomes a permanent resident.**

### Case Law

*Lau v. Canada (Minister of Citizenship & Immigration)* (2009), 84 Imm. L.R. (3d) 261, 356 F.T.R. 206 (Eng.), 2009 FC 1089, 2009 CarswellNat 3343 (F.C.) — This was an application for judicial review of a decision of the Immigration Appeal Division of the Immigration and Refugee Board dismissing the appeal of a decision of a visa officer refusing to approve the permanent resident visa application made to sponsor the applicant's spouse. The IAD dismissed the appeal on the basis that the divorce in question between the applicant and Huang was not undertaken in compliance with Canadian law and was not deemed to be a valid divorce according to the laws of Canada. The Board made no determination whatsoever as to whether the divorce at issue was legally valid in the place where it was granted. Accordingly, the application for judicial review was allowed, the decision under review set aside and the applicant's appeal to the IAD referred back to the Board for rehearing and redetermination.

**131. Sponsorship undertaking — The sponsor's undertaking shall be given**

**(a) to the Minister; or**

**(b) if the sponsor resides in a province that has entered into an agreement referred to in subsection 8(1) of the Act that enables the province to determine and apply financial criteria with respect to sponsorship and the administration of sponsorship undertakings, to the competent authority of the province.**

**132. (1) Undertaking — duration — Subject to subsection (2), the sponsor's undertaking obliges the sponsor to reimburse Her Majesty in right of Canada or a province for every benefit provided as social assistance to or on behalf of the sponsored foreign national and their family members during the period**

**(a) beginning**

**(i) if the foreign national enters Canada with a temporary resident permit, on the day of that entry,**

**(ii) if the foreign national is in Canada, on the day on which the foreign national obtains a temporary resident permit following an application to remain in Canada as a permanent resident, and**

**(iii) in any other case, on the day on which the foreign national becomes a permanent resident; and**

**(b) ending**

**(i) if the foreign national is the sponsor's spouse, common-law partner or conjugal partner, on the last day of the period of three years following the day on which the foreign national becomes a permanent resident,**

**(ii) if the foreign national is a dependent child of the sponsor or of the sponsor's spouse, common-law partner or conjugal partner or is a person referred to in paragraph 117(1)(g), and is less than 22 years of age when they become a permanent resident, on the earlier of**

**(A) the last day of the period of 10 years following the day on which the foreign national becomes a permanent resident, and**

**(B) the day on which the foreign national reaches 25 years of age,**

**(iii) if the foreign national is a dependent child of the sponsor or of the sponsor's spouse, common-law partner or conjugal partner and is 22 years of age or older when they become a permanent resident, on the last day of the period of three years following the day on which the foreign national becomes a permanent resident; and**

**(iv) if the foreign national is a person other than a person referred to in subparagraph (i), (ii) or (iii), on the last day of the period of 10 years**

following the day on which the foreign national becomes a permanent resident.

(2) **Undertaking to province — duration** — In the case of an undertaking to a competent authority of a province referred to in paragraph 131(b), the period referred to in subsection (1) shall end not later than

(a) if the foreign national is a dependent child and is less than 22 years of age on the day on which they become a permanent resident, the later of

(i) the day on which they reach 22 years of age, and

(ii) the last day of the period of 10 years following the day they become a permanent resident; and

(b) if the foreign national is a person other than a dependent child and is less than 22 years of age on the day on which they become a permanent resident, on the last day of the period of 10 years following the day on which the foreign national becomes a permanent resident.

(3) **Undertaking to province — alternate duration** — Notwithstanding subsection (2), the period referred to in subsection (1) shall end on the day provided for by the laws of the province if that day is earlier than the later of the days referred to in subsection (2).

(4) **Agreement** — Subject to paragraph 137(c), if the person is to be sponsored as a member of the family class or of the spouse or common-law partner in Canada class and is at least 22 years of age, or is less than 22 years of age and is the sponsor's spouse, common-law partner or conjugal partner, the sponsor, the co-signer, if any, and the person must, before the sponsorship application is approved, enter into a written agreement that includes

(a) a statement by the sponsor and the co-signer, if any, that they will provide for the basic requirements of the person and their accompanying family members during the applicable period referred to in subsection (1);

(b) a declaration by the sponsor and the co-signer, if any, that their financial obligations do not prevent them from honouring their agreement with the person and their undertaking to the Minister in respect of the person's application; and

(c) a statement by the person that they will make every reasonable effort to provide for their own basic requirements as well as those of their accompanying family members.

(5) **Co-signature — undertaking** — Subject to paragraph 137(c), the sponsor's undertaking may be co-signed by the spouse or common-law partner of the sponsor if the spouse or common-law partner meets the requirements set out in subsection 130(1), except paragraph 130(1)(c), and those set out in subsection 133(1), except paragraph 133(1)(a), and, in that case,

(a) the sponsor's income shall be calculated in accordance with paragraph 134(1)(b) or (c); and

(b) the co-signing spouse or common-law partner is jointly and severally or solidarily bound with the sponsor to perform the obligations in the undertak-

**ing and is jointly and severally or solidarily liable with the sponsor for any breach of those obligations.**

SOR/2004-167, s. 44(2); SOR/2005-61, s. 5

**133. (1) Requirements for sponsor — A sponsorship application shall only be approved by an officer if, on the day on which the application was filed and from that day until the day a decision is made with respect to the application, there is evidence that the sponsor**

**(a) is a sponsor as described in section 130;**

**(b) intends to fulfil the obligations in the sponsorship undertaking;**

**(c) is not subject to a removal order;**

**(d) is not detained in any penitentiary, jail, reformatory or prison;**

**(e) has not been convicted under the *Criminal Code* of**

**(i) an offence of a sexual nature, or an attempt or a threat to commit such an offence, against any person, or**

**(ii) an offence that results in bodily harm, as defined in section 2 of the *Criminal Code*, to any of the following persons or an attempt or a threat to commit such an offence against any of the following persons, namely,**

**(A) a relative of the sponsor, including a dependent child or other family member of the sponsor,**

**(B) a relative of the sponsor's spouse or of the sponsor's common-law partner, including a dependent child or other family member of the sponsor's spouse or of the sponsor's common-law partner, or**

**(C) the conjugal partner of the sponsor or a relative of that conjugal partner, including a dependent child or other family member of that conjugal partner;**

**(f) has not been convicted outside Canada of an offence that, if committed in Canada, would constitute an offence referred to in paragraph (e);**

**(g) subject to paragraph 137(c), is not in default of**

**(i) any undertaking, or**

**(ii) any support payment obligations ordered by a court;**

**(h) is not in default in respect of the repayment of any debt referred to in subsection 145(1) of the Act payable to Her Majesty in right of Canada;**

**(i) subject to paragraph 137(c), is not an undischarged bankrupt under the *Bankruptcy and Insolvency Act*;**

**(j) if the sponsor resides**

**(i) in a province other than a province referred to in paragraph 131(b), has a total income that is at least equal to the minimum necessary income, and**

**(ii) in a province referred to in paragraph 131(b), is able, within the meaning of the laws of that province and as determined by the competent authority of that province, to fulfil the undertaking referred to in that paragraph; and**

**(k) is not in receipt of social assistance for a reason other than disability.**

**(2) Exception — conviction in Canada — Despite paragraph (1)(e), a sponsorship application may not be refused**

**(a) on the basis of a conviction in Canada in respect of which a pardon has been granted and has not ceased to have effect or been revoked under the *Criminal Records Act*, or in respect of which there has been a final determination of an acquittal; or**

**(b) if a period of five years or more has elapsed since the completion of the sentence imposed for an offence in Canada referred to in paragraph (l)(e).**

**(3) Exception — conviction outside Canada — Despite paragraph (1)(f), a sponsorship application may not be refused**

**(a) on the basis of a conviction outside Canada in respect of which there has been a final determination of an acquittal; or**

**(b) if a period of five years or more has elapsed since the completion of the sentence imposed for an offence outside Canada referred to in that paragraph and the sponsor has demonstrated that they have been rehabilitated.**



**(4) Exception to minimum necessary income — Paragraph (1)(j) does not apply if the sponsored person is**

**(a) the sponsor's spouse, common-law partner or conjugal partner and has no dependent children;**

**(b) the sponsor's spouse, common-law partner or conjugal partner and has a dependent child who has no dependent children; or**

**(c) a dependent child of the sponsor who has no dependent children or a person referred to in paragraph 117(1)(g).**

**(5) Adopted sponsor — A person who is adopted outside Canada and whose adoption is subsequently revoked by a foreign authority or by a court in Canada of competent jurisdiction may sponsor an application for a permanent resident visa that is made by a member of the family class only if the revocation of the adoption was not obtained for the purpose of sponsoring that application.**

SOR/2004-167, s. 45; SOR/2005-61, s. 6

## Case Law

### Section 133(1)(e)

*Canada (Minister of Citizenship & Immigration) v. Brar* (2008), 76 Imm. L.R. (3d) 246, 336 F.T.R. 293 (Eng.), 2008 CarswellNat 4260, 2008 FC 1285 — The wording of subparagraph 133(1)(e)(ii) of the Regulations denies the right of sponsorship to Canadian citizens and permanent residents who have committed offences involving bodily harm against only certain enumerated victims. According to the definition in s. 2 of the Regulations, "relative" means a person who is related to another person by blood or adoption. The Board accepted the submission that the respondent's sister-in-law is not a blood relative. Furthermore, the victim does not fit within the definition of "family member" as defined in subs. 1(3) of the Regulations. Section 133 of the Regulations restricts the victims of assaults causing bodily harm to the sponsored spouse or common-law partner and family members of the sponsor's spouse or common-law partner. It does not include all family members on each side of the family and is not worded so as to catch a sponsor who has committed a crime causing bodily harm against a sister-in-law. Therefore, the respondent's sister-in-law does not fit within the narrow definition of victims of offences causing bodily harm in clause 133(1)(e)(ii)(A).

In the end, the Board concluded that the word "sister-in-law" did not fit within the definition of "family member". The Board did not err in its interpretation and the application for judicial review was dismissed.

## Section 133(1)(k)

*Guzman v. Canada (Minister of Citizenship & Immigration)* (2006), 57 Imm. L.R. (3d) 174, 146 C.R.R. (2d) 305, [2007] 3 F.C.R. 411, 2006 CarswellNat 3005, 2006 FC 1134 — This was an application for judicial review of a decision to reject the applicant's sponsorship application under paragraph 133(1)(k) of the *Immigration and Refugee Protection Regulations*, as the applicant, during the processing of the sponsorship application, was a recipient of social assistance for a reason other than disability. The applicant sought to quash paragraph 133(1)(k) of the IRPR on the basis that it violates s. 15 of the *Canadian Charter of Rights and Freedoms*, Pt. 1 of the *Constitution Act*, 1982, being schedule B to the *Canada Act*, 1982 (UK), 1982 c. 1, and it is not justifiable under s. 1 of the *Charter*. The applicant claimed that paragraph 133(1)(k) is discriminatory as it prevents those on social assistance from being able to sponsor a relative they would otherwise be qualified to sponsor.

The Federal Court applied the three-step framework for analyzing a claim for discrimination under subs. 15(1) of the *Charter* known as the *Law v. Canada (MEI)*, [1999] 1 S.C.R. 497 three-step framework. The Court concluded that all three parts of the *Law* test failed and that paragraph 133(1)(k) of the IRPR does not violate s. 15 of the *Charter*.

The following question was certified: "Whether paragraph 133(1)(k) of the IRPR violates subs. 15(1) of the *Charter* in that it discriminates on the basis of the analogous ground of receipt of social assistance?"

**134. (1) Income calculation rules — For the purpose of subparagraph 133(1)(j)(i), the total income of the sponsor shall be determined in accordance with the following rules:**

> **(a) the sponsor's income shall be calculated on the basis of the last notice of assessment, or an equivalent document, issued by the Minister of National Revenue in respect of the most recent taxation year preceding the date of filing of the sponsorship application;**
>
> **(b) if the sponsor produces a document referred to in paragraph (a), the sponsor's income is the income earned as reported in that document less the amounts referred to in subparagraphs (c)(i) to (v);**
>
> **(c) if the sponsor does not produce a document referred to in paragraph (a), or if the sponsor's income as calculated under paragraph (b) is less than their minimum necessary income, the sponsor's Canadian income for the 12-month**

**period preceding the date of filing of the sponsorship application is the income earned by the sponsor not including**

**(i) any provincial allowance received by the sponsor for a program of instruction or training,**

**(ii) any social assistance received by the sponsor from a province,**

**(iii) any financial assistance received by the sponsor from the Government of Canada under a resettlement assistance program,**

**(iv) any amounts paid to the sponsor under the *Employment Insurance Act*, other than special benefits,**

**(v) any monthly guaranteed income supplement paid to the sponsor under the *Old Age Security Act*, and**

**(vi) any Canada child tax benefit paid to the sponsor under the *Income Tax Act*; and**

**(d) if there is a co-signer, the income of the co-signer, as calculated in accordance with paragraphs (a) to (c), with any modifications that the circumstances require, shall be included in the calculation of the sponsor's income.**

**(2) Change in circumstances — If an officer receives information indicating that the sponsor is no longer able to fulfil the sponsorship undertaking, the Canadian income of the sponsor shall be calculated in accordance with paragraph (1)(c) on the basis of the 12-month period preceding the day the officer receives that information rather than the 12-month period referred to in that paragraph.**



## Case Law

*Dokaj v. Canada (Minister of Citizenship & Immigration)* (2009), 82 Imm. L.R. (3d) 239, 2009 FC 847, 2009 CarswellNat 5484, 2009 CarswellNat 2493 (F.C.) — This was an application for judicial review of a decision by an immigration officer at the Case Processing Centre (CPC) in Mississauga, dated February 10, 2009, wherein the immigration officer refused the applicant's application to sponsor a member of the family class. The officer determined that the applicant did not meet the financial requirements to sponsor his family members. The officer found the applicant's co-signer ineligible to co-sign his application as she was not on the application when it was originally received. A co-signer cannot be added to the application once it has been received at the CPC. Therefore, her income could not be considered toward the financial test and the officer also did not have the authority to consider income earned outside the stated 12-month period. The officer found that the income of the applicant's common-law spouse could not be included in the sponsorship undertaking because she was not his common-law spouse when the initial sponsorship application was remitted and therefore she could not be added once the application was received by the CPC.

The immigration officer at the CPC erred in the determination of whether the applicant could sponsor members of the family class. Since the applicant's common-law spouse is to be considered in the calculation of the size of the applicant's family, her income should also be included in the sponsorship undertaking as per subs. 132(5) and paragraph 134(1)(c) of the Regulations. The statutory provisions do not provide for the exclusion of the spouse's income while including her as a dependent member of the applicant's family. Inclusive of his common-law spouse income, the applicant met the Low Income Cut-off at the time the decision was made. The application for judicial review was allowed.

**135. Default — For the purpose of subparagraph 133(1)(g)(i), the default of a sponsorship undertaking**

**(a) begins when**

**(i) a government makes a payment that the sponsor has in the undertaking promised to repay, or**

**(ii) an obligation set out in the undertaking is breached; and**

**(b) ends, as the case may be, when**

**(i) the sponsor reimburses the government concerned, in full or in accordance with an agreement with that government, for amounts paid by it, or**

**(ii) the sponsor ceases to be in breach of the obligation set out in the undertaking.**

## Case Law

*Mavi v. Canada (Attorney General)* (2009), 85 Imm. L.R. (3d) 1, 98 O.R. (3d) 1, 313 D.L.R. (4th) 137, 259 O.A.C. 33, 2009 ONCA 794, 2009 CarswellOnt 6992 (C.A.); additional reasons (2009), 85 Imm. L.R. (3d) 83, 2009 ONCA 909, 2009 CarswellOnt 8048 (Ont. C.A.) — The main issues on this appeal were whether the governments must exercise discretion on a case-by-case basis and comply with a duty of procedural fairness when enforcing undertakings given by citizens or permanent residents of Canada to sponsor a relative's immigration to Canada. The appellants' sponsored relatives all received social assistance in Ontario during the period of their sponsorships and Ontario has requested payment of their sponsorship debts. The appellants claim that circumstances beyond their control left them unable to honour their undertakings. On this basis, each of the appellants applied for a declaration that they are discharged from their sponsorship obligations. The appellants argued that, properly interpreted, the language of the Acts stating that sponsorship debt "may be recovered" indicates the governments have discretion to forgive sponsorship debt. In support of their argument, the appellants relied on the terms of their undertakings which state that the government may choose not to recover in circumstances involving "abuse" or in "other appropriate circumstances." The lower Court judge rejected their contractual defences. She found that the words "may be recovered" are merely enabling in the sense that they do no more than permit the government to enforce the debt. She concluded that they do not impose either an obligation on government to consider appellants' circumstances on a case-by-case basis, or a duty of procedural fairness. On appeal, the appellants claim that the application judge erred in rejecting their arguments concerning discretion and procedural fairness and in failing to make declarations in that regard. The appeal was allowed, and the lower Court decision set aside and the following four declarations were made:

(i) Canada and Ontario have a case-by-case discretion whether to enforce sponsorship debt taking into account a sponsor's submissions concerning the sponsor's circumstances and those of their sponsored relatives:

(ii) Ontario fettered its discretion by adopting policies that are inconsistent with the provisions of the family class immigration regime;

(iii) Canada and Ontario owe the sponsors a duty of procedural fairness when enforcing sponsorship debt; and

(iv) the duty of procedural fairness includes: a) an obligation to provide sponsors with a process for explaining their own and their sponsored relative's relevant personal and financial circumstances; b) an obligation to consider those circumstances; and c) an obligation to inform any sponsor who makes submissions that their submissions have been considered and of the decision that was made.

*Editor's note: The Ontario Government has appealed this decision to the Supreme Court, with leave allowed 2010 CarswellOnt 2435, 2010 CarswellOnt 2436.*

*Manitoba v. Barkman* (2007), 213 Man. R. (2d) 273, 2007 CarswellMan 86, 2007 MBQB 54 (Q.B.) — The plaintiff sued the defendant to recover the amount of income assistance payments which the plaintiff paid to immigrants sponsored by the defendant pursuant to an "undertaking of assistance," whereby the defendant undertook to provide and guaranteed their maintenance or support. The defendant maintains that the immigrants did not need to apply for social assistance; that any application for such was made at the instance of agents of the plaintiff. The defendant had sponsored his wife and four children. His wife and the children abruptly left. The defendant submitted that his wife and the children did not need to go on income assistance because he was always prepared to support them. The plaintiff's officials were quite right in concluding that the defendant's wife was genuinely in need of income assistance. The plaintiff did not follow their policy with respect to notifying the sponsor by registered mail (or at all) that legal action may be taken to recover the assistance as a result of the sponsor's breach of the undertaking. The plaintiff obtained judgment against the defendant.

**136. (1) Suspension during proceedings against sponsor or co-signer — If any of the following proceedings are brought against a sponsor or co-signer, the sponsorship application shall not be processed until there has been a final determination of the proceeding:**

**(a) an application for revocation of citizenship under the *Citizenship Act*;**

**(b) a report prepared under subsection 44(1) of the Act; or**

**(c) a charge alleging the commission of an offence under an Act of Parliament punishable by a maximum term of imprisonment of at least 10 years.**

**(2) Suspension during appeal by sponsor or co-signer — If a sponsor or co-signer has made an appeal under subsection 63(4) of the Act, the sponsorship application shall not be processed until the period for making the appeal has expired or there has been a final determination of the appeal.**

**137. Undertaking — Province of Quebec — If the sponsor resides in the Province of Quebec, the government of which has entered into an agreement referred to in paragraph 131(b),**

**(a) the sponsor's undertaking, given in accordance with section 131, is the undertaking required by *An Act respecting immigration to Québec*, R.S.Q., c. I-0.2, as amended from time to time;**

**(b) an officer shall approve the sponsorship application only if there is evidence that the competent authority of the Province has determined that the sponsor,**

IRP Regulations

**on the day the undertaking was given as well as on the day a decision was made with respect to the application, was able to fulfil the undertaking; and**

**(c) subsections 132(4) and (5) and paragraphs 133(1)(g) and (i) do not apply.**

# PART 8 — REFUGEE CLASSES

## DIVISION 1 — CONVENTION REFUGEES ABROAD AND HUMANITARIAN-PROTECTED PERSONS ABROAD

### *Interpretation*

**138. Definitions — The definitions in this section apply in this Division and in Division 2.**

**"group" means**

**(a) five or more Canadian citizens or permanent residents, each of whom is at least 18 years of age, who are acting together for the purpose of sponsoring a Convention refugee or a person in similar circumstances; or**

**(b) one or more Canadian citizens or permanent residents, each of whom is at least 18 years of age, and a corporation or unincorporated organization or association referred to in subsection 13(2) of the Act, acting together for the purpose of sponsoring a Convention refugee or a person in similar circumstances.**

***("groupe")***

**"referral organization" means**

**(a) the United Nations High Commissioner for Refugees; or**

**(b) any organization with which the Minister has entered into a memorandum of understanding under section 143.**

***("organisation de recommandation")***

**"sponsor" means**

**(a) a group, a corporation or an unincorporated organization or association referred to in subsection 13(2) of the Act, or any combination of them, that is acting for the purpose of sponsoring a Convention refugee or a person in similar circumstances; or**

**(b) for the purposes of section 158, a sponsor within the meaning of the regulations made under *An Act respecting immigration to Québec*, R.S.Q., c. I-0.2, as amended from time to time.**

***("répondant")***

**"undertaking" means an undertaking in writing to the Minister to provide resettlement assistance, lodging and other basic necessities in Canada for a member of a class prescribed by this Division, the member's accompanying family members and any of the member's non-accompanying family members who meet the requirements of section 141, for the period determined in accordance with subsections 154(2) and (3). *("engagement")***

**"urgent need of protection" means, in respect of a member of the Convention refugee abroad, the country of asylum or the source country class, that their life, liberty or physical safety is under immediate threat and, if not protected, the person is likely to be**

**(a) killed;**

**(b) subjected to violence, torture, sexual assault or arbitrary imprisonment; or**

**(c) returned to their country of nationality or of their former habitual residence.**

***("besoin urgent de protection")***

**"vulnerable" means, in respect of a Convention refugee or a person in similar circumstances, that the person has a greater need of protection than other applicants for protection abroad because of the person's particular circumstances that give rise to a heightened risk to their physical safety. *("vulnérable")***



## General

**139. (1) General requirements — A permanent resident visa shall be issued to a foreign national in need of refugee protection, and their accompanying family members, if following an examination it is established that**

**(a) the foreign national is outside Canada;**

**(b) the foreign national has submitted an application in accordance with section 150;**

**(c) the foreign national is seeking to come to Canada to establish permanent residence;**

**(d) the foreign national is a person in respect of whom there is no reasonable prospect, within a reasonable period, of a durable solution in a country other than Canada, namely**

**(i) voluntary repatriation or resettlement in their country of nationality or habitual residence, or**

**(ii) resettlement or an offer of resettlement in another country;**

**(e) the foreign national is a member of one of the classes prescribed by this Division;**

**(f) one of the following is the case, namely**

**(i) the sponsor's sponsorship application for the foreign national and their family members included in the application for protection has been approved under these Regulations,**

**(ii) in the case of a member of the Convention refugee abroad or source country class, financial assistance in the form of funds from a governmental resettlement assistance program is available in Canada for the foreign national and their family members included in the application for protection, or**

**(iii) the foreign national has sufficient financial resources to provide for the lodging, care and maintenance, and for the resettlement in Canada, of**

**themself and their family members included in the application for protection;**

**(g) if the foreign national intends to reside in a province other than the Province of Quebec, the foreign national and their family members included in the application for protection will be able to become successfully established in Canada, taking into account the following factors:**

**(i) their resourcefulness and other similar qualities that assist in integration in a new society,**

**(ii) the presence of their relatives, including the relatives of a spouse or a common-law partner, or their sponsor in the expected community of resettlement,**

**(iii) their potential for employment in Canada, given their education, work experience and skills, and**

**(iv) their ability to learn to communicate in one of the official languages of Canada;**

**(h) if the foreign national intends to reside in the Province of Quebec, the competent authority of that Province is of the opinion that the foreign national and their family members included in the application for protection meet the selection criteria of the Province; and**

**(i) subject to subsection (3), the foreign national and their family members included in the application for protection are not inadmissible.**

**(2) Exception — Paragraph (1)(g) does not apply to a foreign national, or their family members included in the application for protection, who has been determined by an officer to be vulnerable or in urgent need of protection.**

**(3) Financial inadmissibility — exemption — A foreign national who is a member of a class prescribed by this Division, and meets the applicable requirements of this Division, is exempted from the application of section 39 of the Act.**

**(4) Health grounds — exception — A foreign national who is a member of a class prescribed by this Division, and meets the applicable requirements of this Division, is exempted from the application of paragraph 38(1)(c) of the Act.**

**140. Class of family members — Family members of an applicant who is determined to be a member of a class under this Division are members of the applicant's class.**

**141. (1) Non-accompanying family member — A permanent resident visa shall be issued to a family member who does not accompany the applicant if, following an examination, it is established that**

**(a) the family member was included in the applicant's permanent resident visa application at the time that application was made, or was added to that application before the applicant's departure for Canada;**

**(b) the family member submits their application to an officer outside Canada within one year from the day on which refugee protection is conferred on the applicant;**

(c) the family member is not inadmissible;

(d) the applicant's sponsor under subparagraph 139(1)(f)(i) has been notified of the family member's application and an officer is satisfied that there are adequate financial arrangements for resettlement; and

(e) in the case of a family member who intends to reside in the Province of Quebec, the competent authority of that Province is of the opinion that the foreign national meets the selection criteria of the Province.

(2) **Non-application of s. 150(1)** — For greater certainty, subsection 150(1) does not apply to the application of a non-accompanying family member.

142. **Family members** — For the purposes of this Division, to be considered a family member of an applicant, a person must be a family member of the applicant

(a) at the time the application referred to in subsection 150(1) was made; and

(b) at the time of the determination of the application referred to in paragraph 141(1)(b), without taking account of whether the person has attained 22 years of age.

143. (1) **Memorandum of understanding** — The Minister may enter into a memorandum of understanding with an organization for the purpose of locating and identifying Convention refugees and persons in similar circumstances if the organization demonstrates

(a) a working knowledge of the provisions of the Act relating to protection criteria; and

(b) an ability abroad to locate and identify Convention refugees and persons in similar circumstances.

(2) **Content of memorandum of understanding** — The memorandum of understanding shall include provisions with respect to

(a) the geographic area to be served by the organization;

(b) the number of referrals that may be made by the organization and the manner of referral;

(c) the training of members or employees of the organization; and

(d) the grounds for suspending or cancelling the memorandum of understanding.

## *Convention Refugees Abroad*

144. **Convention refugees abroad class** — The Convention refugees abroad class is prescribed as a class of persons who may be issued a permanent resident visa on the basis of the requirements of this Division.

145. **Member of Convention refugees abroad class** — A foreign national is a Convention refugee abroad and a member of the Convention refugees abroad

**class if the foreign national has been determined, outside Canada, by an officer to be a Convention refugee.**

## *Humanitarian-protected Persons Abroad*

**146. (1) Humanitarian-protected persons abroad — For the purposes of subsection 12(3) of the Act, a person in similar circumstances to those of a Convention refugee is a member of one of the following humanitarian-protected persons abroad classes:**

**(a) the country of asylum class; or**

**(b) the source country class.**

**(2) Classes — The country of asylum class and the source country class are prescribed as classes of persons who may be issued permanent resident visas on the basis of the requirements of this Division.**

**147. Member of country of asylum class — A foreign national is a member of the country of asylum class if they have been determined by an officer to be in need of resettlement because**

**(a) they are outside all of their countries of nationality and habitual residence; and**

**(b) they have been, and continue to be, seriously and personally affected by civil war, armed conflict or massive violation of human rights in each of those countries.**

### Case Law

*El Karm v. Canada (Minister of Citizenship & Immigration)*, 2006 CarswellNat 2410, 2006 FC 972 (F.C.) — The applicant was determined, by a visa officer, not to be eligible to be sponsored as a private group-sponsored refugee to Canada because he was not outside his country of habitual residence. The applicant sought judicial review of the visa officer's decision.

The applicant, born in Jordan in 1973, was a stateless Palestinian. His family moved to Egypt in the 1980s where he completed his education. All of his siblings still live in Egypt. In June 1998, the applicant left Egypt for employment in Gaza. He remained in Gaza legally until November 1998 at which point he lost his status for failure to renew his visitor's permit. He also lost his right to return to Egypt by failing to return to Egypt every six months to renew his residency permit. In March 2003, the applicant attempted to re-enter Egypt but was caught and detained for 20 days because of his illegal entry. Since his release, he has remained in Cairo.

The visa officer, in reaching his conclusion, concluded that since the applicant was inside his country of habitual residence he did not meet the requirements of s. 147(a) of the Regulations. The Court found that the visa officer's conclusion was reasonable, since it was based on the fact that the applicant completed all of his education in Egypt, lived in Egypt from the 1980s until 1998, lived in Egypt again from 2003 to 2005, had siblings living in Egypt, the applicant's right to return to Egypt had lapsed but he was allowed to stay in Egypt for the last two years and the Egyptian government has a policy of not removing long-term Palestinian residents from Egypt. Against all of that factual background, it was at least reasonable for the visa officer to conclude that Egypt was a country of habitual residence for the applicant.

**148. (1) Member of the source country class — A foreign national is a member of the source country class if they have been determined by an officer to be in need of resettlement because**

**(a) they are residing in their country of nationality or habitual residence and that country is a source country within the meaning of subsection (2) at the time their permanent resident visa application is made as well as at the time a visa is issued; and**

**(b) they**

**(i) are being seriously and personally affected by civil war or armed conflict in that country,**

**(ii) have been or are being detained or imprisoned with or without charges, or subjected to some other form of penal control, as a direct result of an act committed outside Canada that would, in Canada, be a legitimate expression of freedom of thought or a legitimate exercise of civil rights pertaining to dissent or trade union activity, or**

**(iii) by reason of a well-founded fear of persecution for reasons of race, religion, nationality, political opinion or membership in a particular social group, are unable or, by reason of such fear, unwilling to avail themself of the protection of any of their countries of nationality or habitual residence.**

**(2) Source country — A source country is a country**

**(a) where persons are in refugee-like situations as a result of civil war or armed conflict or because their fundamental human rights are not respected;**

**(b) where an officer works or makes routine working visits and is able to process visa applications without endangering their own safety, the safety of applicants or the safety of Canadian embassy staff;**

**(c) where circumstances warrant humanitarian intervention by the Department in order to implement the overall humanitarian strategies of the Government of Canada, that intervention being in keeping with the work of the United Nations High Commissioner for Refugees; and**

**(d) that is set out in Schedule 2.**

**149. Minister's consultations on Schedule 2 — The Minister may, for the purpose of advising the Governor in Council of circumstances in a country that may justify amending Schedule 2, consult with the Department of Foreign Affairs and International Trade, the United Nations High Commissioner for Refugees, the provinces and non-governmental organizations with substantial knowledge of the country in question.**

**150. (1) Application — An application for a permanent resident visa submitted by a foreign national under this Division must be made at the immigration office**

IRP Regulations

**outside Canada that serves the applicant's place of residence and must be accompanied by either an undertaking or**

**(a) a referral from a referral organization;**

**(b) a referral resulting from an arrangement between the Minister and a government of a foreign state or any institution of such a government relating to resettlement; or**

**(c) a referral resulting from an agreement relating to resettlement entered into by the Government of Canada and an international organization or a government of a foreign state.**

**(2) Exception — requirement for referral or undertaking — A foreign national may submit a permanent resident visa application without a referral or an undertaking if the foreign national resides in a geographic area that the Minister has determined under subsection (3) to be a geographic area in which circumstances justify the submission of permanent resident visa applications not accompanied by a referral or an undertaking.**

**(3) Minister's determination — The Minister may determine on the basis of the following factors that a geographic area is an area in which circumstances justify the submission of permanent resident visa applications not accompanied by a referral or an undertaking:**

**(a) advice from referral organizations with which the Minister has entered into a memorandum of understanding under section 143 that they are unable to make the number of referrals specified in their memorandum of understanding for the area;**

**(b) the inability of referral organizations to refer persons in the area;**

**(c) the resettlement needs in the area, after consultation with referral organizations that have substantial knowledge of the area; and**

**(d) the relative importance of resettlement needs in the area, within the context of resettlement needs globally.**

SOR/2004-167, s. 47

**151. Travel document — An officer shall issue a temporary travel document to a foreign national who has been determined to be a member of a class prescribed by this Division and who**

**(a) holds a permanent resident visa or a temporary resident permit;**

**(b) does not hold a valid passport or travel document issued by their country of nationality or the country of their present or former habitual residence;**

**(c) does not hold a valid travel document issued by the United Nations or the International Committee of the Red Cross and is unable to obtain such a document within a reasonable time; and**

**(d) would be unable to travel to Canada if the temporary travel document were not issued.**

## *Protected Temporary Residents*

[Heading added SOR/2004-167, s. 48.]

**151.1 (1) Protected temporary residents class — The protected temporary residents class is prescribed as a class of persons who may become permanent residents on the basis of the requirements of this section.**

**(2) Member of the class — A foreign national is a protected temporary resident and a member of the protected temporary residents class if the foreign national holds a temporary resident permit and**

**(a) became a temporary resident under a temporary resident permit for protection reasons after making a claim for refugee protection outside Canada under section 99 of the Act; or**

**(b) was issued a Minister's permit under section 37 of the former Act after seeking admission to Canada under section 7 of the former Regulations or section 4 of the *Humanitarian Designated Classes Regulations*.**

**(2.1) Application — A foreign national destined for Quebec does not become a member of the protected temporary residents class described in paragraph (2)(a) if they have not received a selection certificate from the Province of Quebec.**

**(3) Former Act and Regulations — In subsection (2), "former Act" has the same meaning as in section 187 of the Act and "former Regulations" and "*Humanitarian Designated Classes Regulations*" have the same meaning as in subsection 316(1) of these Regulations.**

SOR/2004-167, s. 48

## DIVISION 2 — SPONSORSHIP

**152. (1) Sponsorship agreements — The Minister may enter into a sponsorship agreement with a sponsor for the purpose of facilitating the processing of sponsorship applications.**

**(2) Contents of agreement — A sponsorship agreement shall include provisions relating to**

**(a) settlement plans;**

**(b) financial requirements;**

**(c) assistance to be provided by the Department;**

**(d) the standard of conduct expected of the sponsor;**

**(e) reporting requirements; and**

**(f) the grounds for suspending or cancelling the agreement.**

*[Editor's Note: SOR/2002-227, s. 336 provides that a sponsorship agreement with the Minister made under the former* Immigration Act, *R.S.C. 1985, c. I-2 and the former* Immigration Regulations, 1978, *SOR/78-172 does not cease to have effect for the sole reason of s. 152 of the new* Immigration and Refugee Protection Regulations, *SOR/2002-227 coming into force on June 28, 2002.]*



IRP Regulations

**153.** (1) **Sponsorship requirements** — In order to sponsor a foreign national and their family members who are members of a class prescribed by Division 1, a sponsor

(a) must reside or have representatives in the expected community of settlement;

(b) must make an application that includes a settlement plan and an undertaking; and

(c) must not be — or include — an individual, a corporation or an unincorporated organization or association that was a party to a sponsorship in which they defaulted on an undertaking and remain in default.

(2) **Undertaking** — The undertaking referred to in paragraph (1)(b) shall be signed by each party to the sponsorship.

(3) **Joint and several or solidary liability** — All parties to the undertaking are jointly and severally or solidarily liable.

(4) **End of default** — A party or a sponsor who defaults on an undertaking ceases to be in default

(a) in the case of a sponsor who defaults on a financial obligation, when the sponsor has reimbursed the government concerned, in full or in accordance with an agreement with that government, for amounts paid by the government;

(b) in the case of a party who defaults on a financial obligation, when the defaulting party has reimbursed any other party to the sponsorship, in full or in accordance with an agreement with that party, for amounts paid by that party;

(c) in the case of a sponsor who defaults on a non-financial obligation, when the sponsor satisfies an officer that they are in compliance with the obligation; and

(d) in the case of an organization or association that was a party to a sponsorship and defaulted for any reason, when a period of five years has elapsed from the date of default.

**154.** (1) **Approval of application** — An officer shall approve an application referred to in paragraph 153(1)(b) if, on the basis of the documentation submitted with the application, the officer determines that

(a) the sponsor has the financial resources to fulfil the settlement plan for the duration of the undertaking, unless subsection 157(1) applies; and

(b) the sponsor has made adequate arrangements in anticipation of the arrival of the foreign national and their family members in the expected community of settlement.

(2) **Duration of sponsor's undertaking** — Subject to subsection (3), the duration of an undertaking is one year.

(3) **Officer's determination** — An officer may, on the basis of the assessment made under paragraph 139(1)(g), require that the duration of the undertaking be more than one year but not more than three years.

*[Editor's Note: SOR/2002-227, s. 337(1) provides that, subject to SOR/2002-227, ss. 337(2) and 337(3), a sponsor who made an undertaking within the meaning of paragraph (b) of the definition "undertaking" in s. 2(1) of the* Immigration Regulations, 1978, *SOR/78-172, or of the definition "undertaking" in s. 1(1) of the* Humanitarian Designated Classes Regulations, *SOR/97-183, and in respect of whom an immigration officer was satisfied that the requirements of ss. 7.1(2)(d) or 5(2)(d) of those Regulations, respectively, were met is deemed to be a sponsor whose application has been approved by an officer under s. 154 of the* Immigration and Refugee Protection Regulations, *SOR/2002-227 (the "new Regulations").*

*SOR/2002-227, s. 337(2) provides that SOR/2002-227, s. 337(1) does not apply to a sponsor who requests that a person be added to his or her undertaking.*

*SOR/2002-227, s. 337(3) further provides that SOR/2002-227, s. 337(1) does not apply to a sponsor who is ineligible to be a party to a sponsorship under s. 156 of the new Regulations.]*

IRP Regulations

**155. Revoking approval — An officer shall revoke an approval given in respect of an application under section 154 if the officer determines that the sponsor no longer meets the requirements of paragraph 154(1)(a) or (b) or is ineligible under subsection 156(1).**

**156. (1) Ineligibility to be a party to a sponsorship — The following persons are ineligible to be a party to a sponsorship:**

**(a) a person who has been convicted in Canada of the offence of murder or an offence set out in Schedule I or II to the *Corrections and Conditional Release Act*, regardless of whether it was prosecuted by indictment, if a period of five years has not elapsed since the completion of the person's sentence;**

**(b) a person who has been convicted of an offence outside Canada that, if committed in Canada, would constitute an offence referred to in paragraph (a), if a period of five years has not elapsed since the completion of the person's sentence imposed under a foreign law;**

**(c) a person who is in default of any support payment obligations ordered by a court;**

**(d) a person who is subject to a removal order;**

**(e) a person who is subject to a revocation proceeding under the *Citizenship Act*; and**

**(f) a person who is detained in any penitentiary, jail, reformatory or prison.**

**(2) Exception if pardoned — For the purpose of paragraph (1)(a), a sponsorship application may not be refused on the basis of a conviction in respect of which a pardon has been granted and has not ceased to have effect or been revoked under the *Criminal Records Act*, or in respect of which there has been a final determination of an acquittal.**

SOR/2010-195, s. 14(1)

**157. (1) Joint assistance sponsorship — If an officer determines that special needs exist in respect of a member of a class prescribed by Division 1, the Depart-**

**ment shall endeavour to identify a sponsor in order to make the financial assistance of the Government of Canada available for the purpose of sponsorship. A sponsor identified by the Department is exempt from the financial requirements of paragraph 154(1)(a).**

(2) **Definition of "special needs" — In this section, "special needs" means that a person has greater need of settlement assistance than other applicants for protection abroad owing to personal circumstances, including**

**(a) a large number of family members;**

**(b) trauma resulting from violence or torture;**

**(c) medical disabilities; and**

**(d) the effects of systemic discrimination.**

158. **Settlement in the Province of Quebec — If the foreign national and their family members intend to reside in the Province of Quebec, the sponsor must meet the requirements for sponsorship that are provided by regulations made under *An Act respecting immigration to Québec*, R.S.Q., c. I-0.2, as amended from time to time. In such a case, the requirements of this Division, other than section 156, do not apply.**

## Division 3 — Determination of Eligibility of Claim

159. **Working day — For the purposes of subsections 100(1) and (3) of the Act,**

**(a) a working day does not include Saturdays or holidays;**

**(b) a day that is not a working day is not included in the calculation of the three-day period; and**

**(c) the three-day period begins from the day on which the claim is received.**

159.1 **Definitions — The following definitions apply in this section and sections 159.2 to 159.7.**

**"Agreement" means the Agreement dated December 5, 2002 between the Government of Canada and the Government of the United States of America for Cooperation in the Examination of Refugee Status Claims from Nationals of Third Countries. *("Accord")***

**"claimant" means a claimant referred to in paragraph 101(1)(e) of the Act. *("demandeur")***

**"designated country" means a country designated by section 159.3. *("pays désigné")***

**"family member", in respect of a claimant, means their spouse or common-law partner, their legal guardian, and any of the following persons, namely, their child, father, mother, brother, sister, grandfather, grandmother, grandchild, uncle, aunt, nephew or niece. *("membre de la famille")***

**"legal guardian", in respect of a claimant who has not attained the age of 18 years, means a person who has custody of the claimant or who is empowered to act on the**

**claimant's behalf by virtue of a court order or written agreement or by operation of law.** ***("tuteur légal")***

**"United States" means the United States of America, but does not include Puerto Rico, the Virgin Islands, Guam or any other United States of America possession or territory.** ***("États-Unis")***

SOR/2004-217, s. 2

## Case Law

*Canadian Counsel for Refugees v. R.* (2008), 74 Admin. L.R. (4th) 79, 2008 CarswellNat 1995, 2008 CarswellNat 2197, 2008 FCA 229 (F.C.A.); leave to appeal to S.C.C. refused 2008 CarswellNat 5170, 2008 CarswellNat 5171 (S.C.C.) — This was an appeal from a decision of Phelan J. (the "applications judge"), granting an application for judicial review by the Canadian Council of Refugees, the Canadian Council of Churches, Amnesty International and John Doe ("the respondents"), declaring invalid sections of 159.1 to 159.7 of the Immigration and Refugee Protection Regulations, and the Agreement between the Government of Canada and the Government of the United States of America for Co-operation in the Examination of Refugee Status Claims from Nationals of Third Countries (the "Safe Third Country Agreement"). The Regulations at issue implement into domestic law a Safe Third Country Agreement between Canada and the United States whereby if a refugee enters Canada from the U.S. at a land border port-of-entry, Canada will, subject to specified exceptions, send the refugee back to the U.S. The same applies for refugees crossing by land from Canada to the U.S. The appeal was allowed and the decision of the applications judge set aside. The appropriate standard of review in respect of the decision of the Governor In Council ("GIC") to designate the United States as a "Safe Third Country" pursuant to s. 102 of the Immigration and Refugee Protection Act is correctness. The Federal Court of Appeal took issue with the applications judge's suggestion that unless "compliance" is made a condition precedent to the designation of a country, the GIC would have discretion to designate a country that does not comply. Subsection 101(2) does not refer to "actual" compliance or compliance "in absolute terms" nor does it otherwise specify the type and extent of compliance contemplated. However, Parliament has specified the four factors to be considered in determining whether a country can be designated. These factors are general in nature and are indicative of Parliament's intent that the matter of compliance be assessed on the basis of an appreciation by the GIC of the country's policies, practices and human rights record. Once it is accepted, as it must be in this case, that the GIC has given due consideration to these four factors, and formed the opinion that the candidate country is compliant with the relevant articles of the Conventions, there is nothing left to be reviewed judicially. The Federal Court of Appeal concluded there was no factual basis on which to assess the alleged Charter breaches. The respondents' main contention was directed at a border officer's lack of discretion to forego returning a claimant to the U.S. for reasons other than the enumerated exceptions set out in s. 159.5 of the Regulations. This challenge, however, should be assessed in a proper factual context - that is, when advanced by a refugee who has been denied asylum in Canada pursuant to the Regulations and faces a real risk of refoulement in being sent back to the U.S. pursuant to the Safe Third Country Agreement. In this case the refugee never came to Canada, and instead claimed that he would have sought asylum in Canada but for the Regulations.

IRP Regulations

*Odicho v. Canada (Minister of Citizenship & Immigration)* (2008), 75 Imm. L.R. (3d) 45, 2008 CarswellNat 4011, 2008 CarswellNat 3442, 2008 FC 1039 (F.C.) — The applicants sought judicial review of a visa officer's decision to refuse to issue a permanent resident visa to the wife. The applicants argued that the visa officer erred by failing to consider H&C grounds, pursuant to subs. 25 of the IRPA. They submit that they specifically requested that the wife's application for permanent residence in Canada be considered on the basis of s. 25. The husband had been landed in Canada in January 2005 and his initial application to sponsor his wife in May 2005 was refused on the basis that he had not disclosed his marriage when he was landed. The application on behalf of a dependent child was refused for the same reason but was subsequently reversed. The visa officer, however, maintained the rejection of the application on behalf of the wife on the basis of paragraph 117(9)(d) of the Regulations.

There was no dispute that the husband failed to declare his wife as a non-accompanying dependant when he landed in Canada in January 2005. There is no evidence to challenge the *bona fides* of the marriage of the applicants. There is no evidence to challenge the status of the infant as their child. The failure of the husband to declare the change in marital status when he landed in Canada gave rise to the exclusion of his wife pursuant to the terms of paragraph 117(9)(d). The Court held that the visa officer apparently ignored the material that was submitted concerning the "circumstances" of the husband's failure to declare the change in his marital status at the time he landed in Canada. The applicants carry the burden of establishing the evidence to justify an exercise of discretion, but the discharge of this burden does not require superfluity. The visa officer's decision does not demonstrate an understanding of the purpose of subs. 25(1) of the Act, which is to overcome the consequences of being in breach of statutory requirements. The initial decision which excluded the child, as well as the wife, illustrates an excess of zeal on the part of the original decision maker, if not a misunderstanding of s. 117 of the Regulations. The application for judicial review was allowed. The matter was remitted for reconsideration by a different member of the Canadian Embassy.

**159.2 Non-application — former habitual residence — Paragraph 101(1)(e) of the Act does not apply to a claimant who is a stateless person who comes directly or indirectly to Canada from a designated country that is their country of former habitual residence.**

SOR/2004-217, s. 2

**159.3 Designation — United States — The United States is designated under paragraph 102(1)(a) of the Act as a country that complies with Article 33 of the Refugee Convention and Article 3 of the Convention Against Torture, and is a designated country for the purpose of the application of paragraph 101(1)(e) of the Act.**

SOR/2004-217, s. 2

*Editor's Note*: See also case summaries under s. 101(1) of the Act.

## Case Law

*Mendez v. Canada (Ministre de la Citoyenneté & de l'Immigration)*, 2005 CarswellNat 369, 2005 FC 75, [2005] F.C.J. No. 152 (F.C.) — Following the introduction of the regulations known as "*Safe Third Country Regulations*", as of December 29, 2004, claims made by those who arrive in Canada via the United States or other safe third country, will no longer be referred to the Refugee Protection Division. Prior to the passage of these regulations, the existing jurisprudence stated that the failure to claim in a safe third country could be considered by the Board in examining subjective fear. A short stay in a safe third country *en route* is not necessarily considered a material enough sojourn to oblige the claimant to declare themselves as a refugee on their way to Canada. This was particularly true of the United States since many claimants must travel through the United States to get to Canada.

**159.4 (1) Non-application — ports of entry other than land ports of entry — Paragraph 101(1)(e) of the Act does not apply to a claimant who seeks to enter Canada at**

**(a) a location that is not a port of entry;**

**(b) a port of entry that is a harbour port, including a ferry landing; or**

**(c) subject to subsection (2), a port of entry that is an airport.**

**(2) In transit exception — Paragraph 101(1)(e) of the Act applies to a claimant who has been ordered removed from the United States and who seeks to enter Canada at a port of entry that is an airport while they are in transit through Canada from the United States in the course of the enforcement of that order.**

SOR/2004-217, s. 2

**159.5 Non-application — claimants at land ports of entry — Paragraph 101(1)(e) of the Act does not apply if a claimant who seeks to enter Canada at a location other than one identified in paragraphs 159.4(1)(a) to (c) establishes, in accordance with subsection 100(4) of the Act, that**

**(a) a family member of the claimant is in Canada and is a Canadian citizen;**

**(b) a family member of the claimant is in Canada and is**

**(i) a protected person within the meaning of subsection 95(2) of the Act,**

**(ii) a permanent resident under the Act, or**

**(iii) a person in favour of whom a removal order has been stayed in accordance with section 233;**

**(c) a family member of the claimant who has attained the age of 18 years is in Canada and has made a claim for refugee protection that has been referred to the Board for determination, unless**

**(i) the claim has been withdrawn by the family member,**

**(ii) the claim has been abandonned by the family member,**

**(iii) the claim has been rejected, or**

**(iv) any pending proceedings or proceedings respecting the claim have been terminated under subsection 104(2) of the Act or any decision respecting the claim has been nullified under that subsection;**

IRP Regulations

**(d) a family member of the claimant who has attained the age of 18 years is in Canada and is the holder of a work permit or study permit other than**

**(i) a work permit that was issued under paragraph 206(b) or that has become invalid as a result of the application of section 209, or**

**(ii) a study permit that has become invalid as a result of the application of section 222;**

**(e) the claimant is a person who**

**(i) has not attained the age of 18 years and is not accompanied by their mother, father or legal guardian,**

**(ii) has neither a spouse nor a common-law partner, and**

**(iii) has neither a mother or father nor a legal guardian in Canada or the United States;**

**(f) the claimant is the holder of any of the following documents, excluding any document issued for the sole purpose of transit through Canada, namely,**

**(i) a permanent resident visa or a temporary resident visa referred to in section 6 and subsection 7(1), respectively,**

**(ii) a temporary resident permit issued under subsection 24(1) of the Act,**

**(iii) a travel document referred to in subsection 31(3) of the Act,**

**(iv) refugee travel papers issued by the Minister of Foreign Affairs, or**

**(v) a temporary travel document referred to in section 151;**

**(g) the claimant is a person**

**(i) who may, under the Act or these Regulations, enter Canada without being required to hold a visa, and**

**(ii) who would, if the claimant were entering the United States, be required to hold a visa; or**

**(h) the claimant is**

**(i) a foreign national who is seeking to re-enter Canada in circumstances where they have been refused entry to the United States without having a refugee claim adjudicated there, or**

**(ii) a permanent resident who has been ordered removed from the United States and is being returned to Canada.**

SOR/2004-217, s. 2; SOR/2009-290, s. 2

## Case Law

*Baron v. Canada (Minister of Citizenship & Immigration)*, 2008 CarswellNat 466, 2008 CarswellNat 1923, 2008 FC 245 — This review concerned a decision by a CBSA officer that the applicant did not qualify for exemption under the Safe Third Country Agreement (STCA) between Canada and the United States. He had claimed exemption on the basis of having a family member in Canada. The applicant was interviewed by a CBSA officer to determine if he qualified for exemption under the STCA as a class of persons who would otherwise be returned to the United States. He relied on the fact that his sister had made a refugee claim. The CBSA officer determined that the sister's claim had been rejected by the Immigration and Refugee Board, that there was no stay of her removal and therefore the sister did not qualify as an "anchor relative" to ground the request for exemption. Section 159.5(c)(iii) does not contemplate finality of all appeal processes. The term "rejected" should be given consistent meaning and it is not one that includes "finally rejected". Once the sister's claim was rejected, she ceased to be the anchor relative.

The Court certified the following two questions:

(1) Does the term "rejected" in the phrase "unless the claim has been rejected" in s. 159.5(c)(iii) of the *Immigration and Refugee Protection Regulations* include the final determination of all reviews and appeals which may flow from the initial rejection decision?

(2) What are the consequences to those persons whose claim was denied under s. 159.5(c)(iii) if the decision in *Canadian Council for Refugees v. Canada*, 2007 FC 1262, is upheld in respect of the *ultra vires* of s. 159 of the Regulations.



**159.6 Non-application — claimants at land ports of entry and in transit — Paragraph 101(1)(e) of the Act does not apply if a claimant establishes, in accordance with subsection 100(4) of the Act, that the claimant**

**(a) is charged in the United States with, or has been convicted there of, an offence that is punishable with the death penalty in the United States; or**

**(b) is charged in a country other than the United States with, or has been convicted there of, an offence that is punishable with the death penalty in that country.**

**(c) [Repealed SOR/2009-210, s. 1.]**

SOR/2004-217, s. 2; SOR/2009-210, s. 1

**159.7 (1) Temporal operation — For the purposes of paragraph 101(1)(e) of the Act, the application of all or part of sections 159.1 to 159.6 and this section is discontinued, in accordance with subsections (2) to (6), if**

**(a) a notice of suspension of the Agreement setting out the period of suspension is publicized broadly in the various regions of Canada by the Minister via information media and on the website of the Department;**

**(b) a notice of renewal of the suspension of the Agreement setting out the period of renewal of suspension is published in accordance with subsection (6);**

**(c) a notice of suspension of a part of the Agreement is issued by the Government of Canada and the Government of the United States; or**

**(d) a notice of termination of the Agreement is issued by the Government of Canada or the Government of the United States.**

**(2) Paragraph (1)(a) — notice of suspension of Agreement — Subject to subsection (3), if a notice of suspension of the Agreement is publicized under paragraph (1)(a), sections 159.2 to 159.6 are rendered inoperative for a period of up to three months that shall be set out in the notice, which period shall begin on the day after the day on which the notice is publicized.**

**(3) Paragraph (1)(b) — notice of renewal of suspension of Agreement — If a notice of renewal of the suspension of the Agreement is published**

**under paragraph (1)(b), sections 159.2 to 159.6 are rendered inoperative for the further period of up to three months set out in the notice.**

**(4) Paragraph (1)(c) — suspension of part of Agreement — If a notice of suspension of part of the Agreement is issued under paragraph (1)(c), those provisions of these Regulations relating to the application of the Agreement that are referred to in the notice are rendered inoperative for a period that shall be set out in the notice. All other provisions of these Regulations continue to apply.**

**(5) Paragraph (1)(d) — termination of Agreement — If a notice of termination of the Agreement is issued under paragraph (1)(d), sections 159.1 to 159.6 and this section cease to have effect on the day set out in the notice.**

**(6) Publication requirement — *Canada Gazette* — Any notice referred to in paragraph (1)(b), (c) or (d) shall be published in the *Canada Gazette*, Part I, not less than seven days before the day on which the renewal, suspension in part or termination provided for in the notice is effective.**

SOR/2004-217, s. 2

## Division 4 — Pre-removal Risk Assessment

**160. (1) Application for protection — Subject to subsection (2) and for the purposes of subsection 112(1) of the Act, a person may apply for protection after they are given notification to that effect by the Department.**

**(2) No notification — A person described in section 165 or 166 may apply for protection in accordance with that section without being given notification to that effect by the Department.**

**(3) Notification — Notification shall be given**

**(a) in the case of a person who is subject to a removal order that is in force, before removal from Canada; and**

**(b) in the case of a person named in a certificate described in subsection 77(1) of the Act, when the summary of information and other evidence is filed under subsection 77(2) of the Act.**

**(4) When notification is given — Notification is given**

**(a) when the person is given the application for protection form by hand; or**

**(b) if the application for protection form is sent by mail, seven days after the day on which it was sent to the person at the last address provided by them to the Department.**

SOR/2008-193, s. 1

### Case Law

*Enabulele v. Canada (Ministry of Public Safety & Emergency Preparedness)* (2009), 81 Imm. L.R. (3d) 78, 347 F.T.R. 309 (Eng.), 2009 FC 641, 2009 CarswellNat 1876, 2009 CarswellNat 5904 (F.C.) — The applicant, a citizen of Nigeria married to a Canadian citizen, applied for permanent residence under the Spouse or Common-law Partner in Canada Class, pursuant to the Ministerial Policy, released in February 2005, and contained in Appendix H of the Citizenship and Immigration of Canada's Operational Manual for Inland Processing IP8. This policy is designed to allow spouses or common-law partners in Canada to apply for permanent residence from within Canada in accordance with the same criteria as members of the Spouse or Common-law Partner in Canada Class regardless of their immigration status. The applicant was advised, by reason of having been charged with two counts of sexual assault, that he was not entitled to a 60-day administrative deferral of removal under the policy. The applicant sought to challenge the policy on the basis that it violated his s. 7 and s. 11(d) *Charter* rights. The Court accepted the respondent's submission that the administrative deferral under the policy sought by the applicant would have expired even if the officer had found that the applicant was eligible for it. Notwithstanding this, the Court considered the *Charter* issues raised in the application.

The applicant argued that the policy compromised his security in that it did not allow him to defend his innocence of the charges laid against him. He says the policy stigmatizes those charged but not convicted of criminal charges. The Court found the applicant's argument without merit and concluded his s. 7 *Charter* rights were not engaged in the circumstances. The impugned policy renders the applicant ineligible for an administrative deferral by reason of his criminal charges. It does not follow, however that the applicant will be removed without a proper risk assessment. The PRRA process, to which the applicant is entitled, is designed to assist foreign nationals who may be required to leave Canada. It is the means by which the applicant can have his risk assessed prior to his departure. It is the very process which provides for consideration of the applicant's life, liberty and security interest in a pre-removal context. The applicant's access to that process was in no way affected by the policy. The application for judicial review was dismissed. The following question was certified:

> Does the Minister's policy on administrative deferral of removal found under IP8 offend the applicant's sections 7 and 11(d) rights of the *Canadian Charter of Rights and Freedoms*?

*Revich c. Canada (Ministre de la Citoyenneté & de l'Immigration)* (2005), 280 F.T.R. 201 (Eng.), (sub nom. *Revich v. Canada (Minister of Citizenship & Immigration))* 2005 CarswellNat 5741, 2005 FC 852 — The respondent issued a departure order against the applicant. Under the old legislation, the departure order was conditional and could not become effective until one of the conditions provided in subs. 49(2) had occurred. The applicant's refugee claim was refused and the departure order came into force 15 days after the notification of the rejection of the refugee claim. The Federal Court refused an application for leave against the decision of the RPD. The refusal ended the stay of execution of the departure order. The departure order became enforceable and became a deportation order pursuant to Reg. 224(2). The applicant was then notified of her right to file a pre-removal risk assessment (PRRA) application. The notice resulted in a stay of execution of the deportation order pending the PRRA decision. The PRRA application was rejected and the stay provided for under s. 232 of the Regulations ended with the rejection of the PRRA application.

Under paragraph 160(3)(a) of the Regulations, the department is required to notify the persons subject to a removal order, such as the present applicant, that they are entitled to apply for a PRRA decision. However, neither the Act nor the Regulations states at what time this notice must be issued. Meanwhile, because the person's refugee claim has been rejected, the stay of execution of the removal order is no longer in force. In other words, the removal order is "enforceable" and, after a 30-day period, the order will become a deportation order unless the person voluntarily leaves the country. The Regulations also provide for the stay of execution of a removal order when a person is notified that he or she may file a PRRA application.

The applicant in this case did not attack the combined effect of these statutory provisions but instead targeted the department's decision to send the notice under s. 160 of the Regulations after the removal order became a deportation order, and thereby depriving her of the opportunity to have the stay that the PRRA application would have triggered. So the essential question was whether it was fair for the department to act in this way.

The purpose of the PRRA is to prevent a foreign national whose refugee claim has already been rejected from being required to return to his country of residence or citizenship when the situation has changed in that country and he would be exposed to a risk of persecution. If this review is to be effective and consistent with Parliament's intention when creating it, the PRRA must coincide as closely as possible with the person's departure from the country. The Court concluded that if an interested party voluntarily complies with the removal order under s. 238 of the Regulations, within the requisite period, he or she may avoid the consequences of the deportation order. Requiring the department to issue a notice before the deportation order comes into force would in turn eliminate the main incentive for people to comply voluntarily with the removal order prior to the PRRA decision. The department's decision to send a notice after the departure order became a deportation order does not fail to meet the requirements of procedural fairness having regard to the objective of the PRRA process, which is to serve as a final "safeguard" before the interested party is required to leave the country. There is nothing inequitable in the applicant asking in the future for written authorization to return to Canada since she knew that this was a consequence of her choice to not leave voluntarily. The application for judicial review was dismissed.

The following question was certified: Is the PRRA officer required to send the notice under s. 160 of the *Immigration Refugee Protection Regulations* before the departure order becomes a deportation order, thereby putting the foreign national in an irregular situation? Should the answer to the preceding question be positive, should the deportation order be set aside?

**161. (1) Submissions — A person applying for protection may make written submissions in support of their application and for that purpose may be assisted, at their own expense, by a barrister or solicitor or other counsel.**

**(2) New evidence — A person who makes written submissions must identify the evidence presented that meets the requirements of paragraph 113(a) of the Act and indicate how that evidence relates to them.**

**162. Application within 15-day period — An application received within 15 days after notification was given under section 160 shall not be decided until at least 30 days after notification was given. The removal order is stayed under section 232 until the earliest of the events referred to in paragraphs 232(c) to (f) occurs.**

**163. Applications after the 15-day period — A person who has remained in Canada since being given notification under section 160 may make an application after a period of 15 days has elapsed from notification being given under that sec-**

**tion, but the application does not result in a stay of the removal order. Written submissions, if any, must accompany the application.**

**164. Application that must be received within 15-day period — certificate — Despite section 163, an application by a person who is named in a certificate described in subsection 77(1) of the Act must be received within 15 days after notification was given under section 160. An application received within that period shall not be decided until at least 30 days after notification was given.**

**165. Subsequent application — A person whose application for protection was rejected and who has remained in Canada since being given notification under section 160 may make another application. Written submissions, if any, must accompany the application. For greater certainty, the application does not result in a stay of the removal order.**

**166. Application at port of entry — An application for protection by a foreign national against whom a removal order is made at a port of entry as a result of a determination of inadmissibility on entry into Canada must, if the order is in force, be received as soon as the removal order is made. Written submissions, if any, must accompany the application. For greater certainty, the application does not result in a stay of the removal order.**

**167. Hearing — prescribed factors — For the purpose of determining whether a hearing is required under paragraph 113(b) of the Act, the factors are the following:**

**(a) whether there is evidence that raises a serious issue of the applicant's credibility and is related to the factors set out in sections 96 and 97 of the Act;**

**(b) whether the evidence is central to the decision with respect to the application for protection; and**

**(c) whether the evidence, if accepted, would justify allowing the application for protection.**

## Case Law

*Tekie v. Canada (Minister of Citizenship & Immigration)*, 2005 CarswellNat 190, 2005 CarswellNat 819, 2005 FC 27 (F.C.) — Section 167 becomes operative where credibility is an issue which could result in a negative PRRA decision. The intent of the provision is to allow an applicant to face any credibility concern which may be put at issue. In this case, the Officer had concerns about the applicant's credibility. Although the case was decided principally on the basis of objective fear, if the applicant's contentions had been accepted, a positive PRRA would have resulted. The fact that in the end, the PRRA decision was based on grounds other than credibility, did not lessen the right to an oral hearing.

**168. Hearing procedure — A hearing is subject to the following provisions:**

**(a) notice shall be provided to the applicant of the time and place of the hearing and the issues of fact that will be raised at the hearing;**

(b) the hearing is restricted to matters relating to the issues of fact stated in the notice, unless the officer conducting the hearing considers that other issues of fact have been raised by statements made by the applicant during the hearing;

(c) the applicant must respond to the questions posed by the officer and may be assisted for that purpose, at their own expense, by a barrister or solicitor or other counsel; and

(d) any evidence of a person other than the applicant must be in writing and the officer may question the person for the purpose of verifying the evidence provided.

169. **Abandonment** — An application for protection is declared abandoned

(a) in the case of an applicant who fails to appear at a hearing, if the applicant is given notice of a subsequent hearing and fails to appear at that hearing; and

(b) in the case of an applicant who voluntarily departs Canada, when the applicant's removal order is enforced under section 240 or the applicant otherwise departs Canada.

170. **Withdrawal** — An application for protection may be withdrawn by the applicant at any time by notifying the Minister in writing. The application is declared to be withdrawn on receipt of the notice.

171. **Effect of abandonment and withdrawal** — An application for protection is rejected when a decision is made not to allow the application or when the application is declared withdrawn or abandoned.

172. (1) **Applicant described in s. 112(3) of the Act** — Before making a decision to allow or reject the application of an applicant described in subsection 112(3) of the Act, the Minister shall consider the assessments referred to in subsection (2) and any written response of the applicant to the assessments that is received within 15 days after the applicant is given the assessments.

(2) **Assessments** — The following assessments shall be given to the applicant:

(a) a written assessment on the basis of the factors set out in section 97 of the Act; and

(b) a written assessment on the basis of the factors set out in subparagraph 113(d)(i) or (ii) of the Act; as the case may be.

(2.1) **Certificate** — Despite subsection (2), no assessments shall be given to an applicant who is named in a certificate until a judge under section 78 of the Act determines whether the certificate is reasonable.

(3) **When assessments given** — The assessments are given to an applicant when they are given by hand to the applicant or, if sent by mail, are deemed to be given to an applicant seven days after the day on which they are sent to the last address that the applicant provided to the Department.

**(4) Applicant not described in s. 97 of the Act — Despite subsections (1) to (3), if the Minister decides on the basis of the factors set out in section 97 of the Act that the applicant is not described in that section,**

> **(a) no written assessment on the basis of the factors set out in subparagraph 113(d)(i) or (ii) of the Act need be made; and**
>
> **(b) the application is rejected.**

SOR/2008-193, s. 2

## Case Law

*Jaballah, Re* (2002), [2003] 3 F.C. 85, 2002 CarswellNat 2697, 2002 CarswellNat 3514, [2002] F.C.J. No. 1385, 2002 FCT 1046, 224 F.T.R. 20 (T.D.) — The statute specifically provides, by s. 116, for Regulations relating to the application of Pt. 1, Division 3 of the Act concerning pre-removal risk assessment. Section 116 includes authority to provide by Regulation, "for any matter relating to the application of this division," including "provisions respecting procedures to be followed with respect to applications for protection." Section 172 of the Regulations, on its face, appears to be within the broad grant of regulating authority under s. 116.

IRP Regulations

**173. (1) Re-examination of stay — procedure — A person in respect of whom a stay of a removal order, with respect to a country or place, is being re-examined under subsection 114(2) of the Act shall be given**

> **(a) a notice of re-examination;**
>
> **(b) a written assessment on the basis of the factors set out in section 97 of the Act; and**
>
> **(c) a written assessment on the basis of the factors set out in subparagraph 113(d)(i) or (ii) of the Act, as the case may be.**

**(2) Assessments and response — Before making a decision to cancel or maintain the stay of the removal order, the Minister shall consider the assessments and any written response of the person in respect of whom the stay is being re-examined that is received within 15 days after the assessments are given to that person.**

**(3) When assessments given — The assessments are given to an applicant when they are given by hand to the applicant or, if sent by mail, are deemed to be given to an applicant seven days after the day on which they are sent to the last address that the applicant provided to the Department.**

SOR/2009-290, s. 6

**174. Reasons for decision — On request, an applicant shall be given a copy of the file notes that record the justification for the decision on their application for protection.**

## Division 5 — Protected Persons — Permanent Residence

**175. (1) Application period — For the purposes of subsection 21(2) of the Act, an application to remain in Canada as a permanent resident must be received by the Department within 180 days after the determination by the Board, or the decision of the Minister, referred to in that subsection.**

**(2) Judicial review — An officer shall not be satisfied that an applicant meets the conditions of subsection 21(2) of the Act if the determination or decision is subject to judicial review or if the time limit for commencing judicial review has not elapsed.**

**(3) Quebec — For the purposes of subsection 21(2) of the Act, an applicant who makes an application to remain in Canada as a permanent resident — and the family members included in the application — who intend to reside in the Province of Quebec as permanent residents and who are not persons whom the Board has determined to be Convention refugees, may become permanent residents only if it is established that the competent authority of that Province is of the opinion that they meet the selection criteria of the Province.**

### Case Law

#### Section 175(1)

*Mashtouli v. Canada (Minister of Citizenship & Immigration)*, 2006 CarswellNat 205, 2006 FC 94 (F.C.) — The Regulations set out a 180-day deadline for successful refugee claimants to file an application for permanent residence. The Regulations, however, do not stipulate that incomplete applications submitted on time should be rejected. On the contrary, s. 12 of the Regulations simply says that incomplete applications should be returned to the applicants. Had the Governor in Council intended that incomplete applications be rejected entirely, it would have said so. In contrast, a sponsorship application that is deficient is considered not to be an application filed in the prescribed manner: see s. 10(6) of the *Immigration and Refugee Protection Regulations*.

**176. (1) Family members — An applicant may include in their application to remain in Canada as a permanent resident any of their family members.**

**(2) One-year time limit — A family member who is included in an application to remain in Canada as a permanent resident and who is outside Canada at the time the application is made shall be issued a permanent resident visa if**

> **(a) the family member makes an application outside Canada to an officer within one year after the day on which the applicant becomes a permanent resident; and**
>
> **(b) the family member is not inadmissible on the grounds referred to in subsection (3).**

**(3) Inadmissibility — A family member who is inadmissible on any of the grounds referred to in subsection 21(2) of the Act shall not be issued a permanent resident visa and shall not become a permanent resident.**

177. **Prescribed classes** — For the purposes of subsection 21(2) of the Act, the following are prescribed as classes of persons who cannot become permanent residents:

(a) the class of persons who have been the subject of a decision under section 108 or 109 or subsection 114(3) of the Act resulting in the loss of refugee protection or nullification of the determination that led to conferral of refugee protection;

(b) the class of persons who are permanent residents at the time of their application to remain in Canada as a permanent resident;

(c) the class of persons who have been recognized by any country, other than Canada, as Convention refugees and who, if removed from Canada, would be allowed to return to that country;

(d) the class of nationals or citizens of a country, other than the country that the person left, or outside of which the person remains, by reason of fear of persecution; and

(e) the class of persons who have permanently resided in a country, other than the country that the person left, or outside of which the person remains, by reason of fear of persecution, and who, if removed from Canada, would be allowed to return to that country.



178. (1) **Identity documents** — An applicant who does not hold a document described in any of paragraphs 50(1)(a) to (h) may submit with their application

(a) any identity document issued outside Canada before the person's entry into Canada; or

(b) if there is a reasonable and objectively verifiable explanation related to circumstances in the applicant's country of nationality or former habitual residence for the applicant's inability to obtain any identity documents, a statutory declaration made by the applicant attesting to their identity, accompanied by

(i) a statutory declaration attesting to the applicant's identity made by a person who knew the applicant, a family member of the applicant, or the applicant's father, mother, brother, sister, grandfather or grandmother prior to the applicant's entry into Canada, or

(ii) the statutory declaration of an official of an organization representing nationals of the applicant's country of nationality or former habitual residence attesting to the applicant's identity.

(2) **Alternative documents** — A document submitted under subsection (1) shall be accepted in lieu of a document described in any of paragraphs 50(1)(a) to (h) if

(a) in the case of an identity document, the identity document

(i) is genuine,

(ii) identifies the applicant, and

(iii) constitutes credible evidence of the applicant's identity; and

(b) in the case of a statutory declaration, the declaration

(i) is consistent with any information previously provided by the applicant to the Department or the Board, and

**(ii) constitutes credible evidence of the applicant's identity.**

SOR/2004-167, s. 49

# PART 9 — TEMPORARY RESIDENTS

## DIVISION 1 — TEMPORARY RESIDENT VISA

**179. Issuance — An officer shall issue a temporary resident visa to a foreign national if, following an examination, it is established that the foreign national**

**(a) has applied in accordance with these Regulations for a temporary resident visa as a member of the visitor, worker or student class;**

**(b) will leave Canada by the end of the period authorized for their stay under Division 2;**

**(c) holds a passport or other document that they may use to enter the country that issued it or another country;**

**(d) meets the requirements applicable to that class;**

**(e) is not inadmissible; and**

**(f) meets the requirements of section 30.**

### Case Law

*Groohi v. Canada (Minister of Citizenship & Immigration)* (2009), 83 Imm. L.R. (3d) 129, 2009 FC 837, 2009 CarswellNat 4136, 2009 CarswellNat 2502 (F.C.) — The applicants were sisters who applied for temporary resident visas which were refused by a visa officer. The sisters had been invited by their brother to visit along with their parents. Their brother was a medical doctor practicing in Manitoba and had status in Canada as a permanent resident. The sisters' applications were initially refused in July 2007 on the basis that in the visa officer's estimation both sisters had "weak ties" to Iran and were unable to show that they would leave Canada at the end of an authorized stay. Applications for judicial review were granted and both visa applications were remitted to a different visa officer for determination. The applications were refused again.

These applications must succeed based simply on the absence of any true analysis of the evidence by the visa officer. It is trite law that simply listing a series of factors, and stating a conclusion, is generally insufficient to meet the test of reasonableness, the reason being that it is impossible for a reviewing Court to appreciate and access the train of thought or logical process engaged in by the decision maker.

A visa officer's decision as to whether an applicant has satisfied him or her that the applicant will not overstay the visit to Canada is not one requiring a detailed and lengthy analysis. However, where the officer concludes that the applicant has failed to satisfy the officer of that essential fact, the applicant is entitled to know the facts which the officer considered, the weight accorded to those facts, and the reasoning of the officer as to why the applicant failed to meet the burden. In these decisions there was a complete lack of any explanation of the reasoning process in which the officer engaged. The applications for judicial review were allowed.

*Rudder v. Canada (Minister of Citizenship & Immigration)* (2009), 82 Imm. L.R. (3d) 173, 346 F.T.R. 286 (Eng.), 2009 FC 689, 2009 CarswellNat 1912, 2009 CarswellNat

5866 (F.C.) — The applicant, a citizen of Guyana aged 53, challenged the decision of a visa officer to refuse her application for a temporary residence visa to enable her to come to Canada to visit relatives and view the gravesites of her mother and sister. The Court found the officer's decision to be contrary to paragraph 18.1(4)(d) of the *Federal Courts Act*. The officer's decision was reached ignoring the evidence before him or by drawing inferences from the evidence which are unreasonable in the perspective of the purposes and objectives for Canada granting entry to this country on a temporary resident visa (TRV) in the category of a visitor. While there is no question an application for a foreign national for a TRV triggers a discretionary decision by an officer, administrative law has settled the principles upon which discretionary decisions of officers dealing with TRV decisions must be reviewed. The officer clearly failed to consider many of the factors identified in the ministerial guideline to access the central and only criteria spelled out in IRPA for the issuance of a TRV, namely, whether on the evidence, the officer should be satisfied an applicant will return to his or her country of residence. The application for judicial review was allowed and the matter referred to a different officer with directions that a TRV for the period of one month be issued forthwith to the applicant.

*Hara v. Canada (Minister of Citizenship & Immigration)* (2009), 79 Imm. L.R. (3d) 27, 2009 FC 263, 2009 CarswellNat 739 (F.C.) — This was an application for judicial review of a decision of a visa officer refusing the applicant's application for a work permit. On June 16, 2008, the applicant submitted a third application for a work permit as a live-in-caregiver. This application was refused on June 20, 2008. The reasons for refusal were that the applicant had failed to provide a new employment contract with her employer in Canada and the officer was not satisfied that the applicant would leave Canada at the end of her authorized stay. The officer noted in the CAIPS notes that the applicant had overstayed in Canada, had failed to mention her refusals for work permits in her previous applications, and had weak connections to Japan.

The Court held that the officer was mistaken in his reasoning that the applicant had not declared being refused a visa to Canada on her first application. The first application was the applicant's first refusal of a visa to Canada. The CPC-Vegreville refusal was not a visa refusal to Canada or, in the Court's opinion, analogous. The applicant, however, did give an incorrect answer to a question in her second application, when she indicated that she had not been refused a visa to Canada when, in fact, the first refusal did constitute a refused visa to Canada. However, the officer's mistaken reasoning as to the extent of the applicant's misstatements is sufficient to hold the officer's finding on this point was unreasonable. The Court agrees with the applicant that the officer's finding that she would not leave Canada at the end of the authorized stay was not sufficiently supported by the evidence and was unreasonable. While the applicant did not leave as required by law once she received the September 2007 CPC-Vegreville refusal, possibly for the reason she attested to, she nevertheless did leave Canada once she became aware that she had to apply for the Live-In-Caregiver Program from outside Canada. Having received no notice to leave Canada, she claims to have only later learned after reviewing the CAIPS notes that she should have left Canada after receiving the CPC-Vegreville refusal. The applicant "did not go underground". The officer also breached the duty of procedural fairness by not providing adequate reasons why he rejected the applicant's detailed explanation of her overstay in Canada. The whole history of the applicant's relationship with Canada and her repeated comings and goings were directly against the officer's conclusions on this point. There is nothing in the Act or Regulations that prevent someone from consulting with a lawyer as to the legal means to remain in Canada. The fact that the applicant

IRP Regulations

had a two-year degree from a Canadian college in early childhood education is evidence that her interest in the LIC Program was not simply a utilitarian move to remain in Canada "no matter for which purpose". The decision was set aside and the application for judicial review was allowed.

*Villagonzalo v. Canada (Minister of Citizenship & Immigration)*, 2008 CarswellNat 4937, 2008 CarswellNat 3640, 2008 FC 1127 — This was an application for judicial review of a visa officer's decision that the applicant did not meet the requirements for a work permit. The applicant applied under the Live-In-Caregiver Program. The applicant argued that the officer failed to take into account that throughout her previous stay in Canada, the applicant undertook to maintain valid TRV status and promptly left when her request for an extension was refused. The applicant explained that she originally received a six-month TRV to come to Canada to attend her brother's wedding. Due to her child being sick, she was unable to attend the wedding. She did, however, come to Canada in November 2004 to visit her family. The applicant deposed that she told this to the visa officer at the time of her interview for a work permit. It appears that her failure to attend her brother's wedding and her failure to leave Canada between either May 17, 2005, or May 22, 2005 (the date she received the refusal to extend her status in Canada), and June 1, 2005, caused the visa officer to believe that the applicant in the future would not leave Canada by the end of any period authorized for her stay. The Court concluded that the visa officer's decision was not reasonable and that there should have been some consideration of the applicant's explanations. The application for judicial review was allowed.

*Singh v. Canada (Minister of Citizenship & Immigration)* (2008), 68 Imm. L.R. (3d) 278, 2008 CarswellNat 894, 2008 CarswellNat 12, 2008 FC 15 (F.C.) — This was the judicial review of one of many refusals to grant the applicant a visa based on the fact that he is believed to be a people smuggler. The applicant first applied for a temporary residence visa in August 1996, which was refused. All the subsequent visa refusals have been based on this 1996 refusal. It was unreasonable for the visa officer to continue to rely solely on the 1996 visa refusal without considering the case in its totality. The decision was quashed. The applicant was entitled to have his visa application reviewed fully and fairly — to be able to address in a real manner the allegations (stated and implied).

*Khatoon v. Canada (Minister of Citizenship & Immigration)* (2008), 71 Imm. L.R. (3d) 102, 2008 CarswellNat 558, 2008 CarswellNat 1024, 2008 FC 276 — The applicant was a citizen of Pakistan who applied for a visitor permit in order to attend her granddaughter's wedding. The application was received along with a letter of invitation from the applicant's grandson. The officer refused the application, checking off the boxes corresponding to two reasons on the standard refusal letter, specifically that the applicant had not satisfied the officer that she met the requirements of Regulation s. 179 and would leave Canada at the end of her temporary period if authorized to stay and the applicant had not provided sufficient documentation to support her host's income and assets. The officer's conclusion was found to be patently unreasonable. The fact that the applicant's son was in Canada out of status could not be used to impute similar conduct to the applicant. People are to be judged according to their own behaviour, not on that of their family members. The mere fact that elderly widowed women normally, in the view of the officer, live with their sons and not daughters, could not be used to attack the *bona fides* of the applicant's application. This type of gross generalization is patently unreasonable. Finally, the officer disregarded the applicant's previous trip to Saudi Arabia, stating that "a trip to Saudi Arabia is not usually considered to be major international travel in the context in which the officer assesses applications for temporary residence." The Court held that a trip from Pakistan to Saudi Arabia was international travel. The application for judicial review was allowed and the visa officer's decision was quashed.

*Wang v. Canada (Minister of Citizenship & Immigration)*, 2006 CarswellNat 3482, 2006 FC 1298 (F.C.) — The applicant made two unsuccessful applications to enter Canada as a student. Her second visa application was refused because the visa officer was not satisfied that she was an intending temporary resident to Canada. The applicant argued that the visa officer's finding that the applicant was not well established in China was bizarre because the record disclosed that she "is as well established in China as any 19-year-old who has just finished high school." While there is some merit to the applicant's contention that one's establishment in a country ordinarily requires consideration of many factors, it is also the case that a visa officer has a broad discretion to weigh the evidence submitted in making a decision. Here the visa officer looked for evidence of the financial situation of the applicant's parents. The visa officer considered this to be important to the assessment of the application and she failed to find it. The applicant's parents were retired and their financial situation was unknown. The onus rested on the applicant to establish an entitlement to a student visa. The visa officer was entitled to base the refusal decision solely on the absence of that evidence of family circumstance. If the evidence had been offered and if it sufficiently answered the concerns of the visa officer, the decision may well have been different.

The applicant also complained that the refusal letter was deficient because it did not contain the reasons for the visa refusal. The CAIPS notes were provided to the applicant in compliance with the *Federal Court Immigration and Refugee Protection Rules*. CAIPS notes have been accepted as a constituent part of an administrative decision. Rule 9 contemplates that the provision of detailed reasons for an immigration decision may occur after the commencement of an application for judicial review. The Court concluded that the respondent met its obligation under that Rule and cannot be taken to have breached a natural justice requirement by failure to abide by some other standard.

*Toor v. Canada (Minister of Citizenship & Immigration)*, 2006 CarswellNat 1342, 2006 FC 573 (F.C.) — The applicant applied for judicial review of a decision of an immigration officer at the New Delhi High Commission, wherein the officer refused the applicant's application for a temporary resident visa. The officer was not satisfied as to the *bona fides* of the application. The applicant had been invited to an interview by a provincial government, however, the officer noted that the letter from the province of Manitoba referred to funds claimed by the applicant which could not be verified on documents and accordingly, concluded there were large inconsistencies. The officer also noted the applicant had no previous travel and only previous refusals from the United States and New Zealand.

The applicant argued that it would have been proper for the visa officer to give him an opportunity to reply to his concerns.

The Court concluded that the obligation to confront an applicant with adverse conclusions applies when the conclusions arise from material not known to the applicant. Where the issue arises out of material provided by the applicant, there is no obligation to provide an opportunity for explanation since the provider of the material is taken to know of the contents of the material. There was no breach of procedural fairness.

*Dhillon v. Canada (Minister of Citizenship & Immigration)*, 2003 CarswellNat 3954, 2003 CarswellNat 4433, 2003 FC 1446 (F.C.) — The applicant tried three times to obtain a visa to allow him to visit his ailing mother in Vancouver for one month. His first two applications were turned down because the officers found that "he had no ties to India". The applicant went to considerable effort to address that concern in his third application. He supplied documents showing details of his prosperous farming operation including proof of title to his land and house, financial statements and savings records. He described his responsibility as sole caregiver to his elderly grandmother and his other family connections in India. The officer who turned down the applicant's third request for a visa had an obligation to consider and respond to the new evidence of the applicant's ties to India. The officer either failed to consider the evidence or failed to explain adequately why the third application was being refused and accordingly the decision was set aside.

## *Holders of Temporary Resident Visas*

**180. Authorization — A foreign national is not authorized to enter and remain in Canada as a temporary resident unless, following an examination, it is established that the foreign national and their accompanying family members**

**(a) met the requirements for issuance of their temporary resident visa at the time it was issued; and**

**(b) continue to meet these requirements at the time of the examination on entry into Canada.**

## *Applications for Extension of Authorization to Remain in Canada as a Temporary Resident*

**181. (1) Circumstances — A foreign national may apply for an extension of their authorization to remain in Canada as a temporary resident if**

**(a) the application is made by the end of the period authorized for their stay; and**

**(b) they have complied with all conditions imposed on their entry into Canada.**

**(2) Extension — An officer shall extend the foreign national's authorization to remain in Canada as a temporary resident if, following an examination, it is established that the foreign national continues to meet the requirements of section 179.**

### Case Law

*Lim v. Canada (Minister of Citizenship & Immigration)* (2005), 45 Imm. L.R. (3d) 271, 2005 CarswellNat 1209, 2005 FC 657 (F.C.) — One of the objectives of the IRPA is to facilitate the entry of temporary workers. Live-in caregivers are temporary workers and are needed in Canada. IRPA and the Regulations have established a special program for caregivers. Under that program, live-in caregivers are given an incentive to come to Canada; they can qualify for permanent residency after having worked as live-in caregivers in Canada. The program works on the basis of dual interdependent authorizations; the work permit and the temporary resident status. Both the work permit and the temporary resident status are obtained when the caregiver first arrives in Canada. If the work permit is renewed, the temporary residency status is also extended. If the work permit expires, the temporary resident status expires. Without valid, unexpired temporary residency status, a caregiver cannot apply for renewal of the work permit. Conversely, a valid unexpired work permit is a precondition for extension of the temporary residency status.

To avoid hardship or exploitation, caregivers can change employers but this is dependent on furnishing, with respect to the new employer, a validated job offer and new employment contract.

Due to the fact that there may be timeline issues, the Regulations allow for an extension for two months for those caregivers who anticipate the problem and apply prior to the expiry of their work permit and a 90 day grace period for those caregivers that missed the deadline and apply after the expiry of their work permit.

The discretion of CIC officers is circumscribed by the mandatory requirements of ss. 181 and 182.

The point of the 90 day grace period is to allow live-in caregivers to rectify their status. The applicant in this case applied within the required period. Any bureaucratic delay in handling the application should not be used as justification to curtail the applicant's rights. The applicant made her application to rectify her status within the 90 day grace period established by s. 182. She still had 19 days to correct any deficiencies. In this case, the deficiency was that in the application she did not tick off one box on the form, Box C and failed to tick off Box D and provided the wrong renewal fee.



The date of receipt of the application is to be considered the lock-in date. The applicant did not know, nor could she reasonably be expected to know, that she had also to apply for restoration of status. The CIC booklet entitled, "Applying to Change Conditions or Extend Your Stay in Canada — Worker (IMM 553-E (04-2004)" is extremely hard to understand and contains confusing and questionable statements.

It is necessary to be mindful of the fact that the actions of CIC in refusing the extension have a drastic effect. The applicant has to return to the Philippines and has to reapply which will take a minimum of two years. She has to re-qualify and start from scratch. The time that she has worked in Canada does not count toward the two years working time she needs before applying for permanent status. The rejection of the application in this case serves no discernable policy goal under IRPA, nor does it prevent any abuse of IRPA or the Regulations. It is completely out of tune with the general nature of the Live-in Caregiver Program.

*Stanislavsky v. Canada (Minister of Citizenship & Immigration)* (2003), 237 F.T.R. 27, 2003 CarswellNat 1961, 2003 CarswellNat 2799, 2003 FCT 835 (T.D.) — The applicants sought judicial review of the decision of an Immigration counsellor denying the applicants' request for a restoration of their temporary resident status. The applicants who are married to each other are citizens of Ukraine. They entered Canada in July 2000 as visitors. They have two sons who are Canadian citizens and who live in Canada. In 2000, the purpose of their visit was to look after the mother of one of the applicants who was ill. The mother died in August 2001 leaving property in Canada to one of the applicants. In February 2002, their request for an extension of their visitor status was refused. They applied for a restoration of their visitor status and that was also refused. In May 2002, the applicants made an application for permanent residence sponsored by one of their sons. The Immigration counsellor refused to restore their temporary status and entered a note in the CAIPS notes advising that the immediate departure of the applicants should be effected.

A person seeking a temporary resident permit must have the intention of staying in Canada for a temporary purpose and the officer must be satisfied that such a person will leave

Canada on the expiry of status. The officer did not refuse the application for restoration on the basis that the applicants were not in Canada for a temporary purpose. The officer denied the application because the applicants' stay would be for a "long temporary purpose", that is, while awaiting a decision on their application for permanent residence. The extended delay was attributed to the long processing time in Vegreville, Alberta, relative to inland sponsorship applications.

The fact that the applicants had submitted an inland sponsorship application was relevant to their intention to remain in Canada for a long temporary purpose. That is for the duration of the processing of their landing applications. This was a new and different temporary purpose from their original temporary purpose when they entered Canada in July 2000. The statutory and regulatory scheme does not say that a person's initial temporary purpose must remain constant and unchanged. The only requirement is the existence of a "temporary purpose". In the present case the officer did not address his mind to this question and this was a reversible error.

## *Restoration of Temporary Resident Status*

**182. Restoration — On application made by a visitor, worker or student within 90 days after losing temporary resident status as a result of failing to comply with a condition imposed under paragraph 185(a), any of subparagraphs 185(b)(i) to (iii) or paragraph 185(c), an officer shall restore that status if, following an examination, it is established that the visitor, worker or student meets the initial requirements for their stay and has not failed to comply with any other conditions imposed.**

### Case Law

*Sui v. Canada (Minister of Public Safety & Emergency Preparedness)* (2006), 58 Imm. L.R. (3d) 135, [2007] 3 F.C.R. 218, 2006 CarswellNat 3554, 2006 FC 1314 (F.C.) — The applicant was in Canada for several years as a temporary resident on a study permit. Before his study permit expired, he applied for a post-graduation work permit. He received a letter from CIC informing him that he did not meet the requirements for a work permit and that he should leave Canada immediately, failing which enforcement action would be taken against him. Within 90 days of the expiration of his study permit and within 90 days of losing his temporary resident status, he applied to have his status restored pursuant to Regulation 182. While awaiting a decision on his application for restoration, two immigration officers attended his home and questioned him. Two inadmissibility reports were issued, the first based on paragraph 40(1)(a) of the IRPA and the fact that "there were reasonable grounds to believe that this foreign national was inadmissible for directly or indirectly misrepresenting or withholding material facts relating to a relevant matter that induces or could induce an error in administration of this Act." The second report was based on paragraph 41(a) and subs. 29(2) of the IRPA and the fact that the applicant was inadmissible for failing to comply with his obligation as a temporary resident to leave Canada by the end of the period authorized for his stay. A Minister's delegate decided to issue an exclusion order based on paragraph 41(a) and subs. 29(2) of the IRPA. In light of s. 225 of the Regulations, this meant that the applicant could not come back to Canada without written consent of the Minister for a period of one year following his departure. The applicant left Canada. No decision with respect to the application for restoration was ever made. In this case, the Minister's delegate had the discretion and even the duty to consider the fact that the applicant had applied for restoration well before a s. 44(1) report was issued against him in respect of his failure to leave Canada at the end of his authorized stay. It was an error of law to consider that the applicant was not entitled to make such an application for restoration simply because after the filing of his application in accordance with the Regulations, a s. 44(1) report had been issued on the sole basis of subs. 29(2) of the IRPA. The decision was set aside.

The following questions were certified:

1. Is an application for restoration pursuant to s. 182 of the Regulations a relevant consideration when the Minister's delegate considers whether or not to make an exclusion order based on a failure to comply with s. 29(2) of the IRPA?

2. Does a foreign national who has applied for restoration within the delay set out in s. 182 of the Regulations, automatically lose the benefit of his or her application when an enforcement officer considers issuing a report under s. 44(1) on the basis of a failure to comply with s. 29(2) of the IRPA?



*Zhang v. Canada (Minister of Citizenship & Immigration)* (2006), 59 Imm. L.R. (3d) 165, 2006 CarswellNat 3831, 2006 FC 1381 (F.C.) — The applicant moved to British Columbia in 2002 on a temporary student permit that was valid until August 2004. He applied for and was granted an extension to August 30, 2005. Since he wanted to continue his studies, he applied for a further extension in August 2005. The officer concluded he was not a *bona fide* student and did not intend to leave Canada at the end of his stay. The applicant did not leave Canada, nor did he seek leave of the Court to challenge the decision to refuse his extension application. Instead, the applicant submitted a restoration application seeking to re-acquire the temporary status he had lost. The applicant's restoration application was refused. The officer's letter essentially quoted paragraph 47(a) of the IRPA and s. 182 of its accompanying Regulations, and simply stated that the applicant was refused as he was not satisfied the applicant met those criteria. It was perfectly legitimate for the applicant to apply for restoration instead of judicial review of the initial decision to extend his study permit. While the immigration officer could take the extension decision into consideration, he also had to assess the applicant's new evidence in support of his claim that the initial decision was mistaken or did not reflect his true intentions. It is true that there is nothing in the IRPA requiring an immigration officer to provide reasons to an applicant. But it is well established that the duty of procedural fairness sometimes requires that explanations be given for a particular decision. In the present case, the mere recital of the relevant sections of the IRPA and the Regulations was clearly not sufficient. The applicant submitted further evidence that he was a *bona fide* student. He is certainly entitled to some explanation as to why these further documents were inadequate to show that he was a *bona fide* student. As a result of the negative restoration decision, the applicant was found to be inadmissible to Canada and the decision that he challenged before the Federal Court would have profound implications for him. The more important a decision is to the lives of those affected and the greater its impact on that person or those persons, the more stringent the procedural protections that will be mandated. Although a relatively low degree of procedural fairness is warranted in an immigration officer's decision to grant or deny an application to restore temporary resident status, a low level of procedural fairness still imposes some obligations on officers to provide reasons for negative decisions. The application for judicial review was granted.

*Patel v. Canada (Minister of Citizenship & Immigration)* (2006), 54 Imm. L.R. (3d) 180, 2006 CarswellNat 454, 2006 CarswellNat 2375, 2006 FC 224 (F.C.) — The applicant was aged 79 and a citizen of India. She had five children and 11 grandchildren living in

Canada, all of whom were Canadian citizens. Her husband was deceased and she had no more family living in India. She first came to Canada to attend the wedding of her granddaughter. Subsequently, her Canadian children decided they would sponsor her to stay in Canada as she would be alone in her mother country. She obtained three extensions of her status as a temporary resident. Her request for a fourth extension was denied after consideration of dual intent and determination that she was not a *bona fide* temporary resident. An application for restoration was denied.

The standard of review applicable to a decision refusing restoration of status is that of reasonableness *simpliciter*.

A permanent residence application does not necessarily preclude a temporary purpose for being in Canada. The current statutory and regulatory scheme does not say that a person's initial temporary purpose must remain constant and unchanged. The only requirement is the existence of a temporary purpose. The application for restoration of temporary status was not refused on the basis that the applicant would not be in Canada for a temporary purpose. On the contrary, it was denied because the applicant's stay in Canada would be for a "longer" temporary purpose, that is, while awaiting a decision on the application for permanent residence. The conclusion reached by the officer contained a reviewable error. The application was granted and the matter referred back to a different officer for redetermination.

*Radics v. Canada (Minister of Citizenship & Immigration)* (2004), 262 F.T.R. 211, 2004 CarswellNat 4093, 2004 FC 1590 (F.C.) — This is an application to review a decision refusing the applicant's request for the restoration of his status. The applicant entered as a visitor and was authorized to remain until December 18, 2003. On December 22, 2003, the applicant applied for a restoration of his temporary resident status. The applicant said that he had inadvertently failed to apply for an extension within the necessary time period.

Pursuant to s. 182, an immigration officer is required to restore an applicant's temporary resident status if he meets the initial requirements for a stay and if he has not failed to comply with any conditions imposed. Section 179 sets out the initial requirements for the issuance of a temporary visa. The applicant must have applied as either a visitor, worker or student and it must be established that the applicant will leave Canada by the end of his authorized stay. In determining whether an applicant will leave Canada, an officer will usually consider the applicant's purpose for wanting to be in Canada. The fact that an applicant applied to restore his visitor's status, and did not evade authorities, suggests that he is law abiding and that he will leave by the end of the period authorized. This fact was ignored by the officer. The officer's decision was set aside.

*Duong v. Canada (Minister of Citizenship & Immigration)*, 2003 CarswellNat 4029, 2003 CarswellNat 3066, 2003 FC 1131 (F.C.) — The applicant came to Canada pursuant to a Minister's permit issued under s. 37 of the former Act. The permit was valid for 6 months. The permit expired and relying on Regulation 182, the applicant applied for restoration. The applicant wants to remain in Canada because she is now married to a Canadian citizen and has submitted an H&C application.

The applicant was not a visitor, worker or student, she was a permit holder. The Minister's delegate was accordingly without jurisdiction to restore her temporary resident status.

*Stanislavsky v. Canada (Minister of Citizenship & Immigration)*, 2003 CarswellNat 1961, 2003 CarswellNat 2799, 237 F.T.R. 27, 2003 FCT 835 (T.D.) — The applicants sought judicial review of the decision of an Immigration counsellor denying the applicants' request for a restoration of their temporary resident status. The applicants who are married to each other are citizens of Ukraine. They entered Canada in July 2000 as visitors. They have two sons who are Canadian citizens and who live in Canada. In 2000, the purpose of their visit was to look after the mother of one of the applicants who was ill. The mother died in August 2001 leaving property in Canada to one of the applicants. In February 2002, their request for an extension of their visitor status was refused. They applied for a restoration of their visitor status and that was also refused. In May 2002, the applicants made an application for permanent residence sponsored by one of their sons. The Immigration counsellor refused to restore their temporary status and entered a note in the CAIPS notes advising that the immediate departure of the applicants should be effected.

A person seeking a temporary resident permit must have the intention of staying in Canada for a temporary purpose and the officer must be satisfied that such a person will leave Canada on the expiry of status. The officer did not refuse the application for restoration on the basis that the applicants were not in Canada for a temporary purpose. The officer denied the application because the applicants' stay would be for a "long temporary purpose", that is, while awaiting a decision on their application for permanent residence. The extended delay was attributed to the long processing time in Vegreville, Alberta, relative to inland sponsorship applications.

The fact that the applicants had submitted an inland sponsorship application was relevant to their intention to remain in Canada for a long temporary purpose. That is for the duration of the processing of their landing applications. This was a new and different temporary purpose from their original temporary purpose when they entered Canada in July 2000. The statutory and regulatory scheme does not say that a person's initial temporary purpose must remain constant and unchanged. The only requirement is the existence of a "temporary purpose." In the present case the officer did not address his mind to this question and this was a reversible error.



## DIVISION 2 — CONDITIONS ON TEMPORARY RESIDENTS

**183. (1) General conditions — Subject to section 185, the following conditions are imposed on all temporary residents:**

**(a) to leave Canada by the end of the period authorized for their stay;**

**(b) to not work, unless authorized by this Part or Part 11; and**

**Proposed Amendment — 183(1)(b)**

**(b) to not work, unless authorized by this Part or Part 11;**

SOR/2010-172, s. 1 [To come into force April 1, 2011.]

**Proposed Addition — 183(1)(b.1)**

**(b.1) if authorized to work by this Part or Part 11, to not enter into an employment agreement, or extend the term of an employment agreement, with an employer whose name appears on the list referred to in subsection 203(6) if a period of two years has not elapsed since the day on which the determination referred to in subsection 203(5) was made; and**

SOR/2010-172, s. 1 [To come into force April 1, 2011.]

**(c) to not study, unless authorized by this Part or Part 12.**

**(2) Authorized period of stay — Subject to subsections (3) to (5), the period authorized for the stay of a temporary resident is six months or any other period that is fixed by an officer on the basis of**

> **(a) the temporary resident's means of support in Canada;**
>
> **(b) the period for which the temporary resident applies to stay; and**
>
> **(c) the expiry of the temporary resident's passport or other travel document.**

**(3) Authorized period begins — The period authorized for the stay of a temporary resident begins on**

> **(a) if they are authorized to enter and remain in Canada on a temporary basis, the day on which they first enter Canada after they are so authorized; and**
>
> **(b) in any other case, the day on which they enter Canada.**

**(4) Authorized period ends — The period authorized for a temporary resident's stay ends on the earliest of**

> **(a) the day on which the temporary resident leaves Canada without obtaining prior authorization to re-enter Canada;**
>
> **(b) the day on which any work permit or study permit issued to the temporary resident expires;**
>
> **(c) the day on which any temporary resident permit issued to the temporary resident is no longer valid under section 63; or**
>
> **(d) the day on which the period authorized under subsection (2) ends, if paragraphs (a) to (c) do not apply.**

**(5) Extension of period authorized for stay — If a temporary resident has applied for an extension of the period authorized for their stay and a decision is not made on the application by the end of the period authorized for their stay, the period is extended until**

> **(a) the day on which a decision is made, if the application is refused; or**
>
> **(b) the end of the new period authorized for their stay, if the application is allowed.**

**(6) Continuation of status and conditions — If the period authorized for the stay of a temporary resident is extended by operation of paragraph (5)(a) or extended under paragraph (5)(b), the temporary resident retains their status, subject to any other conditions imposed, during the extended period.**

## Case Law

### Section 183(1)

*Editor's note: With respect to the issue of the intention to leave Canada by the end of the period authorized, see also case summaries under Regulation 200(1) and Regulation 216.*

*Boughus v. Canada (Minister of Citizenship & Immigration)*, 2010 FC 210, 2010 CarswellNat 2171, 2010 CarswellNat 404 (F.C.) — The applicant's application for a temporary resident visa was refused. The applicant originally came to Canada on his mother's application as a dependant and became a permanent resident in June, 1992. Despite his permanent residence status, the applicant continued his employment overseas. In September, 1996, an inquiry was held to determine if the applicant was still a permanent resident because of the amount of time he had spent outside Canada. The inquiry found that he was still a permanent resident because he maintained his intention to reside in Canada, as demonstrated by his applying for a returning resident permit. However, the applicant was found inadmissible to Canada upon his attempt to return in July, 1999. At the time, an officer wrote a report against the applicant indicating that he had not met the terms of his residency obligation. The applicant returned to Syria prior to an inquiry being held with regards to his status in Canada. The applicant's mother became sick in 2004 and he sought a temporary resident visa (TRV) to visit her in Canada. Between May, 2004 and April, 2009, the applicant applied for a TRV on five occasions and each application was refused. While making these applications, the applicant was unaware that he retained permanent resident status and, as a result, was ineligible for a TRV. In February, 2009, the applicant was made aware of the questionable status of his permanent residency. The applicant then signed a voluntary relinquishment of permanent resident status. The applicant was advised that he could reapply for a visitor's visa after signing a waiver of appeal with regard to his relinquishment of permanent resident status. The applicant's application for a TRV was refused because the officer was not satisfied that the applicant would leave Canada at the end of his stay.



Procedural fairness did not require an interview in this case.

There was nothing to suggest the officer failed to consider family reunification objectives in making the decision. It is the officer's job to weigh competing factors and reach conclusions based upon what he or she finds to be determinative of the issue in hand. The process does not involve a fettering of discretion. Although the Court concluded that a decision in the applicant's favour would have been reasonable, that in itself did not make the officer's decision unreasonable. The Court cannot interfere unless the decision falls outside the acceptable reasonable range enunciated in *Dunsmuir* (2008), 69 Imm. L.R. (3d) 1 (S.C.C.). Application for judicial review was dismissed.

*Murai v. Canada (Minister of Citizenship & Immigration)* (2006), 53 Imm. L.R. (3d) 218, 2006 CarswellNat 367, 2006 FC 186 (F.C.) — The applicant came to Canada without a visa as it was not required. Her application for an extension of time to remain in Canada was refused. Her subsequent application for refugee status was denied and her leave application for judicial review was refused. Her application to defer the removal order was denied. Her pre-removal risk assessment was denied and leave for judicial review was denied. Her humanitarian and compassionate leave application was denied and leave for judicial review was also denied. She left Canada. She then made an application for a work permit as a live-in caregiver. This application was denied as the visa officer was not satisfied that the applicant would leave Canada at the end of the authorized stay period per s. 183(1)(a) of the Regulations. The officer came to this conclusion on the basis of the applicant's previous immigration history.

The officer was entitled to satisfy himself that the applicant for the Live-In Caregiver Program had an intention of leaving Canada should the application for permanent residence be refused. In this case, however, the Court concluded that the officer's decision was unreasonable since the record revealed that the applicant was a law-abiding citizen, who after exhausting her remedies returned to her home country and subsequently applied under the Live-In Caregiver Program. In fact, the evidence of her previous immigration encounters supported the applicant's contention that she was law abiding and would continue to comply with the rules in the future.

The visa officer should have asked himself "will this person stay illegally in Canada if not successful under the program?" Based on the applicant's past performance, any reasonable person would say "no, she would not stay in Canada illegally."

*Boni c. Canada (Ministre de la Citoyenneté & de l'Immigration)*, [2005] F.C.J. No. 43, 2005 CarswellNat 176, 2005 CarswellNat 4646, 2005 FC 31 (F.C.); affirmed [2006] F.C.J. No. 275, 57 Imm. L.R. (3d) 4, 2006 CarswellNat 414, 2006 FCA 68 (C.A.) — The applicant applied for judicial review of a visa officer's decision to deny the applicant's application for a study permit. The risk that study permit applicants will not leave Canada once the period of their stay ends is a very important factor to be considered. An officer may examine the applicant's long-term objective. That objective is a relevant point which carries some weight, in view of the evidence as a whole on whether a study permit would be granted. A visa officer's conclusions will not be disturbed unless they are so unreasonable as to require the Court's intervention.

## Section 183(5)

*De Brito v. Canada (Minister of Citizenship & Immigration)* (2003), 33 Imm. L.R. (3d) 54, 242 F.T.R. 145, 2003 CarswellNat 3719, 2003 CarswellNat 4192, 2003 FC 1379 (F.C.) — The applicant entered Canada and obtained a temporary work authorization. His authorization was extended on two occasions and was to expire August 31, 2002. In March 2002, the applicant entered into a common-law relationship with a Canadian citizen. The applicant also attended courses in English as a second language which were less than 6 months in duration. In April 2002, the applicant ceased her employment in Canada and was accepted in a full-time 40 week ESL program at a community college. In July 2002, the applicant submitted an application for a student authorization to the Canadian Consulate in Buffalo. The applicant, in August 2002, applied for an extension of her temporary work authorization and for a change of terms and conditions through the Case Processing Centre in Vegreville. In September 2002, the applicant received a letter stating that her application for an extension of her temporary work authorization had been transferred to the respondent's offices in Mississauga. The applicant received no further correspondence from either Mississauga or Vegreville in connection with this application for a work authorization extension. In September 2002, the applicant also received a letter from Buffalo stating that she should attend an interview there on October 1, 2002. On October 1, 2002, when the applicant attempted to enter the United States she was refused entry. Upon her return to Canada the applicant advised the Canadian authorities at the port-of-entry that she had been refused entry into the United States and an immigration officer determined that her temporary authorization to remain in Canada was no longer valid because she had left Canada prior to receiving a decision on her extension request and had not obtained a re-entry visa. The applicant was found to be inadmissible and an exclusion order was issued.

The immigration officer erred in requiring the applicant to obtain a visa prior to re-entry due to the fact that the applicant falls under an exemption found in paragraph 190(3) of the Regulations. The applicant was seeking to enter the US solely for the purpose of attending an interview with the Canadian Consulate. She held a work permit that had been issued prior to departing Canada. The applicant had received no decision from the respondent regarding her application for an extension of her work authorization and pursuant to s. 183(5) of the Regulations retained her status until such a decision was made.

*Figueroa v. Canada (Minister of Citizenship & Immigration)*, 2003 CarswellNat 3657, 2003 CarswellNat 4507, 2003 FC 1339 (F.C.) — The applicant sought to review a decision of an immigration officer refusing the applicant's request for an extension of her temporary resident status.

The applicant is a citizen of Cuba. She met her husband, Mr. Cecil Stein, a Canadian citizen, when he was vacationing there. Mr. Stein continued to visit the applicant in Cuba after his holiday and eventually proposed to her. The applicant sought a Canadian visitor visa but was refused. Mr. Stein contacted his member of Parliament and eventually a Minister's permit was obtained for the applicant in the summer of 2002. This permit allowed the applicant temporary residence in Canada until September 30, 2002. On August 21, 2002, the applicant married Mr. Stein and on August 26, 2002, more than 30 days before the expiration of her temporary resident permit, the applicant sought an extension pending a final determination of her permanent resident application. The permanent resident application was filed in September 2002, the applicant applied as a Member of the Spouse In-Canada class. Her application was supported by Mr. Stein's sponsorship application. In December 2002, the applicant's request for an extension of her temporary resident status was refused.

The covering letter from the immigration officer indicated that she was attaching copies of the decision giving written reasons for the decision. However, it is clear that the decision did not include any written reasons.

The respondent took the position that the immigration officer acted in accordance with the instructions from the Minister. The record, however, was silent as to the content of those instructions. In the absence of any evidence as to those instructions, and without reasons, a question arose as to how the immigration officer followed the instructions. In those circumstances, the lack of reasons raised an appearance of arbitrariness on the part of the officer. Accordingly the officer's decision was set aside.



**184. (1) Condition imposed on members of a crew — A foreign national who enters Canada as a member of a crew must leave Canada within 72 hours after they cease to be a member of a crew.**

**(2) Conditions imposed on foreign nationals who enter to become members of a crew — The following conditions are imposed on a foreign national who enters Canada to become a member of a crew:**

**(a) [Repealed SOR/2004-167, s. 50(2).]**

**(b) to join the means of transportation within the period imposed as a condition of entry or, if no period is imposed, within 48 hours after they enter Canada; and**

**(c) to leave Canada within 72 hours after they cease to be a member of a crew.**

SOR/2004-167, s. 50(1), (2)

**185. Specific conditions — An officer may impose, vary or cancel the following specific conditions on a temporary resident:**

**(a) the period authorized for their stay;**

**(b) the work that they are permitted to engage in, or are prohibited from engaging in, in Canada, including**

**(i) the type of work,**

**(ii) the employer,**

**(iii) the location of the work,**

**(iv) the times and periods of the work, and**

**(v) in the case of a member of a crew, the period within which they must join the means of transportation;**

**(c) the studies that they are permitted to engage in, or are prohibited from engaging in, in Canada, including**

**(i) the type of studies or course,**

**(ii) the educational institution,**

**(iii) the location of the studies, and**

**(iv) the times and periods of the studies;**

**(d) the area within which they are permitted to travel or are prohibited from travelling in Canada; and**

**(e) the times and places at which they must report for**

**(i) medical examination, surveillance or treatment, or**

**(ii) the presentation of evidence of compliance with applicable conditions.**

## Case Law

*Patel v. Canada (Minister of Citizenship & Immigration)* (2006), 54 Imm. L.R. (3d) 180, 2006 CarswellNat 454, 2006 CarswellNat 2375, 2006 FC 224 (F.C.) — The applicant was aged 79 and a citizen of India. She had five children and 11 grandchildren living in Canada, all of whom were Canadian citizens. Her husband was deceased and she had no more family living in India. She first came to Canada to attend the wedding of her granddaughter. Subsequently, her Canadian children decided they would sponsor her to stay in Canada as she would be alone in her mother country. She obtained three extensions of her status as a temporary resident. Her request for a fourth extension was denied after consideration of dual intent and determination that she was not a *bona fide* temporary resident. An application for restoration was denied.

The standard of review applicable to a decision refusing restoration of status is that of reasonableness *simpliciter*.

A permanent residence application does not necessarily preclude a temporary purpose for being in Canada. The current statutory and regulatory scheme does not say that a person's initial temporary purpose must remain constant and unchanged. The only requirement is the existence of a temporary purpose. The application for restoration of temporary status was not refused on the basis that the applicant would not be in Canada for a temporary purpose. On the contrary, it was denied because the applicant's stay in Canada would be for a "longer" temporary purpose, that is, while awaiting a decision on the application for permanent residence. The conclusion reached by the officer contained a reviewable error. The application was granted and the matter referred back to a different officer for redetermination.

## Division 3 — Work Without A Permit

**186. No permit required** — A foreign national may work in Canada without a work permit

(a) as a business visitor to Canada within the meaning of section 187;

(b) as a foreign representative, if they are properly accredited by the Department of Foreign Affairs and International Trade and are in Canada to carry out official duties as a diplomatic agent, consular officer, representative or official of a country other than Canada, of the United Nations or any of its agencies or of any international organization of which Canada is a member;

(c) if the foreign national is a family member of a foreign representative in Canada who is accredited with diplomatic status by the Department of Foreign Affairs and International Trade and that Department has stated in writing that it does not object to the foreign national working in Canada;

(d) as a member of the armed forces of a country that is a designated state for the purposes of the *Visiting Forces Act*, including a person who has been designated as a civilian component of those armed forces;

(e) as an officer of a foreign government sent, under an exchange agreement between Canada and one or more countries, to take up duties with a federal or provincial agency;

(f) if they are a full-time student, on the campus of the university or college at which they are a full-time student, for the period for which they hold a study permit to study at that university or college;

(g) as a performing artist appearing alone or in a group in an artistic performance — other than a performance that is primarily for a film production or a television or radio broadcast — or as a member of the staff of such a performing artist or group who is integral to the artistic performance, if

(i) they are part of a foreign production or group, or are a guest artist in a Canadian production or group, performing a time-limited engagement, and

(ii) they are not in an employment relationship with the organization or business in Canada that is contracting for their services, nor performing in a bar, restaurant or similar establishment;

(h) as a participant in sports activities or events, in Canada, either as an individual participant or as a member of a foreign-based team or Canadian amateur team;

(i) as an employee of a foreign news company for the purpose of reporting on events in Canada;

(j) as a guest speaker for the sole purpose of making a speech or delivering a paper at a dinner, graduation, convention or similar function, or as a commercial speaker or seminar leader delivering a seminar that lasts no longer than five days;

(k) as a member of the executive of a committee that is organizing a convention or meeting in Canada or as a member of the administrative support staff of such a committee;

**(l) as a person who is responsible for assisting a congregation or group in the achievement of its spiritual goals and whose main duties are to preach doctrine, perform functions related to gatherings of the congregation or group or provide spiritual counselling;**

**(m) as a judge, referee or similar official at an international amateur sports competition, an international cultural or artistic event or competition or an animal or agricultural competition;**

**(n) as an examiner or evaluator of research proposals, academic projects or programs or university theses;**

**(o) as an expert who conducts surveys or analyses that are to be used as evidence before a federal or provincial regulatory body, a tribunal or a court of law or as an expert witness before such a body, tribunal or court of law;**

**(p) as a student in a health field, including as a medical elective or clinical clerk at a medical teaching institution in Canada, for the primary purpose of acquiring training, if they have written approval from the body that regulates that field;**

**(q) as a civil aviation inspector of a national aeronautical authority conducting inspections of the flight operation procedures or cabin safety of a commercial air carrier operating international flights;**

**(r) as an accredited representative or adviser participating in an aviation accident or incident investigation conducted under the *Canadian Transportation Accident Investigation and Safety Board Act*;**

**(s) as a member of a crew who is employed by a foreign company aboard a means of transportation that**

**(i) is foreign-owned and not registered in Canada, and**

**(ii) is engaged primarily in international transportation;**

**(t) as a provider of emergency services, including medical services, for the protection or preservation of life or property; or**

**(u) until a decision is made on an application made by them under subsection 201(1), if they have remained in Canada after the expiry of their work permit and they have continued to comply with the conditions set out on the expired work permit, other than the expiry date.**

## Case Law

### Section 186

*Singh v. Canada (Minister of Citizenship & Immigration)*, [2008] F.C.J. No. 65, 2008 CarswellNat 92, 2008 FC 58 (F.C.) — The applicant argued that the visa officer erred in finding that he did not have a work permit allowing him to work in Canada and refusing to award him any points for "arranged employment" or "adaptability". The applicant was a Sikh priest and an Indian citizen who came to Canada on a visitor's visa. His visa explicitly prohibited him from being employed while he was in Canada, but did allow him to perform religious duties in the country. The applicant contended that religious workers do not require a work permit to be allowed to work in Canada, and the fact that he did not have such a permit should not have precluded the consideration of his job offer.

The applicant's argument ignored the explicit condition contained in his visitor's visa that he was "prohibited from engaging in employment in Canada". In the face of this language, the visa cannot reasonably be interpreted as amounting to "a written authorization to work in Canada". There was no evidence that the applicant had complied with the application process required under Divisions 2 and 3 of the Regulations containing extensive provisions governing the granting of work permits. Finally, the applicant's offer of employment was never validated by Human Resources and Skills Development Canada. Consequently, there was no error in the visa officer's assessment.

*Singh v. Canada (Minister of Citizenship & Immigration)*, 2007 CarswellNat 142, 2007 FC 69 (F.C.) — The applicant first arrived in Canada on a visitor's visa, allowing him to temporarily perform religious duties. He subsequently applied for permanent residence as a skilled worker. The applicant fell short of the required 67 points.

The applicant was correct in noting that he was exempt from the requirement to obtain a work permit before coming to Canada to work as a Sikh priest as per subs. 186(l) of the Regulations. However, no further accommodations are made in the Regulations that would grant special privileges for workers that meet the requirements of s. 186 when applying for a permanent resident visa. Given the various scenarios considered under s. 82 of the Regulations to be awarded points for arranged employment, had such an exemption been contemplated by the Canadian Government, it could easily have been included in the Regulations. The applicant argued that no such accommodations were made because the occupations listed under s. 186 have already been determined to have a "neutral and positive affect on the labour market in Canada," as required to issue a work permit under s. 203 of the Regulations, and thus an exemption is implied from a joint reading of ss. 186, 203, and 82 of the Regulations. The Court dismissed this argument. The Court found it was clear on the face of the record that the applicant possessed neither a work permit nor an offer of employment validated by HRSDC, and that the decision of the visa officer not to grant the applicant any points for adaptability or arranged employment, and ultimately to refuse the application for permanent residence, was reasonable pursuant to the existing Regulations. Nevertheless, since it appeared at the time that the applicant submitted his application for permanent residence, that there was confusion at Citizenship and Immigration Canada concerning the proper awarding of points for arranged employment for priests, whose job offers were not validated by HRSDC as evidenced by the visa officer's affidavit and the email from a third party submitted by the applicant, this was sufficient to raise serious concerns that all individuals applying for permanent residence in Canada under circumstances similar to that of the applicant may not be treated alike, a situation contrary to the rules of procedural fairness. On this basis alone, the judicial review was granted.

The Court strongly encouraged the Minister of Citizenship and Immigration to clarify the guidelines concerning the allocation of points in permanent resident applications, for both arranged employment and adaptability, for individuals who are permitted to work in Canada without a work permit under s. 186, and who later seek to become permanent residents under the skilled worker class.

*Duraisami v. Canada (Minister of Citizenship & Immigration)*, 2005 CarswellNat 2005, 2005 CarswellNat 4421, 2005 FC 1008 (F.C.) — The applicant was denied an extension of his temporary resident permit on the grounds that he did not satisfy the requirements of the *Immigration and Refugee Protection Regulations*, s. 186(l), as a religious worker. The immigration officer had not been presented any information relating to his abilities to preach doctrine or any certificates indicating he was ordained or educated in any way to perform spiritual duties. The Court concluded that the officer's decision was reasonable as there was no evidence presented on the ability of the applicant to preach doctrine but instead there was only reference to the applicant's religious fervour which the Court concluded could not necessarily be equated to the ability to preach. Section 186(l) has to be given a meaning and application consistent with its purpose "to grant an exemption from work permits to those who have responsibility to assist a congregation or a group in achieving its spiritual goals." There are rational limitations based on the specific facts as to the scope of the provision. Not every person who assists at a place of worship (ushers, singers, teachers of children's religious studies) *per se*, falls within the scope of s. 186(l).

**187. (1) Business visitors — For the purposes of paragraph 186(a), a business visitor to Canada is a foreign national who is described in subsection (2) or who seeks to engage in international business activities in Canada without directly entering the Canadian labour market.**

**(2) Specific cases — The following foreign nationals are business visitors:**

**(a) foreign nationals purchasing Canadian goods or services for a foreign business or government, or receiving training or familiarization in respect of such goods or services;**

**(b) foreign nationals receiving or giving training within a Canadian parent or subsidiary of the corporation that employs them outside Canada, if any production of goods or services that results from the training is incidental; and**

**(c) foreign nationals representing a foreign business or government for the purpose of selling goods for that business or government, if the foreign national is not engaged in making sales to the general public in Canada.**

**(3) Factors — For the purpose of subsection (1), a foreign national seeks to engage in international business activities in Canada without directly entering the Canadian labour market only if**

**(a) the primary source of remuneration for the business activities is outside Canada; and**

**(b) the principal place of business and actual place of accrual of profits remain predominately outside Canada.**

## Division 4 — Study Without a Permit

**188. (1) No permit required — A foreign national may study in Canada without a study permit**

**(a) if they are a family member or a member of the private staff of a foreign representative who is properly accredited by the Department of Foreign Affairs and International Trade and who is in Canada to carry out official duties as a diplomatic agent, consular officer, representative or official of a country other than Canada, of the United Nations or any of its agencies or of any international organization of which Canada is a member;**

**(b) as a member of the armed forces of a country that is a designated state for the purposes of the *Visiting Forces Act*, including a person who has been designated as a civilian component of those armed forces; or**

(c) if the duration of their course or program of studies is six months or less and will be completed within the period for their stay authorized upon entry into Canada.

(2) **Exception** — Despite paragraph (1)(c), a foreign national may apply for a study permit before entering Canada for a course or program of studies of a duration of six months or less.

189. **Expired study permits** — A foreign national who has made an application under subsection 217(1) is authorized to study without a study permit until a decision is made on the application if they have remained in Canada since the expiry of their study permit and continue to comply with the conditions, other than the expiry date, set out on the expired study permit.



## DIVISION 5 — TEMPORARY RESIDENT VISA EXEMPTIONS

190. (1) **Visa exemption — nationality** — A foreign national does not require a temporary resident visa if they

(a) are a citizen of Andorra, Antigua and Barbuda, Australia, Austria, Bahamas, Barbados, Belgium, Botswana, Brunei Darussalam, Croatia, Cyprus, Denmark, Estonia, Finland, France, Federal Republic of Germany, Greece, Hungary, Iceland, Ireland, Italy, Japan, Republic of Korea, Latvia, Liechtenstein, Luxembourg, Malta, Monaco, Namibia, Netherlands, New Zealand, Norway, Papua New Guinea, Portugal, St. Kitts and Nevis, St. Lucia, St. Vincent, Samoa, San Marino, Singapore, Slovakia, Slovenia, Solomon Islands, Spain, Swaziland, Sweden or Switzerland;

(b) are

(i) a British citizen,

(ii) a British overseas citizen who is re-admissible to the United Kingdom, or

(iii) a citizen of a British overseas territory who derives that citizenship through birth, descent, naturalization or registration in one of the British overseas territories of Anguilla, Bermuda, British Virgin Islands, Cayman Islands, Falkland Islands, Gibraltar, Montserrat, Pitcairn Island, Saint Helena or Turks and Caicos Islands; or

(c) are a national of the United States or a person who has been lawfully admitted to the United States for permanent residence.

(2) **Visa exemption — documents** — A foreign national does not require a temporary resident visa if they

(a) hold a passport that contains a diplomatic acceptance, a consular acceptance or an official acceptance issued by the Chief of Protocol for the Department of Foreign Affairs and International Trade on behalf of the Government of Canada and are a properly accredited diplomat, consular officer, representative or official of a country other than Canada, of the United Nations or any of its agencies, or of any international organization of which Canada is a member;

**(b) hold a passport or travel document issued by the Holy See;**

**(c) hold a national Israeli passport;**

**(d) hold a Special Administrative Region passport issued by the Government of the Hong Kong Special Administrative Region of the People's Republic of China; or**

**(e) hold a British National (Overseas) Passport issued by the Government of the United Kingdom to persons born, naturalized or registered in Hong Kong.**

**(2.1) Visa exemption — nationality and documents — A foreign national who is a citizen of Lithuania or Poland does not require a temporary resident visa if they hold a machine readable passport that contains a contactless integrated circuit chip and that is issued by Lithuania or Poland, as the case may be.**

**(3) Visa exemption — purpose of entry — A foreign national does not require a temporary resident visa if they are seeking to enter and remain in Canada solely**

**(a) subject to an agreement between Canada and one or more foreign countries respecting the obligation to hold such a visa,**

**(i) as a member of a crew of a means of transportation other than a vessel or to become a member of a crew of a means of transportation other than a vessel, or**

**(ii) to transit through Canada after working, or to work, as a member of a crew of a means of transportation other than a vessel, if they possess a ticket for departure from Canada within 24 hours after their arrival in Canada;**

**(b) to transit through Canada as a passenger on a flight stopping in Canada for the sole purpose of refuelling and**

**(i) they are in possession of a visa to enter the United States and their flight is bound for that country, or**

**(ii) they were lawfully admitted to the United States and their flight originated in that country;**

**(c) to transit through Canada as a passenger on a flight if the foreign national**

**(i) is transported by a commercial transporter and there is a memorandum of understanding referred to in subsection (4) in effect between the Minister and the commercial transporter concerning the transit of passengers through Canada without a Canadian visa,**

**(ii) holds a passport or travel document that was issued by the country of which the foreign national is a citizen or national and that country is listed in the memorandum of understanding, and**

**(iii) is in possession of any visa required to enter the country of destination;**

**(d) to carry out official duties as a member of the armed forces of a country that is a designated state for the purposes of the *Visiting Forces Act*, unless they have been designated under that Act as a civilian component of those armed forces;**

**(e) to come to Canada from the United States for an interview with a United States consular officer concerning a United States immigrant visa, if they establish that they will be re-admitted to the United States;**

**(f) to re-enter Canada following a visit solely to the United States or St. Pierre and Miquelon, if they**

**(i) held a study permit or a work permit that was issued before they left Canada on such a visit or were authorized to enter and remain in Canada as a temporary resident, and**

**(ii) return to Canada by the end of the period initially authorized for their stay or any extension to it;**

**(g) to conduct inspections of the flight operation procedures or cabin safety of a commercial air carrier operating international flights, if they are a civil aviation inspector of a national aeronautical authority and possess valid documentation to that effect; or**

**(h) to participate as an accredited representative or as an adviser to an aviation accident or incident investigation conducted under the *Canadian Transportation Accident Investigation and Safety Board Act*, if they possess valid documentation to that effect.**

**(3.1) A foreign national who is a member of a crew and who is carried to Canada by a vessel does not require a temporary resident visa if they are seeking**

**(a) to enter Canada as a member of the crew of the vessel; and**

**(b) to remain in Canada solely as a member of the crew of that vessel or any other vessel.**

**(4) Content of memorandum of understanding — A memorandum of understanding referred to in paragraph (3)(c) shall include provisions respecting**

**(a) the countries to which the memorandum of understanding applies;**

**(b) the scheduled flights to which the memorandum of understanding applies; and**

**(c) the commercial transporter's obligation to control the movement of in-transit passengers.**

SOR/2002-326, s. 1; SOR/2002-332, s. 1; SOR/2003-197, s. 2; SOR/2003-260, s. 2; SOR/2004-111, s. 1; SOR/2004-167, s. 53; SOR/2006-228, s. 1; SOR/2007-238, s. 1; SOR/2008-54, s. 1; SOR/2008-308, s. 1; SOR/2009-105, s. 1; SOR/2009-207, s. 1; SOR/2009-208, s. 1

## Case Law

### Section 190(3)

*De Brito v. Canada (Minister of Citizenship & Immigration)* (2003), 33 Imm. L.R. (3d) 54, 242 F.T.R. 145, 2003 CarswellNat 3719, 2003 CarswellNat 4192, 2003 FC 1379 (F.C.) — The applicant entered Canada and obtained a temporary work authorization. His authorization was extended on two occasions and was to expire August 31, 2002. In March 2002, the applicant entered into a common-law relationship with a Canadian citizen. The applicant also attended courses in English as a second language which were less than six months in duration. In April 2002, the applicant ceased her employment in Canada and was accepted in a full-time 40-week ESL program at a community college. In July 2002, the applicant submitted an application for a student authorization to the Canadian Consulate in Buffalo. The applicant, in August 2002, applied for an extension of her temporary work authorization and for a change of terms and conditions through the case processing centre in Vegreville. In September 2002, the applicant received a letter stating that her application for an extension of her temporary work authorization had been transferred to the respondent's offices in Mississauga. The applicant received no further correspondence from either Mississauga or Vegreville in connection with this application for a work authorization extension. In September 2002, the applicant also received a letter from Buffalo stating that she should attend an interview there on October 1, 2002. On October 1, 2002, when the applicant attempted to enter the United States she was refused entry. Upon her return to Canada the applicant advised the Canadian authorities at the port-of-entry that she had been refused entry into the United States and an immigration officer determined that her temporary authorization to remain in Canada was no longer valid because she had left Canada prior to receiving a decision on her extension request and had not obtained a re-entry visa. The applicant was found to be inadmissible and an exclusion order was issued.

The immigration officer erred in requiring the applicant to obtain a visa prior to re-entry due to the fact that the applicant falls under an exemption found in paragraph 190(3) of the Regulations. The applicant was seeking to enter the U.S. solely for the purpose of attending an interview with the Canadian Consulate. She held a work permit that had been issued prior to departing Canada. The applicant had received no decision from the respondent regarding her application for an extension of her work authorization and pursuant to s. 183(5) of the Regulations retained her status until such a decision was made.

## PART 10 — VISITORS

**191. Class — The visitor class is prescribed as a class of persons who may become temporary residents.**

**192. Visitor — A foreign national is a visitor and a member of the visitor class if the foreign national has been authorized to enter and remain in Canada as a visitor.**

**193. Conditions — A visitor is subject to the conditions imposed under Part 9.**

## PART 10.1

[Heading repealed SOR/2008-309, s. 2.]

**193.1.–193.5. [Repealed SOR/2008-309, s. 2.]**

## PART 11 — WORKERS

### DIVISION 1 — GENERAL RULES

**194. Class — The worker class is prescribed as a class of persons who may become temporary residents.**

**195. Worker — A foreign national is a worker and a member of the worker class if the foreign national has been authorized to enter and remain in Canada as a worker.**

**196. Work permit required — A foreign national must not work in Canada unless authorized to do so by a work permit or these Regulations.**

## Case Law

*Brar v. Canada (Minister of Citizenship & Immigration)* (2006), 59 Imm. L.R. (3d) 293, 2006 CarswellNat 4324, 2006 FC 1502 (F.C.) — The applicants sought judicial review in respect of a decision by a member of the Immigration and Refugee Board of Canada given collectively, but pertaining to each of them, that determined that each of the applicants had contravened the terms of the work permit issued to each of them and therefore each was to be excluded from Canada. The applicants were all adult male citizens of India. They applied for and received temporary work permits. The work permit stated:

Employer: Bombay Paradise

Conditions:

- not authorized to work in any occupation other than stated;
- not authorized to work for any employer other than stated; and
- not authorized for work in any location other than stated.

When the applicants arrived in Calgary, they found that the Bombay Paradise Restaurant was under construction and far from being completed. The owner of that business was a numbered company run by a person known as Vic. He placed them in another establishment known as Bombay Sweet House & Restaurant. Apparently, the ownership was not the same as Bombay Paradise, although pay cheques issued to the applicants were from the numbered company which was the owner of the Bombay Paradise business.

It came to the Minister's attention that the applicants were working for an employer whom the Minister believed to be other than that named in the work permit. As a result, an exclusion order was issued. Following that order, an admissibility hearing was held on March 1, 2006. The issue of the hearing was whether each of the applicants was inadmissible under s. 41(a) of the IRPA, as having contravened s. 29(2) of that Act.

The Court concluded that Bombay Paradise paid the applicants and the applicants worked in Calgary, and therefore, no term as set out in the work permit had been breached. A work permit should be understandable to all interested persons, not just the worker or the government, on the face of it. The Minister has the resources to ensure that the permit is complete and understandable. If it is not, the Minister cannot be seen to rely on self-created ambiguities to derive a beneficial interpretation. It is the same concept as *contra proferentum* in the interpretation of a contract. If the contract was prepared by a party, any ambiguity must be interpreted against the interests of that party.

The applicants did not breach the terms of their work permits. Their employer, the person who pays them, was Bombay Paradise. They worked in Calgary. As a result, the exclusion order was set aside and the matter was returned to be determined by a different person.

## Division 2 — Application for Work Permit

**197. Application before entry — A foreign national may apply for a work permit at any time before entering Canada.**

### Case Law

*Villagonzalo v. Canada (Minister of Citizenship & Immigration)*, 2008 CarswellNat 4937, 2008 CarswellNat 3640, 2008 FC 1127 — This was an application for judicial review of a visa officer's decision that the applicant did not meet the requirements for a work permit. The applicant applied under the Live-In-Caregiver Program. The applicant argued that the officer failed to take into account that throughout her previous stay in Canada, the applicant undertook to maintain valid TRV status and promptly left when her request for an extension was refused. The applicant explained that she originally received a six-month TRV to come to Canada to attend her brother's wedding. Due to her child being sick, she was unable to attend the wedding. She did, however, come to Canada in November 2004 to visit her family. The applicant deposed that she told this to the visa officer at the time of her interview for a work permit. It appears that her failure to attend her brother's wedding and her failure to leave Canada between either May 17, 2005, or May 22, 2005 (the date she received the refusal to extend her status in Canada), and June 1, 2005, caused the visa officer to believe that the applicant in the future would not leave Canada by the end of any period authorized for her stay. The Court concluded that the visa officer's decision was not reasonable and that there should have been some consideration of the applicant's explanations. The application for judicial review was allowed.

*da Silva v. Canada (Minister of Citizenship & Immigration)* (2007), 68 Imm. L.R. (3d) 312, 2007 CarswellNat 4883, 2007 CarswellNat 5486, 2007 FC 1138 — The duty to provide reasons is lower in the context of applications for temporary residence status. A number of factors would suggest that the duty to provide reasons is minimal: the applicant has no legal right to obtain a visa, and bears the burden of establishing the merits of his claim; the refusal of a work permit on an application from outside of Canada has less impact on the applicant than would the removal of a benefit; and the officer is better placed to evaluate the cultural and economic benefits of the applicant's prospective employment than the applicant.

**198. (1) Application on entry — Subject to subsection (2), a foreign national may apply for a work permit when entering Canada if the foreign national is exempt under Division 5 of Part 9 from the requirement to obtain a temporary resident visa.**

**(2) Exceptions — A foreign national may not apply for a work permit when entering Canada if**

**(a) a determination under section 203 is required, unless**

**(i) the Department of Human Resources Development has provided an opinion under paragraph 203(2)(a) in respect of an offer of employment — other than seasonal agricultural employment or employment as a live-in caregiver — to the foreign national, or**

**Proposed Amendment — 198(2)(a)(i)**

**(i) the Department of Human Resources and Skills Development has provided an opinion under paragraph 203(2)(a) in respect of an offer of employment — other than seasonal agricultural employment or employment as a live-in caregiver — to the foreign national, or**

SOR/2010-172, s. 5(d) [To come into force April 1, 2011.]

**(ii) the foreign national is a national or permanent resident of the United States or is a resident of Greenland or St. Pierre and Miquelon;**

**(b) the foreign national does not hold a medical certificate that they are required to hold under subsection 30(4); or**

**(c) the foreign national is a participant in an international youth exchange program, unless they are a national or permanent resident of the United States or their application for a work permit was approved before their entry into Canada.**

SOR/2004-167, s. 54



**199. Application after entry — A foreign national may apply for a work permit after entering Canada if they**

**(a) hold a work permit;**

**(b) are working in Canada under the authority of section 186 and are not a business visitor within the meaning of section 187;**

**(c) hold a study permit;**

**(d) hold a temporary resident permit issued under subsection 24(1) of the Act that is valid for at least six months;**

**(e) are a family member of a person described in any of paragraphs (a) to (d);**

**(f) are in a situation described in section 206 or 207;**

**(g) applied for a work permit before entering Canada and the application was approved in writing but they have not been issued the permit;**

**(h) are applying as a trader or investor, intra-company transferee or professional, as described in Section B, C or D of Annex 1603 of the Agreement, within the meaning of subsection 2(1) of the *North American Free Trade Agreement Implementation Act*, and their country of citizenship — being a country party to that Agreement — grants to Canadian citizens who submit a similar application within that country treatment equivalent to that accorded by Canada to citizens of that country who submit an application within Canada, including treatment in respect of an authorization for multiple entries based on a single application; or**

**(i) hold a written statement from the Department of Foreign Affairs and International Trade stating that it has no objection to the foreign national working at a foreign mission in Canada.**

SOR/2004-167, s. 55

## Division 3 — Issuance of Work Permits

**200. (1) Work permits — Subject to subsections (2) and (3), an officer shall issue a work permit to a foreign national if, following an examination, it is established that**

**Proposed Amendment — 200(1) opening words**

**(1) Work permits — Subject to subsections (2) and (3) — and, in respect of a foreign national who makes an application for a work permit before entering Canada, subject to section 87.3 of the Act — an officer shall issue a work permit to a foreign national if, following an examination, it is established that**

SOR/2010-172, s. 2(1) [To come into force April 1, 2011.]

**(a) the foreign national applied for it in accordance with Division 2;**

**(b) the foreign national will leave Canada by the end of the period authorized for their stay under Division 2 of Part 9;**

**(c) the foreign national**

**(i) is described in section 206, 207 or 208,**

**(ii) intends to perform work described in section 204 or 205, or**

**Proposed Amendment — 200(1)(c)(ii)**

**(ii) intends to perform work described in section 204 or 205 but does not have an offer of employment to perform that work,**

SOR/2010-172, s. 2(2) [To come into force April 1, 2011.]

**Proposed Addition — 200(1)(c)(ii.1)**

**(ii.1) intends to perform work described in section 204 or 205, has an offer of employment to perform that work and an officer has determined**

**(A) that the offer is genuine under subsection (5), and**

**(B) that during the two-year period preceding the day on which the application for the work permit is received by the Department,**

**(I) the employer making the offer provided each foreign national employed by the employer with wages, working conditions and employment in an occupation that were substantially the same as the wages, working conditions and occupation set out in the employer's offer of employment to the foreign national, or**

**(II) in the case where the employer did not provide wages, working conditions or employment in an occupation that were substantially the same as those offered, the failure to do so was justified in accordance with subsection 203(1.1), or**

SOR/2010-172, s. 2(2) [To come into force April 1, 2011.]

**(iii) has been offered employment and an officer has determined under section 203 that the offer is genuine and that the employment is likely to result in a neutral or positive effect on the labour market in Canada; and**

**Proposed Amendment — 200(1)(c)(iii)**

(iii) has been offered employment, and an officer has made a positive determination under paragraphs 203(1)(a) to (e); and

SOR/2010-172, s. 2(2) [To come into force April 1, 2011.]

(d) [Repealed SOR/2004-167, s. 56(2).]

(e) the requirements of section 30 are met.

(2) **Non-application of par. (1)(b)** — Paragraph (1)(b) does not apply to a foreign national who satisfies the criteria set out in section 206 or paragraph 207(c) or (d).

(3) **Exceptions** — An officer shall not issue a work permit to a foreign national if

(a) there are reasonable grounds to believe that the foreign national is unable to perform the work sought;

(b) in the case of a foreign national who intends to work in the Province of Quebec and does not hold a *Certificat d'acceptation du Québec*, a determination under section 203 is required and the laws of that Province require that the foreign national hold a *Certificat d'acceptation du Québec*;

(c) the specific work that the foreign national intends to perform is likely to adversely affect the settlement of any labour dispute in progress or the employment of any person involved in the dispute, unless all or almost all of the workers involved in the labour dispute are not Canadian citizens or permanent residents and the hiring of workers to replace the workers involved in the labour dispute is not prohibited by the Canadian law applicable in the province where the workers involved in the labour dispute are employed;

(d) the foreign national seeks to enter Canada as a live-in caregiver and the foreign national does not meet the requirements of section 112; or

**Proposed Amendment — 200(3)(d)**

(d) the foreign national seeks to enter Canada as a live-in caregiver and the foreign national does not meet the requirements of section 112;

SOR/2010-172, s. 2(3) [To come into force April 1, 2011.]

(e) the foreign national has engaged in unauthorized study or work in Canada or has failed to comply with a condition of a previous permit or authorization unless

(i) a period of six months has elapsed since the cessation of the unauthorized work or study or failure to comply with a condition,

(ii) the study or work was unauthorized by reason only that the foreign national did not comply with conditions imposed under paragraph 185(a), any of subparagraphs 185(b)(i) to (iii) or paragraph 185(c),

(iii) section 206 applies to them, or

(iv) the foreign national was subsequently issued a temporary resident permit under subsection 24(1) of the Act.

**Proposed Addition — 200(3)(f)–(h)**

**(f) in the case of a foreign national referred to in subparagraphs (1)(c)(i) to (iii), the issuance of a work permit would be inconsistent with the terms of a federal-provincial agreement that apply to the employment of foreign nationals;**

**(g) the foreign national has worked in Canada for one or more periods totalling four years, unless**

**(i) a period of forty-eight months has elapsed since the day on which the foreign national accumulated four years of work in Canada,**

**(ii) the foreign national intends to perform work that would create or maintain significant social, cultural or economic benefits or opportunities for Canadian citizens or permanent residents, or**

**(iii) the foreign national intends to perform work pursuant to an international agreement between Canada and one or more countries, including an agreement concerning seasonal agricultural workers; or**

**(h) the foreign national intends to work for an employer whose name appears on the list referred to in subsection 203(6) and a period of two years has not elapsed since the day on which the determination referred to in subsection 203(5) was made.**

SOR/2010-172, s. 2(3) [To come into force April 1, 2011.]

**Proposed Addition — 200(4), (5)**

**(4) Cumulative work periods — students — A period of work in Canada by a foreign national shall not be included in the calculation of the four-year period referred to in paragraph (3)(g) if the work was performed during a period in which the foreign national was authorized to study on a full-time basis in Canada.**

**(5) Genuineness of job offer — A determination of whether an offer of employment is genuine shall be based on the following factors:**

**(a) whether the offer is made by an employer, other than an employer of a live-in caregiver, that is actively engaged in the business in respect of which the offer is made;**

**(b) whether the offer is consistent with the reasonable employment needs of the employer;**

**(c) whether the terms of the offer are terms that the employer is reasonably able to fulfil; and**

**(d) the past compliance of the employer, or any person who recruited the foreign national for the employer, with the federal or provincial laws that regulate employment, or the recruiting of employees, in the province in which it is intended that the foreign national work.**

SOR/2010-172, s. 2(4) [To come into force April 1, 2011.]

SOR/2004-167, s. 56

## Case Law

### Section 200(1)

*Editor's note: With respect to the issue of the intention to leave Canada by the end of the period authorized, see also case summaries under Regulation 183(1) and Regulation 216.*

*Singh v. Canada (Minister of Citizenship & Immigration)* (2009), 82 Imm. L.R. (3d) 205, 2009 FC 621, 2009 CarswellNat 1820, 2009 CarswellNat 5881, [2009] F.C.J. No. 798 (F.C.) — The applicant, a native of Punjab province in India, is the 26-year old brother-in-law of the principal owner of the Mahek Restaurant and Lounge in Surrey, British Columbia, his prospective Canadian employer. The applicant was offered a position as a food preparer for a two-year term in connection with a positive Labour Market Opinion (LMO) issued by Service Canada valid through September 4, 2010. This was the applicant's third failed application for a work permit for employment with Mahek Restaurant. Two previous applications were refused because of a visa officer's concerns that the applicant would not be able to perform the work of cook described in the relevant LMO, and because he was "unable to adequately clarify inconsistencies raised in [the] application" and failed to satisfy the visa officer that "his stated reasons for visiting Canada were genuine." The most recent work permit application was for a position as a food preparer and not for cook, as in the two previous applications.

The visa officer seems to have made much of the fact that the applicant had made previous work permit applications in connections with job offers from the same employer, and that this employer is his brother-in-law. There are two potential problems with this: firstly, there is no obvious justification for treating work permit applications like credit card applications, where one's credibility diminishes with every application made; and second, the visa officer's suspicion concerning the "modification" of the LMO was entirely speculative. It is fully possible, and indeed likely, that the employer was in need of both cooks and food preparers. It is not as if the two occupations are unrelated. And it is hardly surprising that a Canadian business in need of workers from India would look to family members living there. There is no obvious connection between the fact that the applicant is being offered a job by a relative and whether he is likely to return to India and the officer fails to explain why she thought this was a relevant fact.

While the officer is entitled to substantial deference in reaching her opinion, when these concerns were examined, the Court found the decision reached did not fall within a range of possible, acceptable outcomes which were defensible in respect of the facts and the law, as set out by the Supreme Court in *Dunsmuir v. New Brunswick* (2008), 69 Imm. L.R. (3d) 1. The Court concluded that the same result may not have been reached had the officer not placed weight on the applicant's history of previous work permits and the fact that the employer was a relative. The application for judicial review was allowed.

*Baylon v. Canada (Minister of Citizenship & Immigration)* (2009), 84 Imm. L.R. (3d) 24, 2009 FC 938, 2009 CarswellNat 2914, 2009 CarswellNat 4471, [2009] F.C.J. No. 1147 (F.C.) — The applicants are young citizens of the Philippines, part of a group of approximately 40 persons who applied for a temporary resident visa in order to come and work at a fish processing plant in Richmond, B.C. The applications were refused because they did not convince the visa officers that they would leave Canada at the end of their visas' terms. They then sought judicial review of the officers' decisions.

In her affidavit, the visa officer states that leaving family behind is not a strong incentive to return to the Philippines, as "it is not uncommon in the Philippines for one or both



IRP Regulations

parents to work overseas for long periods of time, sometimes totaling several years." She added that "in fact, over a million Filipinos every year reside and work abroad, most of them in low-skilled occupations. Separation from close family members due to overseas work is accepted and common place." The Court found this extraneous evidence to be unsupported and undocumented, and in any event irrelevant. The Court accepted that the local conditions in the applicant's home country can be part of the broader picture which the visa officer ought to consider in assessing whether an applicant will leave Canada at the end of the period authorized for any temporary stay. But the mere fact that many low-skilled workers from the Philippines work overseas does not, in and of itself, mean that they overstay their authorized work permit, let alone that they live illegally in other countries. Oversimplified generalizations cannot, and should not, form the basis of what must always be an individualized assessment based on the particular circumstances of each individual. The applications for judicial review were granted in two of the five cases and dismissed in the balance.

*Thomas v. Canada (Minister of Citizenship & Immigration)* (2009), 85 Imm. L.R. (3d) 133, 2009 FC 1038, 2009 CarswellNat 5014, 2009 CarswellNat 3190 (F.C.) — This was an application for judicial review of a decision of a visa officer who determined that the applicant had not satisfied the requirements for obtaining a temporary work permit on the grounds that the applicant had not shown that he was well established in India and that he had not shown that he would return to India at the end of his authorized period of stay given there were better work conditions and high economic incentives to remain in Canada.

The burden rests on the applicant to provide sufficient information for a visa officer to make a determination that the requirements of the program have been met. Fairness does not require that the officer provide the applicant with an interview to address questions that might arise from the materials submitted. The officer is entitled to proceed to a determination upon considering the application as it was presented. However, to arrive at a determination of insufficient establishment in India that would fall within the range of acceptable and defensible outcomes, it was necessary for the visa officer to consider and analyze the relevant evidence on that question. In this case, the visa officer's failure to consider the applicant's property, holdings and valuations leads to the inference that the visa officer made an erroneous finding of fact without regard to the evidence. It was also difficult to understand why the officer concluded that the applicant would require moderate English language skills to perform the job duties when it was not identified as a requirement in the employment contract. Moreover, the record indicated that he had taken two secondary school courses in English, yet the decision did not explain why the officer thought that this was insufficient. The reasoning process was flawed and the resulting decision fell outside the range of possible, acceptable outcomes. The process adopted by the visa officer and its outcome did not resonate with the principles of justification, transparency, and intelligibility. The application for judicial review was allowed.

*Dhanoa v. Canada (Minister of Citizenship & Immigration)*, 2009 FC 729, 2009 CarswellNat 2159, 2009 CarswellNat 4903 (F.C.) — The application for a temporary resident visa work permit was refused on the grounds that the applicant had failed to satisfy the visa officer that he would leave Canada at the end of the authorized period.

The officer's notes read: "PA has no previous travel. As per info in application form his current income in India is low. Is working as a farmer in India. I note that proposed employment in Canada is unrelated to PA's work experience. Given PA's greater earning power in Canada versus India, combined with better living and working conditions in

Canada, I find that PA would have a strong socio-economic incentive to stay in Canada by any means after the end of his authorized stay. I am cognizant that PA has a wife and kids in India. However, on a balance of probabilities, I am not satisfied that PA would not bear the hardship of being separated from his family in order to take advantage of better socio-economic opportunities in Canada. Not satisfied PA meets requirements of R200(1)(b)."

The lack of previous travel can only at most be a neutral factor. If one had traveled and always returned, the visa officer's concern might be lessened. If one came to Canada, claimed refugee status and was not permitted to stay here on humanitarian and compassionate grounds, an application for a temporary work permit would obviously heighten suspicions. The remark that the employment is unrelated to the applicant's work experience as a farmer did not serve as an indication that he was unable to do the job, as that box was not checked off in the decision form. It was not apparent as to how this would be indicative of his intention not to do the job and not to leave Canada at the end of his employment. The references to greater earning power in Canada and better living and working conditions are somewhat sterile as no analysis was done of his living conditions in India, whether his declared intention to purchase a farm was feasible, and what his standard of living would be in India compared to Canada after he earned some money here. Indeed, the very basis of the pilot project is these workers will only come here if they are going to be paid more than in their home country.

The thought that he would abandon his wife and children in order to take advantage of better socio-economic opportunities here is distasteful. It was "sanctimonious" to suggest that our society is more of a draw for him than India, where he would be in the bosom of his family, simply because he would have 30 pieces of silver in his pocket.

The decision was unreasonable not simply because it was stereotypical, but also because it relied on the very factor which would induce someone to come here temporarily in the first place as a main reason for keeping that person out. The application for judicial review was granted.

*Calma v. Canada (Minister of Citizenship & Immigration)* (2009), 83 Imm. L.R. (3d) 135, 2009 FC 742, 2009 CarswellNat 4152, 2009 CarswellNat 2484 (F.C.) — The applicant sought judicial review of a refusal of his application for a work permit. The officer concluded that the applicant had not satisfied him that he would leave Canada by the end of the period authorized for his stay because he "had not demonstrated ties that would satisfy the officer of the applicant's intention to return."

The assessment of an application for a work permit involves an exercise of statutory discretion and attracts a high degree of deference from the Court. Apart from the procedural fairness issues raised, the applicable standard of review in this case is reasonableness.

There was no evidence before the officer to support either conclusion that the applicant had weak economic ties in the Philippines and that he was not sufficiently well established to ensure his return. The applicant was born in the Philippines, had always lived there, had a wife and four children there, and he had been employed in the same job for 10 years that he could go back to. It was difficult to see how anyone could be more established than this, or why this meant he had weak economic ties. The officer's decision could not be reconciled with the evidence presented by the applicant. The evidence was either entirely overlooked or the decision was unreasonable. The application for judicial review was allowed.

*Baylon v. Canada (Minister of Citizenship & Immigration)*, 2009 FC 743, 2009 CarswellNat 4153, 2009 CarswellNat 2505 (F.C.) — The applicant applied for judicial review of a visa officer's decision refusing his application for a work permit. The officer concluded that the applicant had not satisfied him that he would leave Canada by the end of the period authorized for his stay because he "h[ad] not demonstrated ties that would satisfy [the officer] of [the applicant's] intention to return." The applicant said that he should have had an opportunity to provide an explanation for perceived or apparent deficiencies and respond to the officer's concerns. In the present case, however, the officer was not concerned with deficiencies. He assessed the application materials and exercised his discretion as required by statute. If an officer is not convinced that an applicant will leave Canada at the end of the authorized stay, there is no obligation to interview the applicant and provide an opportunity for the applicant to try and dissuade the officer from that conclusion. The onus was on the applicant to provide all the information necessary for the decision and to convince the officer that he was a visitor and not an immigrant. The application for judicial review was dismissed.

*Minhas v. Canada (Minister of Citizenship & Immigration)* (2009), 82 Imm. L.R. (3d) 210, 2009 FC 696, 2009 CarswellNat 2148, 2009 CarswellNat 5682, [2009] F.C.J. No. 867 (F.C.) — This was an application for judicial review of a decision to refuse an application for a work permit. The only reference to English language skills before the officer was the applicant's own affidavit in which he attested that his intended employer informed him that knowledge of the English language was not necessary to the job, and that the applicant could perform the job without English language skills. There was no evidence before the officer addressing the applicant's level of English language ability; thus it was not reasonable to conclude, based on his English language ability, that he could not perform the work of a construction helper.

While higher salary in Canada is alluded to with the remark "high economic incentive," no consideration was given to the difference in cost of living and living standard between Canada and India. The differences in salary between India and Canada may indicate incentive to stay only when the cost of living is also considered. The standard of living in the home country is also important to determining where the applicant may be better off. While economic incentive to stay in Canada is a reasonable consideration on the part of the officer, the majority of applicants would have some economic incentive to come work in Canada, and this incentive therefore cannot so easily correlate with overstays since it is inconsistent with the work permit scheme. The officer failed to make a serious attempt at evaluating establishment and ties given the evidence before him. The decision was unreasonable. The application for judicial review was allowed.

*Rengasamy v. Canada (Minister of Citizenship & Immigration)* (2009), 86 Imm. L.R. (3d) 106, 2009 FC 1229, 2009 CarswellNat 5505, 2009 CarswellNat 4073 (F.C.) — Persons who apply for temporary work permits in Canada are doing so because they can earn more money here than at home. In that sense, anyone who seeks or is granted a temporary work permit will have a financial incentive to stay in Canada beyond the specified term. Accordingly, a financial incentive to remain in Canada cannot, on its own, justify refusing an application. Otherwise no application could succeed. Here, the applicants submitted evidence of their significant family connections in India where each has a parent, spouse and young children. They only have one distant cousin in Canada. Two officers reviewed the applicant's materials. The Minister suggested that the applicants could have supplemented their applications by giving more information about the quality of their family relationships. The officer stated that the applicants had the burden of proving that the personal hardship of being separated from their families indefinitely would outweigh the financial benefits of remaining in Canada. In other words, they had to show that their families meant more to them than $10.43 an hour. The officer misstated the onus on the applicants and by doing so caused the officers to discount, unreasonably, the significance of the applicants' family ties in India and, therefore, the evidence supporting their undertakings to return to India when their permits expire. As a result, the officers' decision was unreasonable. The application for judicial review was allowed.

*Li v. Canada (Minister of Citizenship & Immigration)*, [2008] F.C.J. No. 1625, 76 Imm. L.R. (3d) 265, 337 F.T.R. 100 (Eng.), 2008 CarswellNat 4261, 2008 CarswellNat 5159, 2008 FC 1284 (F.C.) — Service Canada issued a positive Labour Market Opinion ("LMO") and validated the offer of employment. The applicant then applied to the Canadian Consulate in Shanghai, China for a two-year work permit. Obtaining a positive LMO is one of the requirements for a work permit. The visa officer denied the application because he was not satisfied that the applicant will leave Canada upon the expiry of the work permit.

The visa officer made no serious attempt to determine the strength of the ties of the applicant to China. According to the Act, the burden of proof rests on the applicant, who has attempted to discharge the duty by providing information on his family in China, as well as employment and education information. The officer did not sufficiently take into account the fact that the applicant's family ties to China were strong, since he had no family members elsewhere than there. On this basis, the refusal of the visa was based on an erroneous finding of fact, which did not take into account the material evidence which was presented.

The applicant also had no way of knowing that the officer would rely on the applicant's higher salary in Canada, the fact that he often changed jobs in China, the fact that his employment history was difficult to obtain or that he apparently had limited family ties in PRC. In this case, an interview would have been appropriate for the applicant to explain the extent of his family ties in China. He would have been able to communicate the information which is provided in his further affidavit. The Court found the visa officer's failure to give the applicant an opportunity to respond to his concerns, on the facts of this case, amounted to a breach of the rules of natural justice. Application for judicial review was allowed.

*Vairea v. Canada (Minister of Citizenship & Immigration)*, 2006 CarswellNat 3305, 2006 FC 1238 (F.C.) — This is an application for judicial review of the decision of a visa officer to dismiss the applicant's application for a work permit in Canada. The applicant received an offer of employment to work in Canada as a cement finisher. A positive labour market opinion was obtained. The visa officer was not satisfied that the applicant had a genuine offer of employment or was able to perform the work sought. The visa officer reviewed the notes on file including the electronic correspondence from the HRSDC officer, who expressed his concerns regarding the applicant's prospective employer on the basis of a published newspaper article that mentioned that a group of overseas Filipino workers in Toronto had filed a complaint of recruitment fraud against a Toronto-based employment agency and its owner-operator. The visa officer was concerned that the applicant did not know much about his prospective employer. This was supported by the fact that the applicant had never spoken directly to his prospective employer and that his friend had found the ad through the internet. The visa officer's conclusions in this regard were not patently unreasonable. The visa officer's concerns with respect to the ability of the applicant to perform the work sought were not unreasonable.

The visa officer was entitled to find that the applicant's answers with regard to his work experience were unsatisfactory.

*Nguyen c. Canada (Ministre de la Citoyenneté & de l'Immigration)*, 2005 CarswellNat 2305, 2005 CarswellNat 5511, 2005 FC 1087 (F.C.) — The applicant applied for judicial review of a decision by a visa officer denying the applicant's application for a permit to work in Canada. The visa officer determined that the applicant had not satisfied him he would leave Canada at the end of his authorized stay and determined that he was trying to live in Canada permanently. It was the applicant's responsibility to establish that he was not inadmissible and that he meets the requirements of the IRPA. Specifically, he must establish that he will leave Canada at the end of his stay as provided under paragraph 200(1)(b) of the Regulations.

The visa officer took into account the assets of the applicant held in Vietnam. The officer was of the opinion that because the applicant had left his business for nine months and decided to remain in Canada, there was no strong connection that would force him to return to Vietnam. This was evidence tending to establish the absence of a significant connection with that country. Further, the applicant expressed a desire to remain in Canada with his children, which showed a strong connection with Canada. It was therefore not unreasonable for the visa officer to determine that the applicant had not persuaded him he had strong ties with his native country and that he would leave Canada at the end of his stay.

## Section 200(3)

*Duroseau v. Canada (Minister of Citizenship & Immigration)*, 2008 CarswellNat 130, 2008 CarswellNat 957, 2008 FC 72 — The officer refused to issue a work permit for two reasons:

> (1) She referred to the prohibition against issuing a work permit under subparagraph 200(3)(e)(i) to persons having engaged in unauthorized work in Canada in the past six months. The officer believed that the applicant had engaged in such work since her arrival in Canada by helping Ms. Darius with her children.
>
> (2) The officer determined that the applicant did not meet the requirements of s. 112 of the Regulations because the employment contract was not genuine and constituted an offer of convenience aimed at facilitating the applicant's acquisition of status in Canada.

The definition of "work" set forth in the Regulations does not require compensation to have been received in order for an activity to be considered work. The activity merely has to be "in direct competition with the activities of Canadian citizens or permanent residents in the Canadian labour market". Child care meets the definition of work. The friendship between the applicant and the employer was just one fact among many justifying the officer's doubts as to the *bona fide* character of the contract. The fact that the applicant lived in Ms. Darius' home prior to submitting her application, the length of time before she submitted it, and the fact that the applicant was engaged in child-care activity all provided sufficient support for the officer's decision.

*Randhawa v. Canada (Minister of Citizenship & Immigration)* (2006), 57 Imm. L.R. (3d) 99, 2006 CarswellNat 3481, 2006 FC 1294 (F.C.) — This is an application for judicial review of a decision of a visa officer that refused the applicant's application for a work permit. The applicant was an assistant cook specializing in North Indian cuisine. The visa officer questioned the applicant about food hygiene and decided he was not qualified to perform the cook's job he was offered in Toronto. HRSDC confirmed the job offer and provided a positive Labour Market Opinion.

The Court concluded that the visa officer was not an expert on food hygiene, yet the visa officer "grilled" the applicant. The Court concludes that the intense questioning of the applicant by the visa officer on his ability to "maintain high standards of hygiene and sanitation" was an unreasonable basis to form the conclusion that there were reasonable grounds to believe that the applicant is unable to perform the assistant cook job offered to him in Toronto. There was nothing in the evidence to indicate that the visa officer obtained objective standards against which to assess the applicant's level of fitness. In fact, the only objective measure of fitness was the completion of the food hygiene training course that the applicant had completed at the visa officer's request. The visa officer also refused to consider the training that the applicant would receive in the course of his employment in Toronto. While it is reasonable to require that an applicant satisfy the job requirements of a particular position before obtaining a work permit, it is unreasonable not to take into account some measure of job orientation that would inevitably be provided to the applicant. The application for judicial review was allowed.

*Vairea v. Canada (Minister of Citizenship & Immigration)*, 2006 CarswellNat 3305, 2006 FC 1238 (F.C.) — This is an application for judicial review of the decision of a visa officer to dismiss the applicant's application for a work permit in Canada. The applicant received an offer of employment to work in Canada as a cement finisher. A positive labour market opinion was obtained. The visa officer was not satisfied that the applicant had a genuine offer of employment or was able to perform the work sought. The visa officer reviewed the notes on file including the electronic correspondence from the HRSDC officer, who expressed his concerns regarding the applicant's prospective employer on the basis of a published newspaper article that mentioned that a group of overseas Filipino workers in Toronto had filed a complaint of recruitment fraud against a Toronto-based employment agency and its owner-operator. The visa officer was concerned that the applicant did not know much about his prospective employer. This was supported by the fact that the applicant had never spoken directly to his prospective employer and that his friend had found the ad through the internet. The visa officer's conclusions in this regard were not patently unreasonable. The visa officer's concerns with respect to the ability of the applicant to perform the work sought were not unreasonable. The visa officer was entitled to find that the applicant's answers with regard to his work experience were unsatisfactory.

*Chen v. Canada (Minister of Citizenship & Immigration)*, 2005 CarswellNat 4950, 2005 CarswellNat 3219, 2005 FC 1378 (F.C.) — The applicant was a Chinese national and had applied for a temporary work permit. He only spoke Chinese and had been offered a position as a warehouse manager for a Chinese luxury food company that was owned and operated by his nephew. The visa officer refused to issue a work permit on the basis that the applicant had not satisfied the officer that he would leave Canada by the end of the period authorized for the stay and he had not satisfied the officer that he had qualifications and experience for the employment for which the work permit was sought.

The visa officer's notes indicated that he was of the view that Human Resource Development of Canada (HRDC) had imposed an English knowledge requirement on the position and that was included as one of the reasons for rejecting the application for the work permit. The visa officer was under a duty to examine all the relevant evidence before him in order to come to an independent assessment of whether there are reasonable grounds to believe the applicant is unable to perform the work. The officer could not be bound by a

IRP Regulations

statement by HRDC that English is or is not required and he cannot delegate his decision making to a third party such as HRDC. Conversely, a statement by an applicant or employer that English is not required cannot be binding on the officer. Instead, the officer must carry out his own evaluation based on a weighing of all of the evidence before him.

In this case, the visa officer did not simply state that English was a requirement imposed by HRDC. Rather, the visa officer explains in his notes that he cannot foresee how the applicant would train his replacement, as required to do as part of his duties. Since the visa officer viewed the ability to communicate in English as relevant to his assessment as to whether the applicant would be able to perform his duties, the officer's findings were considered to be logical and were not based upon irrelevant considerations. The officer's decision was upheld even though he may have erred by stating that English was a HRDC requirement and even relied to some extent on this error, because the officer also considered the need for English independently of the HRDC validation.

**201. (1) Application for renewal — A foreign national may apply for the renewal of their work permit if**

**(a) the application is made before their work permit expires; and**

**(b) they have complied with all conditions imposed on their entry into Canada.**

**(2) Renewal — An officer shall renew the foreign national's work permit if, following an examination, it is established that the foreign national continues to meet the requirements of subsection 200(1).**

**Proposed Amendment — 201(2)**

**(2) Renewal — An officer shall renew the foreign national's work permit if, following an examination, it is established that the foreign national continues to meet the requirements of section 200.**

SOR/2010-172, s. 3 [To come into force April 1, 2011.]

**202. Temporary resident status — A foreign national who is issued a work permit under section 206 or paragraph 207(c) or (d) does not, by reason only of being issued a work permit, become a temporary resident.**

**203. (1) Effect on the labour market — On application under Division 2 for a work permit made by a foreign national other than a foreign national referred to in subparagraphs 200(1)(c)(i) and (ii), an officer shall determine, on the basis of an opinion provided by the Department of Human Resources Development, if the job offer is genuine and if the employment of the foreign national is likely to have a neutral or positive effect on the labour market in Canada.**

**Proposed Amendment — 203(1)**

**(1) Assessment of employment offered — On application under Division 2 for a work permit made by a foreign national other than a foreign national referred to in subparagraphs 200(1)(c)(i) to (ii.1), an officer shall determine, on the basis of an opinion provided by the Department of Human Resources and Skills Development, if**

**(a) the job offer is genuine under subsection 200(5);**

**(b) the employment of the foreign national is likely to have a neutral or positive effect on the labour market in Canada;**

**(c) the issuance of a work permit would not be inconsistent with the terms of any federal-provincial agreement that apply to the employers of foreign nationals;**

**(d) in the case of a foreign national who seeks to enter Canada as a live-in caregiver,**

**(i) the foreign national will reside in a private household in Canada and provide child care, senior home support care or care of a disabled person in that household without supervision,**

**(ii) the employer will provide adequate furnished and private accommodations in the household, and**

**(iii) the employer has sufficient financial resources to pay the foreign national the wages that are offered to the foreign national; and**

**(e) during the period beginning two years before the day on which the request for an opinion under subsection (2) is received by the Department of Human Resources and Skills Development and ending on the day on which the application for the work permit is received by the Department,**

**(i) the employer making the offer provided each foreign national employed by the employer with wages, working conditions and employment in an occupation that were substantially the same as the wages, working conditions and occupation set out in the employer's offer of employment, or**

**(ii) in the case where the employer did not provide wages, working conditions or employment in an occupation that were substantially the same as those offered, the failure to do so was justified in accordance with subsection (1.1).**

SOR/2010-172, s. 4(1) [To come into force April 1, 2011.]

**Proposed Addition — 203(1.1)**

**(1.1) Justification — A failure referred to in subparagraph (1)(e)(ii) is justified if it resulted from**

**(a) a change in federal or provincial law;**

**(b) a change to the provisions of a collective agreement;**

**(c) the implementation of measures by the employer in response to a dramatic change in economic conditions that directly affected the business of the employer, provided that the measures were not directed disproportionately at foreign nationals employed by the employer;**

**(d) an error in interpretation made in good faith by the employer with respect to its obligations to a foreign national, if the employer subsequently provided compensation — or if it was not possible to provide compensation, made sufficient efforts to do so — to all foreign nationals who suffered a disadvantage as a result of the error;**

**(e) an unintentional accounting or administrative error made by the employer, if the employer subsequently provided compensation — or if it was**



IRP Regulations

**not possible to provide compensation, made sufficient efforts to do so — to all foreign nationals who suffered a disadvantage as a result of the error; or**

**(f) circumstances similar to those set out in paragraphs (a) to (e).**

SOR/2010-172, s. 4(1) [To come into force April 1, 2011.]

**(2) Opinion on request — The Department of Human Resources Development shall provide the opinion referred to in subsection (1) on the request of an officer or an employer or group of employers. A request may be made in respect of**

**Proposed Amendment — 203(2) opening words**

**(2) Opinion on request — The Department of Human Resources and Skills Development shall provide the opinion referred to in subsection (1) on the request of an officer or an employer or group of employers, other than an employer whose name appears on the list referred to in subsection 203(6), if a period of two years has not elapsed since the day on which the determination referred to in subsection 203(5) was made. A request may be made in respect of**

SOR/2010-172, s. 4(2) [To come into force April 1, 2011.]

**(a) an offer of employment to a foreign national; and**

**(b) offers of employment made, or anticipated to be made, by an employer or group of employers.**

**Proposed Addition — 203(2.1)**

**(2.1) Subject matter of opinion — An opinion provided by the Department of Human Resources and Skills Development shall consider the matters set out paragraphs (1)(a) to (e) but, for the purposes of this subsection, the period referred to in paragraph 1(e) shall be considered to end on the day that the request for the opinion is received by the Department of Human Resources and Skills Development.**

SOR/2010-172, s. 4(3) [To come into force April 1, 2011.]

**(3) Factors — An opinion provided by the Department of Human Resources Development shall be based on the following factors:**

**Proposed Amendment — 203(3) opening words**

**(3) Factors re effect on labour market — An opinion provided by the Department of Human Resources and Skills Development with respect to the matters referred to in paragraph (1)(b) shall be based on the following factors:**

SOR/2010-172, s. 4(4) [To come into force April 1, 2011.]

**(a) whether the employment of the foreign national is likely to result in direct job creation or job retention for Canadian citizens or permanent residents;**

**(b) whether the employment of the foreign national is likely to result in the creation or transfer of skills and knowledge for the benefit of Canadian citizens or permanent residents;**

**(c) whether the employment of the foreign national is likely to fill a labour shortage;**

(d) whether the wages offered to the foreign national are consistent with the prevailing wage rate for the occupation and whether the working conditions meet generally accepted Canadian standards;

(e) whether the employer has made, or has agreed to make, reasonable efforts to hire or train Canadian citizens or permanent residents; and

(f) whether the employment of the foreign national is likely to adversely affect the settlement of any labour dispute in progress or the employment of any person involved in the dispute.

**Proposed Addition — 203(3.1)**

(3.1) **Period of validity of opinion** — An opinion provided by the Department of Human Resources and Skills Development shall indicate the period during which the opinion is in effect for the purposes of subsection (1).

SOR/2010-172, s. 4(5) [To come into force April 1, 2011.]

(4) **Province of Quebec** — In the case of a foreign national who intends to work in the Province of Quebec, the opinion provided by the Department of Human Resources Development shall be made in concert with the competent authority of that Province.

**Proposed Amendment — 203(4)**

(4) **Province of Quebec** — In the case of a foreign national who intends to work in the Province of Quebec, the opinion provided by the Department of Human Resources and Skills Development shall be made in concert with the competent authority of that Province.

SOR/2010-172, s. 5(e) [To come into force April 1, 2011.]

**Proposed Addition — 203(5), (6)**

(5) **Employer's failure not justified** — If an officer determines under subparagraph 200(1)(c)(ii.1) or paragraph (1)(e) that, during the period set out in paragraph (1)(e), an employer did not provide wages, working conditions or employment in an occupation that were substantially the same as those offered and that the failure to do so was not justified in accordance with subsection (1.1), the Department shall notify the employer of that determination.

(6) **List of employers** — A list shall be maintained on the Department's website that sets out

(a) the names and addresses of employers referred to in subsection (5); and

(b) the day on which the determination referred to in that subsection was made in respect of an employer.

SOR/2010-172, s. 4(6) [To come into force April 1, 2011.]

SOR/2004-167, s. 57

## Case Law

*Koo v. 5220459 Manitoba Inc.* (2010), 89 Imm. L.R. (3d) 140, 2010 MBQB 132, 2010 CarswellMan 248 (Man. Q.B.) — The issue on this *de novo* hearing under the *Court of*

*Queen's Bench Small Claims Practices Act* was whether the Labour Market Opinion (LMO) obtained by the defendant and furnished to the plaintiff for submission by him in support of his application for a work permit gives the plaintiff the right to recover from the defendant in contract or tort for failure to pay him the wage referred to in the document. The LMO refers to a salary of $14.50 per hour. The defendant paid less than that to the plaintiff and it was agreed that if the plaintiff succeeded in his claim he was entitled to judgment for $9,057.06.

There is no provision in the statute or regulation expressly spelling out the consequences if incorrect information is given in the application for an LMO or if the employer chooses to pay the foreign national a salary less than indicated in the application.

It would be difficult to find that the LMO in itself or the providing of the LMO creates a contract, express or implied, between the plaintiff and defendant. The LMO is an expression of opinion by Service Canada of the matter set out therein. None of the essentials of a contract is present: offer, acceptance, privity, consideration and intention to create legal relations. The fundamental policy being to protect Canadian citizens or persons who are landed immigrants, it would be impossible for a member of that class to sustain an action against the defendant if the defendant had paid the plaintiff a salary greater than $14.50 per hour. It would be impossible for Service Canada to sustain an action against either party for breach of the terms of the document. There is no basis in contract for allowing the plaintiff to recover on the facts of this case. Nor is there a duty of care sufficient to support a tort action.

Is an employer free to disregard the salary set out in the LMO? Perhaps, perhaps not. If there is a false statement in the LMO, it may make it impossible for the employer to justify a finding of genuineness in a second or later application for an LMO. If there is a misrepresentation made knowingly, an employer may be subject to prosecution. Whatever the answer to the question, the plaintiff could have discussed the proposed salary with the defendant before receiving the LMO. He could have sought clarification from the defendant or refused to come to Canada. As it happens, the Court found the parties did have a discussion, and the plaintiff agreed to accept a lesser salary. He was not entitled to recover from the defendant the difference between the salary stated in the LMO and the salary paid. The claim was dismissed.

**204. International agreements — A work permit may be issued under section 200 to a foreign national who intends to perform work pursuant to**

> **(a) an international agreement between Canada and one or more countries, other than an agreement concerning seasonal agricultural workers;**
>
> **(b) an agreement entered into by one or more countries and by or on behalf of one or more provinces; or**
>
> **(c) an agreement entered into by the Minister with a province or group of provinces under subsection 8(1) of the Act.**

## Case Law

*Garro v. Canada (Minister of Citizenship & Immigration)* (2007), 67 Imm. L.R. (3d) 263, 2007 CarswellNat 1827, 2007 CarswellNat 4509, 2007 FC 670 — This was an application for judicial review of a decision of an immigration officer, refusing the application for a work permit for the applicant and visitor status for his family. The immigration officer concluded that the applicant failed to meet the conditions required to obtain investor status under the North American Free Trade Agreement. The letter of refusal that the officer sent contained no reasons explaining why the application was denied. The officer's notes revealed that he did not consider the initial sum of $20,000 to be a substantial investment for purposes of granting the applicant a permit. However, the evidence in the record showed that the applicant invested $166,000 in commercial premises for the company, $67,000 in book stocks to sell and thousands of dollars in equipment. Given that the applicant's evidence was so compelling, the Court concluded that there was absolutely no reason for the officer's decision and allowed the judicial review.

**205. Canadian interests — A work permit may be issued under section 200 to a foreign national who intends to perform work that**

**(a) would create or maintain significant social, cultural or economic benefits or opportunities for Canadian citizens or permanent residents;**

**(b) would create or maintain reciprocal employment of Canadian citizens or permanent residents of Canada in other countries;**

**(c) is designated by the Minister as being work that can be performed by a foreign national on the basis of the following criteria, namely,**

**(i) the work is related to a research, educational or training program, or**

**(ii) limited access to the Canadian labour market is necessary for reasons of public policy relating to the competitiveness of Canada's academic institutions or economy; or**

**(d) is of a religious or charitable nature.**

**206. No other means of support — A work permit may be issued under section 200 to a foreign national in Canada who cannot support themself without working, if the foreign national**

**(a) has made a claim for refugee protection that has been referred to the Refugee Protection Division but has not been determined; or**

**(b) is subject to an unenforceable removal order.**

**207. Applicants in Canada — A work permit may be issued under section 200 to a foreign national in Canada who**

**(a) is a member of the live-in caregiver class set out in Division 3 of Part 6 and meets the requirements of section 113;**

**(b) is a member of the spouse or common-law partner in Canada class set out in Division 2 of Part 7;**

**(c) is a protected person within the meaning of subsection 95(2) of the Act;**

**(d) has applied to become a permanent resident and the Minister has granted them an exemption under section 25 of the Act; or**

**(e) is a family member of a person described in any of paragraphs (a) to (d).**

IRP Regulations

**208. Humanitarian reasons** — A work permit may be issued under section 200 to a foreign national in Canada who cannot support themself without working, if the foreign national

(a) holds a study permit and has become temporarily destitute through circumstances beyond their control and beyond the control of any person on whom that person is dependent for the financial support to complete their term of study; or

(b) holds a temporary resident permit issued under subsection 24(1) of the Act that is valid for at least six months.

SOR/2004-167, s. 58

**209. Invalidity** — A work permit becomes invalid when it expires or when a removal order that is made against the permit holder becomes enforceable.

# PART 12 — STUDENTS

## DIVISION 1 — GENERAL RULES

**210. Class** — The student class is prescribed as a class of persons who may become temporary residents.

**211. Student** — A foreign national is a student and a member of the student class if the foreign national has been authorized to enter and remain in Canada as a student.

**212. Study permit required** — A foreign national may not study in Canada unless authorized to do so by a study permit or these Regulations.

## DIVISION 2 — APPLICATION FOR STUDY PERMIT

**213. Application before entry** — Subject to sections 214 and 215, in order to study in Canada, a foreign national shall apply for a study permit before entering Canada.

**214. Application on entry** — A foreign national may apply for a study permit when entering Canada if they are

(a) a national or a permanent resident of the United States;

(b) a person who has been lawfully admitted to the United States for permanent residence;

(c) a resident of Greenland;

(d) a resident of St. Pierre and Miquelon; or

(e) a foreign national who applied for a study permit before entering Canada, if the application was approved in writing but the permit has not been issued.

**215. (1) Application after entry** — A foreign national may apply for a study permit after entering Canada if they

(a) hold a study permit;

(b) apply within the period beginning 90 days before the expiry of their authorization to engage in studies in Canada under subsection 30(2) of the Act, or paragraph 188(1)(a) of these Regulations, and ending 90 days after that expiry;

(c) hold a work permit;

(d) are subject to an unenforceable removal order;

(e) hold a temporary resident permit issued under subsection 24(1) of the Act that is valid for at least six months;

(f) applied for a study permit before entering Canada and the application was approved in writing but the permit has not been issued; or

(g) are in a situation described in section 207.

**(2) Family members** — A family member of a foreign national may apply for a study permit after entering Canada if the foreign national resides in Canada and the foreign national

(a) holds a study permit;

(b) holds a work permit;

(c) holds a temporary resident permit issued under subsection 24(1) of the Act that is valid for at least six months;

(d) is subject to an unenforceable removal order;

(e) is a member of the armed forces of a country that is a designated state described in paragraph 186(d);

(f) is an officer of a foreign government described in paragraph 186(e);

(g) is a participant in sports activities or events, as described in paragraph 186(h);

(h) is an employee of a foreign news company as described in paragraph 186(i); or

(i) is a person who is responsible for assisting a congregation or group, as described in paragraph 186(l).



## DIVISION 3 — ISSUANCE OF STUDY PERMITS

**216. (1) Study permits** — Subject to subsections (2) and (3), an officer shall issue a study permit to a foreign national if, following an examination, it is established that the foreign national

(a) applied for it in accordance with this Part;

(b) will leave Canada by the end of the period authorized for their stay under Division 2 of Part 9;

(c) meets the requirements of this Part; and

(d) meets the requirements of section 30.

(e) [Repealed SOR/2004-167, s. 59(1).]

**(2) Exception — Paragraph (1)(b) does not apply to persons described in section 206 and paragraphs 207(c) and (d).**

**(3) Study in Quebec — An officer shall not issue a study permit to a foreign national who intends to study in the Province of Quebec — other than under a federal assistance program for developing countries — and does not hold a *Certificat d'acceptation du Québec*, if the laws of that Province require that the foreign national hold a *Certificat d'acceptation du Québec*.**

SOR/2004-167, s. 59

## Case Law

*Editor's note: With respect to the issue of the intention to leave Canada by the end of the period authorized, see also case summaries under Regulation 183(1) and Regulation 200(1).*

*Patel v. Canada (Minister of Citizenship & Immigration)* (2009), 82 Imm. L.R. (3d) 186, 344 F.T.R. 313 (Eng.), 2009 FC 602, 2009 CarswellNat 1786, 2009 CarswellNat 4049 (F.C.) — The applicant, a citizen of India, applied for a study permit and restoration of his temporary resident status to pursue a fourth diploma in information technology, this time from an accredited and statutorily recognized institution. His application was refused on the basis that the officer was not satisfied of the *bona fides* of the applicant as a genuine student and doubted whether he would leave Canada at the end of his authorized stay. In his five years since coming to Canada, the applicant had been awarded three post-secondary diplomas. In April 2008 the applicant applied for a post-graduate work permit on the strength of his certificate from the Canadian Career College and arranged employment. This permit was refused because the Canadian Career College was not a recognized degree-conferring institution. Following this refusal, the applicant applied for a new study permit in June 2008, and also a restoration of his temporary resident status which had by that time expired. It is the refusal of this application which formed the basis of the judicial review.

The officer offered a very thin explanation for the decision to refuse to extend the applicant's student visa, stating only that he was not satisfied the applicant would leave Canada following completion of his studies, and that the applicant's pursuit of an additional degree "seems redundant" in light of previously completed studies. The applicant, however, offered a very plausible explanation. In light of this explanation, it was unreasonable for the officer to conclude that the applicant's further studies were redundant. It was clear the decision was made without regard to the evidence. Furthermore, there was no explanation as to why the officer concluded the applicant would not leave Canada at the end of the authorized study period. There was no rational basis or sufficient explanation offered by the officer for why he doubted the applicant's *bona fides* as a student, and the officer failed to address the applicant's specific evidence on this point. The application for judicial review was allowed.

*Gu v. Canada (Minister of Citizenship & Immigration)*, 2010 FC 522, 2010 CarswellNat 2333, 2010 CarswellNat 1337 (F.C.) — The applicant's application for a study permit was refused. The officer found that the applicant's intentions in Canada did not appear to be of a temporary nature. The applicant first came to Canada as a visitor and subsequently obtained a study permit which was extended. She also obtained a work permit and applied for permanent residence under the live-in caregiver class but was refused in April 2009.

The CAIPS notes indicated the officer was concerned that the applicant did not establish that she had completed any studies in Canada under previously issued study permits or worked in Canada under the work permits issued to her. The Court held that these past permits had been issued and renewed by Canadian immigration authorities and there was no evidence of non-compliance with the Act and the Regulations on the part of the applicant. In circumstances where past compliance issues have never been raised, if an officer has concerns about compliance with past permits, the officer should inform the applicant of the concern and provide them with an opportunity to respond.

*Onyeka v. Canada (Minister of Citizenship & Immigration)* (2009), 80 Imm. L.R. (3d) 56, 2009 CarswellNat 780, 2009 CarswellNat 2094, 2009 FC 336 — This was an application for judicial review of a decision to refuse the applicant's application for a study permit. The officer found that the applicant did not have adequate funds available to him to pay for his tuition and living expenses while in Canada and to return to his country of residence. Also, the officer was not convinced that the applicant would leave Canada by the end of the period authorized for his stay. While the Court accepted the respondent's position that the decision attracted a high degree of deference from the Court, the exercise of discretion in this case approached the arbitrary and capricious. The refusal of a study permit was based upon two grounds. One was that the applicant did not satisfy the officer that he would leave Canada at the end of the authorized stay. The reasons given for this are as follows:

> applicant is single, has no dependant, low paid job. Considering PA's ties to Nigeria balanced against factors which might motivate to stay in Canada, I am not satisfied PA would leave the country at the end of an authorized stay.

Although the Court could see some connection between being single and having no dependants and the issue of whether, under Regulation 216(1)(b), the applicant will leave Canada at the end of the authorized period, it held that these factors merely place the applicant in the position of most students applying for study permits. The applicant had no family connections in Canada: his family was in the UK or Nigeria, and he had a highly responsible job in Nigeria. The officer did give reasons — being single and having no dependants — but these reasons were hardly sufficient to amount to a reasonable exercise of discretion when the other factors are taken into account. There was simply nothing on the facts that suggests that the applicant was not a *bone fide* student or that he would stay in Canada illegally at the end of the authorized period.

The officer's approach to the other ground of refusal — "You have not satisfied me that you have adequate funds available to you to pay for your tuition and living expenses while in Canada and to return to your country of residence" were more significant. The applicant had confirmed financial support of $12,000 per year as well as assurances that the College of Engineering at the University of Saskatchewan makes available $3,000 per year in the form of a "teaching assistant" payment for graduate students with the applicant's qualifications. In addition, the applicant provided evidence of personal savings. The officer, for no apparent reason, simply disregarded this money. The reasons appear entirely arbitrary in light of the evidence that was before the officer. The application for judicial review was allowed.

*Ogbonnaya v. Canada (Minister of Citizenship & Immigration)*, 2008 CarswellNat 1525, 2008 FC 317 — The applicant sought judicial review of a visa officer's decision to refuse his application for a student visa. The visa officer's decision was patently unreasonable. In concluding that the applicant did not satisfy the visa officer that he would return to

Nigeria by the end of the authorized period, the visa officer's notes suggest that this was because the applicant lacked ties to Nigeria, and would therefore have no incentive to return upon the completion of his schooling. The Court found such a conclusion patently unreasonable in light of the fact that the applicant's visa application listed a large and extensive family in Nigeria consisting of his mother, father, and six siblings, all of whom are older than the applicant. As well, the applicant stated that he did not have any relatives in Canada, thereby suggesting a strong incentive to return to Nigeria upon the completion of his studies. Moreover, the applicant demonstrated strong ties to the Presbyterian Church of Nigeria, which would no doubt influence his decision to return to the country. In light of these strong connections to Nigeria, it was also patently unreasonable that the visa officer would conclude that the applicant was not a *bona fide* student. This is especially the case in view of the fact that the applicant proffered a letter of acceptance from York University demonstrating that he had been accepted into the economics programme. The visa officer's decision was set aside.

*Odewole v. Canada (Minister of Citizenship & Immigration)*, 2008 CarswellNat 1667, 2008 CarswellNat 2786, 2008 FC 697 (F.C.) — The applicant sought judicial review of a visa officer's decision to refuse an application for a study permit. The application was refused because the applicant failed to demonstrate that her obligations or ties to her home country are such that they would compel her to leave Canada following the completion of her studies and because the officer was not satisfied that the applicant had dual intent pursuant to s. 22(2) of the Act. The applicant's sister had applied to sponsor the applicant's mother and the applicant was included as a dependant child in her mother's application for permanent residence.

Pursuant to subs. 22(2) of the Act, a person seeking a temporary entry into Canada may also hold the intention of establishing permanent residence. The officer was therefore required to weigh the evidence in connection with the application for a study permit and assess the applicant's intention to leave Canada at the end of her studies under paragraph 20(1)(b) of the Act and subs. 216(1) of the Regulations. The officer was not dealing with the family application for permanent residence, and the issue of dual intent arose only in relation to that application. The application for permanent residence was an irrelevant consideration for the purposes of the applicant's application for a study permit. Although in her affidavit the officer acknowledged that she lacked jurisdiction to assess the applicant's eligibility for permanent residence under the family class sponsorship, she nevertheless took this factor into account. Thus, the officer committed a reviewable error. The decision was set aside.

*Bonilla v. Canada (Minister of Citizenship & Immigration)*, 2007 CarswellNat 26, 2007 FC 20 (F.C.) — The applicant applied for a study permit. The application was refused. The visa officer found that living in Canada during her formative high school years would have a negative impact upon the applicant's ability to function in Colombia. The applicant was therefore unable to establish that she would return to her home country following the expiration of her study permit, should she be given one. The officer concluded that the applicant's separation from her family, community, language and Colombia's education system, for such a long period of time, would result in the severance of her ties to Colombia.

The visa officer relied upon a generalization when he refused the applicant's application. The generalization in question is that all applicants who apply for a study permit which cover four years of high school should be denied, since they would automatically be unlikely to return to their home country due to long-term separation from their families and cultures. Clearly, any individual who applies to study in Canada for four years of high school would be away from the aspects of their home country noted by the visa officer. However, it is not necessarily the case that all young people in these circumstances would become unable to function in their home countries following the four-year period, and as a result, would be unlikely to leave Canada. The officer subjectively formed an opinion and should have allowed the applicant an opportunity to respond to his concerns. The applicant had no way of knowing that the visa officer would act upon his view that those in their "formative years" may not study in Canada for a four-year period, since they would be unlikely to leave the country. The visa officer's failure to give the applicant an opportunity to respond to his concerns, on the facts of this case, amounted to a breach of the rules of natural justice. The application for judicial review was allowed.

*Zuo v. Canada (Minister of Citizenship & Immigration)*, 2007 CarswellNat 182, 2007 FC 88 (F.C.) — The applicant's application for a study permit was refused because he had not satisfied the officer that he was a genuine visitor who would leave Canada by the end of the authorized period of stay. It is not unreasonable for a visa officer to consider the availability of similar programs offered elsewhere at a lower cost; however, this fact will not necessarily be determinative. If this factor were determinative then many, if not most, study permit applications could be denied on this ground. Moreover, people choosing educational programs may base their choices on more than the price of a program. The availability of similar programs elsewhere at a lower cost is simply one factor to be considered by a visa officer in assessing an applicant's motives for applying for a study permit.

The applicant's father clearly believed that the ability to work in English is a valuable asset. The visa officer's determination that it would be an illogical decision for the applicant's parents to spend approximately $30,000 of their $80,000 savings on their son's education is patently unreasonable. Furthermore, her conclusion on this matter is not relevant to the issue she needed to determine, namely whether there is evidence that the applicant would stay past the authorized period. Similarly, the officer's conclusion that the applicant would not leave Canada before the authorized period given the economic opportunities and the high standard of living in Canada is also patently unreasonable. The applicant's family is well off in China and has a high standard of living. The applicant has an education as well as a family with significant ties in local government. The applicant does not lack support or opportunities in China. This Court has, in a number of cases, considered the status of an applicant's family in assessing whether an applicant will leave Canada before the authorized period of stay is over, such that if an applicant's family is well established and well off then the applicant is more likely to leave Canada before the end of the authorized period of stay. This is based on the assumption that there is less incentive for applicants with high standards of living in their home countries to seek to establish themselves in Canada. Here the officer determined that there was a risk the applicant may try to stay in Canada past the authorized period because he is attracted by the high standard of living in Canada without considering the standard of living that the applicant actually enjoyed in China. The application for judicial review was allowed.

*Tran v. Canada (Minister of Citizenship & Immigration)* (2006), 59 Imm. L.R. (3d) 217, 2006 CarswellNat 3833, 2006 FC 1377 (F.C.) — The applicant sought to overturn the decision of an immigration officer who denied his application for a study permit. The visa officer was not satisfied that he was either a *bona fide* student or a *bona fide* temporary resident, sufficiently well established in Vietnam, that he would leave Canada after his authorized stay in Canada. Procedural protection that arises in the context of a student

IRP Regulations

visa application is "relaxed." In other words, there is no clear requirement that an applicant be permitted to respond to an officer's concerns as they arise. Immigration manuals are primary guidelines for the assistance of the visa officers in the assessment of applications for either permanent residence or temporary visas. As such, manuals cannot be relied upon by applicants to argue lack of fairness simply because the officer did not strictly adhere to the guidelines found in the manual in question. It is trite law that the onus is on the applicant to provide a visa officer with all relevant information and documentation to satisfy the visa officer that the applicant meets the statutory requirements of the IRPA and the Regulations. In this case, the visa officer conducted a fulsome and diligent assessment of the applicant's application for a study permit. The visa officer considered a variety of factors in her assessment, including the low income of the applicant's parents in Vietnam and no proof of their employment, income or any assets. The fact that the same type of education is available locally and at a fraction of the cost is a relevant factor in determining the credibility and intentions of a potential foreign student. It was not patently unreasonable for the visa officer to consider the availability of similar courses in Vietnam and South Asia at a much less cost. The applicant's very weak English and his inability to carry even a basic conversation in English, as was revealed during his telephone conversation with the case analyst and reflected in the CAIPS notes, was a relevant factor for the visa officer to consider, given that his acceptance into Algonquin College was conditional upon him meeting the English language requirement. There were no reviewable errors in the visa officer's refusal to issue a study permit. The application for judicial review was dismissed.

*Boni c. Canada (Ministre de la Citoyenneté & de l'Immigration)*, [2005] F.C.J. No. 43, 2005 CarswellNat 176, 2005 CarswellNat 4646, 2005 FC 31 (F.C.); affirmed [2006] F.C.J. No. 275, 57 Imm. L.R. (3d) 4, 2006 CarswellNat 414, 2006 FCA 68 (C.A.) — The applicant applied for judicial review of a visa officer's decision to deny the applicant's application for a study permit. The risk that study permit applicants will not leave Canada once the period of their stay ends is a very important factor to be considered. An officer may examine the applicant's long-term objective. That objective is a relevant point which carries some weight, in view of the evidence as a whole on whether a study permit would be granted. A visa officer's conclusions will not be disturbed unless they are so unreasonable as to require the Court's intervention.

**217. (1) Application for renewal — A foreign national may apply for the renewal of their study permit if**

**(a) the application is made before the expiry of their study permit;**

**(b) they have complied with all conditions imposed on their entry into Canada; and**

**(c) they are in good standing at the educational institution at which they have been studying.**

**(2) Renewal — An officer shall renew the foreign national's study permit if, following an examination, it is established that the foreign national continues to meet the requirements of section 216.**

SOR/2004-167, s. 60

## Case Law

*Dang v. Canada (Minister of Citizenship & Immigration)*, 2007 CarswellNat 25, 2007 FC 15 (F.C.) — The immigration officer's decision not to grant a study permit was based on a factual finding that the applicant had not established that she would leave Canada at the end of her authorized stay. To obtain a renewal of a study permit, the Regulations require that applicants maintain good standing at their educational institution, have sufficient and available financial resources to support their studies, and establish that they will leave Canada after the expiry of their authorized stay. The evidence before the immigration officer, which included progress reports issued to the applicant by the Canadian Conversation College, indicated that the applicant maintained satisfactory standing in her classes. The immigration officer's finding of fact that the applicant was progressing slowly was patently unreasonable. Moreover, the immigration officer erroneously found that the applicant has been studying for 4 1/2 years, when in fact it was three years. The fact that the applicant had pursued an application to permanently reside in Canada with her husband does not establish that she would not leave Canada at the end of the period authorized for her study permit as required under paragraph 216(1)(b) of the Regulations. The visa officer failed to recognize that the IRPA expressly allows the applicant to simultaneously seek permanent resident status and temporary resident status as a student. Without an evidentiary basis on which to support the immigration officer's findings, the conclusion that the applicant would not leave Canada at the end of the period authorized for her stay was patently unreasonable. By determining that the applicant had taken an unreasonable amount of time to learn the English language, the immigration officer based her conclusion on irrelevant factors. The Regulations in this respect only require that an applicant maintain "good standing" at her educational institution, which she had done. The application for judicial review was allowed.



**218. Temporary resident status — A foreign national referred to in paragraph 215(1)(d) and their family members do not, by reason only of being issued a study permit, become temporary residents.**

## Division 4 — Restrictions on Studying in Canada

**219. (1) Acceptance letter — Subject to subsection (2), a study permit shall not be issued to a foreign national unless they have written documentation from the educational institution at which they intend to study that states that they have been accepted to study there.**

**(2) Exception — Subsection (1) does not apply to**

> **(a) a family member of a foreign national whose application for a work permit or a study permit is approved in writing before the foreign national enters Canada; or**
>
> **(b) a foreign national who is applying to renew their study permit and has received notification in writing from the college or university at which they have been studying of successful completion of the requirements for a degree or diploma.**

**(3) Foreign national described in par. (2)(b) — An officer who issues a study permit to a foreign national described in paragraph (2)(b) shall not authorize**

**a period of study that exceeds 90 days following the date of the notification in writing.**

SOR/2004-167, s. 61

**220. Financial resources — An officer shall not issue a study permit to a foreign national, other than one described in paragraph 215(1)(d) or (e), unless they have sufficient and available financial resources, without working in Canada, to**

> **(a) pay the tuition fees for the course or program of studies that they intend to pursue;**
>
> **(b) maintain themself and any family members who are accompanying them during their proposed period of study; and**
>
> **(c) pay the costs of transporting themself and the family members referred to in paragraph (b) to and from Canada.**

**221. Failure to comply with conditions — Despite Division 2, a study permit shall not be issued to a foreign national who has engaged in unauthorized work or study in Canada or who has failed to comply with a condition of a permit unless**

> **(a) a period of six months has elapsed since the cessation of the unauthorized work or study or failure to comply with a condition;**
>
> **(b) the work or study was unauthorized by reason only that the foreign national did not comply with conditions imposed under paragraph 185(a), any of subparagraphs 185(b)(i) to (iii) or paragraph 185(c); or**
>
> **(c) the foreign national was subsequently issued a temporary resident permit under subsection 24(1) of the Act.**

SOR/2004-167, s. 62

## Division 5 — Validity and Expiry of Study Permits

**222. Invalidity — A study permit becomes invalid when it expires or when a removal order made against the permit holder becomes enforceable.**

# Part 13 — Removal

## Division 1 — Removal Orders

**223. Types of removal order — There are three types of removal orders, namely, departure orders, exclusion orders and deportation orders.**

**224. (1) Departure order — An enforced departure order is prescribed as a circumstance that relieves a foreign national from having to obtain authorization under subsection 52(1) of the Act in order to return to Canada.**

**(2) Requirement — A foreign national who is issued a departure order must meet the requirements set out in paragraphs 240(1)(a) to (c) within 30 days after the or-**

der becomes enforceable, failing which the departure order becomes a deportation order.

(3) **Exception — stay of removal and detention** — If the foreign national is detained within the 30-day period or the removal order against them is stayed, the 30-day period is suspended until the foreign national's release or the removal order becomes enforceable.

225. (1) **Exclusion order** — For the purposes of subsection 52(1) of the Act, and subject to subsections (3) and (4), an exclusion order obliges the foreign national to obtain a written authorization in order to return to Canada during the one-year period after the exclusion order was enforced.

(2) **Prescribed circumstance** — For the purposes of subsection 52(1) of the Act, the expiry of a one-year period following the enforcement of an exclusion order, or a two-year period if subsection (3) applies, is prescribed as a circumstance that does not oblige the foreign national to obtain an authorization in order to return to Canada.

(3) **Misrepresentation** — A foreign national who is issued an exclusion order as a result of the application of paragraph 40(2)(a) of the Act must obtain a written authorization in order to return to Canada within the two-year period after the exclusion order was enforced.

(4) **Application of par. 42(b) of the Act** — For the purposes of subsection 52(1) of the Act, the making of an exclusion order against a foreign national on the basis of inadmissibility under paragraph 42(b) of the Act is prescribed as a circumstance that relieves the foreign national from having to obtain an authorization in order to return to Canada.

226. (1) **Deportation order** — For the purposes of subsection 52(1) of the Act, and subject to subsection (2), a deportation order obliges the foreign national to obtain a written authorization in order to return to Canada at any time after the deportation order was enforced.

(2) **Application of par. 42(b) of the Act** — For the purposes of subsection 52(1) of the Act, the making of a deportation order against a foreign national on the basis of inadmissibility under paragraph 42(b) of the Act is prescribed as a circumstance that relieves the foreign national from having to obtain an authorization in order to return to Canada.

(3) **Removal order — certificate** — For the purposes of subsection 52(1) of the Act, a removal order referred to in paragraph 81(b) of the Act obliges the foreign national to obtain a written authorization in order to return to Canada at any time after the removal order was enforced.

227. (1) **Report — family members** — For the purposes of section 42 of the Act, a report prepared under subsection 44(1) of the Act against a foreign national is also a report against the foreign national's family members in Canada.

(2) **Removal — family members** — A removal order made by the Immigration Division against a foreign national is also a removal order against their family members in Canada to whom subsection (1) applies if

(a) an officer informed the family member of the report, that they are the subject of an admissibility hearing and of their right to make submissions and be represented, at their own expense, at the admissibility hearing; and

(b) the family member is subject to a decision of the Immigration Division that they are inadmissible under section 42 of the Act on grounds of the inadmissibility of the foreign national.

## DIVISION 2 — SPECIFIED REMOVAL ORDER

228. (1) **Subsection 44(2) of the Act — foreign nationals** — For the purposes of subsection 44(2) of the Act, and subject to subsections (3) and (4), if a report in respect of a foreign national does not include any grounds of inadmissibility other than those set out in the following circumstances, the report shall not be referred to the Immigration Division and any removal order made shall be

(a) if the foreign national is inadmissible under paragraph 36(1)(a) or (2)(a) of the Act on grounds of serious criminality or criminality, a deportation order;

(b) if the foreign national is inadmissible under paragraph 40(1)(c) of the Act on grounds of misrepresentation, a deportation order;

(c) if the foreign national is inadmissible under section 41 of the Act on grounds of

(i) failing to appear for further examination or an admissibility hearing under Part 1 of the Act, an exclusion order,

(ii) failing to obtain the authorization of an officer required by subsection 52(1) of the Act, a deportation order,

(iii) failing to establish that they hold the visa or other document as required under section 20 of the Act, an exclusion order,

(iv) failing to leave Canada by the end of the period authorized for their stay as required by subsection 29(2) of the Act, an exclusion order, or

(v) failing to comply with subsection 29(2) of the Act to comply with any condition set out in section 184, an exclusion order; and

(d) if the foreign national is inadmissible under section 42 of the Act on grounds of an inadmissible family member, the same removal order as was made in respect of the inadmissible family member.

(2) **Subsection 44(2) of the Act — permanent residents** — For the purposes of subsection 44(2) of the Act, if a removal order is made against a permanent resident who fails to comply with the residency obligation under section 28 of the Act, the order shall be a departure order.

(3) **Eligible claim for refugee protection** — If a claim for refugee protection is made and the claim has been determined to be eligible to be referred to the Refugee Protection Division or no determination has been made, a departure order is the

**applicable removal order in the circumstances set out in any of subparagraphs (1)(c)(i) and (iii) to (v).**

**(4) Reports in respect of certain foreign nationals — For the purposes of subsection (1), a report in respect of a foreign national does not include a report in respect of a foreign national who**

**(a) is under 18 years of age and not accompanied by a parent or an adult legally responsible for them; or**

**(b) is unable, in the opinion of the Minister, to appreciate the nature of the proceedings and is not accompanied by a parent or an adult legally responsible for them.**

SOR/2004-167, s. 63



**229. (1) Paragraph 45(d) of the Act — applicable removal order — For the purposes of paragraph 45(d) of the Act, the applicable removal order to be made by the Immigration Division against a person is**

**(a) a deportation order, if they are inadmissible under subsection 34(1) of the Act on security grounds;**

**(b) a deportation order, if they are inadmissible under subsection 35(1) of the Act on grounds of violating human or international rights;**

**(c) a deportation order, in the case of a permanent resident inadmissible under subsection 36(1) of the Act on grounds of serious criminality or a foreign national inadmissible under paragraph 36(1)(b) or (c) of the Act on grounds of serious criminality;**

**(d) a deportation order, if they are inadmissible under paragraph 36(2)(b), (c) or (d) of the Act on grounds of criminality;**

**(e) a deportation order, if they are inadmissible under subsection 37(1) of the Act on grounds of organized criminality;**

**(f) an exclusion order, if they are inadmissible under subsection 38(1) of the Act on health grounds, unless subsection (2) or (3) applies;**

**(g) an exclusion order, if they are inadmissible under section 39 of the Act for financial reasons, unless subsection (2) or (3) applies;**

**(h) an exclusion order, if they are inadmissible under paragraph 40(1)(a) or (b) of the Act for misrepresentation, unless subsection (3) applies;**

**(i) a deportation order, if they are inadmissible under paragraph 40(1)(d) of the Act for misrepresentation;**

**(j) an exclusion order, if they are inadmissible under paragraph 41(a) of the Act for failing to comply with the requirement to appear for examination, unless subsection (2) or (3) applies;**

**(k) a departure order, if they are inadmissible under paragraph 41(b) of the Act;**

**(l) an exclusion order, if they are inadmissible under paragraph 41(a) of the Act for failing to establish that they have come to Canada in order to establish permanent residence, unless subsection (3) applies;**

**(m) an exclusion order, if they are inadmissible under paragraph 41(a) of the Act for failing to establish that they will leave Canada by the end of the period authorized for their stay, unless subsection (2) applies; and**

**(n) an exclusion order, if they are inadmissible under paragraph 41(a) of the Act for any other failure to comply with the Act, unless subsection (2) or (3) applies.**

**(2) Eligible claim for refugee protection — If a claim for refugee protection is made and the claim has been determined to be eligible to be referred to the Refugee Protection Division or no determination has been made, a departure order is the applicable removal order in the circumstances set out in paragraph (1)(f), (g), (j), (m) or (n).**

**(3) Exception — The applicable removal order in the circumstances set out in paragraph (1)(f), (g), (h), (j), (l) or (n) is a deportation order if the person**

**(a) was previously subject to a removal order and they are inadmissible on the same grounds as in that order;**

**(b) has failed to comply with any condition or obligation imposed under the Act or the *Immigration Act*, chapter I-2 of the Revised Statutes of Canada, 1985, unless the failure is the basis for the removal order; or**

**(c) has been convicted in Canada of an offence under an Act of Parliament punishable by way of indictment or of two offences under any Act of Parliament not arising out of a single occurrence, unless the conviction or convictions are the grounds for the removal order.**

**(3.1) Punishable by way of indictment — For the purposes of paragraph (3)(c), an offence that may be prosecuted either summarily or by way of indictment is deemed to be an offence punishable by way of indictment, even if it has been prosecuted summarily.**

**(4) Section 228 circumstances — If the Immigration Division makes a removal order against a foreign national with respect to any grounds of inadmissibility that are circumstances set out in section 228, the Immigration Division shall make**

**(a) the removal order that the Minister would have made if the report had not been referred to the Immigration Division under subsection 44(2) of the Act; or**

**(b) in the case of a foreign national described in paragraph 228(4)(a) or (b), the removal order that the Minister would have made if the foreign national had not been described in that paragraph.**

SOR/2004-167, s. 64(2)–(4)

## DIVISION 3 — STAY OF REMOVAL ORDERS

### Author's Note

*[All of the decisions of the Federal Court setting out the requirements an applicant must meet in order to obtain a Court Order staying the removal of the applicant from Canada which were collected under section 48 of the former Act may still be relevant and have been reproduced under Section 18.2 of the Federal Courts Act in this text.]*

**230. (1) Considerations — The Minister may impose a stay on removal orders with respect to a country or a place if the circumstances in that country or place pose a generalized risk to the entire civilian population as a result of**

**(a) an armed conflict within the country or place;**

**(b) an environmental disaster resulting in a substantial temporary disruption of living conditions; or**

**(c) any situation that is temporary and generalized.**

**(2) Cancellation — The Minister may cancel the stay if the circumstances referred to in subsection (1) no longer pose a generalized risk to the entire civilian population.**

**(3) Exceptions — The stay does not apply to a person who**

**(a) is inadmissible under subsection 34(1) of the Act on security grounds;**

**(b) is inadmissible under subsection 35(1) of the Act on grounds of violating human or international rights;**

**(c) is inadmissible under subsection 36(1) of the Act on grounds of serious criminality or under subsection 36(2) of the Act on grounds of criminality;**

**(d) is inadmissible under subsection 37(1) of the Act on grounds of organized criminality;**

**(e) is a person referred to in section F of Article 1 of the Refugee Convention; or**

**(f) informs the Minister in writing that they consent to their removal to a country or place to which a stay of removal applies.**



## Case Law

### Section 230(1)

*Adviento v. Canada (Minister of Citizenship & Immigration)*, [2003] F.C.J. No. 1837, 33 Imm. L.R. (3d) 13, 9 Admin. L.R. (4th) 314, 242 F.T.R. 295, 2003 CarswellNat 3955, 2003 CarswellNat 4980, 2003 FC 1430 (F.C.) — It is well-established law that the discretion to defer a removal is very limited. It would be contrary to the purposes and objects to the Act to expand, by judicial declaration, a removal officer's limited discretion so as to mandate "a mini H&C" review prior to removal.

An officer is entitled to take into account a range of factors, such as whether any required travel documents are missing, whether the applicant is subject to a Court Order requiring his or her presence in Canada, or whether there is a health related impediment to the applicant travelling and finally whether the failure to defer will otherwise expose the applicant to the risk of death, extreme sanction or inadequate treatment. These are all factors which could result in a removal being rescheduled.

### Section 230(3)

*Hasan v. Canada (Minister of Citizenship & Immigration)* (2008), 75 Imm. L.R. (3d) 64, 180 C.R.R. 286, 2008 CarswellNat 3445, 2008 FC 1069 (F.C.) — The applicant was reported as an inadmissible permanent resident because of serious criminality pursuant to s. 44 of the IRPA. The CBSA informed the applicant of their intention to seek the opinion, pursuant to s. 115(2)(a) of the IRPA, from the Minister of Citizenship and Immigration that he was a danger to the public and, thus, could be returned to Iraq. There is no requirement in s. 115(2) that the Minister must assess the risk to the person who has been found to be a danger. That obligation arises from the operation of s. 7 of the *Charter*, as decided by the Supreme Court of Canada in *Suresh* (2002), 18 Imm. L.R. (3d) 1. Thus, there is no parallel between the cessation provisions of s. 108, which explicitly require the Minister to demonstrate that the reasons for which the person sought refugee protection have ceased to exist, and s. 115, where the only obligation arises as a result of the *Charter*. The jurisprudence is clear that, once the applicant is found to be a danger to the public, he must establish that he would be at risk.

Therefore, the delegate did not erroneously place the onus on the applicant to prove that he faced the risk of torture or risk to life if returned to Iraq. The delegate properly engaged in an assessment of the current risks facing the applicant should he be removed to Iraq. The applicant was told that he could make written representations or arguments deemed necessary and relevant, including those related to whether his life or freedoms were threatened by removal from Canada. This was adequate notice to the applicant.

The applicant also argued that the delegate failed to have regard to the fact that the Minister had imposed a stay on removals to Iraq pursuant to s. 230 of the Regulations. Not only had the applicant not initially raised this argument in his submissions to the CBSA, but more importantly, the s. 230(1) moratorium does not apply to the applicant since s. 230(3) explicitly states that the stay under s. 230(1) does not apply to a person who is inadmissible on grounds of serious criminality or criminality. In this case, the applicant had been found to be inadmissible on grounds of serious criminality and he could not rely on the stay provisions of s. 230. The application for judicial review was dismissed.

**231. (1) Stay of removal — judicial review — Subject to subsections (2) to (4), a removal order is stayed if the subject of the order has filed an application for leave for judicial review in accordance with subsection 72(1) of the Act with respect to a determination of the Refugee Protection Division to reject a claim for refugee protection, and the stay is effective until the earliest of the following:**

> **(a) the application for leave is refused,**
>
> **(b) the application for leave is granted, the application for judicial review is refused and no question is certified for the Federal Court of Appeal,**
>
> **(c) if a question is certified by the Federal Court — Trial Division,**
>
> > **(i) the appeal is not filed within the time limit, or**
> >
> > **(ii) the Federal Court of Appeal decides to dismiss the appeal, and the time limit in which an application to the Supreme Court of Canada for leave to appeal from that decision expires without an application being made,**
>
> **(d) if an application for leave to appeal is made to the Supreme Court of Canada from a decision of the Federal Court of Appeal referred to in paragraph (c), the application is refused, and**
>
> **(e) if the application referred to in paragraph (d) is granted, the appeal is not filed within the time limit or the Supreme Court of Canada dismisses the appeal.**

(2) **No credible basis exception** — **Subsection (1) does not apply if the Refugee Protection Division states in its decision, in accordance with subsection 107(2) of the Act, that there is no credible basis for the claim.**

(3) **Other exceptions** — **There is no stay of removal if**

**(a) the person is subject to a removal order because they are inadmissible on grounds of serious criminality; or**

**(b) the subject of the removal order resides or sojourns in the United States or St. Pierre and Miquelon and is the subject of a report prepared under subsection 44(1) of the Act on their entry into Canada.**

(4) **Non-application** — **Subsection (1) does not apply if the person applies for an extension of time to file an application referred to in that subsection.**



232. **Stay of removal — pre-removal risk assessment** — **A removal order is stayed when a person is notified by the Department under subsection 160(3) that they may make an application under subsection 112(1) of the Act, and the stay is effective until the earliest of the following events occurs:**

**(a) the Department receives confirmation in writing from the person that they do not intend to make an application;**

**(b) the person does not make an application within the period provided under section 162;**

**(c) the application for protection is rejected;**

**(d) if a decision to allow the application for protection is made under paragraph 114(1)(a) of the Act and the person has not made an application within the period provided under subsection 175(1) to remain in Canada as a permanent resident, the expiry of that period;**

**(e) if a decision to allow the application for protection is made under paragraph 114(1)(a) of the Act, the decision with respect to the person's application to remain in Canada as a permanent resident is made; and**

**(f) in the case of a person to whom subsection 112(3) of the Act applies, the stay is cancelled under subsection 114(2) of the Act.**

233. **Stay of removal — humanitarian and compassionate considerations** — **A removal order made against a foreign national, and any family member of the foreign national, is stayed if the Minister is of the opinion under subsection 25(1) of the Act that there exist humanitarian and compassionate considerations, or public policy considerations, and the stay is effective until a decision is made to grant, or not grant, permanent resident status.**

## Case Law

*Level (Litigation Guardian of) v. Canada (Minister of Public Safety & Emergency Preparedness)* (2008), 71 Imm. L.R. (3d) 52, 2008 CarswellNat 423, 2008 FC 227 (F.C.) — This is an application for judicial review of an enforcement officer's decision to deny the applicant's request for a deferral of removal pending a decision on his application for permanent residence based on an H&C application.

An enforcement officer is statutorily bound to remove an applicant as soon as reasonably practicable. However, if the officer relies on extrinsic evidence not brought forward by the applicant, the applicant must be given an opportunity to respond to that evidence. This is a minimal duty of procedural fairness. In the application at bar, the enforcement officer relied on detailed evidence about medical conditions in Jamaica that the applicant contested in an affidavit filed in support of the applicant's successful motion for a stay of removal. With respect to tight time frames, the applicant had been in Canada for 20 years, and the duty of fairness should not be sacrificed because of an artificial deadline established by the respondent for the applicant's removal. There is no harm in allowing the applicant another week or two in order to respond to extrinsic evidence upon which the enforcement officer intends to rely. If that extrinsic evidence is incorrect, the applicant will suffer great harm. The application for judicial review was allowed.

*Adviento v. Canada (Minister of Citizenship & Immigration)*, [2003] F.C.J. No. 1837, 33 Imm. L.R. (3d) 13, 9 Admin. L.R. (4th) 314, 242 F.T.R. 295, 2003 CarswellNat 3955, 2003 CarswellNat 4980, 2003 FC 1430 (F.C.) — It is well-established law that the discretion to defer a removal is very limited. It would be contrary to the purposes and objects to the Act to expand, by judicial declaration, a removal officer's limited discretion so as to mandate "a mini H&C" review prior to removal.

An officer is entitled to take into account a range of factors, such as whether any required travel documents are missing, whether the applicant is subject to a Court Order requiring his or her presence in Canada, or whether there is a health related impediment to the applicant travelling and finally whether the failure to defer will otherwise expose the applicant to the risk of death, extreme sanction or inadequate treatment. These are all factors which could result in a removal being rescheduled.

*Brown (Litigation Guardian of) v. Canada (Minister of Citizenship & Immigration)* (2003), 26 Imm. L.R. (3d) 192, 2003 CarswellNat 532, 2003 CarswellNat 1526, 2003 FCT 269 (Fed. T.D.) — The applicant applied for an order declaring that it would be a violation of the principles of fundamental justice to deport him back to Jamaica.

The declaratory action is discretionary and the two factors which will influence the Court in the exercise of its discretion are the utility of the remedy if granted and whether, if it is granted, it will settle the questions at issue between the parties. The first factor is directed to the reality of the dispute. A declaration will not normally be granted when the dispute is over and has become academic, or where the dispute has yet to arise and may not arise.

The Court was satisfied the dispute was real and not hypothetical.

The applicant had received approval in principle of an H&C application and by virtue of s. 233 of the IRPA regulations the removal order was stayed until a decision was made to grant, or not grant, permanent resident status. Accordingly the Court concluded that the declaration if granted would have no practical effect as the applicant may be deported if his humanitarian and compassionate application is unsuccessful and in any event cannot be deported until a decision is made to grant or not grant permanent resident status. Therefore no useful purpose would be accomplished by granting a declaration at this time.

**234. Application of par. 50(a) of the Act — For greater certainty and for the purposes of paragraph 50(a) of the Act, a decision made in a judicial proceeding would not be directly contravened by the enforcement of a removal order if**

**(a) there is an agreement between the Department and the Attorney General of Canada or the attorney general of a province that criminal charges will be withdrawn or stayed on the removal of the person from Canada; or**

**(b) there is an agreement between the Department and the Attorney General of Canada or the attorney general of a province to withdraw or cancel any summons or subpoena on the removal of the person from Canada.**

## Division 4 — Enforcement of Removal Orders



**235. Not void — For greater certainty, and subject to section 51 of the Act, a removal order does not become void by reason of any lapse of time.**

**236. Providing copies — A person against whom a removal order is made shall be provided with a copy of the order when it is made.**

**237. Modality of enforcement — A removal order is enforced by the voluntary compliance of a foreign national with the removal order or by the removal of the foreign national by the Minister.**

**238. (1) Voluntary compliance — A foreign national who wants to voluntarily comply with a removal order must appear before an officer who shall determine if**

**(a) the foreign national has sufficient means to effect their departure to a country that they will be authorized to enter; and**

**(b) the foreign national intends to voluntarily comply with the requirements set out in paragraphs 240(1)(a) to (c) and will be able to act on that intention.**

**(2) Choice of country — Following the appearance referred to in subsection (1), the foreign national must submit their choice of destination to the officer who shall approve the choice unless the foreign national is**

**(a) a danger to the public;**

**(b) a fugitive from justice in Canada or another country; or**

**(c) seeking to evade or frustrate the cause of justice in Canada or another country.**

### Case Law

*Revich c. Canada (Ministre de la Citoyenneté & de l'Immigration)* (2005), 280 F.T.R. 201 (Eng.), (sub nom. *Revich v. Canada (Minister of Citizenship & Immigration))* 2005 CarswellNat 5741, 2005 FC 852 — The respondent issued a departure order against the applicant. Under the old legislation, the departure order was conditional and could not become effective until one of the conditions provided in subs. 49(2) had occurred. The applicant's refugee claim was refused and the departure order came into force 15 days after the notification of the rejection of the refugee claim. The Federal Court refused an application for leave against the decision of the RPD. The refusal ended the stay of execution of the departure order. The departure order became enforceable and became a deportation order pursuant to Reg. 224(2) of the Regulations. The applicant was then notified of her right to file a pre-removal risk assessment (PRRA) application. The notice resulted in a stay of execution of the deportation order pending the PRRA decision. The PRRA application was rejected and the stay provided for under s. 232 of the Regulations ended with the rejection of the PRRA application.

Under paragraph 160(3)(a) of the Regulations, the department is required to notify the persons subject to a removal order, such as the present applicant, that they are entitled to apply for a PRRA decision. However, neither the Act nor the Regulations states at what time this notice must be issued. Meanwhile, because the person's refugee claim has been rejected, the stay of execution of the removal order is no longer in force. In other words, the removal order is "enforceable" and, after a 30-day period, the order will become a deportation order unless the person voluntarily leaves the country. The Regulations also provide for the stay of execution of a removal order when a person is notified that he or she may file a PRRA application.

The applicant in this case did not attack the combined effect of these statutory provisions but instead targeted the department's decision to send the notice under s. 160 of the Regulations after the removal order became a deportation order, and thereby depriving her of the opportunity to have the stay that the PRRA application would have triggered. So the essential question was whether it was fair for the department to act in this way.

The purpose of the PRRA is to prevent a foreign national whose refugee claim has already been rejected from being required to return to his country of residence or citizenship when the situation has changed in that country and he would be exposed to a risk of persecution. If this review is to be effective and consistent with Parliament's intention when creating it, the PRRA must coincide as closely as possible with the person's departure from the country. The Court concluded that if an interested party voluntarily complies with the removal order under s. 238 of the Regulations, within the requisite period, he or she may avoid the consequences of the deportation order. Requiring the department to issue a notice before the deportation order comes into force would in turn eliminate the main incentive for people to comply voluntarily with the removal order prior to the PRRA decision. The department's decision to send a notice after the departure order became a deportation order does not fail to meet the requirements of procedural fairness having regard to the objective of the PRRA process, which is to serve as a final "safeguard" before the interested party is required to leave the country. There is nothing inequitable in the applicant asking in the future for written authorization to return to Canada since she knew that this was a consequence of her choice to not leave voluntarily. The application for judicial review was dismissed.

The following question was certified: Is the PRRA officer required to send the notice under s. 160 of the *Immigration Refugee Protection Regulations* before the departure order becomes a deportation order, thereby putting the foreign national in an irregular situation? Should the answer to the preceding question be positive, should the deportation order be set aside?

**239. Removal by Minister — If a foreign national does not voluntarily comply with a removal order, a negative determination is made under subsection 238(1) or**

**the foreign national's choice of destination is not approved under subsection 238(2), the removal order shall be enforced by the Minister.**

**240. (1) When removal order is enforced — A removal order against a foreign national, whether it is enforced by voluntary compliance or by the Minister, is enforced when the foreign national**

**(a) appears before an officer at a port of entry to verify their departure from Canada;**

**(b) obtains a certificate of departure from the Department;**

**(c) departs from Canada; and**

**(d) is authorized to enter, other than for purposes of transit, their country of destination.**

**(2) When removal order is enforced by officer outside Canada — If a foreign national against whom a removal order has not been enforced is applying outside Canada for a visa or an authorization to return to Canada, an officer shall enforce the order if, following an examination, the foreign national establishes that**

**(a) they are the person described in the order;**

**(b) they have been lawfully admitted to the country in which they are physically present at the time that the application is made; and**

**(c) they are not inadmissible on grounds of security, violating human or international rights, serious criminality or organized criminality.**



## Case Law

*Umlani v. Canada (Minister of Citizenship & Immigration)* (2008), 77 Imm. L.R. (3d) 179, 2008 CarswellNat 5454, 2008 CarswellNat 4806, 2008 FC 1373 (F.C.) — The applicant withdrew his refugee claim and advised the Immigration Refugee Board about his departure from Canada. He did not, however, confirm his departure by checking out with CIC officials at the airport when he was leaving. This meant that a departure order came into effect when he withdrew his claim, which eventually turned into a deportation order. The applicant was then called in for a meeting with CIC. He informed CIC by telephone that he had left Canada. CIC advised him to attend at a Canadian Consulate to show evidence that he had left Canada. The applicant attended the Canadian Consulate in New York and provided the requested information. The Canadian Consulate advised him that he would require authorization to return to Canada. The applicant applied for authorization to return to Canada and this application was refused.

Given the highly discretionary and fact-driven nature of ARC decisions, the Court should extend considerable deference in reviewing any such decision against the reasonableness standard. The visa officer refused the applicant's ARC request because:

1. The applicant is a failed refugee claimant;

2. A departure order was issued against the applicant and his departure was never confirmed; and

3. The stated reason for wishing to enter Canada (tourism) did not outweigh the serious import of a removal order and the applicant's non-compliance with the IRPA.

The Court pointed out that the officer gives no explanation as to why the six-year gap between the date of the removal order and the decision was not of any significance or relevance. Also the Court points out that the applicant was not a failed refugee claimant, but that he voluntarily withdrew his refugee application for legitimate reasons.

The only reason why the applicant had to apply for an ARC is because of his inadvertence in failing to appear before an officer to obtain the relevant certificate when he left the country. There was nothing to suggest that the applicant poses any kind of risk, that he had not dealt openly with immigration authorities at all relevant times, or that his re-entry would be undesirable in any way. In fact, the applicant had gone out of his way to correct the mistake and to keep authorities fully informed of why and when it came about. It is obvious that, from time to time, people make the same mistake as the applicant and forget to comply with the technicalities upon leaving Canada. In fact, it happens often enough that CIC has seen fit to address the issue and provide advice on how it should be dealt with in ENF 11 Verifying Departure. Direction is given regarding the circumstances in which officers outside of Canada should enforce an unenforced removal order. Officers are cautioned to keep in mind the "CBSA's overriding priority . . . to maintain control of the removal process", but officers are also advised on what they should do regarding precisely the kind of oversight that occurred in this case. Precisely why the applicant did not receive the benefit of these guidelines was unclear. The applicant's reasons for wanting to re-enter Canada were hardly compelling (tourism) but he was forced to make an ARC request because of a harmless and inadvertent mistake that, in the Court's view, fell under the "oversight" provisions of CIC's own guidelines. The application was allowed.

**241. (1) Country of removal — If a removal order is enforced under section 239, the foreign national shall be removed to**

**(a) the country from which they came to Canada;**

**(b) the country in which they last permanently resided before coming to Canada;**

**(c) a country of which they are a national or citizen; or**

**(d) the country of their birth.**

**(2) Removal to another country — If none of the countries referred to in subsection (1) is willing to authorize the foreign national to enter, the Minister shall select any country that will authorize entry within a reasonable time and shall remove the foreign national to that country.**

**(3) Exception — Despite section 238 and subsection (1), the Minister shall remove a person who is subject to a removal order on the grounds of inadmissibility referred to in paragraph 35(1)(a) of the Act to a country that the Minister determines will authorize the person to enter.**

**242. Mutual Legal Assistance in Criminal Matters Act — A person transferred under an order made under the *Mutual Legal Assistance in Criminal Matters Act* is not, for the purposes of paragraph 240(1)(d), a person who has been authorized to enter their country of destination.**

**243. Payment of removal costs — Unless expenses incurred by Her Majesty in right of Canada have been recovered from a transporter, a foreign national who is removed from Canada at Her Majesty's expense shall not return to Canada if the foreign national has not paid to Her Majesty the removal costs of**

**(a) $750 for removal to the United States or St. Pierre and Miquelon; and**

**(b) $1,500 for removal to any other country.**

## PART 14 — DETENTION AND RELEASE

**244. Factors to be considered — For the purposes of Division 6 of Part 1 of the Act, the factors set out in this Part shall be taken into consideration when assessing whether a person**

**(a) is unlikely to appear for examination, an admissibility hearing, removal from Canada, or at a proceeding that could lead to the making of a removal order by the Minister under subsection 44(2) of the Act;**

**(b) is a danger to the public; or**

**(c) is a foreign national whose identity has not been established.**



### Case Law

*Dehghani v. Canada (Minister of Employment & Immigration*, [1993] 1 S.C.R. 1053, 18 Imm. L.R. (2d) 245, 10 Admin. L.R. (2d) 1, 20 C.R. (4th) 34, 101 D.L.R. (4th) 654, 150 N.R. 241, 14 C.R.R. (2d) 1, 1993 CarswellNat 57, 1993 CarswellNat 1380, EYB 1993-67290, [1993] S.C.J. No. 38 — The appellant, a citizen of Iran, arrived in Canada without valid travel or identity documents and claimed Convention refugee status. He was interviewed at the secondary examination and extensive written notes were made by an immigration officer, which notes were later entered in evidence at the credible-basis hearing. At the conclusion of that hearing the first level tribunal decided that there was no credible basis to the appellant's claim.

When the appellant was taken to a secondary examination at Canadian Immigration at Pearson International Airport, he was not detained in the sense contemplated by s. 10(b) of the *Charter*. Further, the principles of s. 10(b) do not require that the appellant be provided with counsel at the pre-inquiry or pre-hearing stage of the refugee claim determination process. The secondary examination of the appellant at the port-of-entry is not analogous to a hearing. The purpose of the port-of entry interview was to aid in the processing of the appellant's application for entry and to determine the appropriate procedures which should be invoked in order to deal with the appellant's application for Convention refugee status. The principles of fundamental justice do not include a right to counsel in these circumstances of routine information gathering.

*[Editor's Note: Although* Dehghani *was decided under the former Act it may still be relevant.]*

**245. Flight risk** — For the purposes of paragraph 244(a), the factors are the following:

(a) being a fugitive from justice in a foreign jurisdiction in relation to an offence that, if committed in Canada, would constitute an offence under an Act of Parliament;

(b) voluntary compliance with any previous departure order;

(c) voluntary compliance with any previously required appearance at an immigration or criminal proceeding;

(d) previous compliance with any conditions imposed in respect of entry, release or a stay of removal;

(e) any previous avoidance of examination or escape from custody, or any previous attempt to do so;

(f) involvement with a people smuggling or trafficking in persons operation that would likely lead the person to not appear for a measure referred to in paragraph 244(a) or to be vulnerable to being influenced or coerced by an organization involved in such an operation to not appear for such a measure; and

(g) the existence of strong ties to a community in Canada.

**246. Danger to the public** — For the purposes of paragraph 244(b), the factors are the following:

(a) the fact that the person constitutes, in the opinion of the Minister, a danger to the public in Canada or a danger to the security of Canada under paragraph 101(2)(b), subparagraph 113(d)(i) or (ii) or paragraph 115(2)(a) or (b) of the Act;

(b) association with a criminal organization within the meaning of subsection 121(2) of the Act;

(c) engagement in people smuggling or trafficking in persons;

(d) conviction in Canada under an Act of Parliament for

(i) a sexual offence, or

(ii) an offence involving violence or weapons;

(e) conviction for an offence in Canada under any of the following provisions of the *Controlled Drugs and Substances Act*, namely,

(i) section 5 (trafficking),

(ii) section 6 (importing and exporting), and

(iii) section 7 (production);

(f) conviction outside Canada, or the existence of pending charges outside Canada, for an offence that, if committed in Canada, would constitute an offence under an Act of Parliament for

(i) a sexual offence, or

(ii) an offence involving violence or weapons; and

(g) conviction outside Canada, or the existence of pending charges outside Canada, for an offence that, if committed in Canada, would constitute an offence

**under any of the following provisions of the *Controlled Drugs and Substances Act*, namely,**

**(i) section 5 (trafficking),**

**(ii) section 6 (importing and exporting), and**

**(iii) section 7 (production).**

## Case Law

*Capra v. Canada (Attorney General)* (2008), 76 Imm. L.R. (3d) 21, 335 F.T.R. 299 (Eng.), 2008 CarswellNat 3875, 2008 CarswellNat 5267, 2008 FC 1212 (F.C.) — This was an application for a declaration that subs. 128(4) of the *Corrections and Conditional Release Act*, S.C. 1992, c. 20 ("CCRA") is invalid on the ground that it breaches ss. 7, 9 and 15 of the *Canadian Charter of Rights and Freedoms*, Part 1 of the *Constitution Act, 1982*. The applicant had been granted Convention refugee status and became a permanent resident on December 2, 1992. The applicant was subsequently convicted of 80 counts of fraud in connection with credit cards and automatic bank teller machines in 2001. A deportation order was issued on the grounds of serious criminality. Both the appeal of the deportation order and his application were dismissed and the applicant lost his permanent residence status. However, because of his refugee status, he could not be removed to Romania unless the Minister of Citizenship and Immigration issued an opinion that the applicant constitutes a danger to the public. The CBSA sought the opinion of the Minister that he was a danger to the public in Canada. In the meantime, the applicant served his sentence in a medium security federal correctional facility and underwent a rehabilitation program. He became eligible for an unescorted temporary absence ("UTA") and day parole on July 2008. The CBSA informed the sentence management office of the deportation order previously issued against the applicant. As a result, by operation of subs. 128(4) of the CCRA, the applicant was ineligible for release on a UTA or day parole until his full parole eligibility date. The applicant believed that he was being treated differently in relation to day parole eligibility because he was not a Canadian citizen. He claimed that he was the subject of discrimination and regardless of whether he was allowed to stay in Canada or not, he perceived that he was being denied an opportunity to work towards his own rehabilitation simply because of his identity.

The Court held that s. 128(4) of the CCRA was directed at inmates subject to removal. The operation of the subsection is triggered by the issuance of a removal order. A stay of that removal order suspends the section's effect. The application of the section is rationally tied to its purpose and cannot be called arbitrary in relation to the objectives sought to be attained. Accordingly this was not arbitrary detention within the meaning of s. 9. Furthermore, the Supreme Court of Canada had made it clear that a "change in the form in which a sentence is served, whether it be favourable or unfavourable to the prisoner, is not, in itself, contrary to any principle of fundamental justice."

Parliament has decided that offenders subject to removal should serve their sentences in different ways from other offenders, including Canadian citizens. This is to ensure that their status as offenders does not enhance their access to Canadian society over that of non-offenders who face deportation; it is also intended to ensure that their removal status does not result in their serving shorter sentences than either Canadian citizens or non-citizens who are not subject to removal. Parliament has chosen to deal with these issues by suspending day parole and UTA for offenders who are subject to removal. It is possible to disagree with this approach and with whether it achieves the objectives it is in-

IRP Regulations

tended to achieve, but that was not the issue before the court. What is relevant is that the variation in the form of the sentence that comes about as a result of subs. 128(4) of CCRA is triggered by the existence of a removal order and whether this fact makes it part of a deportation scheme.

The Court was not convinced that, if the purpose of parole is to protect society, that the loss of the possibility of that protection because of the loss of eligibility for day parole under subs. 128(4) was a disadvantage to the applicant, whether or not he was removed from Canada. Furthermore if parole was a benefit to offenders, the Court was not convinced that the applicant had been disadvantaged by the loss of any such benefit in a situation where the evidence showed his deportation was being actively pursued and he did not fall into one of the exceptions specifically provided for under subs. 128(6). The applicant failed to demonstrate differential treatment between citizens and non-citizens. The application was dismissed.

*Canada (Minister of Citizenship & Immigration) v. Thanabalasingham*, [2004] 3 F.C.R. 572, 38 Imm. L.R. (3d) 1, [2004] F.C.J. No. 15, 247 F.T.R. 159 (note), 236 D.L.R. (4th) 329, 10 Admin. L.R. (4th) 285, 315 N.R. 91, 2004 CarswellNat 22, 2004 CarswellNat 782, 2004 FCA 4 (C.A.) — This was an appeal on a certified question from a decision of the motions judge. The certified question asked whether detention reviews were hearings *de novo* and whether the detained person bears the burden of establishing that he or she was not a danger to the public or a flight risk. The respondent was arrested in October 2001 on an immigration warrant and detained on grounds that he was a danger to the public because he was the leader of a Tamil gang. His detention was reviewed under the former Act and, after it came into force, under ss. 57 and 58 of IRPA. At his first five reviews the continued detention of the respondent was ordered. At his sixth review the respondent was ordered released. The Minister applied for judicial review and obtained a stay of that order until the next detention review was completed. The next detention review was completed in March 2003 and the respondent was once again ordered released. The Minister once again obtained a stay of that order and sought judicial review and it was this judicial review that was the subject of the matter in this case.

Detention reviews are the kind of essentially fact-based decision to which deference is usually shown. While prior decisions are not binding on a Member, if a Member chooses to depart from prior decisions to detain, clear and compelling reasons for doing so must be set out. The best way for the Member to provide clear and compelling reasons would be to expressly explain what has given rise to the changed opinion. It would be unacceptable for a Member to give a cursory decision which does not advert to the prior reasons for detention in a meaningful way.

Sections 57 and 58 allow persons to be detained for potentially lengthy if not indefinite periods of time without having been charged let alone having been convicted of any crime. As a result, detention decisions must be made with s. 7 of the *Charter* in mind.

It is the Minister who must establish, on a balance of probabilities, that the respondent is a danger to the public if he wants the detention to continue. The onus is always on the Minister to demonstrate that there are reasons which warrant detention or continued detention. Once the Minister has made out a *prima facie* case for the continued detention, the individual must lead some evidence or risk continued detention. The Minister may establish a *prima facie* case in a variety of ways including reliance on reasons for prior detention.

**247.** (1) **Identity not established** — **For the purposes of paragraph 244(c), the factors are the following:**

**(a) the foreign national's cooperation in providing evidence of their identity, or assisting the Department in obtaining evidence of their identity, in providing the date and place of their birth as well as the names of their mother and father or providing detailed information on the itinerary they followed in travelling to Canada or in completing an application for a travel document;**

**(b) in the case of a foreign national who makes a claim for refugee protection, the possibility of obtaining identity documents or information without divulging personal information to government officials of their country of nationality or, if there is no country of nationality, their country of former habitual residence;**

**(c) the destruction of identity or travel documents, or the use of fraudulent documents in order to mislead the Department, and the circumstances under which the foreign national acted;**

**(d) the provision of contradictory information with respect to identity at the time of an application to the Department; and**

**(e) the existence of documents that contradict information provided by the foreign national with respect to their identity.**

(2) **Non-application to minors** — **Consideration of the factors set out in paragraph (1)(a) shall not have an adverse impact with respect to minor children referred to in section 249.**

SOR/2004-167, s. 65

**248.** **Other factors** — **If it is determined that there are grounds for detention, the following factors shall be considered before a decision is made on detention or release:**

**(a) the reason for detention;**

**(b) the length of time in detention;**

**(c) whether there are any elements that can assist in determining the length of time that detention is likely to continue and, if so, that length of time;**

**(d) any unexplained delays or unexplained lack of diligence caused by the Department or the person concerned; and**

**(e) the existence of alternatives to detention.**

## Case Law

*Walker v. Canada (Minister of Citizenship & Immigration)* (2010), 89 Imm. L.R. (3d) 151, 2010 FC 392, 2010 CarswellNat 1050, 2010 CarswellNat 2161 (F.C.) — Section 248 of the Regulations adds the length of detention as a consideration to be taken into account even if the person detained is considered to be a flight risk, as in this case. The length of the applicant's detention has to be considered against other factors besides his refusal to cooperate with immigration officials and to reveal his true identity. These other factors would include the immigration status of the applicant, the fact that this was the 38th detention review, the passage of time since his last criminal conviction, etc. A close reading of the Member's reasons reveals that the three-year detention of the applicant was not considered against these factors. The application for judicial review to set aside the decision of the Immigration Division of the Immigration and Refugee Board to order the applicant remain in detention, was allowed.

*Canada (Minister of Public Safety & Emergency Preparedness) v. Welch*, 2006 CarswellNat 2416, 2006 FC 924 (F.C.) — The Minister sought judicial review of the decision of a member of the Immigration Division of the Immigration and Refugee Board, allowing the conditional release from detention of the respondents. This was the fifth review of the detention of the respondents. The Minister argued that the member did not provide clear and compelling reasons as to why he should depart from the four previous decisions and release the respondents on terms and conditions. The Minister's view was that these terms and conditions were less stringent than those considered at the previous reviews.

The respondents are citizens of the United States and are wanted in the State of Colorado on a number of charges. They fled to Canada following release on bail pending their trial in the United States. Shortly after their arrival in Canada, they were arrested by the RCMP and a decision was made to detain them, and a removal order pursuant to s. 44 of the IRPA was issued against them. The respondents claimed refugee status and this claim had yet to be determined. At the first detention hearing, it was determined that they were a flight risk but the duration of the detention contemplated was very short. It was mentioned that they had two children. At a second detention hearing, the member came to the same conclusion and continued the detention. The two respondents' children were in the audience during the second hearing. It became clear that they had been with their parents when the latter were apprehended. The children were by then in the care of their grandmother in Canada, having been in the custody of the Ministry of Children and Families. It was argued that it was not in the best interest of the children to be separated from their parents. However, the presence of the children was not found to supersede the other factors listed in s. 245 of the Regulations. A proposal for release including a curfew and a $4,000 bond was rejected. At the third detention hearing, the member considered physical restriction to an area, $25,000 cash bond for each of the respondents, a prohibition to carry weapons, daily reporting and, alternatively, the release of only one of the respondents to enable the children, who were back in the United States with their grandmother, to visit and spend some time with her. At this hearing, the Minister argued for the first time that the respondents posed a danger to the public. This argument was rejected. The member concluded that even a release subject to cash bond and very stringent reporting conditions would not be effective considering that the respondents failed to appear for their trial in the United States in spite of significant bail bonds in existence there (US$25,000 and US$100,000).

At the fourth hearing, the member concluded the detention was necessary to ensure the respondents would appear for their removal. At that time, in addition to the three conditions of release discussed earlier, the respondents proposed a release be made subject to a review once a decision was made on the refugee claim. They also alluded to the possibility of electronic tracking as an alternative to detention, but had been advised by the Minister that this was not a viable alternative as no such system was currently available. Despite the fact that the respondents were likely to remain in detention for several months pending the determination of their refugee claim, the member concluded that their continued detention was necessary and found he had no authority to give any direction to the Minister with respect to the quality of the detention and the electronic monitoring. At the fifth detention hearing, the respondents called a representative of the company Trace Canada as a witness to explain how Trace Canada would equip them with electronic tracking devices that would keep a record of their movements at all times. The company could then report this information to immigration officials who would know immediately if the respondents had breached their conditions of release. Their submission was that the flight risk would be considerably reduced if such a mechanism were in use. The member took the matter under advisement. When the hearing resumed, the member specified that he was not "reopening" the detention review, but simply wished to obtain some clarification with regard to the services offered by Trace Canada. He questioned the representative about the functioning of the electronic tracking system. The member concluded that he considered electronic monitoring to be more responsive than a self-monitored curfew and no-go zone. He also stated it was more responsive than periodic physical reporting where, according to him, the respondents could be long gone by the time they failed to show up to report. It was thus a more immediate form of reporting. He also noted that, in the end, if the person's intention is to abscond, they will do so whatever the type of monitoring and explained that:

> Alternatives to detention are not meant to provide absolute certainty of appearance for removal. They need only have the effect of reducing the risk to an acceptable degree. The fact that the persons concerned have proposed electronic monitoring and have made the effort to bring a proposal for consideration is an indication of their sincerity in seeking to address the Minister's concerns of flight.

The question the Court considered was not whether or not the member was justified in ordering the release on the conditions he did, but whether he had provided clear, compelling reasons for departing from the previous decisions reached at the detention reviews. Had the superiority of electronic monitoring been the sole basis of the decision, the Court would have concluded that the reasons given by the member met the low threshold set out by the Court of Appeal in *Thanabalasingham*. However, the member clearly distinguishes the situation before him from those reviewed by his colleagues on the basis of the "new evidence" with respect to the respondents' children. Since the member believed the information relating to the existence of the respondents' children was new, he could not properly turn his mind to the decisions of his colleagues on this point and consider why he should depart from the course of action they took. Since the member clearly failed to consider the contrary view expressed by the previous member on this particular point, the decision was set aside.

**249. Special considerations for minor children — For the application of the principle affirmed in section 60 of the Act that a minor child shall be detained only as a measure of last resort, the special considerations that apply in relation to the detention of minor children who are less than 18 years of age are**

**(a) the availability of alternative arrangements with local child-care agencies or child protection services for the care and protection of the minor children;**

**(b) the anticipated length of detention;**

**(c) the risk of continued control by the human smugglers or traffickers who brought the children to Canada;**

**(d) the type of detention facility envisaged and the conditions of detention;**

(e) the availability of accommodation that allows for the segregation of the minor children from adult detainees who are not the parent of or the adult legally responsible for the detained minor children; and

(f) the availability of services in the detention facility, including education, counselling and recreation.

250. **Applications for travel documents** — If a completed application for a passport or travel document must be provided as a condition of release from detention, any completed application provided by a foreign national who makes a claim for refugee protection shall not be divulged to government officials of their country of nationality or, if there is no country of nationality, their country of previous habitual residence, as long as the removal order to which the foreign national is subject is not enforceable.

## PART 15 — THE IMMIGRATION APPEAL DIVISION

251. **Conditions** — If the Immigration Appeal Division stays a removal order under paragraph 66(b) of the Act, that Division shall impose the following conditions on the person against whom the order was made:

(a) to inform the Department and the Immigration Appeal Division in writing in advance of any change in the person's address;

(b) to provide a copy of their passport or travel document to the Department or, if they do not hold a passport or travel document, to complete an application for a passport or a travel document and to provide the application to the Department;

(c) to apply for an extension of the validity period of any passport or travel document before it expires, and to provide a copy of the extended passport or document to the Department;

(d) to not commit any criminal offences;

(e) if they are charged with a criminal offence, to immediately report that fact in writing to the Department; and

(f) if they are convicted of a criminal offence, to immediately report that fact in writing to the Department and the Division.

## PART 16 — SEIZURE

252. **Custody of seized thing** — A thing seized under subsection 140(1) of the Act shall be placed without delay in the custody of the Department.

253. (1) **Notice of seizure** — An officer who seizes a thing under subsection 140(1) of the Act shall make reasonable efforts to

(a) identify the lawful owner; and

(b) give the lawful owner written notice of, and reasons for, the seizure.

(2) **Disposition after seizure** — Subject to subsection (3), a thing seized shall be disposed of as follows:

(a) if it was fraudulently or improperly obtained, by returning it to its lawful owner unless section 256 applies;

(b) if it was fraudulently or improperly used, by disposing of it under section 257 unless section 254, 255 or 256 applies;

(c) if the seizure was necessary to prevent its fraudulent or improper use

(i) by returning it to its lawful owner, if the seizure is no longer necessary for preventing its fraudulent or improper use, or

(ii) by disposing of it under section 257, if returning it to its lawful owner would result in its fraudulent or improper use; or

(d) if the seizure was necessary to carry out the purposes of the Act, by returning it to its lawful owner without delay if the seizure is no longer necessary to carry out the purposes of the Act.

(3) **Additional factor** — A thing seized shall only be returned if its return would not be contrary to the purposes of the Act. If its return would be contrary to the purposes of the Act, it shall be disposed of under section 257.



254. (1) **Application for return** — The lawful owner of a thing seized or the person from whom it was seized may apply for its return.

(2) **Return** — A thing seized, other than a document, shall be returned to the applicant if

(a) paragraph 253(2)(b) applies to the thing and the seizure is no longer necessary to prevent its fraudulent or improper use or to carry out the purposes of the Act; and

(b) the applicant provides cash security equal to the fair market value of the thing at the time of the seizure or, if there is no significant risk of being unable to recover the debt, a combination of cash and guarantee of performance.

(3) **Disposition of security** — Any cash deposit or guarantee of performance provided under paragraph 2(b) replaces the thing seized and, if section 257 applies, any cash deposit is forfeited to Her Majesty in right of Canada and any guarantee of performance becomes a debt due under section 145 of the Act.

255. (1) **Application by lawful owner** — For the purposes of paragraph 253(2)(b), a person who claims to be the lawful owner of a seized thing may apply in writing for its return within 60 days after the seizure.

(2) **Return of thing** — The thing seized shall be returned to an applicant if the applicant demonstrates that they

(a) were the lawful owner prior to its seizure and have remained a lawful owner;

(b) did not participate in the fraudulent or improper use of the thing; and

(c) exercised all reasonable care to satisfy themselves that the person permitted to obtain possession of the thing was not likely to fraudulently or improperly use it.

(3) **Return of vehicle** — A seized vehicle that is not returned under subsection (2) shall be returned on payment of a $5,000 fee if the applicant demonstrates that they

(a) were the lawful owner prior to its seizure and have remained a lawful owner;

(b) did not profit or intend to profit from the fraudulent or improper use of the vehicle; and

(c) are unlikely to contravene the Act in the future.

(4) **Additional factor** — A thing seized shall only be returned if its return would not be contrary to the purposes of the Act.

(5) **Notice of decision** — The applicant shall be notified in writing of the decision on the application and the reasons for it. If the applicant is notified by mail, notification is deemed to have been effected on the seventh day after the day on which the notification was mailed.

256. (1) **Application by person from whom thing was seized** — If a thing was seized on the ground that it was fraudulently or improperly obtained or used, a person from whom it was seized may apply in writing within 30 days after the seizure for its return.

(2) **Return of thing** — The thing seized shall be returned to an applicant if the applicant demonstrates that it was not fraudulently or improperly obtained or used.

(3) **Notice of decision** — An applicant shall be notified in writing of the decision on the application and the reasons for it. If the applicant is notified by mail, notification is deemed to have been effected on the seventh day after the day on which the notification was mailed.

257. (1) **Sale of a seized thing** — Subject to subsections (2) and (3), if a thing seized is not returned to its lawful owner or the person from whom it was seized under section 254, 255 or 256, the thing shall be sold unless the costs of sale would exceed the monetary value of the thing, in which case the thing shall be destroyed.

(2) **Sale suspended** — A thing seized shall not be sold

(a) during the 15 days following notification of a decision not to return it under section 255 or 256; or

(b) before a final decision is made in any judicial proceeding in Canada affecting the seizure or the return of the thing seized.

(3) **Disposition of documents** — If a document is not returned to its lawful owner or the person from whom it was seized, the document shall be retained for as long as is necessary for the administration or enforcement of Canadian laws, after which it is subject to the applicable laws relating to the disposal of public archives.

258. **Limitation period for seizures** — No seizure may be made under subsection 140(1) of the Act in respect of the fraudulent or improper obtaining or use of a thing more than six years after that obtaining or use.

## PART 17 — TRANSPORTATION

259. **Prescribed documents** — For the purposes of subsection 148(1) of the Act, the following documents that a person requires under the Act to enter Canada are prescribed:

(a) a travel document referred to in subsection 31(3) of the Act;

(b) refugee travel papers issued by the Minister of Foreign Affairs;

(c) a document referred to in subsection 50(1) or 52(1);

(d) a temporary travel document referred to in section 151;

(e) a visa referred to in section 6 or subsection 7(1); and

(f) a permanent resident card.



260. (1) **Holding prescribed documentation** — If a transporter has reasonable grounds to believe that the prescribed documents of a person whom it carries to Canada may not be available for examination at a port of entry, the transporter must give the person a receipt for the documents and hold those documents until examination.

(2) **Presenting documents** — A transporter who holds the documents of a person must, when presenting the person for examination under paragraph 148(1)(b) of the Act, present the documents and a copy of the receipt.

261. (1) **Obligation to hold a person** — For the purposes of paragraph 148(1)(b) of the Act, a transporter has complied with the obligation to hold a person until the examination is completed when

(a) an officer informs the transporter that the examination of the person is completed;

(b) the person is authorized to enter Canada under section 23 of the Act; or

(c) the person is detained under any Canadian law.

(2) **Notification** — A transporter must notify an officer without delay if a person whose examination has not been completed leaves or attempts to leave the transporter's vehicle for any other purpose than examination.

262. **Stowaway notification** — On the arrival of a vessel at its first port of call in Canada, the transporter must notify an officer at the nearest port of entry of the presence of any stowaway and, on request of the officer, must without delay provide a written report concerning the stowaway.

263. (1) **Medical examination and treatment** — A transporter's obligations under paragraph 148(1)(c) of the Act apply only in respect of foreign nationals car-

**ried in respect of whom a report is prepared under subsection 44(1) of the Act, or who are members of a crew or who are entering Canada to become members of a crew.**

**(2) Prescribed medical costs — Unless the transporter establishes that the foreign national holds a temporary or permanent resident visa and that their health condition is not a result of the transporter's negligence, any medical costs incurred with respect to the foreign national are prescribed costs and are calculated on the basis of the applicable provincial health insurance system.**

**(3) Arranging medical examination — A transporter must arrange for the medical examination of a foreign national on a request made under subsection 16(2) of the Act, and must arrange for medical treatment and observation if those conditions are imposed on the foreign national under section 32.**

**264. Prescribed information — A transporter must provide without delay any of the following documents that are requested by an officer within 72 hours after the presentation for examination of a person carried by the transporter to Canada:**

**(a) a copy of any ticket issued to the person;**

**(b) a document specifying the person's itinerary, including the place of embarkation and dates of travel; and**

**(c) a document identifying the document number and type of passport, travel document or identity document carried by the person, the country of issue and the name of the person to whom it was issued.**

**265. (1) Crew list — On arrival at the first port of call in Canada of a vessel registered in a foreign country, the transporter must provide an officer at the nearest port of entry with a list of all members of the crew.**

**(2) Amended crew list — The transporter must maintain on board a current list of all members of the crew while the vessel is in Canada.**

**(3) Final crew list — Before the vessel's departure from its final port of call in Canada, the transporter must provide an officer with a copy of the list referred to in subsection (1) that includes any changes made while the vessel was in Canada.**

**266. Assembly — On the request of an officer, a transporter must assemble without delay aboard the vessel all members of the crew.**

**267. Canadian registered vessels — On the arrival of a vessel registered in Canada at its first port of call in Canada, the transporter must notify an officer at the nearest port of entry of all members of the crew who are not Canadian citizens or permanent residents and, on request, provide the officer with a list of all crew members.**

**268. (1) Reporting obligation — A transporter must, without delay, notify an officer at the nearest port of entry of any foreign national who ceases to be a mem-**

**ber of the crew for a reason listed in paragraph 3(1)(b). The transporter must record that information and provide it in writing on the request of the officer.**

**(2) Failure to join the means of transportation — A transporter must, without delay, notify an officer when a foreign national who entered Canada to become a member of the crew of the transporter's vessel fails to join the means of transportation within the period provided in paragraph 184(2)(b).**

SOR/2004-167, s. 66

**269. (1) Advance passenger information — On the request of an officer, a commercial transporter must provide on departure of their commercial vehicle from the last point of embarkation before arriving in Canada the following information in writing on each person carried:**

**(a) their surname, first name and initial or initials of any middle names;**

**(b) their date of birth**

**(c) the country that issued them a passport or travel document or, if they do not have a passport or travel document, their citizenship or nationality;**

**(d) their gender;**

**(e) their passport number or, if they do not have a passport, the number on the travel document that identifies them; and**

**(f) their reservation record locator or file number.**

**(2) Passenger reservation information — At any time after a commercial transporter undertakes to carry a passenger to Canada, the commercial transporter must provide an officer access to its reservation system or, on the request of an officer, provide in writing all reservation information held by the commercial transporter on passengers to be carried to Canada.**

**270. [Repealed SOR/2004-167, s. 67.]**

**271. (1) Facilities for holding and examination — A commercial transporter, and a transporter who operates an airport or an international bridge or tunnel, must without cost to Her Majesty in right of Canada provide and maintain facilities, including areas, offices and laboratories, that are adequate for the proper holding and examination of persons being carried to Canada.**

**(2) Criteria — The facilities referred to in subsection (1) are adequate if they satisfy the applicable requirements of Part II of the *Canada Labour Code*, are secure and, if necessary, sterile, and include equipment and furnishings that permit officers to discharge their duties under the Act.**

**272. Examination on vessels — A commercial transporter carrying persons to Canada aboard its vessel must provide facilities aboard the vessel that permit an officer to conduct examinations.**

**273. (1) Obligation to carry from Canada — A transporter who has carried a foreign national referred to in any of paragraphs (a) to (d) to Canada, or caused**

**such a foreign national to enter Canada, must carry the foreign national from Canada**

**(a) to any other country, in the case of a foreign national directed to leave under subsection 40(1);**

**(b) to the United States, in the case of a foreign national directed back to that country under section 41;**

**(c) to any other country, in the case of a foreign national allowed to withdraw their application under section 42; or**

**(d) to the country to which the foreign national is removed under section 241, in the case of a foreign national who is subject to an enforceable removal order.**

(2) **Conveyance to vehicle** — **The transporter must transport a foreign national who is subject to an enforceable removal order from wherever the foreign national is situated in Canada to the vehicle in which they will be carried to another country.**

274. (1) **Members of a crew** — **If a transporter carries, or causes to be carried, a foreign national to Canada as a member of its crew or to become a member of its crew, and the foreign national is subject to an enforceable removal order, the transporter must carry that foreign national from Canada to the applicable country as determined under Division 4 of Part 13.**

(2) **Conveyance to vehicle** — **The transporter must transport the foreign national referred to in subsection (1) from wherever the foreign national is situated in Canada to the vehicle in which they will be carried to another country.**

275. **Notification** — **A transporter must notify an officer without delay if a foreign national referred to in section 273 or 274 whom they are carrying from Canada leaves or attempts to leave a vehicle before they are carried from Canada.**

276. (1) **Notifying transporters** — **When a foreign national seeking to enter Canada is made subject to a removal order and a transporter is or might be required under the Act to carry that foreign national from Canada, an officer shall**

**(a) notify the transporter that it is or might be required to carry that foreign national from Canada; and**

**(b) when the removal order is enforceable, notify the transporter that it must carry the foreign national from Canada and whether the foreign national must be escorted.**

(2) **Notifying an officer** — **After being notified under paragraph (1)(b), the transporter must without delay notify an officer of arrangements made for carrying the foreign national from Canada.**

(3) **Time period** — **The transporter must carry the foreign national from Canada within 48 hours after giving notification under subsection (2) of the arrangements made.**

(4) **Non-compliance** — If a transporter does not comply with subsection (2) or (3), or notifies an officer that it is unable to comply with that subsection, or if an officer notifies the transporter in writing that the officer does not accept the proposed arrangements, an officer shall cause the foreign national to be carried from Canada and the transporter shall pay the costs under section 278.

(5) **Criteria for non-acceptance of arrangements** — To be acceptable, the arrangements referred to in subsection (2) must meet the following criteria:

(a) the foreign national is not inadmissible to the country of destination and, for the purposes of transit, all countries of transit;

(b) the safety of the foreign national and other persons aboard any vehicle used to reach the country of destination must be ensured; and

(c) the transporter must undertake to comply with any request for an escort or escorts.



277. **Exception** — Despite sections 273 and 276, a transporter is not obliged to carry from Canada, and is not required to pay the costs with respect to, a foreign national, other than a member of a crew or a foreign national who entered Canada to become a member of a crew, who

(a) was authorized to enter and remain in Canada on a temporary basis; or

(b) held a temporary resident or permanent resident visa at the time of their examination.

278. **Removal costs** — A transporter that is required under the Act to carry a foreign national from Canada must pay the following costs of removal and, if applicable, attempted removal:

(a) expenses incurred within or outside Canada with respect to the foreign national's accommodation and transport, including penalties for changes of date or routing;

(b) accommodation and travel expenses incurred by any escorts provided to accompany the foreign national;

(c) fees paid in obtaining passports, travel documents and visas for the foreign national and any escorts;

(d) the cost of meals, incidentals and other expenses as calculated in accordance with the rates set out in the *Travel Directive* published by the Treasury Board Secretariat, as amended from time to time;

(e) any wages paid to escorts and other personnel; and

(f) the costs or expenses incurred with respect to interpreters and medical and other personnel engaged for the removal.

279. (1) **Assessment of administration fee** — Subject to subsection (2), an administration fee shall be assessed against a commercial transporter in respect of

**any of the following foreign nationals it carried to Canada who are subject to a report under subsection 44(1) of the Act:**

**(a) a foreign national who is inadmissible under section 41 of the Act for failing to meet the requirements of section 6 or subsection 7(1), 50(1) or 52(1);**

**(b) a foreign national whom the transporter has been directed not to carry to Canada under paragraph 148(1)(a) of the Act;**

**(c) a foreign national who is exempt, under subsection 52(2), from the requirement to hold a passport or travel document but who fails to produce sufficient evidence of their identity;**

**(d) a foreign national who failed to appear for an examination on entry into Canada; and**

**(e) a foreign national who entered Canada as a member of a crew or to become a member of a crew and is inadmissible.**

**(2) Exceptions — An administration fee shall not be assessed against a commercial transporter in respect of**

**(a) a foreign national who is authorized to enter and remain in Canada on a temporary basis under the Act, other than a foreign national who entered Canada as a member of a crew or to become a member of a crew;**

**(b) a foreign national who is allowed to withdraw their application to enter Canada under section 42 and leaves Canada immediately;**

**(c) a foreign national who is subject to a removal order issued on their arrival at a port of entry and leaves Canada immediately;**

**(d) a person referred to in section 39; and**

**(e) a foreign national who is inadmissible under section 41 of the Act for failing to meet the requirements of section 6 but is exempted under Division 5 of Part 9 from the requirement to have a temporary resident visa.**

SOR/2004-167, s. 68

**280. (1) Administration fee — Subject to subsection (2), the administration fee assessed under section 279 is $3,200.**

**(2) Memorandum of understanding — If a memorandum of understanding in accordance with subsection (3) is in effect between the commercial transporter and the Minister, the administration fee assessed is**

**(a) $3,200, if the transporter does not demonstrate that it complies with the memorandum of understanding or if the administration fee is assessed in respect of a member of the crew of the transporter;**

**(b) $2,400, if the transporter demonstrates that it complies with the memorandum of understanding;**

**(c) $1,600, if the transporter demonstrates that it complies with the memorandum of understanding and has a number of administration fee assessments that is equal to or less than the number specified in the memorandum, for the period specified in the memorandum, for reducing the administration fee by 50%;**

(d) $800, if the transporter demonstrates that it complies with the memorandum of understanding and has a number of administration fee assessments that is equal to or less than the number specified in the memorandum, for the period specified in the memorandum, for reducing the administration fee by 75%; and

(e) $0, if the transporter demonstrates that it complies with the memorandum of understanding and has a number of administration fee assessments that is equal to or less than the number specified in the memorandum, for the period specified in the memorandum, for reducing the administration fee by 100%.

(3) **Content of memorandum of understanding** — A memorandum of understanding referred to in subsection (2) shall include provisions respecting

(a) document screening;

(b) the training of personnel in document screening;

(c) the use of technological aids;

(d) fraud prevention;

(e) gate checks;

(f) information exchange;

(g) performance standards in respect of document screening, the interdiction of inadmissible foreign nationals and administration fee assessments;

(h) compliance monitoring of the provisions of the memorandum of understanding;

(i) holding documents under section 260;

(j) providing information referred to in subsections 269(1) and (2);

(k) stowaways; and

(l) security screening of members of a crew.



281. (1) **Notice of assessment** — The assessment of an administration fee shall be served personally, by registered mail, by facsimile with acknowledgement of receipt or by electronic transmission on a representative of the commercial transporter.

(2) **Service effected** — Service of the assessment by registered mail is deemed to have been effected on the seventh day after the day on which the assessment was mailed.

282. (1) **Submissions concerning assessment** — The commercial transporter may submit written submissions to the Minister within 30 days after being served with an assessment of an administration fee.

(2) **Final assessment and notice** — If submissions are made, the Minister shall consider the submissions, confirm or cancel the assessment and give written notice of the decision to the commercial transporter.

(3) **Liability** — If no submissions are made within the 30-day period, the assessment is final and the commercial transporter is liable for the assessment at the end of that period.

(4) **Liability** — If the Minister confirms an assessment under subsection (2), the commercial transporter is liable for the assessment on the date the notice is sent.

283. (1) **Security** — The Minister may, on the basis of the following factors, require a commercial transporter to provide security for compliance with its obligations under paragraphs 148(1)(a) to (g) of the Act:

(a) the frequency and regularity of arrival, or anticipated arrival, of the transporter's vehicles carrying persons to Canada;

(b) the number of persons carried, or anticipated to be carried, to Canada aboard the transporter's vehicles;

(c) whether the transporter has carried an inadmissible foreign national to Canada; and

(d) the anticipated risk of inadmissible foreign nationals being carried to Canada by the transporter.

(2) **Amount of security** — If the Minister requires security to be provided, the Minister shall determine the amount of security on the basis of the following factors:

(a) the commercial transporter's record of compliance with the Act; and

(b) the anticipated risk of inadmissible foreign nationals being carried to Canada by the transporter and the estimated removal costs.

(3) **Form of security** — A commercial transporter who is required to provide security must provide it in the form of a cash deposit unless

(a) the transporter has entered into a memorandum of understanding referred to in subsection 280(2) that provides for another form of security; and

(b) the transporter demonstrates that there is no significant risk of a debt not being paid if they were to provide another form of security.

(4) **Return of security** — If the Minister determines on the basis of the factors set out in subsection (1) that security is no longer required, the Minister shall return the security to the commercial transporter.

284. **Application of s. 148(2) of the Act** — For the purposes of subsection 148(2) of the Act, a prescribed good is a good that is not land, a building or a transportation facility.

285. **Object detained or seized** — If an object is detained or seized under subsection 148(2) of the Act, that object shall remain detained or seized until

(a) the transporter complies with its obligations under section 148 of the Act; or

(b) the transporter's obligations are discharged by another person.

**286. (1) Notice of seizure** — Following a seizure under subsection 148(2) of the Act, an officer shall make reasonable efforts to

(a) identify the lawful owner of the object seized; and

(b) give notice of the seizure to that person.

**(2) Disposition after seizure** — A thing seized under subsection 148(2) of the Act shall be disposed of by

(a) returning the object to the transporter on receipt of

(i) an amount equal to the value of the object at the time of seizure and any expenses incurred in the seizure and, if applicable, detention,

(ii) the security required under the Act or any costs and fees for which the transporter is liable, as well as an amount equal to any expenses incurred in the seizure and, if applicable, detention, or

(iii) evidence that the transporter is in compliance with its obligations under subsection 148(1) of the Act and has reimbursed Her Majesty in right of Canada for any expenses incurred in the seizure and, if applicable, detention; or

(b) disposing of the object under section 287.



**287. (1) Sale of a seized object** — If a transporter does not comply with paragraph 286(2)(a) within a reasonable time, an officer shall give notice to the transporter that the object will be sold. The object shall then be sold for the benefit of Her Majesty in right of Canada and the proceeds of the sale shall be applied to the transporter's outstanding debt to Her Majesty under the Act. Any surplus shall be returned to the transporter.

**(2) Costs incurred in seizure** — Any expenses incurred by Her Majesty in right of Canada in selling the object, and any expenses incurred in the seizure or, if applicable, detention of the object, shall be deducted from the proceeds of the sale.

SOR/2004-167, s. 69

## PART 18 — LOANS

**288. Definition of "beneficiary"** — In this Part, "beneficiary", in respect of a person, means

(a) the person's spouse, common-law partner or conjugal partner;

(b) a dependent child of the person or of the person's spouse, common-law partner or conjugal partner; and

(c) any other person who, at the time of their application for a permanent resident visa or their application to remain in Canada as a permanent resident, is in a relationship of dependency with the person by virtue of being cared for by or receiving emotional and financial support from the person.

**289. Types of loans** — The Minister may make loans to the following persons for the following purposes:

(a) to a foreign national referred to in Part 1 of the Act for the purpose of

(i) defraying the cost to the foreign national and their beneficiaries of transportation from their point of departure outside Canada to their point of destination in Canada, and related administrative charges,

(ii) assisting the foreign national and their beneficiaries to become established in Canada, or

(iii) defraying the fee, referred to in subsection 303(1), payable for the acquisition by the foreign national and their beneficiaries of permanent resident status;

(b) to a foreign national referred to in Part 2 of the Act for the purpose of

(i) defraying the cost to the foreign national and their beneficiaries of transportation from their point of departure outside Canada to their point of destination in Canada, and related administrative charges,

(ii) defraying the cost to the foreign national and their beneficiaries of transportation to attend any interview relating to their application, and related administrative charges,

(iii) defraying the cost to the foreign national and their beneficiaries of a medical examination under subsection 16(2) of the Act or section 30 of these Regulations, and related costs and administrative charges, or

(iv) assisting the foreign national and their beneficiaries to become established in Canada; and

(c) to a permanent resident or a Canadian citizen for the purpose of

(i) defraying the cost to their beneficiaries of transportation from their point of departure outside Canada to their point of destination in Canada, and related administrative charges,

(ii) defraying the cost to their beneficiaries of a medical examination under subsection 16(2) of the Act or section 30 of these Regulations, and related costs and administrative charges, if the beneficiaries are protected persons within the meaning of subsection 95(2) of the Act, or

(iii) defraying the fee, referred to in subsection 303(1), payable for the acquisition by their beneficiaries of permanent resident status.

**290. (1) Maximum amount** — The maximum amount of advances that may be made under subsection 88(1) of the Act is $110,000,000.

**(2) Total loans** — The total amount of all loans made under this Part plus accrued interest on those loans shall not at any time exceed the maximum amount of advances prescribed by subsection (1).

291. (1) **Repayment** — Subject to section 292, a loan made under section 289 becomes payable

(a) in the case of a loan for the purpose of defraying transportation costs, 30 days after the day on which the person for whose benefit the loan was made enters Canada; and

(b) in the case of a loan for any other purpose, 30 days after the day on which the loan was made.

(2) **Repayment terms** — Subject to section 292, a loan made under section 289, together with all accrued interest, must be repaid in full, in consecutive monthly instalments, within

(a) 12 months after the day on which the loan becomes payable, if the amount of the loan is not more than $1,200;

(b) 24 months after the day on which the loan becomes payable, if the amount of the loan is more than $1,200 but not more than $2,400;

(c) 36 months after the day on which the loan becomes payable, if the amount of the loan is more than $2,400 but not more than $3,600;

(d) 48 months after the day on which the loan becomes payable, if the amount of the loan is more than $3,600 but not more than $4,800; and

(e) 72 months after the day on which the loan becomes payable, if the amount of the loan is more than $4,800.

292. (1) **Deferred repayment** — If repaying a loan, in accordance with the requirements of section 291, that was made to a person under section 289 would, by reason of the person's income, assets and liabilities, cause the person financial hardship, an officer may, to the extent necessary to relieve that hardship but subject to subsection (2), defer the commencement of the repayment of the loan, defer payments on the loan, vary the amount of the payments or extend the repayment period.

(2) **Maximum extension** — A repayment period shall not be extended beyond

(a) an additional 24 months, in the case of a loan referred to in paragraph 289(b); and

(b) an additional six months, in the case of any other loan.

293. (1) **Rate of interest** — A loan made under this Part bears interest at a rate equal to the rate that is established by the Minister of Finance for loans made by that Minister to Crown corporations and that is in effect

(a) on the first day of January in the year in which the loan is made, in the case of a loan made to a person in Canada who has no other outstanding loans under this Part; and

(b) on the first day of January in the year in which the person for whose benefit the loan is made enters Canada, in any other case.

(2) **Interest on loans under paras. 289(a) and (c)** — The interest on a loan made under paragraph 289(a) or (c) accrues beginning

(a) 30 days after the day on which the loan is made, in the case of a loan made to a person in Canada who has no other outstanding loans under this Part; and

(b) 30 days after the day on which the person for whose benefit the loan is made enters Canada, in any other case.

(3) **Interest on loans under par. 289(b)** — The interest on a loan made under paragraph 289(b) accrues

(a) if the amount of the loan is not more than $1,200, beginning on the first day of the thirteenth month after

(i) the day on which the loan is made, in the case of a loan made to a person in Canada who has no other outstanding loans under this Part, and

(ii) the day on which the person for whose benefit the loan is made enters Canada, in any other case;

(b) if the amount of the loan is more than $1,200 but not more than $2,400, beginning on the first day of the twenty-fifth month after

(i) the day on which the loan is made, in the case of a loan made to a person in Canada who has no other outstanding loans under this Part, and

(ii) the day on which the person for whose benefit the loan is made enters Canada, in any other case; and

(c) if the amount of the loan is more than $2,400, beginning on the first day of the thirty-seventh month after

(i) the day on which the loan is made, in the case of a loan made to a person in Canada who has no other outstanding loans under this Part, and

(ii) the day on which the person for whose benefit the loan is made enters Canada, in any other case.

(4) **Existing loan** — If a loan that was made to a person under section 289 has not been repaid and a subsequent loan is made under that section to that person, the subsequent loan bears interest at a rate equal to the rate of interest payable on the previous loan.

(5) The interest on a loan made under section 289 shall be calculated daily and, if a monthly installment referred to in subsection 291(2) is paid late or in part or is not paid, shall be compounded monthly.

(6) For greater certainty, the applicable rate of interest in respect of a loan made under section 289 remains the same until the loan is repaid in full.

SOR/2006-116, s. 1

# PART 19 — FEES

## DIVISION 1 — GENERAL

294. **Interpretation** — In this Part,

(a) a fee payable under this Part is payable per person, and not per application, and accordingly is payable in respect of each person by or on behalf of whom an application is made, up to the maximum fees prescribed by subsections 296(3), 297(2) and 299(3);

(b) subject to subsections 295(3), 301(2), 304(2) and 314(3), a fee payable under this Part for processing an application is payable at the time the application is made; and

(c) subject to subsections 295(4) and 301(3), if the requirement to pay a fee depends on a person's age or the amount of a fee is calculated in accordance with their age, the age of the person shall be determined as of the day the application in respect of which the fee is payable is made.

SOR/2009-163, s. 14



## DIVISION 2 — FEES FOR APPLICATIONS FOR VISAS AND PERMITS

### *Permanent Resident Visas*

295. (1) **Permanent resident visa** — The following fees are payable for processing an application for a permanent resident visa:

(a) if the application is made by a person as a member of the family class

(i) in respect of a principal applicant, other than a principal applicant referred to in subparagraph (ii), $475,

(ii) in respect of a principal applicant who is a foreign national referred to in any of paragraphs 117(1)(b) or (f) to (h), is less than 22 years of age and is not a spouse or common-law partner, $75,

(iii) in respect of a family member of the principal applicant who is 22 years of age or older or is less than 22 years of age and is a spouse or common-law partner, $550, and

(iv) in respect of a family member of the principal applicant who is less than 22 years of age and is not a spouse or common-law partner, $150;

(b) if the application is made by a person as a member of the investor class, the entrepreneur class, the self-employed persons class, the transitional federal investor class, the transitional federal entrepreneur class or the transitional federal self-employed persons class

(i) in respect of a principal applicant, $1,050,

(ii) in respect of a family member of the principal applicant who is 22 years of age or older or is less than 22 years of age and is a spouse or common-law partner, $550, and

**(iii) in respect of a family member of the principal applicant who is less than 22 years of age and is not a spouse or common-law partner, $150; and**

**(c) if the application is made by a person as a member of any other class or by a person referred to in section 71**

**(i) in respect of a principal applicant, $550,**

**(ii) in respect of a family member of the principal applicant who is 22 years of age or older or is less than 22 years of age and is a spouse or common-law partner, $550, and**

**(iii) in respect of a family member of the principal applicant who is less than 22 years of age and is not a spouse or common-law partner, $150.**

(2) **Exception — refugees** — **The following persons are not required to pay the fees referred to in subsection (1):**

**(a) a person who makes an application as a member of the Convention refugees abroad class and the family members included in the member's application; and**

**(b) a person who makes an application as a member of one of the humanitarian-protected persons abroad classes and the family members included in the member's application.**

(2.1) **Exception — transitional skilled worker class** — **The following persons are not required to pay the fees referred to in subsection (1):**

**(a) a person described in paragraph 85.1(2)(a) who makes an application as a member of the transitional federal skilled worker class for a permanent resident visa and the family members included in the member's application who were also included in the application referred to in subsection 85.1(2); and**

**(b) a person described in paragraph 85.1(2)(b) who makes an application as a member of the transitional federal skilled worker class for a permanent resident visa and the family members included in the member's application who were also included in the application referred to in subsection 85.1(2), if the fees for processing their withdrawn application have not been refunded.**

(2.2) **Exception — transitional federal business classes** — **The following persons are not required to pay the fees referred to in subsection (1):**

**(a) a person described in paragraph 109.1(2)(a) who makes an application as a member of the transitional federal investor class, the transitional federal entrepreneur class or the transitional federal self-employed persons class for a permanent resident visa and the family members included in the member's application who were also included in the application referred to in subsection 109.1(2); and**

**(b) a person described in paragraph 109.1(2)(b) who makes an application as a member of the transitional federal investor class, the transitional federal entrepreneur class or the transitional federal self-employed persons class for a permanent resident visa and the family members included in the member's application who were also included in the application referred to in subsection**

**109.1(2), if the fees for processing their withdrawn application have not been refunded.**

(3) **Payment by sponsor — A fee payable under subsection (1) in respect of a person who makes an application as a member of the family class or their family members**

(a) **is payable, together with the fee payable under subsection 304(1), at the time the sponsor files the sponsorship application; and**

(b) **shall be repaid in accordance with regulations referred to in subsection 20(2) of the *Financial Administration Act* if, before the processing of the application for a permanent resident visa has begun, the sponsorship application is withdrawn by the sponsor.**

(4) **Age — For the purposes of paragraph (1)(a), the age of the person in respect of whom the application is made shall be determined as of the day the sponsorship application is filed.**

SOR/2003-383, s. 6; SOR/2005-61, s. 7; SOR/2009-163, s. 15



## *Temporary Resident Visas*

**296.** (1) **Single entry — $75 — A fee of $75 is payable for processing an application for a temporary resident visa to enter Canada once.**

(2) **Exception — The following persons are not required to pay the fee referred to in subsection (1):**

(a) **a properly accredited diplomat, consular officer, representative or official of a country other than Canada, of the United Nations or any of its agencies or of any intergovernmental organization of which Canada is a member, the members of the suite of such a person and the family members of such a person;**

(b) **a member of the armed forces of a country that is a designated state for the purposes of the *Visiting Forces Act*, including a person who has been designated as a civilian component of that visiting force under paragraph 4(c) of that Act, and their family members;**

(c) **a person who is a member of the clergy, a member of a religious order or a lay person who is to assist a congregation or a group in the achievement of its spiritual goals, if the duties to be performed by the person are to consist mainly of preaching doctrine, presiding at liturgical functions or spiritual counselling, and their family members;**

(d) **persons, other than a group of performing artists and their staff, who apply at the same time and place for a work permit or a study permit;**

(e) **a person who is seeking to enter Canada**

(i) **for the purpose of attending a meeting hosted by the Government of Canada, an organization of the United Nations or the Organization of American States, as a participant,**

(ii) **for the purpose of attending a meeting as a representative of the Organization of American States or the Caribbean Development Bank, or**

(iii) for the purpose of attending a meeting hosted by the Government of Canada, an organization of the United Nations or the Organization of American States, at the invitation of the Government of Canada;

(f) a person who is seeking to enter Canada as a competitor, coach, judge, team official, medical staff member or member of a national or international sports organizing body participating in the Pan-American Games, when held in Canada, or as a performer participating in a festival associated with any of those Games;

(g) a person who is seeking to enter Canada for a period of less than 48 hours and who is

(i) travelling by transporter's vehicle to a destination other than Canada, or

(ii) transiting through or stopping over in Canada for refuelling or for the continuation of their journey in another transporter's vehicle; and

(h) a person who is seeking to enter Canada as a competitor, coach, judge, team official, medical staff member or member of a national or international sports organizing body participating in the XI FINA (Fédération internationale de natation) World Championships to be held in Montreal, Quebec, during the period beginning on July 17, 2005 and ending on July 31, 2005.

(3) **Maximum fee** — The total amount of fees payable under subsection (1) by an applicant and their family members who apply at the same time and place shall not exceed $400.

SOR/2005-63, s. 1; SOR/2010-121, s. 1

297. (1) **Multiple entry — $150** — A fee of $150 is payable for processing an application for a temporary resident visa to enter Canada more than once.

(1.1) **Exception** — The persons referred to in any of paragraphs 296(2)(a) to (e) or (g) are not required to pay the fee referred to in subsection (1).

(2) **Maximum fee** — The total amount of fees payable under subsection (1) by an applicant and their family members who apply at the same time and place shall not exceed $400.

SOR/2004-167, s. 70

## *Temporary Resident Permits*

298. (1) **Fee — $200** — A fee of $200 is payable for processing an application for a temporary resident permit.

(2) **Exception** — The following persons are not required to pay the fee referred to in subsection (1):

(a) a person referred to in subsection 295(2) or any of paragraphs 296(2)(c) and (d), 299(2)(a), (b), (d) to (f) and (h) to (k) and 300(2)(f) to (i);

(a.1) a properly accredited diplomat, consular officer, representative or official of a country other than Canada, of the United Nations or any of its agencies or of any intergovernmental organization of which Canada is a member, the

**members of the suite of such a person and the family members of such a person;**

**(a.2) a member of the armed forces of a country that is a designated state for the purposes of the *Visiting Forces Act*, including a person who has been designated as a civilian component of that visiting force under paragraph 4(c) of that Act, and their family members;**

**(a.3) a person whose work in Canada would create or maintain reciprocal employment for Canadian citizens or permanent residents of Canada in other countries and who is a family member of a person referred to in subparagraph 299(2)(g)(iii);**

**(b) a person in respect of whom an application for a permanent resident visa, an application to remain in Canada as a permanent resident or an application for authorization under subsection 25(1) of the Act is pending;**

**(c) a citizen of Costa Rica seeking to enter and remain in Canada during the period beginning on May 11, 2004 and ending on May 12, 2004, if the person does not hold a temporary resident visa but is not otherwise inadmissible;**

**(d) a person who is seeking to enter Canada**

> **(i) for the purpose of attending a meeting hosted by the Government of Canada, an organization of the United Nations or the Organization of American States, as a participant,**
>
> **(ii) for the purpose of attending a meeting as a representative of the Organization of American States or the Caribbean Development Bank, or**
>
> **(iii) for the purpose of attending a meeting hosted by the Government of Canada, an organization of the United Nations or the Organization of American States, at the invitation of the Government of Canada; and**

**(e) a person who, while they are in transit to Canada, ceases to be exempt under paragraph 190(1)(a) from the requirement for a temporary resident visa, if, during the first 48 hours after they cease to be exempt from that requirement, they seek to enter and remain in Canada and are inadmissible to Canada for the sole reason that they do not have a temporary resident visa.**

SOR/2003-197, s. 3; SOR/2004-111, s. 2; SOR/2004-167, s. 71; SOR/2010-121, s. 2

## *Work Permits*

**299. (1) Fee — $150 — A fee of $150 is payable for processing an application for a work permit.**

**(2) Exception — The following persons are not required to pay the fee referred to in subsection (1):**

**(a) a person in Canada who has made a refugee claim that has not yet been determined by the Refugee Protection Division, and their family members;**

**(b) a person in Canada on whom refugee protection has been conferred, and their family members;**

IRP Regulations

(c) a person who is a member of the Convention refugees abroad class or a member of one of the humanitarian-protected persons abroad classes, and their family members;

(d) a person who holds a study permit and is temporarily destitute, as described in paragraph 208(a);

(e) a person whose work in Canada is designated under subparagraph 205(c)(i);

(f) a person who works in Canada for a Canadian religious or charitable organization, without remuneration;

(g) a person whose work in Canada would create or maintain reciprocal employment for Canadian citizens or permanent residents of Canada in other countries and who is a family member of

(i) a properly accredited diplomat, consular officer, representative or official of a country other than Canada, of the United Nations or any of its agencies or of any intergovernmental organization of which Canada is a member,

(ii) a member of the armed forces of a country that is a designated state for the purposes of the *Visiting Forces Act*, including a person who has been designated as a civilian component of that visiting force under paragraph 4(c) of that Act, or

(iii) an officer of a foreign government sent, under an exchange agreement between Canada and one or more countries, to take up duties with a federal or provincial agency;

(h) a person who works in Canada under an agreement entered into with a country by Canada or by or on behalf of a province, that provides for reciprocal employment opportunities of an artistic, cultural or educational nature;

(i) a person whose work in Canada is pursuant to an international student or young workers reciprocal employment program;

(j) a person who works in Canada as an officer of the United States Immigration and Naturalization Service or of United States Customs carrying out pre-inspection duties, as an American member of the International Joint Commission or as a United States grain inspector, and their family members; and

(k) a United States Government official in possession of an official United States Government passport who is assigned to a temporary posting in Canada, and their family members.

(3) **Maximum fee** — The total amount of fees payable under subsection (1) by a group of three or more persons, consisting of performing artists and their staff, who apply at the same time and place for a work permit is $450.

## *Study Permits*

300. (1) **Fee — $125** — A fee of $125 is payable for processing an application for a study permit.

(2) **Exception** — The following persons are not required to pay the fee referred to in subsection (1):

(a) a person in Canada who has made a refugee claim that has not yet been determined by the Refugee Protection Division, and their family members;

(b) a person in Canada on whom refugee protection has been conferred, and their family members;

(c) a person who is a member of the Convention refugees abroad class or one of the humanitarian-protected persons abroad classes, and their family members;

(d) a properly accredited diplomat, consular officer, representative or official of a country other than Canada, of the United Nations or any of its agencies or of any intergovernmental organization of which Canada is a member, the members of the suite of such a person and the family members of such a person;

(e) a member of the armed forces of a country that is a designated state for the purposes of the *Visiting Forces Act*, including a person who has been designated as a civilian component of that visiting force under paragraph 4(c) of that Act, and their family members;

(f) a person who holds a study permit and is temporarily destitute, as described in paragraph 208(a);

(g) a person whose study in Canada is under an agreement or arrangement between Canada and another country that provides for reciprocity of student exchange programs;

(h) a person who works in Canada as an officer of the United States Immigration and Naturalization Service or of United States Customs carrying out pre-inspection duties, as an American member of the International Joint Commission or as a United States grain inspector, and their family members; and

(i) a United States Government official in possession of an official United States Government passport who is assigned to a temporary posting in Canada, and their family members.



## Division 3 — Fees for Applications to Remain in Canada as a Permanent Resident

301. (1) **Fee** — The following fees are payable for processing an application to remain in Canada as a permanent resident:

(a) if the application is made by a person as a member of the spouse or common-law partner in Canada class

(i) in respect of a principal applicant, $475,

(ii) in respect of a family member of the principal applicant who is 22 years of age or older or is less than 22 years of age and is a spouse or common-law partner, $550, and

(iii) in respect of a family member of the principal applicant who is less than 22 years of age and is not a spouse or common-law partner, $150; and

(b) if the application is made by a person as a member of the live-in caregiver class or as a protected person under subsection 175(1)

(i) in respect of a principal applicant, $550,

(ii) in respect of a family member of the principal applicant who is 22 years of age or older or is less than 22 years of age and is a spouse or common-law partner, $550, and

(iii) in respect of a family member of the principal applicant who is less than 22 years of age and is not a spouse or common-law partner, $150.

(1.1) **Exception** — A person who is a member of the protected temporary residents class and the family members included in their application are not required to pay the fees referred to in subsection (1).

(2) **Payment by sponsor** — The fee payable under subsection (1) in respect of a person who makes an application as a member of the spouse or common-law partner in Canada class or their family members

(a) is payable, together with the fee payable under subsection 304(1), at the time the sponsor files the sponsorship application; and

(b) shall be repaid in accordance with regulations referred to in subsection 20(2) of the *Financial Administration Act* if, before the processing of the application to remain in Canada as a permanent resident has begun, the sponsorship application is withdrawn by the sponsor.

(3) **Age** — For the purposes of paragraph (1)(a), the age of the person in respect of whom the application is made shall be determined as of the day the sponsorship application is filed.

SOR/2004-167, s. 72; SOR/2009-163, s. 16

302. **Fee — $325** — A fee of $325 is payable for processing an application by a person as a member of the permit holder class to remain in Canada as a permanent resident.

SOR/2004-167, s. 73

## Division 4 — Right of Permanent Residence

303. (1) **Fee — $490** — A fee of $490 is payable by a person for the acquisition of permanent resident status.

(2) **Exception** — The following persons are not required to pay the fee referred to in subsection (1):

(a) a person who is a family member of a principal applicant and is a dependent child referred to in paragraph (b) or (c) of the definition "family member" in subsection 1(3);

(b) a principal applicant who is a foreign national referred to in paragraph 117(1)(b), (f) or (g);

**(b.1) a principal applicant in Canada who has made an application in accordance with section 66 and is a dependent child of a permanent resident or of a Canadian citizen;**

**(b.2) a member of the permit holder class who is a dependent child of**

**(i) a member of the permit holder class who has made an application to remain in Canada as a permanent resident, or**

**(ii) a permanent resident or a Canadian citizen;**

**(c) a protected person within the meaning of subsection 95(2) of the Act who has applied to remain in Canada as a permanent resident, and their family members;**

**(c.1) a person who is a member of the protected temporary residents class and is described in paragraph 151.1(2)(b) and the family members included in their application;**

**(d) a person who is a member of the Convention refugees abroad class, and the family members included in their application; and**

**(e) a person who is a member of one of the humanitarian-protected persons abroad classes, and the family members included in their application.**



**(3) Payment — The fee referred to in subsection (1) is payable**

**(a) in the case of an application by or on behalf of a person for a permanent resident visa, before the visa is issued; and**

**(b) in the case of an application by or on behalf of a foreign national to remain in Canada as a permanent resident, before the foreign national becomes a permanent resident.**

**(4) Remission — The fee referred to in subsection (1) is remitted if the person does not acquire permanent resident status, in which case the fee shall be repaid by the Minister to the person who paid it.**

**(5) Transitional — subsection (4) — For the purpose of subsection (4), if the fee was paid before the day on which this subsection comes into force, the amount to be remitted and repaid — except to the extent otherwise remitted — is $975.**

**(6) Transitional — remission — Despite subsections (4) and (5), in the case where the fee of $975 was paid in accordance with paragraph (3)(a), a portion of that fee in the amount of $485 is remitted and shall be repaid — except to the extent otherwise remitted — by the Minister to the person who paid the fee if**

**(a) the person in respect of whom the fee was paid has, on or before the day on which this subsection comes into force, not yet acquired permanent resident status and they are a person referred to in any of paragraphs 117(1)(a), (c), (d) or (h); or**

**(b) the person in respect of whom the fee was paid acquires permanent resident status on or after the day on which this subsection comes into force and they are not a person referred to in any of paragraphs 117(1)(a), (c), (d) or (h).**

SOR/2004-167, s. 74(1), (2); SOR/2005-61, s. 8; SOR/2006-89, s. 1

## DIVISION 5 — FEES FOR OTHER APPLICATIONS AND SERVICES

### *Sponsorship Application for Family Classes*

**304.** (1) **Fee — $75 — A fee of $75 is payable for processing a sponsorship application under Part 7.**

(2) **Payment — The fee referred to in subsection (1) is payable at the time the application is filed.**

### *Extension of Authorization to Remain in Canada as a Temporary Resident*

**305.** (1) **Fee — $75 — A fee of $75 is payable for processing an application under subsection 181(1).**

(2) **Exception — The following persons are not required to pay the fee referred to in subsection (1):**

> **(a) a person who makes an application for a work permit or a study permit at the same time as they make the application referred to in subsection (1);**
>
> **(b) a person who has made a claim for refugee protection that has not yet been determined by the Refugee Protection Division;**
>
> **(c) a person on whom refugee protection has been conferred;**
>
> **(d) a person who has been determined to be a member of the Convention refugees abroad class or one of the humanitarian-protected persons abroad classes;**
>
> **(e) a properly accredited diplomat, consular officer, representative or official of a country other than Canada, of the United Nations or any of its agencies or of any intergovernmental organization of which Canada is a member, the members of the suite of such a person and the family members of such a person;**
>
> **(f) a member of the armed forces of a country that is a designated state for the purposes of the *Visiting Forces Act*, including a person who has been designated as a civilian component of that visiting force under paragraph 4(c) of that Act, and their family members;**
>
> **(g) a person who is a member of the clergy, a member of a religious order or a lay person who is to assist a congregation or a group in the achievement of its spiritual goals, if the duties to be performed by the person are to consist mainly of preaching doctrine, presiding at liturgical functions or spiritual counselling, and their family members;**
>
> **(h) an officer of a foreign government sent, under an exchange agreement between Canada and one or more countries, to take up duties with a federal or provincial agency; and**
>
> **(i) a family member of any of the following persons, namely,**
>
> > **(i) a person who holds a study permit and is temporarily destitute, as described in paragraph 208(a),**

(ii) a person whose work is designated under subparagraph 205(c)(i),

(iii) a person whose work in Canada is for a Canadian religious or charitable organization, without remuneration,

(iv) a person whose presence in Canada is as a participant in a program sponsored by the Canadian International Development Agency, or

(v) a person whose presence in Canada is as a recipient of a Government of Canada scholarship or fellowship.

## *Restoration of Temporary Resident Status*

306. (1) **Fee — $200** — A fee of $200 is payable for processing an application under section 182.

(2) **Exception** — A person who holds an unexpired temporary resident permit is not required to pay the fee referred to in subsection (1).

## *Application under Section 25 of the Act*

307. **Fees** — The following fees are payable for processing an application made in accordance with section 66 if no fees are payable in respect of the same applicant for processing an application to remain in Canada as a permanent resident or an application for a permanent resident visa:

(a) in the case of a principal applicant, $550;

(b) in the case of a family member of the principal applicant who is 22 years of age or older or is less than 22 years of age and is a spouse or common-law partner, $550; and

(c) in the case of a family member of the principal applicant who is less than 22 years of age and is not a spouse or common-law partner, $150.

## *Permanent Resident Cards*

308. (1) **Fee — $50** — A fee of $50 is payable for processing an application made under paragraph 53(1)(b) for a permanent resident card.

(2) **Renewal or replacement fee** — A fee of $50 is payable for processing an application for the renewal of a permanent resident card or for the replacement of a lost, stolen or destroyed permanent resident card.

(3) **Replacement due to error** — No fee is payable for the replacement of a permanent resident card containing an error that is not attributable to the permanent resident.

## Determination of Rehabilitation

**309. Fees — The following fees are payable for processing an application for a determination of rehabilitation under paragraph 36(3)(c) of the Act:**

**(a) in the case of a foreign national inadmissible on grounds of serious criminality under paragraph 36(1)(b) or (c) of the Act, $1,000; and**

**(b) in the case of a foreign national inadmissible on grounds of criminality under paragraph 36(2)(b) or (c) of the Act, $200.**

## Authorization to Return to Canada

**310. Fee — $400 — A fee of $400 is payable for processing an application for authorization to return to Canada under subsection 52(1) of the Act.**

## Certification and Replacement of Immigration Document

**311. (1) Certification — $30 — A fee of $30 is payable for processing an application for the certification of an immigration document, other than a permanent resident card, confirming the date on which a person became a permanent resident.**

**(2) Replacement — $30 — A fee of $30 is payable for processing an application to replace any immigration document, other than a permanent resident card, that is issued by the Department.**

**(3) Exception — The following persons are not required to pay the fee referred to in subsection (1):**

**(a) a federal, provincial or municipal government agency;**

**(b) a person in receipt of provincial social assistance payments; and**

**(c) a person in receipt of assistance under the Resettlement Assistance Program.**

## After-hours Examination

**312. (1) Fee — $100 — The following fees are payable for an examination for the purpose of entering Canada that is made outside the applicable service hours of the port of entry where the officer who conducts the examination is based:**

**(a) a fee of $100 for the first four hours of examination; and**

**(b) a fee of $30 for each additional hour or part of an hour of examination.**

**(2) Payment — The fees are payable at the time of the examination**

**(a) if the transporter's vehicle carrying the person to be examined arrives unscheduled at a port of entry outside service hours, by the transporter; and**

**(b) in any other case, by the person who requests that the examination take place outside service hours.**

## *Alternative Means of Examination*

**313. (1) Fee — $30 — A fee of $30 is payable for processing an application to enroll in a program for an alternative means of examination that is administered solely by the Minister.**

**(2) Payment — The fee is payable in respect of each person to be examined by an alternative means referred to in subsection (1).**

## *Immigration Statistical Data*

**314. (1) Fee for statistical data — The following fees are payable for processing an application for immigration statistical data that have not been published by the Department:**

**(a) $100 for the first 10 minutes or less of access to the Department's database in order to respond to such an application; and**

**(b) $30 for each additional minute or less of such access.**

**(2) Exception — The following persons are not required to pay the fees referred to in subsection (1):**

**(a) an employee of the Department; and**

**(b) an employee of the Data Development Division of the Department of Human Resources Development.**

**Proposed Amendment — 314(2)(b)**

**(b) an employee of the Data Development Division of the Department of Human Resources and Skills Development.**

SOR/2010-172, s. 5(f) [To come into force April 1, 2011.]

**(3) Payment — The fee referred to in subsection (1)(b) is payable at the time the service is rendered.**

SOR/2009-163, s. 17

**315. Travel document — A fee of $50 is payable for processing an application for a travel document issued under subsection 31(3) of the Act.**

# PART 20 — TRANSITIONAL PROVISIONS

## DIVISION 1 — INTERPRETATION

**316. (1) Definitions — The definitions in this subsection apply in this Part.**

**"former Regulations" means the *Immigration Regulations, 1978*, as enacted by Order in Council P.C. 1978-486 dated February 23, 1978 and registered as SOR/78-172. *("ancien règlement")***

IRP Regulations

**"Humanitarian Designated Classes Regulations" means the *Humanitarian Designated Classes Regulations*, as enacted by Order in Council P.C. 1997-477 dated April 8, 1997 and registered as SOR/97-183. *("Règlement sur les catégories d'immigrants précisées pour des motifs d'ordre humanitaire")***

**"Immigration Act Fees Regulations" means the *Immigration Act Fees Regulations*, as enacted by Order in Council P.C. 1996-2003 dated December 19, 1996 and registered as SOR/97-22. *("Règlement sur les prix à payer — Loi sur l'immigration")***

**"Refugee Claimants Designated Class Regulations" means the *Refugee Claimants Designated Class Regulations*, as enacted by Order in Council P.C. 1989-2517 dated December 21, 1989 and registered as SOR/90-40. *("Règlement sur la catégorie admissible de demandeurs du statut de réfugié")***

**(2) Interpretation — former Act — For greater certainty, in this Part "former Act" has the same meaning as in section 187 of the *Immigration and Refugee Protection Act.***

**(3) Interpretation — *Immigration and Refugee Protection Act* — A reference in this Part to the *Immigration and Refugee Protection Act* includes the regulations and rules made under it.**

## DIVISION 2 — GENERAL PROVISIONS

**317. (1) Decisions and orders made under former Act — A decision or order made under the former Act that is in effect immediately before the coming into force of this section continues in effect after that coming into force.**

**(2) Documents issued under former Act — A document, including a visa, that is issued under the former Act and is valid immediately before the coming into force of this section continues to be valid after that coming into force.**

## DIVISION 3 — ENFORCEMENT

**318. Terms and conditions — Terms and conditions imposed under the former Act become conditions imposed under the *Immigration and Refugee Protection Act.***

### Case Law

*Gjoka v. Canada (Minister of Citizenship & Immigration)* (2009), 84 Imm. L.R. (3d) 198, 352 F.T.R. 303, 2009 FC 943, 2009 CarswellNat 3058, 2009 CarswellNat 5358 (Eng.) (F.C.) — The applicant was selected on September 16, 2002, for permanent residence under the entrepreneur category and was issued a permanent resident visa on February 4, 2003, and landed on March 12, 2003. On May 28, 2004, in response to a letter from Canadian Immigration and Citizenship, the applicant submitted a monitoring report and an application to cancel his terms and conditions of landing. No other monitoring reports were submitted. A report pursuant to subs. 41(1) of the Act alleging that the applicant had failed to comply with the terms and conditions of his landing was issued on March 18, 2009. An inadmissibility hearing was held before the ID on May 7, 2008. The respondent submitted that the applicant had not met the conditions imposed on him under the *Immi-*

*gration Regulations* (the former Regulations), specifically paragraphs 23.1(1)(a) to (d). The applicant made his application for permanent residency under the former Act but the selection decision and his permanent resident visa were issued after the coming into force of the current Act. Furthermore, the Confirmation of Permanent Residence form signed by the applicant upon landing specified that the conditions to be met were those of the former Regulations and s. 23.1 of those Regulations was attached to the form. At the admissibility hearing, the ID member found that the conditions imposed on the applicant were of s. 98 of the current Regulations and as such, this subs. 44(1) report alleging a failure to meet the conditions under the former Regulations was unfounded. Following an appeal by the Minister, the IAD set aside the ID's decision and referred the matter back for reconsideration. The IAD accepted the conclusion that the applicant was subject to the conditions set out in s. 98 of the current Regulations and referred the matter back to the ID to determine whether or not the applicant had met the conditions imposed under the Act.

Because of the transitional provisions and s. 318 of the current Regulations, the Court found that the entrepreneur class selected applicants under the former *Immigration Act* are required to comply with post-admission to Canada terms and conditions as set out in paragraphs 23(a) to (d) of the former *Immigration Regulations*. The interpretation of the transitional provisions of the IAD is too restrictive. It implies that s. 98 of the current Regulations can be applied retroactively to entrepreneurial applicants who filed their application prior to January 1, 2002, and were assessed and issued visas as entrepreneur under the former *Immigration Act* and Regulations. Nothing in the Act, the current Regulations or the transitional provisions support such a proposition. The application for judicial review was allowed.

**319. (1) Removal order — Subject to subsection (2), a removal order made under the former Act that was unexecuted on the coming into force of this section continues in force and is subject to the provisions of the *Immigration and Refugee Protection Act*.**

**(2) Stay of removal — The execution of a removal order that had been stayed on the coming into force of this section under paragraphs 49(1)(c) to (f) of the former Act continues to be stayed until the earliest of the events described in paragraphs 231(1)(a) to (e).**

**(3) Exception — Subsection (2) does not apply if**

**(a) the subject of the removal order was determined by the Convention Refugee Determination Division not to have a credible basis for their claim; or**

**(b) the subject of the removal order**

**(i) is subject to a removal order because they are inadmissible on grounds of serious criminality, or**

**(ii) resides or sojourns in the United States or St. Pierre and Miquelon and is the subject of a report prepared under subsection 44(1) of the *Immigration and Refugee Protection Act* on their entry into Canada.**

**(4) Conditional removal order — A conditional removal order made under the former Act continues in force and is subject to subsection 49(2) of the *Immigration and Refugee Protection Act*.**

**(5) Executed removal order** — Section 52 of the *Immigration and Refugee Protection Act* applies to a person who immediately before the coming into force of this section was outside Canada after a removal order was executed against them.

**320. (1) Inadmissibility — security grounds** — A person is inadmissible under the *Immigration and Refugee Protection Act* on security grounds if, on the coming into force of this section, the person had been determined to be a member of an inadmissible class described in paragraph 19(1)(e), (f), (g) or (k) of the former Act.

**(2) Violating human or international rights** — A person is inadmissible under the *Immigration and Refugee Protection Act* on grounds of violating human or international rights if, on the coming into force of this section, the person had been determined to be a member of an inadmissible class described in paragraph 19(1)(j) or (l) of the former Act.

**(2.1) Paragraph 19(1)(l) of the former Act** — For greater certainty, an opinion of the Minister under paragraph 19(1)(l) of the former Act continues as an opinion of the Minister under paragraph 35(1)(b) of the *Immigration and Refugee Protection Act.*

**(3) Serious criminality** — A person is inadmissible under the *Immigration and Refugee Protection Act* on grounds of serious criminality if, on the coming into force of this section, the person had been determined to be a member of an inadmissible class described in paragraph 19(1)(c) or (c.1) of the former Act or had been determined to be inadmissible on the basis of paragraph 27(1)(a.1) of the former Act.

**(4) Criminality** — A person is inadmissible under the *Immigration and Refugee Protection Act* on grounds of criminality if, on the coming into force of this section, the person had been determined to be a member of an inadmissible class described in paragraph 19(2)(a), (a.1) or (b) of the former Act, or had been determined to be inadmissible on the basis of paragraph 27(1)(a.2) or (a.3) or (2)(d) of the former Act.

**(5) Paragraph 27(1)(d) of former Act** — A person who on the coming into force of this section had been determined to be inadmissible on the basis of paragraph 27(1)(d) of the former Act is

(a) inadmissible under the *Immigration and Refugee Protection Act* on grounds of serious criminality if the person was convicted of an offence and a term of imprisonment of more than six months has been imposed or a term of imprisonment of 10 years or more could have been imposed; or

(b) inadmissible under the *Immigration and Refugee Protection Act* on grounds of criminality if the offence was punishable by a maximum term of imprisonment of five years or more but less than 10 years.

**(6) Organized crime** — A person is inadmissible under the *Immigration and Refugee Protection Act* on grounds of organized criminality if, on the coming into force of this section, the person had been determined to be a member of an inadmissible class described in paragraph 19(1)(c.2) or subparagraph 19(1)(d)(ii) of the former Act.

(7) **Health grounds** — A person — other than an applicant described in section 7 of the former Regulations or section 4 of *Humanitarian Designated Classes Regulations* who made an application for admission under the former Act — is inadmissible under the *Immigration and Refugee Protection Act* on health grounds if, on the coming into force of this section, the person had been determined to be a member of the inadmissible class described in paragraph 19(1)(a) of the former Act.

(8) **Financial reasons** — A person is inadmissible under the *Immigration and Refugee Protection Act* for financial reasons if, on the coming into force of this section, the person had been determined to be a member of the inadmissible class described in paragraph 19(1)(b) of the former Act or had been determined to be inadmissible on the basis of paragraph 27(1)(f) or (2)(l) of the former Act.

(9) **Misrepresentation** — A person is inadmissible under the *Immigration and Refugee Protection Act* for misrepresentation if, on the coming into force of this section, the person had been determined to be inadmissible on the basis of paragraph 27(1)(e) or (2)(g) or (i) of the former Act.

(10) **Failing to comply** — A person is inadmissible under the *Immigration and Refugee Protection Act* for failing to comply with that Act if, on the coming into force of this section, the person had been determined to be a member of an inadmissible class described in paragraph 19(1)(h) or (i) or (2)(c) or (d) of the former Act, or had been determined to be inadmissible on the basis of paragraph 27(1)(b) or (2)(b), (e), (f), (h), (i) or (k) of the former Act.

SOR/2004-167, s. 75

321. (1) **Reports** — A report made under section 20 or 27 of the former Act is a report under subsection 44(1) of the *Immigration and Refugee Protection Act*.

(2) **Equivalency** — For the purpose of subsection (1)

(a) inadmissibility as a member of a class described in paragraph 19(1)(e), (f), (g) or (k) of the former Act is inadmissibility on security grounds under the *Immigration and Refugee Protection Act*;

(b) inadmissibility as a member of a class described in paragraph 19(1)(j) or (l) of the former Act is inadmissibility under the *Immigration and Refugee Protection Act* on grounds of violating human or international rights;

(c) inadmissibility as a member of a class described in paragraph 19(1)(c) or (c.1) of the former Act or inadmissibility on the basis of paragraph 27(1)(a.1) of the former Act is inadmissibility under the *Immigration and Refugee Protection Act* on grounds of serious criminality;

(d) inadmissibility as a member of a class described in paragraph 19(2)(a), (a.1) or (b) of the former Act or inadmissibility on the basis of paragraph 27(1)(a.2) or (a.3) or (2)(d) of the former Act is inadmissibility under the *Immigration and Refugee Protection Act* on grounds of criminality;

IRP Regulations

(e) inadmissibility on the basis of paragraph 27(1)(d) of the former Act is inadmissibility under the *Immigration and Refugee Protection Act* on grounds of

(i) serious criminality, if the person was convicted of an offence and a term of imprisonment of more than six months has been imposed or a term of imprisonment of 10 years or more could have been imposed, or

(ii) criminality if the offence was punishable by a maximum term of imprisonment of five years or more but less than 10 years;

(f) inadmissibility as a member of a class described in paragraph 19(1)(c.2) or subparagraph 19(1)(d)(ii) of the former Act is inadmissibility under the *Immigration and Refugee Protection Act* on grounds of organized criminality;

(g) inadmissibility as a member of the inadmissible class described in paragraph 19(1)(a) of the former Act — other than an applicant described in section 7 of the former Regulations or section 4 of the *Humanitarian Designated Classes Regulations* who made an application for admission under the former Act — is inadmissibility under the *Immigration and Refugee Protection Act* on health grounds if, on the coming into force of this section, the person had been determined to be a member of file inadmissible class described in paragraph 19(1)(a) of the former Act;

(h) inadmissibility as a member of a class described in paragraph 19(1)(b) of the former Act or inadmissibility on the basis of paragraph 27(1)(f) or (2)(l) of the former Act is inadmissibility under the *Immigration and Refugee Protection Act* for financial reasons;

(i) inadmissibility on the basis of paragraph 27(1)(e) or (2)(g) or (i) of the former Act is inadmissibility under the *Immigration and Refugee Protection Act* for misrepresentation; and

(j) inadmissibility as a member of a class described in paragraph 19(1)(h) or (i) or (2)(c) or (d) of the former Act or inadmissibility on the basis of paragraph 27(1)(b) or (2)(b), (e), (f), (h), (i) or (k) of the former Act is inadmissibility under the *Immigration and Refugee Protection Act* for failing to comply with the Act.

(3) **Reports forwarded to a senior immigration officer** — A report that was forwarded to a senior immigration officer under the former Act and in respect of which a decision has not been made on the coming into force of this section is a report transmitted to the Minister.

(4) **Inquiry** — The causing by a senior immigration officer of an inquiry to be held under the former Act is the referring by the Minister of a report to the Immigration Division under subsection 44(2) of the *Immigration and Refugee Protection Act* unless that subsection allows the Minister to make a removal order.

(5) **No substantive evidence** — If no substantive evidence was adduced before the Adjudication Division, the causing by a senior immigration officer of an inquiry to be held under the former Act is, if subsection 44(2) of the *Immigration and Refugee Protection Act* allows the Minister to make a removal order, a report on the basis of which the Minister may make a removal order.

322. (1) **Detention** — **The first review of reasons, after the coming into force of this section, for the continued detention of a person detained under the former Act shall be made in accordance with the provisions of the former Act.**

(2) **Period of detention** — **If the review referred to in subsection (1) was the first review in respect of a person's detention, the period of detention at the end of which that review was made shall be considered the period referred to in subsection 57(1) of the *Immigration and Refugee Protection Act*.**

(3) **Subsequent review** — **If a review of reasons for continued detention follows the review referred to in subsection (1), that review shall be made under the *Immigration and Refugee Protection Act*.**

323. **Order issued by Deputy Minister** — **An order issued by a Deputy Minister under subsection 105(1) of the former Act continues in force and the review of reasons for continued detention shall be made under the *Immigration and Refugee Protection Act*.**

324. **Release** — **A release from detention under the former Act is the ordering of release from detention under the *Immigration and Refugee Protection Act* and any terms and conditions imposed under the former Act become conditions imposed under the *Immigration and Refugee Protection Act*.**

325. (1) **Warrants** — **A warrant for arrest and detention made under the former Act is a warrant for arrest and detention made under the *Immigration and Refugee Protection Act*.**

(2) **Detention orders** — **An order for the detention of a person made under the former Act is an order to detain made under the *Immigration and Refugee Protection Act*.**

326. (1) **Danger to the public** — **A claim to be a Convention refugee made by a person described in subparagraph 19(1)(c.1)(i) of the former Act in respect of whom the Minister was of the opinion under subparagraph 46.01(1)(e)(i) of the former Act that the person constitutes a danger to the public in Canada is deemed, if no determination was made by a senior immigration officer under section 45 of the former Act, to be a claim for refugee protection made by a person described in paragraph 101(2)(b) of the *Immigration and Refugee Protection Act* who is inadmissible and in respect of whom the Minister is of the opinion that the person is a danger to the public.**

(2) **Appeals** — **A person in respect of whom subsection 70(5) or paragraph 77(3.01)(b) of the former Act applied on the coming into force of this section is a person in respect of whom subsection 64(1) of the *Immigration and Refugee Protection Act* applies.**

(3) **Removal not prohibited** — **A person whose removal on the coming into force of this section was allowed by the application of paragraphs 53(1)(a) to (d) of the former Act is a person referred to in subsection 115(2) of the *Immigration and Refugee Protection Act*.**

## Case Law

### Section 326(2)

*Townsend v. Canada (Minister of Citizenship & Immigration)* (2004), 41 Imm. L.R. (3d) 1, 2004 CarswellNat 5639, 2004 CarswellNat 4723, 331 N.R. 62, 2004 FCA 436 (F.C.A.) — If a person has been convicted of a crime that was punished in Canada by a term of imprisonment of less than two years, and found to be a danger to the public under subs. 70(5) of the former *Immigration Act* so that person had no right of an appeal to the IAD under the former *Immigration Act*, then s. 326(2) of the *Immigration and Refugee Protection Regulations* bar an appeal to the IAD.

**327. Certificates — A certificate determined to be reasonable under paragraph 40.1(4)(d) of the former Act is deemed to be a certificate determined to be reasonable under subsection 80(1) of the *Immigration and Refugee Protection Act*.**

**328. (1) Permanent residents — A person who was a permanent resident immediately before the coming into force of this section is a permanent resident under the *Immigration and Refugee Protection Act*.**

**(2) Returning resident permit — Any period spent outside Canada within the five years preceding the coming into force of this section by a permanent resident holding a returning resident permit is considered to be a period spent in Canada for the purpose of satisfying the residency obligation under section 28 of the *Immigration and Refugee Protection Act* if that period is included in the five-year period referred to in that section.**

**(3) Returning resident permit — Any period spent outside Canada within the two years immediately following the coming into force of this section by a permanent resident holding a returning resident permit is considered to be a period spent in Canada for the purpose of satisfying the residency obligation under section 28 of the *Immigration and Refugee Protection Act* if that period is included in the five-year period referred to in that section.**

**329. (1) Visitors and permit holders — Any of the following persons who were in Canada immediately before the coming into force of this section are temporary residents under the *Immigration and Refugee Protection Act* and are subject to its provisions:**

**(a) a visitor under the former Act; and**

**(b) a person issued a permit under section 37 of the former Act.**

**(2) Permits — A permit issued by the Minister under section 37 of the former Act is deemed to be a temporary resident permit referred to in section 24 of the *Immigration and Refugee Protection Act*.**

**330. Examination** — Any of the following persons who were in Canada immediately before the coming into force of this section are deemed to have been authorized under section 23 of the *Immigration and Refugee Protection Act* to enter Canada:

(a) a person in respect of whom an examination remains incomplete and whose examination was adjourned and referred to another immigration officer for completion under subsection 12(3) of the former Act;

(b) a person in respect of whom an examination remains incomplete and whose examination was deferred under paragraph 13(1)(a) of the former Act;

(c) a person in respect of whom an examination remains incomplete and who was authorized to come into Canada for further examination under paragraph 14(2)(b) of the former Act;

(d) a person in respect of whom an examination remains incomplete and who was authorized to come into Canada for further examination under paragraph 23(1)(b) of the former Act; and

(e) a person who has made a claim to be a Convention refugee in respect of which a determination of eligibility was not made before the coming into force of this section.

**331. Performance bonds and security deposits** — A performance bond posted or security deposited under the former Act that remains posted or deposited immediately before the coming into force of this section continues as a deposit or a guarantee under the *Immigration and Refugee Protection Act* and is governed by its provisions.

**332. Seizures** — A thing seized under the former Act continues to be seized on the coming into force of this section, and the seizure is governed by the provisions of the *Immigration and Refugee Protection Act.*

**333. Debts** — Any debt under subsection 118(3) of the former Act continues as a debt on the coming into force of this section and is governed by the provisions of the *Immigration and Refugee Protection Act.*

## DIVISION 4 — REFUGEE AND HUMANITARIAN RESETTLEMENT PROGRAM

**334. Applications for protection abroad** — With the exception of subsection 150(1) of these Regulations, the *Immigration and Refugee Protection Act* applies to an applicant described in section 7 of the former Regulations or section 4 of the *Humanitarian Designated Classes Regulations* who made an application for admission under the former Act if the application is pending at the time of the coming into force of this section and no visa has been issued to the applicant.

**335. Family member** — An applicant described in section 7 of the former Regulations or section 4 of the *Humanitarian Designated Classes Regulations* who made an application for admission under the former Act that has not been refused may

**add to their application at any time prior to their departure for Canada a person included in the definition "family member" in subsection 1(3).**

**336. Sponsorship agreements — A sponsorship agreement with the Minister made under the former Act and former Regulations does not cease to have effect for the sole reason of section 152 coming into force.**

**337. (1) Sponsors — Subject to subsections (2) and (3), a sponsor who made an undertaking within the meaning of paragraph (b) of the definition "undertaking" in subsection 2(1) of the former Regulations, or of the definition "undertaking" in subsection 1(1) of the *Humanitarian Designated Classes Regulations*, and in respect of whom an immigration officer was satisfied that the requirements of paragraph 7.1(2)(d) or 5(2)(d) of those Regulations, respectively, were met is deemed to be a sponsor whose application has been approved by an officer under section 154.**

**(2) Additional persons sponsored — Subsection (1) does not apply to a sponsor who requests that a person be added to their undertaking.**

**(3) Ineligibility to sponsor — Subsection (1) does not apply to a sponsor who is ineligible to be a party to a sponsorship under section 156.**

## DIVISION 5 — REFUGEE PROTECTION

**338. Refugee protection — Refugee protection is conferred under the *Immigration and Refugee Protection Act* on a person who**

**(a) has been determined in Canada before the coming into force of this section to be a Convention refugee and**

**(i) no determination was made to vacate that determination, or**

**(ii) no determination was made that the person ceased to be a Convention refugee;**

**(b) as an applicant or an accompanying dependant was granted landing before the coming into force of this section after being issued a visa under**

**(i) section 7 of the former Regulations, or**

**(ii) section 4 of the *Humanitarian Designated Classes Regulations*; or**

**(c) was determined to be a member of the post-determination refugee claimants in Canada class before the coming into force of this section and was granted landing under section 11.4 of the former Regulations or who becomes a permanent resident under subsection 21(2) of the *Immigration and Refugee Protection Act*.**

**339. Rejection of a claim for refugee protection — A determination made in Canada before the coming into force of this section that a person is not a Convention refugee is deemed to be a claim for refugee protection rejected by the Board.**

**340. Ineligibility — A determination made before the coming into force of this section that a person is not eligible to have their Convention refugee claim determined**

by the Convention Refugee Determination Division is deemed to be a determination that the claim is ineligible to be referred to the Refugee Protection Division.

341. **Withdrawal and abandonment** — A claim to be a Convention refugee that was withdrawn or declared to be abandoned before the coming into force of this section is deemed to be a claim determined to be withdrawn or abandoned under the *Immigration and Refugee Protection Act*.

342. **Eligibility** — A claim made in Canada to be a Convention refugee in respect of which a determination of eligibility was not made before the coming into force of this section is deemed to be a claim for refugee protection made in Canada that is received on the day on which this section comes into force.

343. **Redetermination of eligibility** — Subject to section 191 of the *Immigration and Refugee Protection Act*, a claim of a person who was determined eligible before the coming into force of this section to have a claim to be a Convention refugee determined by the Convention Refugee Determination Division, and in respect of which no determination was made by that Division, is a claim that

(a) is referred under the *Immigration and Refugee Protection Act* to the Refugee Protection Division unless an officer gives notice under subsection 104(1) of that Act; and

(b) is subject to the provisions of that Act.

344. **Cessation of refugee protection** — A determination made in Canada before the coming into force of this section that a person has ceased to be a Convention refugee is deemed to be a determination by the Board that refugee protection has ceased.

345. **Vacation** — A decision made in Canada before the coming into force of this section to approve an application to reconsider and vacate a determination that a person is a Convention refugee is deemed to be a determination by the Board to vacate a decision to allow a claim for refugee protection.

346. (1) **Post-determination refugee claimants in Canada class** — An application for landing as a member of the post-determination refugee claimants in Canada class in respect of which no determination of whether the applicant is a member of that class was made before the coming into force of this section is an application for protection under sections 112 to 114 of the *Immigration and Refugee Protection Act* and those sections apply to the application.

(2) **Notification re additional submissions** — Before a decision is made on the application, the applicant shall be notified that they may make additional submissions in support of their application.

(3) **Decision** — A decision on the application shall not be made until 30 days after notification is given to the applicant.

IRP Regulations

(4) **Giving notification** — Notification is given

(a) when it is given by hand to the applicant; or

(b) if it is sent by mail, seven days after the day on which it was sent to the applicant at the last address provided by them to the Department.

(5) **Stay of removal** — For greater certainty, the execution of a removal order made under the former Act against an applicant referred to in subsection (1) is stayed, and the stay is effective until the earliest of the applicable events described in section 232 occurs.

SOR/2004-167, s. 76

347. (1) **Application for landing — Convention refugees** — If landing was not granted before the coming into force of this section, an application for landing submitted under section 46.04 of the former Act is an application to remain in Canada as a permanent resident under subsection 21(2) of the *Immigration and Refugee Protection Act*.

(2) **Application for landing — undocumented Convention refugee in Canada class** — If landing was not granted before the coming into force of this section, an application for landing as a member of the undocumented Convention refugee in Canada class is an application to remain in Canada as a permanent resident under subsection 21(2) of the *Immigration and Refugee Protection Act* and is not subject to the requirement in subsection 175(1) that the application be received within 180 days after a determination is made by the Board.

(3) **Application for landing — post-determination refugee claimants in Canada class** — If landing was not granted before the coming into force of this section, an application for landing submitted by a person pursuant to a determination that the person is a member of the post-determination refugee claimants in Canada class is an application to remain in Canada as a permanent resident under subsection 21(2) of the *Immigration and Refugee Protection Act*.

## Division 6 — Court Proceedings

348. (1) **Judicial review** — On the coming into force of this section, any application for leave to commence an application for judicial review and any application for judicial review or appeal from an application that was brought under the former Act that is pending before the Federal Court or the Supreme Court of Canada is deemed to have been commenced under Division 8 of Part 1 of the *Immigration and Refugee Protection Act* and is governed by the provisions of that Division and section 87.

(2) **Application for non-disclosure** — On the coming into force of this section, any application under subsection 82.1(10) of the former Act that is pending before the Federal Court is deemed to be an application under section 87 of the *Immigration and Refugee Protection Act*.

(3) **Where no leave required** — Despite subsection (1), an application for judicial review that was not subject to the requirement of an application for leave under

**the former Act and was pending on the coming into force of this section does not require such an application under the *Immigration and Refugee Protection Act.***

**(4) Judicial review after coming into force — Any judicial review proceeding brought in respect of any decision or order made or any matter arising under the former Act after the coming into force of this section is governed by Division 8 of Part 1 and section 87 of the *Immigration and Refugee Protection Act.***

**(5) Time for filing — A person in respect of whom the 30-day period provided by section 18.1 of the *Federal Courts Act* for making an application for judicial review from a decision or matter referred to in subsection 82.1(2) of the former Act has not elapsed on the coming into force of this section and who has not made such an application has 60 days from the coming into force of this section to file an application for leave under section 72 of the *Immigration and Refugee Protection Act.***

**(6) Validity or lawfulness of a decision or act — The validity or lawfulness of a decision or act made under the former Act that is the subject of a judicial review procedure or appeal referred to in subsection (1) is determined in accordance with the provisions of the former Act.**

2002, c. 8, s. 182(3)(a)

IRP Regulations

## Case Law

### Section 348(1)

*Dragosin v. Canada (Minister of Citizenship & Immigration)* (2003), 26 Imm. L.R. (3d) 119, 2003 CarswellNat 175, 2003 CarswellNat 988, 2003 FCT 81, 227 F.T.R. 16, 106 C.R.R. (2d) 92 (T.D.) — This was a judicial review of an exclusion order against the applicant who, as a stowaway, arrived in Halifax in November 2001. Upon his arrival ashore in Halifax, the applicant was turned over to the Immigration Department and eventually ordered detained under s. 103.1(a) of the *Immigration Act*. The applicant was interviewed after his detention. He had not, at the time of the second interview, had any contact with counsel. Pursuant to s. 348(1) of IRPA Regulations and s. 190 of IRPA, this proceeding is governed by IRPA, but s. 348(6) of IRPA Regulations provides that the lawfulness or validity of a decision made or done under the *Immigration Act* is to be determined under the provisions of the *Immigration Act*.

The applicant's right to counsel arose at the moment he was ordered detained. The immigration officers who arranged his detention had the responsibility to provide advice about, and to facilitate access to, counsel. It was an error in law not to do so. The exclusion order was set aside because of this failure and an order was issued directing reconsideration of the applicant's circumstances by a different immigration officer.

**349. Other court proceedings — On the coming into force of this section, an appeal made under section 102.17 of the former Act or an application for an order made under section 102.2 of the former Act that is pending remains governed by the provisions of the former Act.**

**350. (1) Decisions referred back — Subject to subsections (2) and (3), if a decision or an act of the Minister or an immigration officer under the former Act is referred back by the Federal Court or Supreme Court of Canada for determination**

**and the determination is not made before this section comes into force, the determination shall be made in accordance with the *Immigration and Refugee Protection Act*.**

(2) **Decisions or acts not provided for by *Immigration and Refugee Protection Act*** — **If the decision or act referred to in subsection (1) was made under paragraph 46.01(1)(e), subsection 70(5) or paragraph 77(3.01)(b) of the former Act and the *Immigration and Refugee Protection Act* makes no provision for the decision or act, no determination shall be made.**

(3) **Skilled workers and self-employed persons** — **If a decision or an act of the Minister or an immigration officer under the former Act in respect of a person described in subparagraph 9(1)(b)(i) or paragraph 10(1)(b) of the former Regulations is referred back by the Federal Court or Supreme Court of Canada for determination and the determination is not made before December 1, 2003, the determination shall be made in accordance with subsections 361(4) and (5.2) of these Regulations.**

(4) **Investors, entrepreneurs and provincial nominees** — **If a decision or an act of the Minister or an immigration officer under the former Act in respect of a person described in subparagraph 9(1)(b)(ii) or (iii) of the former Regulations is referred back by the Federal Court or Supreme Court of Canada for determination and the determination is not made before December 1, 2003, the determination shall be made in accordance with subsections 361(5), (5.1) and (6) of these Regulations.**

(5) **Immigration Appeal Division decisions** — **If a decision of the Immigration Appeal Division made under the former Act is referred back by the Federal Court or Supreme Court of Canada for determination and the determination is not made before the date of the coming into force of this section, the Immigration Appeal Division shall dispose of the matter in accordance with the former Act.**

(6) **Adjudication Division decisions** — **If a decision of the Adjudication Division made under the former Act is referred back by the Federal Court or Supreme Court of Canada for determination and the determination is not made before the date of the coming into force of this section, the immigration Division shall dispose of the matter in accordance with the *Immigration and Refugee Protection Act*.**

SOR/2003-383, s. 7

## Case Law

### Section 350(1)

*Karmali v. Canada (Minister of Citizenship & Immigration)* (2003), 30 Imm. L.R. (3d) 90, 2003 CarswellNat 800, 2003 CarswellNat 2109, 2003 FCT 358, 230 F.T.R. 140 (T.D.) — Section 190 of IRPA and s. 350 of the Regulations do not apply retroactively. They do not state that IRPA should govern as though it was enforced in 1997, rather they state that applications still pending, and specifically applications sent back for re-determination after IRPA came into force, are to be dealt with under IRPA.

The applicant does not have a vested right to have his application re-determined under the law as it existed at the date of the application. Section 190 of IRPA and s. 350 of the

Regulations deal with, in clear terms, the manner in which a matter sent back for re-determination is to be re-considered.

The language of s. 190 is not permissive. When s. 190 of IRPA and s. 350 of the Regulations are read together they clearly provide a complete framework for dealing with applications that are referred back by the Court for re-determination.

Section 350 of the Regulations is not *ultra vires* the framework of s. 190. Section 201 of the IRPA allows for Regulations regarding the transition between the former Act and IRPA.

Finally s. 190 of IRPA does not offend subs. 2(e) of the *Canadian Bill of Rights* as it does not deprive a person of the right to a fair hearing.



### Section 350(3)

*Chen v. Canada (Minister of Citizenship & Immigration)* (2003), 27 Imm. L.R. (3rd) 18, 2003 CarswellNat 804, 2003 CarswellNat 2106, 2003 FCT 368 (Fed. T.D.) — Section 201 of IRPA provides authority for subs. 350(3) of the Regulations and therefore subs. 350(3) of the Regulations is not *ultra vires*.

### Section 350(5)

*Denton-James v. Canada (Minister of Citizenship & Immigration)*, 2004 CarswellNat 2902, 2004 CarswellNat 1942, 254 F.T.R. 290, 2004 FC 911 (F.C.) — Section 350(5) of the IRP Regulations applies to a decision of the IAD that is remitted for re-determination by the Federal Court after June 28, 2002.

## DIVISION 7 — UNDERTAKINGS

**351. (1) Application of the Act to existing undertakings — Subject to subsection (2), an undertaking referred to in section 118 of the former Act that was given before the day on which this section comes into force is governed by the *Immigration and Refugee Protection Act*.**

**(2) Recovery of social assistance payments — Payments that are made to or for the benefit of a person as social assistance or as financial assistance in the form of funds from a government resettlement assistance program referred to in subparagraph 139(1)(f)(ii) as a result of the breach of an undertaking, within the meaning of subparagraph (a)(ii) or paragraph (b) of the definition "undertaking" in subsection 2(1) of the former Regulations or of the definition "undertaking" in subsection 1(1) of the *Humanitarian Designated Classes Regulations*, that was given before the day on which this section comes into force, may be recovered from the person or organization that gave the undertaking as a debt due to Her Majesty in right of Canada or in right of a province.**

**(3) Duration — For greater certainty, the duration of an undertaking referred to in section 118 of the former Act that was given to the Minister before the day on which this section comes into force is not affected by these Regulations.**

**(4) Duration and terms — For greater certainty, if an immigrant visa was issued to a person described in section 7 of the former Regulations or section 4 of the *Humanitarian Designated Classes Regulations* before the day on which this section**

**comes into force, the duration and terms of an undertaking, referred to in section 118 of the former Act, relating to that person are not affected by these Regulations.**

## DIVISION 8 — NON-ACCOMPANYING FAMILY MEMBERS

**352. Not required to be included — A person is not required to include in an application a non-accompanying common-law partner or a non-accompanying child who is not a dependent son or a dependent daughter within the meaning of subsection 2(1) of the former Regulations and is a dependent child as defined in section 2 of these Regulations if the application was made under the former Act before the day on which this section comes into force.**

### Case Law

*Natt v. Canada (Minister of Citizenship & Immigration)*, [2004] F.C.J. No. 997, 254 F.T.R. 122, 36 Imm. L.R. (3d) 292, 2004 CarswellNat 1693, 2004 FC 810 (F.C.) — This was an application to review a decision of the Immigration Appeal Division. The applicant married a Canadian citizen who then sponsored her application for permanent residence. The applicant did not disclose that she had two children and on this basis was granted permanent residence. In May 2001, the applicant sponsored applications for permanent residence for her two children. A visa officer refused these applications and the applicant appealed to the Appeal Division who dismissed her appeal.

The central issue was whether Regulation 117(9)(d) applied to the two children as members of the family class. The purpose of this provision is to ensure that foreign nationals seeking permanent residence do not omit non-accompanying dependent members from their application, thereby avoiding their examination for admissibility at that time, and then, once having obtained their own permanent residence status, seek to sponsor their dependants and benefit from the preferential processing as well as admission treatments given to members of the family class. The sole exception is with respect to the children of sponsors whose applications for permanent residence were made before June 28, 2002, where those children meet the definition of "dependent child" under the Act but do not meet the definition of "dependent child" under the former Act. This exception is articulated in ss. 352 and 355 of the Regulations and reflects the fact that the Act changed the definition of dependent child to include unmarried children as old as age 21, whereas the former Act's definition included only unmarried children up to age 18. The purpose of the exception is to enable family members to sponsor dependants who would have been considered too old to be eligible before the Act came into force.

**353. Requirements not applicable — If a person has made an application under the former Act before the day on which this section comes into force, the following provisions do not apply to the person in respect of any of their non-accompanying dependent children, referred to in section 352, or their non-accompanying common-law partner:**

**(a) paragraph 70(1)(e);**

**(b) subparagraph 72(1)(e)(i); and**

**(c) paragraph 108(1)(a).**

**354. Requirements not applicable — If a person makes an application before the day on which this section comes into force, their non-accompanying dependent children, referred to in section 352, and their non-accompanying common-law partner shall not, for the purposes of that application, be considered inadmissible non-accompanying family members, referred to in paragraph 42(a) of the *Immigration and Refugee Protection Act*, and are not subject to the requirements of paragraph 30(1)(a) or 51(b).**

**355. Family members not excluded from family class — If a person who made an application under the former Act before June 28, 2002 sponsors a non-accompanying dependent child, referred to in section 352, who makes an application as a member of the family class or the spouse or common-law partner in Canada class, or sponsors a non-accompanying common-law partner who makes such an application, paragraph 117(9)(d) does not apply in respect of that dependent child or common-law partner.**

SOR/2004-167, s. 77



## Case Law

*Collier v. Canada (Minister of Citizenship & Immigration)*, [2004] F.C.J. No. 1445, 43 Imm. L.R. (3d) 53, 2004 CarswellNat 5094, 2004 CarswellNat 2993, 260 F.T.R. 266 (Eng.), 2004 FC 1209 (F.C.) — A child who is between 19 and 21, although a dependent under the new Regulations, did not need to be included as a non-accompanying dependent child in the sponsor's application for landing under the former regulations. Section 355 is intended to save an application if it was filed under the former regulatory scheme and in accordance with the former definition of dependant child within that scheme.

*Natt v. Canada (Minister of Citizenship & Immigration)*, [2004] F.C.J. No. 997, 36 Imm. L.R. (3d) 292, 254 F.T.R. 122, 2004 CarswellNat 1693, 2004 FC 810 (F.C.) — This was an application to review a decision of the Immigration Appeal Division. The applicant married a Canadian citizen who then sponsored her application for permanent residence. The applicant did not disclose that she had two children and on this basis was granted permanent residence. In May 2001, the applicant sponsored applications for permanent residence for her two children. A visa officer refused these applications and the applicant appealed to the Appeal Division who dismissed her appeal.

The central issue was whether Regulation 117(9)(d) applied to the two children as members of the family class. The purpose of this provision is to ensure that foreign nationals seeking permanent residence do not omit non-accompanying dependent members from their application thereby avoiding their examination for admissibility at that time, and then, once having obtained their own permanent residence status, seek to sponsor their dependants and benefit from the preferential processing as well as admission treatments given to members of the family class. The sole exception is with respect to the children of sponsors whose applications for permanent residence were made before June 28, 2002, where those children meet the definition of "dependent child" under the Act but do not meet the definition of "dependent child" under the former Act. This exception is articulated in ss. 352 and 355 of the Regulations and reflects the fact that the Act changed the definition of dependent child to include unmarried children as old as age 21, whereas the former Act's definition included only unmarried children up to age 18. The purpose of the exception is to enable family members to sponsor dependants who would have been considered too old to be eligible before the Act came into force.

## Division 9 — Fiancés

**356. Pending applications — If a person referred to in paragraph (f) of the definition "member of the family class" in subsection 2(1) of the former Regulations made an application under those Regulations for a permanent resident visa, or their sponsor submitted a sponsorship application under those Regulations, before June 28, 2002, the person's application or the sponsorship application, as the case may be, is governed by the former Act.**

SOR/2004-167, s. 78

## Division 10 — Fees

**357. Remission — right of landing fee — The fee set out in column III of item 19 of the schedule to the *Immigration Act Fees Regulations* is remitted and shall be repaid by the Minister to the person who paid it if the fee is paid in respect of a person before they become a permanent resident under the *Immigration and Refugee Protection Act* and the person, at the time they made an application for landing under the former Regulations, was**

**(a) a member of the family class and 19 years of age or older and, on the day on which this section comes into force, is a foreign national referred to in paragraph 117(1)(b) or (e) of these Regulations; or**

**(b) an accompanying dependant of an immigrant, within the meaning of subsection 2(1) of the former Regulations, 19 years of age or older and not a spouse of the principal applicant.**

**358. (1) Fees to be reapplied — A fee paid for processing an application in respect of which no decision has been made before the day on which this section comes into force or an application that has been refused but the refusal has not been communicated to the applicant before that day shall be applied to the cost of completing the processing of the application under the *Immigration and Refugee Protection Act*.**

**(2) Exception — Subsection (1) does not apply in respect of an application for a returning resident permit.**

**359. Remission — returning resident permit fee — The fee for a returning resident permit set out in column III of item 3 of the schedule to the *Immigration Act Fees Regulations* is remitted if, before the day on which this section comes into force, no decision has been made on the application for the permit or the application has been refused and the refusal has not been communicated to the applicant. If the fee is remitted, it shall be repaid by the Minister to the person who paid it.**

**360. Remission — fee for review of family business employment offer — The fee set out in column III of item 16 of the schedule to the *Immigration Act Fees Regulations* for the review of an offer of employment made to an applicant in**

respect of a family business is remitted if, before the day on which this section comes into force, no determination has been made on the family business application or the application has been refused and the refusal has not been communicated to the applicant. If the fee is remitted, it shall be repaid by the Minister to the person who paid it.

## DIVISION 11 — ECONOMIC CLASSES

361. (1) **Equivalent assessment** — If, before the day on which this section comes into force, a foreign national referred to in subsection (2) has been assessed by a visa officer and awarded the number of units of assessment required by the former Regulations, that assessment is, for the purpose of these Regulations, an award of points equal or superior to the minimum number of points required of

(a) a skilled worker, in the case of a foreign national described in paragraph (2)(a);

(b) an investor, in the case of a foreign national described in paragraph (2)(b);

(c) an entrepreneur, in the case of a foreign national described in paragraph (2)(c); or

(d) a self-employed person, in the case of a foreign national described in paragraph (2)(a).

(2) **Applicant for immigrant visa** — Subsection (1) applies in respect of a foreign national who submitted an application under the former Regulations, as one of the following, for an immigrant visa that is pending immediately before the day on which this section comes into force:

(a) a person described in subparagraph 9(1)(b)(i) or paragraph 10(1)(b) of the former Regulations;

(b) an investor; or

(c) an entrepreneur.

(3) **Application before January 1, 2002** — During the period beginning on the day on which this section comes into force and ending on March 31, 2003, units of assessment shall be awarded to a foreign national, in accordance with the former Regulations, if the foreign national is an immigrant who,

(a) is referred to in subsection 8(1) of those Regulations, other than a provincial nominee; and

(b) before January 1, 2002, made an application for an immigrant visa under those Regulations that is still pending on the day on which this section comes into force and has not, before that day, been awarded units of assessment under those Regulations.

(4) **Pending applications — skilled workers** — Beginning on December 1, 2003, a foreign national who is an immigrant who made an application under the former Regulations before January 1, 2002 for an immigrant visa as a person described in subparagraph 9(1)(b)(i) or paragraph 10(1)(b) of those Regulations, other than a self-employed person within the meaning of subsection 2(1) of those Regulations, and whose application is still pending on December 1, 2003 and who has not,

before that day, been awarded units of assessment under those Regulations must, in order to become a permanent resident as a member of the federal skilled worker class,

(a) be awarded at least the minimum number of units of assessment required by those Regulations for a person described in subparagraph 9(1)(b)(i) or paragraph 10(1)(b) of those Regulations, other than a self-employed person within the meaning of subsection 2(1) of those Regulations; or

(b) meet the requirements of subsection 75(2) and paragraph 76(1)(b) of these Regulations and obtain a minimum of 67 points based on the factors set out in paragraph 76(1)(a) of these Regulations.

(5) **Pending applications — investors** — Beginning on December 1, 2003, a foreign national who is an immigrant who made an application under the former Regulations before January 1, 2002 for an immigrant visa as an investor and whose application is still pending on December 1, 2003 and who has not, before that day, been awarded units of assessment under those Regulations must, in order to become a permanent resident as a member of the investor class,

(a) be determined to be an investor within the meaning of subsection 2(1) of those Regulations and be awarded at least the minimum number of units of assessment required by those Regulations for an investor; or

(b) be an investor within the meaning of subsection 88(1) of these Regulations and obtain a minimum of 35 points based on the factors set out in subsection 102(1) of these Regulations.

(5.1) **Pending applications — entrepreneurs** — Beginning on December 1, 2003, a foreign national who is an immigrant who made an application under the former Regulations before January 1, 2002 for an immigrant visa as an entrepreneur and whose application is still pending on December 1, 2003 and who has not, before that day, been awarded units of assessment under those Regulations must, in order to become a permanent resident as a member of the entrepreneur class,

(a) be determined to be an entrepreneur within the meaning of subsection 2(1) of those Regulations and be awarded at least the minimum number of units of assessment required by those Regulations for an entrepreneur; or

(b) be an entrepreneur within the meaning of subsection 88(1) of these Regulations and obtain a minimum of 35 points based on the factors set out in subsection 102(1) of these Regulations.

(5.2) **Pending applications — self-employed persons** — Beginning on December 1, 2003, a foreign national who is an immigrant who made an application under the former Regulations before January 1, 2002 for an immigrant visa as a self-employed person and whose application is still pending on December 1, 2003 and who has not, before that day, been awarded units of assessment under those Regulations must, in order to become a permanent resident as a member of the self-employed persons class,

(a) be determined to be a self-employed person within the meaning of subsection 2(1) of those Regulations and be awarded at least the minimum number of units of assessment required by those Regulations for a self-employed person; or

**(b) be a self-employed person within the meaning of subsection 88(1) of these Regulations and obtain a minimum of 35 points based on the factors set out in subsection 102(1) of these Regulations.**

**(6) Provincial nominees — If, before the day on which this section comes into force, a foreign national who was a provincial nominee submitted an application for a permanent resident visa under the former Regulations that is pending immediately before that day, the foreign national shall be assessed, and units of assessment shall be awarded to them, in accordance with those Regulations.**

SOR/2003-383, s. 8

## Case Law

*Kniazeva v. Canada (Minister of Citizenship & Immigration)* (2006), 52 Imm. L.R. (3d) 298, 2006 CarswellNat 472, 2006 FC 268 (F.C.) — The applicant filed an application for permanent residence under the skilled worker class. New legislation was enacted following the applicant's application having been filed. Under subs. 361(4) of the *Immigration and Refugee Protection Regulations*, the applicant could have become a permanent resident as a member of the federal skilled worker class by qualifying under either the former Act's regulation or under the new legislation. Once the visa officer decided to access the applicant under both the old and new Act, he had to inform the applicant of the new requirements with respect to language proficiency. The visa officer's failure to conduct a thorough review of her application under the new Act and failure to provide the applicant with an opportunity to provide him with the language assessment amounted to a clear breach of duty of fairness owed to the applicant.

The visa officer contacted the applicant's former employer with a view to verifying her employment. The employer confirmed the applicant had "practical training at the plant while she was a student and had worked intervals during the period between June 1997 and July 1998. Accordingly, the visa officer had a duty to inform the applicant that he only considered this work experience as part-time and therefore the experience was being disqualified as relevant work experience.

The visa officer breached the duty of procedural fairness and the application for judicial review was allowed.

*Kazi v. Canada (Minister of Citizenship & Immigration)* (2003), 34 Imm. L.R. (3d) 38, [2004] 1 F.C.R. 161, 238 F.T.R. 99, 2003 FC 948, [2003] F.C.J. No. 1212, 2003 CarswellNat 4427, 2003 CarswellNat 2413 (F.C.) — This is an application to review a decision of a visa officer refusing the applicant's application for permanent residence in the skilled worker class category.

A foreign national must, before entering Canada, apply for a visa or for any other document required by the Regulations. The visas or other documents shall be issued if, following an examination, the officer is satisfied that the foreign national is not inadmissible and meets the requirements of the Act and Regulations. A foreign national may be selected as a member of the economic class on the basis of his or her ability to become economically established in Canada.

Subsection 75(1) of the new Regulations creates the "Federal Skilled Worker Class", one of the economic classes for the purposes of subs. 12(2) of the Act. It is defined as a class of persons who are skilled workers and who may become permanent residents on the basis of their ability to become economically established in Canada and who intend to reside in a province other than Quebec. The requirements that a foreign national must meet in order to be considered a skilled worker are listed in subs. 75(2) of the new Regulations. If the foreign worker fails to meet these requirements, the application for permanent residence shall be refused and no further assessment is required. The ability of the foreign national to become economically established must be assessed on the basis of the criteria enumerated at subs. 76(1) of the Regulations. The minimum number of points is to be fixed by the Minister in a manner provided in subs. 76(2). The visa officer has a discretion to substitute his or her evaluation if the number of points awarded is not an accurate indicator of whether the skilled worker may become economically established in Canada. Such an evaluation requires the concurrence of a second officer.

No one has a vested right in the continuation of the laws that stood in the past. The survival provisions of the *Interpretation Act* provide for the continued application of repealed legislation to past situations. However, subs. 43(c) of the *Interpretation Act* is no more than a presumption. This presumption is refutable if the contrary intention is set out in the statute being considered. Section 361 of the Regulations specifically addresses the case where an application has been made before January 1, 2002. Accordingly, it is reasonable to conclude that in so doing it was clearly intended that any application made after January 1, 2002 would be assessed in accordance with the new Act and Regulations.

The new Regulations have a retrospective application in the sense that they change the future legal effect of a past situation. Once the visa officer determined that the applicant's application did not fall within the ambit of the transitional provisions, he should have promptly informed the applicant that he would now be assessed under the changed criteria and given the applicant the opportunity to provide additional information and to complete his application within a reasonable period of time. The lack of proper notice constitutes a breach of rules of fairness.

The decision of the visa officer was set aside and the matter was returned to a different visa officer with directions that the applicant be allowed to complete his application and submit additional information. The Court also directed that three months was a reasonable time to allow for the additional information to be provided.

*Dragan v. Canada (Minister of Citizenship & Immigration)*, [2003] 4 F.C. 189, 27 Imm. L.R. (3d) 157, 2003 CarswellNat 467, 2003 CarswellNat 1525, 2003 FCT 211, 227 F.T.R. 272, 224 D.L.R. (4th) 738, [2003] F.C.J. No. 260; additional reasons at [2003] F.C.J. No. 404, 228 F.T.R. 52, 27 Imm. L.R. (3d) 185, 2003 CarswellNat 588, 2003 CarswellNat 1580, 2003 FCT 281; affirmed (2003), 27 Imm. L.R. (3d) 194, 224 D.L.R. (4th) 764, 2003 CarswellNat 1419, 2003 FCA 233, [2003] F.C.J. No. 813 (C.A.) — This consolidated application involved 124 applicants who applied for permanent residence in Canada before June 28, 2002, the day that the IRPA came into force. The applicants sought a writ of *mandamus* requiring the respondent to assess them in accordance with the former Act and the former Regulations. Sections 190 and 201 of the IRPA indicate that Parliament intended the new Act to apply retrospectively and to authorize regulations with retrospective effect. Parliament can expressly enact retroactive or retrospective legislation. The clear expression of Parliamentary intent in this regard overrides the presumption against retroactivity or retrospectively in s. 43 of the *Interpretation Act*. Section 361 of the IRPA Regulations is validly authorized respective legislation and operates according to its terms, which means that applications filed after January 1, 2002, are to be assessed under the new Regulations and applications filed before January 1, 2002 are to be assessed under the old Regulations up until March 31, 2003.

The following conditions need to be satisfied for the Court to issue a writ of *mandamus*:

1. There must be a public legal duty to act.
2. The duty must be owed to the applicant.
3. There must be a clear right to the performance of that duty, in particular,

    (a) the applicant must have satisfied all conditions precedent giving rise to the duty and;

    b) there was a prior demand for the performance of the duty, a reasonable time to comply with the demand and a subsequent refusal which can either be expressed or implied, e.g. unreasonable delay.

4. No other adequate remedy is available to the applicant.
5. The order sought will be of some practical value or effect.
6. The Court finds no equitable bar to the relief sought.
7. On a balance of convenience an order should issue.

The Court found all of these conditions satisfied and granted a writ of *mandamus* with respect to 102 of the applicants requiring the respondent on or before March 31, 2003 to assess the 102 applicants and award units of assessment in accordance with the former Regulations. Applications for judicial review with respect to applicants who filed after January 1, 2002, will be assessed under the selection criteria in the IRPA. The applicants who applied in this category had notice of the new selection criteria at the time of their application.



**362. Investors — If, before April 1, 1999, a foreign national made an application for an immigrant visa as an investor and signed any document referred to in clause 1(v)(iii)(A) of Schedule X to the former Regulations, as that Schedule read immediately before that date, or, in the case of an investor in a province, either applied for a selection certificate under section 3.1 of *An Act respecting immigration to Québec*, R.S.Q., c. I-0.2, as amended from time to time, or applied for an immigrant visa as an investor, and signed an investment agreement in accordance with the law of that province, the relevant provisions of the former Regulations respecting an applicant for an immigrant visa as an investor, an approved business, an investor in a province, a fund manager, an eligible business, an approved fund, a fund, an escrow agent, a privately administered venture capital fund or a government-administered venture capital fund continue to apply as they read immediately before April 1, 1999 to all persons governed by their application before that date.**

**363. Entrepreneurs — For greater certainty, section 98 does not apply in respect of an entrepreneur within the meaning of subsection 2(1) of the former Regulations who was issued an immigrant visa under subparagraph 9(1)(b)(ii) or (c)(i) of those Regulations.**

# PART 21 — REPEALS AND COMING INTO FORCE

## *Repeals*

**364. Regulations repealed — The following Regulations are repealed:**

**(a) the *Immigration Regulations, 1978*[1];**

**(b) the *Refugee Claimants Designated Class Regulations*[2];**

**(c) the *Immigration Act Fees Regulations*[3]; and**

**(d) the *Humanitarian Designated Classes Regulations*[4].**

## *Coming Into Force*

**365. (1) Coming into force — These Regulations, except paragraph 117(1)(e), subsection 117(5) and paragraphs 259(a) and (f) come into force on June 28, 2002.**

**(2) [Repealed SOR/2005-61, s. 9.]**

**(3) Exception — Paragraphs 259(a) and (f) come into force on December 31, 2003.**
SOR/2003-97, s. 1; SOR/2004-34, s. 1; SOR/2005-61, s. 9

# SCHEDULE 1 — PORTS OF ENTRY

*(Section 2)*

### Division 1 — Ontario

**1. Ambassador Bridge, Windsor**

**2. Detroit and Canada Tunnel, Windsor**

**3. Fort Frances International Bridge, Fort Frances**

**4. Hamilton International Airport, Hamilton**

**5. Lansdowne (Thousand Islands Bridge), Lansdowne**

**6. Lester B. Pearson International Airport, Mississauga**

**7. Lewiston-Queenston Bridge, Queenston**

**8. Peace Bridge, Fort Erie**

**9. Pigeon River Border Crossing at Highway 61, Pigeon River**

**10. Rainbow Bridge, Niagara Falls**

**11. Rainy River International Bridge, Rainy River**

**12. Sarnia Blue Water Bridge, Point Edward**

---

[1]SOR/78-172

[2]SOR/90-40

[3]SOR/97-22

[4]SOR/97-183

13. Sault Ste. Marie International Bridge, Sault Ste. Marie
14. Seaway International Bridge, Cornwall
15. Seaway Skyway International Bridge, Prescott
16. Whirlpool Bridge, Niagara Falls

## Division 2 — Quebec

1. Abercorn, Abercorn
2. Armstrong, Saint-Théophile
3. Beebe, Stanstead
4. Chartierville, Chartierville
5. Clarenceville, Clarenceville
6. Dundee, Sainte-Agnès-de-Dundee
7. East Hereford, East Hereford
8. Frelighsburg, Frelighsburg
9. Glen Sutton, Sutton
10. Hemmingford, Hemmingford
11. Herdman, Athelstan
12. Hereford Road, Saint-Herménégilde
13. Highwater, Highwater
14. Lacolle Highway 15, Saint-Bernard-de-Lacolle
15. Lacolle Highway 221, Notre-Dame Du Mont-Carmel
16. Lacolle Highway 223, Notre-Dame Du Mont-Carmel
17. Montreal International Airport, Dorval
18. Montreal International Airport, Mirabel
19. Noyan, Noyan
20. Rock Island Highway 55, Stanstead
21. Rock Island Highway 143, Stanstead
22. Saint-Armand, Saint-Armand de Philipsburg
23. Stanhope, Stanhope
24. Trout River, Athelstan
25. Woburn, Woburn

## Division 3 — New Brunswick

1. Andover, Carlingford
2. Campobello, Welshpool
3. Centreville, Royalton
4. Clair, Clair
5. Edmundston, Edmundston
6. Gillespie Portage, Gillespie Settlement

**7. Milltown, St. Stephen**

**8. St. Croix, St. Croix**

**9. Saint Leonard, Saint Leonard**

**10. Woodstock Road, Belleville**

**11. Grand Falls, Grand Falls**

### Division 4 — Manitoba

**1. Boissevain, Boissevain**

**2. Emerson West Lynne, Emerson**

**3. Sprague, Sprague**

**4. Winnipeg International Airport, Winnipeg**

### Division 5 — British Columbia

**1. Boundary Bay, Delta**

**2. Douglas, Surrey**

**3. Huntingdon, Huntingdon**

**4. Kingsgate, Kingsgate**

**5. Osoyoos, Osoyoos**

**6. Pacific Highway, Surrey**

**7. Patterson, Rossland**

**8. Roosville, Grasmere**

**9. Stewart, Stewart**

**10. Vancouver International Airport, Richmond**

**11. Victoria International Airport, Sidney**

### Division 6 — Saskatchewan

**1. North Portal, North Portal**

**2. Regway, Regway**

### Division 7 — Alberta

**1. Calgary International Airport, Calgary**

**2. Coutts, Coutts**

**3. Edmonton International Airport, Edmonton**

### Division 8 — Yukon

**1. Beaver Creek, Beaver Creek**

SOR/2004-167, s. 79

# SCHEDULE 2

***(paragraph 148(2)(d) and section 149)***

**1. Colombia**

**2. El Salvador**

**3. Guatemala**

**4. Democratic Republic of Congo**

**5. Sierra Leone**

**6. Sudan**

## Transitional Provisions

— SOR/2010-172, ss. 6–8 [To come into force April 1, 2011.]:

6. For the purposes of section 8, a reference to a former provision of the *Immigration and Refugee Protection Regulations* means a reference to that provision as it read immediately before the coming into force of these Regulations.

7. The calculation of the four-year period referred to in paragraph 200(3)(g), as enacted by subsection 2(3), is not to include work that was performed before the day on which this section comes into force.

8. (1) An application for a work permit that requires an officer's determination based on an opinion referred to in subsection 203(1) of the *Immigration and Refugee Protection Regulations* is to be dealt with under the former sections 200, 201 and 203 if the opinion was requested before the coming into force of this section.

(2) An application under section 197, 198, 199 or 201 of the *Immigration and Refugee Protection Regulations* or a request under subsection 203(2) of those Regulations, that is received before the coming into force of this section, is to be dealt with under the former sections 200, 201 and 203.

# CAN. REG. 2002-228 — REFUGEE PROTECTION DIVISION RULES

## made under the *Immigration and Refugee Protection Act*

SOR/2002-228, as am. S.C. 2002, c. 8, s. 182(3)(a).

### DEFINITIONS

**1. Definitions — The following definitions apply in these Rules.**

**"Act" means the *Immigration and Refugee Protection Act. ("Loi")***

**"contact information" means a person's name, postal address and telephone number, and the person's fax number and electronic mail address, if any. *("coordonnées")***

**"Division" means the Refugee Protection Division. *("Section")***

**"officer" means a person designated as an officer by the Minister under subsection 6(1) of the Act. *("agent")***

**"party" means**

**(a) in a claim for refugee protection, the claimant and, if the Minister intervenes in the claim, the Minister; and**

**(b) in an Application to Vacate Refugee Protection or an Application to Cease Refugee Protection, the protected person and the Minister.**

***("partie")***

**"Personal Information Form" means the form in which a claimant gives the information set out in Schedule 1. *("formulaire sur les renseignements personnels")***

**"proceeding" includes a conference, an application, a hearing and an interview. *("procédure")***

**"refugee protection officer" means an employee of the Board who helps the Division with a proceeding. *("agent de protection des réfugiés")***

**"registry office" means a business office of the Division. *("greffe")***

### COMMUNICATING WITH THE DIVISION

**2. Communicating with the Division — All communication with the Division must be directed to the registry office specified by the Division.**

## INFORMATION AND DOCUMENTS TO BE PROVIDED TO THE DIVISION

### *Claims for Refugee Protection*

3. (1) **Providing Personal Information Form to claimant** — As soon as a claim for refugee protection is referred to the Division, or as soon as possible after it is deemed to be referred, an officer must provide a Personal Information Form to the claimant.

(2) **Providing information and documents to the Division** — After providing the Personal Information Form, the officer must without delay provide to the Division

(a) a written statement of how and when the form was provided to the claimant;

(b) the information required by Schedule 2; and

(c) a copy of any identity or travel documents of the claimant and of any other relevant documents that are in the possession of the officer.

4. (1) **Claimant's contact information** — The claimant must provide the claimant's contact information in writing to the Division and the Minister.

(2) **Time limit** — The claimant's contact information must be received no later than 10 days after the claimant received the Personal Information Form.

(3) **Change to contact information** — If the claimant's contact information changes, the claimant must without delay provide the changes in writing to the Division and the Minister.

(4) **Claimant's counsel** — A claimant who is represented by counsel must, on obtaining counsel, provide the counsel's contact information in writing to the Division and the Minister. If that information changes, the claimant must without delay provide the changes in writing to the Division and the Minister.

### *Personal Information Form*

5. (1) **Personal Information Form** — The claimant must complete the Personal Information Form and sign and date the included declaration that states that

(a) the information given by the claimant is complete, true and correct; and

(b) the claimant knows that the declaration is of the same force and effect as if made under oath.

(2) **Form completed without interpreter** — If the claimant completes the Personal Information Form without an interpreter, the claimant must also sign and date the included declaration that states that the claimant can read the language of the form and understands what information is requested.

(3) **Interpreter's declaration** — If the claimant completes the Personal Information Form with an interpreter, the interpreter must sign and date the included declaration that states

(a) the interpreter is proficient in the languages or dialects used, and was able to communicate fully with the claimant;

(b) the completed form and all attached documents were interpreted to the claimant; and

(c) the claimant assured the interpreter that the claimant understood what was interpreted.

6. (1) **Providing Personal Information Form to Division** — The claimant must provide to the Division the original and two copies of the completed Personal Information Form by one of the means, other than fax or electronic mail, described in rule 33. The completed forms must be received by the Division no later than 28 days after the claimant received the form.

(2) **Extension of time** — A claimant who cannot — or did not — meet the time limit set out in subsection (1) may apply to the Division for more time to provide the Personal Information Form. The claimant must follow rule 44 but is not required to give evidence in an affidavit or statutory declaration.

(3) **Documents to be attached to the form** — The claimant must attach to the original and both copies of the completed Personal Information Form a copy of their identity and travel documents, genuine or not, and a copy of any other relevant documents. The claimant does not have to attach copies of a document that has been seized by an officer.

(4) **Changes to the claimant's information** — If a claimant wants to change any information given in the Personal Information Form, the claimant must provide to the Division three copies of each page of the form to which changes have been made. The claimant must sign and date each new page and underline the change made. This subsection does not apply to a change in the choice of language for the proceedings or the language of interpretation.

(5) **Documents obtained after providing the form** — If the claimant obtains a passport, travel document, identity document or any other relevant document after providing the Personal Information Form, the claimant must provide three copies of the document to the Division without delay.

## *Documents Establishing Identity and Other Elements of the Claim*

7. **Documents establishing identity and other elements of the claim** — The claimant must provide acceptable documents establishing identity and other elements of the claim. A claimant who does not provide acceptable documents must explain why they were not provided and what steps were taken to obtain them.

## *Applications to Vacate or Cease Refugee Protection*

**8. Contact information — If an Application to Vacate Refugee Protection or an Application to Cease Refugee Protection is made, the protected person must without delay notify the Division and the Minister in writing of**

**(a) any change in their contact information; and**

**(b) the contact information of their counsel, if represented by counsel, and any changes to that information.**

## COUNSEL OF RECORD

**9. Becoming counsel of record — As soon as counsel for a claimant or protected person agrees to a date for a proceeding, or as soon as a person becomes counsel after a date for a proceeding has been fixed, the counsel becomes counsel of record for the claimant or protected person.**

### Case Law

*Dvorianova v. Canada (Minister of Citizenship & Immigration)*, 2004 CarswellNat 2390, 2004 CarswellNat 789, 2004 FC 413 (F.C.) — The applicant is a Russian who claims to face political persecution in her home country. She sought to judicially review a decision that her refugee claim was abandoned. Her original refugee hearing was scheduled for November 27, 2002. On the day before the hearing, her immigration consultant advised her that he would seek a postponement. He further advised her not to attend the hearing and that he would do whatever it took to secure the postponement. The panel granted the postponement but scheduled a hearing on April 8, 2003, to give the applicant an opportunity to show cause why her claim should not be abandoned.

The fact that the applicant used an immigration consultant rather than a lawyer is irrelevant. She had a right to do so, but she also must accept the consequences of doing so. An applicant remains bound by the consultant's conduct as would be the case if she had retained counsel. The incompetence of counsel may be a breach of natural justice. It is not necessary that the incompetence be apparent to the decision maker. The claimant must establish the acts or omissions of counsel that are alleged are not the result of professional judgement. The claimant must also establish that there was a miscarriage of justice. Evidence of incompetence must be clear and convincing. In this particular case the application for judicial review was dismissed.

**10. Request to be removed as counsel of record — To be removed as counsel of record, counsel must make a request in writing to the Division and provide a copy of the request to the person represented and to the Minister, if the Minister is a party. If two working days or less remain before the date of a proceeding, counsel must make the request orally at the proceeding.**

**11. (1) Removing counsel of record — To remove counsel as counsel of record, the claimant or protected person must provide written notice to the Division, to counsel and to the Minister, if the Minister is a party, that counsel is no longer counsel for the claimant or protected person.**

**(2) Ceasing to be counsel of record — Counsel is no longer counsel of record when the Division receives the notice.**

## Language of Proceedings

**12. (1) Choice of language — claims for refugee protection — The claimant must choose English or French as the language for the proceedings. The claimant must indicate that choice in the Personal Information Form.**

**(2) Changing the choice of language — The claimant may change the choice of language by notifying the Division in writing. The notice must be received by the Division no later than 20 days before the next proceeding.**

**13. (1) Choice of language — Applications to Vacate or Cease Refugee Protection — The language used by the Minister in an Application to Vacate Refugee Protection or an Application to Cease Refugee Protection is the language of the proceedings.**

**(2) Changing the language of the proceedings — The protected person may change the language of the proceedings by notifying the Division in writing. The notice must be received by the Division no later than 20 days before the next proceeding.**

**14. (1) Need for an interpreter — If a claimant needs an interpreter for the proceedings, the claimant must indicate the language or dialect of the interpreter in the Personal Information Form.**

**(2) Changing the language of interpretation — claimant — If a claimant wants to change the language or dialect of interpretation chosen on their Personal Information Form, the claimant must notify the Division in writing and specify the language or dialect to be interpreted. The notice must be received by the Division no later than 20 days before the next proceeding.**

**(3) Language of interpretation — protected person and witness — If a protected person or any party's witness needs an interpreter for a proceeding, the party must notify the Division in writing and specify the language or dialect of the interpreter. The notice must be received by the Division no later than 20 days before the proceeding.**

**(4) Interpreter's oath — The interpreter must take an oath or make a solemn affirmation to interpret accurately.**

### Case Law

*Lamme v. Canada (Minister of Citizenship & Immigration)*, 2005 CarswellNat 3063, 2005 CarswellNat 4881, 2005 FC 1336 (F.C.) — The general standard to be met with respect to the quality of interpretation is that it must be continuous, precise, impartial and contemporaneous. In addition, for the interpretation to be considered as meeting the standard, it must be established that the applicant understood the interpretation and adequately expressed himself or herself through the interpreter.

## DESIGNATED REPRESENTATIVES

**15. (1) Duty of counsel to notify — If counsel for a party believes that the Division should designate a representative for the claimant or protected person in the proceedings because the claimant or protected person is under 18 years of age or unable to appreciate the nature of the proceedings, counsel must without delay notify the Division in writing. If counsel is aware of a person in Canada who meets the requirements to be designated as a representative, counsel must provide the person's contact information in the notice.**

**(2) Exception — Subsection (1) does not apply in the case of a claimant under 18 years of age whose claim is joined with the claim of a person who is 18 years of age or older.**

**(3) Requirements for being designated — To be designated as a representative, a person must**

**(a) be 18 years of age or older;**

**(b) understand the nature of the proceedings;**

**(c) be willing and able to act in the best interests of the claimant or protected person; and**

**(d) not have interests that conflict with those of the claimant or protected person.**



## REFUGEE PROTECTION OFFICERS

**16. Duties — The duties of refugee protection officers are, as directed by the Division, to**

**(a) review files to identify issues in a claim or other matter;**

**(b) conduct research and collect and provide information;**

**(c) hold interviews, prepare reports and make recommendations;**

**(d) participate in hearings and conferences;**

**(e) present evidence and call and question witnesses;**

**(f) make representations to the Division; and**

**(g) do any other thing that is necessary to ensure a full and proper examination of a claim or other matter.**

## DISCLOSURE OF PERSONAL INFORMATION

**17. (1) Disclosure of information from another claim — Subject to subsection (4), the Division may disclose to a claimant personal and other information that it wants to use from any other claim if the claims involve similar questions of fact or if the information is otherwise relevant to the determination of the claimant's claim.**

**(2) Notice — If the personal or other information of another claimant has not been made public, the Division must make reasonable efforts to notify this person in writing that**

**(a) it intends to disclose the information to a claimant; and**

**(b) the person may object to this disclosure.**

**(3) Request for disclosure — In order to decide whether to object to the disclosure, the person notified may make a written request to the Division for personal and other information relating to the claimant. Subject to subsection (4), the Division may disclose only information that is necessary to permit the person to make an informed decision.**

**(4) Information that may not be disclosed — The Division must not disclose personal or other information if there is a serious possibility that it will endanger the life, liberty or security of any person or is likely to cause an injustice.**

## Case Law

*Seyoboka v. Canada (Minister of Citizenship & Immigration)*, 2009 CarswellNat 237, 2009 FC 104 (F.C.) — This was an application for judicial review of a decision of the Immigration Refugee Board dismissing the applicant's motion to reopen his claim for refugee protection pursuant to s. 72(1) of the IRPA. The applicant contends that the Minister had a duty to disclose exculpatory evidence in vacation proceedings and the Minister breached her duty to disclose the exculpatory evidence.

The Refugee Protection Division of the Immigration and Refugee Protection Board is an administrative tribunal with specialized knowledge, not bound by legal or technical rules of evidence. As a result, the disclosure to standards delineated in *Stinchcombe*, [1991] 3 S.C.R. 326, do not necessarily apply automatically in the context of a refugee hearing and may require some adaptation. On the other hand, the level of disclosure owed to an applicant cannot be decided by a simple invocation of the distinction between criminal and administrative proceedings, and the consequences of an adverse finding on the applicant must be taken into consideration. The application for judicial review was dismissed. The following four questions were certified:

1. Within the context of the judicial review hearing where the Minister intervenes to seek the exclusion of the claimant, is the Minister under a duty to disclose all relevant evidence in his possession including exculpatory evidence subject only to any claims to privilege which would be assessed by the tribunal?

2. Is that duty contingent on any request from the claimant or does the duty exist independently of any request from the claimant?

3. Can the right to disclosure be waived? If so, must the waiver be explicit, or can it be inferred from the conduct of the claimant?

4. If there is a duty to disclose, does that duty include a duty to disclose evidence in the possession of other government agencies when Minister's counsel is aware that that government agency has a file on the person which might contain relevant evidence?

## Specialized Knowledge

**18. Notice to the parties — Before using any information or opinion that is within its specialized knowledge, the Division must notify the claimant or protected person, and the Minister if the Minister is present at the hearing, and give them a chance to**

**(a) make representations on the reliability and use of the information or opinion; and**

**(b) give evidence in support of their representations.**

### Case Law

*Bitala v. Canada (Minister of Citizenship & Immigration)*, 2005 CarswellNat 896, 2005 FC 470 (F.C.) — The RPD did not clearly and unequivocally give notice to the applicants of its intention to rely on its specialized knowledge and provide an opportunity to respond. The specialized knowledge, however, was essentially not in dispute. If the RPD had given, to the applicant, the specific notification required by Rule 18 the applicant's response would not have impacted the final decision. Accordingly, the application for judicial review was dismissed.

## Allowing a Claim Without a Hearing

**19. (1) When a claim may be allowed without a hearing — A claim may be allowed without a hearing only if the Minister has not notified the Division of the Minister's intention to intervene**

**(a) within 15 days after the Minister receives information about the claim, if the Minister has requested information; or**

**(b) within 28 days after the referral of the claim, if the Minister has not requested information about the claim.**

**(2) Interviews — Before allowing a claim without a hearing, the Division may require the claimant to appear at an interview with a refugee protection officer who will prepare a report in which the officer recommends, or does not recommend, that the claim be allowed without a hearing.**

**(3) Recommendation not to hold a hearing — If the refugee protection officer does not recommend that the claim be allowed without a hearing, the Division must provide a copy of the report to the claimant.**

**(4) Allowing a claim without a hearing — If the refugee protection officer recommends that the claim be allowed without a hearing, the Division may allow the claim if**

**(a) there are no issues that should be brought to the attention of the Minister;**

**(b) the claimant's identity is sufficiently established;**

**(c) there are no serious credibility issues; and**

**(d) the information given by the claimant is consistent with information about conditions in their country of nationality or, if they have no country of nation-**

**ality, their country of former habitual residence, and establishes that the claimant is a Convention refugee or a person in need of protection.**

(5) **Decision that hearing is necessary — If the Division decides that a hearing of the claim is necessary, the Division must provide to the claimant a copy of the report in which its decision is recorded.**

## CONFERENCES

**20.** (1) **Requirement to participate at a conference — The Division may require a party to participate at a conference to discuss issues, relevant facts and any other matter in order to make the proceedings more fair and efficient.**

(2) **Information or documents — The Division may require a party to give any information, or provide any document, at or before the conference.**

(3) **Written record — The Division must make a written record of any decisions and agreements made at the conference.**

## FIXING A DATE FOR A PROCEEDING

**21. Fixing a date — The Division may require a party to participate in a scheduling conference or otherwise give information to help the Division fix a date for a proceeding.**

## NOTICE TO APPEAR

**22. Notice to appear — The Division must notify a party in writing of the date, time and location of a proceeding.**

### Case Law

*Canada (Ministre de la Citoyenneté & de l'Immigration) c. Deffo*, 2005 CarswellNat 3924, 2005 CarswellNat 5117, 2005 FC 1589 (F.C.) — The Refugee Protection Division of the Immigration and Refugee Board has a duty to formally notify the counsel representing the Minister pursuant to s. 170(e) of the IRPA and s. 22 of the Rules. There is no discretionary authority for the Board to dispense of this duty. In failing to notify the counsel of record for the Minister after he had filed a notice of intervention in accordance with subs. 25(1) of the Rules, the Board erred in law.

## EXCLUSION, INADMISSIBILITY AND INELIGIBILITY

**23.** (1) **Notice to the Minister of possible exclusion — before a hearing — If the Division believes, before a hearing begins, that there is a possibility that sections E or F of Article 1 of the Refugee Convention applies to the claim, the Division must notify the Minister in writing and provide any relevant information to the Minister.**

(2) **Notice to the Minister of possible exclusion — during a hearing** — If the Division believes, at any time during a hearing, that there is a possibility that section E or F of Article 1 of the Refugee Convention applies to the claim, and the Division is of the opinion that the Minister's participation may help in the full and proper hearing of the claim, the Division must notify the Minister in writing and provide the Minister with any relevant information.

(3) **Disclosure to claimant** — The Division must provide to the claimant a copy of any notice or information provided to the Minister.

24. (1) **Notice to the Minister of possible inadmissibility or ineligibility** — The Division must without delay notify the Minister in writing, and provide the Minister with any relevant information, if the Division believes that

(a) a claimant may be inadmissible on grounds of security, violating human or international rights, serious criminality or organized criminality;

(b) there is an outstanding charge against the claimant for an offence under an Act of Parliament that may be punished by a maximum term of imprisonment of at least 10 years; or

(c) the claimant's claim may be ineligible to be referred under section 101 or paragraph 104(1)(c) or (d) of the Act.

(2) **Disclosure to claimant** — The Division must provide to the claimant a copy of any notice or information that the Division provides to the Minister.

Rules

## INTERVENTION BY THE MINISTER

25. (1) **Notice of intention to intervene** — To intervene in a claim, the Minister must provide

(a) to the claimant, a copy of a written notice of the Minister's intention to intervene; and

(b) to the Division, the original of that notice and a written statement of how and when a copy was provided to the claimant.

(2) **Contents of notice** — In the notice, the Minister must state how the Minister will intervene and give the Minister's counsel's contact information.

(3) **Intervention — exclusion clauses** — If the Minister believes that section E or F of Article 1 of the Refugee Convention may apply to the claim, the Minister must also state in the notice the facts and law on which the Minister relies.

(4) **Time limit** — Documents provided under this rule must be received by the Division and the claimant no later than 20 days before the hearing.

## CLAIMANT OR PROTECTED PERSON IN CUSTODY

26. **Custody** — The Division may order a person who holds a claimant or protected person in custody to bring the claimant or protected person to a proceeding at the location specified by the Division.

## DOCUMENTS

### *Form and Language of Documents*

**27. (1) Documents prepared by party — A document prepared for use by a party in a proceeding must be typewritten on one side of 21.5 cm by 28 cm (8½" × 11") paper and the pages must be numbered.**

**(2) Photocopies — Any photocopy provided by a party must be a clear copy of the document photocopied and be on one side of 21.5 cm by 28 cm (8½" × 11") paper and the pages must be numbered.**

**(3) Numbered documents — A party must number consecutively each document provided by the party.**

**(4) List of documents — If more than one document is provided, the party must provide a list of the documents and their numbers.**

**28. (1) Language of documents — All documents used at a proceeding must be in English or French or, if in another language, be provided with an English or French translation and a translator's declaration.**

**(2) Minister's documents — If the Minister provides a document that is not in the language of the proceedings, the Minister must provide a translation in that language and a translator's declaration.**

**(3) Translator's declaration — A translator's declaration must include the translator's name, the language of the document translated and a statement signed by the translator that the translation is accurate.**

### *Disclosure of Documents*

**29. (1) Disclosure of documents by a party — If a party wants to use a document at a hearing, the party must provide one copy to any other party and two copies to the Division, unless these Rules require a different number of copies.**

**(2) Disclosure of documents by the Division — If the Division wants to use a document at a hearing, the Division must provide a copy to each party.**

**(3) Proof that document was provided — Together with the copies provided to the Division, the party must provide a written statement of how and when a copy was provided to any other party.**

**(4) Time limit — Documents provided under this rule must be received by the Division or a party, as the case may be, no later than**

**(a) 20 days before the hearing; or**

**(b) five days before the hearing if the document is provided to respond to another document provided by a party or the Division.**

## Case Law

*Flores v. Canada (Minister of Citizenship & Immigration)*, 2005 CarswellNat 2332, 2005 FC 1138 (F.C.) — The applicant claimed refugee protection in Canada, but a panel of the Immigration and Refugee Board dismissed his claim because it felt he had not provided acceptable evidence of identity. On the day of his hearing, the applicant provided two documents he hoped would constitute good evidence of his identity and nationality. The first was a photocopy of one page of a Salvadoran passport. The second was a faxed copy of a birth certificate. The Board found that the applicant had failed to prove his identity and, therefore, that it was unnecessary to consider the merits of the claim. The Board stated that it "rejected" the applicant's identity documents for the following reasons: the photocopy of the passport did not resemble the applicant; the documents were mere photocopies; the originals were not available, and the applicant could not provide a reasonable explanation why he could not get them; the applicant had nearly a year between making his refugee claim and the date of his hearing to obtain acceptable identity documents; the documents were filed very late, on the date of the hearing; and the applicant claimed to have spent a period of time in the United States but, without a complete passport, it was impossible to verify the duration of his stay there. Since the Board did not reject the documents solely because they were photocopies, its decision was not out of keeping with the requirements of the IRPA or the Rules.

*Hasan v. Canada (Minister of Citizenship & Immigration)*, 2004 CarswellNat 5000, 2004 CarswellNat 3864, 2004 FC 1537 (F.C.) — The applicant sought to review a negative determination of his application for refugee status and for protection. The Board in rejecting the application, refused to admit as evidence more than 550 pages of documents. The Board paid particular attention to Rule 29 which sets out the 20-day and five-day deadlines.

The decision of the Board was set aside. The Board failed to pay attention to Rule 30, which gives it the discretion to admit documents filed outside the prescribed time. The exercise of the Board's discretion resulted in a denial of natural justice and a breach of principles of fairness. There would have been no offsetting prejudice to the respondent had the evidence been admitted.

**30. Use of undisclosed documents — A party who does not provide a document as required by rule 29 may not use the document at the hearing unless allowed by the Division. In deciding whether to allow its use, the Division must consider any relevant factors, including**

**(a) the document's relevance and probative value;**

**(b) any new evidence it brings to the hearing; and**

**(c) whether the party, with reasonable effort, could have provided the document as required by rule 29.**

## Case Law

*Flores v. Canada (Minister of Citizenship & Immigration)*, 2005 CarswellNat 2332, 2005 FC 1138 (F.C.) — The applicant claimed refugee protection in Canada, but a panel of the Immigration and Refugee Board dismissed his claim because it felt he had not provided acceptable evidence of identity. On the day of his hearing, the applicant provided two documents he hoped would constitute good evidence of his identity and nationality. The



Rules

first was a photocopy of one page of a Salvadoran passport. The second was a faxed copy of a birth certificate. The Board found that the applicant had failed to prove his identity and, therefore, that it was unnecessary to consider the merits of the claim. The Board stated that it "rejected" the applicant's identity documents for the following reasons: the photocopy of the passport did not resemble the applicant; the documents were mere photocopies; the originals were not available, and the applicant could not provide a reasonable explanation why he could not get them; the applicant had nearly a year between making his refugee claim and the date of his hearing to obtain acceptable identity documents; the documents were filed very late, on the date of the hearing; and the applicant claimed to have spent a period of time in the United States but, without a complete passport, it was impossible to verify the duration of his stay there. Since the Board did not reject the documents solely because they were photocopies, its decision was not out of keeping with the requirements of the IRPA or the Rules.

*Behaz v. Canada (Minister of Citizenship & Immigration)*, 2005 CarswellNat 1583, 2005 FC 791 (F.C.) — At the applicant's refugee hearing, his counsel attempted to have the Board admit a package of approximately 87 pages of documentary evidence that had not previously been disclosed by the applicant. The Board initially refused to accept any documents, but ultimately agreed to accept only the identity documents. The decision was set aside. The member, in refusing to admit the applicant's documents did not consider the factors outlined in Rule 30. The only reasons given by the Board for not allowing the late filing was the size of the package of documents and the lateness of the request. It was a denial of natural justice for the presiding member not to take the listed factors in Rule 30 into consideration.

## *Providing a Document*

**31. General provision — Rules 32 to 35 apply to any document, including a notice or a request in writing.**

**32. (1) Providing documents to the Division — A document provided to the Division must be provided to the registry office specified by the Division.**

**(2) Providing documents to the Minister — A document provided to the Minister must be provided to the Minister's counsel.**

**(3) Providing documents to claimant or protected person — A document provided to a claimant or a protected person must be provided to the claimant or protected person or, if the claimant or protected person has counsel, to their counsel.**

### Case Law

#### Section 32(3)

*Sharma v. Canada (Minister of Citizenship & Immigration)*, 2006 CarswellNat 206, 2006 FC 95 (F.C.) — The Board has a duty to give a refugee claimant an opportunity, at a hearing, to show why his or her claim should not be abandoned. Before declaring a claim abandoned, the Board must consider the explanation the claimant provides at the hearing, the claimant's readiness to proceed with his or her claim, as well as other relevant information. Obviously, these obligations would be meaningless if there were no duty to inform the claimant when and where a hearing was to take place. The Board must give a claimant notice in writing of an abandonment hearing. There is no obligation on the Board to send out a new notice when the applicant changes counsel.

**33. How to provide a document — A document can be provided in any of the following ways:**

**(a) by hand;**

**(b) by regular mail or registered mail;**

**(c) by courier or priority post;**

**(d) by fax if the recipient has a fax number and the document has no more than 20 pages, unless the recipient consents to receiving more than 20 pages; and**

**(e) by electronic mail if the Division allows.**

**34. (1) If document cannot be provided under rule 33 — If a party is unable to provide a document in a way required by rule 33, the party may make an application to the Division to be allowed to provide the document in another way or to be excused from providing the document.**

**(2) Form of application — The application must be made under rule 44.**

**(3) Allowing the application — The Division may allow the application if the party has made reasonable efforts to provide the document to the other party.**

Rules

**35. (1) When a document is considered received by the Division — A document provided to the Division is considered to be received by the Division on the day the document is date stamped by the Division.**

**(2) When a document provided by regular mail is considered received by a party — A document provided by regular mail to a party is considered to be received seven days after the day it was mailed. If the seventh day is a Saturday, Sunday or other statutory holiday, the document is considered to be received on the next working day.**

## *Original Documents*

**36. (1) Original documents — A party who has provided a copy of a document to the Division must provide the original document to the Division**

**(a) without delay, on the request in writing of the Division; or**

**(b) if the Division does not make a request, no later than the beginning of the proceeding at which the document will be used.**

**(2) Documents mentioned in paragraph 3(2)(c) — On the request in writing of the Division, the Minister must without delay provide to the Division the original of any document mentioned in paragraph 3(2)(c) that is in the possession of an officer.**

## *Additional Documents*

**37. (1) Additional documents after the hearing has ended — A party who wants to provide a document as evidence after a hearing must make an application to the Division.**

**(2) Written application — The party must attach a copy of the document to the application. The application must be made under rule 44, but the party is not required to give evidence in an affidavit or statutory declaration.**

**(3) Factors — In deciding the application, the Division must consider any relevant factors, including:**

> **(a) the document's relevance and probative value;**
>
> **(b) any new evidence it brings to the proceedings; and**
>
> **(c) whether the party, with reasonable effort, could have provided the document as required by rule 29.**

### Case Law

*Nagulesan v. Canada (Minister of Citizenship & Immigration)*, [2004] F.C.J. No. 1690, 44 Imm. L.R. (3d) 99, 2004 CarswellNat 5903, 2004 CarswellNat 3637, 2004 FC 1382 (F.C.) — The applicant sought to review a negative decision respecting his claim under ss. 96 and 97. A few days after his hearing, the applicant delivered to the RPD a letter addressed to the member presiding at his hearing indicating that he wished to file additional evidence to corroborate his testimony. The proposed evidence was attached to the letter. The letter and the documents attached thereto were not in the certified copy of the tribunal record and the RPD did not refer to the evidence at all in its decision.

The applicant's letter satisfied the requirement of Rule 37. This meant that the RPD had to deal with the applicant's request. It could simply mention that having reviewed the letter, it decided not to consider the evidence because of factors listed in Rule 37(3), or it could accept the new evidence and deal with it in its decision. The failure to deal with the matter at all was a breach of procedural fairness and the decision was set aside.

## WITNESSES

**38. (1) Providing witness information — If a party wants to call a witness, the party must provide in writing to any other party and the Division the following witness information:**

> **(a) the witness's contact information;**
>
> **(b) the purpose and substance of the witness's testimony or, in the case of an expert witness, the expert witness's signed summary of the testimony to be given;**
>
> **(c) the time needed for the witness's testimony;**
>
> **(d) the party's relationship to the witness;**
>
> **(e) in the case of an expert witness, a description of the expert witness's qualifications; and**

**(f) whether the party wants the witness to testify by videoconference or telephone.**

**(2) Proof that document was provided — The witness information must be provided to the Division together with a written statement of how and when it was provided to any other party.**

**(3) Time limit — A document provided under this rule must be received by its recipient no later than 20 days before the hearing.**

**(4) Failure to provide witness information — If a party does not provide the witness information as required under this rule, the witness may not testify at the hearing unless the Division allows the witness to testify.**

## Case Law

*R. v. Laboucan*, [2010] S.C.J. No. 12, 73 C.R. (6th) 235, (sub nom. *R. v. Briscoe)* 400 N.R. 200, 22 Alta. L.R. (5th) 62, 253 C.C.C. (3d) 129, [2010] 6 W.W.R. 13, 316 D.L.R. (4th) 590, (sub nom. *R. v. Briscoe)* 477 A.R. 70, 483 W.A.C. 70, 2010 SCC 12, 2010 CarswellAlta 591, 2010 CarswellAlta 590 — The fact that a witness has an interest in the outcome of the proceedings is common sense and a relevant factor, among others, to take into account when assessing the credibility of the witness's testimony. A trier of fact, however, should not place undue weight on the status of a person in the proceeding as a factor going to credibility. For example, it would be improper to base a finding of credibility regarding a parent's or a spouse's testimony solely on the basis of a witness's relationship to the complainant or to the accused. Regard should be given to all relevant factors in assessing credibility.

Rules

**39. (1) Requesting a summons — A party who wants the Division to order a person to testify at a hearing must make a request to the Division for a summons, either orally at a proceeding or in writing.**

**(2) Factors — In deciding whether to issue a summons, the Division must consider any relevant factors, including**

**(a) the necessity of the testimony to a full and proper hearing;**

**(b) the ability of the person to give that testimony; and**

**(c) whether the person has agreed to be summoned as a witness.**

**(3) Using the summons — If a party wants to use a summons, the party must**

**(a) provide the summons to the summoned person by hand;**

**(b) provide a copy of the summons to the Division with a written statement of how and when the summons was provided; and**

**(c) pay or offer to pay the summoned person the applicable witness fees and travel expenses set out in Tariff A of the *Federal Courts Rules*.**

## Case Law

*Canada (Minister of Public Safety & Emergency Preparedness) v. Kahlon* (2005), 35 Admin. L.R. (4th) 213, 2005 CarswellNat 2255, 2005 CarswellNat 5610, 2005 FC 1000 (F.C.) — The proper procedure when there is a requirement to produce documents, whether by subpoena or otherwise, and there is a genuine dispute as to their relevance or as to whether they are privileged, is to have the documents produced, so that the tribunal charged with determining their relevance will have them available for examination. If any of the documents then turned out to be irrelevant, the privacy interest of the owner would be protected as the documents would not then be provided to the party making the demand. In this case, the Refugee Protection Division improperly exercised its powers to compel evidence and did not follow its own procedural rules.

**40. (1) Cancelling a summons — If a person summoned to appear as a witness wants the summons cancelled, the person must make an application in writing to the Division.**

**(2) Application — The person must follow rule 44, but is not required to give evidence in an affidavit or statutory declaration.**

**41. (1) Arrest warrant — If a person does not obey a summons to appear as a witness, the party who requested the summons may make a request to the Division orally at a hearing, or in writing, to issue a warrant for the arrest of the person.**

**(2) Written request — A party who makes a written request for a warrant must provide supporting evidence by affidavit or statutory declaration.**

**(3) Requirements for issue of arrest warrant — The Division may issue a warrant if**

> **(a) the person summoned was provided the summons by hand or the person is avoiding being provided the summons;**
>
> **(b) the person was paid or offered the applicable witness fees and travel expenses set out in Tariff A of the *Federal Courts Rules*;**
>
> **(c) the person did not appear at the hearing as required by the summons; and**
>
> **(d) the person's testimony is still needed for a full and proper hearing.**

**(4) Content of a warrant — A warrant issued by the Division for the arrest of a person must include directions concerning detention and release.**

**42. Excluded witness — Unless allowed by the Division, a person must not communicate to a witness excluded from a hearing room any testimony given while the witness was excluded until that witness has finished testifying.**

## APPLICATIONS

**43. General provision — Unless these Rules provide otherwise**

> **(a) a party who wants the Division to make a decision on any matter in a proceeding, including the procedure to be followed, must make an application to the Division under rule 44;**
>
> **(b) a party who wants to respond to the application must respond under rule 45; and**
>
> **(c) a party who wants to reply to a response must reply under rule 46.**

## How to Make an Application

44. (1) **Form of application and time limit** — Unless these Rules provide otherwise, an application must be made in writing and without delay. The Division may allow a party to make an application orally at a proceeding if the party with reasonable effort could not have made a written application before the proceeding.

(2) **Content of application** — Unless these Rules provide otherwise, in a written application the party must

(a) state what decision the party wants the Division to make;

(b) give reasons why the Division should make that decision; and

(c) if there is another party and the views of that party are known, state whether the other party agrees to the application.

(3) **Affidavit or statutory declaration** — Unless these Rules provide otherwise, any evidence that the party wants the Division to consider with a written application must be given in an affidavit or statutory declaration that accompanies the application.

(4) **Providing the application to another party and the Division** — A party who makes a written application must provide

(a) to any other party, a copy of the application and any affidavit or statutory declaration; and

(b) to the Division, the original application and any affidavit or statutory declaration, together with a written statement of how and when the party provided the copy to any other party.

Rules

## How to Respond to a Written Application

45. (1) **Responding to a written application** — A response to a written application must be in writing. In a response the party must

(a) state the decision the party wants the Division to make; and

(b) give reasons why the Division should make that decision.

(2) **Evidence in a written response** — Any evidence that the party wants the Division to consider with the written response must be given in an affidavit or statutory declaration that accompanies the response. Unless the Division requires it, an affidavit or statutory declaration is not required if the party who made the application was not required to give evidence in an affidavit or statutory declaration.

(3) **Providing the response** — A party who responds to a written application must provide

(a) to the other party, a copy of the response and any affidavit or statutory declaration; and

(b) to the Division, the original response and any affidavit or statutory declaration, together with a written statement of how and when the party provided the copy to the other party.

(4) **Time limit** — Documents provided under this rule must be received by their recipients no later than seven days after the party received the copy of the application.

## *How to Reply to a Written Response*

46. (1) **Replying to a written response** — A reply to a written response must be in writing.

(2) **Evidence in the reply** — Any evidence that the party wants the Division to consider with the written reply must be given in an affidavit or statutory declaration together with the reply. Unless the Division requires it, an affidavit or statutory declaration is not required if the party was not required to give evidence in an affidavit or statutory declaration with the application.

(3) **Providing the reply** — A party who replies to a written response must provide

(a) to the other party, a copy of the reply and any affidavit or statutory declaration; and

(b) to the Division, the original reply and any affidavit or statutory declaration, together with a written statement of how and when the party provided the copy to the other party.

(4) **Time limit** — Documents provided under this rule must be received by their recipients no later than five days after the party received the copy of the response.

## Changing the Location of a Proceeding

47. (1) **Application to change the location of a proceeding** — A party may make an application to the Division to change the location of a proceeding.

(2) **Form of application** — The party must follow rule 44, but is not required to give evidence in an affidavit or statutory declaration.

(3) **Time limit** — Documents provided under this rule must be received by their recipients no later than 20 days before the proceeding.

(4) **Factors** — In deciding the application, the Division must consider any relevant factors, including

(a) whether the party is residing in the location where the party wants the proceeding to be held;

(b) whether a change of location would allow the proceeding to be full and proper;

(c) whether a change of location would likely delay or slow the proceeding;

(d) how a change of location would affect the operation of the Division; and

(e) how a change of location would affect the parties.

**(5) Duty to appear at the proceeding — Unless a party receives a decision from the Division allowing the application, the party must appear for the proceeding at the location fixed and be ready to start or continue the proceeding.**

## Case Law

*Sundaram v. Canada (Minister of Citizenship & Immigration)*, 2006 CarswellNat 499, 2006 CarswellNat 2426, 2006 FC 291 (F.C.) — When the IRB receives requests for a change of venue because a person cannot attend at a scheduled hearing location, it has an obligation to consider all relevant matters including its own discretionary powers relevant to the request. In this case, the applicant had moved from Toronto to Vancouver. As there was no indication in the conclusionary reasons that the Refugee Protection Division ever turned its mind to the issue of alternative means and locations of hearing, the decision not to reopen the dismissal of the applicant's refugee claim was quashed.

## CHANGING THE DATE OR TIME OF A PROCEEDING

**48. (1) Application to change the date or time of a proceeding — A party may make an application to the Division to change the date or time of a proceeding.**

**(2) Form and content of application — The party must**

**(a) follow rule 44, but is not required to give evidence in an affidavit or statutory declaration; and**

**(b) give at least six dates, within the period specified by the Division, on which the party is available to start or continue the proceeding.**

**(3) If proceeding is two working days or less away — If the party wants to make an application two working days or less before the proceeding, the party must appear at the proceeding and make the application orally.**

**(4) Factors — In deciding the application, the Division must consider any relevant factors, including**

**(a) in the case of a date and time that was fixed after the Division consulted or tried to consult the party, any exceptional circumstances for allowing the application;**

**(b) when the party made the application;**

**(c) the time the party has had to prepare for the proceeding;**

**(d) the efforts made by the party to be ready to start or continue the proceeding;**

**(e) in the case of a party who wants more time to obtain information in support of the party's arguments, the ability of the Division to proceed in the absence of that information without causing an injustice;**

**(f) whether the party has counsel;**

**(g) the knowledge and experience of any counsel who represents the party;**

**(h) any previous delays and the reasons for them;**

**(i) whether the date and time fixed were peremptory;**

Rules

**(j) whether allowing the application would unreasonably delay the proceedings or likely cause an injustice; and**

**(k) the nature and complexity of the matter to be heard.**

**(5) Duty to appear at the proceeding — Unless a party receives a decision from the Division allowing the application, the party must appear for the proceeding at the date and time fixed and be ready to start or continue the proceeding.**

## Case Law

*Chohan v. Canada (Minister of Citizenship & Immigration)*, 2006 CarswellNat 819, 2006 CarswellNat 2501, 2006 FC 390 (F.C.) — The Board has an obligation to deal with a request for an adjournment in a principled way. To have denied the applicant the benefit of a short adjournment was manifestly unfair and contravened the requirement of s. 170 of the IRPA that the applicant be given a reasonable opportunity to present evidence.

The Board's reasons for denying the adjournment request also failed to address the factors required by s. 48 of the *Refugee Protection Division Rules*. Had these factors been considered and applied, the adjournment would also certainly have been granted.

*Herman v. Canada (Minister of Citizenship & Immigration)*, 2005 CarswellNat 1183, 2005 FC 603 (F.C.) — A member of the Immigration and Refugee Protection Board refused a short postponement of the commencement of the applicant's hearing, despite knowing the applicant's counsel had requested the short postponement and that the applicant wanted and expected her counsel to be present. At the time the postponement was refused, counsel was in transit to the Board hearing. The member's decision to refuse to postpone the start time of the hearing was quashed. The member failed to consider the factors set out in Rule 48(4) before ruling on the adjournment. The member did not consider that the applicant wanted counsel present, that counsel had been retained for a long period of time, that counsel was on her way to attend and that the delay was only for about half an hour. The member did not consider the prejudice to the applicant of being denied the right to counsel. Whatever may be said about counsel's actions or the reasonableness of the explanation for the short postponement, the critical matter is that the applicant who was wholly innocent in the matter suffered the consequences of the denied postponement. The Board must, as a minimum, have regard to the consequences of a refusal to postpone and to the relevant factors set out in Rule 48(4).

*Sandy v. Canada (Minister of Citizenship & Immigration)* (2004), 41 Imm. L.R. (3d) 123, 260 F.T.R. 1 (Eng.), 2004 CarswellNat 5110, 2004 CarswellNat 3724, 2004 FC 1468 (F.C.) — The applicant sought to review a negative determination of her refugee claim. The applicant's legal costs were being paid for by Legal Aid. She was sent a notice to appear for September 3, 2003, when her hearing date would be set. Her counsel could not appear on that date, and the panel set a peremptory hearing dated of October 2nd. Counsel could not appear on October 2nd and requested an adjournment on September 24th which request was denied.

The applicant attended the October 2nd hearing alone and when asked whether she was ready to proceed she replied "not to the fullest". The hearing was finished in one hour, and the applicant was found not to be a convention refugee.

The Board's decision was set aside. The Court could not determine from the transcript whether the Board had given consideration to the factors listed in Rule 48(4) of the *Refugee Protection Division Rules*.

## JOINING OR SEPARATING CLAIMS OR APPLICATIONS

**49. (1) Claims automatically joined — The Division must join the claim of a claimant to a claim made by the claimant's spouse or common-law partner, child, parent, brother, sister, grandchild or grandparent.**

**(2) Applications joined if claims joined — Applications to Vacate Refugee Protection or Applications to Cease Refugee Protection are joined if the claims of the protected persons were joined.**

**50. (1) Application to join — A party may make an application to the Division to join claims, Applications to Vacate Refugee Protection or Applications to Cease Refugee Protection.**

**(2) Application to separate — A party may make an application to the Division to separate claims or Applications that are joined.**

**(3) Form of application and providing application — A party who makes an application to join or separate must follow rule 44, but the party is not required to give evidence in an affidavit or statutory declaration. The party must also**

**(a) provide a copy of the application to any person who will be affected by a decision of the Division on the application; and**

**(b) provide the Division with a written statement of how and when the copy of the application was provided to any affected person, together with proof that the party provided the copy to that person.**

**(4) Time limit — Documents provided under this rule must be received by their recipient no later than 20 days before the hearing.**

**(5) Factors — In deciding the application, the Division must consider any relevant factors, including**

**(a) whether the claims or Applications involve similar questions of fact or law;**

**(b) whether allowing the application would promote the efficient administration of the work of the Division; and**

**(c) whether allowing the application would likely cause an injustice.**

## PROCEEDINGS CONDUCTED IN PUBLIC

**51. (1) Application — A person who makes an application to the Division to have a proceeding conducted in public must apply in writing and follow this rule.**

**(2) Content of application — In the application, the person must**

**(a) state what decision the person wants the Division to make;**

**(b) give reasons why the Division should make that decision; and**

**(c) include any evidence that the person wants the Division to consider in deciding the application.**

(3) **Providing the application** — The person must provide the original application and two copies to the Division. The Division must provide a copy of the application to the parties.

(4) **Time limit** — Documents provided under this rule must be received by the Division no later than 20 days before the hearing.

## WITHDRAWAL

52. (1) **Abuse of process** — Withdrawal of a claim, or of an Application to Vacate Refugee Protection or an Application to Cease Refugee Protection, is an abuse of process if withdrawal would likely have a negative effect on the integrity of the Division. If no substantive evidence has been accepted in the proceedings, withdrawal is not an abuse of process.

(2) **Withdrawal if no evidence has been accepted** — If no substantive evidence has been accepted in the proceedings, a party may withdraw the party's claim or Application to Vacate Refugee Protection or Application to Cease Refugee Protection by notifying the Division orally at a proceeding or in writing.

(3) **Withdrawal if evidence has been accepted** — If substantive evidence has been accepted in the proceedings, a party who wants to withdraw the party's claim or Application to Vacate Refugee Protection or Application to Cease Refugee Protection must make an application to the Division under rule 44.

## REINSTATING A WITHDRAWN CLAIM OR APPLICATION

53. (1) **Application to reinstate a withdrawn claim** — A person may apply to the Division to reinstate a claim that was made by that person and withdrawn.

(2) **Form and content of application** — The person must follow rule 44, include their contact information in the application and provide a copy of the application to the Minister.

(3) **Factors** — The Division must allow the application if it is established that there was a failure to observe a principle of natural justice or if it is otherwise in the interests of justice to allow the application.

54. (1) **Application to reinstate an Application to Vacate or Cease Refugee Protection** — The Minister may make an application to the Division to reinstate an Application to Vacate Refugee Protection or an Application to Cease Refugee Protection.

(2) **Form of application** — The application must be made under rule 44.

(3) **Factors** — The Division must allow the application if it is established that there was a failure to observe a principle of natural justice or if it is otherwise in the interests of justice to allow the application.

## REOPENING A CLAIM OR APPLICATION

**55. (1) Application to reopen a claim — A claimant or the Minister may make an application to the Division to reopen a claim for refugee protection that has been decided or abandoned.**

**(2) Form of application — The application must be made under rule 44.**

**(3) Claimant's application — A claimant who makes an application must include the claimant's contact information in the application and provide a copy of the application to the Minister.**

**(4) Factor — The Division must allow the application if it is established that there was a failure to observe a principle of natural justice.**

### Case Law

*Emani v. Canada (Minister of Citizenship & Immigration)*, 2009 CarswellNat 1527, 2009 FC 520 — The applicant sought judicial review of the decision by an officer of the Immigration Refugee Board refusing the applicant's request to have his refugee claim reopened. The jurisprudence appears to be clear that the central consideration in regard to abandonment proceedings is whether the applicant's conduct amounts to an expression of his intention to diligently prosecute his claim. When presented with the application to have the claim reopened, the Board was furnished for the first time with information explaining the applicant's failure to appear, and demonstrating that it was due solely to administrative errors on the part of his counsel. In rejecting the application to reopen his claim, the Board failed to consider evidence before it of the appellant's conduct demonstrating his intention to earnestly pursue his claim. The Board erred in seeing only part of the picture and neglecting this central consideration.

*Matondo v. Canada (Minister of Citizenship & Immigration)*, [2005] F.C.J. No. 509, 44 Imm. L.R. (3d) 225, 2005 CarswellNat 761, 2005 FC 416 (F.C.) — The applicant arrived at Pearson Airport in December 2003 and claimed refugee status. Two days later he was given his personal information form which was due January 20. The accompanying notice said that if the form was not filed in time the applicant would have to show cause why the claim should not be declared abandoned. The applicant provided a Toronto address and acknowledged to Citizenship and Immigration Canada that he would inform it of any change of address. The applicant retained counsel and on January 14, the day after counsel was retained, a letter was faxed to Citizenship and Immigration advising that the applicant was now in Montreal and asking for the address to which the personal information form should be mailed. No PIF form was filed by the deadline of January 20, 2004. On January 26, 2004, counsel's office wrote again to immigration asking for certain information as no reply had been received to the earlier fax communication. On February 2, the Board issued an abandonment decision. Counsel faxed again on March 15 and finally on April 5 went to the Montreal office where they were informed that the refugee claim had been declared abandoned. An application was then made under s. 55 to reopen the claim. The member who declared the claim abandoned made no mention of the futile communications the lawyer's office had with Citizenship and Immigration Canada or the applicant's visit to the immigration offices in Montreal. The member took the approach that counsel should have known better. The word abandon means "to give up absolutely". The applicant had done no such thing. Refugee Protection Division Rule 55 makes reference to the principles of natural justice. The fundamental principle is the right to be heard by an impartial decision maker. The right to be heard is at the heart of our sense of justice and fairness. The Court found this decision of the Refugee Protection Division to be aberrant and abhorrent and set it aside.

*Ahmad v. Canada (Minister of Citizenship & Immigration)*, 2005 CarswellNat 532, 2005 FC 279 (F.C.) — The applicant sought to review a decision of the Refugee Protection Division refusing to reopen his refugee claim. A denial of natural justice is the correct consideration to be employed by the Board in an application to reopen. It is not the Board's function at a hearing for an application to reopen to consider issues that should have been raised in a judicial review application of the abandonment hearing.

*Krishnamoorthy v. Canada (Minister of Citizenship & Immigration)* (2005), 45 Imm. L.R. (3d) 126, 2005 CarswellNat 392, 2005 FC 237 (F.C.) — The applicant sought to review a refusal of his request to reopen his claim for refugee status which had been declared abandoned. Applications to reopen can be allowed only where a breach of natural justice can be demonstrated. Thus, on such an application, the function of the RPD is to review the file to ensure that the abandonment decision was made in a manner that did not breach the principles of natural justice.

*Shahid v. Canada (Minister of Citizenship & Immigration)*, 2004 CarswellNat 5919, 2004 CarswellNat 4311, 2004 FC 1607 (F.C.) — This was an application to review a decision of a Board Member dismissing the applicant's motion to reopen his refugee claim. The decision not to reopen a refugee claim is a final decision. Reasons are required by s. 169(b).

*Javed v. Canada (Minister of Citizenship & Immigration)* (2004), 41 Imm. L.R. (3d) 118, 2004 CarswellNat 3722, 2004 FC 1458 (F.C.) — This was an application to review a decision refusing the applicants' motion to reopen their refugee claim. Reasons are required for refusing an application to reopen a refugee claim. The reasons in this case were not meaningful or sufficient. The Court was unable to determine why the Board made the decision to refuse to reopen.

*Osagie v. Canada (Minister of Citizenship & Immigration)*, 2004 CarswellNat 5055, 2004 CarswellNat 3521, 262 F.T.R. 112, 2004 FC 1368 (F.C.) — The applicant sought to review a decision refusing to reopen her refugee claim. The applicant completed and signed her PIF form within the time period required by the IRB. The form was then given to an employee of her lawyer who was to file the form with the Board. The employee, through inadvertence, failed to do so. Because it had not received the form within the stipulated 28-day period, a notice to appear for abandonment was sent by the Board, both to the applicant and her counsel by ordinary mail. Because her counsel had inadvertently given the Board his office address, as the applicant's personal address, both notices were sent to the applicant's lawyer. The applicant's counsel then failed to appear at her abandonment hearing with a result that her claim was declared abandoned. Counsel then applied to reopen the claim and put before the Board all of the mistakes that had been made by counsel in the matter.

The effect of the various errors committed by the applicant's counsel and his employees denied the applicant natural justice and according to the mandatory language of Rule 55 the request to re-open should have been granted.

*Ali v. Canada (Minister of Citizenship & Immigration)*, [2004] F.C.J. No. 1394, 44 Imm. L.R. (3d) 4, 2004 CarswellNat 5685, 2004 CarswellNat 2742, 258 F.T.R. 226 (Eng.),

2004 FC 1153 (F.C.) — The correct interpretation of Rule 55 is that applications to reopen may only be allowed where a breach of natural justice has been established.

**56. (1) Application to reopen an Application to Vacate or Cease Refugee Protection — The Minister or a protected person may make an application to the Division to reopen an Application to Vacate Refugee Protection or an Application to Cease Refugee Protection that has been decided or abandoned.**

**(2) Form of application — The application must be made under rule 44.**

**(3) Factor to consider — The Division must allow the application if it is established that there was a failure to observe a principle of natural justice.**

## Case Law

*Logeswaren v. Canada (Minister of Citizenship & Immigration)*, [2004] F.C.J. No. 1086, 256 F.T.R. 78, 2004 CarswellNat 1906, 2004 CarswellNat 2983, 2004 FC 886 (F.C.) — The applicants were granted refugee status on May 6, 1993. They applied for permanent residency, which application remains pending. The applicants' respective husband and father was also found to be a refugee and has since become a Canadian citizen. The Minister filed an application to vacate the applicants' refugee status in 1999. That application was dismissed for insufficiency of evidence. Early in 2001, the Minister applied for leave to file a second application to vacate under s. 55 of the *Refugee Protection Division Rules*. The applicants brought a motion to dismiss the application to vacate on the basis of *res judicata*. That motion was dismissed and that decision is the subject of this judicial review application.

The Minister had no right to bring a second application to vary under Rule 55. The appropriate remedy was to be found in Rule 56, which gives the Minister the specific right to apply to reopen the first application to vary, even though it has been decided.

Rules

## APPLICATIONS TO VACATE OR CEASE REFUGEE PROTECTION

**57. (1) Form of Application — An Application to Vacate Refugee Protection or an Application to Cease Refugee Protection made by the Minister must be in writing and follow this rule.**

**(2) Content of application — In the application, the Minister must include**

**(a) the contact information of the protected person and their counsel, if any;**

**(b) the identification number given by the Department of Citizenship and Immigration to the protected person;**

**(c) the date and file number of any Division decision;**

**(d) in the case of a person whose application for protection was allowed abroad, the person's file number, a copy of the decision and the location of the office;**

**(e) what decision the Minister wants the Division to make; and**

**(f) the reasons why the Division should make that decision.**

(3) **Providing the application to the Protected person and Division** — **The Minister must provide**

> **(a) a copy of the Application to the protected person; and**
>
> **(b) the original and one copy of the Application to the registry office that provided the notice of decision in the claim or to the registry office specified by the Division, together with a written statement of how and when a copy was provided to the protected person.**

## ABANDONMENT

**58. (1) Abandonment without hearing the claimant — A claim may be declared abandoned, without giving the claimant an opportunity to explain why the claim should not be declared abandoned, if**

> **(a) the Division has not received the claimant's contact information and their Personal Information Form within 28 days after the claimant received the form; and**
>
> **(b) the Minister and the claimant's counsel, if any, do not have the claimant's contact information.**

**(2) Opportunity to explain — In every other case, the Division must give the claimant an opportunity to explain why the claim should not be declared abandoned. The Division must give this opportunity**

> **(a) immediately, if the claimant is present at the hearing and the Division considers that it is fair to do so; or**
>
> **(b) in any other case, by way of a special hearing after notifying the claimant in writing.**

**(3) Factors to consider — The Division must consider, in deciding if the claim should be declared abandoned, the explanations given by the claimant at the hearing and any other relevant information, including the fact that the claimant is ready to start or continue the proceedings.**

**(4) Decision to start or continue the proceedings — If the Division decides not to declare the claim abandoned, it must start or continue the proceedings without delay.**

### Case Law

*Sharma v. Canada (Minister of Citizenship & Immigration)*, 2006 CarswellNat 206, 2006 FC 95 (F.C.) — The Board has a duty to give a refugee claimant an opportunity, at a hearing, to show why his or her claim should not be abandoned. Before declaring a claim abandoned, the Board must consider the explanation the claimant provides at the hearing, the claimant's readiness to proceed with his or her claim, as well as other relevant information. Obviously, these obligations would be meaningless if there were no duty to inform the claimant when and where a hearing was to take place. The Board must give a claimant notice in writing of an abandonment hearing. There is no obligation on the Board to send out a new notice when the applicant changes counsel.

*Abrazaldo v. Canada (Minister of Citizenship & Immigration)*, 2005 CarswellNat 2928, 2005 CarswellNat 4995, 2005 FC 1295 (F.C.) — The applicable standard of review to be applied to a decision of the Refugee Protection Division declaring a refugee claim to be abandoned is reasonableness *simpliciter*. This means that the Court is not to decide whether it agrees with the decision of the Refugee Protection Division. The Court must not interfere unless the applicant shows that the decision was unreasonable.

*Tajadodi v. Canada (Minister of Citizenship & Immigration)* (2005), 49 Imm. L.R. (3d) 129, 2005 CarswellNat 2436, 2005 CarswellNat 5087, 2005 FC 1096 (F.C.) — The test of "exceptional circumstances" applies for considering a request for an extension of time to file a personal information form, and those "exceptional circumstances," if they exist, are among the relevant factors to be considered, but not the decisive test to be applied in declaring a claim abandoned.

*Khan v. Canada (Minister of Citizenship & Immigration)* (2005), 47 Imm. L.R. (3d) 278, 2005 CarswellNat 1716, 2005 CarswellNat 5405, 2005 FC 833 (F.C.) — There is no doubt that the onus of notifying immigration of change of addresses rests with the refugee claimant. However, where the negligence of counsel is egregious and there has been no contributing negligence or fault on the part of the applicant, the Immigration Refugee Board's decision to refuse to reopen the applicant's claim after it had been declared abandoned when the applicant failed to appear for a hearing and failed to appear at an abandonment show cause hearing can be set aside. In this case, the applicants put their trust in a consultant who led them to believe that he would take care of all correspondence with the Board, that they need not contact the Board directly and that he would advise them of any scheduled proceedings. Consequently, the Court was prepared to accept that their fault was not of such a degree that the applicants should be held accountable for their counsel's failures.

*Andreoli v. Canada (Ministre de la Citoyenneté & de l'Immigration)*, 2004 CarswellNat 5550, 2004 CarswellNat 2680, 2004 FC 1111 (F.C.) — The applicant came to Canada with her family in July 2002. In August 2002 the applicant and her family moved and following the advice of their counsel and the interpreter, they gave their change of address to the interpreter who was working for their counsel. The interpreter had promised that she would inform the IRB of the change of address. The panel of the IRB declared the applicant's claim abandoned when the IRB was unable to reach the applicant because the interpreter had failed to notify them of the change of address. The applicant sought to review that decision.

The evidence established that the interpreter forgot to advise the panel and that it was this error alone that led to the dismissal of the applicant's claim. The applicants do not speak French or English and were therefore particularly vulnerable and dependent on the interpreter. Finding that the applicants were the authors of their own misfortune amounts to punishing them for the carelessness of a third party which is not only unfair but also disregards s. 3(2) of the Act. The decision of the Board declaring the claim abandoned was set aside.

*Revich v. Canada (Ministre de la Citoyenneté & de l'Immigration)* (2004), 44 Imm. L.R. (3d) 129, 2004 CarswellNat 5036, 2004 CarswellNat 2631, 2004 FC 1064 (F.C.) — The *Refugee Protection Division Rules* clearly provide how the Division must proceed in order to declare a claim abandoned. The Division must give the claimant the opportunity to explain why the claim should not be declared abandoned, must take into account the claimant's explanations and must take into account any other relevant factor, in particular the claimant's intention to pursue the matter. The standard of review to apply to abandonment claim decisions is that of reasonableness *simpliciter*. The case law provides that the question the Division must ask itself is whether the applicant truly intended to abandon the claim.

The claimant did not behave like a person indifferent to the outcome of her claim. She informed her counsel of her absence, consulted a physician who confirmed the seriousness of her state of health. She came to the abandonment proceeding with the necessary documentary evidence. The chairperson dismissed the applicant's explanation but did not explain why. The chairperson drew an invalid inference from the evidence in declaring that the claim had been abandoned.

*Anjum v. Canada (Minister of Citizenship & Immigration)* (2004), 39 Imm. L.R. (3d) 157, 250 F.T.R. 311, 2004 CarswellNat 2394, 2004 CarswellNat 917, 2004 FC 496 (F.C.) — The decision of a member of the Refugee Division declaring a claim to be abandoned was set aside. The member did not ask the right question. This was an abandonment case where the inquiry must be directed at the true intention and actions of the claimant, in order to conclude that the claim is abandoned. The question is whether the applicants were ready to proceed with their claim.

## NOTICE OF CONSTITUTIONAL QUESTION

**59. (1) Notice of constitutional question — A party who wants to challenge the constitutional validity, applicability or operability of a legislative provision must complete a notice of constitutional question.**

**(2) Form and content of notice — The party must provide notice using either Form 69, "Notice of Constitutional Question", set out in the *Federal Courts Rules*, or any other form that includes**

> **(a) the name of the party;**
>
> **(b) the Division file number;**
>
> **(c) the date, time and place of the hearing;**
>
> **(d) the specific legislative provision that is being challenged;**
>
> **(e) the relevant facts relied on to support the constitutional challenge; and**
>
> **(f) a summary of the legal argument to be made in support of the constitutional challenge.**

**(3) Providing the notice — The party must provide**

> **(a) a copy of the notice of constitutional question to the Attorney General of Canada and to the attorney general of every province and territory of Canada, in accordance with section 57 of the *Federal Courts Act*;**
>
> **(b) a copy of the notice to the Minister;**
>
> **(c) a copy of the notice to any other party; and**
>
> **(d) the original notice to the Division, together with a written statement of how and when a copy of the notice was provided under paragraphs (a) to (c).**

**(4) Time limit — Documents provided under this rule must be received by their recipients no later than 10 days before the day the constitutional argument will be made.**

2002, c. 8, s. 182(3)(a)

## Oral Representations

**60. Oral representations — Representations made by a party or a refugee protection officer must be made orally at the end of a hearing unless the Division orders otherwise.**

## Decisions

**61. (1) Notice of decision — When the Division makes a decision, other than an interlocutory decision, it must provide a notice of decision in writing to the claimant or the protected person, as the case may be, and to the Minister.**

**(2) Written reasons if claim rejected — If it rejects a claim, the Division must provide the notice of decision, together with written reasons for the decision, to the claimant and the Minister.**

**(3) Written reasons if claim allowed — If the reasons of the Division indicate that it has allowed a claim for refugee protection after determining that sections E or F of Article 1 of the Refugee Convention do not apply, the Division must provide the notice of decision and written reasons for the decision to the claimant and the Minister.**

**(4) Written reasons for a decision on an Application to Vacate or Cease Refugee Protection — When the Division makes a decision on an Application to Vacate Refugee Protection or an Application to Cease Refugee Protection, the Division must provide to the parties, together with the notice of decision, written reasons for the decision.**

### Case Law

*Gutierrez v. Canada (Minister of Citizenship & Immigration)* (2005), 47 Imm. L.R. (3d) 238, 2005 CarswellNat 1706, 2005 CarswellNat 5356, 2005 FC 841 (F.C.) — This was an application for judicial review of the Refugee Protection Division's decision not to reopen the abandonment decision in respect of the applicant's Convention refugee claim. An abandonment decision has dramatic, potentially even fatal, implications for persons. The fact that the Refugee Protection Division did not have an address for the applicant so that it could comply with its obligation to give him notice of its abandonment decision did not relieve the RPD of its obligation under Rule 61(1) to give notice of its decision. The right to be heard is at the heart of our sense of justice and fairness. The RPD failed to observe a principle of natural justice arising out of the failure to give the applicant timely notice of the abandonment decision. The application was allowed and the decision of the RPD was set aside.

*Agalliu v. Canada (Minister of Citizenship & Immigration)* (2005), 49 Imm. L.R. (3d) 1, 34 Admin. L.R. (4th) 214, 2005 CarswellNat 2112, 2005 FC 1035 (F.C.) — The Board's reasons disclosed a number of superficial errors, in footnotes and in references to the documentary evidence. However, the Board's other errors and its failure to explain its conclusions adequately disclosed more fundamental problems. Taken together, these errors led to the conclusion that the Board's decision was not in keeping with the evidence before it. Sometimes, little errors in a written decision represent no more than a lack of final polishing. Other times, they are symptomatic of inadequate care on the part of the decision maker.

*Karakeeva v. Canada (Minister of Citizenship & Immigration)* (2004), 35 Imm. L.R. (3d) 219, 2004 CarswellNat 2142, 2004 CarswellNat 705, 2004 FC 416 (F.C.) — A tribunal may make adverse findings of credibility based on the implausibility of an applicant's story, provided the inferences drawn can be reasonably said to exist. However, plausibility findings should be made only in the clearest cases, i.e. if the facts as presented are outside the realm of what could reasonably be expected or where the documentary evidence demonstrates that the events could not have happened in the manner asserted by the claimant. A tribunal must be careful when rendering a decision based on a lack of plausibility because refugee claimants come from diverse cultures. Actions which appear implausible by Canadian standards might be plausible when considered from within the claimant's milieu.

*Vlad v. Canada (Minister of Citizenship & Immigration)* (2004), 38 Imm. L.R. (3d) 44, 2004 CarswellNat 2874, 2004 CarswellNat 404, 12 Admin. L.R. (4th) 150, 2004 FC 260 (F.C.) — This was an application to review a negative decision of a panel of the Refugee Protection Division.

Questions of procedural fairness are reviewed against a standard of correctness.

The job of a member of the Refugee Protection Division is a difficult one. The Board deals with a very significant volume of cases. Members are required to listen to tales of human misery on a daily basis, sometimes of unimaginable proportions. Their task is complicated by the fact that many claimants speak neither English nor French and must testify with the assistance of an interpreter. Many claimants suffer from psychological trauma which makes it more difficult for them to get their story across. Further, claimants come from a range of different ethnic backgrounds, each with their own cultural norms and attributes.

Sometimes, it may be necessary for Board members to take a somewhat active role in refugee hearings. Board interventions that amount to an energetic exercise in attempting to clear up inconsistencies will not necessarily result in an unfair hearing. If, at the conclusion of the examination, a Board member has concerns about a claimant's testimony the member is entitled to question the applicant in order to clarify the situation.

In this case what happened went beyond what was appropriate. Questions or comments from the Board appear on 111 pages of the 118 pages of the applicant's testimony. The majority of the interventions go beyond benign questions and come closer to what would normally be characterized as cross-examination. Questions were not reserved to the end of the applicant's examination, rather the Board's questions were interspersed throughout the examination in chief and cross-examination. Board members interrupted both the applicant, the applicant's counsel and the refugee protection officer in order to pursue their own line of questions. The Board's intervention did not clarify the situation with respect to the applicant's testimony but just added to the confusion.

The decision of the Board was set aside.

*Mihajlovics v. Canada (Minister of Citizenship & Immigration)*, 2004 CarswellNat 1289, 2004 CarswellNat 348, 2004 FC 215 (F.C.) — This was an application to review a negative decision of a panel of the Refugee Protection Division.

It is well established that on findings of fact the panel is to be accorded a standard of review of patent unreasonableness. On the issue of bias or reasonable apprehension of bias, little deference is paid to the panel and the standard of review is correctness. On the issue of persecution and discrimination, which is a question of mixed law and fact, the standard of review is reasonableness *simpliciter*.

*Murji v. Canada (Minister of Citizenship & Immigration)*, [2004] F.C.J. No. 211, 36 Imm. L.R. (3d) 314, 2004 CarswellNat 297, 2004 FC 148 (F.C.) — The Board stipulated that the only issues on which it wanted to hear submissions were credibility and delay, then proceeded to decide on the ground of state protection. This amounted to a gross denial of natural justice. The applicant was denied the opportunity to know and answer the case against him by the deliberate decision of the Board member presiding over the hearing.

*Kilic v. Canada (Minister of Citizenship & Immigration)*, [2004] F.C.J. No. 84, 245 F.T.R. 52, 2004 CarswellNat 1374, 2004 CarswellNat 428, 2004 FC 84 (F.C.) — The applicant sought to review a negative decision of the Refugee Protection Division. The decision was set aside because the panel's reasons did not demonstrate an analysis of s. 97. Despite the Board's negative credibility finding a separate analysis having regard to the wording of s. 97 may have produced a finding that the applicant was a person in need of protection. Accordingly the applicant's application was sent back for redetermination on this ground.

*Castillo v. Canada (Minister of Citizenship & Immigration)*, 2004 CarswellNat 73, 2004 CarswellNat 873, 2004 FC 56 (F.C.) — The Refugee Protection Division failed to explain why it discounted the applicants' evidence and referred solely to the evidence submitted by the Refugee Protection Officer. This created the impression that the RPD had ignored evidence that went to the crux of the matter. The application for judicial review was allowed.

*Nozem v. Canada (Minister of Citizenship & Immigration)* (2003), 244 F.T.R. 135, 10 Admin. L.R. (4th) 158, 2003 CarswellNat 4620, 2003 FC 1449, 2003 CarswellNat 4119 (F.C.) — The principle of *functus officio* has no application where the final decision in respect of the matter was issued in error.

The principle of *functus officio* is based on policy grounds which favour finality of proceedings.

Justice may require the re-opening of administrative proceedings in order to provide relief which would otherwise be available on appeal.

If the error which renders the decision a nullity is one that taints the whole proceeding then the tribunal must start afresh.

*Ben Ghribi v. Canada (Minister of Citizenship & Immigration)*, [2003] F.C.J. No. 1502, 2003 CarswellNat 3452, 2003 FC 1191, 2003 CarswellNat 3144 (F.C.) — This was an application to review a negative decision of the Refugee Panel. A tribunal is not required to address arguments concerning refugee "sur place" where the applicant has been judged not to have presented any credible evidence substantiating his claim.

*Ibrahimov v. Canada (Minister of Citizenship & Immigration)* (2003), 32 Imm. L.R. (3d) 135, 2003 CarswellNat 3166, 2003 CarswellNat 3871, 2003 FC 1185 (F.C.) — The appli-

Rules

cant sought to review a negative decision of a panel of the Refugee Protection Division. The alleged delay in the applicant's departure from Azerbaijan was a critical reason for the Board's rejection of his claim. Delay not only affected the Board's assessment of the subjective element but also was a significant factor underlying its assessment of the applicant's credibility.

When a claim is based on a number of discriminatory or harassing incidents which culminate in an event which forces a person to leave his country, then the issue of delay cannot be used as a significant factor to doubt that person's subjective fear of persecution.

*Shah v. Canada (Minister of Citizenship & Immigration)*, [2003] F.C.J. No. 1418, 240 F.T.R. 15, 2003 CarswellNat 4768, 2003 CarswellNat 2983, 2003 CFPI 1121, 2003 FC 1121 (F.C.) — The applicant sought to review a negative decision of a panel of the Refugee Protection Division.

The Board's reasons are insufficient; the Board failed to deal with the documentary evidence which corroborated the applicant's claim that he was a person in need of protection. The reasons given amount to no more than an unsupported conclusion with respect to that claim.

*Editor's note: The following case summaries were collected under the provisions of the former Act relating to procedural decisions interpreting the former s. 69.1(11). They may still be relevant.*

*Badal v. Canada (Minister of Citizenship & Immigration)*, [2003] F.C.J. No. 440, 26 Imm. L.R. (3d) 132, 2003 CarswellNat 645, 2003 CarswellNat 1471, 2003 FCT 311, 2003 CFPI 27, 231 F.T.R. 26 (T.D.) — The applicant claimed refugee status based on the fear of persecution in Iran because of his religion. His first claim before a panel of the IRB was denied. That decision was quashed. The evidence before the panel at the second hearing included some documents previously thought to have been lost, a transcript of the first hearing and the decisions and reasons of the first panel. The applicant did not testify at the second hearing due to post-traumatic stress disorder and related memory problems. The Board adjourned and gave counsel an opportunity to file a medical assessment of the applicant. Counsel filed the assessment and stated that he would not be calling the applicant. The Board never resumed hearing. It rendered the decision now under review.

Transcripts of previous hearings are generally admissible before the Board. A transcript should be considered trustworthy in the sense that it represents an accurate record of the oral testimony. It may be considered by the Board for the purpose of fact finding, including, where justified, making conclusions about credibility. When a panel considers a transcript from a previous hearing and relies on it to make credibility findings, its reasons should make the basis for those findings clearer. A panel can rely on the fact finding of another panel. It can for example adopt another panel's conclusions in respect of the conditions in the applicant's country of origin or the feasibility of seeking refuge within its borders. A panel may also admit in evidence and read the written reasons of a previous panel dealing with the same applicant. The question will arise, however, when this happens, concerning whether a reasonable observer would think that the Board had carried out a thorough independent and impartial analysis of all the evidence. It must be clear that the Board considered the matter afresh. A Board must not simply attach to its decisions the reasons of another panel.

*Adjibi v. Canada (Minister of Citizenship & Immigration)*, 2002 CarswellNat 1011, 2002 CarswellNat 2756, 2002 FCT 525, [2002] F.C.J. No. 680, 219 F.T.R. 54 (Fed. T.D.) —

Persecution, by definition, requires maltreatment which rises to the level of serious harm. Meaningful reasons require that a claimant and a reviewing court receive a sufficiently intelligible explanation as to why persecutory treatment does not constitute persecution. This requires a thorough consideration of the level of atrocity of the Acts inflicted upon the applicant, the effect upon the applicant's physical and mental state and whether the experiences constituted a compelling reason not to return the applicant to his/her country of origin.

*Mukwaya v. Canada (Minister of Citizenship & Immigration)* (2001), 15 Imm. L.R. (3d) 258, 2001 CarswellNat 1251, 2001 FCT 650, 209 F.T.R. 28 — The applicant's claim for refugee status was refused on the basis of his involvement with the ADF in Uganda and his complicity in war crimes and crimes against humanity. The following principles should direct a tribunal where the Minister seeks the claimant's exclusion on the basis of the claimant's role as an accomplice to an entity guilty of war crimes or crimes against humanity.

1. The Minister always has the legal burden of establishing that the refugee claimant is complicit in the commission of international crimes.

2. Complicity requires the claimant's personal and knowing participation in the commission of international crimes.

3. As a general rule mere membership in an organization involved in international crimes does not establish personal and knowing participation.

4. An exception to this general rule may arise when the tribunal is "free from doubt" that the Minister has established that the organization is "principally directed to a limited, brutal purpose".

5. Where the exception applies, mere membership in such an organization may place on the refugee claimant the evidentiary burden of showing that he had no personal and knowing participation in the commission of the organization's international crimes.

6. Mere membership in an organization principally directed to a limited, brutal purpose may allow the tribunal to infer the claimant's personal and knowing participation in the international crimes in the absence of any reliable evidence proffered by that person to explain otherwise their role in the organization.

The decision of the panel was set aside. The tribunal made no specific finding that the ADF was an organization principally directed to a limited, brutal purpose. In the absence of such a finding, the tribunal could not infer that the applicant had personal and knowing participation in the international crimes attributed to the ADF, let alone suggest that the claimant had to rebut a presumption of complicity. No properly instructed panel on this evidence could conclude that the ADF was principally directed to a limited, brutal purpose while the applicant was still in Uganda, nor that the applicant could have known that the ADF had such a purpose. The finding of the panel was set aside.

*Hidri v. Canada (Minister of Citizenship & Immigration)*, 2001 CarswellNat 1977, [2001] F.C.J. No. 1362, 2001 FCT 949 (Fed. T.D.) — The applicants sought to review a decision of a panel of the CRDD denying their claim to refugee status. The applicants argued that the Board required them to meet a standard of proof well beyond that of the civil balance of probabilities, when it maintained that it was not "convinced" of the applicants' allegations. It cannot be assumed that using the word "convince" automatically connotes a higher burden of proof without a careful examination of the contextual basis

Rules

of the decision. The Court held that on reading the reasons of the panel and reviewing the materials it was satisfied that the civil standard of proof was applied and that the applicants merely failed to meet that threshold.

*Thanni c. Canada (Ministre de la Citoyenneté & l'Immigration)* (2001), 203 F.T.R. 117, 2001 CarswellNat 2236, 2001 CarswellNat 771, 2001 FCT 353, 2001 CFPI 353 (Fed. T.D.) — This was an application to review a negative decision of a panel of the CRDD. The decision was rendered orally and confirmed at a later date with written reasons. There were some additions in the written reasons which were not part of the oral decision. Some conformity is required between written and oral reasons. The test to be applied is whether the differences between the written and oral reasons are substantial. Decisions in which it has been held that the difference was substantial related to cases in which the panel's conclusion was no longer the same in the written decision, or where some findings appeared in the oral reasons and not in the written reasons. In the present case, the panel's conclusion was the same in both the written and oral reasons. Some written reasons were added in support of the panel's conclusion. Furthermore, the panel did not reserve the right when it gave its oral reasons to make some alterations or additions to those reasons when they appeared in written form.

There was a substantial difference between the oral and written reasons in this case because a number of written reasons were added to the panel's conclusions. If a panel chooses to render its decision at the conclusion of a hearing, it must be concluded that the panel has completed its thinking about the case and that it is prepared to present its decision and the reasons for it. If the panel continues to deliberate afterward on the question and adds reasons to its decision, then one can easily be led to believe that its thinking had not ended when it gave its decision.

A panel may make some corrections in its written decision for the purposes of syntax and comprehension. To accept that a panel could perfect its decision in written reasons because it had forgotten to address one or two questions that it thought were important to the review of the case when it gave its oral reasons would constitute a miscarriage of justice.

Accordingly, the application for judicial review was allowed.

*Bodokia v. Canada (Minister of Citizenship & Immigration)*, 2001 FCT 227, 2001 CarswellNat 552 (Fed. T.D.) — The applicant sought to review a negative decision of a panel of the CRDD. It was reasonable for the panel to conclude that the silence of recent reports monitoring and reporting human rights abuses in Georgia was an indication that there were no current serious problems for Abkhazians in Georgia.

*Chen v. Canada (Minister of Citizenship & Immigration)* (2001), 14 Imm. L.R. (3d) 82, 2001 FCT 500, 2001 CarswellNat 1019 (Fed. T.D.) — The applicant sought to review a negative decision of a panel of the CRDD. The applicant claimed to be adherent of the Tian Dao religion.

Judicial deference to findings of credibility cannot serve to excuse the failure of a panel to clearly express itself on primary findings of fact. It was reasonable to expect that a panel would clearly express itself on primary issues arising from a claim for refugee status. Here, the Board could not conclude that the applicant had a well-founded fear of persecution on religious grounds, unless it found she was a member of the religion in question. The Board failed to address this "primary issue" in its reasons and therefore the decision was set aside.

*Koroz v. Canada (Minister of Citizenship & Immigration)* (2000), 9 Imm. L.R. (3d) 12, 261 N.R. 71, 186 F.T.R. 295 (note), 2000 CarswellNat 2347, [2000] F.C.J. No. 1593 (Fed. T.D.) — The appellant was denied refugee status on the basis of the existence of an internal flight alternative in Moldova.

A panel of the Board may adopt the same reasoning as another panel faced with the same documentary evidence as a basis for finding the existence of an internal flight alternative in the same country. This does not mean that a panel can blindly adopt factual findings of other panels. Where the question is one of fact-finding concerning general country conditions at approximately the same time, however, a panel may rely on the reasoning of an earlier panel on the same documentary evidence. Where the analysis of one panel on the same evidence on such a question commends itself to a later panel, there is no legal bar to the second panel relying upon it. The technique of appending part of the reasons of the first panel to the reasons of the second one is a shortcut practice that should not be used.

*Hartley v. Canada (Minister of Citizenship & Immigration)* (2000), 189 F.T.R. 296, 2000 CarswellNat 912 (Fed. T.D.) — A person's political beliefs do not have to conform to the beliefs ascribed to him or her by the persecutor. Additionally, they do not have to be explicitly stated, but the perception may be based upon the actions of the claimant. It is not incumbent upon the claimant to identify the precise reasons for the persecution, it is for the examiner to decide whether the convention definition is met. Lack of a precedent is no reason to decline to consider whether the claim of an applicant for refugee status falls within the definition.

Natural justice and procedural fairness require the panel to consider the arguments put forward by the claimant. The claimant argued that he was the subject of persecution because of a perception that he was a member of a particular social group. The panel did not address whether perceived membership could give rise to Convention protection, an issue critical to the applicant's claim.

Accordingly, the application for judicial review was allowed.

*Berete v. Canada (Minister of Citizenship & Immigration)* (1999), 1999 CarswellNat 986 (Fed. T.D.) — When documentary evidence is presented that could influence the way in which the panel handles a refugee claim, the panel must indicate its impact on the applicant's claim. The panel must comment on documentary evidence when it directly contradicts the decision made.

*Numbi v. Canada (Minister of Citizenship & Immigration)* (1999), 163 F.T.R. 319 (Fed. T.D.) — The failure of the Board to address the specific and relevant documentary evidence which appeared to corroborate important aspects of the applicant's claim in its analysis constituted a reviewable error.

*Miral v. Canada (Minister of Citizenship & Immigration)* (1999), 161 F.T.R. 213 (Fed. T.D.) — The applicant challenged a negative decision of the CRDD. The applicant who was from Sri Lanka was found not to be a credible witness by the panel.

Considerable deference is given on judicial review to credibility findings made by the CRDD. It is perfectly acceptable for a tribunal to find an applicant lacking in credibility according to implausibilities in the applicant's testimony. Where the tribunal finds a lack of credibility based on inferences, there must be a basis in the evidence to support the inferences. Such inferences must be reasonably open to this tribunal based on the evidence of the applicant. Where the tribunal's inferences are based on what seem to be "common sense or rational perceptions about how a government regime in another country might be expected to act", there is an obligation to provide an opportunity for the applicant to address those inferences on which the tribunal relies. In the case at bar, the tribunal found that the applicant's evidence was perfunctory and lacked the kind of detail that could be expected of someone as articulate and well educated as the claimant.

The Court found that the panel had engaged in speculation as to regular or normal police procedures in Sri Lanka and had no evidence before it on which to base such conclusions. The applicant offered a plausible explanation for the police's repeated acceptance of bribes. The panel, in making its finding regarding probable police procedure, made no references to any documentary evidence to support such a finding. While there may have been a basis in the evidence for such a finding, the panel neglected to point to it. In addition, the panel referred to a lack of corroborating evidence regarding the applicant's detention as significant in the negative determination of her claim. A failure to offer documentation cannot be linked to an applicant's credibility in the absence of evidence to contradict the applicant's testimony. It is not open to the CRDD to require documentary evidence to support an applicant's uncontradicted testimony regarding her arrest and detention.

The decision of the tribunal was set aside.

*Gill v. Canada (Minister of Citizenship & Immigration)*, [1998] F.C.J. No. 1139, 1998 CarswellNat 1561 (Fed. T.D.) — The applicant sought to review a negative decision of the IRB. The panel found that the applicant was persecuted by the Punjabi police in the past. The sole issue framed by the panel was whether the applicant had an internal flight alternative. The panel's analysis, however, did not proceed. The actual analysis dealt with whether conditions had changed sufficiently in India and in particular in the Punjab such that the applicant was no longer at risk of persecution. In making its assessment of the profiles of people currently at risk, the panel relied on documentary evidence. A panel is entitled to accept, reject and weigh documentary evidence. If a panel states that it is relying on specific documentary evidence however, it cannot arbitrarily disregard integral portions of that evidence.

**62. Request for written reasons — A request made by a claimant, or the Minister, for written reasons for a decision allowing a claim must be in writing. The request must be received by the Division no later than 10 days after the claimant or the Minister, as the case may be, received the notice of decision.**

**63. (1) When decisions take effect — decision allowing claim — A decision allowing a claim takes effect**

**(a) if given orally at a hearing, when a Division member states the decision; and**

**(b) if made in writing, when a Division member signs and dates the decision.**

**(2) When decisions take effect — decision rejecting claim — A decision rejecting a claim takes effect**

**(a) if given orally at a hearing, when a Division member states the decision and gives reasons; and**

**(b) if made in writing, when a Division member signs and dates the reasons for the decision.**

**64. When decisions take effect — Application to Vacate or Cease Refugee Protection** — A decision on an Application to Vacate Refugee Protection or an Application to Cease Refugee Protection takes effect

(a) if given orally at a hearing, when a Division member states the decision and gives reasons; and

(b) if made in writing, when a Division member signs and dates the reasons for the decision.

**65. When decisions take effect — decision on abandonment** — A decision on the abandonment of a claim, an Application to Vacate Refugee Protection or an Application to Cease Refugee Protection takes effect

(a) if given orally at a hearing, when a Division member states the decision and gives reasons; and

(b) if made in writing, when a Division member signs and dates the reasons for the decision.

**66. When decisions take effect — allowing application to withdraw** — A decision allowing an application to withdraw a claim, an Application to Vacate Refugee Protection or an Application to Cease Refugee Protection takes effect

(a) if given orally at a hearing, when a Division member states the decision and gives reasons; and

(b) if made in writing, when a Division member signs and dates the reasons for the decision.

**67. (1) When decisions take effect — three member panel allowing claim** — A decision made by a panel of three members allowing a claim takes effect

(a) if given orally at a hearing, when all the members state their decision; and

(b) if made in writing, when all the members sign and date their decision.

**(2) When decisions take effect — other decisions of three member panel** — A decision made by a panel of three members that is a decision rejecting a claim, or allowing an application to withdraw, a decision on the abandonment of a claim or an Application to Vacate Refugee Protection or Application to Cease Refugee Protection, or a decision on an Application to Vacate Refugee Protection or an Application to Cease Refugee Protection, takes effect

(a) if given orally at a hearing, when all the members state their decision and give reasons; and

(b) if made in writing, when all the members sign and date the reasons for their decision.

## General Provisions

**68. No applicable rule** — In the absence of a provision in these Rules dealing with a matter raised during the proceedings, the Division may do whatever is necessary to deal with the matter.

## Case Law

*Benitez v. Canada (Minister of Citizenship & Immigration)*, 2007 CarswellNat 1393, 2007 FCA 199 (Fed. C.A.) — The Federal Court consolidated a number of applications for judicial review impugning the validity of Guideline 7. Guideline 7 was issued by the Chairperson of the Board in 2003, pursuant to the power conferred by paragraph 159(1)(h) of the Immigration and Refugee Protection Act, S.C. 2001, c. 27, to issue guidelines to assist members of the Board in carrying out their duties ("the Guideline 7 issue"). Guideline 7 provides that the standard order of questioning at a refugee protection hearing by the Refugee Protection Division of the Board will be that the claimant is questioned first by the Refugee Protection officer and/or by the Refugee Protection Division member conducting the hearing. However, in exceptional cases members may permit claimants to be questioned first by their own counsel.

Guideline 7 does not breach the duty of fairness by either denying the claimants an effective opportunity to make representations or so distorting the role of the member of the Refugee Protection Division hearing the claim as to give rise to a reasonable apprehension of bias. Nor is it an unlawful fetter on member's discretion, and it was not legally required to have been issued under the chairperson's statutory power to issue rules of procedure, subject to cabinet approval.

*Thamotharem v. Canada (Minister of Citizenship & Immigration)*, 2006 CarswellNat 1588, 2006 FCA 218 (Fed. C.A.) — This appeal concerns the validity of Guideline 7 (preparation and conduct of a hearing in the Refugee Protection Division) issued in 2003 by the Chairperson of the Board pursuant to the statutory power to "issue guidelines. . .to assist members in carrying out their duties": Immigration and Refugee Protection Act, S.C. 2001, c. 27, paragraph 159(1)(h). The key paragraphs of Guideline 7 provide as follows:

> "In a claim for refugee protection, the standard practice will be for the Refugee Protection Officer to start questioning the claimant," although the member of the Refugee Protection Division hearing the claim "may vary the order of questioning in exceptional circumstances."

Guideline 7 is not, on its face, invalid on the ground of procedural unfairness, although, as the Minister and the Board conceded, fairness may require that, in certain circumstances particular claimants should be questioned first by their own counsel. Guideline 7 is not incompatible with the impartiality required of a member when conducting a hearing which is inquisitorial in form. Guideline 7 is not an unlawful fetter on the exercise of members' discretion on the conduct of refugee protection hearings. The Guideline expressly directs members to consider the facts of the particular case before them to determine whether there are exceptional circumstances warranting a deviation from the standard order of questioning. The evidence did not establish that members disregarded this aspect of Guideline 7 and slavishly adhered to the standard order of questioning, regardless of the facts of the case before them. Nor does it follow that the fact that Guideline 7 could have been issued as a statutory rule of procedure that it is invalid because it was not approved by the Governor in Council. The Minister's appeal was allowed, the appellant's cross-appeal was dismissed, the order of the Federal Court set aside, and the application for judicial review dismissed.

69. **Powers of the Division** — The Division may

(a) act on its own initiative, without a party having to make an application or request to the Division;

(b) change a requirement of a rule;

(c) excuse a person from a requirement of a rule; and

(d) extend or shorten a time limit, before or after the time limit has passed.

70. **Failing to follow a rule** — Unless proceedings are declared invalid by the Division, a failure to follow any requirement of these Rules does not make the proceedings invalid.

## COMING INTO FORCE

71. **Coming into force** — These Rules come into force on the day on which section 161 of the Act comes into force.

## SCHEDULE 1 — CLAIMANT'S PERSONAL INFORMATION

*(Rule 1)*

| Item | Information |
|---|---|
| 1. | Any objections the claimant has to the disclosure of personal information in the Personal Information Form to another claimant. |
| 2. | Claimant's name at birth and any other name used by the claimant or by which the claimant is known. |
| 3. | Claimant's gender. |
| 4. | Claimant's date and place of birth. |
| 5. | Claimant's country or countries of citizenship at birth. |
| 6. | Claimant's present country or countries of citizenship. If different from citizenship at birth, date of obtaining present citizenship. |
| 7. | If stateless, the countries in which the claimant has resided since birth and the claimant's status in each country. |
| 8. | Claimant's nationality, ethnic group or tribe. |
| 9. | Claimant's religion and denomination. |
| 10. | The language the claimant first learned and still speaks, and any other languages or dialects spoken and understood by the claimant. |
| 11. | Whether the claimant is single, married, separated, divorced, widowed or is a common-law partner; the date of marriage, separation, divorce, common-law partnership or of becoming a widow or widower; and the name of any spouse, common-law partner or former spouse. |

| Item | Information |
| --- | --- |
| 12. | The date of birth, citizenship and address of the claimant's spouse or common-law partner, and the names, dates of birth, citizenship and place and country of residence of the claimant's children, parents, brothers, sisters and, if the claimant is under 18 years of age, guardian. |
| 13. | If a relative of the claimant has requested refugee protection or asylum in Canada or any other country, at a Canadian office abroad or from the United Nations High Commissioner for Refugees, the details of the request including the name and date of birth of the relative and the date, location and result of the request. |
| 14. | The details of the claimant's formal education or professional training, including the number of years of education or training, the name and location of the schools or educational institutions attended, the dates of attendance, and the level, degree, diploma or certificate obtained. |
| 15. | The details of the claimant's work history, including the dates of employment, the name of the employer, the place and type of employment and the claimant's occupation and title. |
| 16. | Details of any service by the claimant in the armed forces of any country, including<br>(a) if military service is compulsory, at what age;<br>(b) the country served, the dates of service and the rank obtained;<br>(c) if the claimant received a call-up notice but did not serve, the date of the notice and the reasons why the claimant did not serve;<br>(d) if the claimant did not complete their service, the reasons why;<br>(e) whether the claimant volunteered for military service;<br>(f) if the claimant participated in any combat, where and when; and<br>(g) if the claimant received any paramilitary or security training that was not part of regular military service, the dates and type of training received, and who provided the training. |
| 17. | Claimant's addresses within the last 20 years and their status in the country of address. |
| 18. | The details of the claimant's travel to any countries during the past 10 years, including the dates and purpose of travel to those countries. |
| 19. | The route used to come to Canada, including the countries and places of departure and arrival, the dates of arrival and departure and the means of transportation used. |

| Item | Information |
| --- | --- |
| 20. | If the claimant has returned to a country or countries in which they fear persecution, torture or a risk to their life or a risk of cruel and unusual treatment or punishment since making their present claim for refugee protection in Canada, the place and country to which they returned, the dates the claimant returned and left, and the reason why the claimant returned. |
| 21. | The details of all passports or travel documents that have been issued to the claimant in the last twenty years. |
| 22. | The details of all passports or travel documents used by the claimant to travel to Canada, including passports or travel documents that are not genuine or were improperly obtained, and the current location of the documents. If any of those documents has been lost, destroyed or disposed of, the details of the loss, destruction or disposal. |
| 23. | If the claimant has not obtained a passport or travel document, the reason why the claimant did not do so. |
| 24. | If the claimant required an exit visa or special permission to leave their country, the details of any visa or permission obtained by the claimant or, if not obtained, the reason why the claimant did not do so. |
| 25. | The details of any application made by the claimant for a visa to enter Canada, including the type of visa requested and the date and result of the application. |
| 26. | If the claimant entered Canada from the United States of America, a list of the documents that the claimant presented on entry to that country and the current location of those documents. If any of those documents has been lost, destroyed or disposed of, the details of the loss, destruction or disposal. |
| 27. | If the claimant had a visa to enter the United States of America, the place and date of issue of the visa. |
| 28. | If the claimant renewed a passport or travel document since making the present claim for refugee protection in Canada, the details of the document renewed including the date of renewal. |
| 29. | Details — including current location — of the claimant's other identity documents, including documents that the claimant believes they can obtain and the expected date of receipt. |
| 30. | Details of all claims for refugee protection made by the claimant in Canada or at a Canadian office abroad, including the date, location and result. |
| 31. | Details of all claims for refugee protection or asylum made by the claimant in any other country or to the United Nations High Commissioner for Refugees, including the country, date and result of the claim and any document issued. |
| 32. | If the United Nations High Commissioner for Refugees has recognized the claimant as a refugee, the date and place of recognition, and the number and date of issue and current location of any document issued. |

Rules

| Item | Information |
|---|---|
| 33. | Details of any crime or offence that the claimant has committed, including the date, the place and the type of crime or offence. If the claimant has been charged, acquitted or convicted of a crime or offence, the details of the proceedings including dates, verdict and any sentence imposed. |
| 34. | If the claimant has been arrested or is wanted by the police or military or any other authorities in any country, including Canada, the reason why the claimant was arrested or is wanted and the relevant dates and places. |
| 35. | If the claimant has been refused an entry visa by any country or ordered to leave any country, the name of the country, date and reason. |
| 36. | The country or countries against which the claimant is making a claim for refugee protection. |
| 37. | Reasons why the claimant is making a claim for refugee protection and the facts that support the claim. |
| 38. | Whether the claimant has received medical or psychological treatment or evaluation, in Canada or elsewhere, for harm resulting from the events that caused the claimant to make a claim for refugee protection. |
| 39. | The claimant's contact information, and the contact information of any counsel for the claimant. |

## SCHEDULE 2 — INFORMATION TO BE PROVIDED ABOUT THE CLAIMANT BY AN OFFICER

*(Paragraph 3(2)(b))*

| Item | Information |
|---|---|
| 1. | Name, sex and date of birth. |
| 2. | Department of Citizenship and Immigration Client ID Number. |
| 3. | If the claimant is detained, the name of the place of detention. |
| 4. | Claimant's contact information in Canada, if any. |
| 5. | Contact information of any counsel for the claimant. |
| 6. | Official language chosen by the claimant to communicate with the Division. |
| 7. | Name of the officer referring the claim. |
| 8. | Date the claim was referred or deemed to be referred to the Division. |
| 9. | Section of the Act under which the claim is being referred. |
| 10. | Officer's decision about the claim's eligibility under section 100 of the Act, if a decision has been made. |

| Item | Information |
|---|---|
| 11. | **Name of the country or countries in which the claimant fears persecution, torture, a risk of cruel or unusual treatment or punishment, or a risk to their life.** |
| 12. | **Whether the claimant needs an interpreter, including a sign language interpreter, during any proceeding, and the language or dialect to be interpreted.** |
| 13. | **Whether the Minister has asked for any information about the claim.** |
| 14. | **If a claim of the claimant's spouse, common-law partner or any relative has been referred to the Division, the names and Department of Citizenship and Immigration client identification numbers of those persons.** |
| 15. | **When and how the officer notified the claimant of the referral of the claim to the Division.** |

# CAN. REG. 2002-229 — IMMIGRATION DIVISION RULES

## made under the *Immigration and Refugee Protection Act*

SOR/2002-229, as am. S.C. 2002, c. 8, s. 182(3)(a).

### DEFINITIONS

**1. Definitions — The following definitions apply in these Rules.**

**"Act" means the *Immigration and Refugee Protection Act. ("Loi")***

**"admissibility hearing" means a hearing held under subsection 44(2) of the Act. *("enquête")***

**"contact information" means a person's name, postal address and telephone number and the person's fax number and electronic mail address, if any. *("coordonnées")***

**"detention review" means a forty-eight hour review, a seven-day review and a thirty-day review. *("contrôle des motifs de détention")***

**"Division" means the Immigration Division. *("Section")***

**"forty-eight hour review" means the review of the reasons for continued detention under subsection 57(1) of the Act. *("contrôle des quarante-huit heures")***

**"party" means a permanent resident or foreign national, as the case may be, and the Minister. *("partie")***

**"proceeding" means an admissibility hearing, a detention review, a conference or an application. *("procédure")***

**"registry office" means a business office of the Division. *("greffe")***

**"seven-day review" means the review of the reasons for continued detention required to be held during the seven days following a forty-eight hour review, under subsection 57(2) of the Act. *("contrôle des sept jours")***

**"thirty-day review" means the review of the reasons for continued detention required to be held during the thirty days following each previous review, under subsection 57(2) of the Act. *("contrôle des trente jours")***

### COMMUNICATING WITH THE DIVISION

**2. Communicating with the Division — All communication with the Division must be directed to the registry office specified by the Division.**

# Part 1 — Rules Applicable to Admissibility Hearings

## *Information*

**3. Information provided by the Minister — When the Minister requests the Division to hold an admissibility hearing, the Minister must provide to the Division and the permanent resident or foreign national, as the case may be, any relevant information or document that the Minister may have, including**

**(a) the name and other contact information in Canada of the permanent resident or foreign national;**

**(b) the person's date of birth, sex and citizenship;**

**(c) whether the person is single, married, separated or divorced or is a common-law partner;**

**(d) the inadmissibility report and the Minister's referral;**

**(e) whether the person has made a claim for refugee protection;**

**(f) the name and address of the place of detention, if the person is detained;**

**(g) the language — English or French — chosen by the person for communicating with the Division;**

**(h) if an interpreter is required, the language or dialect to be interpreted;**

**(i) if the person has counsel, the counsel's contact information;**

**(j) the client identification number given to the person by the Department of Citizenship and Immigration;**

**(k) the names, sex, date of birth, citizenship, and other contact information of any family member whose case has been referred to the Division, and the client identification number given to them by the Department of Citizenship and Immigration;**

**(l) the date on which the Minister makes the request;**

**(m) the name and title of the Minister's counsel;**

**(n) whether the Minister has made an application for non-disclosure of information;**

**(o) whether the Minister believes that the person is less than 18 years of age or is unable to appreciate the nature of the proceedings; and**

**(p) the evidence to be presented by the Minister.**

**4. Change to contact information — If the contact information changes, the permanent resident or foreign national, unless detained, must without delay provide the changes in writing to the Division and the Minister.**

Rules

## *Withdrawing a Request by the Minister for an Admissibility Hearing*

**5. (1) Abuse of process — Withdrawal of a request for an admissibility hearing is an abuse of process if withdrawal would likely have a negative effect on the integrity of the Division. If no substantive evidence has been accepted in the proceedings, withdrawal of a request is not an abuse of process.**

**(2) Withdrawal if no evidence has been accepted — If no substantive evidence has been accepted in the proceedings, the Minister may withdraw a request by notifying the Division orally at a proceeding or in writing. If the Minister notifies in writing, the Minister must provide a copy of the notice to the other party.**

**(3) Withdrawal if evidence has been accepted — If substantive evidence has been accepted in the proceedings, the Minister must make a written application to the Division in order to withdraw a request.**

### Case Law

*Sheremetov v. Canada (Minister of Citizenship & Immigration)* (2004), 40 Imm. L.R. (3d) 9, 2004 CarswellNat 5184, 2004 CarswellNat 3920, 331 N.R. 163, 2004 FCA 373 (F.C.A.) — The respondent was a landed immigrant. In March 2002, an officer reported to the Deputy Minister that, in his opinion, the respondent had committed an act that constituted a criminal offence both in Canada and Ukraine. The respondent was given notice to attend a hearing scheduled for September 20, 2002. The hearing resumed on November 6, 2002, when both parties requested an adjournment. The hearing then resumed on February 5, 2003 when the Minister withdrew his request for the admissibility hearing. The Immigration Division accepted the withdrawal. The judicial review judge set aside that decision and found that the division should have taken into account the fact that the documents at the heart of the Ukraine charges had not been produced.

Under Rules 5 and 6 the Minister only had to notify the Immigration Division and the respondent of withdrawal of his request for an admissibility hearing because no evidence at all had been accepted in the proceeding. The adjudicator had no jurisdiction to exercise discretion or proceed with the matter. It is only when the Minister applies to reinstate a request for an inadmissibility hearing under Rule 6 that jurisdiction is conferred on the Immigration Division to determine if it is in the interest of justice to allow the application for reinstatement.

## *Reinstating a Request by the Minister for an Admissibility Hearing*

**6. (1) Application for reinstatement of withdrawn request — The Minister may make a written application to the Division to reinstate a request for an admissibility hearing that was withdrawn.**

**(2) Factors — The Division must allow the application if it is established that there was a failure to observe a principle of natural justice or if it is otherwise in the interests of justice to allow the application.**

## Case Law

*Sheremetov v. Canada (Minister of Citizenship & Immigration)* (2004), 40 Imm. L.R. (3d) 9, 2004 CarswellNat 5184, 2004 CarswellNat 3920, 331 N.R. 163, 2004 FCA 373 (F.C.A.) — The respondent was a landed immigrant. In March 2002, an officer reported to the Deputy Minister that, in his opinion, the respondent had committed an act that constituted a criminal offence both in Canada and Ukraine. The respondent was given notice to attend a hearing scheduled for September 20, 2002. The hearing resumed on November 6, 2002, when both parties requested an adjournment. The hearing then resumed on February 5, 2003 when the Minister withdrew his request for the admissibility hearing. The Immigration Division accepted the withdrawal. The judicial review judge set aside that decision and found that the division should have taken into account the fact that the documents at the heart of the Ukraine charges had not been produced.

Under Rules 5 and 6 the Minister only had to notify the Immigration Division and the respondent of withdrawal of his request for an admissibility hearing because no evidence at all had been accepted in the proceeding. The adjudicator had no jurisdiction to exercise discretion or proceed with the matter. It is only when the Minister applies to reinstate a request for an inadmissibility hearing under Rule 6 that jurisdiction is conferred on the Immigration Division to determine if it is in the interest of justice to allow the application for reinstatement.

## *Decision*

**7. (1) Favourable decision — If the decision at the conclusion of an admissibility hearing is in favour of the permanent resident or foreign national, the member making the decision must date and sign a notice of decision and provide a copy to the parties.**

**(2) Unfavourable decision — If the decision is not in favour of the permanent resident or foreign national, the member must date and sign an order indicating the applicable provisions of the Act and provide a copy to the parties. The member must also notify the permanent resident or foreign national of**

> **(a) their right to appeal to the Immigration Appeal Division; or**
>
> **(b) if they do not have the right to appeal, their right to file an application for judicial review in the Federal Court.**

**(3) When decision takes effect — A decision made orally at a hearing takes effect when a Division member states the decision. A decision made in writing takes effect when the member signs and dates it.**

**(4) Request for written reasons — A request made by a party for written reasons for a decision may be made orally at the end of an admissibility hearing or in writing. A request in writing must be received by the Division no later than 10 days after the decision takes effect.**

Rules

## PART 2 — RULES APPLICABLE TO DETENTION REVIEWS

### *Information*

**8. (1) Information provided by the Minister — If a foreign national or a permanent resident is subject to a detention review, the Minister must provide the Division and the person detained with the following information:**

**(a) the person's name, sex, date of birth and citizenship;**

**(b) whether the person is single, married, separated or divorced or is a common-law partner;**

**(c) whether the person has made a claim for refugee protection;**

**(d) the language — English or French — chosen by the person for communicating with the Division;**

**(e) if an interpreter is required, the language or dialect to be interpreted;**

**(f) if the person has counsel, the counsel's contact information;**

**(g) the date and time that the person was first placed in detention;**

**(h) the name and address of the place where the person is being detained;**

**(i) whether the Minister is seeking a detention review after the first forty-eight hour detention or after a seven-day or thirty-day review;**

**(j) the identification number given to the person by the Department of Citizenship and Immigration;**

**(k) the provision of the Act under which the review of the reasons for continued detention is required;**

**(l) whether an application for non-disclosure of information has been made; and**

**(m) whether the Minister believes that the person is less than 18 years of age or is unable to appreciate the nature of the proceedings.**

**(2) Time limit — The information must be received by the Division and the person detained**

**(a) in the case of a forty-eight hour review, as soon as possible; and**

**(b) in the case of a seven-day or thirty-day review, at least three days before the date fixed for the review.**

**9. (1) Application for early review — A party may make a written application to the Division requesting a detention review before the expiry of the seven-day or thirty-day period, as the case may be.**

**(2) Factor — The Division may allow the application if the party sets out new facts that justify an early review of the detention.**

**10. Removal before detention review — The Minister must notify the Division as soon as a permanent resident or foreign national is removed from Canada prior to a scheduled detention review.**

### *Decisions*

**11. (1) Notice to the parties — At the conclusion of a detention review, the member must notify the parties of the member's decision.**

**(2) Order — The member must date and sign an order for detention or release indicating the applicable provisions of the Act and provide a copy to the parties.**

**(3) When decision takes effect — A decision made orally at a hearing takes effect when a Division member states the decision. A decision made in writing takes effect when the member signs and dates it.**

**(4) Request for written reasons — A request made by a party for written reasons for a decision may be made orally at the end of a detention review or in writing. A request in writing must be received by the Division no later than 10 days after the decision takes effect.**

## PART 3 — RULES THAT APPLY TO BOTH ADMISSIBILITY HEARINGS AND DETENTION REVIEWS

### *Information Relating to Counsel*

**12. Counsel's contact information — A permanent resident or foreign national who is represented by counsel must, on obtaining counsel, provide the counsel's contact information in writing to the Division and the Minister. If that information changes, the permanent resident or foreign national must without delay provide the changes in writing to the Division and the Minister.**

Rules

### *Counsel of Record*

**13. Becoming counsel of record — As soon as counsel for a permanent resident or foreign national agrees to a date for a proceeding, or becomes counsel after a date has been fixed, the counsel becomes counsel of record.**

**14. Withdrawal as counsel of record — To withdraw as counsel of record, counsel must notify the Division and the Minister in writing as soon as possible. Counsel is no longer counsel of record as soon as the Division receives the notice.**

**15. Removal of counsel of record — To remove counsel as counsel of record, the permanent resident or foreign national must notify the Division and the Minister in writing as soon as possible. Counsel is no longer counsel of record when the Division receives the notice.**

## *Language of Proceedings*

**16. (1) Changing the language of proceedings — A permanent resident or foreign national may make an application to the Division to change the language of the proceedings to English or French**

> **(a) orally or in writing in the case of a forty-eight hour or seven-day review or an admissibility hearing held at the same time; and**
>
> **(b) in writing in all other cases.**

**(2) Time limit — A written application must be received by the Division**

> **(a) as soon as possible, in the case of a forty-eight hour or seven-day review or an admissibility hearing held at the same time; and**
>
> **(b) in all other cases, at least five days before the hearing.**

**17. (1) Requesting an interpreter — If a party or a party's witness needs an interpreter for a proceeding, the party must notify the Division in writing and specify the language or dialect of the interpreter. The notice must be received by the Division**

> **(a) as soon as possible, in the case of a forty-eight hour or seven-day review or an admissibility hearing held at the same time; and**
>
> **(b) in all other cases, at least five days before the hearing.**

**(2) Interpreter's oath — The interpreter must take an oath or make a solemn affirmation to interpret accurately.**

### Case Law

*Lamme v. Canada (Minister of Citizenship & Immigration)*, 2005 CarswellNat 3063, 2005 CarswellNat 4881, 2005 FC 1336 (F.C.) — The general standard to be met with respect to the quality of interpretation is that it must be continuous, precise, impartial and contemporaneous. In addition, for the interpretation to be considered as meeting the standard, it must be established that the applicant understood the interpretation and adequately expressed him- or herself through the interpreter.

## *Designated Representatives*

**18. Duty of counsel to notify the Division — If counsel for a party believes that the Division should designate a representative for the permanent resident or foreign national in the proceedings because they are under 18 years of age or unable to appreciate the nature of the proceedings, counsel must without delay notify the Division and the other party in writing. If counsel is aware of a person in Canada who meets the requirements to be designated as a representative, counsel must provide the person's contact information in the notice.**

**19. Requirements for being designated — To be designated as a representative, a person must**

> **(a) be 18 years of age or older;**

(b) understand the nature of the proceedings;

(c) be willing and able to act in the best interests of the permanent resident or foreign national; and

(d) not have interests that conflict with those of the permanent resident or foreign national.

## *Conference*

20. (1) **Requirement to participate at a conference** — The Division may require the parties to participate at a conference to discuss issues, relevant facts and any other matter that would make the proceedings more fair and efficient.

(2) **Information or documents** — The Division may require the parties to give any information or document at or before the conference.

(3) **Decisions noted** — The Division must make a written record of any decisions and agreements made at the conference or state them orally at the hearing.

## *Fixing a Date*

21. **Fixing a date** — The Division must fix the date for a hearing and any other proceeding relating to the hearing. The Division may require the parties to participate in the preparation of a schedule of proceedings by appearing at a scheduling conference or otherwise providing information.

## *Notice to Appear*

22. **Notice to appear** — The Division must notify the parties, orally or in writing, of the date, time and location of a hearing.

## *Permanent Resident or Foreign National in Custody*

23. **Order** — The Division may order the person who holds a permanent resident or foreign national in custody to bring the permanent resident or foreign national to a hearing at a location specified by the Division.

## *Documents*

### Form and Language of Documents

24. (1) **Documents prepared by party** — A document prepared for use by a party in a proceeding must be typewritten on one side of 21.5 cm by 28 cm (8½" x 11") paper and the pages must be numbered.

(2) **Photocopies** — Any photocopy provided by a party must be a clear copy of the document photocopied and be on one side of 21.5 cm by 28 cm (8½" x 11") paper and the pages must be numbered.

Rules

(3) **Numbered documents** — A party must number consecutively each document provided by the party.

(4) **List of documents** — If more than one document is provided, the party must provide a list of the documents and their numbers.

25. (1) **Language of documents** — All documents used at a proceeding must be in English or French or, if in another language, be provided with an English or French translation and a translator's declaration.

(2) **Language of Minister's documents** — If the Minister provides a document that is not in the language of the proceedings, the Minister must provide a translation and a translator's declaration.

(3) **Translator's declaration** — A translator's declaration must include the translator's name, the language translated and a statement signed by the translator that the translation is accurate.

### Disclosure of Documents

26. **Disclosure of documents by a party** — If a party wants to use a document at a hearing, the party must provide a copy to the other party and the Division. The copies must be received

(a) as soon as possible, in the case of a forty-eight hour or seven-day review or an admissibility hearing held at the same time; and

(b) in all other cases, at least five days before the hearing.

### How to Provide A Document

27. **General provision** — Rules 28 to 31 apply to any document, including a notice or a written request or application.

28. (1) **Providing documents to the Division** — A document provided to the Division must be provided to a Division member at a proceeding or to the registry office specified by the Division.

(2) **Providing documents to the Minister** — A document provided to the Minister must be provided to the Minister's counsel.

(3) **Providing documents to a permanent resident or foreign national** — A document provided to a permanent resident or foreign national must be provided to them or, if they have counsel, to their counsel.

29. **How to provide a document** — A document can be provided in the following ways:

(a) by hand;

(b) by regular mail or registered mail;

**(c) by courier or priority post;**

**(d) by fax if the recipient has a fax number and the document has no more than 20 pages, unless the recipient consents to receiving more than 20 pages; and**

**(e) by electronic mail if the Division allows.**

**30. If document cannot be provided under rule 29 — If a party after making reasonable efforts is unable to provide a document in a way required by rule 29, the party may make an application to the Division to be allowed to provide the document in another way or to be excused from providing the document.**

**31. (1) When a document Is considered received by the Division — A document provided to the Division is considered received by the Division on the day the document is date stamped by the Division.**

**(2) When a document provided by regular mail is considered received by a party — A document provided by regular mail to a party is considered to be received seven days after the day it was mailed. If the seventh day is a Saturday, Sunday or other statutory holiday, the document is considered to be received on the next working day.**

Rules

## *Witnesses*

**32. (1) Providing witness information — If a party wants to call a witness, the party must provide in writing to the other party and the Division the following witness information:**

**(a) the purpose and substance of the witness's testimony or, in the case of an expert witness, a summary of the testimony to be given signed by the expert witness;**

**(b) the time needed for the witness's testimony;**

**(c) the party's relationship to the witness;**

**(d) in the case of an expert witness, a description of their qualifications;**

**(e) whether the party wants the witness to testify by videoconference or telephone; and**

**(f) the number of witnesses that the party intends to call.**

**(2) Time limit — The witness information must be received by the Division and the other party**

**(a) as soon as possible in the case of a forty-eight hour or seven-day review or an admissibility hearing held at the same time; and**

**(b) in all other cases, at least five days before the hearing.**

### Case Law

*R. v. Laboucan*, [2010] S.C.J. No. 12, 73 C.R. (6th) 235, (sub nom. *R. v. Briscoe)* 400 N.R. 200, 22 Alta. L.R. (5th) 62, 253 C.C.C. (3d) 129, [2010] 6 W.W.R. 13, 316 D.L.R.

(4th) 590, (sub nom. *R. v. Briscoe)* 477 A.R. 70, 483 W.A.C. 70, 2010 SCC 12, 2010 CarswellAlta 591, 2010 CarswellAlta 590 — The fact that a witness has an interest in the outcome of the proceedings is common sense and a relevant factor, among others, to take into account when assessing the credibility of the witness's testimony. A trier of fact, however, should not place undue weight on the status of a person in the proceeding as a factor going to credibility. For example, it would be improper to base a finding of credibility regarding a parent's or a spouse's testimony solely on the basis of a witness's relationship to the complainant or to the accused. Regard should be given to all relevant factors in assessing credibility.

**33. (1) Application for a summons — A party who wants the Division to order a person to testify at a hearing must make an application to the Division for a summons, either orally at a proceeding or in writing.**

**(2) Factors — In deciding whether to issue a summons, the Division must consider any relevant factors, including**

**(a) the necessity of the testimony to a full and proper hearing; and**

**(b) the ability of the person to give that testimony.**

**(3) Using the summons — If a party wants to use a summons, the party must**

**(a) provide the summons to the summoned person by hand;**

**(b) provide a copy of the summons to the Division with a written statement of how and when the summons was provided; and**

**(c) pay or offer to pay the summoned person the applicable witness fees and travel expenses set out in Tariff A of the *Federal Courts Rules*.**

**34. Cancelling a summons — A person summoned to appear may make a written application to the Division to cancel the summons.**

**35. (1) Arrest warrant — If a person does not obey a summons to appear, the party who requested the summons may make a written application to the Division to issue a warrant for the arrest of the person.**

**(2) Supporting evidence — The party must provide supporting evidence for the written application by affidavit or statutory declaration.**

**(3) Requirements for issue of arrest warrant — The Division may issue a warrant if**

**(a) the person was provided the summons by hand or the person is avoiding being provided the summons;**

**(b) the person was paid or offered the applicable witness fees and travel expenses set out in Tariff A of the *Federal Courts Rules*;**

**(c) the person did not appear at the hearing as required by the summons; and**

**(d) the person's testimony is still needed for a full and proper hearing.**

**(4) Content of a warrant — A warrant issued by the Division for the arrest of a person must include directions concerning detention and release.**

**36. Excluded witness** — **Unless allowed by the Division, no person shall communicate to a witness excluded from a hearing room any testimony given while the witness was excluded until that witness has finished testifying.**

## *Applications*

**37. General provision** — **Unless these Rules provide otherwise, a party**

**(a) who wants the Division to make a decision on any matter in a proceeding, including the procedure to be followed, must make an application to the Division under rule 38;**

**(b) who wants to respond to the application must respond under rule 39; and**

**(c) who wants to reply to a response must reply under rule 40.**

### How to Make an Application

**38. (1) Application to the Division** — **Unless these Rules provide otherwise, an application must follow this rule.**

**(2) Time limit and form of application** — **The application must be made orally or in writing, and as soon as possible or within the time limit provided in the Act or these Rules.**

**(3) Procedure in oral application** — **For an application made orally, the Division determines the applicable procedure.**

**(4) Content of written application** — **A party who makes a written application must**

**(a) state the decision that the party wants the Division to make;**

**(b) give reasons why the Division should make that decision;**

**(c) include any evidence that the party wants the Division to consider in deciding the application; and**

**(d) in the case of an application that is not specified in these Rules, include supporting evidence in the form of a statutory declaration or affidavit.**

**(5) Providing the application** — **A party who makes a written application must provide**

**(a) to the other party, a copy of the application; and**

**(b) to the Division, the original application, together with a written statement of how and when the party provided the copy to the other party.**

### How to Respond to a Written Application

**39. (1) Responding to a written application** — **A response to a written application must be in writing. In a response the party must**

**(a) state the decision the party wants the Division to make;**

**(b) give reasons why the Division should make that decision;**

(c) include any evidence that the party wants the Division to consider when it decides the application; and

(d) include supporting evidence in the form of a statutory declaration or affidavit, if the response is to an application that is not provided for by these Rules.

(2) **Providing the response** — A party who responds to a written application must provide

(a) to the other party, a copy of the response; and

(b) to the Division, the original response, together with a written statement of how and when the party provided the copy to the other party.

(3) **Time limit** — Documents provided under this rule must be received by their recipients

(a) as soon as possible, in the case of a forty-eight hour or seven-day review or an admissibility hearing held at the same time; and

(b) in all other cases, no later than five days after the party received a copy of the application.

### How to Reply to a Written Response

40. (1) **Replying to a written response** — A reply to a written response must be in writing.

(2) **Providing the reply** — A party who replies must provide

(a) to the other party, a copy of the reply; and

(b) to the Division, the original reply, together with a written statement of how and when the party provided the copy to the other party.

(3) **Time limit** — Documents provided under this rule must be received by their recipients

(a) as soon as possible, in the case of a forty-eight hour or seven-day review or an admissibility hearing held at the same time; and

(b) in all other cases, no later than three days after the party received a copy of the response.

## *Non-disclosure of Information*

41. (1) **Application to prohibit disclosure** — An application made by the Minister for non-disclosure of information must be made in writing as soon as possible.

(2) **Exclusion from hearing room** — If an application is made during a hearing, the Division must exclude the permanent resident or foreign national, and their counsel, from the hearing room.

(3) **Providing summary to the Minister** — The summary that the Division proposes to provide to the permanent resident or foreign national under paragraph

78(h) of the Act may be provided to the Minister by any means that ensures its confidentiality.

## *Changing the Location of a Hearing*

42. (1) **Application to change the location of a hearing** — A party may make an application to the Division to change the location of a hearing.

(2) **Factors** — In deciding the application, the Division must consider any relevant factors, including

(a) whether a change of location would allow the hearing to be full and proper;

(b) whether a change of location would likely delay or slow the hearing;

(c) how a change of location would affect the operation of the Division;

(d) how a change of location would affect the parties; and

(e) whether a change of location would endanger public safety.

(3) **Duty to appear at the hearing** — Unless a party receives a decision from the Division allowing the application, the party must appear for the hearing at the location fixed and be ready to start or continue the hearing.

## *Changing the Date or Time of a Hearing*

43. (1) **Application to change the date or time of a hearing** — A party may make an application to the Division to change the date or time of a hearing.

(2) **Factors** — In deciding the application, the Division must consider any relevant factors, including

(a) in the case of a date and time that was fixed after the Division consulted or tried to consult the party, the existence of exceptional circumstances for allowing the application;

(b) when the party made the application;

(c) the time the party has had to prepare for the hearing;

(d) the efforts made by the party to be ready to start or continue the hearing;

(e) the nature and complexity of the matter to be heard;

(f) whether the party has counsel;

(g) any previous delays and the reasons for them;

(h) whether the time and date fixed for the hearing was peremptory; and

(i) whether allowing the application would unreasonably delay the proceedings or likely cause an injustice.

(3) **Duty to appear at the hearing** — Unless a party receives a decision from the Division allowing the application, the party must appear for the hearing at the date and time fixed and be ready to start or continue the hearing.

## Case Law

*Fox v. Canada (Minister of Citizenship & Immigration)* (2009), 397 N.R. 222, 2009 FCA 346, 2009 CarswellNat 3936, 2009 CarswellNat 4896 (F.C.A.) — The appellant brought a motion for an order staying the resumption of his inadmissibility hearing before the Immigration Division. The appellant was a citizen of the United States and a permanent resident of Canada who had been convicted of importing cocaine into Canada and was sentenced to seven years and 10 months of imprisonment. A s. 44 report was prepared stating that the enforcement officer was of the opinion that the appellant was inadmissible pursuant to s. 36(a) [*sic*] of the Act on the ground of serious criminality for conviction and imprisonment in Canada. An admissibility hearing was commenced but subsequently adjourned to allow the appellant to seek legal representation. The appellant was then released from incarceration by reason of the National Parole Board's decision to grant him day parole. He was delivered to the custody of a CBSA officer by reason of a warrant issued by the CBSA for his arrest, in accordance with s. 55(1) and s. 59 of the Act. The admissibility hearing resumed and the appellant was represented by his wife who immediately sought an adjournment of the hearing to April 14, 2010, the date being the appellant's full parole eligibility date. The obvious purpose of his wife's request was to prevent her husband's re-incarceration should he be found inadmissible and thus subject to a removal order. Specifically, the appellant sought to avoid application of s. 128(5) of the *Corrections and Conditional Release Act* which provides that if a removal order is made against a person who has received day parole prior to that person's full parole eligibility, the day parole becomes inoperative on the day the removal order is made, and as a result the offender will be re-incarcerated until his full parole eligibility.

In the present matter, a determination of the stay application will likely determine the appeal in that the relief sought by the appellant in this motion is the relief which he is seeking to obtain in his appeal. The Court concluded that the appellant was unable to demonstrate a serious issue. It was not possible to argue that the Immigration Division can adjourn the appellant's admissibility hearing on the ground that a finding of inadmissibility on its part, which would lead to the issuance of a removal order, would cause injustice to the appellant. There is no statutory basis to support the Immigration Division's decision to adjourn the inadmissibility hearing. The motion for the stay was dismissed.

## *Joining or Separating Hearings*

**44. (1) Application to join hearings — A party may make an application to the Division to join hearings.**

**(2) Application to separate hearings — A party may make an application to the Division to separate hearings that are joined.**

**(3) Factors — Before deciding an application, the Division must consider any information provided by the applicant and any other relevant information, including**

> **(a) whether the hearings involve similar questions of law or fact;**
>
> **(b) whether allowing the application would promote the efficient administration of the work of the Division; and**
>
> **(c) whether allowing the application would likely cause an injustice.**

## *Proceedings Conducted in Private*

**45. (1) Application for proceeding conducted in private — A person who makes an application to the Division to have a proceeding conducted in private must apply in writing and follow this rule.**

**(2) Content of application — In the application, the person must state the decision that the person wants the Division to make, and may request that the hearing of the application be conducted in private.**

**(3) Providing the application — The person must provide a copy of the application to the parties and the original application to the Division.**

**(4) Time limit — A document provided under this rule must be received by its recipient**

**(a) as soon as possible, in the case of a forty-eight hour or seven-day review or an admissibility hearing held at the same time; and**

**(b) in all other cases, at least five days before the hearing.**

**(5) Hearing of the application — At the hearing, the person must give reasons why the Division should conduct the proceeding in private and present any evidence that the person wants the Division to consider in deciding the application.**

## *Proceeding Conducted in Public*

**46. (1) Application for proceeding conducted in public — A person who makes an application to the Division to have a proceeding conducted in public must apply in writing and follow this rule.**

**(2) Content of application — In the application, the person must**

**(a) state the decision that the person wants the Division to make;**

**(b) give reasons why the Division should make that decision; and**

**(c) include any evidence that the person wants the Division to consider in deciding the application.**

**(3) Providing the application — The person must provide the original application and two copies to the Division. The Division must provide a copy of the application to the parties.**

**(4) Time limit — A document provided under this rule must be received by the Division**

**(a) as soon as possible, in the case of a forty-eight hour or seven-day review or an admissibility hearing held at the same time; and**

**(b) in all other cases, at least five days before the hearing.**

## *Notice of Constitutional Question*

**47. (1) Notice of constitutional question — A party who wants to challenge the constitutional validity, applicability or operability of a legislative provision must complete a notice of constitutional question.**

**(2) Form and content of notice — The party must provide notice using either Form 69, "Notice of Constitutional Question", set out in the *Federal Courts Rules*, or any other form that includes**

**(a) the name of the party;**

**(b) the Division file number;**

**(c) the date, time and place of the hearing;**

**(d) the specific legislative provision that is being challenged;**

**(e) the relevant facts relied on to support the constitutional challenge; and**

**(f) a summary of the legal argument to be made in support of the constitutional challenge.**

**(3) Providing the notice — The party must provide**

**(a) a copy of the notice of constitutional question to the Attorney General of Canada and to the attorney general of every province and territory of Canada, in accordance with section 57 of the *Federal Courts Act*;**

**(b) a copy of the notice to the other party; and**

**(c) the original notice to the Division, together with a written statement of how and when a copy of the notice was provided under paragraphs (a) and (b).**

**(4) Time limit — Documents provided under this rule must be received by their recipients no later than 10 days before the day the constitutional argument will be made.**

2002, c. 8, s. 182(3)(a)

## *Oral Representations*

**48. Oral representations — Representations made by a party must be made orally at the end of a hearing unless the Division orders otherwise.**

## *General Provisions*

**49. No applicable rule — In the absence of a provision in these Rules dealing with a matter raised during the proceedings, the Division may do whatever is necessary to deal with the matter.**

**50. Powers of the Division — The Division may**

**(a) act on its own, without a party having to make an application or request to the Division;**

**(b) change a requirement of a rule;**

(c) excuse a person from a requirement of a rule; and

(d) extend or shorten a time limit, before or after the time limit has passed.

**51. Failing to follow a rule** — Unless proceedings are declared invalid by the Division, a failure to follow any requirement of these Rules does not make the proceedings invalid.

## *Coming Into Force*

**52. Coming into force** — These Rules come into force on the day on which section 161 of the Act comes into force.

# CAN. REG. 2002-230 — IMMIGRATION APPEAL DIVISION RULES

## made under the *Immigration and Refugee Protection Act*

SOR/2002-230, as am. S.C. 2002, c. 8, s. 182(3)(a).

*[Editor's Note: S.C. 2001, c. 27, s. 192 provides that if a notice of appeal has been filed with the Immigration Appeal Division immediately before June 28, 2002, the appeal shall be continued under the* Immigration Act, *R.S.C. 1985, c. I-2 (the "former Act") by the Immigration Appeal Division of the Immigration and Refugee Board.*

*However, S.C. 2001, c. 27, s. 193 provides that every application, proceeding or matter before the Adjudication Division under the former Act that is pending or in progress immediately before June 28, 2002, in respect of which substantive evidence has been adduced but no decision has been made, shall be continued under the* Immigration and Refugee Protection Act, *S.C. 2001, c. 27 (the "new Act"), by the Immigration Division of the Immigration and Refugee Board.*

*S.C. 2001, c. 27, s. 196 further provides that despite S.C. 2001, c. 27, s. 192, an appeal made to the Immigration Appeal Division before June 28, 2002 shall be discontinued if the appellant has not been granted a stay under the former Act and the appeal could not have been made because of s. 64 of the new Act.*

*S.C. 2001, c. 27, s. 197 still further provides that despite S.C. 2001, c. 27, s. 192, if an appellant who has been granted a stay under the former Act breaches a condition of the stay, the appellant shall be subject to the provisions of s. 64 and s. 68(4) of the new Act.]*

### DEFINITIONS

**1. Definitions — The following definitions apply in these Rules.**

**"Act" means the *Immigration and Refugee Protection Act. ("Loi")***

**"appellant" means the person who makes an appeal to the Division. *("appelant")***

**"contact information" means a person's name, postal address and telephone number, and the person's fax number and electronic mail address, if any. *("coordonnées")***

**"Division" means the Immigration Appeal Division. *("Section")***

**"officer" means a person designated as an officer by the Minister under subsection 6(1) of the Act. *("agent")***

**"party" means the appellant or the respondent. *("partie")***

**"proceeding" includes a hearing, a conference, an application or an alternative dispute resolution process. *("procédure")***

"registry office" means a business office of the Division. *("greffe")*

"respondent" means the Minister or, if the Minister is appealing a decision of the Immigration Division, the person who was the subject of the Immigration Division proceeding. *("intimé")*

## COMMUNICATING WITH THE DIVISION

2. **Communicating with the Division** — All communication with the Division must be directed to the registry office specified by the Division.

## APPEAL BY A SPONSOR

3. (1) **Notice of appeal** — A person who has filed an application to sponsor a foreign national as a member of the family class and who wants to appeal a decision not to issue a permanent resident visa to the foreign national must provide to the Division a notice of appeal and the officer's written reasons for the refusal.

(2) **Time limit** — The notice of appeal and the written reasons for refusal must be received by the Division no later than 30 days after the appellant received the written reasons for the refusal.

(3) **Documents provided to the Minister** — The Division must provide the notice of appeal and the written reasons for the refusal to the Minister without delay.

4. (1) **Appeal record** — The Minister must prepare an appeal record that contains

(a) a table of contents;

(b) the application for a permanent resident visa that was refused;

(c) the application for sponsorship and the sponsor's undertaking;

(d) any document that the Minister has that is relevant to the applications, to the reasons for the refusal or to any issue in the appeal; and

(e) the written reasons for the refusal.

(2) **Providing the appeal record** — The Minister must provide the appeal record to the appellant and the Division.

(3) **Proof that record was provided** — The Minister must provide to the Division, together with the appeal record, a written statement of how and when the appeal record was provided to the appellant.

(4) **Time limit** — Documents provided under this rule must be received by their recipients no later than 120 days after the Minister received the notice of appeal.

Rules

**(5) Late appeal record — If the Division does not receive the appeal record within the time limit set out in subrule (4), the Division may**

**(a) ask the Minister to explain, orally or in writing, why the appeal record was not provided on time and to give reasons why the appeal record should be accepted late; or**

**(b) schedule and start the hearing without the appeal record or with only part of the appeal record.**

## Appeal from a Removal Order Made at an Admissibility Hearing

**5. (1) Notice of appeal — If a foreign national who holds a permanent resident visa, a permanent resident, or a protected person wants to appeal a removal order made at an admissibility hearing, they must provide a notice of appeal**

**(a) by hand to the Immigration Division member who made the removal order; or**

**(b) to the Immigration Appeal Division, together with the removal order.**

**(2) Time limit — Immigration Division member — An appellant who provides a notice of appeal to an Immigration Division member must provide the notice at the end of the admissibility hearing. The Immigration Division must provide the notice to the Immigration Appeal Division without delay.**

**(3) Time limit — Immigration Appeal Division — If an appellant provides a notice of appeal to the Immigration Appeal Division, the notice of appeal and the removal order must be received by the Division no later than 30 days after the appellant received the removal order. The Immigration Appeal Division must provide the notice to the Immigration Division without delay.**

**(4) Documents provided to the Minister — The Immigration Appeal Division must provide the notice of appeal and the removal order to the Minister without delay.**

*[Editor's Note: S.C. 2001, c. 27, s. 190 provides that every application, proceeding or matter under the* Immigration Act, *R.S.C. 1985, c. I-2 (the "former Act") that is pending or in progress immediately before June 28, 2002 shall be governed by the* Immigration and Refugee Protection Act, *S.C. 2001, c. 27 (the "new Act"), effective June 28, 2002.*

*S.C. 2001, c. 27, s. 192 provides that if a notice of appeal has been filed with the Immigration Appeal Division immediately before June 28, 2002, the appeal shall be continued under the former Act by the Immigration Appeal Division of the Immigration and Refugee Board.*

*S.C. 2001, c. 27, s. 196 further provides that despite S.C. 2001, c. 27, s. 192, an appeal made to the Immigration Appeal Division before June 28, 2002 shall be discontinued if the appellant has not been granted a stay under the former Act and the appeal could not have been made because of s. 64 of the new Act.*

*S.C. 2001, c. 27, s. 197 still further provides that despite S.C. 2001, c. 27, s. 192, if an appellant who has been granted a stay under the former Act breaches a condition of the stay, the appellant shall be subject to the provisions of s. 64 and s. 68(4) of the new Act.]*

**6. (1) Appeal record — The Immigration Division must prepare an appeal record that contains**

**(a) a table of contents;**

**(b) the removal order;**

**(c) a transcript of the admissibility hearing;**

**(d) any document accepted as evidence at the admissibility hearing; and**

**(e) any written reasons for the Immigration Division's decision to make the removal order.**

**(2) Providing the appeal record — The Immigration Division must provide the appeal record to the appellant, the Minister and the Immigration Appeal Division.**

**(3) Time limit — The appeal record must be received by its recipients no later than 45 days after the Immigration Division received the notice of appeal.**

## APPEAL FROM A REMOVAL ORDER MADE AT AN EXAMINATION

**7. (1) Notice of appeal — If a foreign national who holds a permanent resident visa, a permanent resident, or a protected person wants to appeal a removal order made at an examination, they must provide a notice of appeal to the Division together with the removal order.**

**(2) Time limit — The notice of appeal and the removal order must be received by the Division no later than 30 days after the appellant received the removal order.**

**(3) Documents provided to the Minister — The Division must provide the notice of appeal and the removal order to the Minister without delay.**

*[Editor's Note: S.C. 2001, c. 27, s. 190 provides that every application, proceeding or matter under the* Immigration Act, *R.S.C. 1985, c. I-2 (the "former Act") that is pending or in progress immediately before June 28, 2002 shall be governed by the* Immigration and Refugee Protection Act, *S.C. 2001, c. 27 (the "new Act"), effective June 28, 2002.*

*S.C. 2001, c. 27, s. 192 provides that if a notice of appeal has been filed with the Immigration Appeal Division immediately before June 28, 2002, the appeal shall be continued under the former Act by the Immigration Appeal Division of the Immigration and Refugee Board.*

*S.C. 2001, c. 27, s. 196 further provides that despite S.C. 2001, c. 27, s. 192, an appeal made to the Immigration Appeal Division before June 28, 2002 shall be discontinued if the appellant has not been granted a stay under the former Act and the appeal could not have been made because of s. 64 of the new Act.*

*S.C. 2001, c. 27, s. 197 still further provides that despite S.C. 2001, c. 27, s. 192, if an appellant who has been granted a stay under the former Act breaches a condition of the stay, the appellant shall be subject to the provisions of s. 64 and s. 68(4) of the new Act.]*

Rules

## Case Law

*Canada (Minister of Citizenship & Immigration) v. Rumpler* (2008), 76 Imm. L.R. (3d) 237, 336 F.T.R. 285 (Eng.), 2008 CarswellNat 4258, 2008 CarswellNat 5085, 2008 FC 1264, 2008 CarswellNat 4258 — This was an application for judicial review of the decision of the IAD wherein the IAD concluded it had jurisdiction to hear an appeal of the respondent's removal order. Returning to Canada from Israel, an immigration officer determined that the respondent did not satisfy the residency requirements of s. 28 of the Act and undertook measures to have him removed. The period to appeal the removal order expired and the respondent voluntarily left Canada for the United States. The respondent then requested of the IAD an extension of the period, to allow him to lodge an appeal of the removal order. The IAD decided that, according to subs. 63(3) of the Act, it did not have the competence to extend the period of appeal after its expiration, because the respondent had lost his status as permanent resident by failing to appeal. Justice Blanchard of the Federal Court granted the respondent's application for judicial review, and held that the IAD did have competence under the said provision to grant the extension. Accordingly, an extension was granted by a different member of the IAD and at a new hearing before the IAD, the Minister asked the tribunal to reject the appeal of the removal order on the ground of mootness, because the respondent had voluntarily left the country and thus executed the order. The Minister's motion was rejected and the Minister brought an application for judicial review of the IAD's decision.

The IAD erred in law in finding that it had continuing jurisdiction in spite of the fact that the respondent had left Canada and had executed the removal order before he filed a notice of appeal. It is trite law that the IAD does not have jurisdiction to reopen an appeal where the motion to reopen has been filed after an appellant is removed from Canada. Since the IAD did not have the jurisdiction to cancel the removal order once it had already been executed, it necessarily had no jurisdiction to grant a request (filed after such an execution) for an extension of time to lodge an appeal of the removal order. Consequently, the application for judicial review was allowed.

**8. (1) Appeal record — The Minister must prepare an appeal record that contains**

**(a) a table of contents;**

**(b) the removal order;**

**(c) any document that the Minister has that is relevant to the removal order or to any issue in the appeal; and**

**(d) any written reasons for the Minister's decision to make the removal order.**

**(2) Providing the appeal record — The Minister must provide the appeal record to the appellant and the Division.**

**(3) Proof that record was provided — The Minister must provide to the Division, together with the appeal record, a written statement of how and when the appeal record was provided to the appellant.**

**(4) Time limit — Documents provided under this rule must be received by their recipients no later than 45 days after the Minister received the notice of appeal.**

**(5) Late appeal record — If the Division does not receive the appeal record within the time limit set out in subrule (4), the Division may**

**(a) ask the Minister to explain, orally or in writing, why the appeal record was not provided on time and to give reasons why the appeal record should be accepted late; or**

**(b) schedule and start the hearing without the appeal record or with only part of the appeal record.**

## Appeal from a Decision Made Outside Canada on the Residency Obligation

**9. (1) Notice of appeal — If a permanent resident wants to appeal a decision made outside Canada on the residency obligation, the permanent resident must provide to the Division a notice of appeal and the officer's written decision. The documents must be provided to the Division registry office for the region in Canada where the appellant last resided.**

**(2) Return to Canada — If the appellant wants to return to Canada for the hearing of the appeal, the appellant must state this in the notice of appeal.**

**(3) Time limit — The notice of appeal and the written decision must be received by the Division no later than 60 days after the appellant received the written decision.**

**(4) Documents provided to the Minister — The Division must provide the notice of appeal and the written decision to the Minister without delay.**

*[Editor's Note: S.C. 2001, c. 27, s. 190 provides that every application, proceeding or matter under the* Immigration Act, *R.S.C. 1985, c. I-2 (the "former Act") that is pending or in progress immediately before June 28, 2002 shall be governed by the* Immigration and Refugee Protection Act, *S.C. 2001, c. 27 (the "new Act"), effective June 28, 2002.*

*S.C. 2001, c. 27, s. 192 provides that if a notice of appeal has been filed with the Immigration Appeal Division immediately before June 28, 2002, the appeal shall be continued under the former Act by the Immigration Appeal Division of the Immigration and Refugee Board.*

*S.C. 2001, c. 27, s. 196 further provides that despite S.C. 2001, c. 27, s. 192, an appeal made to the Immigration Appeal Division before June 28, 2002 shall be discontinued if the appellant has not been granted a stay under the former Act and the appeal could not have been made because of s. 64 of the new Act.*

*S.C. 2001, c. 27, s. 197 still further provides that despite S.C. 2001, c. 27, s. 192, if an appellant who has been granted a stay under the former Act breaches a condition of the stay, the appellant shall be subject to the provisions of s. 64 and s. 68(4) of the new Act.]*

**10. (1) Appeal record — The Minister must prepare an appeal record that contains**

**(a) a table of contents;**

**(b) any document that the Minister has that is relevant to the decision on the residency obligation or any issue in the appeal; and**

Rules

**(c) the officer's written decision and written reasons.**

**(2) Providing the appeal record — The Minister must provide the appeal record to the appellant and the Division.**

**(3) Proof that record was provided — The Minister must provide to the Division, together with the appeal record, a written statement of how and when the appeal record was provided to the appellant.**

**(4) Time limit — Documents provided under this rule must be received by their recipients no later than 120 days after the Minister received the notice of appeal.**

**(5) Late appeal record — If the Division does not receive the appeal record within the time limit set out in subrule (4), the Division may**

> **(a) ask the Minister to explain, orally or in writing, why the appeal record was not provided on time and to give reasons why the appeal record should be accepted late; or**
>
> **(b) schedule and start the hearing without the appeal record or with only part of the appeal record.**

## APPEAL BY THE MINISTER FROM A DECISION OF THE IMMIGRATION DIVISION IN AN ADMISSIBILITY HEARING

**11. (1) Notice of Appeal — If the Minister wants to appeal a decision of the Immigration Division in an admissibility hearing, the Minister must provide a notice of appeal to the respondent, the Immigration Division and the Immigration Appeal Division.**

**(2) Proof that document was provided — The Minister must provide to the Immigration Appeal Division, together with the notice of appeal, a written statement of how and when the notice of appeal was provided to the respondent and the Immigration Division.**

**(3) Time limit — Documents provided under this rule must be received by their recipients no later than 30 days after the Immigration Division decision was made.**

*[Editor's Note: S.C. 2001, c. 27, s. 190 provides that every application, proceeding or matter under the* Immigration Act, *R.S.C. 1985, c. I-2 (the "former Act") that is pending or in progress immediately before June 28, 2002 shall be governed by the* Immigration and Refugee Protection Act, *S.C. 2001, c. 27 (the "new Act"), effective June 28, 2002.*

*S.C. 2001, c. 27, s. 192 provides that if a notice of appeal has been filed with the Immigration Appeal Division immediately before June 28, 2002, the appeal shall be continued under the former Act by the Immigration Appeal Division of the Immigration and Refugee Board.*

*S.C. 2001, c. 27, s. 196 further provides that despite S.C. 2001, c. 27, s. 192, an appeal made to the Immigration Appeal Division before June 28, 2002 shall be discontinued if the appellant has not been granted a stay under the former Act and the appeal could not have been made because of s. 64 of the new Act.*

*S.C. 2001, c. 27, s. 197 still further provides that despite S.C. 2001, c. 27, s. 192, if an appellant who has been granted a stay under the former Act breaches a condition of the stay, the appellant shall be subject to the provisions of s. 64 and s. 68(4) of the new Act.]*

**12. (1) Appeal record — The Immigration Division must prepare an appeal record that contains**

**(a) a table of contents;**

**(b) the Immigration Division decision;**

**(c) a transcript of the admissibility hearing;**

**(d) any document accepted as evidence at the admissibility hearing; and**

**(e) any written reasons for the Immigration Division decision.**

**(2) Providing the appeal record — The Immigration Division must provide the appeal record to the respondent, the Minister and the Immigration Appeal Division.**

**(3) Time limit — The appeal record must be received by its recipients no later than 45 days after the Immigration Division received the notice of appeal.**

## Contact Information

**13. (1) Contact information for the subject of the appeal — A person who is the subject of an appeal must provide their contact information in writing to the Division and the Minister.**

**(2) Time limit — The contact information must be received by the Division and the Minister**

**(a) with the notice of appeal, if the person is the appellant; and**

**(b) no later than 20 days after the person received a notice of appeal, if the Minister is the appellant.**

**(3) Counsel's contact information — A person who is represented by counsel must, on obtaining counsel, provide without delay the counsel's contact information in writing to the Division and the Minister.**

**(4) Change to contact information — If the contact information of the person or their counsel changes, the person must without delay provide the changes in writing to the Division and the Minister.**

### Case Law

*Dubrezil c. Canada (Ministre de la Sécurité publique & de la Protection civile)*, 2006 CarswellNat 918, 2006 FC 441 (F.C.) — The applicant applied for judicial review of the Immigration and Appeal Division's decision to refuse to reopen an appeal on the ground that the applicant had not established he was a victim of a breach of a principle of natural justice. The applicant never sent his change in contact information to the IAD. It was his obligation to do so and he could not attempt to impose that obligation on the IAD. To impose such an obligation would imply that each time a person is absent, lacks diligence

Rules

or acts in such a way that clearly suggests the appeal has been abandoned, the IAD would be bound to investigate to find those persons, remind them of their obligations and summon them to a new hearing before deciding that the proceedings are abandoned. The IAD is not bound to act as the applicant's legal counsel or to remind the applicant of the seriousness of the proceedings in which he is involved, or to ensure that he properly understands that he has to show up at his scheduling conference or that he is bound to advise the IAD of his change of address.

## Counsel of Record

**14. Becoming counsel of record — As soon as counsel for a person who is the subject of an appeal agrees to a date for a proceeding, or becomes counsel after a date for a proceeding has been fixed, the counsel becomes counsel of record for the person.**

**15. (1) Request to be removed as counsel of record — To be removed as counsel of record, counsel must make a request in writing to the Division and provide a copy of the request to the person represented and the Minister.**

**(2) Request received two days or less before proceeding — If counsel's request is received by the recipients two working days or less before the date of a proceeding, counsel must appear at the proceeding and make the request orally.**

**16. (1) Removing counsel of record — To remove counsel as counsel of record, the person who is the subject of the appeal must provide written notice to the Division, to counsel and to the Minister that counsel is no longer the person's counsel.**

**(2) Ceasing to be counsel of record — Counsel is no longer counsel of record when the Division receives the notice.**

## Language of the Appeal

**17. (1) Choice of language — A person who is the subject of an appeal must choose English or French as the language of the appeal. If the person is appealing, the person must indicate their choice in the notice of appeal. If the Minister is appealing, the person must notify the Division and the Minister of their choice in writing. The notice must be received by the Division and by the Minister no later than 20 days after the person received the notice of appeal.**

**(2) Changing the choice of language — A person who is the subject of an appeal may change the choice of language by notifying the Division and the Minister in writing. The notice must be received by the Division and the Minister no later than 20 days before the next proceeding.**

**18. (1) Need for an interpreter — If a party or a party's witness needs an interpreter for a proceeding, the party must notify the Division in writing and specify the**

**language or dialect of the interpreter. The notice must be received by the Division no later than 20 days before the proceeding.**

(2) **Interpreter's oath — The interpreter must take an oath or make a solemn affirmation to interpret accurately.**

## Case Law

*Lamme v. Canada (Minister of Citizenship & Immigration).* 2005 CarswellNat 3063, 2005 CarswellNat 4881, 2005 FC 1336 (F.C.) — The general standard to be met with respect to the quality of interpretation is that it must be continuous, precise, impartial and contemporaneous. In addition, for the interpretation to be considered as meeting the standard, it must be established that the applicant understood the interpretation and adequately expressed himself or herself through the interpreter.

## Designated Representative

**19. (1) Duty of counsel to notify — If counsel for either party believes that the Division should designate a representative for the person who is the subject of the appeal because they are under 18 years of age or unable to appreciate the nature of the proceedings, counsel must without delay notify the Division in writing. If counsel is aware of a person in Canada who meets the requirements to be designated as a representative, counsel must provide the person's contact information in the notice.**

**(2) Requirements for being designated — To be designated as a representative, a person must**

> **(a) be 18 years of age or older;**
>
> **(b) understand the nature of the proceedings;**
>
> **(c) be willing and able to act in the best interests of the person to be represented; and**
>
> **(d) not have interests that conflict with those of the person to be represented.**

## Proceedings in an Appeal

### *Alternative Dispute Resolution Process*

**20. (1) Participation in the alternative dispute resolution process — The Division may require the parties to participate in an alternative dispute resolution process in order to encourage the parties to resolve an appeal without a hearing.**

**(2) Dispute resolution officer — The Division must assign a member of the Division or any other person to act as a dispute resolution officer for an appeal that uses the alternative dispute resolution process. A member who acts as a dispute resolution officer for an appeal must not hear that appeal.**

**(3) Obligations of parties and counsel — The parties and their counsel must**

> **(a) participate in the alternative dispute resolution process in good faith;**

Rules

**(b) follow the directions given by the Division with respect to the process, including the manner of participation;**

**(c) disclose to each other and the Division any document to be relied on in the process, and any document that the Division requires to be prepared or disclosed; and**

**(d) be prepared as a party, or have authority as counsel, to resolve the appeal.**

**(4) Confidentiality — Any information, statement or document that any person gives in an alternative dispute resolution process is confidential. It must not be disclosed later in the appeal or made public unless**

**(a) it was obtained in a way that was not part of the alternative dispute resolution process;**

**(b) it relates to an offence under the Act, or a breach of these Rules; or**

**(c) the person who gave the information, statement or document agrees to its disclosure.**

**(5) Agreement — An agreement to resolve an appeal that is reached through the alternative dispute resolution process must be in writing, signed by the parties or their counsel and approved by the Division. An agreement to resolve an appeal is not confidential under subrule (4).**

## Conference

**21. (1) Requirement to participate at a conference — The Division may require the parties to participate at a conference to discuss issues, relevant facts and any other matter that would make the appeal more fair and efficient.**

**(2) Information or documents — The Division may require the parties to give any information, or provide any document, at or before the conference.**

**(3) Written record — The Division must make a written record of any decision or agreement made at the conference.**

## Fixing a Date for a Proceeding

**22. Fixing a date — The Division may require the parties to participate in a scheduling conference or otherwise give information to help the Division fix a date for a proceeding.**

## Notice to Appear

**23. Notice to appear — The Division must notify the parties of the date, time and location of a proceeding.**

## Subject of an Appeal in Custody

**24. Custody — The Division may order a person who holds a person who is the subject of an appeal in custody to bring the person in custody to a proceeding at the location specified by the Division.**

## Proceeding in Writing

**25. (1) Proceeding in writing — Instead of holding a hearing, the Division may require the parties to proceed in writing if this would not be unfair to any party and there is no need for the oral testimony of a witness.**

**(2) Exception — Subsection (1) does not apply to an appeal against a decision made outside Canada on the residency obligation.**

## Stay of Removal Order

**26. (1) Application to reconsider an appeal — If the Division has stayed a removal order, a party who makes an application to the Division to reconsider the appeal must**

**(a) follow rule 43, but the party is not required to give evidence in an affidavit or statutory declaration; and**

**(b) provide with their application a written statement of whether the subject of the appeal has complied with the conditions of the stay.**

**(2) Response — The other party must respond to the application and provide with their response a written statement of whether the subject of the appeal has complied with the conditions of the stay.**

**(3) Reconsideration on Division's own initiative — If the Division reconsiders an appeal on its own initiative, the Division must notify the parties. The parties must provide to the Division and each other, within the time period specified by the Division, a written statement of whether the subject of the appeal has complied with the conditions of the stay.**

**27. (1) Notice requirement — cancellation of stay — If a stay of removal is cancelled under subsection 68(4) of the Act, the Minister must provide the Division and the subject of the appeal with written notice of the cancellation.**

**(2) Content of notice — In the notice, the Minister must state**

**(a) the name of the person convicted;**

**(b) the date and place of conviction;**

**(c) the offence and relevant provision of an Act of Parliament; and**

**(d) if the offence is not punishable by a maximum term of imprisonment of at least 10 years, the term of imprisonment that was imposed.**

Rules

**(3) Proof that document was provided — The Minister must provide to the Division, together with the written notice, a written statement of how and when the notice was provided to the subject of the appeal.**

## DOCUMENTS

### *Form and Language of Documents*

**28. (1) Documents prepared by party — A document prepared for use by a party in a proceeding must be typewritten on one side of 21.5 cm by 28 cm (8½" × 11") paper and the pages must be numbered.**

**(2) Photocopies — Any photocopy provided by a party must be a clear copy of the document photocopied and be on one side of 21.5 cm by 28 cm (8½" × 11") paper and the pages must be numbered.**

**(3) Numbered documents — A party must number consecutively each document provided by the party.**

**(4) List of documents — If more than one document is provided, the party must provide a list of the documents and their numbers.**

**29. (1) Language of documents — subject of the appeal — All documents used at a proceeding by a person who is the subject of an appeal must be in English or French or, if in another language, be provided with an English or French translation and a translator's declaration.**

**(2) Language of documents — Minister — All documents used by the Minister at a proceeding must be in the language of the appeal, or be provided with a translation and the translator's declaration.**

**(3) Translator's declaration — A translator's declaration must include the translator's name, the language translated and a statement signed by the translator that the translation is accurate.**

### *Disclosure of Documents*

**30. (1) Disclosure of documents by a party — If a party wants to use a document at a hearing, the party must provide a copy to the other party and the Division.**

**(2) Proof that document was provided — Together with the copy provided to the Division, the party must provide a written statement of how and when a copy was provided to the other party.**

**(3) Time limit — general — Subject to subrule (4), documents provided under this rule must be received by the Division and the other party**

**(a) no later than 20 days before the hearing; or**

(b) if the document is provided to respond to another document provided by the other party, no later than 10 days before the hearing.

(4) **Time limit — medical documents** — A medical document provided in an appeal based on inadmissibility on health grounds must be received by the Division and the other party no later than 60 days before the hearing or, if the document is provided to respond to another medical document, no later than 30 days before the hearing.

31. **Use of undisclosed documents** — A party who does not provide a document as required by rule 30 may not use the document at the hearing unless allowed by the Division.

## *Providing a Document*

32. **General provision** — Rules 33 to 36 apply to any document, including a notice or request in writing.

33. (1) **Providing documents to the Division** — A document provided to the Division must be provided to the registry office specified by the Division.

(2) **Providing documents to the Minister** — A document provided to the Minister must be provided to the Minister's counsel.

(3) **Providing documents to the subject of an appeal** — A document provided to a person who is the subject of an appeal must be provided to the person or, if the person has counsel, to their counsel.

34. **How to provide a document** — A document can be provided in any of the following ways:

(a) by hand;

(b) by regular mail or registered mail;

(c) by courier or priority post;

(d) by fax if the recipient has a fax number and the document has no more than 20 pages, unless the recipient consents to receiving more than 20 pages; and

(e) by electronic mail if the Division allows.

35. (1) **If document cannot be provided under rule 34** — If a party is unable to provide a document in a way required by rule 34, the party may make an application to the Division to be allowed to provide the document in another way or to be excused from providing the document.

(2) **Form of application** — The application must be made under rule 43.

(3) **Factor** — The Division may allow the application if the party has made reasonable efforts to provide the document to the other party.

**36. (1) When a document is considered received by the Division — A document provided to the Division is considered to be received by the Division on the day the document is date stamped by the Division.**

**(2) When a document sent by regular mail is considered received by a party — A document sent to a party by regular mail is considered to be received seven days after the day it was mailed. A document sent to a party by regular mail to or from a place outside Canada is considered to be received 20 days after the day it was mailed. If the seventh day or the twentieth day, as the case may be, is a Saturday, Sunday or statutory holiday, the document is considered to be received on the next working day.**

## WITNESSES

**37. (1) Providing witness information — If a party wants to call a witness, the party must provide in writing to the other party and the Division the following witness information:**

> **(a) the witness's contact information;**
>
> **(b) the time needed for the witness's testimony;**
>
> **(c) the party's relationship to the witness;**
>
> **(d) whether the party wants the witness to testify by videoconference or telephone; and**
>
> **(e) in the case of an expert witness, a report signed by the expert witness giving their qualifications and summarizing their evidence.**

**(2) Proof that document was provided — The witness information must be provided to the Division together with a written statement of how and when it was provided to the other party.**

**(3) Time limit — Documents provided under this rule must be received by their recipients no later than 20 days before the hearing.**

**(4) Failure to provide witness information — If a party does not provide the witness information as required under this rule, the witness may not testify at the hearing unless the Division allows the witness to testify.**

### Case Law

*R. v. Laboucan*, [2010] S.C.J. No. 12, 73 C.R. (6th) 235, (sub nom. *R. v. Briscoe)* 400 N.R. 200, 22 Alta. L.R. (5th) 62, 253 C.C.C. (3d) 129, [2010] 6 W.W.R. 13, 316 D.L.R. (4th) 590, (sub nom. *R. v. Briscoe)* 477 A.R. 70, 483 W.A.C. 70, 2010 SCC 12, 2010 CarswellAlta 591, 2010 CarswellAlta 590 — The fact that a witness has an interest in the outcome of the proceedings is common sense and a relevant factor, among others, to take into account when assessing the credibility of the witness's testimony. A trier of fact, however, should not place undue weight on the status of a person in the proceeding as a factor going to credibility. For example, it would be improper to base a finding of credibility regarding a parent's or a spouse's testimony solely on the basis of a witness's relationship to the complainant or to the accused. Regard should be given to all relevant factors in assessing credibility.

*Kamtasingh v. Canada (Minister of Citizenship & Immigration)* (2010), 87 Imm. L.R. (3d) 118, 2010 FC 45, 2010 CarswellNat 801, 2010 CarswellNat 101 (F.C.) — This was an application for judicial review challenging a decision of the Immigration Appeal Division which determined the applicant's marriage was not genuine. The applicant states that the IAD member denied him procedural fairness by preventing him from calling all of his proposed witnesses.

The IAD has the right to limit repetitive testimony, but not by effectively excluding witnesses who could offer evidence going to the central issues of the case. The place to control excessive or repetitive evidence on issues of controversy which are central or determinate is generally not at the entrance to the witness box, but once the witness is testifying — and even then the member must grant some latitude to ensure that all important matters are covered. The IAD can, of course, limit the scope of evidence by stipulating certain points that are not in dispute. In a case like this one where the credibility of the applicant is clearly an issue and where the genuineness of a marriage is in doubt, the evidence of immediate family and close acquaintances is highly relevant and should be heard without reservation. Indeed, it was difficult to see how this matter could be fairly determined after only two hours of evidence, particularly when the applicant was self-represented and was initially intending to lead evidence from several witnesses. This was a situation where the duty to allow the applicant to fully present his case was sacrificed for the desire for administrative efficiency. That is not a permissible trade-off. The application for judicial review was allowed.

*Ayele v. Canada (Minister of Citizenship & Immigration)* (2007), 60 Imm. L.R. (3d) 197, 2007 CarswellNat 253, 2007 FC 126 (F.C.) — The duty of fairness requires that a party to a proceeding should have the opportunity to present his or her case fully and fairly. This generally includes the right to call witnesses in order to establish the evidentiary basis of a claim or defense. The applicant applied to sponsor his wife. A visa officer rejected the wife's application for permanent residence on the ground that the marriage was not genuine and was entered into for immigration purposes. The applicant appealed to the Immigration Appeal Division (IAD). After hearing the applicant's testimony, the IAD was anxious to conclude the hearing and to dismiss the appeal. In the words of the presiding member, "[i]t will be a waste of the tribunal's time to continue to indulge the appellant in this waste of taxpayer's money." The IAD refused to hear a witness that the applicant wished to call. The Minister claimed that the IAD refused to allow the witness to testify because the applicant was in breach of Rule 37 of the *Immigration Appeal Division Rules* which required the applicant to have provided, in writing, witness information.

The Minister's reliance upon Rule 37 in order to justify the refusal of the IAD to hear the witness was misplaced. At the outset of the hearing, after hearing submissions with respect to the applicant's late disclosure of information, including late disclosure of witness information, the presiding member ruled "I will allow you to deal with the witness, but obviously the identity and credibility of the witness will be an issue." Any hurdle posed by Rule 37 was overcome when the IAD ruled it would exercise its discretion to allow the witness to testify. When the IAD later ruled it would not allow the witness to testify, it did not refer to Rule 37. Instead, the presiding member stated, "Even if the witness corroborates the testimony, in assessing the testimony it's not credible. So, there's no point in calling the witness and even if it is characterized as a breach of natural justice, there is no prejudice suffered when the evidence is of no use and calling the witness is futile."



Rules

It is not within the purview of a tribunal bound by the requirement of procedural fairness to dispense with those requirements because, in its view, the result of the hearing will be the same. Rather, it is for a court reviewing a decision of the tribunal that has erred to determine whether, as a matter of administrative law, the consequences of a failure to comply with the requirements of procedural fairness are such that the discretionary remedy available to the reviewing court should be withheld.

The withholding of relief in the face of a breach of procedural fairness is exceptional. One can never rule on the credibility of evidence that has not yet been heard. The presiding member violated the principle when he stated that even if the witness corroborated the applicant's testimony that subsequent testimony would not be credible.

The essence of adjudication is the ability to keep an open mind until all evidence has been heard. The reliability of evidence is to be determined in light of all the evidence in a particular case. The application for judicial review was allowed.

**38. (1) Requesting a summons — A party who wants the Division to order a person to testify at a hearing must make a request to the Division for a summons, either orally at a proceeding or in writing.**

**(2) Factors — In deciding whether to issue a summons, the Division must consider any relevant factors, including**

> **(a) the necessity of the testimony to a full and proper hearing;**
>
> **(b) the ability of the person to give that testimony; and**
>
> **(c) whether the person has agreed to be summoned as a witness.**

**(3) Using the summons — If a party wants to use a summons, the party must**

> **(a) provide the summons to the summoned person by hand;**
>
> **(b) provide a copy of the summons to the Division with a written statement of how and when the summons was provided; and**
>
> **(c) pay or offer to pay the summoned person the applicable witness fees and travel expenses set out in Tariff A of the *Federal Courts Rules*.**

**39. (1) Cancelling a summons — If a person summoned to appear as a witness at a proceeding wants the summons cancelled, the person must make an application in writing to the Division.**

**(2) Application — The person must follow rule 43, but is not required to provide an affidavit or statutory declaration with the application.**

**40. (1) Arrest warrant — If a person does not obey a summons to appear, the party who requested the summons may make a request to the Division orally at a hearing, or in writing, to issue a warrant for the arrest of the person.**

**(2) Written request — A party who makes a written request for a warrant must provide supporting evidence by affidavit or statutory declaration.**

**(3) Requirements for issue of arrest warrant — The Division may issue an arrest warrant if**

**(a) the person summoned was provided the summons by hand or the person is avoiding being provided the summons;**

**(b) the person was paid or offered the applicable witness fees and travel expenses set out in Tariff A of the *Federal Courts Rules*;**

**(c) the person did not appear at the hearing as required by the summons; and**

**(d) the person's testimony is still needed for a full and proper hearing.**

**(4) Content of a warrant — A warrant issued by the Division for the arrest of a person must include directions concerning detention and release.**

**41. Excluded witness — Unless allowed by the Division, a person must not communicate to a witness excluded from a hearing room any testimony given while the witness was excluded until that witness has finished testifying.**

## APPLICATIONS

**42. General provision — Unless these Rules provide otherwise**

**(a) a party who wants the Division to make a decision on any matter in an appeal, including the procedure to be followed, must make an application to the Division under rule 43;**

**(b) a party who wants to respond to the application must respond under rule 44; and**

**(c) a party who wants to reply to a response must reply under rule 45.**



### Case Law

*Malfeo v. Canada (Minister of Citizenship & Immigration)*, 2010 CarswellNat 372, 2010 CarswellNat 2169, 2010 FC 193 (F.C.) — The main question raised by this judicial review application was whether a member of the Immigration Appeal Division (IAD) breached the principles of natural justice and/or the requirements of the law when she dismissed the applicant's request to stay his deportation to Italy. This application had been made pursuant to s. 67(1)(c) of IRPA, which enables the tribunal to grant relief if sufficient humanitarian and compassionate considerations are demonstrated in light of the circumstances.

The use of joint submissions is a concept well known in criminal law where the Crown and the defense make joint submissions, for example, in sentencing. It is not unknown in administrative law cases and has been applied by this Court in the context of immigration law (see *Nguyen v. Canada (Minister of Citizenship & Immigration)* (2000), 10 Imm. L.R. (3d) 252), a case which bears similarity with the case at hand since it involved an application by Mr. Nguyen to the then Appeal Division for the exercise of its humanitarian and compassionate jurisdiction under a provision of the now repealed *Immigration Act* similar to paragraph 67(1)(c) of IRPA. That case involved the failure of the tribunal to explain why the joint submissions of counsel proposing a five-year stay was not endorsed. The purpose of staying the deportation is, in that case as it is in this one, to give the applicant an opportunity to demonstrate, on the ground so to speak, becoming a decent law-abiding resident of the country.

Having received the joint submission albeit unexpectedly, the tribunal breached procedural fairness by rejecting it outright without asking for further input. The applicant in these circumstances was not given a fair hearing. The tribunal provided no analysis and did not even refer to the proposed terms and conditions. It was also clear that the tribunal did not give serious consideration to the joint submissions. Again, it provided no analysis of its terms and dismissed the joint submission in a perfunctory manner. The reasons put forward for rejecting the joint submission also lacked analysis. The application for judicial review was granted.

## *How to Make an Application*

**43. (1) Form of application and time limit — An application must be made in writing and without delay unless**

> **(a) these Rules provide otherwise; or**
>
> **(b) the Division allows it to be made orally at a proceeding after considering any relevant factors, including whether the party with reasonable effort could have made the application in writing before the proceeding.**

**(2) Content of application — Unless these Rules provide otherwise, in a written application the party must**

> **(a) state what decision the party wants the Division to make;**
>
> **(b) give reasons why the Division should make that decision; and**
>
> **(c) if there is another party and the views of that party are known, state whether the other party agrees to the application.**

**(3) Affidavit or statutory declaration — Unless these Rules provide otherwise, any evidence that the party wants the Division to consider with an application in writing must be given in a statutory declaration or affidavit that is provided together with the application.**

**(4) Providing the application — A party who makes an written application must provide**

> **(a) to the other party, a copy of the application and any affidavit or statutory declaration; and**
>
> **(b) to the Division, the original application and any affidavit or statutory declaration, together with a written statement of how and when the party provided the copy to any other party.**

## *How to Respond to a Written Application*

**44. (1) Responding to a written application — A response to a written application must be in writing. In a response the party must**

> **(a) state what decision the party wants the Division to make; and**
>
> **(b) give reasons why the Division should make that decision.**

(2) **Evidence in a written response** — Any evidence that the party wants the Division to consider with the written response must be given in an affidavit or statutory declaration that accompanies the response. Unless the Division requires it, an affidavit or statutory declaration is not required if the party who made the application was not required to provide an affidavit or statutory declaration.

(3) **Providing the response** — A party who responds to a written application must provide

(a) to the other party, a copy of the response and any affidavit or statutory declaration; and

(b) to the Division, the original response and any affidavit or statutory declaration, together with a written statement of how and when the party provided the copy to the other party.

(4) **Time limit** — Documents provided under this rule must be received by the recipients no later than seven days after the party received the copy of the application.

### *How to Reply to a Written Response*

45. (1) **Replying to a written response** — A reply to a written response must be in writing.

(2) **Evidence in the reply** — Any evidence that the party wants the Division to consider with the written reply must be given in an affidavit or statutory declaration together with the reply. Unless the Division requires it, an affidavit or statutory declaration is not required if the party was not required to provide a statutory declaration or affidavit with the application.

(3) **Providing the reply** — A party who replies to a written response must provide

(a) to the other party, a copy of the reply and any affidavit or statutory declaration; and

(b) to the Division, the original reply and any affidavit or statutory declaration, together with a written statement of how and when the party provided the copy to the other party.

(4) **Time limit** — Documents provided under this rule must be received by their recipients no later than five days after the party received the copy of the response.

## RETURN TO CANADA TO APPEAR AT A HEARING

46. (1) **Application for an order to appear** — A permanent resident who appeals a decision made outside Canada on the residency obligation may make an application to the Division for an order that they physically appear at the hearing.

(2) **Form of application** — The application must be made under rule 43.

(3) **Time limit** — Documents provided under this rule must be received by their recipients no later than 60 days after the Division received the notice of appeal.

## CHANGING THE LOCATION OF THE PROCEEDING

**47. (1) Application to change the location of a proceeding** — A party may make an application to the Division to change the location of a proceeding.

(2) **Form of application** — The party must follow rule 43, but is not required to give evidence in an affidavit or statutory declaration.

(3) **Time limit** — Documents provided under this rule must be received by their recipients no later than 30 days before the proceeding.

(4) **Factors** — In deciding the application, the Division must consider any relevant factors, including

(a) whether the party is residing in the location where the party wants the proceeding to be held;

(b) whether a change of location would allow the proceeding to be full and proper;

(c) whether a change of location would likely delay or slow the proceeding;

(d) how a change of location would affect the operation of the Division; and

(e) how a change of location would affect the parties.

(5) **Duty to appear at the proceeding** — Unless a party receives a decision from the Division allowing the application, the party must appear for the proceeding at the location fixed and be ready to start or continue the proceeding.

## CHANGING THE DATE OR TIME OF A PROCEEDING

**48. (1) Application to change the date or time of a proceeding** — A party may make an application to the Division to change the date or time of a proceeding.

(2) **Form and content of application** — The party must

(a) follow rule 43, but is not required to give evidence in an affidavit or statutory declaration; and

(b) give at least six dates, within the period specified by the Division, on which the party is available to start or continue the proceeding.

(3) **Application received two days or less before proceeding** — If the party's application is received by the recipients two working days or less before the date of a proceeding, the party must appear at the proceeding and make the request orally.

(4) **Factors** — In deciding the application, the Division must consider any relevant factors, including

(a) in the case of a date and time that was fixed after the Division consulted or tried to consult the party, any exceptional circumstances for allowing the application;

(b) when the party made the application;

**(c) the time the party has had to prepare for the proceeding;**

**(d) the efforts made by the party to be ready to start or continue the proceeding;**

**(e) in the case of a party who wants more time to obtain information in support of the party's arguments, the ability of the Division to proceed in the absence of that information without causing an injustice;**

**(f) the knowledge and experience of any counsel who represents the party;**

**(g) any previous delays and the reasons for them;**

**(h) whether the time and date fixed for the proceeding were peremptory;**

**(i) whether allowing the application would unreasonably delay the proceedings; and**

**(j) the nature and complexity of the matter to be heard.**

**(5) Duty to appear at the proceeding — Unless a party receives a decision from the Division allowing the application, the party must appear for the proceeding at the date and time fixed and be ready to start or continue the proceeding.**

## Case Law

*Quindiagan v. Canada (Minister of Citizenship & Immigration)*, 2005 CarswellNat 1499, 2005 FC 769 (F.C.) — Before the Appeal Division, counsel on behalf of the applicant requested a postponement on the basis that he wished to raise a constitutional question but had failed to complete and serve a notice of constitutional question within the time limit required by s. 52 of the *Immigration Appeal Division Rules*. The Appeal Division denied the request. Counsel for a party to a case is that party's agent. He or she acts on behalf of the party and assumes a number of obligations including those of conduct of the proceedings and receipt and issue of documents required by the proceedings. The only instance where a Court could disrupt an administrative tribunal's decision due to errors committed by counsel would be in a case where extraordinary incompetence on the part of counsel was shown to have resulted in a breach of natural justice.

## PROCEEDING TO BE HELD IN PRIVATE

**49. (1) Form of application — A person who wants to have a proceeding held in private, or who wants the Division to take any other measure to ensure the confidentiality of the proceedings, must make an application to the Division under rule 43.**

**(2) Time limit — Documents provided under this rule must be received by their recipients no later than 20 days before the proceeding.**

**(3) Response by non-party — Any person may make a written request to the Division to be allowed to respond to an application by another person or a party to have a proceeding held in private. If the Division allows the request, the person must respond under rule 44.**

**(4) Temporary confidentiality — The Division may do anything to ensure the confidentiality of the information in the application.**



Rules

## Withdrawing an Appeal

**50. (1) Abuse of process — Withdrawal of an appeal is an abuse of process if it would likely have a negative effect on the integrity of the Division. If no substantive evidence has been accepted in the appeal, withdrawal is not an abuse of process.**

**(2) Withdrawal if no substantive evidence has been accepted — If no substantive evidence has been accepted in the appeal, a party may withdraw their appeal by notifying the Division orally at a proceeding or in writing.**

**(3) Withdrawal if subtantive evidence has been accepted — If substantive evidence has been accepted in the appeal, a party who wants to withdraw their appeal must make an application under rule 43.**

## Reinstating an Appeal After Withdrawal

**51. (1) Application to reinstate a withdrawn appeal — A person may apply to the Division to reinstate an appeal that was made by that person and withdrawn.**

**(2) Form and content of application — The person must follow rule 43 and include their contact information in the application.**

**(3) Factors — The Division must allow the application if it is established that there was a failure to observe a principle of natural justice or if it is otherwise in the interests of justice to allow the application.**

## Notice of Constitutional Question

**52. (1) Notice of constitutional question — A party who wants to challenge the constitutional validity, applicability or operability of a legislative provision must complete a notice of constitutional question.**

**(2) Form and content of notice — The party must provide notice using either Form 69, "Notice of Constitutional Question", set out in the *Federal Courts Rules*, or any other form that includes**

**(a) the name of the party;**

**(b) the Division file number;**

**(c) the date, time and place of the hearing;**

**(d) the specific legislative provision that is being challenged;**

**(e) the relevant facts relied on to support the constitutional challenge; and**

**(f) a summary of the legal argument to be made in support of the constitutional challenge.**

**(3) Providing the notice — The party must provide**

**(a) a copy of the notice of constitutional question to the Attorney General of Canada and to the attorney general of every province and territory of Canada, according to section 57 of the *Federal Courts Act*;**

**(b) a copy of the notice to the other party; and**

**(c) the original notice to the Division, together with a written statement of how and when a copy of the notice was provided under paragraphs (a) and (b).**

**(4) Time limit — Documents provided under this rule must be received by their recipients no later than 10 days before the day the constitutional argument will be made.**

2002, c. 8, s. 182(3)(a)

## DECISIONS

**53. Notice of decision — When the Division makes a decision, other than an interlocutory decision, it must provide a notice of decision to the parties.**

**54. (1) Written reasons for decision on appeal by a sponsor or that stays a removal order — The Division must provide to the parties, together with the notice of decision, written reasons for a decision on an appeal by a sponsor or for a decision that stays a removal order.**

**(2) Written reasons provided on request — A request made by a party for written reasons for a decision, other than a decision referred to in subrule (1) or an interlocutory decision, must be in writing. The request must be received by the Division no later than 10 days after the party received the notice of decision.**

### Case Law

*Sandhu v. Canada (Minister of Citizenship & Immigration)* (2005), 48 Imm. L.R. (3d) 104, 34 Admin. L.R. (4th) 307, 2005 CarswellNat 2101, 2005 CarswellNat 5263, 2005 FC 1046 (F.C.) — The Immigration Appeal Division dismissed the applicant's appeal of a visa officer's decision to refuse the applicant's application to sponsor his son as a member of the family class. The IAD concluded that the applicant had not shown that the visa officer's refusal was wrong in law. Accordingly, the IAD concluded that the person who was sponsored by the applicant was not a member of the family class and therefore under s. 65 of the IRPA, the IAD had no discretionary jurisdiction to consider humanitarian and compassionate considerations. The application for judicial review was allowed as the IAD provided no explanation or analysis whatsoever to conclude that the visa officer's refusal of the applicant's sponsorship application was wrong in law. Accordingly, the reasons provided by the IAD were entirely insufficient to allow the applicant and his family members to understand why they had been denied the opportunity to unite their family in Canada. The reasons were equally insufficient to allow the Federal Court to determine whether or not the tribunal was justified in deciding as it did.

*Singh v. Canada (Minister of Citizenship & Immigration)*, [2005] F.C.J. No. 2071, 2005 CarswellNat 4126, 2005 CarswellNat 4892, 2005 FC 1673 (F.C.) — An appeal heard under s. 63(1) of the IRPA results in a hearing *de novo*. In such a hearing, the IAD does not need to comment on every piece of new evidence that is proffered, but it must deal with evidence that directly contradicts, or at least addresses, the concerns of the original decision maker.

Rules

*Agalliu v. Canada (Minister of Citizenship & Immigration)* (2005), 49 Imm. L.R. (3d) 1, 34 Admin. L.R. 1 (4th) 214, 2005 CarswellNat 2112, 2005 FC 1035 (F.C.) — The Board's reasons disclosed a number of superficial errors, in footnotes and in references to the documentary evidence. However, the Board's other errors and its failure to explain its conclusions adequately disclosed more fundamental problems. Taken together, these errors led to the conclusion that the Board's decision was not in keeping with the evidence before it. Sometimes, little errors in a written decision represent no more than a lack of final polishing. Other times, they are symptomatic of inadequate care on the part of the decision maker.

*Mann v. Canada (Minister of Citizenship & Immigration)* (2004), 43 Imm. L.R. (3d) 230, 2004 CarswellNat 5099, 2004 CarswellNat 3438, (sub nom. *Canada (Minister of Citizenship & Immigration) v. Mann)* 258 F.T.R. 139 (Eng.), 2004 FC 1338 (F.C.) — This was an application to review a decision of the Immigration Appeal Division wherein the Appeal Division allowed an appeal from a visa officer's refusal to grant the respondent's wife an immigrant visa.

In dealing with the adequacy of reasons, the Court relied upon the Federal Court of Appeal decision in *VIA Rail Canada Inc. v. Canada (National Transportation Agency)* (2000), [2001] 2 F.C. 25, 2000 CarswellNat 2531, 2000 CarswellNat 3453, 261 N.R. 184, 193 D.L.R. (4th) 357, 26 Admin. L.R. (3d) 1, [2000] F.C.J. No. 1685 (Fed. C.A.). Reasons foster better decision making. By ensuring that issues and reasoning are well articulated and therefore more carefully thought out, the process of writing reasons for a decision by itself may be a guarantee of a better decision. Reasons provide the parties with the assurance that their representations have been considered.

Reasons allow the parties to effectuate any right of appeal or judicial review that they might have. They provide a basis for an assessment of possible grounds of appeal or review. They allow the appellate or reviewing body to determine whether the decision maker erred and thereby render him or her accountable. This is particularly important when the decision is subject to a deferential standard of review.

In a case of a regulated industry, the regulator's reasons provide guidance to others who are subject to the regulator's jurisdiction.

The duty to give reasons is only fulfilled if the reasons provided are adequate. What constitutes adequate reasons is a matter to be determined in the light of the circumstances of each case. As a general rule, adequate reasons are those that serve the functions for which the duty to provide them was imposed.

The obligation to provide adequate reasons is not satisfied by merely reciting the submissions and evidence of the parties and stating a conclusion. The decision maker must set out its findings of fact and the principal evidence upon which those findings were based. The reasons must address the major points in issue. The reasoning process followed by the decision maker must be set out and must reflect consideration of the main relevant factors.

In this case, s. 4 of the *Hindu Marriage Act* was an important factor in the case. The interpretation of this section is a matter on which the IAD's reasons are silent, and due to this silence, the reasons are inadequate.

**55. When decision of single member takes effect — A decision of the Division made orally by one Division member at a proceeding takes effect when the**

**member states the decision. A decision made in writing takes effect when the member signs and dates the decision.**

**56. When decision of three-member panel takes effect — A decision of the Division made orally by a panel of three members takes effect when all the members state their decision. A decision made in writing takes effect when all members of the panel sign and date the decision.**

## GENERAL PROVISIONS

**57. No applicable rule — In the absence of a provision in these Rules dealing with a matter raised during an appeal, the Division may do whatever is necessary to deal with the matter.**

**58. Powers of the Division — The Division may**

> **(a) act on its own initiative, without a party having to make an application or request to the Division;**
>
> **(b) change a requirement of a rule;**
>
> **(c) excuse a person from a requirement of a rule; and**
>
> **(d) extend or shorten a time limit, before or after the time limit has passed.**

Rules

### Case Law

*Canada (Minister of Citizenship & Immigration) v. Rumpler* (2008), 76 Imm. L.R. (3d) 237, 336 F.T.R. 285 (Eng.), 2008 CarswellNat 4258, 2008 CarswellNat 5085, 2008 FC 1264, 2008 CarswellNat 4258 — This was an application for judicial review of the decision of the IAD wherein the IAD concluded it had jurisdiction to hear an appeal of the respondent's removal order. Returning to Canada from Israel, an immigration officer determined that the respondent did not satisfy the residency requirements of s. 28 of the Act and undertook measures to have him removed. The period to appeal the removal order expired and the respondent voluntarily left Canada for the United States. The respondent then requested of the IAD an extension of the period, to allow him to lodge an appeal of the removal order. The IAD decided that, according to subs. 63(3) of the Act, it did not have the competence to extend the period of appeal after its expiration, because the respondent had lost his status as permanent resident by failing to appeal. Justice Blanchard of the Federal Court granted the respondent's application for judicial review, and held that the IAD did have competence under the said provision to grant the extension. Accordingly, an extension was granted by a different member of the IAD and at a new hearing before the IAD, the Minister asked the tribunal to reject the appeal of the removal order on the ground of mootness, because the respondent had voluntarily left the country and thus executed the order. The Minister's motion was rejected and the Minister brought an application for judicial review of the IAD's decision.

The IAD erred in law in finding that it had continuing jurisdiction in spite of the fact that the respondent had left Canada and had executed the removal order before he filed a notice of appeal. It is trite law that the IAD does not have jurisdiction to reopen an appeal where the motion to reopen has been filed after an appellant is removed from Canada. Since the IAD did not have the jurisdiction to cancel the removal order once it had already been executed, it necessarily had no jurisdiction to grant a request (filed after such an execution) for an extension of time to lodge an appeal of the removal order. Consequently, the application for judicial review was allowed.

*Rumpler v. Canada (Minister of Citizenship & Immigration)* (2006), 60 Imm. L.R. (3d) 71, 2006 CarswellNat 4492, 2006 FC 1485 (F.C.) — The applicant sought judicial review of a decision of the Appeal Division wherein the Appeal Division decided it did not have jurisdiction to extend time to hear an appeal from a removal order issued at an examination pursuant to s. 63(3) of the IRPA. The Board found that it did not have jurisdiction to extend the time to file an appeal under s. 63(3) once the prescribed delay had expired because the applicant was no longer a permanent resident of Canada. The Board reasoned that since no appeal had been filed in the 30-day period pursuant to paragraph 49(1)(b) of the IRPA, the removal order came into force the day the appeal period expired, and the applicant contemporaneously lost his permanent resident status, pursuant to paragraph 46(1)(c) of the IRPA. Moreover, pursuant to ss. 237 and 240 of the *Immigration and Refugee Protection Regulations* the order had been enforced by the voluntary departure of the applicant to the United States. The Court found that the Appeal Division does have jurisdiction to hear the request to extend time and then decide in the exercise of its discretion if the request is justified. If the extension is granted then the effect of such determination by the Appeal Board would be to allow the appeal to be made in time and the removal order would be vitiated. As a consequence, the applicant would retain his permanent resident status and the Appeal Division would have jurisdiction to hear the appeal. This interpretation is in keeping with the statutory scheme and intention of Parliament to provide a right of appeal, a significant guarantee against arbitrary decisions when important rights are in play. Parliament could not have intended to deprive a person of his or her right to appeal from a deportation order because of a failure to respect the delay to appeal no matter the circumstances, absent express language to that effect.

The IAD Rules passed under authority of the IRPA expressly provide that the Appeal Division can extend time when time has passed. There may well be instances where an applicant is able to adequately explain the delay. Applicants have a right to appeal provided for in law. The Appeal Division's decision was set aside and remitted for re-determination in accordance with the reasons of the Court.

The Court certified the following question:

> Would it be lawful for the Immigration Appeal Division to entertain an application for an extension of time pursuant to subs. 58(d) of the *Immigration Appeal Division Rules* made by an individual who has no right of appeal through the combined effect of paragraphs 48(1)(b) and 46(1)(c), ss. 2 and 63 of the IRPA?

**59. Failing to follow a rule — Unless proceedings are declared invalid by the Division, a failure to follow any requirement of these Rules does not make the proceedings invalid.**

## COMING INTO FORCE

**60. Coming into force — These Rules come into force on the day on which section 161 of the Act comes into force.**

# Can. Reg. 2002-231 — Oath or Solemn Affirmation of Office Rules (Immigration and Refugee Board)

## made under the *Immigration and Refugee Protection Act*

SOR/2002-231

### Oath or Solemn Affirmation of Office

**1. Text of the oath or solemn affirmation of office** — The oath or solemn affirmation of office to be taken by the Chairperson of the Immigration and Refugee Board and members of the Refugee Protection Division, the Refugee Appeal Division and the Immigration Appeal Division pursuant to paragraph 153(1)(b) of the *Immigration and Refugee Protection Act* shall be in the following form:

I, .........., do swear (*or* solemnly affirm) that:

(a) I will, during the term of my appointment, and any re-appointments, faithfully, impartially and to the best of my knowledge and ability, properly carry out the duties of a (full-time *or* part-time) (*title*) of the Immigration and Refugee Board;

(b) I will comply with the *Code of Conduct for Members*;

(c) I will not disclose or make known, unless authorized, any matter that comes to my knowledge because I am holding that office.

(*In the case of an oath, add:* So help me (*Name of Deity*).)

### Coming Into Force

**2. Coming into force** — These Rules come into force on the day on which section 161 of the Act comes into force.

# Federal Courts Act

## An Act respecting the Federal Court of Appeal and the Federal Court

R.S.C. 1985, c. F-7, as am. R.S.C. 1985, c. 41 (1st Supp.), s. 11; R.S.C. 1985, c. 30 (2nd Supp.), s. 61; R.S.C. 1985, c. 16 (3rd Supp.), s. 7; R.S.C. 1985, c. 51 (4th Supp.), ss. 10–12; S.C. 1990, c. 8, ss. 1–14(2), (3) (Fr.), (4), 15–19 [s. 7(2) amended 1990, c. 8, s. 78(1).]; 1990, c. 37, s. 34; 1992, c. 1, s. 68; 1992, c. 26, s. 17; 1992, c. 33, s. 69; 1992, c. 49, ss. 127, 128; 1993, c. 27, s. 214; 1993, c. 34, ss. 68 (Fr.), 69 (Fr.), 70; 1996, c. 10, s. 229; 1996, c. 22, s. 1; 1996, c. 23, s. 187(c); 1996, c. 31, ss. 82–84; 1998, c. 26, s. 73; 1999, c. 31, s. 92; 2001, c. 6, s. 115; 2001, c. 41, ss. 95, 144(2); 2002, c. 8, ss. 13–58; 2003, c. 22, ss. 167, 225(w) [s. 167 amended 2003, c. 22, s. 262; s. 225(w) amended 2003, c. 22, s. 263.]; 2004, c. 7, s. 7 [Amended 2004, c. 7, s. 38.]; 2005, c. 46, s. 56.1 [Added 2006, c. 9, s. 222.]; 2006, c. 9, ss. 5, 6, 38; 2006, c. 11, ss. 20–24; 2008, c. 22, s. 46; 2009, c. 21, s. 18; 2010, c. 8, s. 41 [To come into force June 29, 2012, or earlier by order.].

*[Note: The short title of this Act was changed from "Federal Court Act" to "Federal Courts Act" by S.C. 2002, c. 8, s. 14. The long title of this Act was changed from "An Act respecting the Federal Court of Canada" to "An Act respecting the Federal Court of Appeal and the Federal Court" by S.C. 2002, c. 8, s. 13.]*

.....

### Barristers, Advocates, Attorneys and Solicitors

**11. (1) Barrister or advocate — Every person who is a barrister or an advocate in a province may practise as a barrister or an advocate in the Federal Court of Appeal or the Federal Court.**

**(2) Attorney or solicitor — Every person who is an attorney or a solicitor in a superior court of a province may practise as an attorney or a solicitor in the Federal Court of Appeal or the Federal Court.**

**(3) Officers of court — Every person who may practise as a barrister, an advocate, an attorney or a solicitor in the Federal Court of Appeal or the Federal Court is an officer of that Court.**

2002, c. 8, s. 19

### Case Law

*Obando v. Canada (Minister of Citizenship & Immigration)*, 2003 CarswellNat 1554, 2003 CarswellNat 2613, 2003 FCT 668, 2003 CFPI 668 (Fed. T.D.) — The Court dismissed this application for a stay of execution of a removal order. At the commencement of the hearing, the applicant, who was representing himself, sought approval of the Court to be represented by a consultant who was not a lawyer. The Minister objected based on the Court's own rules permitting representation by persons themselves or by solicitors retained on their behalf. The Court examined the applicant and determined 1), that he was not proficient in English and would not have been able to represent himself; 2), that he had no submissions to make on his own behalf but wished submissions to be made by his consultant; and 3) that he was prepared to adopt submissions made on his behalf by his consultant as his own after those submissions were made. The Court authorized the consultant to make submissions and at the conclusion asked the applicant to affirm that the submissions were adopted by him as his own. The Court, at the conclusion of the submissions, dismissed the request for a stay.

*Salinas v. Canada (Minister of Citizenship & Immigration)* (2000), 2000 CarswellNat 1414, 2000 CarswellNat 3202, [2000] F.C.J. No. 1004 (Fed. T.D.) — The respondent Minister appealed an order of a prothonotary who dismissed the Minister's motion asking that the application for leave and judicial review be dismissed on the ground that no one acting on behalf of the applicants was qualified to represent them.

The Court should not approve of third parties who are not lawyers doing things which are within the exclusive jurisdiction of members of the bar.

It is the Court's role and duty to guarantee compliance with the Act and the Rules and to ensure that those who appear before it, or draft proceedings for the purpose of asserting rights, are officers of the Court. Facts put in evidence in each of the respondent Minister's motions constituted evidence which pointed inexorably to the conclusion that in each case the application for leave and judicial review by the applicants had been prepared and drafted by an agent who could not act as a representative in this Court. If an applicant decides to be represented, Rule 119 is clear: he or she must be represented by a solicitor.

Accordingly, the respondent Minister's appeal was allowed and the application for judicial review dismissed.

*Parmar c. Canada (Ministre de la Citoyenneté & de l'Immigration)* (2000), 12 Imm. L.R. (3d) 178, 2000 CarswellNat 1432, 2000 CarswellNat 3429 (Fed. T.D.) — The defendant Minister appealed an order dismissing its motion asking the Court to dismiss an application for leave and judicial review. The motion had been brought on the ground that the person acting on the plaintiff's behalf was not qualified to represent him.

It is the Court's function and duty to ensure that its Act and its Rules are observed and that those who appear before it or prepare pleadings to be used in asserting rights are officers of the Court. The facts in this matter lead inexorably to the conclusion that the plaintiff's application for leave and judicial review had been prepared and drafted by an agent. It is true that a plaintiff may act in person, but if he or she decides to be represented then the rule is clear that he or she must be represented by a barrister or advocate.

The Court concluded that the plaintiff had been represented by a person who was not authorized to do so and accordingly allowed the Minister's appeal and dismissed the plaintiff's application for leave and for judicial review.

.....

## JURISDICTION OF FEDERAL COURT

[Heading amended 2002, c. 8, s. 24.]

.....

**18. (1) Extraordinary remedies, federal tribunals — Subject to section 28, the Federal Court has exclusive original jurisdiction**

**(a) to issue an injunction, writ of *certiorari,* writ of prohibition, writ of *mandamus* or writ of *quo warranto,* or grant declaratory relief, against any federal board, commission or other tribunal; and**

**(b) to hear and determine any application or other proceeding for relief in the nature of relief contemplated by paragraph (a), including any proceeding brought against the Attorney General of Canada, to obtain relief against a federal board, commission or other tribunal.**

**(2) Extraordinary remedies, members of Canadian Forces — The Federal Court has exclusive original jurisdiction to hear and determine every application for a writ of *habeas corpus ad subjiciendum*, writ of *certiorari,* writ of prohibition or writ of *mandamus* in relation to any member of the Canadian Forces serving outside Canada.**

**(3) Remedies to be obtained on application — The remedies provided for in subsections (1) and (2) may be obtained only on an application for judicial review made under section 18.1.**

1990, c. 8, s. 4; 2002, c. 8, s. 26

### Case Law

### Section 18(1)

*John Doe v. Canada (Minister of Citizenship & Immigration)* (2006), 54 Imm. L.R. (3d) 212, 2006 CarswellNat 1105, 2006 CarswellNat 1543, 2006 FC 535 (F.C.) — The applicant came to Canada in 1984 and was granted refugee status in 1986. He then applied for permanent residence. There ensued many interviews, security checks, etc., without any decision being taken on his application. In 1998, the immigration officers raised security concerns. The applicant made an application for ministerial relief under what would now be subs. 34(2) of the IRPA, which would have the effect of relieving him of possible inadmissibility that might otherwise be a bar to grant permanent residence. In nearly eight years no decision had been taken on the application for ministerial relief. The applicant brought an application for *mandamus* to require the Minister to make a decision with respect to the applicant's permanent residence in Canada.

On the eve of the hearing, the Minister made an offer to settle. The Minister was prepared not to oppose the *mandamus* application but was to agree to an order that would set out time limits for progressive steps leading to an ultimate decision. The applicant found the proposal unacceptable as it contemplated steps totaling some 240 days and did not set out any limit as to how long the Minister of Public Security and Emergency Preparedness might take to decide the application for ministerial relief, which was first made in 1998. The Court directed that a decision on permanent residence be made by a specific date.

Other Relevant Legislation

The Court also awarded costs, finding special reasons — specifically that the Minister failed to take a decision which was requested almost 20 years previous, while the applicant had endured interview after interview, acquired a good deal of legal advice and was forced to bring the Minister to court. Even when faced with this matter being set down for hearing the Minister waited until the afternoon of the day before the hearing to offer a settlement.

*Seyoboka c. Canada (Ministre de la Citoyenneté & de l'Immigration)*, 2005 CarswellNat 5690, 2005 FC 1290 (F.C.) — This was an application for judicial review in order to obtain a writ of *mandamus*, ordering the respondent to determine and make a definitive decision on the applicant's application for permanent residence which had been dated August 12, 1996. The applicant was a citizen of Rwanda and had arrived in Canada on January 17, 1996, and claimed refugee status. The IRB recognized the applicant as a Convention refugee on October 25, 1996. On August 12, 1996, the applicant filed an application for permanent residence. To date, the respondent has still not processed that application. On several occasions, the applicant tried to find out the status of his application. The respondent always replied that the security check was ongoing.

Even though at first glance nine years is a long time for someone who is waiting to be given permanent residence status, *mandamus* applications must be assessed in accordance with the particular facts of the case; the case law is used only to outline the parameters. In this case, the applicant made some significant additions to his file over the last nine years. Considering the facts presented by the applicant since his initial permanent residence application, the respondent was justified in completing its security check. When it is a matter of security, the Court must not issue an order of *mandamus* having the effect of an aborted or abbreviated investigation. Further, the Minister of Public Safety applied to the IRB to annul the applicant's refugee status. That application, though late, is certainly not frivolous. If it is granted, any right to permanent residence would be annulled. In the interim, therefore, until the application by the Minister of Public Safety is decided, issuing a writ of *mandamus* would serve no purpose.

*Uppal v. Canada (Minister of Citizenship & Immigration)*, 2005 CarswellNat 2437, 2005 CarswellNat 4845, 2005 FC 1133 (F.C.) — Costs are generally not awarded in applications for leave and for judicial review brought in a context of the *Immigration and Refugee Protection Act*. This is because Rule 22 of the *Federal Court Immigration and Refugee Protection Rules* provides that no costs shall be awarded in proceedings under the Rules "unless the Court, for special reasons, so orders." The finding that an order of *mandamus* is warranted is not, by itself, sufficient to justify the award of costs.

Although none of the steps required to process the applicant's application were concluded expediently, and an embarrassing gaffe occurred, the pace was not so slow or lax as to give rise to special circumstances and an award of costs.

*Marshall v. R.*, 2002 CarswellNat 2901, 2002 CarswellNat 3965, 2002 FCT 1099, 2002 CFPI 1099 (Fed. T.D.) — The applicant applied to the Court for an order restraining an adjudicator from continuing a hearing against the applicant until the action commenced by the applicant was heard and determined. The Court concluded that it did not have jurisdiction to issue the order requested because no application for judicial review had been filed with the Court. Section 18(1) of the *Federal Court Act* grants the Federal Court the jurisdiction to grant certain remedies but subs. 18(3) requires that the application for judicial review be commenced. In the present motion, the motion for an interim injunction is made incidental to an action, not an application for judicial review. The Court has jurisdiction to grant a stay pursuant to s. 18.2 of the *Federal Courts Act*, but only if a judicial review application has been filed. Subs. 50(1) of the *Federal Courts Act* gives the Court jurisdiction to grant a stay but only provides for stays in proceedings being conducted before the Federal Court. Accordingly the motion for an injunction was dismissed.

*Atlantic Prudence Fund Corp. v. Canada (Minister of Citizenship & Immigration)* (2000), 2000 CarswellNat 531 (Fed. T.D.) — The applicant sought to amend notices of application so as to seek declaratory relief in lieu of *mandamus* and to add to the grounds of their application for judicial review allegations of bad faith.

A notice of application may be amended at any time. The governing principle is that in the absence of prejudice to the opposing party, amendments should be allowed if they will assist in determining the real issue between the parties. Applicants must adduce some evidence to convince the Court that it would be fair in the circumstances to allow them to add a further ground to their applications for judicial review. The Court found that there was some evidence to convince the Court that it was fair to allow the amendments. This evidence included the dissemination of rumours by representatives of the Minister around the time of the decisions which are the subject of the proceedings to the effect that one of the persons associated with the applicants had attempted to bribe an official of the respondent, and that two of the persons associated with the applicants were connected with Chinese organized crime. Further, there was evidence of an e-mail sent by an official of the Ministry which suggested a course of action which ". . . would be far more effective, in our opinion, and would be more likely to hurt the group where it really hurts".

The Court found an absence of any evidence of prejudice and accordingly allowed the amendments.

*Popal v. Canada (Minister of Citizenship & Immigration)*, [2000] 3 F.C. 532, 184 F.T.R. 161, 2000 CarswellNat 459, [2000] F.C.J. No. 352, 2000 CarswellNat 3417 (Fed. T.D.) — The applicant alleged that he was a citizen of Afghanistan, and was determined by a panel of the Convention Refugee Determination Division (CRDD) to be a refugee from that country. Since November 15, 1994, the date of the CRDD decision, the applicant's wife and children have been residing in Pakistan under, what the applicant attested to were, "deplorable conditions". In December 1994, the applicant submitted an application for permanent residence as a Convention refugee. More than 5 years have passed and the applicant remains in suspended animation in Canada. His children continue to grow older and one of his children is now of an age where he can no longer be sponsored. The applicant provided a valid passport, Afghan driver's licence, an Ontario driver's licence and Ontario Health Insurance Card as identity documents. The respondent rejected these identity documents and provided no explanation to the applicant for this decision.

The decision to reject these documents was critical to the future of the principal applicant and his family members. Accordingly, the Court found that the respondent erred in a reviewable manner in not providing reasons for the rejection of the various documents.

The decision to reject these documents was set aside. The respondent was urged to make a redetermination about the satisfactory nature of the applicant's identity documents as expeditiously as possible.

*Gosal v. Canada (Minister of Citizenship & Immigration)* (2000), 2000 CarswellNat 433 (Fed. T.D.) — During the course of processing the applicant's application for permanent residence, the visa officer requested that the applicant undergo DNA testing to establish family relationships. The applicant sought to quash this decision. The decision to require DNA testing was interlocutory in nature and did not in any sense dispose of the proceedings. The Court's jurisdiction under s. 18 is not restricted to final substantive decisions. The Court can, in special circumstances, review an interlocutory decision.

The Court decided not to intervene. If ultimately the applicant was refused, she could apply for judicial review and raise any argument she might have, including the DNA testing. Accordingly, the application for review was dismissed.

*Van Nguyen v. R.* (1997), (sub nom. *Van Nguyen v. Canada)* 134 F.T.R. 241 (T.D.) — The defendant moved pursuant to Rule 324 to strike out the plaintiff's action, which was for damages for wrongful detention by immigration authorities, on the basis of want for a reasonable cause of action.

The plaintiff, a permanent resident, came from Hong Kong as a stateless person in 1991. He married a Canadian permanent resident with whom he had 3 children. He subsequently acquired a criminal record and was ordered deported. In January 1996, he was declared a danger to the public in Canada. On completing his jail sentence the plaintiff remained in immigration custody pending his removal. However, the Vietnamese government would not provide travel documents and the plaintiff was released. The plaintiff obeyed the terms of his release, but was nevertheless arrested by immigration authorities and was in custody at the time this motion was heard. The present statement of claim set out briefly and in the clearest language that the claim was one for damages for arbitrary and unlawful arrest and detention. The absence of some new wrongdoing at the time of the plaintiff's re-arrest made it impossible for the Court to say that the plaintiff's action was futile, devoid of merit, and could not possibly succeed.

Due to the fact that the plaintiff was not seeking any form of declaratory relief, the defendant could not gain any comfort from s. 18(1) of the *Federal Court Act.*

*Chesters v. Canada (Minister of Citizenship & Immigration)* (1997), 38 Imm. L.R. (2d) 269, 45 C.R.R. (2d) 233, 134 F.T.R. 151 (T.D.) — A party may, in an action, seek a declaration that legislation of Parliament is contrary to the *Charter of Rights*. The type of declaration mentioned in s. 18 of the *Federal Courts Act*, is one which impugns the decision of a board, commission or other tribunal. Such a declaration can only be sought in judicial review proceedings.

## Section 18(3)

*Marshall v. R.*, 2002 CarswellNat 2901, 2002 CarswellNat 3965, 2002 FCT 1099, 2002 CFPI 1099 (Fed. T.D.) — The applicant applied to the Court for an order restraining an adjudicator from continuing a hearing against the applicant until the action commenced by the applicant was heard and determined. The Court concluded that it did not have jurisdiction to issue the order requested because no application for judicial review had been filed with the Court. Section 18(1) of the *Federal Court Act* grants the Federal Court the jurisdiction to grant certain remedies but subs. 18(3) requires that the application for judicial review be commenced. In the present motion, the motion for an interim injunction is made incidental to an action, not an application for judicial review. The Court has jurisdiction to grant a stay pursuant to s. 18.2 of the *Federal Courts Act*, but only if a judicial review application has been filed. Subs. 50(1) of the *Federal Courts Act* gives the Court jurisdiction to grant a stay but only provides for stays in proceedings being conducted before the Federal Court. Accordingly the motion for an injunction was dismissed.

*Moktari v. Canada (Minister of Citizenship & Immigration)* (1999), 70 C.R.R. (2d) 133, 249 N.R. 385, [2000] 2 F.C. 341, 12 Imm. L.R. (3d) 12, 1999 CarswellNat 2522, [1999] F.C.J. No. 1864, 1999 CarswellNat 3045 (C.A.) — The Federal Court possesses jurisdiction to hear constitutional challenges to legislation in judicial review proceedings. This is true whether or not the decision-maker possesses the jurisdiction to make constitutional rulings. The Court possesses jurisdiction to grant declaratory relief in judicial review proceedings brought pursuant to s. 18 of the *Federal Court Act*. The cases in which statements of claim have been struck for disclosing no reasonable cause of action where the relief being sought in the action was by declaration and a parallel judicial review application had been brought seeking the same result are to be followed.

To permit parallel proceedings arising from a single decision would diminish the capacity of the Federal Court to dispense justice in an expedient and efficient manner.

*Sivaraj v. Canada (Minister of Citizenship & Immigration)*, [1996] F.C.J. No. 700, 1996 CarswellNat 1040 (Fed. C.A.) — The Court of Appeal upheld the motion judge's ruling, striking the appellant's statement of claim as disclosing no reasonable cause of action. The motions judge had done so on the basis that the declaratory and injunctive relief sought must be pursued by way of judicial review, as opposed to an action, pursuant to subs. 18(1) and 18(3) of the *Federal Courts Act*.

The Court of Appeal was in agreement with the reasons of the motions judge.

*Zelzle v. Canada (Minister of Citizenship & Immigration)*, [1996] 3 F.C. 20, 34 Imm. L.R. (2d) 24, 110 F.T.R. 161 (T.D.) — This was an application to review an interlocutory decision of a panel of the CRDD, wherein it was determined that a previous CRDD panel had failed to render a decision, leaving the CRDD open to hear the applicant's refugee claim *de novo*.

The applicant made a claim for refugee status on November 26, 1992. The applicant appeared for a hearing on the 15th of November 1993. At the commencement of the hearing, a positive Notice of Decision was found in the CRDD file. This Notice of Decision was dated May 10, 1993. The decision had apparently been made pursuant to the expedited hearing process. The November 15, 1993 panel adjourned the matter pending an inquiry to the registrar. On May 4, 1994, the applicant received a letter stating that the May 10th decision had been signed and left in the file as a result of an administrative error and, as such, that the case would proceed *de novo*. At the *de novo* hearing on January 9, 1995, the applicant made a motion that the panel did not have jurisdiction. On May 29, 1995, this motion was dismissed.

Once the tribunal has rendered a final decision, that tribunal's jurisdiction ceases and the tribunal becomes *functus officio*. In the case of the administrative tribunals, however, justice may require the reopening of administrative proceedings in order to provide relief which would otherwise be available on appeal. This exception was established to allow an administrative tribunal to re-open proceedings where, if the hearing of an application had not been held according to the rules of natural justice, the administrative tribunal may treat its decision as a nullity and reconsider the matter. This exception has usually been invoked by unsuccessful refugee claimants where, for example, the CRDD failed to consider evidence of changed country conditions. While the principal of *functus officio* favours the finality of proceedings, its application is flexible in the case of administrative tribunals.

In the instant case, the CRDD discharged the function committed to it by its enabling legislation by issuing the May 10, 1993 decision, which decision was valid on its face.

The decision on May 29, 1995 resulted in the panel exceeding its jurisdiction in looking beyond the decision and determining that it was an "administrative error". The panel had no jurisdiction to question a decision validly made in conformity with the Act. Once such a decision was made, the November 15th and May 29th panels were *functus officio*, since the decision in respect of the applicant's refugee status had been made. If the Minister had concerns regarding the legitimacy of the May 10, 1993 decision, the proper method by which to address those concerns would have been by way of an application for judicial review.

**18.1 (1) Application for judicial review — An application for judicial review may be made by the Attorney General of Canada or by anyone directly affected by the matter in respect of which relief is sought.**

**(2) Time limitation — An application for judicial review in respect of a decision or an order of a federal board, commission or other tribunal shall be made within 30 days after the time the decision or order was first communicated by the federal board, commission or other tribunal to the office of the Deputy Attorney General of Canada or to the party directly affected by it, or within any further time that a judge of the Federal Court may fix or allow before or after the expiration of those 30 days.**

**(3) Powers of Federal Court — On an application for judicial review, the Federal Court may**

**(a) order a federal board, commission or other tribunal to do any act or thing it has unlawfully failed or refused to do or has unreasonably delayed in doing; or**

**(b) declare invalid or unlawful, or quash, set aside or set aside and refer back for determination in accordance with such directions as it considers to be appropriate, prohibit or restrain, a decision, order, act or proceeding of a federal board, commission or other tribunal.**

**(4) Grounds of review — The Federal Court may grant relief under subsection (3) if it is satisfied that the federal board, commission or other tribunal**

**(a) acted without jurisdiction, acted beyond its jurisdiction or refused to exercise its jurisdiction;**

**(b) failed to observe a principle of natural justice, procedural fairness or other procedure that it was required by law to observe;**

**(c) erred in law in making a decision or an order, whether or not the error appears on the face of the record;**

**(d) based its decision or order on an erroneous finding of fact that it made in a perverse or capricious manner or without regard for the material before it;**

**(e) acted, or failed to act, by reason of fraud or perjured evidence; or**

**(f) acted in any other way that was contrary to law.**

**(5) Defect in form or technical irregularity — If the sole ground for relief established on an application for judicial review is a defect in form or a technical irregularity, the Federal Court may**

**(a) refuse the relief if it finds that no substantial wrong or miscarriage of justice has occurred; and**

**(b) in the case of a defect in form or a technical irregularity in a decision or an order, make an order validating the decision or order, to have effect from any time and on any terms that it considers appropriate.**

1990, c. 8, s. 5; 2002, c. 8, s. 27

## Case Law

### Section 18.1(1)

*New Brunswick (Board of Management) v. Dunsmuir*, [2008] 1 S.C.R. 190, (sub nom. *Dunsmuir v. New Brunswick)* [2008] S.C.J. No. 9, 372 N.R. 1, 69 Admin. L.R. (4th) 1, 2008 C.L.L.C. 220-020, D.T.E. 2008T-223, 329 N.B.R. (2d) 1, 170 L.A.C. (4th) 1, 291 D.L.R. (4th) 577, 64 C.C.E.L. (3d) 1, 2008 CarswellNB 124, 2008 CarswellNB 125, 2008 SCC 9 — The operation of three standards of review has not been without practical and theoretical difficulties, neither has it been free of criticism. One major problem lies in distinguishing between the patent unreasonableness standard and the reasonableness simpliciter standard. The difficulty in distinguishing between those standards contributes to the problem of choosing the right standard of review. An even greater problem lies in the application of the patent unreasonableness standard, which at times seems to require parties to accept an unreasonable decision.

Even if one could conceive of a situation in which a clearly or highly irrational decision were distinguishable from a merely irrational decision, it would be unpalatable to require parties to accept an irrational decision simply because, on a deferential standard, the irrationality of the decision is not clear enough. It is also inconsistent with the rule of law to retain an irrational decision. A simpler test is needed.

In judicial review, reasonableness is concerned mostly with the existence of justification, transparency and intelligibility within the decision-making process. But it is also concerned with whether the decision falls within a range of possible, acceptable outcomes which are defensible in respect of the facts and law. The move towards a single reasonableness standard does not pave the way for a more intrusive review by courts and does not represent a return to pre-*Southam* formalism. In this respect, the concept of deference, so central to judicial review in administrative law, has perhaps been insufficiently explored in the case law.

Deference is both an attitude of the Court and a requirement of the law of judicial review. It does not mean that courts are subservient to the determinations of decision makers, or that courts must show blind reverence to their interpretations, or that they may be content to pay lip service to the concept of reasonableness review while in fact imposing their own view. Rather, deference imports respect for the decision-making process of adjudicative bodies with regard to both the facts and the law. The notion of deference "is rooted in part in a respect for governmental decisions to create administrative bodies with delegated powers." There are now only two standards, reasonableness and correctness. The process of judicial review involves two steps. First, courts ascertain whether the jurisprudence has already determined in a satisfactory manner the degree of deference to be accorded with regard to a particular category of question. Secondly, where the first inquiry proves unfruitful, courts must proceed to an analysis of the factors making it possible to identify the proper standard of review.

The existing approach to determining the appropriate standard of review has in the past commonly been referred to as "pragmatic and functional". In the future, it should simply be referred to as the "standard of review analysis". The analysis must be contextual. It is dependent on the application of a number of relevant factors, including: (1) the presence or absence of a privative clause; (2) the purpose of the tribunal as determined by interpretation of enabling legislation; (3) the nature of the question at issue; and (4) the expertise of the tribunal.

The existence of a privative or preclusive clause gives rise to a strong indication of review pursuant to the reasonableness standard. Where the question is one of fact, discretion or policy, as well as questions where the legal issues cannot be easily separated from the factual issues, a standard of reasonableness is appropriate. Where an administrative tribunal has developed particular expertise, a reasonableness test is applied. A question of law that is of "central importance to the legal system. . .and outside the. . .specialized area of expertise" of the administrative decision maker will always attract a correctness standard, while a question of law that does not rise to this level may be compatible with a reasonableness standard.

*Thanabalasingham v. Canada (Minister of Citizenship & Immigration)*, [2006] F.C.J. No. 20, 51 Imm. L.R. (3d) 1, 263 D.L.R. (4th) 51, 345 N.R. 388, 2006 CarswellNat 1416, 2006 CarswellNat 25, 2006 FCA 14 (C.A.) — This was an appeal by the Minister of Citizenship & Immigration from a decision of a Federal Court judge who granted an application for judicial review by Mr. Thanabalasingham to set aside the danger opinion given by the Minister's delegate. The judge granted the application on the ground that the delegate's assessment of risk was based solely on the evidence of country conditions in Sri Lanka and had no regard to the risk resulting from Mr. Thanabalasingham's personal circumstances, and that her reasons did not adequately explain why she accepted the material submitted by the Minister and rejected that favourable to Mr. Thanabalasingham. The judge certified the following question for appeal:

> When an applicant comes to the Court without clean hands on an application for judicial review, should the Court in determining whether to consider the merits of the application, consider the consequences that might befall the applicant if the application is not considered on its merits?

The Minister's principal concern was the judge's decision to hear and grant the application for judicial review in the face of an admission by Mr. Thanabalasingham during the IAD proceedings that he had knowingly made false representations in earlier proceedings to review his detention following his arrest in 2001.

The jurisprudence cited by the Minister does not support the proposition that, "where it appears that an applicant has not come to the Court with clean hands, the Court must initially determine whether in fact the party has unclean hands, and if that is proven, the Court *must* refuse to hear or grant the application on its merits." Rather, the case law suggests that, if satisfied that an applicant has lied, or is otherwise guilty of misconduct, a reviewing court may dismiss the application without proceeding to determine the merits or, even though having found reviewable error, decline to grant relief.

In exercising its discretion, the Court should attempt to strike a balance between, on the one hand, maintaining the integrity of, and preventing the abuse of, judicial and administrative processes, and, on the other, the public interest in ensuring the lawful conduct of government and the protection of fundamental human rights. The factors to be taken into account in this exercise include: the seriousness of the applicant's misconduct and the extent to which it undermines the proceeding in question; the need to deter others from similar conduct; the nature of the alleged administrative unlawfulness and the apparent strength of the case; the importance of the individual rights affected; and the likely impact upon the applicant if the administrative action impugned is allowed to stand.

These factors are not intended to be exhaustive, nor are they necessarily relevant in every case. While this discretion must be exercised on a judicial basis, an appellate court should not lightly interfere with a judge's exercise of the broad discretion afforded by public law proceedings and remedies.

In this case, the judge erred in the exercise of his discretion by failing to take into account the remedy provided to Mr. Thanabalasingham by his right to appeal to the IAD against his removal and the relevance of that appeal to an assessment of the consequences if the Minister's opinion stood. The appeal was allowed. The opinion of the Minister's delegate was restored. The consideration of the consequences of not determining the merits of an application for judicial review is within a judge's overall discretion with respect to the hearing of an application and the grant of relief.

*Chen v. Canada (Minister of Citizenship & Immigration)* (1999), 168 F.T.R. 179, 1999 CarswellNat 943 (Fed. T.D.) — The applicant sought to review a decision of the counsellor, the operations manager, of the Canadian High Commission in Singapore. The applicant submitted an application for permanent residence. At the time of this application, the applicant lived in Taiwan. The applicant listed her intended occupation as supervisor, Organization and Methods Analyst. After paper screening, an interview was scheduled. Based on the information provided in the interview, the visa officer concluded that the applicant had less than one year of experience which was the minimum required for assessment at the time of this application. In response to the refusal letter, the applicant wrote at length requesting a reversal of the visa officer's decision. Upon receiving no response the applicant contacted a Canadian lawyer who sent a fax to the regional program centre in Singapore asking for a review of the issues raised in the applicant's letters. The operations manager reviewed the applicant's correspondences and her lawyer's letter in addition to the entire file and also questioned the visa officer. In the result, the manager concluded that the officer's decision was reasonable and so informed the applicant.

The manager's decision was more than merely a courtesy response. The manager was very thorough in his review and this thoroughness clearly implied that his review was more than a matter of courtesy. The conclusion that the manager reached not to propose that the visa officer's decision be changed constituted a decision which was subject to review pursuant to s. 18.1 of the *Federal Court Act*.

On the merits the Court dismissed the application for judicial review.

*Henry Global Immigration Services v. Canada (Minister of Citizenship & Immigration)* (1998), 158 F.T.R. 110 (T.D.) — The applicant was advised by a visa officer at the Cana dian Consulate General in Hong Kong that all correspondence regarding the applicant's clients would be sent directly to the clients' residential addresses. The respondent advised this was being done due to the fact that over the past several months, "we have received a number of serious complaints from your clients . . .". This communication in a letter from the respondent to the applicant constituted a decision for purposes of an application for judicial review.

The Court found that the decision ran the risk of putting the applicant out of business, at least in relation to applicants for landing from the People's Republic of China and thus the applicant was found to have standing to bring an application for judicial review.

*Gonzalez c. Canada (Ministre de la Citoyenneté & de l'Immigration)* (1998), 1 Imm. L.R. (3d) 144, 158 F.T.R. 290 (T.D.) — This was an application to review the decision of a senior immigration officer. The officer informed the applicant by letter that the department could not take further action on her claim since her claim was ineligible under subs. 44(1) of the *Immigration Act.*

On June 6, 1997, prior to the letter in question being sent, a senior immigration officer had issued a departure order against the applicant which was not contested. The departure order was deemed to be a deportation order on July 17, 1997. The applicant claimed refugee status on July 30, 1997 and received the letter, dated August 15, 1997, which was the subject of this application, informing her that her claim was ineligible.

The application was dismissed on the basis that the letter in question was not a decision which may be reviewed by way of an application for judicial review.

*Cross v. Canada (Minister of Citizenship & Immigration)* (1996), 33 Imm. L.R. (2d) 251, 111 F.T.R. 304 (T.D.) — This was an application to review a decision of an immigration officer who arrested the applicant at the Vancouver pre-trial detention centre and removed him to the U.S. on the same date. The applicant, an American citizen, pleaded guilty to simple assault in the state of Vermont. Upon his release from the detention centre in that state, the applicant came to Canada. At this time, there was a warrant outstanding for the applicant in the state of Vermont. As well, the applicant was a prime suspect in a rape/murder investigation occurring in that state.

The issue of mootness is to be decided in two stages. The first stage requires consideration of whether a live controversy remains. The second stage applies if no live controversy remains. The court must then consider whether to exercise its discretion to hear the appeal, notwithstanding that it is moot. With respect to the second stage, there are three criteria for the exercise of the discretion to hear a matter. One, the existence of an adversarial context; two, the concern for judicial economy; and three, the need for the court to demonstrate a measure of awareness of its proper law-making function.

At the date of the hearing of this motion, the applicant was no longer under arrest by Canadian authorities. He had been freed and then immediately turned over to the U.S. authorities sometime earlier. The applicant's removal from Canada in no way altered his legal standing within Canada. There was therefore no live controversy in this matter. Further, there was no reason to believe that this was a case of a recurring nature. Accordingly, the court declined to hear the matter.

*Sivaraj v. Canada (Minister of Citizenship & Immigration)* (1996), 107 F.T.R. 64 (T.D.); affirmed [1996] F.C.J. No. 700, 1996 CarswellNat 1040 (Fed. C.A.) — The respondent was attempting to remove the applicant to Sri Lanka. The applicant applied for a stay of the execution of the removal order and the respondent took the position that the statement of claim, which the applicant had used to commence these proceedings, did not disclose a reasonable cause of action.

The applicants came to Canada from Sri Lanka. They unsuccessfully claimed refugee status with the result that removal orders were issued. The applicants then filed a statement of claim in order to obtain declaratory relief that the removal orders violated ss. 7 and 12 of the *Canadian Charter of Rights and Freedoms*, and that they contravened the *Geneva Conventions Act.*

The Minister's decision in determining the country of removal was, in fact, a decision made by a federal board, commission, or other tribunal within the meaning of s. 18, and is therefore subject to review under s. 18.1.

The applicants should not have proceeded by way of action to obtain declaratory relief under the *Charter*. The proper procedure was by way of application for judicial review. The Court has often, under the rules of judicial review, examined the constitutionality under the *Charter* of decisions made by federal boards.

The Court did, however, stay the execution of the removal orders, and to avoid a vacuum being created whereby the applicants would have no proceedings before the Court, the Court exercised its jurisdiction under rules 2 and 303 of the *Federal Court Rules* and presumed the proceedings to have been commenced as applications for judicial review.

*Thillaiyampalam v. Canada (Minister of Citizenship & Immigration)* (1994), 1994 CarswellNat 1622 (Fed. T.D.) — This application to set aside a negative determination of a panel of the CRDD was unsuccessful. Although the panel made errors on the face of its reasons, those errors did not "go to the heart of its conclusion that this applicant had, on the particular facts of his situation, a viable internal flight alternative". Accordingly, notwithstanding the errors, the application for judicial review was dismissed.

*Rodrigues v. Canada (Secretary of State)* (1994), 82 F.T.R. 111 (T.D.) — Pedro Rodrigues came from Brazil to Canada and made a refugee claim in 1987. He was subsequently ordered excluded. His application for judicial review was dismissed. In July, 1992, he married a Canadian citizen. John Rodrigues was born a little over a year later. In the spring of 1994, Immigration Canada advised that there were insufficient humanitarian and compassionate factors to intervene in a decision that Pedro Rodrigues must leave the country.

Pedro Rodrigues then brought the present proceedings under s. 18.1 of the *Federal Courts Act*. The infant son, John Rodrigues, was held to be a person directly affected under s. 18.1 of the *Federal Courts Act* and, therefore, an order was issued that he be joined as a party and that the style of cause be amended to reflect the addition of Assis John Rodrigues, a minor through his litigation guardian, Assis Pedro Rodrigues.

*Sitsabeshan v. Canada (Secretary of State)* (1994), 82 F.T.R. 29 (T.D.) — The applicants sought to review a negative determination of the CRDD. The Court found two findings of fact that were erroneous. It was not for the Court to speculate whether the CRDD would have reached the same conclusion if it had not erred in making those two findings of fact. If the decision of the CRDD might have been different, and in this case the Court was satisfied that it very well might have, then the decision of the CRDD will be set aside.

*Singh (R.) v. Canada (Secretary of State)* (1994), 27 Imm. L.R. (2d) 176, (sub nom. *Singh c. Canada (Secrétaire d'Etat))* 82 F.T.R. 68 (T.D.) — The applicant claimed refugee status in a false name. He later approached the Immigration Commission and properly identified himself and sought to have the Commission amend his name on the documents that had already been placed in his file. The Commission refused.

The decision refusing to amend documents in the applicant's file did not constitute a decision within the meaning of s. 18.1 of the *Federal Court Act* and, therefore, the Court had no jurisdiction to consider an application for judicial review of that decision.

*Chen v. Canada (Minister of Employment & Immigration)* (1994), 76 F.T.R. 235 — The applicant sought to overturn a negative decision of the CRDD. The tribunal accepted the applicant's testimony as trustworthy. In the course of giving its reasons, the tribunal misidentified the principal issue. The respondent urged that, despite this error, the conclusions of the tribunal were reasonable on the basis of the evidence before it and the decision as a whole was supportable.

The tribunal did err by not assessing the very basis claimed by the applicant as the grounds of his fear of persecution. While the evidence before the tribunal may be said to support the conclusion it reached, such an assessment is not for the Court on an application for judicial review. Aside from procedural issues, the Court, on a judicial review application, must be concerned with the decision rendered by the tribunal and the reasons expressed for its conclusion.

*Alfred v. Canada (Minister of Employment & Immigration)* (1994), 76 F.T.R. 231 — In this application to review a negative decision of the CRDD, the applicant argued that the tribunal erred in misconstruing "persecution" and that the tribunal erred in law by ignoring or misconstruing the evidence before it. The respondent made reference to portions of the transcript of the hearing and to the documentary evidence before the tribunal, which it argued would warrant the conclusion that the findings of the tribunal were reasonable. The Court must review the decision as rendered by the tribunal and not the evidence to which the decision itself makes no reference but which would have warranted the conclusions reached by the tribunal if the tribunal had expressed reasons relying upon such evidence. The simple statement that the tribunal had reached its decision "after careful consideration of all the evidence adduced at the hearing" was not sufficient when the decision made little or no reference to the principal basis of the applicant's claim. The application was allowed in this case and the matter sent back for rehearing before a differently constituted panel of the CRDD.

## Section 18.1(2)

*Brar v. Canada (Minister of Citizenship & Immigration)* (1997), 140 F.T.R. 163 (Fed. T.D.) — The applicant applied for permanent residence. The application was made in a self-employed category and his application was refused in January 1996. Counsel wrote to the visa officer in March 1996 asking for a review. Counsel wrote again in June, enclosing an affidavit from the applicant's cousin. In July 1996, the visa officer faxed a letter to counsel referring counsel to the refusal letter in January 1996. The July letter was a courtesy letter and did not constitute a decision as that phrase is employed in s. 18.1 of the *Federal Courts Act*.

The *Immigration Act* makes no provision for reconsideration of decisions by a visa officer. There is, however, a clear provision for judicial review of alleged errors. On the concept of *functus officio* and its application to administrative tribunals, the Court adopted the remarks of Sopinka J. in *Chandler v. The Association of Architects*, [1989] 2 S.C.R. 848 at p. 861. The application for judicial review was dismissed.

*Chan v. Canada (Minister of Citizenship & Immigration)*, [1996] F.C.J. No. 1393, 1996 CarswellNat 1876 (Fed. T.D.) — The applicant sought to review a decision of a visa officer refusing the applicant's application for permanent residence. This application for judicial review raises an issue of timeliness. The decision was made on October 23, 1995. The applicant's counsel, instead of proceeding to commence a judicial review application, elected to seek reconsideration. There was no evidence of reconsideration by the respondent. The applicant filed its application for judicial review on February 19, 1996, without seeking an extension of time until three weeks after the respondent had served its motion to dismiss.

The applicant's attempt to provoke a reconsideration from the respondent could not result in extending the date of the refusal and, accordingly, the application for judicial review was dismissed as being untimely.

*Soimu v. Canada (Secretary of State)* (1994), 83 F.T.R. 285 (T.D.) — In a letter dated February 8, 1994, a visa officer refused the applicant's application for permanent residence. On February 14, 1994, counsel for the applicant wrote to the visa officer requesting that she review her decision. On April 20, 1994, the visa officer replied. The April 20 letter, on the facts of this particular case, constitutes a decision by the visa officer and the applicant had, therefore, 30 days pursuant to s. 18.1 of the *Federal Courts Act*, to seek judicial review. The originating notice was filed on May 19, 1994, within 30 days. Accordingly, the respondent's motion to strike the applicant's originating notice of motion was dismissed.

The Court pointed out that the procedural difficulty occasioned in these proceedings might have been avoided if the applicant had sought judicial review of the February 8, 1994 decision in a timely manner. This would not have precluded the applicant from seeking a review by the visa officer. Had the April 20 letter not resulted from a true review, but merely been a "courtesy response", the applicant might well have been out of time to seek judicial review of the February 8, 1994 decision.

## Section 18.1(3)

*Bawa v. Canada (Minister of Citizenship & Immigration)* (2002), 19 Imm. L.R. (3d) 320, 2002 CarswellNat 637, 2002 CarswellNat 3402, 2002 FCT 300, 2002 CFPI 300 (Fed. T.D.) — The applicant's application for permanent residence was refused. The applicant was assessed at 67 points. An error was made under the education factor. Correction of this error resulted in the applicant receiving 69 points. The Court nevertheless ordered that the matter be sent back for reconsideration. The Court was not satisfied "that the error could have made no difference to the officer's decision". The Court declined to speculate on the ultimate disposition by the officer had she understood correctly the extent of the applicant's education in India.

*Lin v. Canada (Minister of Citizenship & Immigration)*, 2001 CarswellNat 2957, 2001 FCT 1368 (Fed. T.D.) — This was an appeal from the decision of the Appeal Division to dismiss an appeal from the issuance of a departure order against the applicants. The applicants were admitted from Taiwan as entrepreneurs and were granted conditional visas. They did not comply with the conditions in their visas and the department commenced an inquiry at which an adjudicator found that the conditions had not been obeyed. The Appeal Division of the IRB dismissed their appeal. An appeal by a person holding a visa to the Appeal Division of the IRB is a hearing *de novo*. The Federal Court in this proceeding was reviewing the Appeal Board's decision. The Court was not reviewing the administrative actions of the visa officer who interviewed the applicants for the purpose of determining whether they had complied with the terms and conditions of their visa. The Court will only review errors which were allegedly committed by the Board. It will not review an alleged breach of procedural fairness by the immigration officer who interviewed the applicants.

*Du v. Canada (Minister of Citizenship & Immigration)* (2001), 15 Imm. L.R. (3d) 64, 2001 FCT 485, 2001 CarswellNat 945 (Fed. T.D.) — The applicant sought to review the rejection of his application for permanent residence. The applicant objected to the units that were awarded for personal suitability. The visa officer had concerns stemming from the applicant's work for the same employer and lack of experience in a competitive labour market. This flowed from her own perception of the applicant's employment record. The officer's concerns were not shared with the applicant and accordingly, the applicant was denied procedural fairness.

The respondent argued that, despite this error, it was inconceivable that the applicant would have obtained the additional units for personal suitability that were required.

Reviewing courts have been warned not to withhold relief for a breach of the duty of fairness on the basis put forward by the respondent because it is dangerous to speculate on what might have happened if a person had been allowed to present relevant evidence and because of the importance of the values which underlie the duty of fairness.

*Mohamed v. Canada (Minister of Citizenship & Immigration)* (2000), 10 Imm. L.R. (3d) 90, 2000 CarswellNat 2551, 195 F.T.R. 137 (T.D.) — This was an application for *mandamus* and the question was whether the delay in processing the applicant's application was so unreasonable as to justify the granting of relief.

Each application for *mandamus* turns upon its own facts. Prior jurisprudence is not particularly helpful except for the purpose of outlining the parameters within which the Court has issued an order in the nature of *mandamus*, where it has found an unusual delay which has not been reasonably explained.

The conditions that have to be met for granting an order are:

1. The delay in question has been longer than the nature of the process required, *prima facie*;
2. The applicant and his counsel are not responsible for the delay; and
3. The authority responsible for the delay has not provided satisfactory justification.

*Gwala v. Canada (Minister of Citizenship & Immigration)*, [1999] 3 F.C. 404, 3 Imm. L.R. (3d) 26, 68 C.R.R. (2d) 48, 242 N.R.173, 1999 CarswellNat 908, 1999 F.C.J. No. 792 (C.A.) — Senior immigration officers do not have the implied jurisdiction to decide questions of law. The Trial Division of the Federal Court has jurisdiction in judicial review proceedings to decide constitutional questions which a senior immigration officer could not entertain.

*San Vicente Freitas v. Canada (Minister of Citizenship & Immigration)* (1999), 49 Imm. L.R. (2d) 33, (sub nom. *Freitas v. Canada (Minister of Citizenship & Immigration))* [1999] 2 F.C. 432, (sub nom. *Freitas v. Canada (Minister of Citizenship & Immigration))* 161 F.T.R. 310, 1999 CarswellNat 50 (T.D.) — These reasons arose out of an application for judicial review of a decision of a panel of the CRDD where they determined the applicant not to be a Convention refugee. The applicant was born in Trinidad, but moved to Venezuela at a very young age. In Venezuela he was a political activist. The applicant came to Canada in 1967 and became a landed immigrant. The applicant was steadily employed in Canada for a period of 10 years and then returned to Venezuela as a visitor in 1981. The applicant found conditions had changed and decided to remain there. After the presidential election in 1983, the applicant ceased any political activities in Venezuela and ultimately in 1986, obtained a false passport and returned to Canada. After being back in Canada, the applicant was convicted of a serious criminal offence and sentenced to nine years. The applicant claimed refugee status against Venezuela.

The applicant's claim was refused, and he applied for leave to review that decision. Leave was granted. However, an application to stay execution of the removal order was refused. The decision of the Supreme Court of Canada in *Pushpanathan v. Canada (Minister of Citizenship & Immigration)*, [1998] 1 S.C.R. 982, mandated that in this case the interpretation of the panel of Article 1F(c) of the Convention was wrong. Accordingly, the decision of the panel was set aside. The execution of the removal order did not render the judicial review proceedings moot.

The Court refused to provide a meaningless remedy in the form of a reference back to the CRDD for redetermination that could only be a determination that the applicant is not a Convention refugee because he is not outside the country of his nationality. Similarly, the Court was not prepared to order the respondent to return the applicant to Canada if the return of the applicant should prove to be unnecessary to an effective redetermination by the CRDD. The Court ordered that if the panel of the CRDD determined that it was necessary for the applicant to appear again to allow it to comply with the order of the Court directing a rehearing, the respondent was ordered forthwith to make best efforts to return the applicant to Canada at the respondent's expense. If the panel, without requiring the return of the applicant, working on the assumption that the applicant was in Canada, was able to determine that the applicant was a Convention refugee, then the respondent was ordered forthwith to make best efforts to return the applicant to Canada at the respondent's expense.

*Vuong v. Canada (Minister of Citizenship & Immigration)* (1998), 47 Imm. L.R. (2d) 129, 153 F.T.R. 207 (T.D.) — This was an application to review and set aside a decision of the Appeal Division wherein the applicant's appeal was dismissed for lack of jurisdiction. The applicant applied to sponsor his adopted daughter. In support of his application he obtained from the People's Committee of the Socialist Republic of Vietnam in the district where he formally resided and where the adoption took place, a document confirming that Xuan was his adopted daughter. The application for landing was refused on the grounds that there was no proof that Xuan was the legally adopted daughter of the applicant. Prior to the hearing before the Appeal Division, the applicant obtained further confirmation from the People's Court of the Socialist Republic of Vietnam that Xuan was his adopted daughter. Prior to the hearing of the appeal, the Minister had also made inquiries through the Canadian Embassy. The government of Vietnam replied that according to the present law of adoption, all adoptions were required to be approved by the People's Committee and recorded in the household register. Since the adoption of the applicant's daughter was not recorded in the household register, the Vietnamese government advised that it could not confirm that the child had been adopted. The Appeal Division determined that the daughter was not a member of the family class and dismissed the appeal for want of jurisdiction.

At the hearing, the Appeal Division had considered documentary evidence and it heard from four witnesses, one of whom was a former lawyer practicing in Vietnam between 1969 and 1975 in the area of public adoption. This witness made it quite clear that customary adoption was a usual and frequent practice among the Vietnamese people and that there was apparently a lax approach to making changes in the household registers. The panel of the Appeal Division found that the applicant's own attempts to have the register changed were genuine, but were thwarted by the nature of the administrative and bureaucratic processes.

The Court allowed the appeal and noted that it was the law applicable at the time of the adoption that was relevant for the purpose of determining whether there had been a valid adoption. The Court noted the uncontradicted evidence of the Vietnamese lawyer and then referred the matter back to a differently constituted panel of the Appeal Division with directions to find that Xuan was the adopted daughter and a member of the family class pursuant to s. 2 of the *Immigration Regulations*.

*Alleti c. Canada (Ministre de la Citoyenneté & de l'Immigration)* (1998), 147 F.T.R. 310 (T.D.) — The scope of the powers conferred on the Court under paragraph 18.1(3)(b) of the *Federal Courts Act* do not permit the Court to issue a visa to the applicant. The Court can set aside a visa officer's decision and refer the matter back for re-determination in accordance with certain directions. The Court cannot issue specific and conclusive directions with respect to the decision a visa officer must make, unless the conclusion is simple, obvious and inescapable. The directions that the Court is authorized to make will vary with the circumstances of each case. If facts remain to be established, it is the officer who must determine them. If the Court finds an error in law, all the visa officer can do is to act accordingly when re-determining the matter.

*Montenegro v. Canada (Minister of Citizenship & Immigration)* (1996), 108 F.T.R. 55 (T.D.) — This was a successful application for judicial review to set aside a negative decision of the CRDD. The applicant was 12 years old at the time the Court's decision was given. The applicant's mother and father married in 1988. They were ultimately divorced in 1992 after their arrival in Canada from El Salvador. The applicant lives with her mother and two younger brothers, both of whom were born in Canada. The applicant's mother married a Canadian citizen and did not want to return to El Salvador. The applicant's father remains in Canada, his claim for refugee status having been successful, but has little, or no, continuing relationship with the applicant or her sibling.

The Court felt it was appropriate to refer this matter for review by the Minister to determine whether or not the applicant should remain in Canada on humanitarian and compassionate grounds, or some other grounds in accordance with the *Immigration Act*. This review was to take place prior to a reconsideration of the applicant's refugee claim. In the event that there was no favourable administrative decision to permit the applicant to remain in Canada, the Court directed that her claim for refugee status be reconsidered by the CRDD.

*Marquez v. Canada (Minister of Citizenship & Immigration)* (1996), 32 Imm. L.R. (2d) 286 (Fed. T.D.) — The judge in this case reconsidered two of his own previous decisions and came to the conclusion that pursuant to s. 18.1(3) of the *Federal Courts Act*, the Court has jurisdiction, when allowing an application for judicial review, to provide directions for the decision maker who has to reconsider the matter, which directions may even be specific in relation to the ultimate outcome of the matter.

On the facts of this case, the Court declined to refer the matter for reconsideration with directions that the tribunal determine the applicant to be a Convention refugee. The record was not so clearly conclusive that the only possible conclusion on reconsideration was that the applicant was a Convention refugee, nor was the sole issue one of law which left the ultimate outcome uncontroverted.

*Abdullahi v. Canada (Minister of Citizenship & Immigration)*, [1996] F.C.J. No. 31, 1996 CarswellNat 31 (Fed. T.D.) — The applicants sought to overturn a negative decision of a panel of the IRB. After determining that there was at least one instance in which there was no evidence to support the Board's conclusion, the Court then had to consider what would be the disposition of the judicial review application.

The Court concluded that once the Board's decision is based on a substantial error, which if it had not been made, might have caused the Board to decide otherwise, the decision of the Board should be quashed and referred back for reconsideration by another panel.

In this case the Court found the errors to be substantial and that the decision of the Board might have been different had it not made those errors and, accordingly, the application was allowed.

*Turanskaya v. Canada (Minister of Citizenship & Immigration)* (1995), 111 F.T.R. 314 (T.D.); affirmed (1997), 145 D.L.R. (4th) 259, 125 F.T.R. 240 (note), 210 N.R. 235 (C.A.) — The applicant was found by a panel of the CRDD to be a stateless person.

The respondent conceded that the Board had erred in law in requiring the applicant to demonstrate a well-founded fear of persecution in respect of both countries of former habitual residence.

The applicant had asked the Court to refer the matter back to the Board, with a direction that it declare the applicant to be a Convention refugee.

There will sometimes be situations in which by giving specific directions, the Court will be able to accomplish indirectly what it is not authorized to do directly. It will be able to compel the Board to reach a specific conclusion, thereby, in effect, substituting its decision for that made by the Board. Specific directions of this type are within the jurisdiction of the Court.

The discretion to give directions should be exercised in the context of the Board's decision. The Court should not go behind that decision on matters unrelated to the error brought forward on judicial review.

But for the error which caused the Board to require the applicant to demonstrate a well-founded fear in respect of both countries of former habitual residence, the Board would have declared the applicant to be a Convention refugee.

Accordingly, the Court issued an order directing the Board to declare the applicant to be a Convention refugee.

*Memarpour v. Canada (Minister of Citizenship & Immigration)* (1995), 104 F.T.R. 55 — At the opening of the hearing of the applicant's refugee claim, the presiding Board member made a statement which indicated that certain evidence about events in Iran was accepted for purposes of the hearing. The Board then, in rendering its decision, made an adverse credibility finding in respect of those events. This was held to be a failure of natural justice. There is no general duty to confront a witness with issues of credibility. Such a requirement exists if credibility becomes an issue for the Board when it has previously been deleted by the Board as a relevant issue.

Having decided that there was a denial of a fair hearing, the Court then must ask itself whether it is nonsensical and contrary to notions of finality and the effective use of public funds and the Board's resources to require a re-hearing. The Court relied upon *Mobile Oil Canada Ltd. v. Canada-Newfoundland Off Shore Petroleum Board*, [1994] 1 S.C.R. 202 at p. 205. In this case, the Court concluded that even if the applicant were to be believed about the events in Iran which were the subject matter of the application, a panel of the IRB would certainly conclude that the applicant did not have a subjective fear of persecution. In those circumstances, the application was dismissed.

*Efremov v. Canada (Minister of Citizenship & Immigration)* (1995), 90 F.T.R. 259 (T.D.) — The applicant sought to quash a negative decision of a panel of the CRDD. In order to quash a decision it must be shown that the Board made an error which was material to the decision. The cumulative effect of a number of errors can also constitute a material error. A microscopic examination of the reasons for the decision is not appropriate. The word "patently" adds nothing to the applicable test. For a decision to be unreasonable it must be plain and obvious that it is so.

*Argueta v. Canada (Minister of Employment & Immigration)*, 1994 CarswellNat 1582 (Fed. T.D.) — The applicant sought judicial review contending that the trier of fact had made three errors of law which warranted the setting aside of the decision. The respondent conceded that the law had been misstated or misapplied in two respects, but suggested that applying the law correctly would support the conclusion of the tribunal and, implicitly, that the same result would follow any reconsideration of the matter. In an application for judicial review, aside from procedural issues, the jurisdiction of the Court is concerned with the decision as it has been rendered, not with a decision that might have been but was not given. The Court may review the evidence before the tribunal only in relation to the decision rendered. It is not for the Court to assess what its decision might be on the evidence before the tribunal nor to speculate on the result if the matter is referred back for reconsideration, the outcome of which will be dependent upon the evidence and argument then before the reconsidering tribunal.

*Ali v. Canada (Minister of Employment & Immigration)* (1994), 24 Imm. L.R. (2d) 289, 76 F.T.R. 182, [1994] 3 F.C. 73, 27 Admin. L.R. (2d) 110 — Section 18.1(3) of the *Federal Courts Act* provides jurisdiction for the Court to issue directions of such specificity that they require the CRDD to declare an applicant to be a Convention refugee.

The Court should only exercise this jurisdiction after asking itself questions of this type:

1. Is the evidence on the record so clearly conclusive that the only possible conclusion is that the claimant is a Convention refugee?
2. Is the sole issue to be decided a pure question of law which will be dispositive of the case?
3. Is the legal issue based on uncontroverted evidence and accepted facts?
4. Is there a factual issue that involves conflicting evidence which is central to the claim?

*Popov v. Canada (Minister of Employment & Immigration)* (1994), 75 F.T.R. 90 (T.D.) — The applicant emigrated to Israel from Russia under the Law of Return. He was entitled to do so because one of his grandparents was Jewish. He suffered discrimination in Israel because he was a new immigrant from Russia and because, while he was Jewish as a matter of racial ancestry, he was a member of the Russian Orthodox Christian church. The applicant applied for refugee status in Canada. The CRDD did not accept his claim, but that decision was rendered before the Supreme Court decision in *Ward v. Canada (Minister of Employment & Immigration)*, (sub nom. *Canada (Attorney General) v. Ward*) [1993] 2 S.C.R. 689 and the Federal Court decision in *Zolfagharkhani v. Canada (Minister of Employment & Immigration)*, [1993] 3 F.C. 540, 20 Imm. L.R. 1, 155 N.R. 311 (C.A.).

The application was dismissed from the bench due to the fact that notwithstanding the errors complained of, no properly instructed Board could have found the applicant to be a Convention refugee. The authority of the Court on a judicial review application is not the same as on an appeal. Even though one might find errors in a Board's decision, that does not, on a judicial review application, result in a decision to send the matter back for rehearing when the Court is convinced that no real purpose will be served by so doing. One does not quash and send it back just for the sake of having a new hearing. When it is clear from the evidence on the record and from the decision that no different result could be reached, the appropriate course of action is to refuse an order requiring that such be done.

The Court noted that the intertwined nature of "appeals" and "judicial review" was found in a recent paper by Madame Justice Desjardins: *Review of Administrative Action in the*

*Federal Court of Canada: The New Style in a Pluralistic Setting*, Law Society of Upper Canada Special Lectures, 1992, at 404.

*Xie v. Canada (Minister of Employment & Immigration)* (1994), 75 F.T.R. 125 — The Court's jurisdiction on applications for judicial review is found in s. 18.1(3) of the *Federal Courts Act*. There is nothing in the subs. that indicates that the Court has the jurisdiction to substitute its opinion for that of the tribunal whose decision is under judicial review and make the decision that the tribunal should have made. As such words do not appear in the Act, the Court does not have jurisdiction to substitute its decision for that of the tribunal in a judicial review application.

The Court does have jurisdiction to refer a matter back for redetermination in accordance with such directions as it considers appropriate. The Court should only issue directions to a tribunal in the nature of a directed verdict where the case is straightforward and the decision of the Court on the judicial review would be dispositive of the matter before the tribunal.

*Siad v. Canada (Minister of Employment & Immigration)* (1993), 21 Imm. L.R. (2d) 6, 64 F.T.R. 271 — This was an application for a judicial review of the decision of the CRDD determining that the applicant was not a Convention refugee.

Two errors of law were cited: (1) the Refugee Division erred by not correctly identifying the social group to which the applicant belonged in deciding that her claim did not come within a group recognized in the definition; and (2) it erred in finding that her fear was not related to being a member of the social group that the Board placed her in.

These errors, if that is what they were, were not errors of law. The Refugee Division addressed the question of whether or not the applicant fell within a particular social group but did not identify that group correctly based on the evidence. Such an error is not an error in law. Similarly, a finding that an applicant's fear is based on a fear of random violence and is not a fear arising from being a member of a social group, may be an error, but it is not an error of law. Further, in this case, these findings of fact could not be characterized as having been made in a perverse or capricious manner or without regard to the material before the tribunal. Accordingly, the judicial review application was dismissed.

*Nueda v. Canada (Minister of Employment & Immigration)* (1993), 21 Imm. L.R. (2d) 211, 65 F.T.R. 24 — The applicant came to Canada on the Foreign Domestic Programme. She was negatively reviewed in November 1983 and December 1984. She did not leave Canada when her employment authorization expired and a warrant for her arrest was executed in October 1987. The applicant claimed refugee status and obtained a work permit and she was employed from July 1988 to June 24, 1992.

It was found that there were no humanitarian and compassionate considerations in her case and a departure notice was issued requiring her to leave Canada by August 1992.

The Court emphasized that it was its responsibility to review the decision of the officers but that it was not sitting in appeal from that decision. The officers had all of the information before them and it could not be found that they had ignored any of it.

Counsel submitted that where a *prima facie* case of a *Charter* infringement has been made out, the Court must substantially review the decision and go beyond the common law grounds of judicial review. The Court agreed with this submission. It found, however, in this case that no *Charter* right of the applicant had been breached. The Court went on to observe that even where there is a substantive review of a decision, s. 18.1(3) of the *Federal Courts Act* still governs the Trial Division's power on judicial review. In terms of a humanitarian and compassionate review, the Trial Division can direct that the review be conducted and that certain factors or directions be considered. It is not for the Court to conduct a review, but simply to indicate what is required to make a proper decision.

## Section 18.1(4)

*Abbasi v. Canada (Minister of Citizenship & Immigration)* (2010), 88 Imm. L.R. (3d) 174, 2010 FC 288, 2010 CarswellNat 1675, 2010 CarswellNat 560 (F.C.) — The applicant challenged a refusal of a visa officer to grant him a permanent resident visa as a member of the family class. The applicant was a Pakistan national being sponsored for landing in Canada by his wife. The refusal of the sponsorship application was based on the finding that the marriage was not genuine. Two grounds were advanced for setting aside the visa officer's decision: the finding that the marriage is not genuine is unreasonable; and that the process applied to reaching the decision offends the *Official Languages Act*, R.S.C. 1985, c. 31 ($4^{th}$ Supp.), because the visa officer's interview of the applicant was conducted in Urdu.

The circumstances of the marriage were unusual which, not surprisingly, raised suspicion. But the unusual circumstances should give cause for very careful consideration. A marriage is a union between two individuals, and where suspicion exists as to the genuineness of the union because an expected standard of conduct is not met, to fairly and properly deal with the suspicion, the evidence of each individual must be carefully considered. There is no evidence on the record that the visa officer provided the applicant's spouse with an opportunity to give her evidence with respect to the quality of the marriage before the decision under review was made. In a case such as this, the visa officer was required to interview both the applicant and his spouse by the best means available whether by teleconference, video conference, or personal interview. The decision under review was unreasonable.

In this case there was no breach of the *Official Languages Act*. The interview was conducted in Urdu at the applicant's request. This choice was confirmed by the visa officer at the opening of the interview. No interpreter was required as the visa officer was fluent in this language. The applicant argued that as a matter of law the visa officer was required to conduct the interview in either English or French through an interpreter who could interpret the visa officer's questions to the applicant in Urdu and his answers back in English or French to the visa officer.

Section 20(1) of the *Charter* provides a right to any member of the public in Canada to communicate with and receive available services from federal institutions in English and French. This right imposes an obligation and practical requirement on federal institutions to comply with the right. This rights based concept does not inhibit federal institutions to offer services in languages other than English or French if the members of the public involved do not wish to exercise their right under s. 20(1) of the *Charter*, and, indeed wish to conduct business in any other language to which the institution's officials are capable of reliably communicating without an interpreter. This point was made by Justice Pinard in *Toma v. Canada (Minister of Citizenships & Immigration)*, [2006] F.C.J. No.

1000 at paragraph 33 where a visa officer conducted an interview in Arabic without an interpreter:

> If the officer speaks the applicant's language — as was the case here — it would be strange indeed for the officer to use an interpreter. There would be no need to do so. The preferable options, as the Manual suggests [Overseas Processing Manual (OP) 5], is to conduct the interview in the applicant's language.

The application for judicial review was allowed on the first ground. The following question was certified:

> Is it a breach of the *Official Languages Act* for a visa officer to conduct an interview with respect to a visa application when, at the applicant's request, the language of the interview was other than English or French and the visa officer is able to comply with the request?

*Zhong v. Canada (Minister of Citizenship & Immigration)* (2009), 350 F.T.R. 43 (Eng.), 2009 FC 632, 2009 CarswellNat 1867 (F.C.) — This application exposes a fundamental fault in the refugee claim process applied at the time the applicant made his initial statements claiming refugee protection. The initial interview was conducted through a Cantonese interpreter. The applicant gave his statements in Cantonese which were in turn given in English by the interpreter and written in English by the interviewing officer. No independent means, such as a recording, was used to verify what was said by either the applicant or the interpreter, or whether the interviewing officer's writing accurately recorded what the Cantonese interpreter said. This "Record of Examination" is the centre of a fundamental controversy in the present application. Following the preparation of the Personal Information Form (PIF) by the applicant with the help of legal counsel, the Record of Examination was made available to the applicant and his counsel. The applicant immediately asserted to his counsel that the Record of Examination did not correctly record what he said in the interview, and, as a result, counsel for the applicant made this known to the Refugee Protection Division well in advance of the hearing. Nevertheless, the RPD Member who conducted the hearing chose to use the Record of Examination as accurate and relied on the statements made in it to find contradictions between it and the PIF and oral evidence produced at the hearing. This process resulted in a negative credibility finding made against the applicant. This process constituted a breach of due process.

In the absence of a verifiable record of what was said by the applicant at his interview, it is a breach of due process for the RPD to have accepted the Record of Examination as accurate in the face of the applicant's sworn statement that it was not accurate. The Record of Examination is the result of a fundamentally flawed record keeping process and should not be used with respect to the applicant's claim for refugee protection. The application for judicial review was allowed. Counsel for the respondents requested a question for certification, however, the applicant objected and the Court agreed that the finding of breach of due process in the present case was based on the facts.

*Kamtasingh v. Canada (Minister of Citizenship & Immigration)* (2010), 87 Imm. L.R. (3d) 118, 2010 FC 45, 2010 CarswellNat 801, 2010 CarswellNat 101 (F.C.) — This was an application for judicial review challenging a decision of the Immigration Appeal Division which determined the applicant's marriage was not genuine. The applicant states that the IAD member denied him procedural fairness by preventing him from calling all of his proposed witnesses.

The IAD has the right to limit repetitive testimony, but not by effectively excluding witnesses who could offer evidence going to the central issues of the case. The place to control excessive or repetitive evidence on issues of controversy which are central or determinate is generally not at the entrance to the witness box, but once the witness is testifying — and even then the member must grant some latitude to ensure that all important matters are covered. The IAD can, of course, limit the scope of evidence by stipulating certain points that are not in dispute. In a case like this one where the credibility of the applicant is clearly an issue and where the genuineness of a marriage is in doubt, the evidence of immediate family and close acquaintances is highly relevant and should be heard without reservation. Indeed, it was difficult to see how this matter could be fairly determined after only two hours of evidence, particularly when the applicant was self-represented and was initially intending to lead evidence from several witnesses. This was a situation where the duty to allow the applicant to fully present his case was sacrificed for the desire for administrative efficiency. That is not a permissible trade-off. The application for judicial review was allowed.

*Khan v. Canada (Minister of Citizenship & Immigration)* (2009), 88 Imm. L.R. (3d) 61, 2009 FC 1312, 2009 CarswellNat 5532, 2009 CarswellNat 4569 (F.C.) — The applicant applied for a permanent resident visa as a federal skilled worker. He only listed English, and professed no proficiency in French. The application needed to be accompanied by test results by an accredited language institution or by other evidence in writing of the applicant's proficiency in his selected language. The High Commission requested further documentation and strongly advised the applicant to provide the International English Language Testing System (IELTS) test results. The applicant was unable to secure a seat for the exam until February 2009. He requested a 60-day extension, through his consultant, to supply the IELTS test results. The CAIPS notes reflect the request but do not state if the consultant gave a reason for the request. The refusal to grant an extension of time was unreasonable. Administrative efficiency is important, and necessary. The underlying consideration on an application to extend time is that justice be done. Consideration should be given to the reason for the requested delay and whether there is an arguable case on the merits. Certainly the applicant had a continuing intention to pursue his application, his application had some merit, there was no prejudice to the Minister arising from the delay and a reasonable explanation existed. Thus the decision arises from procedural unfairness, upon which no deference is owed. However, in any event, the decision on the merits not to award any points for English language ability was also unreasonable. The applicant obtained both an undergraduate degree and a Masters of Administration in England, and had worked in Dubai for a number of years in English. The Regulation does not require an IELTS report and so the visa officer failed to discharge his duty by not accessing the material which was on hand. Not only did the applicant study in the UK, he was awarded 25 out of 25 points for education. It was "ludicrous" to suggest that someone who has obtained both an undergraduate and a Master's degree in England from an English language university has no ability in the English language. The application for judicial review was allowed.

*Zhang v. Canada (Minister of Citizenship & Immigration)* (2010), 89 Imm. L.R. (3d) 75, 2010 FC 75, 2010 CarswellNat 118 (F.C.) — The question for determination was whether the applicant had created a reasonable expectation that important written communication would only be conducted by regular mail. Although the language of the visa application form and the use of representative form could be more clear with respect to the potential use of e-mail communication, when those documents are considered together, no reasonable expectation could arise that the Embassy would not use e-mail to communicate with the applicant's lawyer; even if such an expectation could arise it was surely displaced when the lawyer received an e-mail from the Embassy and did nothing about it at the time. The application for judicial review was dismissed.

*Kaur v. Canada (Minister of Citizenship & Immigration)*, [2009] F.C.J. No. 1530, 2009 FC 935, 2009 CarswellNat 3870, 2009 CarswellNat 4918 (F.C.) — This application for judicial review challenges a decision to refuse the applicant's request for a skilled worker visa. The applicant failed to provide additional evidence to support the application as requested by the Canadian High Commission because of an apparent failed communication between them.

The assumption that the High Commission would continue to communicate by regular mail was, as the facts attest, a dangerous one. It was not reasonable to expect the High Commission to figure out from the absence of an e-mail address on the last communication that his e-mail was no longer functioning. This was a risk which the applicant and her Canadian representative could have avoided by the simple step of advising the High Commission that the previously identified e-mail address was no longer valid, just as the representative had done for his postal address. E-mail is, after all, a standard method of business communication. It is fast, efficient and reliable and it is not unreasonable or unfair for the High Commission to have relied upon it. In these circumstances the failed e-mail delivery was solely caused by the repreentative's unwarranted assumption and by the failure to provide complete and accurate contact information to the High Commission.

In summary, when a communication is correctly sent by a visa officer to an address (e-mail or otherwise) that has been provided by an applicant which has not been revoked or revised and where there has been no indication received that the communication may have failed, the risk of non-delivery rests with the applicant and not with the respondent.

*Sebahtu v. Canada (Minister of Citizenship & Immigration)*, 2010 FC 200, 2010 CarswellNat 1136, 2010 CarswellNat 408 (F.C.) — This was a judicial review of a decision denying the applicant a permanent resident's visa on the grounds that she was a security risk pursuant to s. 34(1)(f) of IRPA. The applicant was already a UN Convention Refugee living in Sudan having fled Ethiopia with her family. Her husband was a member of the Ethiopian Democratic Union (EDU), a group which had fought against the Derg regime in the 1970s. The applicant had a UN form filled out — she being illiterate — which indicated that she had fled Ethiopia in 1977 and her husband in 1978. The form also indicated that she had been a member of the EDU, had participated in meetings and made financial contributions. The applicant contended that she was never a member of the EDU but had merely supported her husband. The visa officer held that the applicant was not forthcoming about her EDU membership and therefore denied her application.

It is within the purview of a visa officer to make a credibility finding but the reasons for that decision must disclose, even in a summary way, the basis for the adverse findings. This is an issue which goes to the fairness of the process and the reasonableness of the result. The second difficulty in this case was the fairness of the process particularly as regards to the translation of her narrative. On the balance of probabilities, there was confusion in the translation — not the fault of either party. Nevertheless it resulted in an unfair process and an unfairness which had serious consequences. The application for judicial review was allowed.

*Healey v. Canada (Minister of Citizenship & Immigration)* (2009), 80 Imm. L.R. (3d) 138, 2009 CarswellNat 891, 2009 FC 355 (F.C.) — This was an application for judicial review of a decision of a visa officer refusing the applicant's application for permanent residence under the federal skilled worker category. There was an error made on the applicant's application in that two years of college were not accurately indicated in the educational history boxes on the application form. The applicant accidentally wrote "0" instead of "2" in the box labeled "University/College." The officer concluded that the applicant had only completed 13 years of education, and 15 points was appropriate. Counsel for the applicant attempted to clarify the mistake but received no response.

It was not possible to tell from the record why the officer felt the applicant only had 13 years of education, and the fact that the officer had recently provided a detailed affidavit justifying his calculations is a clear confirmation that the letter and CAIPS notes do not explain that issue. The officer's affidavit was given no weight by the Court as it went well beyond an elaboration of the reasons and instead provided an after-the-fact rationale for the central issue in this application concerning the way that the points were calculated.

In all the circumstances of this case, the reasons were inadequate. This was a decision of importance for the applicant's future. He could not surmise from the decision why the Thurrock and BTEC certificates had been awarded 0 points. The officer's position was simply that he had no obligation to explain to the applicant why he had taken a position on the facts that the two certificates in question would not be credited. This prevented any understanding or questioning of the officer's position on the facts. It was a denial of the applicant's right to comprehend why he had been refused and an attempt to thwart any action he might take to question the officer's decision. It left him to choose between incomprehension and legal action. In fairness to the applicant, he should have the matter reviewed by someone else who will explain to him what his certificates represent and how they merit, or do not merit, points under the Regulations. A simple explanation by the officer could have prevented what became a significant waste of time and resources on both sides. The application for judicial review was allowed.

*Shapovalov v. Canada (Minister of Citizenship & Immigration)* (August 27, 2007), IMM-784-06 (F.C.) — The applicant sought judicial review of an immigration officer's decision to refuse the applicant's request to have counsel present at his inadmissibility interview. The respondent relied primarily on the fact that the questions posed to the applicant were not of a legal or complex nature and did not warrant the presence of counsel at the interview. The Court held that other factors identified by the applicant outweighed this consideration. Specifically, this interview was not occurring at the early stages of the process, since the applicant had previously been interviewed and a finding had been made that he met the selection criteria; the interview was to determine whether he was inadmissible and was a last crucial step in the process. Further, the rejection of an application on the ground of inadmissibility identified in this case may well hinder any future chance of success and therefore was of importance to the applicant. Thirdly, permitting counsel to attend in these circumstances to observe would not unduly encumber the efficient administration of the process. Finally, given the nature of the inquiry at which the questions were directed coupled with the fact that the application had already been the subject of a judicial review proceeding weighed in favour of concluding that the duty of fairness in these circumstances encompasses the right to have counsel present at the interview. The application for judicial review was allowed.

*Chadha v. Canada (Minister of Citizenship & Immigration)*, 2008 CarswellNat 294, 2008 CarswellNat 1119, 2008 FC 170 — A visa officer is not obligated to take the initiative to transfer a file where there is no request. Had the applicant made a clear and reasoned request for the interview to be held in the applicant's home country, for example, this might well have been done. In *obiter*, the Court indicated that the visa officer did propose one option — the withdrawal of the application and the submission of a new application — and therefore the possibility of simply arranging an interview at a different office could have been suggested.

*da Silva v. Canada (Minister of Citizenship & Immigration)* (2007), 68 Imm. L.R. (3d) 312, 2007 CarswellNat 4883, 2007 CarswellNat 5486, 2007 FC 1138 — The duty to provide reasons is lower in the context of applications for temporary residence status. A number of factors would suggest that the duty to provide reasons is minimal: the applicant has no legal right to obtain a visa, and bears the burden of establishing the merits of his claim; the refusal of a work permit on an application from outside of Canada has less impact on the applicant than would the removal of a benefit; and the officer is better placed to evaluate the cultural and economic benefits of the applicant's prospective employment than the applicant.

*Tantash v. Canada (Minister of Citizenship & Immigration)*, 2008 CarswellNat 1366, 2008 FC 565 — The applicant sought judicial review of a decision to refuse his application for permanent residence in Canada under the economic skilled workers class, on the ground that he had not submitted the requested documents and was therefore inadmissible. Although the applicant made a request for an extension of time to submit an FBI clearance, at no time did the applicant attempt to provide the officer with reasons for the lengthy wait in providing the FBI clearance, nor did he provide her with any timeframe in which he anticipated receiving the documents.

The refusal resulted from the applicant's failure to provide the officer with the evidence and documents that were reasonably required. Reasonable timeframes must be respected in order to allow that applications be processed in an expeditious manner. Therefore, the officer's decision to refuse the application and refuse any further extension of time was free of any breach of procedural fairness or natural justice.

*Level (Litigation Guardian of) v. Canada (Minister of Public Safety & Emergency Preparedness)* (2008), 71 Imm. L.R. (3d) 52, 2008 CarswellNat 423, 2008 FC 227 (F.C.) — This was an application for judicial review of an enforcement officer's decision to deny the applicant's request for a deferral of removal pending a decision on his application for permanent residence based on an H&C application.

An enforcement officer is statutorily bound to remove an applicant as soon as reasonably practical. However, if the officer relies on extrinsic evidence not brought forward by the applicant, the applicant must be given an opportunity to respond to that evidence. This is a minimal duty of procedural fairness. In the application at bar, the enforcement officer relied on detailed evidence about medical conditions in Jamaica that the applicant contested in an affidavit filed in support of the applicant's successful motion for a stay of removal. With respect to tight timeframes, the applicant has been in Canada for 20 years, and the duty of fairness should not be sacrificed because of an artificial deadline established by the respondent for the applicant's removal. There is no harm in allowing the applicant another week or two in order to respond to extrinsic evidence upon which the enforcement officer intends to rely. If that extrinsic evidence is incorrect, the applicant will suffer great harm. The application for judicial review was allowed.

*Thandal v. Canada (Minister of Citizenship & Immigration)*, 2008 CarswellNat 1085, 2008 CarswellNat 1958, 2008 FC 489 — The applicant sought judicial review of a decision to refuse her application for permanent residence as a skilled worker and her H&C application from outside Canada. With the Supreme Court of Canada's decision in *New Brunswick (Board of Management) v. Dunsmuir*, 2008 SCC 9, it is settled that procedural fairness is to be reviewed on a correctness standard while the H&C decision is to be reviewed on a reasonableness standard. The reasonableness standard admits a range of reasonable outcomes. The Court was aware that an H&C decision is discretionary, an exception to the normal rules. The officer, by virtue of familiarity and having interviewed the applicant, was in an excellent position to assess the merits of the applicant's story.

It is well established that an applicant has the burden of establishing her case. Generally, an applicant is to do that once, rather than on the basis of some sort of rolling story of reply, sur-reply and so forth. The applicant had an interview at which all the relevant issues were canvassed. There is nothing unfair in the officer deciding the case on the evidence as provided by the applicant at that time. The judicial review was dismissed.

*Zheng v. Canada (Minister of Citizenship & Immigration)*, 2008 CarswellNat 1864, 2008 CarswellNat 880, 2008 FC 430 — A visa officer rejected an application for landing by a skilled worker from China. The visa officer's entry in the CAIPS system identifies a stark conflict in the evidence the applicant tendered in obvious error: the standard application form was completed to say that the applicant attended Kunming University at the same time she completed high school there, which, of course, is impossible. Because of the conflict, and the fact that the applicant failed to file a diploma to prove her attendance at the university, the applicant's application was rejected. It was remarkably unfair for the visa officer not to have asked for clarification of the obvious error which drove the rejection of the applicant's application. The visa officer's decision was set aside.

*Mekonen v. Canada (Minister of Citizenship & Immigration)* (2007), 66 Imm. L.R. (3d) 222, 2007 CarswellNat 3655, 2007 FC 1133 (F.C.) — Mr. Mekonen brought an application for judicial review of a decision of a visa officer that, as a member of the Eritrean Liberation Front, Mr. Mekonen was captured by paragraph 34(1)(f) of the IRPA, and therefore was inadmissible to Canada. The Court found that the officer should have provided Mr. Mekonen with a CBSA memorandum and an open source document, to allow Mr. Mekonen to make submissions that were responsive to that material. The Court adopted the Federal Court of Appeal decision in *B. (S.) v. Canada (Minister of Citizenship & Immigration)*, 2001 CarswellNat 2008, that the question is not whether the report is or contains extrinsic evidence of facts unknown to the person affected by the decision, but whether the disclosure of the report is required to provide the person with a reasonable opportunity to participate in a meaningful manner in the decision-making process. In this case, meaningful participation included the right to highlight weaknesses in the material before the officer. Because the officer breached the duty of procedural fairness, the application for judicial review was allowed.

*Garro v. Canada (Minister of Citizenship & Immigration)* (2007), 67 Imm. L.R. (3d) 263, 2007 CarswellNat 1827, 2007 CarswellNat 4509, 2007 FC 670 — This was an application for judicial review of a decision of an immigration officer, refusing the application for a work permit for the applicant and visitor status for his family. The immigration officer concluded that the applicant failed to meet the conditions required to obtain investor status under the North American Free Trade Agreement. The letter of refusal that the officer sent contained no reasons explaining why the application was denied. The officer's notes revealed that he did not consider the initial sum of $20,000 to be a substantial investment for purposes of granting the applicant a permit. However, the evidence in the record showed that the applicant invested $166,000 in commercial premises for the company, $67,000 in book stocks to sell and thousands of dollars in equipment. Given that the applicant's evidence was so compelling, the Court concluded that there was absolutely no reason for the officer's decision and allowed the judicial review.

*Somasundram v. Canada (Minister of Citizenship & Immigration)* (2006), 56 Imm. L.R. (3d) 105, 2006 CarswellNat 2180, 2006 FC 925 (F.C.) — The applicant, a single, Tamil female citizen of Sri Lanka, fled Colombo where she was seized and detained by the police who abused her and demanded information as to the warring factions in her local area. Upon her release by the police she fled to Canada claiming refugee protection. Once in Canada, she took up residence with relatives in the Toronto area, has been steadily employed as a cashier in a local business and settled into the community without incident. Her refugee claim was rejected in July of 2001 and in November 2001 she made a claim for exemption from visa requirements on humanitarian and compassionate grounds. This application was dismissed in October 2005 and she sought judicial review of that decision.

The application for judicial review was allowed on the basis that the reasons for the decision did not stand up to a reasonably probative examination as required. The Court found that the last of the quotations from the reasons were nothing more than a recital of the general categories of materials reviewed following which was a recital of the criteria set out by the guidelines and of the decision made. The reasons failed to address any consideration given to the major points at issue. No issues were stated, no points of evidence were discussed, and no explanation of the thought process engaged by the officers was given.

*Sandhu v. Canada (Minister of Citizenship & Immigration)* (2006), 55 Imm. L.R. (3d) 203, 2006 CarswellNat 2360, 2006 FC 941 (F.C.) — The principal applicant, a citizen of India, was sponsored for permanent residence by her daughter in Canada. The applicant included in her permanent residence application her dependant children. Following an interview, the immigration officer expressed concerns about the application because two of the children did not have birth certificates and, in addition, supporting letters issued by the particular public school had, in the past, been found to be fraudulent. Following the interview, the applicant wrote to the Canadian High Commission responding to the concerns regarding the school certificates. She attached documentary evidence corroborating that the school documents provided were genuine. These documents were received by the Canadian High Commission on May 10, 2005. The immigration officer allegedly reviewed all the information in the file, including the post-interview information, and in June 2005 sent the file to the Canadian High Commission Visa Section with her recommendation that the application for permanent residence be refused on the grounds that the applicant had misrepresented or withheld material facts. The application was refused for those reasons. There was no mention of the post-interview documents in the refusal letter.

The applicant sought leave for judicial review of the decision. The respondent took the position that the applicant had misaddressed the correspondence and post-interview documents and therefore had not proven that the Canadian High Commission ever received those post-interview documents. Leave was granted and during the subsequent judicial review proceedings, including the necessary cross-examination of the respondent's representatives, the respondent admitted that it had had the documents from the very time that the applicant had claimed. The respondent, having been "caught out", turned its argument around and through evidence and submission claimed that the documents were considered and given no weight. The immigration officer currently claimed that she had read the documents and gave them no weight — the visa officer could not recall the evidence but said that it would have had made no difference to his decision.

The failure to cite this material in the decision letter counters any weight that might be given to the officer's evidence that the material was considered. For this reason alone, the judicial review was granted. The applicant also asked for costs because of the respondent's conduct of this matter. The Court concluded that the respondent's conduct was misleading to the applicant and was simply unacceptable. Therefore, "special reasons" under Rule 22 of the *Federal Courts Immigration and Refugee Protection Rules* were shown to justify an award of costs. The applicant was awarded solicitor-client costs of the whole of the matter.

*Velasquez v. Canada (Minister of Citizenship & Immigration)*, 2006 CarswellNat 2616, 2006 FC 1024 (F.C.) — A decision to deny the applicant a visa to enter Canada as a permanent resident was set aside, since the officer did not give notice of concerns respecting the nature and scope of the applicant's activities nor was the applicant given a reasonable opportunity to respond. Specifically, the visa officer concluded that the applicant was involved or complicit in crimes against humanity following disclosure by the applicant during a telephone interview that he was with Mobile Brigade #2 in a particular location in Colombia in October 1992. The applicant was never confronted with the opinion formed, and was never asked questions as to what he was doing or what others known to him were doing at the relevant time or place. The visa officer concluded he was inadmissible under subs. 35(1)(a) of the IRPA.

*Dhoot v. Canada (Minister of Citizenship & Immigration)*, [2006] F.C.J. No. 1625, 57 Imm. L.R. (3d) 153, 2006 CarswellNat 3480, 2006 FC 1295 (F.C.) — This is an application for judicial review of a visa officer's decision of the applicant's application for a permanent resident visa which was denied on the basis that the applicant failed to attend an interview scheduled on October 26, 2005. The applicant states that he was never informed of the interview. The visa officer insisted that the notice of the interview was provided to the applicant by letter dated August 19, 2005.

The visa officer, for whatever reason, did not send the notice by mail as would be expected given the significantly prejudicial impact non-delivery would have on the applicant's interest in obtaining a permanent resident visa. It is reasonable to expect that there will be mistakes by the respondent when dealing with thousands of immigration files. When the evidence shows that there has been such a mistake the Court expects that the respondent cure the mistake, *i.e.*, invite the applicant to attend another interview. It was wrong for the respondent, in a case such as this, to oppose the applicant's court case. The application for judicial review was allowed and the applicant was awarded legal costs.

*Zhen v. Canada (Minister of Citizenship & Immigration)*, 2006 CarswellNat 758, 2006 CarswellNat 1854, 2006 FC 408 (F.C.) — The applicant was given only three weeks to comply with the visa officer's request for additional financial records. The visa officer's request for 20 years of financial records supported, in part, by third party verifications, went beyond what is normally required by the department. Since the visa officer requested the documentary history and then failed to afford a reasonable opportunity to the applicant to comply with the request, the handling of the application did not conform to the obligation to allow the applicant to present his case fully and fairly.

*Kniazeva v. Canada (Minister of Citizenship & Immigration)* (2006), 52 Imm. L.R. (3d) 298, 2006 CarswellNat 472, 2006 FC 268 (F.C.) — The applicant filed an application for permanent residence under the skilled worker class. New legislation was enacted following the applicant's application having been filed. Under subs. 361(4) of the *Immigration and Refugee Protection Regulations*, the applicant could have become a permanent resident as a member of the federal skilled worker class by qualifying under either the former Act's regulation or under the new legislation. Once the visa officer decided to access the applicant under both the old and new Act, he had to inform the applicant of the new requirements with respect to language proficiency. The visa officer's failure to conduct a thorough review of her application under the new Act and failure to provide the applicant with an opportunity to provide him with the language assessment amounted to a clear breach of duty of fairness owed to the applicant.

The visa officer contacted the applicant's former employer with a view to verifying her employment. The employer confirmed the applicant had "practical training" at the plant while she was a student and had worked intervals during the period between June 1997 and July 1998. Accordingly, the visa officer had a duty to inform the applicant that he only considered this work experience as part-time and therefore the experience was being disqualified as relevant work experience.

The visa officer breached the duty of procedural fairness and the application for judicial review was allowed.

*Keymanesh v. Canada (Minister of Citizenship & Immigration)*, 2006 CarswellNat 1392, 2006 FC 641 (F.C.) — The applicant challenged a decision made by the officer denying his application for permanent resident status because of a failure to obtain a pardon from a conviction for impaired driving in 1998. In the absence of a pardon, the applicant was ineligible for landing and, in the result, subject to removal. The Court considered whether the department owed a duty to give notice to the applicant that it was intending to determine his application for permanent residence in the absence of proof of a pardon, and if so, did it fulfil that duty. The department advised the applicant that he had been approved in principle for a visa exemption but that landing would be subject to meeting other immigration requirements including health and security assessments. When the department learned of the applicant's criminal conviction, it notified him of the need for a pardon. They also advised him that he would not be eligible to apply for a pardon for three years. This extension of time afforded by the department was generous because the applicant could have been removed immediately on the basis of his criminal conviction. The department, quite rightly, was not prepared to hold the applicant's case for landing in abeyance indefinitely. The department wrote the applicant giving him a notice to respond to its request for the pardon which was returned "undeliverable." Not hearing from the applicant, they sent him a "final notice" which was also returned as "undeliverable." The department refused the application for permanent residence. The applicant claimed not to have received the three notification letters and deposed that he had advised the department of his change of address. The applicant had a clear indication that the department required proof of a pardon before his application for landing would be finalized. However, when the department began to contemplate the possibility of revoking his interim status, it did have a duty to inform him of that risk. Indeed, the department's lengthy acquiescence may well have created some expectation in the mind of the applicant that time was not of the essence and that he would be informed of any change in the department's position.

It is difficult to contemplate any decision by the department which would have greater significance to the applicant than the one taken here. The finalization of his application for permanent residence without the required pardon had only one possible outcome: deportation. The obligation to give effective notice of a potentially adverse administrative decision is different than a situation involving the obligation to produce evidence or to meet a burden of proof. From the department's record, it was not clear that the officer who decided to refuse the application for landing was even aware that its notification correspondence had been returned as undelivered. Although the department need not exhaust every tracing possibility, some effort to that end is essential in cases like this, at least to the extent recognized by the department's own guidelines.

IP5-Immigration Application in Canada Made on Humanitarian and Compassionate Grounds, s. 17.3, suggests that where contact has been lost, some effort should be made to locate the subject. Those guidelines indicate that where an applicant does not respond to requests for information or fails to provide an updated address, a decision can be taken "based on information on file as long as previous correspondence has informed the applicant of how and when to apply and included the consequences of failing to respond." Those guidelines go on to indicate that officers should indicate in their computer notes any attempts to verify the applicant's current address such as looking in the local telephone directory, calling the most recent telephone number provided on the application form or calling other persons listed as contacts or representatives. The recommendations imply that where the department is aware that its notification letters have not been received there is some responsibility to make some enquiries with respect to whereabouts.

The department did not meet the duty of fairness owed to the applicant with respect to giving effective notice. The failure was entirely inadvertent but does require that the decision to refuse the applicant's application for permanent residence be set aside.

*Shaker v. Canada (Minister of Citizenship & Immigration)*, [2006] F.C.J. No. 201, 2006 CarswellNat 271, 2006 CarswellNat 2244, 2006 FC 185 (F.C.) — The applicant submitted an application for permanent residence as a skilled worker in December 1999. An interview date was set for July 2004 and the applicant was instructed to submit additional information regarding his financial situation, employment history and identity. However, before the applicant received the notice, his counsel sent a letter to the embassy requesting that his file be transferred to the Canadian High Commission in Singapore. The Canadian Embassy in Manila sent the file to the Canadian High Commission in Singapore, returned the documents the applicant's counsel had submitted and instructed him to send them directly to the High Commission in Singapore. The applicant was then informed by the High Commission of the coming into effect of the IRPA and that his application would be processed under the new requirements. The applicant was asked to provide proof of his current level of official language proficiency. In August 2004, the applicant sent the High Commission in Singapore the documents that had been sent back by the embassy in Manila, as well as proof of his English language proficiency in the form of school transcripts, a letter from a company stating that he had taken an English course, and six pages of manuscript narrative regarding his use of English in the workplace and at home.

In September 2004, the officer stated in her assessment under the old and new Acts and Regulations that under the old Act she was not satisfied the applicant had performed the essential duties of his intended occupation in Canada, and she consequently would not award him any units of assessment under the "occupational factor" or "experience" headings. In addition to the overall pass mark of 70 units, at least one unit under these headings was necessary for an application to be granted. The officer also stated that in the context of her assessment under the new Act, there was insufficient evidence to determine the applicant's work experience or his proficiency in the English language. She instructed the applicant to submit employment references, work contracts, or any other information/documentation which demonstrates experience in the occupation described by the National Occupational Classification No. 0611, and either IELTS test results or more written evidence that can permit measurement of proficiency in the English language. In addition, the visa officer asked the applicant to pay the cost recovery fee for his wife and child and to submit proof of financial capacity to resettle in Canada. In fact, the High Commission had already sent the applicant a receipt for payment of the processing fees regarding his spouse and child on August 28, 2004.

Since the applicant had sent documents regarding all four of these subjects in August of 2004, he inferred that the officer did not have them when she assessed his application. The Minister argued that the officer did not violate procedural fairness, in that her letter of September 2, 2004, gave the applicant a chance to respond to her concerns regarding his professional qualifications and his proficiency in English. The Court disagreed and held that the fact that the officer requested items that the applicant had already submitted reasonably led him to believe that she did not have any of the evidence he had submitted in the same package. In light of the ambiguity caused by her letter and the applicant's effort to notify her that he had already sent the items she requested, the duty of procedural fairness required the officer to inform the applicant that the evidence he submitted regarding his employment history and proficiency in English was still insufficient, and that she explain the confusion. The officer's decision was found to be unreasonable as she failed to offer any explanation as to why the applicant was awarded no points under the "experience" and "arranged employment" headings. Furthermore, the visa officer's decision to award zero points for English was found to be patently unreasonable. While the presence of mistakes in the applicant's manuscript evidencing his English skills and the relatively poor grades he obtained while studying English may not have warranted the attribution of full marks for English skills, he clearly demonstrated the ability to communicate in English at some level.

*Karanja v. Canada (Minister of Citizenship & Immigration)*, 2006 CarswellNat 1265, 2006 CarswellNat 2533, 2006 FC 574 (F.C.) — Pursuant to the Gender Guidelines (Women Refugee Claimants Fearing Gender-Related Persecution, 9 March 1993, by the chairperson of the Immigration and Refugee Board pursuant to paragraph 159(1)(h) of the *Immigration Act*), the Board should be particularly sensitive to a female applicant's difficulty in testifying. However, the Gender Guidelines, in and of themselves, are not intended to serve as a cure for all deficiencies in the applicant's claim or evidence. The applicant bears the onus of proving her claim. The Guidelines cannot be treated as corroborating any evidence of gender-based persecution so that the giving of the evidence becomes proof of its truth.

Instead, the Guidelines are an aid for the panel in the assessment of the evidence of women who allege that they have been victims of gender-based persecution. The Guidelines do not create new grounds for finding a person to be a victim of persecution. A board's failure to specifically mention the Gender Guidelines does not mean that they were not considered and is not material or fatal to the Board's decision.

The Gender Guidelines specifically state that the female refugee claimant must demonstrate that the harm feared is sufficiently serious to amount to persecution. In this case, there were numerous negative credibility findings by the Board and such findings are open to the Board to make. Accordingly, the applicant failed to demonstrate that the Board's decision was patently unreasonable so as to warrant the intervention of the Court.

*Bortey v. Canada (Minister of Citizenship & Immigration)*, 2006 CarswellNat 327, 2006 CarswellNat 2422, 2006 FC 190 (F.C.) — The Board found that the applicant obtained refugee status on the basis of misrepresentations and the withholding of material facts. The Board also concluded that once these misrepresentations were set aside, there was no other sufficient evidence considered at the time of the first determination on which a decision in favour of the applicant could have been based. The Board was required, under subs. 109(2) of the IRPA, to decipher whether any of the evidence cited in support of the original positive determination is left "untainted" by the fact of the newly discovered material misrepresentations.

*Apaza v. Canada (Minister of Citizenship & Immigration)*, 2006 CarswellNat 606, 2006 CarswellNat 1415, 2006 FC 313 (F.C.) — The applicant's inland application for permanent residence based on humanitarian and compassionate grounds was rejected. The decision letter also stated that the case had been assessed under the spouse or common-law partner in Canada class and was rejected on that ground as well. In the opinion of the immigration officer, there was little evidence to show there was a genuine marriage and that the marriage had not been entered into primarily for the purpose of acquiring permanent residence status in Canada. The refusal letter provided no detailed reasons. The immigration officer's lengthy notes were produced only in the course of the application for judicial review. The court concluded that the officer ignored relevant evidence that, if believed, would have significant probative value. Specifically, the immigration officer ignored evidence about the ages of the applicants, the period of cohabitation before marriage, and supporting documents, including doctors' notes, employer reference letters and the filing of joint income tax returns, in reaching her conclusion about the genuineness of the marriage. Instead, the officer focused on irrelevant matters, for example the contents of bedside tables and the timing of the wife's divorce from her previous husband, and details of the mode of transportation used for their first date, in assessing the genuineness of the marriage. The application for judicial review was allowed and referred to a different officer for redetermination.

*Boni c. Canada (Ministre de la Citoyenneté & de l'Immigration)*, [2005] F.C.J. No. 43, 57 Imm. L.R. (3d) 4, 2005 CarswellNat 176, 2005 CarswellNat 4646, 2005 FC 31 (F.C.); affirmed [2006] F.C.J. No. 275, 2006 CarswellNat 414 (C.A.) — The applicant applied for judicial review of a visa officer's decision to deny the applicant's application for a study permit. The risk that study permit applicants will not leave Canada once the period of their stay ends is a very important factor to be considered. An officer may examine the applicant's long-term objective. That objective is a relevant point which carries some weight, in view of the evidence as a whole on whether a study permit would be granted. A visa officer's conclusions will not be disturbed unless they are so unreasonable as to require the Court's intervention.

*Iliev v. Canada (Minister of Citizenship & Immigration)*, 2005 CarswellNat 2010, 2005 FC 395 (F.C.) — The applicant, a citizen of Bulgaria, made a claim to be a Convention refugee and was found to be a Convention refugee. However, the Minister of Citizenship and Immigration obtained leave to vacate the determination of the Convention Refugee Determination Division pursuant to s. 109 of the IRPA on the basis that the applicant had obtained refugee status on fraudulent means, misrepresentation, suppression and concealment of material facts, specifically with respect to the entry of two criminal convictions in Bulgaria. The Minister relied on certificates of conviction that had been issued by the Bulgarian court. The Board accepted the Minister's argument and concluded that pursuant to Article 1F(b) of the *Refugee Convention*, the applicant was a person who was excluded from consideration as a Convention refugee as a result of having committed a serious non-political offence. The Board's conclusion was set aside by the Federal Court as it was made in the absence of any evidence about the equivalency between the Bulgarian criminal law and the Canadian criminal law. A factual finding made without evidence is a ground for judicial intervention, pursuant to s. 18.1(4) of the *Federal Courts Act*, R.S.C. 1985, c. F-7, as amended.

*Qazi v. Canada (Minister of Citizenship & Immigration)*, [2005] F.C.J. No. 2069, 2005 CarswellNat 4129, 2005 CarswellNat 5566, 2005 FC 1667 (F.C.) — The question of when a PRRA becomes unreasonably stale is not solely dependent on the length of time that has passed, but also depends on the applicant establishing that he has been prejudiced by the delay. In this case, nearly two years had elapsed from the time the applicant replied to the negative risk assessment. While the delay was unfortunate, nevertheless there was no evidence that the applicant had been prejudiced by it. The Court concluded that he had not been denied procedural fairness or natural justice.

*Huiqiao v. Canada (Minister of Citizenship & Immigration)* (2000), 10 Imm. L.R. (3d) 132, 2000 CarswellNat 2509 (Fed. T.D.) — Although not made in the context of an immigration matter, the Federal Court of Appeal stated in *Stelco Inc. v. British Steel Canada Inc.*, [2000] 3 F.C. 282, 20 Admin. L.R. (3d) 159, 252 N.R. 364, 2000 CarswellNat 230, [2000] F.C.J. No. 286, 2000 CarswellNat 3248 (Fed. C.A.) , at p. 284[F.C.]:

> When a tribunal bases a discretionary decision on findings of fact, a reviewing court must examine those findings to ensure that they are rationally based on the material before the tribunal . . . in order to establish that the tribunal committed a reviewable error the applicant and the interveners had to demonstrate on the balance of probabilities that the tribunal's finding was not rationally supported by any material before it.

*Sinnathamby v. Canada (Minister of Citizenship & Immigration)*, 2001 FCT 473, 2001 CarswellNat 1012 (Fed. T.D.) — In cases seeking to review a decision of a panel of the CRDD, the standard of review is twofold. Questions of law are governed by the standard of correctness. Factual findings are regulated by the patently unreasonable standard.

*Singh (S.) v. Canada (Minister of Citizenship & Immigration)* (1999), 2 Imm. L.R. (3d) 191, 173 F.T.R. 280, 1999 CarswellNat 1579, [1999] F.C.J. No. 1283 (T.D.) — The standard of review for a panel of the Convention Refugee Determination Division (CRDD) is patent unreasonableness. Citing *Canada (Director of Investigation & Research) v. Southam*, [1997] 1 S.C.R 748, the Court concluded that the difference between unreasonable and patently unreasonable lies in the immediacy or obviousness of the defect. If the defect is apparent on the face of the tribunal's reasons then the tribunal's decision is patently unreasonable. If it takes some significant searching or testing to find the defect then the decision is unreasonable, but not patently unreasonable.

*Gengeswaran v. Canada (Minister of Citizenship & Immigration)* (1999), 169 F.T.R. 148 (T.D.) — Although there is no obligation on the Board to discuss every piece of evidence, it is required to address those pieces which contradict the Board's finding on key issues. The absence of any analysis of documentary evidence which directly contradicts the Board's finding, permits the Court to infer, from the silence, that the tribunal made an erroneous finding of fact without regard to evidence.

*Cepeda-Gutierrez v. Canada (Minister of Citizenship & Immigration)* (1998), 157 F.T.R. 35 (T.D.) — This was an application to set aside a decision of a panel of the CRDD. The applicant relied on s. 18.1(4)(d) of the *Federal Courts Act*. The applicant was a citizen of Mexico who arrived in Canada and claimed refugee status. The Refugee Division found that while he was a taxi driver in Mexico City he had been the subject of beatings and threats of violence by the federal police. The panel found that the claimant's evidence was credible and held that the claimant had a well-founded fear of persecution in Mexico City; however, they rejected his claim on the basis that he had an internal flight alternative.

Section 18.1(4)(d) of the *Federal Courts Act* does not authorize the Court to substitute its view of the facts for that of the Board which has the benefit of not only seeing and hearing the witnesses, but also of the expertise of its members in assessing evidence relating to facts that are within their area of specialized expertise. The efficient allocation of decision-making resources between administrative agencies and the Courts strongly indicates that the role to be played in fact-finding by the Court on an application for judicial review should be nearly residual. Thus, in order to attract judicial intervention, the applicant must satisfy the Court not only that the Board made a palpably erroneous finding of material fact, but also that the finding was made without regard to the evidence. The Court may infer that the administrative agency made the erroneous finding of fact without regard to the evidence from the agency's failure to mention in its reasons some evidence before it that was relevant to the finding and pointed to a different conclusion from that reached by the agency. Just as a Court will only defer to an agency's interpretation of its constituent statute if it provides reasons for its conclusion, so a Court will be reluctant to defer to an agency's factual determinations in the absence of express findings and an analysis of the evidence that shows how the agency reached its results. Reasons given by an administrative agency are not to be read hypercritically, nor are agencies to be required to refer to every piece of evidence that they received that is contrary to their finding and to explain how they dealt with it. A statement by the agency in its reasons for decision that in making its findings it considered all of the evidence before it will often suffice to assure a reviewing Court that the agency directed itself to the totality of the evidence. The more important the evidence that is not mentioned specifically, the more willing a Court will be to infer from the silence that the agency made an erroneous finding of fact without regard to the evidence. When the agency refers in some detail to evidence supporting its finding, but is silent on evidence pointing to the opposite conclusion, it will be easier to infer that the agency overlooked the contradictory evidence when making its finding of fact. The Court was not persuaded that the Board erred when it found that the applicant faced no serious possibility of persecution outside Mexico City and therefore it was unnecessary to consider whether the Board's finding was made without regard to the evidence.

The applicant called a psychologist as a witness to explain why it was not reasonable to require the applicant to return to Mexico. In making its decision the panel did not refer to the psychologist's evidence. This evidence was so important to the applicant's case that it can be inferred from the refugee division's failure to mention it that the finding made by the panel was made without regard to this evidence. This inference was made easier by the fact that the Board's reasons dealt with other items of evidence indicating that return would not be unduly harsh. The inclusion of the "boilerplate" assertion that the Board considered all the evidence was not sufficient to prevent this inference from being drawn. Accordingly, the decision of the panel was set aside and the matter remitted to a differently constituted panel.

*Khakh v. Canada (Minister of Citizenship & Immigration)* (1996), 116 F.T.R. 310 (T.D.) — The applicant was determined not to be a Convention refugee on the basis that he had fabricated incidents of persecution in order to try to obtain refugee status.

The Court commented on judicial decisions about s. 18.1(4)(d) and found authority for the proposition that three conditions precedent must be met to justify judicial intervention: (1) the finding of fact must be truly erroneous; (2) the finding must be made capriciously or without regard to the evidence; and (3) the decision must be based on the erroneous finding. Further, the subs. permits review where there was no evidence to support the finding, or where, on an assessment of the evidence as a whole, the finding was unreasonable.

Further, the Court adopted Webster's Third New International Dictionary definition of "capricious", which defined the word as "marked or guided by caprice: given to changes of interest or attitude according to whims or passing fancies: not guided by steady judgment, intent, or purpose".

*Osaloun v. Canada (Minister of Citizenship & Immigration)* (June 12, 1996), Doc. IMM-3649-95 (Fed. T.D.) — The issue in this case was whether a panel of the IRB committed an error of natural justice, and if so, whether the breach should be disregarded.

The denial of a right to a fair hearing will render a decision with respect to a refugee claim invalid, unless it can be demonstrated that the claim would in any case be hopeless.

*Singh (A.) v. Canada (Minister of Citizenship & Immigration)* (1995), 30 Imm. L.R. (2d) 211, 98 F.T.R. 58 — This was an application to review a decision of the Appeal Division of the IRB upholding a deportation order issued against the applicant.

The applicant, his parents and his three sisters were sponsored to come to Canada as members of the family class. The applicant completed the statutory declaration in which he declared that he had never been married and that he had no children. The applicant received an immigrant visa in July, 1990 and returned for a visit to Guyana in 1992. In fact, the applicant had fathered a son in Guyana in 1990, and on his return there in 1992, he married the son's mother and then sponsored his wife and son for entrance to Canada. An adjudicator determined that the applicant had been granted landing by misrepresentation of a material fact (ie. — non-disclosure of the birth of his son).

At the outset of the proceedings before the Appeal Division, counsel for the applicant advised the Tribunal that the appeal was being taken pursuant to paragraph 70(3)(b) of the *Immigration Act* on the ground that having regard to the existence of compassionate or humanitarian considerations, the applicant should not be removed from Canada.

The Appeal Division dismissed the appeal and this application for judicial review related to that dismissal. In the proceedings before the Trial Division, the applicant submitted that Immigration Regulations 6(1)(a), 9(1)(a), and 10(1)(a) are *ultra vires* the *Immigration Act*.

The Trial Division is not entitled to pronounce itself on a question not faced by the administrative authority whose decision it is reviewing. This principle applies when the *vires* of regulations passed pursuant to the enabling statute is in issue. Accordingly, due to the fact that counsel before the Appeal Division did not challenge the validity of the regulations in question, that issue could not be raised before the Trial Division and the application for judicial review was dismissed.

*Rehman v. Canada (Secretary of State)* (1995), 92 F.T.R. 297 — The Court was satisfied that there had been a breach of the duty to act fairly. The Court then noted that there was an added requirement before a new hearing could be ordered. Specifically, the Court was required to address its mind to the question of whether the nature of the applicant's claim to refugee status is such that the claim might be described as hopeless or one where the outcome was inevitable, in which case it would be inappropriate to set aside the decision. The Court could not conclude on the facts of this matter that a differently constituted panel of the CRDD would inevitably conclude that these claims must fail. The Court therefore directed that there be a new hearing before a differently constituted panel of the CRDD.

*Indrani v. Canada (Secretary of State)* (1994), 89 F.T.R. 31 — The applicant arrived in Canada with false documents and claimed refugee status. The applicant married a Canadian permanent resident who sought an exemption for her pursuant to s. 114(2). This request was refused.

Three conditions precedent must be met to justify judicial intervention for an erroneous finding of fact. First, the finding must be truly erroneous; second, the finding must be made capriciously or without regard to the evidence; third, the decision must be based upon the erroneous finding. Even if the Court is convinced that a decision is based on an erroneous finding of fact, it cannot intervene unless it is of the view that the tribunal, in making its finding, acted in a perverse and capricious manner, or without regard to the evidence before it.

A reviewing Court should not interfere with the exercise of discretion by an Immigration Officer who is authorized by statute to exercise the discretion unless it is clear that the discretion has been exercised in bad faith or on grounds unrelated to the purposes for which the discretion is granted. In this particular case, the application was dismissed.

*Nguy v. Canada (Minister of Employment & Immigration)* (1994), 80 F.T.R. 53 — The applicant was determined not to be a Convention refugee. The applicant challenged a finding of fact by the Board that he was not stateless as he had alleged, but was a citizen of Vietnam. The application was dismissed.

In order for an alleged error of fact to be reviewable, the finding must be truly erroneous or the finding must be made capriciously or without regard to the evidence, and the decision must be based on that erroneous finding. The decision that the applicant was eligible for Vietnamese citizenship was not erroneous or capricious and was not central to the negative determination of the applicant's refugee claim.

*Alfred v. Canada (Minister of Employment & Immigration)* (1994), 76 F.T.R. 231 — In this application to review a negative decision of the CRDD, the applicant argued that the tribunal erred in misconstruing "persecution" and that the tribunal erred in law by ignoring or misconstruing the evidence before it. The respondent made reference to portions of the transcript of the hearing and to the documentary evidence before the tribunal, which it argued would warrant the conclusion that the findings of the tribunal were reasonable. The Court must review the decision as rendered by the tribunal and not the evidence to which the decision itself makes no reference but which would have warranted the conclusions reached by the tribunal if the tribunal had expressed reasons relying upon such evidence. The simple statement that the tribunal had reached its decision "after careful consideration of all the evidence adduced at the hearing" was not sufficient when the decision made little or no reference to the principal bases of the applicant's claim. The application was allowed in this case and the matter sent back for rehearing before a differently constituted panel of the CRDD.

*Bogdanov v. Canada (Minister of Employment & Immigration)*, 1994 CarswellNat 1614 (Fed. T.D.) — This was an application to set aside a negative determination of the CRDD. The applicants were all citizens of Bulgaria and the sole ground urged by the applicants was that the tribunal erred in its assessment that the cumulative effects of the various incidents of discrimination and harassment, as reported by the claimants, did not amount to persecution. The testimony of the applicants, according to the tribunal, "seemed credible, appeared to be given in good faith and without exaggeration".

The standard for the Court to intervene is set out in s. 18.1(4)(c) and (d) of the *Federal Courts Act*, R.S.C. 1985, c. F-7. The Court must be satisfied that the tribunal "erred in law in making a decision" or "based its decision . . . on an erroneous finding of fact that it made in a perverse or capricious manner or without regard to the material before it". The appellants' argument was essentially that the tribunal reached the wrong conclusion in its assessment of the cumulative effect of the evidence. Even if the Court were inclined to share that view, there was no basis for finding that the tribunal's conclusion was unreasonable in law. Further, the tribunal's conclusion that the incidents of harassment did not individually or cumulatively constitute persecution could not be said to be perverse or capricious or made without regard to the material before the tribunal. The conclusion of the tribunal was one open to it on the evidence adduced. Accordingly, the application was dismissed.

*Gholam-Nejad v. Canada (Minister of Employment & Immigration)* (1994), 25 Imm. L.R. (2d) 51, 77 F.T.R. 44 — This application to review a negative decision of the CRDD was based on the denial to the applicant of her right to counsel because of the alleged manifest incompetence of her representative at the Refugee Board hearing. Section 18.1(4) of the *Federal Courts Act* provides for relief where the CRDD acted or failed to act, or failed to observe a principle of natural justice, procedural fairness or other procedure that it was required by law to observe, or erred in law, or based its decision or order on an erroneous finding of fact made in a perverse or capricious manner. Nothing on the face of that subs. would authorize the intervention of the Court where the issue is the failure on the part of the applicant's representative, rather than on the part of the CRDD itself. This is particularly true where the failure of the representative was not at all apparent to the CRDD and, therefore, the representative's failure could not be identified as a failure of the CRDD to ensure natural justice and fairness. Accordingly, this ground of attack could not succeed and the application was dismissed.

*Su v. Canada (Minister of Employment & Immigration)* (1994), [1994] F.C.J. No. 70, 1994 CarswellNat 1599 (Fed. T.D.) — This was an application to review a negative determination with respect to a refugee claim. Counsel for the respondent argued that there was evidence on the record that could have led the Board to conclude that the applicant's involvement in the pro-democracy movement prior to 1989 was not of such a nature that it would likely result in repercussions leading to persecution in the Convention refugee sense.

The Court's responsibility on a judicial review application is to review the decision in question on the basis on which it was given. In this case, the decision was based on a finding that the applicant was not credible, and not on a finding that even if the story the applicant was telling was true, the facts recounted would not lead to a finding of persecution.

The Court found that the decision that the applicant was not credible was based on a significant misunderstanding of the evidence and quashed the decision.

*Pal v. Canada (Minister of Employment & Immigration)* (1993), 70 F.T.R. 289 — The applicant sought review of a decision denying him Convention refugee status.

The applicant was not granted a recess, when he requested one, in order to review documents which were introduced into evidence and which he had not seen previously. The documents were introduced to contradict evidence which he had given. They were written in English. The applicant was testifying through an interpreter. The Court found that in refusing to allow the applicant and his counsel an opportunity to review the evidence, the applicant was denied the opportunity to answer the case against him and a breach of natural justice occurred.

The Court pointed out that relief under s. 18.1(4) of the *Federal Courts Act* is discretionary and thus, if no prejudice is caused by an erroneous procedure or decision, an order quashing that decision will not normally be given. If no real purpose will be served by requiring another hearing, one will not be ordered.

The Court was unable to conclude that the breach of natural justice that occurred in the context of this case was minor and could not appreciably affect the final decision. The breach was not cured by subsequent actions and accordingly, the decision of the tribunal was quashed.

*Singh (G.) v. Canada (Minister of Employment & Immigration)* (1993), 69 F.T.R. 142 — The applicants sought to set aside a decision that they were not Convention refugees. This case discusses how findings on the evidence can be successfully challenged in the Trial Division.

The Court commented that s. 18.1(4)(d) of the *Federal Courts Act* set out disjunctive conditions under which a decision will be set aside. For purposes of paragraph (c) of that section, the Court noted that findings of fact which are unsupported by adequate evidence are errors in law — the so-called "no evidence rule". Section 18.1(4)(d) allows the Court to set aside a decision which is made "without regard for the material before it". This grants a broader right of review than the traditional "no evidence" test. It compels the setting aside of tribunal decisions where they are unreasonable. The phrase "perverse or capricious manner or without regard for the material before it" is accurately discussed in J.A. Kavanagh, *A Guide to Judicial Review* (1978) at 57–58.

The findings of fact can be divided into two classifications: findings of primary facts and inferences of fact which are drawn from the primary facts. Courts are reluctant to interfere with findings of primary facts made by tribunals. In areas where a tribunal has a particular expertise in drawing inferences, courts are inclined to treat those inferences with deference. If, however, the inference is of a type which is based on common experience, then the Court is in equally as good a position as the tribunal to draw the inference and in that case deference is not shown.

In this particular case, the inferences of fact drawn by the Board did not stand up upon a review of the evidence and the decision refusing refugee status was set aside.

*Muhammed v. Canada (Minister of Employment & Immigration)* (1993), 67 F.T.R. 152 — The applicant applied to set aside a decision which determined that the applicant was not a Convention refugee. Section 18.1(4)(d) of the *Federal Courts Act* provides that in an application for judicial review the Court may grant relief, *inter alia*, where the tribunal based its decision or order on an erroneous finding of fact that it made in a perverse or capricious manner or without regard for the material before it. This is the standard set by the Act and it emphasizes that it is not the role of the Court to substitute its decision for that of the tribunal, especially where the decision is based on an assessment of credibility. The decision of the Court of Appeal in *Giron v. Canada (Minister of Employment & Immigration)* (1992), 143 N.R. 238 (Fed. C.A.) was rendered at a time when the jurisdiction of the Court of Appeal included the authority to make the decision the Immigration and Refugee Board should have made, as well as the jurisdiction to refer the matter back to the Board for reconsideration.

The applicant claimed to be a Sudanese national who had been kidnapped by an insurgent force and compelled to train as a rebel. The applicant claimed that when he escaped from the guerrillas, they returned to his parents' home and shot and killed his father and mother. The Board had difficulty believing that the applicant was a national native of Sudan. Secondly, they found implausibilities in aspects of his story. For example, the assumption that the persons who killed his parents were rebel forces looking for him after he deserted. While the Court might have reached a different conclusion on either of these aspects, the panel's findings could not be said to be unreasonable and, therefore, the findings could not be characterized as perverse or capricious or made without regard to the material before the panel. Therefore, the application was dismissed.

*Naikar v. Canada (Minister of Employment & Immigration)*, 1993 CarswellNat 1717 (Fed. T.D.) — This was an application for judicial review to set aside a determination of the Convention Refugee Determination Division of the IRB that the applicant did not meet the Convention refugee test.

The application was dismissed. The Court noted that on a judicial review application, it must sometimes balance seeming errors in the Board's decision with the more substantive findings the Board has made. To determine whether the errors are of such a nature that, if not committed, the Board's conclusions would have been substantially different, the true test is the reading of the transcript in an attempt to establish whether any purported errors are of a nature to vitiate the ultimate conclusion.

*Boateng v. Canada (Minister of Employment & Immigration)* (1993), 65 F.T.R. 81 — The Refugee Division decided that the applicant was not a Convention refugee. There was evidence that persons returning to Ghana were subject to detention for several months. The panel found that this treatment did not amount to persecution. The Court disagreed with this conclusion but declined to upset the panel's decision because this conclusion had no particular relevance to the applicant's case as there was no evidence that the government of Ghana would have reason to believe that the applicant had sought refugee status in Canada.

**18.2 Interim orders — On an application for judicial review, the Federal Court may make any interim orders that it considers appropriate pending the final disposition of the application.**

1990, c. 8, s. 5; 2002, c. 8, s. 28



## Case Law

*Adolph v. Canada (Minister of Public Safety & Emergency Preparedness)* (2009), 357 F.T.R. 216 (Eng.), 2009 FC 1271, 2009 CarswellNat 4277 (F.C.) — This "sad and disturbing" case involved a minor child who remains alone in Canada after having been sent to Toronto by his mother and aunt on a one-way ticket from St. Lucia, purportedly to offer him an opportunity for a better life. To compound this unacceptable situation, two government agencies are working at cross purposes from each other in this case, each claiming to be taking into account the true best interest of the child. A motion to stay the removal procedure was brought pursuant to s. 18.2 of the *Federal Courts Act*. The applicant argued that the enforcement officer ignored compelling factors demonstrating that the best interests of the applicant were such that his removal should be deferred and that the officer failed to take into account Canada's obligations under the *Convention on the Rights of the Child* to provide protection and assistance to the applicant and act in his best interest. The Minister argued that contrary to the allegations of the Children's Aid Society of Toronto the best interests of the applicant do not include an entitlement to remain in Canada to obtain a better life than he would otherwise have in St. Lucia. The Minister also adds that non-citizen parents from foreign countries should not be encouraged to send and abandon their children in Canada in the hopes of better opportunities for them.

The interpretation and application of the *Convention on the Rights of the Child* in circumstances where a child without immigration status is abandoned, and how the Convention is to be taken into account for immigration purposes in such circumstances pursuant to paragraph 3(3)(f) of IRPA raised a serious issue including who should determine the best interest of an abandoned child in such circumstances, the Children's Aid Society or the immigration authorities? Since the Social Services Agency of St. Lucia had not been contacted in order to secure an onsite report on the applicant's family situation and on potential alternative placement solutions in St. Lucia should the return to the family not be deemed feasible, the applicant was deemed to be facing irreparable harm. In light of the fact that a minor child is involved, the Court preferred to act cautiously. Although the Court strongly supported the Minister's contention that citizens from foreign countries should not be encouraged to send and abandon their children in Canada and although the Minister must carry out a removal order as soon as reasonably practical pursuant to subs. 48(2) of IRPA, the particular circumstances of this case required a finding that the balance of convenience lies at this time with the applicant. The stay was granted.

*Baron v. Canada (Minister of Public Safety & Emergency Preparedness)*, [2009] F.C.J. No. 314, 387 N.R. 278, 79 Imm. L.R. (3d) 157, 2009 CarswellNat 596, 2009 FCA 81 (C.A.) — The Court considered whether an application for judicial review of an enforcement officer's decision not to defer an applicant's scheduled removal from Canada becomes moot where the Court has stayed the removal and the applicant has remained in Canada.

The jurisprudence is conclusive that the enforcement officer's discretion is limited. However, ultimately an enforcement officer is intended to do nothing more than enforce a removal order. While enforcement officers are granted the discretion to fix new removal dates, they are not intended to defer removal to an indeterminate date. On the facts before the Court, the date of the decision on the H&C application was unknown and unlikely to be imminent, and thus, the enforcement officer was being asked to delay removal indeterminately. An indeterminate deferral was simply not within the enforcement officer's powers.

Over the years, the duties of enforcement officers have not changed, and yet, the basis upon which applicants rely to obtain deferrals have dramatically increased. The scope of the enforcement officer's discretion cannot be changed by virtue of the request made. An enforcement officer's role is not to assess the best interest of the children or the probability of success of any application. The enforcement officer's role should remain limited and deferral should be contemplated in very limited circumstances. The legislation has not provided a new step to claimants who desire yet another assessment of their circumstances. Claimants already have the refugee application process, the pre-removal risk assessment process and the H&C application in addition to judicial reviews of these processes and the stay before removal. In this case, it appears that the claimants want to open yet another avenue of review by asking the enforcement officer to reassess information that has already been examined by administrative tribunals and that was a subject of judicial review. For the enforcement officer to comply with this request for reassessment would be akin to the enforcement officer making a quasi-judicial order without the benefit of hearing from opposing counsel. It is time to stop this abusive cycle.

The appeal was dismissed. The removal date having passed, the determination of the reasonableness of the enforcement officer's refusal to defer the removal date in January 2007 was without consequence; the matter was rendered moot.

*Palka v. Canada (Minister of Public Safety & Emergency Preparedness)*, 2008 CarswellNat 1309, 2008 FCA 165 (F.C.A.) — The appellants appealed from a decision of the Federal Court dismissing their application for judicial review of a refusal by an enforcement officer to defer their removal from Canada until their application for permanent residence on humanitarian and compassionate grounds had been decided. The lower Court judge held that the application for judicial review was moot, and did not consider its merits. She based her finding of mootness on the fact that another judge of the Federal Court had stayed the appellants' removal scheduled for June 13, 2007, pending the disposition of their application for judicial review of the officer's refusal to defer their removal. The lower Court judge rejected the position taken by both the appellants and the respondent, the Minister of Public Safety and Emergency Preparedness, that the passing of the scheduled removal date did not render the application for judicial review moot because an application for permanent residence on H&C grounds was outstanding. The lower Court judge certified a question for appeal on the mootness issue. The appellants then brought a motion for a stay of removal to their country of nationality, pending the disposition of the appeal.

They argued that, if they were denied a stay, their appeal on the mootness decision will be nugatory. They claimed that this would constitute irreparable harm. The Court did not agree. Even if their appeal was moot, the Court may decide to hear it in its discretion, on the ground that the question certified may arise repeatedly and be evasive of review. Even if a refusal of a stay does not render the appeal nugatory, this does not necessarily constitute irreparable harm. It all depends on the facts of the individual case.

Despite numerous attempts, through administrative and legal channels, the appellants have been denied status in Canada. There has to be some finality. To grant yet another deferral of their removal was contrary to the public interest as expressed in the Act. Motion to defer removal was dismissed.

See also *Islami v. Canada (Minster of Citizenship & Immigration)*, 2008 CarswellNat 702

*Maruthalingam v. Canada (Minister of Public Safety & Emergency Preparedness)*, [2007] F.C.J. No. 1079, 63 Imm. L.R. (3d) 242, 2007 CarswellNat 3088, 2007 CarswellNat 2278, 2007 FC 823 (F.C.) — The applicants were ordered to report for deportation and an enforcement officer refused the applicants' request that the removal from Canada be deferred. The applicants filed a notice of application for leave and judicial review of the enforcement officer's decision and brought a motion for a stay of their removal until the Court had disposed of the application for judicial review. The motion for the stay was granted. The applicants were not removed. By the time this judicial review application was heard by the Court, the serious issues identified in the stay motion were, in practical terms, academic. This application for judicial review was dismissed. The applicants raised the issue of whether the Court should still rule that the issue was moot where it was asked to stay the removal until the outcome of another process. The Court refused to opine as to whether the Court could grant a remedy to the applicants on a free-standing basis. The applicants had not sought an order to stay the removal until the final determination of their outstanding application on humanitarian and compassionate grounds. Instead, their sole request was that the matter be referred to another enforcement officer for reconsideration. The Court certified the following question:

> Where an applicant has filed an application for leave and judicial review of a decision not to defer the implementation of a removal order outstanding against him or her, does the fact that the applicant's removal is subsequently halted by operation of a stay order issued by this Court render the underlying judicial review application moot?

See also *Vu v. Canada (Minister of Citizenship & Immigration)*, 2007 CarswellNat 3591 (FC)

*Higgins v. Canada (Minister of Public Safety & Emergency Preparedness)*, [2007] F.C.J. No. 516, 64 Imm. L.R. (3d) 98, 2007 CarswellNat 1841, 2007 CarswellNat 832, 2007 FC 377 (F.C.)

By order dated June 29, 2006, the Court stayed the removal of the applicant from Canada pending final determination of the current application for judicial review. The granting of the stay gave the applicant his remedy before the merits of the application for judicial review were addressed.

If the respondent remains determined to remove the applicant before his humanitarian and compassionate grounds application is determined, it would be open to the applicant to request a new deferral of removal, based on all of the current circumstances and evidence. If that request is denied, a further application for leave and for judicial review would be open to him together with a further motion before the Court seeking a stay of removal pending the final determination of that new application for leave and for judicial review.

The application for judicial review was moot. The Court refused to exercise discretion to hear the matter.

*Kovacs v. Canada (Minister of Public Safety & Emergency Preparedness)*, [2007] F.C.J. No. 1625, 68 Imm. L.R. (3d) 218, 2007 CarswellNat 4247, 2007 CarswellNat 5009, 2007 FC 1247 (F.C.) — There will no doubt be cases where the Court can provide an important precedent; in such a situation the Court may decide to exercise its discretion. This is not such a case. The issue in this judicial review is simply whether the Enforcement Officer had regard to the evidence before him. A ruling on this issue would not have any practical side effects on the rights of the parties.

The judicial review was dismissed. The following question was certified:

> Where an applicant has filed an application for leave and judicial review of a decision not to defer the implementation of a removal order outstanding against him or her, does the fact that the applicant's removal is subsequently halted by operation of a stay order issued by this Court render the underlying judicial review application moot?

*Higgins v. Canada (Minister of Public Safety & Emergency Preparedness)* (2006), 55 Imm. L.R. (3d) 30, 2006 CarswellNat 1899, 2006 FC 831 (F.C.) — The applicant entered Canada in June 2004 on a seasonal farm worker visa. Within a few days he left his employment and went into hiding. An arrest warrant and an exclusion order were issued in

February of 2005. In June of 2005, he presented himself to immigration authorities with the intention of making a refugee claim. Such an application could not be entertained because of the outstanding exclusion order. He was arrested and released on a $3,000 bail posted by his eventual spouse. The applicant married and his wife, a Canadian citizen, made an in-land spousal sponsorship application. The Canadian spouse has a nine-year-old son from a previous relationship who has no contact with the biological father and instead calls the applicant his father. There was unchallenged affidavit evidence that the child had recently been diagnosed with behavioural and social disabilities. The applicant, prohibited from working, was the primary caregiver to the child. The applicant's spouse was the only breadwinner in the family and is currently pregnant. The Court was satisfied that the harm to the family and particularly the harm to the child would be irreparable in the long run. The applicant is of invaluable assistance and the primary caregiver to the child. Without his presence, the mother would have to give up her employment and any possible employment insurance benefits she could enjoy come the birth of her child in December of 2006. This stay was granted.

*Clark v. Canada (Minister of Public Safety & Emergency Preparedness)* (2006), 59 Imm. L.R. (3d) 299, 2006 CarswellNat 4518, 2006 FC 1512 (F.C.) — The applicant brought a motion for an order staying a deportation order against him. The applicant has lived in Canada for all of his 59 years, and was the son of Canadian-born parents. The applicant did not register the fact of his birth within two years of its occurrence as required under s. 5(1)(b) of the former *Citizenship Act*. The applicant was currently incarcerated; he was convicted of several offences. The Minister's delegate wrote a report under s. 44(1) of the IRPA stating that the applicant was a foreign national or permanent resident for whom there were reasonable grounds to believe was inadmissible. The Minister's delegate issued a deportation order stating the applicant was inadmissible on grounds of serious criminality. The applicant claimed that he is a citizen of Canada and that the issuance of the deportation order triggered a serious consequence, specifically, the automatic ineligibility for day parole for which the applicant would otherwise be eligible. The applicant raised a serious issue as to whether he was a Canadian citizen. There was a minimal prejudice to the respondents in staying the deportation order since the applicant had lived in Canada for 59 years. Therefore the balance of convenience favoured the applicant and the deportation order was stayed.

*Medawatte v. Canada (Minister of Public Safety & Emergency Preparedness)*, [2005] F.C.J. No. 1672, 52 Imm. L.R. (3d) 109, 2005 CarswellNat 4486, 2005 CarswellNat 3218, 2005 FC 1374 (F.C.) — The applicants were ill-served by their former lawyer. They were ordered to leave Canada. However, had their lawyer filed an application permitting them to remain in Canada based on humanitarian and compassionate grounds, that decision would have been rendered prior to the deportation orders being enforced. When the applicants attended at the immigration office to receive the PRRA decision, they mentioned their pending humanitarian and compassionate application, to which the immigration officer indicated she knew nothing about it. She told the applicants they would not be removed until the H&C application was decided. Shortly thereafter, the applicants were told to report for their removal and discovered there was no pending H&C application as it had never been filed. The removals officer, after having reviewed a great deal of information, concluded that the deportation order was enforceable. The applicants brought an application for a stay of that decision to enforce the removal order. The removal order was stayed on the basis that there was evidence of irreparable harm in that if the H&C application were granted, the effect of children being removed from school in Canada and going to Sri Lanka to be educated in another language, only to come back to Canada in a matter of months or a year could prove devastating.

*Williams v. Canada (Minister of Citizenship & Immigration)*, 2004 CarswellNat 1405, 2004 FC 683, 2004 CarswellNat 3274 (F.C.) — In order to grant the stay of a removal order, the onus is on an applicant to establish each of the elements of the tripartite test. An elevated standard applies to a stay motion arising out of a refusal to defer an applicant's removal, because the stay, if granted, effectively grants the relief sought in the underlying judicial review application. Accordingly, rather than simply applying the serious issue test, it is necessary to closely examine the merits of the underlying application.

*Chen v. Canada (Minister of Citizenship & Immigration)*, 2003 CarswellNat 4124, 2003 CarswellNat 4370, 2003 FC 1464 (F.C.) The applicant was denied refugee status in 2000 and his application for leave and judicial review was also denied in December 2000. He only came to the attention of immigration authorities as a result of a routine check following a traffic accident in October 2003. According to his own affidavit the applicant has had legal counsel since October 2003 and had known since December 3, 2003 about his removal scheduled for December 13, 2003. The applicant brought his motion to stay his removal late on December 11, 2003 and only on December 12, 2003 did he provide the respondent with an application record.

The Court exercised its discretion and declined to hear the motion.

*Almrei v. Canada (Minister of Citizenship & Immigration)*, [2003] F.C.J. No. 1790, 2003 CarswellNat 4244, 2003 CarswellNat 3787, 2003 FC 1394 (F.C.) — The applicant sought an order granting a stay of the removal order in force against him which provided for the applicant's removal to Syria, his country of nationality. The issue of irreputable harm can be answered in one of two ways. The first involves an assessment of the risk of personal harm if a person is deported to a particular country which is one of the key questions at issue in the underlying application to his stay application. The second involves assessing the effect of a denial of a stay application on a person's right to have the merits of his or her case determined and to reap the benefits associated with a positive ruling.

*Antablioghli v. Canada (Minister of Citizenship & Immigration)*, 2003 CarswellNat 3325, [2003] F.C.J. No. 1576, 2003 FC 1245, 2003 CarswellNat 5192, 2003 C.F. 1245 (F.C.) — This was a motion to stay the execution of a removal order. The applicant was a medical doctor from Syria. He was also a Fullbright Scholar, and had obtained two post-graduate degrees in the United States. The applicant had been living in Canada since 1998 and was married to a Canadian. The applicant's Canadian wife was expecting her first child and was financially dependent on the applicant. The applicant was employed as a supervisor of community support workers with the Canadian Red Cross.

The applicant made an application for permanent residence at the Canadian Consulate General in Buffalo. The respondent knew at the time that the applicant was living in Canada. When this matter came on before the Court, the applicant's application for permanent residence as a skilled worker had been outstanding for 21 months. The relevant factor in this case was obviously pertinent and compelling and it only made common sense for the removal officer to check with his own department before removing the applicant from Canada.

A stay of execution of the removal order was granted.

*Marshall v. R.*, 2002 CarswellNat 2901, 2002 CarswellNat 3965, 2002 FCT 1099, 2002 CFPI 1099 (Fed. T.D.) — The applicant applied to the Court for an order restraining an adjudicator from continuing a hearing against the applicant until the action commenced by the applicant was heard and determined. The Court concluded that it did not have jurisdiction to issue the order requested because no application for judicial review had been filed with the Court. Section 18(1) of the *Federal Courts Act* grants the Federal Court the jurisdiction to grant certain remedies, but subs. 18(3) requires that the application for judicial review be commenced. In the present motion, the motion for an interim injunction is made incidental to an action, not an application for judicial review. The Court has jurisdiction to grant a stay pursuant to s. 18.2 of the *Federal Courts Act*, but only if a judicial review application has been filed. Subsection 50(1) of the *Federal Courts Act* gives the Court jurisdiction to grant a stay, but only provides for stays in proceedings being conducted before the Federal Court. Accordingly, the motion for an injunction was dismissed.

*Cruz v. Canada (Minister of Citizenship & Immigration)*, 2001 FCT 491, 2001 CarswellNat 1016 (Fed. T.D.) — This was a motion for an interim order for the issuance of an employment authorization. The applicant based her motion on the fact that she had no other recourse available that would enable her to legally earn a living while waiting for the final disposition of her case. In the judicial review proceeding within which the interim order was sought, the applicant was seeking to quash a decision of a visa officer refusing her an employment authorization pursuant to the live-in caregiver program.

It is not within the purview of the Court, pursuant to s. 18.2 of the *Federal Courts Act*, to issue the order sought by the applicant.

*Ibrahim v. Canada (Minister of Citizenship & Immigration)*, 2000 CarswellNat 3070 (Fed. T.D.) — The respondent moved to strike out an affidavit filed by someone other than the applicant as well as the exhibits and arguments based upon that affidavit.

The aspects that the respondent is seeking to have corrected by this motion are not aspects that, even in the event that the respondent is correct, may be seen as so incorrect or unacceptable that there should be an intervention in the process of an application for judicial review. Any motion to strike out that is made in the course of an application for judicial review must be an exception, so that one of the primary objectives of such an application, which is to hear the applications on the merits as quickly as possible, may be met.

*Muncan v. Canada (Minister of Citizenship & Immigration)* (1998), 141 F.T.R. 241 (T.D.) — The applicant applied for a stay of a pending removal order. The applicant was convicted of a number of criminal offences and was ordered deported. The applicant appealed to the Appeal Division of the IRB against the deportation order. The Minister declared the applicant to be a danger to the public and the applicant sought to set aside the danger opinion and to stay the execution of the deportation order pending review of the opinion.

There is no jurisdictional limit to the discretion that the Court is empowered to apply under s. 18.2. The whole question of whether the discretion should be exercised relates to the merits of each individual case. Regarding an application for a stay of a removal order, the issue is whether it is fair and just to grant it. In considering the entire context in deciding whether to exercise the discretion provided under s. 18.2, the Court found that it was far too technical a perspective to require the deportation order to be challenged on judicial review or to limit the application of the appropriate injunctive test to the circumstances of the deportation order itself.

*Solis v. Canada (Minister of Citizenship & Immigration)*, [1997] 2 F.C. 693, 127 F.T.R. 218 (T.D.) — The applicant sought to stay the execution of a removal order. The applicant came to Canada as a refugee. In 1990, he and his family were granted landed immigrant status. Since 1992, the applicant has been convicted of a number of criminal offences. On the basis of some of the convictions an inquiry was held and a conditional deportation order issued against the applicant. The applicant filed an appeal to the Appeal Division which was still outstanding at the time of this application. While the appeal was pending, the Minister determined that the applicant constituted a danger to the public in Canada. The applicant sought leave to review this opinion, and that application was pending when this application for a stay was heard. The Appeal Division, notwithstanding the issuance of the Minister's opinion, had not decided that it had no jurisdiction to entertain the applicant's appeal with the result that the appeal before the Appeal Division was still outstanding at the time this application was heard.

The application for a stay pursuant to s. 18.2 of the *Federal Courts Act* was dismissed on the basis that there already existed a statutory stay pursuant to paragraph 49(1)(b). In reaching this decision the Court declined to follow the decision of the Court of Appeal in *Tsang v. Canada (Minister of Citizenship & Immigration)* (1997), 37 Imm. L.R. (2d) 1(Fed. C.A.) on the basis that the application of s. 49(1)(b) was not before the Court of Appeal in that case.

*Forde v. Canada (Minister of Citizenship & Immigration)* (1997), 210 N.R. 194 (Fed. C.A.) — The Minister appealed against a decision of the Trial Division in which a judge ordered that "a stay currently exists in this case and the respondent's application [for reconsideration] is dismissed with costs in the cause".

In December 1994, a deportation order was made against the respondent. He appealed to the Appeal Division of the IRB, but before the appeal was heard, a delegate of the Minister decided that the respondent was a danger to the public in Canada. In February 1996, the respondent applied for leave to judicially review that opinion but at no time did he file an application for leave to review the deportation order.

In March 1996, the Trial Division issued a stay of the deportation order "until such time as the application for judicial review is finally disposed of". This order was clearly ancillary to the leave application then pending and was authorized by s. 18.2 of the *Federal Courts Act*. In August 1996, the Trial Division dismissed the application for leave, thus terminating any judicial review proceeding. The original stay, granted in March 1996, thus came to an end, however, the Trial Division in September 1996, granted a "continuation" of the already terminated stay, and when the Minister applied for reconsideration of this order and a declaration that the stay no longer existed, the learned judge of the Trial Division made the order which is now the subject of this appeal.

The Trial Division has a carefully defined judicial review jurisdiction in respect of "any decision or order made or any matter arising under the *[Immigration] Act*". The decision of the Minister pursuant to subs. 70(5) is such a decision. During the course of disposing of an application for leave to seek judicial review of such a decision, the Court is authorized by s. 18.2 to make ancillary orders, such as a stay. Once the leave application was disposed of there was no longer a leave or review proceeding to which a stay could be ancillary under s. 18.2. Section 50(1)(b) of the *Federal Courts Act* was never intended to give a general mandate to the Trial Division to stop deportations which are no longer under attack in the Court.

This appeal was properly brought without a question having been certified as the putative stay was no longer related to any application for leave, proceeding under subs. 82.1(1), and thus an appeal was not barred by s. 82.2.

*Huseyinov v. Canada (Minister of Employment & Immigration)* (1994), 174 N.R. 233 (Fed. C.A.) — The appellants requested an adjournment in order that counsel may have time to consider the implications of proposed new regulations concerning failed refugee claimants.

The adjournment was refused. No such regulations had been adopted. A press release cannot create accrued rights in the appellants. It is the duty of the Court to apply the law as it is, not as it might be, and to hear appeals at the time for which they are set down.

*Yamani v. Canada (Solicitor General)* (1994), 27 Imm. L.R. (2d) 116, 80 F.T.R. 307 — The applicant applied for injunctive relief, pursuant to s. 18.2 of the *Federal Courts Act*. The injunction was granted and the Court had to consider, among other issues, whether the balance of convenience favoured the granting of the stay. The public interest in the maintenance of processes must be considered even where the stay is considered an exemption from the general public requirement in question and not one involving a suspension of that requirement generally.

The Court referred to *RJR-MacDonald Inc. v. Canada (Attorney General)* (1994), 164 N.R. 1 (S.C.C) at pages 38-39. It noted that in the case of a public authority the onus of demonstrating irreparable harm is less than that of a private applicant. The test will nearly always be satisfied upon proof that the authority is charged with the duty of promoting or protecting the public interest and upon some indication that the impugned legislation, regulation or activity was undertaken pursuant to that responsibility. Once these requirements have been met the Court should, in most cases, assume that irreparable harm to the public interest would result from restraint of that action.

In this case deciding that the balance of convenience favoured granting a stay, the Court noted that important as the public interest is in maintaining the statutory processes, the case had not been pursued by the Crown as a matter of great urgency. Further, the grant of the stay preserved the status quo as far as the applicant was concerned and did not interfere significantly with the exercise of their lawful responsibilities by the authorities. This case, if a stay was granted, would not result in a "cascade of stays and exemptions".

The Court granted a stay but only to the extent of ordering that no removal or deportation order be issued against the applicant pending the final determination of the various applications for judicial review now scheduled to be heard by the Court. This interfered as little as possible with the inquiry process as established under the *Immigration Act*.

## Section 48 — former *Immigration Act* (The *Immigration Act*, R.S.C. 1985, c. I-2)

*[Editor's Note: What appears below are the cases which were collected under section 48 of the former Act and which deal with the requirements that an applicant must meet in order to obtain a Court Ordered stay.]*

**48. Time of Execution — Subject to sections 49 and 50, a removal order shall be executed as soon as reasonably practicable.**

*John v. Canada (Minister of Citizenship & Immigration)* (2003), 231 F.T.R. 248, 2003 FCT 420, [2003] F.C.J. No. 583, 2003 CarswellNat 942 (Fed. T.D.) — The applicants sought to review the decision of a removals officer to defer the removal of the applicant from Canada. A removals officer is entitled to rely on what the applicant's counsel determines to be the overriding factor warranting deferral. Counsel must be very selective about what he or she chooses to point out to a removals officer. The *Immigration Act* does not give a removals officer the discretion to consider the various H&C factors in determining whether or not to defer removal. There is no requirement that the removals officer consider the impact of the removal on the Canadian citizen child.

In this case, the overriding factor warranting deferral was the availability of medical treatment for the child. The officer confirmed that a pediatrician in St. Vincent would be able to treat the child with the exact medication referred to by the professionals from Sick Children's Hospital.

Accordingly, the application was dismissed.

*Ahani v. R.* (2002), 19 Imm. L.R. (3d) 231, (sub nom. *Ahani v. Canada (Attorney General))* 58 O.R. (3d) 107, 2002 CarswellOnt 364, (sub nom. *Ahani v. Canada (Attorney General))* 208 D.L.R. (4th) 66, (sub nom. *Ahani v. Canada (Attorney General))* 156 O.A.C. 37, (sub nom. *Ahani v. Canada (Minister of Citizenship & Immigration))* 91 C.R.R. (2d) 145, [2002] O.J. No. 431 (C.A.); leave to appeal refused (2002), 2002 CarswellOnt 1651, 2002 CarswellOnt 1652, (sub nom. *R. v. Ahani)* 92 C.R.R. (2d) 188 (note), 293 N.R. 331 (note), (sub nom. *Ahani v. Canada (Attorney General))* 169 O.A.C. 197 (note) (S.C.C.) — The appellant challenged a decision of the Minister of Citizenship and Immigration to the effect that he was a terrorist and a danger to the security of Canada. The appellant challenged this order alleging that he would face torture in Iran. His appeal was dismissed by the Supreme Court of Canada on January 11, 2002. He then filed a communication with the United Nations Human Rights Committee for relief under the Optional Protocol to the international Covenant on civil and political rights which Canada has ratified but not incorporated into its domestic law. The appellant/applicant applied to the Superior Court for an injunction restraining his deportation pending the committee's consideration of his communication. This application was dismissed and the applicant appealed to the Court of Appeal which stayed his deportation pending the hearing of his appeal.

The applicant's mere removal from Canada does not establish a deprivation of life, liberty or security of the person. Convention refugees and other non-citizens do not have an unqualified constitutional right to remain in Canada. To trigger the principles of fundamental justice the applicant must show a potential risk of serious harm if he is deported. The Supreme Court of Canada has found that the applicant only faces a minimal risk of harm and thus it is not open to the Court in this proceeding to come to a different conclusion.

The content of the principles of fundamental justice can only be determined by balancing individual and state interests. The applicant's interest is reflected in the opportunity to seek the committee's views on whether Canada's treatment of him breached the Covenant which Canada signed. Canada's interest is reflected in the fact that Canada has never incorporated the Covenant or the Protocol into Canadian law by implementing legislation. Further, in signing the Protocol, Canada did not agree to be bound by the final views of the committee. It was decided as a matter of policy by all of the party states to the Covenant, that they each be free, on a case by case basis, to accept or reject the committee's final views.

Section 7 of the *Charter* cannot be used to enforce Canada's international commitments in a domestic court. International treaties and conventions not incorporated into Canadian law have no domestic legal consequences.

This case demonstrates the difference between the proper role of the executive and the proper role of the judiciary. Judges are not competent to assess whether Canada is acting in bad faith by rejecting the committee's interim measures request and instead deporting the applicant immediately. Canada has many international obligations to balance, not the least of which is to ensure that it does not become a safe haven for terrorists.

*Dias v. Canada (Minister of Citizenship & Immigration)*, 2001 CarswellNat 1327, 2001 FCT 677 (Fed. T.D.) — The applicant sought to stay his removal from Canada to Jamaica. The applicant was the subject of two danger opinions issued by the Minister.

By virtue of s. 70(5) of the *Immigration Act*, the applicant loses the benefit of an appeal of his deportation order where the Minister is of the opinion the applicant constitutes a danger to the public in Canada. Should the applicant be successful on the underlying judicial review and have the danger opinion quashed, then his right to appeal the removal order would be restored, but this would be of very little assistance to the applicant if the removal order was already executed. The execution of the removal order before the hearing of the underlying judicial review of the issuance of the danger opinion will effectively render the judicial review nugatory. The loss of the benefit of the judicial review proceedings amounts to irreparable harm for the purposes of the tripartite test for a stay.

*Romans v. Canada (Minister of Citizenship & Immigration)*, 2001 CarswellNat 1622, 2001 FCA 244, 273 N.R. 329 (Fed. C.A.) — This was an application for a stay of a deportation order pending the disposition of the applicant's appeal from an order of the Trial Division dismissing his application for judicial review. The Trial Division judge had certified a question for appeal. The Court found irreparable harm because there was a substantial likelihood that the appellant would suffer irreparable harm if removed to Jamaica. The Court found that the appellant was a mentally incompetent person who was unable to support himself and who had lived in Canada nearly all of his life. If such a person were deported, pending the disposition of his appeal, he would be effectively denied the benefit of a decision that he had a constitutional right to under s. 7 of the *Charter*.

With respect to the balance of convenience test, the Court noted that the appellant will remain in detention pending the disposition of his appeal and that to stay his removal posed no threat to the safety of anyone in Canada. It was true that the Canadian public would bear the cost of this detention. In the Court's view this was a price worth paying. The appellant was a vulnerable person who, in truth, although not a citizen of Canada, was more the product and responsibility of Canadian than of Jamaican society.

*Cheema v. Canada (Minister of Citizenship & Immigration)*, 2001 CarswellNat 1417, 2001 FCT 740 (Fed. T.D.) — The applicants applied to stay their deportation from Canada. The discretion to defer removal is a discretion vested in the Minister notwithstanding the fact that the discretion is exercised by the removal officer. The Minister, pursuant to the Act, is under a positive obligation to execute removal orders. The discretion to be exercised by a removal officer does not consist of assessing risk, but rather of assessing whether there are special circumstances that would justify deferring removal.



The removal officer properly exercised her discretion in deferring removal to allow the children to complete their school year, and at the same time refusing to defer removal pending the disposition of an outstanding H & C application.

There was, accordingly, no serious issue to be tried and the motion for a stay was refused.

*Williams v. Canada (Minister of Citizenship & Immigration)*, 2001 CarswellNat 1713, 2001 FCT 851 (Fed. T.D.) — The applicant applied for a stay of the decision of a removals officer refusing to defer the removal of the applicant pending his submission of an H & C application. With respect to the first part of the three-part test to be met in order to obtain a stay, the Court concluded that it is necessary only to demonstrate that an applicant's case is neither frivolous nor vexatious. The Court relied upon *Turbo Resources Ltd. v. Petro-Canada Inc.*, [1989] 2 F.C. 451, [1989] F.C.J. No. 14, 91 N.R. 341, 22 C.I.P.R. 172, 24 C.P.R. (3d) 1, 39 F.T.R. 240 (note), 1989 CarswellNat 579, 1989 CarswellNat 626 (C.A.)

*Odumosu v. Canada (Minister of Citizenship & Immigration)*, 2001 CarswellNat 2477, 2001 FCT 1174 (Fed. T.D.) — This was an application to stay a removal order. The applicant achieved a negative H&C decision. She had failed to update her H&C application and had failed to disclose that her second child had developed asthma. Thus, the officer who rejected the application was not aware of this fact and therefore had not taken it into consideration.

Injunctions are matters of discretion. The traditional test for an injunction did not address the interests of this ill child. The Court was not comfortable removing this 16-month-old baby to Nigeria without proper evidence about the severity of the child's condition and the facilities for his care in Nigeria. Accordingly, the execution of the removal order was stayed and the applicant was given a deadline by which she was to submit a fresh H&C application. The stay order further provided that the removal order was not to be executed until the disposition of this second H & C application.

*Hussein v. Canada (Minister of Citizenship & Immigration)*, 2001 CarswellNat 2417, 2001 FCT 1172 (Fed. T.D.) — The applicant sought to stay a removal order. This application was brought two days after a similar motion by the applicant was heard and dismissed by another judge of the Federal Court. The Court applied the principle of *res judicata*. The Court observed that even if it were to consider the matter on its merits out of judicial comity, it would not reach a different conclusion than that reached on the earlier application unless it were convinced that the judge was clearly wrong on the basis of the evidence before him. Accordingly, the application was dismissed.

*Essiaw v. Canada (Minister of Citizenship & Immigration)*, 2001 CarswellNat 2312, 2001 FCT 1108, 2001 CarswellNat 3670, 2001 CFPI 1108 (Fed. T.D.) — The Court dismissed a motion for a stay of execution of a departure order. There is an important distinction between a departure order and a deportation order. If a person subject to a departure order leaves voluntarily he or she will be provided, upon request, with a certificate confirming her departure. The effect of the certificate is that the departure is recognized as voluntary and has no implications for the applicant's right to return to Canada in the future. If the person does not leave Canada or leaves but does not obtain the certificate, the departure order is deemed to become a deportation order. As a result, the person may then be forcibly removed if she has remained in Canada. If she is removed or leaves voluntarily but does not obtain a certificate, the result is the same. The person cannot reenter Canada without a permit from the Minister.

The issuance of a departure order represents the exercise of a discretion in favour of the applicant based upon a belief that the applicant will leave the country within the period provided by the Act and Regulations. If applicants choose not to take the benefit of that favourable discretion, then they are treated as they would have been if it had been determined that they were not likely to leave Canada. One cannot get the benefit of a departure order by agreeing to leave Canada and then seek to retain the benefit of that order when one refuses to leave by attempting to stay the order.

At the time of the bringing of the motion, the departure order had not yet changed into a deportation order. The application for a stay was therefore refused on the basis that it was premature.

*Benitez v. Canada (Minister of Citizenship & Immigration)*, [2001] F.C.J. No. 1802, 214 F.T.R. 282, 2001 FCT 1307, 2001 CarswellNat 3468, 2001 CarswellNat 2773, 2001 CFPI 1307 (T.D.) — The applicant sought to review the decision of a removals officer refusing to defer the applicant's removal from Canada. The applicant's refugee claim was refused, his PDRCC was refused and then the applicant appeared for the purpose of making removal arrangements. The applicant's counsel asked the removals officer to defer removal pending the determination of the applicant's H&C application. The submissions of the applicant amounted to calling for a full H&C application to be heard by a removals officer. This is not what s. 48 of the current *Immigration Act* provides. The proper place for the full consideration of all of an applicant's H&C factors is before the H&C officer. The removals officer is entitled to rely on what the applicant's counsel determines to be the overriding factor warranting deferral. As such, counsel must be very selective about what he or she chooses to point out to a removals officer.

The doctrine of legitimate expectation does not override the very limited statutory discretion that the statute makes available to a removals officer. Possible suicidal tendencies should be given consideration by the officer and that was done in the present case. The officer took into account the three psychological reports provided by the applicant in making his decision. The application was dismissed.

*Adel c. Canada (Ministre de la Citoyenneté & de l'Immigration)* (2001), [2002] 2 F.C. 73, 2001 CarswellNat 2022, 2001 CarswellNat 3085, 2001 CFPI 1017, 2001 FCT 1017 (Fed. T.D.) — This was an application for a stay which failed. It often happens that counsel who represent immigrants are themselves consulted at the last minute by clients who live in hope that the removal date will never arrive. Moreover, the Federal Court frequently sees cases in which there is very little time between the applicant's summons and the date of removal. What this means is that often the choice of the hearing date for such applications is outside the control of applicants' counsel. But there are other cases in which counsel know in advance that they will have to make an application for a stay. In those cases, the Court has a hard time understanding why the application for a stay is tendered at the last moment. This does not do justice to either the respondent or the Court, both of whom must comply with the applicants' deadlines. The respondent is often unable to file its evidence. The Court, for its part, must determine complex questions on the basis of an incomplete record and without the benefit of any period of reflection.

When an application to stay an exclusion order is presented at the last minute, certain facts must be taken into consideration. The first is that the Court may very well refuse to hear the application. If the Court is persuaded that it should hear the case, that does not mean that everything will happen in the usual way. The applicant still has the burden of satisfying the Court that he or she is entitled to the order being sought. That burden is eased if the applicant is credible. Generally speaking, a judge hearing an application to stay is not, considering the state of the record, in a position to determine issues of credibility. But when the judge agrees to hear an application to stay on the ground that there was no assessment of the risk of return, and that the risk of return is based solely on the applicant's allegations, the judge must be satisfied that there is reason for concern about the fate of the applicant. The fact that there are others who would perhaps be in a better position to assess the applicant's situation, does not mean that the judge hearing the application for a stay must accept everything that he or she is told without exercising his or her critical faculties.

The Court is in a position to decide questions of credibility, even in the context of an application to stay a removal order. The Court must exercise prudence and maintain a certain reserve in regard to these questions of credibility because the opportunities for a careful analysis of the evidence are frequently lacking. But when the evidence before the court gives rise to some serious questions of credibility, the Court should not ignore the possibility of bad faith.

The Court concluded that the applicant's evidence in this case was not trustworthy and dismissed the application for a stay.

*Nabut v. Canada (Minister of Citizenship & Immigration)*, 2001 CarswellNat 3002, 2001 FCT 1392 (Fed. T.D.) — The denial of bail to an accused, upon his return to the United States, is not irreparable harm. Neither is it irreparable harm to be subjected to questioning in the United States in the course of an investigation into the terrorist attacks of September 11, 2001.

*Chambers v. Canada (Minister of Citizenship & Immigration)*, 2001 FCT 84, 2001 CarswellNat 212 (Fed. T.D.) — This was an application to stay a removal order and in the course of giving reasons the Court agreed that the discretion that a removal officer may exercise is very limited, and in any case, is restricted to when a removal order will be executed. In deciding when it is "reasonably practicable" for a removal order to be executed, a removal officer may consider various factors such as illness, other impediments to travelling, and pending H&C applications that were brought on a timely basis but have yet to be resolved due to backlogs in the system.

*Obasohan v. Canada (Minister of Citizenship & Immigration)* (2001), 13 Imm. L.R. (3d) 82, 2001 FCT 92, 2001 CarswellNat 325 (Fed. T.D.) — This was an application to stay the execution of a removal order arguing irreparable harm to the infant child of the applicant. The infant child was a Canadian citizen, born in Canada in July of 1999. While a Court is normally concerned with irreparable harm to the applicant, the interests of the infant child are inseparably linked with those of the applicant. The Court considered that pending a full consideration of the serious issue, or a full consideration of the child's interests, that the applicant and her daughter were *de facto* inseparable. Accordingly, the issue of irreparable harm was made out and an order was issued staying the removal of the applicant.

*Wang v. Canada (Minister of Citizenship & Immigration)* (2001), 13 Imm. L.R. (3d) 289, [2001] 3 F.C. 682, 204 F.T.R. 5, 2001 FCT 148, [2001] F.C.J. No. 295, 2001 CarswellNat 406, 2001 CarswellNat 2626 (T.D.) — Where a motion for a stay is made from a removal officer's refusal to defer removal, the judge hearing the motion ought not simply to apply the "serious issue" test, but should go further and closely examine the merits of the underlying application. Except in the case of a person overstaying a Ministerial permit, all removal orders are made by officials acting pursuant to a specific authority conferred upon them under the *Immigration Act*. Removal orders are not administrative arrangements made by the Minister, which the Minister is at liberty to change. They are orders which have the force of law which the Minister is called upon to execute. Aside from questions of travel arrangements and fitness to travel, the execution of the order can only be effected by some other process occurring within the framework of the Act since the Minister has no authority to refuse to execute the order. Accordingly, a request for deferral can only be made in the context of some collateral process which might impinge upon the enforceability of the removal order. The appropriate inquiry is whether the process in question could result in a situation in which the execution of the removal order was no longer mandatory.

Section 46.07(4) provides that where a person who has been found to be a Convention refugee is subject to a removal order, an immigration officer or an adjudicator shall inquire whether the person has a right to remain in Canada, and if so, shall quash the removal order and allow the person to remain. Section 53 provides that no Convention refugee or a person who has been found to be a Convention refugee in another country shall be removed to a country where they face a risk to life or freedom, unless they fall within certain enumerated classes of persons. This section contemplates the existence of a removal order which cannot be executed.

Legally, the mere presence of an outstanding H&C claim is not grounds for a stay of execution and by extension a deferral of a removal order. Further, declining the discretion to defer too broadly risks creating the equivalent of a statutory stay where Parliament declined to do so.

*Frankowski v. Canada (Minister of Citizenship & Immigration)* (2000), 2000 CarswellNat 1360 (Fed. T.D.) — The issue on this stay application was whether irreparable harm would result to the applicant if he were deported to Poland. For the purpose of a stay application, irreparable harm implies the serious likelihood of jeopardy to the applicant's life or safety. Irreparable harm must be very grave and more than the unfortunate hardship associated with the break-up or relocation of a family.

*Giwa v. Canada (Minister of Citizenship & Immigration)* (2000), 2000 CarswellNat 1176 (Fed. T.D.) — The applicant sought a stay of the execution of a removal order. The applicant was approximately 13 months late in seeking leave from the Refugee Division's negative decision of April 1999. The Court supports the view that it is without jurisdiction on a stay application where the underlying application for leave is subject to a decision extending time before consideration. The Court noted that some judges have adopted the practice on consent on stay applications deciding the extension of time question first. The Court was not satisfied that an extension of time was warranted and denied the request for an extension.

*Canada (Minister of Citizenship & Immigration) v. Varela* (2000), 6 Imm. L.R. (3d) 182, 185 F.T.R. 258, 2000 CarswellNat 1463 (T.D.) — The Minister sought an injunction preventing the continuation of an adjudicator's inquiry on the inadmissibility of the applicant under s. 19(1)(j). The Court granted the injunction and stayed the inquiry until the judicial review application in this matter was heard.

The courts will not, except in special circumstances, entertain judicial review of interlocutory evidentiary rulings made in the middle of a dually mandated inquiry. One such special circumstance is jurisdiction. The respondent served in the military of Nicaragua from 1983 to 1989. He came to Canada in 1991 and made a refugee claim but was excluded from protection because of Article 1(F)(A). In 1993, the Minister authorized the issuance of a permit to the respondent permitting him and his family to proceed to landing after they had complied with all statutory requirements. In 1999, a report was made to the Deputy Minister stating that the respondent was a person described in paragraph 19(1)(j). When the inquiry commenced, the Minister's counsel argued that the Refugee Division had resolved the issue of there being reasonable grounds to believe that the respondent had committed an act outside of Canada that constituted a war crime. Counsel for the Minister contended that the Minister was only required to lead evidence at the inquiry to the effect that if such an act had been committed in Canada it would have constituted an offence against the laws of Canada. The adjudicator declined to give effect to the Minister's argument and the Minister then applied to judicially review the adjudicator's decision and sought this injunction.

The adjudicator's ruling cannot simply be characterized as an evidentiary ruling made during the course of the tribunal's inquiry. The ruling dealt with the fundamental and basic aspect of the inquiry. Concerning the evidentiary structure or framework of an important element of the inquiry, the adjudicator's decision disposed of a substantial question before him. Viewed in this light the ruling was jurisdictional in nature, determining as it did the essence and scope of the inquiry.

*Harry v. Canada (Minister of Citizenship & Immigration)* (2000), 9 Imm. L.R. (3d) 159, 195 F.T.R. 221, 2000 CarswellNat 2522, [2000] F.C.J. No. 1727 (T.D.) — The applicants sought the stay of a removal order while their humanitarian and compassionate application was pending. If the applicants were returned to Trinidad or remained in Canada in the care of other persons, whichever course of action might be followed, irreparable harm would result to the child even in the possibly brief period that it might take to complete the humanitarian and compassionate application review. The length of that period was entirely at the discretion of the respondent. The applicants and their child have a relatively secure life in Canada. Their future in Trinidad is uncertain at best, both economically and socially. Such uncertainty represents irreparable harm for the young child, as would leaving her in Canada without the care and attention of either of her parents. The other aspects of the test were also found to be made out in this case and, accordingly, a stay was granted.

*Ilyas v. Canada (Minister of Citizenship & Immigration)* (2000), 2000 CarswellNat 2998 (Fed. T.D.) — The applicant was served with a direction to report for removal on November 3, 2000. His removal was scheduled for November 10, 2000 and the applicant failed to appear. The applicant was arrested on November 23, 2000 and received a direction to report informing him that his removal was scheduled for December 3, 2000. At that point, the applicant filed an application for a stay.

The applicant chose not to file a motion to stay during the time between November 3, 2000 and November 10, 2000 but rather decided to disobey a valid deportation order.

The Court refused to hear this application for a stay on the basis that to do so would just reward someone who chose to disobey a valid deportation order.

*Abazi v. Canada (Minister of Citizenship & Immigration)* (2000), 2000 CarswellNat 529 (Fed. T.D.) — The Court found irreparable harm in the fact that the applicants were operating their own business which supported them and enabled them to accumulate savings. If deported, the applicants would lose their business and their savings would be consumed for various purposes associated with their removal. The Court reasoned that if the applicants were successful ultimately in their H&C application, they would be entitled to apply for landing from within Canada but would have lost their business and their savings.

*Fabian v. R.* (2000), (sub nom. *Fabian v. Canada (Minister of Citizenship & Immigration))* 255 N.R. 367, (sub nom. *Fabian v. Canada (Minister of Citizenship & Immigration))* 179 F.T.R. 153 (note), 2000 CarswellNat 93 (C.A.) — The balance of convenience favoured the appellant. The motions judge erred when she concluded that the fact that the appellant had committed crimes in Canada as opposed to abroad weighed against him and in favour of the public interest. The motions judge failed to consider whether the public was in any danger from the appellant given the fact that the appellant was detained and that as long as he so remained there was no evidence that he was endangering the public. It is not sufficient to look at the concept of "public danger" or "danger to the public" when there is in fact no likelihood of contact between the public and the "dangerous" person during the time for which interlocutory relief is sought.

*Aquila v. Canada (Minister of Citizenship & Immigration)* (2000), 2000 CarswellNat 131 (Fed. T.D.) — The test for determining the balance of convenience was affirmed in *R.J.R. - MacDonald Inc.* as a determination of which of the parties will suffer greater harm from the granting or refusal of a stay. One important factor in this comparison is the public interest in the maintenance of both statutory programs and the efforts of those responsible for carrying them out. If the stay is refused, the applications for landing or for leave to seek judicial review of the deportation order will not be prejudiced in any legal sense. Without any other evidence concerning the disruption which will be visited on the applicants if no stay is granted, the Court found that the respondent would suffer greater inconvenience if the stay was granted and accordingly the application to stay the order was dismissed.

*Anderson v. Canada (Minister of Citizenship & Immigration)* (2000), 2000 CarswellNat 520 (Fed. T.D.) — The applicant commenced two proceedings. In one, he requested that his H&C application be determined, and in the other, he sought to review a negative decision of a panel of the Convention Refugee Determination Division (CRDD). The applicant brought a notice of motion for a stay in each of the proceedings. The two applications were heard together. Section 49(1)(c)(i) provides a Statutory Stay of a deportation order when a person has been determined not to be a Convention refugee and has filed an application for leave to commence a judicial review. The statutory stay does not apply to an application compelling a decision on an H&C application. The motions were dismissed because of the statutory stay provided in s. 49(1)(c)(i).

*Melo v. Canada (Minister of Citizenship & Immigration)* (2000), 188 F.T.R. 39, 2000 CarswellNat 526, [2000] F.C.J. No. 403 (T.D.) — The applicant faced deportation to his native Portugal as a result of his criminality. The applicant, however, was also the father of two teenage daughters who resided with their mother in British Columbia and with whom the applicant visits monthly and to whom he speaks on the telephone frequently. He was also the father of a 3-year-old by his relationship with another woman.

The issue of irreparable harm does not turn upon the possibility of serious physical harm to the applicant. If deported, the applicant will be returned to a western European country. Damage to economic and other interests of the applicant can satisfy the requirement of irreparable harm. The applicant will lose a position that is apparently much better than any he has previously been able to obtain. Further, deportation will affect the applicant's ongoing psychiatric treatment which may well result in a loss of the therapeutic gains which the applicant has achieved over a long period of time. Finally, there was evidence that the applicant's children would be devastated by his departure. If the phrase "irreparable harm" is to retain any meaning at all, it must refer to some prejudice beyond that which is inherent in the notion of deportation itself. To be deported is to lose your job, to be separated from familiar faces and places, and it is accompanied by enforced separation and heartbreak. There was nothing in the applicant's circumstances which took it out of the usual consequences of deportation. This was not the case of deporting an elderly woman who cared for and in turn was cared for by an elderly husband, nor was it the case of deporting someone who was the sole caregiver for a blind and sick grandparent.

In this case, the serious issue revolved around the extent to which the children's interests were considered in the proceedings before the Appeal Division. If the applicant is deported, the children's interests will be affected prior to a ruling being made on the extent to which their interests must be considered. This will effectively render the judicial review nugatory. If there is to be any reality to the judicial review application, the *status quo* must be maintained and accordingly, the loss of the benefit of the application for judicial review constitutes irreparable harm.

*S. (R.V.) v. Canada (Minister of Citizenship & Immigration)* (2000), 7 Imm. L.R. (3d) 181, 188 F.T.R. 58, 2000 CarswellNat 524 (T.D.) — This was a motion pursuant to s. 18.2 of the *Federal Courts Act*, for a stay of an exclusion order and a stay of the execution of a removal order until such time as an application for judicial review had been dealt with by the Court.

The law surrounding irreparable harm is treated somewhat differently in the immigration law context than it is when other areas, such as intellectual property, are involved. The high burden of proof has been downgraded so that a moving party merely has to prove that there is a reasonable likelihood that irreparable harm will be suffered. What constitutes irreparable harm has also been modified. Courts have looked to whether a moving party's life or safety will be put in jeopardy, noting that any harm from deportation must be grave, that is, more than the mere unfortunate hardship which inevitably accompanies any removal from Canada. Irreparable harm is not a mere inconvenience which may be managed, nor is it a hardship which may be overcome, or damage which may be readily repaired.

With respect to psychological trauma, a moving party's suicidal tendencies can constitute irreparable harm. Whereas there is no evidence in this case showing that the moving party's psychological problems would lead to similarly irrevocable harm, then the evidence points to the severity of the harm but not to its irrevocability or irreparable nature. The Court was not prepared to consider irreparable harm being constituted by removing the applicant from the supports that he had garnered in Canada in his battle against alcohol until evidence was adduced that no such help was available to the applicant in the country to which he was being removed.

*Panchoo (Litigation Guardian of) v. Canada (Minister of Citizenship & Immigration)* (2001), 3 Imm. L.R. (3d) 206, (sub nom. *Panchoo v. Canada (Minister of Citizenship & Immigration))* [2000] 3 F.C. 18, (sub nom. *Panchoo v. Canada (Minister of Citizenship & Immigration))* 255 N.R. 369, 2000 CarswellNat 165, 2000 CarswellNat 1753, [2000] F.C.J. No. 143 (Fed. C.A.) — The appellant's father was scheduled for deportation after his request to be processed for landing within Canada on humanitarian and compassionate grounds was denied. The Minister sought to deport the appellant's father prior to the Trial Division's consideration of the father's application for leave to commence judicial review proceedings. An application to stay the order was dismissed, and in response the appellant, through her litigation guardian, commenced an action seeking various forms of declaratory relief. The appellant sought a stay with respect to her father's deportation pending the disposition of the action. Her motion for a stay was dismissed. The appellant appealed the dismissal of the interlocutory stay request to the Court of Appeal.

There is no right of appeal from a refusal to grant a stay of a deportation order pending the disposition of an application for leave to commence judicial review proceedings. The Court expressed serious doubts that ss. 82 and 83 of the *Immigration Act* operated to preclude any appeal of a Trial Division's refusal to grant a stay pending perfection and consideration of a leave application. The Minister's decision to effect deportation was taken before the application for leave to commence had been perfected. The Minister knew full well that in proceeding in this manner, the intended deportee would be forced to seek a stay in which it would be argued that there was a serious issue to be addressed in the judicial review proceedings. That argument is for all intents and purposes the very one that will be addressed by a Trial Division judge when considering whether to grant the leave application. The Minister's insistence that deportation be carried out forthwith effectively short-circuits the leave application. The Court expressed its frustrations with respect to the Minister's refusal to allow persons to have their day in court. The Court expressed the view that the Minister should only pursue deportation in the clearest and most compelling of cases.

Because s. 82.2 has been interpreted to the effect that there is no appeal from a motions judge's decision, counsel for the deportee initiated an action in the name of the daughter seeking a declaration that the deportation would not be in the best interest of the daughter.

There was no serious issue in this case because the appellant had no standing to challenge the deportation order. A child has no independent legal right to launch an action to prevent her parent from being removed from Canada. Further, the appellant was seeking a remedy pursuant to s. 24(1) of the *Charter.* A person seeking a remedy under s. 24(1) must personally have been the victim of an infringement. Such a person cannot base her application on an infringement of the rights of third parties. Accordingly, it was with regret, that the stay application was dismissed.

*Antonio (Litigation Guardian of) v. Canada (Minister of Citizenship & Immigration)* (1999), 1999 CarswellOnt 4098 (Ont. S.C.J.) — The Minister moved for a stay of these proceedings on the ground that the Superior Court should decline jurisdiction in favour of the Federal Court. The motion was allowed, however, the Court noted that there was currently an application for consideration on humanitarian and compassionate grounds (H&C) which had not been heard. Given the fact that there were Canadian children in this case, the Court stayed the operation of its order for 120 days to allow the applicant and her children to remain in Canada until the H&C application had been concluded. The Court also allowed that any party could apply to abridge or extend the stay if the circumstances required it.

*Villareal v. Canada (Minister of Citizenship & Immigration)* (1999), 1999 CarswellNat 2314, [1999] F.C.J. No. 1754 (Fed. T.D.) — The applicant sought to stay execution of a removal order that had been made pending the determination of an application for consideration on humanitarian and compassionate (H&C) grounds by an immigration officer. The applicant had applied for H&C considerations in June of 1999. No decision had been made on that application, but the applicant had been advised that it might be some months before an interview could take place if an interview was needed. Irreparable harm, in the context of this application, must be harm which will occur in the interim between the time the applicant is removed and the time when her H&C application is determined. The court was not persuaded that the applicant or her son would suffer irreparable harm in the limited time that could reasonably be expected before a decision was made on the H&C application.

*Lawson v. Canada (Minister of Citizenship & Immigration)* (1999), 178 F.T.R. 147, 1999 CarswellNat 2254 (T.D.) — The applicant was ordered deported by reason of his criminal convictions and his failure to disclose his prior conviction and period of residence in

Canada when applying for admission as a sponsored candidate. The applicant's appeal to the Immigration Appeal Division (IAD) was dismissed without reasons given. The applicant asked for reasons and at the date of this application for a stay, those reasons had not been provided.

The Court concluded that the applicant was entitled to have the reasons of the IAD in hand before arguing his application for his stay. Accordingly, the Court issued a stay on an interim basis against the deportation order. This stay was for a period ending 7 days after the applicant received the reasons of the IAD.

*Ahani v. R.* (1999), 1999 CarswellNat 968 (Fed. C.A.) — The motions judge issued a stay preventing the deportation of the respondent pending the determination of an action before the Court. The Minister appealed. The appeal was dismissed. The jurisdiction of the Court of Appeal to interfere from a decision regarding whether to issue a stay is well established. It is only where the motions judge has misapplied the law, misapprehended the evidence or where circumstances have substantially changed after the motions judge made his or her order — in such a manner as to justify interfering with the order — that the Court of Appeal will exercise its jurisdiction to intervene.

*Suresh v. Canada (Minister of Citizenship & Immigration)*, [1999] 4 F.C. 206, 176 D.L.R. (4th) 296, 249 N.R. 28, [1999] F.C.J. No. 1180, 1999 CarswellNat 1466 (C.A.) — This was an expedited motion for an order staying the removal of the appellant pending the disposition of his appeal. Sri Lankan authorities indicated that the appellant would be detained upon his arrival in Sri Lanka, but that he would not be subjected to torture or degrading treatment. Assuming that the appellant is deported and detained, and assuming that he is successful on his appeal, the appellant's constitutional challenge would be a hollow victory. The authorities in Sri Lanka would be unlikely to release him and he would be unable to avail himself of the fruits of his victory. This was found to constitute irreparable harm.

If judges of the Trial Division are prepared to certify questions of general importance as a condition precedent to the Court of Appeal hearing an unrestricted appeal on the merits, then it is not unreasonable to defer the execution of a deportation or removal order in circumstances where it may ultimately be found that persons such as the appellant have not been dealt with as required by law. While there may be instances in which a person can return to Canada following a successful appeal, this is not one of those cases.

The Court, in concluding that the balance of convenience favoured the public interest, did not wish to be viewed as undermining the legitimate attempts of the Minister to deport those who actively support terrorist organizations. Allowing the appellant to remain in Canada until such time as his appeal had been heard would not adversely affect Canada's reputation in the international community with respect to fighting terrorism.

*Francis (Litigation Guardian of) v. Canada (Minister of Citizenship & Immigration)* (1999), (sub nom. *Francis v. Canada (Minister of Citizenship & Immigration))* 125 O.A.C. 248, 179 D.L.R. (4th) 421, 49 O.R. (3d) 136, 1999 CarswellOnt 3229, [1999] O.J. No. 3853 (C.A.); leave to appeal allowed (2000), [1999] S.C.C.A. No. 558, (sub nom. *Francis v. Canada (Minister of Citizenship & Immigration))* 138 O.A.C. 199 (note), 257 N.R. 200 (note), 2000 CarswellOnt 1961, 2000 CarswellOnt 1962 (S.C.C.) — This was an appeal from an order of McNeely J. who had quashed a deportation order against the respondent and directed that no further order should be made against the respondent until proceedings in which her Canadian-born children had notice, and in which their best interests were considered.

The appeal was allowed. The *lis* of the application before McNeely J. was properly characterized as an immigration matter. This Court has expressed the view that, generally, immigration matters are best dealt with under the comprehensive scheme established under that Act. A provincial superior court will not always yield jurisdiction to the Federal Court. There will be situations in which the Federal Court is not an effective and appropriate forum in which to seek the relief claimed. In those rare cases the Superior Court can properly exercise its jurisdiction. Since the decision of *Baker v. Canada*, 174 D.L.R. (4th) 193, 243 N.R. 22, 1 Imm. L.R. (3d) 1, 14 Admin. L.R. (3d) 173, [1999] 2 S.C.R. 817, [1999] S.C.J. No. 39, 1999 CarswellNat 1124, 1999 CarswellNat 1125 (S.C.C.), it is clear that the interests of the Canadian-born children can be considered under an application made under s. 114(2). Accordingly, the order of McNeely J. was set aside.

The order of the Court of Appeal, however, was stayed for 120 days to ensure that the respondents' s. 114(2) application was dealt with while they were still in Canada.

*Charles v. Canada (Minister of Citizenship & Immigration)* (1999), 171 F.T.R. 304 (T.D.) — The Court did not agree that irreparable harm for the purposes of a stay application implied a serious likelihood of jeopardy to an applicant's life or safety. The Court found that the execution of the deportation order on the facts of this case more than 2 months after the applicant made his application for landing on humanitarian and compassionate grounds would result in irreparable harm.

The respondent has an obligation in law to execute an outstanding deportation order as soon as reasonably practicable. This is a flexible test. The fact that the respondent has a backlog of applications for landing from within Canada on humanitarian and compassionate grounds that has precluded her from dealing with the applicant's application, a backlog which will apparently continue to preclude her from dealing with it for a number of months, should not work against the applicant. Accordingly, in this case a stay was granted.

*Umukoro v. Canada (Minister of Citizenship & Immigration)* (1999), 1999 CarswellNat 505, [1999] F.C.J. No. 436 (Fed. T.D.) — The applicant sought to stay the execution of a removal order. A removal officer has some discretion concerning removal once the officer has become involved in making deportation arrangements. In appropriate circumstances a legitimate consideration in the exercise of that discretion might include the fact that it would be reasonable to await a pending decision on a humanitarian and compassionate application. The fact that such an application is outstanding is not, in and of itself, a bar to the execution of an order. Whether it is appropriate for a removal officer to take into account the fact that there is an outstanding humanitarian and compassionate application will depend on the circumstances of each case. In the present case, the Court found that the evidence on irreparable harm was speculative and hypothetical and refused to grant a stay.

*Mahadeo v. Canada (Minister of Citizenship & Immigration)* (1999), 166 F.T.R. 315, 1999 CarswellNat 347, [1999] F.C.J. No. 294 (Fed. T.D.) — The applicants sought to stay a removal order made against them. On the question of irreparable harm, the applicants who were 17 and 18 years of age respectively, argued that the disruption of their education due to the execution of the removal order before the end of the school year would constitute irreparable harm. Personal difficulties of this nature, although inconvenient, do not constitute irreparable harm, as serious as they may be to the applicant.

*San Vicente Freitas v. Canada (Minister of Citizenship & Immigration)* (1999), 49 Imm. L.R. (2d) 33, (sub nom. *Freitas v. Canada (Minister of Citizenship & Immigration))* [1999] 2 F.C. 432, (sub nom. *Freitas v. Canada (Minister of Citizenship & Immigration))* 161 F.T.R. 310 (T.D.) — These reasons arose out of an application for judicial review of a decision of a panel of the CRDD in which they determined the applicant not to be a Convention refugee. The applicant was born in Trinidad, but moved to Venezuela at a very young age. In Venezuela he was a political activist. The applicant came to Canada in 1967 and became a landed immigrant. The applicant was steadily employed in Canada for a period of 10 years and then returned to Venezuela as a visitor in 1981. The applicant found conditions had changed and decided to remain there. After the presidential election in 1983, the applicant ceased any political activities in Venezuela and ultimately in 1986, obtained a false passport and returned to Canada. After being back in Canada, the applicant was convicted of a serious criminal offence and sentenced to 9 years imprisonment. The applicant claimed refugee status against Venezuela.

The applicant's claim was refused, and he applied for leave to review that decision. Leave was granted. However, an application to stay execution of the removal order was refused. The decision of the Supreme Court of Canada in *Pushpanathan v. Canada (Minister of Citizenship & Immigration)*, [1998] 1 S.C.R. 982, mandated that in this case the interpretation of the panel of Article 1F(c) of the Convention was wrong. Accordingly the decision of the panel was set aside. The execution of the removal order did not render the judicial review proceedings moot.

The Court refused to provide a meaningless remedy in the form of a reference back to the CRDD for redetermination that could only be a determination that the applicant is not a Convention refugee because he is not outside the country of his nationality. Similarly, the Court was not prepared to order the respondent to return the applicant to Canada if the return of the applicant should prove to be unnecessary to an effective redetermination by the CRDD. The Court ordered that if the panel of the CRDD determined that it was necessary for the applicant to appear again to allow it to comply with the order of the Court directing a rehearing, the respondent was ordered forthwith to make best efforts to return the applicant to Canada at the respondent's expense. If the panel, without requiring the return of the applicant, working on the assumption that the applicant was in Canada was able to determine that the applicant was a Convention refugee, then the respondent was ordered forthwith to make best efforts to return the applicant to Canada at the respondent's expense.

*Torres-Samuels (Guardian ad litem of) v. Canada (Minister of Citizenship & Immigration)* (1998), 47 Imm. L.R. (2d) 9, 57 B.C.L.R. (3d) 357, [1999] 6 W.W.R. 207, (sub nom. *Torres-Samuels v. Canada (Minister of Citizenship & Immigration))* 113 B.C.A.C. 214, (sub nom. *Torres-Samuels v. Canada (Minister of Citizenship & Immigration))* 184 W.A.C. 214, 166 D.L.R. (4th) 611 (C.A.) — This petition was brought on behalf of the children of Jose Lino Torres Hurtado who were aged 7 and 2 at the time the petition was launched. They were seeking to enjoin or prohibit the deportation of their father, under a valid order of deportation, on the ground that it would not be in their best interests to be deprived of his attention and care. The petition invoked the *parens patriae* jurisdiction of the Supreme Court of British Columbia. The petitioners appealed from the dismissal of their petition by Mr. Justice Paris.

One of the underlying principles by which the discretion must be exercised is that it is not to be used to override a statutory provision, although it may be used to fill a gap in a legislative scheme.

There is no indication in the *Immigration Act* or elsewhere of a legislative intent to leave with the provincial superior courts, a power to review the validity of a deportation order under the *parens patriae* jurisdiction. Accordingly, the appeal was dismissed.

*Ukponmwan v. Canada (Minister of Citizenship & Immigration)* (1998), 151 F.T.R. 317 (Fed. T.D.) — On August 10, 1998, the applicant applied for leave to review a decision of an immigration enforcement officer directing the applicant to report for removal on August 13, 1998. This decision gave effect to a deportation order dated January 29, 1996, that became executory when the applicant's claim for refugee status was denied and leave to review that decision was refused.

The applicant's grounds for his application were that he would likely be subject to detention and torture by the Nigerian authorities on return, both because he is a member of a particular tribe and a member of a resistance group. Since it would undermine the jurisdiction of the Court over this application if the applicant were removed to Nigeria prior to its disposition, the Court held that it had jurisdiction to stay a removal until the application had been determined.

Secondly, the Court found that it had jurisdiction to review the validity of the directions for the applicant's removal to Nigeria.

*Saini v. Canada (Minister of Citizenship & Immigration)* (1998), 45 Imm. L.R. (2d) 279, [1998] 4 F.C. 325, 150 F.T.R. 148 (T.D.) — The applicant sought to review a decision which was in the form of a communication from a removal officer to the applicant, to the effect that the applicant would be removed from Canada on May 5, 1997.

Removal officers do not have jurisdiction to conduct risk assessments and make risk determinations in the course of making destination decisions. The options open to removal officers in making destination decisions are circumscribed by s. 52 of the Act.

Pursuant to s. 48 of the *Immigration Act,* removal officers have a discretion to delay the execution of a deportation order. In principle, a removal officer can delay a removal to await the determination of a humanitarian and compassionate application. A removal officer may have regard to cogent evidence of risk in removal to a particular destination and as to whether or not an appropriate risk assessment has been conducted and evaluated for the purpose of informing his or her exercise of discretion regarding deferral.

In this case, the applicant's materials in respective risk filed before the removals officer were properly before that officer, but only for the limited purpose of determining whether or not an appropriate assessment had been conducted and evaluated, and whether or not a delay in making removal arrangements was warranted. The representations in respective risk properly constitute part of a certified record in this application.

The material indicates that no appropriate risk assessment was done or determination made. The material disclosed is not evidence that an exercise of discretion to delay was considered. The removal officer's failure to consider whether or not to exercise his or her discretion under s. 48 pending an appropriate risk assessment and risk determination constituted a reviewable error in the nature of a failure or refusal to exercise jurisdiction.

*Muncan v. Canada (Minister of Citizenship & Immigration)* (1998), 141 F.T.R. 241 (T.D.) — The applicant applied for a stay of a pending removal order. The applicant was convicted of a number of criminal offences and was ordered deported. The applicant appealed to the Appeal Division of the IRB against the deportation order. The Minister declared the applicant to be a danger to the public and the applicant sought to set aside the danger opinion and to stay the execution of the deportation order pending review of the opinion.

There is no jurisdictional limit to the discretion that the Court is empowered to apply under s. 18.2. The whole question of whether the discretion should be exercised relates to the merits of each individual case. Regarding an application for a stay of a removal order, the issue is whether it is fair and just to grant it. In considering the entire context in deciding whether to exercise the discretion provided under s. 18.2, the Court found that it was far too technical of a perspective to require the deportation order to be challenged on judicial review or to limit the application of the appropriate injunctive test to the circumstances of the deportation order itself.

*Paszkowski v. R.* (1998), (sub nom. *Paszkowski v. Canada (Minister of Citizenship & Immigration))* 141 F.T.R. 149 (Fed. T.D.) — This was an application for an interlocutory injunction pending the resolution of an action brought by the applicant by way of a statement of claim seeking a declaration that the applicant was granted landed immigrant status in 1984 and therefore had the right to enter and remain in Canada.

Counsel for the Crown argued that the Court did not have jurisdiction to grant the relief claimed due to the fact that this was an immigration matter and accordingly the proper procedure was by way of judicial review. This position was rejected. The cases relied upon by the Crown involved matters where decisions had been rendered by an administrative tribunal and were therefore subject to the *Immigration Rules*, which required that the parties proceed by way of judicial review after having obtained leave. In this case, there was no decision being challenged that had already been dealt with in previous proceedings. The issue in this action was the applicant's permanent status, a question which had never been debated, nor had any decision ever been rendered, from which one could seek judicial review. The only remedy available to the plaintiff in this case was by way of statement of claim.

On the question of the balance of convenience, even though the Court accepted there would be no threat to the applicant's security or freedom if he were returned to Poland, the Court considered the applicant had been in Canada for 12 years, had been employed, had not been involved in any wrongdoing, had a wife and two children residing in Canada and concluded that the balance of convenience was in favour of the applicant.

*Parasidis v. Canada (Minister of Citizenship & Immigration)* (1997), 38 Imm. L.R. (2d) 288, 133 F.T.R. 73 (T.D.) — The applicant sought to stay the execution of a removal order on the basis that there was a statutory stay by virtue of s. 49(1)(b) of the *Immigration Act*. The applicant was a citizen of Greece who had been ordered deported by reason of his having been convicted of a criminal offence. The applicant appealed to the Appeal Division of the IRB and while his appeal was pending the applicant was certified as a danger to the public under s. 70(5) of the *Immigration Act*.

The applicant was not seriously asking the Court for a judicial stay but rather a declaration that a statutory stay operated to preclude his removal. This was a final determination which should properly be left to the judge hearing the judicial review application.

If the Court had been required to render a decision it would have concluded that there was no statutory stay. Assuming for the moment that all requirements of s. 70(5) have been met, the danger opinion has the effect of discharging the statutory stay.

The applicant's counsel also argued that there was no evidence that the adjudicator had determined that the applicant had been convicted of an offence for which a term of imprisonment of 10 years or more may be imposed. It is preferable that the adjudicator state expressly in the words of that provision, that an individual has been convicted of an offence for which a term of imprisonment of 10 years or more may be imposed. That is not, however, a statutory requirement. It may be obvious from the material that such a determination has been made. In the present case, the material submitted by the applicant led the Court to infer that the evidence before the adjudicator caused him to issue the deportation order because the applicant was convicted under subs. 4(2) of the *Narcotic Control Act* — an indictable offence punishable by a maximum punishment of life imprisonment. Accordingly, the application for stay was dismissed.

*Darboe v. Canada (Minister of Citizenship & Immigration)* (1996), 37 Imm. L.R. (2d) 72, 123 F.T.R. 1 (Fed. T.D.) — The applicant had been ordered deported and was also facing outstanding criminal charges in the Ontario Court (General Division). A representative from the Ministry of the Attorney General of Ontario indicated that immediately upon the applicant's removal from Canada, a criminal charge outstanding against the applicant would be withdrawn. In addition, it was also indicated that bail could be varied to provide for the accused's release provided that immigration would continue to detain the accused under the *Immigration Act*. Pursuant to the outstanding criminal charge, the accused was required to report for court subsequent to the date on which the immigration officials proposed to remove him from Canada.

Section 50(1)(a) of the *Immigration Act* operated to stay the removal order so long as the criminal charge remained outstanding. The Court directed, however, that the respondent could immediately execute the removal order upon the withdrawal of the Ontario court charges.

*Kandasamy v. Canada (Minister of Citizenship & Immigration)* (1996), 36 Imm. L.R. (2d) 237, 119 F.T.R. 262 (T.D.) — The applicant is aged 16, male, and a citizen of Sri Lanka. In 1983, he moved with his mother to the Federal Republic of Germany to join his father who fled Sri Lanka in 1981. In June 1995, the applicant left Germany and arrived in Canada by himself. Upon arriving at Fort Erie the applicant was questioned by an immigration officer who concluded that the applicant was a Convention refugee in Germany. Subsequently, the applicant claimed refugee status in Canada. In August 1995, the applicant was determined to be ineligible to have his claim considered on a basis that he was a convention refugee in Germany. The applicant was ordered removed from Canada. Subsequently, the applicant learned that he had not been accepted as a Convention refugee in Germany and the applicant sought to have his eligibility reconsidered in 1996. The request to reconsider was refused and the applicant applied for judicial review of that determination and a stay of the execution of the removal order.

The Court found irreparable harm. The applicant was 16; it was the respondent's intention to remove the applicant to the United States. The evidence before the Court indicated that throughout his entire life and since his arrival in Canada the applicant had continued to live under the care and supervision of adults: his parents in Germany and an uncle in this country. There was no evidence that the applicant was experienced in looking after himself or an individual who had demonstrated himself to be capable of surviving on his own. Should the applicant be removed to the United States, there was no evidence before the Court to suggest that arrangements existed there, so that the applicant could receive the support and care to which he was accustomed. Thus, removal to the United States in those circumstances would create irreparable harm pending determination of the application for judicial review.

*Rizzo v. Canada (Minister of Citizenship & Immigration)* (1996), [1996] F.C.J. No. 1111, 1996 CarswellNat 1252 (Fed. T.D.) — The issue on this stay application was the question of irreparable harm. The applicant had over 20 criminal convictions and was addicted to drugs. His irreparable harm submission was based on his need for continuing medical attention in Canada. The need for such medical attention and support has been caused by the applicant's criminal activities and his drug addiction. Criminal activities and drug addiction cannot be the foundation upon which a claim of irreparable harm can be based for purposes of staying the execution of a deportation order.

*Calabrese v. Canada (Minister of Citizenship & Immigration)* (1996), 115 F.T.R. 213 (T.D.) — The applicant sought to quash a decision of the respondent that the applicant constituted a danger to the public in Canada.

The applicant was born in Italy in 1961, came to Canada with his family at the age of three and became a permanent resident, but never acquired Canadian citizenship. The applicant's family members live in Canada, the applicant does not speak Italian, the applicant has lived in a common law relationship for the past 14 years and has an 11-year-old son who is a Canadian citizen. The applicant's companion is expecting their second child.

The applicant had a long criminal record that included a number of convictions for serious offences. The applicant acknowledged a substance abuse problem.

The basis for the claim of irreparable harm was that the applicant, if deported, would be separated from the professional and community base support, upon which he was relying to remain drug-free and as a consequence crime-free. In addition, it was submitted that there was a lack of equivalent support in the country to which the applicant would be deported and that because of the applicant's inability to speak Italian, the applicant would be faced with significant difficulties in attempting to establish himself again in that country.

The loss of family, professional and community support are capable of constituting irreparable harm. The Court found the elements in this case parallel to those in *Toth v. Canada (M.E.I.)* (1988), 6 Imm L.R. (2d) 123 (Fed. C.A.). The Court disagreed with the decision of Simpson J. in *Calderon v. Canada (Minister of Citizenship & Immigration)* (1995), 92 F.T.R. 107 (Fed. T.D.) which decision concluded that irreparable harm implied the serious likelihood of jeopardy to the applicants life or safety.

*Shayesteh v. Canada (Minister of Citizenship & Immigration)* (1996), 34 Imm. L.R. (2d) 101, 112 F.T.R. 161 (T.D.) — This was an application to stay the execution of a deportation order pending determination of an application for leave and for judicial review of a decision made pursuant to subs. 70(5) of the *Immigration Act*. In dealing with the balance of convenience test, the Court noted that there was inconvenience to the respondent if the stay was granted and acknowledged that there was a public interest in having the respondent's duties under the *Immigration Act* fulfilled in a timely manner. The Court found the balance to lie in the applicant's favour, noting that the deportation order was issued in November 1984 and the process which lead to the issuing of the Minister's opinion was not implemented until September 1995, and the opinion not communicated to the applicant until March 28, 1996. On those facts the balance of convenience was held to lie in favour of granting the stay.

*Duve v. Canada (Minister of Citizenship & Immigration)*, [1996] F.C.J. No. 387, 1996 CarswellNat 390 (Fed. T.D.) — The Court accepted the reasoning of Simpson J. in *Calderon v. Canada (Minister of Citizenship & Immigration)* (1995), 92 F.T.R. 107 (Fed.

T.D.), on the question of irreparable harm. For purposes of a stay, irreparable harm implies the serious likelihood of jeopardy to the applicant's life or safety. This is a very strict test and it is premised upon the fact that the irreparable harm must be more than the unfortunate hardship associated with the breakup or relocation of a family.

*Hogan v. Canada (Minister of Citizenship & Immigration)* (1996), 32 Imm. L.R. (2d) 97, 108 F.T.R. 143 (T.D.) — This was an application to stay the execution of a Deportation Order pending the determination of an application for leave and for judicial review of a decision of the respondent pursuant to subs. 70(5) of the *Immigration Act*. The Court allowed the application. The Court concluded that the balance of convenience test had been met, after noting that the deportation order was outstanding in July 1995 when s. 70(5) came into effect. Since that time there was no evidence to indicate that the applicant was evading implementation of the order. The evidence was to the contrary. It was only on the eve of the hearing of the applicant's appeal that the respondent turned to subs. 70(5) and it then took the respondent from mid-November 1995 to mid-February 1996 to execute the order. This led the Court to conclude that the applicant did not rank high on the respondent's list of individuals constituting a danger to the public.

The Court also referred to, with approval, *Yhap v. Canada (Minister of Employment & Immigration)* (1989), 29 F.T.R. 231 (Fed. T.D.), to the effect that the amendments which brought about s. 70(5) had not yet been tested as to constitutionality, legality or fairness which had the effect of leaving the federal law in the area in a state of imprecision and flux.

*Singh (R.) v. Canada (Minister of Citizenship & Immigration)* (1995), 31 Imm. L.R. (2d) 281, 104 F.T.R. 35 (T.D.) — This was a successful application to stay a removal order. There were three applicants. The first applicant was a citizen of Sri Lanka, the second applicant was his 5-year-old son, and the third applicant was the wife of the first applicant who was a citizen of India. All three made refugee claims. The refugee claim of the father and son was denied and their judicial review application was dismissed. They were, thus, eligible for removal from Canada. For reasons undisclosed by the evidence, the wife's claim had not been concluded at the time of the judicial review application. The Court found irreparable harm in the fact that, if the Minister was allowed to execute the removal order, the 5-year-old child would be separated from his mother. This would occur not as a result of any actions taken by the child, but rather because the processes controlled by the respondent Minister had not dealt with all of the applications at the same time. Removal of an infant child in such circumstances should be avoided. It is a primary goal of the *Immigration Act* to foster family relationships and family unity. The fact that these persons had been treated differently under the administration of the Act raised a serious dilemma for the family. That dilemma results from the department's choice to process the mother's claim at a different time than the other 2 applicants.

The balance of convenience favours the applicants. This order for a stay is temporary pending disposition of the application for leave and judicial review now filed in this court which simply postpones, but does not permanently preclude, the Minister undertaking removal proceedings.

*Muñoz v. Canada (Minister of Citizenship & Immigration)* (1995), 30 Imm. L.R. (2d) 166, 100 F.T.R. 201 (T.D.) — The applicant and his family arrived in Canada from Peru. The applicants were seeking to have their humanitarian and compassionate application determined before their removal. The Court noted that there is a duty cast upon the respondent through its officers to consider H&C applications. The respondent is not entitled to discharge that mandate unjustly, or in a way that neutralizes the legislation. It would be absurd and deleterious to the law's due administration if the Minister was accorded such latitude as would defeat Parliament's intent in enacting s. 114(2). In the extreme circumstances of this case a stay for a deportation order was granted.

*Owusu v. Canada (Minister of Citizenship & Immigration)* (1995), [1995] F.C.J. No. 1166, 1995 CarswellNat 1421 (Fed. T.D.) — The applicants requested a stay of a deportation order in circumstances where they had not directly attacked the validity of the order.

The Court concluded that it had jurisdiction to stay the order but declined to grant relief in this case. The Court commented on the decision in *Shchelkanov v. Canada (Minister of Employment & Immigration)* (1994), 76 F.T.R. 151 (Fed. T.D.) and pointed out that the judge in that case did not suggest any lack of jurisdiction, but rather determined that the applicants had no right to a stay of the order in that case.

*Raman v. Canada (Minister of Citizenship and Immigration)* (1995), 30 Imm. L.R. (2d) 300, 100 F.T.R. 67 — The applicant arrived in Canada from Nigeria in June, 1995. On his arrival, using a Zimbabwean passport, the applicant advised Immigration officials that he had come to Canada to visit a friend in Montreal and would only be staying for a week. The applicant, in response to a specific question, denied that he wished to make a refugee claim. The applicant was, however, excluded from entry. The applicant then advised Immigration officials that the passport he was using was fraudulent, that he was a citizen of Nigeria and that he wished to make a refugee claim. The applicant was advised that, an exclusion order having been made against him, it was too late for him to claim refugee status. The applicant retained counsel and sought to re-open the s. 23(4) inquiry. A senior Immigration officer refused to re-open the inquiry on the basis that she did not have jurisdiction to do so. The applicant sought to judicially review this decision. This application was dismissed on the basis that the applicant would not suffer irreparable harm if the exclusion order were executed. The only evidence that the applicant might suffer irreparable harm was the applicant's own affidavit.

The applicant brought a second application for stay of execution of the exclusion order and this time filed more extensive evidence of irreparable harm. With respect to this second application for a stay, the parties to it were the same as those on the first application. The question was the same as that decided on the first application. The Court indicated that it was satisfied that *res judicata* or issue estoppel applied in respect of the second application. It is an abuse of the process of the court to bring forward the same application a second time with what might prove to be better evidence. Accordingly, this second application for a stay was dismissed.

*Sannes v. Canada (Minister of Citizenship & Immigration)* (1995), 1995 CarswellNat 1429 (Fed. T.D.) — The applicant/plaintiff commenced an action against the respondent/defendant, then applied for a stay of the execution of a deportation order. The plaintiff had maintained in an immigration inquiry that he was a Canadian citizen but had been unable to provide proper proof of that fact. Accordingly, his deportation order was issued and the adjudicator's decision was appealed to the Appeal Division which appeal was dismissed.

The applicant/plaintiff then filed a statement of claim in the Federal Court wherein he claimed status as a Canadian citizen by virtue of the provisions of s. 3(1)(e) of the *Citizenship Act*. The applicant/plaintiff maintained that his situation was similar to the case of

*Benner v. Canada (Secretary of State)* (1993), 155 N.R. 321 (Fed. C.A.) which case was before the Supreme Court of Canada at the time of the commencement of the action.

In the evaluation of irreparable harm, there are three basic elements that must be considered: a) the kind of harm, b) the level of risk, and c) whether the harm is irreparable and not compensable in damages.

Personal inconvenience, even if serious, is not equivalent to irreparable harm. Irreparable harm implies the serious likelihood of jeopardy to the applicant's life and safety if he/she were to be returned to his/her country of origin.

The Court found no irreparable harm. There was no doubt that the applicant would be deprived of an extensive support network of friends in groups which he established in Canada in order to help him deal with his rehabilitation from alcoholic, drug and sexual abuse. This did not constitute irreparable harm. Similarly, being returned to Norway and thrust into a foreign environment also did not constitute irreparable harm. If the applicant requires further treatment for his alcohol and sexual problems, it is admitted that Norway is capable of providing such services.

Merely because the issue raised in the proceedings was a *Charter* issue did not mean that it was necessary for the Court to assume that the harm in question was irreparable. The Court distinguished *RJR-MacDonald Inc. v. Canada (Attorney General)*, [1994] 1 S.C.R. 311 (S.C.C.) on the basis that it dealt with an issue whereby the applicants would incur major expense in altering their packaging. Even though this may be quantifiable, it was determined that because of the *Charter* argument, there were special reasons to conclude there that the harm would be irreparable. Accordingly, the Court found no relation between the facts in *RJR-McDonald* and the case at bar. The application for a stay was denied.

*Calderon v. Canada (Minister of Citizenship & Immigration)* (1995), 1995 CarswellNat 1432 (Fed. T.D.) — In an earlier case the Court dismissed an application for a stay of a departure order on the basis that it could find no irreparable harm. That case concerned a decision made by an adjudicator. At the time of that first application this present application, based on a negative humanitarian and compassionate decision, was outstanding. In this application the issue of irreparable harm could not be relitigated. The doctrine of issue estoppel operated as a bar to the reargument of the issue. Irreparable harm was fundamental to the earlier decision and identical to the issue raised in this application. This conclusion was not dispositive of this application. The tests for injunctive relief are significant guideposts in the decision-making process when a stay is sought. They are not iron shackles. A court must assess all the circumstances and do what is just.

The Court decided to hear submissions about why, quite apart from the question of irreparable harm, it should, or should not, grant a stay of the deportation order.

*Kronenfeld v. Canada (Secretary of State)* (1995), 29 Imm. L.R. (2d) 231 (Fed. T.D.) — The Court declined to grant a stay in this case due to the delay occasioned by counsel for the applicant. The application for a stay was scheduled to be heard on April 10, 1995 at 9:30 in the morning. At approximately 10 a.m. on April 10, 1995 the Court received a 37-page affidavit from the applicant which had been prepared on April 9, 1995.

The Court noted that in urgent matters it will hear an application for a stay on weekends if counsel requests. There was no adequate explanation for counsel's delay in bringing this application and his failure to perfect it in a timely fashion. The lengthy affidavit was sworn the day before the hearing but was only provided to the Court at the very last moment. The Court concluded that this application for a stay was, in fact, an abuse of its processes and refused to hear the application.

*Langner v. Canada (Minister of Employment & Immigration)* (1995), 29 C.R.R. (2d) 184, (sub nom. *Langner v. Ministre de l'Emploi & de l'Immigration)* 184 N.R. 230, 97 F.T.R. 118 (note) (C.A.) — The appellants arrived in Canada with valid visitors visas in 1988. They did not travel to the United States but rather remained in Canada eventually claiming refugee status. While they were waiting for their refugee applications to be disposed of, the parents had two children, both of whom had, by virtue of their birth on Canadian soil, Canadian citizenship and Polish citizenship.

The appellant parents' refugee claims had been rejected. They requested a waiver under s. 114(2) of the requirement that they leave Canada in order to make an application for permanent residence. This request was refused and requests for a review of that decision were also refused. Deportation orders were issued against the parents in October 1992.

The parents proceeded by way of an action for a declaratory judgment seeking a declaration that by virtue of the fact that they had 2 children who were Canadian citizens the Canadian government was prevented from executing the deportation orders made against them.

The Canadian *Charter of Rights and Freedoms* has no application in this case. The appellant parents' decision to take their children to Poland with them, or to leave them with family members in Canada, is a decision which is their own to make. The Canadian government has nothing to do with this decision. There is no government action which could bring the *Charter* into play. The appellant children's rights and freedoms, which attach to their Canadian citizenship are not an issue. Regardless of the decision made by their parents, the children will retain their Canadian citizenship and will be subject to no constraints in the exercise of the rights and liberties associated with their citizenship other than the constraints the parents impose in the exercise of their parental authority.

*Rajan v. Canada (Minister of Employment & Immigration)* (1994), 86 F.T.R. 70 — The applicant applied for a stay in circumstances where the applicant had been issued a departure order and intended to remain in Canada, with the result that the departure order would become a deportation order.

The Court does not have jurisdiction pursuant to s. 18(2) to prevent the departure order from becoming a deportation order.

*Rambharose (Litigation Guardian of) v. R.* (1994), 28 Imm. L.R. (2d) 109 (Fed. T.D.) — This was a motion for an order to stay the execution of a removal order issued against the plaintiff's litigation guardian (mother). The plaintiff was a Canadian born child whose parents came to Canada from Trinidad in 1988. The plaintiff's mother was the subject of a s. 20 report for not having obtained an immigrant visa prior to appearing at a port-of-entry as required by s. 9 of the Act. A subsequent humanitarian and compassionate grounds review was rejected. The mother then applied for Convention refugee status but was found not to have a credible basis for her claim and an exclusion order was issued against her. A second humanitarian and compassionate review was rejected. The plaintiff's father is still awaiting a decision on his humanitarian and compassionate review.

This action was commenced to prevent the Minister from removing the plaintiff's parents. The plaintiff, through a litigation guardian, argued that his rights under the Canadian *Charter of Rights and Freedoms* would be violated if his mother was removed from Canada and he was forced to either depart from Canada or be separated from his mother.

The Court found that the plaintiff would suffer irreparable harm as a result of being separated from his mother at such a tender age. Given the serious prejudice which the plaintiff would likely suffer if the removal order was executed, the balance of convenience favoured granting a stay.

*Bajwa v. Canada (Secretary of State)* (1994), 1994 CarswellNat 1595 (Fed. T.D.) — The applicant applied for a stay of a deportation order, which was refused.

The granting of a stay of a deportation order is a discretionary matter. In that regard, the conduct of the applicant is a relevant consideration. The applicant's conduct in its total context is relevant. It is not merely a question of whether there has been an excessive delay.

The applicant voluntarily undertook expanded family responsibilities knowing there was an outstanding deportation order issued against him. He had not even met his wife prior to the issuance of that order. He was married in February 1993, but did not seek an H & C review until November 1993 and, at the time he sought a stay of a deportation order, his wife was pregnant.

It was not appropriate for the Court to exercise its discretion to grant a stay because the applicant was now trying to rely on a situation in which he purposely placed himself.

*De Medeiros v. Canada (Minister of Employment & Immigration)*, [1994] F.C.J. No. 11, 1994 CarswellNat 1598 (Fed. T.D.) — The Court granted the stay of the execution of a deportation order until such time as it had rendered its decision in respect of an application for leave and for judicial review of a decision of the Appeal Division. On the issue of irreparable harm, the Court found that the Appeal Division had an ongoing and continuing equitable jurisdiction with respect to the applicant, which jurisdiction would cease to exist upon the applicant's departure from Canada. This cessation of the Appeal Division's equitable jurisdiction was held to constitute irreparable harm.

*Boquoi v. Canada (Minister of Employment & Immigration)* (1993), 67 F.T.R. 232 — The applicant and his wife sought to stay departure notices requiring them to leave Canada for Germany before the end of September 1993. The application failed because the applicants were unable to establish irreparable harm. The application for a stay contained affidavits swearing to the fact that the applicants had become very attached to the persons in their community and wished to prevent the separation of their two sons from the community which the sons knew as home. The youngest son was a Canadian citizen born in Prince Edward Island and, further, the applicants alleged that they had no home in Germany to go to and were fearful for their children's safety and security if they were required to return there. This was not a fear of persecution, but rather a fear of the stress and uncertainty of removal to Germany at this time. The applicants stated that prior to their arrival in Canada, there was no work available for them in Germany and that since their arrival they had managed to establish a home here and had been accepted and strongly supported by the community in Prince Edward Island, where they were living. Such factors did not establish irreparable harm. Mere economic dislocation or difficulties or inconvenience do not establish irreparable harm in circumstances where neither applicant has a right to remain in Canada.

*Da Costa v. Canada (Minister of Employment & Immigration)* (1993), 19 Imm. L.R. (2d) 295, 64 F.T.R. 233 — This was an application for a stay of execution of a removal order. The application was filed on Friday, June 4, 1993 and removal was scheduled for 7:30 a.m. Monday, June 7, 1993. The request for a stay of the removal order was denied on the ground of delay by the applicant in bringing the application.

The removal order was issued on January 23, 1992. Before the end of that month the applicant married a Canadian citizen and assumed parental responsibility for a young child. The applicant received a "call in notice" from Immigration dated February 2, 1992 to attend an interview on April 2, 1992. This interview, however, did not take place. Thus, the applicant was aware before his marriage of his precarious situation in Canada and did nothing to attempt to resolve his problem, except to continue to expand his family responsibilities. It was only when he was confronted with a specific date for his removal that he began to examine options open to him to prolong his stay or regularize his status.

The applicant had from January 23, 1992, more than an adequate opportunity to seek legal advice.

No risk to the applicant's life or safety was alleged if he were deported to Jamaica. It was acknowledged, however, that his wife and children would be substantially prejudiced. His wife was expecting a third child and had been hospitalized from time to time because of the pregnancy and thus was disabled from working within or outside the home.

The Court concluded that the magnitude of the harm faced here derived in large part from the failure of the applicant to do anything in the interval since January 23, 1992 to mitigate the problem. Therefore it did not rest easily with him to plead now for an extraordinary remedy. Accordingly, the request for a stay was dismissed.

*Grar v. Canada (Minister of Employment & Immigration)* (1993), 20 Imm. L.R. (2d) 301, 64 F.T.R. 6 — The fact that the applicant's removal from Canada before May 28, 1993 would mean that the applicant was not able to complete a three-year program of studies and receive a diploma, constituted irreparable harm. Deportation would mean that those studies would never be completed; if they were to be completed, it would only be after several years.

There would be no irreparable harm caused to the applicant if he were removed from Canada after the date that the studies were expected to be concluded (May 28) and for that reason the stay of execution of the deportation order was not to extend beyond May 28, when the applicant's studies were expected to be completed.

*Bal v. Canada (Minister of Employment & Immigration)*, [1993] 2 F.C. 199, 63 F.T.R. 226 — The applicant sought a stay of a removal order pending an application for leave to seek judicial review of a decision refusing special treatment on humanitarian and compassionate grounds. Sukhjinder Bal brought his two nephews to Canada because their natural father had received demands for money from members of the All Sikh Student Federation coupled with threats against the children's lives. Upon their entry into Canada the children's citizenship was not disclosed and the immigration officer wrongly assumed them to be their uncle's children. When the true citizenship of the two young children was discovered by Immigration, a conditional deportation order was obtained. The claim for refugee status on the children's behalf was dismissed. The uncle then petitioned for an order of adoption in the Supreme Court of British Columbia. When this was completed the uncle sponsored an application for permanent residence on behalf of the children and requested that the applications be processed from within Canada. This latter request was denied and it was that decision which the applicant sought to question.

Mr. Justice Noel had previously held that the Court did not have jurisdiction to issue a stay in the circumstances of this case. Other judges of the Court had expressed the opposite view. His Lordship was of the view that if he had jurisdiction to grant a stay he would have done so on the facts of this case. The Court determined that it was imperative that there be consistency in the manner in which fundamental issues of jurisdiction are dealt with by the Court. There was an open question as to the jurisdiction to grant relief. Accordingly, the Court determined that the uncertainty about the Court's jurisdiction should be resolved in favour of the party seeking the relief. To do otherwise would deprive a party of a remedy on the assumption that those members of the Court who have assumed the jurisdiction to grant the remedy were wrong. The Court was of the view that the contrary assumption should be made unless and until the Court of Appeal decides otherwise.

Accordingly, a stay in the execution of the removal orders was granted.

*Agyakwa v. Canada (Minister of Employment & Immigration)* (1993), 62 F.T.R. 118 — This was an application to stay the execution of a removal order. The applicant arrived in Canada from Ghana and made a claim for refugee status. While the applicant was in Canada he met and married a Canadian citizen. The marriage occurred before his refugee claim was dismissed. After getting married the applicant applied for landing from within Canada. The refugee claim was dismissed and the applicant was advised that there would be no recommendation that he be landed from within Canada because the immigration officer had serious reservations about whether the marriage was for immigration purposes.

The request for a stay was granted. Irreparable harm was found to be established, not only to the applicant, but to his family. Uncontradicted affidavit evidence established that the applicant's spouse had three children by a previous marriage and that the applicant had in effect become a father to those children. Further, the whole family was heavily dependent upon the applicant for support. The Court found more than personal inconvenience to the applicant at stake.

*Harper v. Canada (Minister of Employment & Immigration)* (1993), 19 Imm. L.R. (2d) 233, 62 F.T.R. 96 — This was an application to stay a deportation order. The applicant claimed refugee status, which claim was found to have no credible basis. The applicant had applied for leave to review a decision finding sufficient humanitarian and compassionate grounds in the applicant's case to warrant a positive recommendation under s. 114(2). In support of the application for a stay, the applicant's counsel filed an affidavit from his personal assistant. In the affidavit the personal assistant reiterated facts about the case that had been told to her by counsel for the applicant. There was no direct evidence from the applicant and no explanation as to why such direct evidence could not be provided. A stay application is in the nature of an interlocutory motion and an affidavit based on belief is acceptable. However, it will have little weight when it consists of hearsay upon hearsay. The courts can only make decisions on the basis of evidence. The affidavit of an employee in which the employee purports to truly believe certain facts of which she has no personal knowledge, in circumstances where she has not even spoken to the person who would have such personal knowledge, is evidence of little probative value.

Information comes to the Court by way of evidence and counsel should ensure that they present evidence that the Court may rely upon with confidence. This is of heightened importance when motions are brought on short notice and the respondent has no practical opportunity to cross-examine on the affidavit or to present an affidavit in response.

One of the attachments to the legal assistant's affidavits was a nine-page letter from counsel to the manager of the Central Removals Unit in Mississauga, Ontario. She also referred to this letter during argument to establish some of the facts relating to the applicant. This raises the difficulty of counsel who was appearing before the Court relying on a letter that counsel has written to establish the truth about facts relating to the client.

Evidence and submissions of counsel are not one and the same. Merely because counsel has written a letter containing information about the client and attached it to an affidavit, does not make it evidence of the truth of what is contained in it. The application for a stay was refused.

*Petit v. Canada (Minister of Employment & Immigration)* (1993), 19 Imm. L.R. (2d) 133 (Fed. T.D.) — The applicant arrived in Canada with her two children and claimed refugee status. She married her present husband while she was in Canada. A number of requests were made by the applicant after the date of her marriage for a determination of whether there were sufficient humanitarian and compassionate grounds to allow her to apply for landing from within Canada, on the ground that she was married to a Canadian citizen. On February 5, 1993 the applicant and her husband were asked to attend a marriage interview. On February 9, 1993 the applicant was notified that she would be required to leave Canada by February 26, 1993 and that there were insufficient humanitarian and compassionate grounds to justify allowing her to apply for landing from within Canada. It is in respect of that decision that leave to commence an application for judicial review was being sought. In those circumstances, s. 18.2 of the *Federal Courts Act* gave the Court jurisdiction to grant a stay.

On the question of whether the applicant would suffer irreparable harm, the Court noted that generally when a person is being returned to a country where there is no threat of physical danger or persecution, it would be hard to argue that irreparable harm exists. However, the Court noted that the applicant and her children found themselves in an "eleventh hour" situation created by the respondent. The applicant had written to the respondent on two or perhaps three occasions requesting a marriage interview. Had the interview been conducted in a timely manner, the applicant would have had an opportunity to test the validity of any decision made before being required to leave Canada. On the facts, the applicant had been called in for a marriage interview on the eve of deportation. She was told by the interviewer that "everything looked good". That decision was reversed by a supervisor with no explanation. The Court found that the execution of the removal order in those circumstances, before the applicant had an opportunity to obtain leave to challenge the decision, was unfair.

The Court does not look favourably upon applicants who appear at the last minute, before a removal order is to be executed, with a new spouse or with new requests for humanitarian and compassionate reviews. The position in which they put themselves in those circumstances is largely of their own making. In this case, the position in which the applicant and her children found themselves was largely of the respondent's making and thus, it was appropriate to grant a stay of the removal order.

*Seegobin v. Canada (Minister of Employment & Immigration)* (1993), 59 F.T.R. 310 (Fed. T.D.) — The Court lacks jurisdiction to grant the stay of a deportation order in circumstances where its validity is not in dispute.

*Membreno-Garcia v. Canada (Minister of Employment & Immigration)* (1992), 7 Admin. L.R. (2d) 38, 17 Imm. L.R. (2d) 291, 55 F.T.R. 104, [1992] 3 F.C. 306 (Fed. C.A.) — The applicant had applied for refugee status but a first-level tribunal found that there was no credible basis to the applicant's claim. The applicant applied for leave to commence an application for judicial review, which leave was granted. The applicant then sought a stay of the deportation order pending the outcome of the appeal.

In the present case, the deportation order flowed from and was underpinned by the decision finding no credible basis to the applicant's claim. If that decision was invalid then the deportation order was invalid. In such circumstances, a challenge has in fact been made to the validity of the deportation order.

In *Lodge v. Canada (Minister of Employment & Immigration)*, [1979] 1 F.C. 775 (C.A.), the Court stated the principle to be applied in deciding whether a permanent injunction should be granted to restrain a Minister of the Crown from performing his statutory duty. In *Toth v. Canada (Minister of Employment & Immigration)* (1988), 6 Imm. L.R. (2d) 123 (Fed. C.A.), the Court held that it had jurisdiction to grant a stay in cases such as this one. Since that time the Trial Division's jurisdiction has been made clear by the addition of s. 18.2 of the *Federal Courts Act.*

The only requirement under s. 18.2 is that the judge consider the interim order "appropriate". It may be that in the absence of at least an indirect attack on the deportation order the Court would not consider a stay appropriate.

In determining when a stay order is "appropriate" the Court referred to the criteria set out in *Toth*. Given that leave had been granted, the applicant clearly had an arguable case. On the basis of the applicant's affidavit evidence it would be hard to reach any other conclusion than that the applicant would suffer irreparable harm if he was returned to El Salvador. Insofar as the balance of convenience is concerned, the test set out in *Metropolitan Stores (MTS) Ltd. v. Manitoba Food & Commercial Workers, Local 832*, [1987] 1 S.C.R. 110 (S.C.C.), is not relevant. In that case, the validity of one section of the statute was under attack and thus an interlocutory injunction order in favour of one litigant would by implication lead to similar orders respecting all individuals covered by the allegedly unconstitutional section in question. The section itself would in fact be rendered inoperative pending the determination of its validity. In the present case, the legislative provisions of the statute were not challenged. One decision by an adjudicative body operating under the statute with respect to one specific individual was being challenged. Rendering an injunction or a stay order in such a case will not suspend the operation of any part of the legislation. Thus, the public interest considerations expressed in *Metropolitan Stores Ltd.* are not in issue.

When considering the balance of convenience in these types of cases, the extent to which the granting of the stay might become a practice which thwarts the efficient operation of the immigration legislation is a valid consideration. The present procedures were put in place because a practice had grown up in which cases totally devoid of merit were initiated in court for the sole purpose of buying the applicants further time in Canada. There is a public interest in having a system which operates in an efficient, expeditious and fair manner and which, to the greatest extent possible, does not lend itself to abusive practices. This is the public interest which must be weighed against the potential harm to the applicant if a stay is not granted.

The situation in this case is quite different from that which exists, for example, when applicants seek humanitarian and compassionate reviews on the eve of the execution of a deportation order and then argue that a stay should be granted because of the uncompleted nature of that review. Such a case is the type of situation in which there is a potential for creating a practice which undermines the orderly operation of the legislation.

Another significant factor in considering the balance of convenience test is the degree of delay which is incurred, if any, in prosecuting the applicant's appeal. Similarly, when the applicant knows of the decision which underlies the challenge to the deportation order and does not seek leave to commence a s. 18 proceeding until the very last moment, there is reason to assume that the seeking of leave and the subsequent request for the staying of the deportation order are primarily time-buying manoeuvres.

In the present case, the balance of convenience was said to lie with the applicant and the stay was granted.

*Editor's Note: Although the refugee procedures have changed, the principle stated herein may still be useful.*

*Khan v. Canada (Minister of Employment & Immigration)* (1992), 53 F.T.R. 158 (Fed. T.D.) — An earlier inquiry concerning the applicant's continuing presence in Canada was quashed by decision of the Court (*Khan v. Canada (Minister of Employment & Immigration)* (1989), 9 Imm. L.R. (2d) 107 (Fed. T.D.)). The preliminary question was whether the application for a stay was properly before the Court in light of the decision in *Ontario Khalsa Darbar Inc. v. Canada (Minister of Employment & Immigration)* (1991), 15 Imm. L.R. (2d) 179 (Fed. T.D.), which held that leave is required to bring an application for a stay in immigration proceedings pursuant to 82.1 of the *Immigration Act*. Previously, *Toth v. Canada (Minister of Employment & Immigration)* (1988), 6 Imm. L.R. (2d) 123, 86 N.R. 302 (Fed. C.A.) acknowledged the inherent jurisdiction of the court to deal with an application for a stay in appropriate circumstances without the necessity of leave being applied for. Section 18.2 of the *Federal Courts Act*, enforced since February 1, 1992, provided authority for the issuance of interim orders in relation to the matters before the Court and was sufficient to give jurisdiction to consider an application for a stay which in this case was interrelated with an application for leave to seek judicial review.

In this case there was no evidence of irreparable harm and the application for a stay was dismissed. The inquiry in question might result in a departure notice and, further, even if a deportation order were issued, removal would only occur after a pre-removal review. This review could result in a decision that there were humanitarian or compassionate considerations which justified permanent residence. Accordingly, the concerns of the applicant about the outcome of the inquiry were speculative and as such not evidence of irreparable harm.

*Hosein v. Canada (Minister of Employment & Immigration)* (1992), 17 Imm. L.R. (2d) 125, 4 Admin. L.R. (2d) 162, 53 F.T.R. 86 (Fed. T.D.) — This was an application for an order staying an inquiry until the applicant's application for leave to commence judicial review proceedings was determined, and, if leave be granted, until those proceedings were finally disposed of by the Court. This application was accompanied by an application for leave pursuant to 82.1. The orders in question were sought in respect of a decision by a first-level tribunal to the effect that it would not hear evidence and argument in relation to s. 7 of the *Charter*. The tribunal then proceeded to find the applicant did not have a credible basis for his claim to being a Convention refugee. The tribunal adjourned and then scheduled a resumption of its hearing. The application for leave to seek judicial review was not considered when this application for a stay was heard.

The Court's jurisdiction to order a stay of proceedings was not limited by s. 18.2 of the *Federal Courts Act* by the necessity to apply for leave to seek judicial review. In an appropriate case, particularly one where the issue raised in an application for leave is arguable but would be moot or the jurisdiction of the Court would be rendered nugatory by failure to grant a stay, a stay may be ordered within the discretion of the Court.

The Court was not persuaded that a stay of proceedings was required at the time the application was heard. Further steps in the process of consideration of the applicant's situation were required before he would be excluded from Canada. The leave for judicial review now sought by the application could proceed in the ordinary course. If the leave application was not completed before steps were taken to remove the applicant, the applicant could apply for leave to stay implementation of those procedures at that time. The test for intervention is set out in the *Toth* case (*Toth v. Canada (Minister of Employment & Immigration)* (1988), 6 Imm. L.R. (2d) 123, 86 N.R. 302 (Fed. C.A.)).

It was determined that it was inappropriate at this stage to stay proceedings of the tribunal and the application was dismissed.

*Pavlov v. Canada (Minister of Employment & Immigration)*, 16 Imm. L.R. (2d) 105, [1992] 2 F.C. 289, 53 F.T.R. 253 — The requirements for issuing stays of deportation orders in the context of applications filed pursuant to s. 82.1 seeking leave to commence a proceeding under s. 18 of the *Federal Courts Act* are as follows:

1. the applicant must demonstrate that there is a serious question to be determined;
2. that the applicant would suffer irreparable harm if the stay were not granted; and
3. that as between the applicant and the respondent Minister the harm to the applicant would be greater if a stay were not granted than to the respondent if one were granted.

In the context of this particular case the application for stay was granted.

The Court in arriving at these requirements applied the decision of *Toth v. Canada (Minister of Employment & Immigration)* (1988), 6 Imm. L.R. (2d) 123 (Fed. C.A.).

*Mathura (Litigation Guardian of) v. Canada (Minister of Employment & Immigration)*, 1992 CarswellNat 819 (Fed. T.D.) — This application to stay the adjudication proceedings was refused. The stay which was sought hinged on a constitutional challenge to certain provisions of the *Immigration Act* and regulations. Leave had not yet been granted to commence a proceeding based on those challenges. No challenge was made by the motion to the validity of the proceedings. Granting a stay in such circumstances would have set a precedent that could have had significant detrimental effects on the integrity of immigration proceedings. The Court ordered disposition of the application for leave within seven days so that the request for a stay might be determined after the decision to grant leave had been made.

*Bada v. Canada (Minister of Employment & Immigration)* (1992), 17 Imm. L.R. (2d) 233, 56 F.T.R. 106 (T.D.) — The applicant sought to stay a deportation order. The deportation order itself is not an issue in the proceedings. The applicant was seeking to quash a decision that there were no humanitarian or compassionate grounds to allow the applicant to apply for landing from within Canada. The Court observed that whether the Trial Division had jurisdiction to grant a stay of deportation orders in circumstances where the orders themselves were not subject to attack, was an issue that should be taken to the Federal Court of Appeal. In this particular case, the Court did not resolve the issue because it determined that there were not sufficient grounds to grant a stay in the event that the Court had jurisdiction to do so.

The Court observed that one factor which gave concern was that the applicant had effectively been denied a determination of his leave application before the date for the execution of his deportation order because the respondent did not file the documentation respecting his case within the required time limits. These time limits had been extended because an Immigration officer was on vacation and the Court observed that this might not have been a proper basis for extending the time limits if the effect of the extension meant that the applicant would be removed from Canada before his application for leave was decided.

*Mashni v. Canada (Minister of Employment & Immigration)* (1992), 56 F.T.R. 103 (T.D.) — The Court re-affirmed that *Cegarra v. Canada (Minister of Employment & Immigration)* (1992), 56 F.T.R. 241 (Fed. T.D.) decided that a stay would inevitably be issued if the file was incomplete or otherwise not ready for adjudication in terms of the leave application. The Court noted that stay proceedings can always be avoided by a timely undertaking on the Minister's part in regard to the timing of removals. The Court noted that the Minister was not being asked to avoid his duty to remove an illegal immigrant, but only to see that those who wished to question the legality of removal have a proper opportunity to do so. Once the matter of leave is determined, further action may be possible. Those without leave will, of course, be forced to depart Canada. Those with leave may be compelled to leave Canada if they are destined for a country where and from which they can still instruct their solicitors.

*Cegarra v. Canada (Minister of Employment & Immigration)* (1992), 56 F.T.R. 241 — Judges who decide immigration leave applications inevitably need the whole file, including the tribunal's records, so that the judge can determine whether the tribunal apparently went as badly off the rails as the applicant alleges. If the file raises an arguable case for judicial review, leave will be granted.

The applicant applied on July 30, 1992 for an eleventh-hour stay. The Court convoked a telephone hearing so that the respondent could be heard on July 30, before the applicant would have been removed from Canada. The removal order was made on June 9, 1992. The applicant's motion for leave was filed on June 16, 1992. The applicant was notified on July 14, 1992 that he was to be removed from Canada on Sunday, August 2, 1992. The Court observed that it could have been determined on July 14, 1992, or shortly thereafter, that the tribunal's record would not become available before the August 2nd removal date.

The execution of a removal order will inevitably be stayed if the file is not complete, and, in the absence of the tribunal's record, it is not complete and the Court cannot properly determine the leave application. When the removal is scheduled for a time before that at which the Court and the respondent are prepared to address an already launched application for leave to commence proceedings, then, pursuant to s. 18.1 of the *Federal Courts Act*, the execution order will almost always be stayed.

Eleventh-hour emergency applications for a stay will result in a dilatory solicitor being personally ordered to pay the costs of the application. Whenever a client comes to consult a solicitor at the last moment, the client's affidavit should make clear reference to that fact, lest the emergency be seen to be an unnecessary ploy or negligence on the solicitor's part. A solicitor who has acted for an applicant at the tribunal hearing can hardly ever assert tardy consultation by the client.

The Court noted in this case that counsel requesting the stay had only been retained at the last minute and was not responsible for the last-minute application.

*Duggal v. Canada (Minister of Employment & Immigration)* (1992), 18 Imm. L.R. (2d) 20 (Fed. C.A.) — The Court of Appeal has no power to stay the execution of a removal order where it is deprived of jurisdiction by s. 82.2(1) of the *Immigration Act* to entertain an appeal from a decision of the Trial Division. The power to stay can only be implied from the Court's power to hear an appeal. If such jurisdiction is denied, then the power to stay is absent. Not even the allegation that its *Charter* right is being violated can give the

Court of Appeal a statutory jurisdiction to hear an appeal where Parliament has seen fit to withhold it.

*Nananso v. Canada (Minister of Employment & Immigration)* (1992), 56 F.T.R. 234 (Fed. T.D.) — The applicant sought an interim order for prohibition pursuant to s. 18 of the *Federal Courts Act*, to prohibit his removal from Canada. The failure of the applicant to perfect his application for a stay in a timely manner did not deprive the Court of jurisdiction. There was no legitimate reason for the application being brought a mere two hours before the applicant's removal from Canada. The Court disapproved of the practice of bringing applications to stay deportation orders on an emergency basis and agreed with the proposition that the bringing of an application for a stay of a deportation order at the very last minute may constitute a sufficient basis for rejecting the application. No adequate explanation for the failure to perfect this application was forthcoming in the affidavit material and, therefore, the application was dismissed.

*Berhan v. Canada (Minister of Employment & Immigration)* (1992), 56 F.T.R. 183 (T.D.) — The applicant sought a stay of a deportation order pending a decision by the Immigration and Refugee Board on an application to re-open the claim to refugee status. Leave to review the decision denying refugee status had been sought and denied.

No decision on the application to re-open had been given prior to the date of this application, which was immediately before the date of the applicant's deportation.

No stay was granted because the Court did not have the authority to do so. Stays can be granted when the validity of a deportation order is itself being challenged. It is also arguable that stays can be given when there is a proceeding before the Court to which s. 18.2 of the *Federal Courts Act* applies. Neither situation pertained in this case and, accordingly, the Court did not have the authority to grant a stay.

*Osei v. Canada (Minister of Employment & Immigration)* (1988), 8 Imm. L.R. (2d) 69, 25 F.T.R. 270 — In this case, the Court reviewed a variety of judicial pronouncements dealing with the Court's jurisdiction to stay an executive order in general or a deportation order in particular:

1. The Court noted that the Minister cannot be enjoined from executing a deportation order when the validity of the order has not been challenged;

2. The Federal Court of Appeal cannot, in the absence of statutory authorization to do so, stay the execution of an order that it has not pronounced, which it has no power to vary, and the validity of which is not challenged;

3. The Immigration Appeal Board has no jurisdiction to reconsider its decision confirming the deportation of a person and the only grounds for so doing would be evidence of new facts; and

4. The Court distinguished the *Toth* case because the issue arose in that case, not out of a refugee status determination, but with respect to a removal order made against a permanent resident of Canada where a statutory right of appeal was provided. Further, the Court noted that, in the *Toth* case, the order itself was being challenged.

*Espinelli v. Canada (Minister of Employment & Immigration)* (1988), 6 Imm. L.R. (2d) 21 (Fed. T.D.) — The applicant had been ordered deported. She then complained to the Human Rights Commission that the deportation proceedings violated the prohibition under the *Canadian Human Rights Act* against discrimination on the basis of marital status. The applicant sought a stay of the deportation order so that she could remain in Canada until her complaint was adjudicated upon. Her application was dismissed. While the *Canadian Human Rights Act* is a fundamental law, it does not clothe the Federal Court Trial Division with the power to stay a deportation order confirmed by the Immigration Appeal Board and maintained by the Federal Court of Appeal. Where the validity of the deportation is not itself an issue, the Trial Division has no jurisdiction under the *Charter* to paralyze an otherwise valid executory order.

*Wood v. Canada (Minister of Employment & Immigration)* (1986), 2 F.T.R. 58 (Fed. T.D.) — The Minister can only defer the execution of a deportation order if the person who is to be deported is subject to a judicial order containing specific provisions that would be violated if the deportation order were to be executed. Accordingly, where the applicant was subject to a probation order, which contained no conditions compelling the presence of the applicant in Canada or his attendance in court at a specified time and place, there was no obligation on the part of the Minister to defer his responsibility to execute the valid deportation order.

*Williams v. Canada (Minister of Employment & Immigration)*, [1985] 2 F.C. 153 (Fed. T.D.) — The applicant was born in Jamaica. She was unmarried and had five children, all of whom lived in Jamaica. The applicant arrived in Canada in September 1979 for a three-week visit and had remained in Canada ever since. The applicant was informed by a lawyer in late 1983 that the long-term illegal migrants' programme did not apply to her because she had not been "underground" for five years. On May 29, 1984, the applicant was apprehended and a deportation order was made June 8, 1984. Judicial review of this order was dismissed in November 1984. The applicant's removal in December 1984 was deferred in order that the applicant's case could be reviewed to determine whether she then qualified under the long-term illegal migrants' programme. The applicant did not qualify under the programme. During the period when the applicant's case was being considered, the long-term illegal migrants' programme was modified in such a way that the applicant would have been eligible for the programme but for the fact of her apprehension. The application to restrain the applicant's removal was dismissed. Where a person has been lawfully ordered deported, and the procedure that he or she wishes to invoke is a purely discretionary one in the hope that he or she might be granted a Minister's permit to stay in Canada, any requirement of fairness in the exercise of the Minister's discretion is minimal. Such a case does not involve a benefit to which the applicant is legally entitled nor denial of any rights legally vested in the applicant. There was no denial of fairness because the applicant did not, albeit for different reasons, come within the old or new guidelines of the long-term illegal programme.

*Mercier v. Canada (Minister of Employment & Immigration)* (April 25, 1985), Doc. T-309-85 (Fed. T.D.); affirmed (1985), 62 N.R. 73 (Fed. C.A.) — On November 17, 1982, following an inquiry, a deportation order was issued against the applicant because he had been convicted of an offence for which a maximum term of imprisonment of 10 years or more may be imposed, pursuant to s. 19(1)(c) of the Act. The applicant's appeal against this deportation order was dismissed on August 14, 1984. On January 30, 1985, the applicant tried to gain admission to the United States without success and returned to Canada with the intention of provoking an inquiry where he might claim refugee status. When the applicant reappeared at the Canadian border, a senior immigration officer issued a Summons to Appear at an inquiry, pursuant to s. 23 of the Act. That decision was countermanded by another senior immigration officer and the applicant's case was withdrawn on the ground that the deportation order, issued against the applicant, had never been executed. It was this decision that was attacked by the applicant, who was seeking a writ of *mandamus* requiring the adjudicator to conduct his inquiry. The decision to countermand the Summons to Inquiry was part of the administrative process. The Court did not intervene because it was of the view that the applicant had not been treated unfairly and that to intervene and issue a writ of *mandamus* would create a situation in which the respondent Minister would, on the one hand, have to execute a deportation order against the applicant and, on the other hand, have to conduct an inquiry with a view to admitting the applicant to the country.

An appeal from this decision was heard on June 28, 1985, and dismissed. The appellant (applicant) sought to raise, for the first time, the assertion that the deportation order had been executed by the appellant himself when he left the country for a 6-week visit to Haiti from May 12, 1984, to June 30, 1984. No consideration was given to the submission on appeal because it was a question which was raised for the first time before the Court of Appeal. It was founded upon an allegation of fact which was never put in issue before the Trial Division. The Court noted that when sitting on appeal of the Trial Division, it sat as a Court of Appeal whose function was to decide whether the issues presented at trial were properly disposed of. It was not the Court's duty to determine other issues which, had they been raised at the Trial Division, might have resulted in a different outcome if the necessary factual basis had been established.

*Farhan v. Canada (Minister of Employment & Immigration)*, 1984 CarswellNat 702 (Fed. T.D.) — The applicant sought an injunction restraining the respondent from effecting her removal to her native Iraq. A deportation order had been made against the applicant. While the order was not attacked, the grounds for the injunction were that returning the applicant to her native land subjected her to cruel and unusual treatment contrary to the Canadian *Charter of Rights and Freedoms*. The applicant had, in Canada, what would be in Iraq an illicit or adulterous relationship and feared members of her family would physically harm her, even to the point of killing her, should she be returned. The Court assumed that it was proper to take into account the particular circumstances of the applicant in deciding the application and held that the evidence fell far short of establishing the applicant's position and, accordingly, the application was dismissed.

*R. v. Gittens* (1982), 68 C.C.C. (2d) 438 (Fed. T.D.) — The applicant came to Canada in 1965 at the age of five. He became a permanent resident but not a Canadian citizen. A deportation order was made based on s. 27(1)(d)(i) and (ii) of the *Immigration Act*. An appeal against the deportation order was dismissed by the Immigration Appeal Board and the Federal Court of Appeal refused leave to appeal the Immigration Appeal Board's decision. The applicant, at the time of the giving of judgment, had completed serving all of the sentences for his criminal offences and was being kept in custody pending the execution of the deportation order. The application for an order quashing the deportation order against the applicant was dismissed because the *Charter* is not retrospective in its operation. The application for an order seeking the release of the applicant was denied on the basis that s. 10 of the *Charter* stipulated that the validity of the detention was to be determined by the way of *habeas corpus* and the Court noted that it had no jurisdiction to grant *habeas corpus*. The Court did not express an opinion whether or not it had jurisdiction to grant *habeas corpus* with *certiorari* in aid, pursuant to the *Charter*. If execution *per se* of a valid deportation order would constitute an infringement or denial of an applicant's fundamental rights and freedoms, the Court had jurisdiction in the first instance to entertain an application for an appropriate remedy. Freedom of association as envisaged by s. 2(d) of the *Charter* will not be violated by the execution of a deportation order. Execution of the order will sever immediate links with family, friends and others. To the extent that these are licit associations, they are social and familial. Assuming that they are the type of associations contemplated by s. 2(d) of the *Charter*, they are subject to such reasonable limits prescribed by law as can demonstrably be justified in a free society. The reasonableness of the right of a free and democratic state to deport alien criminals was held to be self-evident and, therefore, demonstrably justified. Section 11(h) of the *Charter* was not violated because deportation was held not to be punishment for the offences, his conviction for which had rendered him liable to deportation in the first place. In this case, the probative value of the evidence of the conditions in Guyana was minimal. The Court accepted that economic conditions and prospects were not nearly as favourable to the individual there as in Canada, and that the human rights of persons politically opposed to those in power were not, generally, respected by the Government of Guyana. The Court noted that neither the applicant nor his family had in any way been politically active so as to attract the attention of those in power in Guyana and that, therefore, the treatment the applicant could expect in Guyana would depend entirely upon his conduct there. Thus, the Court concluded that the evidence did not support the claim that execution of the deportation order would deprive the applicant of the right to life, liberty and security of the person afforded by s. 7 and, therefore, the Court declined to grant relief.

Finally, the Court noted that the incidents of deportation, whatever their degree, do not render deportation a cruel and unusual treatment of an adult. As a norm, execution of a deportation order is not in the abstract rule an unusual treatment. The Court was not persuaded by the evidence that deportation of the applicant to Guyana would be cruel and unusual treatment in the context of this case. Accordingly, the application was dismissed.

*Lodge v. Canada (Minister of Employment & Immigration)*, [1979] 1 F.C. 775, 94 D.L.R. (3d) 326, 25 N.R. 437 (C.A.) — An application for an order enjoining the Minister from executing the removal order was denied since enforcement of the provisions of the *Immigration Act* was not a denial of access to goods, services, facilities or accommodation customarily available to the general public. Further, the enforcement of the order was not in itself a discriminatory practice within the meaning of the *Canadian Human Rights Act*, S.C. 1976-77, c. 33.

*Pereira v. Canada (Minister of Manpower & Immigration)* (1978), 21 O.R. (2d) 828 (C.A.) — The respondent Minister and various immigration officials were not found to be in contempt of court in attempting to execute the deportation order while an appeal of a dismissal of a *habeas corpus* application and an application for an injunction staying the deportation order were both pending. However, no attempt should have been made at that stage to execute the deportation order which was the subject matter of the *habeas corpus* and injunction applications. The reserved judgment ultimately went against the applicant and his appeal of that judgment was dismissed. The Court held that attempts to execute the deportation order at that stage could not constitute contempt of the Court of Appeal, which had pronounced judgment without ordering a stay of the effect thereof pending any further appeals by the applicant. Service of a notice of motion for leave to appeal to the Supreme Court of Canada and a notice of motion to the Supreme Court of Ontario for an injunction did not have the effect of staying the deportation order. In addition, the Court held that once the notice of motion for leave to appeal to the Supreme Court of Canada was abandoned, the applicant lacked the status to pursue his application to have the respondent Minister and various officials committed for contempt. Such a motion was a motion in the cause, and the cause was ended.

*Denis v. R.*, [1976] 1 F.C. 499 (C.A.) — The appellant appealed from an order dismissing an application for an interlocutory injunction to restrain the execution of a deportation order pending trial of her actions for a permanent injunction and damages. The Court did not decide whether, in a proper case, an injunction could be granted against the Minister of Manpower and Immigration, assuming that the necessary steps were taken to make him a party to the proceedings. The Court refused the injunction because the removal of the appellant would not be a direct and unavoidable result of the application of the law of Canada; rather it would be the result of the decision of the appellant's mother as to whether to take her with her or leave her in Canada.

*Sun v. Canada (Attorney General)* (1960), [1961] S.C.R. 70, 26 D.L.R. (2d) 63 (S.C.C.) — A removal order will not be quashed because the applicant is the mother of a child who is a natural born Canadian citizen and has a right to live in Canada.

**18.3 (1) Reference by federal tribunal — A federal board, commission or other tribunal may at any stage of its proceedings refer any question or issue of law, of jurisdiction or of practice and procedure to the Federal Court for hearing and determination.**

**(2) Reference by Attorney General of Canada — The Attorney General of Canada may, at any stage of the proceedings of a federal board, commission or other tribunal, other than a service tribunal within the meaning of the *National Defence Act*, refer any question or issue of the constitutional validity, applicability or operability of an Act of Parliament or of regulations made under an Act of Parliament to the Federal Court for hearing and determination.**

1990, c. 8, s. 5; 2002, c. 8, s. 28

**18.4 (1) Hearings in a summary way — Subject to subsection (2), an application or reference to the Federal Court under any of sections 18.1 to 18.3 shall be heard and determined without delay and in a summary way.**

**(2) Exception — The Federal Court may, if it considers it appropriate, direct that an application for judicial review be treated and proceeded with as an action.**

1990, c. 8, s. 5; 2002, c. 8, s. 28

## Case Law

*Chen v. Canada (Minister of Citizenship & Immigration)* (2005), 43 Imm. L.R. (3d) 48, 2005 CarswellNat 2045, 2005 CarswellNat 320, 2005 FCA 56, 330 N.R. 387, 4 B.L.R. (4th) 189 (F.C.A.) — This was a motion on behalf of the respondents to quash an appeal by the Minister against a decision directing that an application for judicial review made by the respondents be treated and proceeded with as an action. The litigation from which this motion arose involved claims for injunctive and monetary relief by the respondents, non-Canadian citizens currently outside Canada, who at one time lived here. Their claims allege that the Minister breached their statutory and constitutional rights by unlawfully failing to process their applications for permanent resident cards.

The motion succeeded. The provisions in Division 8 of IRPA effectively preclude an appeal from a decision in an application for a judicial review respecting an immigration matter without a question being certified. The Court noted that once an application for a judicial review has been converted into an action, the proceeding continues subject to the rules governing actions.

*Tihomirovs v. Canada (Minister of Citizenship & Immigration)*, 2005 CarswellNat 906, 2005 FC 479 (F.C.) — The applicant sought an order directing that his application for judicial review be treated as an action. It is the applicant's intention to have the action certified as a class action brought on behalf of all skilled worker, self-employed, entrepreneur and investor applicants who submitted their applications between January 1, 2002 and June 28, 2002. Subs. 18.4(2) of the *Federal Courts Act* places no limits on the factors that can properly be considered on a conversion motion. The desirability of facilitating access to justice and avoiding unnecessary cost and delay is certainly one of them.

Because it has always been the avowed intent of the applicants to seek class action certification, and because the facts that lie behind these motions make it entirely reasonable and appropriate that they should do so, it would be tantamount to a denial of the rights of the applicants and those they seek to represent to deprive them of the opportunity to seek class action certification by denying them conversion at this stage.

*Chen v. Canada (Minister of Citizenship & Immigration)* (2004), 43 Imm. L.R. (3d) 31, 2004 CarswellNat 5730, 2004 CarswellNat 4062, 21 Admin. L.R. (4th) 55, 259 F.T.R. 161 (Eng.), 4 B.L.R. (4th) 172, 2004 FC 1573 (F.C.); affirmed (2005), 43 Imm. L.R. (3d) 48, 2005 CarswellNat 2045, 2005 CarswellNat 320, 2005 FCA 56, 330 N.R. 387, 4 B.L.R. (4th) 189 (F.C.A.) — The principal relief sought in this motion was that the judicial review applications be treated and proceeded with as actions and then these actions be joined with other actions and consolidated into one proceeding. The discretion to direct that judicial review applications be treated and proceeded with as actions is governed by s. 18.4 of the *Federal Courts Act.*

On November 21, 2002, a class action scheme was incorporated into the *Federal Court Rules*, 1998 as Rule 299.1 to Rule 299.42. Significantly, however, this scheme applies only to actions and not to applications. Hence the need for Rule 299.11 that allows for a judicial review application in the Federal Court to come under the class action regime provided it is to be treated and proceeded with as an action under subs. 18.4(2).

The rationale for Rule 299.11 appears to be that the Rules Committee concluded that because judicial review applications in the Court of Appeal, pursuant to s. 28 of the *Federal Courts Act*, should not be heard as class proceedings, a rule was needed to permit applications at the trial division level to benefit from the class action scheme.

Because it has always been the avowed intent of the applicants to seek a class action certification, and because the facts that lie behind these motions make it entirely reasonable and appropriate that they should do so is tantamount to a denial of the rights of the applicants, and those they seek to represent, to deprive them of the opportunity to seek class action certification by denying them conversion under subs. 18.4(2).

This is a fundamental access to justice issue and as such is a legitimate consideration when the Court is asked to exercise its discretion under subs. 18.4(2).

*Gonzalez v. Canada (Minister of Citizenship & Immigration)*, 2001 FCT 25, 2001 CarswellNat 218 (Fed. T.D.) — The applicant sought to convert his application for judicial review into an action. The key test is whether affidavit evidence will be inadequate in all of the circumstances to deal with the issues at hand. The Court found that while *viva voce* evidence would be better than affidavit evidence in the context of this case, it could not be said that affidavit evidence was not adequate so as to allow a proper determination of the relevant issues. Accordingly, the motion was denied.

*Singh (D.) v. R.* (2001), 12 Imm. L.R. (3d) 154, 2001 FCT 32, 2001 CarswellNat 257 (Fed. T.D.) — The plaintiff, Mr. Singh, sought damages and other relief in an action against the defendant. The defendant brought a motion to strike out the statement of claim without leave to amend. The statement of claim arises out of a decision of a visa officer in Buffalo to deny the plaintiff's application for permanent residence.

The proper course of action for a plaintiff is to pursue an application for judicial review pursuant to ss. 18 and 18.1 of the *Federal Courts Act*, and then, if successful, to bring an action for damages. Accordingly, the action was struck out.

*Kozak v. Canada (Minister of Citizenship & Immigration)* (2001), 266 N.R. 158, 12 Imm. L.R. (3d) 123, 2001 CarswellNat 31, 194 F.T.R. 160 (note) (C.A.) — The appellants were unsuccessful refugee claimants. They commenced applications for leave and judicial review and then moved to have their applications converted to actions pursuant to s. 18.4(2) of the *Federal Courts Act*. These motions were denied. Counsel for the appellants then asked the motions judge to certify a question. Counsel for the Crown successfully argued that the motions judge was without jurisdiction to certify a question because the decision was made in the context of the *Federal Courts Act* and not s. 83(1) of the *Immigration Act*. Accordingly, the appellant filed a Notice of Appeal unsupported by a certified question. Counsel for the Crown on the appeal then took the position that the court was without jurisdiction to entertain the appeals because there was no certified question as required by s. 83(1) of the *Immigration Act*.

The Court of Appeal agreed that the decision in question, namely whether an application for judicial review in an immigration matter should be converted to an action, was a decision made under the *Immigration Act*, and accordingly, before an appeal could be filed, a question for appeal had to be certified by the motions judge.

The Court of Appeal awarded costs to the appellant because counsel for the Crown had been inconsistent in this matter, arguing before the motions judge that she had no jurisdiction to certify a question and before the Court of Appeal that subs. 83(1) of the *Immigration Act* applied and that a certified question was required before the decision could be appealed.

*Shao v. Canada (Minister of Citizenship & Immigration)* (1999), 1 Imm. L.R. (3d) 116, 1999 CarswellNat 378 (Fed. T.D.) — The applicant requested an expedited hearing of a permanent residency application. The delay by immigration officials in Hong Kong and the anticipated delay in hearing the matter in the Federal Court had resulted in difficulties and anxieties, both on behalf of the applicant and the applicant's niece and family who now live in Canada.

Where there is a serious issue focusing on irreparable harm and the other side will not be prejudiced, the Court will usually make a judge available, provided a timetable convenient to counsel and the Court can be agreed upon. The applicant in this case had at best shown a serious inconvenience. Absent irreparable harm or some other exceptional circumstances, a hearing ought not to be expedited because there is still a backlog of immigration matters to be heard by the Court. To expedite an individual hearing will mean either a cancellation of an already scheduled hearing or the deferment of a matter which is also waiting for a hearing date.



*Oduro v. Canada (Minister of Employment & Immigration)* (1993), 73 F.T.R. 191 — The applicant sought permission to proceed by way of an action so that the entire document entitled Consistency Project — Final Report on Meetings, dated May 19, 1992, be put before the Court so that Board members could be questioned on their perception of the document. Judicial review is intended to proceed in a summary manner. Proceeding by way of action pursuant to s. 18.4(2) is exceptional and not to be resorted to except in the clearest circumstances. The Court referred to a decision of Pinard J. in *Edwards v. Can-*

*ada (Minister of Agriculture)* (1992), 53 F.T.R. 265 at 267, which allowed an application for an injunction and a declaration to be converted into an action in circumstances where counsel submitted there would be many different issues of fact and law, and that in addition there would be a need for extensive cross-examination on the many affidavits filed by both parties. Further, it was argued that the Court should have the benefit of assessing the demeanour and credibility of witnesses under cross-examination, particularly experts. In this case, the applicant referred to censored evidence. The missing portion of the documents in question was deleted pursuant to the provisions of the *Access to Information Act*. The applicant sought to have the matter treated as an action on the basis of speculation there was further evidence which had been censored which could support the allegation of bias. Such speculation did not constitute a basis upon which the Court could exercise its discretion under s. 18.4(2).

**18.5 Exception to sections 18 and 18.1 — Despite sections 18 and 18.1, if an Act of Parliament expressly provides for an appeal to the Federal Court, the Federal Court of Appeal, the Supreme Court of Canada, the Court Martial Appeal Court, the Tax Court of Canada, the Governor in Council or the Treasury Board from a decision or order of a federal board, commission or other tribunal made by or in the course of proceedings before that board, commission or tribunal, that decision or order is not, to the extent that it may be so appealed, subject to review or to be restrained, prohibited, removed, set aside or otherwise dealt with, except in accordance with that Act.**

1990, c. 8, s. 5; 2002, c. 8, s. 28

. . . . .

## JURISDICTION OF FEDERAL COURT OF APPEAL

**27. (1) Appeals from Federal Court — An appeal lies to the Federal Court of Appeal from any of the following decisions of the Federal Court:**

**(a) a final judgment;**

**(b) a judgment on a question of law determined before trial;**

**(c) an interlocutory judgment; or**

**(d) a determination on a reference made by a federal board, commission or other tribunal or the Attorney General of Canada.**

**(1.1) Appeals from Tax Court of Canada, except from informal procedure — An appeal lies to the Federal Court of Appeal from**

**(a) a final judgment of the Tax Court of Canada, other than one in respect of which section 18, 18.29, 18.3 or 18.3001 of the *Tax Court of Canada Act* applies;**

**(b) a judgment of the Tax Court of Canada, other than one in respect of which section 18, 18.29, 18.3 or 18.3001 of the *Tax Court of Canada Act* applies, on a question of law determined before trial; or**

**(c) an interlocutory judgment or order of the Tax Court of Canada, other than one in respect of which section 18, 18.29, 18.3 or 18.3001 of the *Tax Court of Canada Act* applies.**

**(1.2) Appeals from informal procedure in Tax Court of Canada — An appeal lies to the Federal Court of Appeal from a final judgment of the Tax Court of Canada in respect of which section 18, 18.29, 18.3 or 18.3001 of the *Tax Court of Canada Act* applies.**

**(1.3) Grounds for appeal — The only grounds for an appeal under subsection (1.2) are that the Tax Court of Canada**

> **(a) acted without jurisdiction, acted beyond its jurisdiction or refused to exercise its jurisdiction;**
>
> **(b) failed to observe a principle of natural justice, procedural fairness or other procedure that it was required by law to observe;**
>
> **(c) erred in law in making a decision or an order, whether or not the error appears on the face of the record;**
>
> **(d) based its decision or order on an erroneous finding of fact that it made in a perverse or capricious manner or without regard for the material before it;**
>
> **(e) acted, or failed to act, by reason of fraud or perjured evidence; or**
>
> **(f) acted in any other way that was contrary to law.**

**(1.4) Hearing in summary way — An appeal under subsection (1.2) shall be heard and determined without delay and in a summary way.**

**(2) Notice of appeal — An appeal under this section shall be brought by filing a notice of appeal in the Registry of the Federal Court of Appeal**

> **(a) in the case of an interlocutory judgment, within 10 days after the pronouncement of the judgment or within any further time that a judge of the Federal Court of Appeal may fix or allow before or after the end of those 10 days; and**
>
> **(b) in any other case, within 30 days, not including any days in July and August, after the pronouncement of the judgment or determination appealed from or within any further time that a judge of the Federal Court of Appeal may fix or allow before or after the end of those 30 days.**

**(3) Service — All parties directly affected by an appeal under this section shall be served without delay with a true copy of the notice of appeal, and evidence of the service shall be filed in the Registry of the Federal Court of Appeal.**

**(4) Final judgment — For the purposes of this section, a final judgment includes a judgment that determines a substantive right except as to any question to be determined by a referee pursuant to the judgment.**

R.S.C. 1985, c. 51 (4th Supp.), s. 11; 1990, c. 8, s. 7 [s. 7(2) amended 1990, c. 8, s. 78(1).]; 1993, c. 27, s. 214; 2002, c. 8, s. 34



## Case Law

*Felipa v. Canada (Minister of Citizenship & Immigration)* (2010), 87 Imm. L.R. (3d) 1, 357 F.T.R. 253 (Eng.), 3 Admin. L.R. (5th) 77, 2010 FC 89, 2010 CarswellNat 123, 2010 CarswellNat 124 (F.C.) — The applicant in this interlocutory motion challenged the jurisdiction of a deputy judge over 75 years of age to preside over the hearing of two related applications for judicial review under the *Immigration and Refugee Protection Act*. The applicant challenged the two decisions refusing the relief he sought for H&C consideration and for pre-removal risk assessment. The mandatory age of retirement of 75 years in s. 99(2) of the *Constitution Act, 1867* does not apply to deputy judges of the Federal Court. Section 8(2) of the *Federal Courts Act* does not preclude a person over age 75 from acting as a deputy judge of the Federal Court. This conclusion is consistent with the principles of statutory interpretation, with the limited legislative history and the *obiter* statement of Deputy Judge Grant in *Addy v. Canada*, [1985] 2 F.C. 452. There is no conflict between ss. 8(2) and 10(1.1) of the *Federal Courts Act*. The Court held that the motion was a "separate, divisible judicial act" not subject to s. 74(d) of IRPA. Either party may appeal the interlocutory judgment pursuant to s. 27 of the *Federal Courts Act* without the necessity of a certified question. The applicant's motion was dismissed.

*Charkaoui, Re* (2003), 38 Imm. L.R. (3d) 56, [2004] 3 F.C.R. 32, 253 F.T.R. 22, 2003 CarswellNat 3887, 2003 CarswellNat 4312, 2003 FC 1419 (F.C.) — The applicant was questioning the validity of several provisions of IRPA which establish a procedure for determining whether a permanent resident is a danger to national security or the safety of any person.

One of IRPA's objectives is to maintain the security of Canadian society. One method that Parliament has given the Ministers to accomplish this objective is to sign a certificate that renders the person concerned inadmissible to Canada. The signing of this certificate is a ministerial power that cannot be delegated. The certificate must be signed by the Minister of Citizenship and Immigration and by the Solicitor General, after which it is filed with the Federal Court.

Another method created by Parliament to maintain the security of Canadian society is the signing of an arrest warrant by the Ministers. The signing of this warrant is a non-delegated ministerial power. In order to sign such a warrant both Ministers must have reasonable grounds to believe that the person concerned is a danger to national security or the safety of any person or is unlikely to appear at a proceeding for removal.

Subs. 3(3) and paragraph 78(c) of the IRPA confer on the designated judge the power to decide constitutional questions. IRPA gives the designated judge jurisdiction over the person concerned and the subject matter as well as the power to order a remedy.

The judgement of a designated judge deciding constitutional questions can be appealed under s. 27 of the *Federal Courts Act*.

Given the distinction that the *Charter* draws between citizens and non-citizens, Parliament is entitled to enact a policy establishing rules that a permanent resident must follow in order to be able to enter and remain in Canada. Sections 33 *et seq*. of the IRPA provide that a permanent resident can be declared inadmissible if there are reasonable grounds to believe that the permanent resident is a danger to the security of Canada; that he has participated directly in war crimes or crimes against humanity; was a senior official in the government that committed war crimes or crimes against humanity; he has been convicted of an offence punishable by a term of imprisonment of at least 10 years, or for which a term of imprisonment of more than 6 months was imposed; he has been the member of an organization that has engaged in or is engaging in organized crime; or he made misrepresentations on his application for immigration or was sponsored by a person who made misrepresentations about him.

National security is essential for the preservation of our democratic society. We live in an era when threats to our democracy frequently come from unconventional acts that cannot be detected by unsophisticated investigations or traditional means. The methods used to obtain protected information must not be revealed. At the same time, a permanent resident must be reasonably informed of the reasons for which the Ministers have determined that he is a danger to national security. This is essential to ensure that the person concerned has the opportunity to defend himself.

The procedures established by ss. 76 to 85 of the IRPA take the existence of opposing interests into consideration and strike an acceptable balance between those interests. The fact that a designated judge is involved in striking this balance adds credibility to the procedure and ensures objectivity in achieving the result.

The designated judge must analyze the evidence as a whole and determine whether it provides reasonable grounds to believe there are reasons justifying the inadmissibility or arrest warrant and continued detention of the person concerned. There must be a serious possibility that the facts exist based on reliable, credible evidence.

The system of preventative detention established by Parliament in the IRPA in regard to persons concerned who in the opinion of the Ministers represent a danger to national security or to the safety of any person are consistent with the *Charter*.

Sections 77, 80, 81,82,83 and 85 of the IRPA do not contravene the rights guaranteed by s. 15 of the *Charter* or the rights guaranteed by paragraph 1(b) of the Canadian Bill of Rights.

The expressions "danger to the national security of Canada" and "members" referred to in subs. 83(3) and paragraph 34(1)(d) of the IRPA are not vague or overbroad. Subs. 80(3) and 84 of the IRPA does not contravene s. 96 of the *British North America Act*.

. . . . .

## PROCEDURE

. . . . .

**48. (1) How proceeding against Crown instituted — A proceeding against the Crown shall be instituted by filing in the Registry of the Federal Court the original and two copies of a document that may be in the form set out in the schedule and by payment of the sum of $2 as a filing fee.**

**(2) Procedure for filing originating document — The original and two copies of the originating document may be filed as required by subsection (1) by being forwarded, together with a remittance for the filing fee, by registered mail addressed to "The Registry, The Federal Court, Ottawa, Canada".**

**(3) [Repealed 2002, c. 8, s. 45.]**

**(4) [Repealed 2002, c. 8, s. 45.]**

**(5) [Repealed 2002, c. 8, s. 45.]**

2002, c. 8, s. 45

### Case Law

*Torres-Samuels (Guardian ad litem of) v. Canada (Minister of Citizenship & Immigration)* (1998), 42 Imm. L.R. (2d) 290 (B.C. S.C.); affirmed (1998), 47 Imm. L.R. (2d) 9, 57 B.C.L.R. (3d) 357, [1999] 6 W.W.R. 207, 166 D.L.R. (4th) 611, (sub nom. *Torres-*

*Samuels v. Canada (Minister of Citizenship & Immigration))* 113 B.C.A.C. 214, (sub nom. *Torres-Samuels v. Canada (Minister of Citizenship & Immigration))* 184 W.A.C. 214 (C.A.) — This was a petition brought by two Canadian children of Jose Torres, who was the subject of a deportation order under the *Immigration Act*.

The *parens patriae* jurisdiction of the Court is founded on the obvious necessity that the law should place, somewhere, the care of persons who are not able to care for themselves. The interests of the children are engaged only incidentally in the legal process that is unfolding with respect to their father. The Court questioned the extent to which it could, using its *parens patriae* jurisdiction alone, frustrate an otherwise lawful and constitutional process, the focus of which is the legal status or rights of third parties.

The Court found that the petitioners wanted it, pursuant to its *parens patriae* jurisdiction, to substitute a system of immigration with respect to foreign persons who have children born in Canada whereby it will be the superior courts of the provinces that will decide which of such persons shall be permitted to remain in the country. The Court found that its *parens patriae* jurisdiction did not extend that far.

The *parens patriae* jurisdiction of the Court should not be resorted to in a manner that flies in the face of a legislative scheme unless there is a gap in the scheme. Section 114(2) of the *Immigration Act* permits the Minister to exempt a person from deportation, owing to the existence of compassionate or humanitarian consideration; thus there is provision under the *Immigration Act* for the best interests of the children of prospective deportees to be considered. There is no gap justifying the Court's intervention on behalf of the children. The petitioners also asked for a remedy pursuant to s. 24(1) of the *Charter*. The Court declined to exercise its jurisdiction in favour of the Federal Court.

.....

**50. (1) Stay of proceedings authorized — The Federal Court of Appeal or the Federal Court may, in its discretion, stay proceedings in any cause or matter**

**(a) on the ground that the claim is being proceeded with in another court or jurisdiction; or**

**(b) where for any other reason it is in the interest of justice that the proceedings be stayed.**

**(2) Stay of proceedings required — The Federal Court of Appeal or the Federal Court shall, on application of the Attorney General of Canada, stay proceedings in any cause or matter in respect of a claim against the Crown if it appears that the claimant has an action or proceeding in respect of the same claim pending in another court against a person who, at the time when the cause of action alleged in the action or proceeding arose, was, in respect of that matter, acting so as to engage the liability of the Crown.**

**(3) Lifting of stay — A court that orders a stay under this section may subsequently, in its discretion, lift the stay.**

2002, c. 8, s. 46

## Case Law

*Charkaoui c. Canada (Ministre de la Citoyenneté & de l'Immigration)* (2004), 42 Imm. L.R. (3d) 159, 2004 CarswellNat 3342, 2004 CarswellNat 3884, (sub nom. *Charkaoui,*

*Re)* 328 N.R. 39, 2004 FCA 319 (F.C.A.) — A security certificate had been issued against the moving party. The hearing on the reasonableness of the certificate was to be held in November and December. The appellant asked the Court to issue an order temporarily staying the hearings until the appeal currently before the Federal Court was heard and decided.

Subs. 50(1)(b) of the *Federal Courts Act*, gives the Court the discretion to stay proceedings in any cause or matter. Rule 398, which establishes the procedure to follow for stays, does not strip the Federal Court of Appeal of its power to stay a proceeding if it is in the interests of justice. If an appeal before the Court of Appeal were to be rendered unnecessary, futile or illusory, as the result of an ongoing proceeding before a Federal tribunal or the Federal Court, there is no doubt that the Court of Appeal can order a stay of that proceeding to ensure that its appellate jurisdiction and process are not impeded.

*Forde v. Canada (Minister of Citizenship & Immigration)* (1997), 210 N.R. 194 (Fed. C.A.) — The Minister appealed against a decision of the Trial Division in which a judge ordered that "a stay currently exists in this case and the respondent's application [for reconsideration] is dismissed with costs in the cause".

In December 1994, a deportation order was made against the respondent. He appealed to the Appeal Division of the IRB, but before the appeal was heard, a delegate of the Minister decided that the respondent was a danger to the public in Canada. In February 1996, the respondent applied for leave to judicially review that opinion but at no time did he file an application for leave to review the deportation order.

In March 1996, the Trial Division issued a stay of the deportation order "until such time as the application for judicial review is finally disposed of". This order was clearly ancillary to the leave application then pending and was authorized by s. 18.2 of the *Federal Courts Act*. In August 1996, the Trial Division dismissed the application for leave, thus terminating any judicial review proceeding. The original stay, granted in March 1996, thus came to an end, however, the Trial Division in September 1996 granted a "continuation" of the already terminated stay, and when the Minister applied for reconsideration of this order and a declaration that the stay no longer existed, the learned judge of the Trial Division made the order which is now a subject of this appeal.

The Trial Division has a carefully defined judicial review jurisdiction in respect of "any decision or order made or any matter arising under the *[Immigration] Act*." The decision of the Minister pursuant to subs. 70(5) is such a decision. During the course of disposing of an application for leave to seek judicial review of such a decision, the Court is authorized by s. 18.2 to make ancillary orders, such as a stay. Once the leave application was disposed of there was no longer a leave or review proceeding to which a stay could be ancillary under s. 18.2. Section 50(1)(b) of the *Federal Courts Act* was never intended to give a general mandate to the Trial Division to stop deportations which are no longer under attack in the Court.

This appeal was properly brought without a question having been certified as the putative stay was no longer related to any application for leave, proceeding under subs. 82.1(1), and thus an appeal was not barred by s. 82.2.

.....

## JUDGMENTS OF FEDERAL COURT OF APPEAL

[Heading amended 2002, c. 8, s. 49.]

52. **Powers of Federal Court of Appeal — The Federal Court of Appeal may**

**(a) quash proceedings in cases brought before it in which it has no jurisdiction or whenever those proceedings are not taken in good faith;**

**(b) in the case of an appeal from the Federal Court,**

**(i) dismiss the appeal or give the judgment and award the process or other proceedings that the Federal Court should have given or awarded,**

**(ii) in its discretion, order a new trial if the ends of justice seem to require it, or**

**(iii) make a declaration as to the conclusions that the Federal Court should have reached on the issues decided by it and refer the matter back for a continuance of the trial on the issues that remain to be determined in the light of that declaration; and**

**(c) in the case of an appeal other than an appeal from the Federal Court,**

**(i) dismiss the appeal or give the decision that should have been given, or**

**(ii) in its discretion, refer the matter back for determination in accordance with such directions as it considers to be appropriate.**

**(d) [Repealed 1990, c. 8, s. 17.]**

1990, c. 8, s. 17; 2002, c. 8, s. 50

## Case Law

*Punniamoorthy v. Canada (Minister of Employment & Immigration)* (1994), 166 N.R. 49 (Fed. C.A.) — The appellant, a citizen of Sri Lanka, was a Tamil who claimed refugee status on the grounds that he had a well-founded fear of persecution by the LTTE. The appellant testified that the EPRLF started forcibly recruiting young men into the Tamil Army. As a result of his standing in the community and long association with the commander of the EPRLF army camp, the appellant was repeatedly asked by parents to obtain their conscripted sons' releases. As a result of his frequent visits to the EPRLF camp, the appellant believed that members of the LTTE thought that he had become a spy or informer. When the LTTE seized control of Jaffna, the appellant was arrested and released after two days in custody. He subsequently fled the country.

The Board offered no reasons for disregarding the appellant's testimony on two of the three grounds upon which it based its decision. Applying the reasoning in *Hilo v. Canada (Minister of Employment & Immigration)* (1991), 15 Imm. L.R. (2d) 199, 130 N.R. 236 (Fed. C.A.), the decision of the Board was quashed. This portion of the appeal went on consent. The parties disagreed on whether the Court should exercise its discretion under s. 52(c)(i) of the *Federal Courts Act* and declare the appellant a Convention refugee. This decision reviews all of the relevant cases in the last three years on this question.

In order for the Court to exercise its jurisdiction under s. 52(c)(i), the evidence on the record must be "so clearly conclusive" that the "only possible conclusion" is that the claimant is a Convention refugee. If the sole issue to be decided involves a pure question of law, which is ultimately decided in favour of the claimant, the Court has no difficulty in declaring a claimant to be a Convention refugee. If the issue revolves around uncontroverted evidence and accepted facts upon which a legal conclusion must be drawn, the Court may be compelled to declare a claimant a Convention refugee.

The Court will not invoke s. 52(c)(i) when the factual matter involves conflicting evidence which is central to the refugee determination or the claimant's credibility. It is not necessary, however, for the Board to make positive findings of credibility before the Court will exercise its jurisdiction under s. 52(c)(i). The Court may exercise its discretion and declare a claimant to be a Convention refugee where the inconsistencies in the testimony, although not insignificant, were not central to the claim.

The weight of authority is that it is highly improbable that a claimant will be declared a Convention refugee by the Court if the Board has made an overall negative assessment with respect to credibility. The same holds true when the Board disbelieves aspects of the claimant's case which are central or critical to the making of a refugee determination. In this case, the fact that the Court is dealing with matters of credibility critical to the refugee claim is sufficient for it to be cautious in exercising its discretion under s. 52(c)(i). Simply because a tribunal falls into error by failing to give adequate reasons for rejecting testimony does not of itself establish the truth of what was said.

The appeal was allowed on consent, the decision of the Board set aside and the matter remitted for rehearing.

*Vakeesan v. Canada (Minister of Employment & Immigration)*, 1993 CarswellNat 1712 (Fed. C.A.) — The Court commented that it would not exercise its jurisdiction under paragraph 52(c) of the *Federal Courts Act*. The evidence before the Board was not so clearly conclusive of the issue that the Board ought to declare the appellant a Convention refugee, nor was it clear that such a declaration was the only possible conclusion that the Board could reach. The Court referred to two of its own cases in determining when it would exercise its jurisdiction under paragraph 52(c). Those cases were *Nadarajah v. Canada (Minister of Employment & Immigration)*, [1992] 2 F.C. 394, 17 Imm. L.R. (2d) 1, 142 N.R. 161 (Fed. C.A.) and *Mahathmasseelan v. Canada (Minister of Employment & Immigration)* (1991), 15 Imm. L.R. (2d) 29, 137 N.R. 1 (Fed. C.A.)

.....

## GENERAL

**57. (1) Constitutional questions — If the constitutional validity, applicability or operability of an Act of Parliament or of the legislature of a province, or of regulations made under such an Act, is in question before the Federal Court of Appeal or the Federal Court or a federal board, commission or other tribunal, other than a service tribunal within the meaning of the *National Defence Act*, the Act or regulation shall not be judged to be invalid, inapplicable or inoperable unless notice has been served on the Attorney General of Canada and the attorney general of each province in accordance with subsection (2).**

**(2) Time of notice — The notice must be served at least 10 days before the day on which the constitutional question is to be argued, unless the Federal Court of Appeal or the Federal Court or the federal board, commission or other tribunal, as the case may be, orders otherwise.**

**(3) Notice of appeal or application for judicial review — The Attorney General of Canada and the attorney general of each province are entitled to notice of any appeal or application for judicial review made in respect of the constitutional question.**

**(4) Right to be heard — The Attorney General of Canada and the attorney general of each province are entitled to adduce evidence and make submissions to the Federal Court of Appeal or the Federal Court or the federal board, commission or other tribunal, as the case may be, in respect of the constitutional question.**

**(5) Appeal — If the Attorney General of Canada or the attorney general of a province makes submissions, that attorney general is deemed to be a party to the proceedings for the purpose of any appeal in respect of the constitutional question.**

1990, c. 8, s. 19; 2002, c. 8, s. 54

## Case Law

*Gervasoni v. Canada (Minister of Citizenship & Immigration)* (1995), 101 F.T.R. 150 — This case involves a constitutional challenge to subparagraph 46.01(1)(e)(i). Notice to the Attorney General was given prior to leave having been granted but no returnable date was set forth in the notice. A notice contemplated under s. 57 of the *Federal Courts Act* must contain a returnable day, date, time and location. In immigration judicial reviews such particulars are not known until leave has been granted. The proper practice, therefore, is to give notice after leave has been granted with the notice containing the appropriate information.

. . . . .

# CAN. REG. 98-106 — FEDERAL COURTS RULES

## made under the *Federal Courts Act*

## Rules for regulating the practice and procedure in the Federal Court of Appeal and the Federal Court

SOR/98-106, as am. S.C. 2002, c. 8, ss. 182(3)(a), 183(2)(a); SOR/2002-417, ss. 1–20, 21 (Fr.), 22–24, 25 (Fr.), 26–30; SOR/2004-283, ss. 1–20, 21 (Fr.), 22–41; SOR/2005-340; SOR/2006-219, ss. 1–10, 11 (Fr.), 12–17; SOR/2007-130; SOR/2007-214; SOR/2007-301, ss. 1(1), (2) (Fr.), 2(1) (Fr.), (2), (3), (4) (Fr.), 3–11, 12 (Fr.); SOR/2009-331; SOR/2010-176, ss. 1, 2, 3 (Fr.), 4–13 [Corrected Can. Gaz. 15/09/10 Vol. 144:19.]; SOR/2010-177 [Corrected Can. Gaz. 15/09/10 Vol. 144:19.].

*[Note: The short title of these Rules was changed from "Federal Court Rules, 1998" to "Federal Courts Rules" by SOR/2004-283, s. 2. The long title of these Rules was added by SOR/2004-283, s. 1.]*

. . . . .

## PART 2 — ADMINISTRATION OF THE COURT

. . . . .

### *Court Records*

. . . . .

**22. (1) Caveat register — The Administrator shall keep in the Registry a caveat register, in which all caveats, withdrawals of caveats and orders affecting caveats shall be entered.**

**(2) Entry of caveat — On the filing of a caveat under subsection 493(1), (2) or (3), the Administrator shall enter the caveat in the caveat register.**

. . . . .

### *Summoning of Witnesses or Other Persons*

**41. (1) Subpoena for witness — Subject to subsection (4), on receipt of a written request, the Administrator shall issue, in Form 41, a subpoena for the attendance of a witness or the production of a document or other material in a proceeding.**

**(2) Issuance in blank — A subpoena may be issued in blank and completed by a solicitor or party.**

**(3) Multiple names — Any number of names may be included in one subpoena.**

**(4) Where leave required — No subpoena shall be issued without leave of the Court**

**(a) for the production of an original record or of an original document, if the record or document may be proven by a copy in accordance with an Act of Parliament or of the legislature of a province;**

**(b) to compel the appearance of a witness who resides more than 800 km from the place where the witness will be required to attend under the subpoena; or**

**(c) to compel the attendance of a witness at a hearing other than a trial or a reference under rule 153.**

**(5) *Ex parte* motion — Leave may be granted under subsection (4) on an *ex parte* motion.**

## Case Law

*Zündel, Re* (2004), 259 F.T.R. 249 (Eng.), 2004 CarswellNat 1904, 2004 CarswellNat 2792, 2004 FC 798 (F.C.) — The applicant wanted to issue subpoenas to compel certain persons to attend the hearing being held pursuant to s. 80 of the Act on the reasonableness of a security certificate issued against him.

There are two main considerations which apply to a motion to quash a subpoena:

1. Is there a privilege or other legal rule which applies such that the witness should not be compelled to testify?

2. Is the evidence from the witnesses subpoenaed relevant and significant in regard to the issues the Court must decide?

With respect to two of the witnesses, the applicant sought to compel them to provide evidence of the extent to which they had lobbied ministers of the Crown to deport the applicant. Lobbying ministers is a legitimate exercise in an open and democratic society. The organizations, which two of the witnesses represented, have been rather vocal about the applicant's removal from Canada and so the testimony of the two individuals would add little to the public record. The two witnesses would not be able to testify as to their true influence on the decision of the two Ministers to issue a certificate in this case since only the decision makers know how the decision was made.

Questioning the background knowledge or intent of the ministers at the time of their decision, in this case, would merely be a fishing expedition. The Court held that the evidence of two of the witnesses was not relevant to the determination and quashed the subpoena. A third subpoena was issued in respect of the author of a book. The book purported to expose a number of dealings within CSIS. In deciding whether a journalist should be compelled to testify, the following factors should be considered: the relevance and materiality of the evidence to the issues at trial; the necessity of the evidence to the accused's case and his ability to make full answer in defence; the probative value of the evidence; whether the evidence was available through other means; whether the media's ability to gather and report news would be impaired by the journalist being called to give evidence and the degree of such impairment; and finally, whether the necessity of the evidence outweighs the impairment, if any, and whether the impairment of the media's function can be minimized by confining the evidence adduced to only that which is necessary.

The subpoena issued to the journalist was also quashed.

. . . . .

# PART 3 — RULES APPLICABLE TO ALL PROCEEDINGS

## *General*

. . . . .

### Appeals of Prothonotaries' Orders

**51. (1) Appeal — An order of a prothonotary may be appealed by a motion to a judge of the Federal Court.**

**(2) Service of appeal — Notice of the motion shall be served and filed within 10 days after the day on which the order under appeal was made and at least four days before the day fixed for the hearing of the motion.**

SOR/2004-283, s. 33(e); SOR/2007-130, s. 3

### Case Law

*Zhou v. Canada (Minister of Citizenship & Immigration)* (2003), 31 Imm. L.R. (3d) 136, 2003 CarswellNat 4487, 2003 CarswellNat 2736, 242 F.T.R. 161, 2003 FC 1060 (F.C.) — This was a motion to appeal a decision of the prothonotary dismissing the applicant's motion to introduce additional evidence.

Discretionary orders of prothonotaries are not to be disturbed on appeal unless they are clearly wrong, in the sense that the exercise of discretion by the prothonotary was based upon a wrong principle or upon a misapprehension of the law or they raise questions vital to the final issue in the case. In such circumstances the judge ought to exercise his or her own discretion *de novo*.

. . . . .

### Orders and Directions

. . . . .

**54. Motion for directions — A person may at any time bring a motion for directions concerning the procedure to be followed under these Rules.**

### Case Law

*Patel v. Canada (Minister of Citizenship & Immigration)*, 1999 CarswellNat 1536 (Fed. T.D.) — The applicant made a motion for directions pursuant to Rule 54 with respect to a case summary sworn by the respondent's officer and the inclusion of that summary in the tribunal record.

It would be inappropriate to include the case summary as part of the tribunal record because it was prepared after the impugned decision. The summary, however, will assist the reviewing judge and so it was ordered, on this motion, that the respondent serve and file the original or a copy of the case summary including all exhibits identified within 10 days of the date of these directions.

. . . . .

## *Court Documents*

. . . . .

### Filing of Documents

. . . . .

**72. (1) Irregular documents — Where a document is submitted for filing, the Administrator shall**

**(a) accept the document for filing; or**

**(b) where the Administrator is of the opinion that the document is not in the form required by these Rules or that other conditions precedent to its filing have not been fulfilled, refer the document without delay to a judge or prothonotary.**

**(2) Acceptance, rejection or conditional filing — On receipt of a document referred under paragraph (1)(b), the judge or prothonotary may direct the Administrator to**

**(a) accept or reject the document; or**

**(b) accept the document subject to conditions as to the making of any corrections or the fulfilling of any conditions precedent.**

**(3) Deemed time of filing — A document that is accepted for filing shall be considered to have been filed at the time the document was submitted for filing, unless the Court orders otherwise.**

## Case Law

*Alavinejad v. Canada (Minister of Citizenship & Immigration)*, 2005 CarswellNat 1042, 2005 F.C. 553 (F.C.) — This was a motion for an extension of time. The legal assistant to the applicant's lawyer miscalculated the time for filing by one day. On the day that the record was due to be served and filed, counsel realized the error. He and a student left their office at 4:15 and reached the registry at 4:45, a quarter of an hour after closing time. The registry let them in, however, the registrar refused to accept the document. Such behaviour was not in keeping either with the position of the Federal Court as a service organization or with Federal Courts Rule 72.

It is common procedure where a registrar can be made available and the circumstances are special or warrant such, to hold the Registry open or indeed to open the Registry in an emergency or perhaps as an accommodation, in order to avoid the embarrassment of counsel and extra unnecessary work. The registrar being opened, it is unseemly to deny services. If the Registry felt concern about whether or not to file the tendered material, the Registry is required, by Rule 72, which is mandatory, either to accept a document for filing or to refer it to a judge or prothonotary without delay. In this instance an order was made accepting the application record for filing.

*Chung v. Canada (Minister of Citizenship & Immigration)*, 2003 CarswellNat 4233, 2003 CarswellNat 3055, 2003 FC 1150 (F.C.) — A letter from counsel for the applicants was referred to the Court for directions pursuant to Rule 72. The applicants wanted to file a memorandum of argument exceeding 30 pages in length.

A general rule limiting the length of written submissions is clearly justified otherwise the Court would be unable to control its own process and the parties would be free to submit prolix and redundant submissions.

Accordingly, as a general rule, a memorandum of argument cannot exceed 30 pages in length unless a party has first obtained leave by motion in writing.

. . . . .

## *Affidavit Evidence and Examinations*

### Affidavits

. . . . .

**84. (1) When cross-examination may be made — A party seeking to cross-examine the deponent of an affidavit filed in a motion or application shall not do so until the party has served on all other parties every affidavit on which the party intends to rely in the motion or application, except with the consent of all other parties or with leave of the Court.**

**(2) Filing of affidavit after cross-examination — A party who has cross-examined the deponent of an affidavit filed in a motion or application may not subsequently file an affidavit in that motion or application, except with the consent of all other parties or with leave of the Court.**

### Case Law

*Zhu v. Canada (Minister of Citizenship & Immigration)*, 2000 CarswellNat 2518 (Fed. T.D.) — The applicant sought leave to file additional affidavits and to add material which ought to have been part of the tribunal record from the Canadian Embassy in Manila. The applicant applied for permanent residence as an investor. When it came time to cross-examine the visa officer, which was done by telephone, about half of the documents which ought to have formed part of the tribunal record were missing. Additional affidavits may be filed if such will serve the interests of justice and assist the Court in making a final determination. The applicant was required also to satisfy Rule 84(2) which requires leave to file additional material following cross-examination. The test requires a consideration of the following three items:

1. Was the information in the affidavit available before the cross-examination?
2. Are the facts to be established in the supplemental material relevant?
3. Might the supplementary material cause serious prejudice to other parties?

The Court allowed the filing of extra material in this case.

. . . . .

## *Joinder, Intervention and Parties*

### Joinder

. . . . .

**104. (1) Order for joinder or relief against joinder — At any time, the Court may**

> **(a) order that a person who is not a proper or necessary party shall cease to be a party; or**
>
> **(b) order that a person who ought to have been joined as a party or whose presence before the Court is necessary to ensure that all matters in dispute in the proceeding may be effectually and completely determined be added as a party, but no person shall be added as a plaintiff or applicant without his or her consent, signified in writing or in such other manner as the Court may order.**

**(2) Directions — An order made under subsection (1) shall contain directions as to amendment of the originating document and any other pleadings.**

## Case Law

*Pelishko v. Canada (Minister of Citizenship & Immigration)*, [2003] 3 F.C. 517, 2003 CarswellNat 188, 2003 CarswellNat 1149, 2003 FCT 88, 2003 CFPI 88, 227 F.T.R. 21 (Fed. T.D.) — The applicant brought a motion for an order joining Mr. H. Watson as a party to the proceeding. The Minister is a proper party to the proceedings in which an applicant challenges a decision made in the name of the Minister by one of his agents. Immigration officers authorized to perform the functions for which discretion is given to them under the Immigration Act do so in the name of the Minister. It is the usual practice in actions against the Minister, to have the decision maker file an affidavit on behalf of the Minister and to be available for cross-examination by the applicant. Watson can participate as an affiant on behalf of the Minister should the applicant seek judicial review. This is not a case in which Watson must be added as a party in order to have the issues "effectually and completely" settled. It is not appropriate to add Watson as a party in order to render him personally bound by the determination of the Court. The relief sought is against the Minister and it is only the Minister who is bound by such an order. The Minister carries out what such orders require him to do, such as having applications redetermined through his representatives. Watson is only one such representative.

**105. Consolidation of proceedings — The Court may order, in respect of two or more proceedings,**

> **(a) that they be consolidated, heard together or heard one immediately after the other;**
>
> **(b) that one proceeding be stayed until another proceeding is determined; or**
>
> **(c) that one of the proceedings be asserted as a counterclaim or cross-appeal in another proceeding.**

## Case Law

*Kathirkamu v. Canada (Minister of Citizenship & Immigration)*, 2003 CarswellNat 651, 2003 FCT 308 (Fed. T.D.) — The applicant sought to consolidate separate Federal Court proceedings pursuant to Rule 105. The policy behind consolidation is the avoidance of a multiplicity of proceedings and a promotion of expeditious and inexpensive determination of proceedings. Among the factors that a court should look at to determine if there is sufficient commonality of legal and factual issues to warrant consolidation are common parties, common legal and factual issues, similar causes of action, parallel evidence, and the likelihood that the outcome of one case will resolve the other.

.....

# *Representation of Parties*

### General

**119. Individuals — Subject to rule 121, an individual may act in person or be represented by a solicitor in a proceeding.**

## Case Law

*Salinas v. Canada (Minister of Citizenship & Immigration)*, [2000] F.C.J. No. 1004, 2000 CarswellNat 3202, 2000 CarswellNat 1414 (Fed. T.D.) — The respondent Minister appealed an order of a prothonotary who dismissed the Minister's motion asking that the application for leave and judicial review be dismissed on the ground that no one acting on behalf of the applicants was qualified to represent them.

The Court should not approve of third parties who are not lawyers doing things which are within the exclusive jurisdiction of members of the bar.

It is the Court's role and duty to guarantee compliance with the *Act* and the Rules and to ensure that those who appear before it, or draft proceedings for the purpose of asserting rights, are officers of the Court. Facts put in evidence in each of the respondent Minister's motions constituted evidence which pointed inexorably to the conclusion that in each case the application for leave and judicial review by the applicants had been prepared and drafted by an agent who could not act as a representative in this Court. If an applicant decides to be represented, Rule 119 is clear, he or she must be represented by a solicitor.

Accordingly, the respondent Minister's appeal was allowed and the application for judicial review dismissed.

*Parmar c. Canada (Ministre de la Citoyenneté & de l'Immigration)* (2000), 12 Imm. L.R. (3d) 178, 2000 CarswellNat 1432, 2000 CarswellNat 3429 (Fed. T.D.) — The defendant Minister appealed an order dismissing its motion asking the Court to dismiss an application for leave and judicial review. The motion had been brought on the ground that the person acting on the plaintiff's behalf was not qualified to represent him.

It is the Court's function and duty to ensure that its Act and its Rules are observed and that those who appear before it or prepare pleadings to be used in asserting rights are officers of the Court. The facts in this matter lead inexorably to the conclusion that the plaintiff's application for leave and judicial review had been prepared and drafted by an agent. It is true that a plaintiff may act in person, but if he or she decides to be represented then the rule is clear, he or she must be represented by a barrister or advocate.

The Court concluded that the plaintiff had been represented by a person who was not authorized to do so, and accordingly, allowed the Minister's appeal and dismissed the plaintiff's application for leave and for judicial review.

.....

## *Filing of Confidential Material*

**151. (1) Motion for order of confidentiality — On motion, the Court may order that material to be filed shall be treated as confidential.**

**(2) Demonstrated need for confidentiality — Before making an order under subsection (1), the Court must be satisfied that the material should be treated as confidential, notwithstanding the public interest in open and accessible court proceedings.**

### Case Law

*Harkat, Re*, [2009] F.C.J. No. 228, 80 Imm. L.R. (3d) 89, 2009 CarswellNat 436, 2009 FC 167 — Special advocates do not have the jurisdiction to act in public on behalf of a named person, nor are they permitted to communicate with him while acting as special advocate. They are not counsel of record in the proceeding. They do not, therefore, have standing to seek a confidentiality order which would prevent public access to court records; only counsel for the applicant may seek such an order. The objection made by the special advocates that the three summaries of conversation be kept confidential was granted on an interim basis. The three summaries of conversations were disclosed to the applicant and his counsel. The applicant and his counsel were given 10 days to serve and file a motion asking the Court to continue treating the three summaries of conversations confidentially. In the absence of any such motion, the three summaries of conversations would become part of the public amended security intelligence report.

*C. (A.) v. Canada (Minister of Citizenship & Immigration)* (2003), 33 Imm. L.R. (3d) 45, 2003 CarswellNat 3976, 2003 CarswellNat 4558, 2003 FC 1452, 243 F.T.R. 211, 2003 CFPI 1452 (F.C.) — As an ancillary matter to their judicial review application, the applicants brought a motion for an order sealing the record in this case. The grounds for the motion were that the applicants, as well as the witnesses who testified at the refugee hearing, face a risk of harm if returned to their country of origin, as do their relatives in that country. The harm alleged is in the form of reprisals for their having testified on behalf of the applicants at the refugee hearing. Witnesses who testify before the Refugee Division, after receiving assurances that their evidence will be treated in confidence, should not be exposed to serious and substantial risk of harm if the matter proceeds to the judicial review stage.

The Supreme Court of Canada in *Sierra Club of Canada v. Canada (Minister of Finance)*, [2002] 2 S.C.R. 522, 2002 CarswellNat 823, [2002] S.C.J. No. 42, 2002 SCC 41, (sub nom. *Atomic Energy of Canada Ltd. v. Sierra Club of Canada)* 211 D.L.R. (4th) 193, (sub nom. *Atomic Energy of Canada Ltd. v. Sierra Club of Canada)* 18 C.P.R. (4th) 1, 44 C.E.L.R. (N.S.) 161, 287 N.R. 203, 20 C.P.C. (5th) 1, 40 Admin. L.R. (3d) 1, (sub nom. *Atomic Energy of Canada Ltd. v. Sierra Club of Canada)* 93 C.R.R. (2d) 219, 223

F.T.R. 137 (note), 2002 CarswellNat 822 (S.C.C.), set out a two-part test for a confidentiality order: a) a confidentiality order should only be granted when the order is necessary to prevent a serious risk to an important interest including a commercial interest, in the context of litigation because reasonable alternative measures will not prevent the risk; and b) the salutary effects of the confidentiality order, including the effects on the right of civil litigants to a fair trial, outweigh its deleterious effects, including the effects on the open right to free expression, which in this context includes the public interest in open and accessible court proceedings.

The Court was satisfied that the applicants and their witnesses genuinely felt at risk, but was not satisfied that the applicants had met the onus that would justify a departure from the principle of an open and accessible court.

The Court ordered that the record of the proceeding as is maintained on the Court's website should be amended to show the style of cause as set out in the order that the Court was issuing. Secondly, by deleting from the text the names of the applicants and replacing those names with the initials and finally, by deleting the names of the applicant's witnesses and other identifying features from the text of any order or reasons and replacing them with such alternatives as the Court considered appropriate in the circumstances.

**152. (1) Marking of confidential material — Where the material is required by law to be treated confidentially or where the Court orders that material be treated confidentially, a party who files the material shall separate and clearly mark it as confidential, identifying the legislative provision or the Court order under which it is required to be treated as confidential.**

**(2) Access to confidential material — Unless otherwise ordered by the Court,**

**(a) only a solicitor of record, or a solicitor assisting in the proceeding, who is not a party is entitled to have access to confidential material;**

**(b) confidential material shall be given to a solicitor of record for a party only if the solicitor gives a written undertaking to the Court that he or she will**

**(i) not disclose its content except to solicitors assisting in the proceeding or to the Court in the course of argument,**

**(ii) not permit it to be reproduced in whole or in part, and**

**(iii) destroy the material and any notes on its content and file a certificate of their destruction or deliver the material and notes as ordered by the Court, when the material and notes are no longer required for the proceeding or the solicitor ceases to be solicitor of record;**

**(c) only one copy of any confidential material shall be given to the solicitor of record for each party; and**

**(d) no confidential material or any information derived therefrom shall be disclosed to the public.**

**(3) Order to continue — An order made under subsection (1) continues in effect until the Court orders otherwise, including for the duration of any appeal of the proceeding and after final judgment.**

### Case Law

*Harkat, Re*, [2009] F.C.J. No. 228, 80 Imm. L.R. (3d) 89, 2009 CarswellNat 436, 2009 FC 167 — Special advocates do not have the jurisdiction to act in public on behalf of a named person, nor are they permitted to communicate with him while acting as special advocate. They are not counsel of record in the proceeding. They do not, therefore, have standing to seek a confidentiality order which would prevent public access to court records; only counsel for the applicant may seek such an order. The objection made by the special advocates that the three summaries of conversation be kept confidential was granted on an interim basis. The three summaries of conversations were disclosed to the applicant and his counsel. The applicant and his counsel were given 10 days to serve and file a motion asking the Court to continue treating the three summaries of conversations confidentially. In the absence of any such motion, the three summaries of conversations would become part of the public amended security intelligence report.

. . . . .

## *Summary Disposition*

. . . . .

167. **Dismissal for delay — The Court may, at any time, on the motion of a party who is not in default of any requirement of these Rules, dismiss a proceeding or impose other sanctions on the ground that there has been undue delay by a plaintiff, applicant or appellant in prosecuting the proceeding.**

### Case Law

*Bensalah v. Canada (Ministre de la Citoyenneté & de l'Immigration)* (2000), 184 F.T.R. 311 (note), 2000 CarswellNat 476, 2000 CarswellNat 1956 (Fed. C.A.) — The appellant was benefiting from a statutory stay of execution of a removal order pending disposition of his appeal. Under the Federal Courts Rules the appellant was required to file his memorandum on or before November 25, 1999, but had not done so. The respondent filed a motion to dismiss the appeal alleging as the reason, undue delay. The motion was allowed. The fact that in filing a Notice of Appeal the appellant may benefit from an automatic stay of the removal order, imposes a corresponding duty to prosecute the appeal with diligence and at the very least to comply with the deadlines specified in the rules.

. . . . .

## PART 4 — ACTIONS

. . . . .

## *Summary Judgment and Summary Trial*

[Heading amended SOR/2009-331, s. 3.]

### Motion and Service

[Heading added SOR/2009-331, s. 3.]

**213. (1) Motion by a party — A party may bring a motion for summary judgment or summary trial on all or some of the issues raised in the pleadings at any time after the defendant has filed a defence but before the time and place for trial have been fixed.**

**(2) Further motion — If a party brings a motion for summary judgment or summary trial, the party may not bring a further motion for either summary judgment or summary trial except with leave of the Court.**

**(3) Obligations of moving party — A motion for summary judgment or summary trial in an action may be brought by serving and filing a notice of motion and motion record at least 20 days before the day set out in the notice for the hearing of the motion.**

**(4) Obligations of responding party — A party served with a motion for summary judgment or summary trial shall serve and file a respondent's motion record not later than 10 days before the day set out in the notice of motion for the hearing of the motion.**

SOR/2009-331, s. 3

## Case Law

*Samimifar v. Canada (Minister of Citizenship & Immigration)*, [2006] F.C.J. No. 1626, 58 Imm. L.R. (3d) 24, 2006 CarswellNat 5309, 2006 FC 1301 (F.C.) — The applicant was granted approval-in-principle to accept and process an application for permanent residence from within Canada. He submitted his application in 1994 and until January 2003, his application appears to have been subject to inattention, inaction and delay for reasons which he alleges amount to negligence and breach of his s. 7 *Charter* rights. In January 2003, he was informed that his PR application was refused on the basis of inadmissibility to Canada under s. 34(1)(f) of the IRPA because there were reasonable grounds to believe he was a member of a terrorist organization.

In addition to pursuing his administrative efforts to become a permanent resident, the applicant commenced an action against the Minister of Citizenship and Immigration by filing a Statement of Claim. The respondent brought a motion seeking summary judgment to dismiss all or part of the claim. The Court concluded that the policy considerations did not preclude the imposition of the duty of care where an immigration officer completely ignores a file. At trial, it may be possible for the defendant to be able to provide a satisfactory explanation as to why this matter languished for at least seven years. However, given the unusual nature of the claim involving allegations against a particular immigration officer in the context of the harm allegedly suffered by the applicant, the action should not be summarily dismissed on broad policy grounds.

. . . . .

## *Striking Out Pleadings*

**221. (1) Motion to strike — On motion, the Court may, at any time, order that a pleading, or anything contained therein, be struck out, with or without leave to amend, on the ground that it**

**(a) discloses no reasonable cause of action or defence, as the case may be,**

**(b) is immaterial or redundant,**

**(c) is scandalous, frivolous or vexatious,**

**(d) may prejudice or delay the fair trial of the action,**

**(e) constitutes a departure from a previous pleading, or**

**(f) is otherwise an abuse of the process of the Court,**

**and may order the action be dismissed or judgment entered accordingly.**

**(2) Evidence — No evidence shall be heard on a motion for an order under paragraph (1)(a).**

. . . . .

# PART 5 — APPLICATIONS

. . . . .

## *General*

. . . . .

**302. Limited to single order — Unless the Court orders otherwise, an application for judicial review shall be limited to a single order in respect of which relief is sought.**

### Case Law

*Lee v. Canada (Minister of Citizenship & Immigration)* (1999), 177 F.T.R. 210, 1999 CarswellNat 2174 (Fed. T.D.) — The notice of application referred to two decisions and accordingly the applicant was found not to have complied with Rule 302 of the Federal Courts Rules, which limits an application for judicial review to one order. The Court then dismissed the request to review one of the two decisions and amended the application for judicial review so that it only referred to the decision that was going to be reviewed by the Court.

. . . . .

**312. Additional steps — With leave of the Court, a party may**

**(a) file affidavits additional to those provided for in rules 306 and 307;**

**(b) conduct cross-examinations on affidavits additional to those provided for in rule 308; or**

**(c) file a supplementary record.**

## Case Law

*Zhu v. Canada (Minister of Citizenship & Immigration)*, 2000 CarswellNat 2518 (Fed. T.D.) — The applicant sought leave to file additional affidavits and to add material which ought to have been part of the tribunal record from the Canadian Embassy in Manila. The applicant applied for permanent residence as an investor. When it came time to cross-examine the visa officer, which was done by telephone, about half of the documents which ought to have formed part of the tribunal record were missing. Additional affidavits may be filed if such will serve the interests of justice and assist the Court in making a final determination. The applicant was required also to satisfy Rule 84(2) which requires leave to file additional material following cross-examination. The test requires a consideration of the following three items:

1. Was the information in the affidavit available before the cross-examination?
2. Are the facts to be established in the supplemental material relevant?
3. Might the supplementary material cause serious prejudice to other parties?

The Court allowed the filing of extra material in this case.

.....

# PART 7 — MOTIONS

.....

**369. (1) Motions in writing — A party may, in a notice of motion, request that the motion be decided on the basis of written representations.**

**(2) Request for oral hearing — A respondent to a motion brought in accordance with subsection (1) shall serve and file a respondent's record within 10 days after being served under rule 364 and, if the respondent objects to disposition of the motion in writing, indicate in its written representations or memorandum of fact and law the reasons why the motion should not be disposed of in writing.**

**(3) Reply — A moving party may serve and file written representations in reply within four days after being served with a respondent's record under subsection (2).**

**(4) Disposition of motion — On the filing of a reply under subsection (3) or on the expiration of the period allowed for a reply, the Court may dispose of a motion in writing or fix a time and place for an oral hearing of the motion.**



## Case Law

*Padda v. Canada (Minister of Citizenship & Immigration)*, 2006 CarswellNat 2516, 2006 FC 995 (F.C.) — The applicants brought a motion for an extension of time within which to perfect their record in support of their application for leave and for judicial review. Rather than bringing their motion in writing pursuant to Rule 369 of the *Federal Courts Rules*, as is the norm in immigration leave applications, the applicants elected to proceed orally, making their motion returnable at the general sittings. Such practice should be discouraged. To allow an applicant to obtain an oral hearing for an interlocutory motion in a leave application that is intended to be conducted entirely in writing appears antithetical to the statutory and regulatory objectives of efficiency and expediency. It could easily be abused by an unscrupulous applicant who could obtain an extended stay of removal pending determination of the application for leave by making his or her motion for extension of time returnable in the distant future. The registry should, as a rule, seek directions from the Court with respect to any motion in an immigration leave application that is not brought in writing pursuant to Rule 369 of the *Federal Courts Rules*.

*Desouky v. Canada (Minister of Citizenship & Immigration)* (1999), 176 F.T.R. 302, 1999 CarswellNat 2083 (Fed. T.D.) — This was a motion made pursuant to Rule 369 to allow the applicant to file an application record. The applicant filed, in June 1999, an application for leave to review the decision of an officer refusing an application for consideration on humanitarian and compassionate grounds (H&C). The application for leave was filed out of time, and the applicant requested an extension of time pursuant to subsection 82.1(15). The applicant failed to perfect the application for leave by serving and filing an application record. Therefore, on September 1, 1999, the Court dismissed the application for leave due to the failure of the applicant to file a record.

The only reason given for not having filed the record was that the applicant's lawyer was "new in the practice of law and particularly in the area of immigration law." The inexperience of the applicant's lawyer is not a reason to set aside a final judgement of the Court. To set aside or vary a final judgement the Court requires evidence pursuant to Rule 399(2). Accordingly, the application was dismissed.

*Askar v. Canada (Minister of Citizenship & Immigration)* (1999), 179 F.T.R. 1, 1999 CarswellNat 2230, [1999] F.C.J. No. 1670 (Fed. T.D.) — The test on a motion to strike an application for judicial review seeking a declaration and mandamus, is whether the application is so clearly improper as to be bereft of any possibility of success.

. . . . .

# Part 9 — Case Management and Dispute Resolution Services

## *Case Management*

. . . . .

### Specially Managed Proceedings

. . . . .

**384. Order for special management — The Court may at any time order that a proceeding continue as a specially managed proceeding.**

SOR/2007-214, s. 3

### Case Law

*Huang v. Canada (Minister of Citizenship & Immigration)* (2003), 34 Imm. L.R. (3d) 33, 2003 CarswellNat 412, 2003 CarswellNat 1415, 2003 FCT 196, 2003 CFPI 196 (Fed. T.D.) — The applicant sought to have his action managed as a special managed proceeding. The applicant wanted to expedite judicial review of an interlocutory ruling from the Immigration Appeal Division to adjourn a hearing. The purpose of the adjournment was to permit the tribunal to consider whether the Minister's case may be split so that after all the evidence is in, the Minister's case might be bolstered.

In order to constitute a substantial reason for special management, special circumstances must exist to warrant judicial review intervention at the interlocutory stage. The category of special circumstances is open ended. In the present instance the special circumstance is an allegation of bias on the basis that bias goes to the very function of the tribunal which is to render impartial decisions. The transcript of the adjournment decision leads one to the view that it is most likely that rather than exhibiting bias the tribunal became confused on a number of issues, some of which the Minister's representatives could have sorted out. Accordingly, the motion for special management was dismissed.

.....

# PART 10 — ORDERS

.....

**397. (1) Motion to reconsider — Within 10 days after the making of an order, or within such other time as the Court may allow, a party may serve and file a notice of motion to request that the Court, as constituted at the time the order was made, reconsider its terms on the ground that**

**(a) the order does not accord with any reasons given for it; or**

**(b) a matter that should have been dealt with has been overlooked or accidentally omitted.**

**(2) Mistakes — Clerical mistakes, errors or omissions in an order may at any time be corrected by the Court.**

## Case Law

*Ismail v. Canada (Minister of Citizenship & Immigration)* (2006), 58 Imm. L.R. (3d) 179, 358 N.R. 160, 2006 CarswellNat 4247, 2006 FCA 396 (Fed. C.A.) — The statutory prohibition on appeals in immigration matters unless a question is certified pursuant to paragraph 74(d) of the IRPA would be meaningless if it could be circumvented simply by filing a motion under Rule 397 or 399 (*Federal Courts Rules*).

*Lee v. Canada (Minister of Citizenship & Immigration)*, 2003 CarswellNat 2350, 2003 FC 867 (F.C.) — The applicant sought reconsideration of an Order. Rule 397(1)(b) is a technical rule, designed to address situations where a matter that should have been addressed was overlooked or accidentally omitted. The applicant, in this case, was arguing that a point raised in argument was not addressed in the Reasons for Order and, therefore, the matter should be reconsidered. This is not a proper basis for invoking Rule 397(1)(b).

*Samarraie v. Canada (Minister of Citizenship & Immigration)*, 2003 CarswellNat 1947, 2003 FCT 755 (Fed. T.D.) — Rule 397 is not intended to be used as a method of appeal. The issue is "whether there was some matter the Court overlooked in reaching its decision and if so determine if the overlooked matter changes its decision." In the present case there were two errors of fact in the order. First, the order stated that the applicant applied under the independent and assisted relative categories where, in fact, the applicant applied only as an independent. Secondly, the order has the wrong date of the applicant's immigration interview. Neither of these errors resulted in the order not being in accord with the reasons given or that a matter that should have been dealt with had been overlooked or accidentally omitted. There is no inconsistency between the reasons and the order. Accordingly, the application for reconsideration was dismissed.

*Grant v. Canada (Minister of Citizenship & Immigration)*, 2001 CarswellNat 2770, 2001 FCT 1343 (Fed. T.D.) — The applicant applied for an extension of time to bring a motion for the reconsideration by the Court of one of its orders. Due to the fact that the judge who made the original order was leaving the Court after long and distinguished service, the duty judge elected to deal with the application. The extension of time for the filing of the application and the application record was granted, however, the application itself was dismissed. Jurisprudence existing at the date of the order in question, whether then known or later discovered, does not qualify as a new matter within Rule 397.

*Dan v. Canada (Minister of Citizenship & Immigration)* (2000), 6 Imm. L.R. (3d) 84, 189 F.T.R. 301, [2000] F.C.J. No. 638, 2000 CarswellNat 892 (Fed. T.D.) — The oversight or accidental omission contemplated by Rule 397 must be in the terms of the order, and not in the parties' submissions to the Court prior to the issuance of the order. Rule 397 protects the finality of a court order while allowing for its reconsideration where a matter that should have been dealt with in the order was overlooked or accidentally omitted.

*Haque v. Canada (Minister of Citizenship & Immigration)* (2000), 188 F.T.R. 154, 2000 CarswellNat 1516, [2000] F.C.J. No. 1141 (Fed. T.D.) — This was an application for reconsideration. The application of Rule 397 to a failure by a judge to deal with an argument made before him or her has been considered by two different judges with different results. In *Klockner Namasco Corp. v. Federal Hudson*, [1991] F.C.J. No. 1073, the Court held that the failure to consider an argument came within the meaning of the rule. In *Balasingam v. M.E.I.* (1994), 77 F.T.R. 79, 28 Imm. L.R. (2d) 107, 1994 CarswellNat 256 (Fed. T.D.), the Court considered that failure to consider an argument did not come within the meaning of the rule. To permit what are intended to be final orders to be opened up because an argument has not been dealt with, undermines the finality of the decision. The Court should not have imposed upon it the obligation of dealing with every argument made without regard for its significance or its merit.

*Sizov v. Canada (Minister of Citizenship & Immigration)* (2000), 189 F.T.R. 317, 2000 CarswellNat 1911 (Fed. T.D.) — This was an application for reconsideration of a decision dismissing the applicant's application for leave due to the failure of the applicant to file a Record.

On March 17, 2000, the applicant commenced an application for leave and judicial review. In that application the applicant sought an extension of time. The Application Record was due on April 17, 2000. On May 1, 2000, the applicant obtained, with the consent of the respondent, an order extending the time for service and proof of service of the Application Record to May 6, 2000. The applicant failed to file his Record within that time. Consequently, on June 14, 2000, the Court dismissed his application. The instant motion for reconsideration was not filed within the 10 days stipulated under Rule 397. The order in question does accord with the failure of the applicant to file his Record and no matter that should have been dealt with was overlooked by the judge. Rule 397 provides for an extension of time "within such other time as the Court may allow". The applicant deposed in his affidavit for reconsideration that he had retained a lawyer to proceed with his application and has been unable to contact the lawyer to find out why nothing was done with respect to the filing of his Application Record. The applicant further deposed that he had retained a new solicitor in July 2000. The Court considered that it had jurisdiction on this motion for reconsideration to reconsider its earlier decision and grant an extension of time for the applicant to file his Record.

*McFarlane v. Canada (Minister of Citizenship & Immigration)* (2000), 2000 CarswellNat 1907 (Fed. T.D.) — This was a motion for an order extending the time to reconsider a judgement of the Court dismissing an application for leave due to the failure of the applicant to file an application record.

Rule 397 allows the Court to reconsider an order if it does not accord with the reasons given, or a matter that should have been dealt with has been overlooked or accidentally omitted. There was no suggestion by the applicant that the Court's decision was in any way inconsistent with the material before it at the time it rendered its decision. Therefore, nothing was overlooked and Rule 397 does not apply.

*Velupillai v. Canada (Minister of Citizenship & Immigration)* (2000), 188 F.T.R. 314, 2000 CarswellNat 1898 (Fed. T.D.) — When the Court signed its decision on June 15, 2000, it was not aware of a decision rendered by the Federal Court of Appeal three days before. Given the number of decisions rendered by the Trial Division and by the Appeal Division, it takes a few days to become aware of these decisions. The Federal Court of Appeal decision in question could have had an impact on the Court's decision and accordingly, the Court reconsidered its earlier decision refusing leave and granted leave. The Court of Appeal decision constituted a matter that arose subsequent to the making of the order.

*Chaudhary v. Canada (Minister of Citizenship & Immigration)* (November 2, 1999), Doc. IMM-2002-99, 1999 CarswellNat 2312 (Fed. T.D.) — The applicant was a failed refugee claimant. He filed an application for judicial review of that decision. The record was not filed in time and an extension of time was granted. Once again, the applicant failed to file a record and the Court dismissed the application for lack of an application record. Counsel then filed a notice of motion asking the Court to reconsider its order.

This was not an appropriate case for reconsideration. Nothing was overlooked or accidentally omitted when the Court ordered the dismissal of the application. The material in support of the motion for reconsideration reveals that the cause of the dismissal of the application was the failure of counsel for the applicant to pursue the matter with anything approaching reasonable diligence. Accordingly, the motion for reconsideration was dismissed.

*Sivakumar v. Canada (Minister of Citizenship & Immigration)* (1998), 150 F.T.R. 299 (T.D.) — The defendants sought an extension of time with which to serve and file a Notice of Appeal to the Federal Court of Appeal from a disclosure order made by a judge of the Trial Division. The Notice of Appeal was not filed within 10 days of the decision, rather the defendants brought a motion for reconsideration within the 10-day period. This motion was dismissed. The defendants argued that in filing a reconsideration application they evidenced a continuing intention to appeal and that they brought the extension application within a reasonable period of time after the dismissal of the reconsideration application. Rule 337(5) (now Rule 397), provides that the Court can reconsider a judgement on the grounds that it did not accord with the reasons or that some matter was overlooked or accidentally omitted. The grounds for reconsideration are narrow. Generally they involve inadvertent mistakes or omissions that should be rectified by the judge who rendered the original judgement. Very often the mistake or omission is obvious. Except in these narrow and often obvious circumstances a dissatisfied litigant's recourse is an appeal. Reconsideration applications and appeals are not interchangeable forms of relief.

Reconsideration deals with inadvertent mistakes or omissions. An appeal involves acceptance of the lower court judgement as is, but disagreement with its conclusion. Litigants must decide which recourse to seek.

Where there is doubt, it is likely that reconsideration is not the appropriate course. In any event, a Notice of Appeal should be filed in a timely manner. The application for an extension of time was dismissed.

**398. (1) Stay of order — On the motion of a person against whom an order has been made,**

> **(a) where the order has not been appealed, the court that made the order may order that it be stayed; or**
>
> **(b) where a notice of appeal of the order has been issued, a judge of the court that is to hear the appeal may order that it be stayed.**

**(2) Conditions — As a condition to granting a stay under subsection (1), a judge may require that the appellant**

> **(a) provide security for costs; and**
>
> **(b) do anything required to ensure that the order will be complied with when the stay is lifted.**

**(3) Setting aside of stay — A judge of the court that is to hear an appeal of an order that has been stayed pending appeal may set aside the stay if the judge is satisfied that the party who sought the stay is not expeditiously proceeding with the appeal or that for any other reason the order should no longer be stayed.**

SOR/2004-283, s. 40

## Case Law

*Charkaoui c. Canada (Ministre de la Citoyenneté & de l'Immigration)* (2004), 42 Imm. L.R. (3d) 159, 2004 CarswellNat 3342, 2004 CarswellNat 3884, (sub nom. *Charkaoui, Re)* 328 N.R. 39, 2004 FCA 319 (F.C.A.) — A security certificate had been issued against the moving party. The hearing on the reasonableness of the certificate was to be held in November and December. The appellant asked the Court to issue an order temporarily staying the hearings until the appeal currently before the Federal Court was heard and decided.

Subsection 50(1)(b) of the *Federal Courts Act*, gives the Court the discretion to stay proceedings in any cause or matter. Rule 398, which establishes the procedure to follow for stays, does not strip the Federal Court of Appeal of its power to stay a proceeding if it is in the interests of justice. If an appeal before the Court of Appeal were to be rendered unnecessary, futile or illusory, as the result of an ongoing proceeding before a Federal tribunal or the Federal Court, there is no doubt that the Court of Appeal can order a stay of that proceeding to ensure that its appellate jurisdiction and process are not impeded.

**399. (1) Setting aside or variance — On motion, the Court may set aside or vary an order that was made**

> **(a) *ex parte*; or**

**(b) in the absence of a party who failed to appear by accident or mistake or by reason of insufficient notice of the proceeding,**

**if the party against whom the order is made discloses a *prima facie* case why the order should not have been made.**

**(2) Setting aside or variance — On motion, the Court may set aside or vary an order**

**(a) by reason of a matter that arose or was discovered subsequent to the making of the order; or**

**(b) where the order was obtained by fraud.**

**(3) Effect of order — Unless the Court orders otherwise, the setting aside or variance of an order under subsection (1) or (2) does not affect the validity or character of anything done or not done before the order was set aside or varied.**

## Case Law

*Ismail v. Canada (Minister of Citizenship & Immigration)* (2006), 58 Imm. L.R. (3d) 179, 358 N.R. 160, 2006 CarswellNat 4247, 2006 FCA 396 (Fed. C.A.) — The statutory prohibition on appeals in immigration matters unless a question is certified pursuant to paragraph 74(d) of the IRPA would be meaningless if it could be circumvented simply by filing a motion under Rule 397 or 399 (*Federal Courts Rules*).

*Velupillai v. Canada (Minister of Citizenship & Immigration)* (2000), 188 F.T.R. 314, 2000 CarswellNat 1898 (Fed. T.D.) — When the Court signed its decision on June 15, 2000, it was not aware of a decision rendered by the Federal Court of Appeal three days before. Given the number of decisions rendered by the Trial Division and by the Appeal Division, it takes a few days to become aware of these decisions. The Federal Court of Appeal decision in question could have had an impact on the Court's decision and accordingly, the Court reconsidered its earlier decision refusing leave and granted leave. The Court of Appeal decision constituted a matter that arose subsequent to the making of the order.

# PART 11 — COSTS

## *Awarding of Costs Between Parties*

.....

**404. (1) Liability of solicitor for costs — Where costs in a proceeding are incurred improperly or without reasonable cause or are wasted by undue delay or other misconduct or default, the Court may make an order against any solicitor whom it considers to be responsible, whether personally or through a servant or agent,**

**(a) directing the solicitor personally pay the costs of a party to the proceeding; or**

**(b) disallowing the costs between the solicitor and the solicitor's client.**

**(2) Show cause by solicitor — No order under subsection (1) shall be made against a solicitor unless the solicitor has been given an opportunity to be heard.**

**(3) Notice to client — The Court may order that notice of an order against a solicitor made under subsection (1) be given to the solicitor's client in a manner specified by the Court.**

## Case Law

*Hafeez v. Canada (Minister of Citizenship & Immigration)* (1998), 45 Imm. L.R. (2d) 195 — When this matter came on for hearing, counsel for the applicant advised the Court that there was no evidence upon which the application was based. Both the Court and representative of the respondent wasted their time preparing for a hearing when in fact there was no basis for the application proceeding. Furthermore, counsel for the applicant did not appear on the matter but retained another counsel to appear one day before the hearing was scheduled to proceed. Accordingly, the Court ordered costs of $1,000 in favour of the Crown payable personally by the applicant's counsel of record.

*Channa v. Canada (Minister of Citizenship & Immigration)* (1996), 124 F.T.R. 290 (Fed. T.D.) — The applicant sought to review a decision of a visa officer refusing his application for permanent residence. The applicant scored 59 points, was at the pre-interview stage, and was not granted an interview.

In the absence of a specific statutory provision, reasons are not required when an interview is denied. Further, where the statute only requires reasons when positive discretion is exercised under section 11(3) of the regulations, the Court is not prepared to conclude that reasons are also required when that discretion is not exercised.

Counsel for the applicant acknowledged that, before the hearing, he received more than one telephone call from the respondent's counsel pointing out that arguments in the memorandum of argument were without merit. The applicant abandoned those arguments when the judicial review application was heard, but substituted for them new arguments which came as a total surprise to the respondent's counsel. Counsel is not entitled to proceed without notice and, whether he was asked or not, counsel ought to have advised the respondent's counsel that he was abandoning the applicant's memorandum of argument and planning to present new arguments. There were no special reasons under Rule 16 which would justify a costs award against the applicant. It was the solicitor's conduct which brought the case forward without notice. Accordingly, the court ordered that counsel for the applicant personally pay to the respondent $100 in court costs.

.....

# CAN. REG. 93-22 — FEDERAL COURTS IMMIGRATION AND REFUGEE PROTECTION RULES

## made under the *Immigration Act*

SOR/93-22, as am. SOR/98-235, ss. 1–6, 7 (Fr.), 8 (Fr.); S.C. 2002, c. 8, ss. 182(3)(a), 183(2)(a); SOR/2002-232; SOR/2005-339; SOR/2007-301, s. 13.

*[Note: The long title of these Rules was changed from "Federal Court Immigration and Refugee Protection Rules" to "Federal Courts Immigration and Refugee Protection Rules" by SOR/2005-339, s. 1. It had previously been changed from "Rules of the Federal Court of Canada Respecting the Practice and Procedure for Applications for Leave, Applications for Judicial Review and Appeals Under the Immigration Act" by SOR/2002-232, s. 1. The short title of these Rules was repealed by SOR/2002-232, s. 2.]*

*[Editor's Note: The amending rules came into force on April 25, 1998. Rule 4 applies to all proceedings including further steps taken in proceedings already commenced. See SOR/98-235, ss. 9 and 11.]*

*[Editor's Note: S.C. 2001, c. 27, s. 198 provides that the Refugee Protection Division has jurisdiction to consider decisions of the Convention Refugee Determination Division that are set aside by the Federal Court or the Supreme Court of Canada, and shall dispose of those matters in accordance with the provisions of the* Immigration and Refugee Protection Act, *S.C. 2001, c. 27 (the "new Act").*

*S.C. 2001, c. 27, s. 199 further provides that sections 112 to 114 of the new Act apply to a redetermination of a decision set aside by the Federal Court with respect to an application for landing as a member of the post-determination refugee claimants in Canada class within the meaning of the* Immigration Regulations, 1978, *SOR/78-172.]*

[Heading repealed SOR/2002-232, s. 2.]

**1. [Repealed SOR/2002-232, s. 2.]**

### INTERPRETATION

**2. The following definitions apply in these Rules.**

**"Act" means the *Immigration and Refugee Protection Act*; *("Loi")***

**"appeal" means an appeal referred to in paragraph 74(d) of the Act; *("appel")***

**"application for judicial review" means an application under section 74 of the Act; *("demande de contrôle judiciaire")***

**"application for leave" means an application under section 72 of the Act; *("demande d'autorisation")***

**"Court" means, as the circumstances require,**

**(a) the Federal Court of Appeal, including, in respect of a motion, a single judge of that court; or**

**(b) the Federal Court, including a prothonotary acting within his or her jurisdiction.**

*("Cour")*

**"Registry" means a registry within the meaning of the *Federal Courts Act*. *("greffe")***

**"tribunal" means a person or body who has disposed of a matter referred to in subsection 72(1) of the Act which is the subject of an application for leave or an application for judicial review; *("tribunal administratif")***

**"written reasons" includes a transcript of reasons given orally. *("motifs écrits")***

SOR/98-235, s. 1; SOR/2002-232, s. 3; SOR/2005-339, s. 2

## Application

**3. [Repealed SOR/98-235, s. 2.]**

**4. (1) Subject to subrule (2), except to the extent that they are inconsistent with the Act or these Rules, Parts 1 to 3, 5.1, 6, 7, 10 and 11 and rules 383 to 385 of the *Federal Courts Rules* apply to applications for leave, applications for judicial review and appeals.**

**(2) Rule 133 of the *Federal Courts Rules* does not apply to the service of an application for leave or an application for judicial review.**

SOR/98-235, s. 2; SOR/2002-232, s. 4; SOR/2005-339, s. 3; SOR/2007-301, s. 13

## Case Law

*Zheng v. Canada (Minister of Citizenship & Immigration)*, 1998 CarswellNat 1909 (Fed. T.D.) — Appearing on your own affidavit, in addition to being in breach of a principle of the common law, is now contrary to Rule 82 which prohibits a solicitor from both deposing to an affidavit and presenting arguments based on that affidavit.

*Yazdanian v. Canada (Minister of Citizenship & Immigration)* (1998), 150 F.T.R. 297 (T.D.) — The respondent sought to strike out the affidavit of Soheil Javid and paragraphs of a supplementary affidavit of Shirin Drudian. An affidavit may be struck out where it is abusive or clearly irrelevant, or where a party has obtained leave to admit evidence which turns out to be obviously inadmissible, or where the Court is convinced that the matter of admissibility should be resolved at an early date so that a hearing may proceed in an orderly manner.

The respondent's motion was dismissed. While some of the material in the affidavit may border on conjecture and speculation, there was much more to the affidavit than that. At the stage when this motion was brought, before cross-examination, it was inappropriate to strike out the whole of one affidavit and substantially all of the second affidavit. These were matters that should be determined by the trial judge.

*Sivakumar v. Canada (Minister of Citizenship & Immigration)* (1998), 150 F.T.R. 299 (T.D.) — The defendants sought an extension of time with which to serve and file a Notice of Appeal to the Federal Court of Appeal from a disclosure order made by a judge of the Trial Division. The Notice of Appeal was not filed within 10 days of the decision, rather the defendants brought a motion for reconsideration within the 10-day period. This motion was dismissed. The defendants argued that in filing a reconsideration application they evidenced a continuing intention to appeal, and that they brought the extension application within a reasonable period of time after the dismissal of the reconsideration application. Rule 337(5) (now Rule 397), provides that the Court can reconsider a judgement on the grounds that it did not accord with the reasons or that some matter was overlooked or accidentally omitted. The grounds for reconsideration are narrow. Generally they involve inadvertent mistakes or omissions that should be rectified by the judge who rendered the original judgement. Very often the mistake or omission is obvious. Except in these narrow and often obvious circumstances a dissatisfied litigant's recourse is an appeal. Reconsideration applications and appeals are not interchangeable forms of relief. Reconsideration deals with inadvertent mistakes or omissions. An appeal involves acceptance of the lower court judgement as is, but disagreement with its conclusion. Litigants must decide which recourse to seek.

Where there is doubt, it is likely that reconsideration is not the appropriate course. In any event, a Notice of Appeal should be filed in a timely manner. The application for an extension of time was dismissed.

*International Chartering Services Ltd. v. Canada (Minister of Citizenship & Immigration)* (1998), 45 Imm. L.R. (2d) 305, 148 F.T.R. 151 (T.D.) — A motion to strike out an application for leave and for judicial review can only be successful in those exceptional cases where the application is so clearly improper as to be bereft of any possibility of success.

*Vilus c. Canada (Ministre de la Citoyenneté & de l'Immigration)* (1998), 50 Imm. L.R. (2d) 319 (Fed. T.D.) — This was a motion by the applicant for leave to amend his application for leave to commence an application for judicial review. On March 26, 1997, the applicant applied for permanent residence as the spouse of a Canadian citizen. On February 19, 1998, the applicant was advised that his application for a ministerial exemption could not be granted and that a report had been issued against him pursuant to s. 27. After this report was issued a departure order was made on March 5, 1998. On March 18, 1998, the applicant submitted a claim for Convention refugee status. On March 27, 1998, the applicant was notified pursuant to s. 44(1) of the Act that he was not eligible to have his claim determined because a departure order had been previously made against him. On April 3, 1998, the applicant commenced his application for judicial review of the March 27th decision. Through the instant motion, the applicant sought to have the March 5th decision also set aside by means of this application.

The motion was dismissed. It would be incongruous to allow the applicant to challenge the March 5th decision when he had not previously sought such a remedy. The affidavit filed in support of the motion was silent as to why the March 5th decision had not yet been challenged in a separate application for judicial review.

## Form of Application for Leave

[Heading amended SOR/2002-232, s. 15(a).]

**5. (1) An application for leave shall be in accordance with Form IR-1 as set out in the schedule and shall set out**

**(a) the full names of the parties;**

**(b) the date and the details of the matter — the decision, determination or order made, measure taken or question raised — in respect of which relief is sought and the date on which the applicant was notified of or otherwise became aware of the matter;**

**(c) the name of the tribunal and, if the tribunal was composed of more than one person, the name of each person who was on the tribunal;**

**(d) the tribunal's file number, if any;**

**(e) the precise relief to be sought on the application for judicial review;**

**(f) the grounds on which the relief is sought, including a reference to any statutory provision or Rule to be relied on;**

**(g) the proposed place and language of the hearing of the application for judicial review;**

**(h) whether or not the applicant has received the written reasons of the tribunal; and**

**(i) the signature, name, address and telephone number of the individual solicitor filing the application for leave, or where the applicant acts in person, his or her signature, name, address for service in Canada, and telephone number.**

**(2) Unless he or she is the applicant, the Minister responsible for the administration of the *Immigration and Refugee Protection Act* in respect of the matter for which leave is sought shall be the respondent in an application for leave.**

SOR/2002-232, ss. 5, 15(b), (c); SOR/2005-339, s. 4

## Extension of Time to File and Serve Application for Leave

[Heading amended SOR/2002-232, s. 6.]

**6. (1) A request for an extension of time referred to in paragraph 72(2)(c) of the Act shall be made in the application for leave in accordance with Form IR-1 set out in the schedule.**

**(2) A request for an extension of time shall be determined at the same time, and on the same materials, as the application for leave.**

SOR/2002-232, s. 6

### Case Law

*Bains v. Canada (Minister of Employment & Immigration)* (1999), 47 Admin. L.R. 317, 109 N.R. 239 (Fed. C.A.) — The only question to be considered in disposing of an application for leave under s. 82.1(1) or 82.3(1) is whether or not a fairly arguable case is disclosed for the relief proposed to be sought if leave is granted. Further, the need for material not immediately available has to be established by the applicant and the mere stated intention to rely on such material does not, without an application and an order to that end, operate to extend the time provided by the *Federal Court Immigration Rules* for the applicant to file an affidavit and/or representations in support of the leave application. The requirement for leave is, in reality, the other side of the coin of the traditional jurisdiction to summarily terminate proceedings that disclose no reasonably arguable case. The requirement for leave does not deny refugee claimants access to the Court. The right to apply for leave is, itself, a right of access to the Court and the requirement that leave be obtained before an appeal or application for judicial review may proceed does not impair the right guaranteed to refugee claimants under either s. 7 or 15 of the *Charter.*

*Baig v. Canada (Minister of Citizenship & Immigration)* (1997), 136 F.T.R. 78, 41 Imm. L.R. (2d) 237 (T.D.) — In July 1997, the applicant filed an originating Notice of Motion seeking to set aside a decision of a visa officer which denied his application for permanent residence in Canada. In support of that motion, the applicant, with the assistance of counsel, filed an affidavit in which he swore that he received the refusal in June 1997, notwithstanding that the refusal letter was dated in March 1997. At a conference call in September 1997, the applicant and his counsel disclosed to the Court that the visa officer's letter had been received by the applicant's counsel in April 1997. The contents had only been communicated to the applicant in June 1997, due to the fact that the applicant was travelling and unavailable to his counsel. Subsequent to the conference call in September 1997, the applicant filed a request for an extension of time and filed a further affidavit which disclosed that the applicant's counsel had been unable to contact him and for that reason had not brought the refusal letter to his attention.

The application for an extension of time was refused. If applicants and their counsel wish the Court to exercise its discretion in their favour, it is imperative that full and frank disclosure be made. The Court indicated to counsel for the applicant that if this type of behaviour were to recur, the Court would consider ordering costs against counsel personally.

*Abdi-Egeh v. Canada (Minister of Citizenship & Immigration)* (1995), 29 Imm. L.R. (2d) 254, 99 F.T.R. 279 (T.D.) — The applicant applied for an order extending the time to perfect her application for leave and for an order requiring the respondent to produce all documents in its possession and control. The applicant, in fact, had made a request under the *Privacy Act* and was waiting for the Minister's response to that request at the time the application for an extension was made. The applicant had received from the respondent, pursuant to Rule 9, an indication that no reasons had been given for the decision under review.

The Court denied the request for production. According to s. 82.1(8), applications for leave to commence applications for judicial review are to be determined without delay and in a summary way. It would be contrary to the objective of subs. 82.1(8) to allow the *Privacy Act* procedure to be invoked to frustrate the regime for dealing with applications for leave. For similar reasons, the "gap rule" in the general rules and orders of this Court cannot be resorted to achieve the applicant's objective.

The letter containing the immigration officer's decision contained the following: ". . . we regret to inform you that you do not meet the eligibility criteria for this program due to the following reason(s): You hindered or delayed your removal from Canada." This sentence identified the "reason" why the applicant failed to qualify under DROC. Despite the view of the applicant and of the respondent, the applicant here did receive "reasons" for the impugned decision. That is not to say that the "reasons" given constitute an explanation of the reasoning of the Immigration officer. Such an explanation is not necessary to constitute "reasons."

The Court granted the extension because both the applicant and the respondent were under the mistaken impression that reasons had not been given.

*Mendoza v. Canada (Secretary of State)* (1994), 24 Imm. L.R. (2d) 317, 82 F.T.R. 92 (T.D.) — The applicant sought and obtained an extension of time to file and serve her record on the grounds that Legal Service Society of British Columbia approval had just been obtained, and that the Court reporters could not prepare a transcript of the proceedings before the CRDD in time to permit the applicant to meet the deadline for filing and serving a record.

In granting the extension, the Court considered first whether the request for an extension had been made in a timely fashion; secondly, the fact that the reason for the extension did not relate exclusively to counsel's work load, but rather at least one factor beyond the control of counsel, namely the preparation of the transcript of the CRDD hearing; and finally, the Court considered whether the leave application had any merit.

*Chin v. Canada (Minister of Employment & Immigration)* (1993), 22 Imm. L.R. (2d) 136, 69 F.T.R. 77 (T.D.) — On September 1, 1993, the applicant sought an extension of time for filing the application record. On July 28, 1993, he had filed an application for leave. The application record, according to the rules, was required to be filed before August 27, 1993. The application for an extension of time was filed on August 20, 1993. The reason given for seeking an extension was because counsel was going out of town from August 21 to August 27 and was unable to complete the application record. The application for an extension of time was refused. The time limits set out in the rules are meant to be complied with. If they are too short, then requests should be made to have the rules amended. Extensions are not granted because it is the first time that counsel has asked for one, or because the work load which counsel has assumed is too great. In order for an application to be successful, some reason for the delay, which is beyond the control of counsel or the applicant, must be given, for example, illness or some other unexpected or unanticipated event. There was no such unanticipated delay in the present case. Courts are often reluctant to disadvantage individuals because their counsel missed deadlines. In matters of this nature, however, counsel is acting in the shoes of his or her client. Client and counsel are one for such purposes. It is too easy a justification for non-compliance with the rules for counsel to say the delay was not in any way caused by the client, and that if an extension is not granted the client will be prejudiced.

The comments of the Court occurred when counsel, after having been apprised of the Court's refusal to extend the time, filed a motion for reconsideration. Such a motion is filed pursuant to Rule 337(5). The Court declined the motion for reconsideration. There was no oversight on the part of the Court respecting the evidence. Accordingly, the motion for reconsideration was dismissed.

*Espinoza v. Canada (Minister of Employment & Immigration)* (1992), 142 N.R. 158 (Fed. C.A.) — An order for an extension of the time to comply with Rule 9 does not finally dispose of any matter and issue. Such an order is always open to reconsideration whether made peremptorily or not. The policy of the *Immigration Act* and *Federal Court Immigration Rules* is transparently clear and is one of deciding leave applications expeditiously. The dilatory initiation of Legal Aid applications, delays in providing opinion letters, which counsel know will be required, and the ever slower processing of such applications by Legal Aid cannot be permitted to defeat the policy of the Act and rules. Failure to make a Legal Aid application promptly can be good reason to deny an extension.

*Kazi v. Kalusny* (1991), 13 Imm. L.R. (2d) 258 (Fed. T.D.) — Counsel sought an extension of the time limits provided by s. 9 of the rules. One of the bases for the request was that counsel had occupied himself with a longstanding client who was in a more difficult situation than the applicant. The extension was refused. Counsel had an obligation to delegate the file to someone else or to make sure, in some other manner, that the deadlines which apply to these clients were met. With respect to the main motion for leave to commence a proceeding, it was dismissed. There was no material on the file to support the application for leave.

## Filing and Service of Application for Leave

[Heading amended SOR/2002-232, s. 15(d).]

**7. (1) Service under paragraph 72(2)(b) of the Act is effected by serving a certified copy of the application for leave on the respondent.**

**(2) Proof of service of an application on the other parties shall be filed within 10 days after the application is served.**

SOR/98-235, s. 3; SOR/2002-232, s. 7

## Notice of Appearance

**8. (1) A respondent who is served with an application for leave shall serve a notice of appearance in accordance with Form IR-2 as set out in the schedule on the applicant and the tribunal, and file it, together with proof of service, within 10 days after service of the application.**

**(2) A respondent who has failed to file a notice of appearance in accordance with subrule (1) shall not be entitled to any further notice or service of any further document in the proceeding.**

SOR/2002-232, s. 15(e)

## Obtaining Tribunal's Decision and Reasons

**9. (1) Where an application for leave sets out that the applicant has not received the written reasons of the tribunal, the Registry shall forthwith send the tribunal a written request in Form IR-3 as set out in the schedule.**

**(2) Upon receipt of a request under subrule (1) a tribunal shall, without delay,**

**(a) send a copy of the decision or order, and written reasons therefor, duly certified by an appropriate officer to be correct, to each of the parties, and two copies to the Registry; or**

**(b) if no reasons were given for the decision or order in respect of which the application is made, or reasons were given but not recorded, send an appropriate written notice to all the parties and the Registry.**

**(3) A tribunal shall be deemed to have received a request under subrule (1) on the tenth day after it was sent by mail by the Registry.**

**(4) The applicant shall be deemed to have received the written reasons, or the notice referred to in paragraph 9(2)(b), as the case may be, on the tenth day after it was sent by mail by the tribunal.**

SOR/2002-232, s. 15(f)

## Case Law

*Wang v. Canada (Minister of Citizenship & Immigration)*, 2006 CarswellNat 3482, 2006 FC 1298 (F.C.) — The applicant made two unsuccessful applications to enter Canada as a student. Her second visa application was refused because the visa officer was not satisfied that she was an intending temporary resident to Canada. The applicant argued that the visa officer's finding that the applicant was not well established in China was bizarre because the record disclosed that she "is as well established in China as any 19-year-old who has just finished high school." While there is some merit to the applicant's contention that one's establishment in a country ordinarily requires consideration of many factors, it is also the case that a visa officer has a broad discretion to weigh the evidence submitted in making a decision. Here the visa officer looked for evidence of the financial situation of the applicant's parents. The visa officer considered this to be important to the assessment of the application and she failed to find it. The applicant's parents were retired and their financial situation was unknown. The onus rested on the applicant to establish an entitlement to a student visa. The visa officer was entitled to base the refusal decision solely on the absence of that evidence of family circumstance. If the evidence had been offered and if it sufficiently answered the concerns of the visa officer, the decision may well have been different.

The applicant also complained that the refusal letter was deficient because it did not contain the reasons for the visa refusal. The CAIPS notes were provided to the applicant in compliance with the *Federal Court Immigration and Refugee Protection Rules*. CAIPS notes have been accepted as a constituent part of an administrative decision. Rule 9 contemplates that the provision of detailed reasons for an immigration decision may occur after the commencement of an application for judicial review. The Court concluded that the respondent met its obligation under that Rule and cannot be taken to have breached a natural justice requirement by failure to abide by some other standard.

*Paul v. Canada (Minister of Employment & Immigration)* (1994), 28 Imm. L.R. (2d) 37, 81 F.T.R. 14, 1994 CarswellNat 247 (T.D.) — This was a motion on behalf of the applicant for an order compelling the Appeal Division to provide written reasons for its denial of the applicant's appeal of a deportation order. Section 69.4(5) requires reasons to be given, where they are requested, within 10 days of the disposition of the appeal. The applicant did not request written reasons within that period of time, but nevertheless argued that Rule 9 of the *Federal Court Rules* must take precedence over the *Immigration Act*. The application was dismissed.

The true purpose of Rule 9 is to ensure that all parties are provided with reasons when they are available, and notified when they are not available. Neither the *Immigration Act* nor the rules compel the Board to produce written reasons, unless requested to do so by one of the parties within 10 days following the communication of the decision. Absent an attack on the vires of s. 69.4(5), the Board's refusal to provide written reasons, where none were requested, must be upheld.

## PERFECTING APPLICATION FOR LEAVE

**10. (1) The applicant shall perfect an application for leave by complying with subrule (2)**

**(a) where the application sets out that the applicant has received the tribunal's written reasons, within 30 days after filing the application; or**

**(b) where the application sets out that the applicant has not received the tribunal's written reasons, within 30 days after receiving either the written reasons, or the notice under paragraph 9(2)(b), as the case may be.**

**(2) The applicant shall serve on every respondent who has filed and served a notice of appearance, a record containing the following, on consecutively numbered pages, and in the following order**

**(a) the application for leave,**

**(b) the decision or order, if any, in respect of which the application is made,**

**(c) the written reasons given by the tribunal, or the notice under paragraph 9(2)(b), as the case may be,**

**(d) one or more supporting affidavits verifying the facts relied on by the applicant in support of the application, and**

**(e) a memorandum of argument which shall set out concise written submissions of the facts and law relied upon by the applicant for the relief proposed should leave be granted,**

**and file it, together with proof of service.**

## Case Law

### Section 10(1)

*Mishak c. Canada (Ministre de la Citoyenneté & de l'Immigration)* (1999), 173 F.T.R. 144, 1999 CarswellNat 1582, 1999 CarswellNat 2157 (T.D.) — The applicant attempted, at the last minute, to add to her *factum* and argue an issue that had not been set out in the applicant's material. Permission to raise this argument was refused. The Court relied on *Lanlehin v. Canada (Minister of Employment & Immigration)*, [1993] F.C.J. No. 207, 1993 CarswellNat 2301 (Fed. C.A.).

*Bhui v. Canada (Minister of Citizenship & Immigration)*, 1996 CarswellNat 567 (Fed. T.D.) — The Court had before it a motion by the applicant for an extension of the time limits set out in Rule 10(1) for serving and filing the applicant's record.

In January, 1996, the applicant filed his record within the time required by the rules. The record did not include a memorandum of argument. Counsel provided the court with an affidavit indicating that he did not feel it was necessary to include a memorandum of argument in the record, and therefore did not do so.

The respondent took the position that the applicant's record was not complete and not perfected within the time period provided by the rules.

The filing and service of the applicant's record are official in the court file. There cannot, therefore, be in this case an extension of time to perform acts that have already been done.

If the motion were granted allowing the inclusion of the memorandum of argument in the applicant's record, there would be no additional delays in dealing with the application and no evidence to suggest that the respondent would otherwise be prejudiced. There was nothing in the evidence to support the suggestion that counsel for the applicant was seeking to file the applicant's record in successive steps in order to avoid the time limits set out in Rule 10.

Accordingly, the memorandum of argument was permitted to be filed with the court as part of the applicant's record.

*Moreno v. Canada (Minister of Citizenship & Immigration)* (1996), 33 Imm. L.R. (2d) 84, (sub nom. *Moreno c. Canada (Ministre de la Citoyenneté & de l'Immigration))* 110 F.T.R. 57 (T.D.) — This was a motion pursuant to Rule 21(2) of the *Federal Court Immigration Rules* for an extension of the time limit under Rule 10(1) for serving and filing the applicant's record.

The Court expects the time limit set out in the rules to be complied with and an automatic extension is not available merely because it is requested. An applicant must show that there was some justification for the delay throughout the whole period of the delay and that the applicant has an arguable case. The applicant must demonstrate some reason for the delay which was beyond its control or the control of its counsel, for example, illness, or some other unexpected or unanticipated event. This motion failed because there was a lack of an explanation for the extension and, furthermore, there were no arguments advanced to show that the applicants had an arguable case.

*Amevenu v. Canada (Solicitor General)* (1994), 27 Imm. L.R. (2d) 157, 88 F.T.R. 142 (T.D.) — The applicant failed to file a record within 30 days after the filing of the leave application. The respondent submitted that the application for judicial review should therefore be dismissed. This argument was not considered. The Court granted leave despite the fact that the application record was not filed on time. The respondent, at the time the leave application was pending, did not raise the argument that the record was filed outside of the time limit. To raise the issue of the time limit over two months after leave was granted, and only a week before the judicial review application was to be argued, was unfair and the Court declined to consider the respondent's argument.

## Section 10(2)

*Balouch v. Canada (Minister of Citizenship & Immigration)* (2004), 18 Admin. L.R. (4th) 174, 2004 CarswellNat 5389, 2004 CarswellNat 4087, 2004 FC 1599 (F.C.) — The applicant sought to review the negative decision respecting his application for protection. Leave was granted. At the opening of the hearing, counsel for the respondent argued that the applicant had sworn a false affidavit and placed it before the Court as the underpinning to the application for leave. An applicant's affidavit is critical to the just determination of the leave stage of an application. In the preparation and swearing of an affidavit, great care is required of the applicant and, where appropriate, his or her counsel, to ensure that the respondent's counsel and the Court are not misled. The Court found that both respondent's counsel and the Court had been misled through the swearing by the applicant of a false affidavit, and therefore dismissed the application for judicial review without considering the merits of the application.

*Chan v. Canada (Minister of Citizenship & Immigration)*, 2001 CarswellNat 2857, 2001 FCT 1339 (Fed. T.D.) — The applicant sought to file additional evidence in the judicial review proceedings to point out official records, relied upon by the visa officer in reaching a decision that the applicant was not a dependant, were wrong. Where it is alleged that the evidence before the visa officer which may have been the determining factor was false, whether or not that evidence was in fact false, is a decision that cannot be made on an interluctory motion. Accordingly, the Court allowed the evidence to be filed so that the judge hearing the application can determine its relevance.

*Parveen v. Canada (Minister of Citizenship & Immigration)* (1999), 1 Imm. L.R. (3d) 305, 168 F.T.R. 103, 1999 CarswellNat 772, [1999] F.C.J. No. 660 (T.D.) — This was an application to review and set aside a visa officer's decision denying the applicant a permanent visa. The record that was provided to the Court by the respondent was incomplete. It had been "stripped". Counsel for the respondent advised the Court that this occurred because of a "thin file" policy and the difficulty of retaining the full files for all the individuals applying for immigration to Canada in the various embassies abroad.

The period of time within which a person can file an appeal from a visa officer's decision is limited. The Court could not accept that the administrative burden of retaining the full file for that period of time was unduly onerous. The respondent controls the record that is put before the Court, thus any disputes that arise as a result of deficiency in the record should, in general, be interpreted against the respondent. An incomplete record alone could be grounds, in some circumstances, for setting aside a decision.

Finally, the Court refused to adopt the approach suggested by counsel for the respondent to the effect that visa officers have no interest in these applications. The Court observed that once a visa officer's decision is challenged, he or she has an interest in justifying his or her decision. This was an entirely natural reaction and at that point the visa officer was not, in the Court's view, a disinterested person.

*Chen v. Canada (Minister of Citizenship & Immigration)* (1999), 49 Imm. L.R. (2d) 161, 17 Admin. L.R. (3d) 11, 240 N.R. 376, 174 D.L.R. (4th) 165, 1999 CarswellNat 577 (Fed. C.A.) — This was an appeal from a judgement of the Trial Division dismissing an application to review a determination of a panel of the CRDD that the appellant was not a Convention refugee. The motions judge did not err in refusing to make the audio-tape of the proceedings part of the record, or listen to it, in coming to his decision on the matter before him. Neither the *Immigration Act* nor the relevant Rules require audio tapes to be made part of the record. The witness whose credibility was questioned by the refugee division was seen and heard by that body as the trier of fact. They enjoyed unique advantages in coming to their findings and especially so in making findings upon an assessment of the witnesses' credibility. This principle applies even where a court has asked us to review a decision in the light of an audio-taped record. The advantage of having seen the witness is lost to the reviewing court. A tape recording of a proceeding may be accepted to establish some fundamental unfairness in the conduct of a hearing amounting to a denial of natural justice.

The motions judge was under no obligation to make the audio-tape part of the record or to listen to it, so as to allow himself to make an independent assessment of the appellant's credibility.

*Ou v. Canada (Minister of Citizenship & Immigration)* (1999), 48 Imm. L.R. (2d) 131, 1999 CarswellNat 281 (Fed. T.D.) — In December 1996, the applicant arrived in Canada from China. He made a claim to refugee status. In July of 1997, he notified the Board of his address and telephone number in Toronto. On that same date, he was informed that his claim would be referred to the Board for determination and that he would be required to appear in September 1997. On September 18, 1997, the Board sent a notice to appear for conference to the applicant at his address. On September 25, 1997, the applicant personally delivered to the Board's registry a letter indicating that he wished to delay his hearing date in order to retain counsel. On October 7, 1997, a Board employee attempted to telephone the applicant to advise him that it was not sufficient for him to deliver a letter requesting a delay and that he was required to attend in person. The employee was told that there was "no such person at that telephone number". On October 30, 1997, the Board sent the applicant a notice to appear for abandonment of a Convention refugee claim. The applicant immediately retained counsel. On December 1, 1997, the applicant attended the abandonment hearing. The Board decided that the applicant had abandoned his claim. It is with respect to that decision that the applicant sought judicial review.

The applicant filed a supplementary affidavit from his landlord's daughter, who indicated that she had received a telephone call from Canadian immigration offices and at the time did not know the applicant's name and, as well, that her parent's had a number of tenants in the house at that time.

On an application for judicial review, an applicant, in an attempt to justify his absence from the Board hearing, may tender fresh evidence. The Court noted that a finding of abandonment precludes a consideration of a Convention refugee claim on its merits. The Court set aside the Board's decision that the applicant's claim had been abandoned and ordered a new hearing on that question.

*Bains v. Canada (Minister of Employment & Immigration)* (1999), 47 Admin. L.R. 317, 109 N.R. 239 (Fed. C.A.) — The only question to be considered in disposing of an application for leave under s. 82.1(1) or 82.3(1) is whether or not a fairly arguable case is disclosed for the relief proposed to be sought if leave is granted. Further, the need for material not immediately available has to be established by the applicant and the mere stated intention to rely on such material does not, without an application and an order to that end, operate to extend the time provided by the *Federal Court Immigration Rules* for the applicant to file an affidavit and/or representations in support of the leave application. The requirement for leave is, in reality, the other side of the coin of the traditional jurisdiction to summarily terminate proceedings that disclose no reasonably arguable case. The requirement for leave does not deny refugee claimants access to the court. The right to apply for leave is, itself, a right of access to the court and the requirement that leave be obtained before an appeal or application for judicial review may proceed does not impair the right guaranteed by refugee claimants under either s. 7 or 15 of the *Charter*.

*Yau v. Canada (Minister of Citizenship & Immigration)* (1998), 1998 CarswellNat 1634 (Fed. T.D.) — The applicant was seeking to review a decision of a visa officer and brought two motions. The first, requested permission to file an additional affidavit, and the second, for an extension of time within which to file the record including the additional affidavit. When the applicant commenced his application for judicial review, he was of the opinion that he had been turned down as a self-employed person for two reasons mentioned by the visa officer in his letter of rejection. These reasons were that the applicant had no experience as a self-employed person and that the landing of the applicant would result in no significant economic benefit to Canada. However, in his affidavit filed in opposition to the applicant, the visa officer suggested additional reasons, namely that the applicant had not supplied him with up-to-date financial data, that the applicant's financial assets were insufficient for his purposes, that the applicant had not conducted any research into the Canadian market, and that the applicant had no business plan.

Assuming that the visa officer refused the applicant, relying on facts that were not drawn to the applicant's attention, and with respect to which the applicant at the interview was given no opportunity to comment, it was appropriate that the applicant be given an opportunity to supplement the information supplied at the original interview. The proposed affidavit was offered for the purpose of showing that evidence of such a nature was available had the visa officer indicated a need to produce it. The affidavit also explained why a business plan and a proof of net worth were not placed before the visa officer, namely, because they had been stolen some two days earlier in San Francisco.

The proposed affidavit was admitted, not for the purpose of showing that the decision of the visa officer was wrong, but for the purpose of supporting an attack on the process.

*Kuchin v. Canada (Minister of Citizenship & Immigration)*, 1995 CarswellNat 1420 (Fed. T.D.) — The applicant sought an extension of time to file a reply. There is no provision for any reply evidence, only reply argument. If reply evidence were to be permitted, it would result in the respondent having to give its final argument before all the evidence was filed.

*Awogbade v. Canada (Minister of Citizenship & Immigration)* (1995), 29 Imm. L.R. (2d) 281, 94 F.T.R. 184 (T.D.) — The applicant applied for leave to take judicial review proceedings against a decision of the CRDD. One month after filing the originating motion, the applicant's solicitors sought to extend the time for filing her application record. Additional time was refused by the Court and the applicant brought an application for reconsideration of that order.

In a solicitor/client relationship, there is a strong fiduciary obligation on the solicitor's part to act in a professional, timely manner in order to advance the client's interests. The Ontario Legal Aid plan merely authorizes the payment of fees for the lawyer's services. A professional ethical lawyer will not leave his or her client in the lurch merely because fees are not secured.

It may be that allowing a client's case to turn to ashes while awaiting spurious authorization from legal aid is contempt of Court.

There are several valid reasons for which a judge could extend the time to file an applicant's record, but waiting for a legal aid certificate is not one of them.

The absence of an application record is a substantive defect as well as a procedural one, and an order disallowing additional time for the filing of an application is a final one.

It is a species of professional misconduct for a lawyer to prefer the securing of his or her own fees over the client's interests.

The Court noted that the reasons of the CRDD had not been filed with the original request for an extension of time, and considered that this failure on the part of the applicant's solicitors provided it with a reason to relieve the applicant of the prejudice created by the conduct of her solicitors, and accordingly, reconsidered its order and granted to the applicant a short extension to file her application record.

*Abdullahi v. Canada (Minister of Employment & Immigration)* (1995), 91 F.T.R. 309 (T.D.) — The applicant sought to review a negative decision of the CRDD. Certain evidence referred to by counsel for the applicant was filed under cover of counsel's own affidavit. This documentary evidence post-dated the date of the hearing. The Court was not satisfied of the relevance of the material on the issue of the well-foundedness of the claim in question. The issue before the Court was the relevance of the material in the context of a judicial review application. The documentary evidence covered by counsel's affidavit post-dating the date of the hearing was clearly not before the CRDD and not relevant to the judicial review application and the Court would not take it into account.

*Lieu v. Canada (Minister of Employment & Immigration)*, [1994] F.C.J. No. 857, 1994 CarswellNat 2224 (Fed. T.D.) — This application for an extension of time for the filing of a record in support of an application for leave and for judicial review was denied. The applicant's record was due on March 9. The applicant's lawyer required a legal aid certificate and as the next monthly meeting of the Area Committee was on March 15, he filed his opinion with the Area Committee on March 12. The affidavit of the applicant's lawyer did not disclose whether or not the opinion was received in time for inclusion on the Area Committee's March 15 agenda. This seemed unlikely as March 12 was a Saturday. No justification for the last-minute filing of the opinion was offered. It could have been prepared as early as mid-February.

The material further disclosed that as of May 23 the Area Committee had not decided whether to issue a legal aid certificate and the Court was asked to grant an open-ended indefinite extension of time. In addition, the material filed did not sufficiently address the merits of the application so as to demonstrate a good case on the merits. Finally, the Court noted that bald allegations of *Charter* violations without more would not suffice when the onus was on the applicant to show a good case to justify an extension.

Accordingly, the application for an extension of time was dismissed.

*Koulibaly v. Canada (Solicitor General)* (1993), 93 F.T.R. 241 (T.D.) — The Court granted an order permitting the applicant to serve and file the applicant's record outside the time allowed under s. 10(2) of the *Immigration Rules* of the Federal Court. In support of the motion, the applicant filed the affidavit of his counsel stating that he had been unable to contact the applicant within the time required. It would have been preferable to file the affidavit of the applicant himself, on this question, stating in the affidavit that the applicant had not been available.

## Respondent's Affidavits and Memorandum of Argument

**11. A respondent who opposes an application for leave**

**(a) may serve on the other parties one or more affidavits, and**

**(b) shall serve on the other parties a memorandum of argument which shall set out concise written submissions of the facts and law relied upon by the respondent,**

**and file them, together with proof of service, within 30 days after service of the documents referred to in subrule 10(2).**

SOR/2002-232, s. 15(g)

### Case Law

*Li v. Canada (Minister of Citizenship & Immigration)*, [1999] F.C.J. No. 1398, 1999 CarswellNat 1746 (Fed. T.D.) — The applicant commenced an application for judicial review on October 2, 1998, and filed his application record on November 2, 1998. On November 23, 1998, the respondent wrote to the Court stating that the respondent would not be filing any submissions with respect to the application for leave but reserving the right to do so if leave was granted. On May 27, 1999, the Court granted the applicant leave to commence the judicial review proceeding. The applicant filed no further affidavit material and no further memorandum of argument. The respondent filed no affidavits but did file a memorandum of argument suggesting that the applicant's affidavit, sworn in the previous October, should be declared inadmissible. The Court refused to entertain the respondent's argument that the applicant's affidavit be declared inadmissible. It was too late for the respondent to take that position. The affidavit was part of the record when the respondent chose not to make submissions on the leave application the previous November. It was part of the record that formed the basis for the Court's order granting leave to proceed. It was now too late to suggest that the affidavit was inadmissible.

## AFFIDAVITS

**12. (1) Affidavits filed in connection with an application for leave shall be confined to such evidence as the deponent could give if testifying as a witness before the Court.**

**(2) Unless a judge for special reasons so orders, no cross-examination of a deponent on an affidavit filed in connection with an application is permitted before leave to commence an application for judicial review is granted.**

SOR/2002-232, s. 15(h)

## Case Law

### Section 12(1)

*Ling v. Canada (Minister of Citizenship & Immigration)*, 2003 CarswellNat 3261, 2003 CarswellNat 4323, 2003 FC 1198 (F.C.) — This was an application to set aside a decision of a visa officer. Preliminary objection was taken to the nature of the affidavit provided by the applicant in support of the application. The applicant did not file her own affidavit. She submitted instead an affidavit of an immigration consultant based in Canada.

The failure to file a proper affidavit does not lead to the automatic dismissal of an application. An affidavit must be based on matters of personal knowledge. Portions of the affidavit in question consisted of arguments and conclusions rather than facts and some matters were not within the personal knowledge of the immigration consultant.

There was in the affidavit sufficient evidence to establish the application and its rejection by the visa officer. Where there is no evidence based on personal knowledge to support the application, any error asserted by the applicant must appear on the face of the record. The Court proceeded with the application and dismissed it on the merits.

*Zheng v. Canada (Minister of Citizenship & Immigration)*, 2002 CarswellNat 3199, 2002 CarswellNat 4430, 2002 FCT 1152, 2002 CFPI 1152 (Fed. T.D.) — This was an application to review the refusal of the applicant's application for permanent residence as a self-employed chef. A person who files an application for judicial review does not himself or herself have to file an affidavit. An affidavit filed in support of the application shall be confined to facts within the personal knowledge of the deponent. The general rule against hearsay does not displace the long-standing common-law exceptions to the hearsay rule, nor the reliability and necessity exception of more recent vintage. To admit hearsay, evidence or argument relative to necessity and reliability is required. Where hearsay evidence does not pass the necessity and reliability test, the error said to vitiate the decision must appear on the face of the record. An application will not be dismissed for want of a

Other Relevant Legislation

proper affidavit where the affidavit is sufficient to establish the fact of the application and its rejection.

*Murugappah v. Canada (Minister of Citizenship & Immigration)* (2000), 7 Imm. L.R. (3d) 134, 184 F.T.R. 267, 2000 CarswellNat 1367, [2000] F.C.J. No. 1075 (T.D.) — The applicant sought to stay the execution on a deportation order. Before dealing with the substance of the application, the Court addressed a procedural issue and affirmed that counsel should not appear on a matter in which he or she has deposed an affidavit or in which a partner or associate of counsel has deposed an affidavit.

*Tajgardoon v. Canada (Minister of Citizenship & Immigration)* (2000), 8 Imm. L.R. (3d) 310, [2001] 1 F.C. 591, 193 F.T.R. 230, 2000 CarswellNat 2087, [2000] F.C.J. No. 1450, 2000 CarswellNat 3408 (T.D.) — The applicant applied to immigrate to Canada as an independent applicant and was refused because it was determined that he lacked the personal characteristics which would permit him to establish himself economically in Canada. The applicant is a graduate civil engineer, a former Iranian Ambassador to the Netherlands from 1984 to 1987, the Chief of Protocol in the Iranian Ministry of Foreign Affairs from 1987 to 1990, the former Managing Director of Iran's largest car manufacturer from 1991 to 1994, and since 1994 the Deputy Managing Director for the Iranian Offshore Engineering and Construction Company. The applicant was interviewed by a visa officer in Syria. The interview was conducted entirely in English with no interpreter. The visa officer had no difficulty understanding the applicant, who was able to answer all questions put to him. The applicant was asked to read a paragraph in English and summarize it and was awarded 6 points out of a possible 9 for English language proficiency.

The visa officer assessed the applicant's personal suitability and questioned why he had not learned the local languages during his foreign postings. The applicant replied that he was able to function in English. The visa officer recorded that this reflected negatively upon the applicant's adaptability. The visa officer determined that the applicant had made no efforts to contact prospective employers and indicated that this showed a lack of initiative. The applicant was awarded 5 out of 10 points for personal suitability. Overall the applicant received 69 points. The visa officer indicated that if the applicant had scored 70 points or more he would have exercised negative discretion.

The visa officer's notes were part of the record filed on the judicial review application but there was no affidavit from the visa officer. In these circumstances, the officer's notes are not evidence but are capable of being received as reasons for the officer's decision. Using the traditional language of the law of evidence, the applicant can be said to rely upon the admissions against interest found in the notes, while the respondent seeks to use the notes as self-serving statements made in an out-of-court document whose author is not available for cross-examination. The conclusion flowing from a traditional analysis of the law is that the notes would be admissible at the instance of the applicant and not admissible in the hands of the respondent. The Court then referred to the requirements of necessity and reliability, which if demonstrated, would make the notes admissible as exceptions to the hearsay rule. The Court noted that it is likely easier for the respondent to get an affidavit from its officer then it is for the applicant who is also abroad to find someone to prepare and commission his affidavit. Thus, the requirement of necessity would not normally be satisfied. The requirement of some circumstantial guarantee of trustworthiness was more problematic. The facts necessary to show a circumstantial guarantee of trustworthiness must be found in the document itself. This amounts to relying upon a document of unknown reliability to prove that the same document is reliable.

Accordingly, the notes, absent an affidavit from a visa officer, are not admissible as a principled exception to the hearsay rule.

The applicant's failure to learn local languages was not indicative of adaptability because the applicant was able to learn English and function in that language. In considering adaptability, a visa officer is not free to consider only one factor in isolation and to ignore the balance of an applicant's employment history. The Court noted the irony of a man who had been an ambassador of a major Middle Eastern nation to a European capital, managing director of a significant industrial concern and deputy manager of a large construction and engineering firm, should be reproached for lack of adaptability. The applicant's linguistic failings, such as they are, seem trivial compared to the breadth of the applicant's experience in a number of diverse environments. Finally, the Court noted that age, a factor also taken into account by the officer, was not relevant to adaptability, motivation, initiative, ingenuity or other similar qualities. The labour market realities which confront older workers are already accounted for in the reduced points awarded to immigrants over the age of 44.

The decision of the visa officer was set aside.

*Samolenko v. Canada (Minister of Citizenship & Immigration)*, 1997 CarswellNat 1220 (Fed. T.D.) — The applicant sought to review a negative decision by a visa officer with respect to her application for permanent residence under the independent category. The applicant listed her occupation as a computer graphics specialist. In addition, the applicant alleged that she sent a supplementary application to the visa officer prior to the refusal that was the subject matter of this proceeding. That supplementary application was said to have contained an additional occupational category, namely that of an arts supervisor. The respondent disputed receipt of the supplementary application. The applicant was not assessed as an arts supervisor.

A visa officer has a duty to assess an application with reference to each occupation represented by the applicant as one for which he or she is qualified and prepared to pursue in Canada. Further, there is the clear responsibility on the part of a visa officer to assess alternative occupations inherent in the applicant's work experience.

There was no evidence to establish that the supplementary application was in fact before the visa officer. The copy of the supplementary application submitted by the applicant as part of its application for judicial review did not contain any evidence to suggest receipt of it by the respondent. The respondent specifically denied that any supplementary application was received by the embassy. The only evidence submitted by the applicant was an affidavit of a solicitor who practised in association with counsel for the applicant. This solicitor's affidavit deposed that the source of his information and belief was the applicant's solicitor, who could not reasonably be expected to have personal knowledge of the matter.

Accordingly, the applicant had failed to prove that the supplementary application was before the visa officer and the application for judicial review was therefore dismissed.

*Prajapati v. Canada (Minister of Citizenship & Immigration)* (1995), 31 Imm. L.R. (2d) 182, 103 F.T.R. 37 (T.D.) — This was an application to review a decision of a visa officer rejecting the applicant's application for permanent residence.

The sole affidavit filed in support of the application was that of the solicitor of record. The affidavit attested to the filing of the applicant's application. It further attested to the submissions of the undertaking of assistance and annexed that document and attested to the acknowledgement of receipt of the undertaking of assistance, also annexed. The affidavit attested to the fact that the applicant was invited to a personal interview and a copy of the invitation letter was annexed. It also deposed to the fact that the applicant attended the interview and thereafter informed his solicitor that the visa officer was "fully satisfied with the applicant's answers and congratulated him". The applicant's letter to his solicitor in this regard setting out the applicants report of the interview was also annexed. Finally, the affidavit deposed to the rejection of the applicant's application and an annexed copy of the rejection letter. The paragraph referring to the applicant's report of the interview was numbered 6 in the affidavit.

Hearsay evidence is now admissible on a principle basis, the governing principles being the reliability of the evidence and its necessity. Paragraph 6 was clearly hearsay. Its reliability was brought into question by the divergencies between it and the affidavit of the visa officer filed by the respondent. Accordingly, paragraph 6 was struck out.

Due to the fact that the challenge to the affidavit in support of the applicant's application was, in fact, a challenge to the application itself, because if the affidavit was struck out the application would be without a supporting factual basis, it was appropriate for the respondent to argue this issue at the hearing of the motion itself.

*Patel v. Canada (Minister of Citizenship & Immigration)* (1995), 31 Imm. L.R. (2d) 24, 103 F.T.R. 21 (T.D.) — This was an application to set aside a decision of a visa officer refusing an application for permanent residence. The application for judicial review was supported by the affidavit of the applicant's solicitor of record. The solicitor's affidavit provided no basis for reviewing the visa officer's decision. The affidavit presented only sworn statements about the application process and a confirmation of a negative reply. There was no information about the conduct of the interview, nor any grounds for disputing the visa officer's assessment. It is wholly inappropriate for solicitors to submit their own affidavits in support of an application for judicial review. The court considered the application on its merits but accorded the solicitor's affidavit very little weight.

## Section 12(2)

*Kanes v. Canada (Minister of Employment & Immigration)* (1993), 22 Imm. L.R. (2d) 223, 72 F.T.R. 226 (T.D.) — The applicant brought an interlocutory motion in the course of prosecuting an application for leave seeking permission to cross-examine one Lalita Jeethan on an affidavit she filed on the leave application.

The applicant alleged that there were inaccuracies in the affidavit. The inaccuracies in this case could not be clarified further by cross-examination. The answer, if any, must be found in the documentary evidence attached to the affidavit, namely the applicant's application for permanent residence wherein he answered "No" to the question "Have you . . . ever been convicted of or currently charged with any crime or offence. . ." Further, the deponent, Jeethan, claimed no personal involvement in the handling of the file, therefore, the Court could not appreciate how it would be further enlightened by her cross-examination. On the question of when documents were received by the Commission, this issue would be resolved better, the Court felt, by examining the document.

Finally, the Court noted that a judge dealing with an application for leave is not required to make factual findings, but simply to determine whether a serious issue has been raised. The application for leave process is designed to provide a relatively simple and speedy process for the Court to determine whether there is a serious question that should be dealt with by a normal judicial review process. Judges are not expected to make findings of fact or resolve conflicts in the evidence at that stage.

The Court declined to order costs against the applicant in this case because this was a matter of first impression. It did indicate, however, that it would consider ordering costs where future interlocutory motions were brought on such an insubstantial basis.

## Reply Memorandum

**13. Where a respondent serves a memorandum of argument, an applicant may serve a memorandum of argument in reply thereto, and shall file it, together with proof of service, within 10 days after the day of service of the respondent's memorandum of argument.**

### Case Law

*Beci v. Canada (Minister of Citizenship & Immigration)* (1997), 130 F.T.R. 267 (T.D.) — The applicant sought leave to file an affidavit in reply to prove certain allegations contained in the applicant's reply.

There is no provision in the *Federal Court Immigration Rules* for evidence in reply. Where it comes to the applicant's attention after the record has been filed, that certain material was before the tribunal at the hearing which is not mentioned in the record, leave can be given for affidavit evidence to be filed in reply or alternatively, the time may be extended within which to file an amended record.

In this case, new evidence had come to the attention of the applicant's counsel, which might have altered the decision of the tribunal had it been considered. The fact that such information had been uncovered since the tribunal's decision is irrelevant to a judicial review of that decision. Accordingly, the motion for leave was dismissed.

## Disposition of Application for Leave

**14. (1) Where**

**(a) any party has failed to serve and file any document required by these Rules within the time fixed, or**

**(b) the applicant's reply memorandum has been filed, or the time for filing it has expired,**

**a judge may, without further notice to the parties, determine the application for leave on the basis of the materials then filed.**

**(2) Where the judge considers that documents in the possession or control of the tribunal are required for the proper disposition of the application for leave, the judge may, by order, specify the documents to be produced and filed and give such other directions as the judge considers necessary to dispose of the application for leave.**

**(3) The Registry shall send to the tribunal a copy of an order made under subrule (2) forthwith after it is made.**

**(4) Upon receipt of an order under subrule (2), the tribunal shall, without delay, send a copy of the materials specified in the order, duly certified by an appropriate officer to be correct, to each of the parties, and two copies to the Registry.**

**(5) The tribunal shall be deemed to have received a copy of the order on the tenth day after it was sent by mail by the Registry.**

## Case Law

*Karakulak v. Canada (Minister of Employment & Immigration)* (1995), 98 F.T.R. 81 (T.D.) — This was an application for an extension of time to file a reply and it arose because the notes of the immigration officer who made the impugned decision were not available and there were no written reasons for the decision. The notes had been refused pursuant to the provisions of the *Privacy Act*. The Court would not order the missing pages produced, nor would it agree to extend the time to file a reply for an unlimited period. The applicant industriously pursued the pages, and if this had not been the case, the applicant would have been required to proceed without them. Immigration Rule 14 enables a judge to order the production of documents refused by a tribunal claiming *quasi*-judicial privilege, but it does not permit a judge to order the production of documents protected by the *Privacy Act*.

*Nguyen v. Canada (Minister of Employment & Immigration)* (1993), 66 F.T.R. 75, [1994] 1 F.C. 96, 107 D.L.R. (4th) 186 (T.D.) — The applicant filed an application for leave to challenge a decision of the CRDD denying the applicant refugee status. The applicant obtained a letter from the official reporter of the Board disclosing that no official transcript of the proceedings had been prepared and questioning the accuracy of the Board's quotations of the evidence. The letter from the official reporter was included in the applicant's record. The respondent Minister took the position that there was no evidence that the portions of the testimony quoted were inaccurate. The applicant filed a reply memorandum to which was attached, under cover of an affidavit of the official reporter, a transcript of the proceedings. The respondent Minister objected to the filing of the transcript in reply.

*Federal Court Immigration Rule* 13 states that an applicant may file a memorandum of argument in reply, but it does not specifically state that no other material may be filed. Federal Court Immigration Rule 4(1) provides that Part I, and other parts of the *Federal Court Rules*, apply to immigration applications, except to the extent that they are inconsistent with the *Federal Court Immigration Rules*. *Federal Court Rules* 5 and 6 are sufficient authority for the granting of leave to the applicant to file a copy of the official transcript under cover of the affidavit of the official reporter. In addition, Federal Court Immigration Rule 14(2) provides authority to direct the filing of the transcript.

**15. (1) An order granting an application for leave**

**(a) shall specify the language and the date and place fixed under paragraphs 74(a) and (b) of the Act for the hearing of the application for judicial review;**

**(b) shall specify the time limit within which the tribunal is to send copies of its record required under Rule 17;**

**(c) shall specify the time limits within which further materials, if any, including affidavits, transcripts of cross-examinations, and memoranda of argument are to be served and filed;**

**(d) shall specify the time limits within which cross-examinations, if any, on affidavits are to be completed; and**

**(e) may specify any other matter that the judge considers necessary or expedient for the hearing of the application for judicial review.**

**(2) The Registry shall send to the tribunal a copy of an order granting leave forthwith after it is made.**

**(3) The tribunal shall be deemed to have received a copy of the order on the tenth day after it was sent by mail by the Registry.**

SOR/2002-232, s. 8

## Case Law

*Mishak c. Canada (Ministre de la Citoyenneté & de l'Immigration)* (1999), 173 F.T.R. 144, 1999 CarswellNat 1582, 1999 CarswellNat 2157 (T.D.) — The applicant attempted, at the last minute, to add to her *factum* and argue an issue that had not been set out in the applicant's material. Permission to raise this argument was refused. The Court relied on *Lanlehin v. Canada (Minister of Employment & Immigration)*, [1993] F.C.J. No. 207 (Fed. C.A.).

**16. Where leave is granted, all documents filed in connection with the application for leave shall be retained by the Registry for consideration by the judge hearing the application for judicial review.**

## Case Law

*Law Society of Upper Canada v. Canada (Minister of Citizenship & Immigration)* (2006), 55 Imm. L.R. (3d) 238, 2006 CarswellNat 2717, 2006 FC 1042 (F.C.) — The basic approach of the *Federal Courts Immigration and Refugee Protection Rules* is to adopt a seamless procedural route to obtain judicial review, consisting of one application for both the leave request and the judicial review itself. With respect to any documents filed in connection with the application for leave, Rule 16 specifically provides that they will form part of the record for consideration by the judge hearing the application for judicial review. The purpose of Rule 16 is to ensure that all the documents filed in connection with the leave application, including affidavits, form part of the judicial review record. The affidavit filed in connection with the leave application forms part of the record for the application for judicial review and the opposing party has a *prima facie* right to cross-examine the deponent of any such affidavit.

An order permitting the withdrawal of an affidavit is in the discretion of the Court. The key determining factor when a request for withdrawal is made is a clear existence of prejudice to the party seeking to withdraw if leave is not given. The Court should not permit a withdrawal of an affidavit merely to prevent cross-examination. The Court concluded that the affiant's current views appear to be diametrically opposed to the respondent's position and supportive of the applicant's position and, therefore, it would be unfair and prejudicial to the respondent should the respondent be bound by the affiant's answers and cross-examinations. In contrast, there was no harm or prejudice to the applicant should the affiant's affidavit be allowed to be withdrawn. The respondent had filed another affidavit that was in all material respects identical to the initial affidavit. The second affiant appeared to be as knowledgeable and well versed regarding the issues and was a proper substitute.

## Obtaining Tribunal's Record

**17. Upon receipt of an order under Rule 15, a tribunal shall, without delay, prepare a record containing the following, on consecutively numbered pages and in the following order:**

> **(a) the decision or order in respect of which the application for judicial review is made and the written reasons given therefor,**
>
> **(b) all papers relevant to the matter that are in the possession or control of the tribunal,**
>
> **(c) any affidavits, or other documents filed during any such hearing, and**
>
> **(d) a transcript, if any, of any oral testimony given during the hearing, giving rise to the decision or order or other matter that is the subject of the application for judicial review,**

**and shall send a copy, duly certified by an appropriate officer to be correct, to each of the parties and two copies to the Registry.**

SOR/2002-232, s. 14

## Case Law

*Machalikashvili v. Canada (Minister of Citizenship & Immigration)* (2006), 55 Imm. L.R. (3d) 33, 2006 CarswellNat 1601, 2006 FC 622 (F.C.) — This was an application for judicial review of the decision of a visa officer who rejected the applicant's application for permanent residence as a non-accompanying family member of a refugee under the One Year Window of Opportunity program. The applicant's wife and two children were granted refugee status in October 2004. The visa officer concluded that he was not satisfied that the applicant was not inadmissible to Canada. The visa officer's decision was set aside since the Court was unable to assess the legality of the decision because the certified record filed pursuant to Rule 17 of the *Federal Courts Immigration and Refugee Protection Rules* did not include any of the materials in the applicant's wife's file that was considered by the visa officer and upon which he based his final assessment of the applicant's credibility. A breach of Rule 17 will justify setting the decision aside when the evidence missing from the certified record was particularly material to the finding under review.

*Liao v. Canada (Minister of Citizenship & Immigration)* (2000), 6 Imm. L.R. (3d) 26, 2000 CarswellNat 1461, [2000] F.C.J. No. 1098 (Fed. T.D.) — The applicant sought to review the refusal of his application for permanent residence.

In the course of the judgement the Court adopted the comments of Reed J. in *Chou v. Canada* (2000), 3 Imm. L.R. (3d) 212, [2000] F.C.J. No. 314, 190 F.T.R. 78, 2000 CarswellNat 405 (Fed. T.D) as follows:

> I accept then that the CAIPS notes should be admitted as part of the record, that is, as the reasons for the decision under review. However, the underlying facts on which they rely must be independently proven. In the absence of a visa officer's affidavit attesting to the truth of what he or she recorded as having been said at the interview the notes have no status as evidence of such.

*Liang v. Canada (Minister of Citizenship & Immigration)*, [1999] F.C.J. No. 1301, 1999 CarswellNat 1592 (Fed. T.D.) — The applicant sought to overturn the rejection of his application for permanent residence in the assisted relative category. The Minister is under no obligation to file an affidavit from a visa officer. A visa officer's notes are part of the tribunal's record submitted to the Court under Rule 317 of the *Federal Court Rules*. The notes form part of the application record on which the decision is reviewed.

*Parveen v. Canada (Minister of Citizenship & Immigration)* (1999), 1 Imm. L.R. (3d) 305, 168 F.T.R. 103, 1999 CarswellNat 772, [1999] F.C.J. No. 660 (T.D.) — This was an application to review and set aside a visa officer's decision denying the applicant a permanent visa. The record that was provided to the Court by the respondent was incomplete. It had been "stripped". Counsel for the respondent advised the Court that this occurred because of a "thin file" policy and the difficulty of retaining the full files for all the individuals applying for immigration to Canada in the various embassies abroad.

The period of time within which a person can file an appeal from a visa officer's decision is limited. The Court could not accept that the administrative burden of retaining the full file for that period of time was unduly onerous. The respondent controls the record that is put before the Court, thus any disputes that arise as a result of deficiency in the record should, in general, be interpreted against the respondent. An incomplete record alone could be grounds, in some circumstances, for setting aside a decision.

Finally, the Court refused to adopt the approach suggested by counsel for the respondent to the effect that visa officers have no interest in these applications. The Court observed that once a visa officer's decision is challenged he or she has an interest in justifying his or her decision. This was an entirely natural reaction and at that point the visa officer was not, in the Court's view, a disinterested person.

*Bertold v. Canada (Minister of Citizenship & Immigration)* (1997), 126 F.T.R. 216 (T.D.) — On December 3, 1996, the court granted leave for the applicant to institute judicial review. The Acting Director General, Case Management Branch, failed or neglected to comply with Federal Court Immigration Rule 17 in accordance with the Court's order that certified copies of the tribunal record be sent before or on December 30, 1996.

Section 82.1(7) requires that a judicial review hearing must be set down for hearing no later than 90 days after leave for judicial review was granted. There is nothing in the *Immigration Act* or the *Federal Court Immigration Rules* which allows this time limit to be extended. Due to the fact that neither the *Immigration Act* nor the *Federal Court Immigration Rules* contemplate such an extension, reference may be had to the *Federal Court Rules*. However, Rule 3(1)(c) applies only to extensions of time prescribed by the Rules and to any order. It is clear that the Court cannot extend the period of time prescribed by statute.

It would be unjust to leave the applicant without recourse and, of course, both parties need to have the opportunity to file further affidavits and to cross-examine in regard to the tribunal's record. It would be unjust to let the tribunal (the Acting Director General Case Management Branch) abort the applicant's right to institute judicial review through the tribunal's own failure, neglect or refusal to obey Immigration Rule 17.

The tribunal was found to have perpetrated an injustice upon the applicant by frustrating the Court's powers, and was required to show cause why it ought not to be punished for contempt of Court. The Court ordered that either party may prosecute the contempt application under Rule 355(3).

The Court observed that in the event the judicial review application was commenced on the date previously fixed, it would be open to the judge seized of the matter to adjourn the application to a later date for completion.

*Sajjan v. Canada (Minister of Citizenship & Immigration)* (1997), 125 F.T.R. 198 (T.D.); reversed (1997), 39 Imm. L.R. (2d) 56, (sub nom. *Canada (Minister of Citizenship & Immigration) v. Sajjan)* 216 N.R. 150 (Fed. C.A.) — The applicant sought judicial review of a decision of the Immigration Appeal Division of the IRB, to the effect that the applicant's adopted son was not a member of the family class and that therefore the panel was without jurisdiction to hear an appeal, under subs. 77(3), of a decision of a visa officer under subs. 77(1).

Leave of a judge of the Federal Court is not required to commence this type of application for judicial review. The Appeal Division is not under an obligation to prepare a record, including a transcript, of the oral hearing before the panel and to provide a copy of that record to the applicant. Such an obligation arises under s. 17 of the *Federal Court Immigration Rules*. The obligation under s. 17 arises "upon receipt of an order under rule 15. . ..". An order under Rule 15 is an order granting an application for leave. No application for leave is required in these circumstances and, accordingly, in the absence of such an application, no obligation is placed on the Board by Rule 17. In the result, the Board was correct in concluding that it had no obligation in law to provide to the applicant a record of the proceedings before the panel. This creates an anomalous situation under which neither an applicant nor the Court has a right to require of the Board a record of its proceedings. The Court observed that an amendment to the *Immigration Act* or the *Federal Court Immigration Rules* may be required.

*Vergara v. Canada (Minister of Employment & Immigration)* (1994), 25 Imm. L.R. (2d) 197, (sub nom. *Ortiz Vergara c. Canada (Ministre de l'Emploi & l'Immigration))* 84 F.T.R. 34 (T.D.) — The applicant obtained leave to file an application for judicial review from a decision of a panel of the CRDD. The applicant wanted to enter in evidence on the leave application "the Peru File". This file was entered as an exhibit at the refugee hearing.

The interests of justice do not, however, require that all documents entered at the refugee hearing be reproduced in their entirety for purposes of the judicial review application. A party wishing to use documents on the judicial review application which were part of the Standardized Country File, should draw the Court's attention to the exhibits which it intends to use by attaching them to its submission. It should send a copy to the Court and to the other party before the hearing, thus informing them of the documents to which it intends to refer at the hearing. The opposing party, in turn, can append to its own submission documents taken from the Standardized Country File which it intends to use.

*Lemiecha v. Canada (Minister of Employment & Immigration)* (1993), 72 F.T.R. 49 (T.D.) — This was an application to review a decision that there were no humanitarian or compassionate grounds to permit the applicants to remain in Canada. The applicants were a married couple and their two children. They arrived in Canada during the summer and autumn of 1989. They claimed Convention refugee status and these claims were denied in August, 1990. In April, 1991, through a solicitor, they applied for a review on humanitarian and compassionate grounds. A medical update on their nine-year old son was completed in September, 1991, but not forwarded to the Immigration Centre. Without either of the medical reports having been brought to their attention, through no fault of the respondent, the humanitarian and compassionate review resulted in a negative decision. A further review was conducted on the eve of what was to be the applicants' departure for Poland. One of the medical reports that had been prepared with respect to the son was forwarded to the officer conducting that review. The officer, after seeking advice from a

Canada Immigration physician, refused humanitarian and compassionate relief, and it was that decision that was the subject of this application.

The application failed. The applicants were aware of their nine-year old son's medical condition and its relevance to a humanitarian and compassionate review. The applicants had many months to supply information regarding medical expertise, services and facilities available in Poland and environmental conditions in that country and their relationship to the son's asthmatic condition. The applicants did not submit this information.

Judicial review of a decision of a federal board, commission or other tribunal should proceed on the basis of the evidence that was before the decision-maker. Accordingly, the evidence of the medical experts which was tendered on the judicial review application but not submitted to the officer whose decision was under attack, was not admissible. There was essentially no evidence before the officer whose decision was under attack regarding any link between conditions in Poland, environmental or otherwise, and the nine-year old son's medical difficulties. Accordingly, the application for judicial review was dismissed.

## Disposition of Application for Judicial Review

**18. (1) Before rendering a judgment in respect of an application for judicial review, a judge shall give the parties an opportunity to request that the judge certify that a serious question of general importance is involved as referred to in paragraph 74(d) of the Act.**

**(2) A party who requests that the judge certify that a serious question of general importance is involved shall specify the precise question.**

**(3) [Repealed SOR/2002-232, s. 9(2).]**

SOR/2002-232, s. 9

## Appeals

**19. [Repealed SOR/98-235, s. 4.]**

**20. (1) An appeal to the Federal Court of Appeal shall be commenced by filing a notice of appeal in Form IR-4 as set out in the schedule within**

**(a) 30 days after the pronouncement of the judgment under appeal; or**

**(b) such further time as may be ordered by a judge of the Federal Court.**

**(2) A notice of appeal shall be served on all parties and proof of service filed within 15 days after the notice of appeal is filed.**

SOR/98-235, s. 4; SOR/2002-232, s. 10; 2002, c. 8, s. 183(2)(a); SOR/2005-339, s. 5

### Case Law

*Dasent v. Canada (Minister of Citizenship & Immigration)* (1995), 28 Imm. L.R. (2d) 28, 92 F.T.R. 103 (T.D.) — The respondent moved to extend the time for filing a notice of appeal. The order that was being appealed was signed by the judge on December 8, 1994, but not entered in the registry until December 13, 1994. The order in question was pronounced upon the date on which the judge signed it, namely December 8, 1994.

The notice of appeal must be filed within 15 days after the pronouncement of the judgment which includes the order. The time in this case expired on December 23, 1994. The respondent attempted to file the notice of appeal on December 28, 1994.

In arriving at the decision to extend the time the Court considered, firstly, special circumstances. In this case the Court found that the respondent's counsel was probably misled by the date stamp on the judgment. The Court then considered whether there was prejudice to the applicant in extending the time, whether the respondent had an intention to appeal within the 15 days, whether the delay in requesting an extension was undue, and finally whether the interests of justice mandated the granting of an extension.

## Time Limits

**21. (1) [Repealed SOR/98-235, s. 5.]**

**(2) No time limit prescribed by these Rules may be varied except by order of a judge or prothonotary.**

SOR/98-235, s. 5

## Case Law

### Section 21(2)

*Muhammed v. Canada (Minister of Citizenship & Immigration)* (2003), 30 Imm. L.R. (3d) 145, 2003 CarswellNat 2602, 2003 CarswellNat 2235, 237 F.T.R. 8, 2003 FC 828 (F.C.) — The applicants sought a nominal extension of time in which to serve and file a record.

The test for a time extension is:

1) a continuing intention to pursue the application;

2) there must be some merit in the application;

3) no prejudice to the respondent arises from the delay; and

4) that a reasonable explanation for the delay exists.

*Canada (Minister of Citizenship & Immigration) v. Simakov*, 2001 FCT 469, 2001 CarswellNat 952 (Fed. T.D.) — This was a motion by the respondent for an order allowing an extension of time for serving and filing an appearance pursuant to Rule 305, an extension of time for serving and filing the respondent's affidavits pursuant to Rule 307, and an extension of time for serving and filing the respondent's application record pursuant to Rule 310.

The criteria to be met by a party seeking an extension of time are as follows:

1. a continuing intention to pursue his or her application;
2. that the application has some merit;
3. that no prejudice to the respondent arises from the delay; and
4. that a reasonable explanation for the delay exists.

In addition, the following factors must also be considered: firstly, in the circumstances presented, to do justice between the parties an extension should be granted; and secondly, whether or not the explanation justifies the necessary extension must depend on the facts of the particular case and it would be wrong to attempt to lay down rules which would fetter a discretionary power which Parliament has not fettered.

*Nguyen v. Canada (Minister of Citizenship & Immigration)* (1999), 1999 CarswellNat 1687 (Fed. T.D.) — This was a motion to appeal an order refusing an extension of time. A voluntary change of counsel will not normally justify an extension of time to enable new counsel to submit additional material on an application for leave after the first counsel has filed and served a complete application record in a timely fashion.

*Kurian v. Canada (Minister of Citizenship & Immigration)* (1999), 1999 CarswellNat 1735 (Fed. T.D.) — The applicant sought an order extending the time for filing an application for judicial review. The applicant commenced an application for judicial review on March 9, 1999. The Minister filed a motion in response for an order dismissing the application on the basis that it was filed late. The first application was dismissed in July 1999, and no reasons for the order were given. The Court concluded that, in dismissing the application, the judge implicitly rejected the argument that an extension of time was warranted, and that the application before the Court was subject to the doctrine of *res judicata* and, therefore, it must be dismissed.

Counsel for the applicant could and should have filed a motion for an extension of time in response to the Minister's motion for summary dismissal of the first application so that both motions could be dealt with at the same time. It was not open for counsel to attempt that step after the Minister's motion for summary dismissal had succeeded.

*Abaev v. Canada (Minister of Citizenship & Immigration)* (1999), 49 Imm. L.R. (2d) 29, 163 F.T.R. 149, 1999 CarswellNat 438 (T.D.) — The applicant brings a motion for an extension of time to file affidavits and extensions of time for the completion of other steps in this proceeding. This was an application to review a visa officer's decision. Pursuant to Federal Court Rule 318, the tribunal (a visa officer in the Immigration Section of the Canadian Consulate General in New York) was required to "transmit" the material in its possession within 20 days of the request for such being made. Transmit means more than merely depositing in the post without regard to the amount of time it might take to reach the applicant or his counsel. The Rules intend that the applicant have access to the relevant tribunal material before his or her affidavits are required to be filed in order to review that material to see if it is relevant for the purpose of preparing the affidavits. The Rules allow for a 10-day difference between the transmitting of the material and the filing of the affidavits. The action taken in this case did not constitute the transmitting of the material to the applicant within the required time. In addition to allowing the application, the Court awarded costs on the motion fixed in the amount of $1,000.

*Bains v. Canada (Minister of Employment & Immigration)* (1999), 47 Admin. L.R. 317, 109 N.R. 239 (Fed. C.A.) — The only question to be considered in disposing of an application for leave under s. 82.1(1) or 82.3(1) is whether or not a fairly arguable case is disclosed for the relief proposed to be sought if leave is granted. Further, the need for material not immediately available has to be established by the applicant and the mere stated intention to rely on such material does not, without an application and an order to that end, operate to extend the time provided by the *Federal Court Immigration Rules* for the applicant to file an affidavit and/or representations in support of the leave application. The requirement for leave is, in reality, the other side of the coin of the traditional jurisdiction to summarily terminate proceedings that disclose no reasonably arguable case. The requirement for leave does not deny refugee claimants access to the Court. The right to apply for leave is, itself, a right of access to the Court and the requirement that leave be obtained before an appeal or application for judicial review may proceed does not impair the right guaranteed by refugee claimants under either s. 7 or 15 of the *Charter*.

*Shaker v. Canada (Minister of Citizenship & Immigration)*, 1998 CarswellNat 1817 (Fed. T.D.) — The applicant filed a motion for an extension of time within which to file her application record. The applicant filed, in support, an affidavit evidencing the delay and exhibiting only the cover page of the application record. There was no evidence of an arguable case and so the motion was refused with leave to reapply. The applicant reapplied and this time supported the application by the very record for which leave to file was sought. This material was filed to show an arguable case. In the ordinary course the Court would have returned the record to the applicant. It may well be that all of the evidence of an arguable case is to be found in certain documents and affidavits in the application record. Those documents and affidavits, however, have an independent existence and duplicates could have been exhibited to affidavits with the appropriate explanations in the motion record. Notwithstanding the Court's reservations about the materials, the Court allowed an extension of time to file the application record.

*Mikhail v. Canada (Minister of Citizenship & Immigration)* (1998), 46 Imm. L.R. (2d) 93, 150 F.T.R. 318 (T.D.) — This motion sought an extension of time within which to file a reply. The motion is supported by an affidavit exhibiting the reply sought to be filed. The filing of a reply as an exhibit to an affidavit when the reply cannot be filed without leave is improper.

*Canada (Minister of Citizenship & Immigration) v. Singh (S.M.)* (1997), 140 F.T.R. 102, 41 Imm. L.R. (2d) 284 (T.D.) — The respondent sought to have the applicant Minister's application for leave struck out, on the grounds that the applicant failed to file an application record within the time allowed. The applicant sought an extension of time within which to file his record.

The applicant failed to satisfy either branch of the test for a time extension set out in *Beilin v. Canada (Minister of Employment & Immigration)* (1994), 88 F.T.R. 132 at 134. The Court can grant an extension notwithstanding this fact for the purpose of doing justice between the parties.

If there had been some indication in the material that the applicant had an arguable case, then the Court would have considered whether, to do justice between the parties, a time extension ought to be allowed. The absence of such evidence required that the application for an extension be dismissed and the respondent's motion seeking a dismissal of the application for judicial review was allowed.

*Avalos v. Canada (Minister of Citizenship & Immigration)* (1997), (sub nom. *Avalos c. Canada (Ministre de la Citoyenneté & de l'Immigration))* 136 F.T.R. 125 (T.D.) — The applicants sought an extension of time for filing their records. An application for an extension of time in order to be successful must be accompanied by material which shows some justification for the delay throughout the whole period of the delay, and secondly that the applicant has an arguable case. With respect to the explanation as to why it was not possible to comply with the whole of the time limit set out in subs. 10 of the Rules, the Court noted that the reason must be beyond the control of counsel or the applicant, for example, illness or some other unexpected or unanticipated event.

The Court was not satisfied that this case involved an unexpected event. The Court noted that less than 5 months before, counsel for the applicants approached the Court in two other cases seeking extensions of time allowed by Rule 10 and citing difficulty in filing the records on time. The Court noted that neither the applicant nor counsel gave any details by affidavit which would suggest that the case was arguable on the merits and accordingly the motion for an extension of time was dismissed.

The Court noted that it would have considered awarding costs against the solicitor personally had there been a request to that effect.

*Iakolev v. Canada (Minister of Citizenship & Immigration)*, [1996] F.C.J. No. 640, 1996 CarswellNat 630, 1996 CarswellNat 3124 (Fed. T.D.) — This was an application for an extension of time to perfect an application for judicial review.

The ultimate responsibility to compute time limits under the rules rests with the party and its counsel, regardless of any conversation between a counsel's secretary and a registry officer of the court. Most of the supporting affidavits in this matter referred to what was understood by the applicant's counsel from a conversation with the registry of the court. Such evidence was of no assistance in a motion for an extension of time.

When a deadline is missed, what is required is an explanation of the efforts spent throughout the entire period prescribed by the time limit.

On the basis of the affidavit material, the application for an extension was dismissed.

*Bhui v. Canada (Minister of Citizenship & Immigration)*, 1996 CarswellNat 567 (Fed. T.D.) — The Court had before it a motion by the applicant for an extension of the time limits set out in Rule 10(1) for serving and filing the applicant's record.

In January, 1996, the applicant filed his record within the time required by the rules. The record did not include a memorandum of argument. Counsel provided the Court with an affidavit indicating that he did not feel it was necessary to include a memorandum of argument in the record, and therefore did not do so.

The respondent took the position that the applicant's record was not complete and not perfected within the time period provided by the rules.

The filing and service of the applicant's record are official in the Court file. There cannot, therefore, be in this case an extension of time to perform acts that have already been done.

If the motion were granted allowing the inclusion of the memorandum of argument in the applicant's record, there would be no additional delays in dealing with the application and no evidence to suggest that the respondent would otherwise be prejudiced. There was nothing in the evidence to support the suggestion that counsel for the applicant was seeking to file the applicant's record in successive steps in order to avoid the time limits set out in Rule 10.

Accordingly, the memorandum of argument was permitted to be filed with the Court as part of the applicant's record.

*Moreno v. Canada (Minister of Citizenship & Immigration)* (1996), 33 Imm. L.R. (2d) 84, (sub nom. *Moreno c. Canada (Ministre de la Citoyenneté & de l'Immigration))* 110 F.T.R. 57 (T.D.) — This was a motion pursuant to Rule 21(2) of the *Federal Court Immigration Rules* for an extension of the time limit under Rule 10(1) for serving and filing the applicant's record.

The Court expects the time limit set out in the rules to be complied with and an automatic extension is not available merely because it is requested. An applicant must show that there was some justification for the delay throughout the whole period of the delay and that the applicant has an arguable case. The applicant must demonstrate some reason for the delay which was beyond its control or the control of its counsel, for example, illness, or some other unexpected or unanticipated event. This motion failed because there was a lack of an explanation for the extension and, furthermore, there were no arguments advanced to show that the applicants had an arguable case.

*Milon v. Canada (Minister of Citizenship & Immigration)* (1995), 100 F.T.R. 1 (T.D.) — The applicant sought an extension of time within which to serve and file his record. An applicant seeking an extension of time must demonstrate (1) a continuing intention to pursue his appeal, (2) that there is some merit in his application, (3) that no prejudice to the respondents arises as a result of the delay, and (4) that a reasonable explanation for the delay exists.

On an application for judicial review, the issue before the court is whether sufficient information existed in front of the decision maker to justify the decision that was made. It would be an error of law to take into account any evidence arising subsequent to the making of the decision under review.

The material in this application did not at all deal with the merits of the case, and so the application for an extension was refused.

*Karakulak v. Canada (Minister of Employment & Immigration)* (1995), 98 F.T.R. 81 (T.D.) — This was an application for an extension of time to file a reply and it arose because the notes of the immigration officer who made the impugned decision were not available and there were no written reasons for the decision. The notes had been refused pursuant to the provisions of the *Privacy Act*. The Court would not order the missing pages produced, nor would it agree to extend the time to file a reply for an unlimited period. The applicant industriously pursued the pages, and if this had not been the case the applicant would have been required to proceed without them. Immigration Rule 14 enables a judge to order the production of documents refused by a tribunal claiming quasi-judicial privilege, but it does not permit a judge to order the production of documents protected by the *Privacy Act*.

*Awogbade v. Canada (Minister of Citizenship & Immigration)* (1995), 29 Imm. L.R. (2d) 281, 94 F.T.R. 184 (T.D.) — The applicant applied for leave to take judicial review proceedings against a decision of the CRDD. One month after filing the originating motion the applicant's solicitors sought to extend the time for filing her application record. Additional time was refused by the Court and the applicant brought an application for reconsideration of that order.

In a solicitor/client relationship, there is a strong fiduciary obligation on the solicitor's part to act in a professional, timely manner in order to advance the client's interests. The Ontario Legal Aid plan merely authorizes the payment of fees for the lawyer's services. A professional, ethical lawyer will not leave his or her client in the lurch merely because fees are not secured.

It may be that the allowing of a client's case to turn to ashes, while awaiting spurious authorization from legal aid, is contempt of Court.

There are several valid reasons for which a judge could extend the time to file an applicant's record, but waiting for a legal aid certificate is not one of them.

The absence of an application record is a substantive defect as well as a procedural one, and an order dismissing additional time for the filing of an application is a final one.

It is a species of professional misconduct for a lawyer to prefer the securing of his or her own fees over the client's interests.

The Court noted that the reasons of the CRDD had not been filed with the original request for an extension of time and considered that this failure on the part of the applicant's solicitors provided it with a reason to relieve the applicant of the prejudice created by the conduct of her solicitors, and accordingly, reconsidered its order and granted to the applicant a short extension to file her application record.

*Valyenegro v. Canada (Secretary of State)* (1994), 88 F.T.R. 196 (T.D.) — This was a motion for an extension of time to file the applicant's records. An application for an extension is an interlocutory application, even if in certain circumstances a resulting order refusing an extension might be final in nature.

The burden of justifying an extension of time is on the applicant. It is not incumbent on the respondent to show there is prejudice, but rather the onus is on the applicant to show that there is prejudice to the applicant and that there is no prejudice to the respondent.

It may be assumed that an applicant would be prejudiced if he or she is denied the right to put forward their case. If, however, the applicant does not have a case, he or she cannot be prejudiced if an extension of time is denied. Here the applicant tendered no evidence of an arguable case. There was, therefore, no evidence of any prejudice to the applicant if the request was refused. Accordingly, the application for an extension of time was dismissed.

*Subuncuo v. Canada (Minister of Employment & Immigration)*, 1992 CarswellNat 818 (Fed. T.D.) — The respondent Minister sought an order extending the time within which the respondent would be allowed to file and serve written submissions in response to the applicant's application for leave pursuant to s. 82.1. The adjudicator in this case had delayed in forwarding a copy of the transcript of the hearing and this delay was determined not to be justifiable. In requesting an extension of time in such a situation, the respondent is essentially using its own conduct as a ground for delay — something an applicant would not be allowed to do. There are no good reasons why tapes could not be used to avoid the delay which arises as a result of waiting for the preparation of a transcript. In this case, however, the applicant had requested a transcript and not a copy of the tape and, accordingly, an extension of time was granted. The result would have been different had the applicant requested a copy of the tape rather than a transcript.

*Espinoza v. Canada (Minister of Employment & Immigration)* (1992), 142 N.R. 158 (Fed. C.A.) — An order for an extension of the time to comply with Rule 9 does not finally dispose of any matter in issue. Such an order is always open to reconsideration whether made peremptorily or not. The policy of the *Immigration Act* and *Federal Court Immigration Rules* is transparently clear and is one of deciding leave applications expeditiously. The dilatory initiation of Legal Aid applications, delays in providing opinion letters, which counsel know will be required, and the ever slower processing of such applications by Legal Aid cannot be permitted to defeat the policy of the Act and Rules. Failure to make a Legal Aid application promptly can be good reason to deny an extension.



*Metodieva v. Canada (Department of Employment & Immigration)* (1991), (sub nom. *Metodieva v. Ministre de l'emploi et de l'immigration)* 132 N.R. 38 (Fed. C.A.) — The Convention Refugee Determination Division dismissed the applicant's claim for refugee status. An initial application for leave to appeal was dismissed in December 1990. In May 1991, the applicant made a subsequent application for leave to appeal and for an extension of the 15-day deadline imposed by s. 82.3(4) of the *Immigration Act*. This application was a request to the Court to disregard the final order made by the Court previously refusing leave to appeal. Once an order has been signed by a judge, it is a final order. Apart from clerical mistakes or errors arising from accidental slips or omissions, a party who is not satisfied with such an order may only challenge the order in a manner prescribed by the *Federal Courts Act* or by the Rules of the Court and, in immigration matters, by the *Immigration Act* and the *Federal Court Immigration Rules*. Further, in immigration matters, no appeal lies to the Supreme Court of Canada from a judgment of a Federal Court of Appeal judge on an application for leave to commence proceedings or an application for leave to appeal.

The proceedings defined by the Rules of Court are also available to a dissatisfied party. These proceedings are an application to rehear a motion dismissed in the absence of a party, an application to rescind an order made *ex parte* or, in the absence of a party, an application to reconsider the terms of the pronouncement on the grounds (a) that the pronouncement does not accord with the reasons that were given, or (b) that some matter that should have been dealt with has been overlooked or accidentally omitted, an application for a rehearing under Rule 1103(3), or an application setting aside a judgment for a new matter or fraud (Rule 1733). Apart from these cases, the Court does not have jurisdiction to reconsider a final order. In the case at bar, the original order dismissing the application for leave to appeal was based on the fact that the application was unsupported by affidavit or other material. The fact that an application was dismissed for a procedural defect does not in any way change the fact that the order made is final and not subject to reconsideration except in the allowable cases referred to above. The absence of an affidavit is a substantive defect as well as a procedural one. Rule 9(1) of the *Federal Court Immigration Rules* makes the filing of an affidavit an integral part of an application, and an application for leave not supported by an affidavit is not complete and cannot be allowed by the Court. The fact that the applicant is a foreigner in Canada does not confer any privilege to be ignorant of Canadian law or any special status in respect of errors which may be made by one's counsel. Accordingly, the application for leave to appeal was dismissed.

## Costs

**22. No costs shall be awarded to or payable by any party in respect of an application for leave, an application for judicial review or an appeal under these Rules unless the Court, for special reasons, so orders.**

SOR/2002-232, s. 11

### Case Law

*Bageerthan v. Canada (Minister of Citizenship & Immigration)* (2009), 83 Imm. L.R. (3d) 111, 2009 FC 513, 2009 CarswellNat 4030, 2009 CarswellNat 2555 (F.C.) — This was an application for judicial review of a visa officer's decision to reject the applicant's application for her husband to be granted permanent residence. Section 22 of the *Federal Courts Immigration and Refugee Protection Rules* requires special reasons to award costs. Special reasons include the unnecessary and unreasonable prolongation of proceedings. The file revealed an excess of delay in processing this matter due to the First Secretary in Colombo's lack of sensitivity to the situation of a Tamil who feared returning to Sri Lanka and being killed in a war. A *mandamus* was issued on May 7, 2008, ordering the respondent to process the matter within 90 days. This was not done. Seven days later the officer reviewed the file and raised concerns which he had refused to raise with the applicant or her counsel before and required an in-person interview instead of an interview by video conference or by telephone. This was a special case which justified the awarding of cost. In effect, the officer circumvented a direct court order, which requires a sanction. A sum of $3,000 was awarded. The application for judicial review was granted.

*Ndererehe v. Canada (Minister of Citizenship & Immigration)*, [2007] F.C.J. No. 1144, 317 F.T.R. 23, 63 Imm. L.R. (3d) 291, 2007 CarswellNat 3756, 2007 CarswellNat 2754, 2007 FC 880 (F.C.) — The applicants' application for permanent residence in Canada as members of the Convention Refugee Abroad Class or the Humanitarian-Protected Persons Abroad Class was filed in January, 2005. It was denied in a letter from the visa officer dated October 5, 2006. The operative portions of the decision letter consist of no more than the officer's bald assertion of her conclusions and do not provide the applicants with any explanation as to why their application had been rejected. The requirement for reasons would have been met had an adequate explanation been set out in the officer's notes and provided to the applicants upon request. But the notes did not record any analysis or the sources of information consulted, merely a record of the interview and the decision.

It should have been apparent from a review of the file that the officer's reasons for decision would not withstand judicial review and that the matter should have been brought to a rapid conclusion. It was not necessary to wait for the production of a lengthy tribunal record. Because of the risk to their personal safety, the applicants were forced to incur additional costs in bringing a motion for an expedited leave determination and hearing. While the respondent is entitled to rely on her right to defend a proceeding as she sees fit, she should not be surprised that the Court may conclude that such defence unnecessarily prolonged the proceedings and required the applicants to incur additional and needless expense. It was appropriate to attribute a portion of the applicant's costs thus far to the respondent in light of the unnecessary delay in resolving the application. A lump sum of $5,000 was ordered to be paid by the respondent.

*Sandhu v. Canada (Minister of Citizenship & Immigration)* (2006), 55 Imm. L.R. (3d) 203, 2006 CarswellNat 2360, 2006 FC 941 (F.C.) — The principal applicant, a citizen of India, was sponsored for permanent residence by her daughter in Canada. The applicant included in her permanent residence application her dependant children. Following an interview, the immigration officer expressed concerns about the application because two of the children did not have birth certificates and, in addition, supporting letters issued by the particular public school had, in the past, been found to be fraudulent. Following the interview, the applicant wrote to the Canadian High Commission responding to the concerns regarding the school certificates. She attached documentary evidence corroborating that the school documents provided were genuine. These documents were received by the Canadian High Commission on May 10, 2005. The immigration officer allegedly reviewed all the information in the file, including the post-interview information, and in June 2005 sent the file to the Canadian High Commission Visa Section with her recommendation that the application for permanent residence be refused on the grounds that the applicant had misrepresented or withheld material facts. The application was refused for those reasons. There was no mention of the post-interview documents in the refusal letter.

The applicant sought leave for judicial review of the decision. The respondent took the position that the applicant had misaddressed the correspondence and post-interview documents and therefore had not proven that the Canadian High Commission ever received those post-interview documents. Leave was granted and during the subsequent judicial review proceedings, including the necessary cross-examination of the respondent's representatives, the respondent admitted that it had had the documents from the very time that the applicant had claimed. The respondent, having been "caught out" turned its argument around and through evidence and submission claimed that the documents were considered and given no weight. The immigration officer currently claimed that she had read the documents and gave them no weight — the visa officer could not recall the evidence but said that it would have had made no difference to his decision.

The failure to cite this material in the decision letter counters any weight that might be given to the officer's evidence that the material was considered. For this reason alone, the judicial review was granted. The applicant also asked for costs because of the respondent's conduct of this matter. The Court concluded that the respondent's conduct was misleading to the applicant and was simply unacceptable. Therefore "special reasons" under Rule 22 of the *Federal Courts Immigration and Refugee Protection Rules* were shown to justify an award of costs. The applicant was awarded solicitor-client costs of the whole of the matter.

*Nalbandian v. Canada (Minister of Citizenship & Immigration)* (2006), 56 Imm. L.R. (3d) 67, 2006 CarswellNat 2899, 2006 FC 1128 (F.C.) — The applicant sought judicial review of the decision that humanitarian and compassionate considerations did not justify granting the applicant permanent residence in Canada. The applicant was a citizen of Iraq in her late 60s or early 70s. She was a Christian and fled to Jordan with her daughter in 1990 due to horrific circumstances in Iraq. She did not have permanent status in Jordan. The applicant's daughter and her son subsequently fled to the Netherlands and claimed refugee status. Neither was in a position to support immigration of the applicant to the Netherlands. The applicant's three brothers and sisters all fled directly to Canada and were all citizens of Canada. They were well established in Canada and providing economic support to the applicant. They provided a detailed plan to support the applicant's settlement in Canada. The applicant also has 13 nephews and nieces who are all Canadian citizens. While the decision arrived at by the officer might well be open to her, against a standard of review of reasonableness *simpliciter*, and against the terms of paragraph 3(1)(d) of the Act, and the guidance provided in OP4 to persons such as the officer, the officer erred in a reviewable manner in not documenting her decision against the prescribed criteria. The judicial review was allowed and the applicant's application for permanent residence in Canada referred back for reconsideration.

Six years elapsed between the filing of the application and a decision which represented "special circumstances" justifying an award of costs.

*Dhoot v. Canada (Minister of Citizenship & Immigration)*, [2006] F.C.J. No. 1625, 57 Imm. L.R. (3d) 153, 2006 CarswellNat 3480, 2006 FC 1295 (F.C.) — This is an application for judicial review of a visa officer's decision of the applicant's application for a permanent resident visa which was denied on the basis that the applicant failed to attend an interview scheduled on October 26, 2005. The applicant states that he was never informed of the interview. The visa officer insisted that the notice of the interview was provided to the applicant by letter dated August 19, 2005.

The visa officer, for whatever reason, did not send the notice by mail as would be expected given the significantly prejudicial impact non-delivery would have on the applicant's interest in obtaining a permanent resident visa. It is reasonable to expect that there will be mistakes by the respondent when dealing with thousands of immigration files. When the evidence shows that there has been such a mistake the Court expects that the respondent cure the mistake, *i.e.*, invite the applicant to attend another interview. It was wrong for the respondent, in a case such as this, to oppose the applicant's court case. The application for judicial review was allowed and the applicant was awarded legal costs.

*John Doe v. Canada (Minister of Citizenship & Immigration)* (2006), 54 Imm. L.R. (3d) 212, 2006 CarswellNat 1105, 2006 CarswellNat 1543, 2006 FC 535 (F.C.) — The applicant came to Canada in 1984 and was granted refugee status in 1986. He then applied for permanent residence. There ensued many interviews, security checks, etc., without any decision being taken on his application. In 1998, the immigration officers raised security concerns. The applicant made an application for ministerial relief under what would now be subs. 34(2) of the IRPA, which would have the effect of relieving him of possible inadmissibility that might otherwise be a bar to grant permanent residence. In nearly eight years no decision had been taken on the application for ministerial relief. The applicant brought an application for *mandamus* to require the Minister to make a decision with respect to the applicant's permanent residence in Canada.

On the eve of the hearing, the Minister made an offer to settle. The Minister was prepared not to oppose the *mandamus* application but was to agree to an order that would set out time limits for progressive steps leading to an ultimate decision. The applicant found the proposal unacceptable as it contemplated steps totaling some 240 days and did not set out any limit as to how long the Minister of Public Security and Emergency Preparedness might take to decide the application for ministerial relief, which was first made in 1998. The Court directed that a decision on permanent residence be made by a specific date.

The Court also awarded costs, finding special reasons — specifically that the Minister failed to take a decision which was requested almost 20 years previous, while the applicant had endured interview after interview, acquired a good deal of legal advice and was forced to bring the Minister to court. Even when faced with this matter being set down for hearing the Minister waited until the afternoon of the day before the hearing to offer a settlement.

*Uppal v. Canada (Minister of Citizenship & Immigration)*, 2005 CarswellNat 2437, 2005 CarswellNat 4845, 2005 FC 1133 (F.C.) — Costs are generally not awarded in applications for leave and for judicial review brought in a context of the *Immigration and Refugee Protection Act*. This is because Rule 22 of the *Federal Court Immigration and Refugee Protection Rules* provides that no costs shall be awarded in proceedings under the Rules "unless the Court, for special reasons, so orders." The finding that an order of *mandamus* is warranted is not, by itself, sufficient to justify the award of costs.

Although none of the steps required to process the applicant's application were concluded expediently, and an embarrassing gaffe occurred, the pace was not so slow or lax as to give rise to special circumstances and an award of costs.

*Mugesera c. Canada (Ministre de la Citoyenneté & de l'Immigration)*, [2004] 1 S.C.R. xi, 2004 CarswellNat 2750, 2004 CarswellNat 1105, 325 N.R. 134, 40 Imm. L.R. (3d) 1, 2004 FCA 157 (F.C.A.) — The award of a lump sum in lieu of costs can serve various purposes. It is usually meant to simplify the assessment process and reduce its cost in relatively simple matters, when, for example, the parties are representing themselves or when counsel are ready, at the hearing, to submit their representations to the Court, or even in particularly complex matters where a precise calculation of costs would be unnecessarily complicated. It may also, on occasion, be used to give a party costs higher than the maximum provided for by the Tariff.

The Court must be prudent in exercising its discretion, if only to prevent parties whose conduct is not reprehensible from being ordered to pay costs of an unforeseen quantum.

To ensure that the discretion exercised by the Court is not overly dependant on the perspective of a given panel of judges, I believe that the Court should be guided as much as possible by the standards established in the table to Tariff B when awarding a lump sum in lieu of assessed Courts.

*Jaballah v. Canada (Minister of Citizenship & Immigration)* (2003), 32 Imm. L.R. (3d) 140, 2003 CarswellNat 3164, 2003 CarswellNat 4032, 240 F.T.R. 155, 2003 FC 1182 (F.C.) — The long delay on the part of the Immigration and Refugee Board in complying with a Court Order constituted "special reasons for an award of costs". While the delay could not be attributed directly to the Minister, the Minister nonetheless, on two separate motions before the Court, defended the delay. It would have been open to the Minister to negotiate an agreement in the nature of the directions from the Court. Accordingly, costs were awarded against the Minister on a solicitor and client basis.

*Huang v. Canada (Minister of Citizenship & Immigration)* (2003), 25 Imm. L.R. (3d) 116, 2003 CarswellNat 257, 2003 CarswellNat 991, 2003 FCT 126, 2003 CFPI 126 (Fed. T.D.) — The applicant sought judicial review of her application for permanent residence in the independent category. The visa officer improperly limited her consideration of the applicant's experience to the period 1996 to 2000 without any regard for the evidence before her addressing prior and extensive experience from the period 1988 onward.

The respondent was ordered to pay $4,500 in costs inclusive of disbursements and GST. The applicant was entitled to have her application fairly and reasonably assessed and this did not happen in this case.

*Behagan v. Canada (Minister of Citizenship & Immigration)*, 14 Imm. L.R. (3d) 154, 2001 FCT 301, 2001 CarswellNat 675, 202 F.T.R. 259, [2001] F.C.J. No. 532 (T.D.) — The applicant sought an award of costs in view of the repeated failure of the Minister's representatives to have proper regard to the jurisprudence of the Court dealing with medical inadmissibility and to s. 22 of the Regulations.

The Court has on many occasions stated that a medical officer is not entitled to presume that a particular medical condition must necessarily result in excessive demand and that a medical opinion without an evidentiary foundation cannot be justified.

While it may well be that, in future, costs will flow from a failure to have regard to the requirements set out in the jurisprudence and in s. 22 of the Regulations, the Court was not persuaded to do so in this case.

*Platonov v. Canada (Minister of Citizenship & Immigration)* (2000), 192 F.T.R. 260, 2000 CarswellNat 2060, [2000] F.C.J. No. 1438 (T.D.) — The applicant sought an order in the nature of *mandamus* requiring the completion of the applicant's application within 90 days. The applicant applied under the Immigrant Investor Program at the Buffalo Consulate office. The applicant was interviewed in Warsaw in 1997, advised in 1997 that the case had been provisionally approved, medical examinations were completed and by December of 1997 the applicant had deposited $79,000 in an investor fund as a deposit towards $350,000 which he pledged to invest if admitted to permanent residence. In March of 1998, the applicant was called in for a second interview and in July of 1998 the Embassy requested specific information from his counsel in relation to certain of the applicant's business relations. This information was provided in July of 1998. The application was held in abeyance pending background checks. Finally, in September 1999, the applicant filed this application as there was no further indication of when a decision might be made. The only advice forthcoming had been to the effect that the security checks were not completed.

Each case of this type turns on its own facts. The jurisprudence simply outlines some parameters within which the Court has issued an order in the nature of *mandamus* where it has found that there has been an unusual, unexplained delay. The respondent agreed to an order and an agreement was reached as to a date by which a decision would be made.

Counsel were unable to agree on the question of costs. The applicant requested that in the event that the application was refused, the sum of $23,000 Canadian, said to be the amount of loss from an investment of $79,000 in the Immigrant Investor Fund, be paid to the applicant.

The Court declined to award this amount as costs being of the view that such an amount was more in the nature of damages.

*Naroditskiy v. Canada (Minister of Citizenship & Immigration)*, 1999 CarswellNat 2517 (Fed. T.D.) — The applicant applied for permanent residence and submitted a forged letter in support of his application. After dismissing the application for judicial review, the Court found that this constituted special reasons for awarding $1,100 in costs payable to the respondent.

*Wong v. Canada (Minister of Citizenship & Immigration)* (1999), 3 Imm. L.R. (3d) 120, 1999 CarswellNat 2056 (Fed. T.D.) — Costs in this matter were awarded on a solicitor and client basis. The assessment officer reduced the item in the account that charged for the presence of two counsel at the hearing on behalf of the applicant. The officer concluded that the appearance of either one of the counsel, both of whom were very experienced in their profession, would had sufficed. The applicant's bill of costs was assessed at $5,500 for fees.

*Lam v. Canada (Minister of Citizenship & Immigration)* (1999), 1 Imm. L.R. (3d) 196, 169 F.T.R. 153, 1999 CarswellNat 1187 (T.D.) — An order had been made that the cross-examination of the respondent be video-taped. Counsel for the respondent wanted a copy of the tape but argued that the applicant should pay for the cost of producing that copy.

There is no reason to depart from the usual convention that should the examined party wish a transcript it is for the account of the examined party. Accordingly, the respondent Minister was ordered to pay the costs of making a video-tape of the cross-examination.

*D'Almeida v. Canada (Minister of Citizenship & Immigration)* (1999), 1 Imm. L.R. (3d) 309, 1999 CarswellNat 1114 (Fed. T.D.) — The applicant sought to review the refusal of his application for permanent residence. After the applicant commenced proceedings and filed his records the respondent agreed that the application should be allowed. The applicant then opposed the respondent's motion, he wanted his application heard on the merits so there would be a decision establishing the point of law he thought important.

The Court found nothing novel in the issues of law raised by the applicant. The Court found therefore that the applicant had unreasonably prolonged the proceedings and awarded costs in the amount of $1,500 against the applicant.

*Said v. Canada (Minister of Citizenship & Immigration)* (1999), 246 N.R. 283, 1999 CarswellNat 770, [1999] F.C.J. No. 663 (Fed. C.A.) — The applicant, who came to Canada as a Convention refugee, was found guilty in 1992, on five counts of trafficking in heroin and sentenced to five years in jail. A deportation order was issued as a result of the convictions and subsequently the appellant was found to be a danger to the public. While the appellant's appeal to the Court of Appeal was pending, he was informed that a removal order had been signed against him by the Minister and a motion for a stay was brought on an urgent basis.

The stay was granted and the Court awarded costs in the amount of $1,000. The Court could not understand why the removal order was brought to the appellant's attention only four days before its execution. The appellant was in custody and therefore could not flee upon service of the document. The very fact of detention made it more difficult and time consuming for his counsel to prepare the motion for stay and gather the necessary supporting material.

*Akinsola v. Canada (Minister of Citizenship & Immigration)* (1997), 138 F.T.R. 229 (T.D.) — The Court determined that counsel for the applicant had acted either in bad faith or incompetently. Counsel's actions wasted the court's time and caused serious inconvenience to opposing counsel. The Court awarded costs against counsel personally in the amount of $200.

*Singh (J.) v. Canada (Minister of Citizenship & Immigration)* (1996), 35 Imm. L.R. (2d) 303, 121 F.T.R. 184 (T.D.) — The applicant, an Indian national, had resided in Canada continuously since 1981, pursuant to a series of student authorizations, a minister's permit and two visitor's visas. At the time of this application, the applicant was without status. Since 1981, the applicant had lived with his aunt who had adopted him in accordance with Sikh tradition and culture. After the adoption, the aunt submitted an undertaking of assistance which was approved in June 1992. The applicant then applied for permanent residence as a sponsored member of the family class. The applicant was interviewed by an officer at the Canadian Consulate in Buffalo in January 1993. Although a decision was made to refuse the application approximately 9 months after the interview, this decision was not disclosed to the applicant until April 1996 some two and a half years later.

In the period from April, 1993 to February, 1996, the applicant's counsel wrote 10 letters asking for the status of the application. Seven were written to the officer's attention. The officer personally responded to the first letter and thereafter two form letters were sent to the applicant, neither of which provided accurate information. In addition, three more letters were sent by the applicant's counsel to the senior immigration officer at the consulate describing the circumstances of the case and the extraordinary delay. The senior immigration officer did not respond to counsel's letters.

Costs were awarded for the following three reasons:

1. The delay, caused by the fact that the officer did not address the file between October 1993 and September 1995.
2. The two form letters which were sent contained inaccurate information.
3. The senior immigration officer did not respond to correspondence from the applicant's counsel.

*Marques v. Canada (Minister of Citizenship & Immigration)* (1996), 35 Imm. L.R. (2d) 81, (sub nom. *Marques v. Canada (Minister of Citizenship & Immigration) (No. 2)*) 116 F.T.R. 243 (T.D.) — The respondent consented to an application to review a s. 114(2) decision of an immigration officer. The issue in this matter was a question of costs under Rule 22. The Court found special reasons for an award of costs.

The applicant had first filed an application for a visa exemption invoking s. 114(2) in April 1994. This application was refused. However, the refusal was the subject of a successful application for judicial review. Following the successful judicial review application, the file was returned to Mississauga CIC, where no action was taken on the file until the fall of 1995. The immigration officer conducting this second interview had before her the previous decision and the notes of the review conducted in July 1994, which had been set aside by the Court. Despite the fact that the Court had ordered an entirely new review, the matter was not considered afresh. The immigration officer considered merely whether there had been a change of circumstances since the date of the first s. 114(2) decision. The officer therefore did not comply with the order of the Court. Immigration officers have a duty to act in accordance with decisions from the Federal Court, as well as in a courteous and professional manner.

Accordingly, the Court found special reasons to award costs to the applicant.

*Barbu v. Canada (Secretary of State)*, 1996 CarswellNat 1054 (Fed. T.D.) — This application was to review a decision of a visa officer. Specifically, the visa officer intended to use the discretion conferred by s. 11(3) of the Act to deny an application, and did so without consulting a senior immigration officer and without providing that officer with written reasons.

The only issue in this application was whether the applicant was entitled to costs pursuant to rule 1618 of the *Federal Court Rules*. Rule 1618 provides that no cost shall be payable in respect of an application for judicial review unless the Court for special reason so orders. The Court noted that costs have been awarded in cases where there has been an abuse of process. In very unusual cases, circumstances outside the conduct of the judicial review application could be relevant to costs. A simple fact of an error, without more, does not justify a costs award. Such a conclusion would make rule 1618 meaningless, accordingly, no costs were ordered.

*Chan v. Canada (Minister of Employment & Immigration)* (1994), 82 F.T.R. 244 (T.D.) — This was an application for costs by the respondent. Costs can be awarded only in special circumstances.

Special circumstances existed in this case. The respondent, from a very early date in the proceedings, was prepared to consent to an application for judicial review. However, the applicant, believing in the strength of the case, insisted that the matter be fully litigated to establish that certain regulations applicable to his landed immigrant status were *ultra vires*. He was unsuccessful.

The Court did not think that an applicant can force a respondent, who is willing to consent, to continue proceedings thereby expending time and resources, without being accountable, at least to some extent, for the costs incurred.

*Canada (Minister of Employment & Immigration) v. Ermeyev* (1994), 83 F.T.R. 158 (T.D.) — Costs were awarded against the Minister because the Court viewed that the respondents had been put through a great deal of unnecessary trouble and expense by the way that the Minister's officials had dealt with the respondents. There was, at worst, a technical error committed by the respondents at the time the events giving rise to these proceedings occurred. Once this mistake was discovered, it should not have strained the imagination of immigration officials to find a simple solution, such as the departure of the entire family temporarily to the United States from which they could return together to Canada. Instead, the entire family was put through a series of removal hearings, appeals and court applications over a 4 year period.

Accordingly, at the discontinuance of the Minister's application in this matter, costs were awarded to the respondents.

## FEES

**23. A fee of $50 shall be paid to the Registry in order to file an application for leave or a notice of appeal.**

SOR/2002-232, s. 15(i)

## COMING INTO FORCE

**24. These Rules shall come into force on the day on which sections 73, 114, 115, 116, 117 and 118 of *An Act to amend the Immigration Act and other Acts in consequence thereof*, S.C. 1992, c. 49, come into force.**

# SCHEDULE

## Form IR-1

**(Rules 5 and 6)**

**Court File No.**

**FEDERAL COURT**

**Between**

**(*Insert full name of party or the Minister responsible for the administration of the* Immigration and Refugee Protection Act *in respect of the matter for which leave is sought*)**

**Applicant(s)**

**and**

**(*The Minister responsible for the administration of the* Immigration and Refugee Protection Act *in respect of the matter for which leave is sought or full name of the other party if the Minister is the Applicant*)**

**Respondent(s)**

### Application for Leave and for Judicial Review

**TO THE RESPONDENT(S)**

**AN APPLICATION FOR LEAVE TO COMMENCE AN APPLICATION FOR JUDICIAL REVIEW UNDER SUBSECTION 72(1) OF THE *IMMIGRATION AND REFUGEE PROTECTION ACT* has been commenced by the applicant.**

**UNLESS A JUDGE OTHERWISE DIRECTS, THIS APPLICATION FOR LEAVE will be disposed of without personal appearance by the parties, in accordance with paragraph 72(2)(d) of the *Immigration and Refugee Protection Act*.**

**IF YOU WISH TO OPPOSE THIS APPLICATION FOR LEAVE, you or a solicitor authorized to practice in Canada and acting for you must immediately prepare a Notice of Appearance in Form IR-2 prescribed by the *Federal Courts Immigration and Refugee Protection Rules*, serve it on the tribunal and the applicant's solicitor or, if the applicant does not have a solicitor, serve it on the applicant, and file it,**

**with proof after service, at the Registry, within 10 days after the service of this application for leave.**

**IF YOU FAIL TO DO SO, the Court may nevertheless dispose of this application for leave and, if the leave is granted, of the subsequent application for judicial review without further notice to you.**

**Note: Copies of the relevant Rules of Court, information on the local office of the Court and other necessary information may be obtained from any local office of the Federal Court or the Registry in Ottawa, telephone: (613) 992-4238.**

**The applicant seeks leave of the Court to commence an application for judicial review of:**

> *(Set out the date and details of the matter — the decision, determination or order made, measure taken or question raised — in respect of which a judicial review is sought and the date on which the applicant was notified or otherwise became aware of the matter.)*
>
> *(Set out the name, address and telephone number of the tribunal and, if the tribunal was composed of more than one person, the name of each person who was on the tribunal.)*
>
> *(Set out the tribunal's file number(s), if applicable.)*

*(Add the following paragraph if applicable.)*

*[The applicant further applies to the Court to allow an extension of time under paragraph 72(2)(c) of the* **Immigration and Refugee Protection Act** *on the following grounds:*

*(Set out the grounds for the request for the extension of time to file the application for leave.)]*

**In the event that the leave is granted, the applicant seeks the following relief by way of a judicial review:**

*(Set out the precise relief sought should leave be granted, including any statutory provision or rule relied on.)*

**In the event that the leave is granted, the application for judicial review is to be based on the following grounds:**

*(Set out the grounds to be argued, including a reference to any statutory provision or rule to be relied on.)*

**The applicant has (*has not*) received written reasons from the tribunal.**

**In the event that the leave is granted, the applicant proposes that the application for judicial review be heard at.........., in the (*English and/or French*) language.**

*(Signature of Solicitor/Applicant)*
*Name of Solicitor/Applicant*
*Address*
*Telephone Number*

**To: (*Name(s) and address(es) of respondent(s)*)**

SOR/98-235, s. 6; SOR/2002-232, s. 12; SOR/2005-339, s. 6

## Form IR-2

**(Rule 8)**

**Registry No.**

**FEDERAL COURT**

**Between:**

**Applicant(s)**

**and**

**Respondent(s)**

### Notice of Appearance

**THE RESPONDENT(s) (*name(s)*) intend(s) to respond to this application for leave.**

**The tribunal's file number(s), as set out in the application for leave is (*are*):**

**(*Date*)**

***(Name, address and telephone number of respondent's solicitor, or respondent if acting in person)***

**TO: (*Name and address of applicant's solicitor, or applicant if acting in person*)**

**AND TO: (*Name and address of tribunal*)**

SOR/2002-232, s. 15(j); SOR/2005-339, s. 6

## Form IR-3

**(Rule 9)**

**Court File No.**

**FEDERAL COURT**

**Between:**

**Applicant(s)**

**and**

**Respondent(s)**

### Request to Tribunal

**TO: (*Name and address of tribunal*)**

**RE: (*Set out the complete particulars of the matter — decision, determination or order made, measure taken or question raised — as they appear in the application, with the tribunal's file number(s), if any.*)**

**DATE:**

**In an application filed on .........., 20.........., the applicant set out that he/she had not received written reasons for the above-captioned matter.**

**Pursuant to rule 9 of the *Federal Courts Immigration and Refugee Protection Rules*, you are hereby requested, without delay, to**

**(a) send a copy of the matter — the decision, determination or order made, measure taken or question raised — and written reasons for it, duly certified by an appropriate officer to be correct, to each of the parties, and two copies to the Registry; or**

**(b) send written notice to all the parties and the Registry indicating either that no reasons were given for the matter — decision, determination or order made, measure taken or question raised — in respect of which the application is made, or that reasons were given but not recorded.**

*(Signature of Registry Officer)*
*Name of Registry Officer*
*Telephone Number*
SOR/2002-232, s. 13; SOR/2005-339, s. 6

## Form IR-4

**(Rule 20)**

**Court File No.**

FEDERAL COURT OF APPEAL

**Between:**

**Appellant**
*(Applicant (Respondent) in the Federal Court)*
**and**
*(name)*
**Respondent**
*(Applicant (Respondent) in the Federal Court)*

### Notice of Appeal

**THE APPELLANT (*name*) appeals from the judgment of the Honourable (*name of judge*) of the Federal Court, delivered on (*date*).**

**Pursuant to paragraph 74(d) of the *Immigration and Refugee Protection Act*, the learned Federal Court Judge certified that the following serious question(s) of general importance was(*were*) involved:**

***(Set out question(s) certified by Federal Court Judge.)***

**The appellant seeks the following relief on the determination of the question(s) under section 52 of the *Federal Courts Act*:**

***(Set out the relief sought, with reference to the specific provisions in section 52 of the* Federal Courts Act *relied on.)***

**The appellant requests that this appeal be heard at ..........(*place*), in the (*English and/or French*) language.**

**Dated at.........., this.......... of.........., 20...........**

***(Name, address and telephone number of appellant's solicitor)***

**TO:** ***(Name and address of respondent's solicitor or respondent if acting in person)***

SOR/2002-232, s. 13; 2002, c. 8, s. 182(3)(a); SOR/2005-339, s. 6

# CANADA EVIDENCE ACT

## An Act respecting Witnesses and Evidence

R.S.C. 1985, c. C-5, as am. R.S.C. 1985, c. 27 (1st Supp.), s. 203; R.S.C. 1985, c. 19 (3rd Supp.), ss. 17, 18; S.C. 1992, c. 1, ss. 142 (Sched. V, item 9), 144 (Sched. VII, item 5) (Fr.); 1992, c. 47, s. 66; 1993, c. 28, s. 78 (Sched. III, item 8); 1993, c. 34, s. 15; 1994, c. 44, ss. 85–93; 1995, c. 28, s. 47; 1997, c. 18, ss. 116–118; 1998, c. 9, s. 1; 1999, c. 18, ss. 89–91; 1999, c. 28, ss. 149, 150; 2000, c. 5, ss. 52–57; 2001, c. 41, ss. 43, 44 (Sched. 2), 124, 140, 141(1), (3)–(7); 2002, c. 1, s. 166; 2002, c. 7, s. 96; 2002, c. 8, ss. 118, 119, 183(1)(b) [s. 119 repealed 2001, c. 41, s. 141(3)(a).]; 2003, c. 22, ss. 104, 105; SOR/2004-19; 2004, c. 12, ss. 18, 19; 2005, c. 32, ss. 26, 27; 2005, c. 46, s. 56 [Amended 2006, c. 9, s. 222.]; SOR/2006-80; SOR/2006-335; 2008, c. 3, s. 11.

. . . . .

# PART I

. . . . .

### *Specified Public Interest*

[Heading amended 2001, c. 41, s. 43.]

**37. (1) Objection to disclosure of information — Subject to sections 38 to 38.16, a Minister of the Crown in right of Canada or other official may object to the disclosure of information before a court, person or body with jurisdiction to compel the production of information by certifying orally or in writing to the court, person or body that the information should not be disclosed on the grounds of a specified public interest.**

**(1.1) Obligation of court, person or body — If an objection is made under subsection (1), the court, person or body shall ensure that the information is not disclosed other than in accordance with this Act.**

**(2) Objection made to superior court — If an objection to the disclosure of information is made before a superior court, that court may determine the objection.**

**(3) Objection not made to superior court — If an objection to the disclosure of information is made before a court, person or body other than a superior court, the objection may be determined, on application, by**

> **(a) the Federal Court, in the case of a person or body vested with power to compel production by or under an Act of Parliament if the person or body is not a court established under a law of a province; or**

(b) the trial division or trial court of the superior court of the province within which the court, person or body exercises its jurisdiction, in any other case.

(4) **Limitation period** — An application under subsection (3) shall be made within 10 days after the objection is made or within any further or lesser time that the court having jurisdiction to hear the application considers appropriate in the circumstances.

(4.1) **Disclosure order** — Unless the court having jurisdiction to hear the application concludes that the disclosure of the information to which the objection was made under subsection (1) would encroach upon a specified public interest, the court may authorize by order the disclosure of the information.

(5) **Disclosure order** — If the court having jurisdiction to hear the application concludes that the disclosure of the information to which the objection was made under subsection (1) would encroach upon a specified public interest, but that the public interest in disclosure outweighs in importance the specified public interest, the court may, by order, after considering both the public interest in disclosure and the form of and conditions to disclosure that are most likely to limit any encroachment upon the specified public interest resulting from disclosure, authorize the disclosure, subject to any conditions that the court considers appropriate, of all of the information, a part or summary of the information, or a written admission of facts relating to the information.

(6) **Prohibition order** — If the court does not authorize disclosure under subsection (4.1) or (5), the court shall, by order, prohibit disclosure of the information.

(6.1) **Evidence** — The court may receive into evidence anything that, in the opinion of the court, is reliable and appropriate, even if it would not otherwise be admissible under Canadian law, and may base its decision on that evidence.

(7) **When determination takes effect** — An order of the court that authorizes disclosure does not take effect until the time provided or granted to appeal the order, or a judgment of an appeal court that confirms the order, has expired, or no further appeal from a judgment that confirms the order is available.

(8) **Introduction into evidence** — A person who wishes to introduce into evidence material the disclosure of which is authorized under subsection (5), but who may not be able to do so by reason of the rules of admissibility that apply before the court, person or body with jurisdiction to compel the production of information, may request from the court having jurisdiction under subsection (2) or (3) an order permitting the introduction into evidence of the material in a form or subject to any conditions fixed by that court, as long as that form and those conditions, comply with the order made under subsection (5).

(9) **Relevant factors** — For the purpose of subsection (8), the court having jurisdiction under subsection (2) or (3) shall consider all the factors that would be relevant for a determination of admissibility before the court, person or body.

2001, c. 41, ss. 43, 140; 2002, c. 8, s. 183(1)(b)

## Case Law

*Moumdjian v. Canada (Security Intelligence Review Committee)* (1997), (sub nom. *Moumdjian v. Security Intelligence Review Committee)* 221 N.R. 188, 141 F.T.R. 80 (note), 6 Admin. L.R. (3d) 239 (Fed. C.A.) — This was an appeal from an order of a judge of the Trial Division, sitting as a judge designated by the Chief Justice pursuant to s. 38(1) of the *Canada Evidence Act*. The issue was whether the designated judge erred in sustaining an objection to the disclosure of information that had been placed before the Security Intelligence Review Committee (SIRC) during the course of an investigation by SIRC pursuant to s. 39 of the *Immigration Act*.

In the course of its investigation and in the absence of the appellant and his counsel, SIRC received evidence in the form of oral testimony and documents. The disclosure of this evidence was objected to in the certificate filed pursuant to s. 37(1) of the *Canada Evidence Act*. The disclosure of correspondence between SIRC and CSIS containing information supplied to SIRC and miscellaneous documents containing other information supplied to SIRC by CSIS was also objected to. All of this evidence was listed in a schedule attached to the s. 37(1) certificate. The appellant was provided with a summary of the evidence that was submitted to SIRC in his absence and also with a summary of the argument that was presented to SIRC.

The Court referred to *Henrie v. Canada*, [1989] 2 F.C. 229 (T.D.) for a description of the competing interests at stake and the proper balancing of these interests where an application for judicial review of a SIRC decision is brought. This decision described the balancing that must occur between the principles of openness in the judicial process and the public interest in not disclosing evidence in certain types of cases.

In order to succeed on the appeal, the appellant must satisfy the Court that the Trial Division judge erred in law in refusing to order disclosure. The function of the Court of Appeal in this instance is limited to reviewing the decision of the designated judge so as to be satisfied that it does not disclose an error of the sort enumerated in subs. 18.1(4) of the *Federal Court Act*. If the decision does not reveal such an error, the matter ends and the Court is not entitled to examine any of the information which the judge found ought not to be disclosed.

.....

## *International Relations and National Defence and National Security*

[Heading added 2001, c. 41, s. 43.]

**38. Definitions — The following definitions apply in this section and in sections 38.01 to 38.15.**

**"judge" means the Chief Justice of the Federal Court or a judge of that Court designated by the Chief Justice to conduct hearings under section 38.04. *("juge")***

**"participant" means a person who, in connection with a proceeding, is required to disclose, or expects to disclose or cause the disclosure of, information. *("participant")***

**"potentially injurious information" means information of a type that, if it were disclosed to the public, could injure international relations or national defence or national security. *("renseignements potentiellement préjudiciables")***

**"proceeding" means a proceeding before a court, person or body with jurisdiction to compel the production of information.** ***("instance")***

**"prosecutor" means an agent of the Attorney General of Canada or of the Attorney General of a province, the Director of Military Prosecutions under the** ***National Defence Act*** **or an individual who acts as a prosecutor in a proceeding.** ***("poursuivant")***

**"sensitive information" means information relating to international relations or national defence or national security that is in the possession of the Government of Canada, whether originating from inside or outside Canada, and is of a type that the Government of Canada is taking measures to safeguard.** ***("renseignements sensibles")***

2001, c. 41, ss. 43, 141(4)

. . . . .

# PRIVACY ACT

## An Act to extend the present laws of Canada that protect the privacy of individuals and that provide individuals with a right of access to personal information about themselves

R.S.C. 1985, c. P-21, as am. R.S.C. 1985, c. 22 (1st Supp.), s. 11; 1985, c. 27 (1st Supp.), s. 187; 1985, c. 44, s. 5; 1985, c. 46 (1st Supp.), s. 9; SOR/85-612; 1985, c. 8 (2nd Supp.), s. 27; 1985, c. 19 (2nd Supp.), s. 52; 1985, c. 20 (2nd Supp.), s. 13; 1985, c. 1 (3rd Supp.), s. 12; 1985, c. 3 (3rd Supp.), s. 2; 1985, c. 18 (3rd Supp.), s. 39; 1985, c. 20 (3rd Supp.), s. 39; 1985, c. 24 (3rd Supp.), s. 53; 1985, c. 28 (3rd Supp.), s. 308; 1985, c. 1 (4th Supp.), s. 48; 1985, c. 7 (4th Supp.), s. 7; 1985, c. 10 (4th Supp.), s. 22; 1985, c. 11 (4th Supp.), s. 15; 1985, c. 21 (4th Supp.), s. 5; 1985, c. 28 (4th Supp.), s. 36; 1985, c. 31 (4th Supp.), s. 101; 1985, c. 41 (4th Supp.), s. 53; 1985, c. 47 (4th Supp.), s. 52; SOR/86-136; SOR/88-110; S.C. 1989, c. 3, s. 47; 1989, c. 27, s. 22; 1990, c. 1, s. 31; 1990, c. 3, s. 32; 1990, c. 13, s. 25; SOR/90-326; SOR/90-345; 1991, c. 3, s. 12; 1991, c. 6, s. 24; 1991, c. 16, s. 23; 1991, c. 38, ss. 29, 38; SOR/91-592; 1992, c. 1, ss. 114, 143, 144 (Fr.), 145 (Fr.), 155; 1992, c. 21, ss. 34–37; 1992, c. 33, s. 70; 1992, c. 37, s. 78; SOR/92-97; SOR/92-99; 1993, c. 1, ss. 10, 20, 32, 42; 1993, c. 3, ss. 17, 18; 1993, c. 28, s. 78; 1993, c. 31, s. 26; 1993, c. 34, ss. 104, 148; 1994, c. 26, ss. 56–58; 1994, c. 31, s. 20; 1994, c. 35, s. 39; 1994, c. 38, ss. 21, 22; 1994, c. 41, ss. 29, 30; 1994, c. 43, s. 91; 1995, c. 1, ss. 54–56; 1995, c. 5, ss. 20, 21; 1995, c. 11, ss. 31, 32; 1995, c. 12, s. 11; 1995, c. 18, ss. 89, 90; 1995, c. 28, ss. 54, 55; 1995, c. 29, ss. 15, 31, 35, 75, 84; 1995, c. 45, s. 24; 1996, c. 8, ss. 27, 28; 1996, c. 9, s. 28; 1996, c. 10, ss. 253, 254; 1996, c. 11, ss. 77–80; 1996, c. 16, ss. 46–48; SOR/96-357; SOR/96-539; 1997, c. 6, s. 84; 1997, c. 9, ss. 112, 113; 1997, c. 20, s. 55; 1998, c. 9, ss. 44, 45; 1998, c. 10, ss. 190–194; 1998, c. 25, s. 167; 1998, c. 26, ss. 77, 78; 1998, c. 31, s. 57; 1998, c. 35, s. 123; SOR/98-119; SOR/98-150; SOR/98-321 [Amended SOR/99-402.] [Repealed SOR/2001-144, s. 2.]; SOR/98-567; 1999, c. 17, ss. 174, 175; 1999, c. 31, ss. 177, 178; SOR/99-402; 2000, c. 6, ss. 45, 46; 2000, c. 7, s. 26; 2000, c. 17, s. 90; SOR/2000-176; 2000, c. 28, s. 50; 2000, c. 34, s. 94(j) (Fr.); SOR/2001-144, s. 1; 2001, c. 9, s. 590; 2001, c. 22, ss. 18, 19; SOR/2001-201; SOR/2001-330; 2001, c. 27, s. 269; 2001, c. 33, ss. 25, 26; 2001, c. 34, ss. 16(f), 78; 2001, c. 41, s. 104; SOR/2002-44; SOR/2002-72; 2002, c. 7, ss. 227, 228 [s. 227 not in force at date of publication.]; 2002, c. 8, ss. 159, 160, 182(1)(z.8), 183(1)(s); 2002, c. 10, s. 191; SOR/2002-175; 2002, c. 17, ss. 14(f), 25; SOR/2002-292; SOR/2002-344; SOR/2003-149; 2003, c. 7, s. 129; 2003, c. 22, ss. 189, 225(z.17), 248, 255, 256; 2003, c. 23, s. 81 [Not in force at date of publication. Repealed 2008, c. 22, s. 52.]; SOR/2003-422; SOR/2003-427; SOR/2003-434; SOR/2003-439; SOR/2004-23; 2004, c. 2, s. 75; 2004, c. 7, s. 35; 2004, c. 11, ss. 37–41; 2004, c. 17, ss. 18, 19; SOR/2004-206; 2005, c. 1, ss.

106, 109; 2005, c. 9, s. 152; 2005, c. 10, ss. 30, 31; 2005, c. 27, s. 21 [Amended 2005, c. 27, s. 25(1).]; 2005, c. 30, s. 90; 2005, c. 34, ss. 72–74; 2005, c. 35, s. 63; SOR/2005-252; 2005, c. 38, s. 138(p); 2005, c. 46, ss. 58, 58.1 [Amended 2006, c. 9, s. 224.]; SOR/2006-25; SOR/2006-29; SOR/2006-33; SOR/2006-71; SOR/2006-100; 2006, c. 4, s. 212; SOR/2006-218; 2006, c. 9, ss. 97, 98, 118, 140, 181–184, 185 (Fr.), 186–193; 2006, c. 10, ss. 33, 34; SOR/2007-216; 2008, c. 9, ss. 10, 11; SOR/2008-131 [s. 2 to come into force June 1, 2013.]; SOR/2008-136; 2008, c. 22, s. 50; 2008, c. 28, s. 99 [Not in force at date of publication.]; 2008, c. 32, s. 30; 2009, c. 18, s. 23 [To come into force April 1, 2011.]; SOR/2009-175; SOR/2009-244; SOR/2009-249; 2010, c. 7, ss. 9, 10 [Not in force at date of publication.]; 2010, c. 12, s. 1677 [Not in force at date of publication.].

.....

## Access to Personal Information

### *Right of Access*

**12. (1) Right of access — Subject to this Act, every individual who is a Canadian citizen or a permanent resident within the meaning of subsection 2(1) of the *Immigration and Refugee Protection Act* has a right to and shall, on request, be given access to**

**(a) any personal information about the individual contained in a personal information bank; and**

**(b) any other personal information about the individual under the control of a government institution with respect to which the individual is able to provide sufficiently specific information on the location of the information as to render it reasonably retrievable by the government institution.**

**(2) Other rights relating to personal information — Every individual who is given access under paragraph (1)(a) to personal information that has been used, is being used or is available for use for an administrative purpose is entitled to**

**(a) request correction of the personal information where the individual believes there is an error or omission therein;**

**(b) require that a notation be attached to the information reflecting any correction requested but not made; and**

**(c) require that any person or body to whom that information has been disclosed for use for an administrative purpose within two years prior to the time a correction is requested or a notation is required under this subsection in respect of that information**

**(i) be notified of the correction or notation, and**

**(ii) where the disclosure is to a government institution, the institution make the correction or notation on any copy of the information under its control.**

(3) **Extension of right of access by order — The Governor in Council may, by order, extend the right to be given access to personal information under subsection (1) to include individuals not referred to in that subsection and may set such conditions as the Governor in Council deems appropriate.**

2001, c. 27, s. 269

## Case Law

*Tunian v. Canada (Chairman of the Immigration & Refugee Board)*, 2004 CarswellNat 1809, (sub nom. *Tunian v. Immigration & Refugee Board (Can.)*) 254 F.T.R. 155, 2004 F.C. 849 (F.C.) — The applicants were refused refugee status on June 25, 2002. The applicants sought to review the decision of the respondent not to disclose draft reasons prepared by the member of the Refugee Protection Division who made the decision determining that the applicants were not refugees. After the hearing of the refugee claim, the Board member dictated his notes using the same equipment that also was used to record the proceeding. The dictation was transcribed but the Board did not retain a copy of the transcription as it was of the opinion that it belonged to the member and accordingly was not part of the official record. Therefore, the request made by the applicants to obtain these notes was denied.

The notes were not under the control of the Board and therefore not subject to production pursuant to section 12(1) of the *Privacy Act*.

.....

# Appendix I
# Guidelines Issued by the Chairperson

## Guideline 1 — Civilian Non-Combatants Fearing Persecution in Civil War Situations

### Guidelines Issued by the Chairperson Pursuant to Section 65(3) of the *Immigration Act*

### The Issue

Claims made by civilian non-combatants fearing return to situations of civil war come before the Refugee Division on a regular basis. These Guidelines address the particular difficulties raised in such claims. In claims involving situations of civil war, as in all other refugee claims, the claimants must satisfy all of the elements of the statutory definition of Convention refugee.[1] A major difficulty encountered in analyzing these claims is determining whether or not a linkage exists between the persecution feared and one or more of the Convention grounds.

The Refugee Division, in interpreting the definition of Convention refugee, has determined in many cases that civilian non-combatants fearing return to situations of civil war are included within the definition of Convention refugee. On the other hand, in a limited number of decisions, the Refugee Division has come to an opposite conclusion. It should be observed that paragraph 164 of the UNHCR *Handbook*,[2] which while persuasive is not

[1]In a claim before the Refugee Division, it is not unusual to address various issues which form part of the assessment of the claim for Convention refugee status. These issues can include: change of circumstances in the home country; internal flight; and the application of Articles 1E or 1F of the Convention (the "exclusion clauses"). Such issues should be dealt with following the appropriate legal principles. Section 2(1) of the *Immigration Act* (the "*Act*") provides that a person who comes within the exclusion clauses is not within the definition of Convention refugee. Similarly, the definition does not include a person who has ceased to be a Convention refugee by virtue of section 2(2) of the *Act*. While these Guidelines do not deal with the application of the exclusion clauses, and for that reason there is no reference to them in the framework of analysis, it must be noted that there may be circumstances where a claimant, even though she was a civilian non-combatant, will come within the exclusion clauses, and as such will be excluded from the definition of Convention refugee.

[2]In paragraph 164 of the *Handbook on Procedures and Criteria for Determining Refugee Status*, Office of the United Nations High Commissioner for Refugees, Geneva, January, 1988 (the "UNHCR *Handbook*"), which while persuasive is not binding on the Refugee Division, it is noted that:

> Persons compelled to leave their country of origin as a result of international or national armed conflicts are not normally considered refugees under the 1951 Convention or 1967 Protocol. They do, however, have the protection provided

binding on the Refugee Division, notes that persons who are compelled to leave their country of origin as a result of international or armed national conflicts are not normally considered Convention refugees. The Federal Court has provided some assistance in dealing with cases that arise within the context of civil war. However, there is still a degree of uncertainty in analyzing these claims; hence the need for these Guidelines.

A general proposition which underlies the analysis of issues in civil war claims is the following:

### General Proposition

*There is nothing in the definition of Convention refugee which excludes its application to claimants fearing return to situations of civil war.*[3] *Conversely, those fearing return to situations of civil war ought not to be deemed Convention refugees by that fact alone.*

- In these Guidelines, the feminine includes the masculine.

These Guidelines specifically seek to address the following issues in relation to claims made by civilian non-combatants fearing return to situations of civil war:

#### First Issue

Does the harm feared constitute "persecution" within the definition of Convention refugee?

#### Second Issue

What principles should decision-makers apply when determining whether the claimant's fear of persecution is based on one or more of the grounds set out in the definition of Convention refugee?

---

> for in other international instruments, e.g. the Geneva Conventions of 1949 on the Protection of War Victims and the 1977 Protocol additional to the Geneva Conventions of 1949 relating to the protection of Victims of International Armed Conflicts.

In considering the intention of the drafters of the Convention, James C. Hathaway in *The Law of Refugee Status* (Toronto: Butterworths, 1991) notes at p. 185, the statement of Mr. Robinson of Israel (U.N. Doc. A/CONF.2/SR.22, at 6, July 16, 1951) as follows:

> The text ... obviously did not refer to refugees from natural disasters, for it was difficult to imagine that fires, flood, earthquakes or volcanic eruptions, for instance, *differentiated between their victims* on the grounds of race, religion, or political opinion. Nor did the text cover all man-made events. There was no provision, for example, for refugees fleeing from hostilities unless they were otherwise covered by Article 1 of the Convention. [emphasis added by Professor Hathaway]

[3]The underlying issue is discussed in *Refugees in Civil War Situations*, UNHCR Branch Office, Ottawa, November, 1990 where the following is set out:

> It should be noted at the outset that individuals are considered refugees when they flee or remain outside a country for reasons pertinent to refugee status. Whether these reasons arise in a civil war situation, in international armed conflict or in peace time, is irrelevant. *There is nothing in the definition itself which excludes its application to persons caught up in a civil war.* [emphasis added]

### *Third Issue*

What factors should be considered in determining whether the claimant's fear of persecution is well-founded?

### *Fourth Issue*

What are the key evidentiary elements that decision-makers should look to when considering a claim arising out of a situation of civil war?

## The Analysis

### *I. — Assessing the Harm Feared*

It is necessary to assess the particular circumstances which have given rise to the claimant's fear of persecution. *Does the harm feared constitute "persecution" within the definition of Convention refugee?*

A person taking no active part in the hostilities associated with a civil war should be treated by the combatants humanely without adverse distinction.[4] Her human rights must be respected. If the combatants treat the person in a manner that is contrary to these principles, such treatment can, depending on the claimant's particular circumstances, constitute persecutory treatment. *When one is determining whether the case is one of "persecution", the question to be addressed is whether there are violations of human rights of sufficient degree and importance to constitute persecution.*[5] The fact that the treatment feared by the claimant arises from the hostility felt, or the violence engaged in,

---

[4]See common article 3(1) of each of the four *Geneva Conventions of 1949* discussed *infra*. These Guidelines relate to civilians with no direct participation in the hostilities. Where a claimant provided indirect support to combatants such as supplying food, money or shelter, these actions should not have taken the claimant outside of the category of non-combatant. Any sanction imposed, or threatened to be imposed, against the claimant would have to be considered in relation to the activity engaged in by the claimant; disproportionate punishment could be found to be persecutory as that could be found not to be a legitimate imposition of a sanction. Generally, a threat to life, liberty or security of the person is persecutory regardless of the context. (However, to be within the definition, there must be a link to a Convention ground.) On the other hand, in *Antonio, Pacato Joao v. M.E.I.* (September 27, 1994), IMM-1072-93, Nadon (F.C.T.D.), the Court, in an Angolan claim, was not prepared to conclude that the death penalty when imposed for treason and sabotage constituted persecution.

[5]As noted in paragraph 51 of the UNHCR *Handbook*: "There is no universally accepted definition of "persecution", and various attempts to formulate such a definition have met with little success." The concept of persecution has been described on a number of occasions in Canadian case law. One such description is "the systemic and persistent infliction of threats and injury" [*Rajudeen v. M.E.I.* (1984), 55 N.R. 129 at pp. 133-4 (C.A.)]; another description requires an element of repetition and relentlessness which an isolated incident can satisfy only in very exceptional circumstances [*Valentin v. M.E.I.*, [1991] 3 F.C. 390 (C.A.)]. The Supreme Court of Canada has stated that persecution, although undefined in the Convention, has been ascribed the meaning of "sustained or systemic violation of basic human rights demonstrative of a failure of state protection." [*Canada (Attorney General) v. Ward*, [1993] 2 S.C.R. 689 at p. 734]. It should be noted that in *Murugiah, Rahjendran v. M.E.I.* (May 5, 1993), no. 92-A-6788, Noël (F.C.T.D.) and *Rajah, Jeyadevan v. M.E.I.* (September 27, 1993), no. 92-A-7341, Joyal (F.C.T.D.) the Federal Court Trial Division certified the following questions for consideration by the Federal Court of Appeal: whether persecution requires systematic and persistent acts, and

by combatants directly involved in the civil war does not exclude the possibility that it could constitute persecution.

International instruments are not binding on the Refugee Division unless they are incorporated into Canadian law.[6] However, even if a particular instrument has not been so incorporated, the principles enunciated in the instrument may assist in the application of the definition of Convention refugee. Also, the standards set out in an instrument may assist the Refugee Division in determining permissible conduct even if the instrument is not binding upon the parties to the conflict. By defining permissible conduct, the instruments may assist the Refugee Division in assessing whether or not the treatment constitutes persecution as that term is understood in Canadian case law.

Accordingly, in determining what are the fundamental human rights that must be considered in assessing persecution within the context of civil war, reference should be made to international human rights instruments which provide a framework of international standards for recognizing the protection needs of individuals. Such international human rights instruments include, but are not limited to:

*i. Universal Declaration of Human Rights*

*ii. International Covenant on Civil and Political Rights*

*iii. International Covenant on Economic, Social and Cultural Rights*

*iv. Convention Against Torture and Other Cruel, Inhuman or Degrading Treatment or Punishment*

In addition, international instruments exist that relate to the protection of civilians in time of war. These instruments should be considered as they may assist the Refugee Division in determining what constitutes permissible conduct by combatants toward non-combatants, and they may therefore assist the Refugee Division in determining whether the conduct constitutes persecution. These instruments include, but are not limited to:

*i. Geneva Convention Relative to the Protection of Civilian Persons in Time of War of August 12, 1949 (the "1949 Convention")*

*ii. Protocol II to the 1949 Convention ("Protocol II")*

Article 3 of the *1949 Convention* prohibits in relation to non-combatants certain acts including:

- violence to life and person, in particular murder of all kinds, mutilation, cruel treatment and torture;
- taking of hostages;
- outrages upon personal dignity, in particular humiliating and degrading treatment.

Article 4 of *Protocol II* prohibits in relation to non-combatants certain acts including:

- violence to the life, health and physical or mental well-being of persons, in particular murder as well as cruel treatment such as torture, mutilation or any form of corporal punishment;
- collective punishments;

---

whether one or two violations of basic and inalienable rights such as forced labour or beatings while in police detention is enough to constitute persecution.

[6]For more on this issue, see Anne F. Bayefsky, *International Human Rights Law -Use in Canadian Charter of Rights and Freedoms Litigation* (Markham: Butterworths, 1992).

- taking of hostages;
- acts of terrorism;
- outrages on the personal dignity, in particular humiliating and degrading treatment, rape, enforced prostitution and any form of indecent assault.

Article 13 of *Protocol II* provides that the "civilian population and individual civilians shall enjoy general protection against the dangers arising from military operations." To give effect to this protection, certain rules, including the following are to be observed:

- the civilian population, as well as individual civilians, shall not be the object of attack;
- acts or threats of violence the primary purpose of which is to spread terror among the civil population are prohibited.

*Excerpts from the above two instruments accompany these Guidelines.*[7]

## *II. — Determining Whether Persecution is Based on a Convention Ground*

### *General principles — Federal Court of Appeal*

The determination of whether there is a link between the persecution experienced or feared by the claimant, or her group, and the grounds for persecution found in the defini-

---

[7]Common article 3 of each of the four *Geneva Conventions of 1949* sets out the minimum conduct of each party to an armed conflict of a non-international character in all circumstances of the conflict. Where a claimant has adduced credible or trustworthy evidence that there is a reasonable chance that she would face a violation of any of the provisions in this article, a panel would need to assess whether the action constituted persecutory treatment. Violations of non-derogable rights found in common article 3 likely would lead to a finding of persecution. See also Report of the Representative of the Secretary-General, Mr. Francis Deng, submitted pursuant to Commission on Human Rights resolution 1993/95, "Legal Analysis based on the needs of Internally Displaced Persons" prepared on behalf of the American Society of International Law and the International Human Rights Law Group, Washington D.C., U.S.A. by Janelle M. Diller, Robert K. Goldman and Cecile E.M. Meijer (Working Draft in Progress), January 30, 1995, U.N. Doc. E/CN.4/1995/CRP.1 at pp. 47–54.

For a discussion on *Protocol II* see Charles Lysaght, "The Scope of Protocol II and its Relation to common article 3 of the *Geneva Conventions of 1949* and other Human Rights Instruments", *The American University Law Review*, Vol. 33, 1983, p. 9 and Sylvie Junod, "Additional Protocol II: History and Scope", *The American University Law Review*, Vol. 33, 1983, p. 29.

In considering the impact of international instruments on the position of children in a civil war situation reference should be made to article 4(3) of *Protocol II* and article 38 of the *Convention on the Rights of the Child*. For more on the issue, see Ilene Cohn, "The Convention on the Rights of the Child: What it means for Children in War", *International Journal of Refugee Law*, Vol. 3, no. 1, 1991, p. 100.

Where the claim involves a fear of gender-related persecution, reference should be made to the additional international instruments described in the Chairperson's *Guidelines on Women Refugee Claimants Fearing Gender-related Persecution*, Immigration and Refugee Board, Ottawa, Canada, March 9, 1993 (*the "Gender Guidelines"*). It may be necessary to use these Guidelines as well as the Gender Guidelines to analyze a claim of a woman fearing persecution within the context of a civil war.

tion, has generally proved to be the most difficult aspect of applying the definition in claims arising from civil war.[8] In considering this issue, it is useful to commence the analysis by reference to the two leading decisions of the Federal Court of Appeal. The first of these is *Salibian v. M.E.I.*,[9] which at p. 258 sets out four general principles:

> It can be said in light of earlier decisions by this Court on claims to Convention refugee status that
>
> (1) the applicant does not have to show that he had himself been persecuted in the past or would himself be persecuted in the future;
>
> (2) the applicant can show that the fear he had resulted not from reprehensible acts committed or likely to be committed directly against him but from reprehensible acts committed or likely to be committed against members of a group to which he belonged;
>
> (3) *a situation of civil war in a given country is not an obstacle to a claim provided the fear felt is not that felt indiscriminately by all citizens as a consequence of the civil war, but that felt by the applicant himself, by a group with which he is associated, or, even, by all citizens on account of a risk of persecution based on one of the reasons stated in the definition*; and
>
> (4) the fear felt is that of a reasonable possibility that the applicant will be persecuted if he returns to his country of origin ... [emphasis added]

The Court goes on to adopt the following statement by Professor Hathaway:[10]

> In sum, while modern refugee law is concerned to recognize the protection needs of particular claimants, the best evidence that an individual faces a serious chance of persecution is usually the treatment afforded similarly situated persons in the country of origin. *In the context of claims derived from situations of generalized oppression, therefore, the issue is not whether the claimant is more at risk than anyone else in her country, but rather whether the broadly based harassment or abuse is sufficiently serious to substantiate a claim to refugee status. If persons like the applicant may face serious harm for which the state is accountable, and if that risk is grounded in their civil or political status, then she is properly considered to be a Convention refugee.* [emphasis added]

---

[8]or a discussion of the approaches taken in the United States of America to the assessment of refugee claims involving civil war, see Peter Butcher, "Assessing Fear of Persecution in a War Zone", *Georgetown Immigration Law Journal*, Vol. 5, no. 1, 1991, p. 435. See also Michael G. Heyman, "Redefining Refugee: A Proposal for Relief for Victims of Civil Strife", *San Diego Law Review*, Vol. 24, 1987, p. 449; T. Alexander Aleinikoff, "The Meaning of "Persecution" in U.S. Asylum Law", *Refugee Policy — Canada and the United States* (Toronto: York Lanes Press Ltd., 1991), p. 292; Walter Kalin, "Refugees and Civil Wars: Only a Matter of Interpretation", *International Journal Of Refugee Law*, Vol. 3, no. 3, 1991, p. 435; and Mark R. Von Sternberg, "Political Asylum and the Law of Internal Armed Conflict: Refugee Status, Human Rights and Humanitarian Law Concerns", *International Journal Of Refugee Law*, Vol. 5., no. 2, 1993, p. 153.

[9]*Salibian v. M.E.I.*, [1990] 3 F.C. 250 (C.A.).

[10]*Salibian* at p. 259.

The second case is the very brief decision in *Rizkallah v. M.E.I.*,[11] where the Court of Appeal held that:

> To succeed, *refugee claimants must establish a link between themselves and persecution for a Convention reason.* In other words, they must be *targeted* for persecution in some way, either personally or collectively.
>
> ... the evidence, as presented to us, falls short of establishing that Christians in the claimant's Lebanese village were collectively targeted in some way different from the general victims of the tragic and many-sided civil war. [emphasis added]

The third general principle set out in *Salibian* was commented upon by the Court of Appeal in *Hersi, Nur Dirie v. M.E.I.*,[12] when the Court, on consent, held that the Refugee Division erred "in holding that refugee claimants must be able to show they are at some greater differential risk than other members of their group", a conclusion which the Court found to be at odds with its decision in *Salibian*.

### *Approaches to Analysis of Civil War Claims*

The case law emanating from the Trial Division of the Federal Court seems to suggest that the Trial Division has taken two different approaches to civil war claims. The differences pertain to the question whether there is a nexus between the harm feared and one of the Convention grounds, and to the application of *Salibian* and *Rizkallah*.

### *Non-comparative Approach*

The non-comparative approach to the assessment of a claim is the approach advocated in these Guidelines. This approach is more in accord with the third principle set out in *Salibian*, the decisions of the Court of Appeal in *Rizkallah* and *Hersi, Nur Dirie*, as well as the wording of the Convention refugee definition.[13] With this approach, instead of an emphasis on comparing the level of risk of persecution between the claimant and other individuals (including individuals in the claimant's own group) or other groups, the Court examines the claimant's particular situation, and that of her group, in a manner similar to any other claim for Convention refugee status.

The issue is not a comparison between the claimant's risk and the risk faced by other individuals or groups at risk for a Convention reason, but whether the claimant's risk is a risk of sufficiently serious harm and is linked to a Convention reason as opposed to the

---

[11]In *Rizkallah v. M.E.I.* (1992), 156 N.R. 1 (F.C.A.), the Court determined that the appellants were merely victims of the civil war and found that there was no linkage between the harm feared and their religious status as Lebanese Christians. Lorne Waldman in *Immigration Law and Practice* (Toronto: Butterworths, 1992), Issue 5-12/93, at p. 8.45 contrasts the result in *Rizkallah* to that of *Salibian* and *Ovakimoglu v. M.E.I.* (1983), 52 N.R. 67 (F.C.A.) in illustrating the difficulty in differentiating between a harm common to all persons living in a state of civil war and one that is linked to a Convention ground.

[12]*Hersi, Nur Dirie v. M.E.I.* (November 4, 1993), no. A-1231-91, MacGuigan, Linden, McDonald (F.C.A.).

[13]Section 3(g) of the *Act* recognizes that Canadian immigration policy and the rules and regulations made under the *Act* should be designed and administered in a manner that fulfils Canada's international legal obligations with respect to refugees and the upholding of its humanitarian tradition with respect to the displaced and the persecuted. The definition of Convention refugee in the *Act* should be interpreted in a manner consistent with these objectives.

general, indiscriminate consequences of civil war.[14] A claimant should not be labelled as a "general victim" of civil war without full analysis of her personal circumstances and that of any group to which she may belong. Using a non-comparative approach results in a focusing of attention on whether the claimant's fear of persecution is by reason of a Convention ground.

### *Comparative Approach*

The other approach to assessment of the claim is comparative. This approach considers whether the claimant, or her group, is at a "differential risk" when compared to other individuals or groups in the country of origin.[15] This approach

---

[14]The Federal Court in *Hersi, Ubdi (Ubdi) Hashi v. M.E.I.* (May 5, 1993), no. 92-A-6574, Joyal (F.C.T.D.) agreed with the Minister's argument that:

> ... The evidence of the applicants themselves speaks of general and indiscriminate shelling of cities and villages. Members of various clans become the victims, whether such clans could otherwise be regarded as friends or foes of the assailants.

A similar result was reached in *Siad v. M.E.I.* (1993), 21 Imm. L.R. (2d) 6 (F.C.T.D.) where the Court upheld the Refugee Division decision as,

> It is clear that the Refugee Division concluded that the fear felt was that felt indiscriminately by all citizens [of Somalia] as a result of the civil war and random violence, and was not related to membership in a social group. (p. 11)

In *Khalib v. M.E.I.* (1994), 24 Imm. L.R. (2d) 149 (F.C.T.D.), the Court upheld a decision of the Refugee Division in which it concluded that the claimants' fear in relation to the danger from land mines was one faced indiscriminately by all people in the area notwithstanding that members of the Issaq clan may be concentrated there and form the majority in the area. It appears that the Refugee Division was not persuaded that "the mines were intended to harm only or even mainly the Issaqs living in the area of Hargeisa, and that the mines placed by a former government and not yet removed constitute grounds for fear, recognized by the Convention, of persecution by a government that is no longer in authority." (at p. 152)

In a brief decision, the Federal Court of Appeal in *Shereen, Agha Agha v. M. E.I.* (March 21, 1994), no. A-913-90, Mahoney, MacGuigan, Linden (F.C.A.) held that a perceived political opinion is not to be ascribed to all individuals who find themselves victimized by government forces in a civil war even if they live in an area of insurgency. This case illustrates the need to provide supporting evidence as to targeting. The need to address the issue of targeting can be seen in Ahmed, Faisa *Talarer v. M.E.I.* (November 2, 1993), no. A-1017-92, Noël (F.C.T.D.) and *Abdi, Jama Osman v. M.E.I.* (November 18, 1993), no. A-1089-92, Simpson (F.C.T.D.) where, in both cases, decisions of the Refugee Division were found to be in error due to the failure to deal with documentary evidence which supported the claimant's position that the fear felt by the claimant was not the general fear felt by all in Somalia.

[15]In a similar fashion, the Refugee Division has applied the concept of "differential risk" and "comparative differential risk" in the analysis of civil war claims. Due to the concerns outlined in these Guidelines, neither mode of analysis is recommended. For a review of the relevant Canadian case law and an in-depth discussion of the issue see CRDD T93-11627, T93-11628, James, Band, March 29, 1994.

For reasons that follow the comparative approach see: CRDD T92-05687, Davis, Thomas, February 9, 1993 (The panel found that the claimant's ethnic group, the Hazara, was not targeted differentially than any other ethnic group in Afghanistan. On judicial appears to involve a consideration of the predicament faced by the claimant, or her group, as compared with the circumstances of other persons in her country of origin who face harm from the same or other agents of persecution. In other words, is the claimant's, or her group's, predicament worse or different than the predicaments of others in her country of origin?[16]

---

review, the application was allowed on consent and the negative decision set aside — IMM-836-93, Reed J., March 23, 1994. A positive determination was made on the re-hearing of the claim.); CRDD T93-09000, T93-09143, Davis, Grice, January 14, 1994 (Positive determinations were made as the panel found that members of the claimant's religious group suffer more frequently from more atrocious human rights violations differentially from any other group.); and CRDD T93-09464, T93-09465, Davis, Wolman, January 6, 1994 (The claimants, ethnic Croatians, were found not to be Convention refugees as they failed to establish that they faced a differential risk when compared to other ethnic groups in the country. A leave application for judicial review was not filed.).

In Abdi, *Jama Osman v. M.E.I.* (November 18, 1993), no. A-1089-92, Simpson (F.C.T.D.), the Court stated at p. 3 that: "As a general matter, when large numbers of civilians are being killed without regards to their beliefs or affiliations, it is difficult to demonstrate a fear of persecution based on a personal belief or membership in a particular group. However, this case was unusual because there was some documentary evidence which corroborated the claimant's fear of persecution at the hands of the Abgal sub-clan." This statement illustrates the need for submission of evidence which shows the targeting of the claimant and/or her group. In addition, it recognizes that even in situations where large numbers of persons suffer harm for reasons not linked to a Convention ground, targeting for a Convention ground can take place.

[16]Requiring a demonstration of greater hardship might mean any one of several things. To succeed, the claimant might have to establish: (i) that the claimant's, or her group's, level of risk is greater than the risk level of persons in other groups [rejected in *Janjicek, Davorin v. M.C.I.* (March 24, 1995), no. IMM-2242-94, Richard (F.C.T.D.), but accepted in other decisions of the Trial Division]; or (ii) that the claimant's level of risk is greater than the risk level of other persons in the claimant's own group (rejected by the Court of Appeal in *Hersi, Nur Dirie*); or (iii) that the claimant is at risk of suffering harm greater than that which threatens others.

With respect to the third alternative, the question which must be addressed by the Refugee Division is whether the treatment feared crosses the threshold of what constitutes persecution, not whether the claimant is at risk of harm greater than that to which some other group, or some other person in the claimant's own group, might be subjected. The threshold should not be raised because the claim arises out of a situation of civil war; generally, it cannot be said that something which would constitute persecution in peacetime does not meet the standard in war time. Moreover, the linkage to a Convention ground should not be negated by the mere fact that the persecution arises within the context of civil war.

In *Janjicek*, the Federal Court Trial Division, on consent, ordered a claim remitted for a new hearing on the basis that "a Convention refugee claimant need not establish that her or his ethnic group is at greater risk than members of other ethnic groups, in accordance with the decision of the Federal Court of Appeal in *Salibian v. M.E.I.*". However, in *Barisic, Rajko v. M.C.I.* (January 26, 1995), no. IMM-7275-93, Noël (F.C.T.D.), the Court held that it could not conclude that the Refugee Division acted unreasonably by holding that, like all Croatians, the claimant was a victim of a civil war. The Refugee Division concluded that the claimant was situated similarly to all citizens of Croatia and had not demonstrated the existence of a serious risk of persecution based on one of the

The clearest adoption of the comparative approach has been in *Isa v. S. S.C.*[17]

### *Conclusion*

> These Guidelines advocate the use of the non-comparative approach, as this approach promotes the case law in *Salibian, Rizkallah* and *Hersi, Nur Dirie*. The Guidelines do not recommend the use of any form of "differential risk" analysis. It can lead to the use of a comparative approach, where the requirement that the claimant, or her group, be exposed to hardship which is greater than the hardship of others in the country of origin, may be difficult to reconcile with certain passages in *Salibian, Rizkallah* and *Hersi, Nur Dirie*. In addition, the comparative approach may be difficult to reconcile with the Convention refugee definition.

---

reasons set out in the Convention. The claimant had been forced out of his village when it was occupied by the Serb army, and had adduced evidence of "ethnic cleansing". The Court noted that the Croats, in the spirit of revenge, were engaging in acts just as reprehensible.

[17]In *Isa v. S.S.C.* (1995), 28 Imm. L.R. (2d) 68 (F.C.T.D.), the Trial Division upheld a decision of the Refugee Division (CRDD T93-01998, Mojgani, Cole, March 8, 1994) in which the panel at p. 4 concluded that:

> Given the totality of the documentary evidence before us, it appears that all clans and sub-clans are both perpetrators and victims of the ongoing violence. We do not find that the claimant's clan has been differentially targeted for persecution from any other clan nor that he had been targeted any differently from any other Somali.

The claimant was found not to be a Convention refugee notwithstanding that documentary evidence described attacks on the claimant's clan. The Court did not take issue with the Refugee Division's finding that the claimant's fear was similar to that of all Somali citizens in general and arose out of the ongoing civil strife in Somalia. In particular, at p. 72 the Court stated that:

> Many, if not most, civil war situations are racially or ethnically based. If racially motivated attacks in civil war circumstances constitute a ground for Convention refugee status, then, all individuals on either side of the conflict will qualify. The passages quoted by the board from [paragraph 164 of] the United Nations Handbook (supra) indicates that this is not the purpose of the 1951 Convention.

See also *Ali, Farhan Omar v. M.C.I.* (June 26, 1995), no. A-1652-92, McKeown (F.C.T.D.) where without referring to any particular passage in Isa, that decision was cited approvingly. In *Ali*, the Court upheld the decision of the Refugee Division which found the claimants not to be Convention refugees as they had not shown that they were "differentially at risk of being persecuted despite the civil war situation" (at p. 3). *Isa* was applied in CRDD T94-06601, T94-06602, T94-06603, T94-06604, T94-06605, T94-06606, Davis, Bubrin, August 2, 1995 where the panel in considering whether an IFA existed for the claimants held at p. 10 that Shi'ite Hazaras did not face "more or different difficulties in Afghanistan." (Application for leave for judicial review filed as IMM-2456-95 with leave granted.) For a similar analysis with respect to Pashtuns in Afghanistan see CRDD T95-02614, Davis, Hope, November 24, 1995. See also, CRDD T95-02034, Davis, Bubrin, October 13, 1995 where the Refugee Division applying a similar analysis determined that members of the Majerteen clan of the Darod tribe do not face a differential risk in Somali from other Somali citizens. (Application for leave for judicial review filed as IMM-3170-95.)

### *Application of the Non-Comparative Approach: Relevant Principles*

To succeed, refugee claimants must establish a link between themselves and persecution on a Convention ground. In other words, they must be targeted for persecution in some way, either personally or collectively.[18] Inasmuch as persecutory measures are often directed at groups rather than individuals, the claimant need not be personally identified ("singled out") or targeted for persecution in order to be determined a Convention refugee.[19]

Where the persecution which has occurred, or the possibility of persecution in the future, is directed at the claimant's group as a whole rather than each individual member of the group, it is the fact of membership in the group which provides the foundation for the fear. Where the targeting is due to the possession of a certain characteristic related to a Convention ground, then all those who possess the characteristic may be at risk of harm by reason of their possession of that characteristic.[20] In such a case, the linkage to a

---

[18]In *Ali, Hassan Isse v. M.E.I.* (June 9, 1994), no. IMM-39-93, MacKay (F.C.T.D.), the Court notes, after referring to *Salibian* and *Rizkallah, that Rizkallah* "is not authority for concluding that the civil war situation in Somalia faces all Somalis indiscriminately" (p. 7) as held by the Refugee Division. In addition, the Refugee Division had concluded "that the situation in Somalia is basically one of civil war, and that the claimant is not targeted, individually or collectively, in some way different from the general victims of civil war." The panel had not provided an explanation related to the evidence for this determination. The Court held that the panel's decision erred in not assessing the claimant's claim to a fear of persecution because of his membership in his clan, and in not referring to the particulars of the claimant's own situation. It is suggested that the Court in this case focused on the fear as it related to a Convention ground as opposed to the "differential risk" analysis found in *Abdulle, Sadia Mohamed v. M.E.I.* (September 16, 1993), no. A-1440-92, Nadon (F.C.T.D.) and *Mohamud, Nasra Ali v. M.E.I.* (January 21, 1994), no. A-614-92, Nadon (F.C.T.D.).

In T94-05955, Rucker, Cram, March 7, 1995 (signed October 11, 1995), the Refugee Division found the claimant, a Darod/Marjerteen from Mogadishu, Somalia, to be a Convention refugee based on the clan-based fighting due to its adverse impact on him personally, and on his clan.

[19]See Suzanne J. Egan, *Civil War Refugees and the Issue of "Singling Out" in a State of Civil Unrest* (Toronto: The Centre for Refugee Studies, 1991). See also David Matas, "Innocent Victims of Civil War as Refugees", Vol. 22, Fall 1993, *Manitoba Law Journal*, p. 1.

In *Osman, Ashu Farah v. M.C.I.* (January 25, 1995), no. IMM-1295-94, Cullen (F.C.T.D.), the Court upheld the Refugee Division's finding that the claimant, a Somali women whose deceased husband was of another clan, did not have a well-founded fear of persecution by reason of her clan membership. However, the decision was overturned due to the panel's failure to consider the particular situation faced by the claimant related to her marriage which put her "at a heightened risk." In coming to its decision, the Court stated at p. 5 that the "Board cannot hide behind the civil war situation and automatically find that claimants from Somalia are not refugees." In *Hotaki, Khalilullah v. M.E.I.* (November 22, 1994), no. IMM-6659-93, Gibson (F.C.T.D.), the Court found that the Refugee Division erred in failing to recognise that the "applicant was personally or differentially targeted and was not simply suffering from the fear felt indiscriminately by all citizens [of Afghanistan] as a consequence of the civil war" (at p. 4).

[20]While the membership of a claimant, who is a non-combatant, in a group which is a combatant in the civil war often forms the basis for her claim of a well-founded fear of

Convention ground is not negated by the fact that the persecutor does not "discriminate" between one possessor of the characteristic and another possessor of the same characteristic. What is important is that the group is targeted, or there is a reasonable possibility of targeting of the claimant or the group in the future. Moreover, the number of persons in the group is irrelevant.

Targeting should be considered from the perspective of the agent of persecution, i.e. the intention of the agent of persecution must be examined. The Supreme Court of Canada has clarified that the examination of the circumstances of a case, including the intention of the agent of persecution, should be approached from the perspective of the agent of persecution, since it is this perspective that is "determinative in inciting the persecution."[21]

> Where the intention of the agent of persecution to target a claimant, or her group, is clear from the evidence, it will be a straightforward matter to determine whether there is a link to one of the Convention grounds. Where the intention is not clear on the particular facts of the case, the link to a Convention ground may be inferred from the effect that the actions of the agent of persecution have on the claimant or her group.

A civilian non-combatant should not be fixed with a share of "collective guilt" because combatant members of the claimant's group are inflicting harm on members of other groups.[22] Such actions should not disqualify a claimant from refugee status if she otherwise fulfils the definition. As noted in *Isa*, there should be a recognition that civil wars are often waged for reasons found in the Convention grounds. *In applying Salibian and Rizkallah, the Guidelines recommend that a decision-maker should exercise caution before determining that a linkage to a Convention ground does not exist in such a case.* The fact that all persons on either side of the conflict may come within the definition, should not disqualify a claimant where that claimant has a well-founded fear of persecution based on a Convention ground.

In considering whether a linkage to a Convention ground exists, it is useful for decision-makers to reflect on the following comments made by Dr. Joachim Henkel, Judge, Ger-

---

persecution, it is clear that it is not determinative of the issue as the claimant must prove that the harm feared is linked to a Convention ground. In *Abdulle, Sadia Mohamed v. M.E.I.* (September 16, 1993), no. A-1440-92, Nadon (F.C.T.D.), the Court rejected the applicant's submission that membership in one of two groups involved in a two-sided conflict is determinative of the issue. The Court, applying a "differential risk" analysis, a mode of analysis not recommended in these Guidelines, required proof of targeting of the applicant or her group, an approach in accord with the Guidelines. See also *Farah, Ali Said v. M.C.I.* (January 13, 1995), no. IMM-1141-94, Dubé (F.C.T.D.). The Court, in concluding that the Refugee Division was not unreasonable in holding that the claimant had not established that he would be targeted for persecution in some way different from the general victims of civil war in Somalia, noted that "the mere fact that the applicant is a member of a tribe or clan in Somalia does not necessarily imply that he has an objectively well-founded fear of persecution" (at pp. 1-2).

[21]*Ward* at p. 747.

[22]However, see *Barisic, Rajko v. M.C.I.* (January 26, 1995), no. IMM-7275-93, Noël (F.C.T.D.), where the Court in dismissing the application for judicial review noted that the Croats, in the spirit of revenge, were engaging in acts just as reprehensible as those committed by the Serb army.

man Federal Administrative Court with respect to the "general consequences" of civil war.[23]

> The general rule that the Geneva Refugee Convention does not provide protection against the general consequences of civil war is correct, but is often applied too broadly. Certainly, the danger of being caught up in the fighting and thus losing ones life more or less by accident is a general consequence of civil war. Furthermore, the danger of loosing [sic] a limb by treading on a land mine is a general consequence of civil war. Lack of food and water, lack of electricity and heating, lack of medical treatment and many other sufferings are general consequences of civil war. But, in my view, it amounts to persecution if one of the waring [sic] parties as part of its strategy subjects the femal[e] members of the enemy community to wide-spread rape; if the waring [sic] parties resort to the practice of "ethnic-cleansing"; if the waring [sic] parties detain all male members of the enemy community in concentration camps in which they are abused and ill-treated; if one of the waring [sic] parties after having captured a city takes to killing even civilian members of the enemy community. Even though such atrocities may be common in today's civil wars they clearly are directed against persons as individuals; they are not just the unavoidable more or less anonymous consequences of a war. Thus, if one of the waring [sic] parties singles out a person or a group of persons for reasons of race, political opinion or one of the other elements enumerated in the refugee definition and subjects it to serious human rights violations this clearly constitutes persecution...

### *Categories of Claims Encountered*

In considering the issue of whether the persecution feared is based on a Convention ground, it is beneficial to highlight the types of claims seen in the civil war context. Claims arising within civil war situations may be divided into three broad categories:

1. *Fear of persecution in a generalized civil war:*
    - *a. Individualized harm that is distinguishable from the general dangers of civil war.*
    - *b. Group-based harm that is distinguishable from the general dangers of civil war.*
    - *c. Harm that is not distinguishable from the general dangers of civil war.*
2. *Fear of persecution arising from a civil war specifically directed against a group with which the claimant is affiliated.*
3. *Fear of persecution from circumstances unrelated to the civil war.*

These categories have been identified as they delineate factual situations within which we find the majority of civil war claims. When such claims are considered within these categories, the linkage between the harm feared and the Convention grounds is more readily discernible. The examples set out below are not meant to be exhaustive of the situations that might come within a particular category.

Other Relevant Legislation

[23] Dr. Joachim Henkel, Judge, German Federal Administrative Court. Excerpt from his contribution to the International Judicial Conference on Asylum Law and Procedures, London, England, November 1995, "Who is a refugee? (Refugees from civil war and other internal armed conflicts)", in section titled "Persecution versus "general consequences" of civil war" at pp. 3-4.

*1. Fear of persecution in a generalized civil war.*

*A) Individualized harm that is distinguishable from the general dangers of civil war:*

Certain individuals, although not taking any part in the hostilities, may nevertheless face a reasonable chance of persecution[24] because of their civil or political status, or due to a status which is imputed to them by combatants in the civil war. For example:

1. persons facing persecution for refusing to join either side in the armed struggle out of a desire to remain neutral, a conscious political choice or other valid reasons of conscience;[25]

2. human rights activists, journalists or other citizens threatened with measures of persecution for investigating and/or criticizing military, paramilitary or guerilla activities and atrocities;

3. persons fearing persecution for certain views attributed or imputed to them, such as "sabotaging the war efforts" or "collaborating with the enemy".[26]

*B) Group-based harm that is distinguishable from the general dangers of civil war:*

Although the civil war has an adverse impact on the entire population, a particular racial, national, religious, social or political group may face a reasonable chance of persecution because of the group's identifying characteristic(s). For example:

1. members of an ethnic group might face persecution as a result of, for example, selective denial of state protection related to their ethnicity;

---

[24] *Adjei v. M.E.I.*, [1989] 2 F.C. 680 (C.A.). In *Chan, Kwong Hung v. M.E.I.* (October 19, 1995), no. 23813, Major, Sopinka, Cory, Iacobucci (majority); La Forest, L'Heureux-Dubé, Gonthier (dissenting) (S.C.C.), Justice Major after citing *Adjei* phrased the test as follows: "The applicable test has been expressed as a "reasonable possibility" or, more appropriately in my view, as a "serious possibility"." (p. 13). Both of these terms, as well as "reasonable chance", are found in *Adjei.*

[25] The claimant in such a situation might fear persecution at the hands of members of her own group for attempting to maintain neutrality in the conflict. Alternatively, her fear could emanate from groups in conflict with her group, as the claimant could be perceived to be a supporter of her own group.

As noted at p. 750 of the decision of the Supreme Court of Canada in *Canada (Attorney General) v. Ward*, [1993] 2 S.C.R. 689: "Not just any dissent to any organization will unlock the gates to Canadian asylum; the disagreement has to be rooted in a political conviction." At p. 749 the Court contrasted its decision in Ward with a recent United States Supreme Court disposition in *I.N.S. v. Elias-Zacarias*, 112 S.Ct. 812 (1992), where the majority was not convinced that the claimant's motive for refusing to join an anti-government guerilla force, nor that perceived by the guerillas to be his motive, was politically based.

[26] In *Antonio, Pacato Joao v. M.E.I.* (September 27, 1994), IMM-1072-93, Nadon (F.C.T.D.), the Court, in an Angolan claim, was not prepared to conclude that the death penalty, when imposed for treason and sabotage, constituted persecution. While providing indirect support to dissident forces may be subject to prosecution by the government, such prosecution must not be carried out in a persecutory manner.

2. women and children may, because of their social or political role or because of their association with certain individuals (including family members) be targets of deliberate violence and abuse;[27]

3. members of a clan might be perceived as associated with another clan that had ruled the country prior to the civil war and might by reason of that perceived association, face persecution.[28]

*C) Harm that is not distinguishable from the general dangers of civil war.*

As noted above, certain individuals and groups may face a reasonable chance of persecution on a Convention ground, notwithstanding the civil war's adverse impact on the entire population. On the other hand, there will be circumstances where the persecution feared may not be linked to a Convention ground. Reference is then made to the unavoidable, more or less anonymous consequences of a civil war. For example:

1. civilians who are the unintentional victims of cross-fire between rival militias. The lack of an intention on the part of either of the rival militias leaves the civilians as "mere victims" of the civil war as there is no linkage between the harm feared and a Convention ground;[29]

2. civilians who are the unintentional victims of arbitrary, general or indiscriminate shelling and bombing or laying of land mines where the fear of such treatment is not linked to a Convention ground;[30]

---

[27]Where the claim involves a fear of gender-related persecution, consideration of the Chairperson's *Guidelines on Women Refugee Claimants Fearing Gender-related Persecution*, Immigration and Refugee Board, Ottawa, Canada, March 9, 1993 (the "*Gender Guidelines*") might be required. Thus, it may be necessary to use these Guidelines as well as the *Gender Guidelines* to analyze a claim of a woman fearing persecution within the context of a civil war. For a case involving a civil war situation where the panel failed to consider the *Gender Guidelines*, see *Hazarat, Ghulam v. S.S.C.* (November 25, 1994), no. IMM-5496-93, MacKay (F.C.T.D.). However, in *Narvaez, Cecilia v. M.C.I.* (February 9, 1995), no. IMM-3660-94, McKeown (F.C.T.D.), the Court had the following to say in a domestic violence case with respect to the *Gender Guidelines*: "While the guidelines are not law, they are authorized by subsection 65(3) of the Act, and intended to be followed unless circumstances are such that a different analysis is appropriate" (p. 6). With respect to the position of children see, *supra*, note 7.

[28]See *Shirwa, Mohamed Mahmoud v. M.E.I.* (December 16, 1993), no. A-1290-92, Denault (F.C.T.D.). Also, members of the clan that had ruled the country prior to the civil war might face persecution by reason of their clan membership.

[29]It is recognized that in a civil war there will be civilian casualties incidental to the fighting; while regrettable, such deaths or injuries are distinct from those resulting from an attack directed at civilian non-combatants or where the combatants show wanton disregard for the safety of civilians. Evidence of such disregard might lead the Refugee Division to find that there is a link between the persecution feared and a Convention ground. For cases illustrating this issue, see, *supra*, note 14.

[30]See *Khalib v. M.E.I.* (1994), 24 Imm. L.R. (2d) 149 (F.C.T.D.), supra, note 14. This example can be contrasted with a situation where one participant in a civil war bombs and shells an area of a town primarily inhabited by civilian non-combatants who are members of another participant in the civil war. Civilians who are not near military targets should not face direct attack by combatants. Where civilians are present in or near military targets, they may be found to have assumed the risk of death or injury incidental to attacks against such military targets.

3. civilians who are subject to random violence, such as looting, where the violence is not related to a Convention ground.[31]

*2. Fear of persecution arising from a civil war specifically directed against a group with which the claimant is affiliated.*

The violence is directed at a group that differs from the rest of the population by virtue of specific racial, national, social or political features. For example:

1. members of an ethnic group against which a genocidal campaign is being waged;

2. members of a religious faith expelled from their homes and suffering other forms of persecutory treatment as part of an "ethnic cleansing" agenda.[32]

*3. Fear of persecution from circumstances unrelated to the civil war.*

Although the claimant comes from a country in civil war, the danger faced by the claimant is not associated, directly or indirectly, with that war. However, the claimant may still be a Convention refugee if the fear of persecution is related to one of the five grounds. In this situation the claim should be determined without reference to the civil war framework. For example:

1. union leaders threatened with measures of persecution for promoting unionism;

2. members of a minority group treated in a persecutory manner, where such treatment or lack of protection is not related to the civil war.

### *III. — Determining whether there is a Well-Founded Fear of Persecution*

It is clear from the case law that a claimant must establish that her fear is well founded, and that the state's inability to protect must be considered at this stage of the analysis of the claim. In addition, the Supreme Court of Canada in *Ward* confirmed that a claimant is to seek out international protection only when national or state protection is unavailable.[33] The claimant must seek the protection of the country of origin before seeking international protection, unless it is objectively unreasonable to do so.[34]

The question, which must be addressed by the Refugee Division, is whether the claimant faces a reasonable chance of persecution by reason of a Convention ground: Is there a subjective fear for which there is an objective basis? As previously stated in these Guidelines, it is not required that the claimant's chance of facing persecution, individually or as a member of a group, be greater than the chance of persecution faced by others in situations of civil war; nor is it required that the persecution feared by the claimant be more severe than that feared by others.

---

[31]This can be contrasted with the intentional infliction of harm described by Dr. Joachim Henkel. In *Abdi, Ascia Hassan v. M.C.I.* (October 27, 1994), no. A-1016-92, Noël (F.C.T.D.), the Court in dismissing the application, concluded that its review of the evidence did not justify its interference with the Refugee Division's finding that "members of the Darod or Hawiye tribes, including the Applicants, were subject to the same risk of random violence as the general population of Somalia" (at p. 7).

[32]In CRDD T92-03148, Miller, Shatzky, September 9, 1992, the Refugee Division determined a Bosnian Moslem to be a Convention refugee as the panel concluded that "Muslims are not merely the victims caught in the crossfire of war, but are a targeted group selected for elimination because of their religion" (p. 5).

[33]*Ward* at p. 709.

[34]*Ward* at p. 724.

### *State Protection*

A state's ability to protect the claimant is a crucial element in determining whether the fear of persecution is well founded, and as such, is not an independent element of the definition of Convention refugee. The Supreme Court of Canada in *Ward* held that there were two presumptions at play in refugee determination. With respect to the first presumption, the Court concluded that it can be presumed that persecution will be likely and the fear well-founded if the fear of persecution is credible and there is an absence of state protection. As a second presumption the Court held that except in situations where the state is in a condition of complete breakdown, states must be presumed capable of protecting their citizens. The Court found that this presumption can be rebutted by "clear and convincing" evidence of the state's inability to protect.[35]

> The presumption that a state must be presumed capable of protecting its citizens can be rebutted where there is a complete breakdown of state apparatus, such as that recognized in *Zalzali v. M.E.I.*[36] in relation to the civil war, then raging, in Lebanon. However, even where there is a breakdown of state apparatus,[37] there may be several established authorities in a country able to provide protection in the part of the country controlled by them.[38] Thus, the Refugee Division must

---

[35]See *Ward* at pp. 722–6.

[36]*Zalzali v. M.E.I.*, [1991] 3 F.C. 605 (C.A.). As noted at p. 614 of the decision, the non-existence of a government cannot be an obstacle to claiming refugee status. It would be an absurd result that the greater the chaos in a given country, the less acts of persecution could be capable of founding a claim for refugee status. However, for the principle in *Zalzali* to apply, the claimant must demonstrate a prospective risk of persecution. Thus, in *Roble, Abdi Burale v. M.E.I.* (April 25, 1994), no. A-1101-91, Heald, Stone, McDonald (F.C.A.), where the agent of persecution (the NSS in Somalia) was no longer a factor, the Court held at p. 9 that "... the inability of the state to protect the [claimant] is not, in itself, a sufficient basis for his claim."

[37]In *Mendivil v. S.S.C.* (1994), 23 Imm. L.R. (2d) 225 (F.C.A.) at p. 232, Desjardins J.A. in analyzing the situation in Peru (on the basis of the evidence filed in the particular case) stated: "Isolated cases of persons having been victimized may not reverse the presumption [of protection]. A state of profound unrest with ineffective protection for the claimant may, however, have reversed it." In *Oblitas, Jorge v. M.C.I.* (February 2, 1995), no. IMM-2489-94, Muldoon (F.C.T.D.), at p. 9, the Court goes so far as to say that while the situation in Peru due to the terrorist activities of the Shining Path is not quite one of state breakdown (as in *Zalzali*), it comes very close.

[38]*Zalzali*, at p. 615 where the Court goes on to state:

> The "country", the "national government", the "legitimate government", the "nominal government" will probably vary depending on the circumstances and the evidence and it would be presumptuous to attempt to give a general definition. I will simply note here that I do not rule out the possibility that there may be several established authorities in the same country which are each able to provide protection in the part of the territory controlled by them, protection which may be adequate though not necessarily perfect.

See also *Sami, Sami Qowdan v. M.E.I.* (June 1, 1994), no. A-629-92, Simpson (F.C.T.D.) and *Saidi, Ahmed Abrar v. M.E.I.* (September 14, 1993), no. A-749-92, Wetston (F.C.T.D.) where, in each case, the Court upheld the Refugee Division's findings that protection was available in northern Somalia.

consider whether there is an established authority from which protection may be sought and adequate protection is available.[39]

### *Internal Flight Alternative*

Even when a claimant otherwise meets all the elements of the Convention refugee definition in her home area of her country of origin,[40] the claimant may have an internal flight alternative (IFA) elsewhere in that country: *If there is an IFA, the claimant is not a Convention refugee.* The question of whether a IFA exists is an integral part of the Convention definition.[41] If it is necessary to consider the availability of an IFA, reference may be made to the *Commentary* on IFA.[42]

The key concepts concerning IFA come from two cases: *Rasaratnam and Thirunavukkarasu.*[43] From these cases it is clear that the test to be applied in determining whether there is a IFA is two-pronged. Both prongs must be satisfied for there to be a finding that the claimant has an IFA. The Court of Appeal in *Rasaratnam* at pp. 709–11 adopts the two-pronged test:

1. The Board must be satisfied on a balance of probabilities that there is no serious possibility of the claimant being persecuted in the part of the country to which it finds a IFA exists.
2. Moreover, conditions in the part of the country considered to be a IFA must be such that it would be not unreasonable, in all the circumstances, including those particular to the claimant, for him to seek refuge there.[44]

In determining whether there is a reasonable chance of persecution in the potential IFA, the factors considered are similar to those evaluated when the panel makes this finding with respect to the claimant's home area of the country. However, some considerations

---

[39]The Supreme Court of Canada in *Ward* did not discuss the standard of protection that a country needs to offer its nationals. In determining what constitutes adequate protection, the Refugee Division may consider as a factor, whether the established authority is able to provide the claimant with protection from the acts prohibited by common article 3 of the *1949 Convention*. For a discussion of the appropriate standard see *M.E.I. v. Villafranca* (1992), 18 Imm. L.R. (2d) 130 (F.C.A.); *Velarde-Alvarez v. S.S.C.* (1995), 27 Imm. L.R. (2d) 88 (F.C.T.D.); *Bobrik, Iouri v. M.C.I.* (September 16, 1994), no. IMM-5519-93, Tremblay-Lamer (F.C.T.D.); *Smirnov v. S.S.C.*, [1995] 1 F.C. 780 (T.D.).

[40]In *Kanagaratnam, Parameswary v. M.E.I.* (January 17, 1996), no. A-356-94, Strayer, Linden, McDonald (F.C.A.), the Court of Appeal in answering "no" to the certified question "Is the determination of whether a claimant has a well founded fear of persecution in the area from which he or she originates a prerequisite to the consideration of an internal flight alternative?", held at p. 2 that "while the Board may certainly do so if it chooses, there was no *need* as a matter of law for the Board to decide whether there was persecution in the area of origin *as a prerequisite* to the consideration of an IFA" (emphasis added by the Court).

[41]*Rasaratnam v. M.E.I.*, [1992] 1 F.C. 706 at p. 710 (C.A.).

[42]*Internal Flight: When is it an Alternative*?, IRB Legal Services, April 1994. The Commentary provides a detailed review of the issue and includes a suggested framework of analysis.

[43]*Thirunavukkarasu v. M.E.I.*, [1994] 1 F.C. 589 (C.A.).

[44]For an elaboration of this statement, reference should be made to *Thirunavukkarasu* at pp. 596–9.

are different in order to account for the fact that the claimant is being expected to seek out alternative refuge in the country of origin.[45]

In dealing with the second prong of the IFA test, "reasonableness in all the circumstances", the Court of Appeal has stated that the circumstances must be relevant to the IFA question: "They cannot be catalogued in the abstract. They will vary from case to case."[46]

> The Trial Division has provided some guidance in assessing the reasonableness of an IFA. In the civil war context, the Court has indicated that relevant factors include the state of infrastructure and economy in the IFA region (i.e. destroyed or not), and the stability or instability of the government that is in place there.[47] In addition, it may be necessary to consider the hardship in travelling to the IFA region.
>
> *A claimant should not be required to suffer great physical danger or undue hardship in travelling to the IFA region or in staying there.*[48] *However, if there is an IFA, the claimant is not a Convention refugee.*

## *IV. — Evidentiary Matters*

When assessing a fear of persecution by a person fearing return to a situation of civil war the evidence must show that what the claimant fears is persecution on a Convention ground and that the fear is well-founded. The burden is on the claimant to provide the Refugee Division with credible or trustworthy evidence to show that all elements of the definition have been met; this includes establishing that there is individual or group targeting on a Convention ground.

Evidence can be provided through the claimant's own testimony. In addition, this can be done by the use of witnesses (including experts) to provide evidence on country conditions relating to targeting; such evidence can be introduced by way of affidavit in lieu of oral testimony.[49] The Refugee Division may take notice of any facts that may be judi-

---

[45]In particular, in determining whether there is an objective basis for fearing persecution in the IFA region, the Refugee Division must consider the personal circumstances of the claimant, and not just general evidence concerning other persons who live there.

[46]*M.E.I. v. Sharbdeen* (1994), 23 Imm. L.R. (2d) 300 at p. 301-2 (F.C.A.).

[47]*Farrah, Sahra Said v. M.E.I.* (October 5, 1993), no. A-694-92 at p. 3, Reed (F.C.T.D.). See also *Megag, Sahra Abdilahi v. M.E.I.* (December 10, 1993), no. A-822-92, Rothstein (F.C.T.D.) at p. 3 where the Court holds that instability alone is not the test of reasonableness. In *Irene, Steve Albert v. M.C.I.* (October 6, 1994), no. IMM-6275-93, Rothstein (F.C.T.D.), the Court in considering an IFA in an area controlled by one of the groups to the conflict, did not disagree with the applicant's submission that the group was not internationally recognized, had lost territory, was not an established force in the country (Liberia) and the applicant could not reasonably claim protection from that group. In those circumstances, the Court rejected the Refugee Division's finding that an IFA existed.

[48]The Trial Division has specifically addressed the issue of at what point in time IFA is to be considered. In *Dubravac v. M.C.I.* (1995), 29 Imm. L.R. (2d) 55 (F.C.T.D.) where the claimants' home town had been surrounded by opposing Serbian forces, the Court commented that the claimants "would not be required to go from their home town to the safe zone of Croatia, but ... from wherever they were relanded upon being sent back" (p. 56).

[49]The *Act* provides in section 68(3) that all proceedings before the Refugee Division shall be dealt with as informally and expeditiously as the circumstances and the considerations of fairness permit.

cially noticed and, subject to giving proper notice, of any other generally recognized facts and any information or opinion that is within its specialized knowledge.[50]

One way for the claimant to establish her case can be through evidence that other similarly situated persons face a reasonable chance of persecution, whether or not that chance is applicable to a specific group only or to large segments of the population similarly situated to the claimant.[51]

> Refugee Claim Officers under the direction of the panel and Counsel should submit documentary evidence to provide evidence of country conditions relating to targeting. *There should be recognition by the Refugee Division of the difficulty that is often encountered in acquiring information on country conditions when a country is embroiled in a civil war.* Notwithstanding that a claimant has the burden of establishing her claim, Refugee Division panels should consider the statements in the UNHCR *Handbook* at paragraph 196 on the shared burden of information gathering.
>
>> ... Thus, while the burden of proof in principle rests on the applicant, the duty to ascertain and evaluate all the relevant facts is shared between the applicant and the examiner. Indeed, in some cases, it may be for the examiner to use all the means at his disposal to produce the necessary evidence in support of the application.[52]

In addition, there should be recognition that, given the rapidly changing country conditions generally associated with civil wars, there may be problems with the timeliness of evidence and problems encountered in obtaining current information with respect to those changes. Accordingly, Refugee Claim Officers under the direction of the panel and Counsel should seek out and submit to the hearing the most current information relating to country conditions.

### *Framework of Analysis*

1. Assess the particular circumstances which have given rise to the claimant's fear of persecution. Does the harm feared constitute persecution?

For the treatment to amount to persecution, it must be a serious form of harm which detracts from the claimant's human rights and fundamental freedoms. The degree and importance of the rights and freedoms violated must be examined in relation to how the concept of persecution has been defined in Canadian jurisprudence. One objective standard is provided by international human rights instruments and international instruments that relate to the position of civilians in non-international armed conflicts. However, Canadian jurisprudence on the definition of persecution is not restricted to the violation of rights or interests protected in such international instruments.

---

[50] In accordance with the requirements of natural justice, section 68(5) of the *Act* provides that before the Refugee Division takes notice of any facts, information or opinion, other than facts that may be judicially noticed, in any proceedings, notice of its intention must be given and a reasonable opportunity to make representations with respect thereto must be afforded to the claimant (and the Minister, if present).

[51] In dismissing the application for judicial review in *Ahmed, Mohamed Hassan v. M.E.I.* (May 20, 1994), no. A-818-92, McKeown (F.C.T.D.), the Court noted that "the onus is on the applicant to show that he is similarly situated to members of a social group who suffered persecution" (at p. 2).

[52] See also paragraphs 195 to 205. The need to ascertain and evaluate all relevant facts is reflected in some of the enhancements to the Convention refugee determination process implemented by the Refugee Division in October 1995.

2. Is the harm feared as a result of the targeting of the claimant or her group on the basis of any one, or a combination, of the grounds in the definition of Convention refugee? Alternatively, the question can be posed: Is the claimant's fear of persecution based on any one, or a combination, of the grounds enumerated in the definition of Convention refugee?

*Considerations*:

- *the intention of the agent of persecution must be assessed*
- *intention may be inferred from the effect that the actions of the agent of persecution have on the claimant or her group*
- *a claimant need not be individually targeted for persecution*
- *it is necessary to ascertain the characteristic which places the claimant or members of her group at risk and the linkage to a Convention ground*
- *the level of risk of persecution should not be compared to that of other individuals or groups in the country of origin*
- *as civil wars are often waged for reasons related to a Convention ground, caution should be exercised before determining that there is not a linkage to a ground*

3. Determine whether, under all the circumstances, the claimant's fear is well-founded. This includes an assessment of the evidence related to the availability of adequate state protection and whether there is an objective basis to the claim.

*Considerations*:

- *is there an established authority from which protection may be sought and adequate protection is available*?
- *recognition of the difficulty of acquiring information on country conditions is important*

4. If required, determine whether there is the possibility of an internal flight alternative (IFA), or whether other issues require analysis.

*Considerations*:

- *the state of infrastructure and economy in the IFA region (i. e. destroyed or not), and the stability or instability of the government that is in place there*
- *whether or not there would be undue hardship on the claimant, both in reaching the location of the IFA and in establishing residence there*
- *if there is an IFA, the claimant is not a Convention refugee*

## *Relevant International Instruments*

### Geneva Convention Relative to the Protection of Civilian Persons in Time of War of August 12, 1949

Article 3 of each of the four *Geneva Conventions of 1949* set out in the schedule to the *Geneva Conventions Act*, R.S.C. 1985, c. G-3, provides as follows:

> 3. In the case of armed conflict not of an international character occurring in the territory of one of the High Contracting Parties, each Party to the conflict shall be bound to apply, as a minimum, the following provisions:
>
> (1) Persons taking no active part in the hostilities, including members of armed forces who have laid down their arms and those placed *hors de combat* by sickness, wounds, detention, or any other cause shall in all circumstances be treated humanely, without adverse distinction founded on race, colour, religion or faith, sex, birth or wealth, or any other similar criteria.

To this end, the following acts are and shall remain prohibited at any time and in any place whatever with respect to the above-mentioned persons:

a. violence to life and person, in particular murder of all kinds, mutilation, cruel treatment and torture;

b. taking of hostages;

c. outrages upon personal dignity, in particular humiliating and degrading treatment;

d. the passing of sentences and the carrying out of executions without previous judgment pronounced by a regularly constituted court, affording all the judicial guarantees which are recognized as indispensable by civilized peoples.

**Protocol II to the Geneva Convention Relative to the Protection of Civilian Persons in Time of War of August 12, 1949**

*(Schedule vi of the Geneva Conventions Act as amended by S.C. 1990, c. 14, s. 1)*

***Article 4***

1. All persons who do not take a direct part or who have ceased to take part in hostilities, whether or not their liberty has been restricted, are entitled to respect for their person, honour and convictions and religious practices. They shall in all circumstances be treated humanely, without any adverse distinction. It is prohibited to order that there shall be no survivors.

2. Without prejudice to the generality of the foregoing, the following acts against the persons referred to in paragraph 1 are and shall remain prohibited at any time and in any place whatsoever:

a. violence to the life, health and physical or mental well-being of persons, in particular murder as well as cruel treatment such as torture, mutilation or any form of corporal punishment;

b. collective punishments;

c. taking of hostages;

d. acts of terrorism;

e. outrages on the personal dignity, in particular humiliating and degrading treatment, rape, enforced prostitution and any form of indecent assault;

f. slavery and the slave trade in all their forms;

g. pillage;

h. threats to commit any of the foregoing acts.

3. Children shall be provided with the care and aid they require, and in particular:

(c) children who have not attained the age of fifteen years shall neither be recruited in the armed forces or groups nor allowed to take part in hostilities;...

***Article 13 — Protection of the Civilian Population***

1. The civilian population and individual civilians shall enjoy general protection against the dangers arising from military operations. To give effect to this protection, the following rules shall be observed in all circumstances.

2. The civilian population as such, as well as individual civilians, shall not be the object of attack. Acts or threats of violence the primary purpose of which is to spread terror among the civilian population are prohibited.

3. Civilians shall enjoy the protection afforded by this Part, unless and for such time as they take a direct part in hostilities.

***Article 14 — Protection of objects indispensable to the survival of the civilian population***

Starvation of civilians as a method of combat is prohibited. It is therefore prohibited to attack, destroy, remove or render useless, for that purpose, objects indispensable to the survival of the civilian population, such as foodstuffs, agricultural areas for the production of foodstuffs, crops, livestock, drinking water installations and supplies and irrigation works.

## Guideline 2 — Guidelines on Detention

### Guidelines Issued by the Chairperson, Pursuant to Section 65(4) of the *Immigration Act*

Canadian law[53] regards preventive detention as an exceptional measure. This general principle emerges from statute and case law, and is enshrined in the *Canadian Charter of Rights and Freedoms*[54] (hereinafter referred to as the Charter). International law,[55] as reflected in the *International Covenant on Civil and Political Rights* and the *Optional Protocol to the International Covenant on Civil and Political Rights*, respects the same principle.

*In the immigration field, Parliament has established two main grounds that justify detention:*[56]

1. *The person is likely to pose a danger to the public.*
2. *The person is not likely to appear for an examination, an inquiry or removal.*

Adjudicators have the power to order the detention or continued detention of a person. They may also order that a person be released from detention, subject to such terms and conditions as they deem appropriate, including the payment of a security deposit or the posting of a performance bond.[57]

These Guidelines deal with the following topics which are intended to help adjudicators achieve greater consistency in exercising their jurisdiction and, thereby, ensure greater fairness:

*(a) long-term detention;*

*(b) the notion of "danger to the public";*

*(c) alternatives to detention; and*



---

[53]For examples, refer to ss. 503(1) and 515(10) of the *Criminal Code*, R.S.C. 1985, c. C-46.

[54]*Canadian Charter of Rights and Freedoms*, Part I of the *Constitution Act, 1982*, Schedule B of the *Canada Act 1982*, 1982, c. 11 (U.K.).

[55]*International Covenant on Civil and Political Rights*, (1976) 999 UNTS 107, in force on March 23, 1976, ss. 9, 10 and 11, and the *Optional Protocol to the International Covenant on Civil and Political Rights*, (1976) 999 UNTS 216, in force on March 23, 1976. These two instruments confer status in law on the civil and political rights set out in the Universal Declaration of Human Rights, U.N. Doc. A/810, p. 71 (1948).

[56]The detention provided for in section 103.1 of the *Immigration Act* is not dealt with in these Guidelines because these specific provisions are infrequently applied.

[57]Sections 80.1 and 103 of the *Immigration Act*.

*(d) evidence and procedure.*

## A. — Long-Term Detention

In immigration matters, a person may be detained for an examination, an inquiry or removal.[58] Consequently, custody is preventive rather than punitive in nature. Furthermore, Parliament has required that the reasons for detention be reviewed at regular intervals, although it has not limited the total detention period. *Adjudicators should, however, be guided by certain general principles arising from the case law*:

- *Detention is an exceptional restraining measure in our society;*[59]
- *Although the Immigration Act does not limit the total duration of detention, there are implicit restrictions on the power of detention;*[60]
- *Detention for a reasonable length of time, given all the circumstances of the case, is the standard applicable to continued detention;*[61] *and*
- *The right guaranteed by section 7 of the Charter*[62] *implies that continued detention must be in accordance with the principles of fundamental justice.*[63]

---

[58]Sections 103(3), 103(6) and 103(8) of the *Immigration Act.*

[59]*Salilar v. Canada (Minister of Citizenship and Immigration)*, [1995] 3 F.C. 150 (T.D.); *Sahin v. Canada (Minister of Citizenship and Immigration)*, [1995] 1 F. C. 214 (T.D.), appeal dismissed on the grounds that the certified question had become hypothetical: *Sahin, Bektas v. M.C.I.* (June 8, 1995), no. A-575-94, Stone, MacGuigan, Robertson (F.C.A.).

[60]In *Sahin* (*supra*, note 7) Rothstein J. quoted, at p. 227, Woolf J. in *R. v. Governor of Durham Prison, ex p. Singh*, [1984] 1 All E.R. 983 (Q.B.) at p. 985: "Since 20 July 1983 the applicant has been detained under the power contained in para. 2(3) of Sch. 3 to the *Immigration Act 1971*. Although the power which is given to the Secretary of State in para 2 to detain individuals is not subject to any express limitation of time, I am quite satisfied that it is subject to limitations. First of all, it can only authorize detention if the individual is being detained in one case pending the making of a deportation order and, in the other case, pending his removal. It cannot be used for any other purpose. Second, as the power is given in order to enable the machinery of deportation to be carried out, I regard the power of detention as being impliedly limited to a period which is reasonably necessary for that purpose. The period which is reasonable will depend on the circumstances of the particular case. What is more, if there is a situation where it is apparent to the Secretary of State that he is not going to be able to operate the machinery provided in the Act for removing persons who are intended to be deported within a reasonable period, it seems to me that it would be wrong for the Secretary of State to seek to exercise his power of detention." In that case, the person had been convicted of a criminal offence and was detained for approximately five months following release on parole. See also, *Lam v. Tai A Chau Detention Centre* (1996), 199 N.R. 30 (J.C.P.C.).

[61]*Sahin*, *supra*, note 7.

[62]*Supra*, note 2, section 7: "Everyone has the right to life, liberty and security of the person and the right not to be deprived thereof except in accordance with the principles of fundamental justice."

[63]*Sahin*, *supra*, note 7, at p. 230: "... an adjudicator must have regard to whether continued detention accords with the principles of fundamental justice under section 7 of the Charter."

Often a person whose detention is continued is under a removal order or a conditional removal order. In such circumstances, continued detention is justified only if the removal order can be executed *within a reasonable period of time.*

The Department of Citizenship and Immigration is responsible for enforcing removal orders as soon as is reasonably practicable.[64] Nonetheless, the enforcement of removal orders can be delayed by reason of a legal impediment,[65] such as a stay of execution.

The existence of a legal impediment to the execution of a removal order does not render removal invalid.[66] However, if a detention appears unduly lengthy, *the reasonableness of the delay* should be considered, in order to ensure that the detention is not in fact an "indefinite detention."[67] Such detentions constitute deprivations of liberty that come into conflict with the principles of fundamental justice.

The fact remains however that in most cases of long-term detention, enforcement of the removal order is delayed despite the absence of any legal impediment. This can be attributed chiefly to the problems immigration authorities encounter in ascertaining the identity of the person in custody and in securing the cooperation of the country to which the person is to be removed.

---

[64]Sections 48 to 53 of the *Immigration Act.*

[65]Sections 49, 50, 52(3), 53(1), 73(1)(c) and 74(2) of the *Immigration Act.*

[66]*Re Rojas and the Queen* (1978), 20 O.R. (2d) 590 (Ont. C.A.). In dismissing a *habeas corpus* application, the Ontario Court of Appeal held as follows: "It is obvious that the problem of finding a country to which the appellant can be deported continues to occupy the bona fide attention and efforts of the immigration authorities, and therefore his detention cannot be characterized as having ceased to be lawful. "In *Sahin* (*supra*, note 7), a person had been detained for fourteen months on the ground that he was not likely to appear for his removal, based on his own statements to the effect that he would not report for removal if required to do so. The Minister applied for a judicial review of a decision of the Convention Refugee Determination Division in which it was held that the person was a Convention refugee. Thus, the person was under a conditional removal order. Rothstein J. of the Federal Court (Trial Division) held at pp. 223-224: "Until all appeals have been disposed of, a person might still be found not to be a Convention refugee and it is that eventuality that justifies the continuance of conditional removal orders against such persons. As long as a conditional removal order may become an effective removal order, section 103 recognizes that the Minister must be in a position to enforce the order. It is consistent with that objective that persons be detained when the Minister is of the opinion that they would not appear for removal if a removal order is to be executed."

[67]An example of such a situation is where the Immigration Appeal Division stays the execution of a removal order based on s. 74(2) of the *Immigration Act*, which provides that the Division "... shall review the case from time to time as it considers necessary or advisable." Given that the time of the execution of the removal cannot be foreseen, the detention should be considered "indefinite." In *Sahin* (*supra*, note 7) the Court held as follows at p. 229: "... when any number of possible steps may be taken by either side and the times to take each step are unknown, I think it is fair to say that a lengthy detention, at least for practical purposes, approaches what might be reasonably termed 'indefinite'." In *Re Rojas and the Queen* (*supra*, note 14) Zuber J.A. made the following remarks: "The *Immigration Act*, R.S.C. 1970, c. I-2, permits detention pending deportation, but this Act does not thereby authorize permanent imprisonment. In some cases it may be that the objective of deportation will become so unlikely or illusory that detention premised on this occurrence cannot be justified and will become unlawful."

Where there is no legal impediment to the execution of the removal order, it is all the more important to consider the *reasonableness of the delay*. With this in mind, the adjudicator should ask the Minister's representative to explain why the removal has not been carried out, since the latter must demonstrate diligent attempts to do so.[68] Depending on the nature of the impediments to removal, it may be appropriate to ask the Minister's representative to estimate the time that will be required to resolve the problems. This will enable the adjudicator to forecast more effectively the expected length of detention.[69]

*The following principles should guide adjudicators when reviewing reasons for detention*:

- *Where a person is being detained pending removal, it is relevant to consider whether the removal will be executed in the foreseeable future;*[70]
- *Each review of the reasons for detention is a hearing de novo. The Minister must, at every hearing, provide adequate reasons for the continued detention.*[71] *However, it should be noted that it is incumbent upon the person concerned to show why detention should not continue (especially in the absence of any new facts);*[72] *and*
- *The decisions of adjudicators must be based on their own analysis and assessment of the facts of the case, not solely on a previous decision of a colleague (although this may be considered)*[73] *or the conclusion of another decision-making body.*[74]

Consequently, when dealing with a continuing detention, adjudicators must consider both grounds for detention as required by the *Immigration Act*. However, their analysis must not end there. In every case where they are called upon to review the reasons for detention, they must consider the reasons for the continued failure to execute the removal, assess — based on the problems identified — whether the person is likely to be removed within a reasonable period of time, and determine — on a balance of probabilities — whether the duration of the detention is reasonable having regard to the circumstances of the particular case.

Adjudicators must also take into account the right to liberty guaranteed by section 7 of the Charter. In *Sahin*,[75] the Federal Court — Trial Division stated as follows: "... it is obvious that section 7 Charter considerations are relevant to the exercise of discretion by an adjudicator under section 103 of the *Immigration Act*." In this case the Court put forth

---

[68]*Cushnie v. M.E.I.* (1988), 54 D.L.R. (4th) 420 (Que. C.A.).

[69]Where the detention appears unduly lengthy, it may, depending on the circumstances of the case, have become unjustified, and therefore illegal, because removal has become illusory. (See the remarks of Zuber J.A. in *Re Rojas and the Queen*, *supra*, note 14.)

[70]*Re Rojas and the Queen*, *supra*, note 14; *Cushnie*, *supra*, note 16; *Sahin*, *supra*, note 7.

[71]*Cushnie*, *supra*, note 16; *Sahin*, *supra*, note 7; *Salilar*, *supra*, note 7.

[72]*Canada (Minister of Citizenship and Immigration) v. Salinas-Mendoza*, [1995] 1 F.C. 251 (T.D.).

[73]*McIntosh v. Canada (Minister of Citizenship and Immigration)* (1996), 30 Imm. L.R. (2d) 314 (F.C.T.D.); *Arruda v. Canada (Minister of Citizenship and Immigration)* (1995), 27 Imm. L.R. (2d) 154 (F.C.T.D.).

[74]*Lin v. Canada (Minister of Citizenship and Immigration)* (1996), 33 Imm. L.R. (2d) 8 (F.C.T.D.); *Salilar*, *supra*, note 7; *Salinas-Mendoza*, *supra*, note 20; *Lam v. Canada (Minister of Employment and Immigration)* (1995), 26 Imm. L. R. (2d) 207 (F.C.T.D.); *Ejim, Chukwudi Prince Chidi v. M.C.I.* (December 1, 1994), no. IMM-4590-94, Rothstein (F.C.T.D.). See also comments on *Williams*, *infra*, note 31.

[75]*Sahin*, *supra*, note 7, at p. 228.

*four factors to be taken into account by adjudicators in determining whether continued detention is in accordance with the principles of fundamental justice as required by section 7 of the Charter*:

1. There is a stronger case for continuing a lengthy detention when an individual is considered a danger to the public;[76]

2. The length of time that a person has already spent in detention and the length of time detention will likely continue, or the fact that the duration of future detention time cannot be ascertained, are factors which should have a bearing on release;

3. Unexplained delay and even unexplained lack of diligence should count against the offending party; and

4. The availability, effectiveness and appropriateness of alternatives to detention must be considered.

The foregoing list of considerations is not exhaustive. The considerations, and the weight to be given to each of them, will depend on the facts of the case.[77] A balance must be struck between the public interest and the person's right to liberty: "The principles of fundamental justice are concerned not only with the interest of the person who claims his liberty has been limited, but with the protection of society. Fundamental justice requires that a fair balance be struck between these interests, both substantively and procedurally."[78] Although detention of asylum-seekers and children is rare, decisions in this regard should be made in a manner that is consistent with not only the Charter but also the UNHCR *Handbook on Procedures and Criteria for Determining Refugee Status*[79] and the *Convention on the Rights of the Child*.[80]

The public does, of course, have an interest in detaining individuals who are not likely to appear at the immigration proceedings that they are required to attend, but that interest undoubtedly weighs more heavily in favour of detention where the individuals are likely to pose a danger to the public. It is the latter ground that usually justifies long-term detention. Hence, the need to examine the notion of danger to the public.

## B. — The Notion of "Danger to the Public"

Neither the *Immigration Act* nor the case law clearly defines the phrase "danger to the public." Evidently this expression relates to the protection of the health, safety and good order of Canadian society.[81]

In general, the detention of persons who are likely to pose a danger to the public is a detention based on criminal grounds. It is possible for people to be detained because they



---

[76] *Sahin, supra*, note 7, at p. 231. See also *Kidane, Derar v. M.C.I.* (July 11, 1997), no. IMM-2044-96, Jerome (F.C.T.D.).

[77] *Sahin, supra*, note 7; *Halm v. Canada (Minister of Employment and Immigration)*, [1996] 1 F.C. 547 (T.D.).

[78] *Cunningham v. Canada*, [1993] 2 S.C.R. 143 at pp. 151-52.

[79] *Handbook on Procedures and Criteria for Determining Refugee Status*, Office of the United Nations High Commissioner for Refugees, Geneva, January 1988.

[80] *Convention on the Rights of the Child* (CRC), which was adopted by the United Nations General Assembly (Resolution no. 44/25) on November 20, 1989, was signed by Canada on May 28, 1990, was ratified on December 13, 1991 and came into force on January 12, 1992.

[81] Section 3(i) of the *Immigration Act*.

represent a threat to public order and health; however, since such cases are relatively infrequent, these Guidelines deal solely with detention on criminal grounds.

*The following propositions may be made on the basis of existing case law*:

- The meaning to be ascribed to "danger to the public" is that there be a present or future danger to the public;[82]
- It is not unreasonable to draw inferences from a person's criminal record in determining whether that person is likely to be a danger to the public;[83]
- Where a person has been convicted of an offence and has served the related sentence, the conviction alone is not sufficient to support a finding that that person is likely to be a danger to the public;[84] and
- The phrase "danger to the public" "must refer to the possibility that a person who has committed a serious crime in the past may seriously be thought to be a potential re-offender."[85]

It follows from these propositions that a person's criminal background is a relevant factor that adjudicators should take into account.

Nevertheless, since they must assess the present and future danger posed by the person, it is incumbent on them to assess the seriousness of the crimes and the likelihood of recidivism. The criminal background is only one of several factors: an adjudicator cannot conclude that a person is likely to be a danger to the public based on this sole, generally insufficient, consideration. This is especially true where the person has been convicted and has served the related sentence in respect of those offences.

Based on the above statements, *the following factors should be weighed when considering whether a person is likely to be a danger to the public*:

1. The seriousness of the offences:
   - their nature[86] (offences against the person vs. offences against property);

---

[82]*Thompson v. Canada (Minister of Citizenship and Immigration)* (1996), 37 Imm. L.R. (2d) 9 (F.C.T.D.); *Bahadori, Amir Hussein v. M.C.I.* (April 25, 1995), no. IMM-4931-94, Wetston (F.C.T.D.).

[83]*McIntosh*, *supra*, note 21.

[84]*Salilar*, *supra*, note 7.

[85]*Williams v. Canada (Minister of Citizenship and Immigration)*, [1997] 2 F.C. 646 at p. 668 (C.A.). In this case, the Court interpreted the phrase "danger to the public" contained in section 70(5) of the *Immigration Act*. It should be noted that the Court was referring to the commission of a crime. Thus, a person who is suspected of having committed a serious offence could be considered to be a person likely to pose a danger to the public. However, in the absence of a conviction, the adjudicator will have to take into account the presumption of innocence guaranteed to the person concerned by the common law and section 11(d) of the Charter. In this case, the person's criminal record is also of relevance and will have to be taken into account by the adjudicator. It should be noted that the Minister's opinion to the effect that the person constitutes a danger to the public is not binding on an adjudicator. The latter's decision must be based on the adjudicator's own analysis and assessment of the facts of the case. Therefore, it is possible that an adjudicator orders a person's release from detention although the Minister has issued a "danger to the public" opinion.

[86]Because of the changing nature of society's values, it is not always easy to assess the seriousness of offences, based on their nature. For example, it is only in recent years that assaults against a spouse (which constitute offences against the person) have been consid-

- the circumstances in which they were committed; and
- the number of offences, their frequency and the pattern of criminal activity.

2. The likelihood of re-offending:
   - the person's criminal record;
   - association with or membership in a criminal organization;
   - willingness to be rehabilitated[87] and possibility of rehabilitation;[88] and
   - family and community support.[89]

These factors are not exhaustive. Whether a person is a danger to the public depends on a multiplicity of factors and on the weight given to them, depending on the circumstances of the case.

## C. — Alternatives to Detention

Parliament has provided that adjudicators may order the release of a person detained pursuant to the *Immigration Act*, subject to such terms and conditions as they deem appropriate, including the payment of a security deposit or the posting of a performance bond. Given these provisions, together with the basic assumption that detention should be an exceptional measure in Canadian society, *adjudicators should, in all cases, consider whether it would not be appropriate to impose certain conditions to reduce the risk of the person concerned failing to appear for an examination, an inquiry or removal from Canada, or to reduce the risk that such a person may pose to the public.*

It should be noted that while Parliament has conferred broad discretionary powers upon adjudicators in this area, it has not given them a free hand; the conditions imposed by adjudicators must be appropriate in the case before them, depending on whether one or both of the grounds of detention exist. The conditions must be designed to secure the presence of the individual at the required proceedings, and/or to ensure the protection of society.

---

ered to be serious offences. As far as offences against property are concerned, by way of a guide, under the *Corrections and Conditional Release Act*, S.C. 1992, c. 20, an offender may be released after having served one-sixth of the related sentence in respect of a first offence other than an offence against the person (ss. 119.1 and 126.1, amended by the *Act to Amend the Criminal Code (offenders with a high risk of recidivism)*, the *Corrections and Conditional Release Act*, the *Criminal Records Act*, the *Prisons and Reformatories Act* and the *Ministry of the Solicitor General Act*, ss. 21 and 25, which came into force by order on July 3, 1997, (1997) 131 *Can. Gaz.* II, 2286).

[87]In order to determine a person's willingness to be rehabilitated, credibility must be assessed. The person's criminal record, conduct following the commission of the offence, behaviour during incarceration and involvement in therapy or rehabilitation programs are some of the factors that may be taken into account.

[88]Depending on the type of problem involved (violence, alcohol or drug abuse, and so on) certain rehabilitation programs may be available. Naturally, despite the desire for rehabilitation shown by the person, the status in Canada of the individual and the imminence of removal may result in the person being unable to take advantage of such programs.

[89]The presence of family members in Canada, the relationship of the person to those family members and ties with the community, as well as the support available from these sources, are all factors that can decrease the likelihood of re-offending.

Consideration of this question requires, first, that the risk posed by the person in relation to the above two grounds be assessed. Next, it must be determined whether any conditions would reduce this risk. If, because of the risk involved, a person would have to be subject to conditions that would be very difficult to abide by, a detention order might be appropriate. If, on the other hand, the level of risk is acceptable, or would become acceptable under certain conditions that would make it possible to exercise real control over the person following release, then a conditional release should be contemplated.

The conditions will, of course, vary depending on the grounds for the detention and the circumstances of the case. *However, the conditions of release should be stated in clear and precise terms, leaving no room for ambiguity in their interpretation.* It is also important to ensure that the conditions do not conflict with those imposed by another decision-making body.[90]

The *Immigration Act* provides expressly for the payment of a security deposit or the posting of a performance bond. This is a condition that precedes release and is intended to guarantee that the other conditions imposed will be complied with.

Generally, if an adjudicator contemplates a person's release subject to the payment of a security deposit or the posting of a performance bond, it is because the adjudicator is of the opinion that the person could be released and that such a security deposit would reduce the risk of that person's failing to attend the related examination, inquiry or removal proceedings. This does not mean, however, that the release of a person who is likely to pose a danger to the public cannot be contemplated. Where the public interest and the person's right to liberty are in the balance, it goes without saying that a detention, even of short duration, is more easily justified if the person concerned is likely to pose a danger to the public.[91] Nevertheless, if all the relevant factors are considered and weighed, including those listed above under the heading "The Notion of 'Danger to the Public'", it should be possible to gauge the level of risk and to determine whether the terms and conditions — namely, the payment of a security deposit or the posting of a performance bond — would reduce the risk to a level where release would be possible.

*It is incumbent on adjudicators to determine whether it is appropriate to impose conditions, including the payment of a security deposit or the posting of a performance bond.* If the latter conditions are imposed, adjudicators should consider the amount of the security deposit and the form that it should take. The amount should always be based on the risk posed by the person and the constraint that the security deposit would achieve in the circumstances of each particular case. *If a security deposit is not available, all other alternatives to detention should be contemplated.*[92]

At first glance, the payment of a security deposit might appear more constraining, but a performance bond provided by a solvent individual may be just as effective. The *Immigration Act* makes no distinction as to the relative value of each. In fact, the relationship between the guarantor and the detainee can sometimes impose a greater constraint on the latter. When examining this question, therefore, adjudicators should consider the availability of a cash security deposit and the suitability of the guarantor, including the guarantor's ability to pay.

---

[90]For example, conditions imposed by a Justice of the Peace, a court of criminal jurisdiction or — in respect of a stay of execution of a removal order — by the Immigration Appeal Division.

[91]*Sahin*, *supra*, note 7, at p. 232.

[92]Family members, the community and even NGOs may be able to exert such influence on a person as to secure the person's presence at the required immigration proceedings.

On occasion, the parties will have come to an agreement on the conditions of release before the hearing and will submit the agreement to the adjudicator. If the parties' proposal seems reasonable, the adjudicator should endorse it. If, however, the proposed conditions are unusual or seem excessive, the adjudicator should determine whether other conditions are more appropriate, having regard to the nature and degree of risk posed by the person, and the constraining effect such conditions would have on the conduct of the person concerned.

## D. — Evidence and Procedure

### *I. — Evidence*

*In the absence of statutory provisions concerning evidence, two general principles apply when it comes to determining whether a person is to be detained or released:*

1. The balance of probabilities constitutes the applicable standard of evidence.[93]
2. Refusal to accept relevant and available evidence when reviewing the reasons for detention constitutes a breach of the principles of natural justice.[94]

### *II — Procedure*

As regards procedure, the *Immigration Act* merely states the principle that the hearing to review the reasons for a person's detention shall be conducted in public, subject to any rules of the place where a person is detained.[95]

Despite the absence of statutory provisions creating a framework for a review of the reasons for detention, the Adjudication Division has implemented a procedure that conforms to the principles of natural justice.[96]

The legal controversy over whether the principles of natural justice and fairness oblige a quasi-judicial tribunal to give reasons for its decision has not yet been settled.[97] *Never-*

---

[93]*Salilar, supra*, note 7, at pp. 157-58. See also *Smith v. Canada (Minister of Employment and Immigration)*, [1991] 3 F.C. 3 (T.D.). In this case, the Court decided on the reasonable nature of a certificate issued in accordance with section 40.1(1) of the *Immigration Act* and whose effect is to compel the adjudicator to issue a detention order. At p. 29, Cullen J., referring to *R. v. Secretary of State for the Home Department, ex p. Khawaj*, [1984] A.C. 74, stated as follows: "As a liberty interest was at stake in the detention, the immigration officer had to satisfy a civil standard of proof to a high degree of probability that the detained person was an illegal immigrant."

[94]*McIntosh, supra*, note 21. See also *Sahin, supra*, note 7, at p. 234: "It is the adjudicator himself or herself who must determine whether he or she is satisfied that the applicant would not pose a danger to the public. ... The issue is an open one on each detention review and must be decided by the adjudicator each time. The applicant and the respondent are free to bring forward whatever evidence or information is relevant to assist the adjudicator in reviewing a detention."

[95]Section 103(9) of the *Immigration Act*.

[96]The review of the reasons for detention is undertaken at a hearing, in the presence of the person concerned, who is entitled to the services of an interpreter. The person is informed of the purpose and consequences of the hearing, and of the right to be represented by a lawyer. The person concerned can submit evidence and present arguments in favour of release. See also rules 18, 28, 29 and 30 of the *Adjudication Division Rules*.

[97]Where a statutory duty to give reasons exists, the courts ensure that it is strictly enforced. See *Northwestern Utilities Limited v. The City of Edmonton*, [1979] 1 S.C.R. 684

*theless, given the serious impact of the Adjudication Division's decisions on the rights of individuals, particularly in the area of detention, detention review hearings must be recorded and the reasons for decision must be given.*[98]

The reasons must be sufficient and adequate. They should allow the person concerned to understand the grounds on which the adjudicator is ordering detention or its continuation, to decide whether the available recourses against the adjudicator's decision should be exercised and, if applicable, to make the most of the case.[99]

*Consequently, the reasons must show the following*:

1. *the nature of the hearing held*;[100]
2. *the applicable criterion or criteria*;[101]
3. *a summary of the facts*;[102]
4. *an analysis and assessment of the facts*;[103] *and*
5. *the decision.*

In order to respect the principles of natural justice and procedural fairness, the reasons of the adjudicator ordering the detention should be transcribed and distributed to the parties before the next hearing is held, whether an initial or continued detention is involved.

---

and *S.E.P.Q.A. v. Canada (Canadian Human Rights Commission)*, [1989] 2 S.C.R. 879. Where such a duty does not exist, however, the case law diverges: see *Proulx v. Public Service Staff Relations Board et al.*, [1978] 2 F.C. 133 (C.A.); *Canadian Arsenals Limited v. C.L.R.B.*, [1979] 2 F.C. 393 (C.A.); *Kindler v. Canada (Minister of Justice)*, [1991] 2 S.C.R. 779; *Taabea v. Refugee Status Advisory Committee*, [1980] 2 F.C. 316 (T.D.); *Torres v. Canada (Minister of Employment and Immigration)*, [1983] 2 F.C. 81 (C.A.).

[98]*Mensinger v. Canada (Minister of Employment and Immigration)*, [1987] 1 F. C. 59 (T.D.), at p. 72: "It is the facts, the circumstances and the nature of the decision being made which will determine whether a decision-maker is required to give reasons in order to comply with the principles of fairness."; *Cardinal v. Director of Kent Institution*, [1985] 2 S.C.R. 643, at p. 659: "... because of the serious effect of the Director's decision on the appellants, procedural fairness required that he inform them of the reasons for his intended decision ...".

[99]*Mehterian, Pierre Antoine v. M.E.I.* (June 17, 1992), no. A-717-90, Hugessen, MacGuigan, Desjardins (F.C.A.); *Syed, Saqlain Mohyuddin v. M.E.I.* (September 13, 1994), no. IMM-2080-93, Jerome (F.C.T.D.).

[100]Detention ordered by an adjudicator in accordance with ss. 103(3), 103(6), 103(8) or 103.1(5) of the *Immigration Act*. In the case of a review of the decision for detention pursuant to s. 103(6) of the Act, it is important to specify the period of time involved — 48 hours, 7 days or 30 days.

[101](1) The person is likely to pose a danger to the public. (2) The person is not likely to appear for the examination, inquiry or removal. In the case of detention pursuant to s. 103.1(2) or (3) of the *Immigration Act*, the applicable criterion is that set out in s. 103.1(5), namely the question whether reasonable efforts are being made by the Minister to investigate the matter.

[102]Unless an initial review of the reasons for detention is involved, the summary of the facts can be very brief, but new facts must necessarily be mentioned.

[103]Since each review of the reasons for detention is a *de novo* hearing, the analysis and assessment of the facts must be those of the adjudicator who held the hearing.

# Guideline 3 — Child Refugee Claimants Procedural and Evidentiary Issues

### Guidelines Issued by the Chairperson Pursuant to Section 65(3) of the *Immigration Act*

Children, persons under 18 years of age,[104] can make a claim to be a Convention refugee and have that claim determined by the Convention Refugee Determination Division (CRDD) of the Immigration and Refugee Board (IRB). *The Immigration Act* does not set out specific procedures or criteria for dealing with the claims of children different from those applicable to adult refugee claimants, except for the designation of a person to represent the child in CRDD proceedings.[105] The procedures currently being followed by the CRDD for an adult claimant may not always be suitable for a child claimant.

The international community has recognized that refugee children have different requirements from adult refugees when they are seeking refugee status. The United Nations *Convention on the Rights of the Child* (CRC)[106] has recognized the obligation of a government to take measures to ensure that a child seeking refugee status receives appropriate protection.[107] In addition, the United Nations High Commissioner for Refugees (UNHCR) has issued guidelines on the protection and care of refugee children.[108]

There are three broad categories of children who make refugee claims at the IRB. In all three categories, there are procedural and evidentiary issues which affect the child claimant:

1. The *first category* consists of *children who arrive in Canada at the same time as their parents or some time thereafter*. In most cases, the parents also seek refugee

---

[104]For the purpose of these *Guidelines*, "child" refers to any person under the age of 18 who is the subject of proceedings before the CRDD.

Section 69(4) provides special protection to refugee claimants under the age of 18 in the form of a designated representative in proceedings before the CRDD. Section 69(4) of the *Immigration Act*, as enacted by R.S.C. 1985 (4th Supp.), c. 28, s. 18, provides in part as follows:

> Where a person who is the subject of proceedings before the Refugee Division is under eighteen years of age ... the Division shall designate another person to represent that person in the proceedings.
>
> The age of 18 is consistent with the provisions of the *Convention on the Rights of the Child* (hereafter the CRC) which provides in Article 1 that "for the purposes of the present Convention, a child means every human being below the age of eighteen years unless, under the law applicable to the child, majority is attained earlier."

[105]*Ibid.*

[106]The CRC was adopted by the United Nations General Assembly on 20 November 1989. It was signed by Canada on 28 May 1990 and ratified on 13 December 1991, and came into force on 12 January 1992.

[107]See Article 22 of the CRC:

> State Parties shall take appropriate measures to ensure that a child who is seeking refugee status or who is considered a refugee in accordance with applicable international or domestic law and procedures shall, whether unaccompanied or accompanied by his or her parents or by any other person, receive appropriate protection ...

[108]"*Refugee Children — Guidelines on Protection and Care*", UNHCR, Geneva 1994.

status. In these situations, the child should be considered an "accompanied" child. If the child arrives at the same time as the parents, then his or her claim is usually heard jointly[109] with the parents but a separate refugee determination is made.

2. The *second category* consists of *children who arrive in Canada with, or are being looked after in Canada by, persons who purport to be members of the child's family.* If the CRDD is satisfied that these persons are related to the child, then the child should be considered an "accompanied" child. If the CRDD is not satisfied as to the family relationship, then the child should be considered an "unaccompanied" child.

3. The *third category* consists of *children who are alone in Canada without their parents or anyone who purports to be a family member.* For example, an older child may be living on his or her own or a child may be in the care of a friend of the child's family. These children should be considered "unaccompanied".

These *Guidelines* will address the specific procedural issue of the designation of a representative and the more general procedural issue of the steps to be followed in processing claims by unaccompanied children. The *Guidelines* will also address the evidentiary issues of eliciting evidence in a child's claim and assessing that evidence.

## A. — Procedural Issues

### *I. — General Principle*

*In determining the procedure to be followed when considering the refugee claim of a child, the CRDD should give primary consideration to the "best interests of the child".*

The "best interests of the child" principle has been recognized by the international community as a fundamental human right of a child.[110] In the context of these Guidelines, this right applies to the process to be followed by the CRDD. *The question to be asked when determining the appropriate process for the claim of a child is "what procedure is in the best interests of this child?"* With respect to the merits of the child's claim, all of the elements of the Convention refugee definition must be satisfied.[111]

The phrase "best interests of the child" is a broad term and the interpretation to be given to it will depend on the circumstances of each case. There are many factors which may

---

[109]Rule 10(2) of the *Convention Refugee Determination Division Rules*, SOR/93-45. These Rules also provide for claims to be heard separately if a joined hearing is likely to cause an injustice.

[110]See Article 3(1) of the CRC:

> In all actions concerning children, whether undertaken by public or private social welfare institutions, courts of law, administrative authorities or legislative bodies, the best interests of the child shall be a primary consideration.
>
> See also UNHCR Executive Committee Conclusion XXXVIII "Refugee Children", 1987:
>
>> The Executive Committee ... [s]tressed that all action taken on behalf of refugee children must be guided by the principle of the best interests of the child ...

[111]In determining the child's fear of persecution, the international human rights instruments, such as the *Universal Declaration of Human Rights*, the *International Covenant on Civil and Political Rights*, the *International Covenant on Economic, Social and Cultural Rights* and the *Convention on the Rights of the Child*, should be considered in determining whether the harm which the child fears amounts to persecution.

affect the best interests of the child, such as the age, gender,[112] cultural background and past experiences of the child, and this multitude of factors makes a precise definition of the "best interests" principle difficult.[113]

### *II. — Designated Representative*

The *Immigration Act* requires[114] the designation of a representative for all child claimants. In cases where the child is accompanied by his or her parents, one of the parents is usually appointed as the designated representative of the child. This designation applies to *all* the "proceedings" of the refugee claim and not only to the hearing of the claim. The role of the designated representative is not the same as that of legal counsel.[115] In addition to the designated representative, the child has a right to be represented by legal or other counsel.[116]

There are certain *mandatory criteria* to apply when designating a representative:

- the person must be over 18 years of age;
- the person must have an appreciation of the nature of the proceedings;
- the person must not be in a conflict of interest situation with the child claimant such that the person must not act at the expense of the child's best interests;
- the person must be willing and able to fulfill the duties of a representative and to act in the "best interests of the child".

In addition, the linguistic and cultural background, age, gender and other personal characteristics of the designated representative are factors to consider.

The *duties* of the designated representative are as follows:

- to retain counsel:
- to instruct counsel or to assist the child in instructing counsel;

---

[112]For female child refugee claimants, reference can also be made to the Chairperson's *Guidelines on Women Refugee Claimants Fearing Gender-Related Persecution*, Immigration and Refugee Board, Ottawa, Canada, March 9, 1993.

[113]Madame Justice McLachlin of the Supreme Court of Canada, in *Gordon v. Goertz* (May 2, 1996), no. 24622, Lamer, LaForest, L'Heureux-Dubé, Sopinka, Gonthier, Cory, McLachlin, Iacobucci, Major (S.C.C.), had occasion to discuss the interpretation to be given to the phrase "best interests of the child" and the difficulty with giving the phrase a concrete definition:

> The best interests of the child test has been characterized as "indeterminate" and "more useful as legal aspiration than as legal analysis"... The multitude of factors that may impinge on the child's best interest make a measure of indeterminacy inevitable. A more precise test would risk sacrificing the child's best interest to expediency and certainty.

[114]See *endnote 1*.

[115]Although legal counsel for the claimant may also be appointed as the designated representative, the roles of the two are distinct.

[116]Section 69(1) of the *Immigration Act*, as enacted by R.S.C. 1985 (4th Supp.), c. 28, s. 18, provides as follows:

> In any proceedings before the Refugee Division ... the person who is the subject of the proceedings may, at that person's own expense, be represented by a barrister or solicitor or other counsel.

- to make other decisions with respect to the proceedings or to help the child make those decisions;
- to inform the child about the various stages and proceedings of the claim;
- to assist in obtaining evidence in support of the claim;
- to provide evidence and be a witness in the claim;
- to act in the best interests of the child.

Before designating a person as a representative for the child, the CRDD panel should inform the proposed designated representative of his or her duties and should make an assessment of the person's ability to fulfill those duties.

There may be situations where the person who was designated to be the representative ceases to be an appropriate representative of the child. For example, the person may prove unwilling or unable to make themselves available for pre-hearing conferences. In these situations, the CRDD should remove the person as designated representative[117] and designate another appropriate representative.

## III. — Processing Claims of Unaccompanied Children

The fact that children claiming refugee status can be unaccompanied raises many unique concerns with respect to the processing of their claims. The UNHCR has recognized that this group of refugees, due to their age and the fact that they are unaccompanied, warrant special attention in the process of determining their claims to refugee status.[118]

The "best interests of the child" should be given primary consideration at all stages of the processing of these claims. This principle is reflected in the following procedures:

> 1. *Claims of unaccompanied children should be identified as soon as possible by Registry staff after referral to the CRDD.* The name of the child and any other relevant information should be referred to the provincial authorities responsible for child protection issues, if this has not already been done by Citizenship and Immigration Canada (CIC).[119] After referral, all notices of hearings and pre-hearing conferences should be forwarded to the provincial authority.
>
> 2. *The CRDD panel and Refugee Claim Officer (RCO) should be immediately assigned to the claim and, to the extent possible, the same individuals should retain responsibility for the claim until completion.* It may also be necessary in some cases to assign an interpreter to the claim as early as possible so that the child can develop

---

[117]Section 69(1) of the *Immigration Act*, as enacted by R.S.C. 1985 (4th Supp.), c. 28, s. 18, provides as follows:

> In any proceedings before the Refugee Division ... the person who is the subject of the proceedings may, at that person's own expense, be represented by a barrister or solicitor or other counsel.

[118]UNHCR Executive Committee Conclusion XXXVIII "Refugee Children", 1987:

> The Executive Committee ... underlined the special situation of unaccompanied children and children separated from their parents, who are in the care of other families, including their needs as regards determination of their status ...

[119]An unaccompanied child claimant is by virtue of that status a child who may be at risk and the authority responsible for children at risk should be notified. Because CRDD proceedings are held in camera and disclosing information about the refugee claim of the child would involve releasing private information, the provisions of the *Privacy Act* (S.C. 1980-81-82-83, c. 111, Sch. II "1") must be complied with.

a relationship of trust with the interpreter.[120] Before the panel, RCO and interpreter are assigned, consideration should be given to their experience in dealing with the claims of children.[121]

3. *The claim should be given scheduling and processing priority*[122] *because it is generally in the best interests of the child to have the claim processed as expeditiously as possible.* There may be circumstances, however, where in the best interests of the child the claim should be delayed. For example, if the child is having a great deal of difficulty adjusting to Canada, he or she may need more time before coming to the CRDD for a hearing.

4. *A designated representative for the child should be appointed as soon as possible following the assignment of the panel to the claim.* This designation would usually occur at the pre-hearing conference referred to below, but it may be done earlier. CRDD panels should refer to Section II above for guidelines on designating an appropriate representative. In determining whether a proposed representative is willing and able to act in the "best interests of the child", the panel should consider any relevant information received from the provincial authorities responsible for child protection as well as any relevant information from other reliable sources.

5. *A pre-hearing conference should be scheduled within 30 days of the receipt of the Personal Information Form (PIF).* The purposes of the conference would include assigning the designated representative (if this has not already been done), identifying the issues in the claim, identifying the evidence to be presented and determining what evidence the child is able to provide and the best way to elicit that evidence. Information from individuals, such as the designated representative, medical practitioners, social workers, community workers and teachers can be considered when determining what evidence the child is able to provide and the best way to obtain the evidence.

6. *In determining what evidence the child is able to provide and the best way to elicit this evidence, the panel should consider, in addition to any other relevant factors, the following: the age and mental development of the child both at the time of the hearing and at the time of the events about which they might have information; the capacity of the child to recall past events and the time that has elapsed since the events; and the capacity of the child to communicate his or her experiences.*

Other Relevant Legislation

---

[120]An appropriate interpreter is vital to the processing of a refugee claim. It is important that the child trust the interpreter and that the interpreter be right for the child. The cultural and linguistic background, age, gender and other personal characteristics of an interpreter may be factors for consideration in selecting an appropriate interpreter for the child. See "*Working with Unaccompanied Minors in the Community: a family-based approach*", UNHCR, 1994.

[121]In the context of interviewing children in emergency situations, the International Social Service in "*Unaccompanied Children in Emergencies*", J. Williamson, A. Moser, 1987, indicated that persons interviewing unaccompanied children need experience in working with children and an understanding of how refugee situations affect children.

[122]The UNHCR document "*Refugee Children — Guidelines on Protection and Care*", endnote 5 above, provides that "the refugee status determination must be made quickly... Keeping children in limbo regarding their status, hence their security and their future, can be harmful to them." (Page 100.)

## B. — Evidentiary Issues

### I. — Eliciting the Evidence

Whether accompanied or unaccompanied, a child claimant may be called upon to provide evidence through oral testimony about his or her claim.[123] Like an adult claimant, a child claimant also has a right to be heard in regard to his or her refugee claim.[124] An assessment should be made as to what evidence the child is able to provide and the best way to elicit that evidence from the child.

In general, children are not able to present evidence with the same degree of precision as adults with respect to context, timing, importance and details. They may be unable, for example, to provide evidence about the circumstances surrounding their past experiences or their fear of future persecution. In addition, children may manifest their fears differently from adults.

If the panel determines that a child is able to give oral evidence and that the panel needs to hear from the child, the following should be considered:

> 1. *The process which is to be followed should be explained to the child throughout the hearing to the extent possible, taking into account the age of the child.* In particular, the various participants and their roles at the hearing should be explained as well as the purpose of questioning the child and the sequence of questioning (that is, the fact that counsel normally questions first, followed by the RCO and then the panel).
>
> 2. *Before hearing testimony from a child, the panel should determine if the child understands the nature of an oath or affirmation to tell the truth and if the child is able to communicate evidence.*[125] If the child satisfies both of these criteria then he

---

[123]A child refugee claimant has a right to be present at his or her refugee proceedings. Section 69(2) of the *Immigration Act*, as enacted by R.S.C. 1985 (4th Supp.), c. 28, s. 18, provides that:

> (2) Subject to subsections (3) and (3.1), proceedings before the Refugee Division shall be held in the presence of the person who is the subject of the proceedings, wherever practicable ...

[124]Section 69.1(5)(a)(i) of the *Immigration Act*, as enacted by R.S.C. 1985 (4th Supp.), c. 28, s. 18, provides that:

> (5) At the hearing into a person's claim to be a Convention refugee, the Refugee Division
>
> > (a) shall give
> >
> > > (i) the person a reasonable opportunity to present evidence, question witnesses and make representations ...

Further, Article 12 of the CRC provides that:

> 1. State Parties shall assure to the child who is capable of forming his or her own views the right to express those views freely in all matters affecting the child, the view of the child being given due weight in accordance with the age and maturity of the child.
>
> 2. For this purpose, the child shall in particular be provided the opportunity to be heard in any judicial and administrative proceeding affecting the child, either directly, or through a representative or an appropriate body, in a manner consistent with the procedural rules of national law.

[125]In the case of a nine-year-old citizen of Russia (CRDD V93-02093, Brisson, Neuenfeldt, May 4, 1994), the CRDD panel agreed that given the young age of the claimant, she

or she can take an oath or solemn affirmation. A child who does not satisfy these criteria can still provide unsworn testimony. The weight to be given to the unsworn testimony depends on the child's understanding of the obligation to be truthful and his or her ability to communicate evidence.

3. *The environment in which the child testifies should be informal.* It may be appropriate to use an interview-style room rather than a hearing room. It may also be appropriate to have an adult whom the child trusts present when the child is providing information about his or her claim. This person may or may not be the designated representative.[126]

4. *Questioning of a child should be done in a sensitive manner and should take into account the type of evidence the child may be able to provide.* Children may not know the specific circumstances that led to their flight from the country of origin and, even if they know the circumstances, they may not know the details of those circumstances.[127] The questions put to a child should be formulated in such a manner that the child will understand the question and be able to answer. Consideration should also be given to choosing the person who is best able to question the child.

5. *Even in an informal environment, some children may find it difficult to testify orally in front of decision-makers.* Where appropriate, the evidence of the child may also be obtained by using videotape evidence or an expert as a liaison between the CRDD and the child. For example, the panel may be able to indicate to a medical expert the questions which the panel would like the child to answer.

6. *The hearing should, if possible, conclude in one sitting. If this is not possible then the earliest possible resumption date should be scheduled.* Notwithstanding the desirability of concluding the hearing in one sitting, a child's possible need for breaks and adjournments should always be taken into consideration.

7. *During the course of the hearing, extensive use may be made of conferences with the hearing participants to resolve issues as they arise.* For example, the panel may hear some testimony on a particular issue from the child and then hold a conference with the hearing participants to determine what further testimony, if any, is required.

In all cases, whether the child provides oral evidence or not, the following alternative or additional evidence may be considered:

- evidence from other family members in Canada or another country;
- evidence from other members of the child's community;
- evidence from medical personnel, teachers, social workers, community workers and others who have dealt with the child;
- documentary evidence of persons similarly situated to the child, or his or her group, and general country conditions.

Other Relevant Legislation

---

would not be asked to swear an oath or make a solemn affirmation. When asked, the child indicated that she understood the necessity of telling the truth during her hearing and added that it was "not nice" to tell a lie. The CRDD found her evidence to be truthful.

[126]The UNHCR document "*Refugee Children — Guidelines on Protection and Care*", endnote 5 above, states that arrangements should be made "to have a trusted adult accompany the child during the interviewing process, either a family member of the child, a friend or an appointed independent person." (Page 102.)

[127]As stated by the CRDD in T92-09383, Wolpert, Hunt, May 4, 1993, "[a] child might well not 'know' certain things: he is not privy to an adult's world."

### *II. — Assessing the Evidence*

The CRDD is not bound by the technical rules of evidence and may base its determination on any evidence it considers credible or trustworthy in the circumstances of the case. When assessing the evidence presented in support of the refugee claim of a child, the panel should take note of the following:

1. If the child has given oral testimony, then the weight to be given to the testimony must be assessed. In determining the weight to be given, the panel should consider the opportunity the child had for observation, the capacity of the child to observe accurately and to express what he or she has observed, and the ability of the child to remember the facts as observed. These factors may be influenced by the age, gender[128] and cultural background of the child as well as other factors such as fear, memory difficulties, post-traumatic stress disorder and the child's perception of the process at the CRDD.[129]

2. A child claimant may not be able to express a subjective fear of persecution in the same manner as an adult claimant. Therefore, it may be necessary to put more weight on the objective rather than the subjective elements of the claim.[130] The Federal Court of Canada (Appeal Division) has said the following on this issue:

> ... I am loath to believe that a refugee status claim could be dismissed solely on the ground that as the claimant is a young child ... he or she was incapable of experiencing fear the reasons for which clearly exist in objective terms.[131]

3. When assessing the evidence presented in the claim of a child refugee claimant, the panel may encounter gaps in the evidence. For example: a child may indicate that men in uniforms came to the house but not know what type of uniforms they were wearing or a child may not know the political views of his or her family. The

---

[128]See endnote 9.

[129]With respect to the assessment of evidence of a child claimant, the CRDD panel in V92-00501, Burdett, Brisco, April, 1993, said as follows:

> I agree that a claimant who is a child may have some difficulty recounting the events which have led him or her to flee their country. Often the child claimant's parents will not have shared distressing events with the claimant, with the intention of protecting the child. As a result, the child claimant, in testifying at his or her refugee hearing, may appear to be vague and uninformed about important events which have led up to acts of persecution. Before a trier of fact concludes that a child claimant is not credible, the child's sources of knowledge, his or her maturity, and intelligence must be assessed. The severity of the persecution alleged must be considered and whether past events have traumatized the child and hindered his or her ability to recount details.

[130]The UNHCR document "*Refugee Children — Guidelines on Protection and Care*", endnote 5 above, provides that where a child is not mature enough to establish a well-founded fear of persecution in the same way as an adult "it is necessary to examine in more detail objective factors, such as the characteristics of the group the child left with[,] the situation prevailing in the country of origin and the circumstances of family members, inside or outside the country of origin." (Page 100 - 101.) The same point is made in the UNHCR *Handbook on Procedures and Criteria for Determining Refugee Status* (Geneva, January 1979) which states in paragraph 217 that "it may be necessary to have a greater regard to certain objective factors."

[131]*Yusuf v. M.E.I.*, [1992] 1 F.C. 629, per Hugessen, J.A.

child may, due to age, gender, cultural background or other circumstances, be unable to present evidence concerning every fact in support of the claim. In these situations, the panel should consider whether it is able to infer the details of the claim from the evidence presented.

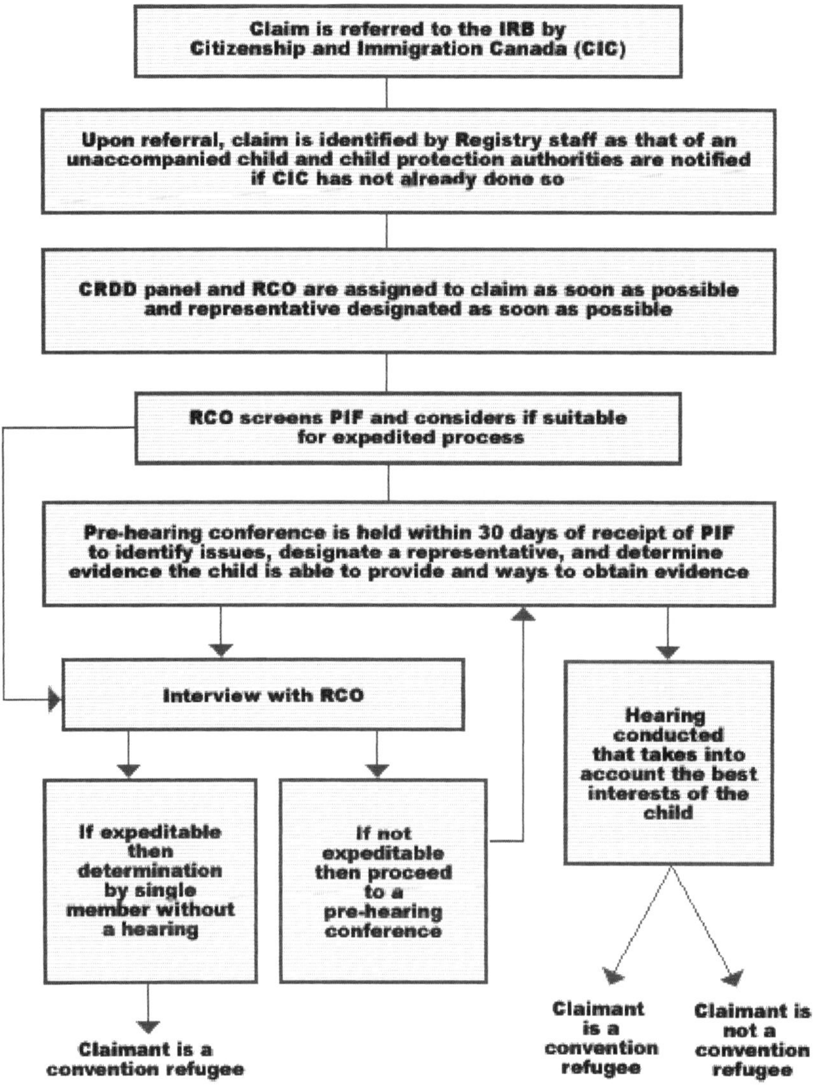

# Guideline 4 — Women Refugee Claimants Fearing Gender-Related Persecution

## Guidelines Issued by the Chairperson Pursuant to Section 65(3) of the *Immigration Act*

### Update

The definition of a Convention refugee in the *Immigration Act* does not include *gender* as an independent enumerated ground for a well-founded fear of persecution warranting the recognition of Convention refugee status. As a developing area of the law, it has been more widely recognized that gender-related persecution is a *form* of persecution which can and should be assessed by the Refugee Division panel hearing the claim. Where a woman claims to have a gender-related fear of persecution, the central issue is thus the need to determine the *linkage* between gender, the feared persecution and one or more of the definition grounds.

*Most gender-related refugee claims brought forward by women raise four critical issues which these Guidelines seek to address*:

1. To what extent can women making a gender-related claim of fear of persecution successfully rely on any one, or a combination, of the five enumerated grounds of the Convention refugee definition?

2. Under what circumstances does sexual violence, or a threat thereof, or any other prejudicial treatment of women constitute persecution as that term is jurisprudentially understood?

3. What are the key evidentiary elements which decision-makers have to look at when considering a gender-related claim?

4. What special problems do women face when called upon to state their claim at refugee determination hearings, particularly when they have had experiences that are difficult and often humiliating to speak about?

### A. — Determining the Nature and the Grounds of the Persecution

Obviously, not all claims brought forward by women are specifically gender-related. Women frequently claim fear of persecution in common with their male fellow citizens, though not necessarily of the same nature or at the same level of vulnerability, for such reasons as belonging to an ethnic or a linguistic minority, or membership in a political movement, a trade union or a religious denomination.

#### *I. — General Proposition*

*Although gender is not specifically enumerated as one of the grounds for establishing Convention refugee status, the definition of Convention refugee may properly be interpreted as providing protection for women who demonstrate a well-founded fear of gender-related persecution by reason of any one, or a combination of, the enumerated grounds.*

Before determining the appropriate ground(s) applicable to the claim, decision-makers must first identify the *nature* of the persecution feared by the claimant.

Generally speaking, women refugee claimants may be put into four broad categories, although these categories are not mutually exclusive or exhaustive:[132]

1. *Women who fear persecution on the same Convention grounds, and in similar circumstances, as men. That is, the risk factor is not their sexual status, per se, but rather their particular identity (i.e. racial, national or social) or what they believe in, or are perceived to believe in (i.e. religion or political opinion).* In such claims, the substantive analysis does not vary as a function of the person's gender, although the nature of the harm feared and procedural issues at the hearing may vary as a function of the claimant's gender.

2. *Women who fear persecution solely for reasons pertaining to kinship, i.e. because of the status, activities or views of their spouses, parents, and siblings, or other family members.* Such cases of *"persecution of kin"* typically involve violence or other forms of harassment against women, who are not themselves accused of any antagonistic views or political convictions, in order to pressure them into revealing information about the whereabouts or the political activities of their family members. Women may also have political opinions imputed to them based on the activities of members of their family.

3. *Women who fear persecution resulting from certain circumstances of severe discrimination on grounds of gender or acts of violence either by public authorities or at the hands of private citizens from whose actions the state is unwilling or unable to adequately protect the concerned persons.* In the refugee law context, such discrimination may amount to persecution if it leads to consequences of a substantially prejudicial nature for the claimant and if it is imposed on account of any one, or a combination, of the statutory grounds for persecution. The acts of violence which a woman may fear include violence inflicted in situations of *domestic violence*[133] and situations of *civil war.*[134]

---

[132] See generally M. Meyer, "Oppression of Women and Refugee Status", in *Proceedings of the International Seminar on Refugee Women* (Amsterdam: Dutch Refugee Council, 1985) at pp. 30–33, and A.B. Johnsson, "The International Protection of Women Refugees — A Summary of Principal Problems and Issues" (1989) 1 *International Journal of Refugee Law* 221, at pp. 223-224, for a more detailed discussion of the different categories of women refugee claimants. Similar categories have been used in the Amnesty International report, *Women in the Front Line: Human Rights Violations Against Women* (New York: Amnesty International Publications, 1991) at pp. 1–3, in enumerating human rights violations against women.

[133] In this context, domestic violence is meant to include violence perpetrated against women by family members or other persons with whom the woman lives.

[134] See C. Niarchos, "Women, War and Rape: Challenges Facing the International Tribunal for the Former Yugoslavia" (1995) 17 *Human Rights Quarterly* 649. With respect to the former Yugoslavia,

> At several levels, the rapes reflect the policy of "ethnic cleansing", rape is used as a means to terrorize and displace the local population, to force the birth of children of mixed "ethnic" descent in the group, and to demoralize and destroy. The rapes are also an expression of misogyny: women are targeted not simply because they are the "enemy" but also because they are women. Gender is essential to the method of assault. (at p. 658)

The author concludes that "Women's suffering in war is specifically related to gender — women are raped, forced into prostitution, forcibly impregnated." (at p. 689)

4. *Women who fear persecution as the consequence of failing to conform to, or for transgressing, certain gender-discriminating religious or customary laws and practices in their country of origin.* Such laws and practices, by singling out women and placing them in a more vulnerable position than men, may create conditions for the existence of a *gender-defined social group*. The religious precepts, social traditions or cultural norms which women may be accused of violating can range from choosing their own spouses instead of accepting an arranged marriage, to such matters as the wearing of make-up, the visibility or length of hair, or the type of clothing a woman chooses to wear.

## II. — Grounds Other Than Membership in a Particular Social Group

*Race*:

There may be cases where a woman claims a fear of persecution because of her race and her gender. For example, a woman from a minority race in her country may be persecuted not only for her race, but also for her gender.

*Religion*:

A woman who, in a theocracy for example, chooses not to subscribe to or follow the precepts of a state religion may be at risk of persecution for reasons of religion. In the context of the Convention refugee definition, the notion of religion may encompass, among other freedoms, the freedom to hold a belief system of one's choice or *not to hold* a particular belief system and the freedom to practise a religion of one's choice or *not to practise* a prescribed religion. In certain states, the religion assigns certain roles to women; if a woman does not fulfill her assigned role and is punished for that, she may have a well-founded fear of persecution for reasons of religion. A woman may also be perceived as expressing a political view (and have a political opinion imputed to her) because of her attitude and/or behaviour towards religion.

*Nationality*:

A gender-related claim of fear of persecution may be linked to reasons of nationality in situations where a national law causes a woman to lose her nationality (i.e. citizenship) because of marriage to a foreign national. What would constitute good grounds for fearing persecution is not the fact of losing her nationality as such (notwithstanding that such laws are discriminatory to the extent that they do not apply to men married to foreign nationals), but the consequences she may suffer as a result.[135]

*Political Opinion*:

A woman who opposes institutionalized discrimination against women, or expresses views of independence from male social/cultural dominance in her society, may be found to fear persecution by reason of her *actual political opinion or a political opinion imputed to her (i.e. she is perceived by the agent of persecu-*

---

See also the Chairperson's *Guidelines on Civilian Non-Combatants Fearing Persecution in Civil War Situations*, Immigration and Refugee Board, Ottawa, Canada, March 7, 1996.

[135]A separate issue to be determined is whether the woman concerned has acquired her spouse's nationality, thereby enabling her to avail herself of the protection of that country.

*tion to be expressing politically antagonistic views).* Two considerations are of paramount importance when interpreting the notion of "political opinion":

1. In a society where women are "assigned" a *subordinate status* and the authority exercised by men over women results in a general oppression of women, their political protest and activism do not always manifest themselves in the same way as those of men.[136]

2. The *political nature* of oppression of women in the context of religious laws and rituals should be recognized. Where tenets of the governing religion in a given country require certain kinds of behaviour exclusively from women, contrary behaviour may be perceived by the authorities as evidence of an unacceptable political opinion that threatens the basic structure from which their political power flows.[137]

### *III. — Membership in a Particular Social Group*

In considering the application of the "membership in a particular social group" ground, decision-makers should refer to the Supreme Court of Canada decision in Ward.[138] *The Ward decision indicated three possible categories of "particular social group":*

*1) groups defined by an innate or unchangeable characteristic;*

*2) groups whose members voluntarily associate for reasons so fundamental to their human dignity that they should not be forced to forsake the association; and*

---

[136]See F. Stairs & L. Pope, "No Place Like Home: Assaulted Migrant Women's Claims to Refugee Status" (1990) 6 *Journal of Law and Social Policy* 148, at p. 163, where the authors assert that, "Where an ostensibly non-political act such as choice of dress is seen to in fact be political in nature, it may provide the basis for a claim to refugee status.""

J. Greatbatch, in "The Gender Difference: Feminist Critiques of Refugee Discourse" (1989) 1 *International Journal of Refugee Law* 518, gives examples of how the refusal by Iranian women to conform to the dress code can be viewed as opposition to the Iranian government, thereby constituting a political act. The author also discusses the development of Chilean communal kitchens and co-operative nurseries and the search for missing relatives as examples of how Chilean women demonstrated their resistance to the Pinochet regime.

See also *Shahabaldin, Modjgan v. M.E.I.* (March 2, 1987), IAB V85-6161, MacLeod, Mawani, Singh, where the former Immigration Appeal Board found the claimant to be a Convention refugee on the basis of her political opinion, because she opposed the Iranian laws governing dress.

In CRDD T90-01845, Jackson, Wright (dissenting in part), December 21, 1990, the Refugee Division was of the view that the claimant's opposition to the government's enforcement of the dress laws, "could possibly result in her being persecuted because of political opinion should she be returned to Iran." The panel noted that Iranian women are subject to "extreme discrimination".

[137]See *Namitabar v. M.E.I.*, [1994] 2 F.C. 42 (T.D.). In this case, the Court said that "I consider that in the case at bar the female applicant has demonstrated that her fear of persecution is connected to her political opinion. In a country where the oppression of women is institutionalized any independent point of view or act opposed to the imposition of a clothing code will be seen as a manifestation of opposition to the established theocratic regime."

[138]*Canada (Attorney General) v. Ward*, [1993] 2 S.C.R. 689.

> *3) groups associated by a former voluntary status, unalterable due to its historical permanence.*

The Court gave examples of the three categories as follows:

> The first category would embrace individuals fearing persecution on such bases as *gender*, linguistic background and sexual orientation, while the second would encompass, for example, human rights activists. The third branch is included more because of historical intentions, although it is also relevant to the anti-discrimination influences, in that one's past is an immutable part of the person.

*Depending on the basis of the claim, women refugee claimants may belong to a group defined in any of these categories.*

*A further holding of the Ward decision is that a particular social group cannot be based solely on the common victimization of its members.* A group is not defined *solely* by common victimization if the claimant's fear of persecution is also based on her gender, or on another innate or unchangeable characteristic of the claimant.[139]

### *Family as a particular social group*

There is jurisprudential authority for recognizing claims grounded in familial affiliation (i.e. where kinship is the risk factor) as coming within the ambit of the "membership in a particular social group" category. See, for example, *Al-Busaidy, Talal Ali Said v. M.E.I.*,[140]

> ... the [Immigration and Refugee] Board has committed reviewable error in not giving due effect to the applicant's uncontradicted evidence with respect to his membership in a particular social group, namely, his own immediate family.

---

[139]The Federal Court of Canada has found "women subject to domestic abuse" to be a particular social group in two cases — *Narvaez v. M.C.I.*, [1995] 2 F.C. 55 (T.D.) and *Diluna v. M.E.I.* (1995), 29 Imm. L.R. (2d) 156 (T.D.). The issue which must then be addressed is whether the claimant's fear of persecution is well-founded.

[140](1992), 16 Imm. L.R. (2d) 119 at 121 (F.C.A.).

The former Immigration Appeal Board also considered the family as constituting a "particular social group" in *Astudillo v. M.E.I.* (1979), 31 N.R. 121 (F.C.A.), *Barra-Velasquez, Marie Mabel De La v. M.E.I.* (April 29, 1981), IAB 80-6330, Hlady, Weselak, Howard, and in Zarketa, *Ignacio v. M.E.I.* (February 6, 1985), IAB M81-9776, D. Davey, Suppa, Tisshaw.

Several Refugee Division decisions have also found women to be members of a particular social group, the family. See, for example, CRDD M89-02465, Hebert, Champoux-Ohrt (dissenting), January 4, 1990, and CRDD T89-03943, Kapasi, Jew, July 25, 1990, where a political opinion was imputed to the Somali claimant because of the actions of her brothers. See also CRDD M89-00057, Wills, Gauthier, February 16, 1989, where the Iranian claimant was found to be a member of the social group, "a pro-Shah family", and CRDD M89-00971, Wolfe, Hendricks, June 13, 1989, where the Refugee Division found the Peruvian claimant to be a member of a particular social group, her family. In CRDD M89-01098, Van der Buhs, Lamarche, June 14, 1989, the Sri Lankan claimant was also found to be a refugee because she was a young Tamil in a Tamil family.

In CRDD T89-02313, T89-02314, T89-02315, Teitelbaum (dissenting), Sri-Skanda-Rajah, October 17, 1990, the Refugee Division found that the Guatemalan claimant was found to be a member of the social group, "targeted family". The Refugee Division, in CRDD C90-00299, C90-00300, Lo, Pawa, December 18, 1990, also found a Salvadoran claimant to belong to a particular social group, her husband's family.

### *Gender-defined particular social group*

There is increasing international support for the application of the particular social group ground to the claims of women who allege a fear of persecution solely by reason of their gender. See *Conclusion no. 39 (XXXVI) Refugee Women and International Protection*, 1985, where the Executive Committee of the United Nations High Commissioner for Refugees (UNHCR)...

> (k) Recognized that States, in the exercise of their sovereignty, are free to adopt the interpretation that women asylum-seekers who face harsh or inhuman treatment due to their having transgressed the social mores of the society in which they live may be considered as a "particular social group" within the meaning of Article 1 A(2) of the 1951 United Nations Refugee Convention.[141]

---

[141]In July 1991, the UNHCR Executive Committee released *Guidelines on the Protection of Refugee Women*, EC/SCP/67 (July 22, 1991). These guidelines stress that women,

> ... fearing persecution or severe discrimination on the basis of their gender should be considered a member of a social group for the purposes of determining refugee status. Others may be seen as having made a religious or political statement in transgressing the social norms of their society.

In an *Information Note* submitted by the High Commissioner with the release of the above *Guidelines*, it was noted that "ensuring the protection of refugee women requires compliance not only with the 1951 *Convention* and its 1967 *Protocol*, but also with other relevant international instruments." (at p. 1)

During its 41st session in 1990, the UNHCR Executive Committee stated that severe discrimination experienced by women, prohibited by the *Convention on the Elimination of all Forms of Discrimination Against Women (CEDAW)*, can form the basis for the granting of refugee status. The importance of documentation regarding gender-based persecution and its consequences in the countries of origin of refugee women was discussed. See, in this regard, the UNHCR Executive Committee, *Note on Refugee Women and International Protection*, EC/SCP/59 (August 28, 1990) at p. 5.

The UNHCR has noted repeatedly that refugee women have special needs in the area of protection. See, for example, the discussion at the 41st session in the *Note on Refugee Women and International Protection*, cited above, at pp. 2–4. See also the United Nations General Assembly, Executive Committee of the High Commissioner's Programme, *Report on Refugee Women*, A/AC.96/727 (July 19, 1989) at p. 2.

It is interesting to observe that the European Parliament, as early as 1984, had passed a resolution similar to the 1985 UNHCR Resolution. The European Parliament called upon member states "to apply the UN treaty of 1951, as well as the 1967 Protocol regarding the status of refugees, in accordance with this interpretation." For a discussion of the resolution of the European Parliament, see the *Proceedings of the International Seminar on Refugee Women* (Amsterdam: Dutch Refugee Council, 1985) at p. 33.

In 1984, the Dutch Refugee Council issued the following policy directive:

It is the opinion of the Dutch Refugee Council that persecution for reasons of membership of a particular social group, may also be taken to include persecution because of social position on the basis of sex. This may be especially true in situations where discrimination against women in society, contrary to the rulings of international law, has been institutionalized and where women who oppose this discrimination, or distance themselves from it, are faced with drastic sanctions, either from the authorities themselves, or from their social environment, where the authorities are unwilling or unable to offer protection.

### *Application of the statutory ground*

*In evaluating the "membership in a particular social group" ground for a fear of gender-related persecution, two considerations are necessary:*

1. Most of the gender-specific claims involving fear of persecution for transgressing religious or social norms may be determined on *grounds of religion or political opinion*. Such women may be seen by the governing authorities or private citizens as having made a religious or political statement in transgressing those norms of their society, even though UNHCR *Conclusion no. 39*, above, contemplates the use of "particular social group" as an appropriate ground.

2. *For a woman to establish a well-founded fear of persecution by reason of her membership in a gender-defined particular social group*[142] *under the first category in Ward (i.e. groups defined by an innate or unchangeable characteristic)*:
   - The fact that the particular social group consists of large numbers of the female population in the country concerned is *irrelevant* — race, religion, nationality and political opinion are also characteristics that are shared by large numbers of people.
   - *Gender is an innate characteristic*[143] *and, therefore, women may form a particular social group within the Convention refugee definition*. The relevant assessment is whether the claimant, as a woman, has a well-founded fear of per-

---

[142]Although the former Immigration Appeal Board decided few claims dealing specifically with gender-related persecution, there is one decision that merits discussion. In *Incirciyan, Zeyiye v. M.E.I.* (August 10, 1987), IAB M87-1541X, M87-1248, P. Davey, Cardinal, Angé, an Armenian claimant and her daughter who had been living in Turkey were found to be refugees on the basis of membership in a particular social group "made up of single women living in a Moslem country without the protection of a male relative (father, brother, husband, son)." Since the claimant had requested and had been refused the protection of the Turkish authorities on several occasions, the Board concluded that there was a lack of adequate state protection.

On several occasions, the Refugee Division has found women refugee claimants to have a well-founded fear of persecution by reason of their membership in a particular social group. In CRDD T89-06969, T89-06970, T89-06971, Nicholson, Bajwa, July 17, 1990, the Refugee Division found that the claimant and her two daughters had a well-founded fear of persecution on the basis of their membership in a particular social group, "consisting of women and girls who do not conform to Islamic fundamentalist norms." In CRDD U91-04008, Goldman, Bajwa, December 24, 1991, the Somali claimant was found to be a refugee on the basis of her membership in a particular social group, "young women without male protection." The Refugee Division, in CRDD T89-02248, Maraj, E.R. Smith, April 3, 1990, found the claimant to be a member of the particular social group composed of women who belong to a "women's organization objecting to the treatment of women in Iran."

[143]In the *Ward* decision, the Court described the first of the three possible categories of particular social group as "groups defined by an innate or unchangeable characteristic." The Court held that this category would include individuals fearing persecution on such basis as gender, linguistic background and sexual orientation. In CRDD T93-05935/36, Liebich, Larke, December 31, 1993, the Refugee Division found that a woman who was a divorced mother living under the jurisdiction of Sharia law had a well-founded fear of persecution by reason of her membership in a particular social group of "women." In CRDD T93-12198/12199/12197, Ramirez, McCaffrey, May 10, 1994 (reasons signed July 13, 1994), the panel found that "women" was a particular social group.

secution in her country of nationality by reason of her membership in this group.

- *Particular social groups comprised of sub-groups of women may also be an appropriate finding in a case involving gender-related persecution.* These particular social groups can be identified by reference to factors, in addition to gender, which may also be innate or unchangeable characteristics. Examples of other such characteristics are age, race, marital status and economic status. Thus, for example, there may be sub-groups of women identified as old women, indigenous women, single women or poor women. In determining whether these factors are unchangeable, consideration should be given to the cultural and social context in which the woman lives, as well as to the perception of the agents of persecution and those responsible for providing state protection.
- *Because refugee status is an individual remedy, the fact that a claim is based on social group membership may not be sufficient in and of itself to give rise to refugee status.* The woman will need to show that she has a genuine fear of harm, that one of the grounds of the definition is the reason for the feared harm, that the harm is sufficiently serious to amount to persecution, that there is a reasonable possibility that the feared persecution would occur if she was to return to her country of origin and that she has no reasonable expectation of adequate national protection.

## B. — Assessing the Feared Harm

Claims involving gender-related fear of persecution often fall quite comfortably within one of the five grounds of the Convention refugee definition. The difficulty sometimes lies in establishing whether the various forms of prejudicial treatment or sanctions imposed on women making such claims come within the scope of the concept of "persecution".

### *Considerations*

*The circumstances which give rise to women's fear of persecution are often unique to women.*[144] The existing bank of jurisprudence on the meaning of persecution is based, for the most part, on the experiences of male claimants. Aside from a few cases of rape, the definition has not been widely applied to female-specific experiences, such as infanticide,

Other Relevant Legislation

[144]Several commentators argue that the *Convention* refugee definition,

> ... ignores the persecution that girls and women endure, even die under, for stepping out of the closed circle of social norms; choosing a husband in place of accepting an arranged marriage; undergoing an abortion where it is illegal; becoming politically active in the women's movement. Women are also abandoned or persecuted for being rape victims, bearing illegitimate children or marrying men of different races. See L. Bonnerjea, *Shaming the World: The Needs of Women Refugees* (London: Change, 1985) at p. 6.

> See also Greatbatch, *supra*, footnote 3, at p. 218, and Stairs and Pope, *supra*, footnote 3, at pp. 163-164.

genital mutilation,[145] bride-burning, forced marriage,[146] domestic violence,[147] forced abortion or compulsory sterilization.[148]

The fact that violence, including sexual and domestic violence, against women is universal is *irrelevant* when determining whether rape, and other gender-specific crimes constitute forms of persecution. *The real issues are whether the violence — experienced or feared — is a serious violation of a fundamental human right for a Convention ground*[149]

---

[145]In CRDD T93-12198/12199/12187, Ramirez, McCaffrey, May 10, 1994 (reasons signed July 13, 1994), the Refugee Division concluded that the claimant's right to personal security would be grossly infringed if she were forced to undergo female genital mutilation. The panel found that this was a contravention of Article 3 of the *Universal Declaration of Human Rights and the United Nations Convention on the Rights of the Child*. The Federal Court of Canada in *Annan v. Canada*, [1995] 3 F.C. 25 (T.D.) in considering the case of a woman fearing female genital mutilation stated that Ghana, "according to the documentary evidence, has failed to demonstrate any intention of protecting its female citizens from the horrific torture of excision practised at various places throughout the country."

[146]In *Vidhani v. M.C.I.*, [1995] 3 F.C. 60 (T.D.), the Court held that "women who are forced into marriages against their will have had a basic human right violated."

[147]The CRDD in C93-00433, Wieler, Lazo, December 3, 1993, in dealing with the case of a woman fearing her husband and her family, found that the claimant's fear of "the violent behaviour of her husband condoned by that society, the traditional rituals which include the searing of her body with a heated instrument and the continuing domination and demands causing her to be enslaved" amounted to persecution.

[148]In L. Heise, "Crimes of Gender" (1989) 2 *Worldwatch* 12, the many forms of violence against women are discussed. The author notes that,

> Every day, thousands of women are beaten in their homes by their partners, and thousands more are raped, assaulted and sexually harassed. And, there are the less recognized forms of violence: In Nepal, female babies die from neglect because parents value sons over daughters; in Sudan, girls' genitals are mutilated to ensure virginity until marriage; and in India, young brides are murdered by their husbands when parents fail to provide enough dowry. In all these instances, women are targets of violence because of their sex. This is not random violence; the risk factor is being female.
>
> With respect to compulsory or forced sterilization, the Federal Court of Canada in *Cheung v. M.E.I.*, [1993] 2 F.C. 314 (C.A.) held that "The forced sterilization of women is a fundamental violation of basic human rights. It violates Articles 3 and 5 of the United Nations Universal Declaration of Human Rights... The forced sterilization of a woman is a serious and totally unacceptable violation of her security of the person. Forced sterilization subjects a woman to cruel, inhuman and degrading treatment."

[149]When considering whether sexual violence or domestic violence (both of which may involve mental and physical suffering) are forms of torture or cruel, inhuman and degrading treatment amounting to persecution, decision-makers should examine th UN *Convention Against Torture and Other Cruel, Inhuman and Degrading Treatment and Punishment*. This Convention which, like the 1951 Refugee Convention, incorporates the principle of non-refoulement, defines "torture" as:

> ... any act by which severe pain or suffering, whether physical or mental, is intentionally inflicted on a person for such purposes as obtaining from [her] or a third person information or a confession, punishing [her] for an act [she] or a third

*and in what circumstances can the risk of that violence be said to result from a failure of state protection.*[150]

The social, cultural, traditional and religious norms and the laws affecting women in the claimant's country of origin ought to be assessed *by reference to human rights instruments which provide a framework of international standards for recognizing the protection needs of women.* What constitutes permissible conduct by the agent of persecution towards women may be determined, therefore, by reference to international instruments such as:

*Universal Declaration of Human Rights*
*International Covenant on Civil and Political Rights*
*International Covenant on Economic, Social and Cultural Rights*

---

person has committed or is suspected of having committed, or intimidating or coercing [her] or a third person, or for any reason based on discrimination of any kind, when such pain or suffering is inflicted by or at the instigation of or with the consent or acquiescence of a public official or other person acting in an official capacity. It does not include pain or suffering arising only from, inherent in or incidental to lawful sanctions. (Article 1)

Reference should also be made to Article 16 as it relates to "... other acts of cruel, inhuman or degrading treatment or punishment which do not amount to torture as defined in Article 1 ...".

[150]In their influential study, *Sexual Violence Against Refugee Women* (The Hague, Ministry for Social Affairs, 1984) at pp. 6 & 7, C.E.J. de Neef & S.J. de Ruiter document the manner in which sexual violence "may have played a role in the flight from the country of origin in any of a variety of ways:

1. It may have been part of the way in which the persecution based on her political conviction was expressed; (When a woman has been imprisoned in the country of origin she may have suffered sexual violence. Both for men and women in a number of countries sexual violence is an integral part of the methods of torture.)

2. It may be that a woman by not conforming to the cultural traditions in the country of origin which prescribe a certain behaviour for women is fearful to be subjected to violence. (An example of this type of violence is decapitating or stoning women who have committed adultery in some Islamic cultures.)

3. It may be that through the threat of, or through actual sexual violence against women, conflicts between different political or religious groups are decided. (... Sexual violence against women here can be a means to hurt an entire group and to reinforce the superiority of the one group over the other.)

4. It may be that women who have fled because of conditions of war or of a reign of terror ... are a victim of sexual violence because they are exceptionally vulnerable when they are deprived of the men's traditional protection and have lost their status of wife."

The Dutch Refugee Council publication, *Sexual Violence: You Have Hardly Any Future Left* (Amsterdam: Dutch Refugee Council, 1987), contains a excellent discussion of the meaning and forms of sexual violence. Excerpts from this publication form part of the documentation for the workshop, "Socio-cultural Context to Refugee Claims made by Women — Case Studies: Iran, Somalia and Latin America," organized by the Toronto I CRDD Working Group on Women Refugee Claimants, Toronto, June 21, 1990. The documentation is available in the Board's regional Documentation Centres.

*Convention on the Elimination of All Forms of Discrimination Against Women*[151]
*Convention on the Political Rights of Women*
*Convention on the Nationality of Married Women*
*Convention Against Torture and other Cruel, Inhuman or Degrading Treatment or Punishment*
*Declaration on the Elimination of Violence Against Women*[152]

A woman's claim to Convention refugee status *cannot be based solely on the fact that she is subject to a national policy or law to which she objects.* The claimant will need to establish that:

(a) the policy or law is inherently persecutory; or

(b) the policy or law is used as a means of persecution for one of the enumerated reasons; or

(c) the policy or law, although having legitimate goals, is administered through persecutory means; or

---

[151]During its 41st session in 1990, the UNHCR Executive Committee stated that severe discrimination experienced by women and prohibited by *Convention on the Elimination of All Forms of Discrimination Against Women (CEDAW)* can form the basis for the granting of refugee status. The importance of documentation regarding gender-based persecution and its consequences in the countries of origin of refugee women was discussed. See, in this regard, the UNHCR Executive Committee, *Note on Refugee Women and International Protection*, EC/SCP/59 (August 28, 1990) at p. 5.

The Refugee Division in T91-01497, T91-01498, Ramirez, Toth, August 9, 1994 (reasons signed November 1, 1994), referred to the *Convention on the Elimination of All Forms of Discrimination Against Women* in finding that the claimants, from Bulgaria, had a well-founded fear of persecution. The adult claimant had been subjected to spousal abuse throughout her marriage in the form of battering, threats of death, and rape. The panel held that despite Bulgaria's signing of the above Convention, the authorities had repeatedly ignored the violence against the adult claimant. The panel also referred to several other international human rights instruments and to the IRB's *Guidelines* on women refugee claimants, and held that the adult claimant had "an internationally protected right to protection from domestic violence and failure to give that protection is a form of gender-based discrimination."

[152]The *Declaration on the Elimination of Violence Against Women* provides in Article 2 that

> Violence against women shall be understood to encompass, but not be limited to, the following:
>
> (a) Physical, sexual and psychological violence occurring in the family, including battering, sexual abuse of female children in the household, dowry-related violence, marital rape, female genital mutilation and other traditional practices harmful to women, non-spousal violence and violence related to exploitation;
>
> (b) Physical, sexual and psychological violence occurring within the general community, including rape, sexual abuse, sexual harassment and intimidation at work, in educational institutions and elsewhere;
>
> (c) Physical, sexual and psychological violence perpetrated or condoned by the State, wherever it occurs.

(d) the penalty for non-compliance with the policy or law is disproportionately severe.[153]

## C. — Evidentiary Matters

When an assessment of a woman's claim of gender-related fear of persecution is made, the evidence must show that what the claimant genuinely fears is persecution for a Convention reason as distinguished from random violence or random criminal activity perpetrated against her as an individual. The central factor in such an assessment is, of course, the claimant's particular circumstances in relation to both the general human rights record of her country of origin and the experiences of other similarly situated women. Evaluation of the weight and credibility of the claimant's evidence ought to include evaluation of the following considerations, among others:

1. *A gender-related claim cannot be rejected simply because the claimant comes from a country where women face generalized oppression and violence and the claimant's fear of persecution is not identifiable to her on the basis of an individualized set of facts.* This so-called "particularized evidence rule" was rejected by the Federal Court of Appeal in *Salibian v. M.E.I.*,[154] and other decisions.

2. *Decision-makers should consider evidence indicating a failure of state protection if the state or its agents in the claimant's country of origin are unwilling or unable to provide adequate protection from gender-related persecution.*[155] If the claimant can demonstrate that it was objectively unreasonable for her to seek the protection of her state, then her failure to approach the state for protection will not defeat her claim. Also, the fact that the claimant did or did not seek protection from non-government groups is irrelevant to the assessment of the availability of state protection.[156]

---

[153] In *Fathi-Rad, Farideh v. S.S.C.*. (April 13, 1994), no. IMM-2438-93, McGillis (F.C.T.D.), the Court had to deal with the issue of whether the Islamic dress code is a policy of general application applied to all citizens of Iran. In the Court's view, "The Islamic dress code is a law applicable only to women in Iran. It dictates the manner in which Iranian women must dress to comply with the religious beliefs of the theocratic governing regime and prescribes punishments for any violation of the law. A law which specifically targets the manner in which women dress may not properly be characterized as a law of general application which applies to all citizens." In the alternative, the Court concluded that the punishment for minor infractions of the Islamic dress code was disproportionate to the objective of the law and, therefore, constituted persecution. Since the decision in *Fathi-Rad*, the Documentation, Information and Research Branch, IRB, has published a document entitled "Human Rights Brief: Women in the Islamic Republic of Iran", June 1994, which indicates that the dress code in Iran applies equally to men and women.

[154] [1990] 3 F.C. 250 at 258 (C.A.).

[155] The Supreme Court of Canada in *Ward* held that except in situations where the state is in a condition of complete breakdown, states must be presumed capable of protecting their citizens. The Court found that this presumption can be rebutted by "clear and convincing" evidence of the state's inability to protect.

[156] It is clear that the claimant's failure to seek protection from non-government groups can have no impact on the assessment of the availability of state protection. In certain circumstances, however, the fact that the claimant did not approach existing non-government organizations in her country of origin may have an impact on her credibility or, more generally, on the well foundedness of her claim.

*When considering whether it is objectively unreasonable* for the claimant not to have sought the protection of the state, *the decision-maker should consider, among other relevant factors, the social, cultural, religious, and economic context in which the claimant finds herself.* If, for example, a woman has suffered gender-related persecution in the form of rape, she may be ostracized from her community for seeking protection from the state. Decision-makers should consider this type of information when determining if the claimant should reasonably have sought state protection.

*In determining whether the state is willing or able to provide protection* to a woman fearing gender-related persecution, *decision-makers should consider the fact that the forms of evidence which the claimant might normally provide as "clear and convincing proof" of state inability to protect, will not always be either available or useful in cases of gender-related persecution.*

For example, where a gender-related claim involves threats of or actual sexual violence at the hands of government authorities (or at the hands of non-state agents of persecution, where the state is either unwilling or unable to protect), the claimant may have difficulty in substantiating her claim with any "statistical data" on the incidence of sexual violence in her country.

In cases where the claimant cannot rely on the more standard or typical forms of evidence as "clear and convincing proof" of failure of state protection, *reference may need to be made to alternative forms of evidence to meet the "clear and convincing" test.* Such alternative forms of evidence might include the testimony of women in similar situations where there was a failure of state protection, or the testimony of the claimant herself regarding past personal incidents where state protection did not materialize.

3. *A change in country circumstances, generally viewed as a positive change, may have no impact, or even a negative impact, on a woman's fear of gender-related persecution.* In situations where a woman's fear is related to personal-status laws or where her human rights are being violated by private citizens, a change in country circumstances may not mean a positive change for the woman, as these areas are often the last to change. An assessment should be made of the claimant's particular fear and of whether the changes are meaningful and effective enough for her fear of gender-related persecution to no longer be well-founded.[157]

4. *In determining the reasonableness of a woman's recourse to an internal flight alternative (IFA), decision-makers should consider the ability of women, because of their gender, to travel safely to the IFA and to stay there without facing undue hardship.*[158] In determining the reasonableness of an IFA, the decision-makers should take into account factors including religious, economic, and cultural factors, and consider whether and how these factors affect women in the IFA.

---

[157]See *Yusuf, Sofia Mohamed v. M.E.I.* (January 9, 1995), no. A-130-92, Hugessen, Strayer, Décary (F.C.A.). See also Legal Services' Commentary on *Change of Circumstances*, IRB Legal Services, September 1994.

[158]See *Thirunavukkarasu v. M.E.I.*, [1994] 1 F.C. 589 at p. 598, where the Court ruled as follows: "The claimant cannot be required to encounter great physical danger or to undergo undue hardship in travelling there or in staying there." See also Legal Services' Commentary "*Internal Flight: When is it an Alternative*?", IRB Legal Services, April 1994.

### D. — Special Problems at Determination Hearings

*Women refugee claimants face special problems in demonstrating that their claims are credible and trustworthy.* Some of the difficulties may arise because of cross-cultural misunderstandings. For example:

1. Women from societies where the preservation of one's virginity or marital dignity is the cultural norm may be reluctant to disclose their experiences of sexual violence in order to keep their "shame" to themselves and not dishonour their family or community.[159]

2. Women from certain cultures where men do not share the details of their political, military or even social activities with their spouses, daughters or mothers may find themselves in a difficult situation when questioned about the experiences of their male relatives.[160]

3. Women refugee claimants who have suffered sexual violence may exhibit a pattern of symptoms referred to as Rape Trauma Syndrome,[161] and may require extremely sensitive handling. Similarly, women who have been subjected to domestic violence may exhibit a pattern of symptoms referred to as Battered Woman Syndrome and may also be reluctant to testify.[162] In some cases it will be appropriate to

---

[159]The UNHCR Executive Committee notes that decision-makers should refrain from asking women refugee claimants for details of sexual abuse. They note that, "the important thing in establishing a well-founded fear of persecution is to establish that some form of it has occurred." *Guidelines on the Protection of Refugee Women*, *supra*, footnote 10, at p. 27.

[160]In two cases in the Federal Court of Canada, the issue of the woman's place within her society and her lack of knowledge about the activities of male family members was addressed. In *Roble v. M.E.I.* (1994), 25 Imm. L.R. (2d) 186 (F.C.T.D.), the Court stated that in Somali culture it is often the case that a wife is not privy to information concerning her husband's occupation. In *Montenegro, Suleyama v. M.C.I.* (February 29, 1996), no. IMM-3173-94, MacKay (F.C.T.D.), the Court faulted the CRDD for ignoring the claimant's explanation that her knowledge of her husband's political involvement in El Salvador was based entirely on what he had been willing to tell her, pointing out that "within their social order wives were not expected to question their husband's activities."

[161]The UNHCR Executive Committee *Guidelines on the Protection of Refugee Women*, *supra*, footnote 10, at p. 27, discuss the symptoms of Rape Trauma Syndrome as including "persistent fear, a loss of self-confidence and self-esteem, difficulty in concentration, an attitude of self-blame, a pervasive feeling of loss of control, and memory loss of distortion."

[162]F. Stairs & L. Pope, supra, footnote 5, at p. 202, stress that decision-makers should be,

> ... sensitive to the fact that women whose children are attached to their claim may also be reticent to describe the details of their persecution in front of their children. Further, if the claimant's culture dictates that she should suffer battering silently, the use of an interpreter from her community may also intimidate her.

For a discussion of the battered woman syndrome see *R. v. Lavallee*, [1990] 1 S.C.R. 852. In *Lavallee*, Madame Justice Wilson addressed the mythology about domestic violence and phrased the myth as "[e]ither she was not as badly beaten as she claims, or she would have left the man long ago. Or, if she was battered that severely, she must have stayed out of some masochistic enjoyment of it." The Court further indicated that a manifestation of the victimization of battered women is a "reluctance to disclose to others the fact or extent of the beatings". In *Lavallee*, the consider whether claimants should be allowed to have the option of providing their testimony outside the hearing room by affidavit or by videotape, or in front of members and refugee claims officers specifically trained in dealing with violence against women. Members should be familiar with the UNHCR Executive Committee *Guidelines on the Protection of Refugee Women.*[163]

## *Framework of Analysis*

1. *Assess the harm feared by the claimant. Does the harm feared constitute persecution?*

(*a*) For the treatment to likely amount to persecution, it must be a serious form of harm which detracts from the claimant's fundamental human rights.

(*b*) To assist decision-makers in determining what kinds of treatment are considered persecution, an objective standard is provided by international human rights instruments. The following instruments, among others, may be considered:

*Universal Declaration of Human Rights,*
*International Covenant on Civil and Political Rights*
*International Covenant on Economic, Social and Cultural Right*
*Convention on the Elimination of All Forms of Discrimination Against Women*
*Convention on the Political Rights of Women,*
*Convention on the Nationality of Married Women*
*Convention Against Torture and other Cruel, Inhuman or*
*Degrading Treatment or Punishment*
*Declaration on the Elimination of Violence Against Women*

2. *Ascertain whether the claimant's fear of persecution is based on any of the grounds, singly or in combination, enumerated in the Convention refugee definition. Considerations*:

- It is necessary to ascertain the characteristic of the claimant which places her or members of her group at risk, and to ascertain the linkage of that characteristic to a Convention ground.
- Gender is an innate characteristic and it may form a particular social group.
- A subgroup of women may also form a particular social group. Women in these particular social groups have characteristics (possibly innate or unchangeable) additional to gender, which make them fear persecution.
- The gender-defined group cannot be defined solely by the fact that its members share common persecution.

3. *Determine whether the claimant's fear of persecution is well-founded. This includes an assessment of the evidence related to the ability or willingness of the state to protect the claimant and, more generally, the objective basis of the claim. Considerations*:

- There may be little or no documentary evidence presented with respect to the inadequacy of state protection as it relates to gender-related persecution. There may be a

---

Court indicated that expert evidence can assist in dispelling these myths and be used to explain why a woman would remain in a battering relationship.

[163]It should be noted that Amnesty International, in *Women in the Front Line: Human Rights Violations Against Women*, *supra*, footnote 1, at p. 54, recommends that:

> In procedures for the determination of refugee status governments should provide interviewers trained to recognize the specific protection needs of women refugee and asylum-seekers.

need for greater reliance on evidence of similarly situated women and the claimant's own experiences.

- The claimant need not have approached non-state organizations for protection.
- Factors including the social, cultural, religious, and economic context in which the claimant finds herself should be considered in determining whether it was objectively unreasonable for the claimant not to have sought state protection.
- Where a woman's fear relates to personal-status laws or where her human rights are being violated by private citizens, an otherwise positive change in country conditions may have no impact, or even a negative impact, on a woman's fear of gender-related persecution.

4. *If required, determine whether there is a possibility of an internal flight alternative. Considerations*:

- Whether there would be undue hardship for the claimant, both in reaching the location of the IFA and in establishing residence there.
- Religious, economic, social and cultural factors, among others, may be relevant in determining the reasonableness of an IFA for a woman fearing gender-related persecution.

## Guideline 5 — Providing the PIF and No PIF Abandonment in the Refugee Protection Division

### Guidelines Issued by the Chairperson Pursuant to Section 159(1)(h) of the *Immigration and Refugee Protection Act*

### Introduction

The Refugee Protection Division (RPD) is the largest division of Canada's largest administrative tribunal, the Immigration and Refugee Board (IRB). Administrative tribunals operate less formally and more expeditiously than courts of law. Accordingly, the *Immigration and Refugee Protection Act (IRPA)* requires the IRB to deal with proceedings before it informally, quickly and fairly.[164] The Chairperson has issued these guidelines because timely and accurate provision of the Personal Information Form (PIF) is necessary for the RPD to carry out its mandate under *IRPA*.

The guidelines apply to most cases heard by the RPD. However, in compelling or exceptional circumstances, the members will use their discretion not to apply some guidelines or to apply them less strictly.

Generally speaking, the RPD will make allowances for unrepresented claimants who are unfamiliar with the Division's processes and rules. Claimants identified as particularly vulnerable will be treated with special sensitivity.

### Time Limit

The PIF must be received by the RPD no later than 28 days after the claimant received it from Citizenship and Immigration Canada.[165] If the RPD does not receive the PIF on time, this may lead to a decision that the claim has been abandoned. The process for

Other Relevant Legislation

[164] *Immigration and Refugee Protection Act*, s. 162(2).

[165] *Refugee Protection Division Rules*, s. 6(1). The 28-day timeframe and the fact that abandonment is a possible consequence of failing to comply is set out in the instructions on the first page of the PIF.

declaring a claim abandoned is set out in the *Refugee Protection Division Rules* (*RPD Rules*).[166]

In normal circumstances 28 days is enough time to provide a PIF. This time limit provides a claimant with a reasonable period to provide information about his or her claim, while also allowing the RPD to operate efficiently. It is expected that this time limit will be followed unless there are exceptional circumstances.

## Extensions of Time to File PIF

1. The claimant may apply to the RPD for an extension of time to provide the PIF.[167] A claimant is expected to act responsibly when seeking an extension of time. This means that the claimant should apply for the extension within the 28-day timeframe. If an extension is requested and not granted, an abandonment hearing will be scheduled automatically as the PIF has not been provided within the 28-day timeframe.[168]

2. A request for an extension of time that is made outside of the 28-day timeframe must be dealt with at the abandonment hearing even if the extension request is filed prior to the abandonment hearing.[169]

3. The fact that a claimant is waiting for an application for legal aid to be approved or has failed to obtain legal aid funding is not, in and of itself, a reason for granting an extension of time to file the PIF.[170]

4. The fact that a claimant has been unable to hire his or her counsel of choice is not, in and of itself, a reason for granting an extension of time to file the PIF. The claimant is expected to retain counsel who is available to assist with PIF completion within the 28-day timeframe set by the RPD.[171]

5. If the claimant has not received a copy of the Port of Entry notes, this is not a reason for granting an extension of time to file the PIF.

6. The granting of an extension of time to file the PIF is only to occur in exceptional circumstances. The particular circumstances of the claimant must be considered in deciding whether to grant an extension of time or to declare a claim abandoned. Most extensions should not be more than 5 working days as the claimant is expected to act even more responsibly once the 28-day timeframe set by the RPD has passed.

7. Where an extension of time to file the PIF is granted by the RPD, the direction to the claimant must include (1) the due date for providing the PIF, and (2) a warning that failure to provide the PIF within the extended timeframe will result in abandonment proceedings being scheduled.

8. Where the PIF is provided after the 28-day timeframe, but before the abandonment hearing, the claimant must still attend the abandonment hearing. The presence of the claimant at the abandonment hearing is necessary so that the claimant can state the reasons why he or she failed to provide the PIF within the 28-day timeframe. This inquiry must take place to ensure that all relevant factors are considered. The fact that the claim-

---

[166]*Immigration and Refugee Protection Act*, s. 168(1); *Refugee Protection Division Rules*, s. 58.

[167]*Refugee Protection Division Rules*, s. 6(2).

[168]*Refugee Protection Division Rules*, s. 58(2); *Commentary* to Rules 5 and 6.

[169]*Commentary* to Rules 5 and 6.

[170]*Shokri, Evette v. M.C.I.* (July 12, 2002), no. IMM-1768-01, Blanchard (F.C.T.D.).

[171]*Pilnitz, Viktor v. M.C.I.* (March 7, 1997), no. IMM-1205-96, Tremblay-Lamer (F.C.T.D.).

ant has provided the PIF by the time this inquiry takes place does not mean that the inquiry is not necessary.

9. When a claimant comes to an abandonment hearing and provides the PIF at the hearing, this is not, in and of itself, a basis for allowing the claim to proceed. The readiness of the claimant to proceed is only one of the factors that must be considered in deciding whether the claim should be declared abandoned. The RPD will consider the explanations given by the claimant and any other relevant information.[172]

# Guideline 6 — Scheduling and Changing the Date or Time of a Proceeding in the Refugee Protection Division

### Guidelines Issued by the Chairperson Pursuant to Section 159(1)(h) of the *Immigration and Refugee Protection Act*

## Introduction

The Refugee Protection Division (RPD) is the largest division of Canada's largest administrative tribunal, the Immigration and Refugee Board (IRB). Administrative tribunals operate less formally and more expeditiously than courts of law. Accordingly, the *Immigration and Refugee Protection Act (IRPA)* requires the IRB to deal with proceedings before it informally, quickly and fairly.[173] The Chairperson has issued these guidelines to explain what the RPD does before and during the hearing to make its proceedings more efficient but still fair. The guidelines also set out what the RPD expects participants to do.

The guidelines apply to most cases heard by the RPD. However, in compelling or exceptional circumstances, the members will use their discretion not to apply some guidelines or to apply them less strictly.

Generally speaking, the RPD will make allowances for unrepresented claimants who are unfamiliar with the Division's processes and rules. Claimants identified as particularly vulnerable will be treated with special sensitivity.

In order to fulfil its mandate, the Refugee Protection Division (RPD) must schedule its hearings so that refugee protection claims are finalized as quickly as possible.

The RPD has the authority to set its own procedures, as long as the principles of natural justice and fairness are followed.[174]

The RPD recognises that a claimant has the right to be represented by counsel.[175] This includes a reasonable opportunity to choose that counsel. However, the choice is not un-

Other Relevant Legislation

[172] *Refugee Protection Division Rules*, s. 58(3). In *Ghassan, Daher v. M.E.I.* (June 22, 1994), no. IMM-2843 93, Denault (F.C.T.D.) the Court held that the very purpose of the abandonment hearing is to allow the person concerned to explain the reasons why he did not abandon the claim. The Court rejected the argument that as long as a claimant produces a PIF at an abandonment hearing this was evidence of intent to proceed with the claim and therefore it was not possible to conclude that the claim had been abandoned.

[173] *Immigration and Refugee Protection Act*, s. 162(2).

[174] *Gorodiskiy, Volodimir v. M.C.I.* (July 7, 1998), no. IMM-3066-97, MacKay (F.C.T.D.); See also: *Siloch, Hancy v. Canada (M.E.I.)* (January 11, 1993), no. A-88-92, 151 N.R. 76 at 78, Stone, Desjardins, Décary (F.C.A.); *Prassad v. M.E.I.*, [1989] 1 S.C.R. 560 at 569.

[175] *Immigration and Refugee Protection Act*, s. 167(1). Representation may be by a barrister or solicitor or other counsel.

limited. Any counsel chosen must be ready and able to appear according to the scheduling requirements of the RPD.[176]

Changes to the time or date for proceedings after the time and date have been set interfere with the RPD's ability to fulfil its obligation to deal with claims quickly and fairly. They result in considerable costs and lost time in the hearing room, and cause more delays in finalizing cases that have already started.

## *1. — Scheduling*

1. The RPD schedules proceedings based on operational requirements and principles of fairness. The RPD does not have to consult counsel on a case-by-case basis as to their availability.

2. The RPD Notice to Appear will advise claimants that they must choose counsel who is available on the hearing date that has been scheduled if they want to be represented at that hearing.

3. Counsels are invited to submit their available dates for scheduling purposes to the RPD in accordance with the directions of the RPD. If Counsel submits available dates then counsel must inform the RPD as soon as possible if counsel is no longer available on those dates. The RPD may also contact counsel for available dates. Although the RPD is not bound by counsel's availability, the RPD tries to accommodate counsel's calendar. However, these attempts cannot interfere with the ability of the RPD to schedule its proceedings efficiently.

4. A claimant who retains counsel after the RPD has scheduled a proceeding is responsible for making sure that their counsel is available on the scheduled date.

5. If counsel represents so many claimants that the Division can not schedule cases efficiently taking counsel's availability into account, the RPD may schedule proceedings on dates when counsel is not available. If this happens then claimants will be notified of the conflict in their counsel's schedule. This provides the claimant with the opportunity to deal with their counsel or to retain new counsel so that the proceeding can take place on the date and time that it is scheduled to proceed.

6. If a date earlier than the scheduled date of a proceeding becomes available, the RPD can proceed with that earlier date if the parties consent.

## *2. — Changing the Date or Time of a Proceeding*

### *2.1 — General Principles*

1. The RPD allows applications to change the date or time of a proceeding only in exceptional circumstances and where such a change is justified. When considering an application, the RPD looks at whether the party making the application has demonstrated good faith and whether the party has made reasonable efforts to proceed as scheduled.[177]

2. All applications to change the date or time of a proceeding are determined on the basis of the evidence and arguments that are made in support of the change. In deciding

---

[176] *Pierre v. Minister of Manpower and Immigration* (April 21, 1978), no. A-936-77, Jackett, Collier, Kelly (F.C.A.); *Aseervatham, Vimalathas v. Minister of Citizenship and Immigration* (June 1, 2000), no. IMM-1091-99, Dubé (F.C.T.D.).

[177] *Yung, Ten Fu v. M.E.I.* (February 24, 1994), no. A-416-92, Stone, Robertson, Craig (F.C.A.).

whether or not to allow such an application, the RPD must take into consideration the factors set out in the *RPD Rules*[178] and reasonable alternatives.

### 2.2 — Specific Cases

3. The RPD must take into account its obligation to deal with proceedings as quickly as possible. Even if it is the first time a party is asking to change the date or time of a proceeding, this is not necessarily sufficient to allow the application. The RPD will consider if the parties have been given notice of the date and time of the proceeding and if the parties have had a reasonable amount of time to prepare for it.

4. The fact that all the parties to the proceedings agree to an application to change the date or time of a proceeding does not, in itself, mean that the application is going to be allowed by the RPD. A party must not expect an application to be allowed simply because the other party also agrees with the application.

5. The RPD makes the effort in each case to provide the parties with reasonable notice of the date and time of a proceeding. Where counsel gets reasonable notice of a hearing date, it is assumed that counsel will be available and prepared to present the client's case at the time and date set by the RPD. Where, for any reason, counsel is unable to appear at a proceeding, counsel is expected to make the necessary arrangements to be replaced by another counsel who is prepared to proceed with the case. If counsel does not appear, the RPD may decide to proceed without counsel, to start abandonment proceedings or to conclude that the claim be abandoned.

6. The RPD informs unrepresented parties of its process in a reasonable period of time before the date that has been set for the proceeding. This includes informing them of the right to be represented by counsel. The RPD expects unrepresented parties to be prepared to present their cases on the date scheduled for the proceeding.

Therefore, where the party was given reasonable notice of the date and time of a proceeding, it will not be a valid reason to allow an application to change the date or time of the proceeding if a claimant has not arranged to have counsel, or if the counsel chosen is not prepared to proceed with the case on the date that has been set by the RPD.[179]

7. The size of counsel's workload or the failure of counsel to manage his schedule appropriately are not valid reasons for allowing an application to change the date or time of a proceeding where reasonable notice was given of the date and time of the hearing.[180] The RPD recognises that there can be unforeseen conflicts that arise in counsel's schedule, such as where the Federal Court sets a date for a proceeding and counsel is also expected to appear before the RPD on that same date. If this happens then it is expected that counsel will advise the RPD as soon as possible about this conflict. Failure to advise the RPD as soon as possible may mean that an application to change the date or time of a proceeding will be denied.

8. If one of the parties claims not to have had enough time to prepare or not to have been able to prepare adequately (for example: waiting for documents), this is not a valid reason to allow an application to change the date or time of a proceeding if the RPD gave the parties reasonable notice of the date and time of a proceeding.

9. The fact that counsel wants to take time off, fulfil other professional duties or attend to personal matters that are neither urgent nor unforeseen are not sufficient reasons to allow



---

[178] *Refugee Protection Division Rules*, s. 48; See *Commentary* to Rule 48.

[179] *Aseervatham*, *supra*, note 4.

[180] *Ibid.*

an application to change the date or time of a proceeding if the RPD gave counsel reasonable notice of the date and time of the proceeding.

10. The fact that a claimant is waiting for an application for legal aid to be approved is not a sufficient reason to allow an application to change the date or time of a proceeding, if the RPD gave reasonable notice of the time and date of the proceeding.[181]

11. The fact that immigration or other proceedings involving the claimant are in progress does not constitute a sufficient reason to allow an application to change the date or time of a proceeding if the RPD gave the claimant and his counsel reasonable notice of the date and time of the proceeding.[182]

12. If a claimant asks for a change of time or date of a proceeding because of illness, the claimant must provide a medical certificate wherever possible; otherwise the RPD may, where it thinks it is appropriate, start abandonment proceedings.

### *2.3 — Procedure*

13. A party who makes an application to change the date or time of a proceeding must do so according to the *RPD Rules*.[183] Where the application is denied before the proceeding or the RPD was not able to communicate its decision to the party before the proceeding, the party and / or their counsel must still appear at the RPD and be prepared to proceed; otherwise the RPD may start abandonment proceedings.

14. If the RPD believes that the party is trying, without valid reason, to delay the proceeding, the RPD may set a peremptory hearing date. The RPD may start abandonment proceedings in all cases where the parties do not appear for a proceeding or otherwise fail to proceed with the case.[184]

## Guideline 7 — Concerning Preparation and Conduct of a Hearing in the Refugee Protection Division

### Guidelines Issued by the Chairperson Pursuant to Section 159(1)(h) of the *Immigration and Refugee Protection Act*

### Introduction

The Refugee Protection Division (RPD) is the largest division of Canada's largest administrative tribunal, the Immigration and Refugee Board (IRB). Administrative tribunals operate less formally and more expeditiously than courts of law. Accordingly, the *Immigration and Refugee Protection Act (IRPA)* requires the IRB to deal with proceedings before it informally, quickly and fairly.[185] The Chairperson has issued these guidelines to explain what the RPD does before and during the hearing to make its proceedings more efficient but still fair. The guidelines also set out what the RPD expects participants to do.

---

[181] *Awogbade, Emeline Karibi v. M.C.I.* (April 10, 1995), no. IMM-165-95, Muldoon (F.C.T.D.).

[182] *M.C.I. v. John Frederick Lundgren* (September 25 1992), no. T-682-92, Dubé (F.C.T.D.).

[183] *Refugee Protection Division Rules*, ss. 44 and 48.

[184] *Fetni, Toufik v. M.C.I.* (March 27, 1997), no. IMM-1230-96, Pinard (F.C.T.D.); *Ressam, Ahmed v. M.C.I.* (February 9, 1996), no. IMM-1271-95, Pinard (F.C.T.D.).

[185] *Immigration and Refugee Protection Act*, s. 162(2).

The guidelines apply to most cases heard by the RPD. However, in compelling or exceptional circumstances, the members will use their discretion not to apply some guidelines or to apply them less strictly.

Generally speaking, the RPD will make allowances for unrepresented claimants who are unfamiliar with the Division's processes and rules. Claimants identified as particularly vulnerable will be treated with special sensitivity.

## The Roles of Members, RPOS and Counsel

Under the *IRPA*, RPD members have the same powers as commissioners who are appointed under the *Inquiries Act*.[186] They may inquire into anything they consider relevant to establishing whether a claim is well-founded.[187] This means that they define what issues must be resolved in order for them to render a decision.

A member's role is different from the role of a judge. A judge's primary role is to consider the evidence and arguments that the opposing parties choose to present; it is not to tell parties how to present their cases. Case law[188] has clearly established that the RPD has control of its own procedures. It decides and gives directions as to how a hearing is to proceed, including who will start the questioning. The members have to be actively involved to make the RPD's inquiry process work properly.

A Refugee Protection Officer (RPO) may be involved in proceedings at the preparation stage, at the hearing, or both. An RPO acts under the direction of the Division to carry out activities necessary for a full and proper examination of a claim or other matter.[189]

The role of counsel is the same whether counsel is representing a claimant or the Minister. Counsel assists the client in presenting the case in an efficient manner within the limits set by the member. Their role is essentially to protect the client's interests and right to a fair hearing.

### *1. — Case Preparation*

To make the best use of hearing time, these guidelines emphasize the importance of case preparation. Issues have to be identified early in the process and the rules have to be strictly followed.

#### *1.1 — Early identification of issues*

1. The RPD will make a preliminary identification of the issues it considers to be central to the claim. A copy of the RPD File Screening Form identifying those issues will be provided to the parties together with the Notice to Appear.

2. After seeing the issues indicated on the RPD File Screening Form, a party is expected to notify the RPD as soon as possible of any issue it wants to add or delete, and explain why.



[186]*Immigration and Refugee Protection Act*, s. 165.

[187]*Immigration and Refugee Protection Act*, s. 170(a).

[188]*Rezaei, Iraj v. M.C.I.* (December 5, 2002), no. IMM-1367-02, Beaudry (F.C.T.D.), which refers to the powers of administrative tribunals according to *Prassad v. Canada (Minister of Manpower and Immigration)*, [1989] 1 S.C.R. 560.

[189]*Refugee Protection Division Rules*, s. 16.

### *1.2 — Disclosure of documents*[190] *and witness information*[191]

3. Parties must disclose documents they want to use and a list of those documents no later than 20 days before the hearing.[192] Unless the member decides otherwise, a document that was not disclosed according to the *RPD Rules* cannot be used at the hearing.[193] The RPD has to follow the same rule.[194] If it does not disclose in time, its documents cannot be used without the member's permission.

4. Members will refuse to accept documents that are not relevant to the proceeding. Members will take such documents off the exhibit list submitted.

5. The RPD will continue to provide information on the country of reference. This means that every case will have some basic documentary evidence.

### *1.3 — Information requests to IRB Research Directorate*

6. The RPD will submit requests for country of origin and claimant-specific information to the IRB Research Directorate only where the RPD considers that the information is necessary to decide the case and cannot be obtained from any other source.

## ***2. — Hearing Preliminaries***

The procedure for opening hearings is standardized to allow more of the hearing time to be spent on the claim itself instead of on opening formalities. Hearings proceed informally, but all the participants must show respect for the RPD and the parties.

### *2.1 — Failure to appear*

7. The hearing will begin promptly as scheduled. Participants must be present and ready to proceed by the scheduled start time.

8. If a party or counsel does not appear by the scheduled start time, the member will note this on the record.

9. If a party or counsel appears within 15 minutes after the scheduled start time, the member will note the explanation for the late arrival on the record.

10. After 15 minutes,

- if it is a claimant who has not appeared, the member will decide whether to adjourn the matter on a peremptory basis or to start abandonment proceedings according to the *RPD Rules*.[195]
- if it is a protected person[196] who has not appeared, the member will decide whether to proceed in the absence of that party or to adjourn the matter on a peremptory basis.

---

[190] *Refugee Protection Division Rules*, s. 29.

[191] *Refugee Protection Division Rules*, s. 38.

[192] *Refugee Protection Division Rules*, s. 27(4), 29(4).

[193] *Refugee Protection Division Rules*, s. 30.

[194] *Refugee Protection Division Rules*, s. 29(2), (4) and *Commentary* to Rules 29, 30 and 37.

[195] *Refugee Protection Division Rules*, s. 58(2).

[196] *Immigration and Refugee Protection Act*, s. 95(2).

- if it is counsel who has not appeared, the member will decide whether to proceed in counsel's absence, adjourn the matter on a peremptory basis or start abandonment proceedings according to the *RPD Rules*.[197]

### *2.2 — Informal conference before the hearing*

11. A brief conference with the parties will be held just before the hearing only where it would help make better use of hearing time.[198] When the claimant is represented, the member, the RPO and all counsel will participate, but the claimant will not usually be present. A represented claimant may be present if the member decides it would be useful. If the claimant was not present at the conference, before the hearing begins, the member will summarize for the claimant what was discussed and what directions the member gave at the conference. The conference will be recorded and form part of the tribunal's record.

### *2.3 — Interpreters*

12. Interpreters are permanently bound by their promise to interpret accurately once they take an oath or make a solemn affirmation to do so. Therefore, a member who knows that an interpreter has been sworn in before by the Division should simply ask the interpreter to confirm that s/he has taken the oath or made the affirmation.

13. At the beginning of the hearing, the interpreter will confirm that s/ he used a standardized script to make sure that the interpreter and claimant are able to speak to and understand each other.

### *2.4 — Affirmation/Oath*

14. Before the claimant starts testifying, the member will ask the claimant to make either a solemn affirmation or an oath on a holy book that the claimant has brought for that purpose.

### *2.5 — Personal Information Form (PIF)*

15. The claimant is responsible for making sure that the PIF was interpreted to him or her before the hearing. At the beginning of the hearing, the member will ask the claimant to confirm that the interpretation was done.

16. The member will not ask the claimant if there are amendments to the PIF. Any changes to the PIF must be submitted 20 days before the hearing, in three copies and underlined, according to the RPD's rules.[199]

### *2.6 — Exhibits*

17. The member will not make an exhibit list or ask if there are any other exhibits. The member will enter into evidence the exhibit lists already submitted by the RPO and the parties.



---

[197] *Refugee Protection Division Rules*, s. 58(2).

[198] For example, where there are complex legal issues to be discussed, or matters related to procedure or to evidence to be settled. A conference should only be held where it would be more practical or efficient to consider such issues before the actual hearing or where it may be more appropriate to discuss certain sensitive issues without the presence of the claimant.

[199] *Refugee Protection Division Rules*, s. 6(4), s. 29(4), s. 30 and *Commentary* to rules 5 and 6.

### 3. — Hearing

It is an essential part of the members' inquisitorial role to be actively involved in the conduct of hearings. The member is in charge of the inquiry and issues directions to make the proceedings more efficient. The member decides the order of the proceedings in accordance with these *Guidelines*, including the order of questioning and representations by the parties and the RPO.

#### 3.1 — Issue agenda

18. Using the File Screening Form as a starting point, the member will consult with the RPO and counsel about the issues and how long the hearing is expected to last. Once the issues have been confirmed by the member, questioning must be limited to those issues. However, if it becomes necessary, the member can add or delete issues even during the course of the hearing.

#### 3.2 — Questioning

19. In a claim for refugee protection, the standard practice will be for the RPO to start questioning the claimant. If there is no RPO participating in the hearing, the member will begin, followed by counsel for the claimant. Beginning the hearing in this way allows the claimant to quickly understand what evidence the member needs from the claimant in order for the claimant to prove his or her case.

20. In a claim for refugee protection where the Minister intervenes on an issue other than exclusion, for example, on a credibility issue, the RPO starts the questioning. If there is no RPO at the hearing, the member will start the questioning, followed by the Minister's counsel and then counsel for the claimant.

21. In proceedings where the Minister intervenes on the issue of exclusion, Minister's counsel will start the questioning, followed by the RPO, the member, and counsel for the claimant. Where the Minister's counsel requests another chance to question at the end, the member will allow it if the member is satisfied that new matters were raised during questioning by the other participants.

22. In proceedings where the Minister is making an application to vacate or to cease refugee protection, Minister's counsel will start the questioning, followed by the member, and counsel for the protected person. Where the Minister's counsel requests another chance to question at the end, the member will allow it if the member is satisfied that new matters were raised during questioning by the other participants.

23. The member may vary the order of questioning in exceptional circumstances. For example, a severely disturbed claimant or a very young child might feel too intimidated by an unfamiliar examiner to be able to understand and properly answer questions. In such circumstances, the member could decide that it would be better for counsel for the claimant to start the questioning. A party who believes that exceptional circumstances exist must make an application to change the order of questioning before the hearing. The application has to be made according to the *RPD Rules*.[200]

24. The member will limit the questioning by the RPO and counsel for the parties according to the nature and complexity of the issues. Questioning must bring out relevant information that will help the member make an informed decision. Questions that are answered by the claimant just repeating what is written in the PIF do not help the member.

---

[200] *Refugee Protection Division Rules*, s. 44.

### *3.3 — Representations*

25. Parties will have a reasonable opportunity to make representations at a hearing.[201] The member will set time limits for the representations after all the evidence has been heard. The time limits will be reasonable in relation to the number of issues and the amount of relevant evidence heard.

26. The RPO and the parties must be prepared to give oral representations after the evidence has been heard.[202] These representations must be relevant, focused and concise so that they help a member to decide the claim efficiently and make it possible for the member to give an oral decision and reasons at the end of the hearing.

27. The member may direct the RPO not to deliver representations if the member considers that representations by the RPO are not necessary.

## Guideline 8 — Guideline on Procedures with Respect to Vulnerable Persons Appearing Before The IRB[203]

### 1. — Introduction

1.1 The intention of this Guideline is to provide procedural accommodation(s) for individuals who are identified as vulnerable persons by the Immigration and Refugee Board of Canada (IRB). Chairperson's Guidelines are issued to assist members in carrying out their duties as decision-makers under the *Immigration and Refugee Protection Act* (IRPA)[204] and to promote consistency, coherence and fairness in the treatment of cases at the IRB.

1.2 Appearing before an IRB hearing is a process that can be difficult due to language and cultural barriers and due to the fact that the outcome of the hearing is so significant for those involved. The IRB makes decisions on immigration and refugee matters, including admissibility, detention, removal, refugee protection, permanent resident status and family reunification — all matters that affect the lives of individuals directly and profoundly.

1.3 The IRB's three divisions, the Immigration Division (ID), the Immigration Appeal Division (IAD) and the Refugee Protection Division (RPD), are committed to providing fair hearings to all persons appearing before them in a manner that is guided and informed by the objectives set out in section 3 of the IRPA. This Guideline is intended to apply to the three divisions of the IRB.

1.4 The IRB occasionally hears cases involving persons for whom a hearing or other case process is a particularly difficult experience because their ability to present their cases is severely impaired due to a physical or psychological frailty or for other reasons. The vulnerability of these persons has always required special consideration and the IRB has in the past adopted case by case procedures to deal with their cases. This Guideline articulates the IRB's commitment to making procedural accommodations for such persons so that they are not disadvantaged in presenting their cases.

1.5 A person's vulnerability may be due to having experienced or witnessed torture or genocide or other forms of severe mistreatment; however, it may also be due to innate or acquired personal characteristics such as a physical or mental illness, or age. What vulnerable persons appearing before the IRB have in common is their severe difficulty in

Other Relevant Legislation

---

[201]*Immigration and Refugee Protection Act*, s. 170(e).

[202]*Refugee Protection Division Rules*, s. 60.

[203]Short title: Guideline on Vulnerable Persons.

[204]S.C. 2001, c. 27.

going through the hearing process or other IRB processes without special consideration being given to their individual situations. Like all persons appearing before the IRB, vulnerable persons need to be treated with sensitivity and respect, but they also need to have their cases processed taking into account their specific vulnerabilities.

## 2. — Definition of Vulnerable Persons

2.1 For the purposes of this Guideline, vulnerable persons are individuals whose ability to present their cases before the IRB is severely impaired. Such persons may include, but would not be limited to, the mentally ill, minors, the elderly, victims of torture, survivors of genocide and crimes against humanity, and women who have suffered gender-related persecution.

2.2 The definition of vulnerable persons may apply to persons presenting a case before the IRB, namely, to refugee protection claimants (in the RPD), appellants (in the IAD), and foreign nationals or permanent residents (in the ID). In certain circumstances, close family members of the vulnerable person who are also presenting their cases before the IRB may qualify as vulnerable persons because of the way in which they have been affected by their loved one's condition.

2.3 Persons who appear before the IRB frequently find the process difficult for various reasons, including language and cultural barriers and because they may have suffered traumatic experiences which resulted in some degree of vulnerability.[205] IRB proceedings have been designed to recognize the very nature of the IRB's mandate, which inherently involves persons who may have some vulnerabilities. In all cases, the IRB takes steps to ensure the fairness of the proceedings. This Guideline addresses difficulties which go beyond those that are common to most persons appearing before the IRB. It is intended to apply to individuals who face particular difficulty and who require special consideration in the procedural handling of their cases. It applies to the more severe cases of vulnerability.

2.4 Wherever it is reasonably possible, the vulnerability must be supported by independent credible evidence[206] filed with the IRB Registry.

## 3. — Objectives

3.1 To recognize that certain individuals face particular difficulties when they appear for their hearings or other IRB processes because their ability to present their cases is severely impaired.

3.2 To ensure that such vulnerable persons are identified and appropriate procedural accommodations are made.

3.3 To the extent possible, to prevent vulnerable persons from becoming traumatized or re-traumatized by the hearing process or other IRB process.

---

[205]For example, paragraph 209 of the *UNHCR Handbook on Procedures and Criteria for Determining Refugee Status under the 1951 Convention and the 1967 Protocol relating to the Status of Refugees* (Geneva, January 1992) states that "some degree of mental disturbance is frequently found in persons who have been exposed to severe persecution." Such persons regularly appear before the IRB, and the processes of the IRB have been designed to ensure that all persons are treated with sensitivity and respect. This Guideline will not necessarily apply to all such persons since it is intended to apply to those individuals whose ability to present their cases before the IRB is severely impaired.

[206]Such as a detailed report by an expert following an in-depth assessment of the person.

3.4 To ensure the on-going sensitization of members and other hearing room participants to the impact of severe vulnerability.

## 4. — Procedural Accommodations

4.1 Depending upon the nature of a person's vulnerability, they may face particular difficulties in presenting or addressing evidence which should be taken into account in determining the procedural accommodations to be made. Such difficulties may include the following:

a. a person's vulnerability may affect memory and behaviour and their ability to recount relevant events;

b. the vulnerable person may be suffering from symptoms that have an impact on the consistency and coherence of their testimony;

c. vulnerable persons who fear persons in a position of authority may associate those involved in the hearing process with the authorities they fear;

d. a vulnerable person may be reluctant or unable to talk about their experiences.

4.2 The Division has a broad discretion to tailor procedures to meet the particular needs of a vulnerable person, and, where appropriate and permitted by law, the Division may accommodate a person's vulnerability by various means, including:

a. allowing the vulnerable person to provide evidence by videoconference or other means;

b. allowing a support person to participate in a hearing;

c. creating a more informal setting for a hearing;

d. varying the order of questioning;[207]

e. excluding non-parties from the hearing room;

f. providing a panel and interpreter of a particular gender;

g. explaining IRB processes to the vulnerable person;

h. allowing any other procedural accommodation that may be reasonable in the circumstances.

## 5. — General Principles

5.1 A person may be identified as vulnerable, and procedural accommodations made, so that the person is not disadvantaged in the presentation of their case. The identification of vulnerability will usually be made at an early stage, before the IRB has considered all the evidence in the case and before an assessment of the person's credibility has been made.

5.2 A person may be identified as vulnerable based, in part, on alleged underlying facts which are also central to the ultimate determination of their case before the IRB. An identification of vulnerability does not indicate the IRB's acceptance of the alleged underlying facts. It is made for the purpose of procedural accommodation only. Thus the identification of a person as vulnerable does not predispose a member to make a particular determination of the case on its merits. Rather, a determination of the merits of the case will be made on the basis of an assessment of all the evidence.

5.3 Similarly, evidence initially used to identify a vulnerable person and to make procedural accommodations may not have been tested through credibility assessments or other means. If such evidence is then used to adjudicate the merits of the case, the member

Other Relevant Legislation

---

[207]See section 3.2 of IRB, *Guideline 7 — Concerning Preparation and Conduct of a Hearing in the Refugee Protection Division*, December 1, 2003.

should ensure that all hearing participants are given an opportunity to address this evidence as it relates to the merits of the case. This means that submissions may be made about the relevance of the evidence and the evidence may be tested through such means as questioning by the parties and the member, and other methods. The credibility and probative value of the evidence may then be assessed by the member, even though the IRB previously accepted the evidence for the purpose of identifying vulnerability and making procedural accommodations.

## 6. — Proceedings with More than One Party

6.1 Some IRB hearings are adversarial in nature, and the rules of natural justice apply equally to both parties. Identification of vulnerable persons and procedural accommodations for vulnerable persons cannot have the effect of denying any party a fair opportunity to present their case. Where the Minister[208] is a party, the Minister's views will be sought on whether a person should be identified as a vulnerable person and, if so, on the nature of any procedural accommodations to be made, except for accommodations of an administrative or minor nature.

## 7. — Early Identification

7.1 A person can be identified as vulnerable at any stage of the proceedings. It is preferable to identify vulnerable persons at the earliest opportunity.

7.2 In the course of early review of the file, the IRB may find information which discloses that the ability of the person to present their case may be severely impaired. The IRB may initiate early contact with the person, the designated representative, counsel or any other person to gather evidence which is relevant to whether the individual should be identified as a vulnerable person and which is relevant to the types of procedural accommodations which might be made.

7.3 Counsel for a person who may be considered vulnerable is best placed to bring the vulnerability to the attention of the IRB, and is expected to do so as soon as possible. Others who are associated with the person or who have knowledge of facts indicating that the person may be vulnerable (counsel for the Minister or any other person) are encouraged to do the same. Wherever it is reasonably possible, independent credible evidence documenting the vulnerability must be filed with the IRB Registry.

7.4 Counsel for a person who wishes to be identified as a vulnerable person must make an application under the Rules of the Division.[209] The application must specify the nature of the vulnerability, the type of procedural accommodations sought and the rationale for the particular accommodations. The IRB will be sensitive to the barriers that may be created by the formal requirements related to making applications in the case of unrepresented persons and other situations and will waive or modify the requirements or time limits set out in the Rules, as appropriate. The IRB may also act on its own initiative.

7.5 A Coordinating Member, Assistant Deputy Chairperson or ID Director may identify an individual as a vulnerable person and may take appropriate measures to accommodate the person at an early stage and before a member has been assigned to conduct a proceeding. The assigned member is not bound by the IRB's early identification. The assigned member will consider this Guideline and whether the identification and any procedural accommodations made will be maintained, amended or discontinued.

---

[208]The Minister of Citizenship and Immigration and the Minister of Public Safety and Emergency Preparedness.

[209]RPD rule 44 (SOR/2002-228), ID rule 38 (SOR/2002-229) and IAD rule 43 (SOR/2002-230).

7.6 To the extent practicable, the same Tribunal Officer will have administrative responsibility for the vulnerable person's file from the beginning of the IRB process to the end.

7.7 The Division may hold conferences prior to and during hearings to assist in identifying vulnerable persons and to establish the nature of the procedural accommodations required.

## 8. — Expert Evidence

8.1 A medical, psychiatric, psychological, or other expert report regarding the vulnerable person is an important piece of evidence that must be considered. Expert evidence can be of great assistance to the IRB in applying this Guideline if it addresses the person's particular difficulty in coping with the hearing process, including the person's ability to give coherent testimony.

8.2 The IRB may suggest that an expert report be submitted but will not order or pay for it.

8.3 Generally, experts' reports should contain the following information:

a. the particular qualifications and experience of the professional that demonstrate an expertise which pertains to the person's particular condition;

b. the questions that were posed to the expert by the person who requested the expert report;

c. the factual foundation underlying the expert's opinion;

d. the methodology used by the expert in assessing the person, including whether an interview was conducted, the number and length of interviews, whether tests were administered, and, if so, what those tests were and the significance of the results;

e. whether the person is receiving treatment and, if so, the nature of the treatment and whether the treatment is controlling the condition;

f. whether the assessing expert was also treating the person at the time of producing the report; and

g. the expert's opinion about the person's condition and ability to participate in the hearing process, including any suggested procedural accommodations and why particular procedural accommodations are recommended.

8.4 Experts should not offer opinions on issues within the exclusive jurisdiction of the decision-maker, such as the merits of the person's case.

8.5 An expert's opinion is not in itself proof of the truthfulness of the information upon which it is based. The weight given to the report will depend, among other things, on the credibility of the underlying facts in support of the allegation of vulnerability.

8.6 The absence of expert evidence does not necessarily lead to a negative inference about whether the person is in fact vulnerable. The IRB will consider whether it was reasonably possible to obtain such evidence.

## 9. — Scheduling

9.1 The IRB has a duty to determine all proceedings before it as informally and quickly as the circumstances and the considerations of fairness and natural justice permit.[210] Moreover, the uncertainty and anxiety caused by delay can be particularly detrimental to vulnerable persons. As a general rule, proceedings involving vulnerable persons will be

[210]IRPA, section 162(2).

given scheduling priority; however, some cases may be reasonably delayed if doing so facilitates meeting the objectives of this Guideline.[211]

## 10. — Questioning the Vulnerable Person

10.1 The IRB ensures that all those who appear at its hearings or other proceedings are questioned with sensitivity and respect. This obligation is all the more important in the case of vulnerable persons. In probing the information provided by the person, the IRB will attempt to avoid traumatizing or re-traumatizing the vulnerable person.[212]

## 11. — Decisions and Reasons

11.1 The uncertainty and anxiety generated by waiting for a decision and reasons for decision may be particularly stressful for vulnerable persons. Generally, decisions and reasons for decisions involving vulnerable persons will be delivered as soon as possible, and orally wherever appropriate. In individual cases, members may determine that written reasons are preferable.

## 12. — Designated Representative

12.1 In some cases, vulnerable persons may be under 18 years of age or unable, in the opinion of the Division, to appreciate the nature of the proceedings. In such cases, the Division shall designate a person to represent the person, as required by section 167(2) of IRPA.[213]

## 13. — Unrepresented Persons

13.1 Unrepresented persons are entitled to the same procedural safeguards as those who are represented, and the IRB will endeavour to ensure that the process outlined in this Guideline is both accessible and understandable to these persons. The IRB will take extra care to ensure that unrepresented vulnerable persons can participate as meaningfully as possible in their own hearings.

## 14. — Gender Issues

14.1 The RPD will consider the IRB *Guideline on Women Refugee Claimants Fearing Gender-Related Persecution* in all cases involving refugee cases based on gender.[214] This Guideline comprehensively sets out the relevant considerations and explicitly recognizes the special problems faced by women who fear gender-related persecution.

---

[211]Scheduling in the RPD will continue to be subject to the Chairperson's *Instructions Governing the Management of Refugee Protection Claims Awaiting Front-end Security Screening* (2006).

[212]For a useful guide on questioning, see the *Training Manual on Victims of Torture* developed by the Professional Development Branch of the IRB in April 2004. The principles suggested in the manual with respect to torture victims can be adopted, with necessary modifications, to the questioning of other vulnerable persons.

[213]See also RPD rule 15 (SOR/2002-228), ID rules 18 and 19 (SOR/2002-229) and IAD rule 19 (SOR/2002•230).

[214]*Update*, November 25, 1996.

## 15. — Minors

15.1 In all cases involving minors, the RPD will continue to consider and apply the IRB *Guideline on Child Refugee Claimants: Procedural and Evidentiary Issues*.[215]

15.2 In all cases involving minors appearing before the Immigration Division or the Immigration Appeal Division, the ID or the IAD will consider and apply the IRB *Guideline on Child Refugee Claimants: Procedural and Evidentiary Issues*, making necessary modifications in respect of any provisions in the Guideline which are not relevant to the ID or the IAD.

## 16. — References

- *Immigration and Refugee Protection Act*, S.C. 2001, c. 27.
- *Refugee Protection Division Rules*, SOR/2002-228.
- *Immigration Appeal Division Rules*, SOR/2002-230.
- *Immigration Division Rules*, SOR/2002-229.
- Immigration and Refugee Board of Canada. *Instructions Governing the Management of Refugee Protection Claims Awaiting Front-end Security Screening*. February 2006.
- Immigration and Refugee Board of Canada. Professional Development Branch. *Training Manual on Victims of Torture*. 2004. *(available upon request)*.
- Immigration and Refugee Board of Canada. *Guideline 3 — Child Refugee Claimants: Procedural and Evidentiary Issues 1996. <http://www.irb-cisr.gc.ca/en/references/policy/guidelines/child_e. htm>*.
- Immigration and Refugee Board of Canada. *Guideline 4 — Women Refugee Claimants Fearing Gender-Related Persecution*. 1996. Update.
- Immigration and Refugee Board of Canada. *Guideline 7 — Concerning Preparation and Conduct of a Hearing in the Refugee Protection Division*. 2003.

## 17. — Inquiries

For information contact:

Director, Policy and Procedures Directorate
Operations Branch
Immigration and Refugee Board of Canada
Canada Building (Minto Place)
344 Slater Street, 14th Floor
Ottawa, Ontario K1A 0K1
Fax: 613-952-9083



[215]*September 30, 1996.*

# Appendix II
# An Act respecting immigration to Québec

R.S.Q., c. I-0.2, as am. S.Q. 1978, c. 82; 1979, c. 32, ss. 9, 10; 1981, c. 9, ss. 1–8; 1981, c. 23, s. 32; U.K. 1982, c. 11, Sched. B, Pt. I, s. 33; S.Q. 1984, c. 44, s. 21; 1984, c. 47, s. 102; 1985, c. 30, s. 55; 1987, c. 75; 1988, c. 41, ss. 69–71; 1990, c. 4, s. 583; 1991, c. 3; 1992, c. 5; 1993, c. 70, ss. 1–18 [ss. 3(1), 8, 9, 11(2), (8), (9) not in force at date of publication; s. 8 repealed 1998, c. 15, s. 14.]; 1994, c. 15, ss. 12–29; 1996, c. 21, ss. 48, 49; 1997, c. 43, s. 302; 1998, c. 15, ss. 1–13; 1999, c. 40, s. 147; 1999, c. 71; 2001, c. 58 [Not in force at date of publication.]; 2004, c. 18 [ss. 2, 6, 10(5) not in force at date of publication.]; 2005, c. 24, ss. 38–40.

*[Note: This Act was formerly entitled "An Act respecting the Ministère de l'immigration". The title was replaced by section 1 of chapter 9 of the statutes of 1981.*

*The Act was formerly entitled "An Act respecting the Ministère des Communautés culturelles et de l'immigration". The title was replaced by 1994, c. 15, s. 12.]*

## Division I — Definition

**1.** [Repealed 1994, c. 15, s. 13.]

**2. "foreign national"** — In this act, **"foreign national"** means a person who is neither a Canadian citizen nor a permanent resident within the meaning of the *Immigration and Refugee Protection Act* (Statutes of Canada, 2001, chapter 27) and the regulations thereunder, who settles temporarily in Québec otherwise than as the representative of a foreign government or as an international civil servant.

1968, c. 68, s. 2; 1974, c. 64, s. 1; 1978, c. 82, s. 1; 1981, c. 9, s. 3; 1994, c. 15, s. 15; 2004, c. 18, s. 1

## Division II — Selection of Foreign Nationals

**3. Selection of foreign nationals** — The selection of foreign nationals wishing to settle permanently or temporarily in Québec is effected within the framework of government policy concerning immigrants and foreign nationals. The selection is intended, in particular,

(a) to contribute to the enrichment of the socio-cultural heritage of Québec, to the stimulation of its economic development and to the pursuit of its demographic objectives;

(b) to facilitate the reuniting, in Québec, of Canadian citizens and permanent residents with their close relatives from abroad;

(c) to enable Québec to assume its share of responsibilities regarding the reception of refugees and other persons in a particularly distressful situation;

(d) to favour the coming, among foreign nationals who apply therefor, of persons who will be able to become successfully established in Québec;

(e) to facilitate the conditions of the stay in Québec of foreign nationals wishing to study, work temporarily or receive medical treatment, having regard to the reasons for their coming and the capacity of Québec to receive them.

**Proposed Amendment — 3(e)**

(e) to facilitate the conditions of the stay in Québec of foreign nationals wishing to study or work temporarily, having regard to the reasons for their coming and the capacity of Québec to receive them.

2004, c. 18, s. 2 [Not in force at date of publication.]

1968, c. 68, s. 3; 1969, c. 9, s. 3; 1974, c. 6, s. 111; 1974, c. 64, s. 2; 1978, c. 82, s. 2; 1988, c. 41, s. 69; 1993, c. 70, s. 1; 1994, c. 15, s. 17

**3.0.0.1** The Minister, having regard to government policy concerning immigrants and foreign nationals, shall formulate guidelines respecting immigration and table them in the National Assembly for examination by the appropriate committee of the Assembly. The National Assembly may, for that purpose, hear any person or organization.

2004, c. 18, s. 3

**3.0.1 Annual immigration plan** — The Minister, having regard to government policy concerning immigrants and foreign nationals and to its guidelines on immigration, shall establish an annual immigration plan.

**Foreign nationals** — The purpose of the plan is to specify planned immigration levels to promote the enrichment of the sociocultural fabric of Québec within the framework of the objectives pursued in the selection of foreign nationals.

**Selection activities** — The plan shall set out the maximum or estimated number of foreign nationals who may settle in Québec or of selection certificates that may be issued, and their distribution by class or within the same class; the maximum or estimated number may also be determined by source area. The plan shall take into account, among other factors, the projected overall demand for selection certificates, the projected admission and selection levels and Québec's capacity to welcome and integrate immigrants.

A source area may comprise a country, a group of countries, a continent or part of a continent.

**Tabling** — The plan shall be tabled in the National Assembly not later than 1 November or, if the Assembly is not sitting on that date, not later than the fifteenth day after resumption.

1998, c. 15, s. 1; 1999, c. 71, s. 1; 2004, c. 18, s. 4

**3.1 Application for permanent residence** — A foreign national wishing to settle permanently in Québec must, except for the classes and cases prescribed by regulation, file an application for a selection certificate with the Minister of Immigration and Cultural Communities in the manner determined by regulation in accordance with the procedure prescribed under paragraph f of section 3.3.

**Process** — The Minister shall process the application, having regard to the annual immigration plan and to the order of priorities prescribed by regulation.

**Selection certificate** — The Minister shall issue a selection certificate to the foreign national who meets the conditions and criteria of selection determined by regulation.

**Suspension of examination** — The Minister shall suspend the examination of applications or cease to issue selection certificates for or within a class until the beginning of the following calendar year if the maximum set out in the annual plan has been reached. The Minister may, for or within a class, suspend the examination of applications or cease to issue selection certificates until the beginning of the following calendar year if the

Minister considers that the maximum number or estimate set out in the annual plan will be reached.

**Selection certificate** — Notwithstanding the third or fourth paragraph, the Minister may, in accordance with the regulations, issue a selection certificate to a foreign national in a particularly distressful situation, in particular, in the case of Convention refugees as defined in the Act respecting immigration to Canada, or in any other case where the Minister considers that the results obtained following the application of the selection criteria do not reflect whether or not the foreign national will be able to become successfully established in Québec. Conversely, the Minister may refuse to issue such a certificate to a foreign national who meets the conditions and criteria of selection if he has reasonable grounds to believe that the foreign national does not intend to settle in Québec or is unlikely to settle successfully in Québec or that the settlement of the foreign national would be contrary to public interest.

*[Editor's Note: SOR/2002-227, s. 362 provides that if, before April 1, 1999, a foreign national made an application for an immigrant visa as an investor and signed any document referred to in clause 1(v)(iii)(A) of Schedule X to the* Immigration Regulations, 1978, *SOR/78-172 (the "former Regulations"), as Schedule X read immediately before April 1, 1999, or, in the case of an investor in a province, either applied for a selection certificate under s. 3.1 of* An Act respecting immigration to Québec, *R.S.Q., c. I-0.2, as amended from time to time, or applied for an immigrant visa as an investor, and signed an investment agreement in accordance with the law of Québec, the relevant provisions of the former Regulations respecting an applicant for an immigrant visa as an investor, an approved business, an investor in a province, a fund manager, an eligible business, an approved fund, a fund, an escrow agent, a privately administered venture capital fund or a government-administered venture capital fund continue to apply as they read immediately before April 1, 1999 to all persons governed by their application before April 1, 1999.]*

1978, c. 82, s. 3; 1992, c. 5, s. 1; 1993, c. 70, s. 2; 1994, c. 15, s. 18; 1996, c. 21, s. 48; 1998, c. 15, s. 2; 1999, c. 71, s. 2; 2005, c. 24, s. 38

**3.1.1 Selection criteria** — In the cases determined by regulation, an undertaking to assist a foreign national to settle in Québec is required.

**Proposed Amendment — 3.1.1**

**3.1.1 Selection Criteria** — Where determined by regulation, an undertaking to assist the foreign national in settling in Québec shall constitute one of the selection criteria prescribed under paragraph b of section 3.3.

1993, c. 70, s. 3(1) [Not in force at date of publication.]

**Application for undertaking** — The application for an undertaking shall be filed by a person or group of persons determined by regulation according to the conditions prescribed thereby. If, in the opinion of the Minister, the person or group of persons meets the conditions prescribed by regulation, the undertaking shall be subscribed to according to the terms determined by regulation. The application for an undertaking and the undertaking shall be made on the forms prescribed by the Minister.

**Certificate of undertaking** — The Minister shall issue a certificate of undertaking to a foreign national in whose respect an undertaking has been made and who is not required to file an application for a selection certificate.

1991, c. 3, s. 1; 1993, c. 70, s. 3; 1998, c. 15, s. 3

**3.1.2 Application** — A foreign national in Québec who does not hold a selection certificate may make an application to the Minister for a certificate of statutory situation. He shall file his application in accordance with the procedure prescribed under paragraph f of section 3.3.

**Certificate of identity** — The Minister shall issue a certificate of statutory situation to any foreign national who meets the conditions determined by regulation.

1992, c. 5, s. 2; 1993, c. 70, s. 4; 1998, c. 15, s. 4

3.1.3 **Conditions** — The Minister may impose conditions prescribed under paragraph f.1.2 of section 3.3 which affect the granting of permanent residence under the *Immigration and Refugee Protection Act* (Statutes of Canada, 2001, chapter 27) to a foreign national who applies for a selection certificate.

**Conditions** — The Minister may, in the cases determined by regulation or at the request of a permanent resident, modify, lift or cancel the conditions imposed.

1993, c. 70, s. 5; 2004, c. 18, s. 5

3.2 **Temporary foreign nationals** — Excepting the classes of foreign nationals excluded by regulation, every foreign national seeking temporary admission to Québec to work, study or receive medical treatment must hold a certificate of acceptance issued by the Minister. He must file an application in accordance with the procedure prescribed under paragraph f of section 3.3.

**Proposed Amendment — 3.2 first para.**

Excepting the classes of foreign nationals excluded by regulation, every foreign national seeking temporary admission to Québec to work or study must hold a certificate of acceptance issued by the Minister. He must file an application in accordance with the procedure prescribed under paragraph f of section 3.3.

2004, c. 18, s. 6 [Not in force at date of publication.]

**Certificate of acceptance** — The Minister shall issue a certificate of acceptance to the foreign national who meets the conditions determined by regulation.

**Certificate of acceptance** — Notwithstanding the second paragraph, the Minister may, in cases provided for by regulation, exempt a foreign national from the application of the conditions contemplated in the second paragraph and issue a certificate of acceptance to him.

1978, c. 82, s. 3; 1979, c. 32, s. 9; 1993, c. 70, s. 6; 1998, c. 15, s. 5

3.2.1 **Truthfulness of declarations** — Where the Minister so requires, any person must, under penalty of refusal of the application for a selection certificate, a certificate of acceptance or a certificate of statutory selection or of the application for an undertaking, demonstrate to the Minister the truthfulness of the declarations made by the person respecting the application and submit to him, in the manner and time determined by him, any document which the Minister deems to be pertinent.

In particular, the Minister may refuse any application containing any false or misleading information or document.

1991, c. 3, s. 2; 1992, c. 5, s. 3; 1993, c. 70, s. 7; 1998, c. 15, s. 6; 2004, c. 18, s. 7

3.2.2 **Cancellation of certificate** — The Minister may cancel a selection certificate, a certificate of acceptance, a certificate of statutory situation, an undertaking or a certificate of undertaking

(a) where the application for a certificate or an undertaking contains any false or misleading information or document;

(b) where the certificate was delivered or the undertaking accepted by error;

(c) where the conditions required for the issue of the certificate or the acceptance of the undertaking cease to exist.

**Minister's decision** — The decision of the Minister shall take effect immediately. It must give reasons and be submitted in writing to the person concerned.

1991, c. 3, s. 2; 1992, c. 5, s. 4; 1998, c. 15, s. 7; 2004, c. 18, s. 8

**3.2.2.1** The Minister may refuse to examine an application for a certificate made by a person who, in the past five years, has provided any false or misleading information or document relating to an application under this Act.

The Minister may also refuse to examine an application for an undertaking made by a person who, in the past two years, has provided such information or such a document.

2004, c. 18, s. 9

## Division III — Integration of Foreign Nationals

**3.2.3 Integration program** — The Minister shall establish and maintain, for those persons who settle in Québec, an integration program for the purpose of favouring their introduction to Québec life.

**Proposed Amendment — 3.2.3**

**3.2.3 Integration program** — The Minister shall establish and be responsible for the implementation of reception services and linguistic, social and economic integration services for immigrants.

2001, c. 58, s. 1 [Not in force at date of publication.]

1991, c. 3, s. 2

**3.2.4 Linguistic integration services** — The Minister, under the integration program, shall provide and take charge of the implementation of linguistic integration services consisting of services of French language instruction and introduction to Québec life.

**Proposed Repeal — 3.2.4**

**3.2.4** [Repealed 2001, c. 58, s. 1. Not in force at date of publication.]

1991, c. 3, s. 2

**3.2.5 Eligibility** — Immigrants domiciled in Québec who are unable to demonstrate, according to the evaluation procedure prescribed by regulation, a knowledge of French adequate to assuring their harmonious integration with the francophone majority of Québec society and who meet the other conditions established by regulation are admissible for linguistic integration services.

**Extension of services** — The maintaining and extension of the services are conditional upon compliance by the student receiving them with the conditions prescribed by regulation.

**Proposed Repeal — 3.2.5**

**3.2.5** [Repealed 2001, c. 58, s. 1. Not in force at date of publication.]

1991, c. 3, s. 2

**3.2.6 Financial assistance** — The Minister may allocate financial assistance to a student receiving linguistic integration services.

**Proposed Amendment — 3.2.6**

**3.2.6 Financial assistance** — The Minister may allocate financial assistance to an immigrant receiving reception or integration services.

2001, c. 58, s. 2 [Not in force at date of publication.]

1991, c. 3, s. 2; 1998, c. 15, s. 8

**3.2.7 Loan** — The Minister may, according to the conditions prescribed by regulation, grant a loan to an immigrant in a particularly distressful situation with a view to enabling him to discharge the cost or a part of the cost of his immigration to Québec or to assisting him to discharge the costs of becoming established in Québec.

1991, c. 3, s. 2; 1993, c. 70, s. 10; 1998, c. 15, s. 9

**3.2.8 Deferment of loan repayment** — The Minister may defer a loan repayment or reduce the obligations of repayment where the borrower shows that he is unable to repay his loan according to the terms and conditions prescribed by regulation.

**Release from debt** — Where it has been impossible to recover a debt resulting from a loan even though the appropriate recovery measures have been applied to it, the Minister may grant a release from the debt.

1991, c. 3, s. 2

## Division IV — Regulations and Agreements

**3.3 Regulations** — The Government may make regulations

(a) determining classes of foreign nationals who have filed an application for a selection certificate referred to in section 3.1;

(a.1) determining the cases where and the classes of foreign nationals for which an application for a selection certificate is not required;

(b) determining the conditions of selection applicable to each of such classes of foreign nationals, having regard, in particular, to criteria such as the vocational or professional training and experience of the foreign national,the needs of the labour market in Québec as regards his profession, the age and personal qualities, education, knowledge of languages, and financial capacity of the foreign national, the assistance he may receive from relatives or friends residing in Québec, his place of destination in Québec, and the place of establishment of his enterprise; such conditions and criteria may vary within the same class, in particular by reason of the foreign national's contribution to enriching the socio-cultural or economic heritage of Québec;

(b.1) determining the classes of foreign nationals which may be exempted from one or several of the conditions and criteria of selection prescribed under paragraph b and providing that such exemptions may vary within the same class;

(b.2) determining the classes of foreign nationals in respect of which paragraph b applies to a family member of a foreign national, as defined by regulation, and providing for cases of total or partial exemption of a family member of a foreign national from conditions or criteria of selection; such conditions and criteria may vary according to the family situation of the foreign national and also within the same class;

(b.3) determining, from among the criteria prescribed under paragraph b, those which apply to a preliminary processing for selection intended to identify the applications which will be processed, prescribing the classes of foreign nationals to which the criteria will apply and determining the cases of total or partial exemption of foreign nationals; the criteria may vary according to the class and also within the same class;

(b.4) prescribing the classes of foreign nationals in respect of which a selection interview must be held, determining the cases of total or partial exemption from this obligation and providing that the obligation may vary within the same class;

(b.5) determining the conditions or criteria applicable to a person whose participation is required for the management of the financial investment of a foreign national;

(c) determining the cases where an undertaking to assist a foreign national to settle in Québec is required and the cases where an undertaking ceases to have effect;

(c.1) determining the persons or groups of persons who may file an application for an undertaking and the conditions of the filing;

(c.2) determining the conditions which must be met by the person or group of persons who subscribe to such an undertaking and prescribing exemptions to one or several conditions by reason of the family situation or minority of the foreign national for whom the undertaking is subscribed;

(c.3) determining the terms of the undertaking and its duration, which may vary according to the age or circumstances of the foreign national or of his family;

**Proposed Addition — 3.3(c.4)**

(c.4) determining the cases in which an undertaking to assist a foreign national in settling in Québec constitutes one of the conditions and one of the criteria of selection referred to in paragraph b;

1993, c. 70, s. 11(2) [Not in force at date of publication.]

(d) determining the cases where and the classes of foreign nationals to whom the Minister may issue a selection certificate referred to in the fifth paragraph of section 3.1, and determining the procedure to be followed in a case where the Minister considers that the results obtained following the application of the selection criteria do not reflect whether or not the foreign national will be able to become successfully established in Québec;

(d.1) determining the cases where a certificate of statutory situation referred to in section 3.1.2 is to be issued and determining, according to the status of the foreign national as established under the *Immigration Act* (Revised Statutes of Canada, 1985, chapter I-2), types of certificates of statutory situation and the conditions applicable to each type;

(e) for the purposes of section 3.2, determining, while having particular regard to labour market conditions in Québec, the conditions that must be met by a foreign national seeking to stay temporarily in Québec to work, determining the conditions that must be met by a foreign national seeking to stay temporarily in Québec to study or receive medical treatment, establishing the cases where the Minister may exempt a foreign national from the application of the conditions referred to in the second paragraph of section 3.2 and issue a certificate of acceptance, and determining the classes of foreign nationals who may be excluded from the application of section 3.2;

**Proposed Amendment — 3.3(e)**

(e) for the purposes of section 3.2, determining, while having particular regard to labour market conditions in Québec, the conditions that must be met by a foreign national seeking to stay temporarily in Québec to work, determining the conditions that must be met by a foreign national seeking to stay temporarily in Québec to study, establishing the cases where the Minister may exempt a foreign national from the application of the conditions referred to in the second paragraph of section 3.2 and issue a certificate of acceptance, and determining the classes of foreign nationals who may be excluded from the application of section 3.2;

2004, c. 18, s. 10(5) [Not in force at date of publication.]

(f) determining the procedure that must be followed in order to obtain a selection certificate under section 3.1, a certificate of statutory situation under section 3.1.2 or a certificate of acceptance under section 3.2, or in order to subscribe an undertaking;

(f.1) determining the conditions of validity and the duration of a selection certificate, which may vary according to the class of foreign nationals or within the same class and according to whether the application is made in Québec or abroad;

(f.1.0.1) determining the conditions of validity of a certificate of acceptance, which may vary according to the class of employment or within the same class, and determining the duration of a certificate of acceptance, which may vary, in the case of a foreign national coming to Québec to study, according to whether the person is a minor or of age or according to the program of study or the duration of the studies, and in the case of a foreign national coming to Québec to work, according to the class of employment or within the same class, the duration of employment, the person's professional experience or labour market needs in the person's profession;

(f.1.0.2) determining the cases in which a selection certificate or certificate of acceptance lapses, which may vary according to the class of foreign nationals or within the same class;

(f.1.1) determining the duration of a certificate of statutory situation and the cases in which it lapses and providing that the duration and cases in which it lapses may vary by reason, in particular, of the type of certificate of statutory situation;

(f.1.2) for the purposes of section 3.1.3, providing conditions affecting the granting of permanent residence under the *Immigration and Refugee Protection Act* to a foreign national who applies for a selection certificate under section 3.1 so as to ensure, in particular, the protection of public health, the meeting of regional or sectorial needs for specialized labour, the regional or sectorial creation of enterprises or the financing of such enterprises, and the socio-economic integration of the foreign national, determining classes of foreign nationals according to which such conditions may vary and providing that such conditions may vary within the same class;

(f.1.3) determining the classes of foreign nationals which may be exempted from one or several conditions prescribed under paragraph f.1.2 and providing that such exemptions may vary within the same class;

(f.1.4) determining the duration of the conditions prescribed under section 3.1.3, determining the classes of foreign nationals according to which the duration may vary and providing that the duration may vary within the same class;

(f.1.5) determining the cases in which the conditions prescribed under section 3.1.3 may be modified, lifted or cancelled;

(f.2) establishing the fees payable for processing an application for an undertaking, a certificate of statutory situation, a selection certificate or a certificate of acceptance, for issuing any such certificate or for subscribing an undertaking, and determining the cases where total or partial exemption from payment is to be granted; the fees may vary in the case of an undertaking according to the family situation of the foreign national, in the case of a certificate of statutory situation according to the authorization allowing the foreign national to be in Canada, in the case of a selection certificate according to the classes of foreign nationals or to the stages in the processing of an application or, in the case of a certificate of acceptance according to the reason for the temporary admission of the foreign national to Québec;

(f.3) establishing the fees payable for processing an application by an employer relating to a temporary or permanent job for a foreign national; the fees may vary according to whether the job is temporary or permanent or according to the class of employment;

(g) prescribing an order of priorities for the processing of applications for a selection certificate referred to in section 3.1;

(h) determining, with regard to linguistic integration services, the services offered, the teaching program, the conditions of admissibility to the services, the form and tenor of an application, the conditions of obtaining, maintaining and extending the said services, the appropriate training period and the procedure for evaluating the knowledge of French; these provisions may vary according to services and classes of immigrants or of students;

**Proposed Amendment — 3.3(h)**

(h) determining the conditions of eligibility for reception services and linquistic, social or economic integration services, according to services or classes of immigrants;

2001, c. 58, s. 3 [Not in force at date of publication.]

**Proposed Amendment — 3.3(h)**

(h) determining, with regard to linguistic integration services, the services offered, the teaching program, the conditions of admissibility to the services, the conditions of obtaining, maintaining and extending the said services, the appropriate training period and the procedure for evaluating the knowledge of French; these provisions may vary according to services and classes of immigrants or of students;

1993, c. 70, s. 11(8) [Not in force at date of publication.]

(i) [Repealed 1998, c. 15, s. 10(8).]

(j) determining, with a view to assisting the reception and settlement of immigrants in a particularly distressful situation, the classes of loans, the conditions of granting and of repayment thereof, and the applicable rate of interest;

(k) defining the expression "immigration consultant", determining classes of consultants and establishing various standards according to such classes;

(l) establishing standards of qualification for the recognition of immigration consultants and determining the conditions to be met and the information or documents to be provided to obtain recognition, the duration of the recognition, the conditions for its renewal and the fees payable for an application for recognition or for its renewal;

(m) determining the functions and powers of the Minister with respect to the recognition of immigration consultants and the supervision of their activities, and the cases in which or conditions under which recognition is to be refused, suspended, revoked or not renewed;

(n) determining conditions or obligations applicable to immigration consultants or activities they are prohibited from engaging in, in particular with respect to advertising their services;

(o) prescribing the content and amount of the professional liability insurance policy that immigration consultants are required to hold;

(p) exempting members or a class of members of a professional order from all or part of the rules applicable to immigration consultants; and

(q) determining the provisions of a regulation whose violation constitutes an offence.

A regulation under any of subparagraphs a to b.5, f.2 and f.3 of the first paragraph is not subject to the publication requirement set out in section 8 of the *Regulations Act* (chapter R-18.1) and, despite section 17 of that Act, comes into force on the date of its publication in the *Gazette officielle du Québec* or on any later date mentioned in the regulation.

1978, c. 82, s. 3; 1979, c. 32, s. 10; 1981, c. 23, s. 32; 1984, c. 47, s. 103; 1987, c. 75, s. 1; 1991, c. 3, s. 3; 1992, c. 5, s. 5; 1993, c. 70, s. 11; 1998, c. 15, s. 10; 2004, c. 18, s. 10(1)–(4), (6)–(9)

**3.4 Regulations** — The Minister may, by regulation,

(a) establish the weighting of selection criteria and the passing score and, where expedient, the cutoff score determined in relation to a selection criterion, applicable to the preliminary stage of selection established under paragraph b.3 of section 3.3 and to the selection established under paragraph b of section 3.3, which weighting and which scores may vary according to the family situation of the foreign national, according to the classes of foreign nationals and within the same class of foreign nationals;

(b) determine that the regulation applies to applications that are being processed, or to applications filed after a particular date that are being processed, or to those that have not yet reached a particular stage on the date of coming into force of the regulation.

**Regulation** — A regulation made under this section is not subject to the requirement to publish contained in section 8 of the *Regulations Act* (R.S.Q., chapter R-18.1) and, notwithstanding section 17 of that Act, comes into force on the date of its publication in the *Gazette officielle du Québec*, or at any later date fixed in the regulation.

1993, c. 70, s. 12

**3.5** The Minister may, with the approval of the Government, suspend the receipt of applications for selection certificates for a specified period particularly if the Minister considers that the number of applications for all countries or a source area, or for a class of foreign nationals or part of a class of foreign nationals, will be significantly greater than the estimate set out in the annual immigration plan, that the number of applications from a source area prevents a fair treatment of applications from other areas or that the number of applications in a class or within a class will be detrimental to other applications in view of Québec's capacity to welcome and integrate immigrants.

The suspension may not exceed one year and may be renewed.

The suspension may apply to all countries or to a source area and to a class of foreign nationals or part of a class of foreign nationals.

A suspension takes effect on the date of the pulication [*sic*] of the suspension notice in the *Gazette officielle du Québec* or on any later date mentioned in the notice. The reason for the suspension must be included in the notice. The same applies to the renewal of a suspension.

A suspension under this section may, if it so specifies, apply to applications for selection certificates received within three months before its effective date that have yet to be examined by the Minister. In such cases, the Minister shall notify the applicant and shall either return the fees sent or reimburse the fees already collected.

2004, c. 18, s. 11

*[Editor's Note: S.Q. 2004, c. 18, s. 16 states that s. 3.5 applies only to applications for selection certificates received after May 13, 2004.]*

**4.** [Repealed 1994, c. 15, s. 21.]

**5.** [Repealed 1988, c. 41, s. 70.]

**6. Agreements** — The Minister may, according to law, make any agreement with the Government of Canada or any body thereof and with any other government or body, in conformity with the interests and rights of Québec, to facilitate the carrying out of this Act.

**Agreements for exchange of information** — He may make any agreement, in the same manner and with the same authorities or with any department or body of the Gouvernement du Québec, for the exchange of information obtained under an Act entrusted to the administration of that Government, department or body, in order to attain the immigration objectives or to discharge the obligations incumbent upon him under this Act.

1968, c. 68, s. 7; 1991, c. 3, s. 4; 1993, c. 70, s. 13; 1994, c. 15, s. 22

**7.–8.** [Repealed 1984, c. 44, s. 21.]

**9.–12.** [Repealed 1994, c. 15, s. 23.]

## Division V — Investigations

**12.1 Inquiries** — The Minister or any person designated by him as an investigator or inspector may make inquiries in order to ensure that this Act and the regulations are being complied with and to prevent, detect or repress contraventions to this Act.

1978, c. 82, s. 5; 1991, c. 3, s. 5; 1992, c. 5, s. 6; 1993, c. 70, s. 14

**12.1.1 Powers and immunity** — In conducting an investigation, the Minister and investigators are vested with the powers and immunity of commissioners appointed under the *Act respecting public inquiry commissions* (R.S.Q., chapter C-37), except the power to order imprisonment.

1993, c. 70, s. 15

**12.1.2 Information** — An inspector may, for the purposes of this Act and the regulations, require any information and any document and examine and make copies of such documents.

1993, c. 70, s. 15

**12.1.3 Immunity** — No inspector may be prosecuted for acts performed in good faith in the carrying out of his duties.

1993, c. 70, s. 15

**12.1.4 Identification** — On request, an inspector or investigator shall identify himself and produce the certificate signed by the Minister and attesting his capacity.

1993, c. 70, s. 15

**12.2 Copy of documents** — Any copy of a book, register or document produced for an investigation and certified by the Minister or an investigator as being a true copy of the original, is admissible as proof and has the same probative force as the original.

1978, c. 82, s. 5; 1991, c. 3, s. 5

## Division VI — Penal Provisions

**12.3 Offence** — Every person is guilty of an offence who communicates information he knows or should have known to be false or misleading to the Minister or to an investigator or inspector in relation to an application

(a) for a selection certificate, a certificate of acceptance, a certificate of statutory situation or an undertaking;

(b) for access to linguistic integration services;

**Proposed Amendment — 12.3(b)**

(b) for access to reception or integration services;

2001, c. 58, s. 4(1) [Not in force at date of publication.]

(c) for financial assistance for a student receiving linguistic integration services;

**Proposed Amendment — 12.3(c)**

(c) for financial assistance for a person receiving reception or integration services;

2001, c. 58, s. 4(2) [Not in force at date of publication.]

(d) for a loan for an immigrant in a particularly distressful situation.

1978, c. 82, s. 5; 1990, c. 4, s. 583; 1991, c. 3, s. 5; 1992, c. 5, s. 7; 1993, c. 70, s. 16; 1998, c. 15, s. 11

**12.4 Offence** — Every person who contributes to the issue of a selection certificate, a certificate of acceptance, a certificate of undertaking or a certificate of statutory situation to a foreign national or to the subscription of an undertaking in favour of a foreign national in contravention of this Act is guilty of an offence.

1991, c. 3, s. 5; 1992, c. 5, s. 8; 1998, c. 15, s. 12

**12.4.1 Offence and penalty** — Every person who obstructs an inspector in the carrying out of his duties is guilty of an offence.

1993, c. 70, s. 17

**12.4.2** Every person who acts as an immigration consultant without being duly recognized by the Minister or while the person's recognition is suspended, non-renewed, revoked or cancelled is guilty of an offence.

2004, c. 18, s. 12

**12.4.3** No person may use or evoke the expression "Immigration-Québec", "Ministère de l'Immigration et des Communautés culturelles" or "Ministère de l'Immigration du Québec" in order to hold out or lead to the belief that the person's conduct, operations or services are approved by the Minister or the Government.

No person may use or evoke the expression "Immigration-Québec", "Ministère de l'Immigration et des Communautés culturelles" or "Ministère de l'Immigration du Québec" in order the [*sic*] hold out or lead to the belief that the person's competence is recognized by the Minister or the Government, unless the person is recognized as an immigration consultant in accordance with this Act.

Every person who contravenes this section is guilty of an offence.

2004, c. 18, s. 12; 2005, c. 24, s. 39

**12.4.4** Every person who contravenes a provision referred to in paragraph q of section 3.3 is guilty of an offence.

2004, c. 18, s. 12

**12.5 Fine** — A natural person is liable to a fine of $500 to $1 000 in the case of an offence under section 12.3, to a fine of $1 000 to $10 000 in the case of an offence under section 12.4, to a fine of $250 to $1 000 in the case of an offence under section 12.4.1 and to a fine of $1,000 to $50,000 in the case of an offence under section 12.4.2, 12.4.3 or 12.4.4.

**Legal person** — Where the offence is committed by a legal person, the fine shall be doubled.

**Subsequent offence** — In the case of a second or subsequent offence, the fine prescribed for a first offence shall be doubled.

1991, c. 3, s. 5; 1993, c. 70, s. 18; 2004, c. 18, s. 13

**12.6 Parties to offence** — Where a legal person is guilty of an offence described by this Act, the director, officer or representative of the legal person who prescribed or authorized the performance of the act or the omission which constitutes the offence or who consented thereto is party to the offence and liable to the penalty prescribed by law.

1991, c. 3, s. 5; 1999, c. 40, s. 147

**12.7 Prescription** — Prescription of penal proceedings begins to run, for an offence contemplated by section 12.3, on the date of examination of the information disclosed to the Minister or investigator and, for an offence contemplated by section 12.4, on the date of examination of the application for the selection certificate, the certificate of acceptance, the undertaking or the certificate of statutory situation.

Prescription of proceedings under section 12.4.2 or 12.4.3 begins to run on the date the Minister becomes aware of the offence.

However, no proceedings may be instituted if more than five years have elapsed from the date of the commission of the offence.

1991, c. 3, s. 5; 1992, c. 5, s. 9; 1998, c. 15, s. 13; 2004, c. 18, s. 14

**13.–16.** [Repealed 1994, c. 15, s. 26.]

## Division VII — Proceeding Before the Administrative Tribunal of Québec

**17.** A decision of the Minister may, within 60 days of notification of the decision, be contested before the Administrative Tribunal of Québec by

(a) any natural person whose application for an undertaking is rejected or whose undertaking is cancelled;

(b) any foreign national whose selection certificate or certificate of acceptance is cancelled;

(c) any person whose recognition as an immigration consultant is refused, suspended, revoked or cancelled.

1982, c. 21, s. 1; U.K., 1982, c. 11, Sched. B, Part I, s. 33; 1991, c. 3, s. 6; 1997, c. 43, s. 302; 2004, c. 18, s. 15

**18.–39.** [Repealed 1997, c. 43, s. 302.]

## Division VIII — Final Provision

**40.** The Minister of Immigration and Cultural Communities is responsible for the administration of this Act.

1994, c. 15, s. 29; 1996, c. 21, s. 49; 2005, c. 24, s. 40

# APPENDIX III

# Chapter 16 of the North American Free Trade Agreement

## Temporary Entry for Business Persons

### Article 1601 — General Principles

Further to Article 102 (Objectives), this Chapter reflects the preferential trading relationship between the Parties, the desirability of facilitating temporary entry on a reciprocal basis and of establishing transparent criteria and procedures for temporary entry, and the need to ensure border security and to protect the domestic labor force and permanent employment in their respective territories.

### Article 1602 — General Obligations

1. Each Party shall apply its measures relating to the provisions of this Chapter in accordance with Article 1601 and, in particular, shall apply expeditiously those measures so as to avoid unduly impairing or delaying trade in goods or services or conduct of investment activities under this Agreement.

2. The Parties shall endeavour to develop and adopt common criteria, definitions and interpretations for the implementation of this Chapter.

### Article 1603 — Grant of Temporary Entry

1. Each Party shall grant temporary entry to business persons who are otherwise qualified for entry under applicable measures relating to public health and safety and national security, in accordance with this Chapter, including the provisions of Annex 1603.

2. A Party may refuse to issue an immigration document authorizing employment to a business person where the temporary entry of that person might affect adversely:

(a) the settlement of any labour dispute that is in progress at the place or intended place of employment; or

(b) the employment of any person who is involved in such dispute.

3. When a Party refuses pursuant to paragraph 2 to issue an immigration document authorizing employment, it shall:

(a) inform in writing the business person of the reasons for the refusal; and

(b) promptly notify in writing the Party whose business person has been refused entry of the reasons for the refusal.

4. Each Party shall limit any fees for processing applications for temporary entry of business persons to the approximate cost of services rendered.

## Article 1604 — Provision of Information

1. Further to Article 1802 (Publication), each Party shall:

(a) provide to the other Parties such materials as will enable them to become acquainted with its measures relating to this Chapter; and

(b) no later than one year after the date of entry into force of this Agreement, prepare, publish and make available in its own territory, and in the territories of the other Parties, explanatory material in a consolidated document regarding the requirements for temporary entry under this Chapter in such a manner as will enable business persons of the other Parties to become acquainted with them.

2. Subject to Annex 1604.2, each Party shall collect and maintain, and make available to the other Parties in accordance with its domestic law, data respecting the granting of temporary entry under this Chapter to business persons of the other Parties who have been issued immigration documentation, including data specific to each occupation, profession or activity.

## Article 1605 — Working Group

1. The Parties hereby establish a Temporary Entry Working Group, comprising representatives of each Party, including immigration officials.

2. The Working Group shall meet at least once each year to consider:

(a) the implementation and administration of this Chapter;

(b) the development of measures to further facilitate temporary entry of business persons on a reciprocal basis;

(c) the waiving of labour certification tests or procedures of similar effect for spouses of business persons who have been granted temporary entry for more than one year under Section B, C or D of Annex 1603; and

(d) proposed modifications of or additions to this Chapter.

## Article 1606 — Dispute Settlement

1. A Party may not initiate proceedings under Article 2007 (Commission — Good Offices, Conciliation and Mediation) regarding a refusal to grant temporary entry under this Chapter or a particular case arising under Article 1602(1) unless:

(a) the matter involves a pattern of practice; and

(b) the business person has exhausted the available administrative remedies regarding the particular matter.

2. The remedies referred to in paragraph (1)(b) shall be deemed to be exhausted if a final determination in the matter has not been issued by the competent authority within one year of the institution of an administrative proceeding, and the failure to issue a determination is not attributable to delay caused by the business person.

## Article 1607 — Relation to Other Chapters

Except for this Chapter, Chapters One (Objectives), Two (General Definitions), Twenty (Institutional Arrangements and Dispute Settlement Procedures) and Twenty-two (Final Provisions) and Articles 1801 (Contacts Points), 1802 (Publication), 1803 (Notification and Provision of Information) and 1804 (Administrative Proceedings), no provision of this Agreement shall impose any obligation on a Party regarding its immigration measures.

### Article 1608 — Definitions

For purposes of this Chapter:

"business person" means a citizen of a Party who is engaged in trade in goods, the provision of services or the conduct of investment activities;

citizen means "citizen" as defined in Annex 1608 for the Parties specified in that Annex;

existing means "existing" as defined in Annex 1608 for the Parties specified in that Annex;

"temporary entry" means entry into the territory of a Party by a business person of another Party without the intent to establish permanent residence.

## ANNEX 1603 — TEMPORARY ENTRY FOR BUSINESS PERSONS

### Section A. — Business Visitors

1. Each Party shall grant temporary entry to a business person seeking to engage in a business activity set out in Appendix 1603.A.1, without requiring that person to obtain an employment authorization, provided that the business person otherwise complies with existing immigration measures applicable to temporary entry, on presentation of:

(a) proof of citizenship of a Party;

(b) documentation demonstrating that the business person will be so engaged and describing the purpose of entry; and

(c) evidence demonstrating that the proposed business activity is international in scope and that the business person is not seeking to enter the local labor market.

2. Each party shall provide that a business person may satisfy the requirements of paragraph 1(c) by demonstrating that:

(a) the primary source of remuneration for the proposed business activity is outside the territory of the Party granting temporary entry; and

(b) the business person's principal place of business and the actual place of accrual of profits, at least predominantly, remain outside such territory.

A Party shall normally accept an oral declaration as to the principal place of business and the actual place of accrual of profits. Where the Party requires further proof, it shall normally consider a letter from the employer attesting to these matters as sufficient proof.

3. Each Party shall grant temporary entry to a business person seeking to engage in a business activity other than those set out in Appendix 1603.A.1, without requiring that person to obtain an employment authorization, on a basis no less favourable than that provided under the existing provisions of the measures set out in Appendix 1603.A.3, provided that the business person otherwise complies with existing immigration measures applicable to temporary entry.

4. No Party may:

(a) as a condition for temporary entry under paragraph 1 or 3, require prior approval procedures, petitions, labour certification tests or other procedures of similar effect; or

(b) impose or maintain any numerical restriction relating to temporary entry under paragraph 1 or 3.

5. Notwithstanding paragraph 4, a Party may require a business person seeking temporary entry under this Section to obtain a visa or its equivalent prior to entry. Before imposing a visa requirement, the Party shall consult, on request, with a Party whose business persons would be affected with a view to avoiding the imposition of the requirement. With respect to an existing visa requirement, a Party shall consult, on request, with a Party whose business persons are subject to the requirement with a view to its removal.

### Section B. — Traders and Investors

1. Each Party shall grant temporary entry and provide confirming documentation to a business person seeking to:

(a) carry on substantial trade in goods or services principally between the territory of the Party of which the business person is a citizen and the territory of the Party into which entry is sought, or

(b) establish, develop, administer or provide advice or key technical services to the operation of an investment to which the business person or the business person's enterprise has committed, or is in the process of committing, a substantial amount of capital, in a capacity that is supervisory, executive or involves essential skills,

provided that the business person otherwise complies with existing immigration measures applicable to temporary entry.

2. No Party may:

(a) as a condition for temporary entry under paragraph 1, require labor certification tests or other procedures of similar effect; or

(b) impose or maintain any numerical restriction relating to temporary entry under paragraph 1.

3. Notwithstanding paragraph 2, a Party may require a business person seeking temporary entry under this Section to obtain a visa or its equivalent prior to entry.

### Section C. — Intra-Company Transferees

1. Each Party shall grant temporary entry and provide confirming documentation to a business person employed by an enterprise who seeks to render services to that enterprise or a subsidiary or affiliate thereof, in a capacity that is managerial, executive or involves specialized knowledge, provided that the business person otherwise complies with existing immigration measures applicable to temporary entry. A Party may require the business person to have been employed continuously by the enterprise for one year within the three-year period immediately preceding the date of the application for admission.

2. No Party may:

(a) as a condition for temporary entry under paragraph 1, require labor certification tests or other procedures of similar effect; or

(b) impose or maintain any numerical restriction relating to temporary entry under paragraph 1.

3. Notwithstanding paragraph 2, a Party may require a business person seeking temporary entry under this Section to obtain a visa or its equivalent prior to entry. Before imposing a visa requirement, the Party shall consult with a Party whose business persons would be affected with a view to avoiding the imposition of the requirement. With respect to an existing visa requirement, a Party shall consult, on request, with a Party whose business persons are subject to the requirement with a view to its removal.

## Section D. — Professionals

1. Each Party shall grant temporary entry and provide confirming documentation to a business person seeking to engage in a business activity at a professional level in a profession set out in Appendix 1603.D.1, if the business person otherwise complies with existing immigration measures applicable to temporary entry, on presentation of:

(a) proof of citizenship of a Party; and

(b) documentation demonstrating that the business person will be so engaged and describing the purpose of entry.

2. No Party may:

(a) as a condition for temporary entry under paragraph 1, require prior approval procedures, petitions, labor certification tests or other procedures of similar effect; or

(b) impose or maintain any numerical restriction relating to temporary entry under paragraph 1.

3. Notwithstanding paragraph 2, a Party may require a business person seeking temporary entry under this Section to obtain a visa or its equivalent prior to entry. Before imposing a visa requirement, the Party shall consult with a Party whose business persons would be affected with a view to avoiding the imposition of the requirement. With respect to an existing visa requirement, a Party shall consult, on request, with a party whose business persons are subject to the requirement with a view to its removal.

4. Notwithstanding paragraphs 1 and 2, a Party may establish an annual numerical limit, which shall be set out in Appendix 1603.D.4, regarding temporary entry of business persons of another Party seeking to engage in business activities at a professional level in a profession set out in Appendix 1603.D.1, if the Parties concerned have not agreed otherwise prior to the date of entry into force of this Agreement for those Parties. In establishing such a limit, the Party shall consult with the other Party concerned.

5. A Party establishing a numerical limit pursuant to paragraph 4, unless the Parties concerned agree otherwise:

(a) shall, for each year after the first year after the date of entry into force of this Agreement, consider increasing the numerical limit set out in Appendix 1603.D.4 by an amount to be established in consultation with the other Party concerned, taking into account the demand for temporary entry under this Section;

(b) shall not apply its procedures established pursuant to paragraph 1 to the temporary entry of a business person subject to the numerical limit, but may require the business person to comply with its other procedures applicable to the temporary entry of professionals; and

(c) may, in consultation with the other Party concerned, grant temporary entry under paragraph 1 to a business person who practices in a profession where accreditation, licensing, and certification requirements are mutually recognized by those Parties.

6. Nothing in paragraph 4 or 5 shall be construed to limit the ability of a business person to seek temporary entry under a Party's applicable immigration measures relating to the entry of professionals other than those adopted or maintained pursuant to paragraph 1.

7. Three years after a Party establishes a numerical limit pursuant to paragraph 4, it shall consult with the other Party concerned with a view to determining a date after which the limit shall cease to apply.

## Appendix 1603.A.1 — Business Visitors

### Research and Design

- Technical, scientific and statistical researchers conducting independent research or research for an enterprise located in the territory of another Party.

### Growth, Manufacture and Production

- Harvester owner supervising a harvesting crew admitted under applicable law.
- Purchasing and production management personnel conducting commercial transactions for an enterprise located in the territory of another Party.

### Marketing

- Market researchers and analysts conducting independent research or analysis or research or analysis for an enterprise located in the territory of another Party.
- Trade fair and promotional personnel attending a trade convention.

### Sales

- Sales representatives and agents taking orders or negotiating contracts for goods or services for an enterprise located in the territory of another Party but not delivering goods or providing services.
- Buyers purchasing for an enterprise located in the territory of another Party.

### Distribution

- Transportation operators transporting goods or passengers to the territory of a Party from the territory of another Party or loading and transporting goods or passengers from the territory of a Party, with no unloading in that territory, to the territory of another Party.
- With respect to temporary entry into the territory of the United States, Canadian customs brokers performing brokerage duties relating to the export of goods from the territory of the United States to or through the territory of Canada.
- With respect to temporary entry into the territory of Canada, United States customs brokers performing brokerage duties relating to the export of goods from the territory of Canada to or through the territory of the United States.
- Customs brokers providing consulting services regarding the facilitation of the import or export of goods.

### After-Sales Service

- Installers, repair and maintenance personnel, and supervisors, possessing specialized knowledge essential to a seller's contractual obligation, performing services or training workers to perform services, pursuant to a warranty or other service contract incidental to the sale of commercial or industrial equipment or machinery, including computer software, purchased from an enterprise located outside the territory of the Party into which temporary entry is sought, during the life of the warranty or service agreement.

## General Service

- Professionals engaging in a business activity at a professional level in a profession set out in Appendix 1603.D.1.
- Management and supervisory personnel engaging in a commercial transaction for an enterprise located in the territory of another Party.
- Financial services personnel (insurers, bankers or investment brokers) engaging in commercial transactions for an enterprise located in the territory of another Party.
- Public relations and advertising personnel consulting with business associates, or attending or participating in conventions.
- Tourism personnel (tour and travel agents, tour guides or tour operators) attending or participating in conventions or conducting a tour that has begun in the territory of another Party.
- Tour bus operators entering the territory of a Party:
  (a) with a group of passengers on a bus tour that has begun in, and will return to, the territory of another Party;
  (b) to meet a group of passengers on a bus tour that will end, and the predominant portion of which will take place, in the territory of another Party; or
  (c) with a group of passengers on a bus tour to be unloaded in the territory of the Party into which temporary entry is sought, and returning with no passengers or reloading with the group for transportation to the territory of another Party.
- Translators or interpreters performing services as employees of an enterprise located in the territory of another Party.

## Definitions

For purposes of this Appendix:

territory of another Party means the territory of a Party other than the territory of the Party into which temporary entry is sought;

tour bus operator means a natural person, including relief personnel accompanying or following to join, necessary for the operation of a tour bus for the duration of a trip; and

transportation operator means a natural person, other than a tour bus operator, including relief personnel accompanying or following to join, necessary for the operation of a vehicle for the duration of a trip.

## Appendix 1603.A.3 — Existing Immigration Measures

1. In the case of Canada, subsection 19(1) of the *Immigration Regulations, 1978*, SOR/78-172, as amended, made under the *Immigration Act*, R.S.C. 1985, c. 1-2, as amended.

2. In the case of the United States, section 101(a)(15)(B) of the *Immigration and Nationality Act*, 1952, as amended.

3. In the case of Mexico, Chapter III of the *Ley General de Poblacion*, 1974, as amended.

## Appendix 1603.D.1 — Professionals

| PROFESSION[1] | MINIMUM EDUCATION REQUIREMENTS AND ALTERNATIVE CREDENTIALS |
|---|---|
| General | |
| Accountant | Baccalaureate or Licenciatura Degree, or C.P.A., C.A., C.G.A., C.M.A. |
| Architect | Baccalaureate or Licenciatura Degree; or state/provincial license[2] |
| Computer Systems Analyst | Baccalaureate or Licenciatura Degree; or Post-Secondary Diploma[3] or Post-Secondary Certificate,[4] and three years experience |
| Disaster Relief Insurance Claims Adjuster (claims adjuster employed by an insurance company located in the territory of a Party, or an independent claims adjuster) | Baccalaureate or Licenciatura Degree, and successful completion of training in the appropriate areas of insurance adjustment pertaining to disaster relief claims; or three years experience in claims adjustment and successful completion of training in the appropriate areas of insurance adjustment pertaining to disaster relief claims |
| Economist | Baccalaureate or Licenciatura Degree |
| Engineer | Baccalaureate or Licenciatura Degree; or state/provincial license |
| Forester | Baccalaureate or Licenciatura Degree; or state/provincial license |
| Graphic Designer | Baccalaureate or Licenciatura Degree; or Post-Secondary Diploma or Post-Secondary Certificate, and three years experience |
| Hotel Manager | Baccalaureate or Licenciatura Degree in hotel/restaurant management; or Post-Secondary Diploma or Post-Secondary Certificate in hotel/restaurant management, and three years experience in hotel/restaurant management |
| Industrial Designer | Baccalaureate or Licenciatura Degree; or Post-Secondary Diploma or Post-Secondary Certificate, and three years experience |
| Interior Designer | Baccalaureate or Licenciatura Degree; or Post-Secondary Diploma or Post-Secondary Certificate, and three years experience |
| Land Surveyor | Baccalaureate or Licenciatura Degree; or state/provincial/federal license |

| PROFESSION[1] | MINIMUM EDUCATION REQUIREMENTS AND ALTERNATIVE CREDENTIALS |
|---|---|
| Landscape Architect | Baccalaureate or Licenciatura Degree |
| Lawyer (including Notary in the Province of Quebec) | LL.B., J.D., LL.L., B.C.L. or Licenciatura Degree (five years); or membership in a state/provincial bar |
| Librarian | M.L.S. or B.L.S. (for which another Baccalaureate or Licenciatura Degree was a prerequisite) |
| Management Consultant | Baccalaureate or Licenciatura Degree; or equivalent professional experience as established by statement or professional credential attesting to five years experience as a management consultant, or five years experience in a field of specialty related to the consulting agreement |
| Mathematician (including Statistician) | Baccalaureate or Licenciatura Degree |
| Range Manager/Range Conservationalist | Baccalaureate or Licenciatura Degree |
| Research Assistant (working in a post-secondary educational institution) | Baccalaureate or Licenciatura Degree |
| Scientific Technician/Technologist[5] | Possession of (a) theoretical knowledge of any of the following disciplines: agricultural sciences, astronomy, biology, chemistry, engineering, forestry, geology, geo-physics, meteorology or physics; and (b) the ability to solve practical problems in any of those disciplines, or the ability to apply principles of any of those disciplines to basic or applied research |
| Social Worker | Baccalaureate or Licenciatura Degree |
| Sylviculturist (including Forestry Specialist) | Baccalaureate or Licenciatura Degree |
| Technical Publications Writer | Baccalaureate or Licenciatura Degree; or Post-Secondary Diploma or Post-Secondary Certificate, and three years experience |
| Urban Planner (including Geographer) | Baccalaureate or Licenciatura Degree |
| Vocational Counsellor | Baccalaureate or Licenciatura Degree |
| Medical/Allied Professional | |
| Dentist | D.D.S., D.M.D., Doctor en Odontologia or Doctor en Cirugia Dental; or state/provincial license |

| PROFESSION[1] | MINIMUM EDUCATION REQUIREMENTS AND ALTERNATIVE CREDENTIALS |
|---|---|
| Dietitian | Baccalaureate or Licenciatura Degree; or state/provincial license |
| Medical Laboratory Technologist (Canada)/Medical Technologist (Mexico and the United States)[6] | Baccalaureate or Licenciatura Degree; or Post-Secondary Diploma or Post-Secondary Certificate, and three years experience |
| Nutritionist | Baccalaureate or Licenciatura Degree |
| Occupational Therapist | Baccalaureate or Licenciatura Degree; or state/provincial license |
| Pharmacist | Baccalaureate or Licenciatura Degree; or state/provincial license |
| Physician (teaching and/or research only) | M.D. or Doctor en Medicina; or state/provincial license |
| Physiotherapist/Physical Therapist | Baccalaureate or Licenciatura Degree; or state/provincial license |
| Psychologist | State/provincial license; or Licenciatura Degree |
| Recreational Therapist | Baccalaureate or Licenciatura Degree |
| Registered Nurse | State/provincial license; or Licenciatura Degree |
| Veterinarian | D.V.M., D.M.V., or Doctor en Veterinaria; or state/provincial license |
| Scientist | |
| Agriculturist (Agronomist) | Baccalaureate or Licenciatura Degree |
| Animal Breeder | Baccalaureate or Licenciatura Degree |
| Animal Scientist | Baccalaureate or Licenciatura Degree |
| Apiculturist | Baccalaureate or Licenciatura Degree |
| Astronomer | Baccalaureate or Licenciatura Degree |
| Biochemist | Baccalaureate or Licenciatura Degree |
| Biologist | Baccalaureate or Licenciatura Degree |
| Chemist | Baccalaureate or Licenciatura Degree |
| Dairy Scientist | Baccalaureate or Licenciatura Degree |
| Entomologist | Baccalaureate or Licenciatura Degree |
| Epidemiologist | Baccalaureate or Licenciatura Degree |
| Geneticist | Baccalaureate or Licenciatura Degree |
| Geologist | Baccalaureate or Licenciatura Degree |
| Geochemist | Baccalaureate or Licenciatura Degree |
| Geophysicist (including Oceanographer in Mexico and the United States) | Baccalaureate or Licenciatura Degree |
| Horticulturist | Baccalaureate or Licenciatura Degree |
| Meteorologist | Baccalaureate or Licenciatura Degree |
| Pharmacologist | Baccalaureate or Licenciatura Degree |
| Physicist (including Oceanographer in Canada) | Baccalaureate or Licenciatura Degree |

| PROFESSION[1] | MINIMUM EDUCATION REQUIREMENTS AND ALTERNATIVE CREDENTIALS |
|---|---|
| Plant Breeder | Baccalaureate or Licenciatura Degree |
| Poultry Scientist | Baccalaureate or Licenciatura Degree |
| Soil Scientist | Baccalaureate or Licenciatura Degree |
| Zoologist | Baccalaureate or Licenciatura Degree |
| Teacher | |
| College | Baccalaureate or Licenciatura Degree |
| Seminary | Baccalaureate or Licenciatura Degree |
| University | Baccalaureate or Licenciatura Degree |

**Notes:**

1 A business person seeking temporary entry under this Appendix may also perform training functions relating to the profession, including conducting seminars.

2 "State/provincial license" and "state/provincial/federal license" mean any document issued by a state, provincial or federal government, as the case may be, or under its authority, but not by a local government, that permits a person to engage in a regulated activity or profession.

3 "Post-Secondary Diploma" means a credential issued, on completion of two or more years of post-secondary education, by an accredited academic institution in Canada or the United States.

4 "Post-Secondary Certificate" means a certificate issued, on completion of two or more years of post-secondary education at an academic institution, by the federal government of Mexico or a state government in Mexico, an academic institution recognized by the federal government or a state government, or an academic institution created by federal or state law.

5 A business person in this category must be seeking temporary entry to work in direct support of professionals in agricultural sciences, astronomy, biology, chemistry, engineering, forestry, geology, geophysics, meterorology or physics.

6 A business person in this category must be seeking temporary entry to perform in a laboratory chemical, biological, hematological, immunologic, microscopic or bacteriological tests and analyses for diagnosis, treatment or prevention of disease.

## Appendix 1603.D.4 — United States

1. Beginning on the date of entry into force of this Agreement as between the United States and Mexico, the United States shall annually approve as many as 5,500 initial petitions of business persons of Mexico seeking temporary entry under Section D of Annex 1603 to engage in a business activity at a professional level in a profession set out in Appendix 1603.D.1.

2. For purposes of paragraph 1, the United States shall not take into account:

(a) the renewal of a period of temporary entry;

(b) the entry of a spouse or children accompanying or following to join the principal business person;

(c) an admission under section 101(a)(15)(H)(i)(b) of the *Immigration and Nationality Act*, 1952, as may be amended, including the worldwide numerical limit established by section 214(g)(1)(A) of that Act; or

(d) an admission under any other provision of section 101(a)(15) of that Act relating to the entry of professionals.

3. Paragraphs 4 and 5 of Section D of Annex 1603 shall apply as between the United States and Mexico for no longer than:

(a) the period that such paragraphs or similar provisions may apply as between the United States and any other Party other than Canada or any non-Party; or

(b) 10 years after the date of entry into force of this Agreement as between such Parties,

whichever period is shorter.

## ANNEX 1604.2 — PROVISION OF INFORMATION

The obligations under Article 1604(2) shall take effect with respect to Mexico one year after the date of entry into force of this Agreement.

## ANNEX 1608 — COUNTRY — SPECIFIC DEFINITIONS

For purposes of this Chapter:

citizen means, with respect to Mexico, a national or a citizen according to the existing provisions of Articles 30 and 34, respectively, of the Mexican Constitution; and

existing means, as between:

(a) Canada and Mexico, and Mexico and the United States, in effect on the date of entry into force of this Agreement; and

(b) Canada and the United States, in effect on January 1, 1989.

# APPENDIX IV

# CANADA–CHILE FREE TRADE AGREEMENT (CCFTA) DECEMBER 5, 1996

# Chapter K — Temporary Entry for Business Persons

## Article K-01 — General Principles

Further to Article A-02 (Objectives), this Chapter reflects the preferential trading relationship between the Parties, the desirability of facilitating temporary entry on a reciprocal basis and of establishing transparent criteria and procedures for temporary entry, and the need to ensure border security and to protect the domestic labour force and permanent employment in their respective territories.

## Article K-02 — General Obligations

Each Party shall apply its measures relating to the provisions of this Chapter in accordance with Article K-01 and, in particular, shall apply expeditiously those measures so as to avoid unduly impairing or delaying trade in goods or services or conduct of investment activities under this Agreement.

## Article K-03 — Grant of Temporary Entry

1. Each Party shall grant temporary entry to business persons who are otherwise qualified for entry under applicable measures relating to public health and safety and national security, in accordance with this Chapter, including the provisions of Annex K-03 and Annex K-03.1.

2. A Party may refuse to issue an immigration document authorizing employment to a business person where the temporary entry of that person might affect adversely:

(a) the settlement of any labour dispute that is in progress at the place or intended place of employment; or

(b) the employment of any person who is involved in such dispute.

3. When a Party refuses pursuant to paragraph 2 to issue an immigration document authorizing employment, it shall:

(a) inform in writing the business person of the reasons for the refusal; and

(b) promptly notify the other Party in writing of the reasons for the refusal.

4. Each Party shall limit any fees for processing applications for temporary entry of business persons to the approximate cost of services rendered.

## Article K-04 — Provision of Information

1. Further to Article L-02 (Publication), each Party shall:

(a) provide to the other Party such materials as will enable it to become acquainted with its measures relating to this Chapter; and

(b) no later than one year after the date of entry into force of this Agreement, prepare, publish and make available in its own territory, and in the territory of the other Party, explanatory material in a consolidated document regarding the requirements for temporary entry under this Chapter in such a manner as will enable business persons of the other Party to become acquainted with them.

2. Each Party shall collect and maintain, and make available to the other Party in accordance with its domestic law, data respecting the granting of temporary entry under this Chapter to business persons of the other Party who have been issued immigration documentation, including data specific to each occupation, profession or activity.

## Article K-05 — Working Group

The Parties hereby establish a Temporary Entry Working Group, comprising representatives of each Party, including immigration officials, to consider the implementation and administration of this Chapter and any measures of mutual interest.

## Article K-06 — Dispute Settlement

1. A Party may not initiate proceedings under Article N-07 (Commission — Good Offices, Conciliation and Mediation) regarding a refusal to grant temporary entry under this Chapter or a particular case arising under Article K-02 unless:

(a) the matter involves a pattern of practice; and

(b) the business person has exhausted the available administrative remedies regarding the particular matter.

2. The remedies referred to in paragraph (1)(b) shall be deemed to be exhausted if a final determination in the matter has not been issued by the competent authority within one year of the institution of an administrative proceeding, and the failure to issue a determination is not attributable to delay caused by the business person.

## Article K-07 — Relation to Other Chapters

Except for this Chapter, Chapters A (Objectives), B (General Definitions), N (Institutional Arrangements and Dispute Settlement Procedures) and P (Final Provisions) and Articles L-01 (Contacts Points), L-02 (Publication), L-03 (Notification and Provision of Information) and L-04 (Administrative Proceedings), no provision of this Agreement shall impose any obligation on a Party regarding its immigration measures.

## Article K-08 — Definitions:

For purposes of this Chapter:

business person means a citizen of a Party who is engaged in trade in goods, the provision of services or the conduct of investment activities; and

temporary entry means entry into the territory of a Party by a business person of the other Party without the intent to establish permanent residence.

# ANNEX K-03 — TEMPORARY ENTRY FOR BUSINESS PERSONS

## Section I — Business Visitors

1. Each Party shall grant temporary entry to a business person seeking to engage in a business activity set out in Appendix K-03.I.1, without requiring that person to obtain an employment authorization, provided that the business person otherwise complies with existing immigration measures applicable to temporary entry, on presentation of:

(a) proof of citizenship of a Party;

(b) documentation demonstrating that the business person will be so engaged and describing the purpose of entry; and

(c) evidence demonstrating that the proposed business activity is international in scope and the business person is not seeking to enter the local labour market.

2. Each Party shall provide that a business person may satisfy the requirements of paragraph 1(c) by demonstrating that:

(a) the primary source of remuneration for the proposed business activity is outside the territory of the Party granting temporary entry; and

(b) the business person's principal place of business and the actual place of accrual of profits, at least, predominantly, remain outside such territory.

A Party shall normally accept an oral declaration as to the principal place of business and the actual place of accrual of profits. Where the Party requires further proof, it shall normally consider a letter from the employer attesting to these matters as sufficient proof.

3. Each Party shall grant temporary entry to a business person seeking to engage in a business activity other than those set out in Appendix K-03.I.1, without requiring that person to obtain an employment authorization, on a basis no less favourable than that provided under the existing provisions of the measures set out in Appendix K-03.I.3, provided that the business person otherwise complies with existing immigration measures applicable to temporary entry.

4. Neither Party may:

(a) as a condition for temporary entry under paragraph 1 or 3, require prior approval procedures, petitions, labour certification tests or other procedures of similar effect; or

(b) impose or maintain any numerical restriction relating to temporary entry under paragraph 1 or 3.

5. Notwithstanding paragraph 4, a Party may require a business person seeking temporary entry under this Section to obtain a visa or its equivalent prior to entry. Before imposing a visa requirement, the Party shall consult with the other Party with a view to avoiding the imposition of the requirement. With respect to an existing visa requirement, a Party shall consult, on request, with the other Party with a view to its removal.

## Section II — Traders and Investors

1. Each Party shall grant temporary entry and provide confirming documentation to a business person seeking to:

(a) carry on substantial trade in goods or services principally between the territory of the Party of which the business person is a citizen and the territory of the other Party into which entry is sought, or

(b) establish, develop, administer or provide advice or key technical services to the operation of an investment to which the business person or the business person's enterprise has committed, or is in the process of committing, a substantial amount of capital,

in a capacity that is supervisory, executive or involves essential skills, provided that the business person otherwise complies with existing immigration measures applicable to temporary entry.

2. Neither Party may:

(a) as a condition for temporary entry under paragraph 1, require labour certification tests or other procedures of similar effect; or

(b) impose or maintain any numerical restriction relating to temporary entry under paragraph 1.

3. Notwithstanding paragraph 2, a Party may require a business person seeking temporary entry under this Section to obtain a visa or its equivalent prior to entry.

### Section III — Intra-Company Transferees

1. Each Party shall grant temporary entry and provide confirming documentation to a business person employed by an enterprise who seeks to render services to that enterprise or a subsidiary or affiliate thereof, in a capacity that is managerial, executive or involves specialized knowledge, provided that the business person otherwise complies with existing immigration measures applicable to temporary entry. A Party may require the business person to have been employed continuously by the enterprise for one year within the three-year period immediately preceding the date of the application for admission.

2. Neither Party may:

(a) as a condition for temporary entry under paragraph 1, require labour certification tests or other procedures of similar effect; or

(b) impose or maintain any numerical restriction relating to temporary entry under paragraph 1.

3. Notwithstanding paragraph 2, a Party may require a business person seeking temporary entry under this Section to obtain a visa or its equivalent prior to entry. Before imposing a visa requirement, the Party shall consult with the other Party with a view to avoiding the imposition of the requirement. With respect to an existing visa requirement, a Party shall consult, on request, with the other Party with a view to its removal.

### Section IV — Professionals

1. Each Party shall grant temporary entry and provide confirming documentation to a business person seeking to engage in a business activity at a professional level in a profession set out in Appendix K-03.IV.1, if the business person otherwise complies with existing immigration measures applicable to temporary entry, on presentation of:

(a) proof of citizenship of a Party; and

(b) documentation demonstrating that the business person will be so engaged and describing the purpose of entry.

2. Neither Party may:

(a) as a condition for temporary entry under paragraph 1, require prior approval procedures, petitions, labour certification tests or other procedures of similar effect; or

(b) impose or maintain any numerical restriction relating to temporary entry under paragraph 1.

3. Notwithstanding paragraph 2, a Party may require a business person seeking temporary entry under this Section to obtain a visa or its equivalent prior to entry. Before imposing a visa requirement, the Party shall consult with the other Party with a view to avoiding the imposition of the requirement. With respect to an existing visa requirement, a Party shall consult, on request, with the other Party with a view to its removal.

4. Notwithstanding paragraphs 1 and 2, a Party may establish an annual numerical limit, which shall be set out in Appendix K-03.IV.4, regarding temporary entry of business persons of the other Party seeking to engage in business activities at a professional level in a profession set out in Appendix K-03.IV.1, if the Parties have not agreed otherwise prior to the date of entry into force of this Agreement. In establishing such a limit, the Party shall consult with the other Party.

5. A Party establishing a numerical limit pursuant to paragraph 4, unless the Parties agree otherwise:

(a) shall, for each year after the first year after the date of entry into force of this Agreement, consider increasing the numerical limit set out in Appendix K-03.IV.4 by an amount to be established in consultation with the other Party, taking into account the demand for temporary entry under this Section;

(b) shall not apply its procedures established pursuant to paragraph 1 to the temporary entry of a business person subject to the numerical limit, but may require the business person to comply with its other procedures applicable to the temporary entry of professionals; and

(c) may, in consultation with the other Party, grant temporary entry under paragraph 1 to a business person who practices in a profession where accreditation, licensing, and certification requirements are mutually recognized by the Parties.

6. Nothing in paragraph 4 or 5 shall be construed to limit the ability of a business person to seek temporary entry under a Party's applicable immigration measures relating to the entry of professionals other than those adopted or maintained pursuant to paragraph 1.

7. Three years after a Party establishes a numerical limit pursuant to paragraph 4, it shall consult with the other Party with a view to determining a date after which the limit shall cease to apply.

## Annex K-03.1

1. Business persons who enter Chile under any of the categories set out in Annex K-03 shall be deemed to be engaged in activities which are in the country's interest.

2. Business persons who enter Chile under any of the categories set out in Annex K-03 and are issued a temporary visa shall have that temporary visa extended for subsequent periods provided the conditions on which it is based remain in effect, without requiring that person to apply for permanent residence.

3. Business persons who enter Chile may also obtain an identity card for foreigners.

## Appendix K-03.I.1 — Business Visitors

### Research and Design

- Technical, scientific and statistical researchers conducting independent research or research for an enterprise located in the territory of the other Party.

### Growth, Manufacture and Production

- Purchasing and production management personnel conducting commercial transactions for an enterprise located in the territory of the other Party.

### Marketing

- Market researchers and analysts conducting independent research or analysis or research or analysis for an enterprise located in the territory of the other Party.
- Trade fair and promotional personnel attending a trade convention.

### Sales

- Sales representatives and agents taking orders or negotiating contracts for goods or services for an enterprise located in the territory of the other Party but not delivering goods or providing services.
- Buyers purchasing for an enterprise located in the territory of the other Party.

### Distribution

- Customs brokers providing consulting services regarding the facilitation of the import or export of goods.

### After-sales Service

- Installers, repair and maintenance personnel, and supervisors, possessing specialized knowledge essential to a seller's contractual obligation, performing services or training workers to perform services, pursuant to a warranty or other service contract incidental to the sale of commercial or industrial equipment or machinery, including computer software, purchased from an enterprise located outside the territory of the Party into which temporary entry is sought, during the life of the warranty or service agreement.

### General Service

- Professionals engaging in a business activity at a professional level in a profession set out in Appendix K-03.IV.1.
- Management and supervisory personnel engaging in a commercial transaction for an enterprise located in the territory of the other Party.
- Financial services personnel (insurers, bankers or investment brokers) engaging in commercial transactions for an enterprise located in the territory of the other Party.
- Public relations and advertising personnel consulting with business associates, or attending or participating in conventions.
- Tourism personnel (tour and travel agents, tour guides or tour operators) attending or participating in conventions or conducting a tour that has begun in the territory of the other Party.
- Translators or interpreters performing services as employees of an enterprise located in the territory of the other Party.

### Definitions

For purposes of this Appendix:

territory of the other Party means the territory of the Party other than the territory of the Party into which temporary entry is sought.

## Appendix K-03.I.3 — Existing Immigration Measures

1. In the case of Canada, subsection 19(1) of the *Immigration Regulations*, 1978, SOR/78-172, as amended, made under the *Immigration Act* R.S.C. 1985, c. I-2, as amended.

2. In the case of Chile, Title I, paragraph 6 of *Decree Law 1094*, Official Gazette, July 19, 1975, *Immigration Law ("Decreto Ley 1094,* Diario Oficial, julio 19, 1975, *Ley de Extranjería"),* and *Title III of Immigration Regulation ("Decreto Supremo 597 del Ministerio del Interior,* Diario Oficial noviembre 24, 1984, *Reglamento de Extranjería*").

## Appendix K-03.IV.1 — Professionals

| PROFESSION[1] | MINIMUM EDUCATION REQUIREMENTS AND ALTERNATIVE CREDENTIALS[2] |
|---|---|
| *General* | |
| Accountant | Baccalaureate or Licenciatura Degree; or C.P.A., C.A., C.G.A. or C.M.A.; or Contador auditor or Contador público (University Title)[3] |
| Architect | Baccalaureate or Licenciatura Degree; or state/provincial licence[4] |
| Computer Systems Analyst | Baccalaureate or Licenciatura Degree; or Post-Secondary Diploma[5] or Post-Secondary Certificate[6], and three years experience |
| Disaster Relief Insurance Claims Adjuster (claims adjuster employed by an insurance company located in the territory of a Party, or an independent claims adjuster) | Baccalaureate or Licenciatura Degree, and successful completion of training in the appropriate areas of insurance adjustment pertaining to disaster relief claims; or three years experience in claims adjustment and successful completion of training in the appropriate areas of insurance adjustment pertaining to disaster relief claims |
| Economist (including Commercial Engineer in Chile) | Baccalaureate or Licenciatura Degree |
| Engineer | Baccalaureate or Licenciatura Degree; or state/provincial licence |
| Forester | Baccalaureate or Licenciatura Degree; or state/provincial licence |
| Graphic Designer | Baccalaureate or Licenciatura Degree; or Post-Secondary Diploma or Post-Secondary Certificate, and three years experience |

| PROFESSION[1] | MINIMUM EDUCATION REQUIREMENTS AND ALTERNATIVE CREDENTIALS[2] |
|---|---|
| Hotel Manager | Baccalaureate or Licenciatura Degree in hotel/restaurant management; or Post-Secondary Diploma or Post-Secondary Certificate in hotel/restaurant management, and three years experience in hotel/restaurant management |
| Industrial Designer | Baccalaureate or Licenciatura Degree; or Post-Secondary Diploma or Post-Secondary Certificate, and three years experience |
| Interior Designer | Baccalaureate or Licenciatura Degree; or Post-Secondary Diploma or Post-Secondary Certificate, and three years experience |
| Land Surveyor | Baccalaureate or Licenciatura Degree; or state/provincial/national licence |
| Landscape Architect | Baccalaureate or Licenciatura Degree |
| Lawyer (including Notary in the Province of Quebec) | LL.B., J.D., LL.L., B.C.L. or Licenciatura Degree (five years) or Abogado, or membership in a state/provincial bar |
| Librarian | M.L.S. or B.L.S. or Magister en Bibliotecología (for which another Baccalaureate or Licenciatura Degree was a prerequisite) |
| Management Consultant | Baccalaureate or Licenciatura Degree; or equivalent professional experience as established by statement or professional credential attesting to five years experience as a management consultant, or five years experience in a field of specialty related to the consulting agreement |
| Mathematician (including Statistician) | Baccalaureate or Licenciatura Degree |
| Range Manager/Range Conservationalist | Baccalaureate or Licenciatura Degree |
| Research Assistant (working in a post- secondary educational institution) | Baccalaureate or Licenciatura Degree |

| PROFESSION[1] | MINIMUM EDUCATION REQUIREMENTS AND ALTERNATIVE CREDENTIALS[2] |
| --- | --- |
| Scientific Technician/Technologist[7] | Possession of (a) theoretical knowledge of any of the following disciplines: agricultural sciences, astronomy, biology, chemistry, engineering, forestry, geology, geophysics, meteorology or physics; and (b) the ability to solve practical problems in any of those disciplines, or the ability to apply principles of any of those disciplines to basic or applied research |
| Social Worker | Baccalaureate or Licenciatura Degree or Asistente Social/Trabajador social (University Title) |
| Sylviculturist (including Forestry Specialist) | Baccalaureate or Licenciatura Degree |
| Technical Publications Writer | Baccalaureate or Licenciatura Degree; or Post-Secondary Diploma or Post-Secondary Certificate, and three years experience |
| Urban Planner (including Geographer) | Baccalaureate or Licenciatura Degree |
| Vocational Counsellor | Baccalaureate or Licenciatura Degree |
| *Medical/Allied Professional* | |
| Dentist | D.D.S., D.M.D., Doctor en Odontologia or Doctor en Cirugia Dental or Licenciatura en Odontologia; or state/provincial licence |
| Dietitian | Baccalaureate or Licenciatura Degree or Dietista Nutricional (University Title); or state/provincial licence |
| Medical Laboratory Technologist (Canada)/Medical Technologist (Chile, Mexico and the United States of America)[8] | Baccalaureate or Licenciatura Degree; or Post-Secondary Diploma or Post-Secondary Certificate, and three years experience |
| Nutritionist | Baccalaureate or Licenciatura Degree or Nutricionista/Dietista Nutricional (University Title) |
| Occupational Therapist | Baccalaureate or Licenciatura Degree or Terapeuta Ocupacional (University Title); or state/provincial licence |
| Pharmacist | Baccalaureate or Licenciatura Degree; or state/provincial licence |
| Physician (teaching or research only) | M.D. or Doctor en Medicina or Médico Cirujano/Médico (University Title); or state/provincial licence |

| **PROFESSION**[1] | **MINIMUM EDUCATION REQUIREMENTS AND ALTERNATIVE CREDENTIALS**[2] |
|---|---|
| Physiotherapist/Physical Therapist | Baccalaureate or Licenciatura Degree or Kinesiólogo/Kinesioterapeuta (University Title); or state/provincial licence |
| Psychologist | State/provincial licence; or Licenciatura Degree |
| Recreational Therapist | Baccalaureate or Licenciatura Degree |
| Registered Nurse | State/provincial licence, or Licenciatura Degree, or Enfermera (University Title) |
| Veterinarian | D.V.M., D.M.V. or Doctor en Veterinaria or Médico Veterinario (University Title); or state/provincial licence |
| *Scientist* | |
| Agriculturist (including Agronomist) | Baccalaureate or Licenciatura Degree |
| Animal Breeder | Baccalaureate or Licenciatura Degree |
| Animal Scientist | Baccalaureate or Licenciatura Degree |
| Apiculturist | Baccalaureate or Licenciatura Degree |
| Astronomer | Baccalaureate or Licenciatura Degree |
| Biochemist | Baccalaureate or Licenciatura Degree |
| Biologist | Baccalaureate or Licenciatura Degree |
| Chemist | Baccalaureate or Licenciatura Degree |
| Dairy Scientist | Baccalaureate or Licenciatura Degree |
| Entomologist | Baccalaureate or Licenciatura Degree |
| Epidemiologist | Baccalaureate or Licenciatura Degree |
| Geneticist | Baccalaureate or Licenciatura Degree |
| Geologist | Baccalaureate or Licenciatura Degree or Geólogo (University Title) |
| Geochemist | Baccalaureate or Licenciatura Degree |
| Geophysicist (including Oceanographer in Mexico and the United States of America) | Baccalaureate or Licenciatura Degree |
| Horticulturist | Baccalaureate or Licenciatura Degree |
| Meteorologist | Baccalaureate or Licenciatura Degree |
| Pharmacologist | Baccalaureate or Licenciatura Degree |
| Physicist (including Oceanographer in Canada and Chile) | Baccalaureate or Licenciatura Degree for Physicist; Oceanógrafo (University Title)for Oceanographer |
| Plant Breeder | Baccalaureate or Licenciatura Degree |
| Poultry Scientist | Baccalaureate or Licenciatura Degree |
| Soil Scientist | Baccalaureate or Licenciatura Degree |
| Zoologist | Baccalaureate or Licenciatura Degree |
| *Teacher* | |
| College | Baccalaureate or Licenciatura Degree |

| PROFESSION[1] | MINIMUM EDUCATION REQUIREMENTS AND ALTERNATIVE CREDENTIALS[2] |
|---|---|
| Seminary | Baccalaureate or Licenciatura Degree |
| University | Baccalaureate or Licenciatura Degree |

**Notes:**

1 A business person seeking temporary entry under this Appendix may also perform training functions relating to the profession, including conducting seminars.

2 *Accountant*:

C.P.A.: Certified Public Accountant; C.A.: Chartered Accountant; C.G.A.: Certified General Accountant; C.M.A.: Certified Management Accountant

*Dentist*:

D.D.S.: Doctor of Dental Surgery; D.M.D.: Doctor of Dental Medicine

*Lawyer*:

LL.B.: Bachelor of Laws; J.D.: Doctor of Jurisprudence (not a doctorate); LL.L: Licence en Droit (Québec universities and University of Ottawa); BCL: Bachelor of Civil Law

*Librarian*:

M.L.S.: Master of Library Science; B.L.S.: Bachelor of Library Science

*Physician*:

M.D.: Medical Doctor

*Veterinarian*:

D.V.M.: Doctor of Veterinary Medicine; D.M.V.: Docteur en Médicine Vétérinaire

3 "University Title" means any document conferred by universities recognized by the Government of Chile and shall be deemed to be equivalent to the Minimum Education Requirements and Alternative Credentials for that profession. In the case of the profession of Lawyer (Abogado), the title is conferred by the Supreme Court of Chile.

4 "State/provincial licence" and "state/provincial/national licence" mean any document issued by a provincial or national government, as the case may be, or under its authority, but not by a local government, that permits a person to engage in a regulated activity or profession.

5 "Post-Secondary Diploma" means a credential issued, on completion of two or more years of post-secondary education, by an accredited academic institution in Canada or the United Sates of America.

6 "Post-Secondary Certificate" means a certificate issued, on completion of two or more years of post-secondary education at an academic institution:

— in the case of Mexico, by the federal government or a state government, an academic institution recognized by the federal government or a state government, or an academic institution created by federal or state law; and

— in the case of Chile, by an academic institution recognized by the Government of Chile.

7 A business person in this category must be seeking temporary entry to work in direct support of professionals in agricultural sciences, astronomy, biology, chemistry, engineering, forestry, geology, geophysics, meteorology or physics.

8 A business person in this category must be seeking temporary entry to perform in a laboratory chemical, biological, hematological, immunologic, microscopic or bacteriological tests and analyses for diagnosis, treatment or prevention of disease.

Notwithstanding Annex K-03.IV.4, for the purposes of this Agreement, neither Party shall establish an annual numerical limit regarding temporary entry of business persons of the other Party seeking to engage in business activities at a professional level set out in Appendix K-03.IV.1.

# APPENDIX V

# CANADA–PERU FREE TRADE AGREEMENT

# Chapter 12 — Temporary Entry For Business Persons

## Article 1201: General Principles

Further to Article 1202, this Chapter reflects the preferential trading relationship between the Parties, the mutual objective to facilitate temporary entry for business persons on a reciprocal basis and in accordance with Annex 1203, the need to establish transparent criteria and procedures for temporary entry and the need to ensure border security and to protect the domestic labour force and permanent employment in their respective territories.

## Article 1202: General Obligations

1. Each Party shall apply its measures relating to the provisions of this Chapter in accordance with Article 1201 and, in particular, shall expeditiously apply those measures so as to avoid unduly impairing or delaying trade in goods or services or conduct of investment activities under this Agreement.

2. Nothing in this Chapter shall be construed to prevent a Party from applying measures to regulate the entry of natural persons into, or their temporary stay in, its territory, including those measures necessary to protect the integrity of, and to ensure the orderly movement of natural persons across, its borders, provided that such measures are not applied in such a manner as to unduly impair or delay trade in goods or services or conduct of investment activities under this Agreement.

## Article 1203: Grant of Temporary Entry

1. Each Party shall grant temporary entry to business persons who comply with existing immigration measures applicable to temporary entry such as those relating to public health and safety and national security, in accordance with this Chapter, including the provisions of Annex 1203.

2. Subject to each Party's labour legislation, a Party may refuse to issue a work permit or authorization to a business person where the temporary entry of that person might adversely affect:

(a) the settlement of any labour dispute that is in progress at the place or intended place of employment; or

(b) the employment of any person who is involved in such dispute.

3. Each Party shall limit any fees for processing applications for temporary entry of business persons so as to not unduly impair or delay trade in goods or services or the conduct of investment activities under this Agreement.

Other Relevant Legislation

## Article 1204: Provision of Information

1. Further to Article 1901 (Transparency — Publication), and recognizing the importance to the Parties of transparency of temporary entry information, each Party shall:

(a) provide to the other Party relevant materials that will enable it to become acquainted with its measures relating to this Chapter; and

(b) no later than six months after the date of entry into force of this Agreement, make available explanatory material regarding the requirements for temporary entry under this Chapter in such a manner that will enable business persons of the other Party to become acquainted with them.

2. Each Party shall collect and maintain, and, on request, make available to the other Party in accordance with its domestic law, data respecting the granting of temporary entry under this Chapter to business persons of the other Party who have been issued immigration documentation.

## Article 1205: Contact Points

1. The Parties hereby establish Contact Points:

(a) in the case of Canada, the Contact Point is:

*Director*

*Temporary Resident Policy*

*Immigration Branch*

*Citizenship and Immigration Canada*

(b) in the case of Peru, the Contact Point is:

*Director*

*Directorate of Immigrations*

*General Directorate of Immigration and Naturalization*

*Ministry of Interior,*

or the occupant of any successor position.

2. The Contact Points shall exchange information as described in Article 1204 and shall meet as required to consider matters pertaining to this Chapter, such as:

(a) the implementation and administration of the Chapter;

(b) the development and adoption of common criteria and interpretations for the implementation of the Chapter;

(c) the development of measures to further facilitate temporary entry of business persons on a reciprocal basis;

(d) proposed modifications to the Chapter; and

(e) measures that affect the temporary entry of business persons under this Chapter.

## Article 1206: Dispute Settlement

1. A Party may not initiate proceedings under the general dispute settlement provisions of this Agreement regarding a refusal to grant temporary entry under this Chapter unless:

(a) the matter involves a pattern of practice; and

(b) the business person has exhausted the available administrative remedies regarding the particular matter.

2. The remedies referred to in subparagraph 1(b) shall be deemed to be exhausted if a final determination in the matter has not been issued by the competent authority within one year of the institution of an administrative proceeding, and the failure to issue a determination is not attributable to delay caused by the business person.

## Article 1207: Relation to Other Chapters

1. No provision of this Agreement shall be interpreted to impose any obligation on a Party regarding its immigration measures, except as specifically identified in this Chapter and Chapters One and Nineteen to Twenty-Three (Initial Provisions and General Definitions, Transparency, Administration of the Agreement, Dispute Settlement, Exceptions and Final Provisions).

2. Nothing in this Chapter shall be construed to impose obligations or commitments with respect to other Chapters of this Agreement.

## Article 1208: Transparency in Processing of Applications

1. Further to Chapter Nineteen (Transparency), each Party shall establish or maintain appropriate mechanisms to respond to inquiries from interested persons regarding applications and procedures relating to the temporary entry of business persons.

2. Each Party shall endeavour to, within a reasonable period that should not exceed 45 days after an application requesting temporary entry is considered complete under its domestic laws and regulations, inform the applicant of the decision concerning the application. At the request of the applicant, the Party shall endeavour to provide, without undue delay, information concerning the status of the application.

## Article 1209: Definitions

For purposes of this Chapter:

*business person* means a national of a Party who is engaged in trade in goods, the supply of services or the conduct of investment activities;

*contract service supplier* means an employee who is a professional or technician of a foreign based company, partnership, or firm who enters the territory of the other Party temporarily in order to perform a service pursuant to a contract between his/her employer and a service consumer in the territory of the other Party, when the employer:

(a) has no commercial presence in the territory of the other Party;

(b) is a juridical person that has obtained a contract for the provision of a service in the territory of the other Party that does not consist exclusively in the supply of personnel; and

(c) provides the employee's remuneration;

*executive* means a business person within an organisation who primarily directs the management of the organisation, exercises wide latitude in decision-making, and receives only general supervision or direction from higher level executives, the board of directors, and/or stockholders of the business;

*independent professional or technician* means a professional or technician who enters the territory of the other Party temporarily in order to perform a service pursuant to a contract with a service consumer located in the territory of the other Party when:

(a) the professional or technician supplies the service as a self-employed person;

(b) the professional or technician has obtained a service contract in the territory of the Party where the service is to be supplied; and

(c) the remuneration for the contract is to be paid solely to the professional or technician in the territory of the Party where the service is to be supplied;

*labour dispute* means a strike between a union and employer relating to terms and conditions of employment;

*management trainee on professional development* means an employee with a post-secondary degree who is on a temporary work assignment intended to broaden that employee's knowledge of and experience in a company in preparation for a senior leadership position within the company;

*manager* means a business person within an organisation who primarily directs the organisation or a department or sub-division of the organisation, supervises and controls the work of other supervisory, professional or managerial employees, has the authority to hire and fire or take other personnel actions (such as promotion or leave authorisation), and exercises discretionary authority over day-to-day operations;

*professional* means a national of a Party who is engaged in a specialty occupation[216] requiring:

(a) theoretical and practical application of a body of specialized knowledge, and who is eligible to obtain the certification or license to practice, if required; and

(b) attainment of a post-secondary degree in the specialty requiring four, or more years of study as a minimum for entry into the occupation[217];

*professional or technician in a subordinate relationship* means a professional or technician who enters the territory of the other Party temporarily in order to perform a service under the direction of an employer in the other Party, who has the authority to regulate, direct and sanction the activities of the employee;

*specialist* means an employee who possesses specialized knowledge of the company's products or services and its application in international markets, or an advanced level of expertise or knowledge of the company's processes and procedures. A specialist may include, but is not limited to, professionals and technicians;

*technician* means a national of a Party who is engaged in a specialty occupation[218] requiring:

(a) theoretical and practical application of a body of specialized knowledge, and who is eligible to obtain the certification/license to practice, if required; and

(b) attainment of a post-secondary or technical degree requiring one, or more years of study, or the equivalent of such a degree, as a minimum for entry into the occupation;[219] and

*temporary entry* means entry into the territory of a Party by a business person of the other Party without the intent to establish permanent residence.

---

[216]With respect to Canada, a professional specialty occupation shall mean an occupation which falls within the National Occupation Classification (NOC) levels O and A.

[217]With respect to Canada, these requirements shall be those defined in the NOC. With respect to Peru, requirements for regulated professions shall be provided in accordance with Article 1204.

[218]With respect to Canada, a technical specialty occupation shall mean an occupation which falls within the NOC level B.

[219]With respect to Canada, these requirements shall be those defined in the NOC. With respect to Peru, requirements for regulated technician occupations shall be provided in accordance with Article 1204.

## Annex 1203 — Temporary Entry for Business Persons

### Section A — Business Visitors

1. Each Party shall grant temporary entry to a business person seeking to engage in a business activity set out in Appendix 1203.A.1, without requiring that person to obtain a work permit or an employment authorization, provided that the business person otherwise complies with existing immigration measures applicable to temporary entry, on presentation of:

(a) proof of nationality, citizenship or permanent residency status of a Party;

(b) documentation demonstrating that the business person will be engaged in a business activity set out in Appendix 1203.A.1 and describing the purpose of entry; and

(c) evidence demonstrating that the proposed business activity is international in scope and the business person is not seeking to enter the local labour market.

2. Each Party shall provide that a business person may satisfy the requirements of subparagraph 1(c) by demonstrating that:

(a) the primary source of remuneration for the proposed business activity is outside the territory of the Party granting temporary entry; and

(b) the business person's principal place of business and the actual place of accrual of profits, at least predominantly, remain outside the territory of the Party granting temporary entry.

A Party shall normally accept an oral declaration as to the principal place of business and the actual place of accrual of profits. Where the Party requires further proof, it shall normally consider a letter from the employer or the representing organization attesting to these matters as sufficient proof.

3. Neither Party may:

(a) as a condition for temporary entry under paragraph 1, require prior approval procedures, labour certification tests or other procedures of similar effect; or

(b) impose or maintain any numerical restriction relating to temporary entry under paragraph 1.

4. Notwithstanding paragraph 3, a Party may require a business person seeking temporary entry under this Section to obtain a visa or an equivalent requirement prior to entry. Before imposing a visa or an equivalent requirement, the Party shall consult with the other Party whose business persons would be affected with a view to avoiding the imposition of the requirement.

### Section B — Traders and Investors

1. Each Party shall grant temporary entry and provide a work permit or other authorization to a business person seeking to:

(a) carry on substantial trade in goods or services principally between the territory of the Party of which the business person is a national and the territory of the other Party into which entry is sought; or

(b) establish, develop or administer an investment to which the business person or the business person's enterprise has committed, or is in the process of committing, a substantial amount of capital,

in a capacity that is supervisory, executive or involves essential skills, provided that the business person otherwise complies with existing immigration measures applicable to temporary entry.

2. Neither Party may:

(a) as a condition for temporary entry under paragraph 1, require labour certification tests or other procedures of similar effect; or

(b) impose or maintain any numerical restriction relating to temporary entry under paragraph 1.

3. Notwithstanding paragraph 2, a Party may require a business person seeking temporary entry under this Section to obtain a visa or an equivalent requirement prior to entry. Before imposing a visa or an equivalent requirement, the Party shall consult with the other Party whose business persons would be affected with a view to avoiding the imposition of the requirement.

## Section C — Intra-Company Transferees

1. Each Party shall grant temporary entry and provide a work permit or other authorization to a business person employed by an enterprise who seeks to render services to that enterprise or a subsidiary or affiliate thereof as an executive or manager, a specialist, or a management trainee on professional development, provided that the business person otherwise complies with existing immigration measures applicable to temporary entry. A Party may require the business person to have been employed continuously by the enterprise for six months within the three-year period immediately preceding the date of the application for admission.

2. Neither Party may:

(a) as a condition for temporary entry under paragraph 1, require labour certification tests or other procedures of similar effect; or

(b) impose or maintain any numerical restriction relating to temporary entry under paragraph 1.

3. Notwithstanding paragraph 2, a Party may require a business person seeking temporary entry under this Section to obtain a visa or an equivalent requirement prior to entry. Before imposing a visa or an equivalent requirement, the Party shall consult with the other Party whose business persons would be affected with a view to avoiding the imposition of the requirement.

## Section D — Professionals and Technicians

1. Each Party shall grant temporary entry and provide a work permit or other authorization to a business person seeking to engage in a business activity at a professional or technical level in accordance with Appendix 1203.D.1, either as an independent professional and technician, as a professional and technician in a subordinate relationship, or as a contract service supplier, including training activities related to a particular profession, if the business person otherwise complies with existing immigration measures applicable to temporary entry, on presentation of:

(a) proof of nationality, citizenship or permanent residency status of a Party; and

(b) documentation demonstrating that the business person is seeking to enter the territory of the other Party to provide pre-arranged professional services in the field for which he/she has the appropriate qualifications.

2. Neither Party may:

(a) as a condition for temporary entry under paragraph 1, require prior approval procedures, labour certification tests or other procedures of similar effect; or

(b) impose or maintain any numerical restriction relating to temporary entry under paragraph 1.

3. Notwithstanding paragraph 2, a Party may require a business person seeking temporary entry under this Section to obtain a visa or an equivalent requirement prior to entry. Before imposing a visa or an equivalent requirement, the Party shall consult with the other Party whose business persons would be affected with a view to avoiding the imposition of the requirement.

## Annex 1203.A.1 Business Visitors

### Meetings and Consultations

Business persons attending meetings, seminars, or conferences; or engaged in consultations with business associates.

### Research and Design

Technical, scientific and statistical researchers conducting independent research or research for an enterprise located in the territory of the other Party.

### Growth, Manufacture and Production

Purchasing and production management personnel, conducting commercial transactions for an enterprise located in the territory of the other Party.

Harvester owner supervising a harvesting crew.

### Marketing

Market researchers and analysts conducting independent research or analysis or research or analysis for an enterprise located in the territory of the other Party.

Trade-fair and promotional personnel attending a trade convention.

### Sales

Sales representatives and agents taking orders or negotiating contracts for goods or services for an enterprise located in the territory of the other Party but not delivering goods or providing services.

Buyers purchasing for an enterprise located in the territory of the other Party.

### Distribution

Transportation operators transporting goods or passengers to the territory of a Party from the territory of the other Party or loading and transporting goods or passengers from the territory of a Party, with no unloading in that territory, to the territory of the other Party.

Customs brokers providing consulting services regarding the facilitation of the import or export of goods.

### After-Sales or After-Lease Service

Installers, repair and maintenance personnel, and supervisors, possessing specialized knowledge essential to a seller's contractual obligation, performing services or training workers to perform services, pursuant to a warranty or other service contract incidental to the sale or lease of commercial or industrial equipment or machinery, including computer software, purchased or leased from an enterprise located outside the territory of the Party into which temporary entry is sought, during the life of the warranty or service agreement.

### General Service

Professionals and technicians engaging in a business activity at a professional or technical level as set out in Appendix 1203.D.1.

Management and supervisory personnel engaging in a commercial transaction for an enterprise located in the territory of the other Party.

Financial services personnel of an enterprise located in the territory of the other Party, engaging in the area of financial services, where the provision of such financial services does not require the authorization of the competent authority of the Party or where such financial services are listed in Annex 1105.

Public relations and advertising personnel consulting with business associates, or attending or participating in conventions.

Tourism personnel (tour and travel agents, tour guides or tour operators) attending or participating in conventions or conducting a tour that has begun in the territory of the other Party.

Cook personnel (cookers and assistants) attending or participating in gastronomic events or exhibitions, or consulting with business associates.

Translators or interpreters performing services as employees of an enterprise located in the territory of the other Party.

Information and communication technology service providers attending meetings, seminars or conferences, or engaged in consultations with business associates.

Franchise traders and developers which seek to offer their services in the territory of the other Party.

## Annex 1203.D.1 Professionals

The professionals listed below, as defined in Article 1209, are not covered under this Chapter:

1. All Health, Education, and Social Services occupations and related occupations including:

    (a) Managers in Health/Education/Social & Community Services;

    (b) Physicians/Dentists/Optometrists/Chiropractors/Other Health Professions;

    (c) Pharmacists, Dietians & Nutritionists;

    (d) Therapy & Assessment Professionals;

    (e) Nurse Supervisors & Registered Nurses;

    (f) Psychologists/Social Workers;

    (g) University Professors & Assistants;

    (h) College & Other Vocational Instructors; and

    (i) Secondary/Elementary School Teachers & Counsellors.

2. All professional occupations related to cultural industries as defined in Article 2207 (Exceptions — Definitions), including:

    (a) Managers in Libraries, Archives, Museums and Art Galleries;

    (b) Managers in Publishing, Motion Pictures, Broadcasting and Performing Arts; and

    (c) Creative & Performing Artists.

3. Recreation, Sports and Fitness Program and Service Directors.

4. Managers in Telecommunication Carriers.

5. Managers in Postal and Courier Services.
6. Managers in Manufacturing.
7. Managers in Utilities.
8. Managers in Construction and Transportation.
9. Judges, Lawyers and Notaries except foreign legal consultants.

### Technicians

The technicians listed below, as defined in Article 1209, are covered under this chapter:

1. Civil Engineering Technologists and Technicians;
2. Electrical and Electronics Engineering Technologists and Technicians;[220]
3. Mechanical Engineering Technologists and Technicians;
4. Industrial Engineering and Manufacturing Technologists and Technicians;
5. Construction Inspectors and Estimators;
6. Engineering Inspectors, Testers and Regulatory Officers;
7. Supervisors in the following: Machinists and Related Occupations; Printing and Related Occupations; Mining and Quarrying; Oil and Gas Drilling and Service; Mineral and Metal Processing; Petroleum, Gas and Chemical Processing and Utilities; Food, Beverage and Tobacco Processing; Plastic and Rubber Products Manufacturing; Forest Products Processing; and Textile Processing;
8. Contractors and Supervisors in the following: Electrical Trades and Telecommunications Occupations; Pipefitting Trades; Metal Forming, Shaping and Erecting Trades; Carpentry Trades; Mechanic Trades; Heavy Construction Equipment Crews; and Other Construction Trades, Installers, Repairers and Servicers;
9. Electricians;[221]
10. Plumbers;
11. Industrial Instrument Technicians and Mechanics;
12. Aircraft Instrument, Electrical and Avionics Mechanics, Technicians and Inspectors;
13. Underground Production and Development Miners;
14. Oil and Gas Well Drillers, Servicers and Testers;
15. Graphic Designers and Illustrators;
16. Interior Designers;
17. Chefs;
18. Computer and Information System Technicians; and
19. International Selling and Purchasing Agents.



[220]This includes electronic service technicians.

[221]This includes industrial electricians.

## Annex 1203

### For Peru:

| Category | Migratory Condition | Length of Stay |
| --- | --- | --- |
| Business Visitor | Negocios (business) | Up to 90 days, renewable for 30 days. |
| Traders | Negocios (business) | Up to 90 days, renewable for 30 days. |
| Investor (in the process of committing an investment) | Negocios (business) | Up to 90 days, renewable for 30 days. |
| Investor | Independiente-inversionista (Investor) | Up to 1 year, renewable for consecutive periods, the number of times that it is requested, to the extent that the conditions which motivated its granting are maintained. |
| Intra-Company Transferees | Trabajador (Worker) | Up to 1 year, renewable for consecutive periods, the number of times that it is requested, to the extent that the conditions which motivated its granting are maintained. |
| Professionals and Technicians (in a subordinate relationship) | Trabajador (Worker) | Up to 1 year, renewable for consecutive periods, the number of times that it is requested, to the extent that the conditions which motivated its granting are maintained. |
| Professionals and Technicians (Independent) | Independiente — Profesional (Independent — Professional) | Up to 1 year, renewable for consecutive periods, the number of times that it is requested, to the extent that the conditions which motivated its granting are maintained. |
| Professionals and Technicians (Contract service supplier) | | Up to 6 months. |

### For Canada:

| Category | Length of Stay |
| --- | --- |
| Business Visitors | Up to six months, extensions are possible. |
| Traders and Investors | Up to one year, extensions are possible. |
| Intra-Company Transferees | Up to three years, extensions are possible. |
| Professionals and Technicians | Up to one year, extensions are possible. |

# APPENDIX VI

## CONSTITUTION ACT, 1982

Canada Act 1982 (U.K.), c. 11 R.S.C. 1985, Appendix II, No. 44, as am. Constitution Amendment Proclamation, 1983, SI/84-102, Schedule, SI/93-54.

. . . . .

## PART I — CANADIAN CHARTER OF RIGHTS AND FREEDOMS

Whereas Canada is founded upon principles that recognize the supremacy of God and the rule of law:

### Guarantee of Rights and Freedoms

1. **Rights and freedoms in Canada** — The *Canadian Charter of Rights and Freedoms* guarantees the rights and freedoms set out in it subject only to such reasonable limits prescribed by law as can be demonstrably justified in a free and democratic society.

### Fundamental Freedoms

2. **Fundamental freedoms** — Everyone has the following fundamental freedoms:

(a) freedom of conscience and religion;

(b) freedom of thought, belief, opinion and expression, including freedom of the press and other media of communication;

(c) freedom of peaceful assembly; and

(d) freedom of association.

### Democratic Rights

3. **Democratic rights of citizens** — Every citizen of Canada has the right to vote in an election of members of the House of Commons or of a legislative assembly and to be qualified for membership therein.

4. (1) **Maximum duration of legislative bodies** — No House of Commons and no legislative assembly shall continue for longer than five years from the date fixed for the return of the writs at a general election of its members.

(2) **Continuation in special circumstances** — In time of real or apprehended war, invasion or insurrection, a House of Commons may be continued by Parliament and a legislative assembly may be continued by the legislature beyond five years if such contin-

uation is not opposed by the votes of more than one-third of the members of the House of Commons or the legislative assembly, as the case may be.

5. **Annual sitting of legislative bodies** — There shall be a sitting of Parliament and of each legislature at least once every twelve months.

## Mobility Rights

6. (1) **Mobility of citizens** — Every citizen of Canada has the right to enter, remain in and leave Canada.

(2) **Rights to move and gain livelihood** — Every citizen of Canada and every person who has the status of a permanent resident of Canada has the right

(a) to move to and take up residence in any province; and

(b) to pursue the gaining of a livelihood in any province.

(3) **Limitation** — The rights specified in subsection (2) are subject to

(a) any laws or practices of general application in force in a province other than those that discriminate among persons primarily on the basis of province of present or previous residence; and

(b) any laws providing for reasonable residency requirements as a qualification for the receipt of publicly provided social services.

(4) **Affirmative action programs** — Subsections (2) and (3) do not preclude any law, program or activity that has as its object the amelioration in a province of conditions of individuals in that province who are socially or economically disadvantaged if the rate of employment in that province is below the rate of employment in Canada.

## Legal Rights

7. **Life, liberty and security of person** — Everyone has the right to life, liberty and security of the person and the right not to be deprived thereof except in accordance with the principles of fundamental justice.

8. **Search or seizure** — Everyone has the right to be secure against unreasonable search or seizure.

9. **Detention or imprisonment** — Everyone has the right not to be arbitrarily detained or imprisoned.

10. **Arrest or detention** — Everyone has the right on arrest or detention

(a) to be informed promptly of the reasons therefor;

(b) to retain and instruct counsel without delay and to be informed of that right; and

(c) to have the validity of the detention determined by way of *habeas corpus* and to be released if the detention is not lawful.

11. **Proceedings in criminal and penal matters** — Any person charged with an offence has the right

(a) to be informed without unreasonable delay of the specific offence;

(b) to be tried within a reasonable time;

(c) not to be compelled to be a witness in proceedings against that person in respect of the offence;

(d) to be presumed innocent until proven guilty according to law in a fair and public hearing by an independent and impartial tribunal;

(e) not to be denied reasonable bail without just cause;

(f) except in the case of an offence under military law tried before a military tribunal, to the benefit of trial by jury where the maximum punishment for the offence is imprisonment for five years or a more severe punishment;

(g) not to be found guilty on account of any act or omission unless, at the time of the act or omission, it constituted an offence under Canadian or international law or was criminal according to the general principles of law recognized by the community of nations;

(h) if finally acquitted of the offence, not to be tried for it again and, if finally found guilty and punished for the offence, not to be tried or punished for it again; and

(i) if found guilty of the offence and if the punishment for the offence has been varied between the time of commission and the time of sentencing, to the benefit of the lesser punishment.

12. **Treatment or punishment** — Everyone has the right not to be subjected to any cruel and unusual treatment or punishment.

13. **Self-crimination** — A witness who testifies in any proceedings has the right not to have any incriminating evidence so given used to incriminate that witness in any other proceedings, except in a prosecution for perjury or for the giving of contradictory evidence.

14. **Interpreter** — A party or witness in any proceedings who does not understand or speak the language in which the proceedings are conducted or who is deaf has the right to the assistance of an interpreter.

## Equality Rights

15. (1) **Equality before and under law and equal protection and benefit of law** — Every individual is equal before and under the law and has the right to the equal protection and equal benefit of the law without discrimination and, in particular, without discrimination based on race, national or ethnic origin, colour, religion, sex, age or mental or physical disability.

(2) **Affirmative action programs** — Subsection (1) does not preclude any law, program or activity that has as its object the amelioration of conditions of disadvantaged individuals or groups including those that are disadvantaged because of race, national or ethnic origin, colour, religion, sex, age or mental or physical disability.

## Official Languages of Canada

16. (1) **Official languages of Canada** — English and French are the official languages of Canada and have equality of status and equal rights and privileges as to their use in all institutions of the Parliament and government of Canada.

(2) **Official languages of New Brunswick** — English and French are the official languages of New Brunswick and have equality of status and equal rights and privileges as to their use in all institutions of the legislature and government of New Brunswick.

(3) **Advancement of status and use** — Nothing in this Charter limits the authority of Parliament or a legislature to advance the equality of status or use of English and French.

16.1 (1) **English and French linguistic communities in New Brunswick** — The English linguistic community and the French linguistic community in New Brunswick have equality status and equal rights and privileges, including the right to distinct educational institutions and such distinct cultural institutions as are necessary for the preservation and promotion of those communities.

(2) **Role of the legislature and government of New Brunswick** — The role of the legislature and government of New Brunswick to preserve and promote the status, rights and privileges referred to in subsection (1) is affirmed.

SI/93-54, Sched., s. 1

17. (1) **Proceedings of Parliament** — Everyone has the right to use English or French in any debates and other proceedings of Parliament.

(2) **Proceedings of New Brunswick legislature** — Everyone has the right to use English or French in any debates and other proceedings of the legislature of New Brunswick.

18. (1) **Parliamentary statutes and records** — The statutes, records and journals of Parliament shall be printed and published in English and French and both language versions are equally authoritative.

(2) **New Brunswick statutes and records** — The statutes, records and journals of the legislature of New Brunswick shall be printed and published in English and French and both language versions are equally authoritative.

19. (1) **Proceedings in courts established by Parliament** — Either English or French may be used by any person in, or in any pleading in or process issuing from, any court established by Parliament.

(2) **Proceedings in New Brunswick courts** — Either English or French may be used by any person in, or in any pleading in or process issuing from, any court of New Brunswick.

20. (1) **Communications by public with federal institutions** — Any member of the public in Canada has the right to communicate with, and to receive available services from, any head or central office of an institution of the Parliament or government of Canada in English or French, and has the same right with respect to any other office of any such institution where

(a) there is a significant demand for communications with and services from that office in such language; or

(b) due to the nature of the office, it is reasonable that communications with and services from that office be available in both English and French.

(2) **Communications by public with New Brunswick institutions** — Any member of the public in New Brunswick has the right to communicate with, and to receive available services from, any office of an institution of the legislature or government of New Brunswick in English or French.

21. **Continuation of existing Constitutional provisions** — Nothing in sections 16 to 20 abrogates or derogates from any right, privilege or obligation with respect to the

English and French languages, or either of them, that exists or is continued by virtue of any other provision of the Constitution of Canada.

22. **Rights and privileges preserved** — Nothing in sections 16 to 20 abrogates or derogates from any legal or customary right or privilege acquired or enjoyed either before or after the coming into force of this Charter with respect to any language that is not English or French.

## Minority Language Educational Rights

23. (1) **Language of instruction** — Citizens of Canada

(a) whose first language learned and still understood is that of the English or French linguistic minority population of the province in which they reside, or

(b) who have received their primary school instruction in Canada in English or French and reside in a province where the language in which they received that instruction is the language of the English or French linguistic minority population of the province,

have the right to have their children receive primary and secondary school instruction in that language in that province.

(2) **Continuity of language instruction** — Citizens of Canada of whom any child has received or is receiving primary or secondary school instruction in English or French in Canada, have the right to have all their children receive primary and secondary school instruction in the same language.

(3) **Application where numbers warrant** — The right of citizens of Canada under subsections (1) and (2) to have their children receive primary and secondary school instruction in the language of the English or French linguistic minority population of a province

(a) applies wherever in the province the number of children of citizens who have such a right is sufficient to warrant the provision to them out of public funds of minority language instruction; and

(b) includes, where the number of those children so warrants, the right to have them receive that instruction in minority language educational facilities provided out of public funds.

## Enforcement

24. (1) **Enforcement of guaranteed rights and freedoms** — Anyone whose rights or freedoms, as guaranteed by this Charter, have been infringed or denied may apply to a court of competent jurisdiction to obtain such remedy as the court considers appropriate and just in the circumstances.

(2) **Exclusion of evidence bringing administration of justice into disrepute** — Where, in proceedings under subsection (1), a court concludes that evidence was obtained in a manner that infringed or denied any rights or freedoms guaranteed by this Charter, the evidence shall be excluded if it is established that, having regard to all the circumstances, the admission of it in the proceedings would bring the administration of justice into disrepute.

25. **Aboriginal rights and freedoms not affected by Charter** — The guarantee in this Charter of certain rights and freedoms shall not be construed so as to abrogate or

derogate from any aboriginal treaty or other rights or freedoms that pertain to the aboriginal peoples of Canada including

(a) any rights or freedoms that have been recognized by the Royal Proclamation of October 7, 1763; and

(b) any rights or freedoms that now exist by way of land claims agreements or may be so acquired.

26. **Other rights and freedoms not affected by Charter** — The guarantee in this Charter of certain rights and freedoms shall not be construed as denying the existence of any other rights or freedoms that exist in Canada.

27. **Multicultural heritage** — This Charter shall be interpreted in a manner consistent with the preservation and enhancement of the multicultural heritage of Canadians.

28. **Rights guaranteed equally to both sexes** — Notwithstanding anything in this Charter, the rights and freedoms referred to in it are guaranteed equally to male and female persons.

29. **Rights respecting certain schools preserved** — Nothing in this Charter abrogates or derogates from any rights or privileges guaranteed by or under the Constitution of Canada in respect of denominational, separate or dissentient schools.

30. **Application to Territories and territorial authorities** — A reference in this Charter to a province or to the legislative assembly or legislature of a province shall be deemed to include a reference to the Yukon Territory and the Northwest Territories, or to the appropriate legislative authority thereof, as the case may be.

31. **Legislative powers not extended** — Nothing in this Charter extends the legislative powers of any body or authority.

## Application of Charter

32. (1) **Application of Charter** — This Charter applies

(a) to the Parliament and government of Canada in respect of all matters within the authority of Parliament including all matters relating to the Yukon Territory and Northwest Territories; and

(b) to the legislature and government of each province in respect of all matters within the authority of the legislature of each province.

(2) **Exception** — Notwithstanding subsection (1), section 15 shall not have effect until three years after this section comes into force.

33. (1) **Exception where express declaration** — Parliament or the legislature of a province may expressly declare in an Act of Parliament or of the legislature, as the case may be, that the Act or a provision thereof shall operate notwithstanding a provision included in section 2 or sections 7 to 15 of this Charter.

(2) **Operation of exception** — An Act or a provision of an Act in respect of which a declaration made under this section is in effect shall have such operation as it would have but for the provision of this Charter referred to in the declaration.

(3) **Five year limitation** — A declaration made under subsection (1) shall cease to have effect five years after it comes into force or on such earlier date as may be specified in the declaration.

(4) **Re-enactment** — Parliament or a legislature of a province may re-enact a declaration made under subsection (1).

(5) **Five year limitation** — Subsection (3) applies in respect of a re-enactment made under subsection (4).

## Citation

34. **Citation** — This Part may be cited as the *Canadian Charter of Rights and Freedoms.*

# Index — Immigration and Refugee Protection Act, Regulations and Rules

*Most references in this index are as follows: Immigration Appeal Division Rules -- IADR; Immigration and Refugee Protection Act - IRPA; Immigration and Refugee Protection Regulations - IRPR; Federal Courts Act - FCA; Immigration Division Rules - IDR; Federal Courts Rules - FCR; Federal Courts Immigration and Refugee Protection Rules - FCIRP; and Refugee Protection Division Rules - RPDR. A "p." designation refers to a specific page of the text.*



Index

Index

Index

Index

Index

Index

Index

## J

Index

Index

Index

## S

Index

Index